AN INTRODUCTION TO
BRAIN AND BEHAVIOR

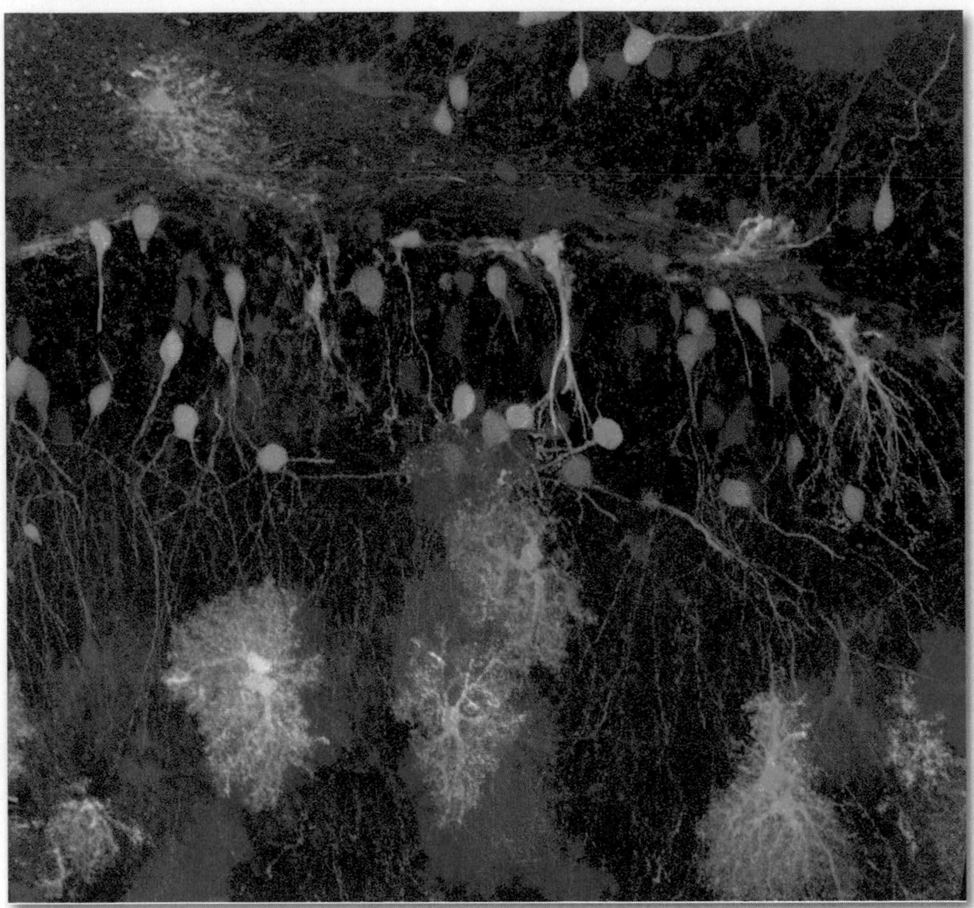

The image on the cover illustrates a cell-staining technique called Brainbow developed by Jean Livet and his colleagues at Harvard University. (The name is a play on the word "rainbow.") In this Brainbow image of a mouse hippocampus, the brain cells are expressing fluorescent proteins. The Brainbow technique, which labels cells by highlighting them with distinct colors, involves introducing into mice genes that produce cyan (blue), green, yellow, and red fluorescent proteins. The "red" gene is obtained from coral and the "blue" and "green" genes are obtained from jellyfish. The extent to which each gene is activated varies somewhat, owing to chance factors, and by mixes of the primary colors produces fluorescence in one hundred or more different hues. Brainbow offers a way to image the shape and location of cells and to describe neuronal circuits—that is, where each neuron sends its processes and how it interconnects with other neurons. Lichtman Laboratory/Harvard University

AN INTRODUCTION TO BRAIN AND BEHAVIOR

Third Edition

BRYAN KOLB
University of Lethbridge

IAN Q. WHISHAW
University of Lethbridge

WORTH PUBLISHERS

To the first neuron, our ancestors, our families, and students who read this book

Senior Publisher: Catherine Woods
Senior Acquisitions Editor: Charles Linsmeier
Development Editor: Barbara Brooks
Marketing Coordinator: Jennifer Bilello
Senior Project Editor: Georgia Lee Hadler
Manuscript Editors: Patricia Zimmerman and Penelope Hull
Production Manager: Sarah Segal
Media and Supplements Editor: Peter Twickler
Text and Cover Design: Vicki Tomaselli
Photo Editor: Ted Szczepanski
Senior Illustration Coordinator: Bill Page
Illustrations: Dragonfly Media Group and Northeastern Graphic, Inc.
Composition: Northeastern Graphic, Inc.
Printing and Binding: Worldcolor Versailles

Library of Congress Control Number: 2009936819

ISBN-13: 9780716776918
ISBN-10: 071677691X

First printing

Worth Publishers
41 Madison Avenue
New York, NY 10010
www.worthpublishers.com

About the Authors

Bryan Kolb received his Ph.D. from the Pennsylvania State University in 1973. He conducted postdoctoral work at the University of Western Ontario and the Montreal Neurological Institute. He moved to the University of Lethbridge in 1976, where he is currently Professor of Neuroscience and holds a Board of Governors Chair in Neuroscience. His current research examines how neurons of the cerebral cortex change in response to various factors, including hormones, experience, psychoactive drugs, neurotrophins, and injury, and how these changes are related to behavior in the normal and diseased brain. Kolb is a Fellow of the Royal Society of Canada, the Canadian Psychological Association (CPA), the American Psychological Association, and the Association of Psychological Science. He is a recipient of the Hebb Prize from CPA and from the Canadian Society for Brain, Behaviour, and Cognitive Science (CSBBCS) and has received honorary doctorates from the University of British Columbia and Thompson Rivers University. He is currently a member of the Experience-Based Brain and Behavioral Development program of the Canadian Institute for Advanced Research.

Ian Q. Whishaw received his Ph.D. from the University of Western Ontario in 1971. He moved to the University of Lethbridge in 1970, where he is currently Professor of Neuroscience and holds a Board of Governors Chair in Neuroscience. He has held visiting appointments at the University of Texas, University of Michigan, Cambridge University, and the University of Strasbourg, France. He is a Fellow of Clair Hall, Cambridge. His current research examines how the precise details of movements are influenced by injury or disease to the motor systems of rodents and humans and how animals and humans move through real and mental space. Whishaw is a Fellow of the Canadian Psychological Association, the American Psychological Association, and the Royal Society of Canada, and the Institute for Scientific Information includes him in its list of most cited neuroscientists. He is a recipient of a Bronze medal from the Canadian Humane Society, and a recipient of the Ingrid Speaker medal for research. He has received honorary doctorates from Thompson Rivers University and the University of Lethbridge.

Index of Disorders

*Name of disorder is followed by chapter number(s) where information appears; * indicates a Focus box.*

For a summary of general treatment categories, see the table on page 577.

For a summary of research techniques, see Chapter 6.

Contents in Brief

Contents

Jeff Minton

Katsuycshi Tanaka

© Alessandra Sanguinetti/Magnum

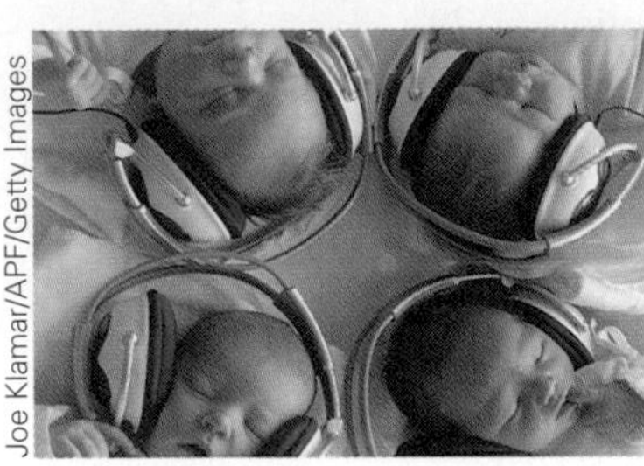
Joe Klamar/APF/Getty Images

Courtesy of Cognitive Evolution Group, University of Louisiana at Lafayette, New Iberia Research.

Gordon Parks/Time & Life Pictures/Getty Images

Preface

The Third Edition of *An Introduction to Brain and Behavior* continues to reflect the evolution of the field of behavioral neuroscience. Perhaps the two biggest developments are the rapid emergence of noninvasive imaging to study cognitive processing in human and nonhuman subjects as well as the burgeoning evidence of the plasticity of brain structure and function. We have thus added more imaging and plasticity concepts and research to the text and in Focus boxes.

The biggest change in the book has been the addition of a chapter dedicated to methods. Chapter 6, "How Do We Study the Brain's Structure and Functions?" was a response to requests from instructors to have a dedicated discussion showcasing the range of methods used by behavioral neuroscientists to study brain and behavior. The chapter includes both traditional methods as well as newer techniques such as optical tomography and epigenetics. Material from the Second Edition's Appendix on animal welfare has been incorporated in Chapter 6 in the context of how we develop animal models of human disorders. Expanded discussions of other techniques appear in other chapters where appropriate. For example, Chapter 16 includes a discussion of the new methods of virtual-reality therapies for anxiety-related disorders.

Several new features have been added throughout the book. We had originally included background material such as anatomical orientation (Chapter 2) and basic chemistry (Chapter 3) within the main text. This material is now separated into boxes called "The Basics." So the material is still there for readers who are not familiar with it, and readers familiar with the information can easily skip it.

Another new feature is margin notes that increase the reader's ease in finding related information elsewhere in the book. This should be especially helpful when concepts are introduced early in the text and then elaborated on in later chapters. Readers can return quickly to the earlier discussion to refresh their knowledge of the basic concept. The margin notes should also allow instructors to move through the book to preview later discussions.

Much of the book remains familiar. Throughout, we continue to examine the nervous system with a focus on function, on how our behavior and our brains interact. We structured the First Edition of *An Introduction to Brain and Behavior* on key questions that students and neuroscientists ask about the brain:

- Why do we have a brain?
- How is the nervous system organized?
- How do drugs affect our behavior?
- How does the brain learn?
- How does the brain think?

As it was then, our goal in the new edition is to bring coherence to a vast subject by helping students understand the big picture. Asking fundamental questions about the brain has another benefit: it piques students' interest in the subject and challenges them to join us on the journey of discovery that is brain science.

Scientific understanding of the brain and human behavior continues to grow at an exponential pace. We want to communicate the excitement of recent breakthroughs in brain science and to relate some of our own experiences in studying the brain for the past 40 years, both to make the field's developing core concepts and latest revelations understandable and meaningful and to take uninitiated students to the frontiers of physiological psychology.

Chapter-by-Chapter Updates in the Third Edition

Chapter 1 now opens with a Clinical Focus on traumatic brain injury (TBI) and its treatments (Research Focus 1-2) and is refocused, briefer, and more inviting.

Chapter 2 includes a streamlined emphasis on neuroplasticity and nervous-system anatomy and function, providing a road map for the rest of the book.

Chapter 3 streamlines the coverage of the nervous system and adds a "The Basics" feature on its most referenced material. Clinical Focus 3-3 provides updated coverage of multiple sclerosis, and new Research Focus 3-5 covers Brainbow imaging.

Chapter 4 improves the presentation of electrical activity at the cell membrane, including back propagation. It also features new Research Focus 4-2 on light-sensitive ion channels.

Chapter 5 expands coverage of neural activating systems and streamlines coverage of learning at the synapse.

Chapter 6 showcases a state-of-the-art range of techniques and topics including optimal tomography and epigenetics and includes new Research Focus 6-4 on ADHD.

Chapter 7 begins with new Research Focus 7-1 on SIDS, and new Research Focus 7-3 discusses cortical representation of second languages.

Chapter 8 includes new Clinical Focus 8-1 on addiction and a new section on sex differences in and treatments for drug abuse. It also includes a new section on anabolic steroids.

Chapter 9 expands coverage of sensation and perception. The coverage of vision is more streamlined than it was in the previous edition for more balance with the other senses. New Research Focus 9-3 covers color-deficient vision.

Chapter 10 includes new coverage of "bilingual" brains and a new Research Focus on the neural basis of musical ability. The chapter also includes a new example from Oliver Sacks's *Musicophilia.*

Chapter 11 includes new Research Focus 11-1 on the computer–brain interface (BCI) and new Research Focus 11-5 on treating phantom limb pain. Clinical Focus 11-2 on autism spectrum disorder has been updated.

Chapter 12 includes a new section on unconscious olfactory processing in humans and updated coverage on weight-loss strategies based on results from comparative research on diets.

Chapter 13 features new information on why some of us are morning people and others evening people. It also presents expanded discussion of how genes influence daily biorhythms and of a neural basis for cataplexy, and it updates clinical coverage of SAD, RLS, and sleep apnea.

Chapter 14 emphasizes seven principles of neuroplasticity. Clinical Focus 14-1 includes a technique, featured in *The New Science of Learning* on PBS, for remediating dyslexia. Coverage of patient H. M. is updated and includes his photo, which was released after his death. Also illustrated is dramatic cortical healing of a stroke lesion.

Chapter 15 discusses research on the role of the human mirror-neuron system in social cognition and the implications of its dysfunction in autism spectrum disorder. The chapter includes a new section on multisensory integration, and it updates coverage of the binding problem and incidence of synesthesia.

Chapter 16 includes research on the neural basis of PTSD; success of virtual reality simulations as therapy; a new section on age-related cognitive loss; updated treatment therapies using TMS, DBS, growth factors, and stem cells. Emphasis is on the efficacy of talking therapies—including real-time fMRI and cognitive-behavioral therapy—used in conjunction with drugs or in lieu of them.

We feature the relation between the brain and behavior in every chapter. For example, when we first describe how neurons communicate in Chapter 5, we also describe how plasticity in connections between neurons can serve as the basis of learning. Later, in Chapter 14, which is directed to the question of how we learn and remember, we explore how interactions among different parts of the brain enable our more complex behaviors.

Emphasis on Evolution, Genetics, Plasticity and Psychopharmacology

To make sure that this book conveys the excitement of current neuroscience as researchers understand it, we emphasize evolution, genetic research, neural plasticity, and psychopharmacology throughout. After all, evolution results from the complex interplay of genes and environment. This ongoing interplay influences a person's brain and behavior from earliest infancy through old age.

We cover the evolution of the brain in depth in Chapters 1 and 2 and return to this perspective of neuroscience in an evolutionary context in almost every chapter. Examples:

- Evolution of the synapse in Chapter 5
- Evolution of the visual pathways in Chapter 9
- How natural selection might promote overeating in Chapter 12
- Evolutionary theories of sleeping and dreaming in Chapter 13
- Evolution of sex differences in spatial cognition and language in Chapter 15
- Links between our evolved reactions to stress and the development of anxiety disorders in Chapter 16

The foundations of genetic research, including knockout technology, are introduced in depth in Chapter 3. Chapter 5 includes discussions of metabotropic receptors and DNA and of learning and genes. The role of genes in development is integral to Chapter 7, as is the topic of genes and drug action in Chapter 8. Chapter 9 explains the genetics of color vision, and the genetics of sleep disorders is a major topic in Chapter 13. Chapter 16 considers the role of genetics in understanding the causes of behavioral disorders.

We have updated and expanded the Research Focus boxes to showcase new and interesting developments on topics relevant to each chapter. In Chapter 6, for example, we explore research on attention-deficit/hyperactivity disorder (ADHD) in the context of developing animal models of disease. In Chapter 12 we investigate brain activation in response to physical and emotional pain and find their effects to be surprisingly similar. We have added special emphasis in this edition on common behavioral disorders such as traumatic brain injury (TBI), addiction, Alzheimer's disease, Parkinson's disease, autism spectrum disorder (ASD), and posttraumatic stress disorder (PTSD). In Chapter 16, for example, we review new approaches to the treatment of PTSD in veterans of the wars in Iraq and Afghanistan.

Chapter 8 deals with drugs and behavior, and we turn to this topic in many other chapters as well. You will find coverage of drugs and information transfer in Chapter 4, drugs and cellular communication in Chapter 5, drugs and motivation in Chapter 12, drugs and sleep disorders in Chapter 13, neuronal changes with drug use in Chapter 14, and drugs as treatments for a range of disorders in Chapter 16.

Neural plasticity continues as a hallmark of the book. We introduce the concept in Chapter 2 and expand on it throughout, including an elaboration of basic principles in Chapter 14.

Scientific Background Provided

We describe the journey of discovery that is neuroscience in a way that students just beginning to study the brain and behavior can understand. We have found that this course can sometimes be daunting, largely because understanding brain function requires information from all the basic sciences. If we are ultimately interested in how the brain understands language or music, for example, the properties of sound waves and the functioning of the ear become relevant because the ear is where auditory information enters the brain.

These encounters with basic science can be both a surprise and a shock to introductory students, who often come to the course without the necessary background. Our approach provides all the background students require to understand an introduction to brain science. We provide the philosophical and anatomical background needed to understand modern evolutionary theory, offer a short introduction to chemistry before describing the chemical activities of the brain, and briefly discuss electricity before exploring the brain's electrical activity. Because some of this information is very familiar to students with an extensive science background, we have separated some basic material from the main text into boxes called "The Basics." Readers already comfortable with the material can easily skip it, and less experienced readers can still review it.

Similarly, we review basic psychological facts such as behavioral development in Chapter 7 and the forms of learning and memory in Chapter 14. In these ways, students can tackle brain science with greater confidence. Students in social science disciplines often remark on the amount of biology and chemistry in the book, whereas an equal number of students in biological sciences remark on the amount of psychology. More than half the students enrolled in our Bachelor of Science in Neuroscience program have switched from biochemistry or psychology majors after taking this course. We must be doing something right!

Clinical Focus Maintained

We repeatedly emphasize that neuroscience is a human science—that everything in this book is relevant to our lives. Neuroscience helps us understand how we learn, how we develop, and how we can help people who suffer from sometimes deadly and destructive brain and behavioral disorders. We have found that emphasizing the clinical aspects of neuroscience is especially useful in motivating introductory students and in demonstrating to them the relevance of our field.

Clinical material helps to make neurobiology particularly relevant to those who are going on to careers in psychology, social work, or other professions related to mental health, as well as to students pursuing careers in the biological sciences. For this reason, we not only integrate clinical information throughout this textbook and feature it in Clinical Focus boxes but also expand on it in Chapter 16 at the end of the book.

As in the First Edition, the placement of some topics in *An Introduction to Brain and Behavior* is novel relative to traditional treatments. For example, we include brief descriptions of brain diseases close to discussions of basic processes that may be associated with the diseases. The integrated coverage of Parkinson's disease in Chapter 5 is an example.

This strategy helps first-time students repeatedly see the close links between what they are learning and real-life problems. The integration of real-life problems, especially behavioral disorders, into every chapter is further accomplished by our many Clinical Focus boxes. These boxes typically describe interesting case studies to highlight specific disorders that are related to a chapter's content.

In this new edition, the range of disorders we cover has expanded to more than 130 disorders, all indexed on page vi, opposite the Contents in Brief. Our capstone Chapter 16 expands on the nature of neuroscience research and the multidisciplinary treatment methods described in the preceding chapters' coverage of neurological and psychiatric disorders, including a discussion of causes and classifications of abnormal behavior. Certainly the most common questions from students who contact us, sometimes years after they have completed our courses, concern the major behavioral disorders that people are likely to encounter in their lifetimes that are reviewed in Chapter 16.

Another area of emphasis in this book is questions that relate to the biological basis of behavior. For us, the excitement of neuroscience is in understanding how the brain explains what we do, whether it is talking, sleeping, seeing, or learning. Readers will therefore find nearly as many illustrations about behavior as there are illustrations about the brain. This emphasis on explaining behavior's biological foundation is another reason that we have included both Clinical Focus and Research Focus boxes throughout the text.

Abundant Chapter Pedagogy

In addition to the innovative teaching devices just described, you will find numerous other in-text pedagogical aids. Every chapter begins with a chapter outline and a Focus box that draws students into the topic by connecting brain and behavior to relevant clinical or research experience. Within the chapters, end-of-section Reviews help students remember major points, summary illustrations help them visualize or review concepts, and terms are defined in the margins to reinforce their importance.

Each chapter ends with a Summary, consisting of topical key questions and their answers, and a list of Key Terms, which includes the page numbers on which the terms are defined. In contrast to the previous editions, Review Questions and For Further Thought can be found on the Companion Web Site at www.worthpublishers.com/kolb. Other material on the Web site will broaden students' understanding of chapter topics.

Superb Visual Reinforcement

Our most important learning aid, which you can see by simply paging through the book, continues to be an expansive and, we believe, exceptional set of illustrations. Hand in hand with our words, these illustrations describe and illuminate the world of the brain. In response to advice from instructors and readers, important anatomical diagrams have been enlarged to ease perusal.

The illustrations in every chapter are consistent and reinforce one another. For example, throughout the book, we consistently color-code diagrams that illustrate each aspect of the neuron and those that depict each structural region in the brain. We often include micrographic images to show what a particular neural structure actually looks like when viewed through a microscope. You will also find these images on our PowerPoint presentations and integrated as labeling exercises in our study guide and testing materials.

Teaching Through Metaphors, Examples, and Principles

We've developed this book in a style that students enjoy because, if a textbook is not enjoyed, it has little chance of teaching well. We heighten students' interest in the material they are reading through abundant use of metaphors and examples. Students read about patients whose brain injuries are sources of insight into brain function, and we examine car engines, robots, and prehistoric flutes for the same purpose. Frequent comparative biology examples and representative Comparative Focus boxes help students understand how much we humans have in common with creatures as far distant from us as sea slugs.

We also facilitate learning by reemphasizing main points and by distilling sets of principles about brain function that can serve as a framework to guide students' thinking. Thus, Chapter 2 concludes by introducing ten key principles that explain how the various parts of the nervous system work together. Chapter 14 summarizes seven guiding principles of neuroplasticity, a concept fundamental to understanding brain–behavior relationships. These principles form the basis of many discussions throughout the book, and marginal notes remind readers when they encounter the principles again.

Big-Picture Emphasis

One challenge in writing an introductory book on any topic is deciding what to include and what to exclude. We decided to organize discussions to focus on the bigger picture. A prime example is the discussion of general principles of nervous-system function introduced in Chapter 2 and echoed throughout the book. Although any set of principles may be a bit arbitrary, it nevertheless gives students a useful framework for understanding the brain's activities.

Similarly, in Chapters 7 through 16, we tackle behavioral topics in a more general way than most contemporary books do. For instance, in Chapter 12, we revisit the experiments and ideas of the 1960s as we try to understand why animals behave in the way they do, after which we consider emotional and motivated behaviors as diverse as eating and anxiety attacks in humans. Another example of our focus on the larger picture is the discussion of learning and memory in Chapter 14, which is presented alongside a discussion of recovery from brain damage.

We believe that this broader focus helps students grasp the larger problems that behavioral neuroscience is all about. Broadening our focus, however, has required us to leave out some details that might be found in other textbooks. But we think that discussions of larger problems and issues in the study of brain and behavior are of greater interest to students who are new to this field and are more likely to be remembered.

As in preceding editions, we have been selective in our citation of the truly massive literature on the brain and behavior because we believe that numerous citations can disrupt the flow of a textbook and distract students from the task of mastering what they read. We provide citations to classic works by including the names of the researchers and by mentioning where the research was performed. In areas where there is controversy or new breakthroughs, we also include detailed citations to current papers, citing papers from the years 2006 to 2009 when possible. A References section at the end of the book lists all the literature used in developing the book.

Supplements

Materials of various kinds, for students and instructors and thoroughly checked for accuracy, are available to supplement our book.

For Students

***New!* Online Neuroscience Tool Kit** The Neuroscience Tool Kit gives instructors and students access to a dozen, high-quality, interactive tutorials covering important brain and nervous-system structures and important functions (e.g., eating, language, movement). Clips from the Worth Neuroscience Video Series are integrated into the Tool Kit to provide a real-world context for the material discussed in the tutorials.

***Revised!* An Introduction to Brain and Behavior, Third Edition, Companion Web Site** Created by Joe Morrissey, Binghamton University, and available at www.worthpublishers.com/kolb, the companion Web site is an online educational setting for students that provides a virtual study guide, 24 hours a day, 7 days a week. Best of all, the resources are free and do not require any special access codes or passwords. Tools on the site include chapter outlines and summaries; learning objectives; annotated Web links; interactive flashcards; research exercises; selections from PsychSim 5.0 by Thomas Ludwig, Hope College; and online quizzes with immediate feedback and instructor notification.

For the instructor, the site offers online quizzing (with access to a quiz gradebook for viewing student results), a syllabus posting service, PowerPoint presentation files, electronic versions of illustrations in the book (through Worth Publishers' Image and Lecture Gallery), and links to additional tools including the WebCT E-pack and Blackboard course cartridge.

***Revised!* Study Guide** Written by Terrence J. Bazzett, State University of New York at Geneseo, the revised *Study Guide* is carefully crafted, with the use of a variety of engaging exercises and tools, to enhance student interest in the material presented in the textbook. To aid learning and retention, each chapter includes a review of key concepts and terms, practice tests, short-answer questions, illustrations for identification and labeling, Internet activities, and crossword puzzles. Students who have completed the tests and exercises can better organize and apply what they have studied.

Scientific American Explores the Hidden Mind: A Collector's Edition On request, this reader is free of charge when packaged with the textbook. In the past decade, we have learned more about the brain and how it creates the mind than we have in the entire preceding century. In a special collector's edition, *Scientific American* provides a must-have compilation of updated feature articles that explore and reveal the mysterious inner workings of our minds and brains.

Improving the Mind and Brain: A Scientific American Special Issue On request, this reader is free of charge when packaged with the textbook. This new single-topic issue from *Scientific American* magazine features the latest findings from the most distinguished researchers in the field.

***Ronald J. Comer's* Psychological Disorders: A Scientific American Reader** On request, this reader is free of charge when packaged with the textbook. Drawn from *Scientific American,* this full-color collection of articles enhances coverage of the disorders covered in the physiological psychology course. The selections have been hand-picked by Worth author and clinical psychologist Ronald Comer, who provides a preview and discussion questions for each article.

Scientific American: Clinical Neuroscience Reader On request, this reader is free of charge when packaged with the textbook. Drawn from *Scientific American* and *Scientific American Mind,* the reader offers 15 full-color articles on cutting-edge science in clinical neuroscience. The selections have been hand-picked by neuroscientists actively teaching the biological psychology course.

For Instructors

***Revised!* Instructor's Resources** Revised by Debora Baldwin, University of Tennessee, Knoxville, the resources include chapter-by-chapter learning objectives and chapter overviews, detailed lecture outlines, thorough chapter summaries, chapter key terms, in-class demonstrations and activities, springboard topics for discussion and debate, ideas for research and term-paper projects, homework assignments and exercises, and suggested readings for students (from journals and periodicals). Course-planning suggestions and a guide to videos and Internet resources also are included.

Assessment Tools

***Revised!* Test Bank** Prepared by Robert Sainsbury, University of Calgary, the revised Test Bank includes a battery of more than 1500 multiple-choice and short-answer test questions as well as diagram exercises tied to the major illustrations in each chapter. Each item is keyed to the page in the textbook on which the answer can be found. The wide variety of applied, conceptual, and factual questions have been thoroughly reviewed and edited for accuracy.

Diploma Computerized Test Bank The Test Bank is also available on a dual-platform CD-ROM. Instructors are guided step-by-step through the process of creating a test and can quickly add an unlimited number of questions, edit, scramble, or resequence items, and format a test. The accompanying gradebook enables them to record students' grades throughout the course and to sort student records and view detailed analyses of test items, curve tests, generate reports, and add weights to grades. The CD-ROM is the access point for Diploma Online Testing, allowing instructors to create and administer secure exams over a network and over the Internet, as well as Blackboard- and WebCT-formatted versions of each item in the Test Bank.

Online Quizzing—Powered by Questionmark This supplement is accessed through the companion Web site at www.worthpublishers.com/kolb. Instructors can easily and securely quiz students online by using prewritten multiple-choice questions for each chapter. Students receive instant feedback and can take the quizzes multiple times. Using the online quiz gradebook, instructors can view results by quiz, student, or question, or they can obtain weekly results by e-mail.

Presentation

Chapter Illustrations and Outline PowerPoint Slides Available at www.worthpublishers.com/kolb, these PowerPoint slides can be either used directly or customized to fit an instructor's needs. There are two prebuilt, customizable slide sets for each chapter of the book—one featuring chapter section headings and the other featuring all chapter figures, tables, and illustrations.

Worth Publishers' Image and Lecture Gallery Available at www.worthpublishers.com/ilg, the Image and Lecture Gallery is a convenient way to access electronic versions of lecture materials. Instructors can browse, search, and download illustrations from every book published by Worth Publishers, as well as prebuilt PowerPoint presentations that contain all chapter illustrations or chapter section headings in text form. Users can also create personal folders on a personalized home page for easy organization of the materials.

Video

Worth Publishers' Neuroscience Video Collection Edited by Ronald J. Comer, Princeton University, and available on VHS, DVD, and CD-ROM (in MPEG format), this video collection consists of dozens of video segments, each from 1 to 10 minutes in length. Clinical documentaries, television news reports, and archival footage constitute only a small part of the exciting source material for each video. Each segment has been created to provide illustrations that can help bring a lecture to life, engaging students and enabling them to apply neuroscience theory to the real world. This collection offers powerful and memorable demonstrations such as the links between the brain and behavior, neuroanatomical animations, cutting-edge neuroscience research, brain assessment in action, important historical events, interviews, and a wide sampling of brain phenomena and brain dysfunction. A special cluster of segments reveals the range of research methods used to study the brain. The accompanying Faculty Guide offers a description of each segment so that instructors can make informed decisions about how to best use the videos to enhance their lectures.

The Brain and Behavior Video Segments Available on VHS, this special collection includes targeted selections from the revised edition of the highly praised *Scientific American Frontiers* series. Hosted by Alan Alda, these video clips provide instructors with an excellent tool for showing how neuroscience research is conducted. The 10- to 12-minute modules focus on the work of Steve Sumi, Renée Baillargeon, Car Rosengren, Laura Pettito, Steven Pinker, Barbara Rothbaum, Bob Stickgold, Irene Pepperberg, Marc Hauser, Linda Bartoshuk, and Michael Gazzaniga.

The Mind—Video Teaching Modules, Second Edition Edited by Frank J. Vattano, Colorado State University, in consultation with Charles Brewer, Furman University, and David Myers, in association with WNET, these 35 brief, engaging video clips dramatically enhance and illustrate lecture topics and are available on VHS and DVD. This collection of short clips contains segments on language processing, infant cognitive development, heredity factors in alcoholism, and living without memory (featuring a dramatic interview with Clive Wearing). The accompanying Faculty Guide offers descriptions for each module and suggestions for incorporating them into class presentations.

The Brain—Video Teaching Modules, Second Edition Edited by Frank J. Vattano, Thomas L. Bennet, and Michelle Butler, all of Colorado State University, and available on VHS and DVD, this collection is a great source of classroom discussion ideas. It includes 32 short clips that provide vivid examples of brain development, function, disorders, and research. Individual segments range from 3 to 15 minutes in length, providing flexibility in highlighting specific topics. The accompanying Faculty Guide offers descriptions for each module and suggestions for incorporating them into class presentations.

Course Management Aids

Online Course Materials (WebCT and Blackboard) As a service for adopters who use WebCT or Blackboard course management systems, the various resources for this textbook are available in the appropriate format for their systems. The files can be customized to fit specific course needs or they can be used as is. Course outlines, prebuilt quizzes, links, and activities are included, eliminating hours of work for instructors. For more information, please visit our Web site at www.worthpublishers.com/mediaroom and click "course management."

Acknowledgments

As in the past with this text and *Fundamentals of Human Neuropsychology,* we have a special debt to Barbara Brooks, our development editor. She has learned how to extract the best from each of us by providing a firm guiding hand to our thinking. While we don't always initially agree with her (or our wives), we have learned to listen carefully and discover that she is usually right. Her sense of humor is infectious and her commitment to excellence has again left a strong imprint on the entire book. Thank you, Barbara.

We must sincerely thank the many people who contributed to the development of this edition. The staff at Worth and W. H. Freeman and Company are remarkable and make the revision a joy to do. We thank our sponsoring editor, Charles Linsmeier, our long-time project editor Georgia Lee Hadler, and our production manager Sarah Segal. Our manuscript editors Patricia Zimmerman and Penelope Hull ensured the clarity and consistency of the text. We also thank Vicki Tomaselli for the inviting and accessible design and Ted Szczepanski for coordinating the photo research and the various specialists who found photographs and other illustrative materials that we would not have found on our own. We remain indebted to the illustrators at Dragonfly Media and Northeastern Graphic for their excellent work in updating the artwork.

Our colleagues, too, helped in the development of this edition. We are especially indebted to those reviewers who provided extensive comments on selected chapters and illustrations: Chana Akins, *University of Kentucky;* Michael Anch, *Saint Louis University;* Maura Mitrushina, *California State University, Northridge;* Paul Wellman, *Texas A & M University;* and Ilsun White, *Morehead State University.* New chapters are always a challenge because they are inserted into an existing storyline and must fit in seamlessly. The new methods chapter had the additional challenge of taking what could read like a seed catalogue and making it engaging to readers. We therefore are indebted to Margaret G. Ruddy, *The College of New Jersey*, and Ann Voorhies, *University of Washington*, for providing extensive advice on Chapter 6.

We'd also like to thank those that contributed their thoughts to the Second Edition: Barry Anton, *University of Puget Sound;* R. Bruce Bolster, *University of Winnipeg;* James Canfield, *University of Washington;* Edward Castañeda, *University of New Mexico;* Darragh P. Devine, *University of Florida;* Kenneth Green, *California State University, Long Beach;* Eric Jackson, *University of New Mexico;* Sheri Mizumori, *University of Washington;* Michael Nelson, *University of Missouri, Rolla;* Joshua S. Rodefer, *University of Iowa;* Charlene Wages, *Francis Marion University;* Doug Wallace, *Northern Illinois University;* Patricia Wallace, *Northern Illinois University;* and Edie Woods, *Madonna University.* Sheri Mizumuri deserves special mention here for reading the entire manuscript for accuracy and providing fresh ideas that proved invaluable.

Finally, we must thank our tolerant wives for putting up with us during the revision of *An Introduction to Brain and Behavior* immediately after completing the revision of *Fundamentals of Human Neuropsychology.* We also thank our graduate students, technicians, and postdoctoral fellows, who kept our research programs moving forward when were engaged in revising the book.

Bryan Kolb and Ian Q. Whishaw

William West/AFP/Getty Images

CHAPTER 1

What Are the Origins of Brain and Behavior?

CLINICAL FOCUS 1-1

Living with Brain Injury

Fred Linge, a clinical psychologist with a degree in brain research, wrote this description 12 years after his injury occurred.

> In the second it took for my car to crash head-on, my life was permanently changed, and I became another statistic in what has been called "the silent epidemic."
>
> During the next months, my family and I began to understand something of the reality of the experience of head injury. I had begun the painful task of recognizing and accepting my physical, mental, and emotional deficits. I couldn't taste or smell. I couldn't read even the simplest sentence without forgetting the beginning before I got to the end. I had a hair-trigger temper that could ignite instantly into rage over the most trivial incident. . . .
>
> Two years after my injury, I wrote a short article: "What Does It Feel Like to Be Brain Damaged?" At that time, I was still intensely focusing on myself and my own struggle. (Every head-injured survivor I have met seems to go through this stage of narcissistic preoccupation, which creates a necessary shield to protect them from the painful realities of the situation until they have a chance to heal.) I had very little sense of anything beyond the material world and could only write about things that could be described in factual terms. I wrote, for example, about my various impairments and how I learned to compensate for them by a variety of methods.
>
> At this point in my life, I began to involve myself with other brain-damaged people. This came about in part after the publication of my article. To my surprise, it was reprinted in many different publications, copied, and handed out to thousands of survivors and families. It brought me an enormous outpouring of letters, phone calls, and personal visits that continue to this day. Many were struggling as I had struggled, with no diagnosis, no planning, no rehabilitation, and most of all, no hope. . . . The catastrophic effect of my injury was such that I was shattered and then remolded by the experience, and I emerged from it a profoundly different person with a different set of convictions, values, and priorities. (Linge, 1990)

Vinnie Malhortra/ABC (American Broadcasting Companies, Inc.)

Steve Fenn/ABC (American Broadcasting Companies, Inc.)

(*Left*) Bob Woodruff of ABC News in Iraq in 2006, speaking with U.S. soldiers moments before the vehicle from which he was reporting triggered a roadside bomb. Woodruff sustained a severe head injury and was subjected to brain surgery and kept in a medically induced coma for several weeks. In the months that followed, he relearned to walk and talk. (*Right*) A year after his surgery, he was able to resume limited work. Woodruff and his wife, Lee, have published an account of their lives and his recovery.

Neuroscience in the Twenty-First Century

In the years after his injury, Fred Linge made a journey. Before the car crash, he gave little thought to the relation between his brain and his behavior. At the end of his journey, adapting to his injured brain and behavior dominated his life.

The purpose of this book is to take you on a journey toward understanding the link between brain and behavior: how the brain is organized to create behavior. Evidence comes from studying three sources: (1) the evolution of brain and behavior in diverse animal species, (2) how the brain is related to behavior in normal people, and (3) how the brain changes in people who suffer brain damage or other brain abnormalities. The knowledge emerging from these lines of study is changing how we think about ourselves, how we structure education and our social interactions, and how we aid those with brain injury, disease, and disorder.

On our journey, we will learn how the brain stores and retrieves information, why we engage in the behaviors that we do, and how we are able to read the lines on this page and generate ideas and thoughts. The coming decades will be exciting times for the study of brain and behavior. They will offer an opportunity for us to broaden our understanding of what makes us human.

We will marvel at the potential for future discoveries. We will begin to understand how genes control neural activity. The development of new imaging techniques will reveal how our own brains think. One day, we will be able to arrest the progress of brain disease. One day, we will be able to stimulate processes of repair in malfunctioning brains. One day, we will be able to make artificial brains that extend the functions of our own brains. One day, we will understand ourselves and other animals.

Why Study Brain and Behavior?

The *brain* is a physical object, a living tissue, a body organ. *Behavior* is action, momentarily observable, but fleeting. Brain and behavior differ greatly but are linked. They have evolved together: one is responsible for the other, which is responsible for the other, which is responsible for the other, and so on and on. There are three reasons for linking the study of brain and behavior:

1. *A growing list of behavioral disorders can be explained and cured by understanding the brain.* Indeed, more than 2000 disorders may in some way be related to brain abnormalities. As indexed in the table that appears in the front matter on page vi, we detail relations between brain disorders and behavioral disorders in every chapter, especially in the "Focus" sections. A classic example of the control exerted by the brain on behavior is illustrated in Research Focus 1-2, "Recovering Consciousness."
2. *The brain is the most complex living organ on Earth and is found in many different groups of animals.* Students of the brain want to understand its place in the biological order of our planet. Chapter 1 describes the basic structure and evolution of the brain, especially the human brain, Chapter 2 overviews its structures and functions, and Chapters 3 through 5 describe the functioning of brain cells—the building blocks of the brains of all animals.
3. *How the brain produces both behavior and human consciousness is a major unanswered scientific question.* Scientists and students study the brain from the philosophical perspective of understanding humanity. Many chapters in this book touch on the relation between psychological questions related to brain and behavior and philosophical questions related to humanity. For example, in Chapters 14 and 15, we address questions related to how we become conscious, how we speak, and how we remember.

None of us can predict the ways in which knowledge about the brain and behavior may prove useful. A former psychology major wrote to tell us that she took our course because she was unable to register in a preferred course. She felt that, although our course was interesting, it was "biology and not psychology." After graduating and getting a job in a social agency, she has found to her delight that an understanding of the links between brain and behavior is a source of insight into the disorders of many of her clients and the treatment options for them.

What Is the Brain?

For his postgraduate research, our friend Harvey chose to study the electrical activity given off by the brain. He said that he wanted to live on as a brain in a bottle after his body died. He expected that his research would allow his bottled brain to communicate with others who could "read" his brain's electrical signals. Harvey mastered the

RESEARCH FOCUS 1-2

Recovering Consciousness

The patient, a 38-year-old man, had lingered in a **minimally conscious state** (MCS) for more than 6 years after an assault. He was occasionally able to communicate with single words, occasionally able to follow simple commands, but otherwise able to make few movements and could not feed himself despite 2 years of inpatient rehabilitation and four years in a nursing home.

This patient is one of approximately 1.4 million people each year in the United States who contend with **traumatic brain injury** (TBI), a wound to the brain that results from a blow to the head. Of them, as many as 100,000 may become comatose, and only as few as 20 percent recover consciousness.

Among the remaining patients, some are diagnosed as being in a **persistent vegetative state** (PVS), alive but unable to communicate or to function independently at even the most basic level, because they have such extensive brain damage that no recovery can be expected. Others, such as the assault victim heretofore described, are diagnosed as being in an MCS because behavioral observation and brain-imaging studies suggest that they do have a great deal of functional brain tissue remaining.

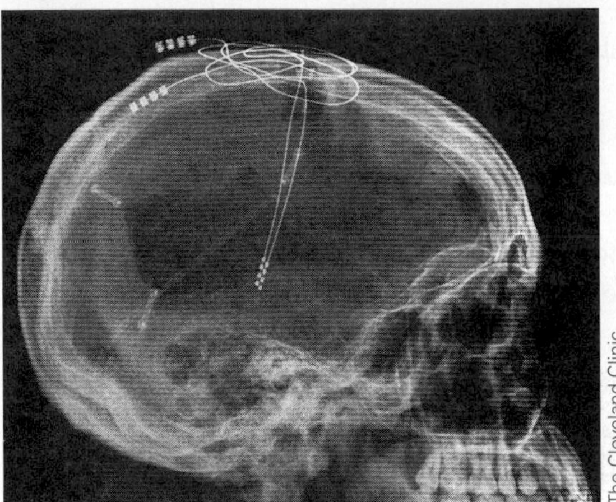
The Cleveland Clinic

X-ray of a human brain showing electrodes implanted in the thalamus for deep brain stimulation.

Nicholas Schiff and his colleagues (2007) reasoned that, if they could stimulate the brain of their MCS patient, they could enhance his level of consciousness and improve his behavioral abilities. As part of a **clinical trial** (an approved experiment directed toward developing a treatment), they implanted thin wire electrodes into his thalamus, a brainstem structure that normally arouses the cortex.

Through these electrodes, which are visible in the accompanying x-ray image, the investigators could electrically stimulate the thalamus with a low-voltage electrical current for 12 hours each day. The procedure is called **deep brain stimulation** (DBS). They found dramatic improvement in the patient's level of arousal and his ability to follow commands, and he was, for the first time, able to feed himself and swallow food. He could even interact with his caregivers and watch television, and he showed further improvement in response to rehabilitation.

Neuroscientists are experimenting with many techniques, including drug therapies, DBS, and transplantation of new brain cells to improve the function of people who have suffered TBI. As illustrated by the patient described here, even small improvements such as the ability to eat are huge steps in improving the function of a damaged brain.

techniques of brain electrical activity but failed in his objective, not only because the goal was technically impossible but also because he lacked a full understanding of what "brain" means.

Brain is the Anglo-Saxon word for the tissue found within the skull, and it is this tissue that Harvey wanted to put into a bottle. The brain comprises two major sets of structures. The *forebrain* is prominent in birds and mammals with big brains, including ourselves. The *brainstem* is the source of behavior in simpler animals such as fish, amphibians, and reptiles. The forebrain enfolds the brainstem and is responsible for most of our conscious behaviors. The brainstem is responsible for most of our unconscious behaviors.

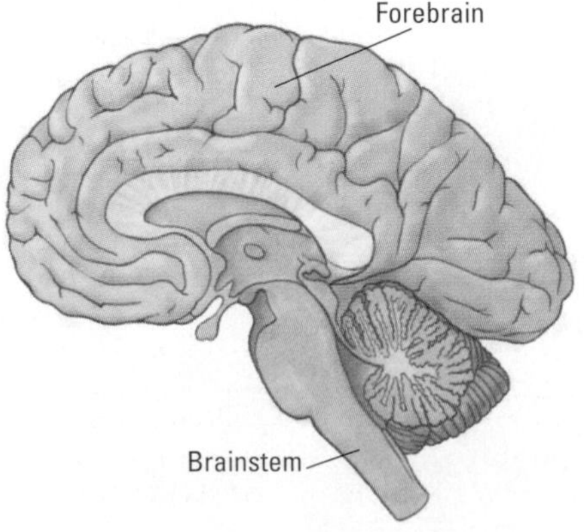

Major structural divisions of the human brain

The forebrain has two nearly symmetrical halves, called **hemispheres,** one on the left and one on the right. Just as your body is symmetrical, having two arms and two legs, so is your brain. **Figure 1-1** shows the left hemisphere of a typical human forebrain oriented in the upright human skull.

The entire outer layer of the forebrain consists of a thin, folded layer of nerve tissue, the **cerebral cortex,** detailed in the sectional view in Figure 1-1. The word *cortex,* Latin for the bark of a tree, is apt, considering the cortex's heavily folded surface and

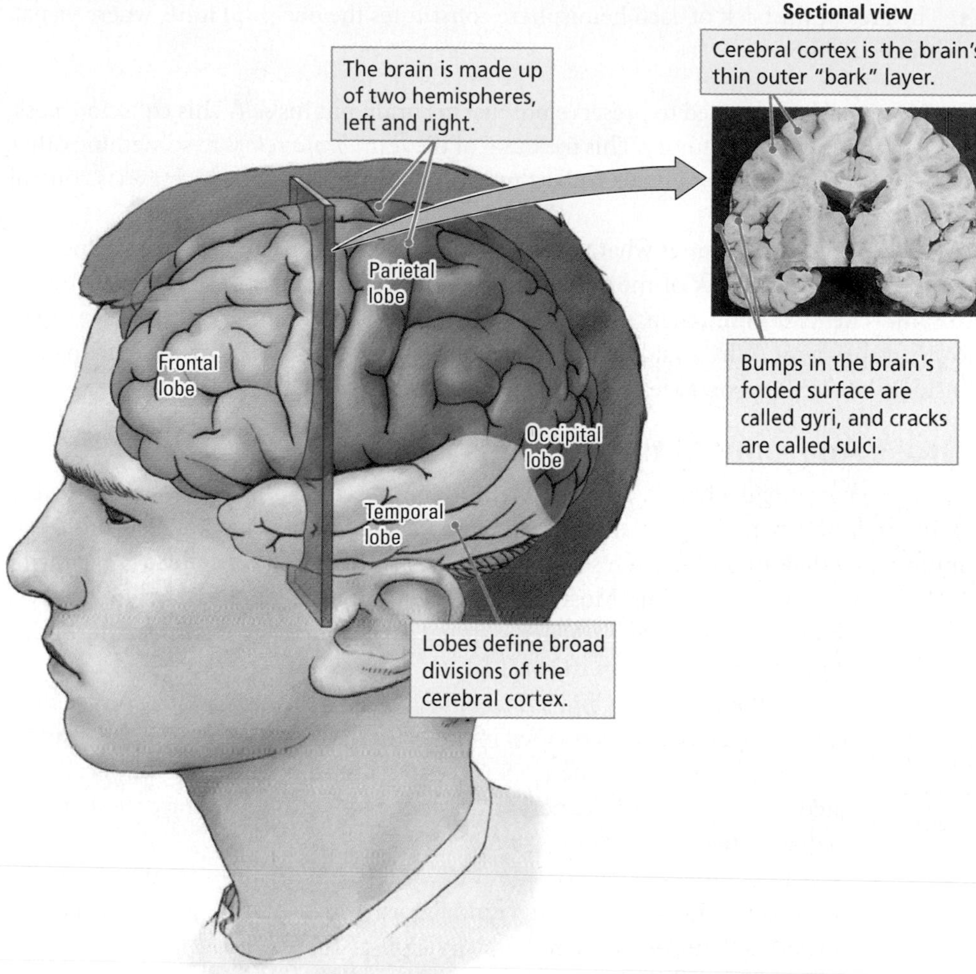
The brain is made up of two hemispheres, left and right.
Parietal lobe
Frontal lobe
Occipital lobe
Temporal lobe
Lobes define broad divisions of the cerebral cortex.
Sectional view
Cerebral cortex is the brain's thin outer "bark" layer.
Bumps in the brain's folded surface are called gyri, and cracks are called sulci.
Glauberman/Photo Researchers.

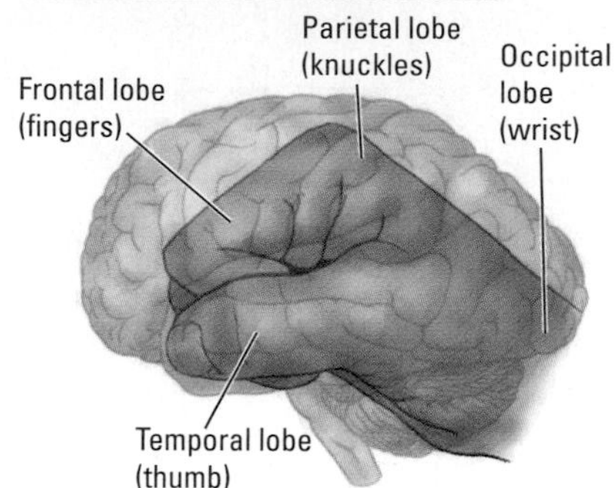
Your right hand, if made into a fist, represents the positions of the lobes of the left hemisphere of your brain.
Parietal lobe (knuckles)
Frontal lobe (fingers)
Occipital lobe (wrist)
Temporal lobe (thumb)

FIGURE 1-1 The Human Brain. The nearly symmetrical hemispheres of the brain, shown here as oriented in the head, are divided into four lobes. The surface of the brain, or cerebral cortex, is a thin sheet of nerve tissue that is folded many times to fit inside the skull, as shown in the sectional view. Your fist can serve as a guide to the orientation of the brain's left hemisphere and its lobes.

its location, covering most of the rest of the brain. Unlike the bark on a tree, the brain's folds are not random but rather demarcate its functional zones.

If you make a fist with your right hand and hold it up, the fist can represent the positions of the forebrain's broad divisions, or *lobes,* within the skull, as diagrammed in Figure 1-1. Each lobe is named for the skull bone that it lies beneath:

- The forward-pointing **temporal lobe** is located at the side of the brain, approximately the same place as the thumb on your upraised fist. The temporal lobe functions in connection with hearing and language and musical abilities.
- Immediately above your thumbnail, your fingers correspond to the location of the **frontal lobe,** often characterized as performing the brain's "executive" functions, such as decision making.
- The **parietal lobe** is located at the top of the skull, behind the frontal lobe and above the temporal lobe. Parietal functions include directing our movements toward a goal or to perform a task, such as grasping an object.

Minimally conscious state (MCS) Condition in which a person can display some rudimentary behaviors, such as smiling, or utter a few words but is otherwise not conscious.
Traumatic brain injury (TBI) Wound to the brain that results from a blow to the head.
Persistent vegetative state (PVS) Condition in which a person is alive but unable to communicate or to function independently at even the most basic level.
Clinical trial Approved experiment directed toward developing a treatment.
Deep brain stimulation (DBS) Neurosurgery in which electrodes implanted in the brain stimulate a targeted area with a low-voltage electrical current to facilitate behavior.
Hemisphere Literally, half a sphere, referring to one side of the cerebral cortex or one side of the cerebellum.
Cerebral cortex Outer layer of brain-tissue surface composed of neurons; the human cerebral cortex is heavily folded.
Temporal lobe Cortex that functions in connection with hearing, language, and musical abilities and lies below the lateral fissure, beneath the temporal bone at the side of the skull.
Frontal lobe Cerebral cortex often generally characterized as performing the brain's "executive" functions, such as decision making, lying anterior to the central sulcus and beneath the frontal bone of the skull.
Parietal lobe Cerebral cortex that functions to direct movements toward a goal or to perform a task, such as grasping an object, lying posterior to the central sulcus and beneath the parietal bone at the top of the skull.

- The area at the back of each hemisphere constitutes the **occipital lobe,** where visual processing begins.

Harvey clearly wanted to preserve not just his brain but his *self*—his consciousness, his language, and his memory. This meaning of the term *brain* refers to something other than the organ found inside the skull. It refers to the brain as that which exerts control over behavior.

This meaning of brain is what we intend when we talk of someone smart being "the brain" or when we speak of the computer that guides a spacecraft as being the vessel's "brain." The term brain, then, signifies both the organ itself and the fact that this organ controls behavior. Why could Harvey not manage to preserve his control-exerting self inside a bottle? Read on to learn one answer to this question.

Gross Anatomy of the Nervous System

The nervous system, charted in **Figure 1-2,** is composed of cells, as is the rest of the body, and these nerve cells, or **neurons,** most directly control behavior. Neurons communicate with one another, with sensory receptors on the body, with muscles, and with internal body organs. Most of the connections between the brain and the rest of the body are made through the **spinal cord,** which descends from the brainstem through a canal in the backbone.

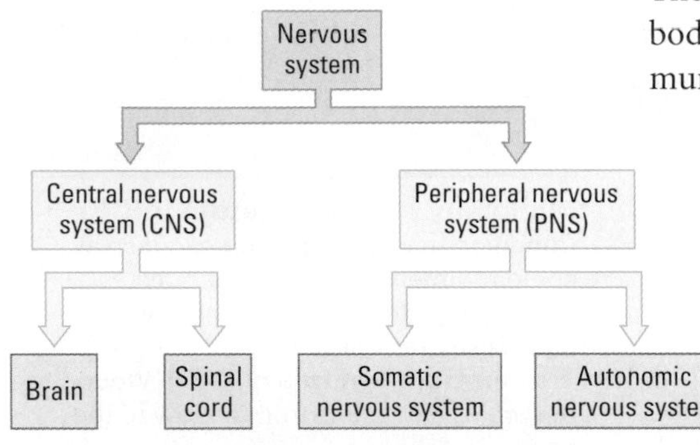

FIGURE 1-2 Anatomical Divisions of the Human Nervous System.

Together, the brain and spinal cord make up the **central nervous system** (CNS). Thus the CNS is encased in bone, the brain by the skull, and the spinal cord by the vertebrae. The CNS is "central" both because it is physically located to be the core of the nervous system and because it is the core structure mediating behavior.

All the processes radiating out beyond the brain and spinal cord as well as all the neurons outside the brain and spinal cord constitute the **peripheral nervous system** (PNS). Neurons in the *somatic* division of the PNS connect to receptors on the body's surface and on its muscles to gather sensory information for the CNS and to convey information from the CNS to move muscles of the face, body, and limbs. Similarly, the *autonomic* division of the PNS enables the CNS to govern the workings of your body's internal organs—such as the beating of your heart, the contractions of your stomach, and the movement of your diaphragm to inflate and deflate your lungs.

To return to Harvey's brain-in-a-bottle experiment, the effect of placing the brain or even the entire CNS in a bottle would be to separate it from the PNS and thus to separate it from the sensations and movements mediated by the PNS. How would the brain function without sensory information and without the ability to produce movement?

In the 1920s, Edmond Jacobson wondered what would happen if our muscles completely stopped moving, a question relevant to Harvey's experiment. Jacobson believed that, even when we think we are entirely motionless, we still make subliminal movements related to our thoughts. The muscles of the larynx subliminally move when we "think in words," for instance, and we make subliminal movements of our eyes when we imagine or visualize a scene. So, in Jacobson's experiment, people practiced "total" relaxation and were later asked what the experience was like. They reported a condition of "mental emptiness," as if the brain had gone blank (Jacobson, 1932).

In 1957, Woodburn Heron investigated the effects of sensory deprivation, including feedback from movement, by having each subject lie on a bed in a bare, soundproof room and remain completely still. Tubes covered the subjects' arms so that they had no sense of touch, and translucent goggles cut off their vision. The subjects reported that the experience was extremely unpleasant, not just because of the social isolation

Occipital lobe Cerebral cortex where visual processing begins, lying at the back of the brain and beneath the occipital bone.
Neuron A specialized "nerve cell" engaged in information processing.
Spinal cord Part of the central nervous system encased within the vertebrae (spinal column) that provides most of the connections between the brain and the rest of the body.
Central nervous system (CNS) The brain and spinal cord that together mediate behavior.
Peripheral nervous system (PNS) All the neurons in the body located outside the brain and spinal cord; provides sensory and motor connections to and from the central nervous system.
Embodied consciousness Hypothesis that the movements that we make and those that we perceive in others are essential features of our conscious behavior.

but also because they lost their normal focus in this situation. Some subjects even hallucinated, as if their brains were somehow trying to create the sensory experiences that they suddenly lacked. Most asked to be released from the study before it ended.

One line of research and philosophical argument, called **embodied consciousness,** proposes that the movements that we make and those that we perceive in others are central to consciousness (Prinz, 2008). That is, we understand one another not only by listening to words but also by observing gestures and other body language, and we think not only with silent language but also with overt gestures and body language.

Findings from these lines of research suggest that the CNS needs ongoing sensory stimulation from the world and from its own body's movement if it is to maintain its intelligent activity. Thus, when we use the term brain to mean an intelligent, functioning organ, we should refer to an active brain that is connected to the rest of the nervous system and can therefore produce behavior. Unfortunately for Harvey, that a brain in a bottle, disconnected from the PNS, would continue to function normally seems unlikely.

What Is Behavior?

Irenäus Eibl-Eibesfeldt began his textbook *Ethology: The Biology of Behavior,* published in 1970, with the following definition: "Behavior consists of patterns in time." These patterns can be made up of movements, vocalizations, or changes in appearance, such as the facial movements associated with smiling. The expression "patterns in time" includes thinking. Although we cannot directly observe someone's thoughts, techniques exist for monitoring changes in the brain's electrical and biochemical activity that may be associated with thought. So, thinking, too, is a behavior that forms patterns in time.

The behavioral patterns of some animals are relatively fixed: most of their behaviors are inherited ways of responding. The behavioral patterns of other animals are both inherited and learned. If all members of a species display the same behavior under the same circumstances, that species has probably inherited a nervous system evolved to produce that relatively fixed behavioral pattern automatically. In contrast, if each member of a species displays a somewhat different response in a similar situation, that species has inherited a much more flexible nervous system that is capable of changes in behavior due to learning.

An example of the difference between a relatively fixed behavioral pattern and a more flexible one is the contrast in the eating behavior of two different animal species—crossbills and roof rats—illustrated in **Figure 1-3.** A crossbill is a bird with a beak that seems to be awkwardly crossed at the tips; yet this beak is exquisitely evolved to eat certain kinds of pine cones. If the shape of a crossbill's beak is changed even slightly, the bird is unable to eat preferred pine cones until its beak grows back.

When eating these pine cones, crossbills use largely fixed behavioral patterns that are inherited and do not require much modification through learning. Roof rats, in contrast, are rodents with sharp incisor teeth that appear to have evolved to cut into anything. But roof rats can eat pine cones efficiently only if they are taught to do so by an experienced mother.

The mixture of inherited and learned behaviors varies considerably in different species. Generally, animals with smaller, simpler nervous systems have a narrow range of behaviors dependent on *heredity.* Animals with complex nervous systems have more behavioral options that depend on *learning.* We humans believe that we are the animal species with the most-complex nervous system and the greatest capacity for learning new responses.

Species that have evolved greater complexity have not thrown away their simpler nervous systems. Rather, complexity emerges in part because new nervous-system structures are added to old ones. For this reason, although human behavior depends mostly

A crossbill's beak is specifically designed to open pine cones. This behavior is innate.

A baby roof rat must learn from its mother how to eat pine cones. This behavior is learned.

FIGURE 1-3 Innate and Learned Behaviors. Some animal behaviors are largely innate and fixed (*top*), whereas others are largely learned (*bottom*). This learning is a form of cultural transmission. Adapted from (*top*) *The Beak of the Finch* (p. 183), by J. Weiner, 1995, New York: Vintage; and from (*bottom*) "Cultural Transmission in the Black Rat: Pinecone Feeding," by J. Terkel, 1995, *Advances in the Study of Behavior, 24,* p. 122.

on learning, we, like other species, still possess many inherited ways of responding. The sucking response of a newborn infant is an inherited eating pattern in humans, for example.

REVIEW: Neuroscience in the Twenty-First Century

- ✔ Traumatic brain injury can be caused by a blow to the head. After severe brain injury, the brain demonstrates a remarkable ability to recover; but, after either mild or severe injury, a person can be left with a permanent disability that prevents full recovery to former levels of function.
- ✔ Brain and behavior are linked, and behavioral disorders can be explained and possibly cured by understanding the brain. Understanding how the brain produces both behavior and consciousness remains a major unanswered scientific question. Students of the brain want to understand its place in the biological order of our planet.
- ✔ The human brain consists of a forebrain and a brainstem connected to the spinal cord. The forebrain has nearly symmetrical left and right cerebral hemispheres, each with a folded outer layer called the cortex, which is divided into four lobes: temporal, frontal, parietal, and occipital.
- ✔ The brain and spinal cord together make up the central nervous system. All the nerve fibers radiating out beyond the brain and spinal cord as well as all the neurons outside the brain and spinal cord form the peripheral nervous system.
- ✔ A simple definition of behavior is any kind of movement in a living organism. Although all behaviors have both a cause and a function, they vary in complexity and in the degree to which they are inherited, or automatic, and the degree to which they depend on learning.

Perspectives on Brain and Behavior

Returning to the central question in the study of brain and behavior—how the two are related—we now survey three classic theories about the cause of behavior: mentalism, dualism, and materialism. You will recognize familiar "common sense" ideas that you might have about behavior as being derived from one or another of these long-standing perspectives.

E. Lessing/Art Resource, New York

François Gerard, *Psyche and Cupid* (1798).

Aristotle and Mentalism

The hypothesis that the mind (or soul or psyche) is responsible for behavior can be traced back more than 2000 years to ancient Greece. In classical mythology, Psyche was a mortal who became the wife of the young god Cupid. Venus, Cupid's mother, opposed his marriage to a mortal, and so she harassed Psyche with countless, almost impossible tasks.

Psyche performed the tasks with such dedication, intelligence, and compassion that she was made immortal, thus removing Venus's objection to her. The ancient Greek philosopher Aristotle was alluding to this story when he suggested that all human intellectual functions are produced by a person's **psyche.** The psyche, Aristotle argued, is responsible for life, and its departure from the body results in death.

Aristotle's account of behavior had no role for the brain, which Aristotle thought existed to cool the blood. To him, the nonmaterial psyche was responsible for human thoughts, perceptions, and emotions and for such processes as imagination, opinion, desire, pleasure, pain, memory, and reason. The psyche was an entity independent of the body. Aristotle's view that a nonmaterial psyche governs our behavior was adopted by Christianity in its concept of the soul and has been widely disseminated throughout the world.

Mind is an Anglo-Saxon word for memory and, when "psyche" was translated into English, it became mind. The philosophical position that a person's mind, or psyche, is responsible for behavior is called **mentalism,** meaning "of the mind."

Because the mind is nonmaterial, it cannot be studied with scientific methods. Just the same, mentalism has influenced modern behavioral science because many terms—*sensation, perception, attention, imagination, emotion, motivation, memory,* and *volition* among them—remain in use for patterns of behavior today, and matters related to these behaviors are the focus of contemporary research in psychology.

Psyche Synonym for mind, an entity once proposed to be the source of human behavior.
Mind Proposed nonmaterial entity responsible for intelligence, attention, awareness, and consciousness.
Mentalism Of the mind; an explanation of behavior as a function of the nonmaterial mind.
Dualism Philosophical position that holds that both a nonmaterial mind and the material body contribute to behavior.
Mind–body problem Quandary of explaining a nonmaterial mind in command of a material body.

Descartes and Dualism

In the first book on brain and behavior, René Descartes (1596–1650), a French physiologist, mathematician, and philosopher, proposed a new explanation of behavior in which the brain played an important role. Descartes placed the seat of the mind in the brain and linked the mind to the body. In the first sentence of *Treatise on Man* (1664), he stated that mind and body "must be joined and united to constitute people. . . ."

To Descartes, most of the activities of the body and brain, such as motion, digestion, and breathing, could be explained by mechanical and physical principles. The nonmaterial mind, on the other hand, is responsible for rational behavior. Descartes's proposal that an entity called the mind directs a machine called the body was the first serious attempt to explain the role of the brain in controlling behavior.

The philosophical position that behavior is controlled by two entities, a mind and a body, is called **dualism.** Descartes's theory posed the problem of how a nonmaterial mind and a physical brain might interact, and it has come to be called the **mind–body problem.** To Descartes, the mind receives information from the body through the brain. The mind also directs the body through the brain. The rational mind, then, depends on the brain both for information and to control behavior.

Descartes was also aware of the many new machines being built, including gears, clocks, and water wheels. He saw mechanical gadgets on public display in parks. In the water gardens in Paris, one device caused a hidden statue to approach and spray water when an unsuspecting stroller walked past it. The statue's actions were triggered when the person stepped on a pedal hidden in the sidewalk. Influenced by these mechanical devices, Descartes developed mechanical principles to explain the functions of the body.

Descartes developed a mechanical explanation of how the mind produces movement. He suggested that the mind resides in a small structure in the center of the brain, the pineal body (now called the *pineal gland*), which is located beside fluid-filled cavities called *ventricles* **(Figure 1-4).** According to Descartes, the pineal body directs fluid from the ventricles through nerves and into muscles. When the fluid expands those muscles, the body moves.

FIGURE 1-4 Dualist Hypothesis. To explain how the mind controls the body, Descartes suggested that the mind resides in the pineal gland, where it directs the flow of fluid through the ventricles and into the body to investigate objects and to become informed about their properties.

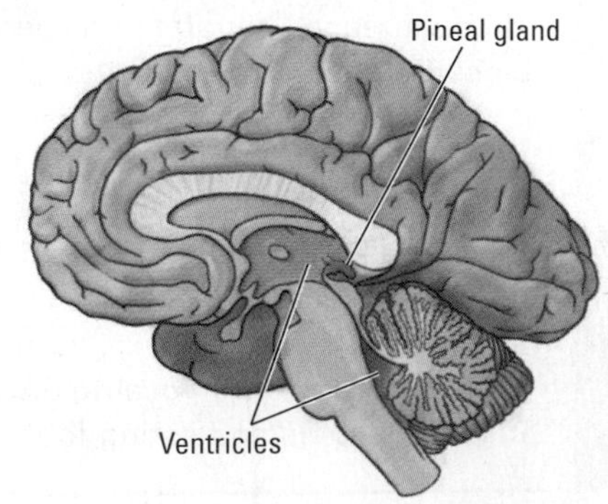

Many problems in detail and logic corrupt Descartes's theory. It quickly became apparent to scientists that people who have damaged pineal bodies or even no pineal body at all still display normal intelligent behavior. Today, we understand that the pineal gland plays a role in behavior related to biological rhythms, but it does not govern human behavior. We now know that fluid is not pumped from the brain into muscles when they contract. Placing an arm in a bucket of water and contracting the arm's muscles does not cause the water level in the bucket to rise, as it should if the volume of the muscle increased because fluid had been pumped into it. We now also know that there is no obvious way that a nonmaterial entity can influence the body, because doing so requires the spontaneous creation of energy, which violates the physical law of conservation of matter and energy.

Nevertheless, Descartes proposed scientific tests of his theory. To determine if an organism possesses a mind, Descartes proposed the language test and the action test. To pass the language test, an organism must use language to describe and reason about things that are not physically present. The action test requires the organism to display behavior that is based on reasoning and is not just an automatic response to a particular situation.

Descartes proposed that nonhuman animals and machines would be unable to pass the tests. Experimental research is casting doubt on these assumptions. For example, studies of language in apes and other animals are partly intended to find out whether animals can describe and reason about things that are not present and so pass the language and action tests. Comparative Focus 1-3, "The Speaking Brain," summarizes a contemporary approach to studying language in animals. Computer specialists are also trying to create robots with artificial intelligence—robots that think and remember.

Descartes's theory of mind led to a number of unfortunate results. On the basis of it, some people argued that young children and the insane must lack minds, because they often fail to reason appropriately. We still use the expression "he's lost his mind" to describe someone who is "mentally ill." Some proponents of this view also reasoned that, if someone lacked a mind, that person was simply a machine not due normal

COMPARATIVE FOCUS 1-3

The Speaking Brain

Language is such a striking characteristic of our species that it was once thought to be a trait unique to humans. Nevertheless, evolutionary theory predicts that language is unlikely to have appeared full blown in modern humans. Language does have antecedents in other species. Many species lacking a cerebral cortex, including fish and frogs, are capable of elaborate vocalizations, and vocalization is still more elaborate in species having a cerebral cortex, such as birds, whales, and primates. But can nonhuman animals speak?

In 1969, Beatrice and Alan Gardner taught a version of American Sign Language to a chimpanzee named Washoe, showing that nonverbal forms of language might have preceded verbal language. Sue Savage-Rumbaugh and her coworkers (1999) then taught a pygmy chimpanzee named Malatta a symbolic language called Yerkish. (The pygmy chimpanzee, or *bonobo,* is a species thought to be an even closer relative of humans than the common chimp.)

Malatta and her son Kanzi were caught in the wild, and Kanzi accompanied his mother to class. It turned out that, even though he was not specifically trained, Kanzi learned more Yerkish than his mother did. Remarkably, Kanzi also displayed clear evidence of understanding complex human speech.

While recording vocalizations made by Kanzi interacting with people and eating food, Jared Taglialatela and coworkers (2003, 2008) found that Kanzi made many sounds associated with their meanings, or semantic context. For example, various peeps were associated with specific foods. The research group also found that chimps use a "raspberry" or "extended grunt" sound in a specific context to attract the attention of others, including people.

Great Ape Trust of Iowa

Jared Taglialatela and Kanzi.

Imaging of blood flow in the brain associated with the use of "chimpanzeeish" indicates that the same frontal cortex regions that are activated when humans speak are also activated when the chimpanzees speak. These findings strongly support the idea that language has antecedents in nonhuman animals.

respect or kindness. Cruel treatment of animals, children, and the mentally ill has been justified by Descartes's theory for centuries. It is unlikely that Descartes himself intended these interpretations. He was reportedly very kind to his own dog, Monsieur Grat.

Darwin and Materialism

By the mid–nineteenth century, another theory of brain and behavior was emerging. This theory was the perspective of **materialism**—the idea that rational behavior can be fully explained by the workings of the brain and the rest of the nervous system, without any need to refer to an immaterial mind. This perspective became prominent when supported scientifically by the evolutionary theories of Alfred Russel Wallace and Charles Darwin.

Wallace and Darwin independently arrived at the same conclusion—the idea that all living things are related. Each outlined this view in papers presented at the Linnaean Society of London in July 1858. Darwin further elaborated on the topic in his book *On the Origin of Species by Means of Natural Selection,* published in 1859. This book presented a wealth of supporting detail, which is why Darwin is regarded as the founder of modern evolutionary theory.

Both Darwin and Wallace had looked carefully at the structure of animals and at animal behavior. Despite the diversity of living animals, both men were struck by the myriad characteristics common to so many species. For example, the skeleton, muscles, and body parts of humans, monkeys, and other mammals are remarkably similar.

Such observations led first to the idea that living organisms must be related, an idea widely held even before Wallace and Darwin. But, more importantly, these same observations led to Darwin's explanation of how the great diversity in the biological world could have evolved from common ancestry. Darwin proposed that animals have traits in common because these traits are passed from parents to their offspring.

Natural selection is Darwin's theory for explaining how new species evolve and existing species change over time. A **species** is a group of organisms that can breed among themselves but not with members of other species. Individual organisms within any species vary extensively in their characteristics *(phenotypes),* with no two members of the species being exactly alike. Some are big, some are small, some are fat, some are fast, some are lightly colored, and some have large teeth.

Those individual organisms whose characteristics best help them to survive in their environment are likely to leave more offspring than are less-fit members. This unequal ability of individual members to survive and reproduce leads to a gradual change in a species' population over time, with characteristics favorable for survival in a particular habitat becoming more prevalent in succeeding generations. Natural selection is nature's equivalent of the artificial selection practiced by plant and animal breeders to produce organisms with desirable traits.

Neither Darwin nor Wallace understood the basis of the great variation in plant and animal species. The underlying principles of that variation were discovered by another scientist, Gregor Mendel (a nineteenth-century monk), beginning about 1857, through experiments that he did with pea plants in his monastery garden. Mendel deduced that heritable factors, which we now call *genes,* are related to the various physical traits displayed by the species.

Members of a species that have a particular gene or combination of genes *(genotype)* will express that trait. If the genes for a trait are passed on to offspring, the offspring also will have the same trait. New traits appear because new gene combinations are inherited from parents, because existing genes change or mutate, because suppressed genes are reexpressed, because expressed genes are suppressed, or because genes or parts of genes are deleted or duplicated.

Materialism Philosophical position that holds that behavior can be explained as a function of the nervous system without explanatory recourse to the mind.

Natural selection Darwin's theory for explaining how new species evolve and how existing species change over time. Differential success in the reproduction of different characteristics (phenotypes) results from the interaction of organisms with their environment.

Species Group of organisms that can interbreed.

Thus, the unequal ability of individual organisms to survive and reproduce is related to the different genes that they inherit from their parents and pass on to their offspring. By the same token, similar characteristics within or between species are usually due to similar genes. For instance, genes that produce the nervous system in different kinds of animal species tend to be very similar.

Darwin's theory of natural selection has three important implications for the study of the brain and behavior:

1. *Because all animal species are related, so too must be their brains.* Today, brain researchers study animals as different as slugs, fruit flies, rats, and monkeys, knowing that they can extend their findings to human beings.
2. *Because all species of animals are related, so too must be their behavior.* Darwin was particularly interested in this subject. In his book *On the Expression of the Emotions in Man and Animals,* he argued that emotional expressions are similar in humans and other animals because we inherited these expressions from a common ancestor. Evidence for such inheritance is illustrated in **Figure 1-5.** That people in different parts of the world display the same behavior suggests that the trait is inherited rather than learned.
3. *Both the brain and behavior changed bit by bit in animals that evolved to greater complexity, as humans obviously did.* In the next section, we trace the steps in which the human nervous system evolved from a simple netlike arrangement, to a spinal cord connected to that net, and finally to a nervous system with a brain that controls behavior.

Evidence that the brain controls behavior is today so strong that the idea has the status of a theory: the *brain theory.* Donald O. Hebb in his influential book *The Organization of Behavior,* published in 1949, described the brain theory in a folksy manner:

> Modern psychology takes completely for granted that behavior and neural function are perfectly correlated, that one is completely caused by the other. There is no separate soul or life force to stick a finger into the brain now and then and make neural cells do what they would not otherwise. (Hebb, 1949, p. iii)

Some people question the theory that only the brain is responsible for behavior because they think it denies religion. The theory, however, is neutral with respect to religious beliefs. Fred Linge, whose experience of brain trauma begins this chapter, has strong religious beliefs, as do the other members of his family. They used their reli-

FIGURE 1-5 An Inherited Behavior. People from all parts of the world display the same emotional expressions that they also recognize in others, as is illustrated by these smiles. This evidence supports Darwin's suggestion that emotional expression is inherited.

J. Tisne/Stone Images

O. Benn/Stone Images

A. Cassidy/Stone Images

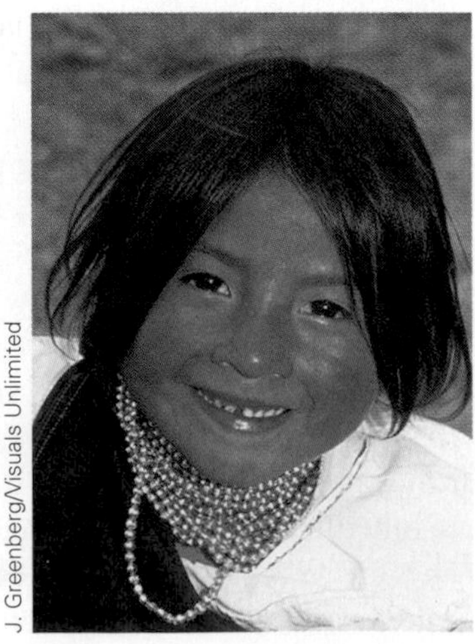
J. Greenberg/Visuals Unlimited

gious strength to aid in his recovery. Yet, despite their religious beliefs, they realize that Linge's brain injury was the cause of his change in behavior and that the process of recovery that his brain underwent is the cause of his restored health. Similarly, many behavioral scientists hold deep religious beliefs and see no contradiction between those beliefs and their use of the scientific method to examine the relations between the brain and behavior.

REVIEW: Perspectives on Brain and Behavior

- ✔ Mentalism is the view that behavior is a product of an intangible entity called the mind (psyche); the brain has little importance.
- ✔ Dualism is the notion that the immaterial mind acts through the material brain to produce language and rational behavior, whereas the brain alone is responsible for the "lower" kinds of actions that we have in common with other animal species.
- ✔ Materialism, the view that brain function fully accounts for all behavior, language and reasoning included, guides contemporary research on the brain and behavior. Support for the materialistic view comes from the study of natural selection—the theory that behaviors such as human language evolved from the simpler language abilities of human ancestors.

Evolution of Brain and Behavior

The study of living organisms shows that nervous systems or brains are not common to all and that nervous systems and behavior built up and changed bit by bit as animals evolved. We trace the evolution of the human brain and behavior by describing (1) those animals that first developed a nervous system and muscles with which to move and (2) how the nervous system became more complex as the brain evolved to mediate complex behavior.

The popular interpretation of human evolution is that we are descended from apes. Actually, apes are not our ancestors, although we are related to them through a **common ancestor,** a forebearer from which two or more lineages or family groups arise. To demonstrate the difference, consider the following story.

Two people named Joan Campbell are introduced at a party, and their names afford a good opening for a conversation. Although both belong to the Campbell lineage (family line), one Joan is not descended from the other. The two women live in different parts of North America, one in Texas and the other in Ontario, and both of their families have been in those locations for many generations.

Nevertheless, after comparing family histories, the two Joans discover that they have ancestors in common. The Texas Campbells are descended from Jeeves Campbell, brother of Matthew Campbell, from whom the Ontario Campbells are descended. Jeeves and Matthew had both boarded the same fur-trading ship when it stopped for water in the Orkney Islands north of Scotland before sailing to North America in colonial times.

The Joan Campbells' common ancestors, then, were the mother and father of Jeeves and Matthew. Both the Texas and the Ontario Campbell family lines are descended from this same man and woman. If the two Joan Campbells were to compare their genes, they would find similarities that correspond to their common lineage.

In much the same way, humans and apes are descended from common ancestors. But, unlike the Joan Campbells, we do not know who those distant relatives were. By comparing the brain and behavioral characteristics of humans and related animals and

Common ancestor Forebearer from which two or more lineages or family groups arise and so is ancestral to both groups.

Cladogram Phylogenetic tree that branches repeatedly, suggesting a taxonomy of organisms based on the time sequence in which evolutionary branches arise.
Nerve net Simple nervous system that has no brain or spinal cord but consists of neurons that receive sensory information and connect directly to other neurons that move muscles.

by comparing their genes, however, scientists are tracing our lineage back farther and farther to piece together the story of our origins. In the following sections, we trace some of the main evolutionary events that led to human brains and human behavior.

Origin of Brain Cells and Brains

Earth formed about 4.5 billion years ago, and the first life forms arose about a billion years later. About 700 million years ago, animals evolved the first brain cells, and, by 250 million years ago, the first brain had evolved. A humanlike brain first developed only about 6 million years ago, and our modern human brain has been around for only the past 200,000 years. Although life evolved very early in the history of our planet, brain cells and the brain evolved only recently, and large complex brains, such as ours, appeared only an eye blink ago in evolutionary terms.

Classification of Life

Taxonomy, the branch of biology concerned with naming and classifying species, groups organisms according to their common characteristics and their relationships to one another. As shown in the top rows of **Figure 1-6,** which illustrates the human

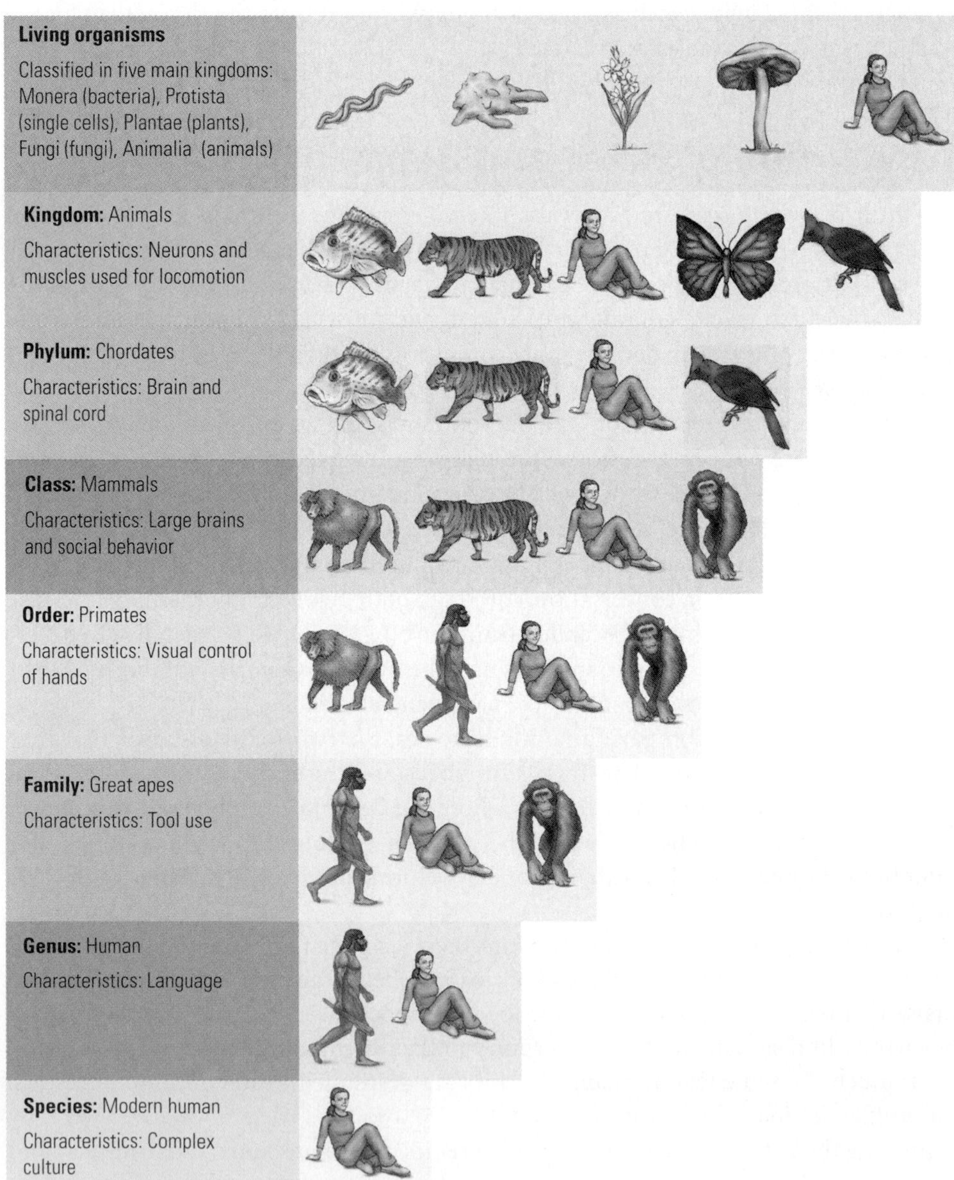

FIGURE 1-6 Taxonomy of Modern Humans. Taxonomy classifies comprehensive groups of living organisms into increasingly specific subordinate groups. Modern humans are the only surviving species of the genus that includes numerous extinct species of humanlike animals.

lineage, the broadest unit of classification is a kingdom, with more subordinate groups being phylum, class, order, family, genus, and species. We humans belong to the animal kingdom, the chordate phylum, the mammalian class, the primate order, the great ape family, the *Homo* genus, and the *sapiens* species. Animals are usually identified by their genus and species name. So we humans are called *Homo sapiens,* meaning "wise humans."

This taxonomic hierarchy is useful in helping us trace the evolution of brain cells and the brain. Brain cells and muscles first evolved in animals, allowing them to move. The brain as an organ first evolved in chordates, allowing more-complex movements. A large brain with many different functions first evolved in the ancestor of birds and mammals, and a brain capable of written language and complex culture first evolved in the primate *Homo sapiens.* Although complex brains and patterns of behavior have evolved in the human lineage, large brains and complex behaviors have also evolved in some other lineages. Highly social dolphins have large brains, and many birds, such as the Galápagos woodpecker finch and the crow have big brains and make and use tools.

Gavin Hunt

Crows are among the animals that make and use tools, often, as here, to obtain food.

Evolution of Animals Having Nervous Systems

A nervous system is not essential for life. In fact, most organisms both in the past and at the present have done without one. Of the five kingdoms of living organisms illustrated in **Figure 1-7,** only one, Animalia, contains species with muscles and nervous systems. It is noteworthy that muscles and nervous systems evolved together to underlie the forms of movement that distinguish members of the animal kingdom.

Figure 1-7 shows the taxonomy of the animal kingdom in a chart called a **cladogram** (from the Greek word *clados,* meaning "branch"). Cladograms display groups of related organisms as branches on a tree. Branch order represents how the groups are related evolutionarily, as well as the traits that distinguish them. A cladogram is read from left to right: the most recently evolved organism (animal) or trait (muscles and neurons) is located farthest to the right.

Figure 1-8A shows the taxonomy of the 15 groups, or *phyla,* of animals, classified according to increasing complexity of nervous systems and movement. At the left, the nervous system representative of evolutionarily older phyla, such as jellyfishes and sea anemones, is extremely simple. It consists of a diffuse **nerve net,** which has no structure that resembles a brain or spinal cord but consists entirely of neurons that receive sensory information and connect directly to other neurons that move muscles. Compare the human nervous system illustrated in Figure 1-8B. Now imagine that the brain and spinal cord have been removed.

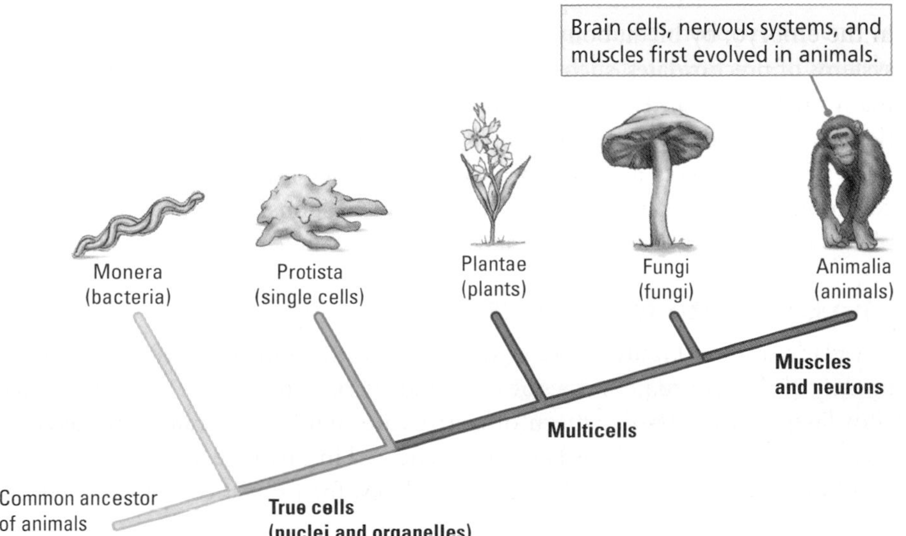

FIGURE 1-7 Cladogram. This chart relates the evolutionary sequence, or phylogeny, connecting the five main kingdoms of living organisms.

We have learned to read, to calculate, to compose and play music, and to develop the sciences. Clearly, the human nervous system evolved long before we mastered these achievements.

In turn, culture now plays a dominant role in shaping our behavior. Because we drive cars, use computers, and watch television, we and our nervous systems must be different from those of our ancestors who did not engage in these activities. The basis for change in the nervous system is the fundamental property of **neuroplasticity,** the nervous system's potential for physical or chemical change that enhances its adaptability to environmental change and its ability to compensate for injury.

Principle 2: The details of nervous-system functioning are constantly changing, an attribute called neuroplasticity.

Functional Organization of the Nervous System

From an anatomical standpoint, the brain and spinal cord together make up the central nervous system, and all the nerve fibers radiating out beyond the brain and spinal cord as well as all the neurons outside the brain and spinal cord form the peripheral nervous system. **Figure 2-1**A charts this anatomical organization. Nerves of the PNS carry sensory information into the CNS and motor instructions from the CNS to the body's muscles and tissues, including those that perform autonomic functions such as digestion and blood circulation.

In a functional organization, little changes, but the focus shifts to how the parts of the system work together (Figure 2-1B). Neurons in the somatic division of the PNS connect through the cranial and spinal nerves to receptors on the body's surface and on its muscles to gather sensory information for the CNS and to convey information from the CNS to move muscles of the face, body, and limbs. Similarly, the autonomic division of the PNS enables the CNS to govern the workings of your body's internal organs—the beating of your heart, the contractions of your stomach, and the movement of your diaphragm to inflate and deflate your lungs.

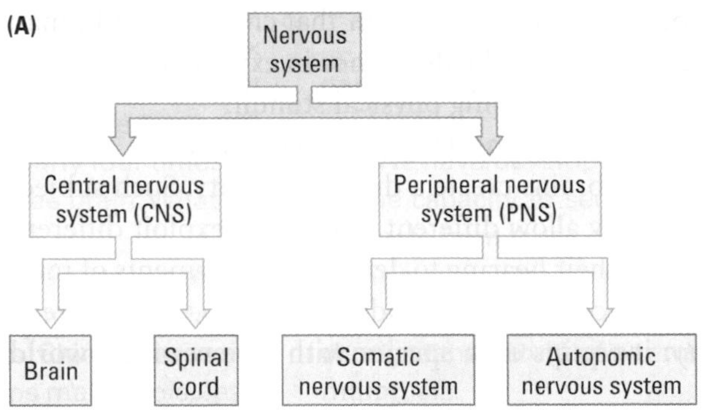

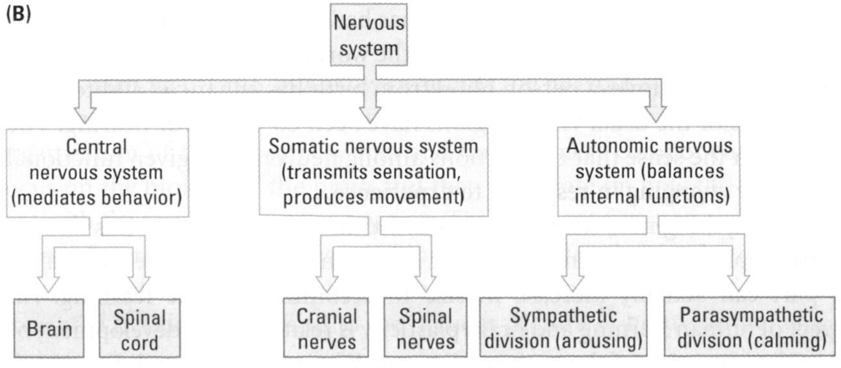

FIGURE 2-1 Parsing the Nervous System. The nervous system can be conceptualized anatomically (A) and functionally (B). The functional approach employed in this book focuses on how the parts of the nervous system interact.

From a functional standpoint, then, the major divisions of the PNS step up to constitute, along with the CNS, an interacting, three-part system:

- The CNS includes the brain and the spinal cord, the structures at the core of the nervous system that mediate behavior.
- The **somatic nervous system** (SNS), all the spinal and cranial nerves carrying sensory information to the CNS from the muscles, joints, and skin, also transmits outgoing motor instructions that produce movement.
- The **autonomic nervous system** (ANS) balances the body's internal organs to "rest and digest" through the *parasympathetic* (calming) *nerves* or to "fight or flee" or engage in vigorous activity through the *sympathetic* (arousing) *nerves.*

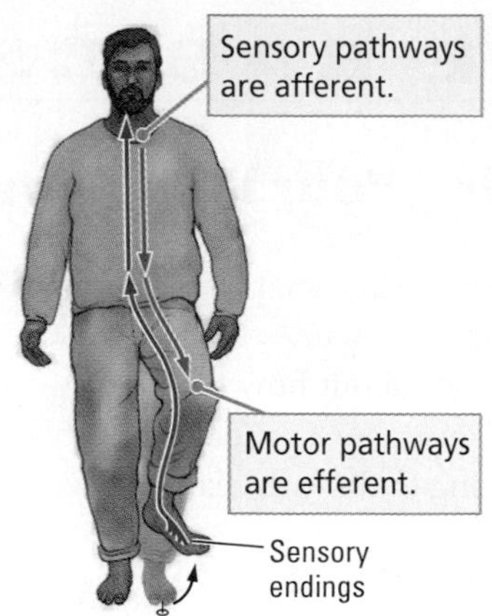

FIGURE 2-2 Information Flow.

The direction of neural information flow is important. **Afferent** (incoming) refers to sensory information coming into the CNS or one of its parts, whereas **efferent** (outgoing) refers to information leaving the CNS or one of its parts. Thus, when you step on a tack, the sensory signals transmitted from the body into the brain are afferent. Efferent signals from the brain trigger a motor response: you lift your foot (**Figure 2-2**).

The words are similar but easy to keep straight. Alphabetically, afferent comes before efferent, and sensory information must come into the brain before an outward-flowing signal can trigger a motor response. Afferent means "incoming" and efferent means "outgoing."

The Brain's Surface Features

When buying a new car, people like to open the hood and examine the engine, the part of the car responsible for most of its behavior—and misbehavior. All most of us can do is gaze at the maze of tubes, wires, boxes, and fluid reservoirs. What we see simply makes no sense, except in the most general way. We know that the engine burns fuel to make the car move and somehow generates electricity to run the radio and lights. But this knowledge tells us nothing about what all the engine's many parts do.

When it comes to behavior, the brain is the engine. In many ways, examining a brain for the first time is similar to looking under the hood of a car. We have a vague sense of what the brain does, but most of us have no sense of how the parts that we see accomplish these tasks. We may not even be able to identify the parts. If you are familiar with the anatomical terms and orientations used in brain drawings and images, read on. If you prefer to review this terminology, consult The Basics on pages 36–37.

The place to start our functional overview is to "open the hood" by observing the brain snug in its home within the skull. The first thing that you encounter is not the brain but rather a tough, triple-layered, protective covering, the **meninges,** illustrated in **Figure 2-3.** The outer *dura mater* (from Latin, meaning "hard mother") is a tough double layer of fibrous tissue that encloses the brain and spinal cord in a kind of loose sack. In the middle is the *arachnoid layer* (from Greek, meaning "like a spider's web"), a very thin sheet of delicate connective tissue that follows the brain's contours. The inner

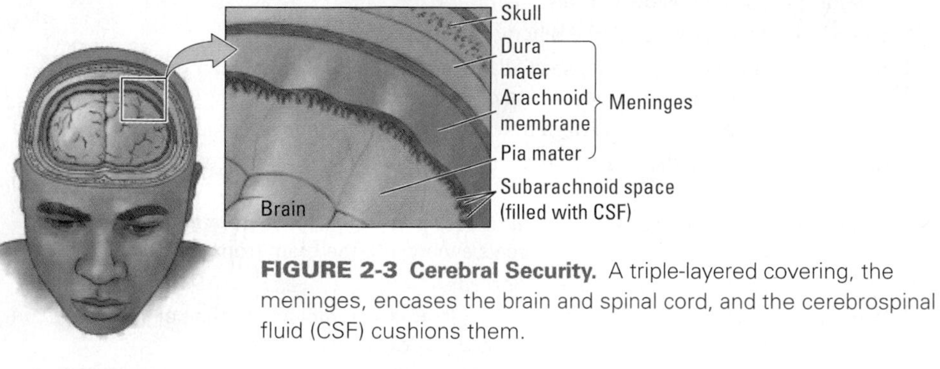

FIGURE 2-3 Cerebral Security. A triple-layered covering, the meninges, encases the brain and spinal cord, and the cerebrospinal fluid (CSF) cushions them.

Neuroplasticity The nervous system's potential for physical or chemical change that enhances its adaptability to environmental change and its ability to compensate for injury.
Somatic nervous system (SNS) Part of the PNS that includes the cranial and spinal nerves to and from the muscles, joints, and skin that produce movement, transmit incoming sensory input, and inform the CNS about the position and movement of body parts.
Autonomic nervous system (ANS) Part of the PNS that regulates the functioning of internal organs and glands.
Afferent Conducting toward a central nervous system structure.
Efferent Conducting away from a central nervous system structure.
Meninges Three layers of protective tissue—dura mater, arachnoid, and pia mater—that encase the brain and spinal cord.

Finding Your Way Around the Brain

When the first anatomists began to examine the brain with the primitive tools of their time, the names that they chose for brain regions often manifest their erroneous assumptions about how the brain works. They named one brain region the *gyrus fornicatus* because they thought that it had a role in sexual function, but most of this region has nothing to do with sexual activity.

A Wonderland of Nomenclature

As time went on, the assumptions and tools of brain research changed, but the naming continued to be haphazard and inconsistent. Many brain structures have several names, and terms are often used interchangeably. This peculiar nomenclature arose because research on the brain and behavior spans several centuries and includes scientists of many nationalities and languages.

Early investigators named structures after themselves or objects or ideas. They used different languages, especially Latin, Greek, and English. More recently, investigators have often used numbers or letters, but even this system lacks coherence, because the numbers may be Arabic or Roman and are often used in combination with Greek or Latin letters.

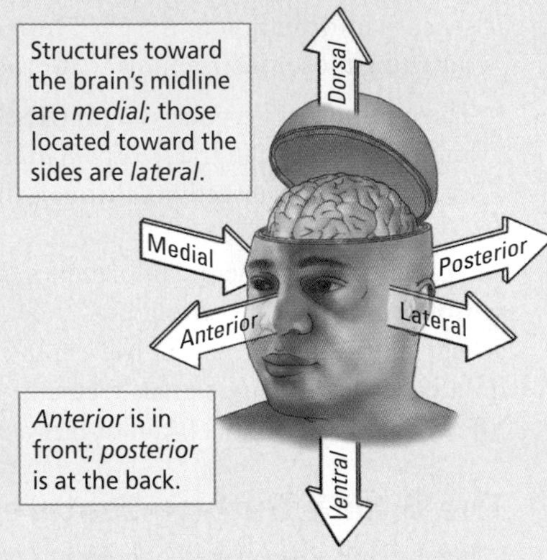
Structures atop the brain or a structure within the brain are *dorsal*.
Structures toward the brain's midline are *medial*; those located toward the sides are *lateral*.
Dorsal
Medial
Posterior
Anterior
Lateral
Anterior is in front; *posterior* is at the back.
Ventral
Structures toward the bottom of the brain or one of its parts are *ventral*.

Brain–Body Orientation.

Describing Locations in the Brain

Many names for nervous-system structures include information about their anatomical locations with respect to other body parts of the animal, with respect to their relative locations, and with respect to a viewer's perspective.

- **Brain–Body Orientation** describes brain-structure location from the frame of reference of the face.
- **Spatial Orientation** describes brain-structure location in relation to other body parts.
- **Anatomical Orientation** describes the direction of a cut, or section, through the brain (part A) from the perspective of a viewer (part B).

The orienting terms are derived from Latin. Consult the Glossary of Anatomical Location and Orientation for easy reference. It is common practice to combine orienting terms. A structure may be described as dorsolateral, for example, meaning that it is located "up and to the side."

Finally, the nervous system, like the body, is symmetrical, with a left side and a right side. Structures that lie on the same side are *ipsilateral;* if they lie on opposite sides, they are *contralateral* to each other. If a structure lies in each hemisphere, it is *bilateral.* Structures close to one another are *proximal;* those far from one another are *distal.*

Glossary of Anatomical Location and Orientation

Term	Meaning with respect to the nervous system
Anterior	Located near or toward the front of the animal or the front of the head (see also *frontal* and *rostral*)
Caudal	Located near or toward the tail of the animal (see also *posterior*)
Coronal	Cut vertically from the crown of the head down; used in reference to the plane of a brain section that reveals a frontal view
Dorsal	On or toward the back of the animal or, in reference to human brain nuclei, located above; in reference to brain sections, a viewing orientation from above
Frontal	"Of the front" (see also *anterior* and *rostral*); in reference to brain sections, a viewing orientation from the front
Horizontal	Cut along the horizon; used in reference to the plane of a brain section that reveals a dorsal view
Inferior	Located below (see also *ventral*)
Lateral	Toward the side of the body or brain
Medial	Toward the middle, specifically the body's midline; in reference to brain sections, a side view of the central structures
Posterior	Located near or toward the tail of the animal (see also *caudal*)
Rostral	"Toward the beak" of the animal; located toward the front (see also *anterior* and *frontal*)
Sagittal	Cut lengthways from front to back of the skull; used in reference to the plane of a brain section that reveals a view into the brain from the side
Superior	Located above (see also *dorsal*)
Ventral	On or toward the belly or the side of the animal where the belly is located; in reference to brain nuclei, located below (see also *inferior*)

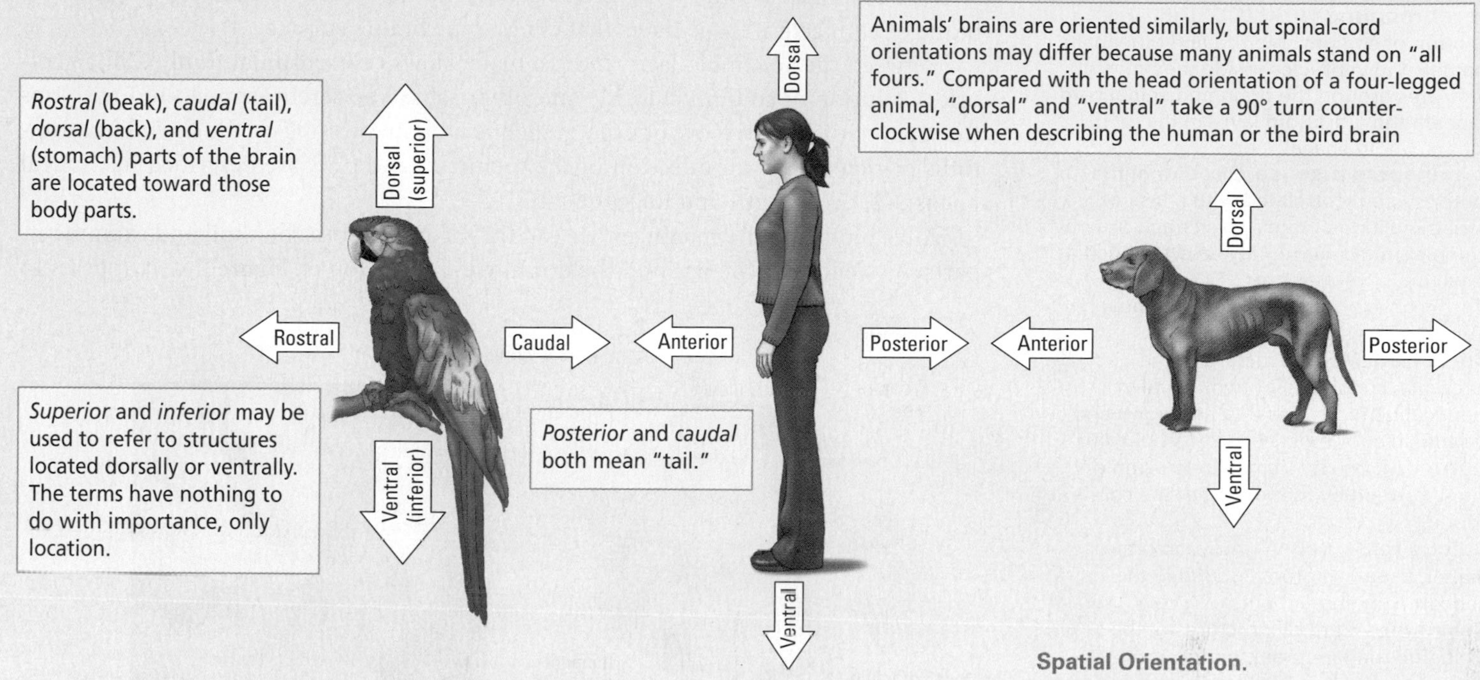

Rostral (beak), *caudal* (tail), *dorsal* (back), and *ventral* (stomach) parts of the brain are located toward those body parts.
Dorsal (superior)
Rostral
Caudal
Ventral (inferior)
Superior and *inferior* may be used to refer to structures located dorsally or ventrally. The terms have nothing to do with importance, only location.
Anterior
Dorsal
Posterior
Ventral
Posterior and *caudal* both mean "tail."
Animals' brains are oriented similarly, but spinal-cord orientations may differ because many animals stand on "all fours." Compared with the head orientation of a four-legged animal, "dorsal" and "ventral" take a 90° turn counter-clockwise when describing the human or the bird brain
Dorsal
Anterior
Posterior
Ventral

Spatial Orientation.

(A) Plane of section | **(B) View of brain**

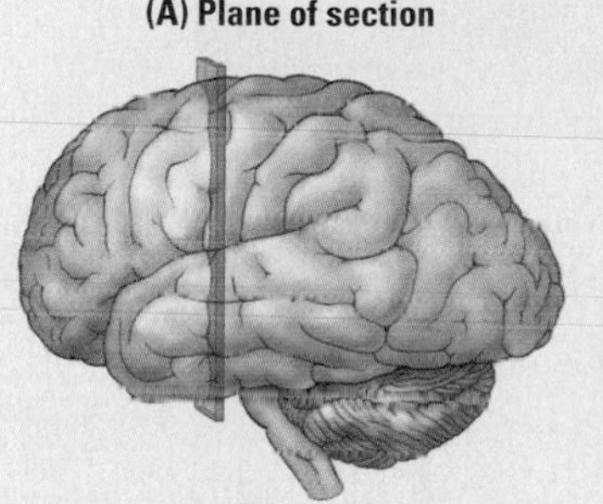

Coronal section

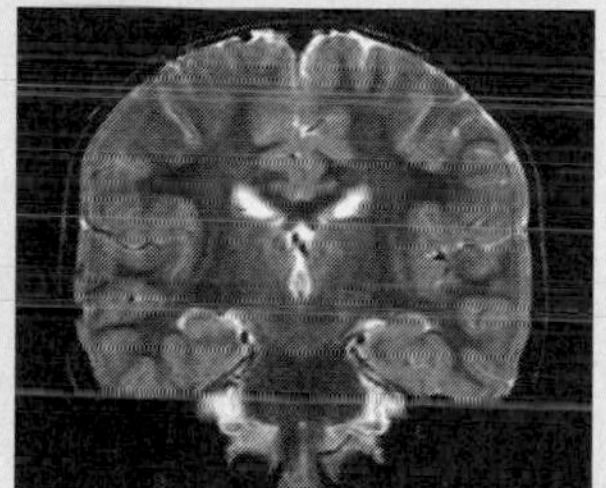

Frontal view

A *coronal section* is cut in a vertical plane, from the crown of the head down, yielding a frontal view of the brain's internal structures.

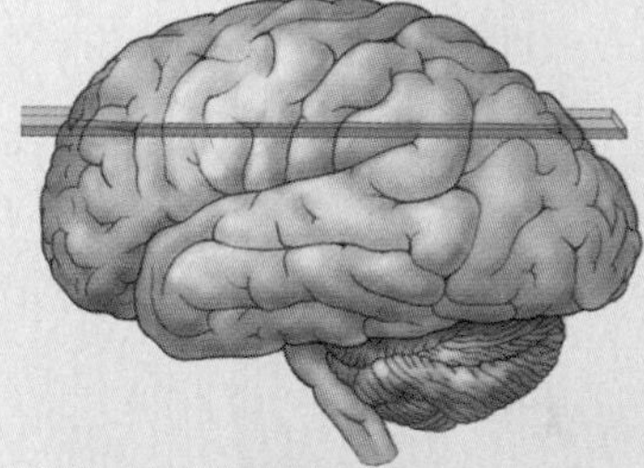

Horizontal section

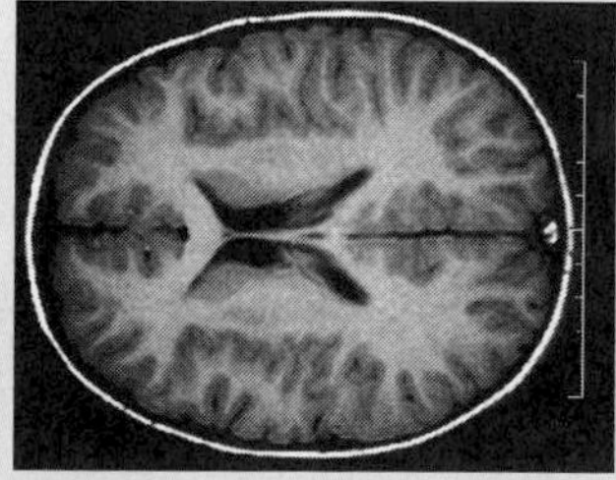

Dorsal view

A *horizontal section*, so-called because the view or the cut falls along the horizon, is usually viewed looking down on the brain from above—a dorsal view.

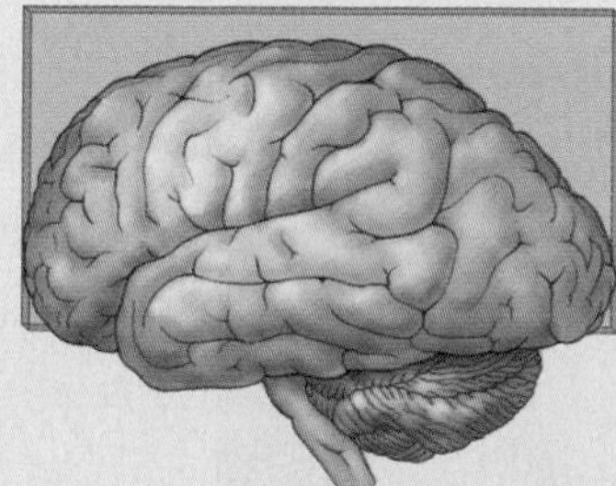

Sagittal section

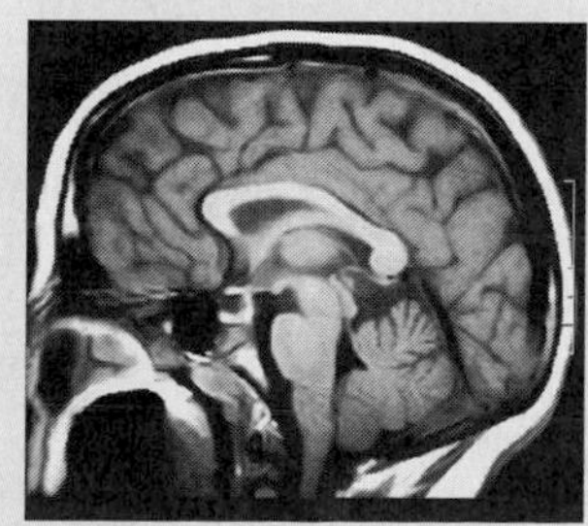

Medial view

A *sagittal section* is cut lengthways from front to back and viewed from the side, a medial view. Imagine the brain oriented as an arrow—in Latin, *sagitta*.

Anatomical Orientation. Photographs courtesy of Dr. D. Armstrong, University of Toronto/Lifeart.

Cerebrospinal fluid (CSF) Clear solution of sodium chloride and other salts that fills the ventricles inside the brain and circulates around the brain and spinal cord beneath the arachnoid layer in the subarachnoid space.
Parkinson's disease Disorder of the motor system correlated with a loss of dopamine in the brain and characterized by tremors, muscular rigidity, and a reduction in voluntary movement.
Hemispherectomy Surgical removal of a cerebral hemisphere.
Cerebrum Major structure of the forebrain, consisting of two virtually identical hemispheres (left and right) and responsible for most conscious behavior.
Gyrus (pl. gyri) A small protrusion or bump formed by the folding of the cerebral cortex.
Sulcus (pl. sulci) A groove in brain matter, usually a groove found in the neocortex or cerebellum.
Brainstem Central structures of the brain, including the hindbrain, midbrain, thalamus, and hypothalamus, responsible for most unconscious behavior.

layer, or *pia mater* (from Latin, meaning "soft mother"), is a moderately tough membrane of connective-tissue fibers that cling to the brain's surface.

Between the arachnoid layer and pia mater flows **cerebrospinal fluid** (CSF), a colorless solution of sodium chloride and other salts. The cerebrospinal fluid cushions the brain so that it can move or expand slightly without pressing on the skull. The symptoms of meningitis, an infection of the meninges and CSF, are described in Clinical Focus 2-2, "Meningitis and Encephalitis."

After removing the meninges, we can lift the brain from the skull and examine its parts. As we look at the brain in the dorsal view at the top of **Figure 2-4,** it appears to

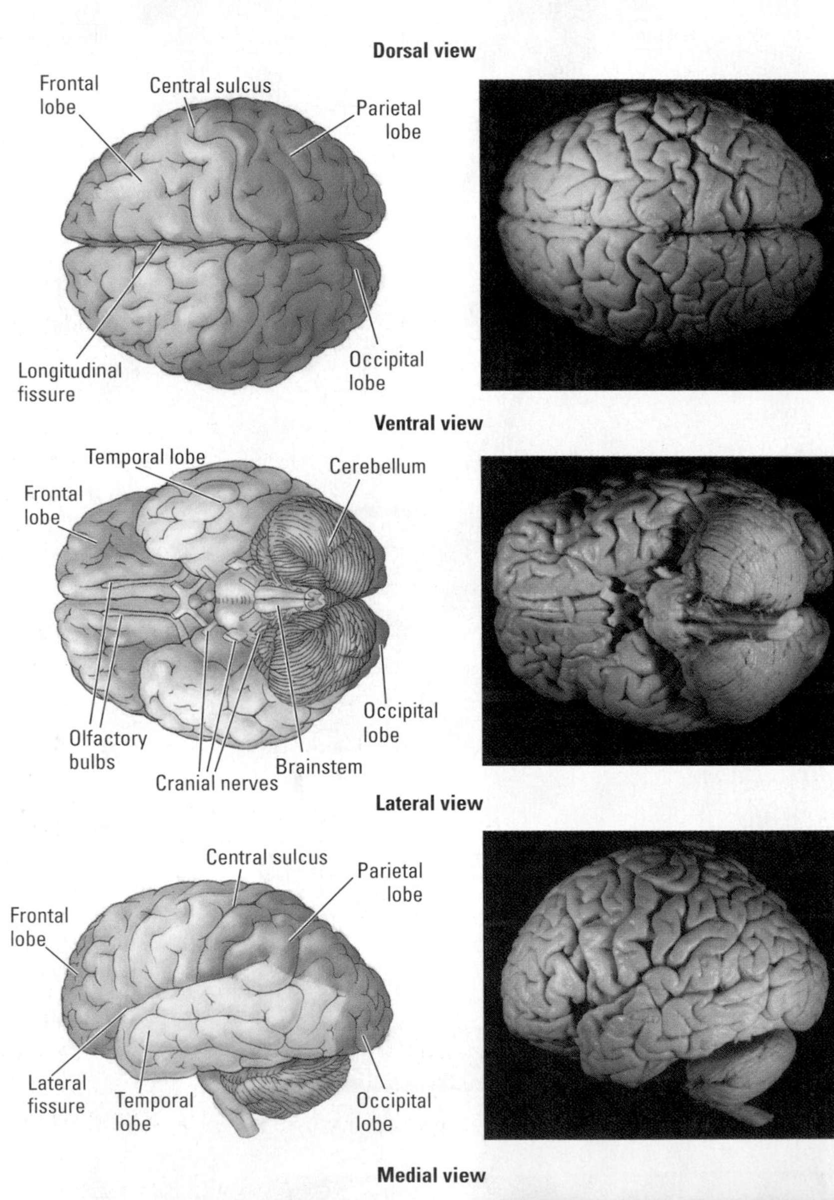

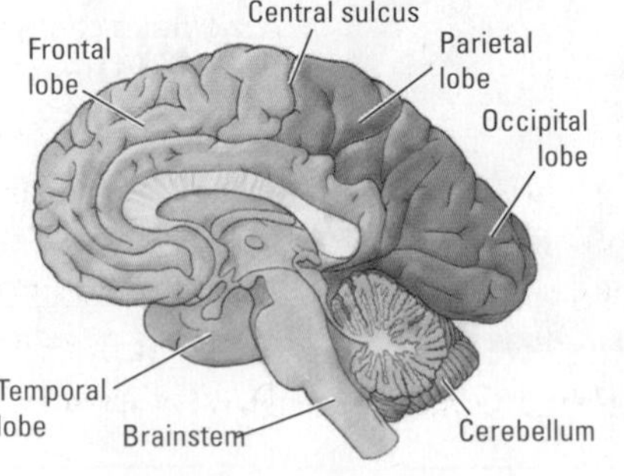

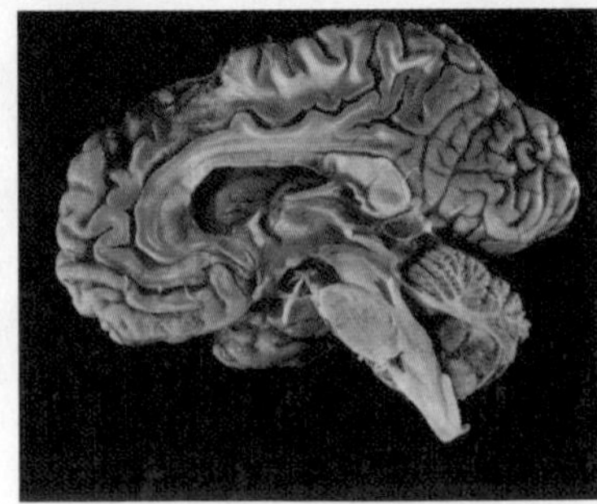

FIGURE 2-4 Examining the Human Brain. Locations of the lobes of the cerebral hemispheres are shown in these top, bottom, side, and midline views, as are the cerebellum and the three major sulci.
Photographs courtesy of Yakolev Collection/AFIP.

CLINICAL FOCUS 2-2

Meningitis and Encephalitis

Harmful microorganisms can invade the layers of the meninges, particularly the pia mater and the arachnoid layer, as well as the CSF flowing between them, and cause a variety of infections that lead to a condition called *meningitis.* One symptom, inflammation, places pressure on the brain. Because the space between meninges and skull is slight, unrelieved pressure can lead to delirium and, if the infection progresses, to drowsiness, stupor, and even coma.

Usually, the earliest symptom of meningitis is severe headache and a stiff neck (cervical rigidity). Head retraction (tilting the head backward) is an extreme form of cervical rigidity. Convulsions, a common symptom in children, indicate that the brain also is affected by the inflammation.

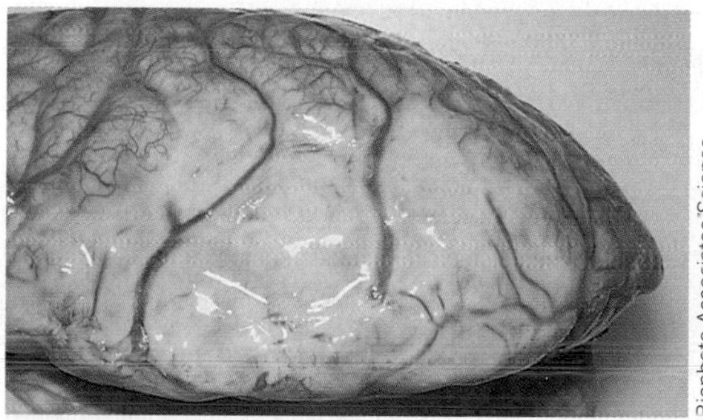

Biophoto Associates/Science Source/Photo Researchers

Pus is visible over the anterior surface of this brain infected with meningitis.

Infection of the brain itself is called *encephalitis.* Some of the many forms of encephalitis have great historical significance. A century ago, in World War I, a form of encephalitis called sleeping sickness *(encephalitis lethargica)* reached epidemic proportions.

Its first symptom is sleep disturbance. People sleep all day and become wakeful, even excited, at night. Subsequently, they show symptoms of **Parkinson's disease**—a disorder of the motor system characterized by severe tremors, muscular rigidity, and difficulty in controlling body movements. Many are completely unable to make any voluntary movements, such as walking or even combing their hair. Survivors of sleeping sickness were immortalized by the neurologist Oliver Sacks in the book and movie *Awakenings.*

The cause of these encephalitis symptoms is the death of an area deep in the brain, the *substantia nigra* ("black substance"), which you will learn about later in this chapter. Other forms of encephalitis may have different effects on the brain. For example, Rasmussen's encephalitis attacks one cerebral hemisphere in children. In most cases, the only effective treatment is radical: **hemispherectomy,** the surgical removal of the entire affected hemisphere.

Surprisingly, some young children who lose a hemisphere adapt rather well. They may even complete college, literally with half a brain. But retardation is a more common outcome of hemispherectomy after encephalitis.

have two major parts, each wrinkly in appearance, resembling a walnut meat taken whole from its shell. These two parts are the left and right hemispheres of the **cerebrum,** the major structure of the forebrain, which is the most recently evolved structure of the central nervous system.

From the opposite, ventral view shown in the second panel in Figure 2-4, the hemispheres of the smaller "little brain," or cerebellum, are visible. Both the cerebrum and the cerebellum are visible in the lateral and medial views shown in the bottom panels of Figure 2-4. These structures appear wrinkled in large-brained animals because their outer surface, or cortex, is a relatively thin sheet of tissue that is crinkled up to fit into the skull.

Thus, much of the cortex is invisible from the brain's surface. All we can see are bumps, or **gyri** (singular: gyrus), and cracks, or **sulci** (singular: sulcus). Some sulci are so very deep that they are called *fissures.* The longitudinal fissure between the cerebral hemispheres and the lateral fissure at the side of the brain are both shown in various views in Figure 2-4, along with the central sulcus at the top of the cerebrum.

If we now look at the bottom of the brain, the ventral view in Figure 2-4, we see something completely different. In the midst of the wrinkled cerebrum and cerebellum emerges a smooth whitish structure with little tubes attached. This central set of structures is the **brainstem,** the area responsible for most unconscious behavior, and the little

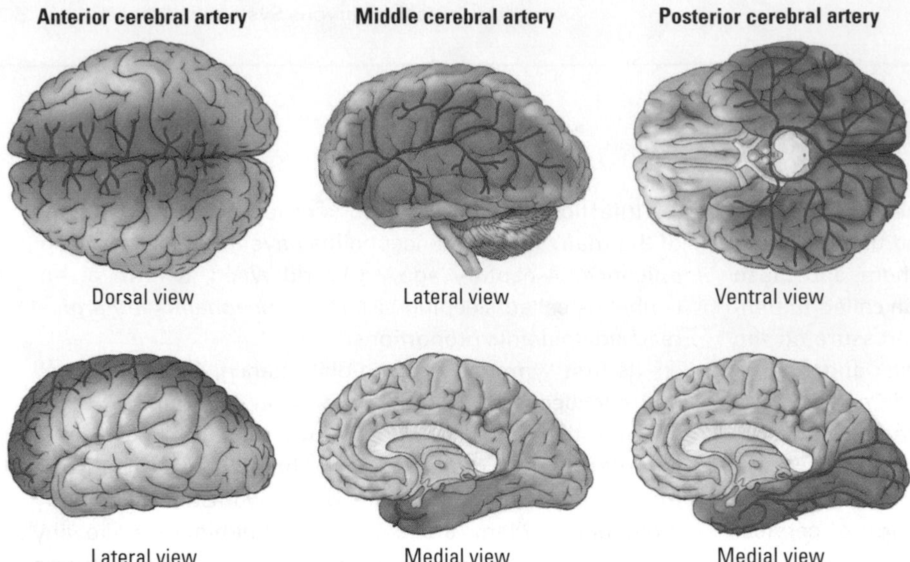

FIGURE 2-5 Major Cerebral Arteries. Each of the three major arteries that feed blood to the cerebral hemispheres branches extensively to service the pink regions.

tubes in the illustration mark out the cranial nerves that run to and from the brain.

One final gross feature is obvious: the brain's surface appears to be covered in blood vessels. Like the rest of the body, the brain receives blood through arteries and sends it back through veins to the kidneys and lungs for cleaning and oxygenation. The cerebral arteries emerge from the neck to wrap around the outside of the brainstem, cerebrum, and cerebellum, finally piercing the brain's surface to nourish its inner regions.

Three major arteries send blood to the cerebrum—namely, the anterior, middle, and posterior cerebral arteries shown in **Figure 2-5.** Because the brain is very sensitive to loss of blood, a blockage or break in a cerebral artery is likely to lead to the death of the affected region, a condition known as **stroke,** the sudden appearance of neurological symptoms as a result of severe interruption of blood flow. Because the three cerebral arteries service different parts of the brain, strokes disrupt different brain functions, depending on the artery affected.

Principle 3: Many of the brain's circuits are crossed.

Because the brain's connections are crossed, stroke in the left hemisphere affects sensation and movement on the right side of the body. The opposite is true for those with strokes in the right hemisphere. Clinical Focus 2-3, "Stroke," describes some disruptions that this condition causes, both to the person who experiences it and to those who care for stroke victims.

The Brain's Internal Features

The simplest way to examine the inside of something is to cut it in half. The orientation in which we cut makes a difference in what we see, however. Consider what happens when we slice through a pear. If we cut from side to side, we cut across the core providing a dorsal view; if we cut from top to bottom, we cut parallel to the core, providing a medial view. Our impression of what the inside of a pear looks like is clearly influenced by the way in which we slice it. The same is true of the brain.

The Macro View

We can reveal the brain's inner features by slicing it downward through the middle, parallel to the front of the body, in a coronal section as shown in **Figure 2-6**A. The resulting frontal view, shown in Figure 2-6B, makes it immediately apparent that the interior is not homogeneous. Both dark and light regions of tissue are visible and,

FIGURE 2-6 Coronal Section Through the Brain. The brain is (A) cut through the middle parallel to the front of the body and then (B) viewed at a slight angle. This frontal view displays white matter, gray matter, and the lateral ventricles. A large bundle of fibers, the corpus callosum, visible above the ventricles joins the hemispheres.

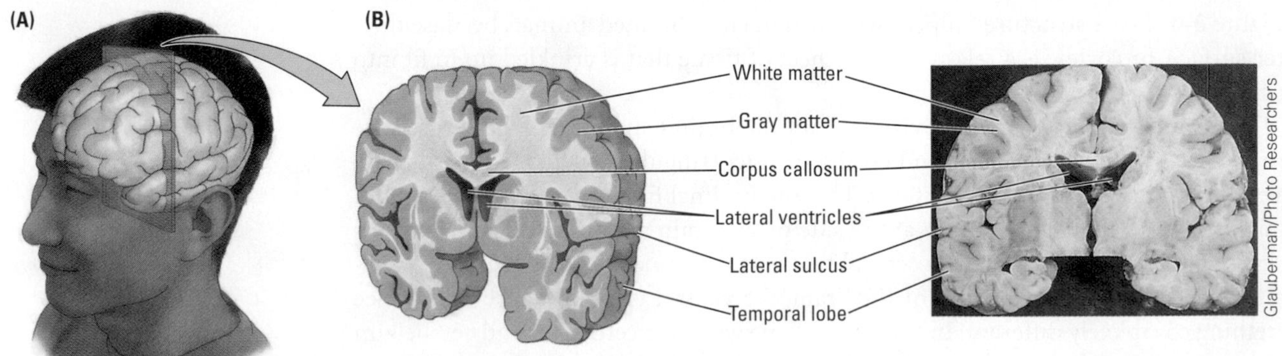

CLINICAL FOCUS 2-3

Stroke

In the United States, someone suffers a stroke with obvious symptoms approximately every minute, producing more than a half million new stroke victims every year. Worldwide, stroke is the second leading cause of death. In addition to the visible strokes, at least twice as many "silent" strokes may occur. These small strokes of the white matter do not produce obvious symptoms.

Even with the best and fastest medical attention, most who endure stroke suffer some residual motor, sensory, or cognitive deficit. For every ten people who have a stroke, two die, six are disabled to varying degrees, and two recover to a degree but still endure a diminished quality of life. One in ten who survive risks further stroke.

The consequences of stroke are significant for victims, their families, and their life styles. Consider Mr. Anderson, a 45-year-old electrical engineer who took his three children to the movies one Saturday afternoon in 1998 and collapsed. Rushed to the hospital, he was diagnosed as having a massive stroke of the middle cerebral artery of his left hemisphere. The stroke has impaired Mr. Anderson's language ever since and, because the brain's connections are crossed, his motor control on the right side as well.

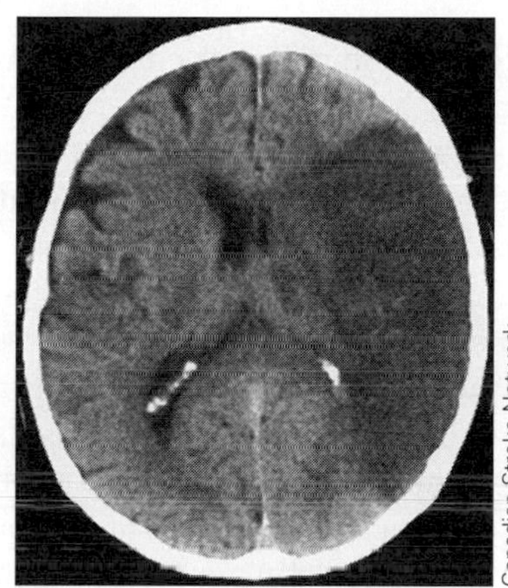

Canadian Stroke Network

In this computer tomographic scan of a brain with a stroke, viewed dorsally, the dark area of the right hemisphere has been damaged by the loss of blood flow.

Seven years after his stroke, Mr. Anderson remained unable to speak, but he could understand simple conversations. Severe difficulties in moving his right leg required him to use a walker. He could not move the fingers of his right hand and so had difficulty feeding himself, among other tasks. Mr. Anderson will probably never return to his engineering career or be able to drive or to get around on his own.

Like Mr. Anderson, most stroke survivors require help to perform everyday tasks. Their caregivers are often female relatives who give up their own careers and other pursuits. Half of these caregivers develop emotional illness, primarily depression or anxiety or both, after a year. Lost income and stroke-related medical bills have a significant effect on the family's standard of living.

Although we tend to speak of stroke as a single disorder, two major types of strokes have been identified. In the more common and often less-severe *ischemic stroke,* a blood vessel is blocked (such as by a clot). The more-severe *hemorrhagic stroke* results from a burst vessel bleeding into the brain.

The hopeful news is that ischemic stroke can be treated acutely with a drug called *tissue plasminogen activator* (t-PA) that breaks up clots and allows a return of normal blood flow to an affected region. Unfortunately, no treatment exists for hemorrhagic stroke, where the use of clot-preventing t-PA would be disastrous.

The results of clinical trials showed that, when patients are given t-PA within 3 hours of suffering an ischemic stroke, the number who make a nearly complete recovery increases by 32 percent compared with those who are given a placebo (Chiu et al., 1998). In addition, impairments are reduced in the remaining patients who survive the stroke.

One difficulty is that many people are unable to get to a hospital soon enough for treatment with t-PA. Most stroke victims do not make it to an emergency room until about 24 hours after symptoms appear, too late for the treatment. Apparently, most people fail to realize that stroke is an emergency.

Other drugs producing an even better outcome than does t-PA will likely become available in the future. The hope is that these drugs will extend the 3-hour window for administering treatment after a stroke. There is also intense interest in developing treatments in the postacute period that will stimulate the brain to initiate reparative processes. Such treatment will facilitate the patient's functional improvement (see a review by Salter et al., 2007).

though these regions may not be as distinctive as the parts of a car's engine, they nevertheless represent different brain components.

The darker regions, called **gray matter,** are largely composed of cell bodies and capillary blood vessels. The cells of the gray matter function either to collect and modify information or to support this activity. The lighter regions, called **white matter,** are mostly nerve fibers with fatty coverings that produce the white appearance, much as

Stroke Sudden appearance of neurological symptoms as a result of severe interruption of blood flow.

Gray matter Areas of the nervous system composed predominantly of cell bodies and blood vessels that function either to collect and modify information or to support this activity.

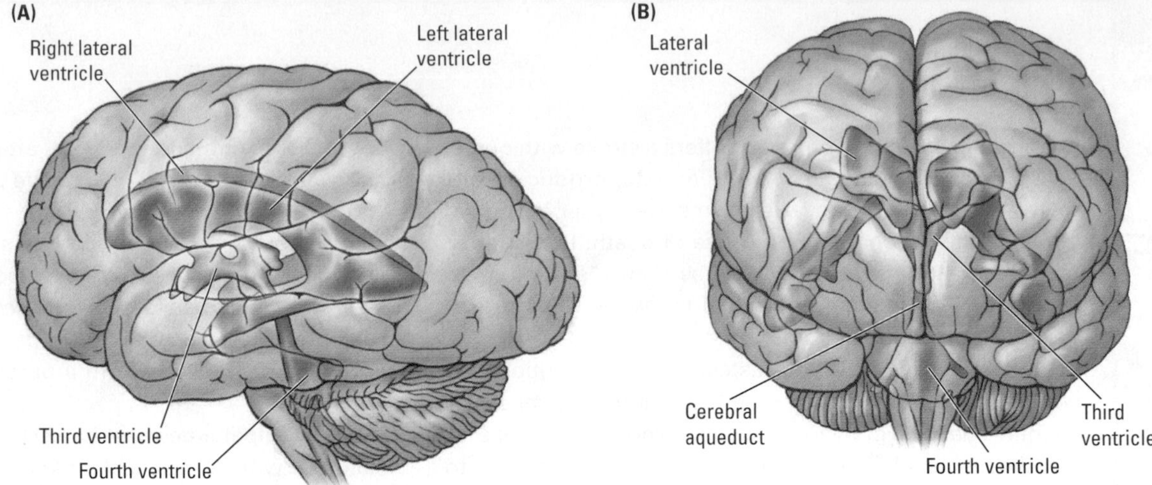

FIGURE 2-7 Cerebral Ventricles. The four ventricles are interconnected. The lateral ventricles are symmetrical, one in each hemisphere. The third and fourth cerebral ventricles lie in the brain's midline and drain into the cerebral aqueduct that runs the length of the spinal cord.

fat droplets in milk make it appear white. The fibers of the white matter form the connections between the cells.

A second feature apparent at the middle of our frontal view in Figure 2-6B consists of two wing-shaped cavities, the **ventricles,** that contain cerebrospinal fluid. The brain contains four ventricles, which are shown in place in **Figure 2-7.** Cells that line the ventricles make the cerebrospinal fluid that fills them. The ventricles are connected; so the CSF flows from the two lateral ventricles to the third and fourth ventricles that lie on the brain's midline and into the cerebral aqueduct, a canal that runs the length of the spinal cord. Recall that CSF is also found in the space between the lower layers of the meninges wrapping around the brain and spinal cord (see Figure 2-3).

Although the functions of the ventricles are not well understood, researchers think that they play an important role in maintaining brain metabolism. The cerebrospinal fluid may allow certain compounds access to the brain, and it probably helps the brain excrete metabolic wastes. In the event of head or spinal trauma, CSF cushions the blow.

Another way to cut through the brain is perpendicularly from front to back, a sagittal section (**Figure 2-8**A). If we make our cut down the brain's midline, we divide the cerebrum into its two hemispheres, revealing several distinctive brain components in a medial view (Figure 2-8B). One feature is a long band of white matter that runs much of the length of the cerebral hemispheres. This band, the **corpus callosum,** contains about 200 million nerve fibers that join the two hemispheres and allow communication between them.

Figure 2-8B clearly shows that the cortex covers the cerebral hemispheres above the corpus callosum, whereas below it are various internal *subcortical regions.* The brainstem is a subcortical structure that generally controls basic physiological functions.

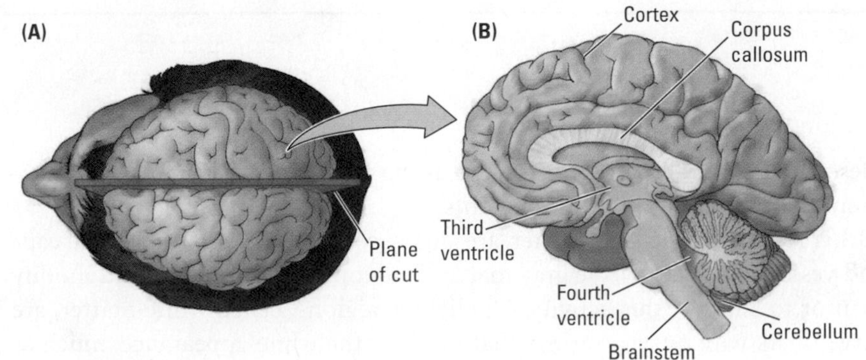

FIGURE 2-8 Sagittal Section Through the Brain. This sagittal section (A) separates the hemispheres, allowing a medial view (B) of the midline structures of the brain, including the subcortical structures that lie below the corpus callosum.

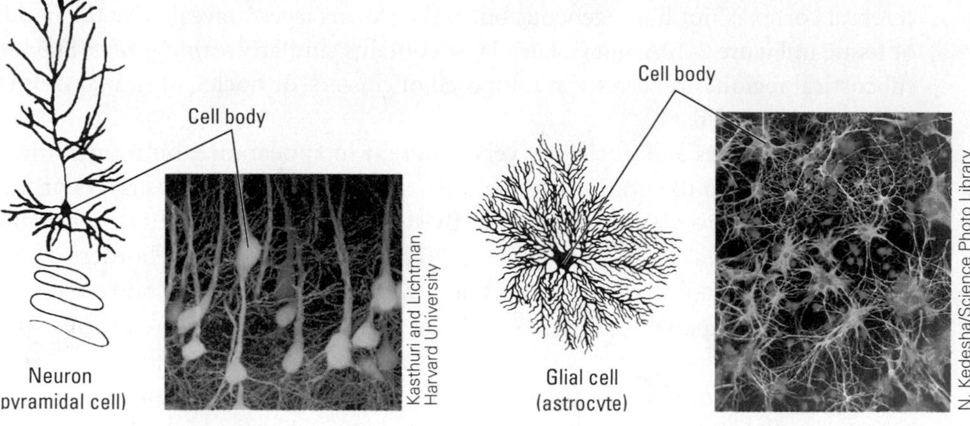

FIGURE 2-9 Brain Cells. A prototypical neuron (*left*) and glial cell (*right*) show that both have branches emanating from the cell body. This branching organization increases the surface area of the cell membrane. The neuron is called a pyramidal cell because the cell body is shaped somewhat like a pyramid; the glial cell is called an astrocyte because of its star-shaped appearance.

But many subcortical regions are forebrain structures intimately related to the cortical areas that process motor, sensory, perceptual, and cognitive functions. This cortical–subcortical relation alerts us to the concept that there is redundancy of function at different levels of the nervous system's organization.

Principle 4: The central nervous system functions on multiple levels.

If you were to compare the left and right hemispheres in sagittal section, you would be struck by their symmetry. The brain, in fact, has two of nearly every structure, one on each side. The few one-of-a-kind structures, such as the third and fourth ventricles, are found along the brain's midline (see Figure 2-7B). Another one-of-a-kind structure is the pineal gland, which Descartes declared the seat of the mind in his theory about how the brain works.

Principle 5: The brain is both symmetrical and asymmetrical.

Microscopic Inspection: Cells and Fibers

The fundamental units of the brain—its cells—are so small that they can be viewed only with the aid of a microscope. By using a microscope, we quickly discover that the brain has two main types of cells, illustrated in **Figure 2-9.** *Neurons* carry out the brain's major functions, whereas *glial cells* aid and modulate the neurons' activities—for example, by insulating neurons. Both neurons and glia come in many forms, each determined by the work that they do.

The human brain contains about 80 billion neurons and 100 billion glia. We examine their structures and functions in detail in Chapter 3.

We can see the internal structures of the brain in much more detail by dyeing their cells with special stains (**Figure 2-10**). For example, if we use a dye that selectively stains

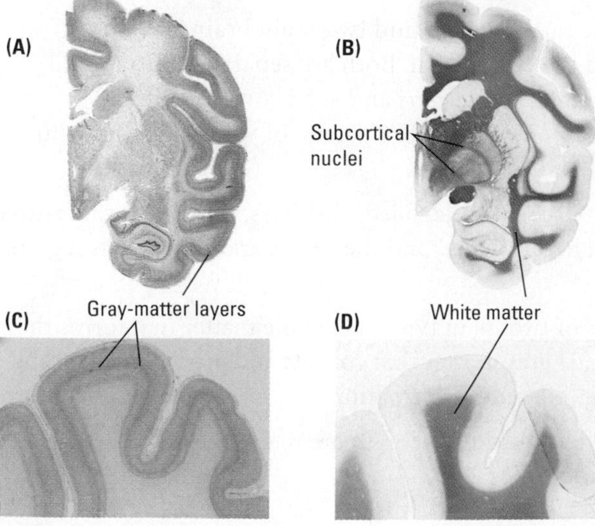

FIGURE 2-10 Cortical Layers and Glia. Brain sections from the left hemisphere of a monkey (midline is to the left in each image). Cells are stained with (A and C) a selective cell-body stain for neurons and (B and D) a selective fiber stain for insulating glial cells, or *myelin*. The images reveal very different pictures of the brain at a microscopic level (C and D).]

White matter Areas of the nervous system rich in fat-sheathed neural axons that form the connections between brain cells.
Ventricle One of four cavities in the brain that contain cerebrospinal fluid that cushions the brain and may play a role in maintaining brain metabolism.
Corpus callosum Fiber system connecting the two cerebral hemispheres to provide a route for direct communication between them.

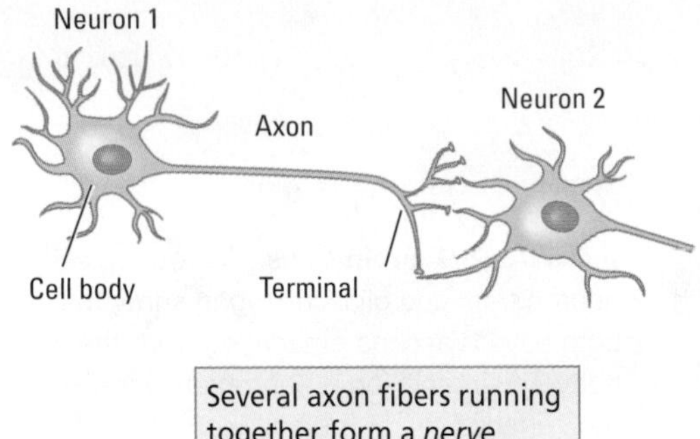

Several axon fibers running together form a *nerve* when outside the CNS or a *tract* within the CNS.

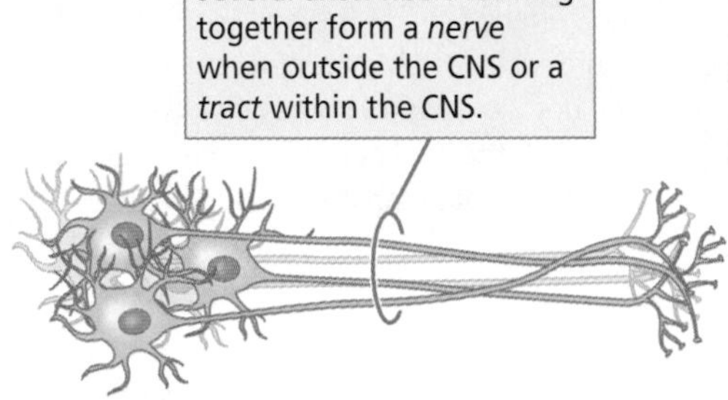

FIGURE 2-11 Neuronal Connections.

cell bodies, we can see that the distribution of cells within the gray matter of the cerebral cortex is not homogeneous but rather forms layers, revealed by the bands of tissue in Figure 2-10A and C. Each layer contains similarly staining cells. Stained subcortical regions are seen to be composed of clusters, or **nuclei,** of similar cells in Figure 2-10 A and B.

Although layers and nuclei are very different in appearance, both form functional units within the brain. Whether a particular brain region has layers or nuclei is largely an accident of evolution. By using a stain that selectively dyes the fibers of neurons, as shown in Figure 2-10B and D, we can see the borders of the subcortical nuclei more clearly. In addition, we can see that the cell bodies stained in the right-hand panels of Figure 2-10 lie in regions adjacent to the regions with most of the fibers.

A key feature of neurons is that they are connected to one another by fibers known as *axons.* When axons run along together, much like the wires that run from a car engine to the dashboard, they form a **nerve** or a **tract** (**Figure 2-11**). By convention, the term *tract* is usually used to refer to collections of nerve fibers found within the brain and spinal cord, whereas bundles of fibers located outside these CNS structures are typically referred to simply as *nerves.* Thus, the pathway from the eye to the brain is known as the optic nerve, whereas the pathway from the cerebral cortex to the spinal cord is known as the corticospinal tract.

REVIEW: An Overview of Brain Function and Structure

✔ The primary functions of the brain are to produce movement and to create a perceptual world in which to move. Because the world is not constant, the brain also needs to be flexible in structure and function, a capacity referred to as neuroplasticity.

✔ To study how the nervous system functions, we abandon the anatomical divisions between the central nervous system and the peripheral nervous system to focus instead on function—on how the CNS interacts with the divisions of the PNS: the somatic and autonomic nervous systems.

✔ Anatomical orientation is most simply referred to as dorsal versus ventral (top versus bottom), anterior versus posterior (front versus back), or medial versus lateral (middle versus side).

✔ Inside the skull and under the meninges we find two main brain structures: the cerebrum (forebrain) and the cerebellum. Both are separated into roughly symmetrical hemispheres that have many gyri and sulci covering their surfaces. At the base of the brain, we see the brainstem, of which the cerebellum is a part.

✔ Cutting open the brain, we observe the fluid-filled ventricles, the corpus callosum that connects the two cerebral hemispheres, and the cortex and subcortical regions below it.

✔ We also see that brain tissue is of two main types: (1) white matter that forms the connections among cells and (2) gray matter that collects and processes incoming (afferent) sensory or outgoing (efferent) information.

✔ The fibers of white matter that lie outside the brain are referred to as nerves, whereas fibers within the brain form tracts.

Nucleus (pl. nuclei) A group of cells forming a cluster that can be identified with special stains to form a functional grouping.
Nerve Large collection of axons coursing together outside the central nervous system.
Tract Large collection of axons coursing together within the central nervous system.

Evolutionary Development of the Nervous System

The developing brain is less complex than the mature adult brain and provides a clearer picture of its basic structural plan. The biological similarity of embryos of vertebrate species as diverse as amphibians and mammals is striking in the earliest stages of development. In the evolution of complex nervous systems, simpler and evolutionarily more primitive forms have not been discarded and replaced but rather have been added to. As a result, all anatomical and functional features of simpler nervous systems are present in the most-complex nervous systems, including ours.

We explore biological and evolutionary similarities in development among humans and other species in Chapter 7.

The bilaterally symmetrical nervous system of simple worms is common to complex nervous systems. Indeed, the spinal cord that constitutes most of the nervous system of the simplest fishes is recognizable in humans, as is the brainstem of more-complex fishes, amphibians, and reptiles. The neocortex, although particularly complex in dolphins and humans, is nevertheless clearly the same organ found in other mammals.

The nervous system of a young vertebrate embryo begins as a sheet of cells that folds into a hollow tube and develops into three regions: forebrain, midbrain, and hindbrain (Figure 2-12A). These three regions are recognizable as a series of three enlargements at the end of the embryonic spinal cord. The adult brain of a fish, amphibian, or reptile is roughly equivalent to this three-part brain. The *prosencephalon* (front brain) is responsible for olfaction, the *mesencephalon* (middle brain) is the seat of vision and hearing, and the *rhombencephalon* (hindbrain) controls movement and balance. The spinal cord is considered part of the hindbrain.

In mammals, the prosencephalon develops further to form the cerebral hemispheres, the cortex and subcortical structures known collectively as the *telencephalon* (endbrain), and the *diencephalon* (between brain) containing the thalamus, among other structures (Figure 2-12B). The hindbrain also develops further into the *metencephalon* (across brain), which includes the enlarged cerebellum, and the *myelencephalon* (spinal brain), including the medulla and the spinal cord.

The human brain is a more-complex mammalian brain, possessing especially large cerebral hemispheres but retaining most of the features of other mammalian brains

FIGURE 2-12 Stages in Brain Evolution and Development. The forebrain grows dramatically in the evolution of the mammalian brain.

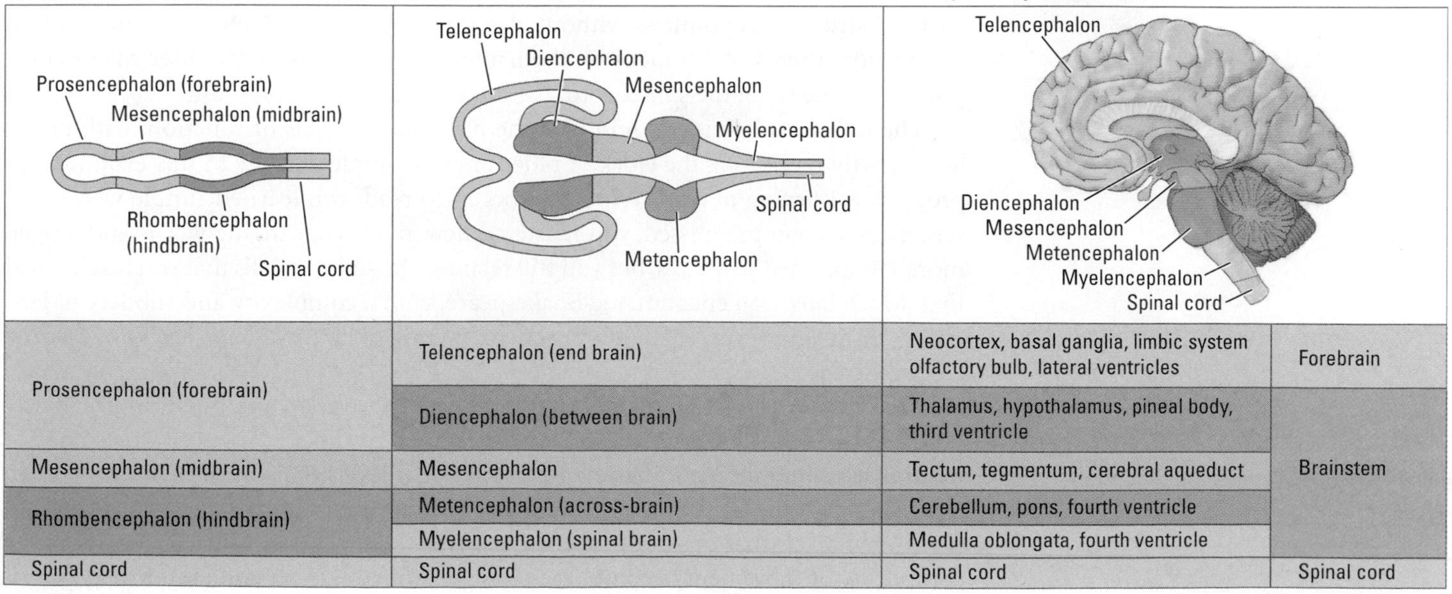

(A) Vertebrate	(B) Mammalian embryo	(C) Fully developed human brain	
Prosencephalon (forebrain)	Telencephalon (end brain)	Neocortex, basal ganglia, limbic system olfactory bulb, lateral ventricles	Forebrain
	Diencephalon (between brain)	Thalamus, hypothalamus, pineal body, third ventricle	Brainstem
Mesencephalon (midbrain)	Mesencephalon	Tectum, tegmentum, cerebral aqueduct	
Rhombencephalon (hindbrain)	Metencephalon (across-brain)	Cerebellum, pons, fourth ventricle	
	Myelencephalon (spinal brain)	Medulla oblongata, fourth ventricle	
Spinal cord	Spinal cord	Spinal cord	Spinal cord

Abnormalities associated with brain injury and brain disease that seem bizarre when considered in isolation are only the normal manifestation of parts of a hierarchically organized brain. Through the principle of hierarchy, we can see that our evolutionary history, our developmental history, and our own personal history are integrated at the various anatomical and functional levels of the nervous system.

(Figure 2-12C). And, as noted in Research Focus 2-1, the human brain shows increases in selected cerebral areas such as the prefrontal cortex.

Most behaviors are not the product of a single locus in the brain but rather of many brain areas and levels. These several nervous-system layers do not simply replicate function; rather, each region adds a different dimension to the behavior. This hierarchical organization affects virtually every behavior in which humans engage.

REVIEW: Evolutionary Development of the Nervous System

- ✔ The brain of vertebrates evolved into three regions: forebrain, midbrain, and hindbrain.
- ✔ The forebrain shows the greatest growth in vertebrate evolution and becomes the largest region of the mammalian brain. The forebrain's growth represents the elaboration of functions already present in the other regions and leads to the brain's functioning on multiple levels.
- ✔ The evolution of levels of control adds flexibility to the control of behavior.

The Central Nervous System: Mediating Behavior

When we look under the hood, we can make some pretty good guesses about what each part of a car engine does. The battery must provide electrical power to run the radio and lights, for example, and, because batteries need to be charged, the engine must contain some mechanism for charging them. We can take the same approach to deduce the functions of the parts of the brain. The part connected to the optic nerve coming from each eye must have something to do with vision. Structures connected to the auditory nerve coming from each ear must have something to do with hearing.

From these simple observations, we can begin to understand how the brain is organized. The real test of inferences about the brain comes in analyzing actual brain function: how this seeming jumble of parts produces behaviors as complex as human thought. The place to start is the brain's anatomy, but learning the name of a particular CNS structure is pointless without also learning something about its function. In this section, therefore, we focus on the names and functions of the three major components of the CNS: the spinal cord, the brainstem, and the forebrain.

These three subdivisions reinforce the principle of levels of function, with newer levels partly replicating the work of older ones. A simple analogy to this evolutionary progress is learning to read. When you began to read, you learned simple words and sentences. As you progressed, you mastered new, more-challenging words and longer, more-complicated sentences, but you still retained the simpler skills that you had learned first. Much later, you encountered Shakespeare, with a complexity and subtlety of language unimagined in elementary school, taking you to a new level of reading comprehension.

Principle 6: Brain systems are organized both hierarchically and in parallel.

Each new level of training adds new abilities that overlap and build on previously acquired skills. Yet all the functional levels deal with reading. Likewise, in the course of natural selection, the brain has evolved functional levels that overlap one another in purpose but allow for a growing complexity of behavior. For instance, the brain has functional levels that control movements. With the evolution of each new level, the complexity of movement becomes increasingly refined. We expand on the principle of evolutionary levels of function later in this chapter.

The Spinal Cord

Although the production of movement is the principle function of the brain, ultimately, the spinal cord produces most body movements, usually following instructions from the brain but at times acting independently. To understand how important the spinal cord is, think of the old saying "running around like a chicken with its head cut off." When a chicken's head is lopped off to provide dinner for the farmer's family, the chicken is still capable of running around the barnyard until it collapses from loss of blood. The chicken accomplishes this feat because the spinal cord can act independently of the brain.

The complexity of the spinal cord can be understood by realizing that it is not a single structure but rather a set of segmented "switching stations." Each segment receives information from a discrete part of the body and sends out commands to that area. Spinal nerves, which are part of the somatic nervous system, carry sensory information to the cord from the skin, muscles, and related structures and, in turn, send motor instructions to control each muscle.

You can demonstrate movement controlled by the spinal cord in your own body by tapping your patellar tendon, just below your kneecap (the patella). The sensory input causes your lower leg to kick out and, try as you might, it is very hard to prevent the movement from occurring. Your brain, in other words, has trouble inhibiting this *spinal reflex,* which is automatic.

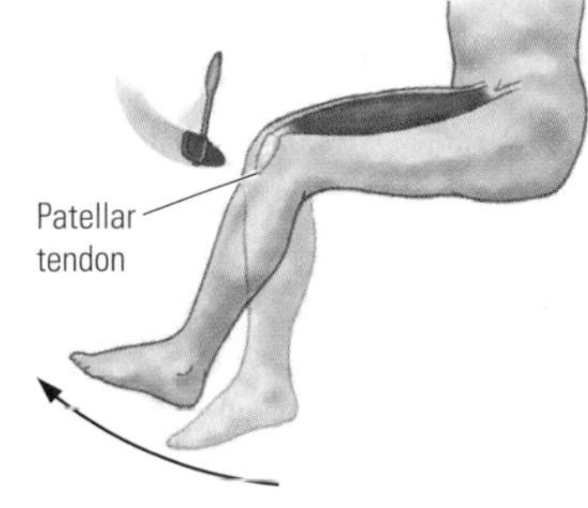

We explain reflexes in Chapter 11.

The Brainstem

The brainstem begins where the spinal cord enters the skull and extends upward into the lower areas of the forebrain. The brainstem receives afferent nerves from all of the body's senses, and it sends efferent nerves to the spinal cord to control virtually all of the body's movements except the most-complex movements of the fingers and toes. The brainstem, then, both directs movements and creates a sensory world.

In some animals, such as frogs, the entire brain is largely equivalent to the mammalian or avian brainstem. And frogs get along quite well, demonstrating that the brainstem is a fairly sophisticated piece of machinery. If we had only a brainstem, we would still be able to create a world, but it would be a far simpler, sensorimotor world, more like what a frog experiences.

An animal's perception of the external world depends on the complexity and organization of its nervous system.

The brainstem can be divided into three regions: hindbrain, midbrain, and diencephalon, meaning "between brain" because it borders upper and lower parts of the brain. In fact, the "between brain" status of the diencephalon can be seen in a neuroanatomical inconsistency: some anatomists place it in the brainstem and others place it in the forebrain. **Figure 2-13**A illustrates the location of these three brainstem regions

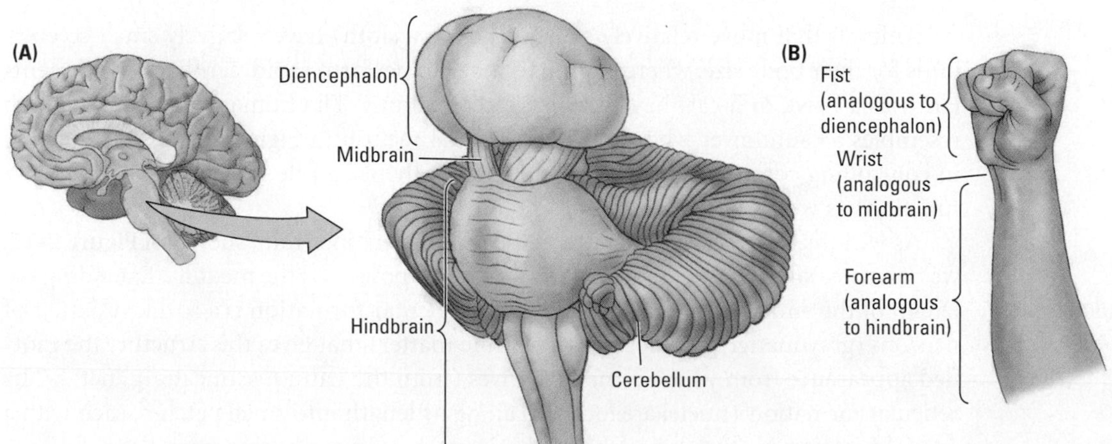

FIGURE 2-13 Brain Structures. (A) Medial view of the brain shows the relation of the brainstem to the cerebral hemisphere. (B) The shapes and relative sizes of the brainstem's parts can be imagined as analogous as to your hand, wrist, and forearm.

under the cerebral hemispheres, and Figure 2-13B compares the shape of the brainstem regions to the lower part of your arm held upright. The hindbrain is long and thick like your forearm, the midbrain is short and compact like your wrist, and the diencephalon at the end is bulbous like your hand forming a fist.

The hindbrain and midbrain are essentially extensions of the spinal cord; they developed first as simple animals evolved a brain at the anterior end of the body. It makes sense, therefore, that these lower brainstem regions should retain a division between structures having sensory functions and those having motor functions, with sensory structures located dorsally and motor ones ventrally.

Principle 7: Sensory and motor divisions exist throughout the nervous system.

Each brainstem region performs more than a single task. Each contains various subparts, made up of groupings of nuclei that serve different purposes. All three regions, in fact, have both sensory and motor functions. However, the hindbrain is especially important in motor functions, the midbrain in sensory functions, and the diencephalon in integrative tasks. Here we consider the central functions of these three regions; later chapters contain more detailed information about them.

The Hindbrain

The **hindbrain** controls various motor functions ranging from breathing to balance to fine movements, such as those used in dancing. Its most distinctive structure, and one of the largest structures of the human brain, is the cerebellum. The relative size of the cerebellum increases with the physical speed and dexterity of a species, as shown in **Figure 2-14A**.

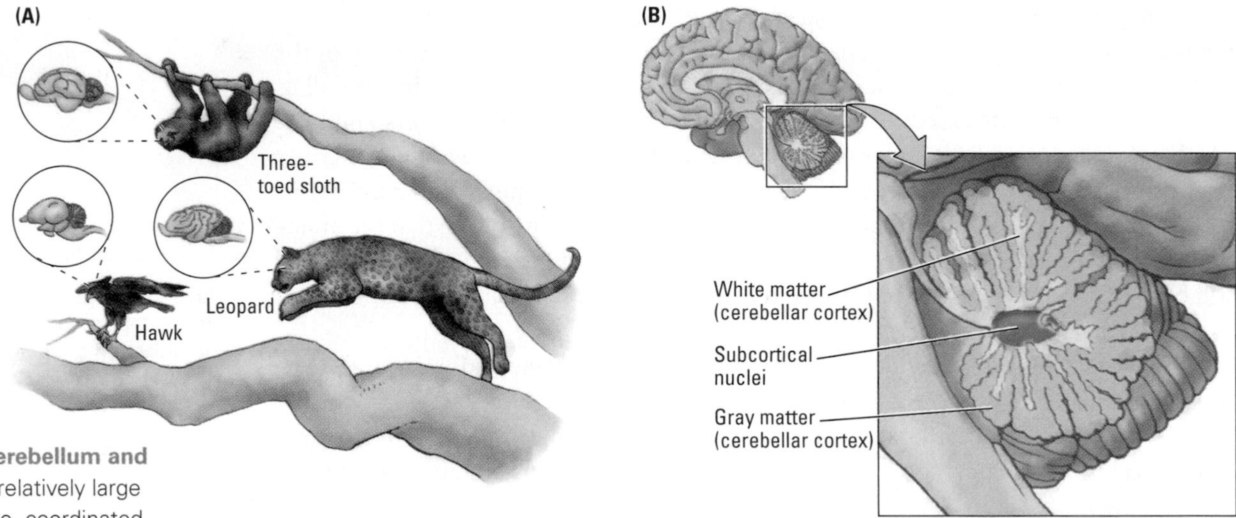

FIGURE 2-14 The Cerebellum and Movement. (A) Their relatively large cerebellums enable fine, coordinated movements such as flight and landing in birds and prey-catching in cats. Slow-moving animals such as the sloth have smaller cerebellums relative to their brain size. (B) Like the cerebrum, the human cerebellum has an extensively folded cortex with gray and white matter and subcortical nuclei.

Animals that move relatively slowly (such as a sloth) have relatively small cerebellums for their body size, whereas animals that can perform rapid, acrobatic movements (such as a hawk or a cat) have very large cerebellums. The human cerebellum, which resembles a cauliflower when viewed in sagittal section in Figure 2-14B, is important in controlling complex movements and apparently has a role in a variety of cognitive functions as well.

As we look below the cerebellum at the rest of the hindbrain, shown in **Figure 2-15**, we find three subparts: the reticular formation, the pons, and the medulla. Extending the length of the entire brainstem at its core, the **reticular formation** is a netlike mixture of neurons (gray matter) and nerve fibers (white matter) that gives this structure the mottled appearance from which its name derives (from the Latin *rete,* meaning "net"). The reticular formation's nuclei are localized along its length into small patches, each with a special function in stimulating the forebrain, such as in awakening from sleep.

Not surprisingly, the reticular formation is sometimes called the *reticular activating system.*

Hindbrain Evolutionarily the oldest part of the brain; contains the pons, medulla, reticular formation, and cerebellum structures that coordinate and control most voluntary and involuntary movements.

Reticular formation Midbrain area in which nuclei and fiber pathways are mixed, producing a netlike appearance; associated with sleep–wake behavior and behavioral arousal.

Midbrain Central part of the brain that contains neural circuits for hearing and seeing as well as orienting movements.

Tectum Roof (area above the ventricle) of the midbrain; its functions are sensory processing, particularly visual and auditory, and the production of orienting movements.

Tegmentum Floor (area below the ventricle) of the midbrain; a collection of nuclei with movement-related, species-specific, and pain-perception functions.

Orienting movement Movement related to sensory inputs, such as turning the head to see the source of a sound.

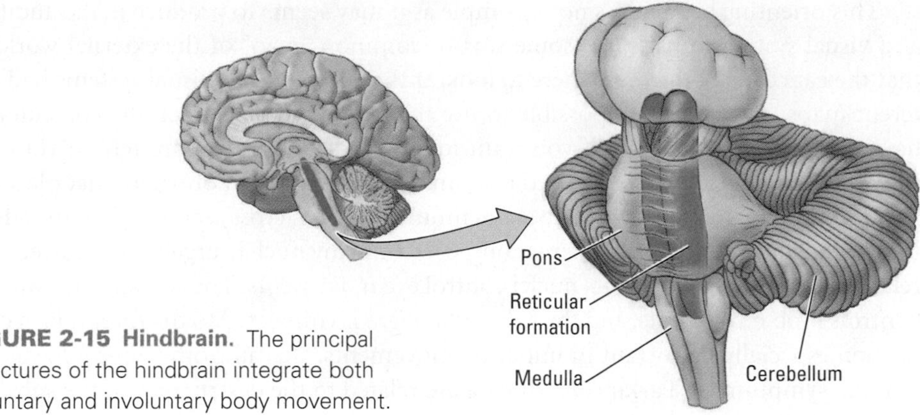

FIGURE 2-15 Hindbrain. The principal structures of the hindbrain integrate both voluntary and involuntary body movement.

The pons and medulla contain substructures that control many vital movements of the body. Nuclei within the pons receive inputs from the cerebellum and actually form a bridge from it to the rest of the brain (the Latin word *pons* means "bridge"). At the rostral tip of the spinal cord, the medulla's nuclei control such vital functions as regulating breathing and the cardiovascular system. For this reason, a blow to the back of the head can kill you: your breathing stops if the control centers in the hindbrain are injured.

The Midbrain

In the **midbrain,** shown in **Figure 2-16A,** the sensory component, the **tectum** (roof), is located dorsally, whereas a motor structure, the **tegmentum** (floor), is ventral. The tectum receives a massive amount of sensory information from the eyes and ears. The optic nerve sends a large bundle of nerve fibers to the *superior colliculus,* whereas the *inferior colliculus* receives much of its input from auditory pathways. The colliculi function not only to process sensory information but also to produce **orienting movements** related to sensory inputs, such as turning your head to see the source of a sound.

Collis in Latin means "hill"; thus the colliculi appear to be four little hills on the dorsal surface of the midbrain.

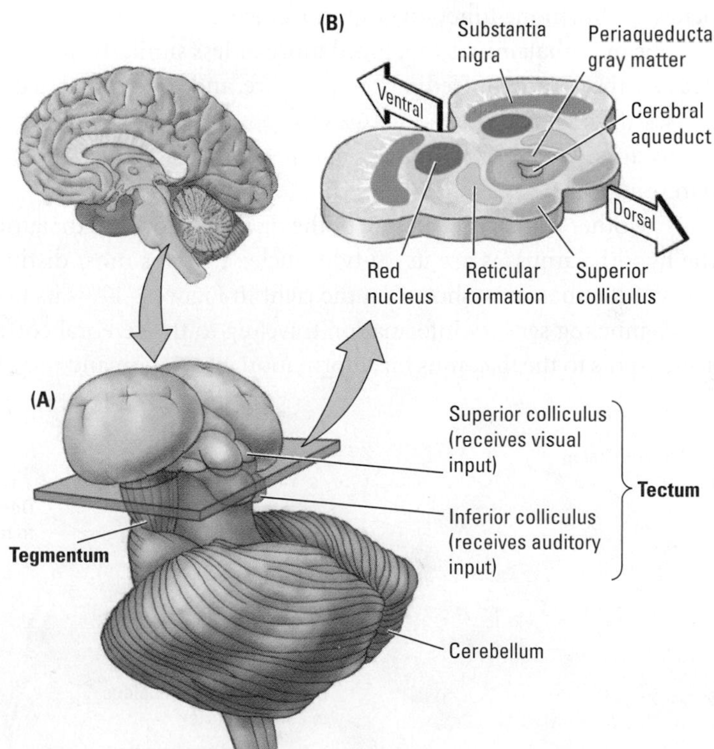

FIGURE 2-16 Midbrain. (A) Structures in the midbrain are critical in producing orienting movements, species-specific behaviors, and the perception of pain. (B) The tegmentum in cross section, revealing various nuclei.

Principle 8: Sensory input to the brain is divided for object recognition and motor control.

This orienting behavior is not as simple as it may seem. To produce it, the auditory and visual systems must share some sort of common "map" of the external world so that the ears can tell the eyes where to look. If the auditory and visual systems had different maps, it would be impossible to use the two together. In fact, the colliculi also have a tactile map. After all, if you want to look at the source of an itch on your leg, your visual and tactile systems need a common representation of where that place is.

Lying ventral to the tectum, the tegmentum (shown in cross section in Figure 2-16B) is not a single structure but rather is composed of many nuclei, largely with movement-related functions. Several of its nuclei control eye movements. The so-called *red nucleus* controls limb movements, and the *substantia nigra* is connected to the forebrain, a connection especially important in initiating movements. (Recall from Clinical Focus 2-2 that the symptoms of Parkinson's disease are related to the destruction of the substantia nigra.) The *periacqueductal gray matter,* made up of cell bodies that surround the aqueduct joining the third and fourth ventricles, contains circuits controlling species-typical behaviors (e.g., female sexual behavior). These nuclei also play an important role in the modulation of pain by opioid drugs.

Diencephalon The "between brain" that integrates sensory and motor information on its way to the cerebral cortex.
Hypothalamus Diencephalon structure that contains many nuclei associated with temperature regulation, eating, drinking, and sexual behavior.
Thalamus Diencephalon structure through which information from all sensory systems is integrated and projected into the appropriate region of the neocortex.
Forebrain Evolutionarily the newest part of the brain; coordinates advanced cognitive functions such as thinking, planning, and language; contains the limbic system, basal ganglia, and the neocortex.
Neocortex (cerebral cortex) Newest, outer layer (new bark) of the forebrain and composed of about six layers of gray matter that creates our reality.

The Diencephalon

The **diencephalon,** shown in sagittal section at the top left in **Figure 2-17,** integrates sensory and motor information on its way to the cerebral cortex. The two principal structures of the diencephalon are the hypothalamus and the thalamus. The thalamus—one in each hemisphere—lies just to the left of the tip of the brainstem, and the hypothalamus lies to the left of the thalamus.

The **hypothalamus** also is found in each hemisphere, lying bilaterally along the brain's midline. It is composed of about 22 small nuclei, as well as nerve-fiber systems that pass through it. A critical function of the hypothalamus is to control the body's production of hormones, which is accomplished by its interactions with the pituitary gland, shown at the bottom left in Figure 2-17. Although constituting only about 0.3 percent of the brain's weight, the hypothalamus takes part in nearly all aspects of behavior, including feeding, sexual behavior, sleeping, temperature regulation, emotional behavior, hormone function, and movement.

The hypothalamus is organized more or less similarly in different mammals, largely because the control of feeding, temperature, and so on, is carried out similarly. But there are sex differences in the structures of some parts of the hypothalamus, owing probably to differences between males and females in activities such as sexual behavior and parenting.

The other principal structure of the diencephalon, the **thalamus,** is much larger than the hypothalamus, as are its 20-odd nuclei. Perhaps most distinctive among the functions of the thalamus, shown on the right in Figure 2-17, is its role as a kind of gateway for channeling sensory information traveling to the cerebral cortex. All sensory systems send inputs to the thalamus for information integration and relay to the appropriate area

FIGURE 2-17 Diencephalon. The diencephalon is composed of the thalamus and hypothalamus, among other structures. The various thalamic regions connect to discrete regions of cortex. Lying below (hypo) the thalamus, at the base of the brain, the hypothalamus and pituitary lie above the roof of the mouth. The hypothalamus is composed of many nuclei, each with distinctly different functions.

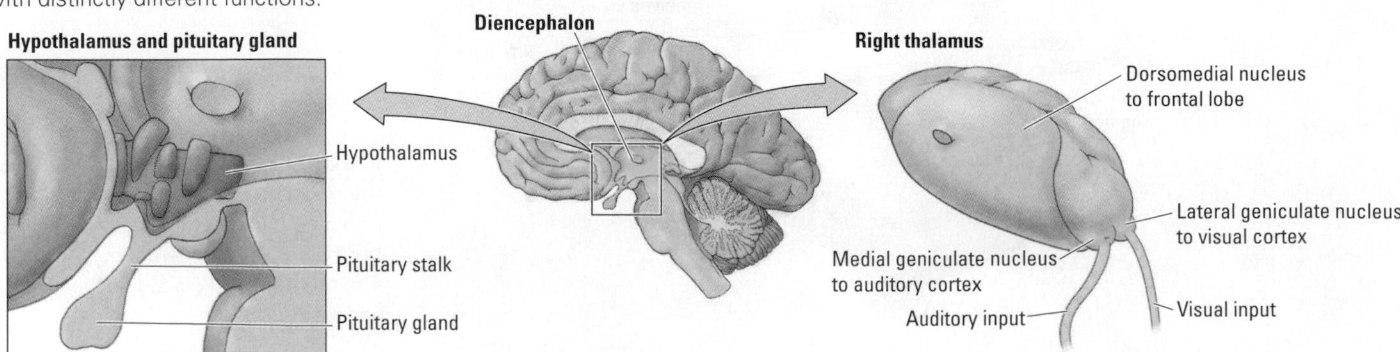

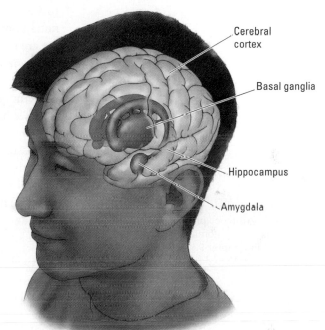

in the cortex. The optic tract, for example, sends information through a large bundle of fibers to a region of the thalamus, the *lateral geniculate nucleus,* shown on the right side of the thalamus in Figure 2-17. In turn, the lateral geniculate nucleus processes some of this information and then sends it to the visual region of the cortex in each hemisphere.

The routes to the thalamus may be indirect. For example, the route for olfaction traverses several synapses before entering the *dorsomedial nucleus* of the thalamus on its way to the forebrain. Analogous sensory regions of the thalamus receive auditory and tactile information, which is subsequently relayed to the respective auditory and tactile cortical regions in each hemisphere. Some thalamic regions have motor functions or perform integrative tasks. One region with an integrative function is the *dorsomedial thalamic nucleus.* It connects to most of the frontal lobe.

We return to the thalamic sensory nuclei in Chapters 9 through 11, where we examine how sensory information is processed. Other thalamic regions are considered in Chapters 12 and 14, where we explore motivation and memory.

The Forebrain

The **forebrain,** whose major internal and external structures are shown in **Figure 2-18,** is the largest region of the mammalian brain. Each of its three principal structures has multiple functions. To summarize briefly, the *neocortex* (another name for the cerebral cortex) regulates a host of mental activities ranging from perception to planning; the *basal ganglia* control voluntary movement; and the *limbic system* regulates emotions and behaviors that create and require memory.

Extending our analogy between the brainstem and your forearm, imagine that the "fist" of the brainstem (the diencephalon) is thrust inside a watermelon. The watermelon represents the forebrain, with the rind being the cortex and the fruit inside being the subcortical limbic system and basal ganglia. By varying the size of the watermelon, we can vary the size of the brain, which in a sense is what evolution has done. The forebrain therefore varies considerably in size across species (recall the photographs in Research Focus 2-1).

Cerebral cortex
Basal ganglia
Hippocampus
Amygdala

FIGURE 2-18 Forebrain Structures. The major structures of the forebrain integrate sensation, emotion, and memory to enable advanced cognitive functions such as thinking, planning, and language.

The Cortex

There are actually two types of cortex, the old and the new. The **neocortex** (new bark) is the tissue that is visible when we view the brain from the outside, as in Figure 2-4. The neocortex is unique to mammals, and its primary function is to create a perceptual world and respond to that world. The older cortex, sometimes called *limbic cortex,* is more primitive than the neocortex. It is found in the brains of other chordates in addition to mammals, especially in birds and reptiles.

The limbic cortex is thought to play a role in controlling motivational states. Although anatomical and functional differences exist between the neocortex and the limbic cortex, the distinctions are not critical for most discussions in this book. Therefore, we will usually refer to both types of tissue simply as cortex.

Measured by volume, the cortex makes up most of the forebrain, comprising 80 percent of the human brain overall. It is the brain region that has expanded the most in the course of mammalian evolution. The human neocortex has a surface area as large as 2500 square centimeters but a thickness of only 1.5 to 3.0 millimeters. This area is equivalent to about four pages of this book. By contrast, a chimpanzee has a cortical area equivalent to about one page.

The pattern of sulci and gyri formed by the folding of the cortex varies across species. Some species, such as rats, have no sulci or gyri, whereas carnivores, such as cats, have gyri that form a longitudinal pattern. In primates, the sulci and gyri form a more diffuse pattern.

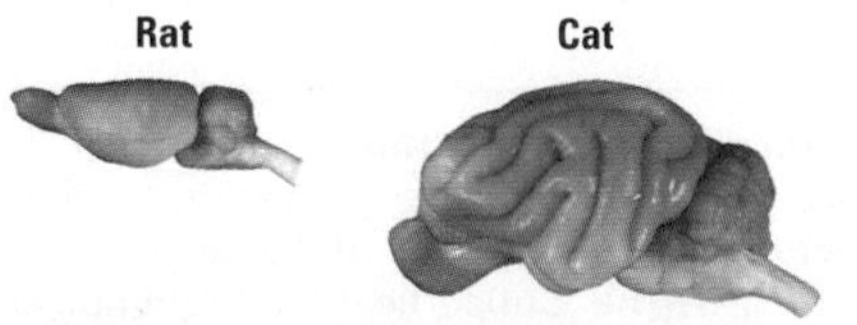

Cortical Lobes The human cortex consists of two nearly symmetrical hemispheres, the left and the right, which are separated by the longitudinal fissure (**Figure 2-19**). Each

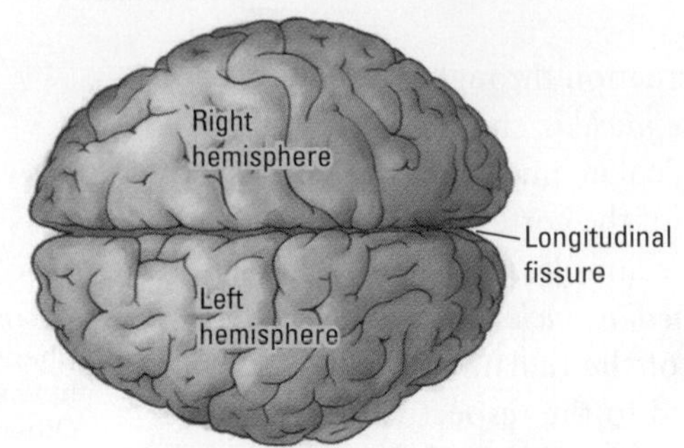

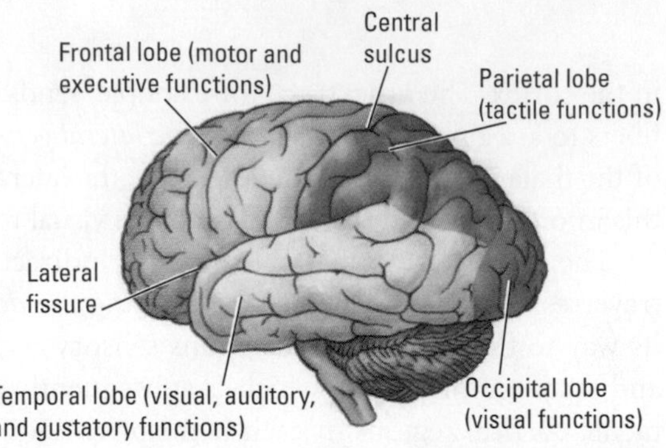

FIGURE 2-19 Cortical Boundaries.

hemisphere is subdivided into the four lobes introduced in Chapter 1, corresponding to the skull bones overlying them: frontal, temporal, parietal, and occipital. Unfortunately, bone location and brain function are unrelated. As a result, the lobes of the cortex are rather arbitrarily defined regions that include many different functional zones.

Principle 9: Functions in the brain are both localized and distributed.

Nonetheless, we can attach some gross functions to each lobe. The three posterior lobes have sensory functions: the occipital lobe is visual; the parietal lobe is tactile; and the temporal lobe is visual, auditory, and gustatory. In contrast, the frontal lobe is motor and is sometimes referred to as the brain's "executive" because it integrates sensory and motor functions and formulates plans of action.

Fissures and sulci often establish the boundaries of cortical lobes. For instance, in humans, the central sulcus and lateral fissure form the boundaries of each frontal lobe. They also form the boundaries of each parietal lobe, which lies posterior to the central sulcus. The lateral fissure demarcates each temporal lobe as well, forming its dorsal boundary. The occipital lobes are not so clearly separated from the parietal and temporal lobes because no large fissure marks their boundaries.

Traditionally, the occipital lobes are defined on the basis of anatomical features that are presented in Chapter 9.

Cortical Layers The neocortex has six layers of gray matter atop a layer of white matter. (In contrast, the limbic cortex has three layers.) The layers of the neocortex have several distinct characteristics:

- Different layers have different types of cells.
- The density of cells in each layer varies, ranging from virtually no cells in layer I (the top layer) to very dense cell packing in layer IV of the neocortex (**Figure 2-20**).
- Other differences in appearance relate to the functions of cortical layers in different regions.

These visible differences led neuroanatomists of the early twentieth century to map the cortex. The map in **Figure 2-21** was developed by Korbinian Brodmann in about 1905. Because these maps are based on cell characteristics, the subject of cytology, they are called **cytoarchitectonic maps.** For example, viewed through a microscope, sensory cortex in the parietal lobe, shown in red in Figure 2-20, has a distinct layer IV. Motor cortex in the frontal lobe, shown in blue in Figure 2-20, has a distinctive layer V. Layer IV is afferent, whereas layer V is efferent. It makes sense that a sensory region would have a large input layer, whereas a motor region would have a large output layer.

Chemical differences in the cells in different cortical layers can be revealed by staining the tissue. Some regions are rich in one chemical, whereas others are rich in another. These differences presumably relate to functional specialization of different areas of the cortex.

The one significant difference between the organization of the cortex and the organization of other parts of the brain is its range of connections. Unlike most structures that connect to only selective brain regions, the cortex is connected to virtually all other parts of the brain. The cortex, in other words, is the ultimate meddler. It takes part in everything. This fact not only makes it difficult to identify specific functions of

Cytoarchitectonic map Map of the neocortex based on the organization, structure, and distribution of the cells.
Basal ganglia Subcortical forebrain nuclei that coordinate voluntary movements of the limbs and body; connected to the thalamus and to the midbrain.

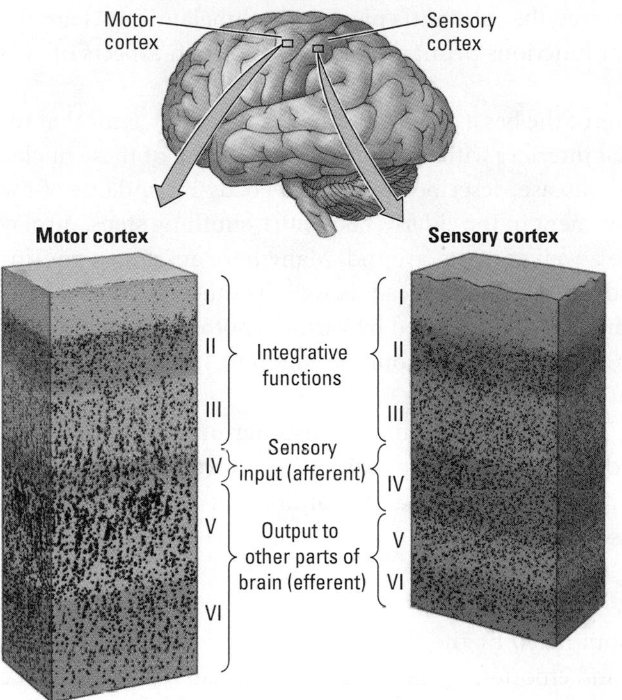

FIGURE 2-20 Layering in the Neocortex. As this comparison of cortical layers in the sensory and motor areas shows, layer IV is relatively thick in the sensory cortex and relatively thin in the motor cortex. Afferents connect to layer IV (from the thalamus) as well as to layers II and III. Efferents in layers V and VI connect to other parts of the cortex and to the motor structures of the brain.

FIGURE 2-21 Early Brain Map. In his cytoarchitectonic map of the cortex, Brodmann defined areas by the organization and characteristics of the cells that he examined. The regions shown in color are associated with the simplest sensory perceptions of touch (red), vision (purple), and hearing (orange). As we shall see, the areas of the cortex that process sensory information are far more extensive than these basic areas.

the cortex but also complicates our study of the rest of the brain because the cortex's role in other brain regions must always be considered.

Consider your perception of clouds. You have no doubt gazed up at clouds on a summer's day and imagined sailing ships, elephants, faces, and countless other objects. Although a cloud does not really look exactly like an elephant, you can concoct an image of one if you impose your frontal cortex—that is, your imagination—on the sensory inputs. This kind of cortical activity is known as *top-down processing* because the top level of the nervous system, the cortex, is influencing how information is processed in lower regions of the hierarchy—in this case, the midbrain and hindbrain.

The cortex influences many behaviors besides the perception of objects. It influences our cravings for foods, our lust for things (or people), and how we interpret the meaning of abstract concepts, words, and images. The cortex is the ultimate creator of our reality, and one reason that it serves this function is that it is so well connected.

The Basal Ganglia

A collection of nuclei that lie within the forebrain just below the white matter of the cortex, the **basal ganglia** consist of three principal structures: the *caudate nucleus,* the *putamen,* and the *globus pallidus,* all shown in **Figure 2-22**. Together with the thalamus

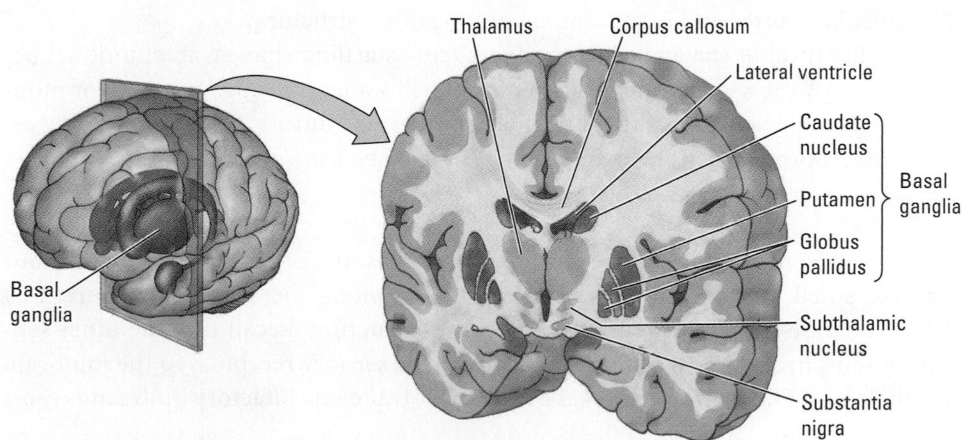

FIGURE 2-22 Basal Ganglia. This frontal section of the cerebral hemispheres shows the basal ganglia relative to surrounding structures. Two associated structures that are instrumental in controlling and coordinating movement, the substantia nigra and subthalamic nucleus, also are shown.

and two closely associated structures, the substantia nigra and subthalamic nucleus, the basal ganglia form a system that functions primarily to control certain aspects of voluntary movement.

Detailed coverage of Parkinson's disease appears in Chapters 5 and 16, and detail on Tourette's syndrome is in Chapter 11.

We can observe the functions of the basal ganglia by analyzing the behavior that results from the many diseases that interfere with the normal functioning of these nuclei. People afflicted with Parkinson's disease, described in Clinical Focus 2-2 and one of the most common disorders of movement in the elderly, take short, shuffling steps, display bent posture, and often require a walker to get around. Many have an almost continual tremor of the hands and sometimes of the head as well. Another disorder of the basal ganglia is **Tourette's syndrome,** characterized by various motor tics, involuntary vocalizations (including curse words and animal sounds), and odd, involuntary movements of the body, especially of the face and head.

Neither Parkinsonism nor Tourette's syndrome is a disorder of *producing* movements, as in paralysis. Rather they are disorders of *controlling* movements. The basal ganglia, therefore, must play a role in the control and coordination of movement patterns, not in activating the muscles to move.

The Limbic System

In the 1930s, psychiatry was dominated by the theories of Sigmund Freud, who emphasized the roles of sexuality and emotion in understanding human behavior. At the time, regions controlling these behaviors had not been identified in the brain, but a group of brain structures, collectively called the "limbic lobe," as yet had no known function. It was a simple step to thinking that perhaps the limbic structures played a central role in sexuality and emotion.

One sign that this hypothesis might be correct came from James Papez, who discovered that people with rabies have infections of limbic structures, and one of the symptoms of rabies is heightened emotionality. We now know that such a simple view is inaccurate. In fact, the **limbic system** is not a unitary system at all, and, although some limbic structures have roles in emotion and sexual behaviors, limbic structures serve other functions, too, including memory and motivation.

The limbic system figures prominently in discussions of addiction in Chapter 8, motivation and emotion in Chapter 12, memory in Chapter 14, and brain disorders in Chapter 16.

The principal limbic structures are shown in **Figure 2-23.** They include the *amygdala,* the *hippocampus,* and the *limbic,* or *cingulate, cortex,* which lies in the cingulate gyrus between the cerebral hemispheres. Recall that limbic cortex, structured in three or four layers of gray matter atop a layer of white matter, is evolutionarily older than the six-layered neocortex.

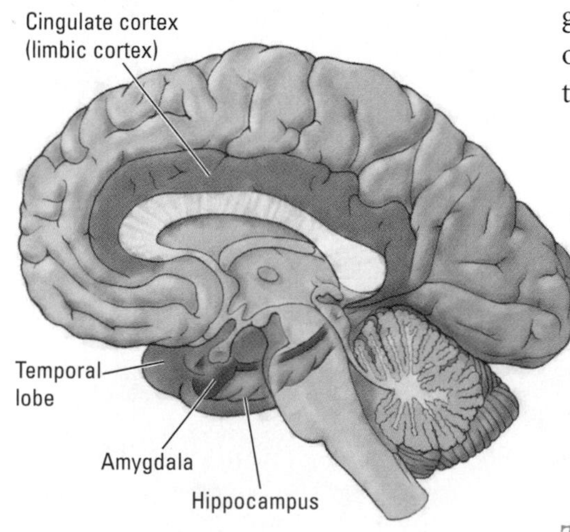

FIGURE 2-23 Limbic System. This medial view of the right hemisphere illustrates the principal structures of the limbic system that play roles in emotional and sexual behaviors, motivation, and memory.

The hippocampus, the cingulate cortex, and associated structures have roles in certain memory functions, as well as in controlling navigation in space. Many limbic structures are also believed to be at least partly responsible for the rewarding properties of psychoactive drugs. Repeated exposure to drugs such as amphetamine or nicotine produces both chemical and structural changes in the cingulate cortex and hippocampus, among other structures.

Removal of the amygdala produces truly startling changes in emotional behavior. A cat with the amygdala removed will wander through a colony of monkeys, completely undisturbed by their hooting and threats. No self-respecting cat would normally be caught anywhere near such bedlam.

The Olfactory System

At the very front of the brain lie the olfactory bulbs, the organs responsible for our sense of smell. The olfactory system is unique among the senses, as **Figure 2-24** shows, because it is almost entirely a forebrain structure. Recall that the other sensory systems project most of their inputs from the sensory receptors to the midbrain and thalamus. Olfactory input takes a less-direct route: the olfactory bulb sends most

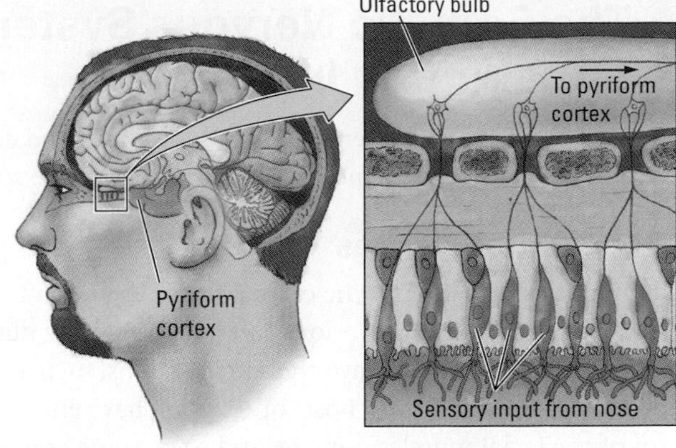

FIGURE 2-24 Sense of Smell. Our small olfactory bulbs lie at the base of the forebrain, connected to receptor cells that lie in the nasal cavity.

of its inputs to a specialized region, the *pyriform cortex* at the bottom of the brain, before progressing to the dorsal medial thalamus, which then provides a route to the frontal cortex.

A curious aspect of the olfactory system is that it is one of the first senses to have evolved in animals, yet it is found at the front of the human brain and considered part of the forebrain (see the ventral view in Figure 2-4). This is partly an "accident" of evolution. The olfactory bulbs lie near the olfactory receptors in the nasal cavity and, although they send their inputs to the pyriform cortex in mammals, the input to the brainstem is more direct in simpler brains.

Compared with the olfactory bulbs of animals such as rats, cats, and dogs, which depend more heavily on the sense of smell than we do, the human olfactory bulb is relatively small. Nonetheless, it is still sensitive and plays an important role in various aspects of our feeding and sexual behavior.

We return to the olfactory system in Chapter 12 in considering the senses of smell and taste in the context of emotional and motivated behavior.

REVIEW: The Central Nervous System: Mediating Behavior

- ✔ The CNS is subdivided into three functionally distinct subsections—the spinal cord, brainstem, and forebrain—that represent the evolution of levels of function. As the brain grows larger, new levels of control are integrated into existing neural systems.
- ✔ The spinal cord can perceive sensations from the skin and muscles and produce movements independent of the brain.
- ✔ The brainstem both directs movements and creates a sensory world through its connections with the sensory systems, the forebrain, and the spinal cord.
- ✔ The brainstem includes three functional regions: the hindbrain, midbrain, and diencephalon. The hindbrain is an extension of the spinal cord, the midbrain is the first brain region to receive sensory inputs, and the diencephalon integrates sensory and motor information on its way to the cerebral cortex.
- ✔ The forebrain's subcortical regions include the basal ganglia, which control voluntary movement, and the limbic system, which controls mood, motivation, and some forms of memory. Overlying the brainstem and subcortical forebrain regions is the cerebral cortex, composed of six layers.
- ✔ The forebrain is the largest part of the mammalian brain. It regulates cognitive activity, including thought and memory, and holds ultimate control over movement.

Tourette's syndrome Disorder of the basal ganglia characterized by tics; involuntary vocalizations (including curse words and animal sounds); and odd, involuntary movements of the body, especially of the face and head.
Limbic system Disparate forebrain structures lying between the neocortex and the brainstem that form a functional system controlling affective and motivated behaviors and certain forms of memory; includes cingulate cortex, amygdala, hippocampus, among other structures.

The Somatic Nervous System: Transmitting Information

The somatic nervous system (SNS) is monitored and controlled by the CNS—the cranial nerves by the brain and the spinal nerves by the spinal cord segments.

The Cranial Nerves

The linkages provided by the **cranial nerves** between the brain and various parts of the head and neck as well as various internal organs are illustrated and tabulated in **Figure 2-25.** Cranial nerves can have afferent functions, such as sensory inputs to the brain from the eyes, ears, mouth, and nose, or they can have efferent functions, such as motor control of the facial muscles, tongue, and eyes. Some cranial nerves have both sensory and motor functions, such as the modulation of both sensation and movement in the face.

The 12 pairs of cranial nerves are known both by their numbers and by their names, as listed in Figure 2-25. One set of 12 controls the left side of the head, whereas the other set controls the right side. This arrangement makes sense for innervating duplicated parts of the head (such as the eyes), but why separate nerves should control the right and left sides of a singular structure (such as the tongue) is not so clear. Yet that is how the cranial nerves work. If you have ever received novocaine for dental work, you know that usually just one side of your tongue becomes anesthetized because the dentist injects the drug into only one side of your mouth. The rest of the skin and muscles on each side of the head are similarly controlled by cranial nerves located on that same side.

We consider many of the cranial nerves in some detail in later chapters in discussions on topics such as vision, hearing, olfaction, taste, and responses to stress. For now, you simply need to know that cranial nerves form part of the somatic nervous system, providing inputs to the brain from the head's sensory organs and muscles and con-

FIGURE 2-25 Cranial Nerves. Each of the 12 pairs of cranial nerves has a different function. A common mnemonic device for learning the order of the cranial nerves is, On old Olympus's towering top, a Finn and German vainly skip & hop. The first letter of each word is, in order, the first letter of the name of each nerve.

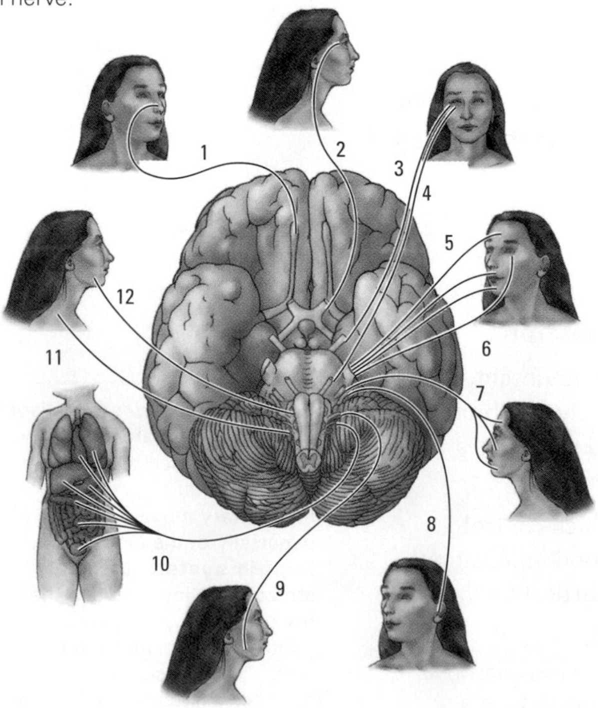

Cranial nerve	Name	Function
1	Olfactory	Smell
2	Optic	Vision
3	Oculomotor	Eye movement
4	Trochlear	Eye movement
5	Trigeminal	Masticatory movements and facial sensation
6	Abducens	Eye movement
7	Facial	Facial movement and sensation
8	Auditory vestibular	Hearing and balance
9	Glossopharyngeal	Tongue and pharynx movement and sensation
10	Vagus	Heart, blood vessels, viscera, movement of larynx and pharynx
11	Spinal accessory	Neck muscles
12	Hypoglossal	Tongue muscles

trolling head and facial movements. The cranial nerves also contribute to maintaining autonomic functions by connecting the brain and internal organs and by influencing other autonomic responses, such as salivation.

Cranial nerve One of a set of 12 nerve pairs that control sensory and motor functions of the head, neck, and internal organs.

Vertebrae (sing. vertebra) The bones, or segments, that form the spinal column.

The Spinal Nerves

The spinal cord lies inside the bony spinal column, which is made up of a series of small bones called **vertebrae,** categorized into five anatomical regions from top to bottom: cervical, thoracic, lumbar, sacral, and coccygeal, as diagrammed in **Figure 2-26**A. You can think of each vertebra within these five groups as a very short segment of the spinal column. The corresponding spinal-cord segment within each vertebral region functions as that segment's "minibrain."

This arrangement may seem a bit odd, but it has a long evolutionary history. Think of a simpler animal, such as a snake, which evolved long before humans did. A snake's body is a tube divided into segments. Within that tube is another tube, the spinal cord, which also is segmented. Each of the snake's nervous-system segments receives nerve fibers from sensory receptors in the part of the body adjacent to it, and that nervous-system segment sends fibers back to the muscles in that body part. Each segment, therefore, works independently.

A complication arises in animals such as humans, who have limbs that may originate at one spinal-segment level but extend past other segments of the spinal column. Your shoulders, for example, may begin at C5 (cervical segment 5), but your arms hang down well past the sacral segments. So, unlike the snake, which has spinal-cord segments that connect to body segments fairly directly adjacent to them, human body segments fall schematically into more of a patchwork pattern, as shown in Figure 2-26B. This arrangement makes sense if the arms are extended as they are when we walk on "all fours."

Spinal-cord segmentation and bilateral symmetry (one half of the body is the mirror image of the other) are two important structural features of human nervous-system evolution noted in Chapter 1.

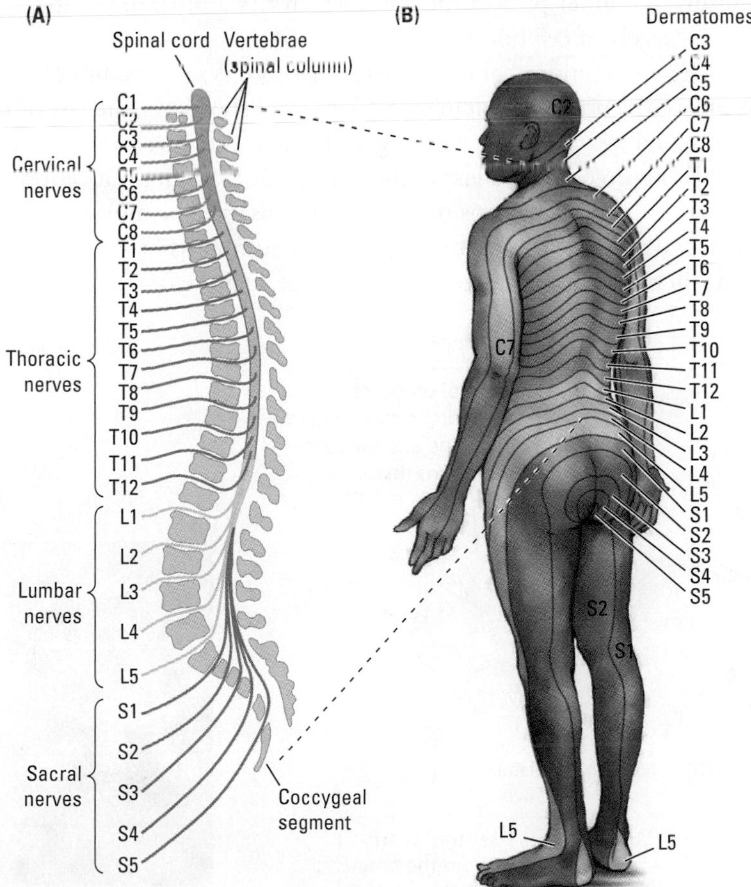

FIGURE 2-26 Spinal Segments and Dermatomes. (A) Medial view of the spinal column, showing the five spinal-cord segments: cervical (C), thoracic (T), lumbar (L), sacral (S), and coccygeal. (B) Each spinal segment corresponds to a region of body surface (a dermatome) identified by the segment number (examples are C5 at the base of the neck and L2 in the lower back).

Dermatome Area of the skin supplied with afferent nerve fibers by a single spinal-cord dorsal root.
Law of Bell and Magendie The general principle that sensory fibers are located dorsally and motor fibers are located ventrally.

Regardless of their complex pattern, however, the segments of our bodies still correspond to segments of the spinal cord. Each of these body segments is called a **dermatome** (meaning "skin cut"). A dermatome has both a sensory nerve, which sends information from the skin, joints, and muscles to the spinal cord, and a motor nerve, which controls the movements of the muscles in that particular segment of the body.

These sensory and motor nerves, known as *spinal* (or *peripheral*) *nerves,* are functionally equivalent to the cranial nerves of the head. Whereas the cranial nerves receive information from sensory receptors in the eyes, ears, facial skin, and so forth, the spinal nerves receive information from sensory receptors in the rest of the body—that is, in the PNS. Similarly, whereas the cranial nerves move the muscles of the eyes, tongue, and face, the peripheral nerves move the muscles of the limbs and trunk.

Connections of the Somatic Nervous System

Like the central nervous system, the somatic nervous system is bilateral (two sided). Just as the cranial nerves control functions on the same side of the head on which they are found, the spinal nerves on the left side of the spinal cord control the left side of the body, and those on the right side of the spinal cord control the body's right side.

Figure 2-27A shows the spinal column in cross section. Look first at the nerve fibers entering the spinal cord's dorsal (back) side. These dorsal fibers are afferent: they carry information from the body's sensory receptors. The fibers collect together as they enter a spinal-cord segment, and this collection of fibers is called a *dorsal root.*

Fibers leaving the spinal cord's ventral (front) side are efferent, carrying information from the spinal cord to the muscles. They, too, bundle together as they exit the spinal cord and so form a ventral root. The outer part of the spinal cord, which is pictured in Figure 2-27B, consists of white matter, or CNS nerve tracts. These tracts are arranged so that, with some exceptions, dorsal tracts are sensory and ventral tracts are motor. The inner part of the cord, which has a butterfly shape, is gray matter composed largely of cell bodies.

Recall that white matter forms the connections among cells, and gray matter collects and processes incoming (afferent) sensory or outgoing (efferent) motor information.

The observation that the dorsal spinal cord is sensory and the ventral side is motor is one of the nervous system's very few established laws, the **law of Bell and Magendie.** Combined with an understanding of the spinal cord's segmental organization, this law enables neurologists to make accurate inferences about the location of spinal-cord damage or disease on the basis of changes in sensation or movement that patients experience. For instance, if a person experiences numbness in the fingers of the left hand but can still move the hand fairly normally, one or more of the dorsal nerves in spinal-cord

FIGURE 2-27 Spinal-Nerve Connections. (A) A cross section of the spinal cord, viewed from the front. The butterfly-shaped inner regions consist of neural cell bodies (gray matter), and the outer regions consist of nerve tracts (white matter) traveling to and from the brain. (B) A dorsal-view photograph shows the intact spinal cord exposed.

(A)

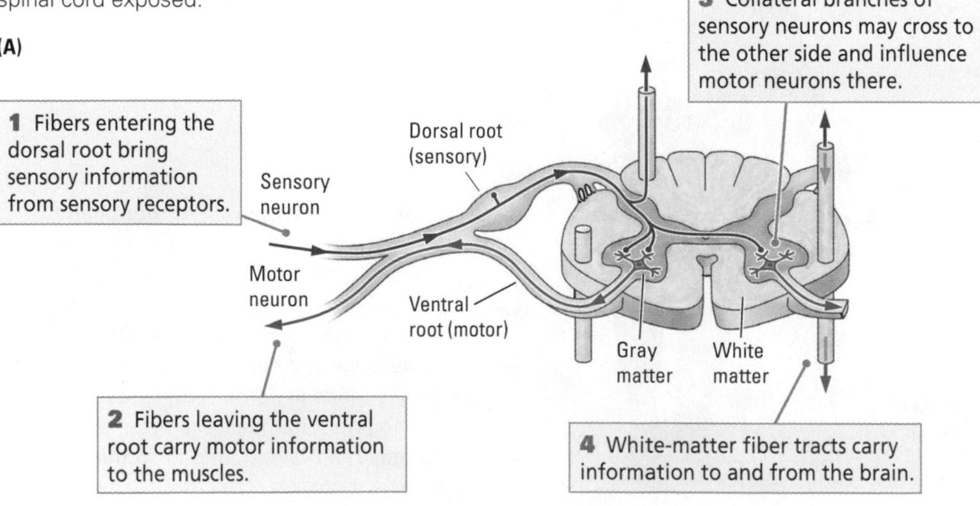

1 Fibers entering the dorsal root bring sensory information from sensory receptors.
Sensory neuron
Motor neuron
Dorsal root (sensory)
Ventral root (motor)
3 Collateral branches of sensory neurons may cross to the other side and influence motor neurons there.
Gray matter
White matter
2 Fibers leaving the ventral root carry motor information to the muscles.
4 White-matter fiber tracts carry information to and from the brain.

(B)

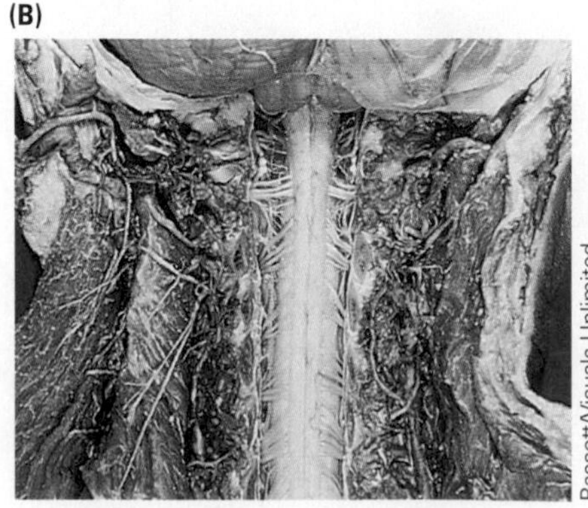

Bassett/Visuals Unlimited

CLINICAL FOCUS 2-4

Magendie, Bell, and Bell's Palsy

François Magendie, a volatile and committed French experimental physiologist, reported in a three-page paper in 1822 that he had succeeded in cutting the dorsal and ventral roots of puppies, animals in which the roots are sufficiently segregated to allow such surgery. Magendie found that cutting the dorsal roots caused loss of sensation, whereas cutting the ventral roots caused loss of movement.

Eleven years earlier, a Scot named Charles Bell had proposed functions for these nerve roots on the basis of anatomical information and the results of somewhat inconclusive experiments on rabbits. Although Bell's findings were not identical with those of Magendie, they were similar enough to ignite a controversy. Bell hotly disputed Magendie's claim to the discovery of dorsal- and ventral-root functions. As a result, the principle of sensory and motor segregation in the nervous system has been named after both researchers: the law of Bell and Magendie.

Magendie's conclusive experiment on puppies was considered extremely important because it enabled neurologists, for the first time, to localize nervous system damage from the symptoms that a patient displays. Bell went on to describe an example of such localized, cranial motor-nerve dysfunction that still bears his name—*Bell's palsy,* a facial paralysis that develops when the motor part of the facial nerve on one side of the head becomes inflamed (see the accompanying photograph).

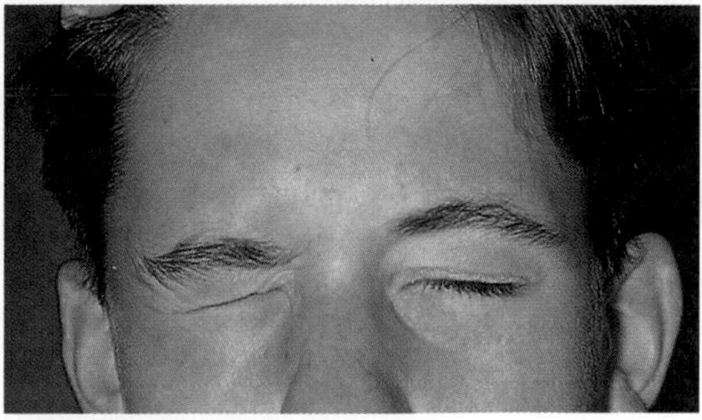

Dr. P. Marazzi/Science Photo Library/Photo Researchers

A young man suffering from Bell's palsy, a paralysis of the facial nerve that causes weakness over one side of the face. He was photographed during an involuntary tic (a nervous reaction) that affects the right side of the face, causing his right eye to close tightly.

The onset of Bell's palsy is typically sudden. Often the stricken person wakes up in the morning and is shocked to discover the face paralyzed on one side. He or she cannot open the mouth on that side of the head or completely close the eye on that side. Most people fully recover from Bell's palsy, although recovery may take several months. But, in rare instances, such as that of Jean Chretien, a former prime minister of Canada, partial paralysis of the mouth is permanent.

segments C7 and C8 must be damaged. In contrast, if sensation in the hand is normal but the person cannot move the fingers, the ventral roots of the same segments must be damaged. Clinical Focus 2-4, "Magendie, Bell, and Bell's Palsy," further explores the topic of diagnosing spinal-cord injury or disease.

Chapter 11 explores causes of spinal-cord injuries and treatments for them. The link between spinal injury and loss of emotion is a topic in Chapter 12.

Integrating Spinal Functions

So far, we have emphasized the segmental organization of the spinal cord, but the spinal cord must also somehow coordinate inputs and outputs across different segments. For example, many body movements require the coordination of muscles that are controlled by different segments, just as many sensory experiences require the coordination of sensory inputs to different parts of the spinal cord. How is this coordination accomplished? The answer is that the spinal-cord segments are interconnected in such a way that adjacent segments can operate together to direct rather complex coordinated movements.

The integration of spinal-cord activities does not require the brain's participation, which is why the headless chicken can run around in a reasonably coordinated way. Still, a close working relation must exist between the brain and the spinal cord. Otherwise, how could we consciously plan and execute our voluntary actions?

Somehow information must be relayed back and forth, and examples of this information sharing are numerous. For instance, tactile information from sensory nerves in the skin travels not just to the spinal cord but also to the cerebral cortex through the

Sympathetic division Part of the autonomic nervous system; arouses the body for action, such as mediating the involuntary fight-or-flight response to alarm by increasing heart rate and blood pressure.
Parasympathetic division Part of the autonomic nervous system; acts in opposition to the sympathetic division—for example, preparing the body to rest and digest by reversing the alarm response or stimulating digestion.

thalamus. Similarly, the cerebral cortex and other brain structures can control movements through their connections to the ventral roots of the spinal cord. So, even though the brain and spinal cord can function independently, the two are intimately connected in their CNS functions.

REVIEW: The Somatic Nervous System: Transmitting Information

- ✔ The cranial and spinal (peripheral) nerves constitute the somatic nervous system. Both sets of SNS nerves function to receive sensory information or to send motor signals to muscles or both.
- ✔ Both sets of SNS nerves have a symmetrical organization, with one set controlling each side of the body.
- ✔ The cranial nerves have both sensory and motor functions, receiving and sending information to the head (e.g., eyes, ears, skin, muscles) and internal body organs (e.g., heart and gut).
- ✔ The spinal nerves contact distinct segments of the spinal cord that are defined by the vertebrae of the spinal column. Each segment is composed of a dorsal (sensory) and ventral (motor) division that together act as a "minibrain" to elicit the rapid responses of basic movement reflexes, independently of the brain.

The Autonomic Nervous System: Balancing Internal Functions

The internal autonomic nervous system is a hidden partner in controlling behavior. Even without our conscious awareness, it stays on the job to keep the heart beating, the liver releasing glucose, the pupils of the eyes adjusting to light, and so forth. Without the ANS, which regulates the internal organs and glands by connections through the SNS to the CNS, life would quickly cease. Although learning to exert some conscious control over some of these vegetative activities is possible, such conscious interference is unnecessary. An important reason is that the ANS must keep working during sleep when conscious awareness is off-duty.

Although we might think that the autonomic system's organization must be pretty simple because it functions outside conscious awareness, the ANS, like the SNS, can be thought of as a collection of minibrains. The autonomic system has a surprisingly complex organization. For example, the gut responds to a range of hormones and other chemicals with exquisite neural responses. Some scientists have even proposed that the central nervous system evolved from the gut of very simple organisms.

Principle 10: The nervous system works by juxtaposing excitation and inhibition.

The two divisions of the ANS, **sympathetic** and **parasympathetic,** work in opposition. The sympathetic system arouses the body for action, for example, by stimulating the heart to beat faster and inhibiting digestion when we exert ourselves during exercise or times of stress—the familiar "fight or flight" response. The parasympathetic system calms the body down, for example, by slowing the heartbeat and stimulating digestion to allow us to "rest and digest" after exertion and during quiet times.

Like the SNS, the ANS interacts with the rest of the nervous system. Activation of the sympathetic division starts in the thoracic and lumbar spinal-cord regions. But the spinal nerves do not directly control the target organs. Rather, the spinal cord is connected to autonomic control centers, which are collections of neural cells called *ganglia.* The ganglia control the internal organs, and each acts as a minibrain for specific organs.

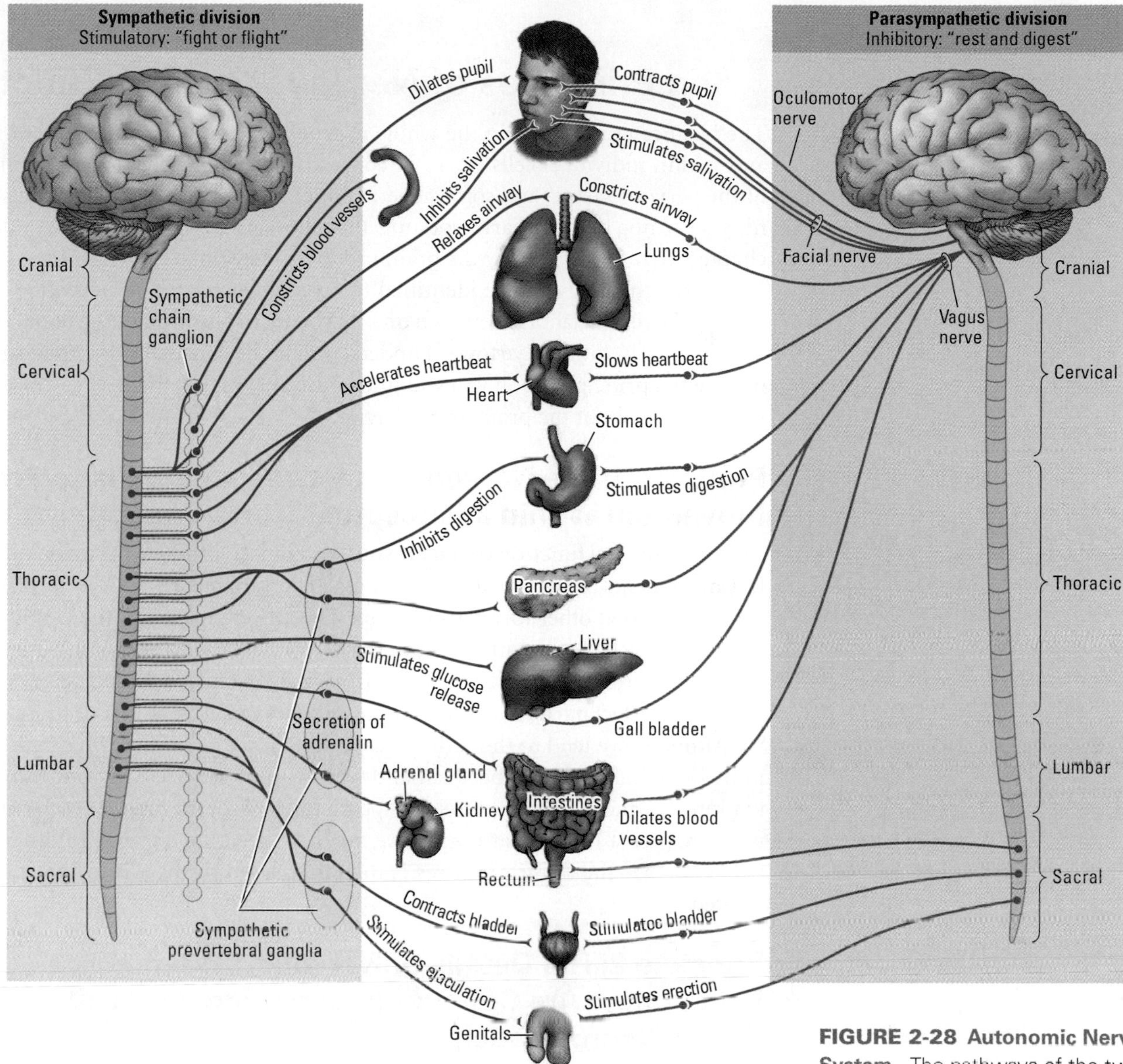

FIGURE 2-28 Autonomic Nervous System. The pathways of the two divisions of the ANS exert opposing effects on the organs that they innervate. All autonomic fibers connect at "stops" en route from the CNS to their target organs. (*Left*) Arousing sympathetic fibers connect to a chain of ganglia near the spinal cord. (*Right*) Calming parasympathetic fibers connect to individual parasympathetic ganglia near the target organs.

The sympathetic ganglia are located near the spinal cord, forming a chain that runs parallel to the cord, as illustrated on the left in **Figure 2-28.** The parasympathetic division also is connected to the spinal cord—specifically, to the sacral region—but the greater part of it derives from three cranial nerves: the vagus nerve, which calms most of the internal organs, and the facial and oculomotor nerves, which control salivation and pupil dilation, respectively (review Figure 2-26). In contrast with the sympathetic division, the parasympathetic division connects with ganglia that are near the target organs, as shown on the right in Figure 2-28.

REVIEW: The Autonomic Nervous System: Balancing Internal Functions

- ✔ The ANS ganglia act as a minibrain outside conscious awareness to control our body glands and organs.
- ✔ The sympathetic division of the ANS arouses the body for action, and the parasympathetic division calms the organs. The two divisions work in opposition to allow for quick defensive responses (fight or flight) and a calming (rest and digest) state.

Ten Principles of Nervous-System Function

The balance created within the whole nervous system, within the functioning brain, and within individual cells works in concert to produce behavior. Knowing the parts of the nervous system and some general notions about what they do is only the beginning. Learning how the parts work together allows us to proceed to a closer look, in the chapters that follow, at how the brain produces behavior.

In this chapter, we have identified ten principles related to nervous-system functioning. Here, we elaborate on each one. As you progress through the book, review these ideas regularly with an eye toward understanding the concept rather than simply memorizing the principle. Soon you will find yourself applying them as you encounter new information about the brain and behavior.

Principle 1: The Nervous System's Function Is to Produce Movement Within a Perceptual World Created by the Brain

The fundamental function of the nervous system is to produce behavior, or movement. But movements are not made in a vacuum. They are related to objects, places, memories, and myriad other forces and factors. The representation of the world depends on the nature of the information sent to the brain. Those who are color-blind have a very different representation of the world from that of those who perceive color. People who have perfect pitch have a different perceptual world from that of those who do not.

Although we tend to think that the world that we perceive is what is actually there, individual realities, both between and within species, are clearly but rough approximations of what is actually present. A special function of the brain of each animal species is to produce a reality that is adaptive for that species to survive. In other words, the behavior that the brain produces is directly related to the world that the brain has created.

Principle 2: The Details of Nervous-System Functioning Are Constantly Changing, an Attribute Called Neuroplasticity

The brain's organization is altered by experience, and neuroplasticity is required for learning and memory functions as well as for survival. In fact, information is stored in the nervous system only if neural connections change. Forgetting is presumably due to a loss of the connections that represented the memory.

Neuroplasticity is a characteristic not just of the mammalian brain; it is found in the nervous systems of all animals, even the simplest worms. Nonetheless, larger brains have more capacity for change and are thus likely to show more-plastic neural organization.

Neuroplasticity is not always beneficial. Analyses of the brains of animals given addicting doses of drugs such as cocaine or morphine reveal large changes in neural connectivity suspected of underlying some maladaptive behaviors related to addiction. Among the many other examples of pathological neuroplasticity are pathological pain, epilepsy, and dementia.

Chapter 14 explores the neural bases of plasticity and drug addiction. Chapter 11 explains how we feel pain. Chapter 4 describes the symptoms of epilepsy, and Chapter 16 details its diagnosis and treatment. Chapter 16 also describes the spectrum of dementias that neuroscientists have identified.

Principle 3: Many of the Brain's Circuits Are Crossed

A most-peculiar organizational feature of the brain is that most of its inputs and outputs are "crossed." Each hemisphere receives sensory stimulation from the opposite (contralateral) side of the body and controls muscles on the contralateral side as well. Crossed organization explains why people who experience strokes or other damage to the left cerebral hemisphere may have difficulty in sensing stimulation to the right side of the body or in moving body parts on the right side. The opposite is true of people with strokes in the right cerebral hemisphere.

The human visual system, explained in Chapter 9, has evolved a fascinating solution to the challenge of representing the world seen through two eyes as a single perception: both eyes connect with both hemispheres.

A crossed nervous system must join the two sides of the perceptual world together somehow. To do so, innumerable neural connections link the left and right sides of the brain. The most prominent connecting cable is the corpus callosum, which joins the left and right cerebral hemispheres with about 200 million nerve fibers.

Two important exceptions to the crossed-circuit principle are the olfactory and somatic nervous systems. Olfactory information does not cross but rather projects directly into the same (ipsilateral) side of the brain. Furthermore, the cranial and spinal nerves do not cross but are connected ipsiliaterally.

Principle 4: The Central Nervous System Functions on Multiple Levels

Sensory and motor functions are carried out at many places in the brain, in the spinal cord and the brainstem as well as in the forebrain. This multiplicity of functions results from the nature of brain evolution.

Simple animals such as worms have a spinal cord, more-complex animals such as fish have a brainstem as well, and more-complex animals have evolved a forebrain. Each new addition to the CNS has added a new level of behavioral complexity without discarding previous levels of control. As animals evolved legs, for example, they also had to add brain structures to move them. Later, when they developed independent digit movements, it, too, required more brainpower.

The addition of new brain areas can be viewed as the addition of new levels of nervous-system control. The new levels are not autonomous but rather must be integrated into the existing neural systems. Each new level can be conceived of as a way of refining and elaborating the control provided by the earlier levels.

The idea of levels of function can be seen not only in the addition of forebrain areas to refine the control of the brainstem but also within the forebrain itself. As mammals evolved, they developed an increased capacity to represent the world in the cortex, an ability that is related to the addition of more "maps." The new maps must be related to the older ones, however, and, again, are simply an elaboration of the sensory world that was there before.

Principle 5: The Brain Is Both Symmetrical and Asymmetrical

Although the left and the right hemispheres look like mirror images, they also have some dissimilar features. Cortical asymmetry is essential for integrative tasks, language and body control among them.

Consider speaking. If a language zone existed in both hemispheres, each connected to one side of the mouth, we would have the strange ability to talk out of both sides of our mouths at once. It would make talking awkward, to say the least. One solution is to locate language control of the mouth on one side of the brain only. Organizing the brain in this way allows us to speak with a single voice.

A similar problem arises in controlling the body's movement in space. We would not want the left and the right hemispheres each trying to take us to a different place. Again, the problem can be solved if a single brain area controls this sort of spatial processing.

In fact, functions such as language and spatial navigation are localized on only one side of the brain. Language is usually on the left side, and spatial functions are usually on the right. The brains of many species have both symmetrical and asymmetrical features. The control of singing is located in one hemisphere in the bird brain. Like human language, birdsong is usually located on the left side. The control of song by two sides of the brain would likely suffer the same problems as the control of language, and birds and humans likely evolved the same solution independently—namely, to place the control only on one side of the brain.

Principle 6: Brain Systems Are Organized Both Hierarchically and in Parallel

When we consider that the CNS comprises multiple levels of function, these levels clearly must be extensively interconnected to integrate their processing and create unified perceptions or movements. The nature of this connectivity leads to the next principle of brain function: the brain has both serial (or hierarchical) and parallel circuitry.

A hierarchical circuit hooks up a linear series of all regions concerned with a particular function. Consider vision. In a serial system, the information from the eyes goes to regions that detect the simplest properties such as color or brightness. This information would then be passed to another region that determines shape and then to another region that measures movement and so on until, at the most-complex level, the information is understood to be, say, your grandmother. Information therefore flows in a hierarchical manner sequentially from simpler to more-complex regions as illustrated in **Figure 2-29**A.

(A)

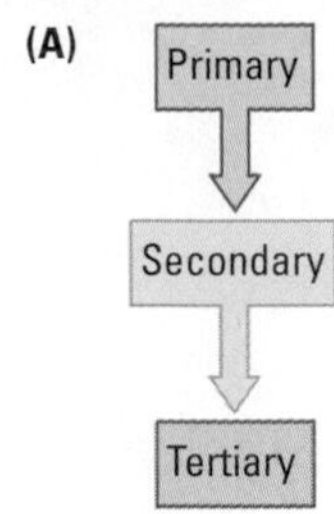

(B)

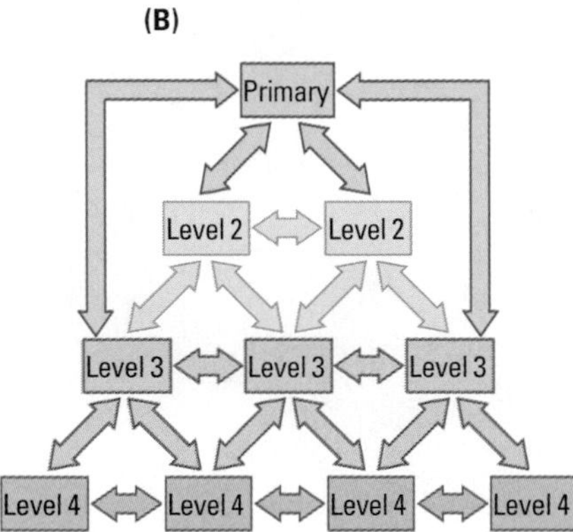

FIGURE 2-29 Models of Neural Information Processing. (A) Simple serial hierarchical model of cortical processing similar to that first proposed by Alexandre Luria in the 1960s. (B) In Daniel Felleman and David van Essen's distributed hierarchical model, multiple levels exist in each of several processing streams. Areas at each level interconnect.

One difficulty with hierarchical models, however, is that functionally related structures in the brain are not always linked in a linear series. Although the brain has many serial connections, many expected connections are missing. For example, within the visual system, not all cortical regions are connected to one another. The simplest explanation is that the unconnected regions must have very different functions.

Parallel circuits operate on a different principle that also is illustrated by the visual system. Imagine looking at a car. As we look at a car door, one set of visual pathways processes information about its nature, such as its color and shape, whereas another set of pathways processes information about door-related movements, such as those required to open it.

These two visual systems are independent of each other, yet they must interact in some manner. Your perception when you pull the door open is not one of two different representations—the door's size, shape, and color on the one hand and the opening movements on the other. When you open the door, you have the impression of unity in your conscious experience.

Figure 2-29B illustrates the flow of information in such a distributed hierarchy. If you trace the information flow from the primary area to levels 2, 3, and 4, you can see the parallel pathways. These multiple parallel pathways are also connected to one another. However, the connections are more selective than those that exist in a purely serial circuit.

Interestingly, the brain is organized into multiple parallel pathways in all its subsystems. Yet our conscious experiences are always unified. As we explore this conundrum throughout the book, keep in mind that your commonsense impressions of how the brain works may not always be correct.

Principle 7: Sensory and Motor Divisions Exist Throughout the Nervous System

The segregation of sensory and motor functions described by the Bell and Magendie law exists throughout the nervous system. However, distinctions between motor and sensory functions become subtler in the forebrain.

Sensory and Motor Divisions in the Somatic Nervous System

You can review cranial- and spinal-nerve connections in Figures 2-26 and 2-27.

The spinal nerves are either sensory or motor in function. Some cranial nerves are exclusively sensory; some are exclusively motor; and some have two parts, one sensory and one motor, much like spinal nerves serving the skin and muscles.

Sensory and Motor Divisions in the Central Nervous System

Brainstem structures are illustrated in Figures 2-13 through 2-17.

The lower brainstem regions—hindbrain and midbrain—are essentially extensions of the spinal cord and retain the spinal-cord division, with sensory structures located dorsally and motor ones ventrally. An important function of the midbrain is to orient the body to stimuli. Orienting movements require both sensory input and motor output. The midbrain's colliculi, which are located dorsally in the tectum, are the sensory component, whereas the tegmentum, which is ventral, is a motor structure that plays a role in controlling various movements, including orienting ones.

Distinct sensory nuclei are present in the thalamus, too, although they are no longer located dorsally. Because all sensory information reaches the forebrain through the thalamus, to find separate nuclei associated with vision, hearing, and touch is not surprising. Separate thalamic nuclei also control movements. Other nuclei have neither sensory nor motor functions but rather connect to cortical areas, such as the frontal lobe, that perform more-integrative tasks.

Finally, sensory and motor functions are divided in the cortex in two ways:

1. Separate sensory and motor cortical regions process particular sensory inputs, such as vision, hearing, or touch. Others control detailed movements of discrete body parts, such as the fingers.
2. The entire cortex is organized around the sensory and motor distinction. Layer IV of the cortex always receives sensory inputs, layers V and VI always send motor outputs, and layers I, II, and III integrate sensory and motor operations.

To review the layered structure of the cortex, see Figure 2-20.

Principle 8: Sensory Input to the Brain Is Divided for Object Recognition and Motor Control

Sensory systems evolved first for controlling motion, not for recognizing things. Simple organisms can detect stimulation such as light and move to or from it. It is not necessary to "perceive" an object to direct movements toward or away from it. As animals, and their behaviors, became more complex, they began to evolve ways of representing their environment. Animals with complex brains, such as ourselves, evolved separate systems for producing movement toward objects and for recognizing them. The visual system exemplifies this separation.

Visual information travels from the eyes to the thalamus to visual regions of the occipital lobe where it follows one of two routes: one route, known as the *ventral stream*, leads to the temporal lobe for identification, whereas the other route, known as the *dorsal stream*, goes to the parietal lobe to guide movements relative to objects (**Figure 2-30**). People with ventral-stream injuries are "blind" for the recognition of objects, yet they nevertheless shape their hands appropriately when asked to reach for the objects that they cannot identify.

In Chapter 9, we review the evidence that led to understanding the functions of the visual streams and how each stream processes visual information.

Consider reaching for a cup. When a normal subject reaches for a cup, his or her hand forms a shape that is different from the shape that it forms when reaching for a spoon. People with ventral-stream injuries can make appropriate hand shapes, yet they do not consciously recognize the object. In contrast, people with dorsal-stream injuries can recognize objects but make clumsy reaching movements because they do not form appropriate hand postures until they contact objects. Only then do they shape the hand on the basis of tactile information.

The recognition that perception for movement and perception for object recognition are independent processes has three important implications for understanding brain organization:

1. The dorsal and ventral systems provide an excellent example of parallel information processing in the brain.
2. Although we may think that we are aware of our entire sensory world, the sensory analysis required for some movements is clearly not conscious.
3. The presence of unconscious and conscious brain processing underlies an important difference in our cognitive functions. The unconscious-movement system is always acting in the present and in response to ongoing sensory input. In

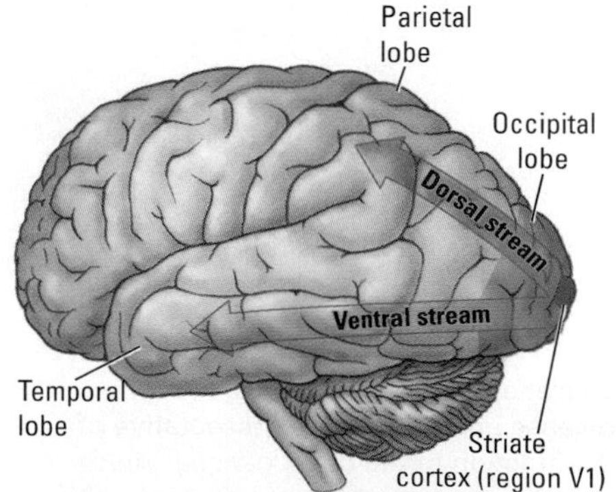

FIGURE 2-30 Neural Streams. The dorsal and ventral streams mediate vision for action and recognition, respectively.

Alzheimer's disease Degenerative brain disorder related to aging that first appears as progressive memory loss and later develops into generalized dementia.
Excitation Increase in the activity of a neuron or brain area.
Inhibition Decrease in the activity of a neuron or brain area.

contrast, the recognition system allows us to escape the present and bring to bear information from the past. Thus, the object-recognition system forms the neural basis of enduring memory.

Principle 9: Functions in the Brain Are Both Localized and Distributed

One of the great debates in the history of brain research has concerned what aspects of different functions are actually localized in specific brain regions. Perhaps the fundamental problem is that of defining a function. Language, for example, includes the comprehension of spoken words, written words, signed words (as in American Sign Language), and even touched words (as in Braille). Language also includes processes of producing words orally, in writing, and by signing, as well as constructing whole linguistic compositions, such as stories, poems, songs, and essays.

Because the function that we call language has many aspects, it is not surprising that these aspects reside in widely separated areas of the brain. We see evidence of this widespread distribution in language-related brain injuries. People with injuries in different locations may selectively lose the abilities to produce words, understand words, read words, write words, and so forth. Specific language-related abilities, therefore, are found in specific locations, but language itself is distributed throughout a wide region of the brain.

Memory provides another example of this same distributed pattern. Memories can be extremely rich in detail and can include sensual feelings, words, images, and much more. Like language, then, aspects of memory are located in many brain regions distributed throughout a vast area of the brain.

Because many functions are both localized and distributed in the brain, damage to a small brain region produces only focal symptoms. Massive brain damage is required to completely remove some functions. Thus, a small injury could impair some aspect of language functioning, but it would take a widespread injury to completely remove all language abilities. In fact, one of the characteristics of dementing diseases is that people can endure widespread deterioration of the cortex yet maintain remarkably normal language functions until late stages of the disease. **Alzheimer's disease** is a degenerative brain disorder related to aging that first appears as progressive memory loss and only much later develops into generalized dementia.

You will find information about the neurochemistry of Alzheimer's disease in Chapter 5, its incidence and possible causes in Chapter 14, and treatments in Chapter 16.

Principle 10: The Nervous System Works by Juxtaposing Excitation and Inhibition

Although we have emphasized the brain's role in making movements, we must also recognize that the brain acts to prevent movements. To make a directed movement, such as picking up a glass of water, we must refrain from other movements, such as waving the hand back and forth. In producing movement, then, the brain produces some action through **excitation** and, through **inhibition,** prevents other action.

Brain injury or disease can produce either a *loss* or a *release* of behavior through changes in the balance between excitation and inhibition. A person with a brain injury to a region that normally initiates speech may render the person unable to talk. This result is a loss of behavior. A person with an abnormality in a region that inhibits inappropriate language (such as swearing) may be unable to inhibit this form of talking. This result is a release of behavior that can be seen in Tourette's syndrome.

Tourette's syndrome and Parkinson's disease are disorders representative of dysfunction in the basal ganglia, which coordinates voluntary movement.

Patients with Parkinson's disease may endure uncontrollable shaking of the hands because the neural system that inhibits such movements has failed. Paradoxically, they often have difficulty initiating movements and appear frozen because they are unable to generate the excitation needed to produce movements.

This juxtaposition of excitation and inhibition is central to how the brain produces behavior and can be seen at the level of individual neurons. All neurons have a spontaneous rate of activity that can be either increased (excitation) or decreased (inhibition). Some neurons excite others, whereas other neurons inhibit. Both effects are produced by specific neurochemicals by which neurons communicate.

REVIEW: Ten Principles of Nervous-System Function

✔ The ten basic principles that form the basis for many discussions throughout this book are listed in the accompanying table. Understanding these principles fully will place you at an advantage in your study of brain and behavior.

Ten Principles of Nervous-System Function

Principle 1: The nervous system's function is to produce movement within a perceptual world created by the brain.
Principle 2: The details of nervous-system functioning are constantly changing, an attribute called neuroplasticity.
Principle 3: Many of the brain's circuits are crossed.
Principle 4: The central nervous system functions on multiple levels.
Principle 5: The brain is both symmetrical and asymmetrical.
Principle 6: Brain systems are organized both hierarchically and in parallel.
Principle 7: Sensory and motor divisions exist throughout the nervous system.
Principle 8: Sensory input to the brain is divided for object recognition and motor control.
Principle 9: Functions in the brain are both localized and distributed.
Principle 10: The nervous system works by juxtaposing excitation and inhibition.

Summary

An Overview of Brain Function and Structure

The primary function of the brain is to produce behavior in a perceptual world that is created by the brain. This perceptual world is ever changing and thus the brain must also change, a property referred to as neuroplasticity.

The human nervous system can be viewed as composed of two semiautonomous functional divisions: the central nervous system, composed of the brain and spinal cord, and the peripheral nervous system, composed of the somatic nervous system and the autonomic nervous system.

Evolutionary Development of the Nervous System

The vertebrate nervous system has evolved from a relatively simple structure mediating reflexlike behaviors to the complex human brain mediating advanced cognitive processes. Primitive forms have not been replaced but rather have been adapted and modified as new structures have been added to allow for the production of more complex behavior in an increasingly sophisticated perceptual world. Thus, the general principles of nervous-system organization and function generalize across vertebrates.

The Central Nervous System: Mediating Behavior

The central nervous system includes the brain and the spinal cord. The brain can be divided into the brainstem and forebrain, each made up of hundreds of parts. The brainstem provides the basic sensory and motor functions that are modified and elaborated by the forebrain. The most-elaborate part of the forebrain is the cerebral cortex, which grows disproportionately large in the human brain.

The Somatic Nervous System: Transmitting Information

The somatic nervous system consists of the spinal nerves that enter and leave the spinal column, going to and from muscles, skin, and joints in the body, and of the cranial nerves that link the muscles of the face and some internal organs to the brain. Some cranial nerves are sensory, some are motor, and some combine both functions. The spinal cord functions as a kind of minibrain for the peripheral (spinal) nerves that enter and leave its five segments. Each spinal segment works independently, although CNS fibers interconnect them and coordinate their activities.

The Autonomic Nervous System: Balancing Internal Functions

The autonomic nervous system controls the body's internal organs. Its sympathetic (arousing) and parasympathetic (calming) divisions work in opposition to each other. The parasympathetic division directs the organs to "rest and digest," whereas the sympathetic division prepares for "fight or flight."

Ten Principles of Nervous-System Function

The nervous system operates according to some simple principles:

1. The function of the brain is to produce movement within a perceptual world created by the brain. This perceptual world is created by the sum of inputs from sensory receptors combining to form neural networks that create our impression of the world.
2. The details of nervous-system functioning are constantly changing, a process called neuroplasticity.
3. Many brain circuits are crossed, meaning that the right cerebral hemisphere is connected to the left side of the body, whereas the left hemisphere is connected to the body's right side.
4. The nervous system functions on multiple levels, with older and newer levels often duplicating tasks.
5. The brain, though largely symmetrical, also has asymmetrical organization appropriate for controlling tasks such as language and spatial navigation.
6. Brain circuits are organized to process information both hierarchically and in parallel.
7. Sensory and motor functions are separated throughout the nervous system, not just in the periphery but in the brain as well.
8. Sensory input to the brain is divided for object recognition and motor control, which means that two distinctly different representations of the perceptual world coexist in the brain.
9. Complex functions exemplified by memory and language are both localized and distributed in the brain.
10. The nervous system works by juxtaposing excitatory and inhibitory signals.

Key Terms

afferent, p. 35
Alzheimer's disease, p. 66
autonomic nervous system (ANS), p. 35
basal ganglia, p. 52
brainstem, p. 38
cerebrospinal fluid (CSF), p. 38
cerebrum, p. 38
corpus callosum, p. 43
cranial nerve, p. 57
cytoarchitectonic map, p. 52
dermatome, p. 58
diencephalon, p. 50
efferent, p. 35
excitation, p. 66
forebrain, p. 50
gray matter, p. 41
gyrus (pl. gyri), p. 38
hemispherectomy, p. 38
hindbrain, p. 49
hypothalamus, p. 50
inhibition, p. 66
law of Bell and Magendie, p. 58
limbic system, p. 55
meninges, p. 35
midbrain, p. 49
neocortex (cerebral cortex), p. 50
nerve, p. 44
neuroplasticity, p. 35
nucleus (pl. nuclei), p. 44
orienting movement, p. 49
parasympathetic division, p. 60
Parkinson's disease, p. 38
reticular formation, p. 49
somatic nervous system (SNS), p. 35
stroke, p. 41
sulcus (pl. sulci), p. 38
sympathetic division, p. 60
tectum, p. 49
tegmentum, p. 49
thalamus, p. 50
Tourette's syndrome, p. 55
tract, p. 44
ventricle, p. 43
vertebrae (sing. vertebra), p. 57
white matter, p. 43

▶*Please refer to the Companion Web Site at* **www.worthpublishers.com/kolbintro3e** *for Interactive Exercises and Quizzes.*

Amanda Voisard/The Palm Beach Post/Zuma Press

CHAPTER 3

What Are the Units of Nervous-System Function?

RESEARCH FOCUS 3-1

Programming Behavior

If we understand how the nervous system produces a behavior, we should be able to produce a nervous-system robot that produces the same behavior. Robots, after all, engage in goal-oriented actions, just as animals do. A robot's computer must guide and coordinate those actions, doing much the same work that an animal's nervous system does. Barbara Webb's cricket robot, constructed from Lego blocks, wires, and a motor and shown in the accompanying photograph, is a nervous-system robot (Reeve et al., 2007) Although far more cumbersome than nature's model, Webb's robot is designed to mimic a female cricket that listens for the source of a male's chirping song and travels to it. These behaviors are not as simple as they may seem.

Robert P. Carr/Bruce Coleman (animal); Barbara Webb (model)

Rules obtained from the study of crickets' behavior can be programmed into robots to be tested. From "A Cricket Robot," by B. Webb, 1996, *Scientific American, 214*(12), p. 99.

In approaching a male, a female cricket must avoid open, well-lit places where a predator could detect her. In addition, the female must often choose between competing males, preferring, for example, the male that makes the longest chirps. All these behaviors must be "wired into" a successful cricket robot, making sure that one behavior does not interfere with another. In simulating cricket behavior in a robot, Webb is duplicating the rules of a cricket's nervous system, which are "programmed" by its genes.

Is the idea of a nervous-system robot disturbing? We are familiar with many machines, including cars, computers, and cell phones. Nervous-system robots are machines that differ only in that they produce a behavior in the same way in which the nervous system does.

Robots help neuroscientists to learn more about the brain and behavior. Researchers such as Webb switch back and forth between studying the nervous system and the behaviors that it enables and writing computer programs and building robots designed to simulate those behaviors. When the animal under study and the computerized robot respond in exactly the same way, researchers can be fairly sure that they understand how some part of the nervous system works.

The construction of robots that display principles of nervous-system function is important to the area of science called artificial intelligence (AI). Artificial-intelligence researchers attempt to produce machines that can think. Future robots may help neuroscientists evaluate the correctness of a complete theory of how the brain works. An additional goal of robotics is to incorporate into the machines human qualities such as emotion and self-awareness so as to expand robots' abilities and usefulness (Riva et al., 2008). The fictional universe of *Star Trek* explores this idea in the character of Lieutenant Commander Data.

Chapter 7 details the origins, growth, and development of neurons and glial cells.

THIS CHAPTER INVESTIGATES the internal structure and functioning of neural cells. If you think of a cell as nature's microscopic robot, its fabrication requires three things: a set of plans, the building blocks that make up its structure, and the assembly of these parts to produce specific functions. The plans for a cell are encoded by its genes; its components are its proteins, each of which is specified by one gene; and the assembly of these proteins into a working organism determines the cell's function.

Not only does an understanding of genes, proteins, and cellular structure allow us to understand normal brain function, it also allows us to understand abnormal function. For example, a gene's workings can go awry, usually with devastating consequences for behavior. Many neurological disorders described in this book result from errors in protein manufacture that are due to errors in genes passed from parent to child. For this reason, we explore the process of both normal and abnormal genetic transmission in this chapter.

Cells of the Nervous System

If Barbara Webb's robot mysteriously arrived in a box on your doorstep, could you guess what it is designed to do? The robot's wheels imply that it is meant to move, and the gears next to the wheels suggest that it can vary its speed or perhaps change directions. The robot's many exposed wires show that it is not intended to go into water. And, because this robot has no lights or cameras, you can infer that it is not meant to see. The structure of the robot suggests its function. So it is with cells.

Nervous-system cells are small, are packed tightly together, and have the consistency of jelly. To see a brain cell, you must first distinguish it from surrounding cells, find a way to make it visible, and then magnify it by using a microscope. Anatomists have many ways of highlighting individual cells. Usually, they remove most of the water from the brain to make it firm by soaking it in formaldehyde. Then the brain can be sliced thinly and stained with various dyes that either color its cells completely or color some of the cells' components. When viewed through a microscope, individual cells can be seen. Anatomists can also "culture" brain cells in a dish where living cells can be viewed and studied in a more-realistic setting that mirrors conditions of a living brain.

There remains, however, the problem of making sense of what you see. Different brain samples can yield different images, and different people can interpret those images in different ways. So began a controversy between two great scientists over what neurons really are. One was the Italian Camillo Golgi and the other the Spaniard Santiago Ramón y Cajal. Both men were awarded the Nobel Prize for medicine in 1906.

Imagine that you are Camillo Golgi hard at work in your laboratory staining and examining cells of the nervous system. You immerse a thin slice of brain tissue in a solution containing silver nitrate and other chemicals, a technique used at the time to produce black-and-white photographic prints. A contemporary method, shown in **Figure 3-1A**, produces a color-enhanced microscopic image that resembles the images seen by Golgi.

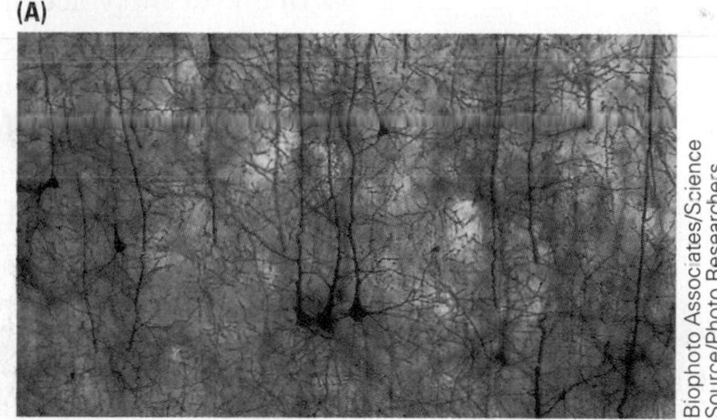

Biophoto Associates/Science Source/Photo Researchers

FIGURE 3-1 Two Views of a Cell. A tissue preparation revealing human pyramidal cells stained by using the Golgi technique (A) offers a far different view from that of (B) Cajal's drawing of a single neuron. (B) From *Histologie du système nerveux de l'homme et des vertebres,* by S. Ramón y Cajal, 1909–1911, Paris: Maloine.

The image is beautiful and intriguing, but what do you make of it? To Golgi, this structure suggested that the nervous system is composed of a network of interconnected fibers. He thought that information, like water running through pipes, somehow flowed around this "nerve net" and produced behavior. His theory was reasonable, given what he saw.

But Santiago Ramón y Cajal came to a different conclusion. He used Golgi's stain to study the brain tissue of chick embryos. He assumed that their nervous systems would be simpler and easier to understand than would an adult nervous system. Figure 3-1B shows one of the images that he rendered from the neural cells of a chick embryo. Cajal concluded that the nervous system is made up of discrete cells that begin life with a rather simple structure that becomes more complex with age. When mature, each cell consists of a main body with extensions projecting from it.

The structure looks something like a plant, with branches coming out of the top and roots coming out of the bottom. Cajal's belief that these complexly shaped cells are the functional units of the nervous system is now universally accepted. The idea proposed by Cajal, that neurons are the units of brain function, is called the *neuron hypothesis.*

Figure 3-2 shows the three basic subdivisions of a neuron. The core region is called the **cell body** or **soma** (Greek, meaning "body" and the root of words such as "somatic"). A neuron's branching extensions, or **dendrites** (from Greek for "tree"), collect information from other cells, and its main "root" is the single **axon** (Greek for "axle") that carries messages to other neurons. So a neuron has only one axon, but most have many dendrites. Some small neurons have so many dendrites that they look like a garden hedge.

No one has counted all 100 billion neurons. Scientists have estimated the total number by counting the cells in a small sample of brain tissue and then multiplying by the brain's volume.

The human nervous system contains about 100 billion neurons. How can we explain how 100 billion cells cooperate, make connections, and produce behavior? Fortunately, examining how one cell works can be a source of insight that we can generalize to other cells. Brain cells are built in accord with a common plan. As you learn to recognize some of their different types, you will also see how their specialized structures contribute to their functions in your body.

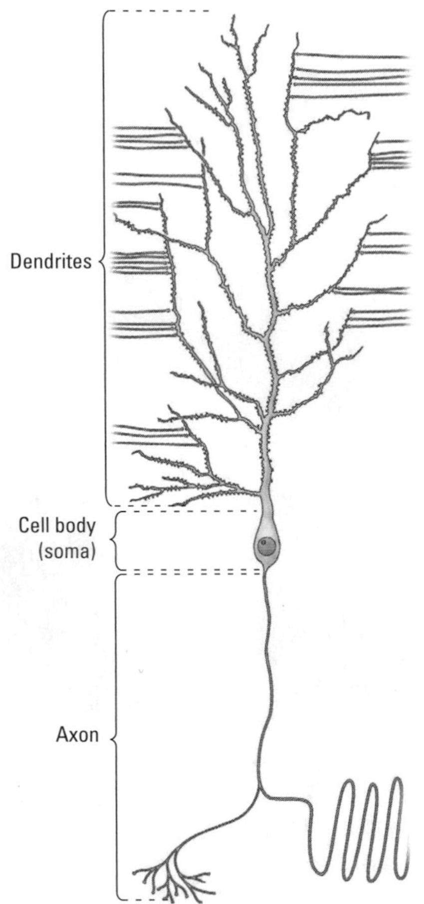

FIGURE 3-2 Basic Structure of a Neuron. Dendrites gather information from other neurons, the cell body (soma) integrates the information, and the axon sends the information to other cells. Note that, though it may have many dendrites, there is only one axon.

Neurons: The Basis of Information Processing

As the information-processing units of the nervous system, neurons acquire information from sensory receptors, pass that information on to other neurons, and make muscles move to produce behaviors. They encode memories and produce our thoughts and emotions. At the same time, they regulate all of the many body processes to which we seldom give a thought, such as breathing, heartbeat, body temperature, and the sleep–wake cycle.

Some scientists think that a specific function is sometimes assigned to a single neuron. For example, Einat Adar and colleagues (2008) studied how birds learn songs and proposed a relation between the number of neurons produced for singing and the complexity of the song that is sung. For most behaviors in most species, scientists think that neurons work together in groups of many hundreds to many thousands to produce some aspect of the behavior.

For complex behaviors, the loss of a neuron or two is no more noticeable than the loss of one or two voices from a cheering crowd. It is the crowd that produces the overall sound, not each individual person. In much the same way, although neuroscientists say that neurons are the information-processing units of the brain, they really mean that large teams of neurons serve this function.

Scientists also speak informally about the structure of a particular neuron, as if that structure never changes. But neurons are the essence of plasticity. If fresh brain tissue is kept alive in a dish of salty water and viewed through a microscope, the neurons reveal themselves to be surprisingly active, both producing new dendrite branches and losing old ones. In fact, when they are watched for a period of time in the brain or in a dish, neurons are continuously growing and shrinking and changing their shape.

These physical changes result from coding and storing our experiences and memories. Neural changes of all kinds are possible because of a special property that neurons possess. Even in a mature, fully grown neuron, the cell's genetic blueprints can be "reopened" to produce new proteins and thus allow the neuron to alter its structure and function.

Another important property of neurons is their longevity. At a few locations in the human nervous system, the ongoing production of new neurons does take place throughout life, and some behavior does depend on the production of new neurons. But most of your neurons are with you for life and are never replaced. If the brain or spinal cord is damaged, for example, the neurons that are lost are not replaced, and functional recovery is poor.

The Neuron's Structure and Function

Figure 3-3 details the external and internal features common to neurons and shows how different stains highlight these aspects. The surface area of the cell is increased immensely by its extensions into dendrites and an axon (Figure 3-3A and B). The den-

(A)

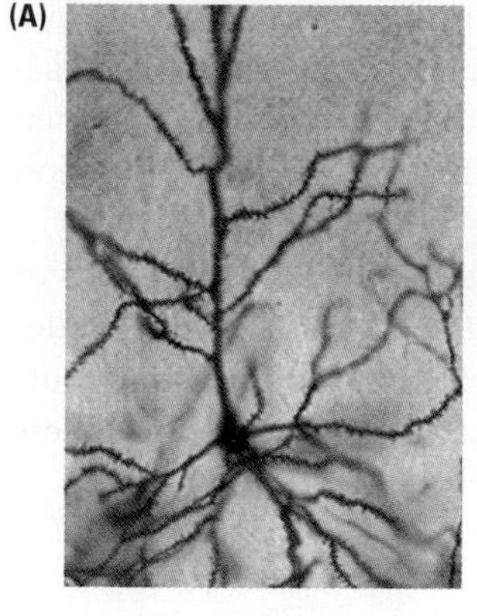

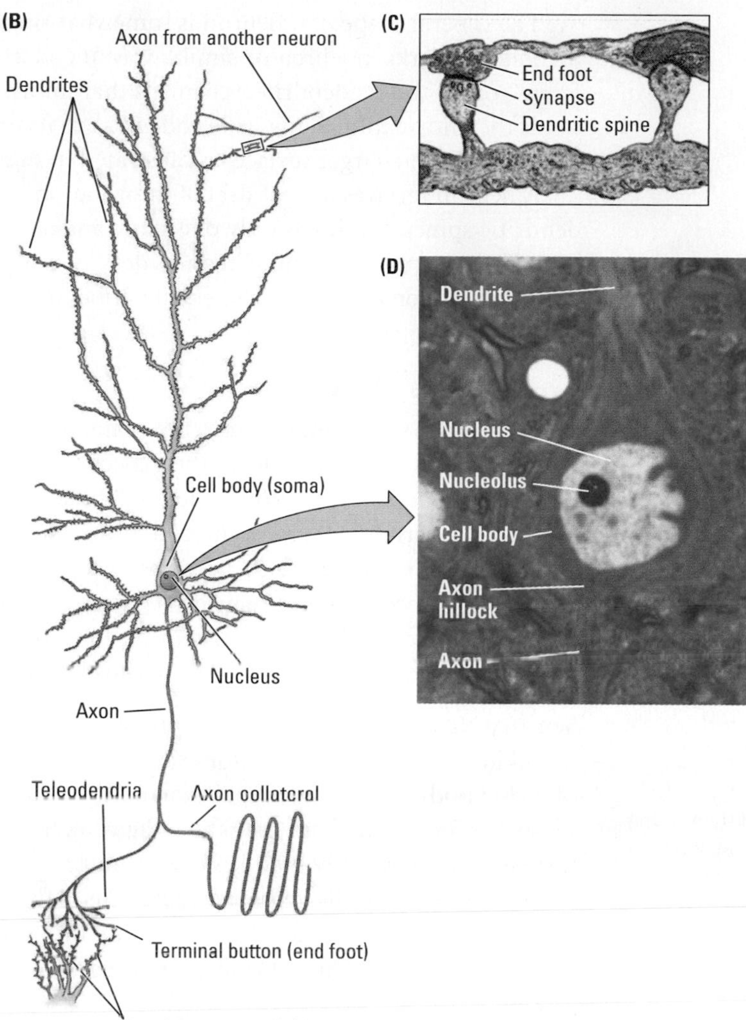

FIGURE 3-3 Major Parts of a Neuron. **(A)** A typical neuron stained with the use of the Golgi technique to reveal its dendrites and cell body. **(B)** The neuron's basic structures identified. **(C)** An electron micrograph captures the synapse between an axon from another neuron and a dendritic spine. **(D)** A high-power light-microscopic view inside the cell body. Note the axon hillock at the junction of the soma and axon.

dritic area is further increased by many small protrusions called **dendritic spines** (Figure 3-3C). A neuron may have from 1 to 20 dendrites, each may have from one to many branches, and the spines on the branches may number in the many thousands. Because dendrites collect information from other cells, their surface area corresponds to how much information the neuron can gather.

Each neuron has but a single axon that carries messages to other neurons. The axon begins at one end of the cell body at an expansion known as the **axon hillock** (little hill) shown in Figure 3-3D. The axon may branch out into one or many **axon collaterals,** which usually emerge from it at right angles as shown at the bottom of Figure 3-3B. Thus, the same message can be sent to a number of locations in the brain.

Note also that the lower tip of an axon may divide into a number of smaller branches (*teleodendria,* or end branches). At the end of each teleodendrion is a knob called an *end foot* or **terminal button.** The terminal button sits very close to a dendritic spine or some other part of another cell, although it does not touch it (see Figure 3-3C). This "almost connection," which includes the surfaces of the end foot and the neighboring dendritic spine as well as the space between them, is called a **synapse.**

Chapter 4 describes how neurons communicate; here, we simply generalize about function by examining shape. Imagine looking at a river system from an airplane. You see many small streams merging to make creeks, which join to form tributaries, which join to form the main river channel. As the river reaches its delta, it breaks up into a number of smaller channels again before discharging its contents into the sea.

Cell body (soma) Core region of the cell containing the nucleus and other organelles for making proteins.
Dendrite Branching extension of a neuron's cell membrane that greatly increases the surface area of the cell and collects information from other cells.
Axon "Root," or single fiber, of a neuron that carries messages to other neurons.
Dendritic spine Protrusion from a dendrite that greatly increases the dendrite's surface area and is the usual point of dendritic contact with the axons of other cells.
Axon hillock Juncture of soma and axon where the action potential begins.
Axon collateral Branch of an axon.
Terminal button (end foot) Knob at the tip of an axon that conveys information to other neurons.
Synapse Junction between one neuron and another neuron, usually between an end foot of the axon of one neuron and a dendritic spine of the other neuron.

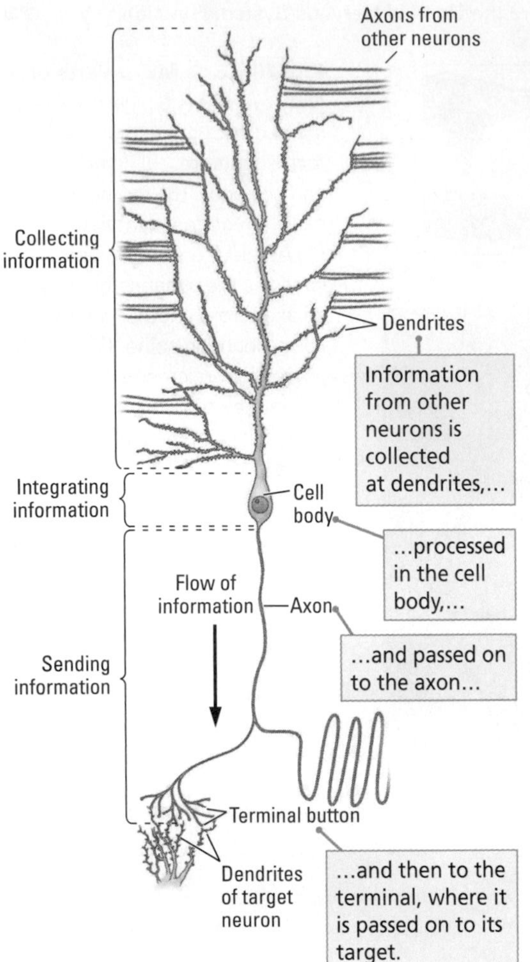

FIGURE 3-4 Information Flow Through a Neuron.

The general shape of a neuron is somewhat similar to such a river system, and the neuron works in a broadly similar way. It collects information from many different sources on its dendrites, channels that information onto its axon, and then sends the information along its teleodendria to its end feet, where the information is released onto a target surface, as illustrated in **Figure 3-4.**

A neuron receives a great deal of information on its hundreds to thousands of dendritic spines, but it has only one axon, and so it acts as a decision-making device. The information coming in on its dendrites is pooled to produce a single outgoing message on the axon. Chapter 4 describes in detail how neurons perform these processes.

Three Types of Neurons

The nervous system contains an array of neurons in varying shapes and sizes and structured differently to perform their specialized tasks. Some appear quite simple and others very complex. With a little practice in looking into a microscope, you can quickly learn to recognize three neuron types by their features and functions. **Sensory neurons** (**Figure 3-5**A) are designed to bring information into the brain from sensory receptors, **interneurons** (Figure 3-5B) to associate sensory and motor activity in the central nervous system, and **motor neurons** (Figure 3-5C) to carry information out of the brain and spinal cord to the body's muscles.

Sensory Neurons These are the simplest neurons structurally. A **bipolar neuron** found in the retina of the eye, for example, has a single short dendrite on one side of its cell body and a single short axon on the other side. Bipolar neurons transmit sensory information from the retina's light receptors to the neurons that carry information into the visual centers of the brain.

A bit more complicated sensory neuron is the **somatosensory neuron,** which brings sensory information from the body into the spinal cord. Structurally, the somatosensory dendrite connects directly to its axon, and so the cell body sits to one side of this long pathway.

Interneurons Generally called *association cells* because they link sensory and motor neurons, interneurons branch extensively, the better to collect information from many sources. A major difference between animals with small brains and animals with large brains is that large-brained animals have more interneurons. A specific association cell, the *stellate* (star-shaped) *cell,* is characteristically small, with many dendrites extending around the cell body. Its axon is difficult to see among the maze of dendrites.

A **pyramidal cell** has a long axon, a pyramid-shaped cell body, and two sets of dendrites, one set projecting from the apex of the cell body and the other from its sides. Pyramidal interneurons carry information from the cortex to the rest of the brain and spinal cord. A **Purkinje cell** (named for its discoverer) is a distinctive output cell with

FIGURE 3-5 Neuron Shape and Function. Sensory neurons **(A)** collect information from a source and pass it on to an interneuron **(B)**. The many branches of interneurons collect information from many sources and link to motor neurons **(C)**, which are distinctively large and pass information on to command muscles to move. Note that these cells are not drawn to scale.

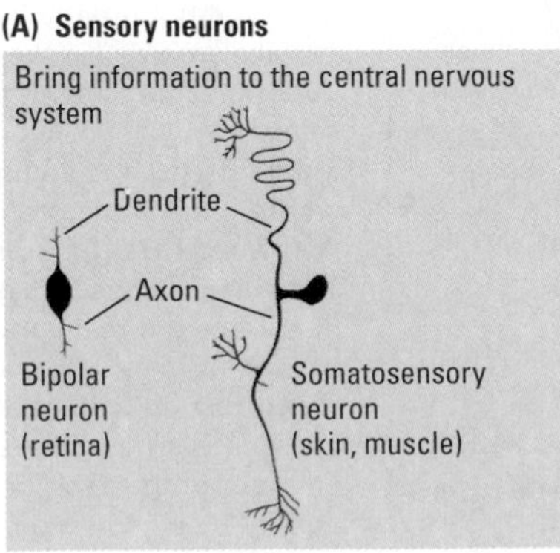

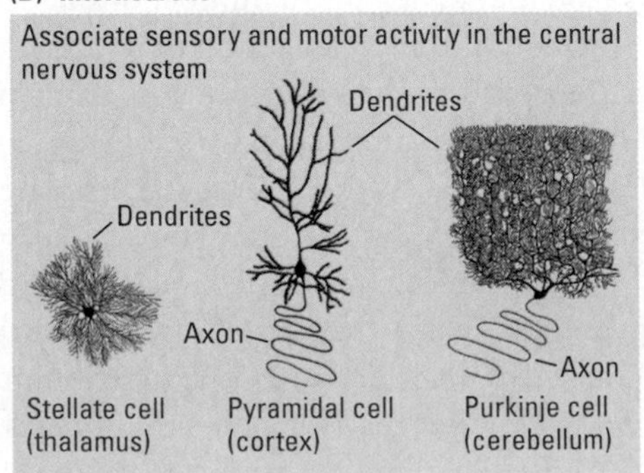

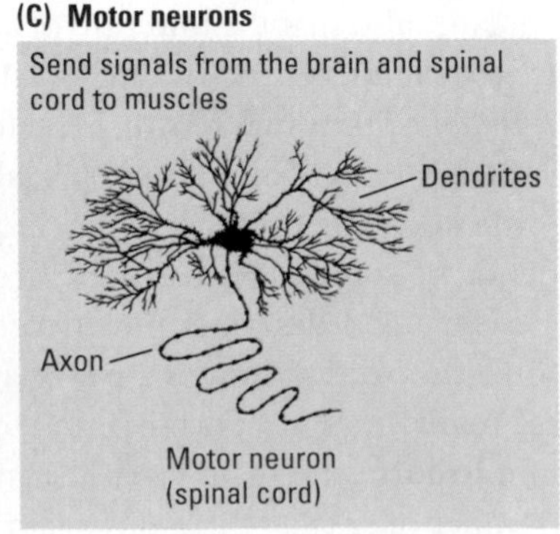

extremely branched dendrites that form a fan shape. It carries information from the cerebellum to the rest of the brain and spinal cord.

Motor Neurons To collect information from many sources, motor neurons have extensive networks of dendrites, large cell bodies, and long axons that connect to muscles. Motor neurons are located in the lower brainstem and spinal cord. All outgoing neural information must pass through them to reach the muscles.

Sensory neuron Neuron that carries incoming information from sensory receptors into the spinal cord and brain.
Interneuron Association neuron interposed between a sensory neuron and a motor neuron; thus, in mammals, interneurons constitute most of the neurons of the brain.
Motor neuron Neuron that carries information from the brain and spinal cord to make muscles contract.
Bipolar neuron Sensory neuron with one axon and one dendrite.
Somatosensory neuron Brain cell that brings sensory information from the body into the spinal cord.
Pyramidal cell Distinctive interneuron found in the cerebral cortex.
Purkinje cell Distinctive interneuron found in the cerebellum.

Neural Connections

Neurons are "networkers" that produce behavior, and the appearance of each neuron tells us something about the connections that it must make. Figure 3-5 illustrates the relation between form and function of neurons but does not illustrate their relative sizes. Neurons that project for long distances, such as somatosensory neurons, pyramidal neurons, and motor neurons, are generally very large relative to other neurons. In general, neurons with large cell bodies have extensions that are very long, whereas neurons with small cell bodies, such as stellate cells, have short extensions.

Long extensions carry information to distant parts of the nervous system; short extensions are engaged in local processing. For example, the tips of the dendrites of some somatosensory neurons are located in your big toe, whereas the target of their axons is at the base of your brain. These sensory neurons send information over a distance as long as 2 meters, or more. The axons of some pyramidal neurons must reach from the cortex as far as the lower spinal cord, a distance that can be as long as a meter. The imposing size of this pyramidal cell body is therefore in accord with the work that it must do in providing nutrients and other supplies for its axons and dendrites.

The Language of Neurons: Excitation and Inhibition

Neurons are in constant communication. Their basic language may remind you of how digital devices work. That is, neurons either excite other neurons (turn them on) or inhibit other neurons (turn them off). Like computers, neurons send "yes" or "no" signals to one another; the "yes" signals are excitatory, and the "no" signals are inhibitory. Each neuron receives thousands of excitatory and inhibitory signals every second.

Recall the principle from Chapter 2: The nervous system works through a combination of excitatory and inhibitory signals.

The neuron's response to all those inputs is democratic: it sums them. A neuron is spurred into action only if its excitatory inputs exceed its inhibitory inputs. If the reverse is true and inhibitory inputs exceed excitatory inputs, the neuron does not activate.

We can apply the principle of the excitation and inhibition of neuron action to the workings of the cricket robot described at the beginning of this chapter. Suppose we could insert a neuron between the microphone for sound detection on each side of this robot and the motor on the opposite side. **Figure 3-6**A shows how the two neurons

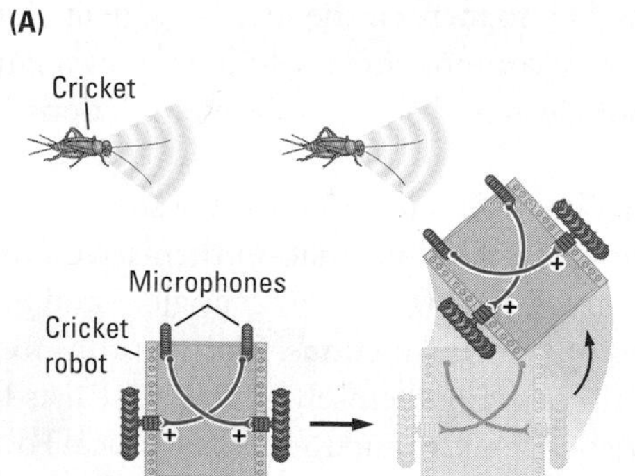

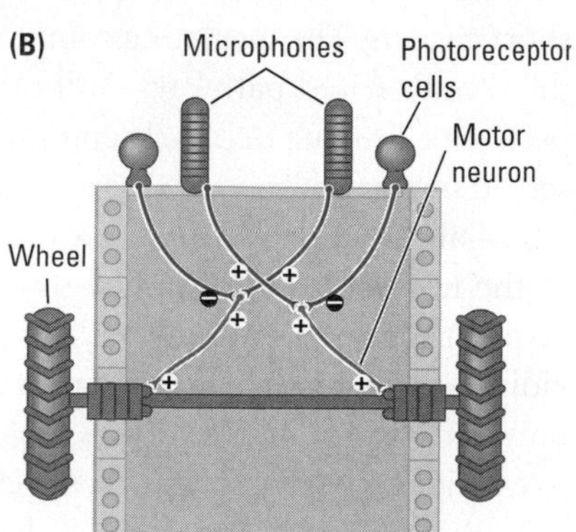

FIGURE 3-6 Excitation and Inhibition. (A) Excitatory inputs from the chirping of a male cricket, picked up by the cricket robot's microphones, activate the robot's wheels to orient toward the chirp. (B) In a slightly more complex cricket robot, sensory neurons from the microphone excite motor neurons, but input from photoreceptors inhibits them.

Glial cell Nervous-system cell that provides insulation, nutrients, and support and that aids in repairing neurons and eliminating waste products.
Ependymal cell Glial cell that makes and secretes cerebrospinal fluid; found on the walls of the ventricles in the brain.
Hydrocephalus Buildup of pressure in the brain and, in infants, swelling of the head caused if the flow of cerebrospinal fluid is blocked; can result in retardation.
Astrocyte Glial cell with a star-shaped appearance that provides structural support to neurons in the central nervous system and transports substances between neurons and capillaries.

would be connected. It would take only two rules to instruct the robot to seek out a chirping male cricket:

Rule 1: Each time that a microphone detects a male cricket's song, an excitatory message is sent to the opposite wheel's motor, activating it. This rule ensures that the robot turns toward the cricket each time that it hears a chirp.

Rule 2: The message sent should be proportional to the intensity of the sound. This rule means that, if the chirp is coming from the robot's left side, it will be detected as being louder by the microphone on the left, which will make the right wheel turn a little faster, swinging the robot to the left. The opposite would happen if the sound came from the right. If the sound comes from straight ahead, both microphones will detect it equally, and the robot will move directly forward. This rule ensures that the robot travels in the correct direction.

To make the robot more "intelligent" requires more neurons. Figure 3-6B shows how we could mimic the idea of sensory and motor neurons. The robot now has two sound-detecting sensory neurons receiving input from its microphones. When activated, each sensory neuron excites a motor neuron that turns on one of the two wheel motors. But now we add sensory neurons coming from photoreceptors on the robot that detect light. These light-detecting sensory neurons, when activated, inhibit the motor neurons leading to the wheels and so prevent the robot from moving toward a male. Now the cricket will only move when it is dark and "safe."

This arrangement gives the robot some interesting properties. For example, at dusk, the excitatory signals from sound and the weak inhibitory signals from the dim light might conflict. The robot might make small "intention" movements that orient it toward the male while not actually searching for it. A researcher might want to examine the behavior of a real female cricket to see if it acts in the same way under these conditions.

This arrangement illustrates the function of sensory and motor neurons and the principle of excitation and inhibition, but bear in mind that it contains only six neurons and each neuron has only one connection with another neuron. We have not even placed interneurons in the robot. Imagine how infinitely more complex a human nervous system is with its hundred billion neurons, most of which are interneurons, each with thousands of connections.

Still, this simple example serves a valuable purpose. It shows the great versatility of function possible from the dual principles of excitation and inhibition. From the simple yes-or-no language of neurons emerges enormous possibilities for behavior.

Five Types of Glial Cells

Imagine how much more efficiently your robot would work if you could add components that enhance the functioning of your simulated neurons. Some could attach the neurons to the appropriate parts of the robot; others could insulate them to prevent short circuits. The insulating components might also increase the speed of signals along the robot's wired pathways. Still other auxiliary components could lubricate moving parts or eliminate debris, keeping your robot clean and shiny. All these functions are served by glial cells.

Glia form the fatty coverings around neurons that show up as white matter in brain images.

Glial cells (from the Greek word for "glue") are often described as the support cells of the nervous system. Although they do not transmit information themselves, they help neurons carry out this task, binding them together (some *do* act as glue) and providing support, nutrients, and protection, among other functions. Most neurons form only early in life, but glial cells are constantly replacing themselves. **Table 3-1** lists the five major types of glia. Each has a characteristic structure and function. Clinical Focus 3-2, "Brain Tumors," on page 78, describes the results of uncontrolled glial cell growth.

TABLE 3-1 Types of Glial Cells

Type	Appearance	Features and function
Ependymal cell		Small, ovoid; secretes cerebrospinal fluid (CSF)
Astrocyte		Star shaped, symmetrical; nutritive and support function
Microglial cell		Small, mesodermally derived; defensive function
Oligodendroglial cell		Asymmetrical; forms myelin around axons in brain and spinal cord
Schwann cell		Asymmetrical; wraps around peripheral nerves to form myelin

Ependymal Cells

On the walls of the ventricles, the cavities inside your brain, are **ependymal cells** that produce and secrete the cerebrospinal fluid that fills the ventricles. Cerebrospinal fluid is constantly being formed and flows through the ventricles toward the base of the brain, where it is absorbed into the blood vessels. Cerebrospinal fluid serves several purposes. It acts as a shock absorber when the brain is jarred; it provides a medium through which waste products are eliminated; it assists the brain in maintaining a constant temperature; it is a source of nutrients for parts of the brain located adjacent to the ventricles.

As CSF flows through the ventricles, it passes through some narrow passages, especially from the cerebral aqueduct into the fourth ventricle, which runs through the brainstem. If the fourth ventricle is fully or partly blocked, the fluid flow is restricted. Because CSF is continuously being produced, this blockage causes a buildup of pressure that begins to expand the ventricles, which in turn push on the surrounding brain.

You can review the location of the cerebral aqueduct and the ventricles in Figure 2-7.

If such a blockage develops in a newborn infant, before the skull bones are fused, the pressure on the brain is conveyed to the skull and the baby's head consequently swells. This condition, called **hydrocephalus** (literally, water brain), can cause severe mental retardation and even death. To treat it, doctors insert one end of a tube, called a *shunt,* into the blocked ventricle and the other end into a vein. The shunt allows the CSF to drain into the bloodstream.

Astroglia

Astrocytes (star-shaped glia shown in Table 3-1), also called *astroglia,* provide structural support within the central nervous system. Their extensions attach to blood vessels and to the brain's lining, creating scaffolding that holds neurons in place. These same extensions provide pathways for the movement of certain nutrients between blood vessels and neurons. Astrocytes also secrete chemicals that keep neurons healthy and help them heal if injured.

CLINICAL FOCUS 3-2

Brain Tumors

One day while she was watching a movie in a neuropsychology class, R. J., a 19-year-old college sophomore, collapsed on the floor and began twitching, displaying symptoms of a brain seizure. The instructor helped her to the university clinic, where she recovered, except for a severe headache. She reported that she had suffered from severe headaches on a number of occasions.

A few days later, computer tomography (CT) was used to scan her brain; the scan showed a tumor over her left frontal lobe. She underwent surgery to have the tumor removed and returned to classes after an uneventful recovery. She successfully completed her studies, finished law school, and has been practicing law for more than 15 years without any further symptoms.

A **tumor** is a mass of new tissue that undergoes uncontrolled growth and is independent of surrounding structures. No region of the body is immune, but the brain is a common site. In 2008, nearly 44,000 Americans were diagnosed with tumors that originated in the brain. Brain tumors do not grow from neurons but rather from glia or other supporting cells. The rate of growth depends on the type of cell affected.

Some tumors are benign, as R. J.'s was, and not likely to recur after removal; others are malignant, likely to progress, and apt to recur after removal. Both kinds of tumors can pose a risk to life if they develop in sites from which they are difficult to remove.

The earliest symptoms are usually due to increased pressure on surrounding brain structures and can include headaches, vomiting, mental dullness, changes in sensory and motor abilities, and seizures such as R. J experienced. Many symptoms depend on the precise location of the tumor. The three major types of brain tumors are classified according to how they originate:

1. *Gliomas* arise from glial cells. They constitute roughly half of all brain tumors. Gliomas that arise from astrocytes are usually slow growing, not often malignant, and relatively easy to treat. In contrast, gliomas that arise from the precursor *blast* or *germinal* cells that grow into glial cells are much more often malignant, grow more quickly, and often recur after treatment. Senator Edward Kennedy was diagnosed with a malignant glioma in his left parietal cortex in 2008. He died a year later. Like R. J.'s, his first symptom was an epileptic seizure.

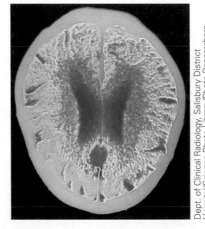

Dept. of Clinical Radiology, Salisbury District Hospital/Science Photo Library/Photo Researchers

The red area in this colored CT scan is a meningioma, a noncancerous tumor arising from the arachnoid membrane covering the brain. A meningioma may grow large enough to compress the brain but usually does not invade brain tissue.

2. *Meningiomas,* the type of tumor that R. J. had, attach to the meninges and so grow entirely outside the brain, as shown in the accompanying CT scan. These tumors are usually well encapsulated, and, if they are located in places that are accessible, recovery after surgery is good.
3. The *metastatic tumor* becomes established by a transfer of tumor cells from one region of the body to another (which is what the term *metastatsis* means). Typically, metastatic tumors are present in multiple locations, making treatment difficult. Symptoms of the underlying condition often first appear when the tumor cells reach the brain. In 2008, 170,000 patients in the United States learned that cancers from other parts of their bodies had spread to their brains.

Treatment for a brain tumor is usually surgery, which also is one of the main means of diagnosing the type of tumor. If possible, the entire tumor is removed. Radiotherapy (treatment with X-rays) is useful for destroying developing tumor cells. Chemotherapy, although common for treating tumors in other parts of the body, is less successful in the treatment of brain tumors because getting the chemicals across the blood–brain barrier is difficult.

At the same time, astrocytes play a role in contributing to a protective partition between blood vessels and the brain, the **blood–brain barrier.** As shown in **Figure 3-7,** the end feet of astrocytes attach to the blood-vessel cells, causing them to bind tightly together. These tight junctions prevent an array of substances, including many toxins, from entering the brain through the blood-vessel walls.

The molecules (smallest units) of these substances are too large to pass between the blood-vessel cells unless the blood–brain barrier is somehow compromised. But the downside to the blood–brain barrier is that many useful drugs, including antibiotics such as penicillin, cannot pass through to the brain either. As a result, brain infections are very difficult to treat.

Yet another important function of astrocytes is to enhance brain activity. When you engage a part of your brain for some behavior, the brain cells of that area require more oxygen and glucose. In response, the blood vessels in the area dilate, allowing greater oxygen- and glucose-carrying blood flow. But what triggers the blood vessels to dilate? This is where the astrocytes come in. They convey signals from the neurons to the blood vessels, stimulating them to expand and so provide more fuel.

Astrocytes also contribute to the process of healing damaged brain tissue. If the brain is injured by a blow to the head or penetrated by some sharp object, astrocytes form a scar to seal off the damaged area. Although the scar tissue is beneficial in healing the injury, it can unfortunately act as a barrier to the regrowth of damaged neurons. One experimental approach to repairing brain tissue seeks to get the axons and dendrites of CNS neurons to grow around or through a glial scar.

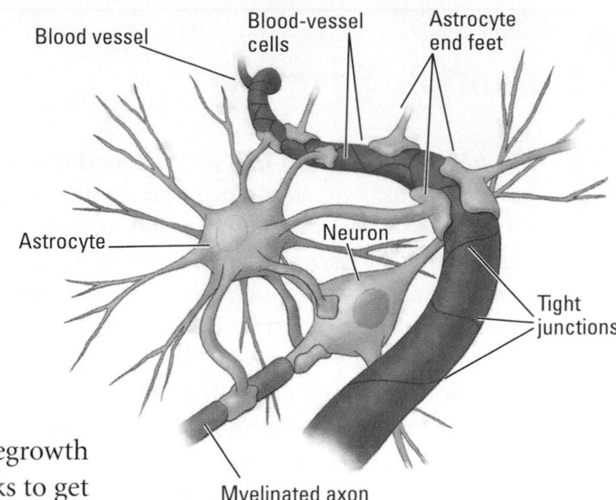

FIGURE 3-7 Functions of Astrocytes. Astrocyte processes attach to neurons and to blood vessels to provide support between different structures in the brain, stimulate the cells on blood vessels to form tight junctions and so form the blood–brain barrier, and transport chemicals excreted by neurons to blood vessels.

Microglia

Unlike other glial cells, which originate in the brain, **microglia** originate in the blood as an offshoot of the immune system and migrate throughout the brain. Microglia monitor the health of brain tissue. When brain cells are damaged, microglia invade the area to provide growth factors that aid in repair and to engulf and remove foreign matter and debris, an immune process called *phagocytosis.* Damage to the brain can be detected in a postmortem examination because, as illustrated in **Figure 3-8,** microglia will be left where neurons were once located.

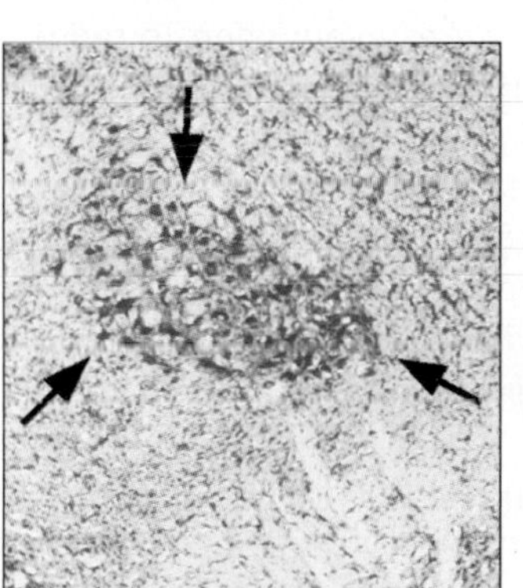
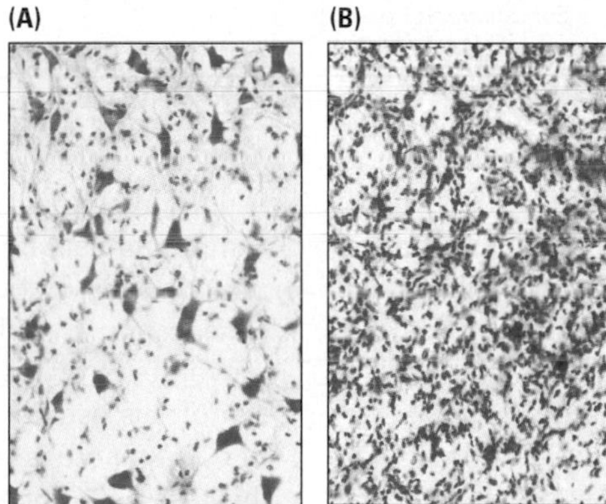
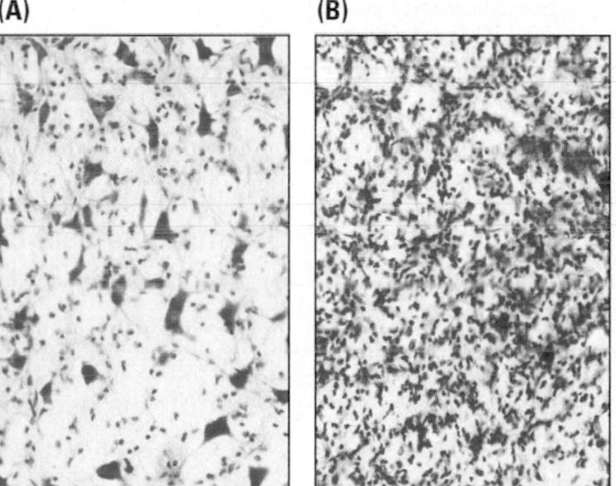

FIGURE 3-8 Detecting Brain Damage. Arrows on the micrograph at the left indicate a brain area called the red nucleus in a rat. (A) Closeup of cresyl-violet-stained neurons in the healthy red nucleus. (B) After exposure to a neurotoxin, only microglia remain.

Oligodendroglia and Schwann Cells

Two kinds of glial cells insulate the axons of neurons. Like the rubber insulation on electrical wires, this **myelin** prevents adjacent neurons from short-circuiting each other's activity. **Oligodendroglia** myelinate axons in the brain and spinal cord by sending out large, flat branches that enclose and separate adjacent axons (the prefix *oligo* means "few" and here refers to the fact that these glia have few branches in comparison with astrocytes; see Table 3-1).

Schwann cells myelinate axons in the peripheral nervous system. Each Schwann cell wraps itself repeatedly around a part of an axon, forming a structure somewhat like a bead on a string. In addition to the myelination, Schwann cells and oligodendroglia contribute to a neuron's nutrition and function by absorbing chemicals that the neuron releases and releasing chemicals that the neuron absorbs.

In Chapter 4, you will learn how myelin speeds up the flow of information along a neuron. Neurons that are heavily myelinated send information much faster than neurons having little or no myelin. Neurons that send messages over long distances quickly, including sensory and motor neurons, are heavily myelinated.

Tumor Mass of new tissue that grows uncontrolled and independent of surrounding structures.
Blood–brain barrier The tight junctions between the cells that compose blood vessels in the brain, providing a barrier to the entry of large molecules into the brain.
Microglia Glial cells that originate in the blood, aid in cell repair, and scavenge debris in the nervous system.
Myelin Glial coating that surrounds axons in the central and peripheral nervous systems.
Oligodendroglia Glial cells in the central nervous system that myelinate axons.
Schwann cell Glial cell in the peripheral nervous system that forms the myelin on sensory and motor axons.

CLINICAL FOCUS 3-3

Multiple Sclerosis

One day J. O., who had just finished university requirements to begin work as an accountant, noticed a slight cloudiness in her right eye that did not go away when she wiped her eye. The area of cloudiness grew over the next few days. Her optometrist suggested that she see a neurologist, who diagnosed optic neuritis, a symptom that could be a flag for multiple sclerosis (MS).

Although we do not yet understand what causes MS, we do know that it is characterized by a loss of myelin (see illustration), both on pathways bringing sensory information to the brain and on pathways taking commands to muscles. This loss of myelin occurs in patches, and scarring is frequently left in the affected areas.

Eventually, a hard scar, or *plaque,* may form in the affected areas, which is why the disease is called sclerosis (from the Greek word meaning "hardness"). Associated with the loss of myelin is impairment in neuron function, causing characteristic MS symptoms of sensory loss and difficulty in moving. Fatigue, pain, and depression are common related symptoms. Bladder dysfunction, constipation, and sexual dysfunction all complicate the condition. Multiple sclerosis greatly affects a person's emotional, social, and vocational functioning. As yet, it has no cure.

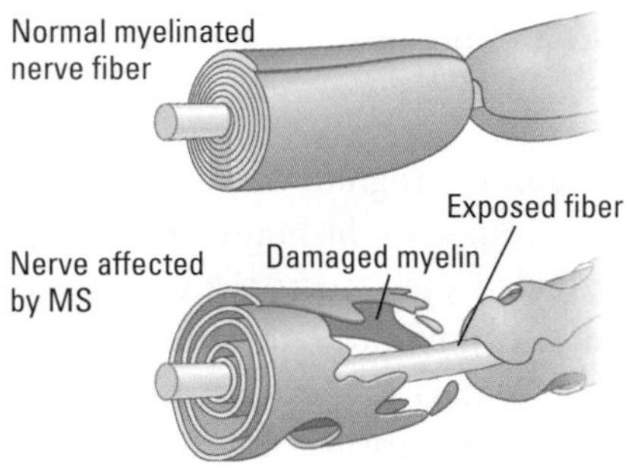

Adapted from Mayo Foundation for Medical Education and Research.

J. O.'s eye cleared over the next few months, and she had no further symptoms until after the birth of her first child 3 years later, when she felt a tingling in her right hand that spread up her arm, until gradually she lost movement in the arm. Movement was restored 5 months later. Then $2\frac{1}{2}$ years later, after her second child was born, she felt a tingling in her left big toe that spread along the sole of her foot and then up to her leg, eventually leading again to loss of movement. J. O. received corticosteroid treatment, which helped, but the condition rebounded when she stopped treatment. Then it subsided and eventually disappeared.

Since then, J. O. has had no major outbreaks of motor impairment, but she still feels occasional tingling in her trunk, some weakness in her left leg, and brief periods of tingling and numbness in different body parts that last a couple of weeks before clearing. The feeling is very similar to the numbness in the face after a dentist gives a local anesthetic.

Although she suffers no depression, J. O. reports enormous fatigue, takes long naps daily, and is ready for bed early in the evening. Her sister and a female cousin have experienced similar symptoms. Computer tomographic scans on both J. O. and her sister revealed scarring in the spinal cord, a condition that helped confirm an MS diagnosis for them. One of J. O.'s grandmothers had been confined to a wheelchair, although the source of her problem was never diagnosed.

J. O. occasionally wears a brace to support her left knee and sometimes wears a collar to support her neck. She makes every effort to reduce stress to a minimum but otherwise lives a normal life that includes exercise and even vigorous sports such as water skiing.

J. O.'s extremely strange symptoms, which are often difficult to diagnose, are typical of multiple sclerosis. The first symptoms usually appear in adulthood, and their onset is quite sudden and swift. These initial symptoms may be loss of sensation in the face, limbs, or body or loss of control over movements or loss of both sensation and control. Motor symptoms usually appear first in the hands or feet.

Often there is remission of early symptoms, after which they may not appear again for years. In some of its forms, however, the disease may progress rapidly over a period of just a few years until the person is reduced to bed care. In cases in which the disease is fatal, the average age of death is between 65 and 84.

You will find statistics on the incidence of MS as well as possible causes and treatments in Chapter 16.

If myelin is damaged, a neuron may be unable to send any messages over its axons. In **multiple sclerosis** (MS), the myelin formed by oligodendroglia is damaged, and the functions of the neurons whose axons it encases are disrupted. Clinical Focus 3-3, "Multiple Sclerosis," describes the course of the disease.

Glial Cells and Neuron Repair

A deep cut on your body—on your arm or leg for instance—may cut the axons connecting your spinal cord to muscles and to sensory receptors. Severed motor-neuron axons will render you unable to move the affected part of your body, whereas severed sensory fibers will result in loss of sensation from that body part. Cessation of both movement and sensation is **paralysis.** In a period of weeks to months after motor and sensory axons are severed, movement and sensation will return. The human body can repair this kind of nerve damage, and so the paralysis is not permanent.

Multiple sclerosis (MS) Nervous-system disorder that results from the loss of myelin (glial-cell covering) around neurons.

Paralysis Loss of sensation and movement due to nervous-system injury.

Both microglia and Schwann cells play a part in repairing damage to the peripheral nervous system. When a PNS axon is cut, it dies back to the cell body. Microglia remove all the debris left by the dying axon. Meanwhile, the Schwann cells that provided the axon's myelin shrink and then divide, forming numerous smaller glial cells along the path that the axon formerly took. The neuron then sends out axon sprouts that search for the path made by the Schwann cells and follow it.

Eventually, one sprout reaches the intended target, and this sprout becomes the new axon; all other sprouts retract. The Schwann cells envelop the new axon, forming new myelin and restoring normal function, as shown in **Figure 3-9.** In the PNS, then, Schwann cells serve as signposts to guide axons to their appropriate end points. Axons can get lost, however, as sometimes happens after surgeons reattach a severed limb. If axons destined to innervate one finger end up innervating another finger instead, the wrong finger will move when a message is sent along that neuron.

Unfortunately, glial cells do not provide much help in allowing neurons in the central nervous system to regrow, and they may actually inhibit regrowth. When the CNS is damaged, as happens, for example, when the spinal cord is cut, function does not return, even though the distance that damaged fibers must bridge is short. That recovery should take place in the peripheral nervous system but not in the central nervous system is both a puzzle and a challenge to treating people with brain and spinal-cord injury.

The absence of recovery after spinal-cord injury is especially frustrating because the spinal cord contains many axon pathways, just like those found in the PNS. Researchers investigating how to encourage the regrowth of CNS neurons have focused on the spinal cord. They have placed tubes across an injured area, trying to get axons to regrow through the tubes. They have also inserted immature glial cells into injured areas to facilitate axon regrowth, and they have used chemicals to stimulate the regrowth of axons. Some success has been obtained with each of these techniques, but none is as yet sufficiently advanced to treat people with spinal-cord injuries.

(A) When a peripheral axon is cut, the axon dies.

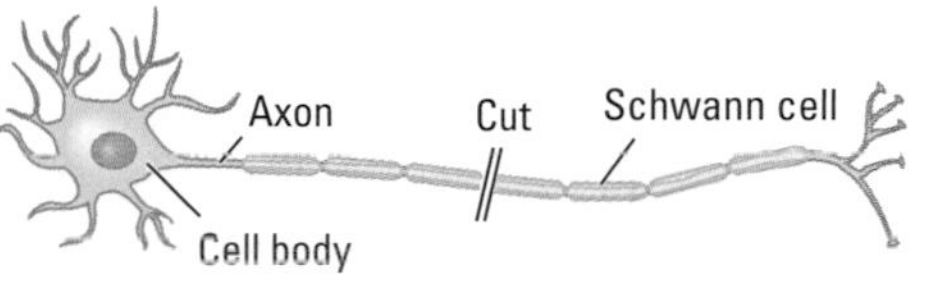

(B) Schwann cells first shrink and then divide, forming glial cells along the axon's former path.

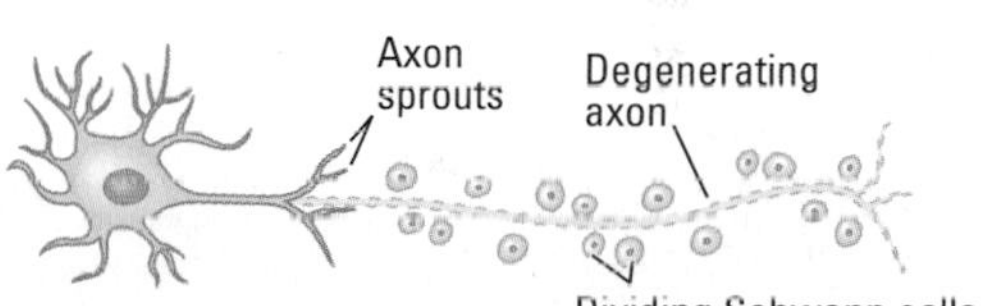

(C) The neuron sends out axon sprouts, one of which finds the Schwann-cell path and becomes a new axon.

(D) Schwann cells envelop the new axon, forming new myelin.

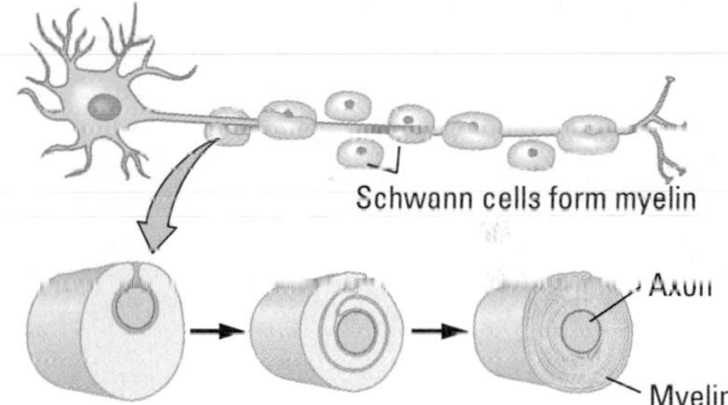

FIGURE 3-9 Neuron Repair. Schwann cells aid the regrowth of axons in the somatic division of the peripheral nervous system.

REVIEW: Cells of the Nervous System

- ✔ The two classes of nervous-system cells are neurons and glia.
- ✔ Neurons are the information-conducting units of the nervous system and either excite or inhibit one another through their connecting synapses. The three types of neurons are sensory neurons, interneurons, and motor neurons.
- ✔ The five types of glial cells are ependymal cells, astrocytes, microglia, oligodendroglia, and Schwann cells. Their function is to nourish and remove waste, insulate, support, and repair neurons.

Internal Structure of a Cell

What is it about the structure of neurons that gives them their remarkable ability to receive, process, store, and send a seemingly limitless amount of information? To answer this question, we must look inside a neuron to see what its components are and understand what they do. The internal features of a neuron can be colored with stains and examined under a light microscope that produces an image by reflecting light waves through the tissue. If the neurons are very small, they can be viewed with an electron microscope, in which electrons take the place of the photons of the light microscope. Just as we can take apart a robot to see how its pieces work, we can view the parts of a cell and take apart a cell to understand how its pieces function.

Because a cell is so small, it is sometimes hard to imagine that it, too, has components. Yet packed inside are hundreds of interrelated parts that do the cell's work. This feature is as true of neurons as it is of any other cell type. A primary function of a cell is to act as a miniature "factory" of work centers that manufacture and transport the proteins that are the cell's products.

To a large extent, the characteristics of cells are determined by their proteins. When researchers ask how a cell performs a certain function, the answer lies in the structure of a certain protein. Each cell can manufacture thousands of proteins, which variously take part in building the cell and in communicating with other cells. When a neuron malfunctions or contains errors, proteins are implicated and so are involved in many kinds of brain disease. In the following sections, we explain how the different parts of a cell contribute to protein manufacture, describe what a protein is, and detail some major functions of proteins.

Water, salts, and ions play prominent parts in the cell's functions, as you will learn throughout this chapter and the next few chapters. If you already understand the structure of water and you know what a salt is and what ions are, read on. If you prefer a brief chemistry review, turn first to The Basics on page 84.

The Cell As a Factory

We have compared a cell to a miniature factory, with work centers that cooperate to make and ship the cell's products—proteins. We now continue this analogy as we investigate the internal parts of a cell, the *organelles,* and how they function, beginning here with a quick overview of the cell's internal structure. **Figure 3-10** displays many cellular components.

A factory's outer wall separates it from the rest of the world and affords some security. Likewise, a cell's double-layered outer wall, or *cell membrane,* separates the cell from its surroundings and allows it to regulate what enters and leaves its domain. The cell membrane surrounds the neuron's cell body, its dendrites and their spines, and its axon and its terminals and so forms a boundary around a continuous intracellular compartment.

Very few substances can enter or leave a cell, because the cell membrane is almost impenetrable. Proteins made by the cell are embedded in the cell membrane to facilitate the transport of substances into and out of the cell. Some proteins thus serve as the cellular factory's gates.

Although the neurons and glia of the brain appear to be tightly packed together, they, like all cells, are separated by *extracellular fluid* composed mainly of water with dissolved salts and many other chemicals. A similar *intracellular fluid* is found inside a cell as well. The important point is that the concentrations of substances inside and outside the cell are different.

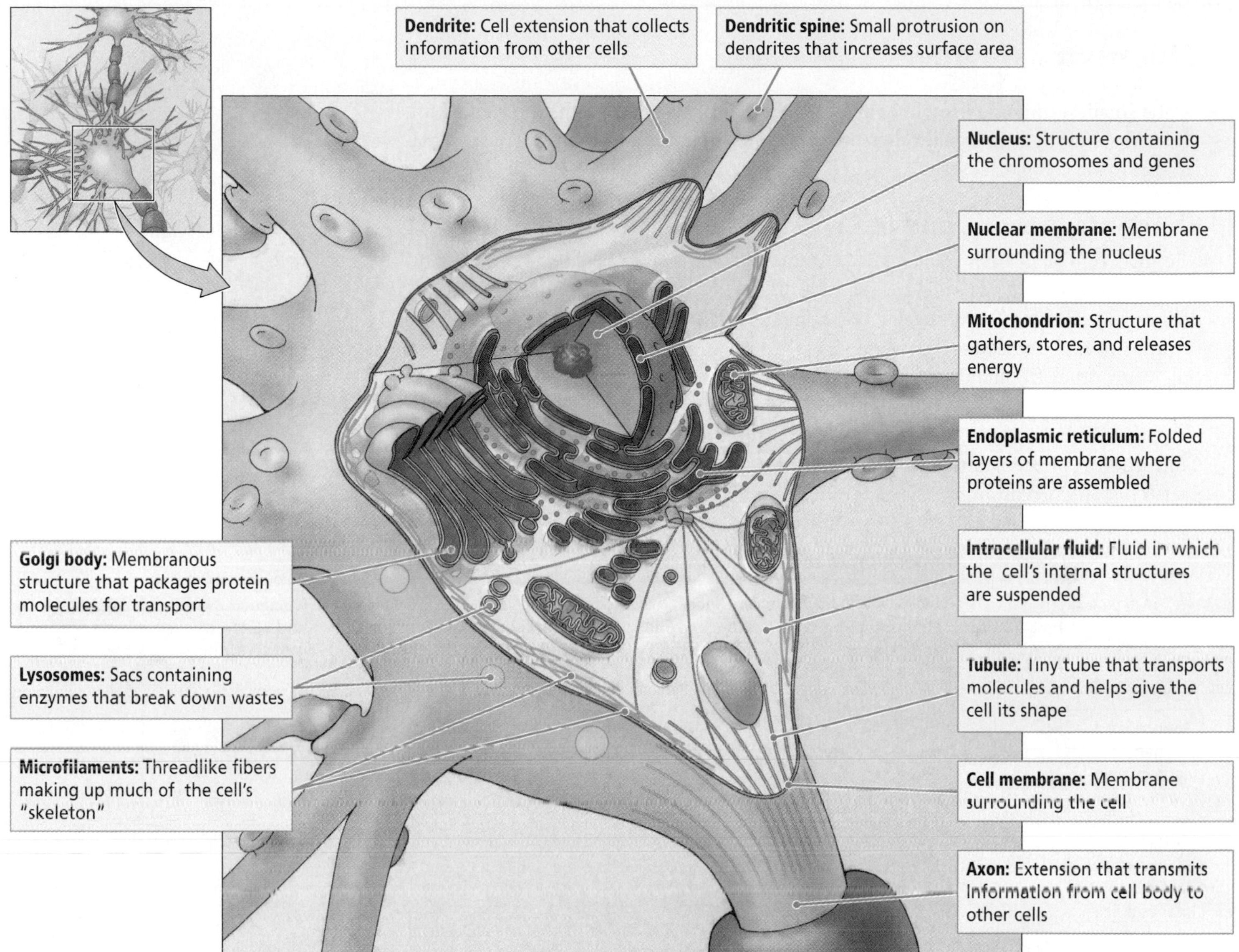
Dendrite: Cell extension that collects information from other cells
Dendritic spine: Small protrusion on dendrites that increases surface area
Nucleus: Structure containing the chromosomes and genes
Nuclear membrane: Membrane surrounding the nucleus
Mitochondrion: Structure that gathers, stores, and releases energy
Endoplasmic reticulum: Folded layers of membrane where proteins are assembled
Intracellular fluid: Fluid in which the cell's internal structures are suspended
Tubule: Tiny tube that transports molecules and helps give the cell its shape
Cell membrane: Membrane surrounding the cell
Axon: Extension that transmits information from cell body to other cells
Golgi body: Membranous structure that packages protein molecules for transport
Lysosomes: Sacs containing enzymes that break down wastes
Microfilaments: Threadlike fibers making up much of the cell's "skeleton"

FIGURE 3-10 Typical Nerve Cell. This view inside a neuron reveals its organelles and other internal components.

Within the cell shown in Figure 13-10 are membranes that surround its interior compartments, similar to the work areas demarcated by the inner walls of a factory. In each inner compartment, the cell concentrates chemicals that it needs while keeping out unneeded ones. The prominent *nuclear membrane* surrounds the cell's *nucleus,* where the genetic blueprints for the cell's proteins are stored, copied, and sent to the "factory floor." The *endoplasmic reticulum* (ER) is an extension of the nuclear membrane; the cell's protein products are assembled in the ER in accord with instructions from the nucleus.

When those proteins are assembled, they are packaged and sent throughout the cell. Parts of the cell called the *Golgi bodies* provide the packaging rooms where the proteins are wrapped, addressed, and shipped. Other cell components are called *tubules,* of which there are a number of kinds. Some *(microfilaments)* reinforce the cell's structure, others aid in the cell's movements, and still others *(microtubules)* form the transportation network that carries the proteins to their destinations, much as roads allow a factory's trucks and forklifts to deliver goods to their destinations.

Two other important parts of the cellular factory shown in Figure 3-10 are the *mitochondria,* the cell's power plants that supply its energy needs, and *lysosomes,* sacklike

Chemistry Review

The smallest unit of a protein or any other chemical substance is the molecule. Molecules and the even smaller elements and atoms that make them up are the raw materials for the cellular factory.

Elements, Atoms, and Ions

Chemists represent each *element*, a substance that cannot be broken down into another substance, by a symbol—for example, O for oxygen, C for carbon, and H for hydrogen. Of Earth's 92 naturally occurring elements, the 10 listed in Chemical Composition of the Brain constitute virtually the entire makeup of an average living cell. Many other elements are vital to the cell but present in minute quantities.

An *atom* is the smallest quantity of an element that retains the properties of that element. The basic structures of a cell's most common atoms are shown in Chemical Composition of the Brain. Ordinarily, atoms are electrically neutral, as illustrated in part A of Ion Formation.

Chemical Composition of the Brain

Percentage of weight	Element name and symbol	Nucleus and electrons (not to scale)	Percentage of weight	Element name and symbol	Nucleus and electrons (not to scale)
65.0	Oxygen, O		0.4	Potassium, K	
18.5	Carbon, C				
9.5	Hydrogen, H				
3.5	Nitrogen, N		0.2	Sulfur, S	
1.5	Calcium, Ca		0.2	Sodium, Na	
1.0	Phosphorus, P		0.2	Chlorine, Cl	

Together, oxygen, carbon, and hydrogen account for more than 90 percent of a cell's makeup.

Some symbols derive from an element's Latin name—K for *kalium* (Latin for potassium) and Na for *natrium* (Latin for sodium), for example.

Atoms of chemically reactive elements such as sodium and chlorine can easily lose or gain electrons. When an atom gives up electrons, it becomes positively charged; when it takes on extra electrons, it becomes negatively charged, as illustrated in part B of Ion Formation. In either case, the charged atom is now an *ion*. The positive and negative charges of ions allow them to interact, a property central to cell function.

Ions Critical to Cell Function

Na^+	sodium
K^+	potassium
Ca^{2+}	calcium
Cl^-	chloride

Ions formed by losing electrons are represented by an element's symbol followed by one or more plus signs.

Ions formed by gaining electrons are represented by an element's symbol followed by a minus sign.

Molecules: Salts and Water

Salt crystals form bonds through the electrical attraction between ions. The formula for table salt, NaCl (sodium chloride), means that this molecule consists of one sodium ion and one chlorine ion. KCl, the formula for the salt potassium chloride, is composed of one potassium ion and one chlorine ion.

Atoms bind together to form *molecules,* the smallest units of a substance that contain all of that substance's properties. A water molecule (H_2O) is the smallest unit of water that still retains the properties of water. Breaking down water any further would release its component elements, the gases hydrogen and oxygen. The formula H_2O indicates that a water molecule is the union of two hydrogen atoms and one oxygen atom.

Charged ionic bonds hold salt molecules together, but water molecules share electrons. As you can see in part A of Chemistry of Water, below, the electron sharing is not equal: H electrons spend more time orbiting the O atom than they do each H atom. This structure gives the oxygen region of the water molecule a slight negative charge and leaves the hydrogen regions with a slight positive charge. Like atoms, most molecules are electrically neutral, but water is a *polar molecule:* it has opposite charges on opposite ends, just as Earth does at the North and South Poles.

(A) Water molecule

Two hydrogen atoms share electrons unequally with one oxygen atom, creating a polar water molecule positively charged on the hydrogen end and negatively charged on the oxygen end.

H H H H O O H_2O

(B) Hydrogen bonds

Hydrogen bonds join water molecules to a maximum of four partners.

H^+ and O^{2-} ions in each water molecule are attracted to nearby water molecules.

Chemistry of Water.

(A) Atoms

Total positive (+) and negative (–) charges in atoms are equal. The nucleus contains *neutrons* (no charge) and *protons* (positive charge). Orbiting the nucleus are *electrons* (negative charge).

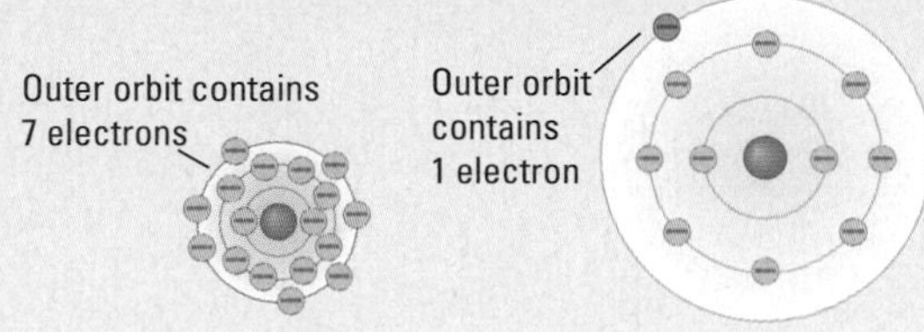

Outer orbit contains 7 electrons
Outer orbit contains 1 electron

Cl atoms have 17 protons and 17 electrons.

Na atoms have 11 protons and 11 electrons.

(B) Ions

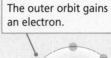

The outer orbit gains an electron.

The outer orbit disappears because it lost its only electron.

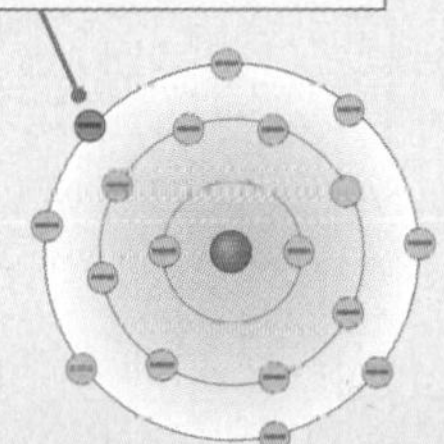

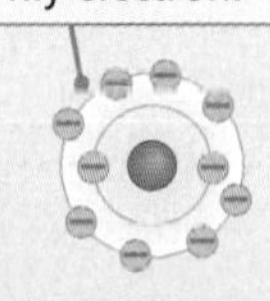

Charged chloride ion (Cl^-)

Charged sodium ion (Na^+)

Ion Formation.

Because water molecules are polar, they are attracted to other electrically charged substances and to one another. Part B of Chemistry of Water, above, illustrates this attracting force, called a *hydrogen bond.* Hydrogen bonding gives water its ability to dissolve electrically neutral salt crystals into their component ions. Salts thus cannot retain their shape in water. As illustrated in Salty Water, the polar water molecules muscle their way into the Na^+ and Cl^- lattice, surrounding and separating the ions.

Sodium chloride is one dissolved salt found in the fluid inside and outside cells. Many other dissolved salts, including KCl (potassium chloride) and $CaCl_2$ (calcium chloride) are found in living tissue as well.

Salty Water.

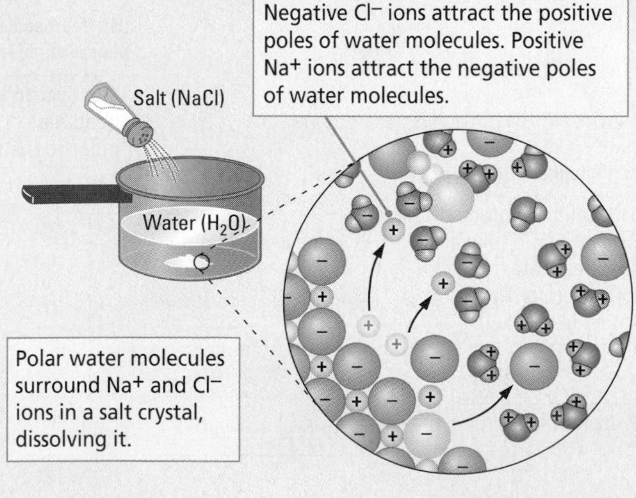

Negative Cl^- ions attract the positive poles of water molecules. Positive Na^+ ions attract the negative poles of water molecules.
Salt (NaCl)
Water (H_2O)
Polar water molecules surround Na^+ and Cl^- ions in a salt crystal, dissolving it.

vesicles that transport incoming supplies and move and store wastes. Interestingly, more lysosomes are found in old cells than in young ones. Cells apparently have trouble disposing of their garbage, just as we do.

With this brief overview of the cell's internal structure in mind, you can now examine its parts in more detail, beginning with the cell membrane.

The Cell Membrane: Barrier and Gatekeeper

The cell membrane separates the intracellular from the extracellular fluid and so allows the cell to function as an independent unit. The double-layered structure of the membrane, shown in **Figure 3-11A**, also regulates the movement of substances into and out of the cell. One of these substances is water. If too much water enters a cell, it will burst, and, if too much water leaves a cell, it will shrivel. The cell membrane's structure helps ensure that neither will happen.

The cell membrane also regulates the differing concentrations of salts and other chemicals on its inner and outer sides. This regulation is important because, if the concentrations of chemicals within a cell become unbalanced, the cell will not function normally. What properties of a cell membrane allow it to regulate water and salt concentrations within the cell? One property is its special molecular construction. These molecules, called *phospholipids,* are named for their structure, shown close up in Figure 3-11B.

The phosopholipid molecule's "head" contains the element phosphorus (P) bound to some other atoms, and its two "tails" are lipids, or fat molecules. The head region is polar, with a slight positive charge in one location and a slight negative charge in another, like water molecules. The tails consist of hydrogen and carbon atoms that are tightly bound to one another by their shared electrons; hence there are no polar regions in the fatty tail. Figure 3-11C shows a chemical model of the phosopholipid molecule.

The polar head and the nonpolar tails are the underlying reasons that a phospholipid molecule can form cell membranes. The heads are hydrophilic (Greek *hydro,* meaning "water," and *philia,* meaning "love") and so are attracted to one another and to polar water molecules. The nonpolar tails have no such attraction for water. They are *hydrophobic,* or water hating (from the Greek word *phobia,* meaning "fear").

Quite literally, then, the head of a phospholipid loves water and the tails hate it. To avoid water, the tails of phospholipid molecules point toward each other, and the hydrophilic heads align with one another and point outward to the intracellular and extracellular fluid. In this way, the cell membrane consists of a bilayer (two layers) of phospholipid molecules (see Figure 3-11A).

FIGURE 3-11 Structure of the Cell Membrane. (A) The double-layered cell membrane close up. (B) Detail of a phospholipid molecule's polar head and electrically neutral tails. (C) Space-filling model shows why the phosphate head's polar regions (positive and negative poles) are hydrophilic, whereas its fatty acid tail, having no polar regions, is hydrophobic.

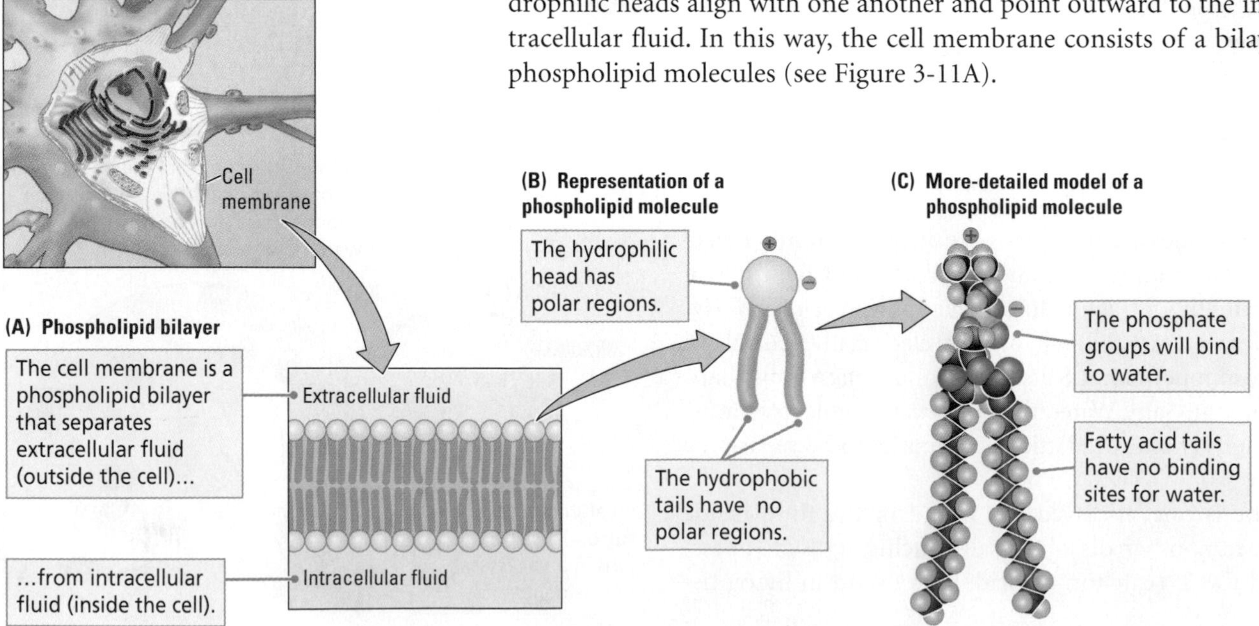
Cell membrane
(A) Phospholipid bilayer
The cell membrane is a phospholipid bilayer that separates extracellular fluid (outside the cell)...
...from intracellular fluid (inside the cell).
Extracellular fluid
Intracellular fluid
(B) Representation of a phospholipid molecule
The hydrophilic head has polar regions.
The hydrophobic tails have no polar regions.
(C) More-detailed model of a phospholipid molecule
The phosphate groups will bind to water.
Fatty acid tails have no binding sites for water.

The bilayer cell membrane is flexible while still forming a remarkable barrier to a wide variety of substances. It is impenetrable to intracellular and extracellular water, because polar water molecules cannot pass through the hydrophobic tails on the interior of the membrane. Ions in the extracellular and intracellular fluid also cannot penetrate this membrane, because they carry charges and thus cannot pass the polar phospholipid heads. In fact, only a few small molecules, such as oxygen (O_2), can pass through a phospholipid bilayer.

Recall that the cell-membrane barrier is punctuated with embedded protein "gates" that receive its supplies, dispose of its wastes, and ship its products. Before we describe these mechanisms in detail, we consider how proteins are manufactured and transported within the cell.

The Nucleus: Site of Gene Transcription

In our factory analogy, the nucleus is the cell's executive office where the blueprints for making proteins are stored, copied, and sent to the factory floor. These blueprints are called *genes,* segments of DNA that encode the synthesis of particular proteins. Genes are contained within the *chromosomes,* the double-helix structures that hold an organism's entire DNA sequence.

The name *chromosome* means "colored body," referring to the fact that chromosomes can be readily stained with certain dyes.

The chromosomes are like a book of blueprints for making a complex building, whereas a gene is like one page of the book containing the plan for a door or a corridor between rooms. Each chromosome contains thousands of genes. The location of the chromosomes in the nucleus of the cell, the appearance of a chromosome, and the structure of the DNA in a chromosome are shown in **Figure 3-12.**

This static picture of chromosomes does not represent the way that they look in living cells. Video recordings of the cell nucleus show that chromosomes are constantly changing shape and moving in relation to one another so as to occupy the best locations within the nucleus for collecting the building blocks of proteins and making proteins. By changing shape, chromosomes expose different genes to the surrounding fluid, thus allowing the processes of protein formation to begin.

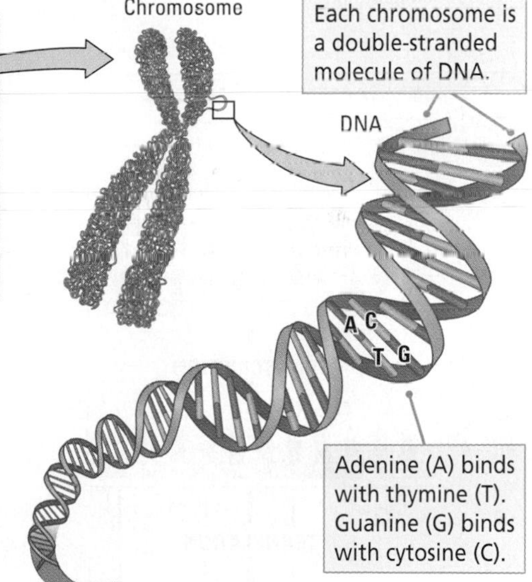
Chromosome
Each chromosome is a double-stranded molecule of DNA.
DNA
A C
T G
Adenine (A) binds with thymine (T). Guanine (G) binds with cytosine (C).

FIGURE 3-12 A Chromosome. The nerve-cell nucleus contains paired chromosomes of double-stranded DNA molecules bound together by a sequence of nucleotide bases.

A human somatic (body) cell has 23 pairs of chromosomes, or 46 chromosomes in all (in contrast, the 23 chromosomes within a reproductive cell are not paired). Each chromosome is a double-stranded molecule of *deoxyribonucleic acid* (DNA), which is capable of replicating and determining the inherited structure of a cell's proteins. The two strands of a DNA molecule coil around each other, as shown in Figure 3-12. Each strand possesses a variable sequence of four *nucleotide bases,* the constituent molecules of the genetic code: *adenine* (A), *thymine* (T), *guanine* (G), and *cytosine* (C).

Adenine on one strand always pairs with thymine on the other, whereas guanine on one strand always pairs with cytosine on the other. The two strands of the DNA helix are bonded together by the attraction that the bases in each pair have for each other, as illustrated in Figure 3-12. Sequences of hundreds of nucleotide bases within the chromosomes spell out the genetic code—for example, ATGCCG, and so forth.

Recall that a gene is a segment of a DNA strand and encodes the synthesis of a particular protein. The code is contained in the sequence of the nucleotide bases, much as a sequence of letters spells out a word. The sequence of bases "spells out" the particular order in which *amino acids,* the constituent molecules of proteins, should be assembled to construct a certain protein.

To initiate the process, the appropriate gene segment of the DNA strands first unwinds. The exposed sequence of nucleotide bases on one of the DNA strands then serves

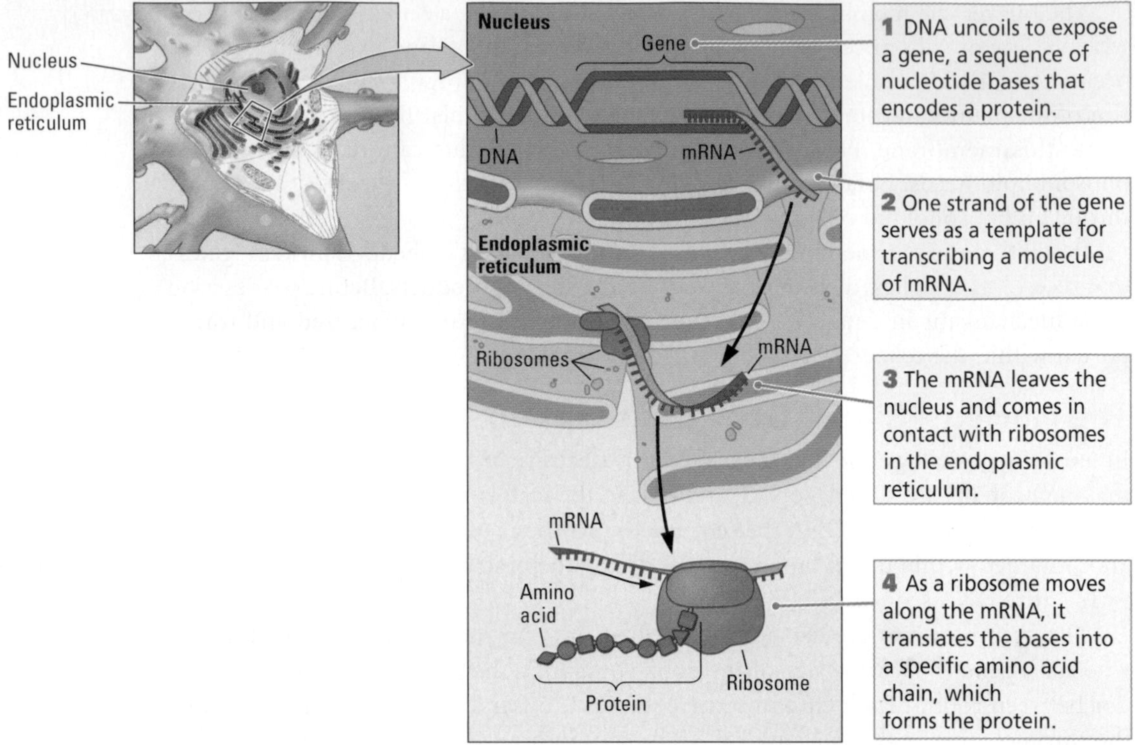

Nucleus
Endoplasmic reticulum
Nucleus
Gene
DNA
mRNA
Endoplasmic reticulum
Ribosomes
mRNA
mRNA
Amino acid
Protein
Ribosome
1 DNA uncoils to expose a gene, a sequence of nucleotide bases that encodes a protein.
2 One strand of the gene serves as a template for transcribing a molecule of mRNA.
3 The mRNA leaves the nucleus and comes in contact with ribosomes in the endoplasmic reticulum.
4 As a ribosome moves along the mRNA, it translates the bases into a specific amino acid chain, which forms the protein.

FIGURE 3-13 Protein Synthesis. The flow of information in a cell is from DNA to mRNA (messenger RNA, one of the three types of ribonucleic acids) to protein (peptide chain).

as a template to attract free-floating molecules called *nucleotides.* The nucleotides thus attached form a complementary strand of *ribonucleic acid* (RNA), the single-stranded nucleic acid molecule required for protein synthesis. This process, called *transcription,* is shown in steps 1 and 2 of **Figure 3-13.** (To transcribe means "to copy," as in copying a piece of text in a word-processing program.)

The Endoplasmic Reticulum: Site of RNA Synthesis

The RNA produced through transcription is much like a single strand of DNA except that the base *uracil* (U, which also is attracted to adenine) takes the place of thymine. The transcribed strand of RNA is called *messenger RNA* (mRNA) because it carries the genetic code out of the nucleus to the endoplasmic reticulum, where proteins are manufactured.

Steps 3 and 4 in Figure 3-13 show that the ER consists of membranous sheets folded to form numerous channels. A distinguishing feature of the ER is that it may be studded with *ribosomes,* protein structures that act as catalysts in the building of proteins. When an mRNA molecule reaches the ER, it passes through a ribosome, where its genetic code is "read."

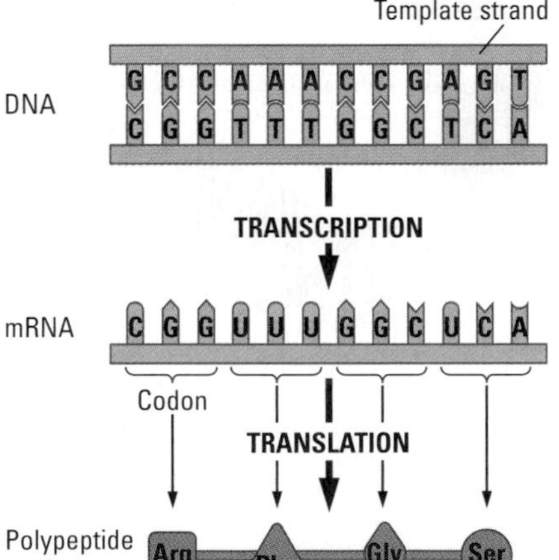

Template strand
DNA
G C C A A A C C G A G T
C G G T T T G G C T C A
TRANSCRIPTION
mRNA
C G G U U U G G C U C A
Codon
TRANSLATION
Polypeptide chain
Arg
Phe
Gly
Ser
Amino acids

FIGURE 3-14 Transcription and Translation. In protein synthesis (see Figure 3-13), a strand of DNA is transcribed into mRNA. Each sequence of three bases in the mRNA strand (a codon) encodes one amino acid. Directed by the codons, the amino acids link together to form a polypeptide chain. The amino acids illustrated are tryptophan (Trp), phenylalanine (Phe), glycine (Gly), and serine (Ser).

In this process, called *translation,* a particular sequence of nucleotide bases in the mRNA is transformed into a particular sequence of amino acids. (To translate means to convert one language into another, in contrast with transcription, in which the language remains the same.) *Transfer RNA* (tRNA) assists in translation. *Proteins* are just long chains of amino acids, folded up to form specific shapes.

The flow of information contained in the genetic code is conceptually quite simple: a DNA strand is transcribed into an mRNA strand, and the mRNA strand is translated by ribosomes into a molecular chain of amino acids. As shown in **Figure 3-14,** each group of three consecutive nucleotide bases along an mRNA molecule encodes one particular amino acid. These sequences of three bases are called *codons.* For example, the base sequence uracil, guanine, guanine (UGG) encodes the amino acid tryptophan (Trp), whereas the base sequence uracil, uracil, uracil (UUU) encodes the amino acid

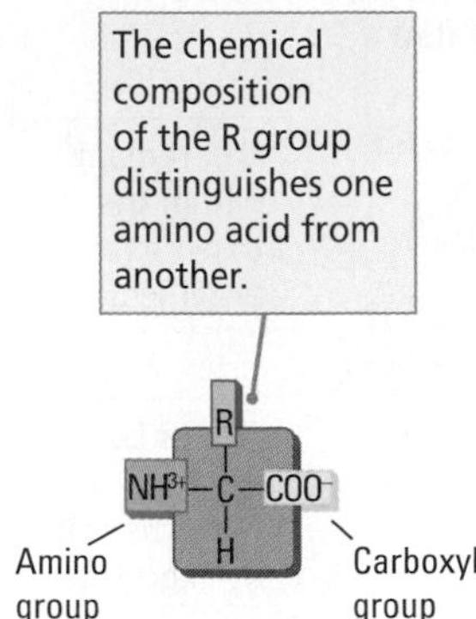
(A) Amino acid structure
The chemical composition of the R group distinguishes one amino acid from another.
R
NH3+ —C—COO−
H
Amino group
Carboxyl group

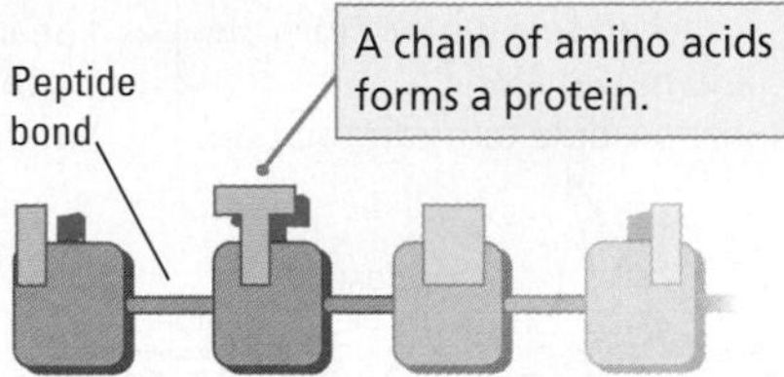
(B) Polypeptide chain
Peptide bond
A chain of amino acids forms a protein.

FIGURE 3-15 Properties of Amino Acids. (A) Each amino acid consists of a central carbon atom (C) attached to an amine group (NH^{3+}), a carboxyl group (COO^{-}), and a distinguishing side chain (R). (B) The amino acids are linked by peptide bonds to form a polypeptide chain.

phenylalanine (Phe). Codons also direct the placement of particular amino acids into a polypeptide chain.

Humans require 20 different amino acids to synthesize proteins. All 20 are structurally similar, as illustrated in **Figure 3-15**A. Each consists of a central carbon atom (C) bound to a hydrogen atom (H), an *amino group* (NH^{3+}), a *carboxyl group* (COO^{-}), and a *side chain* (represented by the letter R). The side chain varies in chemical composition from one amino acid to another, which helps to give different protein molecules their distinctive biochemical properties.

Proteins: The Cell's Product

Amino acids are linked together chemically by a special *peptide bond* (Figure 3-15B). A series of amino acids is called a *polypeptide chain* (meaning "many peptides"). Just as a remarkable number of words can be made from the 26 letters of the English alphabet, a remarkable number of peptide chains can be made from the 20 different amino acids. These amino acids can form 400 (20 × 20) different dipeptides (two-peptide combinations), 8000 (20 × 20 × 20) different tripeptides (three-peptide combinations), and almost countless polypeptides.

A polypeptide chain and a protein are related, but they are not the same. The relation is analogous to that between a length of ribbon and a bow of a particular size and shape that can be made from the ribbon. Long polypeptide chains have a strong tendency to twist into a helix (a spiral) or to form pleated sheets, which, in turn, have a strong tendency to fold together to form more-complex shapes as shown in **Figure 3-16.**

A folded-up polypeptide chain constitutes a protein. In addition, two or more polypeptide chains may combine to form a single protein. Many proteins are globular (round) in shape and others are fibrous, but, within these broad categories, countless variations are possible. A protein's shape and ability to change shape and to combine with other proteins are central to the protein's function.

Any one neuron may use as many as 10,000 protein molecules. Some proteins are destined to be incorporated into the structure of the cell. They become part of the cell membrane, the nucleus, the ER, and so forth. Other proteins remain in the intracellular fluid, where they act as *enzymes*—protein catalysts that facilitate the cell's chemical reactions. Still other proteins are excreted by the cell as "messenger molecules" and so allow the cell to communicate with other cells.

Golgi Bodies and Microtubules: Protein Packaging and Shipment

Getting all these different proteins to the right destinations is the task of the cell components that package, label, and ship them. These components operate much like a postal service.

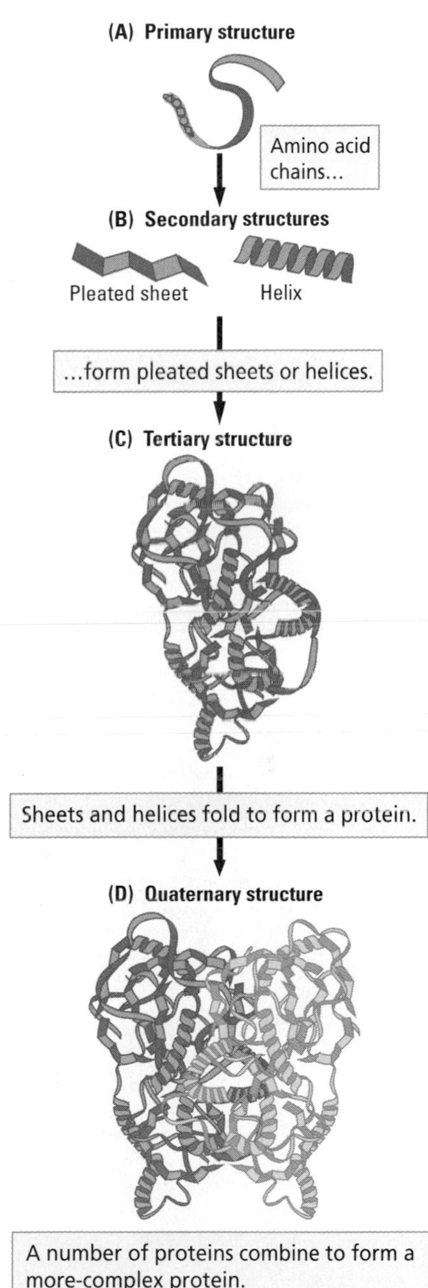
(A) Primary structure
Amino acid chains...
(B) Secondary structures
Pleated sheet
Helix
...form pleated sheets or helices.
(C) Tertiary structure
Sheets and helices fold to form a protein.
(D) Quaternary structure
A number of proteins combine to form a more-complex protein.

FIGURE 3-16 Four Levels of Protein Structure. Whether a polypeptide chain forms a pleated sheet or a helix and its ultimate three-dimensional shape are determined by the sequence of amino acids in the primary structure.

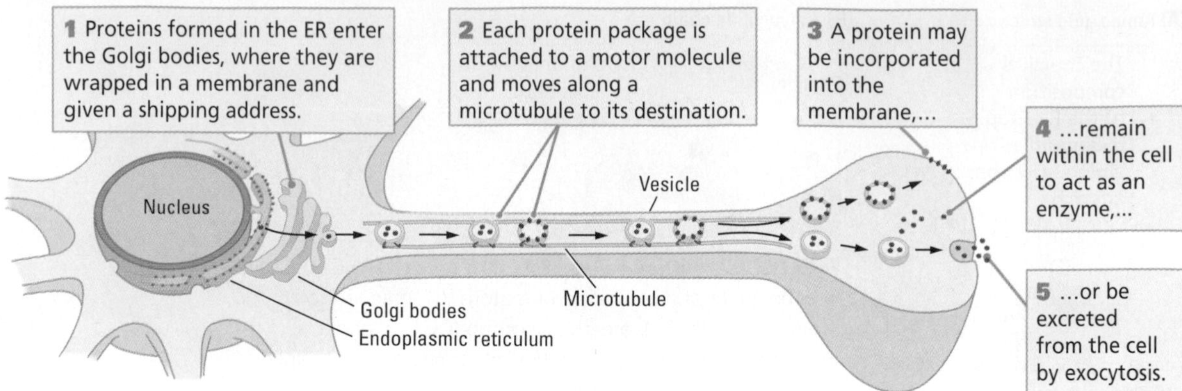

1 Proteins formed in the ER enter the Golgi bodies, where they are wrapped in a membrane and given a shipping address.
2 Each protein package is attached to a motor molecule and moves along a microtubule to its destination.
3 A protein may be incorporated into the membrane,...
4 ...remain within the cell to act as an enzyme,...
5 ...or be excreted from the cell by exocytosis.
Nucleus
Vesicle
Golgi bodies
Endoplasmic reticulum
Microtubule

FIGURE 3-17 Protein Export. Exporting a protein entails packaging, transport, and its function at the destination.

To reach their appropriate destinations, the protein molecules that have been synthesized in the cell must first be wrapped in membranes and marked with their destination addresses to indicate where they are to go. This wrapping and labeling takes place in the organelles called Golgi bodies. The packaged proteins are then loaded onto motor molecules that "walk" along the many microtubules radiating through the cell, thus carrying each protein to its destination. The work of exporting proteins is illustrated in **Figure 3-17.**

If a protein is destined to remain within the cell, it is unloaded into the intracellular fluid. If it is to be incorporated into the cell membrane, it is carried to the membrane, where it inserts itself. Suppose that a particular protein is to be excreted at the cell membrane. In this process, called *exocytosis,* the membrane, or *vesicle,* in which the protein is wrapped first fuses with the membrane of the cell. Now the protein inside the vesicle can be expelled into the extracellular fluid. Many excreted proteins travel to other cells to induce chemical reactions and so serve as messenger molecules.

Crossing the Cell Membrane: Channels, Gates, and Pumps

Knowing something about the structure of proteins will help you to understand other ways that substances can travel across what would otherwise be an impermeable cell membrane. Recall that some proteins are carried to the cell membrane, where they become embedded. Hydrophobic parts of a protein molecule affix themselves within the cell membrane while hydrophilic parts of the protein stick out into the intra- and extracellular fluid. In this way, membrane protein molecules span the cell membrane.

These membrane proteins play a number of important roles, one of which is to transport substances across the membrane. We will consider how three such membrane proteins work: channels, gates, and pumps. In each case, notice how the function of the particular protein is an emergent property of its shape.

Both the shape of a protein and its ability to change shape are emergent properties of the precise sequence of amino acids that compose the protein molecule. Some proteins change shape when other chemicals bind to them, others change shape as a function of temperature, and still others change shape in response to changes in electrical charge. The ability of a protein molecule to change shape is analogous to a lock in a door. When a key of the appropriate size and shape is inserted into the lock and turned, the locking device activates and changes shape, allowing the door to be closed or opened.

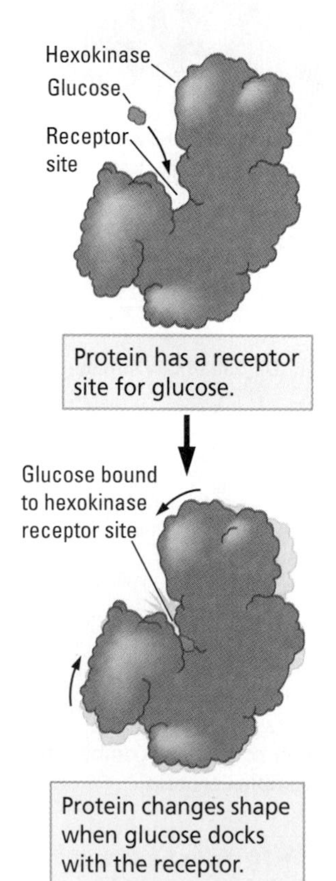

Protein has a receptor site for glucose.
Glucose bound to hexokinase receptor site

FIGURE 3-18 Receptor Binding. When substances bind to a protein's receptors, the protein changes shape, which may change its function.

An example of a shape-changing protein is the enzyme hexokinase, illustrated in **Figure 3-18.** The surface of this protein molecule has a groove, called a *receptor,* which is analogous to a keyhole. When another molecule—in this case, glucose—enters the receptor area, it induces a slight change in the shape of the protein, causing the hexokinase to embrace the glucose. Either small molecules or other proteins can bind to the

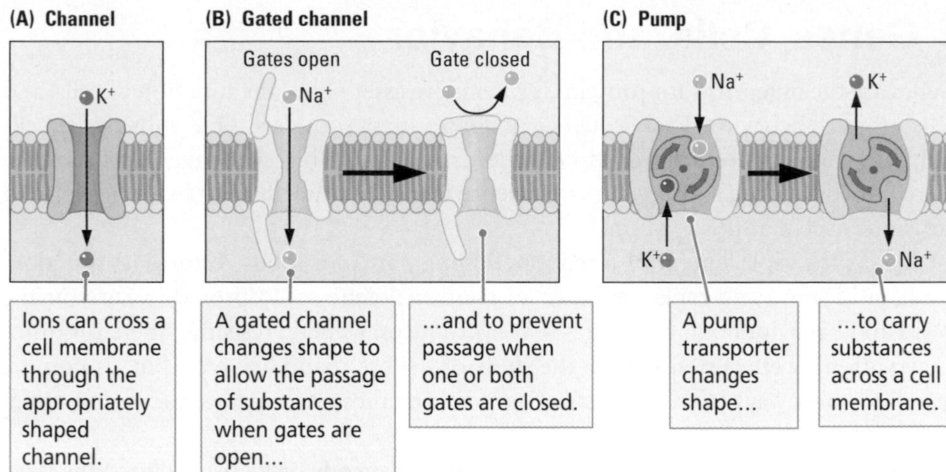

(A) Channel
(B) Gated channel
(C) Pump
Gates open
Gate closed
K^+
Na^+
Na^+
K^+
K^+
Na^+
Ions can cross a cell membrane through the appropriately shaped channel.
A gated channel changes shape to allow the passage of substances when gates are open...
...and to prevent passage when one or both gates are closed.
A pump transporter changes shape...
...to carry substances across a cell membrane.

FIGURE 3-19 Transmembrane Proteins. Channels, gates, and pumps are embedded in the cell membrane.

receptors of proteins and cause them to change shape. Changes in shape then allow the proteins to serve some new function.

A cell-membrane protein's shape or the protein's ability to change shape enable substances to cross the cell membrane. Some membrane proteins create **channels** through which substances can pass. Different-sized channels in different proteins allow the passage of different substances. **Figure 3-19**A illustrates a protein with a particular shape forming a small channel in the cell membrane that is large enough for potassium (K^+) ions, but not other ions, to pass through. Other protein channels allow sodium ions or chloride ions to pass into or out of the cell.

Figure 3-19B shows a protein molecule that acts as a **gate** to regulate the passage of substances across the cell membrane by changing the protein's shape in response to some trigger, as does the protein hexokinase in Figure 3-18. The protein allows the passage of substances when its shape forms a channel and prevents the passage of substances when its shape leaves the channel closed. Thus a part of this protein acts as a gate.

Changes in the shape of a protein can also allow it to act as a **pump.** Figure 3-19C shows a protein that, when Na^+ and K^+ ions bind to it, changes its shape to carry ("pump") the substances across the membrane, exchanging the Na^+ on one side of the membrane for the K^+ on the other side of the membrane.

Channels, gates, and pumps play an important role in allowing substances to enter and leave a cell. This passage of substances is critical in explaining how neurons send messages. Chapter 4 explores the topic of neuron communication in detail.

REVIEW: Internal Structure of a Cell

- ✔ Chemical elements within cells combine to form molecules that in turn organize into the constituent parts of the cell, including the cell membrane, nucleus, endoplasmic reticulum, Golgi bodies, tubules, and vesicles.
- ✔ Important products of the cell are proteins, which serve many functions that include acting at the cell membrane as channels, gates, and pumps to allow substances to cross the membrane.
- ✔ Simply put, the sequence of events in building a protein is as follows: DNA → mRNA → protein.
- ✔ DNA makes mRNA and mRNA makes protein. When formed, the protein molecules are wrapped by the Golgi bodies and transported to their designated sites in the neuron, to its membrane, or for export from the cell by microtubules.

Channel Opening in a protein embedded in the cell membrane that allows the passage of ions.
Gate Protein embedded in a cell membrane that allows substances to pass through the membrane on some occasions but not on others.
Pump Protein in the cell membrane that actively transports a substance across the membrane.

Allele Alternate form of a gene; a gene pair contains two alleles.
Homozygous Having two identical alleles for a trait.
Heterozygous Having two different alleles for the same trait.
Wild type Refers to a normal (most common in a population) phenotype or genotype.
Mutation Alteration of an allele that yields a different version of that allele.

Genes, Cells, and Behavior

Genes are the blueprints for proteins, proteins are essential to the function of cells, and cells produce behavior. That sequence of connections sounds simple enough. But exactly how one connection leads to another is one of the big challenges for future research. If you choose a career in neuroscience research, you will most likely be working out some aspect of this relation.

Just as the replacement of a malfunctioning part of a robot restores its function, the identification and replacement of an abnormal gene could provide a cure for the brain and behavioral abnormalities that it produces. Genetic research, then, promises a revolutionary effect not only on the study of the brain and behavior but also on the search for new ways to treat genetic disorders. For these reasons, we focus on human genetics in the rest of this chapter.

To review, genes are chromosome segments that encode proteins, and proteins serve as enzymes, membrane channels, and messenger molecules. This knowledge does not tell you much about the ultimate structure and function of a cell, because so many genes and proteins take part. The eventual function of a cell is an emergent property of all its many constituent parts.

Similarly, knowing that behaviors result from the activity of neurons does not tell you much about the ultimate form that behaviors will take, because so many neurons participate in them. Your behavior is an emergent property of the action of all your billions of neurons. The challenge for future research is to be able to explain how genes, proteins, cells, and behavior are related.

The field of study directed toward understanding how genes produce proteins is called *genomics.* The exact number of protein-encoding genes in the human genome is under debate, but it is likely between 20,000 and 50, 000. About half of all genes are estimated to contribute to building the brain. Although each gene is a code for one protein, the number of proteins that can be produced is much larger than the number of genes.

The number of proteins produced by the genome is increased in four different ways:

1. Most gene pairs have a number of variants, and each variant will produce a slightly different protein. In addition, in an individual organism, one of the gene variants from one parent may be imprinted so that it is expressed, whereas the other variant is not.
2. Enzymes in the cell nucleus can edit the mRNA that carries the message from a gene to produce a protein, resulting in still more protein variants.
3. After they have been formed, protein molecules can be cleaved by enzymes, producing two or more different proteins.
4. Protein molecules can merge to form still different proteins (see Figure 3-16). The mergers may produce thousands of proteins that form interactions that collaborate to produce biological functions.

In principle, then, there is no upper limit on the number of proteins that a cell could manufacture, but the number of proteins required for normal cell function is likely less than 100,000. Knowing what functions each of those proteins performs advances our understanding of how the brain is constructed and produces behavior. The field of study directed toward understanding what all these proteins do is called *proteomics.*

The Human Genome Project has cataloged the human genome (all the genes in our species), and now the genomes of individual persons are being documented. James Watson, the co-discoverer of DNA and the first person to have his genome documented, has made his genome available to scientists for further study. In addition, the genomes of many other animal and plant species have been described, including the long-extinct Neanderthal human.

Interestingly, genome size and chromosome number seem unrelated to the complexity of the organism (**Table 3-2**), and there are many similarities in the genes of different species. Genes that are necessary for life are highly conserved. Those that are necessary to structural features of the body tend to be highly similar to the extent that the body plan of animals is similar. Genes that are likely to be different are those related to particular physical and behavioral traits of individual animal species. Finally, even single traits in animals may depend on many genes. In a study on the small worm *Caenorhabditis elegans,* for example, Kaveh Ashrafi and colleagues (2003) found 305 genes that contribute to decreased body fat and 112 genes that increase it.

TABLE 3-2 Genome Size and Chromosome Number in Selected Species

Species	Genome size (base pairs)	Chromosome pairs
Ameba	670,000,000,000	Several hundred
Lily	90,000,000,000	12
Mouse	3,454,200,000	20
Human	2,850,000,000	23
Carp	1,700,000,000	49
Chicken	1,200,000,000	39
Housefly	900,000,000	6
Tomato	655,000,000	12

Even though neuroscientists cannot yet explain human behavior in relation to genes and neurons, we know the severe behavioral consequences of about 2000 genetic abnormalities that affect the nervous system. For example, an error in a gene could produce a protein that should be a K^+ channel but will not allow K^+ to pass, it may produce a pump that will not pump, or it may produce a protein that the transportation system of the cell refuses to transport.

With thousands of different proteins in a cell, a genetic mutation that results in an abnormality of any one protein could have a beneficial effect, it could have little noticeable effect, or it could have severe negative consequences. Studying genetic abnormalities is one source of insight into how genes, neurons, and behaviors are linked. Such studies may also help to reduce the negative effects of these abnormalities, perhaps someday even eliminating them completely.

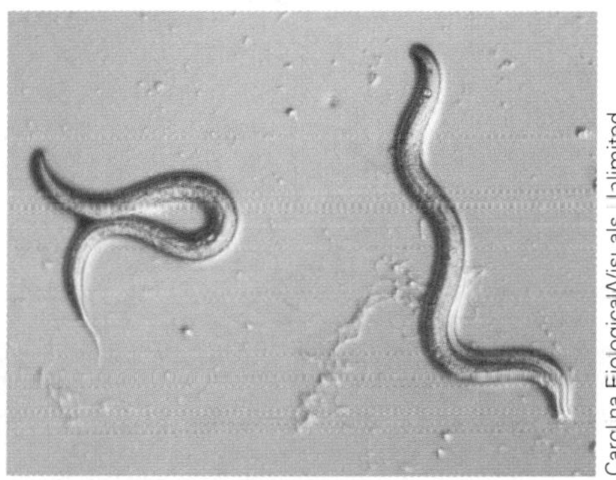

Carolina Biological/Visuals Unlimited

Caenorhabditis elegans is a small roundworm about 1 millimeter long that lives in the soil. It was the first species to have all its neurons and synapses and its genome described.

Chromosomes and Genes

Recall that the nucleus of each human somatic cell contains 23 pairs of chromosomes, or 46 in all. One member of each pair of chromosomes comes from the mother, and the other member comes from the father. The chromosome pairs are numbered from 1 to 23, roughly according to size, with chromosome 1 being the largest (**Figure 3-20**).

Chromosome pairs 1 through 22 are called *autosomes,* and they contain the genes that contribute to most of our physical appearance and behavioral functions. The 23rd pair comprises the *sex chromosomes,* which eventually produce our physical and behavioral sexual characteristics. There are two types of mammalian sex chromosomes, referred to as X and Y because of their appearance. Female mammals have two X chromosomes, whereas males have an X and a Y.

Because your chromosomes are "matched" pairs, a cell contains two copies of every gene, one inherited from your mother, the other from your father. These two matching copies of a gene are called **alleles.** The term "matched" here does not necessarily mean identical. The nucleotide sequences in a pair of alleles may be either identical or different. If they are identical, the two alleles are **homozygous** (*homo* means "the same"). If they are different, the two alleles are **heterozygous** (*hetero* means "different").

The nucleotide sequence that is most common in a population is called the **wild-type** allele, whereas a less frequently occurring sequence is called a **mutation.** Mutant genes often determine genetic disorders.

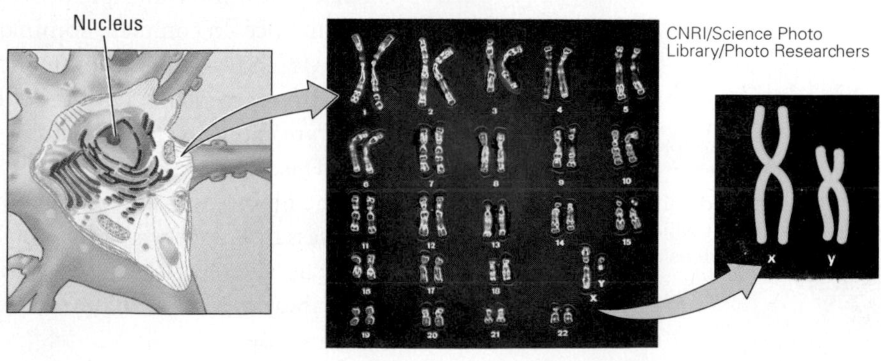

CNRI/Science Photo Library/Photo Researchers

FIGURE 3-20 Human Chromosomes. The nucleus of a human cell contains 23 chromosomes derived from the father and 23 from the mother. Sexual characteristics are determined by the 23rd pair, the X and Y sex chromosomes.

Genotype and Phenotype

The actions of genes give rise to what we call physical or behavioral traits, but these actions are not always straightforward. A gene may be "imprinted" by one parent so that it is not expressed, even though present. The actions of a protein manufactured by one gene may be suppressed or modified by other genes. Developmental age or experiential factors also may influence gene expression. For these reasons, as well as others, some genes are not expressed as traits or may be expressed only incompletely.

The proteins and genes that contribute to human skin color provide a good example. The color expressed depends on the precise complement of a number of different genes. And environmental factors such as exposure to sunlight may modify gene expression. Genes and expressed traits can thus be very different, and so scientists distinguish between them:

- *Genotype* refers to the full set of all the genes that an organism possesses.
- *Phenotype* refers to the appearance of an organism that results from the interaction of genes with one another and with the environment (*pheno* comes from the Greek word meaning "show").

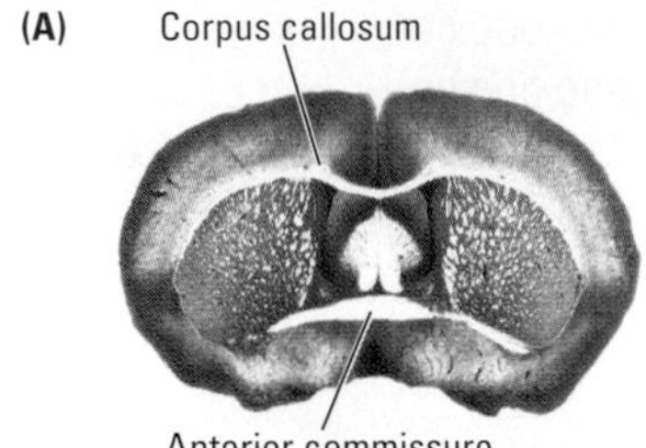

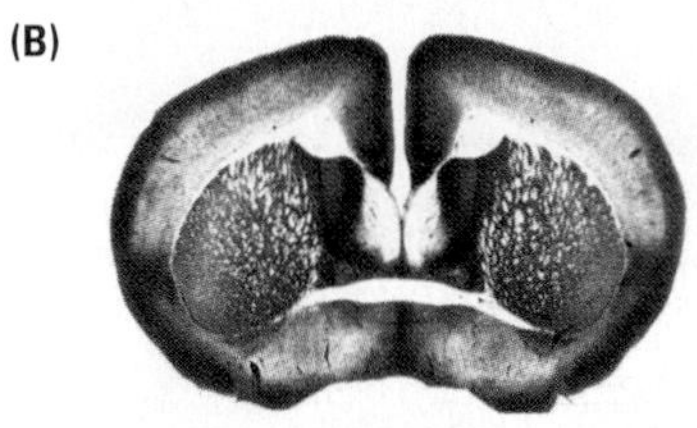

FIGURE 3-21 Gene Expression. Identical coronal sections through the brains of genetically identical mice reveal frontal views of distinctly different phenotypes. The mouse brain in part **(A)** has a corpus callosum, whereas that in part **(B)** does not. Adapted from "Defects of the Fetal Forebrain in Acallosal Mice," by D. Wahlsten and H. W. Ozaki, 1994, in *Callosal Agenesis* (p. 126), edited by M. Lassonde and M. A. Jeeves. New York: Plenum Press.

The extent of phenotypic variation, given the same genotype, can be dramatic. For example, in strains of genetically identical mice, some develop a brain with no corpus callosum, the large band of fibers that connects the two hemispheres (**Figure 3-21**). This abnormality is similar to a disorder in humans. The absence of a corpus callosum has a genetic cause, but something happens in the development of the brain that determines whether the trait is expressed in a particular mouse. Although the precise causal factors are not known, they affect the embryo at about the time at which the corpus callosum should form.

This example illustrates the importance of distinguishing between genotype and phenotype. Having identical genes does not mean that those genes will be identically expressed. By the same token, even if we knew everything about the structure and function of our own genes, predicting how much of our behavior is due to our genotype would be impossible because so much of our behavior is phenotypical.

Dominant and Recessive Alleles

If both alleles in a pair of genes are homozygous, the two encode the same protein, but, if the two alleles in a pair are heterozygous, they encode two different proteins. Three possible outcomes attend the heterozygous condition when these proteins express a physical or behavioral trait: (1) only the allele from the mother may be expressed; (2) only the allele from the father may be expressed; or (3) both alleles may be expressed simultaneously.

A member of a gene pair that is routinely expressed as a trait is called a *dominant* allele; a routinely unexpressed allele is *recessive.* Alleles can vary considerably in their dominance. In complete dominance, only the allele's own trait is expressed in the phenotype. In incomplete dominance, the expression of the allele's own trait is only partial. In *codominance,* both the allele's own trait and that of the other allele in the gene pair are expressed completely.

Mendel was conducting his experiments about the time at which Charles Darwin was developing his ideas about natural selection.

The concept of dominant and recessive alleles was first introduced by Gregor Mendel in the nineteenth century when he studied pea plants. Mendel showed that organisms possess discrete units of heredity, which we now call genes. Each gene makes an independent contribution to the offspring's inheritance, even though that contribution may not always be visible in the offspring's phenotype. When paired with a dominant allele, a recessive allele is often not expressed. Still, it can be passed on to future generations and influence their phenotypes when not masked by the influence of some dominant trait.

Genetic Mutations

The mechanism for reproducing genes and passing them on to offspring is fallible. Errors can arise in the nucleotide sequence when reproductive cells make gene copies. The new versions of the genes are mutations. The number of potential genetic mutations is enormous.

A mutation may be as small as a change in a single nucleotide base. Because the average gene has more than 1200 nucleotide bases, an enormous number of mutations can potentially occur on a single gene. For example, the *BRCA1* gene, found on chromosome 17, predisposes women to breast cancer, but more than 600 different mutations have already been found on this gene. Thus, in principle, there are more than 600 different ways in which to inherit a predisposition to breast cancer from just this gene.

A change in a nucleotide or the addition of a nucleotide in a gene sequence can be either beneficial or disruptive. An example of a mutation that is both causes sickle-cell anemia, a condition in which blood cells have an abnormal sickle shape that offers some protection against malaria, but they also have poor oxygen-carrying capacity, thus weakening the person who possesses them.

Other genetic mutations are more purely beneficial in their results, and still others are seemingly neutral to the functioning of the organism that carries them. Most mutations, however, have a negative effect. If not lethal, they produce in their carriers debilitating physical and behavioral abnormalities.

A mutation may have a specific effect on one particular trait, or it can have widespread effects. Most mutant genes responsible for human hereditary disorders cause multiple symptoms. Because each protein produced by the gene takes part in many different chemical reactions, an affected person is likely to display many different symptoms.

Mendel's Principles Apply to Genetic Disorders

Some disorders caused by mutant genes clearly illustrate Mendel's principles of dominant and recessive alleles. One is **Tay-Sachs disease,** caused by a dysfunctional protein that acts as an enzyme known as HexA (hexosaminidase A), which fails to break down a class of lipids (fats) in the brain. Symptoms usually appear a few months after birth. The baby begins to suffer seizures, blindness, and degenerating motor and mental abilities. Inevitably, the child dies within a few years. The Tay-Sachs mutation appears with high frequency among certain ethnic groups, including Jews of European origin and French Canadians.

The dysfunctional Tay-Sachs enzyme is caused by a recessive allele. Distinctive inheritance patterns result from recessive alleles, because two copies (one from the mother and one from the father) are needed for the disorder to develop. A baby can inherit Tay-Sachs disease only when both parents carry the recessive Tay-Sachs allele.

Because both parents have survived to adulthood, both must also possess a corresponding dominant normal allele for that particular gene pair. The egg and sperm cells produced by this man and woman will therefore contain a copy of one or the other of these two alleles. Which allele is passed on is determined completely by chance.

This situation gives rise to three different potential gene combinations in any child produced by two Tay-Sachs carriers, as diagrammed in **Figure 3-22A**. The child may have two normal alleles, in which case he or she will be spared the disorder and cannot

Tay-Sachs disease Inherited birth defect caused by the loss of genes that encode the enzyme necessary for breaking down certain fatty substances; appears 4 to 6 months after birth and results in retardation, physical changes, and death by about age 5.

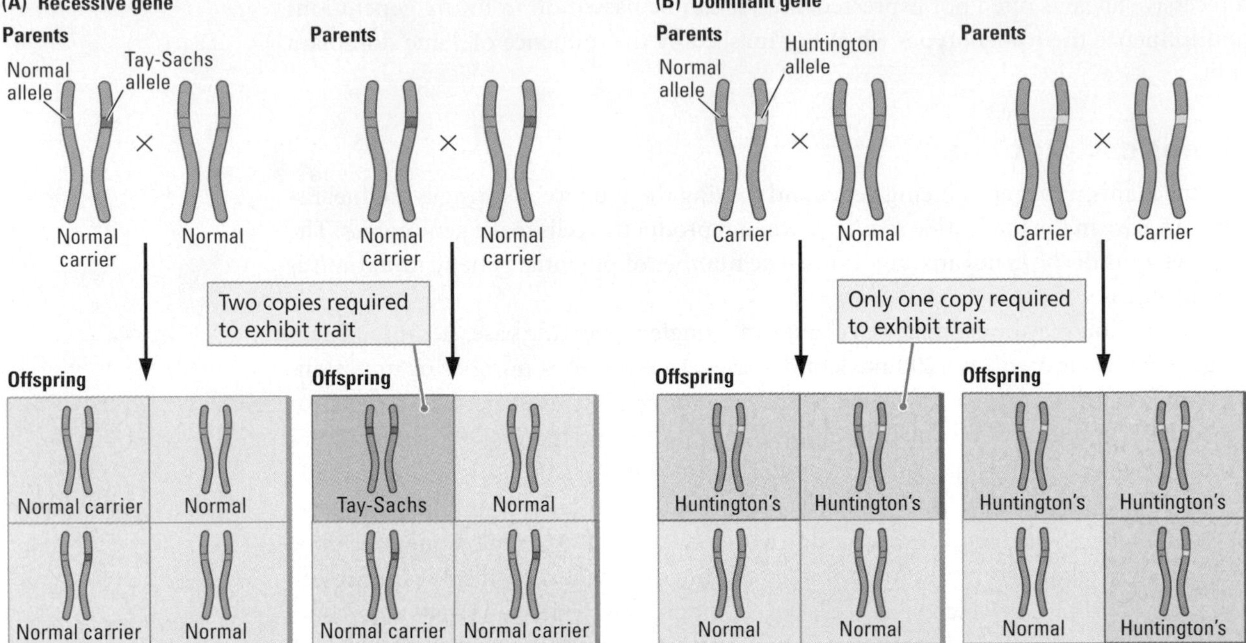

FIGURE 3-22 Inheritance Patterns. (A) Recessive condition: If a parent has one mutant allele, that parent will not show symptoms of the disease but will be a carrier. If both parents carry a mutant allele, each of their offspring stands a 1 in 4 chance of developing the disease. (B) Dominant condition: A person with a single allele will develop the disease. If this person mates with a normal partner, offspring have a 50-50 chance of developing the disease. If both parents are carriers, both will develop the disease, and offspring have a 75 percent chance of developing it.

pass on the disease. The child may have one normal and one Tay-Sachs allele, in which case he or she, like the parents, will be a carrier of the disorder. Or the child may have two Tay-Sachs alleles, in which case he or she will develop the disease.

In the recessive condition, the chance of a child of two carriers being normal is 25 percent, the chance of being a carrier is 50 percent, and the chance of having Tay-Sachs disease is 25 percent. If only one of the parents is a Tay-Sachs carrier and the other is normal, then any of their children has a 50-50 chance of being either normal or a carrier. Such a couple has no chance of conceiving a baby with Tay-Sachs disease.

This allele operates independently of the dominant allele, just as Mendel described. As a result, it still produces the defective HexA enzyme, and so the person who carries it has a higher-than-normal lipid accumulation in the brain. Because this person also has a normal allele that produces a functional enzyme, the abnormal lipid accumulation is not enough to cause Tay-Sachs disease.

Fortunately, a blood test can detect whether a person carries the recessive Tay-Sachs allele. People found to be carriers can make informed decisions about conceiving children. If they avoid having children with another Tay-Sachs carrier, none of their children will have the disorder, although some will probably be carriers.

The one normal allele that a carrier of Tay-Sachs possesses produces enough functional enzyme to enable the brain to operate in a satisfactory way. It would not be the case if the normal allele were dominant, however, as happens with the genetic disorder **Huntington's chorea.** Here, the buildup of an abnormal version of a protein known as *huntingtin* causes the death of brain cells, especially cells in the basal ganglia and the cortex.

Symptoms can begin anytime from infancy to old age, but they most often start in midlife and include abnormal involuntary movements, which is why the disorder is called a *chorea* (from the Greek, meaning "dance"). Other symptoms are memory loss and eventually a complete deterioration of behavior, followed by death. The abnormal huntingtin allele is dominant to a normal allele, and so only one defective allele is needed to cause the disorder, as discussed further in Clinical Focus 3-4, "Huntington's Chorea."

Figure 3-22B illustrates the inheritance patterns associated with a dominant allele that produces a disorder such as Huntington's chorea. If one parent carries the defec-

CLINICAL FOCUS 3-4

Huntington's Chorea

Woody Guthrie, whose protest songs made him a spokesman for farm workers during the Great Depression of the 1930s, is revered as one of the founders of American folk music. His best-known song is "This Land Is Your Land." Bob Dylan was instrumental in reviving Woody's popularity in the 1960s.

Guthrie died in 1967 after struggling with the symptoms of what was eventually diagnosed as Huntingon's chorea. His mother had died of a similar condition, although her illness was never diagnosed. Two of Guthrie's five children, from two marriages, developed the disease, and his second wife, Marjorie, became active in promoting its study.

Huntington's chorea is devastating, characterized by memory impairment, abnormal uncontrollable movements, and marked changes in personality, eventually leading to virtually total loss of normal behavioral, emotional, and intellectual functioning. Fortunately, it is rare, with an incidence of only 5 to 10 victims in 100,000 people; it is most common in people of European ancestry.

Used with permission of the Woody Guthrie Archives. Photograph by Robin Carson

Woody Guthrie, whose unpublished lyrics and artwork are archived at woodyguthrie.org.

The symptoms of Huntington's chorea result from the degeneration of neurons in the basal ganglia and cortex. Those symptoms can appear at any age but typically start in midlife. In 1983, the *huntingtin* gene responsible for Huntington's chorea was located on chromosome 4 and, subsequently the abnormality in the base pairs of the gene have been described.

The study of the *huntingtin* gene has been a source of fascinating insights into the transmission of genetic disorders. A part of the gene contains a number of CAG repeats, and CAG encodes the amino acid glutamine. If the number of CAG repeats exceeds about 40, the carrier may display Huntington symptoms. As the number of CAG repeats increases, the onset of symptoms is earlier in life and progression of the disease becomes more rapid. Typically, non-Europeans have fewer repeats than do Europeans, and so the disease is more common in Europeans. The number of repeats can also increase with transmission from the father but not from the mother.

Why brain cells containing the abnormal Huntington protein die and why symptom onset takes so long are unknown at present. The answers to these questions may be sources of insight into other brain diseases with onsets later in life. Although Huntington's disease is quite rare, Alzheimer's disease, a degenerative disease associated with aging, has many similarities. Alzheimer's disease is most prevalent in people older than 65 and can affect about 1 in 70 people.

tive allele, offspring have a 50 percent chance of inheriting the disorder. If both parents have the defective allele, the chance of inheriting it increases to 75 percent. Because the abnormal *huntingtin* allele is usually not expressed until midlife, after the people who possess it have already had children, it can be passed from generation to generation even though it is lethal.

As with the allele causing Tay-Sachs disease, there is now a test for determining if a person possesses the allele that causes Huntington's chorea. If a person is found to have the allele, he or she can elect not to procreate. A decision not to have children in this case will reduce the incidence of the abnormal *huntingtin* allele in the human gene pool.

Chromosome Abnormalities

Genetic disorders are caused not only by single defective alleles. Some nervous-system disorders are caused by aberrations in a part of a chromosome or even an entire chromosome. Changes in the number of chromosomes, even a doubling of an entire set of chromosomes, is one way in which new species are produced.

Huntington's chorea Hereditary disease characterized by chorea (ceaseless, involuntary, jerky movements) and progressive dementia, ending in death.

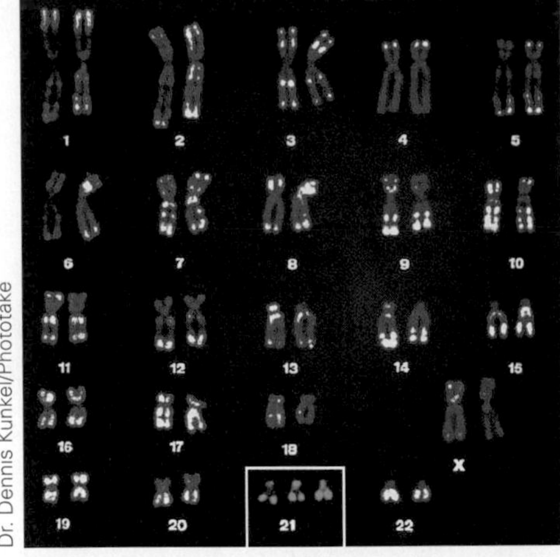

Dr. Dennis Kunkel/Phototake

Walter McBride/Retna Ltd. Image

FIGURE 3-23 Chromosome Aberration. (*Top*) Down syndrome, also known as trisomy 21, is caused by an extra copy of chromosome 21. (*Bottom*) Chris Burke, who lives with Down syndrome, attends a Broadway opening in 2008. Burke played a leading role on the television series *Life Goes On* in the 1990s.

In humans, one condition due to a change in chromosome number is **Down syndrome,** which affects approximately 1 in 700 children. Down syndrome is usually the result of an extra copy of chromosome 21. One parent (usually the mother) passes on two of these chromosomes to the child, rather than the normal single chromosome. Combining these two chromosomes with one from the other parent yields three chromosomes 21, an abnormal number called a *trisomy* (**Figure 3-23**).

Although chromosome 21 is the smallest human chromosome, its trisomy severely alters a person's phenotype. People with Down syndrome have characteristic facial features and short stature. They also endure heart defects, susceptibility to respiratory infections, and mental retardation. They are prone to developing leukemia and Alzheimer's disease. Although people with Down syndrome usually have a much shorter-than-normal life span, some live to middle age or beyond. Improved education for children with Down syndrome shows that they can learn to compensate greatly for the brain changes that cause mental handicaps.

Genetic Engineering

Despite advances in understanding the structure and function of genes, there remains a gap in understanding how genes produce behavior. To investigate gene structure and behavior relations, geneticists have invented a number of methods to influence the traits that genes express. This approach collectively defines the science of *genetic engineering.* In its simplest forms, genetic engineering entails the removal of a gene from a genome, the modification of a gene, or the addition of a gene to the genome.

The oldest means of influencing genetic traits is the *selective breeding* of animals and plants. Beginning with the domestication of wolves into dogs more than 15,000 years ago, many species of animals have been domesticated by selectively breeding males and females that display particular traits. For example, the selective breeding of dogs has produced breeds that can run fast, haul heavy loads, retrieve prey, dig for burrowing animals, climb rocky cliffs in search of sea birds, herd sheep and cattle, or sit on an owner's lap and cuddle.

Selective breeding is an effective way to alter gene expression. As is described by Erik Karlsson and colleagues (2007) in regard to the dog genome, insights into the relations among genes, behavior, and disease can be usefully examined because, as the result of selective breeding, this animal displays the most diverse traits of all animal species.

Maintaining spontaneous mutations is another method of affecting genetic traits. By using this method, researchers create whole populations of animals possessing some unusual trait that originally arose as an unexpected mutation in only one individual animal or in a few of them. In laboratory colonies of mice, for example, large numbers of spontaneous mutations have been discovered and maintained in various mouse strains.

There are strains of mice that have abnormal movements, such as reeling, staggering, and jumping. Some have diseases of the immune system; others have sensory deficits and are blind or cannot hear. Some mice are smart, some mice are not, some have big brains, some small, and many display distinctive behavioral traits. Many of these genetic variations can also be found in humans. As a result, the neural and genetic bases of the altered behavior in the mice can be studied systematically to develop treatments for human disorders.

More-direct approaches to manipulating the expression of genetic traits include altering early embryonic development. One such method is *cloning.* One form of cloning can produce an offspring that is nearly genetically identical with another animal.

To clone an animal, scientists begin with a cell nucleus containing DNA, usually from a living animal, place it into an egg from which the nucleus has been removed, and, after stimulating the egg to start dividing, implant the new embyro into the uterus of a female. Because each individual animal that develops from these cells is genetically identical with the donor of the nucleus, clones can be used to preserve valuable traits, to study the relative influences of heredity and environment, or to produce new tissue or organs for transplant to the donor. Dolly, a female sheep, was the first mammal to be cloned (**Figure 3-24**).

FIGURE 3-24 A Clone and Her Offspring. Dolly (*right*) was cloned in 1996. A team of researchers in Scotland implanted a nucleus from a mammary-gland cell of an adult sheep into another ewe's unfertilized egg from which the nucleus had been removed. The resulting embryo was implanted into a third sheep's uterus. Dolly subsequently mated and bore a lamb (*left*).

Cloning has matured from an experimental manipulation to a commercial enterprise. The first horse to be cloned was derived from a cell belonging to her mother, and so the foal was her mother's identical twin. Cloning provides a way of rapidly producing animals with desired traits, preserving endangered animals, and making copies of favored animals. To this end, Charmayne James, who rode her horse Scamper to 11 world championships in barrel racing, cloned him. She will stand Clayton, the resulting stallion, at stud in an attempt to maintain a "bloodline" that could not be derived from Scamper, because he was gelded. The first cat to be cloned was called Copycat. The first rare species cloned was an Asian gaur, an animal related to the cow.

In genetic engineering, genes can be introduced into an embryo or removed from it. For example, the introduction of a new gene can allow goats to produce medicines in their milk, and those medicines can be extracted from the milk to treat human diseases (Niemann and Kues, 2007). *Chimeric animals,* which have genes from two different species, also can be produced. A cell from one species is introduced into the early embryonic stage of a different species. The resulting animal has cells with genes from both parent species and behaviors that are a product of those gene combinations.

The chimeric animal may display an interesting mix of the behaviors of the parent species. For example, chickens that have received Japanese quail cells in early embryogenesis display some aspects of quail crowing behavior rather than chicken crowing behavior, thus providing evidence for the genetic basis of some bird vocalization (Balaban, 1997). The chimeric preparation provides an investigative tool for studying the neural basis of crowing because quail neurons can be distinguished from chicken neurons when examined under a microscope.

In so-called **transgenic animals,** a gene from one animal is added to the genome of another animal and is passed along and expressed in subsequent generations. One application of genetic engineering is in the study and treatment of human genetic disorders. For instance, researchers have introduced into a line of mice the human gene that causes Huntington's chorea (van Dellen et al., 2008). The mice express the abnormal *huntingtin* allele and display symptoms similar to the disorder in humans. This mouse line is being used to study potential therapies for the Huntington's disorder in humans. Transgenic techniques can be used to introduce new genes in the DNA of an animal not only to study disease but also to examine nervous-system structure and function, as described in Research Focus 3-5, "Brainbow: Rainbow Neurons," on page 100.

Finally, *knockout technology* can be used to inactivate a gene so that a line of mice fails to express it (Eisener-Dorman et al., 2008). That line of mice can then be examined to determine whether the targeted gene is responsible for a human disorder and to examine possible therapies for the disorder. It is potentially possible to knock out genes that are related to certain kinds of memory, such as emotional memory, social memory, or spatial memory. Such technology provides a useful way of investigating the neural basis of memory. So genetic research is directed not only toward finding cures for genetic abnormalities in brain and behavior but also toward studying normal brain function.

Down syndrome Chromosomal abnormality resulting in mental retardation and other abnormalities, usually caused by an extra chromosome 21.

Transgenic animal Product of the genetic-engineering procedure of taking a gene from one species and introducing it into the genome of another species.

RESEARCH FOCUS 3-5

Brainbow: Rainbow Neurons

Most of the genes contained in the human genome are found in other animal and plant species, and so researchers can use other species, including mice, as substitutes for human experimentation. The prime objectives of this work are to find causes and treatments for human disease and to study nervous-system function. Jean Livet (2007) and his colleagues at Harvard University have developed a technique of labeling many different neurons by highlighting them with distinct colors, a technique called Brainbow, a play on the word "rainbow."

In the same way a television monitor produces the full range of colors that the human eye can see by mixing only red, green, and blue, the scientists introduced genes that produce cyan (blue), green, yellow, and red fluorescent proteins into the genomes of mice. The red gene is obtained from coral and the blue and green genes are obtained from jellyfish. (The 2008 Nobel Prize in chemistry was awarded to Roger Tsien, Osamu Shimomura, and Martin Chalfie for their discovery of fluorescent proteins in coral and jellyfish.)

The mice also received a bacterial gene called *Cre*. This gene activates the color genes inside each cell, but, owing to chance factors, the extent to which each gene is activated varies somewhat. As the mice develop, the variable expression of the color-coding genes results in cells that fluoresce in one hundred or more different hues. When viewed through a fluorescent microscope that is sensitive to these wavelengths, individual brain cells and their connections can be visualized because they have slightly different hues, as illustrated in the accompanying micrographs and on the cover of this book.

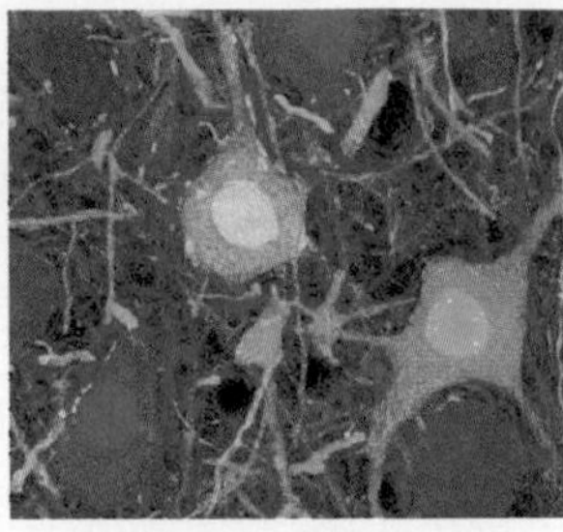
Cell bodies

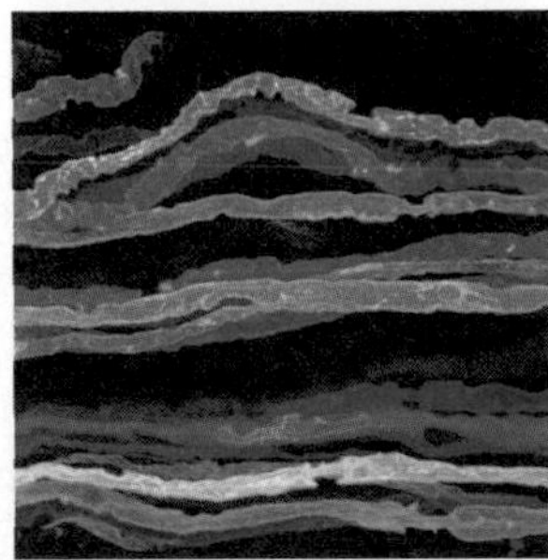
Axons

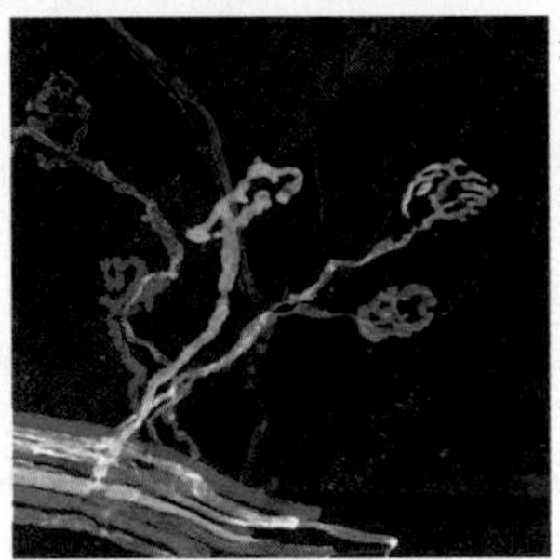
Terminal buttons

Livet, Draft, Sanes, and Lichtman, Harvard University

Because many individual cells can be visualized, Brainbow offers a new way of describing neuronal circuits—that is, a way of describing where each neuron sends its processes and how it interconnects with other neurons. You have probably seen an electrical power cord in which the different wires have different colors (black, white, red) that signify what they do and how they should be connected. By visualizing living brain tissue in a dish, Brainbow provides a method of examining changes in connectivity with the passage of time.

In the future, Brainbow will become useful for examining specific populations of cells—for example, cells that are implicated in specific brain diseases. In principle, Brainbow could be turned on at specific times, such as during development or aging or even during the solving of a particular problem. Brainbow could reveal the pattern of changes associated with behavioral changes in each case.

REVIEW: Genes, Cells, and Behavior

- ✔ Researchers in genomics study how genes produce proteins, whereas those studying proteomics seek to understand what individual proteins do.
- ✔ Each of our 23 chromosome pairs contains thousands of genes, and each gene contains the code for one protein. The genes that we receive from our mothers and fathers may include slightly different versions (alleles) of particular genes, which will be expressed in slightly different proteins.
- ✔ Abnormalities in a gene, caused by mutations, can result in an abnormally formed protein that, in turn, results in the abnormal function of cells. Recessive or dominant alleles can result in neurological disorders such as Tay-Sachs disease and Huntington's chorea, respectively.
- ✔ Chromosomes can be abnormal, resulting in the abnormal function of many genes. Down syndrome is caused by an extra copy of chromosome 21.

- ✔ Selective breeding is the oldest form of genetic manipulation. Genetic engineering is a new science in which the genome of an animal is altered. The genetic composition of a cloned animal is identical with that of a parent or sibling; transgenic animals contain new or altered genes; and knockouts have genomes from which a gene has been deleted.
- ✔ The study of alterations in the nervous systems or in the behavior of animals produced by these manipulations can be a source of insight into how genes produce proteins and how proteins contribute to the structure and function of the nervous system.

Summary

Cells of the Nervous System

The nervous system is composed of two kinds of cells: neurons, which transmit information, and glia, which support brain function. Sensory neurons send information from the body's sensory receptors to the brain, motor neurons send commands enabling muscles to move, and interneurons link sensory and motor activities in the CNS.

Like neurons, glial cells can be grouped by structure and function. Ependymal cells produce cerebrospinal fluid. Astrocytes structurally support neurons, help to form the blood–brain barrier, and seal off damaged brain tissue. Microglia aid in the repair of brain cells, and oligodendroglia and Schwann cells myelinate axons in the CNS and the somatic division of the PNS, respectively.

A neuron is composed of three basic parts: a cell body, or soma; branching extensions called dendrites, designed to receive information; and a single axon that passes information along to other cells. A dendrite's surface area is greatly increased by numerous dendritic spines. An axon may have branches called axon collaterals, which are further divided into teleodendria, each ending at a terminal button, or end foot. A synapse is the "almost connection" between a terminal button and the membrane of another cell.

Internal Structure of a Cell

A surrounding cell membrane protects the cell and regulates what enters and leaves it. Within the cell are a number of compartments, also enclosed in membranes. These compartments include the nucleus (which contains the cell's chromosomes and genes), the endoplasmic reticulum (where proteins are manufactured), the mitochondria (where energy is gathered and stored), the Golgi bodies (where protein molecules are packaged for transport), and lysosomes (which break down wastes). A cell also contains a system of tubules that aid its movements, provide structural support, and act as highways for transporting substances.

To a large extent, the work of cells is carried out by proteins. The nucleus contains chromosomes—long chains of genes, each gene encoding a specific protein needed by the cell. Proteins perform diverse tasks by virtue of their diverse shapes. Some act as enzymes to facilitate chemical reactions; others serve as membrane channels, gates, and pumps; and still others are exported for use in other parts of the body.

A gene is a segment of a DNA molecule and is made up of a sequence of nucleotide bases. Through a process called transcription, a copy of a gene is produced in a strand of messenger RNA. The mRNA then travels to the endoplasmic reticulum, where a ribosome moves along the mRNA molecule, translating it into a sequence of amino acids. The resulting chain of amino acids is a polypeptide. Polypeptides fold and combine to form protein molecules with distinctive shapes that are used for specific purposes in the body.

Genes, Cells, and Behavior

From each parent, we inherit one of each of the chromosomes in our 23 chromosome pairs. Because all but the sex chromosomes are "matched" pairs, a cell contains two alleles of every gene. Sometimes the two alleles of a pair are homozygous (the same), and sometimes they are heterozygous (different).

An allele may be dominant and expressed as a trait; recessive and not expressed; or codominant, in which case both it and the other allele in the pair are expressed in the individual organism's phenotype. One allele of each gene is designated the wild type—that is, the most common one in a population, whereas the other alleles of that gene are called mutations. A person might inherit any of these alleles from a parent, depending on that parent's genotype.

Comprehending the links among genes, cells, and behavior is the ultimate goal of research, but these links are as yet only poorly understood. The structure and function of a cell are properties of all its many genes and proteins, just as behavior is a property of the actions of billions of nerve cells. Learning how such a complex system works will take years. In the meantime, the study of genetic abnormalities is a potential source of insight.

Genes can potentially undergo many mutations, in which their codes are altered by one or more changes in the nucleotide sequence. Most mutations are harmful and may produce abnormalities in nervous-system structure and behavioral function. Genetic research seeks to prevent the expression of genetic and chromosomal abnormalities and to find cures for those that are expressed.

Selective breeding is the oldest form of genetic manipulation. Genetic engineering is a new science in which the genome of an animal is altered. The genetic composition of a cloned animal is identical with that of a parent or sibling; transgenic animals contain new or altered genes; and knockouts have genomes from which a gene has been deleted.

Key Terms

allele, p. 92
astrocyte, p. 76
axon, p. 73
axon collateral, p. 73
axon hillock, p. 73
bipolar neuron, p. 75
blood–brain barrier, p. 79
cell body (soma), p. 73
channel, p. 91
dendrite, p. 73
dendritic spine, p. 73
Down syndrome, p. 99
ependymal cell, p. 76
gate, p. 91
glial cell, p. 76
heterozygous, p. 92
homozygous, p. 92
Huntington's chorea, p. 97
hydrocephalus, p. 76
interneuron, p. 75
microglia, p. 79
motor neuron, p. 75
multiple sclerosis (MS), p. 81
mutation, p. 92
myelin, p. 79
oligodendroglial cell, p. 79
paralysis, p. 81
pump, p. 91
Purkinje cell, p. 75
pyramidal cell, p. 75
Schwann cell, p. 79
sensory neuron, p. 75
soma (cell body), p. 73
somatosensory neuron, p. 75
synapse, p. 73
Tay-Sachs disease, p. 95
transgenic animal, p. 99
terminal button (end foot), p. 73
tumor, p. 79
wild type, p. 92

▶*Please refer to the Companion Web Site at* **www.worthpublishers.com/kolbintro3e** *for Interactive Exercises and Quizzes.*

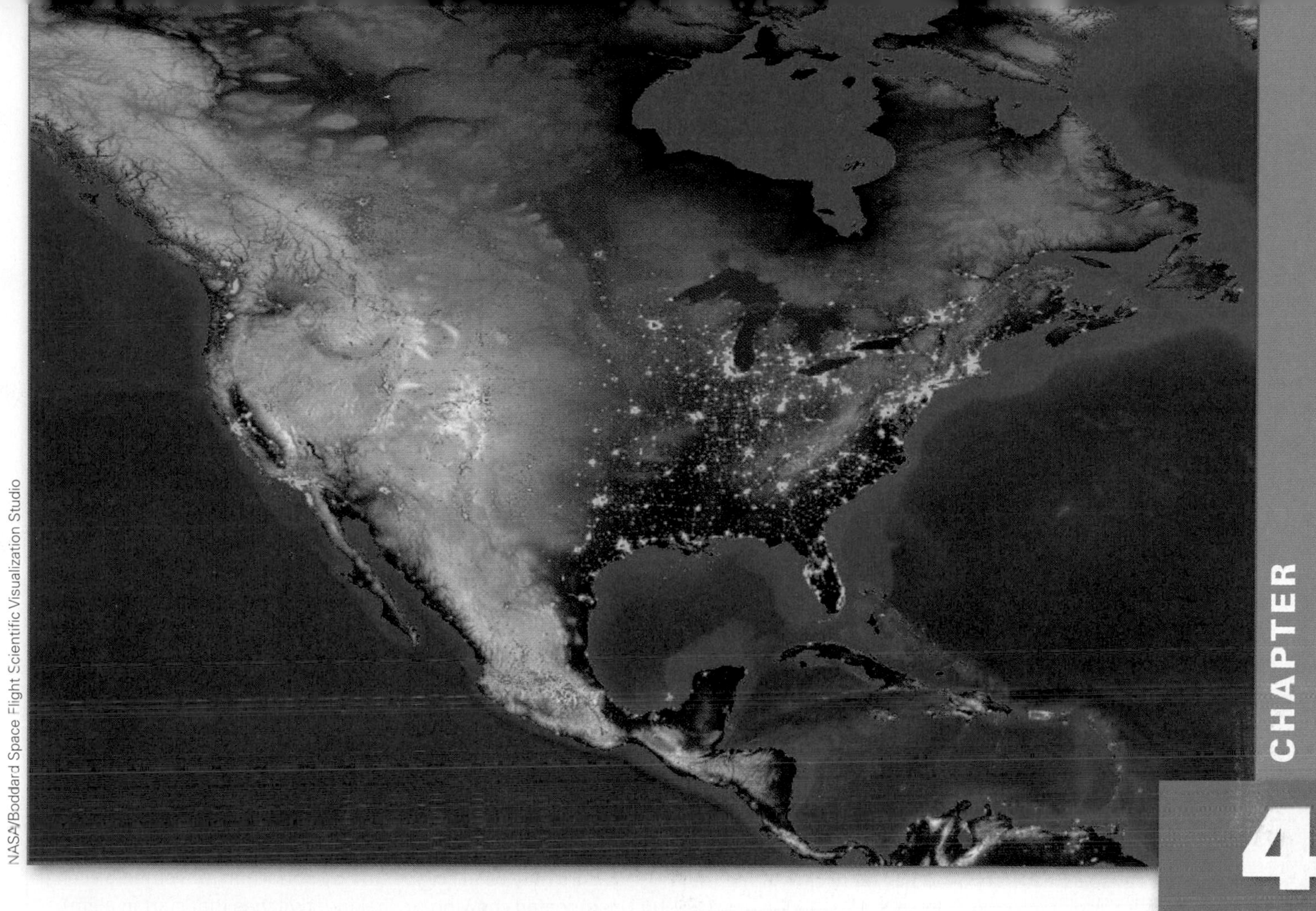

NASA/Boddard Space Flight Scientific Visualization Studio

CHAPTER 4

How Do Neurons Transmit Information?

CLINICAL FOCUS 4-1

Epilepsy

J.D. worked as a disc jockey for a radio station and for parties in his off-hours. One evening, he set up on the back of a truck at a rugby field to emcee a jovial and raucous rugby party. Between musical sets, he made introductions, told jokes, and exchanged toasts with jugs of beer with the crowd.

About one o'clock in the morning, J. D. suddenly collapsed, making unusual jerky motions, and then passed out. He was rushed to a hospital emergency room, where he gradually recovered. The attending physician noted that he was not drunk, released him to his friends, and recommended a series of neurological tests for the next day. Subsequent state-of-the-art brain scans indicated no obvious brain injury or tumor.

When the electrical activity in J. D.'s brain was recorded while a strobe light was flashed before his eyes, an *electroencephalogram,* or EEG, displayed a series of abnormal electrical patterns characteristic of epilepsy. The doctor prescribed Dilantin (diphenylhydantoin), an anesthetic agent given in low doses, and advised J. D. to refrain from drinking. He was required to give up his driver's license to prevent the possibility that an attack while driving could cause an accident. And he lost his job at the radio station.

After 3 months of uneventful drug treatment, he was taken off medication and his driver's license was restored. Eventually, J. D. convinced the radio station that he could resume work, and, in the past 20 years, he has been seizure free.

One person in 20 will experience an epileptic seizure in his or her lifetime. Synchronous stimuli can trigger a seizure; thus, a strobe light is often used in diagnosis. Some epileptic seizures can be linked to a specific symptom, such as infection, trauma, tumor, or other damage to a part of the brain. Others appear to arise spontaneously. Their cause is poorly understood.

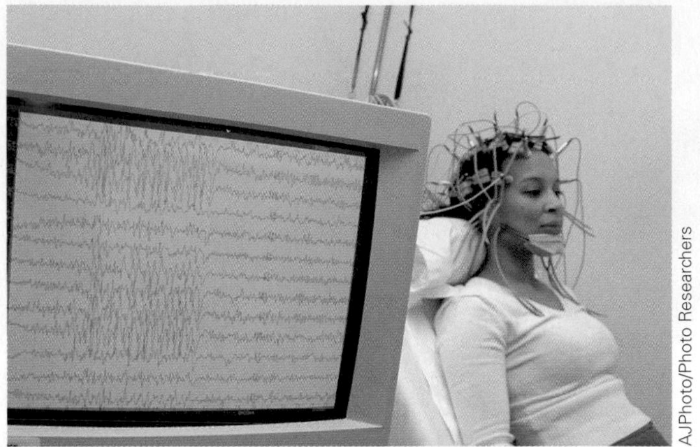

AJPhoto/Photo Researchers

The EEG detects the electrical signals given off by the brain in various states of consciousness, as explained in Chapters 6 and 13. Chapter 16 details the diagnosis and treatment of epilepsy.

Three symptoms are common to many kinds of epilepsy. The victim often experiences an *aura,* or warning, of an impending seizure, which may take the form of a sensation, such as an odor or sound, or may simply be a "feeling." The seizure may be accompanied by abnormal movements such as repeated chewing or shaking; twitches that start in a limb and spread across the body; and, in some cases, a total loss of muscle tone and postural support, causing the person to collapse. The victim may lose consciousness and later be unaware that the seizure ever happened.

If seizures occur repeatedly and cannot be controlled by drug treatment, surgery may be performed. The goal of surgery is to remove damaged or scarred tissue that serves as the focal point of a seizure. Removing this small area prevents seizures from starting and spreading to other brain regions. The condition of epilepsy reveals that the brain is normally electrically active and if this activity becomes abnormal, the consequences are severe.

THE MOST REPRODUCED DRAWING in behavioral neuroscience is nearly 350 years old. Taken from René Descartes's book *Treatise on Man* and reproduced in **Figure 4-1,** it illustrates the first serious attempt to explain how information travels through the nervous system. Descartes proposed that the carrier of information is cerebrospinal fluid flowing through nerve tubes.

When the fire burns the man's toe, Descartes reasoned, it stretches the skin, which tugs on a nerve tube leading to the brain. In response to the tug, a valve in a ventricle of the brain opens and CSF flows down the tube, filling the leg muscles and causing them to contract and pull the toe back from the fire. The flow of fluid through other tubes to other muscles of the body (not shown in Figure 4-1) causes the head to turn toward the painful stimulus and the hands to rub the injured toe.

Descartes's theory was inaccurate, yet it is remarkable because he isolated the three basic questions that underlie a behavioral response:

1. How do our nerves detect a sensory stimulus and inform the brain about it?
2. How does the brain decide what response should be made?
3. How does the brain command muscles to move to produce a behavioral response?

Descartes proposed the idea behind dualism—that the nonmaterial mind controls body mechanics—described in Chapter 1.

Descartes was trying to explain the very same things that we want to explain today. If not by stretched skin tugging on a nerve tube that initiates the message, the message must still be initiated somehow. If not by the opening of valves to initiate the flow of CSF to convey information, the information must still be sent. If not by the filling of muscles with fluid that produces movements, some other mechanism must still cause muscles to contract.

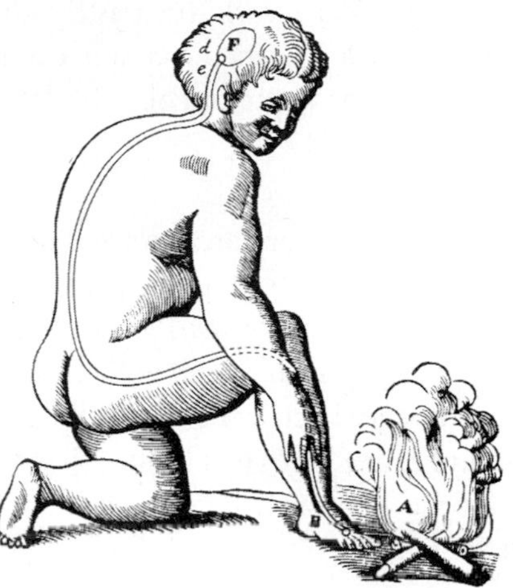

FIGURE 4-1 Descartes's Theory of Information Flow. From Descartes, 1664.

What all these mechanisms in fact are is the subject of this chapter. We examine how neurons convey information from the environment throughout the nervous system and ultimately activate muscles to produce movement. We begin by describing the clues and tools that explained the electrical activity of the nervous system.

Searching for Electrical Activity in the Nervous System

The first hints about how the nervous system conveys its messages came in the eighteenth century, following the discovery of electricity. Early discoveries on the nature of electricity quickly led to proposals that it plays a role in conducting information in the nervous system. We describe a few milestones that lead from this idea to an understanding of how the nervous system really conveys information. If you have a basic understanding of how electricity works and how it is used to stimulate neural tissue, read on. If you prefer to brush up on electricity and electrical stimulation first, turn to The Basics on page 106.

Early Clues That Linked Electricity and Neuronal Activity

In 1731, Stephen Gray, an eighteenth-century amateur English scientist, rubbed a rod with a piece of cloth to accumulate electrons on the rod. Then, he touched the charged rod to the feet of a boy suspended on a rope and brought a metal foil to the boy's nose. The foil bent on approaching the boy's nose, being attracted to it, and, as foil and nose touched, electricity passed from the rod, through the boy, to the foil.

Gray's experiment is similar to accumulating electrons on a comb by combing your hair. If you then hold a piece of paper near the comb, the paper will bend in the comb's direction. The negative charges on the comb have pushed the paper's negative charges to the backside of the paper, leaving the front side positively charged. Because opposite charges attract, the paper bends toward the comb.

Yet the boy was completely unaware that the electricity had passed through his body. Therefore, Gray speculated that electricity might be the messenger that spreads information through the nervous system. Two other lines of evidence, drawn from electrical-stimulation and electrical-recording studies, implicated electrical activity in the nervous system's flow of information.

Electrical-Stimulation Studies

When eighteenth-century Italian scientist Luigi Galvani observed that frogs' legs hanging on a wire in a market twitched during a lightning storm, he surmised that sparks of electricity from the storm were activating the muscles. Investigating this possibility,

THE BASICS

Electricity and Electrical Stimulation

Electricity powers the lights in your home and the batteries that run so many gadgets, including cell phones. *Electricity* is the flow of electrons from a body that contains a higher charge (more electrons) to a body that contains a lower charge (fewer electrons). This electron flow can perform work, such as lighting an unlit bulb. If biological tissue contains an electrical charge, the charge can be recorded; if tissue is sensitive to an electrical charge, the tissue can be stimulated.

How Electricity Works

In the Power Source illustration, negatively charged electrons are attracted to the positive pole because opposite charges attract. The electrons on the negative pole have the potential to flow to the positive pole. This *electrical potential,* or electrical charge, is the ability to do work through the use of stored electrical energy.

Electrical charge is measured in *volts,* the difference in charge between the positive and the negative poles. The positive and negative poles in a battery, like the poles in each wall socket in your home, are separated by an *insulator,* a substance through which electrons cannot flow, such as switch.

Electrical Activity in Cells

If the bare tip of an insulated wire, or *electrode,* from each pole of a battery is brought into contact with biological tissue, current will flow from the electrode connected to the negative pole into the tissue and then from the tissue into the electrode connected to the positive pole. The most-intense stimulation comes from the tip of the electrode. Microelectrodes can record from or stimulate tissue as small as a single living cell.

Electrical stimulation, illustrated in part A of Studying Electrical Activity in Animal Tissue, is most effective when administered in brief pulses. A timer in the stimulator turns the current on and off to produce the pulses. In *electrical recording,* voltage can be displayed by the dial on a *voltmeter,* a recording device that measures the voltage of a battery or of biological tissue (part B of the illustration).

Because electrons are negatively charged, the negative pole has a higher electrical charge (more electrons) than the positive pole.

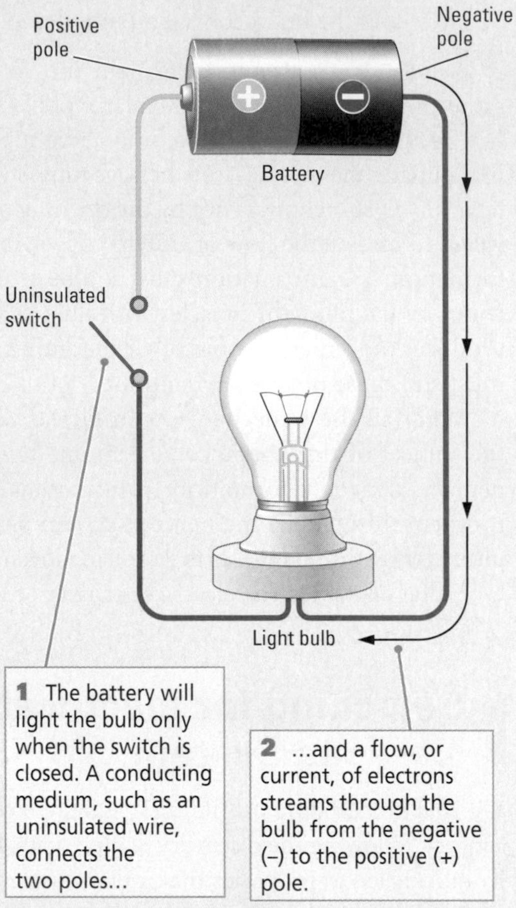

Positive pole
Negative pole
Battery
Uninsulated switch
Light bulb
1 The battery will light the bulb only when the switch is closed. A conducting medium, such as an uninsulated wire, connects the two poles...
2 ...and a flow, or current, of electrons streams through the bulb from the negative (–) to the positive (+) pole.

Power Source.

(A) Electrical stimulation

Current leaves the stimulator through a wire lead (red) that attaches to an electrode. From the uninsulated tip of the electrode, the current enters the tissue and stimulates it. The current flows back to the stimulator through a second lead (green) connected to a reference electrode.

1 A stimulating electrode delivers current (electrons) ranging from 2 to 10 volts, intensities sufficient to produce a response without damaging cells.

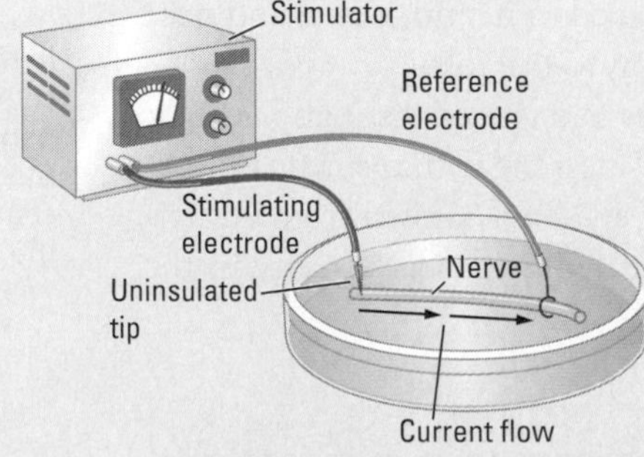

2 The reference electrode contacts a large surface area that spreads out the current and thus does not excite the tissue here.

(B) Electrical recording

The difference in voltage between the tip of a recording electrode and a reference electrode deflects a needle that indicates the current's voltage.

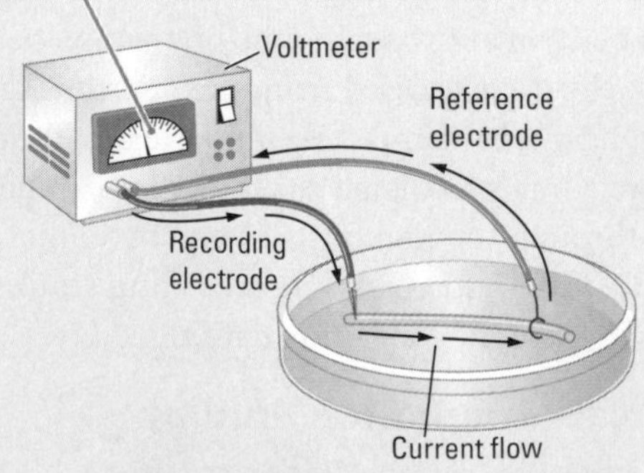

Studying Electrical Activity in Animal Tissue.

he found that, if an electrical current is applied to a dissected nerve, the muscle to which the nerve is connected contracts. It was unclear how the process worked, but Galvani had discovered the technique of **electrical stimulation:** passing an electrical current from the uninsulated tip of an electrode onto a nerve produces a muscular contraction.

Electrical stimulation Passage of an electrical current from the uninsulated tip of an electrode through tissue, resulting in changes in the electrical activity of the tissue.

Voltmeter Device that measures the flow and the strength of electrical voltage by recording the difference in electrical potential between two bodies.

Electroencephalogram (EEG) Graph that records electrical activity through the skull or from the brain and represents graded potentials of many neurons.

Among the many other researchers who used Galvani's technique to produce muscle contraction, two mid-nineteenth-century Prussian scientists, Gustave Theodor Fritsch and Eduard Hitzig, demonstrated that electrical stimulation of the neocortex causes movement. They studied several animal species, including rabbits and dogs, and may even have stimulated the neocortex of a person whom they were treating for head injuries on a Prussian battlefield. They observed movements of the arms and legs of their subjects in response to the stimulation of specific parts of the neocortex.

In 1874, Roberts Bartholow, a Cincinnati physician, wrote the first report describing the effects of human brain stimulation. His patient, Mary Rafferty, had a skull defect that exposed part of her neocortex. Bartholow stimulated her exposed brain tissue to examine the effects. In one of his observations he wrote:

> Passed an insulated needle into the left posterior lobe so that the non-insulated portion rested entirely in the substance of the brain. The reference was placed in contact with the dura mater. When the circuit was closed, muscular contraction in the right upper and lower extremities ensued. Faint but visible contraction of the left eyelid, and dilation of the pupils, also ensued. Mary complained of a very strong and unpleasant feeling of tingling in both right extremities, especially in the right arm, which she seized with the opposite hand and rubbed vigorously. Notwithstanding the very evident pain from which she suffered, she smiled as if much amused. (Bartholow, 1874)

Bartholow's report was not well received. An uproar after its publication forced him to leave Cincinnati. Nevertheless, he had demonstrated that the brain of a conscious person could be stimulated electrically to produce movement of the body.

In the twentieth century, brain stimulation became a standard part of many neurosurgical procedures, such as those described in Chapter 16.

Electrical-Recording Studies

Another, less invasive line of evidence that the flow of information in the brain is partly electrical in nature came from the results of electrical-recording experiments. Richard Caton, a Scottish physician who lived in the early twentieth century, was the first to measure the electrical currents of the brain with a sensitive **voltmeter**, a device that measures the flow and the strength of electrical voltage by recording the difference in electrical potential between two bodies. Caton reported that, when he placed electrodes on the skull of a human subject, he could detect fluctuations in his voltmeter recordings. Today, this type of brain recording, the **electroencephalogram** (EEG), which graphs the brain's electrical activity, is a standard tool used to monitor sleep stages and record waking activity as well as to diagnose disruptions such as those that occur in epilepsy.

Detail on these applications of the EEG appears in Chapters 6, 13, and 16.

The results of electrical-recording studies provided evidence that neurons send electrical messages, but concluding that nerves and tracts carry conventional electrical currents proved to be problematic. Hermann von Helmholtz, a nineteenth-century German scientist, stimulated a nerve leading to a muscle and measured the time that it took the muscle to contract. The time was extremely long. The nerve conducted information at the rate of only 30 to 40 meters per second, whereas electricity flows along a wire at the much faster speed of light (3×10^8 meters per second).

The flow of information in the nervous system, then, is much too slow to be a flow of electricity. To explain the electrical signals of a neuron, Julius Bernstein suggested in 1886 that neurons have an electrical charge that can move as a wave and that this wave has a chemical basis. Bernstein's idea was that successive waves constitute the message conveyed by the neuron.

Oscilloscope Device that serves as a sensitive voltmeter by registering the flow of electrons to measure voltage.
Microelectrode A microscopic insulated wire or a salt-water-filled glass tube of which the uninsulated tip is used to stimulate or record from neurons.

FIGURE 4-2 Wave Effect. Waves created by dropping a stone into still water do not entail the forward movement of the water but rather differences in pressure that change the height of the surface of the water.

Notice that it is not the electrical *charge* but the *wave* that travels along the axon. To understand the difference, consider other kinds of waves. If you drop a stone into a pool of water, the contact produces a wave that travels away from the site of impact, as shown in **Figure 4-2.** The water itself does not travel. Only the change in pressure moves, changing the height of the surface of the water and creating the wave effect.

Similarly, when you speak, you induce pressure waves in air, and these waves carry the "sound" of your voice to a listener. If you flick a towel, a wave travels to the other end of the towel. Just as waves through the air send a spoken message, waves of chemical change travel along an axon to deliver a neuron's message.

Tools for Measuring a Neuron's Electrical Activity

The waves that carry nervous-system messages are very small and are restricted to the surfaces of neurons. Still, we can measure such waves and determine how they are produced, by using electrical-stimulation and -recording techniques. If a single axon is stimulated, it produces a wave of excitation; and, if an electrode connected to a voltmeter is placed on a single axon, the electrode can detect a change in electrical charge on that axon's membrane as the wave passes, as illustrated in **Figure 4-3.**

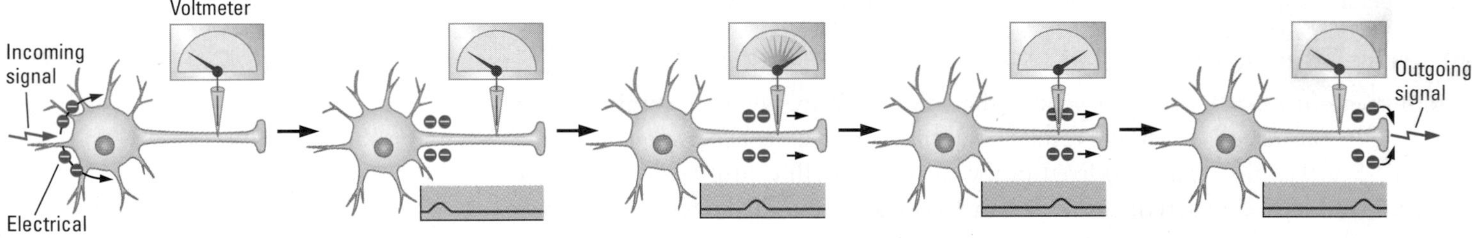

FIGURE 4-3 Wave of Information. Neurons can convey information as a wave induced by stimulation on the cell body traveling down the axon to its terminal. A voltmeter detects the passage of the wave.

As simple as this process may seem, recording a wave and explaining how it is produced requires a neuron large enough to record, a recording device sensitive enough to detect a small electrical impulse, and an electrode small enough to place on the surface of a single neuron. The discovery of the giant axon of the squid, the invention of the oscilloscope, and the development of microelectrodes met all these requirements.

The Giant Axon of the Squid

1 micrometer = one-millionth of a meter or one-thousandth of a millimeter.

The neurons of most animals, including humans, are tiny, on the order of 1 to 20 micrometers in diameter, too small to be seen by the eye and too small on which to perform experiments easily. British zoologist J. Z. Young, when dissecting the North Atlantic squid, *Loligo,* noticed that it has giant axons, as much as a millimeter (1000 micrometers) in diameter. **Figure 4-4** illustrates *Loligo* and the giant axons leading to its body wall, or mantle, which contracts to propel the squid through the water.

Loligo is not a giant squid. It is only about a foot long. But its axons are giants as axons go. Each axon is formed by the fusion of many smaller axons. Because larger axons send messages faster than smaller axons do, these giant axons allow the squid to jet propel away from predators.

(A)

(B)

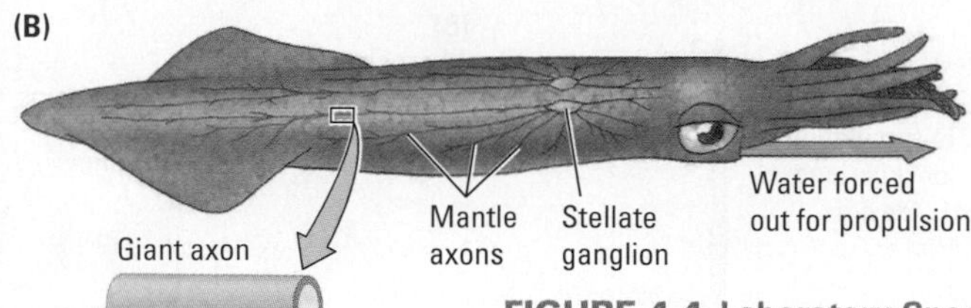

FIGURE 4-4 Laboratory Specimen. (A) The North Atlantic squid propels itself both with fins and by contracting its mantle to force water out for propulsion. (B) The stellate ganglion projects giant axons to contract the squid's mantle.

In 1936, Young suggested to Alan Hodgkin and Andrew Huxley, two neuroscientists at Cambridge University in England, that *Loligo*'s axons were large enough to use for electrical-recording studies. A giant axon could be dissected out of the squid and kept functional in a bath of salty liquid that approximates body fluids. In this way, Hodgkin and Huxley described the neuron's electrical activity, for which they received a Nobel Prize in 1963.

The Oscilloscope

Hodgkin and Huxley's experiments were made possible by the invention of the **oscilloscope,** a device that serves as a sensitive voltmeter. In an oscilloscope, an electron beam leaves a trace on a screen, and deflections of the beam can be used to record voltage changes on an axon. You are familiar with one form of oscilloscope, a boxy analog television set that uses glass vacuum tubes. Today, the digital oscillocope (**Figure 4-5**A) has replaced older cathode-ray oscilloscopes. As illustrated in Figure 4-5B, the scales used when recording the electrical charge from a nerve are millivolts (1 milllivolt is one-one thousandth of a volt) and milliseconds (1 millisecond is one-one thousandth of a second).

Microelectrodes

The final ingredient needed to measure a neuron's electrical activity is a set of electrodes small enough to place on or into an axon. Such **microelectrodes** can deliver an electrical current to a single neuron or record from it. One way to make a microelectrode is to etch the tip of a piece of thin wire to a fine point of about 1 micrometer in size and insulate the rest of the wire. The tip is placed on or into the neuron.

Microelectrodes can also be made from a thin glass tube. If the middle of the tube is heated while the ends of the tube are pulled, the middle stretches as it turns molten, and eventually breaks, producing two pieces of glass tubing, each tapered to a very fine tip. The tip of a glass microelectrode can be as small as 1 micrometer, even though it still remains hollow. When the glass tube is then filled with salty water, which provides the conducting medium through which an electrical current can travel, it acts as an

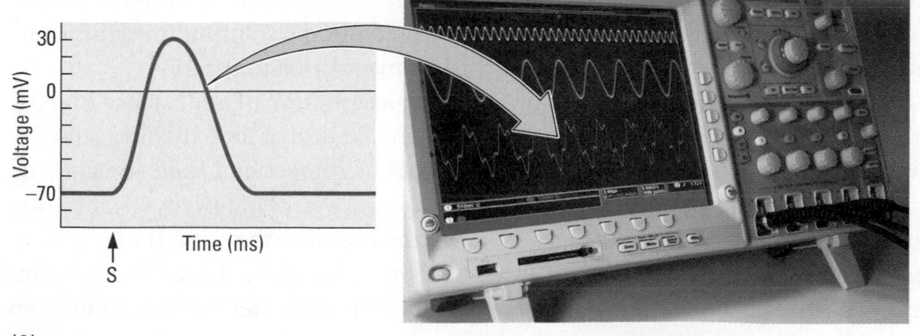

(A)

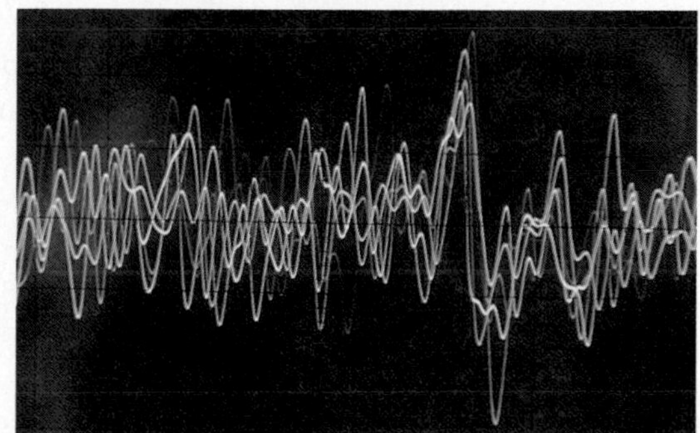

(B)

FIGURE 4-5 Oscilloscope Recording. (A) Basic wave shapes are displayed on a digital oscilloscope, a versatile electronic instrument used to visualize and measure electrical signals changing in time. (B) Neuron traces displayed on an oscilloscope screen. (C) On the graph of a trace produced by an oscilloscope, S stands for stimulation. The horizontal axis measures time, and the vertical axis measures voltage. The voltage of the axon is represented as −70 mV.

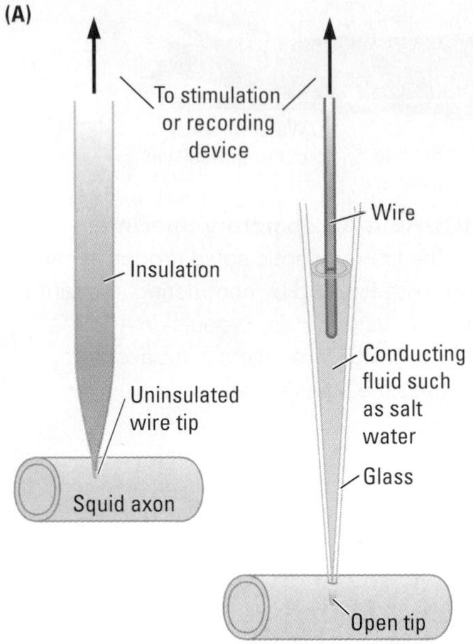

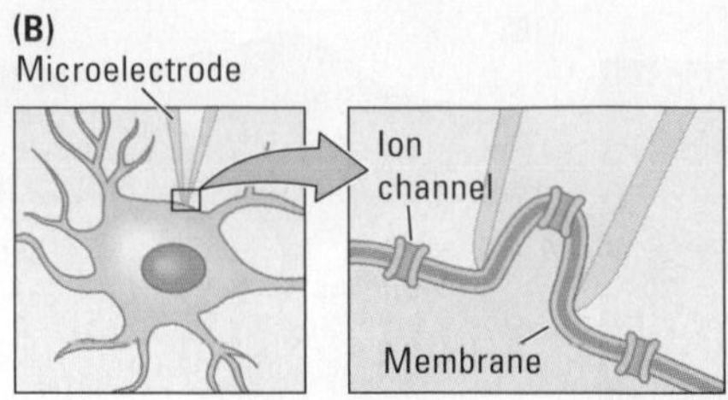

FIGURE 4-6 Uses of Microelectrodes. (A) A squid axon is larger than the tip of either a wire (*left*) or a glass (*right*) microelectrode. Both types of electrodes can be placed on an axon or into it. (Drawings are not to scale.) (B) One way to use a microelectrode is to record from only a small piece of an axon by pulling the membrane up into the glass electrode through suction.

electrode. **Figure 4-6**A shows a glass microelectrode containing a salt solution. A wire placed in the salt solution connects the electrode to a stimulation or recording device.

Microelectrodes are used to record from an axon in a number of different ways. Placing the tip of a microelectrode on an axon provides an extracellular measure of the electrical current from a very small part of the axon. If a second microelectrode is used as the reference, one tip can be placed on the surface of the axon and the other inserted into the axon. This technique provides a measure of voltage across the cell membrane.

A still more refined use of a glass microelectrode is to place its tip on the neuron's membrane and apply a little back suction until the tip becomes sealed to a patch of the membrane, as shown in Figure 4-6B. This technique is analogous to placing the end of a soda straw against a piece of plastic wrapping and sucking to grasp the plastic. This method allows a recording to be made from only the small patch of membrane that is sealed within the perimeter of the microelectrode tip.

Using the giant axon of the squid, an oscilloscope, and microelectrodes, Hodgkin and Huxley recorded the electrical voltage on an axon's membrane and explained the nerve impulse as changes in ion concentration across the membrane. The basis of this electrical activity is the movement of intracellular and extracellular ions, which carry positive and negative charges. So, to understand Hodgkin and Huxley's results, you first need to understand the principles underlying the movement of ions.

How the Movement of Ions Creates Electrical Charges

The intracellular and extracellular fluids of a neuron are filled with various ions, including positively charged Na^+ (sodium) and K^+ (potassium) ions and negatively charged Cl^- (chloride) ions. These fluids also contain numerous negatively charged protein molecules (A^- for short). Positively charged ions are called *cations,* and negatively charged ions, including protein molecules, are called *anions.* Three factors influence the movement of anions and cations into and out of cells: diffusion, concentration gradient, and charge.

Because molecules move constantly, they spontaneously tend to spread out from where they are more concentrated to where they are less concentrated. This spreading out is **diffusion.** Requiring no work, diffusion results from the random motion of molecules as they move and bounce off one another to gradually disperse in a solution. When diffusion is complete, a dynamic equilibrium, with an equal number of molecules everywhere, is created.

The Chemistry Review on pages 84–85 covers the basics on ions, and the Salty Water illustration in that review shows how water molecules dissolve salt crystals.

Smoke from a fire gradually diffuses into the air of a room, until every bit of air contains the same number of smoke molecules. Dye poured into water diffuses in the same way—from its point of contact to every part of the water in the container. Salts placed in water dissolve into ions surrounded by water molecules. Carried by the random motion of the water molecules, these ions diffuse throughout the solution to equilibrium, when every part of the container has exactly the same salty concentration.

Concentration gradient describes the relative concentration of a substance in space or in a solution. As illustrated in **Figure 4-7**A, when you drop a little ink into a beaker of water, the dye starts out concentrated at the site of contact and then spreads out. The ink diffuses from a point of higher concentration to points of lower concentration until it is equally distributed and all the water in the beaker is the same color.

A similar process takes place when a salt solution is placed into water. The salt concentration is initially high in the location where it enters the water, but it then diffuses from that location until its ions are in equilibrium. You are familiar with other kinds

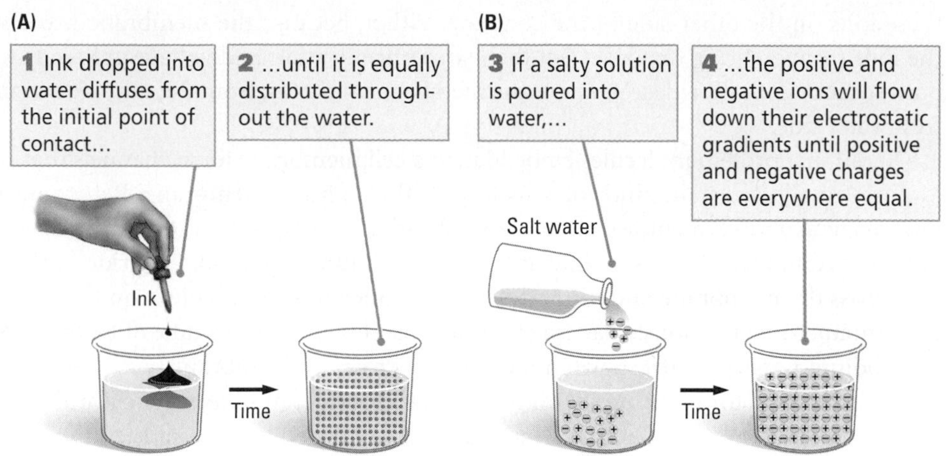

FIGURE 4-7 Moving to Equilibrium. (A) A concentration gradient. (B) A voltage gradient.

of gradients. A car parked on a hill will roll down the grade if it is taken out of gear, a skier will slide down a mountain, and a dropped ball falls to the ground.

Because ions carry an electrical charge and like charges repel one another, ion movement can be described either by a concentration gradient or by a **voltage gradient,** the difference in charge between two regions that allows a flow of current if the two regions are connected. Ions will move down a voltage gradient from an area of higher charge to an area of lower charge, just as they move down a concentration gradient from an area of higher concentration to an area of lower concentration. Figure 4-7B illustrates this process: when salt is dissolved in water, its diffusion can be described either as movement down a concentration gradient (for sodium and chloride ions) or movement down a voltage gradient (for the positive and negative charges). In a container such as a beaker, which allows unimpeded movement of ions, the positive and negative charges eventually balance.

A lack of impediment is not the case in intracellular and extracellular fluid, because the semipermeable cell membrane acts as a partial barrier to the movement of ions between a cell's interior and exterior. An imaginary experiment illustrates how a cell membrane influences the movement of ions. **Figure 4-8**A shows a container of water divided in half by a solid membrane. If we place a few grains of salt (NaCl) in the left half of the container, the salt dissolves. The ions diffuse down their concentration and voltage gradients until the water in the left compartment is in equilibrium.

In the left side of the container, there is no longer a gradient for either sodium or chloride ions, because the water everywhere is equally salty. There are no gradients for

Diffusion Movement of ions from an area of higher concentration to an area of lower concentration through random motion.
Concentration gradient Differences in concentration of a substance among regions of a container that allow the substance to diffuse from an area of higher concentration to an area of lower concentration.
Voltage gradient Difference in charge between two regions that allows a flow of current if the two regions are connected.

The cell membrane is impermeable to salty solutions because the salt ions, which are surrounded by water molecules, will not pass through the membrane's hydrophobic tails (review Figure 3-11).

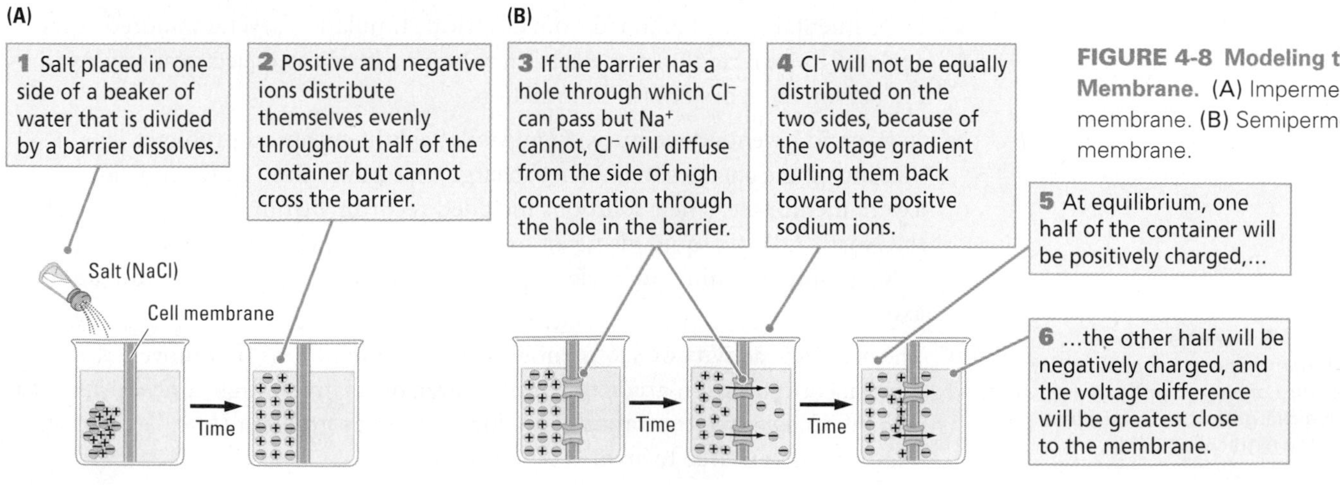

(A)
1 Salt placed in one side of a beaker of water that is divided by a barrier dissolves.
2 Positive and negative ions distribute themselves evenly throughout half of the container but cannot cross the barrier.
Salt (NaCl)
Cell membrane
Time
(B)
3 If the barrier has a hole through which Cl⁻ can pass but Na⁺ cannot, Cl⁻ will diffuse from the side of high concentration through the hole in the barrier.
4 Cl⁻ will not be equally distributed on the two sides, because of the voltage gradient pulling them back toward the positve sodium ions.
5 At equilibrium, one half of the container will be positively charged,...
6 ...the other half will be negatively charged, and the voltage difference will be greatest close to the membrane.
Time
Time

FIGURE 4-8 Modeling the Cell Membrane. (A) Impermeable membrane. (B) Semipermeable membrane.

these ions on the other side of the container either, because the membrane prevents the ions from entering that side. But there are concentration and voltage gradients for both sodium and chloride ions *across* the membrane—that is, from the salty side to the freshwater side.

Recall that protein molecules embedded in a cell membrane form channels that act as pores to allow certain kinds of ions to pass through the membrane. Returning to our imaginary experiment, we place a few chloride channels in the membrane that divides the container of water, as illustrated at the left in Figure 4-8B. Chloride ions will now cross the membrane and move down their concentration gradient on the side of the container that previously had no chloride ions, shown in the middle of Figure 4-8B. The sodium ions, in contrast, will not be able to cross the membrane.

Although sodium ions are smaller than chloride ions, sodium ions have a greater tendency to stick to water molecules and so are bulkier and will not pass through a small chloride channel.

If the only factor affecting the movement of chloride ions were the chloride concentration gradient, the efflux (outward flow) of chloride from the salty to the freshwater side of the container would continue until chloride ions were in equilibrium on both sides. But this outcome is not what actually happens. Because the chloride ions carry a negative charge, they are attracted back toward the positively charged sodium ions (opposite charges attract). Consequently, the concentration of chloride ions remains higher in the left side of the container than in the right, as illustrated on the right in Figure 4-8B.

The efflux of chloride ions down the chloride concentration gradient is counteracted by the influx (inward flow) of chloride ions down the chloride voltage gradient. At some point, equilibrium is reached in which the concentration gradient of chloride ions is balanced by the voltage gradient of chloride ions. In brief:

$$\text{concentration gradient} = \text{voltage gradient}$$

At this equilibrium, there is a differential concentration of the chloride ions on the two sides of the membrane, the difference in ion concentration produces a difference in charge, and so a voltage exists across the membrane. The left side of the container is positively charged because some chloride ions have migrated, leaving a preponderance of positive (Na^+) charges. The right side of the container is negatively charged because some chloride ions (Cl^-) have entered that chamber where no ions were before. The charge is highest on the surface of the membrane, the area at which positive and negative ions accumulate, and is much the same as what happens in a real cell.

REVIEW: Searching for Electrical Activity in the Nervous System

- ✔ Experimental results obtained from electrical stimulation several hundred years ago and, more recently, from electrical recording implicated electrical activity in the nervous system's flow of information.
- ✔ In the mid–twentieth century, scientists solved the technical problems in measuring the changes in electrical charge that travel like a wave along an axon's membrane. Their solutions included recording from the giant axons of the North Atlantic squid, using an oscilloscope to measure small changes in voltage, and obtaining microelectrodes small enough to place on or into an axon.
- ✔ The electrical activity of axons entails the diffusion of ions that move both down a concentration gradient (from an area of relatively high concentration to an area of lower concentration) and down a voltage gradient (from an area of relatively high charge to an area of lower charge).

Resting potential Electrical charge across the cell membrane in the absence of stimulation; a store of energy produced by a greater negative charge on the intracellular side relative to the extracellular side.

✔ The flow of ions in the nervous system is also affected by the semipermeable cell membrane and ion channels in cell membranes, which may open (facilitating ion movement), close (impeding that movement), or pump ions across the membrane.

Electrical Activity of a Membrane

Specific aspects of the cell membrane's electrical activity interact to convey information throughout the nervous system. The movement of ions across neural membranes creates the electrical activity that enables this information to flow.

Resting Potential

Figure 4-9 graphs the voltage difference recorded when one microelectrode is placed on the outer surface of an axon's membrane and another is placed on its inner surface. In the absence of stimulation, the difference is about 70 millivolts. Although the charge on the outside of the membrane is actually positive, by convention it is given a charge of zero. Therefore, the inside of the membrane at rest is −70 mmillivolts *relative to* the extracellular side.

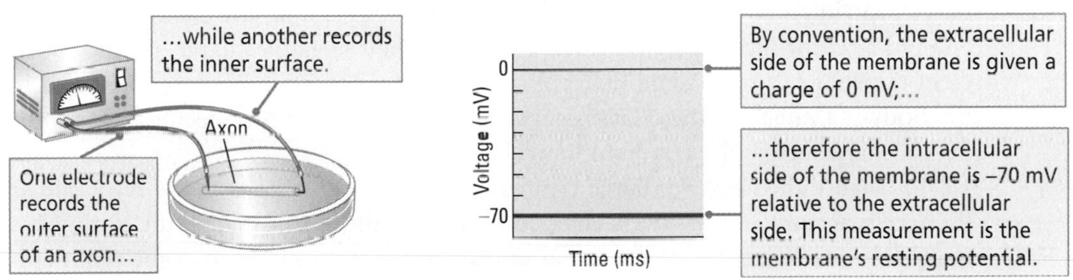

FIGURE 4-9 Resting Potential. The electrical charge across a resting cell membrane creates a store of potential energy.

If we were to continue to record for a long period of time, the charge across the unstimulated membrane would remain much the same. The charge can change, given certain changes in the membrane, but, at rest, the difference in charge on the inside and outside of the membrane creates an electrical potential—the ability to use its stored power. The charge is thus a store of potential energy called the membrane's **resting potential.**

We might use the term *potential* in the same way to talk about the financial potential of someone who has money in the bank—that person can spend the money at some future time.

The resting potential, then, is a store of energy that can be used at a later time. Most of your body's cells have a resting potential, but it is not identical on every axon. A resting potential can vary from −40 to −90 mmillivolts on axons of different animal species.

Four charged particles take part in producing the resting potential: ions of sodium (Na^+) and potassium (K^+), chloride ions (Cl^-), and large protein molecules (A^-), the cations and anions mentioned earlier. As **Figure 4-10** shows, these charged particles are distributed unequally across the axon's membrane, with more protein anions and K^+ ions in the intracellular fluid and more Cl^- and Na^+ ions in the extracellular fluid. Let us consider how the unequal concentrations arise and how each contributes to the membrane's resting potential.

FIGURE 4-10 Ion Distribution Across the Resting Membrane. The number of ions distributed across the resting cell membrane is unequal. Protein ions are represented by A^-.

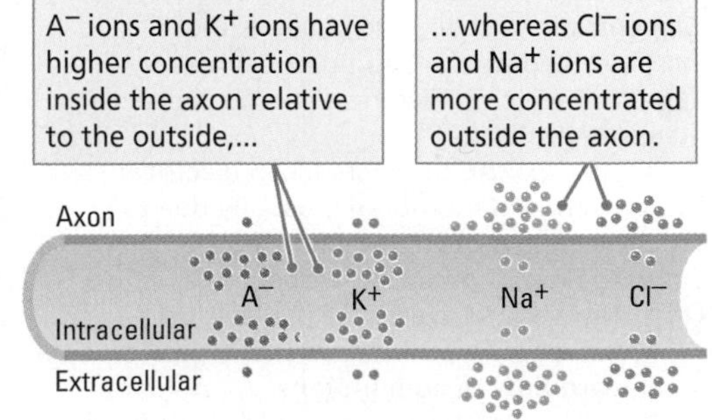

Maintaining the Resting Potential

The cell membrane's channels, gates, and pumps maintain the resting potential. **Figure 4-11**, which shows the resting membrane close up, details these three features of the cell membrane that contribute to its resting charge:

1. Because the membrane is relatively impermeable, large negatively charged protein molecules remain inside the cell.

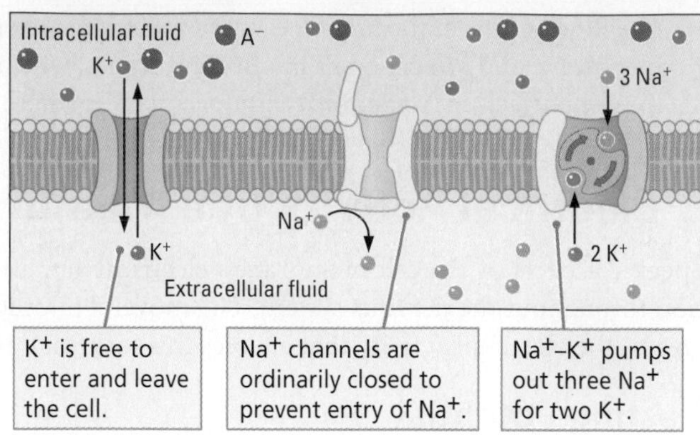
Intracellular fluid
A⁻
K⁺
3 Na⁺
Na⁺
K⁺
2 K⁺
Extracellular fluid
K⁺ is free to enter and leave the cell.
Na⁺ channels are ordinarily closed to prevent entry of Na⁺.
Na⁺–K⁺ pumps out three Na⁺ for two K⁺.

FIGURE 4-11 Maintaining the Resting Potential. Channels, gates, and pumps in the cell membrane contribute to the transmembrane charge.

2. Ungated potassium (and chloride) channels allow K^+ (and Cl^-) ions to pass more freely, but gates on sodium channels keep out positively charged Na^+ ions.
3. Na^+–K^+ pumps extrude Na^+ from the intracellular fluid and inject K^+.

We now describe the workings of each feature in more detail.

Inside the Cell

Large protein anions are manufactured inside cells. No membrane channels are large enough to allow these proteins to leave the cell. Their negative charge alone is sufficient to produce a transmembrane voltage or resting potential. Because most cells in the body manufacture these large, negatively charged protein molecules, most cells have a charge across the cell membrane.

To balance the negative charge created by large protein anions in the intracellular fluid, cells accumulate positively charged K^+ ions to the extent that about 20 times as many K^+ ions cluster inside the cell as outside it. Potassium ions cross the cell membrane through open K^+ channels, as shown in Figure 4-11. With this high concentration of K^+ ions inside the cell, however, the K^+ concentration gradient across the membrane limits the number of K^+ ions entering the cell. In other words, some potassium ions do not enter the cell, because the internal concentration of K^+ ions is much higher than the external K^+ concentration.

A few residual K^+ ions are enough to contribute to the charge across the membrane, adding to the negativity on the intracellular side of the membrane relative to the extracellular side. You may be wondering whether you read the last sentence correctly. If there are 20 times as many positively charged K^+ ions inside the cell as there are outside, why should the inside of the membrane have a negative charge? Should not all those K^+ ions in the intracellular fluid give the inside of the cell a positive charge instead? No, because not quite enough K^+ ions are able to enter the cell to balance the negative charge of the protein anions.

Think of it this way: if the number of K^+ ions that could accumulate on the intracellular side of the membrane were unrestricted, the positively charged K^+ ions inside would exactly match the negative charges on the intracellular protein anions. There would be no charge across the membrane at all. But there is a limit on the number of K^+ ions that accumulate inside the cell because, when the intracellular K^+ ion concentration becomes higher than the extracellular concentration, further K^+ ion influx is opposed by the K^+ concentration gradient.

Outside the Cell

The equilibrium of the potassium voltage gradient and the potassium concentration gradient results in some K^+ ions remaining outside the cell. Only a few K^+ ions staying outside the cell are needed to maintain a negative charge on the inner side of the membrane. As a result, K^+ ions contribute to the charge across the membrane.

Graded potential Small voltage fluctuation in the cell membrane restricted to the vicinity on the axon where ion concentrations change to cause a brief increase (hyperpolarization) or decrease (depolarization) in electrical charge across the cell membrane.
Hyperpolarization Increase in electrical charge across a membrane, usually due to the inward flow of chloride ions or the outward flow of potassium ions.
Depolarization Decrease in electrical charge across a membrane, usually due to the inward flow of sodium ions.

Sodium (Na^+) and chloride (Cl^-) ions also take part in producing the resting potential. If positively charged Na^+ ions were free to move across the membrane, they would diffuse into the cell and eliminate the transmembrane charge produced by the unequal distribution of K^+ ions inside and outside the cell. This diffusion does not happen, because a gate on the Na^+ ion channels on the cell membrane is ordinarily closed (see Figure 4-11), blocking the entry of most Na^+ ions. Still, given enough time, a sufficient number of Na^+ ions could leak into the cell to neutralize its membrane potential. The cell membrane has a different mechanism to prevent this neutralization from happening.

When Na^+ ions do leak into the neuron, they are immediately escorted out again by the action of a *sodium–potassium pump,* a protein molecule embedded in the cell membrane. A membrane's many thousands of pumps continually exchange three intracellular Na^+ ions for two K^+ ions, as shown in Figure 4-11. The K^+ ions are free to leave the cell through open potassium channels, but closed sodium channels slow the reentry of the Na^+ ions. In this way, Na^+ ions are kept out to the extent that about 10 times as many Na^+ ions reside on the extracellular side of the axon membrane as on the membrane's intracellular side. The difference in Na^+ concentrations also contributes to the membrane's resting potential.

Now consider the chloride ions. Unlike Na^+ ions, Cl^- ions move in and out of the cell through open channels in the membrane. The equilibrium at which the chloride concentration gradient equals the chloride voltage gradient is approximately the same as the membrane's resting potential, and so Cl^- ions ordinarily contribute little to the resting potential. At this equilibrium point, there are about 12 times as many Cl^- ions outside the cell as inside it.

All the features of a cell membrane, including its semipermeability and the actions of its channels, gates, and pumps thus creates a voltage across the cell membrane (**Figure 4-12**).

FIGURE 4-12 Resting Transmembrane Charge.

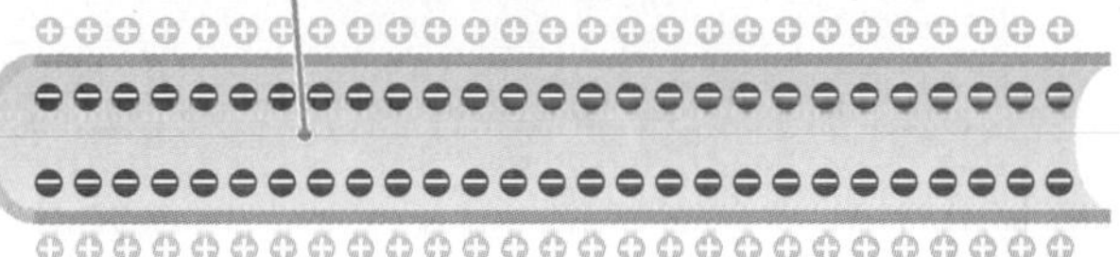

Unequal distribution of different ions causes the inside of the axon to be relatively negatively charged.

Graded Potentials

The resting potential provides an energy store that can be used somewhat like the water in a dam, where small amounts can be released by opening gates for irrigation or to generate electricity. If the concentration of any of the ions across the unstimulated cell membrane changes, the membrane voltage will change. Conditions under which ion concentrations across the cell membrane change produce **graded potentials,** small voltage fluctuations that are restricted to the vicinity on the axon where ion concentrations change.

Just as a small wave produced by dropping a stone into the middle of a large, smooth pond decays before traveling much distance, graded potentials produced on a cell membrane decay before traveling very far. But an isolated axon will not undergo a spontaneous change in charge. For a graded potential to arise, an axon must somehow be stimulated.

Stimulating an axon electrically through a microelectrode mimics the way in which membrane voltage changes to produce a graded potential in the living cell. If the voltage applied to the inside of the membrane is negative, the membrane potential increases in negative charge by a few millivolts. As illustrated in **Figure 4-13**A, it may change from a resting potential of -70 millivolts to a new, slightly greater potential of -73 millivolts.

This change is a **hyperpolarization** because the charge (polarity) of the membrane increases. Conversely, if positive voltage is applied inside the membrane, its potential decreases by a few millivolts. As illustrated in Figure 4-13B, it may change from a resting potential of -70 millivolts to a new, slightly smaller potential of -65 millivolts. This change is a **depolarization** because the membrane charge decreases. Graded potentials are usually brief, lasting only milliseconds.

FIGURE 4-13 Graded Potentials. (A) Stimulation (S) that increases relative membrane voltage produces a hyperpolarizing graded potential. (B) Stimulation that decreases relative membrane voltage produces a depolarizing graded potential.

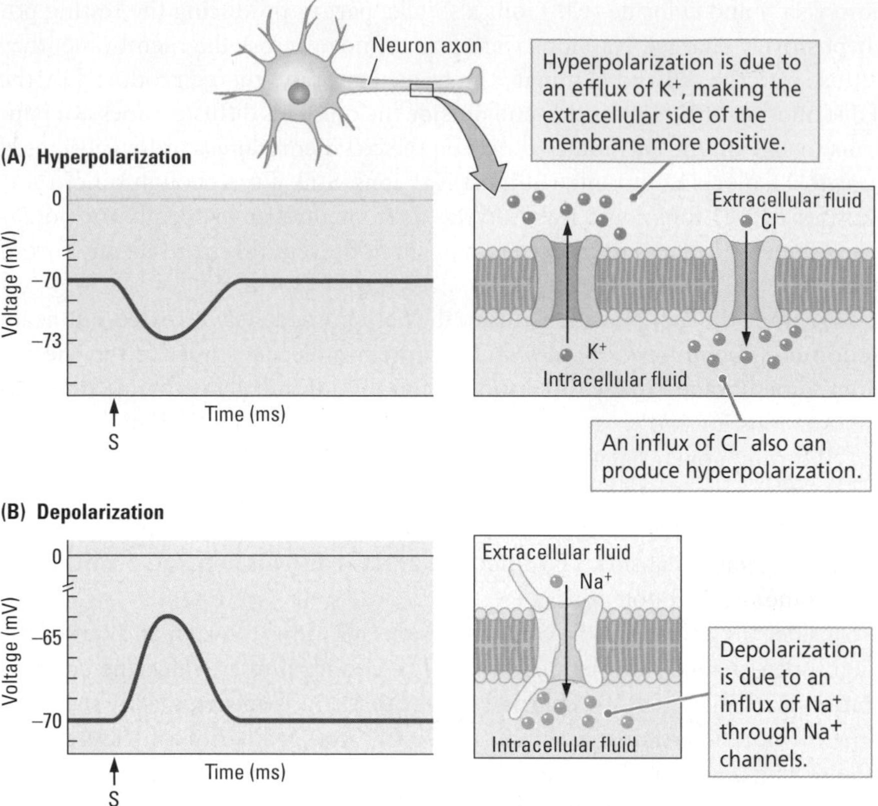

Hyperpolarization and depolarization typically take place on the soma (cell-body) membrane and on the dendrites of neurons. These areas contain channels that can open and close, causing the membrane potential to change as illustrated in Figure 4-13. Three channels, for sodium, potassium, and chloride ions, underlie graded potentials.

For the membrane to become hyperpolarized, its extracellular side must become more positive, which can be accomplished with an efflux of K^+ ions or an influx of Cl^- ions. Evidence that potassium channels have a role in hyperpolarization comes from the fact that the chemical tetraethylammonium (TEA), which blocks potassium channels, also blocks hyperpolarization. But, if potassium channels are ordinarily open, how can a greater-than-normal efflux of K^+ ions take place? Apparently, even though potassium channels are open, there is still some resistance to the outward flow of K^+ ions. Reducing this resistance enables hyperpolarization.

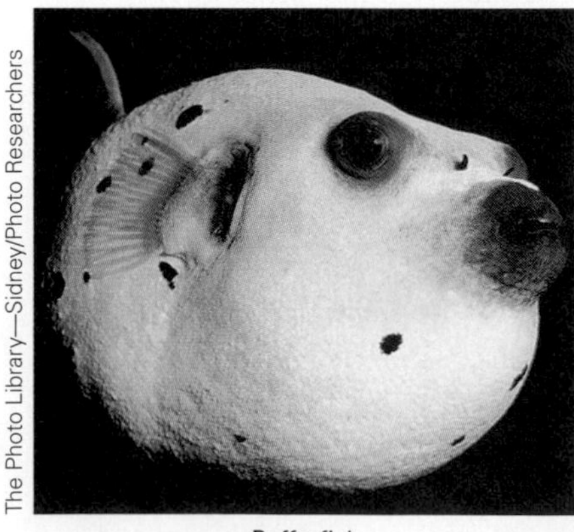

Pufferfish

Depolarization, on the other hand, can be produced by an influx of sodium ions and is produced by the opening of normally closed gated sodium channels. The involvement of sodium channels in depolarization is indicated by the fact that the chemical tetrodotoxin, which blocks sodium channels, also blocks depolarization. The pufferfish, which is considered a delicacy in some countries, especially Japan, secretes this potentially deadly poison; so skill is required to prepare this fish for dinner. The fish is lethal to the guests of careless cooks because its toxin impedes the electrical activity of neurons.

Action potential Large, brief reversal in the polarity of an axon.
Threshold potential Voltage on a neural membrane at which an action potential is triggered by the opening of Na^+ and K^+ voltage-sensitive channels; about −50 millivolts relative to extracellular surround.

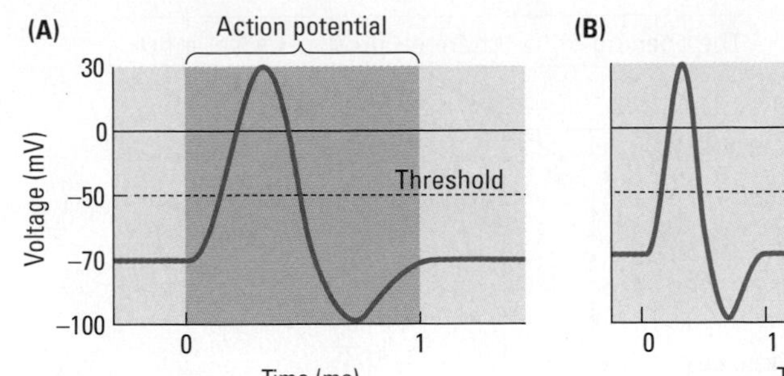

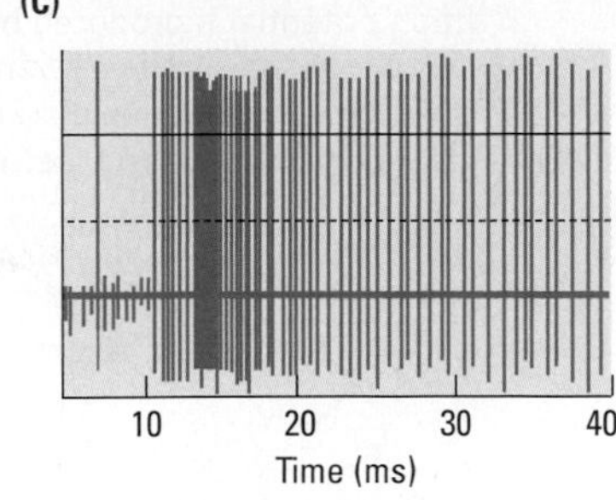

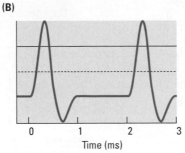

FIGURE 4-14 Measuring Action Potentials. (A) The phases of a single action potential. The time scales on the horizontal axes are compressed to chart (B) each action potential as a discrete event and (C) the ability of a membrane to produce many action potentials in a short time.

The Action Potential

Electrical stimulation of the cell membrane at resting potential produces localized graded potentials on the axon. An **action potential** is a brief but larger reversal in the polarity of an axon's membrane that lasts about 1 millisecond (**Figure 4-14**A). The voltage across the membrane suddenly reverses, making the intracellular side positive relative to the extracellular side, and then abruptly reverses again, after which the resting potential is restored. Because the duration of the action potential is brief, many action potentials can occur within a second, as illustrated in Figure 4-14B and C, where the time scales are compressed.

An action potential occurs when a large concentration of, first, Na^+ ions and, then, K^+ ions crosses the membrane rapidly. The depolarizing phase of the action potential is due to Na^+ influx, and the hyperpolarizing phase to K^+ efflux. In short, Na^+ ions rush in and then K^+ ions rush out. As shown in **Figure 4-15,** the *combined* flow of Na^+ and K^+ ions underlies the action potential.

An action potential is triggered when the cell membrane is depolarized to about −40 millivolts. At this **threshold potential,** the membrane charge undergoes a remarkable further change in with no additional stimulation. The relative voltage of the membrane drops to zero and then continues to depolarize until the charge on the inside of the membrane is as great as +30 millivolts—a total voltage change of 100 millivolts. Then, the membrane potential reverses again, becoming slightly hyperpolarized—a reversal of a little more than 100 millivolts. After this second reversal, the membrane slowly returns to its resting potential at −70 millivolts.

The action potential normally consists of the summed current changes caused, first, by the inflow of Na^+ ions and, then, by the outflow of K^+ ions on an axon. Experimental results reveal that, if an axon membrane is stimulated to produce an action potential while the solution surrounding the axon contains TEA (to block potassium channels), a smaller-than-normal action potential due entirely to a Na^+ influx is recorded. Similarly,

FIGURE 4-15 Triggering an Action Potential.

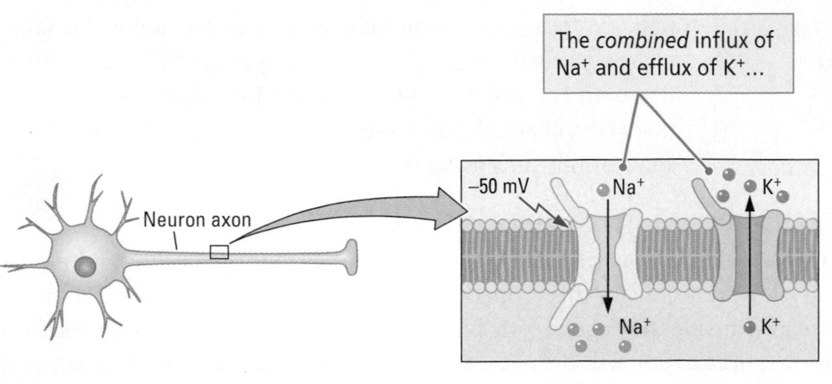

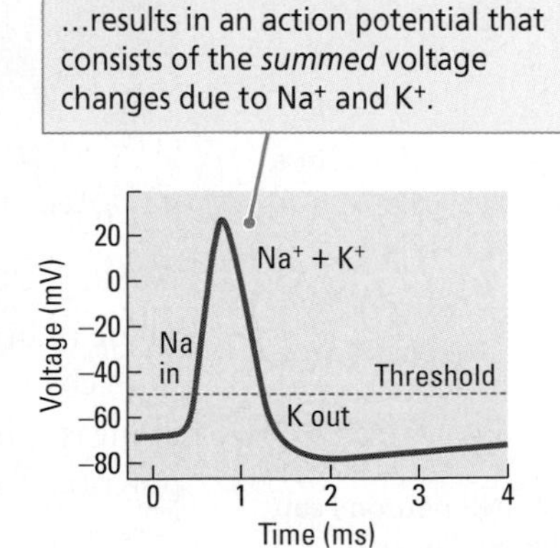

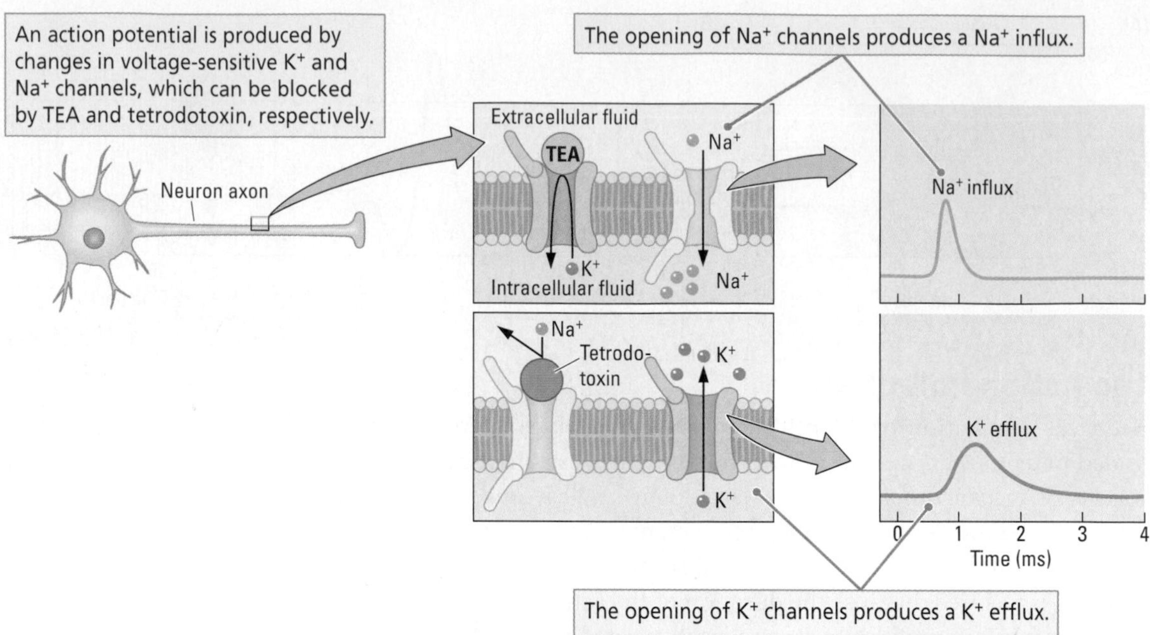

FIGURE 4-16 Blocking an Action Potential.

Voltage-sensitive channel Gated protein channel that opens or closes only at specific membrane voltages.

Absolutely refractory Refers to the state of an axon in the repolarizing period during which a new action potential cannot be elicited (with some exceptions), because gate 2 of sodium channels, which is not voltage sensitive, is closed.

if an axon's membrane is stimulated to produce an action potential while the solution surrounding the axon contains tetrodotoxin (to block sodium channels), a slightly different action potential due entirely to the efflux of potassium is recorded. **Figure 4-16** illustrates these experimental results.

The Role of Voltage-Sensitive Ion Channels

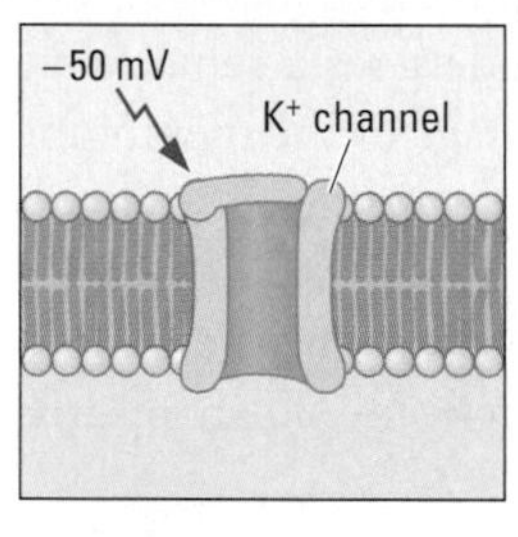

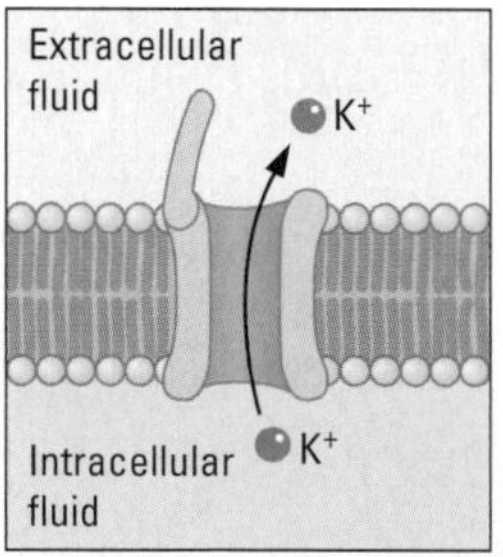

FIGURE 4-17 Voltage-Sensitive Potassium Channel.

What cellular mechanisms underlie the movement of Na^+ and K^+ ions to produce an action potential? The answer lies in the behavior of a class of gated Na^+ and K^+ ion channels that are sensitive to the membrane's voltage (**Figure 4-17**). These **voltage-sensitive channels** are closed when an axon's membrane is at its resting potential, and so ions cannot pass through them. When the membrane reaches threshold voltage, the configuration of the voltage-sensitive channels alters, enabling them to open and let ions pass through. Thus, these gated channels can open to permit the flow of ions or close to restrict their flow.

Voltage-sensitive channels are attuned to the threshold voltage of −50 millivolts. Voltage-sensitive sodium channels are more sensitive than the potassium channels and so open first. As a result, the voltage change due to Na^+ ion influx takes place slightly before the voltage change due to K^+ ion efflux. Research Focus 4-2, "Light-Sensitive Ion Channels," explains that gated channels can be sensitive to stimuli other than voltage, stimuli such as light.

Action Potentials and Refractory Periods

There is an upper limit on how frequently action potentials occur. Sodium and potassium channels are responsible for this property of the action potential. If the axon membrane is stimulated during the depolarizing phase of the action potential, another action potential will not occur. Nor will the axon produce another action potential when it is repolarizing. During these times, the membrane is described as being **absolutely refractory.**

Exceptions do exist: some CNS neurons can discharge again during the repolarizing phase.

RESEARCH FOCUS 4-2

Light-Sensitive Ion Channels

The membrane channels participating in the electrical activity of mammalian neurons are sensitive to voltage changes on the membrane, to stretching of the membrane, or to chemicals. Channels that are responsive to light have been discovered in nonmammalian animal species, and they have been successfully introduced into worms and into mice through transgenic techniques. The introduction of two light-sensitive channels into a species provides a way of exciting the organism's movements with one light wavelength and inhibiting them with another light wavelength.

The channelrhodopsins are a class of light-activated ion channel in the green algae *Chlamydomonas reinhardtii.* Channelrhodopsin-2 (ChR2) absorbs blue light and, in doing so, opens briefly to allow the passage of cations, including sodium and potassium ions. When introduced into animals with the use of transgenic techniques, these light-sensitive channels allow the passage of Na^+ and K^+ ions when a cell is illuminated with blue light. The resulting depolarization excites the cell, resulting in action potentials.

Halorhodopsin (NpHR) is a light-driven ion pump, specific for chloride ions, and found in phylogenetically ancient bacteria *(archaea),* known as halobacteria. When illuminated with green-yellow light, halorhodopsin pumps the anion Cl into the cell. When introduced into animals with the use of transgenic techniques, halorhodopsin pumps Cl^- when the cell is illuminated with green-yellow light, which hyperpolarizes the cell and so inhibits its activity.

Worms, fruit flies, and mice with introduced light-sensitive channels have been controlled in different ways when their nervous-system cells have been illuminated with appropriate wavelengths of light. The accompanying illustration shows these effects on the movement of the roundworm *Caenorhabditis elegans* (A) and diagrams the membrane-channel responses that excite (B) or inhibit (C) movement.

Researchers have identified many potential uses of light-sensitive channels for the treatment of disease and for the regulation of neural activity in humans. The results of one study suggest that people who have suffered the loss of vision due to the loss of the light-sensitive retina of the eye could have their vision restored with light-sensitive channels (Bi et al., 2006). The researchers propose that the introduction of light-sensitive channels into the remaining cells in the eye would allow those cells to stand in for lost retinal cells.

Light is also a less-intrusive means of activating neurons than electrical stimulation is. Thus, the potential exists for using light to treat some brain conditions with light-stimulation methods. Light could potentially be used to activate muscles and so overcome paralysis and to maintain muscle tone when it is lost owing to paralysis.

(A) *C. elegans*

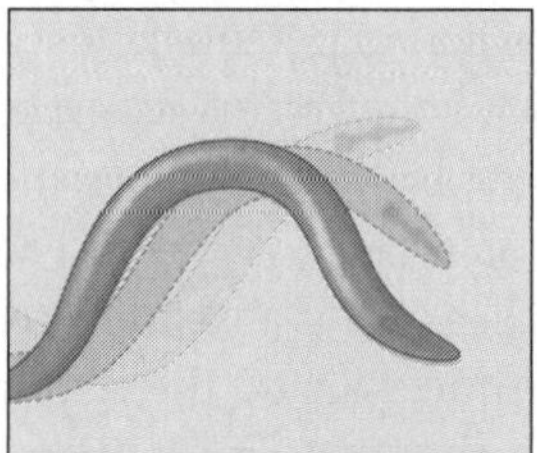

(B) Excitation

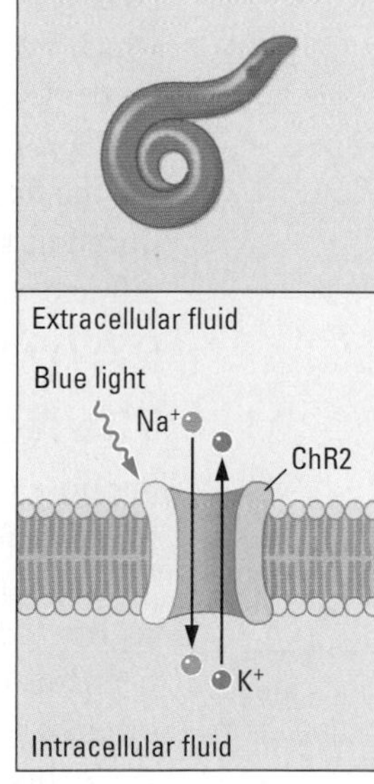

(C) Inhibition

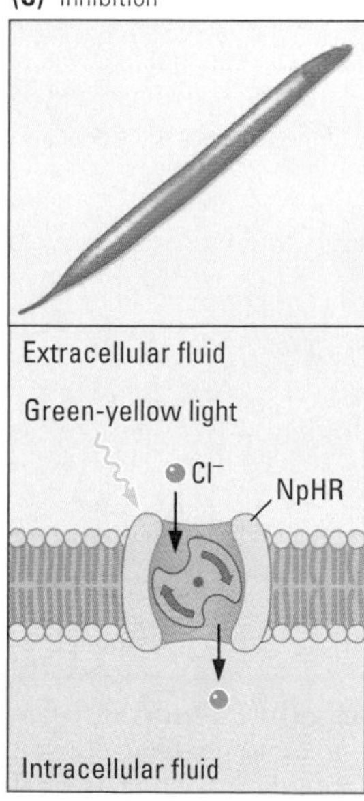

Light-Sensitive Channels. (A) The normal movements of *C. elegans,* pictured on page 93, a popular organism for neuroscience experiments because it is transparent and has a simple nervous system. (B) When channelrhodopsin-2 (ChR2) is introduced into its neurons, *C. elegans* coils when exposed to blue light (Zhang et al., 2007). (C) With halorhodopsin (NpHR) introduced into its muscles, *C. elegans* elongates when exposed to green-yellow light (Liewald et al., 2008).

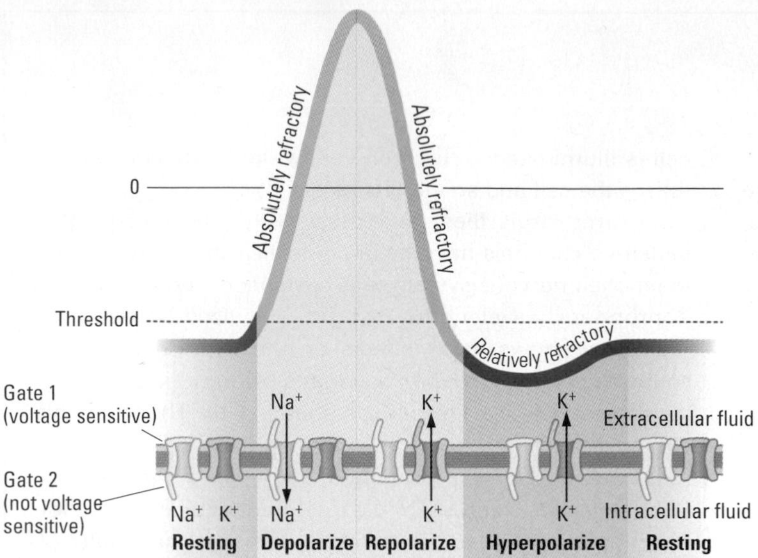

FIGURE 4-18 Phases of an Action Potential. Initiated by changes in voltage-sensitive sodium and potassium channels, an action potential begins with a depolarization (gate 1 of the sodium channel opens and then gate 2 closes). The slower-opening potassium-channel gate contributes to repolarization and hyperpolarization until the resting membrane potential is restored.

If, on the other hand, the axon membrane is stimulated during hyperpolarization, another action potential can be induced, but the stimulation must be more intense than that which initiated the first action potential. During this phase, the membrane is **relatively refractory.**

Refractory periods result from the way in which gates of the voltage-sensitive sodium and potassium channels open and close. Sodium channels have two gates, and potassium channels have one gate. **Figure 4-18** illustrates the position of these gates before, during, and after the various phases of the action potential. We will first describe changes in the sodium channels and then in the potassium channels.

During the resting potential, gate 1 of the sodium channel depicted in Figure 4-18 is closed and only gate 2 is open. At the threshold level of stimulation, gate 1 also opens. Gate 2, however, closes very quickly after gate 1 opens. This sequence produces a brief period during which both sodium gates are open followed by a brief period during which gate 2 is closed. Thus, when gate 1 opens, the membrane depolarizes and, when gate 2 closes, depolarization ends.

Both sodium gates eventually regain their resting-potential positions, with gate 1 closed and gate 2 open. But, while gate 2 of the sodium channel is closed during repolarization, the membrane is absolutely refractory. The opening of the potassium channels repolarizes and eventually hyperpolarizes the membrane. Because the potassium channels open and close more slowly than the sodium channels do, the hyperpolarization produced by a continuing efflux of potassium ions makes the membrane relatively refractory for a period of time after the action potential has passed.

The refractory period has a practical use in conducting information. Because of refractory periods, there is about a 5-millisecond limit on how frequently action potentials can occur. In other words, an axon can produce action potentials at a maximum rate of about 200 per second.

A lever-activated toilet provides an analogy for some of the changes in polarity that take place during an action potential. Pushing the lever slightly produces a slight flow of water, which stops when the lever is released. This activity is analogous to a graded potential. A harder lever press brings the toilet to threshold and initiates flushing, a response that is out of all proportion to the lever press. This activity is analogous to the action potential. During the flush, the toilet is absolutely refractory, meaning that another flush cannot be induced at this time. During the refilling of the bowl, in contrast, the toilet is relatively refractory, meaning that reflushing is possible but harder to bring about. Only after the cycle is over and the toilet is once again "resting," can the usual flush be produced again.

The Nerve Impulse

Suppose you place two recording electrodes at a distance from one another on an axon membrane and then electrically stimulate an area adjacent to one of these electrodes. That electrode would immediately record an action potential. A similar recording would register on the second electrode in a flash. Apparently, an action potential has arisen near this electrode also, even though this second electrode is some distance from the original point of stimulation.

Is this second action potential simply an echo of the first that passes down the axon? No, it cannot be, because the size and shape of the action potential are exactly the same at the two electrodes. The second is not just a faint, degraded version of the first but is equal in magnitude. Somehow the full action potential has moved along the axon. This propagation of an action potential along an axon is called a **nerve impulse.**

Relatively refractory Refers to the state of an axon in the later phase of an action potential during which increased electrical current is required to produce another action potential; a phase during which potassium channels are still open.

Nerve impulse Propagation of an action potential on the membrane of an axon.

Why does an action potential move? Remember that the total voltage change during an action potential is 100 millivolts, far beyond the 20-millivolt change needed to bring the membrane from its resting state of −70 millivolts to the action potential threshold level of −50 millivolts. Consequently, the voltage change on the part of the membrane at which an action potential first occurs is large enough to bring adjacent parts of the membrane to a threshold of −50 millivolts.

When the membrane of an adjacent part of the axon reaches −50 millivolts, the voltage-sensitive channels at that location pop open to produce an action potential there as well. This second occurrence, in turn, induces a change in the voltage of the membrane still farther along the axon, and so on and on, down the axon's length. **Figure 4-19** illustrates this process. The nerve impulse occurs because each action potential propagates another action potential on an adjacent part of the axon membrane. The word *propagate* means "to give birth," and that is exactly what happens. Each successive action potential gives birth to another down the length of the axon.

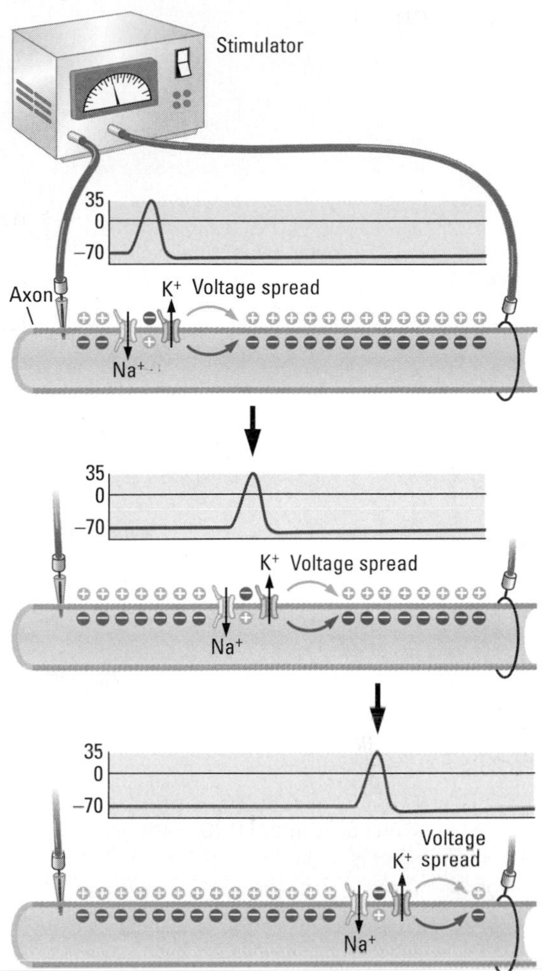

FIGURE 4-19 Propagating an Action Potential. Voltage sufficient to open Na^+ and K^+ channels spreads to adjacent sites of the axon membrane, inducing voltage-sensitive gates to open. Here, voltage changes are shown on only one side of the membrane.

Two main factors ensure that a single nerve impulse of a constant size travels down the axon:

1. Voltage-sensitive channels produce refractory periods, as you know. Although an action potential can travel in either direction on an axon, refractory periods prevent it from reversing direction and returning to the point from which it came. Thus, refractory periods create a single, discrete impulse that travels away from the point of initial stimulation.
2. All action potentials generated as a nerve impulse travels are of the same magnitude. An action potential depends on energy expended at the site where it occurs, and the same amount of energy is expended at every site along the membrane where a nerve impulse is propagated. As a result, there is no such thing as a dissipated action potential. Simply stated, an action potential is either generated completely or it is not generated at all, which means that a nerve impulse always maintains a constant size.

To summarize the action of a nerve impulse, think of the voltage-sensitive channels along the axon as a series of dominoes. When one domino falls, it knocks over its neighbor, and so on down the line. The "wave" cannot return the way that it has come. There is also no decrement in the size of the fall. The last domino travels exactly the same distance and falls just as hard as the first one did.

Essentially, this "domino effect" happens when voltage-sensitive channels open. The opening of one channel produces a voltage change that triggers its neighbor to open, just as one domino knocks over the next. When gate 2 on a voltage-sensitive sodium channel closes, that channel is inactivated, much as a domino is temporarily inactivated after it falls over. Both channel and domino must be reset before they can work again. Finally, the channel-opening response does not grow any weaker as it moves along the axon. The last channel opens exactly like the first, just as the domino action stays constant to the end of the line. Because of this behavior of voltage-sensitive channels, a single nerve impulse of constant size moves in only one direction along an axon.

The domino effect

Saltatory Conduction and Myelin Sheaths

Because the giant axons of squid are so large, they can transmit nerve impulses very quickly, much as a large-diameter pipe can deliver a lot of water at a rapid rate. But large axons take up substantial space, and so a squid cannot accommodate many of them or its body would become too bulky. For us mammals, with our many axons producing repertoires of complex behaviors, giant axons are out of the question. Our axons must be extremely slender because our complex behaviors require a great many of them.

Our largest axons are only about 30 micrometers wide; so the speed with which they convey information should not be especially fast. And yet, like most vertebrate species, we are hardly sluggish creatures. We process information and generate responses with impressive speed. How do we manage to do so if our axons are so thin? The vertebrate nervous system has evolved a solution that has nothing to do with axon size.

You can review all five types of glial cells in Table 3-1.

Glial cells play a role in speeding nerve impulses in the vertebrate nervous system. Schwann cells in the human peripheral nervous system and oligodendroglia in the central nervous system wrap around each axon, insulating it except for a small, exposed gap between each glial cell (**Figure 4-20**). This insulation is referred to as myelin or as a myelin sheath, and insulated axons are said to be myelinated.

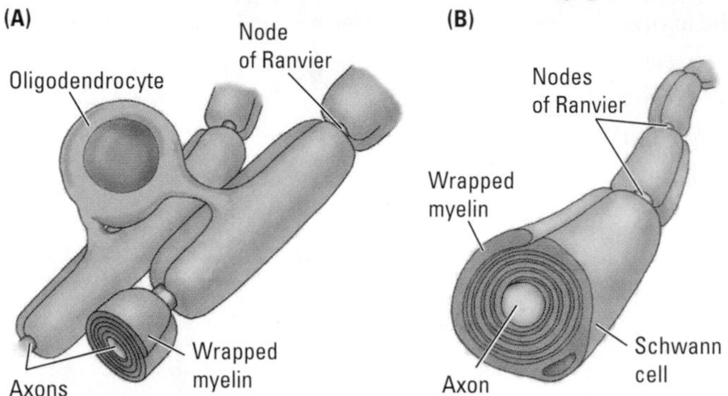

FIGURE 4-20 Myelination. An axon is insulated by (A) oligodendroglia in the CNS and (B) Schwann cells in the PNS. Each glial cell is separated by a gap, or node of Ranvier.

Action potentials cannot occur where myelin is wrapped around an axon. For one thing, the myelin creates an insulating barrier to the flow of ionic current. For another, regions of an axon that lie under myelin have few channels through which ions can flow, and, as you know, such channels are essential to generating an action potential.

But axons are not totally encased in myelin. Unmyelinated gaps on the axon between successive glial cells are richly endowed with voltage-sensitive channels. These tiny gaps in the myelin sheath, the **nodes of Ranvier,** are sufficiently close to one another that an action potential occurring at one node can trigger the opening of voltage-sensitive gates at an adjacent node. In this way, a relatively slow action potential jumps at the speed of light from node to node, as shown in **Figure 4-21.** This flow of energy is called **saltatory conduction** (from the Latin verb *saltare,* meaning "to dance").

Jumping from node to node speeds the rate at which an action potential can travel along an axon. On larger, myelinated mammalian axons, nerve impulses can travel at a rate as high as 120 meters per second, compared with only about 30 meters per second on smaller, uninsulated axons. Think of how a "wave" of consecutively standing spectators travels around a football stadium. As one person rises, the adjacent person rises, producing the wave effect. This wave is like conduction along an unmyelinated axon. Now think of how much faster the wave would complete its circuit around the field if only spectators in the corners rose to produce it, which is analogous to a nerve impulse that travels by jumping from one node of Ranvier to the next. The quick reactions that humans and other mammals are capable of are due in part to this saltatory conduction in their nervous systems.

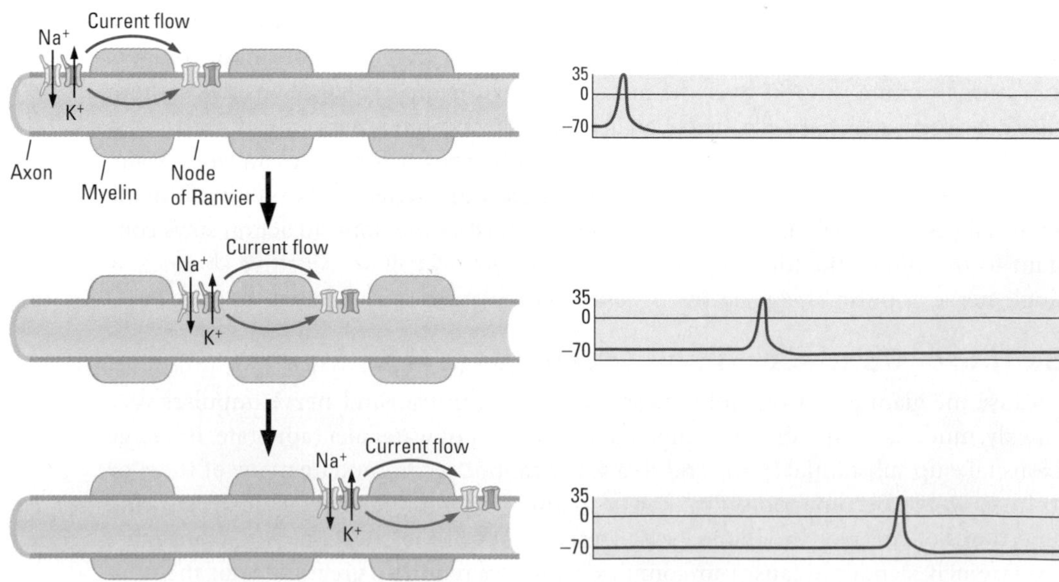

FIGURE 4-21 Saltatory Conduction. Myelinated stretches of axon are interrupted by nodes of Ranvier, rich in voltage-sensitive channels. In saltatory conduction, the action potential jumps from node to node rapidly.

REVIEW: Electrical Activity of a Membrane

- ✔ Microelectrodes connected to a voltmeter and placed on either side of an axon membrane will record a voltage difference across the membrane owing to the unequal distribution of ions inside and outside the cell.
- ✔ The semipermeable cell membrane prevents the efflux of large protein anions, and it pumps sodium ions out of the cell to maintain a slightly negative charge in the intracellular fluid relative to the extracellular fluid.
- ✔ Although potassium ions and chloride ions are relatively free to cross the membrane through their respective channels, the equilibrium at which their concentration gradient matches their voltage gradient contributes to the relative transmembrane charge of −70 millivolts.
- ✔ Some sodium and potassium channels sensitive to the membrane's voltage open their gates when the membrane is electrically stimulated, allowing a brief free flow of ions across the membrane and stimulating an action potential, a brief reversal of charge on the membrane.
- ✔ The voltage change associated with an action potential is sufficiently large to stimulate adjacent parts of the axon membrane to the threshold for propagating the action potential along the length of an axon as a nerve impulse.
- ✔ Along a myelinated axon, the nerve impulse travels by saltatory conduction, jumping from one node of Ranvier to the next, thus greatly increasing the speed at which a nerve impulse travels.

How Neurons Integrate Information

A neuron is more than just an axon connected to microelectrodes by some curious scientist who stimulates it with electrical current. A neuron has an extensive dendritic tree covered with spines, and, through these dendritic spines, it can establish more than 50,000 connections to other neurons. Nerve impulses traveling to each of these synapses from other neurons bombard the receiving neuron with all manner of inputs. In addition, a neuron has a cell body between its dendritic tree and its axon, and this cell body, too, can receive connections from many other neurons.

At the cellular level, the neurons that receive more than one kind of input sum up the information that they get.

How does the neuron integrate this enormous array of inputs into a nerve impulse? In the 1960s, John C. Eccles and his students performed experiments that helped to answer this question, for which Eccles received the Nobel Prize in 1963. Rather than recording from the giant axon of a squid, Eccles recorded from the cell bodies of large motor neurons in the vertebrate spinal cord. He did so by refining the stimulating and recording techniques developed for the study of squid axons.

A spinal-cord motor neuron has an extensive dendritic tree with as many as 20 main branches that subdivide numerous times and are covered with dendritic spines. Motor neurons receive input from multiple sources, including the skin, joints, muscles, and brain, which is why they are ideal for studying how a neuron responds to diverse inputs. Each motor neuron sends its axon directly to a muscle, as you would expect for neurons that produce movement. Clinical Focus 4-3, "Myasthenia Gravis," explains what happens when muscle receptors lose their sensitivity to motor-neuron messages.

Excitatory and Inhibitory Postsynaptic Potentials

To study the activity of motor neurons, Eccles inserted a microelectrode into a vertebrate spinal cord until the tip was located in or right beside a motor neuron's cell body. He then placed stimulating electrodes on the axons of sensory fibers entering the spinal

Node of Ranvier The part of an axon that is not covered by myelin.
Saltatory conduction Propagation of an action potential at successive nodes of Ranvier; saltatory means "jumping" or "dancing."

CLINICAL FOCUS 4-3

Myasthenia Gravis

R.J. was 22 years old when she noticed that her eyelid drooped. She consulted her physician, but he was unable to explain her condition or give her any help. In the course of the next few years, she experienced some difficulty in swallowing, general weakness in her limbs, and terrific fatigue.

Many of the symptoms would disappear for days and then suddenly reappear. R. J. also noted that, if she got a good night's sleep, she felt better but, if she performed physical work or became stressed, the symptoms got worse. About 3 years after the symptoms first appeared, she was diagnosed with myasthenia gravis, a condition that affects the communication between motor neurons and muscles.

A specialist suggested that R. J. undergo a new treatment in which the thymus gland is removed. She underwent the surgery and, within the next 5 years, all her symptoms gradually disappeared. She remained symptom free thereafter.

In myasthenia gravis, the receptors of muscles are insensitive to the chemical messages passed from axon terminals. Consequently, the muscles do not respond to commands from motor neurons. Myasthenia gravis is rare, with a prevalence of 14/100,000, and the disorder is more common in women than in men.

The age of onset is usually in the 30s to 40s for women and after age 50 for men. In about 10 percent of cases, the condition is limited to the eye muscles, but, for the majority of patients, the condition gets worse. At the time when R. J. contracted the disease, about a third of myasthenia gravis patients died from the disease or from complications such as respiratory infections.

Why is removal of the thymus gland sometimes an effective treatment? A gland of the immune system, the thymus takes part in producing antibodies to foreign material and viruses that enter the body. In myasthenia gravis, the thymus may start to make antibodies to the end-plate receptors on muscles.

Blocked by these antibodies, the receptors can no longer produce a normal response to acetylcholine, the chemical transmitter at the muscle synapse; so Na^+ and K^+ do not move through the end-plate pore and the muscle does not receive the signal to contract. Disorders in which the immune system makes antibodies to a person's own body are called **autoimmune diseases.**

Myasthenia gravis has now been modeled almost completely in animals and has become a model for studying other autoimmune diseases—of which there are nearly 80 kinds, including neuromyalgia, multiple sclerosis, and diabetes. A variety of contemporary treatments besides the removal of the thymus gland include thyroid-gland removal and drug treatments, such as those that increase the release of acetylcholine at muscle receptors. As a result, most myasthenia gravis patients today live out their normal life spans.

1 2 3 4

Courtesy of Y. Harati, M.D., Baylor College of Medicine, Houston, Texas

This myasthenia gravis patient was asked to look up (photograph 1). Her eyelids quickly become fatigued and droop (photographs 2 and 3). Photograph 4 shows her eyelids open normally after a few minutes rest.

cord. By teasing apart the fibers of the incoming sensory nerves, he was able to stimulate one fiber at a time.

Figure 4-22 diagrams the experimental setup used by Eccles. He found that stimulating some of the fibers produced a depolarizing graded potential (reduced the charge) on the membrane of the motor neuron to which these fibers were connected. Eccles called these potentials **excitatory postsynaptic potentials** (EPSPs). Because they reduce the charge on the membrane toward the threshold level, they increase the probability that an action potential will result.

In contrast, when Eccles stimulated other incoming sensory fibers, he produced a hyperpolarizing graded potential (increased the charge) on the receiving motor-neuron membrane. Eccles called these potentials **inhibitory postsynaptic potentials** (IPSPs). Because they increase the charge on the membrane away from the threshold level, they decrease the probability that an action potential will result.

Autoimmune disease Illness resulting from the loss of the immune system's ability to discriminate between foreign pathogens in the body and the body itself.

Excitatory postsynaptic potential (EPSP) Brief depolarization of a neuron membrane in response to stimulation, making the neuron more likely to produce an action potential.

Inhibitory postsynaptic potential (IPSP) Brief hyperpolarization of a neuron membrane in response to stimulation, making the neuron less likely to produce an action potential.

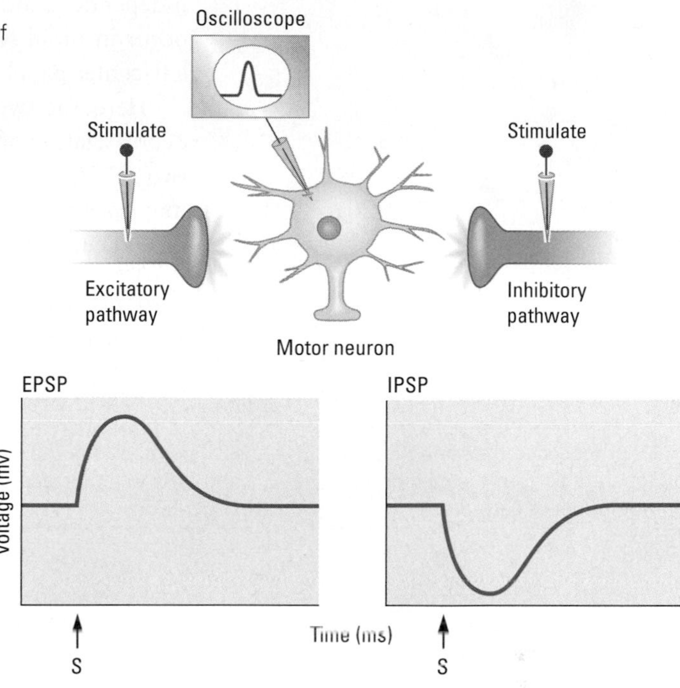

FIGURE 4-22 Eccles's Experiment. To demonstrate how input onto neurons influences their excitability, a recording is made from the cell body of a motor neuron while either an excitatory (*left*) or an inhibitory (*right*) input is delivered. Stimulation **(S)** of the excitatory pathway produces a membrane depolarization, or excitatory postsynaptic potential (EPSP). Stimulation of the inhibitory pathway produces a membrane hyperpolarization, or inhibitory postsynaptic potential (IPSP).

Both EPSPs and IPSPs last only a few milliseconds, after which they decay and the neuron's resting potential is restored. EPSPs are associated with the opening of sodium channels, which allows an influx of Na^+ ions. IPSPs are associated with the opening of potassium channels, which allows an efflux of K^+ ions (or with the opening of chloride channels, which allows an influx of Cl^- ions).

Although the size of a graded potential is proportional to the intensity of the stimulation, an action potential is not produced on the motor neuron's cell-body membrane even when an EPSP is strongly excitatory. The reason is simple: the cell-body membrane of most neurons does not contain voltage-sensitive channels. The stimulation must reach the axon hillock, the area of the cell where the axon begins. The hillock is rich in voltage-sensitive channels.

Summation of Inputs

Remember that a motor neuron has thousands of dendritic spines, allowing for myriad inputs to its membrane, both EPSPs and IPSPs. How do these incoming graded potentials interact? For example, what happens if there are two EPSPs in succession? Does it matter if the time between them is increased or decreased? And what happens when an EPSP and an IPSP arrive together? Answers to such questions provide an understanding of how the thousands of inputs to a neuron might influence its activities.

Temporal Summation

If one excitatory pulse of stimulation is delivered and is followed some time later by a second excitatory pulse, one EPSP is recorded and, after a delay, a second identical EPSP is recorded, as shown at the top left in **Figure 4-23**. These two widely spaced EPSPs are

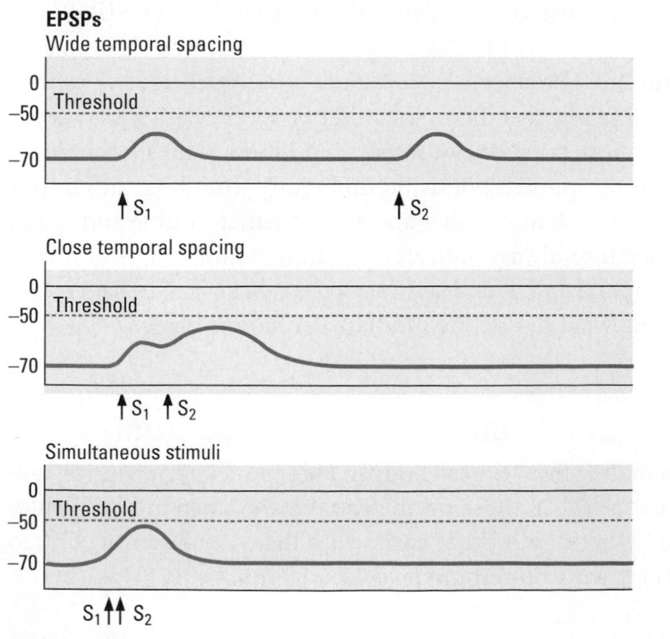

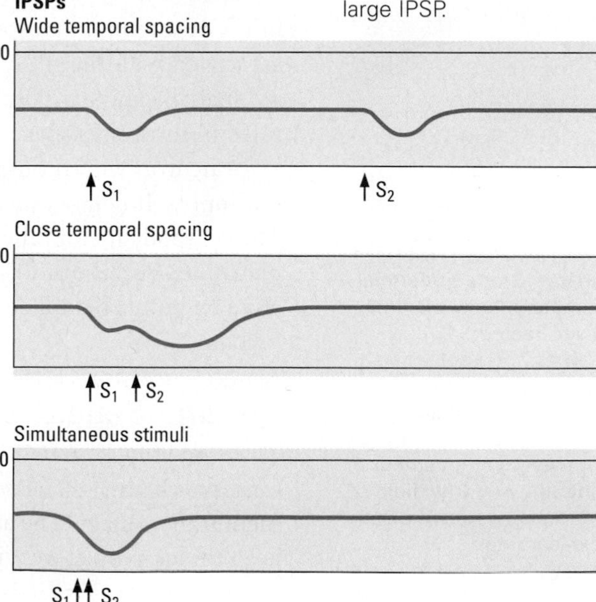

FIGURE 4-23 Temporal Summation. (*Left*) Two depolarizing pulses of stimulation (S_1 and S_2) separated in time produce two EPSPs similar in size. Pulses close together in time partly sum. Simultaneous EPSPs sum as one large EPSP. (*Right*) Two hyperpolarizing pulses (S_1 and S_2) widely separated in time produce two IPSPs similar in size. Pulses in close temporal proximity partly sum. Simultaneous IPSPs sum as one large IPSP.

independent and do not interact. If the delay between them is shortened so that the two occur in rapid succession, however, a single large EPSP is produced, as shown in the left-center panel of Figure 4-23.

Here, the two excitatory pulses are summed (added together to produce a larger depolarization of the membrane than either would induce alone). This relation between two EPSPs occurring close together or even at the same time is called **temporal summation.** The right side of Figure 4-23 illustrates that equivalent results are obtained with IPSPs. Therefore, temporal summation is a property of both EPSPs and IPSPs.

Spatial Summation

What happens when inputs to the cell body's membrane are located close together, and what happens when the inputs are spaced farther apart? By using two recording electrodes (R_1 and R_2) we can see the effects of spatial relations on the summation of inputs.

If two EPSPs are recorded at the same time but on widely separated parts of the membrane (**Figure 4-24A**), they do not influence one another. If two EPSPs occurring close together in time are also close together in location, however, they sum to form a larger EPSP (Figure 4-24B). This **spatial summation** indicates that two separate inputs occurring very close to one another on the cell membrane and in time sum. Similarly, two IPSPs produced at the same time sum if they occur at approximately the same place on the cell-body membrane but not if they are widely separated.

(A)

EPSPs produced at the same time, but on separate parts of the membrane, do not influence each other.

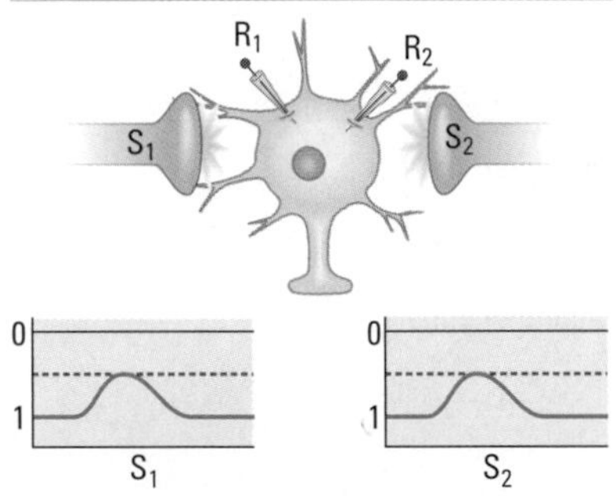

(B)

EPSPs produced at the same time, and close together, add to form a larger EPSP.

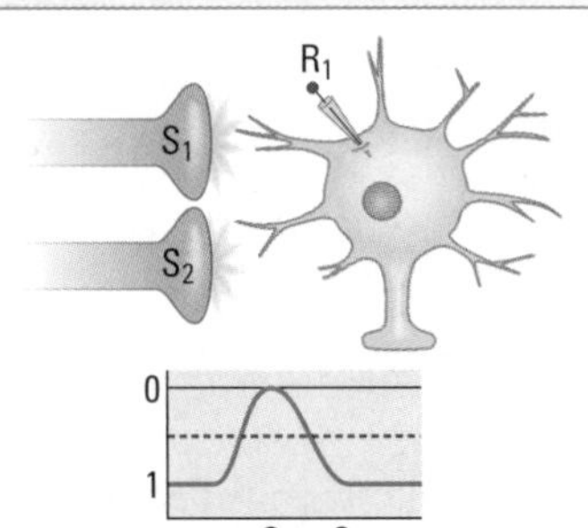

FIGURE 4-24 Spatial Summation. Illustrated here for EPSPs, the process for IPSPs is equivalent.

The Role of Ions in Summation

Summation is a property of both EPSPs and IPSPs in any combination. The interactions between EPSPs and IPSPs make sense when you consider that the influx and the efflux of ions are being summed. The influx of sodium ions accompanying one EPSP is added to the influx of sodium ions accompanying a second EPSP if the two occur close together in time and space. If the two influxes of sodium ions are remote in time or in space or in both, no summation is possible.

The same is true regarding effluxes of potassium ions. When they occur close together in time and space, they sum; when they are far apart in either or both of these ways, there is no summation. The patterns are identical for an EPSP and an IPSP. The influx of sodium ions associated with the EPSP is added to the efflux of potassium ions associated with the IPSP, and the difference between them is recorded as long as they are spatially and temporally close together. If, on the other hand, they are widely separated in time or in space or in both, they do not interact and there is no summation.

A neuron with thousands of inputs responds no differently from one with only a few inputs. It democratically sums all inputs that are close together in time and space. The cell-body membrane, therefore, always indicates the summed influences of multiple inputs. Because of this temporal and spatial summation, a neuron can be said to analyze its inputs before deciding what to do. The ultimate decision is made at the axon hillock.

Voltage-Sensitive Channels and the Action Potential

The axon hillock, shown emanating from the cell body in **Figure 4-25,** is rich in voltage-sensitive channels. These channels, like those on the squid axon, open at a particular membrane voltage. The actual threshold voltage varies with the type of neuron, but, to keep things simple, we will stay with a threshold level of −50 millivolts.

Temporal summation Graded potentials that occur at approximately the same time on a membrane are summated.

Spatial summation Graded potentials that occur at approximately the same location and time on a membrane are summated.

Back propagation Reverse movement of an action potential into the dendritic field of a neuron; postulated to play a role in plastic changes that underlie learning.

To produce an action potential, the summed IPSPs and EPSPs on the cell-body membrane must depolarize the membrane at the axon hillock to −50 millivolts. If that threshold voltage is only briefly obtained, voltage-sensitive channels open, and just one or a few action potentials may occur. If the threshold level is maintained for a longer period, however, action potentials will follow one another in rapid succession, just as quickly as the gates on the voltage-sensitive channels can reset. Each action potential is then repeatedly propagated to produce a nerve impulse that travels down the length of the axon.

Voltage-sensitive channels are not equally concentrated on the axon and dendrites of a neuron. Neurons often have extensive dendritic trees but, because dendrites and dendritic branches do not have many voltage-sensitive channels, they do not ordinarily produce action potentials. There are exceptions: the dendrites of cortical and hippocampal pyramidal cells and a few other brain and spinal-cord neurons can produce action potentials.

The movement of an action potential into the dendritic field of a neuron is called **back propagation** to distinguish it from normal propagation of the axon potential from the axon hillock down the axon. Voltage-sensitive channels enable action potentials to occur on dendrites, just as they occur on the axon. Back propagation serves as a signal to the dendritic field that the neuron is sending an action potential over its axon and is postulated to play a role in plastic changes in the neuron that underlie learning.

We explore the neuronal basis of learning in Chapter 5.

There is another relation between the dendritic field and the action potential initiated at the axon hillock, the typical site of propagation. EPSPs and IPSPs on the distant branches of dendrites may have less influence than do EPSPs and IPSPs that are closer to the axon hillock. Inputs close to the axon hillock are usually much more dynamic in their influence than those occurring some distance away. Those distant inputs usually have a modulating effect. As in all democracies, some inputs have more say than others.

To summarize the relation between EPSPs, IPSPs, and action potentials, imagine a brick standing on end a few inches away from a wall. It can be tilted back and forth over quite a wide range. If it is tilted too far in one direction, it tips against the wall; if it is tilted too far in the other direction, it topples over completely. Movements toward the wall are like IPSPs (inhibitory inputs). No matter how much these inputs sum, the brick never falls. Movements away from the wall are like EPSPs (excitatory inputs). If their sum reaches some threshold point, the brick topples over. With sufficient excitation, then, the brick falls, which is analogous to generating an action potential.

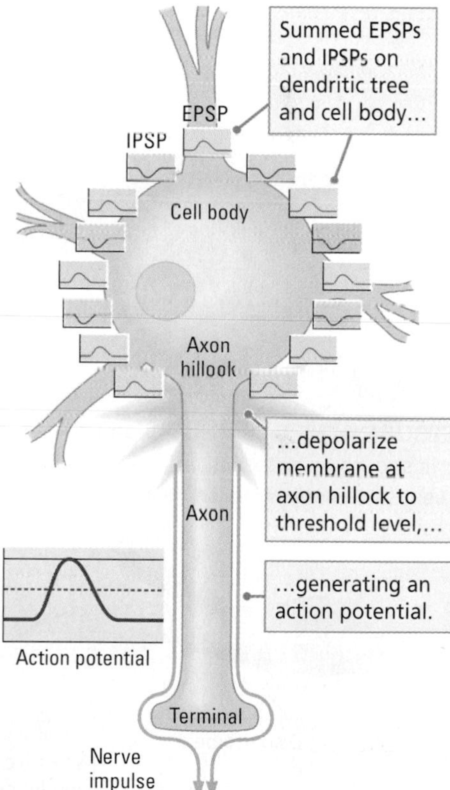

FIGURE 4-25 Triggering an Action Potential. If the summated EPSPs and IPSPs on the dendritic tree and cell body of a neuron charge the membrane to threshold level at the axon hillock, an action potential travels down the axon membrane.

REVIEW: How Neurons Integrate Information

- ✔ Stimulation at synapses produces graded potentials on a neuron's cell body and dendrites.
- ✔ Graded potentials that decrease the charge on the cell membrane, moving it toward the threshold level, are called excitatory postsynaptic potentials because they increase the likelihood that an action potential will occur.
- ✔ Graded potentials that increase the charge on the cell membrane, moving it away from the threshold level, are called inhibitory postsynaptic potentials because they decrease the likelihood that an action potential will result.
- ✔ EPSPs and IPSPs that occur close together in time and space are summed. In this way, a neuron integrates information that it receives from other neurons.

Stretch-sensitive channel Ion channel on a tactile sensory neuron that activates in response to stretching of the membrane, initiating a nerve impulse.
End plate On a muscle, the receptor–ion complex that is activated by the release of the neurotransmitter acetylcholine from the terminal of a motor neuron.
Transmitter-sensitive channel Receptor complex that has both a receptor site for a chemical and a pore through which ions can flow.

- ✔ If summed inputs are sufficiently excitatory to bring the axon hillock to a threshold level, an action potential is triggered and then propagated as it travels along the cell's axon as a nerve impulse.
- ✔ Some neurons have voltage-sensitive channels on their dendrites that allow an action potential to back propagate into the dendritic field.

Into the Nervous System and Back Out

The nervous system allows us to respond to sensory stimuli by detecting them in the environment and sending messages about them to the brain. The brain interprets the information, triggering responses that contract muscles and cause movements of the body, that is, behavior. Until now, we have been dealing only with the middle of this process—how neurons convey information to one another, integrate that information, and generate action potentials. We have not explored the beginning and end of the journey.

To fill in those missing pieces, we now explain how a sensory stimulus initiates a nerve impulse and how a nerve impulse produces a muscular contraction. You will see that ion channels are again important but that these channels are different from those described so far. You will first see how they differ as we examine the production of action potentials by sensory stimuli.

How Sensory Stimuli Produce Action Potentials

We receive information about the world through tactile sensations (body senses such as touch and pain), auditory sensations (hearing), visual sensations (sight), and chemical sensations (taste and olfaction). Each sensory modality has one or more separate functions. For example, the body senses include touch, pressure, joint sense, pain, and temperature. Receptors for audition and balance are modified touch receptors. The visual system has receptors for light and for different colors. And taste and olfactory senses are sensitive to myriad chemical compounds.

To process all these different kinds of sensory inputs requires a remarkable array of different sensory receptors. But one thing that neurons related to these diverse receptors have in common is the presence of ion channels on their cell membranes. When a sensation stimulates these ion channels, it initiates the chain of events that produces a nerve impulse.

Touch provides an example. Each hair on the human body is very sensitive to touch, allowing us to detect an even very slight displacement. You can demonstrate this sensitivity to yourself by selecting a single hair on your arm and bending it. If you are patient and precise in your experimentation, you will discover that some hairs are sensitive to displacement in one direction only, whereas others respond to displacement in any direction. What enables this very finely tuned sensitivity?

FIGURE 4-26 Tactile Stimulation. A hair's touch receptor activated by a feather results in a nerve impulse heading to the brain.

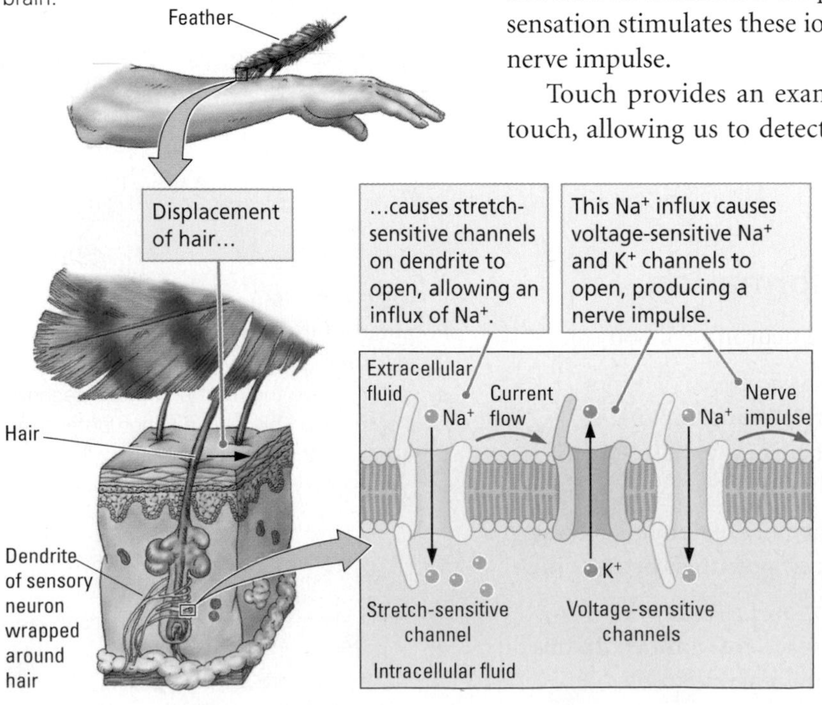
Feather
Displacement of hair...
...causes stretch-sensitive channels on dendrite to open, allowing an influx of Na+.
This Na+ influx causes voltage-sensitive Na+ and K+ channels to open, producing a nerve impulse.
Extracellular fluid
Current flow
Na+
Na+
Nerve impulse
K+
Hair
Dendrite of sensory neuron wrapped around hair
Stretch-sensitive channel
Voltage-sensitive channels
Intracellular fluid

The dendrites of sensory neurons are specialized to conduct nerve impulses, and one of these dendrites is wrapped around the base of each hair on your body. As shown in **Figure 4-26,** when a hair is mechanically displaced, as when you bend it, the encircling dendrite is stretched, initiating the opening of a series of **stretch-sensitive channels** in the dendrite's membrane. When these channels open, they allow an influx of Na^+ ions sufficient to depolarize the dendrite to its threshold level.

At threshold, the voltage-sensitive sodium and potassium channels open to initiate the nerve impulse.

Other kinds of sensory receptors have similar mechanisms for transforming the energy of a sensory stimulus into nervous-system activity. The *hair receptors* for hearing and balance, when displaced, likewise activate stretch-sensitive channels. In the visual system, light particles strike chemicals in receptors within the eye, and the resulting chemical change activates ion channels in the membranes of *relay neurons.* An odorous molecule in the air that lands on an olfactory receptor and fits itself into a specially shaped compartment opens chemical-sensitive ion channels. When tissue is damaged, injured cells release a chemical called bradykinin that activates bradykinin-sensitive channels on a pain nerve. The point here is that, in all our sensory systems, ion channels begin the process of information conduction.

We consider the details of how sensory receptors change, or *transduce,* energy from the external world into action potentials in later chapters:
Sensation, perception, and vision in Chapter 9
Hearing in Chapter 10
Touch, pain, and balance in Chapter 11
Smell and taste in Chapter 12

How Nerve Impulses Produce Movement

What happens at the end of the neural journey? How, after sensory information has traveled to the brain and been interpreted, is a behavioral response that includes the contraction of muscles generated? Behavior, after all, is movement, and, for movement to take place, muscles must contract. If motor neurons fail to work, movement becomes impossible and muscles atrophy, as described in Clinical Focus 4-4, "Lou Gehrig's Disease."

Motor neurons send nerve impulses through their axons. The motor-neuron axons, in turn, generate in muscle cells the action potentials that are instrumental in making the muscle contract. So the question is, How does an action potential on a motor-neuron axon produce an action potential on a muscle?

The axon of each motor neuron makes one or a few contacts (synapses) with its target muscle, similar to those that neurons make with one another (**Figure 4-27**). The part of the muscle membrane that is contacted by the axon terminal is a specialized area called an **end plate**, shown in Figure 4-27A and B. The axon terminal releases onto the end plate a chemical transmitter called *acetylcholine* that activates skeletal muscles.

This transmitter does not enter the muscle but rather attaches to **transmitter-sensitive channels** on the end plate (Figure 4-27C). When these channels open in response to acetylcholine, they allow a flow of ions across the muscle membrane sufficient to depolarize it to the threshold for its action potential. At threshold, adjacent voltage-sensitive channels open. They, in turn, produce an action potential on the muscle fiber, which is the basis for muscular contraction.

The transmitter-sensitive channels on muscle end plates are somewhat different from the channels on axons and dendrites. A single end-plate channel is larger than two sodium and two potassium channels on a neuron combined. When transmitter-sensitive channels open, they allow both Na^+ influx and K^+ efflux through the same pore. The number of channels that open depends on the amount of transmitter released. Therefore, to generate a sufficient depolarization on the end plate to activate neighboring voltage-sensitive channels requires the release of an appropriate amount of acetylcholine.

A wide range of neural events can be explained by the actions of membrane channels. Some channels generate the transmembrane charge. Others mediate graded potentials. Still others trigger the action potential. Sensory stimuli activate channels on neurons to initiate a nerve impulse, and the nerve impulse eventually activates channels on motor neurons to produce muscle contractions.

These various channels and their different functions probably evolved over a long period of time in the same way that new species of animals and their behaviors evolve. So far, not all the different channels that neural membranes possess have been described, but you will learn about some additional channels in subsequent chapters.

(A)

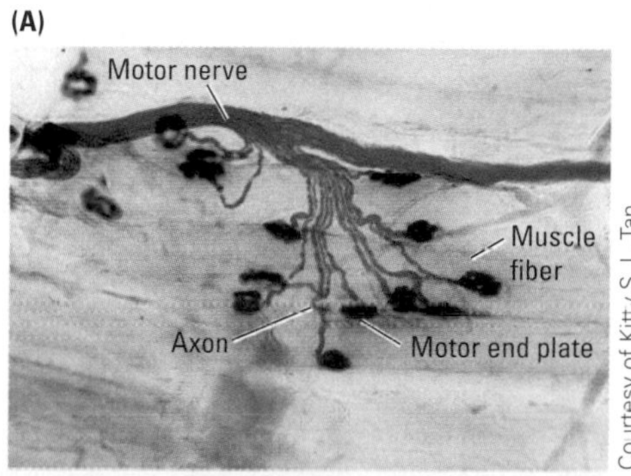

(B)

(C)

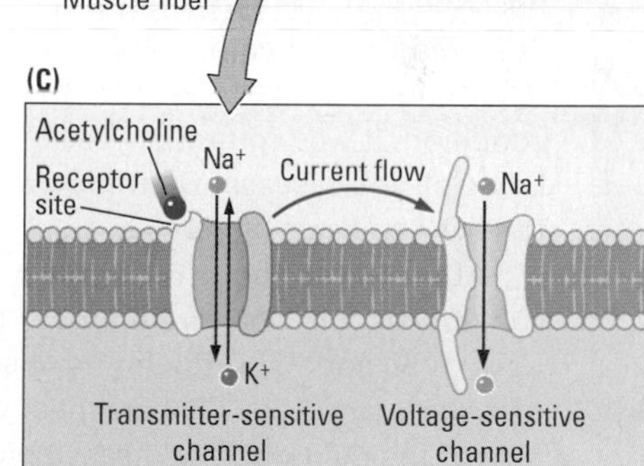

FIGURE 4-27 Muscle Contration. (A) Microscopic view of a motor-neuron's axon collaterals contacting muscle end plates. The dark patches are end plates and the axon terminal buttons are not visible. (B) An axon terminal contacts an end plate. (C) The neurotransmitter acetylcholine attaches to receptor sites on transmitter-sensitive end-plate channels, opening them. These large membrane channels allow the simultaneous influx of sodium ions and efflux of potassium ions, generating a current sufficient to activate voltage-sensitive channels that trigger an action potential on the muscle, causing it to contract.

CLINICAL FOCUS 4-4

Lou Gehrig's Disease

Baseball legend Lou Gehrig played for the New York Yankees from 1923 until 1939. He was a member of numerous World Series championship teams, set a host of individual records, some of which still stand today, and was immensely popular with fans, who knew him as the "Iron Man." His record of 2130 consecutive games was untouched until 1990, when Cal Ripkin, Jr., played his 2131st consecutive game.

In 1938, Gehrig started to lose his strength. In 1939, he played only eight games and then retired from baseball. Eldon Auker, a pitcher for the Detroit Tigers, described Lou's physical decline: "Lou seemed to be losing his power. His walking and running appeared to slow. His swing was not as strong as it had been in past years."

Eldon was not describing the symptoms of normal aging but rather the symptoms of amyotrophic lateral sclerosis (ALS), a diagnosis shortly to be pronounced by Lou's physician. ALS was first described by French physician Jean-Martin Charcot in 1869, but, after Lou Gehrig developed the condition, it was commonly called Lou Gehrig's disease. Gehrig died in 1941 at the age of 38.

Lou Gehrig in his prime, jumping over Yankee teammate Joe DiMaggio's bat.

Baseball Hall of Fame Library, Cooperstown, N.Y.

ALS affects about 6 of every 100,000 people and strikes most commonly between the ages of 50 and 75, although its onset can be as early as the teenage years. About 10 percent of victims have a family history of the disorder. The disease begins with general weakness, at first in the throat or upper chest and in the arms and legs. Gradually, walking becomes difficult and falling common. The patient may lose use of the hands and legs, have trouble swallowing, and have difficulty speaking. The disease does not usually affect any sensory systems, cognitive functions, bowel or bladder control, or even sexual function. Death often occurs within 5 years of diagnosis.

ALS is due primarily to the death of motor neurons, which connect the rest of the nervous system to muscles, allowing movement. Neurons in the brain that connect primarily with motor neurons also can be affected. The technical term, amyotrophic lateral sclerosis, describes its consequences on both muscles (*amyotrophic* means "muscle weakness") and on the spinal cord (*lateral sclerosis* means "hardening of the lateral spinal cord") where motor neurons are located.

Several theories have been advanced to explain why motor neurons suddenly start to die in ALS victims. Recent evidence suggests that ALS can result from head trauma that activates the cell's DNA to produce signals that initiate the neuron's death, a phenomenon known as *apoptosis* (programmed cell death). Genetic factors are also suspected (Siddique and Siddique, 2008).

At the present time, there is no cure for ALS, although some newly developed drugs appear to slow its progression and offer some hope for future treatments. Nascent brain–computer interfaces could potentially allow people with ALS to continue to communicate with others and to maintain muscle tone that is lost with the disease.

REVIEW: Into the Nervous System and Back Out

- ✔ The membrane of a receptor cell contains a mechanism for transducing sensory energy into changes in ion channels that, in turn, allow ion flow to alter the voltage of the membrane to the point that voltage-sensitive channels open, initiating a nerve impulse.
- ✔ The way in which a sensory stimulus initiates a nerve impulse is surprisingly similar for all our sensory systems.

✔ Muscle contraction also depends on ion channels. The axon terminal of a motor neuron releases the chemical transmitter acetylcholine onto the end plate of a muscle-cell membrane. Transmitter-sensitive channels on the end plate open in response, and the subsequent flow of ions depolarizes the muscle membrane to the threshold for its action potential. This depolarization, in turn, activates neighboring voltage-sensitive channels, producing an action potential on the muscle fiber, which brings about contraction of the muscle.

Summary

Searching for Electrical Activity in the Nervous System

Electrical-stimulation studies and electrical-recording studies provided early clues about the electrical activity of the nervous system. Electrical-stimulation studies, which date as far back as the eighteenth century, showed that stimulating a nerve with electrical current could induce a muscle contraction. More recently, electrical-recording studies, in which the brain's electrical current was measured with a voltmeter, showed that electrical activity is continually taking place within the nervous system.

To measure the electrical activity of a single neuron, researchers used giant axons of the squid. They recorded small, rapid electrical changes with an oscilloscope and developed microelectrodes that they could place on or into the cell.

The electrical activity of neurons is generated by the flow of electrically charged ions across the cell membrane. These ions flow both down a concentration gradient (from an area of relatively high concentration to an area of lower concentration) and down a voltage gradient (from an area of relatively high voltage to an area of lower voltage). The distribution of ions is also affected by the opening and closing of ion channels in neural membranes.

Electrical Activity of a Membrane

The resting potential results from an unequal distribution of ions on a membrane's two sides, with the intracellular side registering about −70 millivolts relative to the extracellular side. Negatively charged protein anions are too large to leave the neuron, and the cell membrane actively pumps out positively charged sodium ions. In addition, unequal distributions of potassium cations and chloride anions contribute to the resting potential.

Graded potentials result when the when the neuron is stimulated because ion channels in the membrane are affected, which in turn changes the distribution of ions, suddenly increasing or decreasing the transmembrane voltage by a small amount. A slight increase in the voltage is called hyperpolarization, whereas a slight decrease is called depolarization.

An action potential is a brief but large change in the polarity of an axon membrane that is triggered when the transmembrane voltage drops to a threshold level of about −50 millivolts. The transmembrane voltage suddenly reverses (with the intracellular side becoming positive relative to the extracellular side) and then abruptly reverses again, after which the resting potential is gradually restored. These reversals are due to the behavior of voltage-sensitive channels—sodium and potassium channels that are sensitive to the membrane's voltage.

When an action potential is triggered at the axon hillock, it can propagate along the axon as a nerve impulse. Nerve impulses travel more rapidly on myelinated axons because of saltatory conduction: the action potentials jump between the nodes separating the glial cells that form the axon's myelin sheath.

How Neurons Integrate Information

The summated inputs to neurons from other cells can produce both excitatory postsynaptic potentials and inhibitory postsynaptic potentials. EPSPs and IPSPs are summed both temporally and spatially, which integrates the incoming information. If the resulting sum moves the voltage of the membrane at the axon hillock to the threshold level, an action potential will be produced on the axon.

Into the Nervous System and Back Out

Sensory-receptor cells in the body contain mechanisms for transducing sensory energy into energy changes in ion channels. These changes, in turn, alter the transmembrane voltage to the point at which voltage-sensitive channels open, triggering an action potential and propagating a nerve impulse that transmits sensory information to relevant parts of the nervous system.

Ion channels again come into play to activate muscles because the chemical transmitter acetylcholine, released at the axon terminal of a motor neuron, activates channels on the end plate of a muscle-cell membrane. The subsequent flow of ions depolarizes the muscle-cell membrane to the threshold for its action potential. This depolarization, in turn, activates voltage-sensitive channels, producing an action potential on the muscle fiber. The action potential induces the contraction of muscle fibers that enable movement.

Key Terms

absolutely refractory, p. 118
action potential, p. 116
autoimmune disease, p. 124
back propagation, p. 126
concentration gradient, p. 111
diffusion, p. 111
depolarization, p. 114
electrical stimulation, p. 107
electroencephalogram (EEG), p. 107
end plate, p. 128
excitatory postsynaptic potential (EPSP), p. 124
graded potential, p. 114
hyperpolarization, p. 114
inhibitory postsynaptic potential (IPSP), p. 124
microelectrode, p. 108
nerve impulse, p. 120
node of Ranvier, p. 123
oscilloscope, p. 108
relatively refractory, p. 120
resting potential, p. 112
saltatory conduction, p. 123
spatial summation, p. 126
stretch-sensitive channel, p. 128
temporal summation, p. 126
threshold potential, p. 116
transmitter-sensitive channel, p. 128
voltage gradient, p. 111
voltage-sensitive channel, p. 118
voltmeter, p. 107

▶*Please refer to the Companion Web Site at* **www.worthpublishers.com/kolbintro3e** *for Interactive Exercises and Quizzes.*

Katsuyoshi Tanaka

CHAPTER 5

How Do Neurons Communicate and Adapt?

RESEARCH FOCUS 5-1

The Basis of Neural Communication in a Heartbeat

Discoveries about how neurons communicate stem from experiments designed to study what controls an animal's heart rate. Like that of any animal, your heartbeat quickens if you are excited or exercising; if you are resting, it slows. Heart rate changes to match energy expenditure—that is, to meet the body's nutrient and oxygen needs.

Heartbeat undergoes a most dramatic change when you dive beneath water: it almost completely stops. This drastic slowing, called *diving bradycardia,* conserves the body's oxygen when you are not breathing. Bradycardia (*brady,* meaning "slow," and *cardia,* meaning "heart") is a useful survival strategy. This energy-conserving response under water is common to many animals. But what controls it?

Otto Loewi, a great storyteller, recounted that his classic experiment, for which he was awarded a Nobel Prize in 1936, came to him in a dream. As shown in the Procedure section of Experiment 5-1 on page 135, Loewi first maintained a frog's heart in a salt bath and then electrically stimulated the vagus nerve—the cranial nerve that leads from the brain to the heart. At the same time, he channeled some of the fluid bath from the vessel containing the stimulated heart through a tube to another vessel in which a second heart was immersed but not electrically stimulated.

Loewi recorded the beating rates of both hearts. His findings are represented in the Results section of Experiment 5-1. The electrical stimulation decreased the beating rate of the first heart, but, more important, the second heartbeat also slowed. This finding suggested that the fluid transferred from the first to the second container carried the message "slow down."

Bill Coster/Peter Arnold

Puffins fish by diving underwater, propelling themselves by flapping their short stubby wings, as if flying. During these dives, their hearts display the diving-bradycardia response, just as our hearts do. Here, a puffin emerges from a dive.

But where did the message come from originally? Loewi reasoned that a chemical released from the stimulated vagus nerve must have diffused into the fluid to influence the second heart. The experiment therefore demonstrated that the vagus nerve contains a chemical that tells the heart to slow its rate of beating.

Loewi subsequently identified the messenger chemical. Later, he identified a chemical that tells the heart to speed up. Apparently, the heart adjusts its rate of beating in response to at least two different messages: an excitatory message that says "speed up" and an inhibitory message that says "slow down."

IN THIS CHAPTER, we describe how excitatory and inhibitory signals enable neurons to communicate, the chemicals that carry the neuron's signal, and the receptors on which those chemicals act to produce behavior. Then, we explore the neural bases of learning—that is, how neural synapses adapt physically as a result of an organism's experience.

A Chemical Message

Loewi's successful heartbeat experiment, diagrammed in **Experiment 5-1,** marked the beginning of research into how chemicals carry information from one neuron to another. Loewi was the first to isolate a chemical messenger. We now know the chemical as **acetylcholine** (ACh), the same transmitter described in Chapter 4 that activates skeletal muscles. Yet, here, ACh acts to inhibit heartbeat, to slow it down. It turns out that

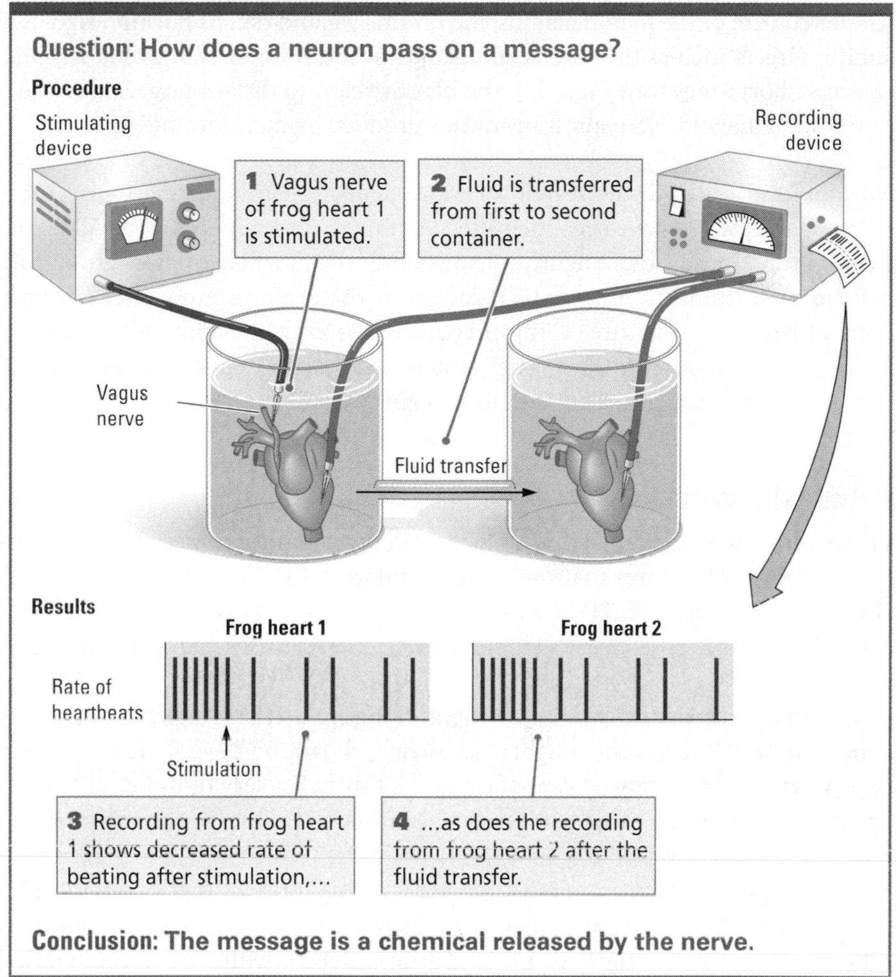
EXPERIMENT 5-1
Question: How does a neuron pass on a message?
Procedure
Stimulating device
Recording device
1 Vagus nerve of frog heart 1 is stimulated.
2 Fluid is transferred from first to second container.
Vagus nerve
Fluid transfer
Results
Frog heart 1
Frog heart 2
Rate of heartbeats
Stimulation
3 Recording from frog heart 1 shows decreased rate of beating after stimulation,...
4 ...as does the recording from frog heart 2 after the fluid transfer.
Conclusion: The message is a chemical released by the nerve.

Acetylcholine (ACh) The first neurotransmitter discovered in the peripheral and central nervous systems; activates skeletal muscles in the somatic nervous system and may either excite or inhibit internal organs in the autonomic system.

Epinephrine (EP, or adrenaline) Chemical messenger that acts as a hormone to mobilize the body for fight or flight during times of stress and as a neurotransmitter in the central nervous system.

Norepinephrine (NE, or noradrenaline) Neurotransmitter found in the brain and in the sympathetic division of the autonomic nervous system.

Neurotransmitter Chemical released by a neuron onto a target with an excitatory or inhibitory effect.

ACh activates skeletal muscles in the somatic nervous system and may either excite or inhibit internal organs in the autonomic system. And, yes, ACh is the chemical messenger that slows the heart in diving bradycardia.

In further experiments, Loewi stimulated another nerve to the heart, the accelerator nerve, and obtained a speeded-up heart rate. As before, the fluid that bathed the accelerated heart increased the rate of beating of a second heart that was not electrically stimulated. Loewi identified the chemical that carries the message to speed up heart rate in frogs as **epinephrine** (EP), also known as *adrenaline*. Adrenaline (Latin) and epinephrine (Greek) are the same substance, produced by the adrenal glands located atop the kidneys. Adrenaline is the name more people know, in part because a drug company used it as a trade name, but EP is common parlance in the neuroscience community.

Further experimentation eventually demonstrated that the chemical that accelerates heart rate in mammals is **norepinephrine** (NE, also *noradrenaline*), a chemical closely related to EP. The results of Loewi's complementary experiments showed that ACh from the vagus nerve inhibits heartbeat, and EP from the accelerator nerve excites it.

Messenger chemicals released by a neuron onto a target to cause an excitatory or inhibitory effect are referred to as **neurotransmitters.** Outside the central nervous system,

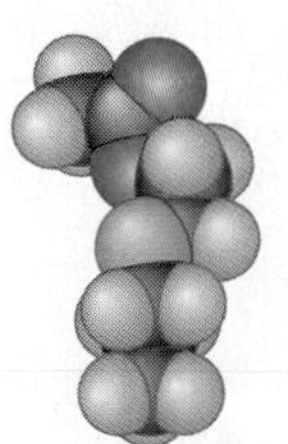
Acetylcholine (ACh)

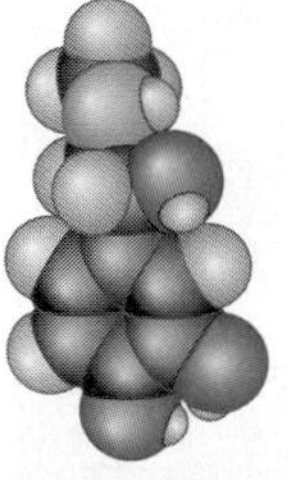
Epinephrine (EP)

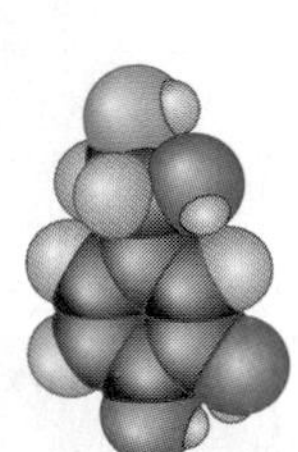
Norepinephrine (NE)

Acetylcholine inhibits heartbeat; epinephrine and norepinephrine excite the heart in frogs and humans, respectively.

Chapter 8 explains how drugs and hormones influence the brain and behavior.

many of these same chemicals, EP among them, circulate in the bloodstream as *hormones.* Under control of the hypothalamus, the pituitary gland directs hormones to excite or inhibit targets such as the organs and glands in the autonomic nervous system. In part because hormones travel through the bloodstream to distant targets, their action is slower than that of CNS neurotransmitters prodded by the lightning-quick nerve impulse.

In addition to treatments directed toward replacing the depleted neurotransmitter, exercise and music are helpful. Parkinson patients who attend dance classes, such as those pictured at the beginning of this chapter, report that moving to music helps them regain muscle control.

Loewi's discoveries led to the search for more neurotransmitters and their functions, and now at least 100 have been identified. As this chapter unfolds, you will learn the names and functions of more neurotransmitters and you will learn how groups of neurons form neurotransmitter systems throughout the brain to modulate, or temper, aspects of behavior. The three Clinical Focus boxes in this chapter tell the fascinating story of one such neurotransmitter system that, when depleted, is associated with a specific neurological disorder. The story begins with Clinical Focus 5-2, "Parkinson's Disease."

Structure of Synapses

Loewi's discovery about the regulation of heart rate by chemical messengers was the first of two important findings that form the foundation for current understanding of how neurons communicate. The second had to wait nearly 30 years, for the invention of the electron microscope, which enabled scientists to see the structure of a synapse.

Figure 4-5 shows a digital oscilloscope and describes how it measures voltage in biological tissue.

The electron microscope, shown on the right in **Figure 5-1,** uses some of the principles of both an oscilloscope and a light microscope, shown on the left. The electron microscope works by projecting a beam of electrons through a very thin slice of tissue. The varying structure of the tissue scatters the beam onto a reflective surface where it leaves an image, or shadow, of the tissue.

FIGURE 5-1 Microscopic Advance. Whereas a light microscope (*left*) can be used to see the general features of a cell, an electron microscope (*right*) can be used to examine the details of a cell's organelles.

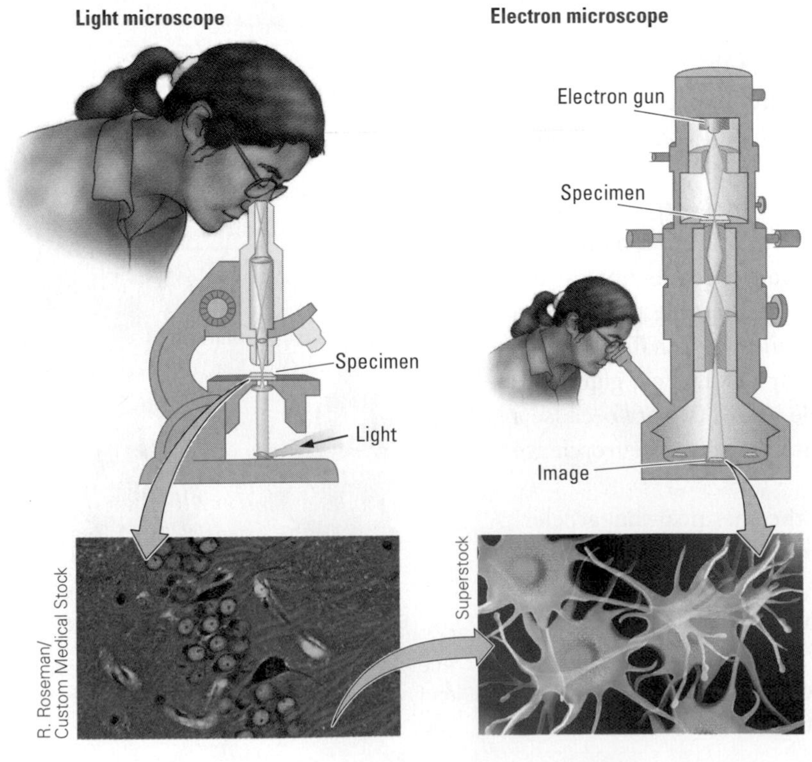

The resolution of an electron microscope is much higher than that of a light microscope because electron waves are smaller than light waves, and so there is much less scatter when the beam strikes the tissue. If the tissue is stained with substances that reflect electrons, very fine structural details can be observed. Compare the images at the bottom of Figure 5-1.

The first good electron micrographs, made in the 1950s, revealed the structure of a synapse for the first time. In the center of the micrograph in **Figure 5-2**A, the upper part of the synapse is the axon end terminal; the lower part is the receiving dendrite. Note the round granular substances in the terminal. They are the **synaptic vesicles** containing the neurotransmitter.

The dark patches on the dendrite consist mainly of protein receptor molecules that receive chemical messages. Dark patches on the axon terminal membrane are protein molecules that serve largely as channels and pumps to release the transmitter or to recapture it after its release. The terminal and the dendrite are separated by a small space, the **synaptic cleft.** The synaptic cleft is central to synapse function because neurotransmitter chemicals must bridge this gap to carry a message from one neuron to the next.

You can also see on the micrograph that the synapse is sandwiched by many surrounding structures. These structures include glial cells, other axons and dendritic

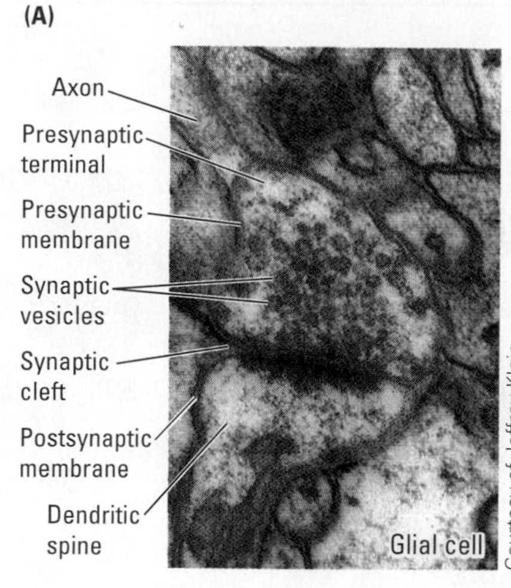

Courtesy of Jeffrey Klein

Mitochondrion: Organelle that provides the cell with energy.

FIGURE 5-2 Chemical Synapse. (A) Electron photomicrograph of a synapse. Surrounding the centrally located synapse are glial cells, axons, dendrites, and other synapses. (B) Characteristic parts of a synapse. Storage granules hold vesicles containing neurotransmitter that, when released, travels to the presynaptic membrane. It is expelled into the synaptic cleft through the process of exocytosis, crosses the cleft, and binds to receptor proteins on the postsynaptic membrane.

processes, and other synapses. The surrounding glia contribute to chemical neuro transmission in a number of ways—by supplying the building blocks for the synthesis of neurotransmitters or by mopping up excess neurotransmitter molecules, for example.

The drawing in Figure 5-2B details the process of neurotransmission at a **chemical synapse,** the junction where messenger molecules are released from one neuron to excite the next neuron. Here the **presynaptic membrane** forms the axon terminal, the **postsynaptic membrane** forms the dendritic spine, and the space between the two is the synaptic cleft. Within the axon terminal are specialized structures, including mitochondria, the organelles that supply the cell's energy needs; **storage granules,** large compartments that hold several synaptic vesicles; and microtubules that transport substances, including the neurotransmitter, to the terminal.

Chemical synapses are the rule in mammalian nervous systems, but they are not the only kind of synapse. Rare in mammals but commonly found in other animals, the **electrical synapse** is a fused presynaptic and postsynaptic membrane that allows an action potential to pass directly from one neuron to the next. This fusion prevents the brief delay in information flow—about 5 milliseconds per synapse—of chemical transmission. For example, the crayfish's electrical synapses activate its tail flick, a response that allows it to quickly escape from a predator.

Why, if chemical synapses transmit messages more slowly, do mammals depend on them almost exclusively? The benefits outweigh the drawback of slowed communication. Probably the greatest benefit is the flexibility that chemical synapses allow in controlling whether a message is passed from one neuron to the next.

Synaptic vesicle Organelle consisting of a membrane structure that encloses a quantum of neurotransmitter.
Synaptic cleft Gap that separates the presynaptic membrane from the postsynaptic membrane.
Chemical synapse Junction at which messenger molecules are released when stimulated by an action potential.
Presynaptic membrane Membrane on the transmitter-output side of a synapse.
Postsynaptic membrane Membrane on the transmitter-input side of a synapse.
Storage granule Membranous compartment that holds several vesicles containing a neurotransmitter.
Electrical synapse Fused presynaptic and postsynaptic membrane that allows an action potential to pass directly from one neuron to the next.

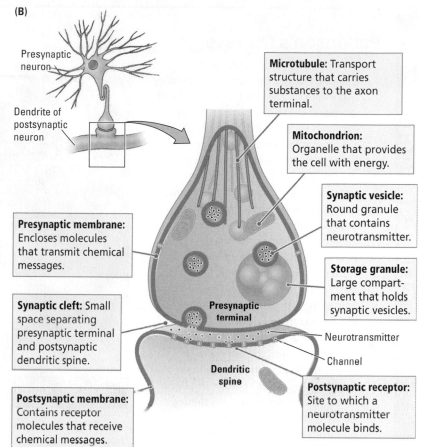

CLINICAL FOCUS 5-2

Parkinson's Disease

Case VI: The gentleman . . . is seventy-two years of age. He has led a life of temperance, and has never been exposed to any particular situation or circumstance which he can conceive likely to have occasioned, or disposed to this complaint: which he rather seems to regard as incidental on his advanced age, than as an object of medical attention. . . . About eleven or twelve, or perhaps more, years ago, he first perceived weakness in the left hand and arm, and soon after found the trembling to commence. In about three years afterwards the right arm became affected in a similar manner: and soon afterwards the convulsive motions affected the whole body and began to interrupt speech. In about three years from that time the legs became affected. Of late years the action of the bowels had been very much retarded. (James Parkinson, 1817/1989)

MCA/Universal Pictures—Courtesy: Everett Collection

AP Photo/David Adame

Actor Michael J. Fox gained wide fame when he starred in the *Back to the Future* movie series in the 1980s (*left*). Fox was diagnosed with young-onset Parkinson's disease in 1991. In 2004, he spoke publicly in support of stem-cell research (*right*).

In his 1817 essay from which this case study is taken, James Parkinson, a British physician, reported similar symptoms in six patients, some of whom he observed only in the streets near his clinic. Shaking was usually the first symptom, and it typically began in a hand. Over a number of years, the shaking spread to include the arm and then other parts of the body.

As the disease progressed, patients had a propensity to lean forward and walk on the forepart of their feet. They also tended to run forward to prevent themselves from falling. In the later stages of the disease, patients had difficulty eating and swallowing. They drooled and their bowel movements slowed. Eventually, the patients lost all muscular control and were unable to sleep because of the disruptive tremors.

More than 50 years after James Parkinson's description, French neurologist Jean-Martin Charcot named the condition **Parkinson's disease.** Three findings have helped researchers understand its neural basis:

1. In 1919, Constantin Tréatikoff studied the brains of nine Parkinson patients on autopsy and found that the substantia nigra, a nucleus in the midbrain taking part in the initiation of movement, had degenerated. In the brain of one patient who had experienced symptoms of Parkinson's disease on one side of the body only, the substantia nigra had degenerated on the side opposite that of the symptoms.
2. Chemical examination of the brains of Parkinson patients showed that symptoms of the disease appear when **dopamine,** then a proposed neurotransmitter, was reduced to less than 10 percent of normal in the basal ganglia (Ehringer and Hornykiewicz, 1960).
3. Confirming the role of dopamine in a neural pathway connecting the substantia nigra to the basal ganglia, Urban Ungerstedt found in 1971 that injecting a neurotoxin called 6-hydroxydopamine into rats selectively destroyed these dopamine-containing neurons and produced the symptoms of Parkinson's disease.

Researchers have now linked the loss of dopamine neurons to an array of causes, including genetic predisposition, the flu, pollution, insecticides and herbicides, and toxic drugs. Dopamine itself has been linked not only to motor behavior but also to some forms of learning and to neural structures that mediate reward and addiction. Thus, this remarkable series of discoveries initiated by James Parkinson has been a source of more insight into the function of the brain than has the investigation of any other disease.

Neurotransmission in Four Steps

The four-step process of chemically transmitting information across a synapse is illustrated in **Figure 5-3** and explained in this section. In brief, the neurotransmitter must be

1. synthesized and stored in the axon terminal;
2. transported to the presynaptic membrane and released in response to an action potential;
3. able to activate the receptors on the target-cell membrane located on the postsynaptic membrane; and
4. inactivated, or it will continue to work indefinitely.

Step 1: Neurotransmitter Synthesis and Storage

Neurotransmitters are derived in two general ways, and these origins define two broad classes of neurotransmitters. Some are synthesized in the axon terminal from building blo[cks] derived from food. **Transporters,** protein molecules that pump substances acros[s] ... absorb the required precursor chemicals from the blood supply ... [abs]orb the neurotransmitter ready-made.) Mit[ochondria] ... both to synthesize precurs[ors] ... branous vesicles.

Other neurotra[nsmitters] ... [i]ons contained in the n[ucleus] ... ported on microt[ubules] ... be manufacture[d] ... ported to the te[rminal] ...

Regardless ... found in thre[e] ... warehoused ... others are a[ttached] ... which a tra[nsmitter] ... released int[o] ...

Step 2: ...

When a[n] ... [cha]nges on the ... (Ca^{2+}) ... [pl]ay an impor[tant] ... volta[ge] ... ing e[vent] ... **ure** ... cha[nnels] ... ax[on] ...

The ... and the resulting ... actions: one releases v[esicles] ... membrane, and the other relea[ses] ... [fil]aments in the axon terminal. The vesic[les] ... the presynaptic membrane empty their cont[ents into] the synaptic cleft through the process of exocytosis. The vesicles from storage granules and on filaments then move up to replace the vesicles that just emptied their contents.

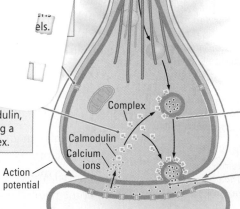

1 Synthesis: Some neurotransmitters are transported from the cell nucleus to the terminal button. Others,...

Precursor chemicals

Neurotransmitter

... made from building blocks imported into the terminal, are packaged into vesicles there.

2 Release: In response to an action potential, the transmitter is released across the membrane by exocytosis.

3 Receptor action: The transmitter crosses the synaptic cleft and binds to a receptor.

4 Inactivation: The transmitter is either taken back into the terminal or inactivated in the synaptic cleft.

FIGURE 5-3 Synaptic Transmission.

For a refresher on protein export, review Figure 3-17.

Parkinson's disease Disorder of the motor system correlated with a loss of dopamine in the brain and characterized by tremors, muscular rigidity, and reduction in voluntary movement.

Dopamine (DA) Amine neurotransmitter that plays a role in coordinating movement, in attention and learning, and in behaviors that are reinforcing.

Transporter Protein molecule that pumps substances across a membrane.

FIGURE 5-4 Neurotransmitter Release.

... [c]almodulin, forming a complex.

Complex

Calmodulin

Calcium ions

Action potential

3 This complex binds to vesicles, releasing some from filaments and inducing others to bind to the presynaptic membrane and to empty their contents by exocytosis.

Step 3: Receptor-Site Activation

After the neurotransmitter has been released from vesicles on the presynaptic membrane, it diffuses across the synaptic cleft and binds to specialized protein molecules embedded in the postsynaptic membrane. These **transmitter-activated receptors** have binding sites for the transmitter substance. Through the receptors, the postsynaptic cell may be affected in one of three ways, depending on the type of neurotransmitter and the kind of receptors on the postsynaptic membrane. The transmitter may

1. depolarize the postsynaptic membrane and so have an excitatory action on the postsynaptic neuron;
2. hyperpolarize the postsynaptic membrane and so have an inhibitory action on the postsynaptic neuron; or
3. initiate other chemical reactions that modulate either effect, inhibitory or excitatory, or that influence other functions of the receiving neuron.

In addition to interacting with the postsynaptic membrane's receptors, a neurotransmitter may interact with receptors on the presynaptic membrane. That is, it may influence the cell that just released it. Presynaptic receptors that may be activated by a neurotransmitter are called **autoreceptors** (self-receptors) to indicate that they receive messages from their own axon terminals.

How much neurotransmitter is needed to send a message? Bernard Katz was awarded a Nobel Prize in 1970 for providing an answer. Recording electrical activity from the postsynaptic membranes of muscles, he detected small, spontaneous depolarizations now called *miniature postsynaptic potentials.* The potentials varied in size, but each size appeared to be a multiple of the smallest potential.

Katz concluded that the smallest postsynaptic potential is produced by the release of the contents of just one synaptic vesicle. This amount of neurotransmitter is called a **quantum.** To produce a postsynaptic potential that is large enough to initiate a postsynaptic action potential requires the simultaneous release of many quanta from the presynaptic cell.

The results of subsequent experiments show that the number of quanta released from the presynaptic membrane in response to a single action potential depends on two factors: (1) the amount of Ca^{2+} that enters the axon terminal in response to the action potential and (2) the number of vesicles docked at the membrane, waiting to be released. Both factors are relevant to synaptic activity during learning, which we consider at the end of the chapter.

Step 4: Neurotransmitter Deactivation

Chemical transmission would not be a very effective messenger system if a neurotransmitter lingered within the synaptic cleft, continuing to occupy and stimulate receptors. If this happened, the postsynaptic cell could not respond to other messages sent by the presynaptic neuron. Therefore, after a neurotransmitter has done its work, it is quickly removed from receptor sites and from the synaptic cleft. Deactivation is accomplished in at least four ways:

1. Diffusion: some of the neurotransmitter simply diffuses away from the synaptic cleft and is no longer available to bind to receptors.
2. Degradation by enzymes in the synaptic cleft.
3. **Reuptake:** membrane transporter proteins may bring the transmitter back into the presynaptic axon terminal for subsequent reuse. The by-products of degradation by enzymes also may be taken back into the terminal to be used again in the cell.
4. Some neurotransmitters are taken up by neighboring glial cells. Potentially, the glial cells can also store transmitter for re-export to the axon terminal.

Transmitter-activated receptor Protein that has a binding site for a specific neurotransmitter and is embedded in the membrane of a cell.
Autoreceptor "Self-receptor" in a neural membrane that responds to the transmitter released by the neuron.
Quantum (pl. quanta) Quantity, equivalent to the contents of a single synaptic vesicle, that produces a just observable change in postsynaptic electric potential.
Reuptake Deactivation of a neurotransmitter when membrane transporter proteins bring the transmitter back into the presynaptic axon terminal for subsequent reuse.

Interestingly, an axon terminal has chemical mechanisms that enable it to respond to the frequency of its own use. If the terminal is very active, the amount of neurotransmitter made and stored there increases. If the terminal is not often used, however, enzymes located within the terminal may break down excess transmitter. The by-products of this breakdown are then reused or excreted from the neuron. Axon terminals may even send messages to the neuron's cell body requesting increased supplies of the neurotransmitter or the molecules with which to make it.

Varieties of Synapses

So far, we have considered a generic chemical synapse, with features possessed by most synapses. In the nervous system, synapses vary widely, with each type specialized in location, structure, function, and target. **Figure 5-5** illustrates this diversity on a single hypothetical neuron.

You have already encountered two kinds of synapses. One is the *axomuscular synapse,* in which an axon synapses with a muscle end plate, releasing acetylcholine. The other synapse familiar to you is the *axodendritic synapse* detailed in Figure 5-2B, in which the axon terminal of a neuron ends on a dendrite or dendritic spine of another neuron.

Figure 4-27 shows both microscopic and schematic views of an axomuscular synapse.

Figure 5-5 diagrams the axodendritic synapse as well as the *axosomatic synapse,* an axon terminal ending on a cell body; the *axoaxonic synapse,* an axon terminal ending on another axon; and the *axosynaptic synapse,* an axon terminal ending on another presynaptic terminal—that is, at the synapse between some other axon and its target. *Axoextracellular synapses* have no specific targets but instead secrete their transmitter chemicals into the extracellular fluid. In the *axosecretory synapse,* a terminal synapses with a tiny blood vessel called a capillary and secretes its transmitter directly into the blood. Finally, synapses are not limited to axon terminals. Dendrites also may send messages to other dendrites through *dendrodendritic synapses.*

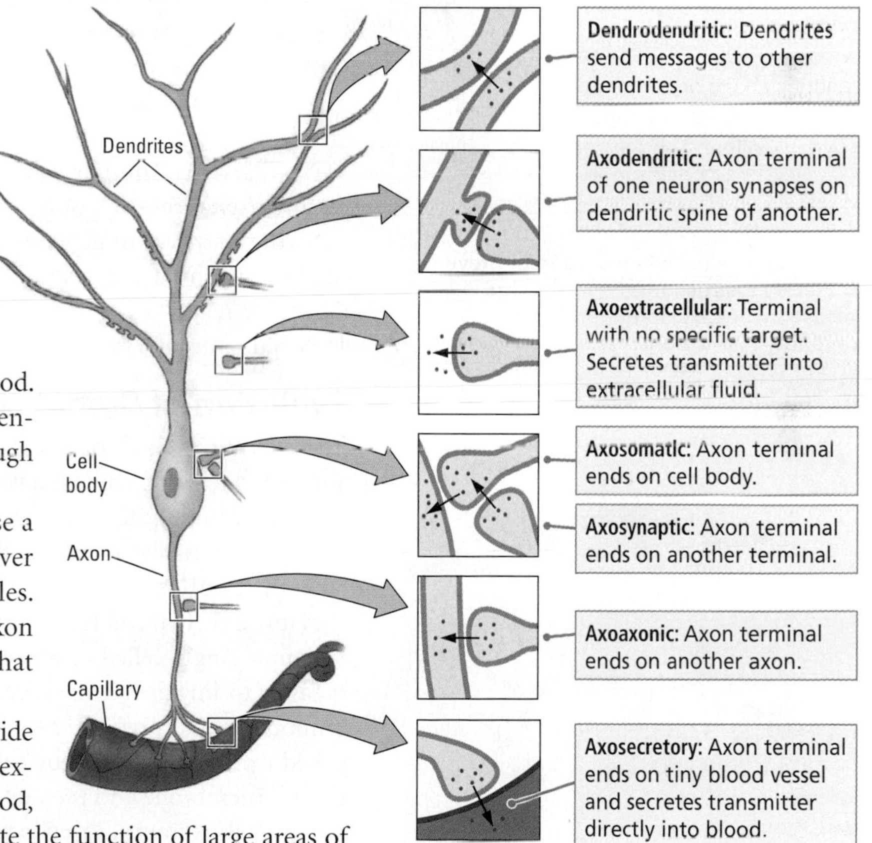

FIGURE 5-5 The Versatile Synapse.

This wide variety of connections makes the synapse a versatile chemical delivery system. Synapses can deliver transmitters to highly specific sites or to diffuse locales. Through connections to the dendrites, cell body, or axon of a neuron, transmitters can control the actions of that neuron in different ways.

Through axosynaptic connections, they can also provide exquisite control over another neuron's input to a cell. By excreting transmitters into extracellular fluid or into the blood, axoextracellular and axosecretory synapses can modulate the function of large areas of tissue or even of the entire body. Recall that many transmitters secreted by neurons act as hormones circulating in your blood, with widespread influences on your body.

Excitatory and Inhibitory Messages

A neurotransmitter can influence the function of a neuron in a remarkable number of ways. In its direct actions in influencing a neuron's electrical excitability, however, a neurotransmitter acts in only one of two ways: either to increase or to decrease the probability that the cell with which it comes in contact will produce an action potential. Thus, despite the wide variety of synapses, they all convey messages of only these two types: excitatory or inhibitory. For simplicity, *Type I synapses* are excitatory in their

Once again we see that the nervous system works through a combination of excitatory and inhibitory signals. Each neuron receives thousands of excitatory and inhibitory signals every second.

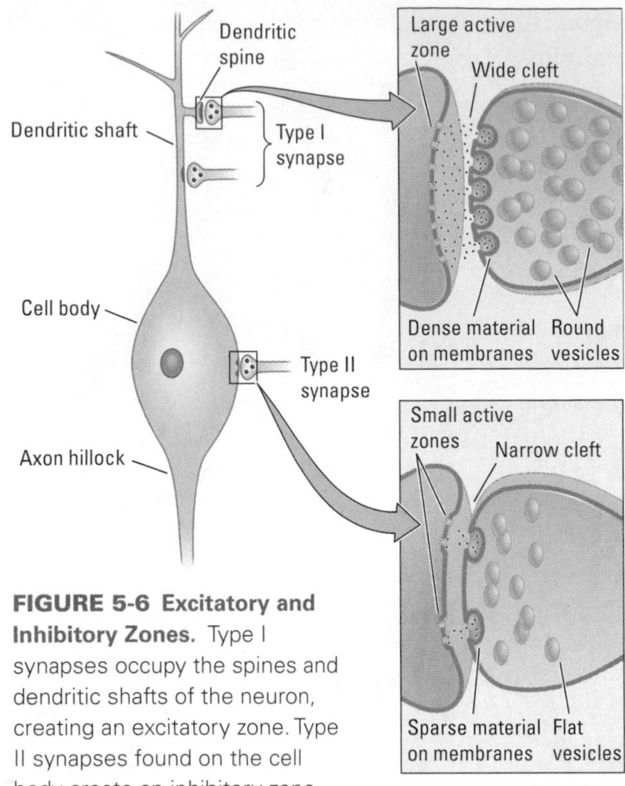

FIGURE 5-6 Excitatory and Inhibitory Zones. Type I synapses occupy the spines and dendritic shafts of the neuron, creating an excitatory zone. Type II synapses found on the cell body create an inhibitory zone.

Behaviors are lost when a disorder prevents excitatory instructions; behaviors are released when a disorder prevents inhibitory instructions.

actions, whereas *Type II synapses* are inhibitory. Each type has a different appearance and is located on different parts of the neurons under its influence.

As shown in **Figure 5-6**, Type I (excitatory) synapses are typically located on the shafts or the spines of dendrites, whereas Type II (inhibitory) synapses are typically located on a cell body. In addition, Type I synapses have round synaptic vesicles, whereas the vesicles of Type II synapses are flattened. The material on the presynaptic and postsynaptic membranes is denser in a Type I synapse than it is in a Type II, and the Type I synaptic cleft is wider. Finally, the active zone on a Type I synapse is larger than that on a Type II synapse.

The different locations of Type I and Type II synapses divide a neuron into two zones: an excitatory dendritic tree and an inhibitory cell body. You can think of excitatory and inhibitory messages as interacting from these two different perspectives.

Viewed from an inhibitory perspective, you can picture excitation coming in over the dendrites and spreading to the axon hillock to trigger an action potential. If the message is to be stopped, it is best stopped by applying inhibition on the cell body, close to the axon hillock where the action potential originates. In this model of excitatory–inhibitory interaction, inhibition blocks excitation by a "cut 'em off at the pass" strategy.

Another way to conceptualize excitatory–inhibitory interaction is to picture excitation overcoming inhibition. If the cell body is normally in an inhibited state, the only way to generate an action potential at the axon hillock is to reduce the cell body's inhibition. In this "open the gates" strategy, the excitatory message is like a racehorse ready to run down the track, but first the inhibitory starting gate must be removed.

Evolution of Complex Neurotransmission Systems

Considering all the biochemical steps required for getting a message across a synapse and the variety of synapses, you may well wonder why—and how—such a complex communication system ever evolved. This arrangement must make up for its complexity in the considerable behavioral flexibility that it affords the nervous system. Flexible behavior is a decided evolutionary advantage.

How did chemical transmitters originate? If you think about the feeding behaviors of simple single-celled creatures, the origin of chemical secretions for communication is easier to imagine. The earliest unicellular creatures secreted juices onto bacteria to immobilize and prepare them for ingestion. These digestive juices were probably expelled from the cell body by exocytosis, in which a vacuole or vesicle attaches itself to the cell membrane and then opens into the extracellular fluid to discharge its contents. The prey thus immobilized is captured through the reverse process of endocytosis.

The mechanism of exocytosis for digestion parallels its use to release a neurotransmitter for communication. Quite possibly the digestive processes of single-celled animals were long ago adapted into processes of neural communication in more-complex organisms.

REVIEW: A Chemical Message

✔ In mammals, the principal form of communication between neurons is chemical. Chemical neurotransmission appears to be an adaptation of processes used by single-celled organisms to immobilize, ingest, and digest food.

✔ Chemical synapses, though slower and more complex than electrical synapses, more than compensate by greatly increasing behavioral flexibility.

✔ When an action potential is propagated on an axon terminal, a chemical transmitter is released from the presynaptic membrane into the synaptic cleft. There the transmitter diffuses across the cleft and binds to receptors on the postsynaptic membrane, after which the transmitter is deactivated.

✔ The nervous system has evolved a variety of synapses, between axon terminals and dendrites, cell bodies, muscles, other axons, and even other synapses. One variety of synapse releases chemical transmitters into extracellular fluid or into the bloodstream as hormones, and still another connects dendrites to other dendrites.

✔ Even though synapses vary in both structure and location, they all do one of only two things: excite their targets (Type I) or inhibit them (Type II).

Varieties of Neurotransmitters

Subsequent to Otto Loewi's discovery, in 1921, that excitatory and inhibitory chemicals control heart rate, many researchers thought that the brain must work under much the same dual-type control. They reasoned that there must be excitatory and inhibitory brain cells and that norepinephrine and acetylcholine were the transmitters through which these neurons worked. They did not imagine what we know today: the human brain employs a large number of neurotransmitters. These chemicals are used in still more versatile ways, as some may be excitatory at one location and inhibitory at another location, and two or more may team up in a single synapse so that one serves to make the other more potent.

Although neuroscientists are now certain of only about 50 substances that act as neurotransmitters, discovery in this field continues. Few scientists are willing to put an upper limit on the eventual number of transmitters that will be found. In this section, you will learn how neurotransmitters are identified and how they fit within three broad categories on the basis of on their chemical structure. The functional aspects of neurotransmitters interrelate and are intricate, with no simple one-to-one relation between a single neurotransmitter and a single behavior.

Four Criteria for Identifying Neurotransmitters

Among the many thousands of chemicals in the nervous system, which of them are neurotransmitters? **Figure 5-7** presents four identifying criteria:

1. The chemical must be synthesized in the neuron or otherwise be present in it.
2. When the neuron is active, the chemical must be released and produce a response in some target.
3. The same response must be obtained when the chemical is experimentally placed on the target.
4. A mechanism must exist for removing the chemical from its site of action after its work is done.

The criteria for identifying a neurotransmitter are fairly easy to apply when examining the somatic nervous system, especially at an accessible nerve–muscle junction with only one main neurotransmitter, acetylcholine. But identifying chemical transmitters in the central nervous system is not so easy. In the brain and spinal cord, thousands of synapses are packed around

FIGURE 5-7 Criteria for Identifying Neurotransmitters.

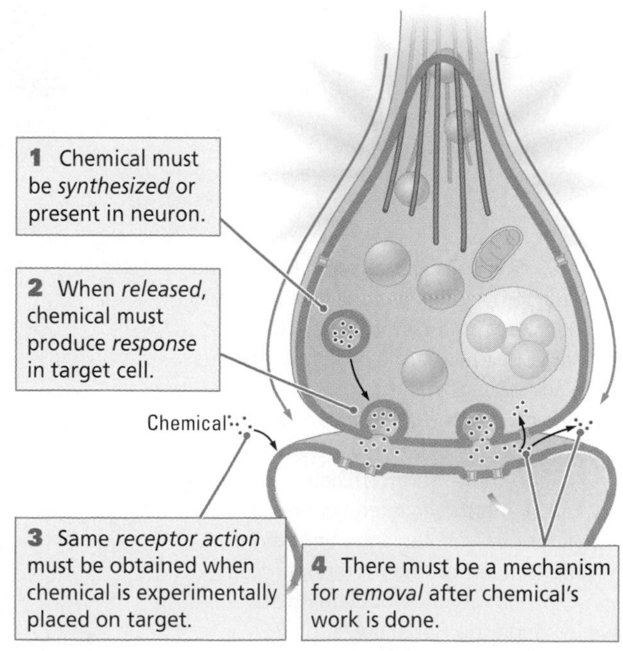
1 Chemical must be *synthesized* or present in neuron.
2 When *released*, chemical must produce *response* in target cell.
Chemical
3 Same *receptor action* must be obtained when chemical is experimentally placed on target.
4 There must be a mechanism for *removal* after chemical's work is done.

every neuron, preventing easy access to a single synapse and its activities. Consequently, a large number of techniques including staining, stimulating, and collecting are used in the search for substances thought to be CNS neurotransmitters. A suspect chemical that has not yet been shown to meet all the criteria is called a *putative* (supposed) *transmitter.*

Researchers trying to identify new CNS neurotransmitters can use microelectrodes to stimulate and record from single neurons. A glass microelectrode is small enough to be placed on specific targets on a neuron. It can be filled with a chemical of interest and, when a current is passed through the electrode, the chemical can be ejected into or onto the neuron to mimic the release of a neurotransmitter onto the cell.

Many staining techniques can identify specific chemicals inside the cell. Methods have also been developed for preserving nervous-system tissue in a saline bath while experiments are performed to determine how the neurons in the tissue communicate. The use of "slices of tissue" simplifies the investigation by allowing the researcher to view a single neuron through a microscope while stimulating it or recording from it.

Brainbow technology, described in Research Focus 3-5, holds promise for aiding in the search for unidentified neurotransmitters.

Acetylcholine was not only the first substance identified as a neurotransmitter but also the first substance identified as a CNS neurotransmitter. A logical argument that predicted its presence even before experimental proof was gathered greatly facilitated the process. As you know, all motor-neuron axons leaving the spinal cord use ACh as a transmitter. Each of these axons has an axon collateral within the spinal cord that synapses on a nearby CNS interneuron. The interneuron, in turn, synapses back on the motor neuron's cell body. This circular set of connections, called a *Renshaw loop* after the researcher who first described it, is shown in **Figure 5-8.**

Because the main axon to the muscle releases acetylcholine, investigators suspected that its axon collateral also might release ACh. For two terminals of the same axon to use different transmitters seemed unlikely. Knowing what chemical to look for made finding and obtaining the required proof that ACh is in fact a neurotransmitter in both locations easier.

The loop made by the axon collateral and the interneuron in the spinal cord forms a feedback circuit that enables the motor neuron to inhibit itself from becoming overexcited if it receives a great many excitatory inputs from other parts of the CNS. Follow the

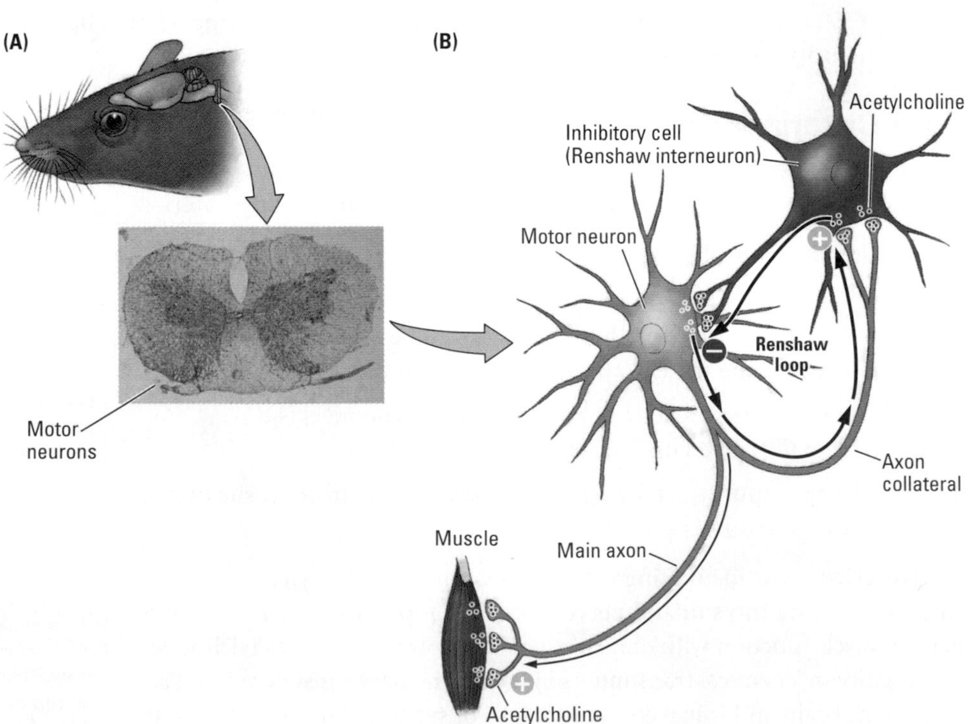

FIGURE 5-8 Renshaw Loop. (A) Location of spinal-cord motor neurons that project to the muscles of the rat's forelimb. (B) Circular connections of a motor neuron in a Renshaw loop: its main axon projects to a muscle and its axon collateral remains in the spinal cord to synapse with a Renshaw interneuron there. The terminals of both the main axon and the collateral contain acetylcholine. The plus and minus signs indicate that, when the motor neuron is highly excited, it can modulate its activity level through the Renshaw loop.

positive and negative signs in Figure 5-8B to see how the Renshaw loop works. If the Renshaw loop is blocked, as can be done with the toxin strychnine, motor neurons become overactive, resulting in convulsions that can choke off respiration and so cause death.

The term "neurotransmitter" is used more broadly now than it was when researchers began to identify these chemicals. The term applies to substances that carry a message from one neuron to another by influencing the voltage on the postsynaptic membrane. And chemicals that have little effect on membrane voltage but rather have a common message-carrying function, such as changing the structure of a synapse, also qualify as neurotransmitters. Furthermore, neurotransmitters can communicate not only by delivering a message from the presynaptic to the postsynaptic membrane but by sending messages in the opposite direction as well. These reverse-direction messages influence the release or reuptake of transmitters.

The definition of what a transmitter is and the criteria used to identify one have become increasingly flexible because neurotransmitters are so diverse and active in such an array of ways. Different kinds of neurotransmitters typically coexist within the same synapse, complicating the question of what exactly each contributes in relaying or modulating a message. To find out, researchers have to apply various transmitter "cocktails" to the postsynaptic membrane. And some transmitters are gases that act so differently from a classic neurotransmitter such as acetylcholine that it is hard to compare the two.

Small-molecule transmitter Belongs to a class of quick-acting neurotransmitters synthesized in the axon terminal from products derived from the diet.

Three Classes of Neurotransmitters

Some order can be imposed on the diversity of neurotransmitters by classifying them into three groups on the basis of their chemical composition: (1) small-molecule transmitters, (2) peptide transmitters, and (3) transmitter gases.

Small-Molecule Transmitters

The first neurotransmitters identified are the quick-acting **small-molecule transmitters** such as acetylcholine. Typically, they are synthesized from dietary nutrients and packaged ready for use in axon terminals. When a small-molecule transmitter has been released from a terminal button, it can be quickly replaced at the presynaptic membrane.

Because small-molecule transmitters or their main components are derived from the food that we eat, their level and activity in the body can be influenced by diet. This fact is important in the design of drugs that act on the nervous system. Many neuroactive drugs are designed to reach the brain by the same route that small-molecule transmitters or their precursor chemicals follow: the digestive tract.

Table 5-1 lists some of the best-known and most extensively studied small-molecule transmitters. In addition to acetylcholine, four amines (related by a chemical structure that contains an amine, or NH, group) and three amino acids are included in this list. A few other substances including histamine also are classified as small-molecule transmitters. In the future, researchers are likely to find more.

TABLE 5-1 Small-Molecule Neurotransmitters

Acetylcholine (ACh)
Histamine (H)
Amines
Dopamine (DA)
Norepinephrine (NE, or noradrenaline, NA)
Epinephrine (EP, or adrenaline)
Serotonin (5-HT)
Amino acids
Glutamate (Glu)
Gamma-aminobutyric acid (GABA)
Glycine (Gly)

Acetylcholine Synthesis Figure 5-9 illustrates how acetylcholine molecules are synthesized and broken down. As you know, ACh is present at the junction of neurons and muscles, including the heart, as well as in the CNS. The molecule is made up of two substances, choline and acetate.

Choline is among the breakdown products of fats in foods such as egg yolk, avocado, salmon, and olive oil; acetate is a compound found in acidic foods, such as vinegar and lemon juice. As depicted in Figure 5-9, inside the cell, acetyl coenzyme A (acetyl CoA) carries acetate to the synthesis site, and the transmitter is synthesized as a second enzyme, choline acetyltransferase (ChAT), transfers the acetate to choline to form ACh. After ACh has been released into the synaptic cleft and diffuses to receptor sites on the postsynaptic membrane, a third enzyme, acetylcholinesterase (AChE), reverses the

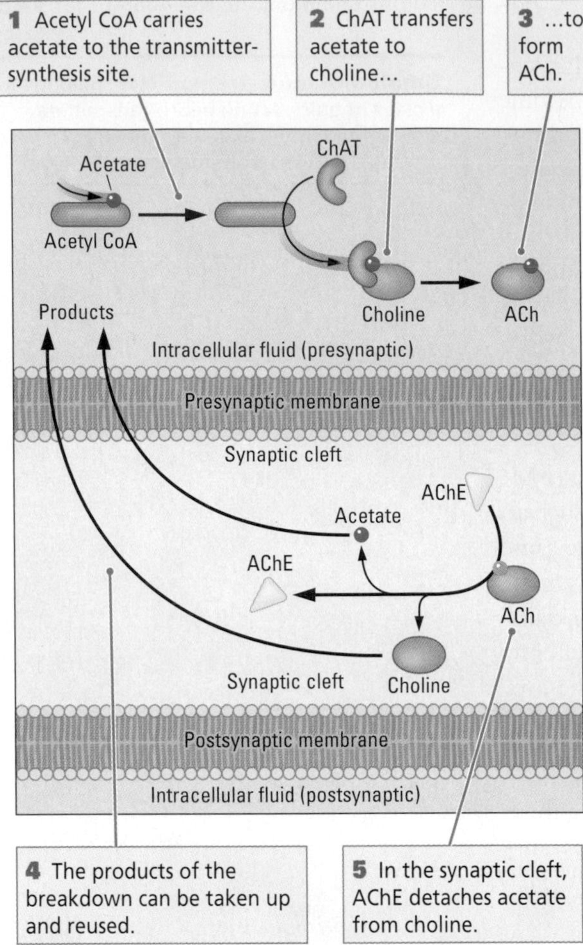

FIGURE 5-9 Chemistry of Acetylcholine. Two enzymes combine the dietary precursors of ACh within the cell, and a third breaks them down in the synapse for reuptake.

process by detaching acetate from choline. These breakdown products can then be taken back into the presynaptic terminal for reuse.

Amine Synthesis Some of the transmitters grouped together in Table 5-1 have common biochemical pathways to synthesis and so are related. You are familiar with the amines dopamine (DA), norepinephrine (NE), and epinephrine (EP). To review, DA loss has a role in Parkinson's disease, EP is the excitatory transmitter at the amphibian heart, and NE is the excitatory transmitter at the mammalian heart.

Figure 5-10 charts the biochemical sequence that synthesizes these amines in succession. The precursor chemical is tyrosine, an amino acid abundant in food. (Hard cheese and bananas are good sources.) The enzyme tyrosine hydroxylase (enzyme 1 in Figure 5-10) changes tyrosine into L-dopa, which is sequentially converted by other enzymes into dopamine, norepinephrine, and, finally, epinephrine.

An interesting fact about this biochemical sequence is that the supply of the enzyme tyrosine hydroxylase is limited. Consequently, so is the rate at which dopamine, norepinephrine, and epinephrine can be produced, regardless of how much tyrosine is present or ingested. This **rate-limiting factor** can be bypassed by the oral administration of L-dopa, which is why L-dopa is a medication used in the treatment of Parkinson's disease, as described in Clinical Focus 5-3, "Awakening with L-Dopa."

The amine transmitter **serotonin** (5-HT, for 5-hydroxytryptamine) is synthesized differently. Serotonin plays a role in regulating mood and aggression, appetite and arousal, respiration, and the perception of pain. Serotonin is derived from the amino acid tryptophan, which is abundant in turkey, milk, and bananas, among other foods.

Amino Acid Synthesis Two amino acid transmitters, **glutamate** (Glu) and **gamma-aminobutyric acid** (GABA), also are closely related. GABA is formed

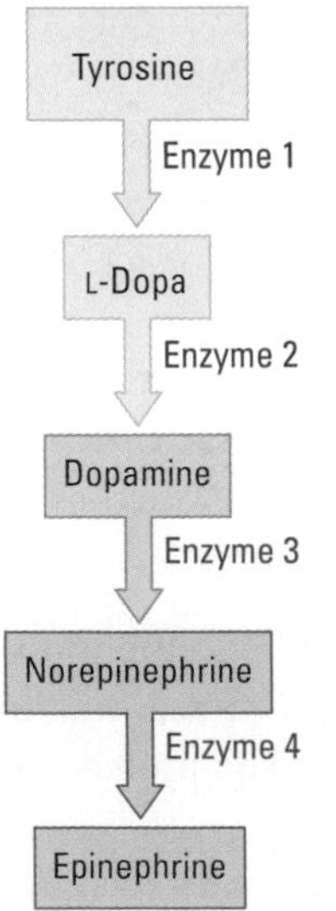

FIGURE 5-10 Sequential Synthesis of Three Amines. A different enzyme is responsible for each successive molecular modification in this biochemical sequence.

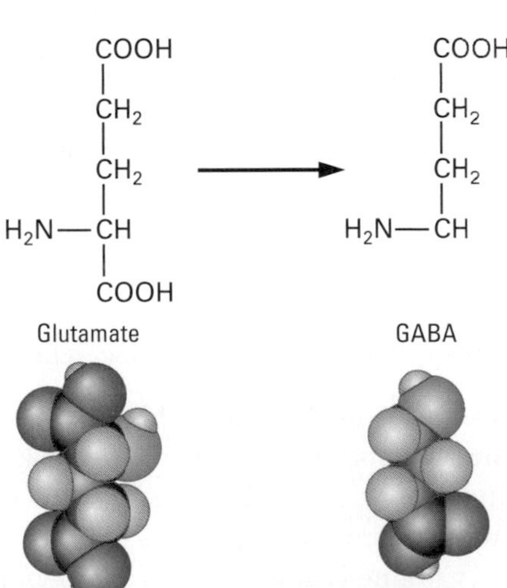

FIGURE 5-11 Amino Acid Transmitters. (*Top*) Removal of a carboxyl (COOH) group from the bottom of the glutamate molecule produces GABA. (*Bottom*) Their different shapes thus allow these amino acid transmitters to bind to different receptors.

by a simple modification of the glutamate molecule, as shown in **Figure 5-11.** These two transmitters are the workhorses of the brain because so many synapses use them.

In the forebrain and cerebellum, glutamate is the main excitatory transmitter and GABA is the main inhibitory transmitter. Type I excitatory synapses thus have glutamate as a neurotransmitter, and Type II inhibitory synapses have GABA as a neurotransmitter. So the appearance of a synapse provides information about the neurotransmitter and its function (review Figure 5-6). Interestingly, glutamate is widely distributed in CNS neurons, but it becomes a neurotransmitter only if it is appropriately packaged in vesicles in the axon terminal. The amino acid transmitter glycine (Gly) is a much more common inhibitory transmitter in the brainstem and spinal cord, where it acts within the Renshaw loop, for example.

Among its many functions, which include the control of arousal and of waking, the transmitter **histamine** (H) can cause the constriction of smooth muscles. When activated in allergic reactions, histamine contributes to asthma, a constriction of the airways. You are probably familiar with antihistamine drugs used to treat allergies.

Rate-limiting factor Any enzyme that is in limited supply, thus restricting the pace at which a chemical can be synthesized.
Serotonin (5-HT) Amine neurotransmitter that plays a role in regulating mood and aggression, appetite and arousal, the perception of pain, and respiration.
Glutamate (Glu) Amino acid neurotransmitter that excites neurons.
Gamma-aminobutyric acid (GABA) Amino acid neurotransmitter that inhibits neurons.
Histamine (H) Neurotransmitter that controls arousal and waking; can cause the constriction of smooth muscles and so, when activated in allergic reactions, contributes to asthma, a constriction of the airways.

CLINICAL FOCUS 5-3

Awakening with L-Dopa

He was started on L-dopa in March 1969. The dose was slowly raised to 4.0 mg a day over a period of three weeks without *apparently* producing any effect. I first discovered that Mr. E. was responding to L-dopa by accident, chancing to go past his room at an unaccustomed time and hearing regular footsteps inside the room. I went in and found Mr. E., who had been chair bound since 1966, walking up and down his room, swinging his arms with considerable vigor, and showing erectness of posture and a brightness of expression completely new to him. When I asked him about the effect, he said with some embarrassment: "Yes! I felt the L-dopa beginning to work three days ago—it was like a wave of energy and strength sweeping through me. I found I could stand and walk by myself, and that I could do everything I needed for myself—but I was afraid that you would see how well I was and discharge me from the hospital." (Sacks, 1976)

Everett Collection

The movie *Awakenings* recounts the L-dopa trials conducted by Oliver Sacks and described in his book of the same title.

In this case history, neurologist Oliver Sacks describes administering L-dopa to a patient who acquired Parkinsonism as an aftereffect of severe influenza in the 1920s. The relation between the influenza and the symptoms of Parkinson's disease suggests that the flu virus entered the brain and selectively attacked dopamine neurons in the substantia nigra. L-Dopa, by increasing the amount of DA in remaining synapses, relieved the patient's symptoms.

Two separate groups of investigators had quite independently given L-dopa to Parkinson patients beginning in 1961 (Birkmayer and Hornykiewicz, 1961; Barbeau et al., 1961). Both research teams knew that the chemical is catalyzed into dopamine at DA synapses (see Figure 5-10). The L-dopa turned out to reduce the muscular rigidity that the patients suffered.

This work was the first demonstration that a neurological condition can be relieved by a drug that aids in replacing a neurotransmitter. L-Dopa has since become a standard treatment for Parkinson's disease. Its effects have been improved by the administration of drugs that prevent L-dopa from being broken down before it gets to dopamine neurons in the brain.

L-Dopa is not a cure. Parkinson's disease still progresses during treatment and, as more and more dopamine synapses are lost, the treatment becomes less and less effective. Eventually, L-dopa begins to produce *dyskinesias*—involuntary, unwanted movements, such as tremors. When these side effects eventually become severe, the treatment must be discontinued.

TABLE 5-2 Peptide Neurotransmitters

Family	Example
Opioids	Enkephaline, dynorphin
Neurohypophyseals	Vasopressin, oxytocin
Secretins	Gastric inhibitory peptide, growth-hormone-releasing peptide
Insulins	Insulin, insulin growth factors
Gastrins	Gastrin, cholecystokinin
Somatostatins	Pancreatic polypeptides
Corticosteroids	Glucocorticoids, mineralocorticoids

Peptide Transmitters

Peptides are proteins (molecular chains of amino acids) connected by peptide bonds, which accounts for the name (see Figure 3-15).

More than 50 amino acid chains of various lengths form the families of the peptide transmitters listed in **Table 5-2. Neuropeptides,** synthesized through the translation of mRNA from instructions contained in the neuron's DNA, are multifunctional chains of amino acids that act as neurotransmitters.

In some neurons, peptide transmitters are made in the axon terminal, but most are assembled on the neuron's ribosomes, packaged in a membrane by Golgi bodies, and transported by the microtubules to the axon terminals. The entire process of neuropeptide synthesis and transport is relatively slow compared with the nearly ready-made formation of small-molecule neurotransmitters. Consequently, peptide transmitters act slowly and are not replaced quickly.

Neuropeptides have an enormous range of functions in the nervous system, as might be expected from the large number that exist there. They act as hormones that respond to stress, allow a mother to bond to her infant, regulate eating and drinking and pleasure and pain, and probably contribute to learning. Opium and related synthetic chemicals such as morphine, long known to produce both euphoria and pain reduction, appear to mimic the actions of three natural brain neurotransmitter peptides: met-enkephalin, leu-enkephalin, and beta-endorphin. (The term *enkephalin* derives from the phrase "in the cephalon," meaning "in the brain or head," whereas the term *endorphin* is a shortened form of "endogenous morphine.")

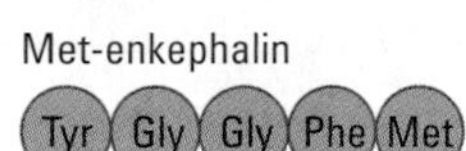

FIGURE 5-12 Opioid Peptides. Parts of the amino acid chains of some neuropeptides that act on brain centers for pleasure and pain are similar in structure and are similar to drugs such as opium and morphine, which mimic their functions.

A part of the amino acid chain in each of these three peptide transmitters is structurally similar to the others, as illustrated for two of these peptides in **Figure 5-12.** Presumably, opium mimics this part of the chain. The discovery of naturally occurring opium-like peptides suggested that one or more of them might take part in the management of pain. Opioid peptides, however, appear in a number of locations and perform a variety of functions in the brain, including the inducement of nausea. Therefore opium-like drugs are still preferred for pain management.

Some CNS peptides take part in specific periodic behaviors, each month or each year perhaps. For instance, neuropeptide transmitters act as hormones specifically to prepare female white-tail deer for the fall mating season (luteinizing hormone). Come winter, a different set of biochemicals facilitates the development of the deer fetus. The mother gives birth in the spring, and yet another set of highly specific neuropeptide hormones such as oxytocin, which enables her to recognize her own fawn, and prolactin, which enables her to nurse, takes control.

The same neuropeptides serve similar, specific hormonal functions in humans. Others, such as neuropeptide growth hormones, have much more general functions in regulating growth. And neuropeptide corticosteroids mediate general responses to stress.

Chapter 8 explains the major ways that drugs are administered, how they reach the CNS, and how the body eliminates them.

Unlike small-molecule transmitters, neuropeptides do not bind to ion channels, and so they have no direct effects on the voltage of the postsynaptic membrane. Instead, peptide transmitters activate synaptic receptors that indirectly influence cell structure and function. Because peptides are amino acid chains that are degraded by digestive processes, they generally cannot be taken orally as drugs, as the small-molecule transmitters can.

Transmitter Gases

The gases **nitric oxide** (NO) and **carbon monoxide** (CO) are the most unusual neurotransmitters yet identified. As water-soluble gases, they are neither stored in synaptic vesicles nor released from them; instead, they are synthesized in the cell as needed. After synthesis, each gas diffuses away, easily crossing the cell membrane and immediately becoming active. Both NO and CO activate metabolic (energy-expending) processes in cells, including those modulating the production of other neurotransmitters.

Nitric oxide, for example, serves as a chemical messenger in many parts of the body. It controls the muscles in intestinal walls, and it dilates blood vessels in brain regions that are in active use, allowing these regions to receive more blood. Because it also dilates blood vessels in the sexual organs, NO is active in producing penile erections. Viagra, a drug used to treat erectile dysfunction in men, acts by enhancing the chemical pathways that make NO. Note that NO does not of itself produce sexual arousal.

Neuropeptide Multifunctional chain of amino acids that acts as a neurotransmitter; synthesized from mRNA on instructions from the cell's DNA; peptide neurotransmitters can act as a hormones and may contribute to learning.

Nitric oxide (NO) Acts as a chemical neurotransmitter gas—for example, to dilate blood vessels, aid digestion, and activate cellular metabolism.

Carbon monoxide (CO) Acts as a neurotransmitter gas in the activation of cellular metabolism.

Ionotropic receptor Embedded membrane protein with two parts: a binding site for a neurotransmitter and a pore that regulates ion flow to directly and rapidly change membrane voltage.

Metabotropic receptor Embedded membrane protein, with a binding site for a neurotransmitter but no pore, linked to a G protein that can affect other receptors or act with second messengers to affect other cellular processes.

G protein Belongs to a family of guanyl-nucleotide-binding proteins coupled to metabotropic receptors that, when activated, bind to other proteins.

Two Classes of Receptors

When a neurotransmitter is released from a synapse, it crosses the synaptic cleft and binds to a receptor. What happens next depends on the receptor type. Each of the two general classes of receptor proteins has a different effect. One directly changes the electrical potential of the postsynaptic membrane, whereas the other induces cellular change indirectly.

Ionotropic receptors allow the movement of ions such as Na^+, K^+, and Ca^{2+}, across a membrane (the suffix *tropic* means "to move toward"). As **Figure 5-13** illustrates, an ionotropic receptor has two parts: (1) a binding site for a neurotransmitter and (2) a pore or channel. When the neurotransmitter attaches to the binding site, the receptor changes shape, either opening the pore and allowing ions to flow through it or closing the pore and blocking the flow of ions. Because the binding of the transmitter to the receptor is quickly followed by the opening or closing of the receptor pore that affects the flow of ions, ionotropic receptors bring about very rapid changes in membrane voltage. Ionotropic receptors are usually excitatory in that they trigger an action potential.

Structurally, ionotropic receptors are similar to the voltage-sensitive channels that propagate the action potential, discussed in Chapter 4.

In contrast, a **metabotropic receptor** has a binding site for a neurotransmitter but lacks its own pore through which ions can flow. Through a series of steps, activated metabotropic receptors indirectly produce changes in nearby ion channels or in the cell's metabolic activity.

Figure 5-14A shows the first of these two indirect effects. The metabotropic receptor consists of a single protein that spans the cell membrane, its binding site facing the synaptic cleft. Receptor proteins are each coupled to one of a family of guanyl-nucleotide-binding proteins, **G proteins** for short, shown on the inner side of the cell membrane in Figure 5-14A.

A G protein consists of three subunits: alpha, beta, and gamma. The alpha subunit detaches when a neurotransmitter binds to the G protein's associated metabotropic receptor. The detached alpha subunit can then bind to other proteins within the cell membrane or within the cytoplasm of the cell.

If the alpha subunit binds to a nearby ion channel in the membrane as shown at the bottom of Figure 5-14A, the structure of the channel changes, modifying the flow of ions through it. If the channel is open, it may be closed by the alpha subunit or, if closed, it may open. Changes in the channel and the flow of ions across the membrane influence the membrane's electrical potential.

FIGURE 5-13 Ionotropic Receptor. When activated, these embedded proteins bring about direct, rapid changes in membrane voltage.

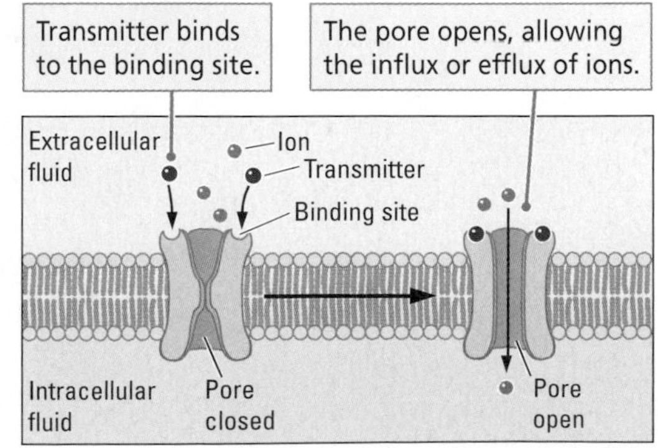
Transmitter binds to the binding site.
The pore opens, allowing the influx or efflux of ions.
Extracellular fluid
Ion
Transmitter
Binding site
Intracellular fluid
Pore closed
Pore open

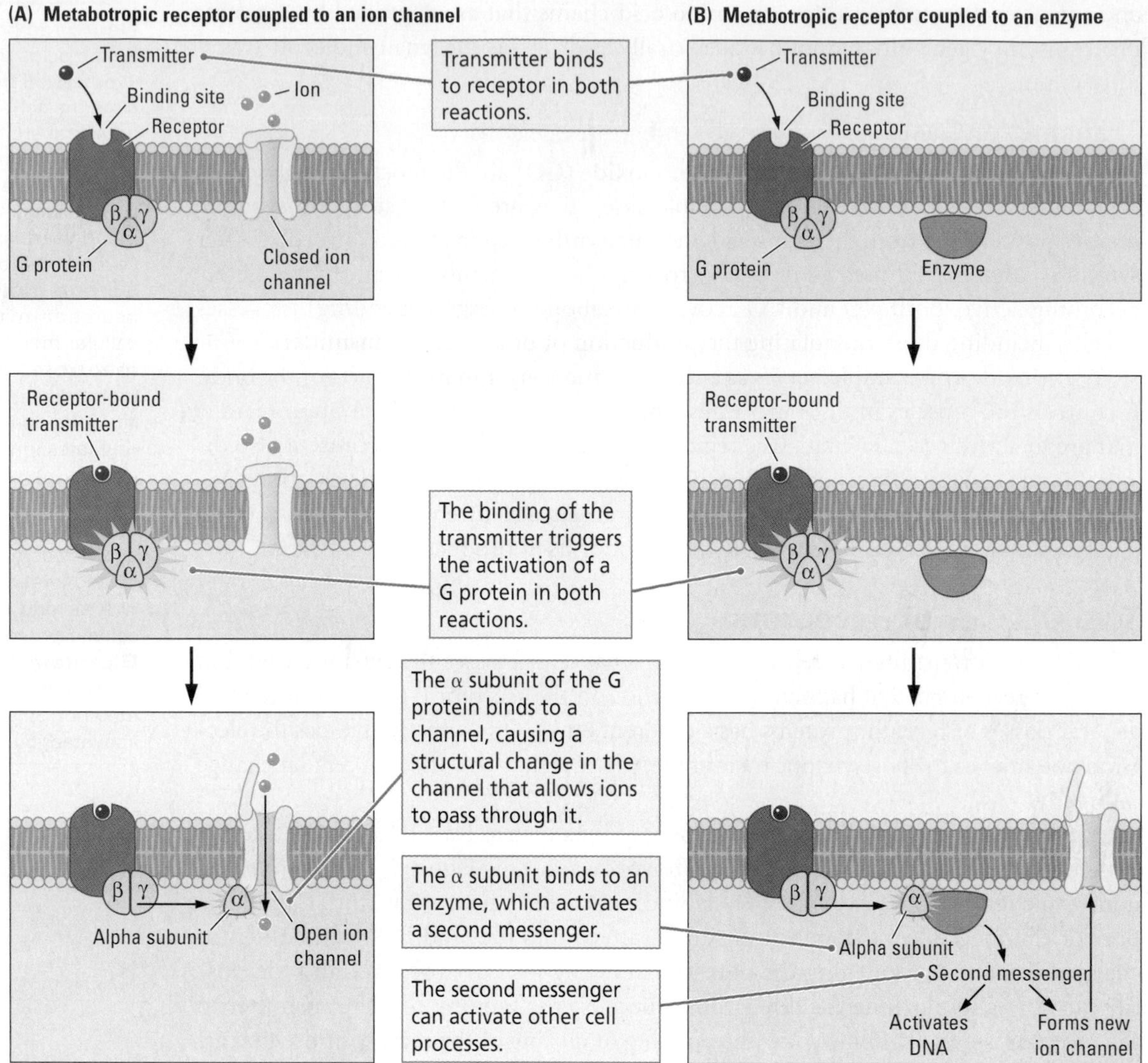
(A) Metabotropic receptor coupled to an ion channel
(B) Metabotropic receptor coupled to an enzyme
Transmitter
Binding site
Ion
Receptor
G protein
Closed ion channel
Transmitter binds to receptor in both reactions.
Transmitter
Binding site
Receptor
G protein
Enzyme
Receptor-bound transmitter
Receptor-bound transmitter
The binding of the transmitter triggers the activation of a G protein in both reactions.
The α subunit of the G protein binds to a channel, causing a structural change in the channel that allows ions to pass through it.
Alpha subunit
Open ion channel
The α subunit binds to an enzyme, which activates a second messenger.
The second messenger can activate other cell processes.
Alpha subunit
Second messenger
Activates DNA
Forms new ion channel

FIGURE 5-14 Metabotropic Receptors. When activated, these embedded membrane proteins trigger associated G proteins, thereby exerting indirect effects (A) on nearby ion channels or (B) in the cell's metabolic activity.

The binding of a neurotransmitter to a metabotropic receptor can also trigger more-complicated cellular reactions, summarized in Figure 5-14B. All these reactions begin when the detached alpha subunit binds to an enzyme. The enzyme in turn activates a **second messenger** (the neurotransmitter is the first messenger) that carries instructions to other structures inside the cell. As illustrated in at the bottom of Figure 5-14B, the second messenger can

- bind to a membrane channel, causing the channel to change its structure and thus alter ion flow through the membrane;
- initiate a reaction that causes protein molecules within the cell to become incorporated into the cell membrane, for example, resulting in the formation of new ion channels; or
- instruct the cell's DNA to initiate the production of a new protein.

In addition, metabotropic receptors allow for the possibility that a single neurotransmitter's binding to a receptor can activate an escalating sequence of events called an *amplification cascade.* The cascade effect causes many downstream proteins (second messengers or channels or both) to be activated or deactivated. Ionotropic receptors do not have such a widespread "amplifying" effect.

No one neurotransmitter is associated with a single receptor type or a single influence on the postsynaptic cell. Typically, a transmitter may bind either to an ionotropic receptor and have an excitatory effect on the target cell or to a metabotropic receptor and have an inhibitory effect.

Recall that acetylcholine has an excitatory effect on skeletal muscles. Here it activates an ionotropic receptor. You know that ACh has an inhibitory effect on the heart rate. Here it activates a metabotropic receptor. In addition, each transmitter may bind with several different kinds of ionotropic or metabotropic receptors. Elsewhere in the nervous system, for example, acetylcholine may activate a wide variety of either receptor type.

REVIEW: Varieties of Neurotransmitters

- ✔ Neurotransmitters are identified using four experimental criteria: synthesis, release, receptor action, and inactivation.
- ✔ The three broad classes of chemically related neurotransmitters are small-molecule transmitters, peptide transmitters, and transmitter gases. All three classes, encompassing the approximately 100 likely neurotransmitters active in the nervous system, are associated with both ionotropic and metabotropic receptors.
- ✔ An ionotropic receptor contains a pore or channel that can be opened or closed to regulate the flow of ions through it, which, in turn, directly brings about rapid and usually excitatory voltage changes on the cell membrane.
- ✔ Metabotropic receptors are generally inhibitory, are slow acting, and activate second messengers to indirectly produce changes in the function and structure of the cell.

Neurotransmitter Systems and Behavior

When researchers began to study neurotransmission, you'll recall, they reasoned that any given neuron would contain only one transmitter at all its axon terminals. New methods of staining neurochemicals, however, reveal that this hypothesis is a simplification.

A single neuron may use one transmitter at one synapse and a different transmitter at another synapse. Moreover, different transmitters may coexist in the same terminal or synapse. Neuropeptides have been found to coexist in terminals with small-molecule transmitters, and more than one small-molecule transmitter may be found in a single synapse. In some cases, more than one transmitter may even be packaged within a single vesicle.

All such findings allow for a number of combinations of neurotransmitters and receptors for them. They caution as well against the assumption of a simple cause-and-effect relation between a neurotransmitter and a behavior. What are the functions of so many combinations? The answer will likely vary, depending on the behavior that is controlled. Fortunately, neurotransmission can be simplified by concentrating on the dominant transmitter located within any given axon terminal. The neuron and its dominant transmitter can then be related to a function or behavior.

We now consider some of the links between neurotransmitters and behavior. We begin by exploring the two parts of the peripheral nervous system: somatic and autonomic. Then we investigate neurotransmission in the central nervous system.

Neurotransmission in the Somatic Nervous System

Motor neurons in the brain and spinal cord send their axons to the body's skeletal muscles, including the muscles of the eyes and face, trunk, limbs, fingers, and toes. Without these SNS (somatic nervous system) neurons, movement would not be possible.

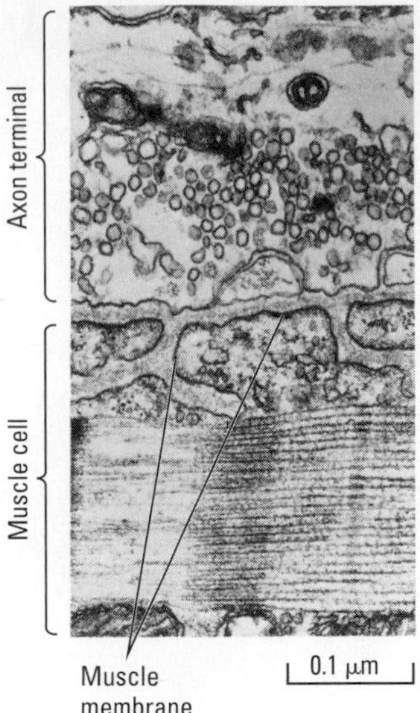

Nicotinic acetylcholine receptor. From J. E. Heuser and T. Reese, 1977, in *The Nervous System,* Vol. 1, *Handbook of Physiology,* edited by E. R. Kandel, Oxford University Press, p. 266.

Motor neurons are also called **cholinergic neurons** because acetylcholine is their main neurotransmitter. At a skeletal muscle, cholinergic neurons are excitatory and produce muscular contractions.

Just as a single main neurotransmitter serves the SNS, so does a single main receptor, an ionotropic, transmitter-activated channel called a *nicotinic ACh receptor* (nAChr). When ACh binds to this receptor, its pore opens to permit ion flow, thus depolarizing the muscle fiber. The pore of a nicotinic receptor is large and permits the simultaneous efflux of K^+ and influx of Na^+. The molecular structure of nicotine, a chemical found in tobacco, activates the nAChr in the same way that ACh does, which is how this receptor got its name. The molecular structure of nicotine is sufficiently similar to ACh that nicotine acts as a mimic, fitting into acetylcholine-receptor binding sites.

Although acetylcholine is the primary neurotransmitter at skeletal muscles, other neurotransmitters also are found in these cholinergic axon terminals and are released onto the muscle along with ACh. One of these neurotransmitters is a neuropeptide called calcitonin-gene-related peptide (CGRP) that acts through CGRP metabotrophic receptors to increase the force with which a muscle contracts.

Two Activating Systems of the Autonomic Nervous System

To review the divisions of the autonomic nervous system in detail, see Figure 2-28.

The complementary divisions of the autonomic nervous system (ANS), sympathetic and parasympathetic, regulate the body's internal environment. The sympathetic division rouses the body for action, producing the fight-or-flight response. Heart rate is turned up, digestive functions are turned down. The parasympathetic division calms the body down, producing an essentially opposite rest-and-digest response. Digestive functions are turned up, heart rate is turned down, and the body is made ready to relax.

Figure 5-15 shows the neurochemical organization of the ANS. Both ANS divisions are controlled by acetylcholine neurons that emanate from the CNS at two levels of the spinal cord. The CNS neurons synapse with parasympathetic neurons that also con-

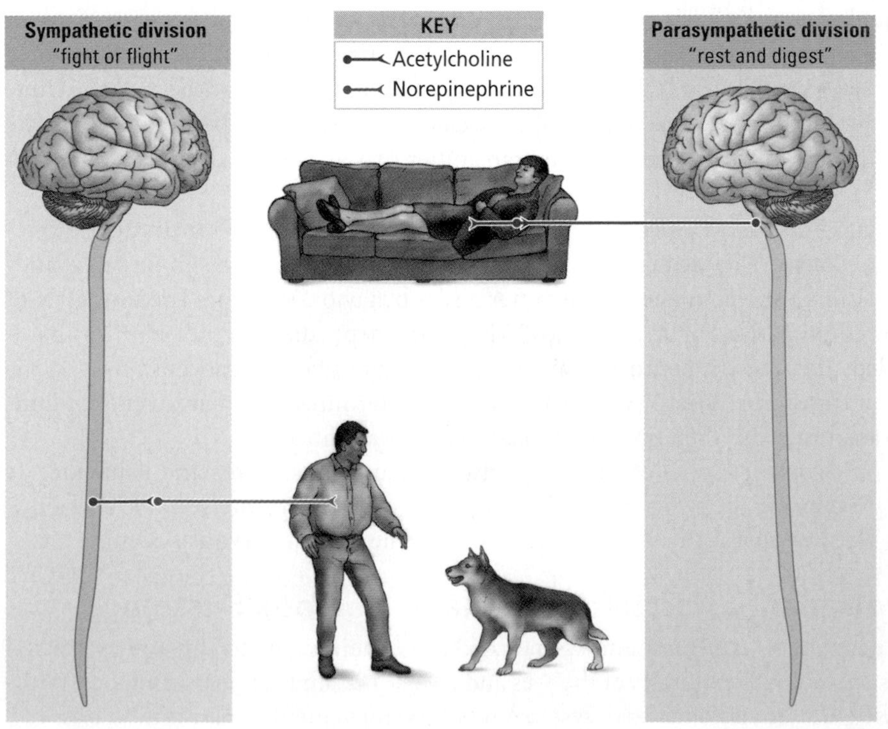

FIGURE 5-15 Controlling Biological Functions in the Autonomic Nervous System. All the neurons leaving the spinal cord have acetylcholine as a neurotransmitter. (*Left*) In the sympathetic division, these ACh neurons activate autonomic norepinephrine neurons, which stimulate organs required for fight or flight and suppress the activity of organs used to rest and digest. (*Right*) In the parasympathetic division, ACh neurons from the spinal cord activate ACh neurons in the ANS, which suppress activity in organs used for fight or flight and stimulate organs used to rest and digest.

tain acetylcholine and with sympathetic neurons that contain norepinephrine. In other words, ACh neurons in the CNS synapse with sympathetic NE neurons to prepare the body's organs for fight or flight. Cholinergic (ACh) neurons in the CNS synapse with autonomic ACh neurons in the parasympathetic division to prepare the body's organs to rest and digest.

Whether acetylcholine synapses or norepinephrine synapses are excitatory or inhibitory on a particular body organ depends on that organ's receptors. During sympathetic arousal, norepinephrine turns up heart rate and turns down digestive functions because NE receptors on the heart are excitatory, whereas NE receptors on the gut are inhibitory. Similarly, acetylcholine turns down heart rate and turns up digestive functions because its receptors on these organs are different. Acetylcholine receptors on the heart are inhibitory, whereas those on the gut are excitatory. The activity of neurotransmitters, excitatory in one location and inhibitory in another, allows the sympathetic and parasympathetic divisions to form a complementary autonomic regulating system that maintains the body's internal environment under differing circumstances.

Second messenger Chemical that carries a message to initiate a biochemical process when activated by a neurotransmitter (the first messenger).
Cholinergic neuron Neuron that uses acetylcholine as its main neurotransmitter. The term *cholinergic* applies to any neuron that uses ACh as its main transmitter.
Activating system Neural pathways that coordinate brain activity through a single neurotransmitter; cell bodies are located in a nucleus in the brainstem and axons are distributed through a wide region of the brain.

Four Activating Systems in the Central Nervous System

Figure 5-16 shows a cross section of a rat brain stained for the enzyme acetylcholinesterase, which breaks ACh down in synapses, as diagrammed earlier in Figure 5-9. The darkly stained areas have high AChE concentrations, indicating the presence of cholinergic terminals. Note that AChE is located throughout the cortex and is especially dense in the basal ganglia. Some AChE terminals belong to neurons that are local. Others come from more-distant cells. Some of these distant neurons are organized in discrete clusters, or nuclei, that distribute their axons and synapses widely in the brain.

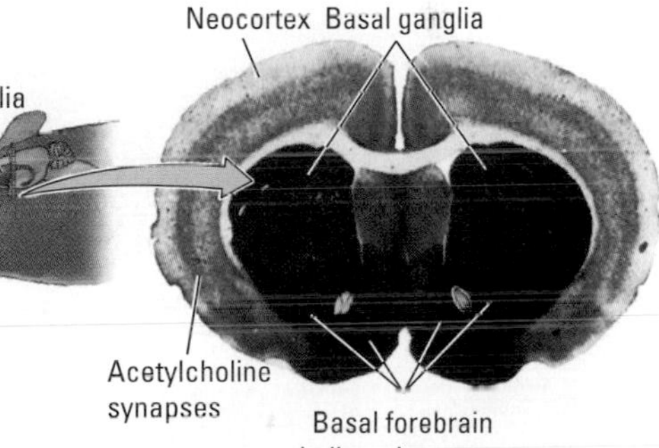

FIGURE 5-16 Cholinergic Activation. The drawing shows the location of the micrograph stained to reveal the enzyme AChE. Cholinergic neurons of the basal forebrain project to the neocortex, and the darkly stained bands in the cortex show areas rich in cholinergic synapses. The darker central parts of the section, also rich in cholinergic neurons, are the basal ganglia.

This anatomical organization, in which a few neurons send axons to widespread brain regions, suggests that these neurons play a role in synchronizing activity throughout the brain. Such a neurochemical organization is referred to as an **activating system.** You can envision an activating system as analogous to the power supply to a house. The fuse box is the source of the house's power and, from it, lines goes to each room.

Just as in the ANS, the precise action of the transmitter depends on the region of the brain that is innervated and on the types of receptors on which the transmitter acts at that region. To continue our analogy, precisely what the activating effect of the power is in each room depends on the electrical devices in the room.

Each of four small-molecule transmitters participates in its own neural activating system—the cholinergic, dopaminergic, noradrenergic, and serotonergic systems. The activating systems are similarly organized in that the cell bodies of their neurons are clustered together in only a few nuclei in the brainstem, whereas the axons are widely distributed in the forebrain, brainstem, and spinal cord. **Figure 5-17** maps the location of each system's nuclei, with arrow shafts mapping the pathways of axons and arrowheads indicating axon-terminal locales.

As summarized on the right in Figure 5-17, each activating system is associated with a number of behaviors. With the exception of dopamine's clear link to Parkinson's disease, however, associations among activating systems, behavior, and brain disorders are far less certain. All these relations are subjects of extensive, ongoing research.

The difficulty in making definitive correlations between activating systems and behavior or activating systems and a disorder is that the axons of these systems connect to almost every part of the brain. They likely have both specific functions and modulatory roles. We will detail some of the documented relations between the systems and behavior and disorders here and in many subsequent chapters.

FIGURE 5-17 Major Activating Systems. Each system's cell bodies are gathered into nuclei (shown as ovals) in the brainstem. The axons project diffusely through the brain and synapse on target structures. Each activating system is associated with one or more behaviors or diseases.

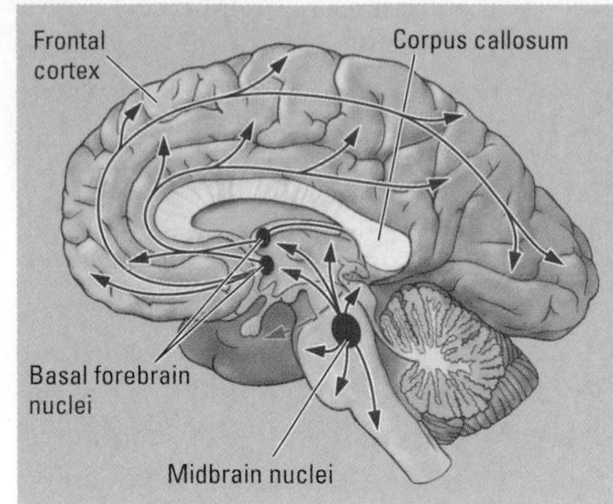

Cholinergic system
(acetylcholine):

- Active in maintaining waking electroencephalographic pattern of the cortex.
- Thought to play a role in memory by maintaining neuron excitability.
- Death of cholinergic neurons and decrease in ACh in the neocortex are thought to be related Alzheimer's disease

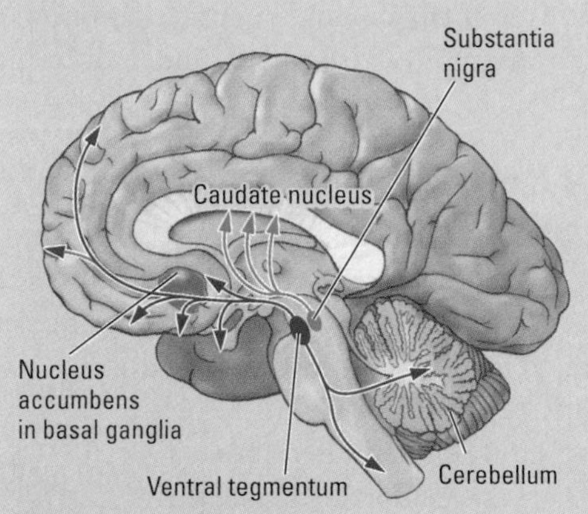

Dopaminergic system
(dopamine):

Nigrostriatial pathways (orange projections)

- Active in maintaining normal motor behavior
- Loss of DA is related to muscle rigidity and dyskinesia in Parkinson's disease

Mesolimbic pathways (purple projections)

- Dopamine release causes feelings of reward and pleasure
- Thought to be the neurotransmitter system most affected by addictive drugs
- Increases in DA activity may be related to schizophrenia

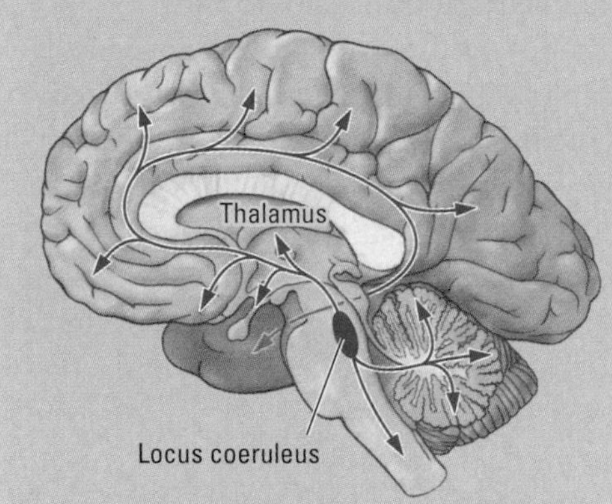

Noradrenergic system
(norepinephrine):

- Active in maintaining emotional tone
- Decreases in NE activity are thought to be related to depression
- Increases in NE are thought to be related to mania (overexcited behavior)

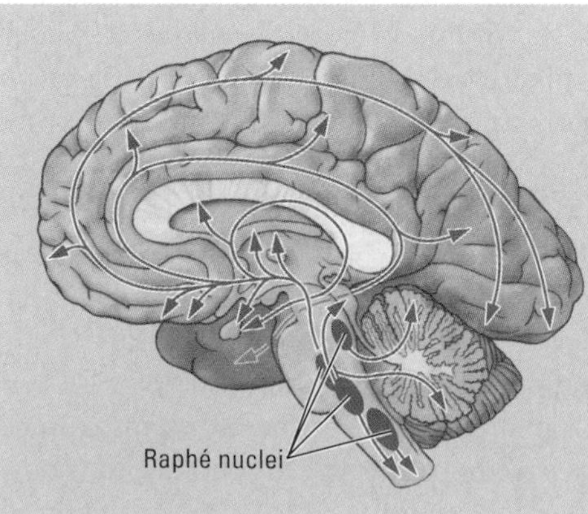

Serotonergic system
(serotonin):

- Active in maintaining waking electroencephalographic pattern
- Changes in serotonin activity are related to obsessive–compulsive disorder, tics, and schizophrenia
- Decreases in serotonin activity are related to depression
- Abnormalities in brainstem 5-HT neurons are linked to disorders such as sleep apnea and SIDS

Alzheimer's disease Degenerative brain disorder related to aging that first appears as progressive memory loss and later develops into generalized dementia.
Schizophrenia Behavioral disorder characterized by delusions, hallucinations, disorganized speech, blunted emotion, agitation or immobility, and a host of associated symptoms.
Noradrenergic neuron From *adrenaline,* Latin for epinephrine; a neuron containing norepinephrine.
Major depression Mood disorder characterized by prolonged feelings of worthlessness and guilt, the disruption of normal eating habits, sleep disturbances, a general slowing of behavior, and frequent thoughts of suicide.
Mania Disordered mental state of extreme excitement.

Cholinergic System

The cholinergic system plays a role in normal waking behavior and is thought to function in attention and in memory. For example, cholinergic neurons take part in producing one form of waking EEG activity. People who suffer from the degenerative **Alzheimer's disease,** which begins with minor forgetfulness, progresses to major memory dysfunction, and later develops into generalized dementia, show a loss of cholinergic neurons at autopsy. One treatment strategy currently being pursued for Alzheimer's is to develop drugs, such as donepezil (Aricept), that stimulate the cholinergic system to enhance alertness. But the beneficial effects of these drugs are not dramatic. Recall that ACh is synthesized from nutrients in food; thus, the role of diet in maintaining ACh levels also is being investigated.

The current state of research on Alzheimer's disease and treatment for it is detailed in Chapters 14 and 16.

The brain abnormalities associated with Alzheimer's disease are not limited to the cholinergic neurons, however. Autopsies reveal extensive damage to the neocortex and other brain regions. As a result, what role the cholinergic neurons play in the progress of the disorder is not yet clear. Perhaps their destruction causes degeneration in the cortex or perhaps the cause-and-effect relation is the other way around, with cortical degeneration causing cholinergic cell death. Then, too, the loss of cholinergic neurons may be just one of many neural symptoms of Alzheimer's disease.

Dopaminergic System

Note in Figure 5-17 that the dopaminergic activating system operates in two distinct pathways. The *nigrostriatial dopaminergic system* plays a role in coordinating movement. As described throughout this chapter in relation to Parkinsonism, when DA neurons in the substantia nigra are lost, the result is a condition of extreme rigidity. Opposing muscles contract at the same time, making it difficult for an affected person to move.

Parkinson patients also exhibit rhythmic tremors, especially of the limbs, which signals a release of formerly inhibited movement. Although Parkinson's disease usually arises for no known cause, it can actually be triggered by the ingestion of certain "toxic" drugs, as described in Clinical Focus 5-4, "The Case of the Frozen Addict." Those drugs may act as selective neurotoxins that kill dopamine neurons.

Dopamine in the *mesolimbic dopaminergic system* may be the neurotransmitter most affected by addictive drugs. Many drugs that people abuse act by stimulating the mesolimbic part of the system, where dopamine release triggers feelings of reward or pleasure. Excessive mesolimbic DA activity has a role in **schizophrenia,** a behavioral disorder characterized by delusions, hallucinations, disorganized speech, blunted emotion, agitation or immobility, and a host of associated symptoms. Schizophrenia is one of the most common and debilitating psychiatric disorders, affecting 1 in 100 people.

Drug effects on the mesolimbic dopaminergic system are described in Chapters 8 and 12. We examine schizophrenia's possible causes in Chapter 8 and its neurobiology in Chapter 16.

Noradrenergic System

The term **noradrenergic** is derived from *adrenaline,* the Latin name for epinephrine. Norepinephrine (noradrenalin) may play a role in learning by stimulating neurons to change their structure. It may also facilitate normal development of the brain and play a role in organizing movements.

In the main, behaviors and disorders related to the noradrenergic system concern the emotions. Some symptoms of **major depression**—a mood disorder characterized by prolonged feelings of worthlessness and guilt, the disruption of normal eating habits, sleep disturbances, a general slowing of behavior, and frequent thoughts of suicide—may be related to decreases in the activity of noradrenergic neurons. Conversely, some symptoms of **mania** (excessive excitability) may be related to increases in the activity of these same neurons.

CLINICAL FOCUS 5-4

The Case of the Frozen Addict

> Patient 1: During the first 4 days of July 1982, a 42-year-old man used 4? grams of a "new synthetic heroin." The substance was injected intravenously three or four times daily and caused a burning sensation at the site of injection. The immediate effects were different from heroin, producing an unusual "spacey" high as well as transient visual distortions and hallucinations. Two days after the final injection, he awoke to find that he was "frozen" and could move only in "slow motion." He had to "think through each movement" to carry it out. He was described as stiff, slow, nearly mute, and catatonic during repeated emergency room visits from July 9 to July 11. He was admitted to a psychiatric service on July 15, 1982, with a diagnosis of "catatonic schizophrenia" and was transferred to our neurobehavioral unit the next day. (Ballard et al., 1985, p. 949)

Patient 1 was one of seven young adults hospitalized at about the same time in California. All showed symptoms of severe Parkinson's disease that appeared very suddenly after drug injection. These symptoms are extremely unusual in this age group. All those affected reportedly injected a synthetic heroin that was being sold on the streets in the summer of 1982.

J. William Langston (2008) and his colleagues found that the heroin contained a contaminant called MPTP (1-methyl-4-phenyl-1,2,3,6-tetrahydropyridine) resulting from poor preparation during its synthesis. The results of experimental studies in rodents showed that MPTP was not itself responsible for the patients' symptoms but was metabolized into MPP^+ (1-methyl-4-phenylpyridinium), a neurotoxin.

In one autopsy of a suspected case of MPTP poisoning, the victim suffered a selective loss of dopamine neurons in the substantia nigra. The rest of the brain was normal. Injection of MPTP into monkeys, rats, and mice produced similar symptoms and a similar selective loss of DA neurons in the substantia nigra. Thus, the combined clinical and experimental evidence indicates that Parkinson's disease can be induced by a toxin that selectively kills dopamine neurons.

In 1988, Patient 1 received an experimental treatment at University Hospital in Lund, Sweden. Dopamine neurons taken from human fetal brains at autopsy were implanted into the caudate nucleus and putamen. Extensive work with rodents and nonhuman primates in a number of laboratories had demonstrated that fetal neurons, which have not yet developed dendrites and axons, can survive transplantation and grow into mature neurons that can secrete neurotransmitters.

Patient 1 had no serious postoperative complications and was much improved 24 months after the surgery. He could dress and feed himself, visit the bathroom with help, and make trips outside his home. He also responded much better to medication.

The transplantation of fetal neurons to treat Parkinson's disease continues as an area of active research into the idea that a damaged brain can be treated with a brain transplant. The treatment does not work in all patients and can produce unwanted side effects in others. Because Parkinson's disease can affect as many as 20 people per 100,000, a successful method of transplantation and a source of transplantation tissue must be found. The solution to both needs is thought to lie in stimulating stem cells in the brains of individual patients to divide, migrate, and mature into dopamine neurons to restore lost brain tissue.

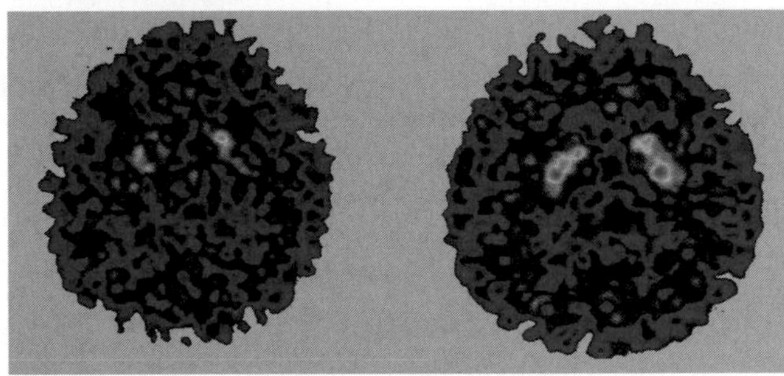

Dr. Hakan Widner, M.D., PhD., Lund University, Sweden

Positron emission tomographic (PET) images of Patient 1's brain before the implantation of fetal dopamine neurons (*left*) and 12 months after the operation (*right*). The increased areas of red and gold show that the transplanted neurons are producing DA. From "Bilateral Fetal Mesencephalic Grafting in Two Patients with Parkinsonism Induced by 1-Methyl-4-phenyl-1,2,3,6-tetrahydropyradine (MPTP)," by H. Widner, J. Tetrud, S. Rehngrona, B. Snow, P. Brundin, B. Gustavii, A. Bjorklund, O. Lindvall, and J. W. Langston, 1992, *New England Journal of Medicine, 327*, p. 151.

Serotonergic System

The serotonergic activating system is active in maintaining a waking EEG in the forebrain when we move and thus plays a role in wakefulness, as does the cholinergic system. Like norepinephrine, serotonin also plays a role in learning, as described in the next section. Some symptoms of depression may be related to decreases in the activity of serotonin neurons, and drugs commonly used to treat depression act on serotonin neurons. Consequently, two forms of depression may exist, one related to norepinephrine and another related to serotonin.

The results of some research suggest that some symptoms of schizophrenia also may be related to increases in serotonin activity, which implies that there may be different forms of schizophrenia as well. Increased serotonergic activity is also related to symptoms observed in **obsessive-compulsive disorder** (OCD), a condition in which a person compulsively repeats acts (such as hand washing) and has repetitive and often unpleasant thoughts (obsessions). Evidence also points to a link between abnormalities in serotonergic nuclei and conditions such as sleep apnea and sudden infant death syndrome (SIDS).

Obsessive-compulsive disorder (OCD) Behavior disorder characterized by compulsively repeated acts (such as hand washing) and repetitive, often unpleasant, thoughts (obsessions).

Learning Relatively permanent change in behavior that results from experience.

Details on the causes of SIDS appear in Chapter 7, and Chapter 13 details sleep apnea.

REVIEW: Neurotransmitter Systems and Behavior

- ✔ Although neurons can synthesize more than one neurotransmitter, they are usually identified by the principal neurotransmitter in their axon terminals.
- ✔ Although no one-to-one relation exists between any neurotransmitter and any behavior, some neurotransmitters take part in specific periodic behaviors, such as acting as hormones to stimulate reproduction. Other CNS neurotransmitters continuously monitor vegetative behaviors.
- ✔ Neural activating systems modulate aspects of behavior. Acetylcholine produces muscular contractions in the somatic nervous system, and acetylcholine and norepinephrine regulate the complementary divisions of the autonomic nervous system.
- ✔ The CNS contains not only widely dispersed glutamate (excitatory) and GABA (inhibitory) neurons but also activating systems of acetylcholine, norepinephrine, dopamine, and serotonin.
- ✔ Neuromodulatory systems are associated both with specific aspects of behavior and with specific neurological disorders.

Role of Synapses in Three Kinds of Learning and in Memory

One of our most cherished abilities is that we can learn and remember. Neuroplasticity, the nervous system's potential for change that enhances its ability to adapt, is a requirement for learning and memory. Neuroplasticity is a characteristic not only of the mammalian brain but also of the nervous systems of all animals, even the simplest worms.

Larger brains, having more connections, have more capacity for change, however, and are thus likely to show more adaptability in neural organization. This greater adaptability happens because experience alters the synapse. Not only are synapses versatile in structure and function, they are also plastic: they can change. The synapse, therefore, provides a site for the neural basis of **learning,** a relatively permanent change in behavior that results from experience.

In Chapter 14, we take up learning, memory, and neuroplasticity again in detail. Experiments and Focus boxes throughout the book often revisit the nervous system's adaptability and potential for self-repair, a principle first introduced in Chapter 2.

Donald O. Hebb (1949) was not the first to suggest that learning is mediated by structural changes in synapses. But the change that he envisioned in his book *The Organization of Behavior* was novel 60 years ago. Hebb theorized, "When an axon of cell A is near enough to excite a cell B and repeatedly or persistently takes part in firing it, some growth process or metabolic change takes place in one or both cells such that A's

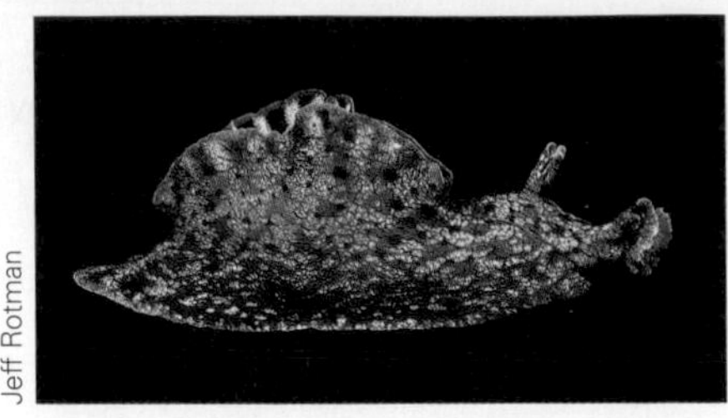
Jeff Rotman

Aplysia californica

efficiency, as one of the cells firing B, is increased" (Hebb, 1949, p. 62). A synapse that physically adapts in this way is called a *Hebb synapse* today.

Eric Kandel was awarded a Nobel Prize in 2000 for his descriptions of the synaptic basis of of learning in which the conjoint activity of nerve cells serves to link them. His subject, the marine snail *Aplysia californica*, is an ideal subject for learning experiments. Slightly larger than a softball and lacking a shell, *Aplysia* has roughly 20,000 neurons, some of which are quite accessible to researchers, who can isolate and study circuits having very few synapses.

When threatened, *Aplysia* defensively withdraws its more-vulnerable body parts—the gill (through which it extracts oxygen from the water to breathe) and the siphon (a spout above the gill that excretes seawater and waste). By touching or shocking the snail's appendages, Kandel and his coworkers produced enduring changes in its defensive behaviors. These behavioral responses were then used to study underlying changes in the snail's nervous system.

We now illustrate the role of synapses in three kinds of learning: habituation, sensitization, and associative learning. For humans, these kinds of learning are called unconscious because they do not depend on a person's knowing precisely when and how they occur. In Chapter 14, we describe forms of conscious learning in which knowing the "Ws," (who, what, when, and where) are important.

In learning how learning takes place you will recognize each of these forms of unconscious behavior as part of your experience. You will also recognize the structural basis of these forms of learning because they entail changes in synaptic function and structure with which you are familiar.

Habituation Response

In **habituation,** the response to a stimulus weakens with repeated presentations of that stimulus. If you are accustomed to living in the country and then move to a city, you might at first find the sounds of traffic and people extremely loud and annoying. With time, however, you stop noticing most of the noise most of the time. You have habituated to it.

Habituation develops with all our senses. When you first put on a shoe, you "feel" it on your foot, but very shortly it is as if the shoe is no longer there. You have not become insensitive to sensations, however. When people talk to you, you still hear them; when someone steps on your foot, you still feel the pressure. Your brain simply has habituated to the customary, "background" sensations.

Aplysia habituates to waves in the shallow tidal zone where it lives. These snails are constantly buffeted by the flow of waves against their bodies, and they learn that waves are just the background "noise" of daily life. They do not flinch and withdraw every time a wave passes over them. They habituate to this stimulus.

A sea snail that is habituated to waves remains sensitive to other touch sensations. Prodded with a novel object, it responds by withdrawing its siphon and gill. The animal's reaction to repeated presentations of the same novel stimulus forms the basis for **Experiment 5-2,** studying its habituation response.

Habituation Learning behavior in which a response to a stimulus weakens with repeated stimulus presentations.

Sensitization Learning behavior in which the response to a stimulus strengthens with repeated presentations of that stimulus because the stimulus is novel or because the stimulus is stronger than normal—for example, after habituation has occurred.

Posttraumatic stress disorder (PTSD) Syndrome characterized by physiological arousal symptoms related to recurring memories and dreams related to a traumatic event for months or years after the event.

Neural Basis of Habituation

The Procedure section of Experiment 5-2 shows the setup for studying what happens to the withdrawal response of *Aplysia*'s gill after repeated stimulation. A gentle jet of water is sprayed on the siphon while movement of the gill is recorded. If the jet of water is presented to *Aplysia*'s siphon as many as 10 times, the gill-withdrawal response is weaker some minutes later when the animal is again tested with the water jet. The decrement in the strength of the withdrawal is habituation, which can last as long as 30 minutes.

The Results section of Experiment 5-2 starts by showing a simple representation of the pathway that mediates *Aplysia*'s gill-withdrawal response. For purposes of illustration, only one sensory neuron, one motor neuron, and one synapse are shown, even though, in actuality, about 300 neurons may take part in this response. The jet of water stimulates the sensory neuron, which in turn stimulates the motor neuron responsible for the gill withdrawal. But exactly where do the changes associated with habituation take place? In the sensory neuron? In the motor neuron? Or in the synapse between the two?

Habituation does not result from an inability of either the sensory or the motor neuron to produce action potentials. In response to direct electrical stimulation, both the sensory neuron and the motor neuron retain the ability to generate action potentials even after habituation. Electrical recordings from the motor neuron show that, accompanying the development of habituation, the excitatory postsynaptic potentials in the motor neuron become smaller.

The most likely way in which these EPSPs decrease in size is that the motor neuron is receiving less neurotransmitter from the sensory neuron across the synapse. And, if less neurotransmitter is being received, then the changes accompanying habituation must be taking place in the presynaptic axon terminal of the sensory neuron.

Calcium Channels Habituate

Kandel and his coworkers measured neurotransmitter output from a sensory neuron and verified that less neurotransmitter is in fact released from a habituated neuron than from a nonhabituated one. Recall that the release of a neurotransmitter in response to an action potential requires an influx of calcium ions across the presynaptic membrane. As habituation takes place, that Ca^{2+} influx decreases in response to the voltage changes associated with an action potential. Presumably, with repeated use, voltage-sensitive calcium channels become less responsive to voltage changes and more resistant to the passage of calcium ions.

The neural basis of habituation lies in the change in presynaptic calcium channels. Its mechanism, which is summarized in the right-hand close-up of Experiment 5-2, is a reduced sensitivity of calcium channels and a consequent decrease in the release of a neurotransmitter. Thus, habituation can be linked to a specific molecular change, as summarized in the Conclusion section of the experiment.

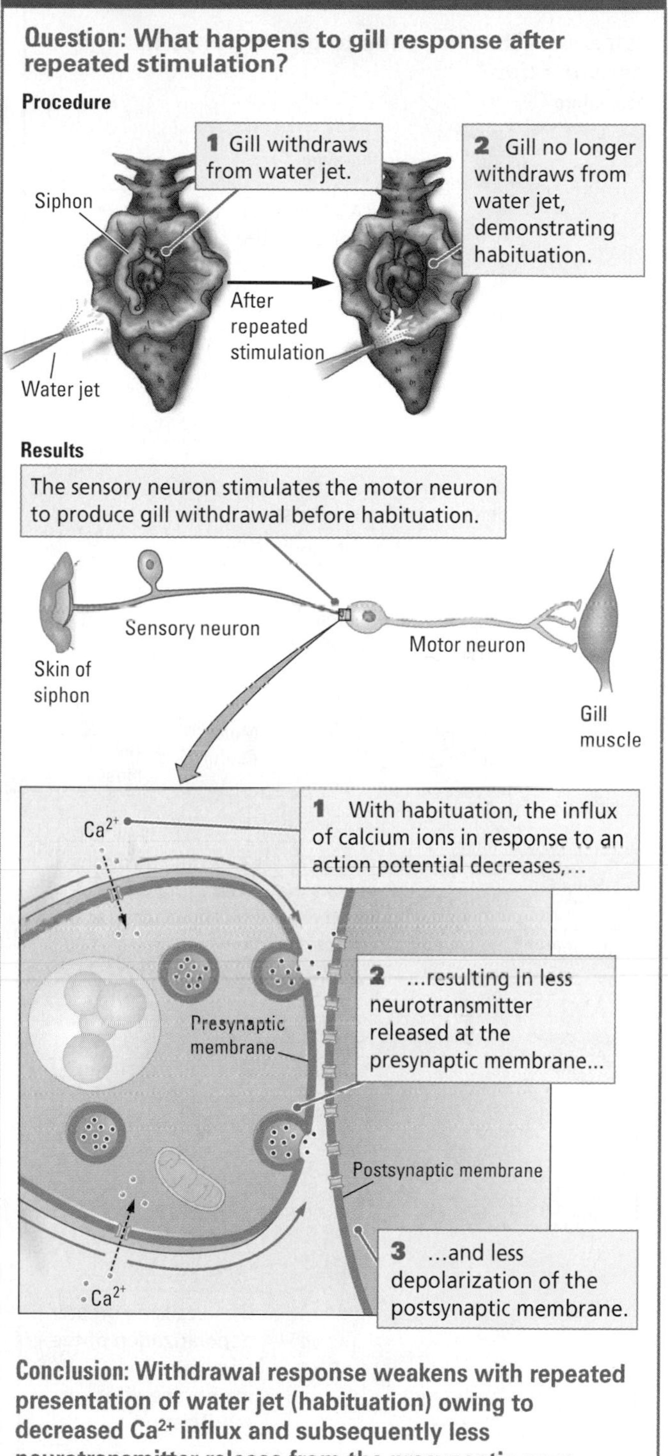
EXPERIMENT 5-2
Question: What happens to gill response after repeated stimulation?
Procedure
1 Gill withdraws from water jet.
2 Gill no longer withdraws from water jet, demonstrating habituation.
Siphon
After repeated stimulation
Water jet
Results
The sensory neuron stimulates the motor neuron to produce gill withdrawal before habituation.
Sensory neuron
Motor neuron
Skin of siphon
Gill muscle
Ca2+
1 With habituation, the influx of calcium ions in response to an action potential decreases,...
2 ...resulting in less neurotransmitter released at the presynaptic membrane...
Presynaptic membrane
Postsynaptic membrane
3 ...and less depolarization of the postsynaptic membrane.
Ca2+
Conclusion: Withdrawal response weakens with repeated presentation of water jet (habituation) owing to decreased Ca2+ influx and subsequently less neurotransmitter release from the presynaptic axon terminal.

Sensitization Response

A sprinter crouched in her starting blocks is often hyperresponsive to the starter's gun: its firing triggers in her a very rapid reaction. The stressful, competitive context in which the race takes place helps to sensitize her to this sound. **Sensitization,** an enhanced response to some stimulus, is the opposite of habituation. The organism becomes hyperresponsive to a stimulus rather than accustomed to it.

Sensitization occurs within a context. Sudden, novel stimulation heightens our general awareness and often results in larger-than-normal responses to all kinds of stimulation. If you are suddenly startled by a loud noise, you become much more responsive to other stimuli in your surroundings, including some to which you had been previously habituated. In **posttraumatic stress disorder** (PTSD), physiological arousal related to recurring memories and dreams surrounding a traumatic event persist for

The role of stress in fostering and prolonging the effects of PTSD are topics in Chapters 8 and 12, and Chapter 16 covers treatment strategies.

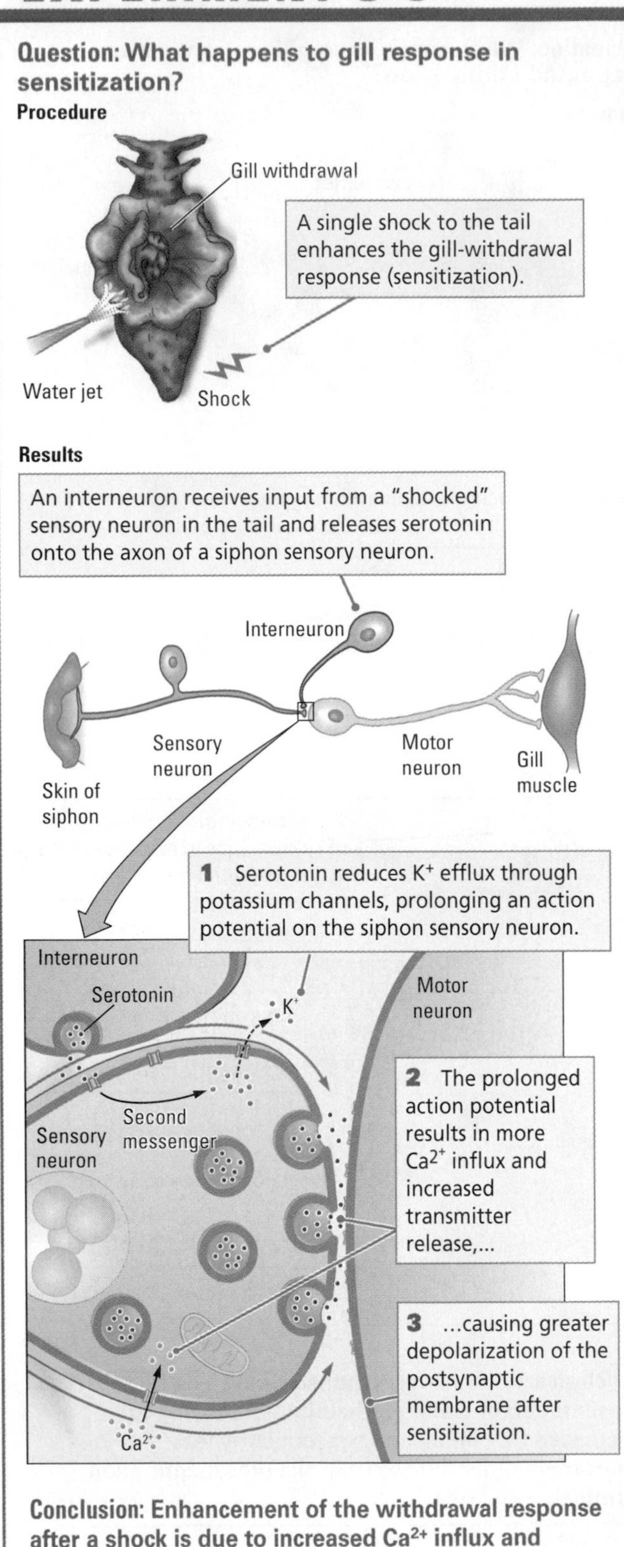
EXPERIMENT 5-3
Question: What happens to gill response in sensitization?
Procedure
Gill withdrawal
A single shock to the tail enhances the gill-withdrawal response (sensitization).
Water jet
Shock
Results
An interneuron receives input from a "shocked" sensory neuron in the tail and releases serotonin onto the axon of a siphon sensory neuron.
Interneuron
Sensory neuron
Motor neuron
Gill muscle
Skin of siphon
1 Serotonin reduces K+ efflux through potassium channels, prolonging an action potential on the siphon sensory neuron.
Interneuron
Serotonin
K+
Motor neuron
Second messenger
Sensory neuron
2 The prolonged action potential results in more Ca2+ influx and increased transmitter release,...
3 ...causing greater depolarization of the postsynaptic membrane after sensitization.
Ca2+
Conclusion: Enhancement of the withdrawal response after a shock is due to increased Ca2+ influx and subsequently more neurotransmitter release from the presynaptic axon terminal.

months or years after the event. One characteristic of PTSD is a heightened response to stimuli, suggesting that the disorder is in part related to sensitization.

The same thing happens to *Aplysia.* Sudden, novel stimuli can heighten a snail's responsiveness to familiar stimulation. When attacked by a predator, for example, the snail becomes acutely aware of other changes in its environment and hyperresponds to them. In the laboratory, a small electric shock to *Aplysia*'s tail mimics a predatory attack and effects sensitization, as illustrated in the Procedure section of **Experiment 5-3.** A single electric shock to the snail's tail enhances its gill-withdrawal response for a period that lasts from minutes to hours.

Neural Basis of Sensitization

The neural circuits participating in sensitization differ from those that take part in a habituation response. The Results section of Experiment 5-3 again shows one of each kind of neuron: the heretofore described sensory and motor neurons that produce the gill-withdrawal response and an interneuron that is responsible for sensitization.

An interneuron that receives input from a sensory neuron in the tail (and so carries information about the shock) makes an axoaxonic synapse with a siphon sensory neuron. The interneuron's axon terminal contains serotonin. Consequently, in response to a tail shock, the tail sensory neuron activates the interneuron, which in turn releases serotonin onto the axon of the siphon sensory neuron. Information from the siphon still comes through the siphon sensory neuron to activate the motor neuron leading to the gill muscle, but the gill-withdrawal response is amplified by the action of the interneuron in releasing serotonin onto the presynaptic membrane of the sensory neuron.

At the molecular level, the serotonin released from the interneuron binds to a metabotropic serotonin receptor on the axon of the siphon sensory neuron. This binding activates second messengers in the sensory neuron. Specifically, the serotonin receptor is coupled through its G protein to the enzyme adenyl cyclase. This enzyme increases the concentration of the second messenger cyclic adenosine monophosphate (cAMP) in the presynaptic membrane of the siphon sensory neuron.

Through a number of chemical reactions, cAMP attaches a phosphate molecule (PO_4) to potassium channels, and the phosphate renders the potassium channels less responsive. The closeup on the right side of the Results section in Experiment 5-3 sums it up. In response to an action potential traveling down the axon of the siphon sensory neuron (such as one generated by a touch to the siphon), the potassium channels on that neuron are slower to open. Consequently, K^+ ions cannot repolarize the membrane as quickly as is normal, and so the action potential lasts longer than it usually would.

Potassium Channels Sensitize

The longer-lasting action potential that occurs because potassium channels are slower to open prolongs the inflow of Ca^{2+} into the membrane. You know that Ca^{2+} influx is necessary for neurotransmitter release. Thus, more Ca^{2+} influx results in more neurotransmitter being released from the sensory synapse onto the motor neuron.

Associative learning Linkage of two or more unrelated stimuli to elicit a behavioral response.

Long-term potentiation (LTP) In response to stimulation at a synapse, changed amplitude of an excitatory postsynaptic potential that lasts for hours to days or longer and plays a part in associative learning.

This increased release of neurotransmitter produces greater activation of the motor neuron and thus a larger-than-normal gill-withdrawal response. The gill withdrawal may also be enhanced by the fact that the second messenger cAMP may mobilize more synaptic vesicles, making more neurotransmitter ready for release into the sensory–motor synapse.

Sensitization, then, is the opposite of habituation at the molecular level as well as at the behavioral level. In sensitization, more Ca^{2+} influx results in more transmitter being released, whereas, in habituation, less Ca^{2+} influx results in less neurotransmitter being released. The structural basis of cellular memory in these two forms of learning is different, however. In sensitization, the change takes place in potassium channels, whereas, in habituation, the change takes place in calcium channels.

Long-Term Potentiation and Associative Learning

The findings from studies of habituation and sensitization in *Aplysia* show that physical changes in synapses do underlie learning. In this section, we look at experiments that demonstrate how adaptive synapses participate in a different kind of learning in the mammalian brain. Such **associative learning,** a response elicited by linking unrelated stimuli together—by learning that A goes with B—is very common.

Associating a face with a person, an odor with a food, or a sound with a musical instrument are everyday examples of associative learning. Your learning that learning takes place at synapses is another example. The phenomenon that underlies associative learning entails a neural change in which an excitatory signal crossing a synapse is enhanced long after use.

Neural Basis of Associative Learning

We begin in the forebrain structure called the hippocampus. Both the relatively simple circuitry of the hippocampus and the ease of recording postsynaptic potentials there make it an ideal structure for studying the neural basis of learning. In 1973, Timothy Bliss and Terje Lømø demonstrated that repeated electrical stimulation of the pathway entering the hippocampus produces a progressive increase in EPSP size recorded from hippocampal cells. This enhancement in the size of these "field potentials" lasts for a number of hours to weeks or even longer. Bliss and Lømø called it **long-term potentiation** (LTP).

The hippocampus is a structure in the limbic system, which is diagrammed in Figure 2-23, and plays a role in memory and navigating in space, among other functions.

The fact that LTP lasts for some time after stimulation suggests two things:

1. At the synapse, a change must take place that allows the field potential to become larger and remain larger.
2. The change at the synapse might be related to everyday learning experiences.

Figure 5-18A illustrates the experimental procedure for obtaining LTP. The presynaptic neuron is stimulated electrically while the electrical activity produced by the

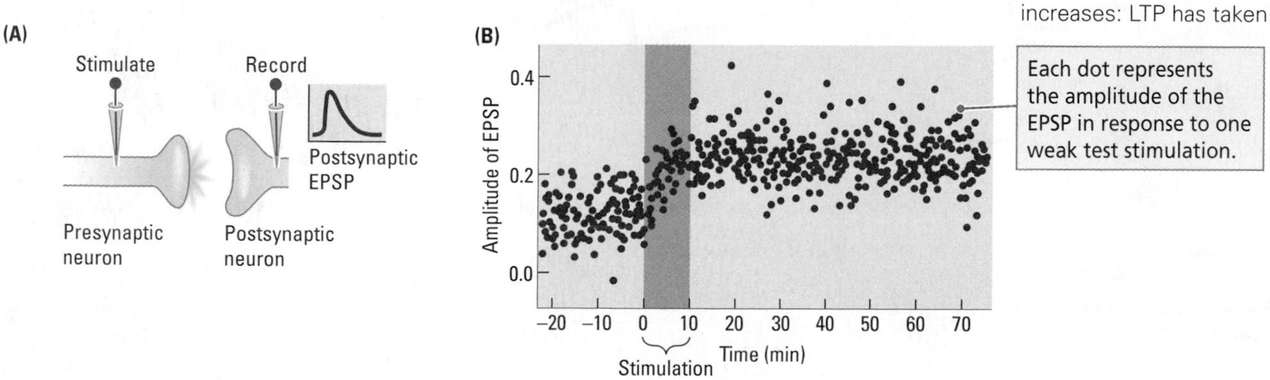

FIGURE 5-18 Recording Long-Term Potentiation. (A) In this experimental setup, the presynaptic neuron is stimulated with a test pulse and the EPSP is recorded from the postsynaptic neuron. (B) After a period of intense stimulation, the amplitude of the EPSP produced by the test pulse increases: LTP has taken place.

stimulation is recorded from the postsynaptic neuron. The readout in Figure 5-18A shows the EPSP produced by a single pulse of electrical stimulation.

In a typical experiment, a number of test stimuli are given to estimate the size of the induced EPSP. Then a strong burst of stimulation, consisting of a few hundred pulses of electrical current per second, is administered (Figure 5-18B). The test pulse is then given again. The increased amplitude of the EPSP endures for as long as 90 minutes after the high-frequency burst of stimulation.

The high burst of stimulation has produced a long-lasting change in the response of the postsynaptic neuron: LTP has taken place. For the EPSP to increase in size, either more neurotransmitter must be released from the presynaptic membrane or the postsynaptic membrane must become more sensitive to the same amount of transmitter or both changes must take place.

Neurochemistry of Long-Term Potentiation

The synapses at which LTP is recorded use glutamate as the neurotransmitter. Glutamate is released from the presynaptic neuron and acts on two different types of receptors on the postsynaptic membrane, the NMDA and AMPA receptors, as shown in **Figure 5-19**A. AMPA receptors ordinarily mediate the responses produced when glutamate is released from a presynaptic membrane, and they allow Na^+ ions to enter, depolarizing and thus exciting the postsynaptic membrane. The initial amplitude of the EPSP in Figure 5-18 is produced by this action of the AMPA receptor.

NMDA is shorthand for *N*-methyl-D-aspartate, and AMPA stands for alpha-amino-3-hydroxy-5-methylisoazole-4-proprionic acid.

NMDA receptors do not usually respond to glutamate, because their pores are blocked by magnesium ions (Mg^{2+}). NMDA receptors are doubly gated channels that can open to allow the passage of calcium ions if two events take place at approximately the same time:

1. The postsynaptic membrane is depolarized, displacing the magnesium ion from the NMDA pore (Figure 5-19B). The strong electrical stimulation delivered by the experimenter serves as a way of displacing magnesium.
2. NMDA receptors are activated by glutamate from the presynaptic membrane (Figure 5-19C).

FIGURE 5-19 Glutamate's Lasting Effects. Enhanced glutamate prompts a neurochemical cascade that underlies synaptic change and LTP.

(A) Weak electrical stimulus

Because the NMDA receptor pore is blocked by a magnesium ion, release of glutamate by a weak electrical stimulation activates only the AMPA receptor.

Glutamate
Calcium ions
Magnesium ion
NMDA receptor
AMPA receptor
Presynaptic neuron
Postsynaptic neuron

(B) Strong electrical stimulus (depolarizing EPSP)

A strong electrical stimulation can depolarize the postsynaptic membrane sufficiently that the magnesium ion is removed from the NMDA receptor pore.

NMDA receptor
AMPA receptor

(C) Weak electrical stimulus

Now glutamate, released by weak stimulation, can activate the NMDA receptor to allow Ca^{2+} influx, which, through a second messenger, increases the function or number of AMPA receptors or both.

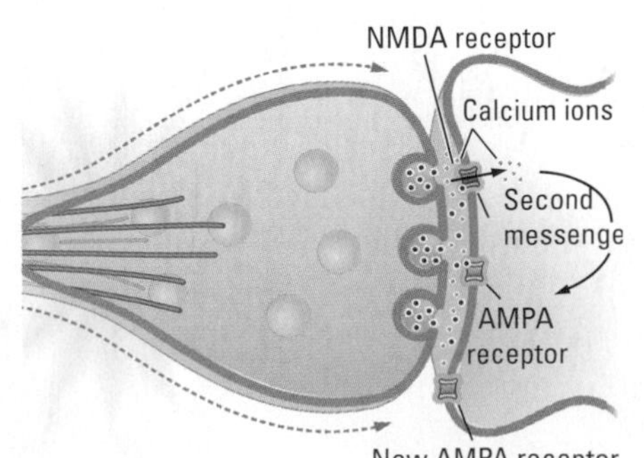

With the doubly gated NMDA channels open, calcium ions enter the postsynaptic neuron and act through second messengers to initiate the cascade of events associated with LTP. These events include an increased responsiveness of AMPA receptors to glutamate, the formation of new AMPA receptors, and even retrograde messages to the presynaptic terminal to enhance the release of glutamate. The final amplitude of the EPSP in Figure 5-18B is produced by one or more of these actions.

The change that takes place in the synapse is associative because two different stimuli (the initial strong electrical stimulation and the weaker test stimulus) activating two different mechanisms are linked. Remember that the NMDA receptor is doubly gated. In order for calcium ions to pass through its pore, the magnesium block must be removed by depolarization of the membrane (the strong stimulus), and then glutamate must bind to the receptor (the weak stimulus).

The demonstration of LTP taking place at a synapse when a weak stimulus is paired with a stronger one provides a model that underlies real-life associative learning. The real-life corollary of weak stimulation may be an environmental event that triggers glutamate-releasing activity into a synapse at the same time as another environmental event is removing the magnesium block. A specific example will help you see how this process relates to associative learning in mammals.

Suppose that, as a rat walks around, a cell fires when the rat reaches a certain location. The stimulus that produces this firing may be the sight of a particular object, such as a light. The neural signal about the light will be carried by the visual system to the cell, the putative site of learning.

Now suppose that, in an excursion to this place where the light is located, the rat encounters a tasty piece of food. Input concerning that food can be carried from the taste area of the neocortex to the same cell that fires in response to the light. As a result, the taste and odor input associated with the food arrives at the cell at the time that it is firing in response to the light, providing a sufficiently strong signal to remove the Mg^{2+} block so LTP can take place.

Subsequently, not only will seeing the light at a particular location fire this cell but so will the odor of this particular food. The cell, in other words, stores an association between the food and the light. If the rat were to smell the odor of this food on the snout of another rat that had eaten it, the same cell would discharge. Because the discharge of this cell is also associated with a particular light and location in the environment, would the rat go to that location, expecting once again to find food there?

Bennett Galef and his coworkers (1990) in fact demonstrated that a rat that smells the odor of a particular food on the breath of a demonstrator rat will go to the appropriate location to obtain the food. This social transmission of food-related information is an excellent example of associative learning.

Long-term potentiation is not the only change in a neuron that can underlie learning. Learning can also be mediated by a neuron that becomes less active in response to repeated stimulation. This process is called *long-term depression* or LTD. The neural basis of LTD may be quite similar to that of LTP in that both require NMDA receptors. In neurons that display LTD, the influx of Ca^{2+} may result not in increased responsiveness or increased numbers of AMPA receptors but rather in decreased responsiveness or decreased numbers of AMPA receptors.

Learning As a Change in Synapse Number

The neural changes associated with learning must be long-lasting enough to account for a relatively permanent change in an organism's behavior. The changes at synapses described in the preceding sections develop quite quickly, but they do not last indefinitely, as memories often do. How, then, can synapses be responsible for the long-term changes in learning and memory?

Repeated stimulation produces habituation and sensitization or associative behaviors that can persist for months. Brief training produces short-term learning, whereas longer training periods produce more enduring learning. If you cram for an exam the night before you take it, you might forget the material quickly, but, if you study a little each day for a week, your learning may tend to endure. What underlies this more-persistent form of learning? It would seem to be more than just a change in the release of glutamate, and, whatever the change is, it must be long-lasting.

Craig Bailey and Mary Chen (see Miniaci et al., 2008) found that the number and size of sensory synapses change in well-trained, habituated, and sensitized *Aplysia.* Relative to a control neuron, the number and size of synapses decrease in habituated animals and increase in sensitized animals, as represented in **Figure 5-20.** Apparently, synaptic events associated with habituation and sensitization can also trigger processes in the sensory cell that result in the loss or formation of new synapses.

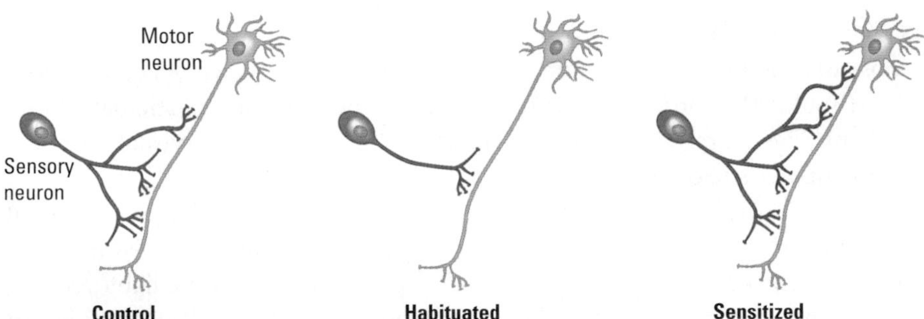

FIGURE 5-20 Physical Basis of Memory. Relative to a control neuronal connection (*left*), the number of synapses between *Aplysia*'s sensory neuron and a motor neuron decline as a result of habituation (*center*) and increase as a result of sensitization (*right*). Such structural changes may underlie enduring memories.

A mechanism through which these processes can take place begins with calcium ions that mobilize second messengers to send instructions to nuclear DNA. The transcription and translation of nuclear DNA, in turn, initiate structural changes at synapses. Research Focus 5-5, "Dendritic Spines, Small but Mighty," summarizes experimental evidence about structural changes in dendritic spines. The second messenger cAMP probably plays an important role in carrying instructions regarding these structural changes to nuclear DNA. The evidence for cAMP's involvement comes from studies of fruit flies.

In the fruit fly, *Drosophila,* two genetic mutations can produce the same learning deficiency. Both render the second messenger cAMP inoperative, but in opposite ways. One mutation, called *dunce,* lacks the enzymes needed to degrade cAMP, and so the fruit fly has abnormally high cAMP levels. The other mutation, called *rutabaga,* reduces levels of cAMP below the normal range for *Drosophila* neurons.

Significantly, fruit flies with either of these mutations are impaired in acquiring habituated and sensitized responses because their levels of cAMP cannot be regulated. New synapses seem to be required for learning to take place, and the second messenger cAMP seems to be needed to carry instructions to form them. **Figure 5-21** summarizes these research findings.

Just as more-enduring habituation and sensitization are mediated by relatively permanent changes in neuronal structure—that is, fewer or more synaptic connections—so associative learning links to changes in synaptic number. LTP and LTD may be associated with increases or decreases in relatively permanent synapses, thus representing enduring associative memories. For example, our memories of our parents and loved ones are enduring because they are encoded in enduring synapses and dendritic spines.

FIGURE 5-21 Genetic Disruption of Learning. Two mutations in the fruit fly, *Drosophila,* inactivate the second messenger cAMP by moving its level above or below the concentration range at which it can be regulated.

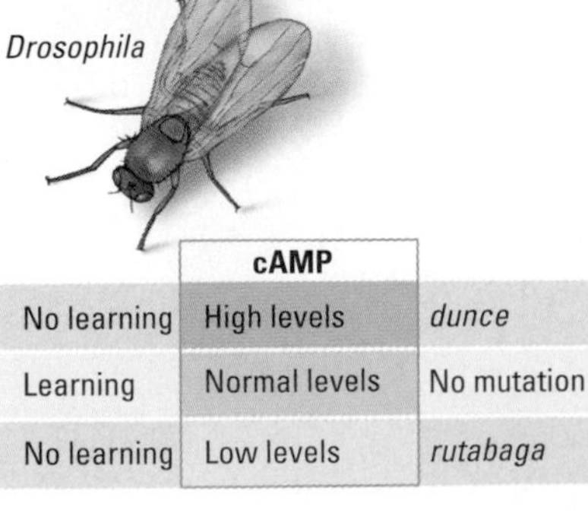

	cAMP	
No learning	High levels	*dunce*
Learning	Normal levels	No mutation
No learning	Low levels	*rutabaga*

RESEARCH FOCUS 5-5

Dendritic Spines, Small but Mighty

Dendritic spines are from about 1 to 3 micrometers long, are less than 1 micrometer in diameter, and protrude from the dendrite shaft. Each neuron may have many thousands of spines. The number of dendritic spines in the human cerebral cortex may be 10^{14}. Dendritic spines provide the structural basis of our behavior, our individual skills, and memories (Debello, 2008). Impairments in forming spines characterize some kinds of mental retardation, and the loss of spines is associated with the dementia of Alzheimer's disease.

Dendritic spines have their origins in *filopodia* (from the Latin *file,* for "thread," and the Greek *podium,* for "foot") that bud out of neurons, especially their dendrites. Microscopic observation of dendrites shows that filopodia are constantly emerging and retracting, over times on the order of seconds.

The budding of filopodia is much more pronounced in developing neurons and in the developing brain. Because filopodia can become dendritic spines, the budding suggests that they are searching for contacts from the end feet of axons so as to form synaptic contacts. When contact with an end foot is made, some of the synapses so formed may have only a short life; others will endure.

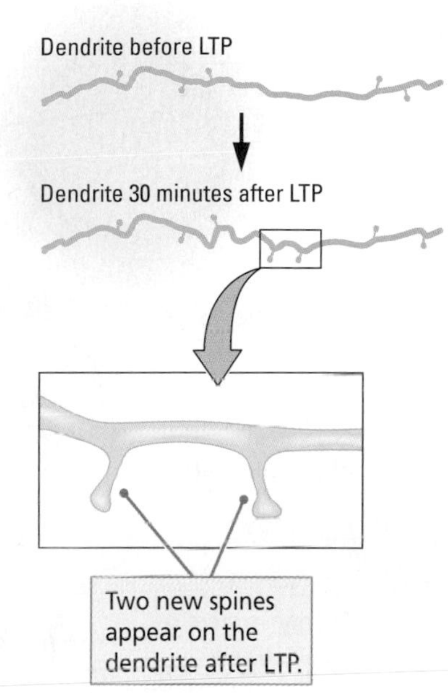
Dendrite before LTP
Dendrite 30 minutes after LTP
Two new spines appear on the dendrite after LTP.

Neural stimulation that produces LTP causes structural changes in neurons: new dendritic spines grow in conjunction with LTP.

A permanent dendritic spine tends to have a large head, giving it a large area of contact with an end foot, and a long stem, giving it an identity apart from that of its dendrite. The heads of spines serve as biochemical compartments that can generate huge electrical potentials and so influence the neuron's electrical messages. The mechanisms that allow spines to appear and to change shape include a number of different cytoskeletal filaments linked to the membrane receptors.

Dendritic spines mediate enduring learning, including habituation, sensitization, and associations. To mediate learning, each spine must be able to act independently, undergoing changes that its neighbors do not undergo.

The influx of calcium ions or other actions of the dendritic receptors can lead to the assembly of larger filaments; some can change the length of the spine, others can change its width, and still others can cause it to divide. The examination of dendritic spines in the nervous system shows that some are simple and others complex. This variety suggests that some mediate skills and memories that we retain only briefly, whereas others mediate memories and skills that endure.

REVIEW: Role of Synapses in Three Kinds of Learning and in Memory

✔ The neural basis for learning and memory resides at the synapse. *Aplysia*'s synaptic function mediates two basic forms of learning: habituation and sensitization.

✔ Presynaptic voltage-sensitive calcium channels mediate habituation by growing less sensitive with use.

✔ Metabotropic serotonin receptors on a sensory neuron can change the sensitivity of presynaptic potassium channels and so increase Ca^{2+} influx to mediate sensitization.

✔ At the same time, these sensory receptors can produce fewer or more synapses to provide a structural, physical basis for long-term habituation and sensitization and for changes in behavior. Mammals also demonstrate structural synaptic changes related to associative learning.

✔ Clearly, many changes in the synapses of neurons can mediate learning, but associative learning takes place only if requisite events take place at nearly the same time and thus become linked. Because associative learning has a neural basis, measurements of synaptic structure and neurochemistry may suggest relations between synaptic change, experience, and behavior.

✔ The illustration below summarizes synaptic structures that can be measured and related to learning and behavior and the structural changes that may subserve learning.

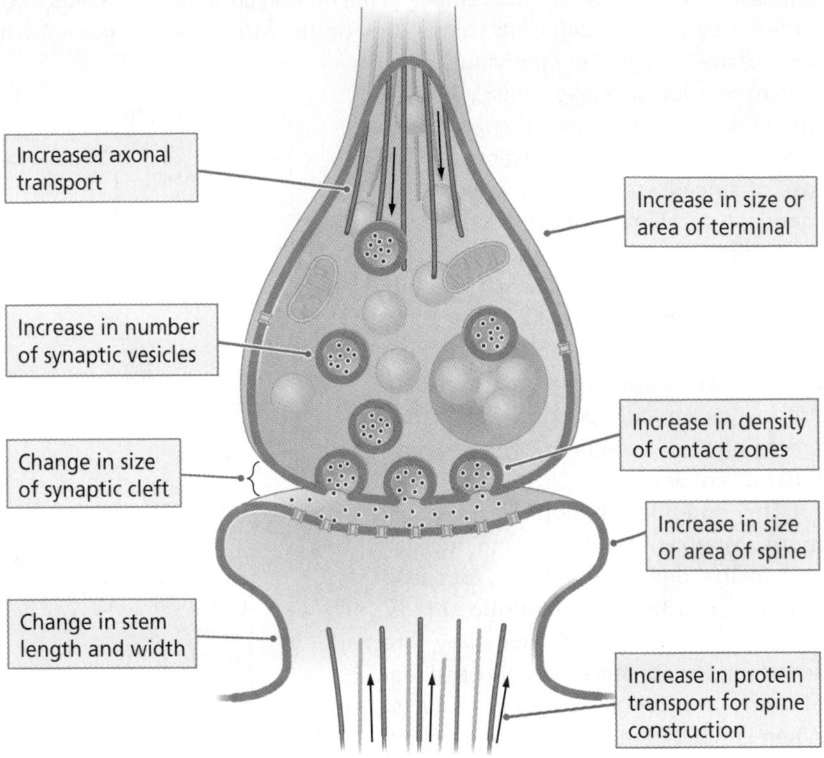

Summary

A Chemical Message

In the 1920s, Otto Loewi suspected that nerves to the heart secrete a chemical that regulates its rate of beating. His subsequent experiments with frogs showed that acetylcholine slows heart rate, whereas epinephrine increases it. This observation provided the key to understanding the basis of chemical neurotransmission.

A synapse consists of the sending neuron's axon terminal (surrounded by a presynaptic membrane), a synaptic cleft (a tiny gap between the two neurons), and a postsynaptic membrane on the receiving neuron. Systems for the chemical synthesis of an excitatory or inhibitory neurotransmitter are located in the presynaptic neuron's axon terminal or its soma, whereas systems for storing the neurotransmitter are in its axon terminal. Receptor systems on which that neurotransmitter acts are located on the postsynaptic membrane.

The four major stages in neurotransmission are (1) synthesis and storage, (2) release from the axon terminal, (3) action on postsynaptic receptors, and (4) inactivation.

After synthesis, the neurotransmitter is wrapped in a membrane to form synaptic vesicles in the axon terminal. When an action potential is propagated on the presynaptic membrane, voltage changes set in motion the attachment of vesicles to the presynaptic membrane and the release of the neurotransmitter by exocytosis.

One synaptic vesicle releases a quantum of neurotransmitter into the synaptic cleft, producing a miniature potential on the postsynaptic membrane. To generate an action potential on the postsynaptic cell requires the simultaneous release of many quanta of transmitter. After a transmitter has done its work, it is inactivated by such processes as diffusion out of the synaptic cleft, breakdown by enzymes, and reuptake of the transmitter or its components into the axon terminal (or sometimes uptake into glial cells).

Varieties of Neurotransmitters

Small-molecule transmitters, neuropeptides, and transmitter gases are broad classes of the perhaps 100 neurotransmitters. Neurons containing these transmitters make a variety of connections with various parts of other neurons as well as with muscles, blood vessels, and extracellular fluid.

Functionally, neurons can be both excitatory and inhibitory, and they can participate in local circuits or in general brain systems. Excitatory synapses, known as Type I, are usually located on a dendritic tree, whereas inhibitory synapses, known as Type II, are usually located on a cell body.

Each neurotransmitter may be associated with both ionotropic and metabotropic receptors. An ionotropic receptor quickly and directly produces voltage changes on the postsynaptic cell membrane as its pore opens or closes to regulate the flow of ions through the cell membrane. Slower-acting metabotropic receptors activate second messengers to indirectly produce changes in the function and structure of the cell.

Neurotransmitter Systems and Behavior

Because neurotransmitters are multifunctional, scientists find it impossible to isolate single-neurotransmitter–single-behavior relations. Rather, systems of neurons that employ the same principal neurotransmitter influence various general aspects of behavior. For instance, acetylcholine, the main neurotransmitter in the somatic nervous system, controls movement of the skeletal muscles, whereas acetylcholine and norepinephrine, the main transmitters in the autonomic system, control the body's internal organs.

The central nervous system contains not only widely dispersed glutamate and GABA neurons but also neural activating systems that employ acetylcholine, norepinephrine, dopamine, or serotonin as their main neurotransmitter. All these systems ensure that wide areas of the brain act in concert, and each is associated with various classes of behaviors and disorders.

Role of Synapses in Three Kinds of Learning and in Memory

Changes in synapses underlie learning and memory. In habituation, a form of learning in which a response weakens as a result of repeated stimulation, calcium channels become less responsive to an action potential. Consequently, less neurotransmitter is released when an action potential is propagated.

In sensitization, a form of learning in which a response strengthens as a result of stimulation, changes in potassium channels prolong the duration of the action potential, resulting in an increased influx of calcium ions and, consequently, release of more neurotransmitter. With repeated training, new synapses can develop, and both of these forms of learning can become relatively permanent.

In associative learning, two or more unrelated stimuli become linked, and this linkage elicits a behavioral response. The formation of new synapses can record this relation for the long term.

In *Aplysia,* the number of synapses connecting sensory neurons and motor neurons decreases in response to repeated sessions of habituation. Conversely, in response to repeated sessions of sensitization, the number of synapses connecting sensory and motor neurons increases. Presumably, these changes in synapse number are related to long-term learning.

Key Terms

acetylcholine (ACh), p. 135
activating system, p. 153
Alzheimer's disease, p. 154
associative learning, p. 161
autoreceptor, p. 140
carbon monoxide (CO), p. 149
chemical synapse, p. 137
cholinergic neuron, p. 153
dopamine (DA), p. 139
electrical synapse, p. 137
epinephrine (EP), p. 135
gamma-aminobutyric acid (GABA), p. 147
glutamate (Glu), p. 147
G protein, p. 149
habituation, p. 158
histamine (H), p. 147
ionotropic receptor, p. 149
learning, p. 157
long-term potentiation (LTP), p. 161
major depression, p. 154
mania, p. 154
metabotropic receptor, p. 149
neuropeptide, p. 149
neurotransmitter, p. 135
nitric oxide (NO), p. 149
noradrenergic neuron, p. 154
norepinephrine (NE), p. 135
obsessive-compulsive disorder (OCD), p. 157
Parkinson's disease, p. 139
postsynaptic membrane, p. 137
posttraumatic stress disorder (PTSD), p. 158
presynaptic membrane, p. 137
quantum (pl. quanta), p. 140
rate-limiting factor, p. 147
reuptake, p. 140
schizophrenia, p. 154
second messenger, p. 153
sensitization, p. 158
serotonin (5-HT), p. 147
small-molecule transmitter, p. 145
storage granule, p. 137
synaptic cleft, p. 137
synaptic vesicle, p. 137
transmitter-activated receptor, p. 140
transporter, p. 139

▶*Please refer to the Companion Web Site at* **www.worthpublishers.com/kolbintro3e** *for Interactive Exercises and Quizzes.*

H. Watanabe, et al., 2008

CHAPTER 6

How Do We Study the Brain's Structure and Functions?

In the span of a century, techniques of neuroscience research have advanced from Brodmann's map of the cortex, based on staining and shown in Figure 2-21, to the confocal microscopic brainbow images that accompany Research Focus 3-5.

selectively stains the complete structure of individual neurons (Figure 6-1 at the right). These techniques allowed researchers such as Korbinian Brodmann to divide the cerebral cortex into many distinct zones. These zones, investigators presumed, had specific functions.

By the dawn of the twenty-first century, dozens of techniques for labeling neurons and their connections, as well as glial cells, had developed. These techniques allow researchers to identify molecular, neurochemical, and morphological (structural) differences among neuronal types and ultimately to relate these characteristics to behavior. Parkinson's disease offers one of the clearest examples of neuronal/behavioral relations. Early analysis of postmortem brain tissue from humans afflicted with the disease showed that cells in the brainstem's midbrain region, the substantia nigra, had died (**Figure 6-2**). Later studies using laboratory animals showed that if the substantia nigra was killed experimentally, the animals showed symptoms remarkably similar to those in human Parkinson's patients, including tremors, muscular rigidity, and a reduction in voluntary movement.

The connection between anatomy and behavior can also be seen in studies of animals trained on various types of learning tasks, such as spatial mazes. Such learning can be correlated with a variety of neuronanatomical changes—modifications in the synaptic organization of cells in specific cortical regions, such as the visual cortex in animals trained in visually guided mazes, for example, or in the number of newly generated cells that survive in the hippocampus, shown in **Figure 6-3.** Although the changes in synaptic organization or cell survival have not yet been proved to be the basis of the new learning, the cellular and behavioral changes presumably are closely linked.

Dorsal view of substantia nigra, a nucleus in the midbrain involved in initiating movement.

A healthy substantia nigra, rich in the cell bodies of dopamine neurons, shown in cross section.

In a weakened substantia nigra, dopamine neurons have degenerated, contributing to symptoms of Parkinson's disease.

FIGURE 6-2 Pathology in Parkinson's Disease. A variety of motor disturbances appear when enough dopamine-producing cells in the substantia nigra die. Adapted from healthguide.howstuffworks.com/substantia-nigra-and-parkinsons-disease-picture.htm

Methods of Behavioral Neuroscience

The ultimate function of any brain region is to produce behavior (movement). It follows that brain dysfunction will alter behavior in some way. The study of brain–behavior relationships began to be called neuropsychology in the 1940s, although the term is now often confined to the study of humans. The broader field, including both human and laboratory animals, is now referred to as **behavioral neuroscience,** the study of the biological basis of behavior.

A major challenge to behavioral neuroscientists is to develop methods for studying both normal and abnormal behavior. Measuring behavior in humans and laboratory

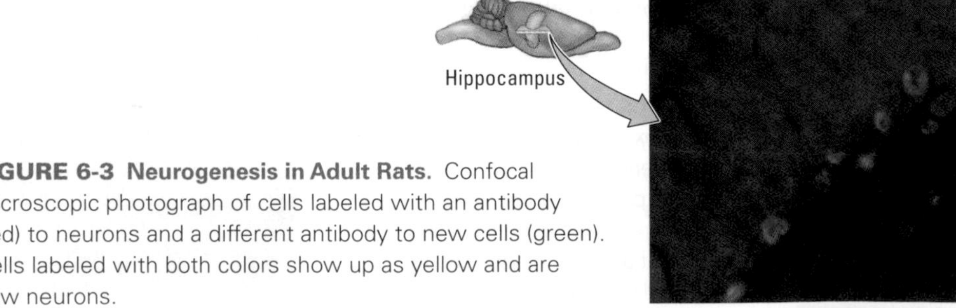

FIGURE 6-3 Neurogenesis in Adult Rats. Confocal microscopic photograph of cells labeled with an antibody (red) to neurons and a different antibody to new cells (green). Cells labeled with both colors show up as yellow and are new neurons.

animals is different, in large part because humans speak: investigators can ask them about their symptoms. It is also possible to use both paper-and-pencil and computer-based tests to identify specific symptoms in people.

Measuring behavior in laboratory animals is more complex. Researchers must learn to speak "ratese" to "talk" to rat subjects or "monkeyese" to "talk" to monkeys. In short, researchers must develop ways to enable the animals to reveal their symptoms. The development of the fields of animal learning and *ethology,* the study of animal behavior, provided the basis for modern behavioral neuroscience (see Whishaw and Kolb, 2005). To illustrate the logic of behavioral neuroscience, we describe some examples of measurement in humans and in rats.

Behavioral neuroscience Study of the biological basis of behavior.

Neuropsychological Testing of Humans

The brain has exquisite control of an amazing array of functions ranging from control of movement and sensory perception to memory, emotion, and language. As a consequence, any analysis of behavior must be tailored to the particular function(s) under investigation. Consider the analysis of memory.

People with damage to the temporal lobes often complain of memory disturbance. But memory is not a single function. We have memory for events, colors, names, places, and motor skills, among other categories, and each must be measured separately. It would be rare indeed for someone to be impaired in all forms of memory. Neuropsychological tests of three distinct forms of memory are illustrated in **Figure 6-4.**

The Corsi block-tapping test shown in Figure 6-4A requires participants to observe an experimenter tap a sequence of blocks—blocks 4-6-1-8-3 for instance. The task is to repeat the sequence correctly. Note that the subject does not see numbers on the blocks but rather must remember the location of the blocks tapped. The Corsi test provides a measure of the short-term recall of spatial position, an ability that we can call *block span.*

The test can be made more difficult by determining the maximum block span of an individual (say, 6 blocks) and then adding one (*span+1*). By definition, the participant will fail on the first presentation, but given the span+1 repeatedly the participant will eventually learn it. Span + 1 identifies a different form of memory from block span, and different types of neurological dysfunction will interfere differentially with tasks

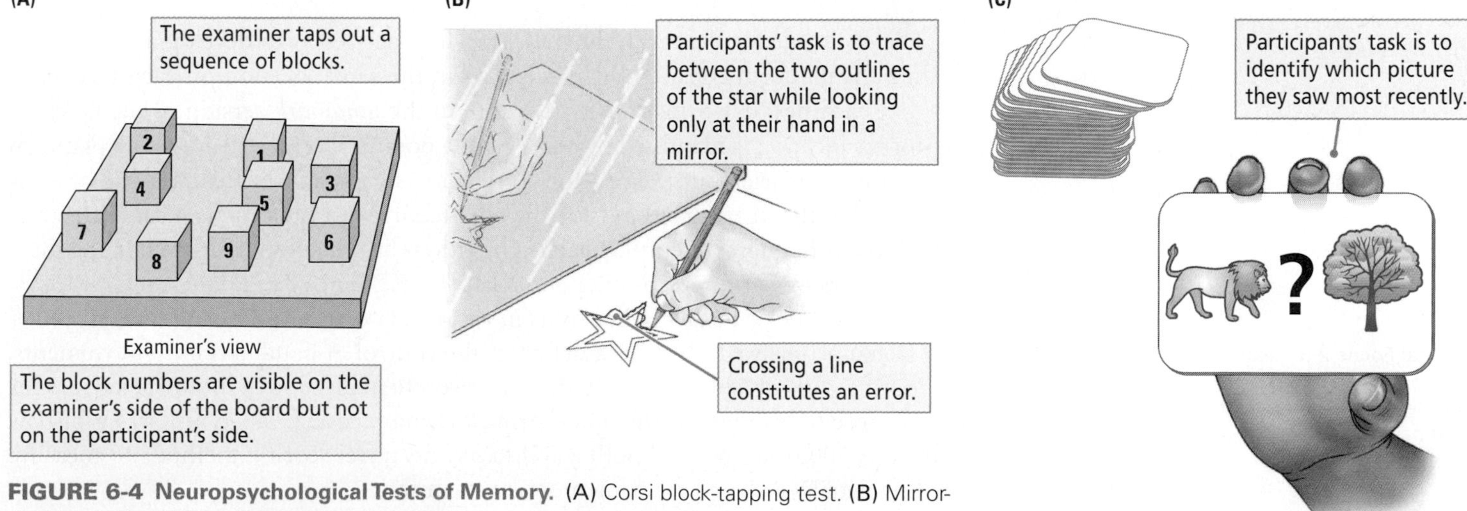
(A)
The examiner taps out a sequence of blocks.
2
1
4
3
5
7
8
9
6
Examiner's view
The block numbers are visible on the examiner's side of the board but not on the participant's side.
(B)
Participants' task is to trace between the two outlines of the star while looking only at their hand in a mirror.
Crossing a line constitutes an error.
(C)
Participants' task is to identify which picture they saw most recently.
?

FIGURE 6-4 Neuropsychological Tests of Memory. (A) Corsi block-tapping test. (B) Mirror-drawing task. (C) Test of recent memory.

that superficially appear to be quite similar. Block span is measuring the short-term recall of information whereas the span+1 task reflects the learning and longer-term memory storage of information.

The *mirror-drawing task* (Figure 6-4B) requires a person to trace a pathway, such as a star, by looking in a mirror. This motor task initially proves quite difficult because our movements are backward in the mirror. With practice, participants learn the task accurately, and they show considerable recall of the skill when retested days later. Curiously, subjects with certain types of memory problems have no recollection of learning the task on the previous day but perform it flawlessly.

In this book, we refer to humans in research studies who are "normal" as *participants* and to people who have a brain or behavioral impairment as *subjects.*

In the *recency memory task* (Figure 6-4C), participants are shown a long series of cards, each bearing two stimulus items that are words or pictures. On some trials a question mark appears between the items. The subjects' task is to indicate whether they have seen the items before and if so, which item they saw most recently. People may be able to correctly recall that they have seen items before but unable to recall which observation was most recent. Conversely, they may not be able to identify the items as being familiar, but when forced to choose the most recent one, they can correctly identify it.

The latter result is counterintuitive and reflects the need for behavioral researchers to develop ingenious ways of identifying memory abilities. It is not enough simply to ask people to recall information verbally, although this, too, measures a form of memory.

Behavioral Analysis of Rats

Learning and memory are the subjects of Chapter 14.

Psychologists interested in the neural basis of memory have devised a vast array of mazes to investigate different forms of memory in rats. **Figure 6-5** illustrates three different tests based on a task originally devised by Richard Morris in 1980. Researchers place rats in a large swimming pool where an escape platform lies just below the surface of the water, invisible to the rats.

In one version of the task, *place learning,* the rat must find the platform from any starting location in the pool (Figure 6-5A). The only cues available are outside the pool, so the rat must learn the relation between several cues in the room and the platform's location. In a second version of the task, *matching-to-place learning,* the rat that has already learned that a platform always lies somewhere in the pool but is moved to a different location every day. The rat is released and searches for the platform (Figure 6-5B). Once the rat finds the platform, the animal is removed from the pool and after a brief delay (such as 10 seconds) is released again. The task is to swim directly to the platform.

The challenge for the rat in the matching-to-place test is to develop a strategy for finding the platform consistently: it is always in the same location on each trial, each day, but each new day brings a new location. In the *landmark* version of the task, the platform's location is identified by a cue on the pool wall (Figure 6-5C). The platform moves on every trial, but the relation to the cue is constant. In this task the brain is learning that the distant cues outside the pool are irrelevant; only the local cue is relevant. Rats with different neurological perturbations are selectively impaired in the three different versions of the swimming pool task.

Clinical Focus 2-3 describes some disruptions strokes cause, both to the people who experience them and to people who care for stroke victims.

Another type of behavioral analysis in rats is related to movement. A major problem facing people with stroke is a deficit in the control of hand and limb movements, prompting considerable interest in devising ways to analyze such motor behaviors for the purpose of testing new therapies for facilitating recovery. Ian Whishaw (Whishaw and Kolb, 2005) has devised both novel tasks and novel scoring methods to measure the fine details of skilled reaching movements in rats.

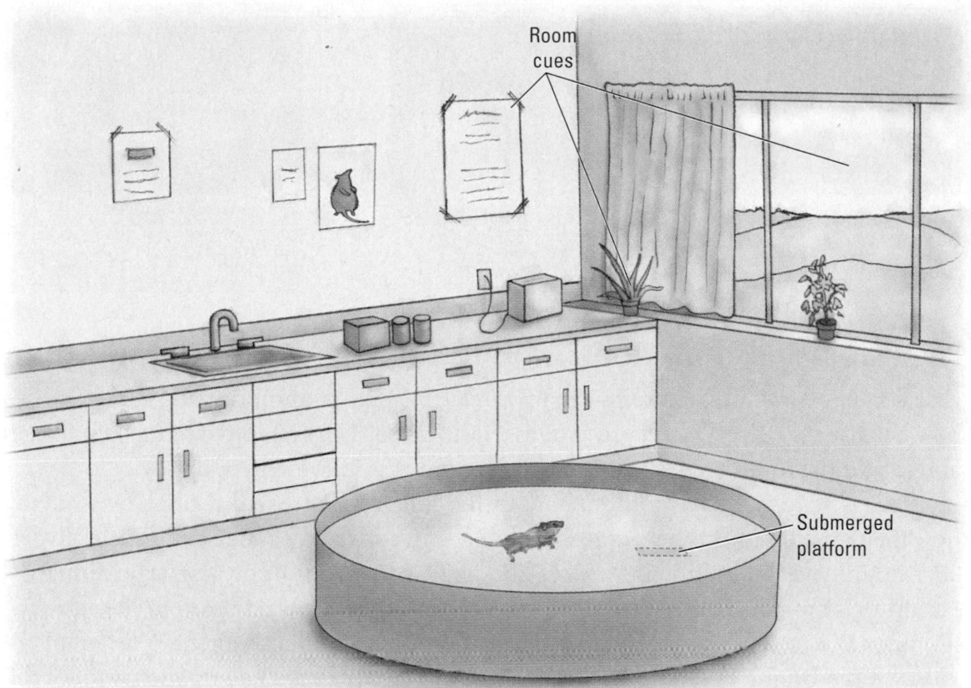

FIGURE 6-5 Swimming Pool Tasks. General arrangement of the swimming pool used in three different visuospatial learning tasks for rats. The red lines in parts A, B, and C mark the rat's swimming path on each trial (T). (A) Adapted from "Spatial Localization Does Not Require the Presence of Local Cues," by R. G. M. Morris et al., 1981, *Learning and Motivation, 12,* 239–260. (B) Adapted from "Dissociating Performance and Learning Deficits in Spatial Navigaion Tasks in Rats Subjected to Cholinergic Muscarinic Blockade," by I. Q. Whishaw, 1989, *Brain Research Bulletin, 23,* 347–358. **(C)** Adapted from "Behavioural and Anatomical Studies of the Posterior Parietal Cortex of the Rat," by B. Kolb and J. Walkey, 1987, *Behavioural Brain Research, 23,* 127–145.

(A) Place-learning task

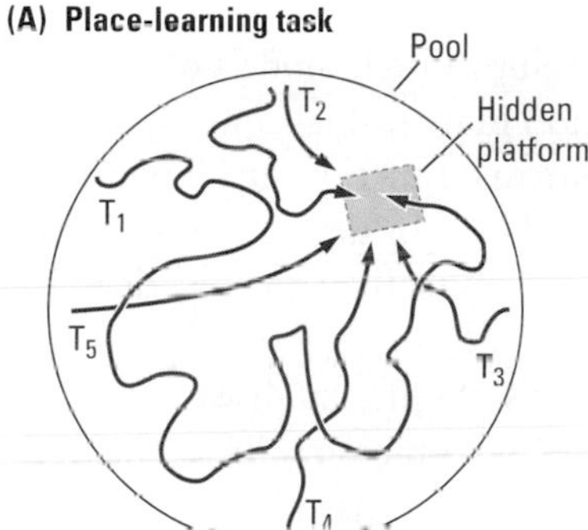

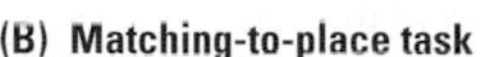

A rat placed in the pool at various starting locations must learn to find a hidden platform. The rat can do this only by considering the configuration of visual cues in the room—windows, wall decorations, potted plants, and the like.

(B) Matching-to-place task

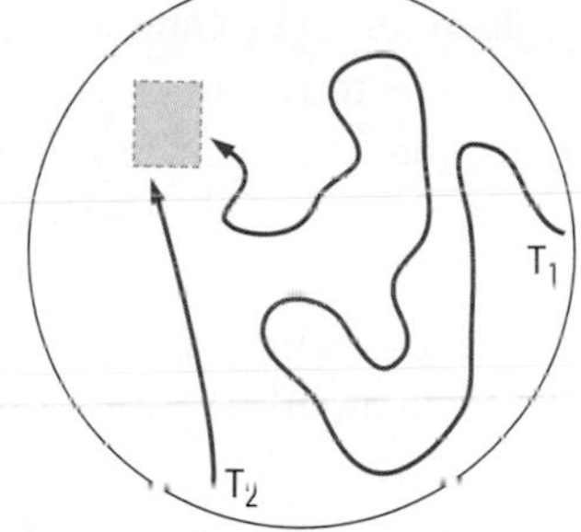

The rat is again put into the pool at random locations, but the hidden platform is in a new location on each test day. The animal must learn that the location where it finds the platform on the first trial day is its location for all trials on that day.

(C) Landmark-learning task

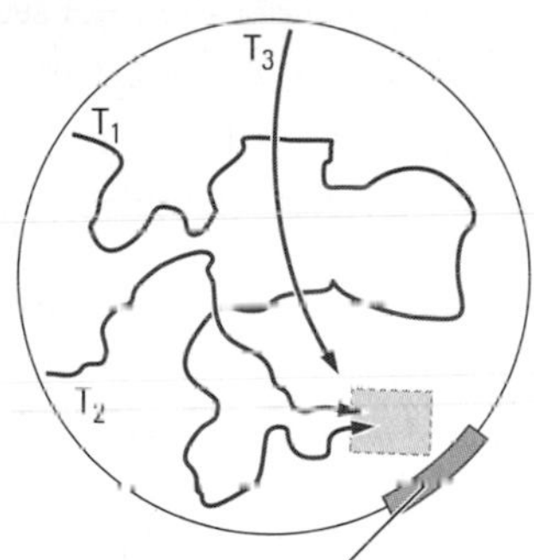

The rat must ignore the room cues and learn that only the cue on the wall of the pool signals the loaction of the platform. The platform and cue are moved on each trial, so the animal is penalized for using room cues to try to solve the problem.

In one test, rats are trained to reach through a slot to obtain a piece of sweet food. The movements are remarkably similar to those people make in a similar task and can be broken down into segments. Investigators can score the segments, which are differentially affected by different types of neurological perturbation, separately.

The photo series in **Figure 6-6** details how a rat orients its body to the slot (A), aims its paw through the slot (B), rotates the paw horizontally to grasp the food (C), then rotates the paw vertically and withdraws the paw to obtain the food (D). Contrary to reports common in neurology textbooks, primates are not the only animals to make fine digit movements, but because the rodent paw is small and moves so quickly, digit dexterity can be seen in rodents only by using high-speed photography.

(A)

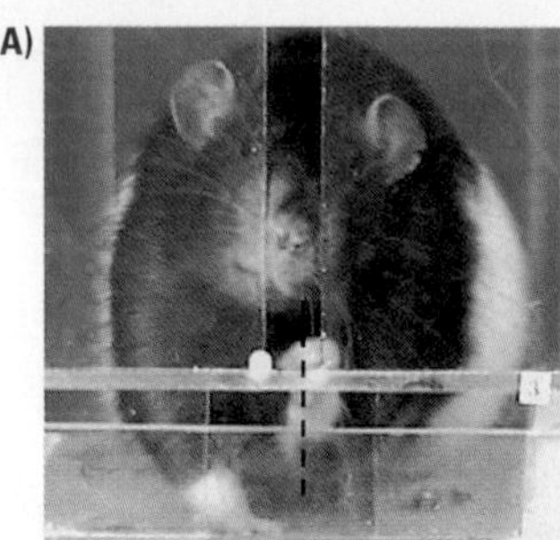

(B)

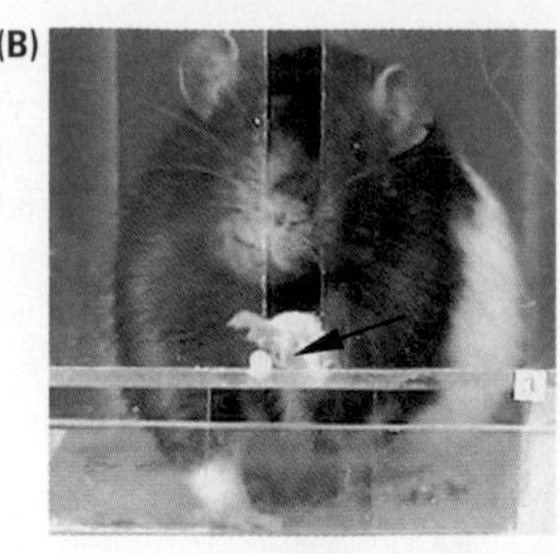

(C)

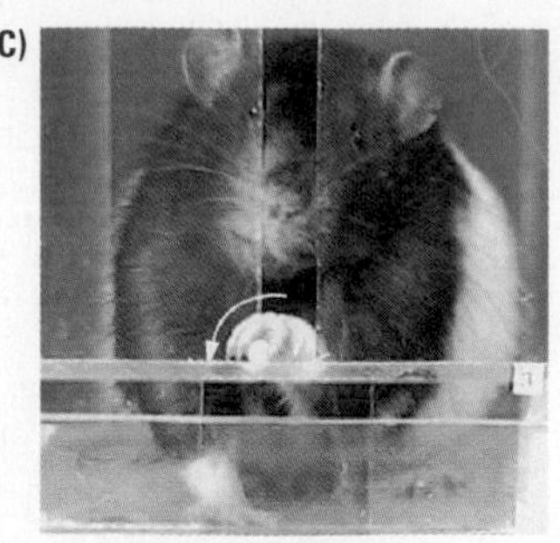

(D)

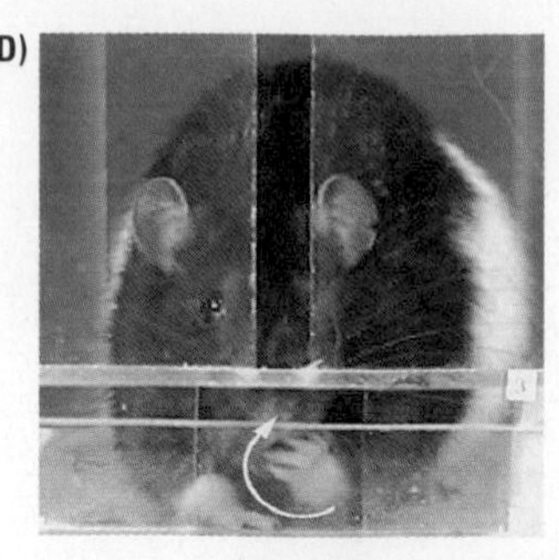

Bryan Kolb

FIGURE 6-6 Skilled Reaching in Rats. Movement series displayed by rats trained to reach through a narrow vertical slot to obtain sweet food: (A) aim the paw, (B) reach over the food, (C) grasp the food, (D) withdraw and move food to the mouth.

Manipulating and Measuring Brain–Behavior Interactions

One strategy for studying brain–behavior relationships is to modify the brain and see how behavior is altered. There are two reasons to do so. The first is to develop hypotheses about how the brain affects behavior; the second is to test the hypotheses.

Neuroscientists can hypothesize about the functions of brain regions by studying how their absence affects behavior. Recall that Broca studied patients with naturally occurring injuries and made inferences about the organization of language. Similarly, Parkinson's patients have motor disturbances and associated cell death in the substantia nigra. It is a small step experimentally to produce specific injuries to different regions in the brains of laboratory animals and study their behavior. Such studies tell investigators not only about the function of the injured region but also what the remaining brain can do in the absence of the injured region.

Three Clinical Focus boxes in Chapter 5 detail many aspects of Parkinson's disease, a disorder of the motor system correlated with a loss of dopamine in the brain.

A second reason to manipulate the brain is to develop animal models of neurological and psychiatric disorders. The general presumption in neurology and psychiatry is that it ought to be possible to restore at least some normal functioning by pharmacological, behavioral, or other interventions. A major problem for developing such treatments, however, is that like most new treatments in medicine, they must be developed in nonhuman subjects first.

For brain disorders, researchers must develop models of different diseases that then can be treated. Consider dementia, a condition of progressive memory impairment that appears to be related to neuronal death in specific brain regions. The goal for treatment is to reverse or prevent cell death, but developing effective treatments requires an animal model that mimics dementia.

Chapters 2 and 5 introduce possible factors that contribute to dementias such as Alzheimer's disease; Chapters 14 and 16 describe, respectively, the current state of research on and treatment for Alzheimer's disease.

Brains can be manipulated in a variety of ways, the precise manner depending on the specific research question being asked. The principal techniques are to lesion the brain or to electrically or chemically (with drugs) stimulate or inactivate the brain.

Brain Lesions

The first—and the simplest—technique used was to ablate (remove or destroy) tissue. Beginning in the 1920s Karl Lashley, a pioneer of neuroscience research, used ablation, and for the next 30 years he tried to find the location of memory in the brain. He trained monkeys and rats on various mazes and motor tasks and then removed bits of cerebral cortex with the goal of producing amnesia for specific memories. To his chagrin, Lashley failed to produce amnesia but instead discovered that memory loss was related to the amount of tissue he removed. The only conclusion Lashley could reach was that memory is distributed throughout the brain and not located in any single place.

Scoville's patient, H. M., who is profiled in Chapter 14, became the most-studied case in neuroscience.

Ironically, just as Lashley was retiring in the 1950s, William Scoville and Brenda Milner (1957) described an amnesic patient from whose brain Scoville had removed the hippocampus for the treatment of epilepsy. During his ablation research, Lashley had never removed the hippocampus because he had no reason to believe that this structure had any role in memory. And because the hippocampus is not accessible on the surface of the brain, other techniques had to be developed before subcortical lesions could be used.

appears that repeated exposu
caine, and nicotine can produ
ity to change in response to e:

REVIEW: Measuri

- ✔ The relationship between neuroanatomy and/or on
- ✔ Behavioral studies were a brain–behavior relationsh animals with different ne compared to postmortem related to brain changes c
- ✔ Anatomical studies rely o their connections. Functi regions electrically or che

Measuring th

The brain is always electricall tivity are important for stud ing the effectiveness of thera for tracking the brain's electr potentials (ERP), magnetoe

In part, these technique tentials and graded potenti cell bodies and dendrites te duct action potentials. Gra as these regions normally d

EEG Recordings o

In the early 1930s, Hans Be recorded simply by placing popularly known as "brain electroencephalogram. An thousands of neurons. EE scope called a polygraph (

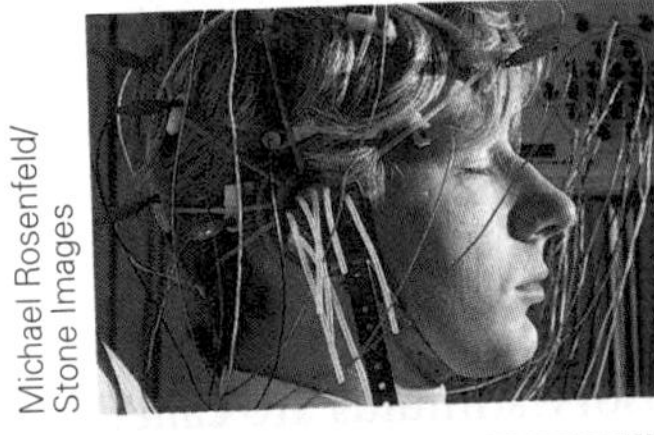
Michael Rosenfeld/ Stone Images

1 Electrodes are attached to the skull, corresponding to specific areas of the brain.

FIGURE 6-7 Neurosurgery. A human patient held in a stereotaxic device for brain surgery. The device allows the precise positioning of electrodes.

Michael English, M.D./Custom Medical Stock

Stereotaxic apparatus Surgical instrument that permits the researcher to target a specific part of the brain.
Akinesia Slowness or absence of movement.

The solution to accessing subcortical regions is to use a **stereotaxic apparatus,** a device that permits a researcher or a neurosurgeon to target a specific part of the brain, as shown in **Figure 6-7.** The head is held in a fixed position and, because brain structures hold a fixed relationship with the location of the junction of the skull bones, it is possible to imagine a three-dimensional map of the brain.

Rostral–caudal (front to back) measurements are made relative to the junction of the frontal and parietal bones (the *bregma*); dorsal–ventral (top to bottom) measurements are made relative to the surface of the brain; medial–lateral measurements are made relative to the midline junction of the cranial bones. Atlases of the brains of humans and laboratory animals have been created from postmortem tissue so that the precise location of any structure can be specified in three-dimensional space.

You can refresh your memory for anatomical locations and orientations in the brain by reviewing "The Basics" in Chapter 2.

Consider the substania nigra. To ablate this region to produce a rat that displays symptoms of Parkinson's disease, the structure and its three-dimensional location in the brain atlas would be located. A small hole would then be drilled in the skull and an electrode lowered to the substantia nigra. If a current were passed through the electrode, the tissue in the region of the electrode tip would be killed, producing an *electrolytic lesion.*

A problem with electrolytic lesions is that not only are the neurons of the tissue (in this case substantia nigra) killed but any nerve fibers passing through the region die as well. One solution is to lower a narrow, metal tube (a cannula) instead of an electrode, infuse a neuron-killing chemical, and thus produce a *neurotoxic lesion.* A selective toxin can be injected that kills only neurons, sometimes only certain types of neurons, and spares the fibers.

To create a Parkinsonian rat, a toxin can be injected that is selectively taken up by dopaminergic neurons, thus leading to a condition that mimics human Parkinson pathology. Animals with such lesions have a variety of motor symptoms including **akinesia** (slowness or absence of movement), short footsteps, and tremor. Drugs such as L-dopa, which enhances dopamine production, and atropine, which blocks acetylcholine production, relieve these symptoms in human patients. Ian Whishaw and his colleagues (Schallert et al., 1978) thus were able to selectively lesion the substantia nigra in rats to produce a behavioral model of Parkinson's disease.

Ian Whishaw/AAAS

Shuffling gait of a Parkinsonian rat, captured in prints left by its ink-stained hind feet.

Brain Stimulaton

The brain operates on both electrical and chemical energy, so it is possible to selectively turn brain regions "on" or "off" by using electrical or chemical stimulation, usually delivered via a stereotaxic apparatus. Electrical stimulation was first used by Wilder Penfield to stimulate the cerebral cortex of humans directly during neurosurgery. Later researchers used the stereotaxic instrument to place an electrode or a cannula in specific brain locations with the objective of enhancing or blocking the activity of neurons and observing the behavioral effects.

You can read more about Penfield's dramatic discoveries in Chapter 10.

Perhaps the most dramatic research example comes from stimulating specific regions of the hypothalamus. Rats with electrodes placed in the lateral hypothalamus

Figure 2-17 diagrams the location c hypothalamus within the brainsten diencephalon. Chapter 12 details it motivated and emotional behavior

Research Focus 1-2 describes how the thalamus dramatically improv responsiveness in a man who hac in a minimally conscious state for following a traumatic brain injury.

LTP, explained in Chapter 5, play: learned associations. Chapter 16 how TMS is used to treat disorde

Chapter 8 examines how drugs hormones affect the brain and t

FIGURE 6-8 Transcranial Mi Stimulation.

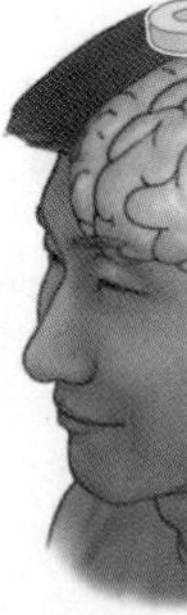

Attention-deficit/hyperactivity disorder (ADHD) Developmental disorder characterized by core behavioral symptoms of impulsivity, hyperactivity, and/or inattention.

Two important issues surface in developing treatments for brain and behavioral disorders with animal models. The first is whether the animals actually contract the same neurological diseases that humans do. The second involves the ethics of using animals in research. We consider each problem separately.

Benefits of Creating Animal Models of Disease

Some disorders—stroke, for example—seem relatively easy to model in laboratory animals because it is possible to interrupt blood supply to the brain and induce cortical injury and subsequent behavioral change. Obviously, it is much more difficult to determine whether behavioral disorders can actually be induced in laboratory animals. Consider **attention-deficit/hyperactivity disorder (ADHD)**, a developmental disorder characterized by core behavioral symptoms of impulsivity, hyperactivity, and/or inattention. The most common issue in children with ADHD is that they have problems in school. Lab animals such as rats and mice do not go to school, so diagnosis is challenging.

Chapter 15 explores the nature of attention and disorders that result in deficits of attention.

ADHD has proved difficult to treat in children, and interest in developing an animal model is high. One way to proceed is to take advantage of the normal variance in the performance of rats on various tests of working memory and cognitive functioning. Many studies have now shown that treating rats with methylphendiate (Ritalin), a common treatment for children diagnosed with ADHD, actually improves the performance of rats that do poorly on tests of attentional processes.

One rat strain, the Kyoto SHR rat, has been proposed as an especially good model for ADHD. The strain presents known abnormalities in prefrontal dopaminergic innervation that correlate with behavioral abnormalities such as hyperactivity. Dopaminergic abnormalities are believed to be one underlying symptom of ADHD in children, as explained in Research Focus 6-4, "Attention-Deficit/Hyperactivity Disorder." Dopamine agonists such as methylphenidate can reverse behavioral abnormalities, both in children with ADHD and in the SHR rats.

An *agonist* is a substance that enhances neurotransmission; an *antagonist* blocks it. Chapter 8 describes substances of both types.

Other models of ADHD focus on manipulating the animal's prefrontal development by perinatal anoxia (oxygen deprivation). This treatment leads to prefrontal abnormalities lateralized to the right hemisphere, which is also seen in humans with ADHD. There is no consistent evidence that perinatal anoxia is related to ADHD in children, however.

TABLE 6-1 Member Organizations in the Canadian Council on Animal Care

Member Organizations
Agriculture Canada
Association of Canadian Faculties of Dentistry
Association of Canadian Medical Colleges
Association of Universities and Colleges of Canada
Canadian Association for Laboratory Animal Medicine
Canadian Association for Laboratory Animal Science
Canadian Federation of Humane Societies
Canadian Institute for Health Research
Canadian Society of Zoologists
Committee of Chairpersons for Departments of Psychology
Confederation of Canadian Faculties of Agriculture and Veterinary Medicine
Department of National Defense
Environment Canada
Fisheries and Oceans Canada
Health and Welfare Canada
Heart and Stroke Foundation of Canada
National Cancer Institute
National Research Council
Natural Sciences and Engineering Research Council
Canada's Research-Based Pharmaceutical Companies (Rx&D)

Animal Welfare and Scientific Experimentation

Using nonhuman animals in scientific research has a long history, but only in the past half-century have ethical issues surrounding animal research gained considerable attention. Just as the scientific community has established ethical standards for research on human subjects, it has also developed regulations governing experimentation on animals. The governments of most developed nations regulate the use of animals in research; most states and provinces have additional legislation. Universities and other organizations engaged in research have their own rules governing animal use, as do professional societies of scientists and the journals in which they publish.

In Canada, the 20 organizations listed in **Table 6-1** make up the Canadian Council on Animal Care. The council is dedicated to enhanced animal care and use through education, voluntary compliance, and codes of ethics. The council is organized to re-

RESEARCH FOCUS 6-4

Attention-Deficit/Hyperactivity Disorder

ADHD is probably the most common disorder of brain and behavior in children, with an incidence of from 4 percent to 10 percent of school-aged children. Although often not recognized, an estimated 50 percent of ADHD children still show symptoms in adulthood, where its behaviors are associated with family breakups, substance abuse and driving accidents.

The neurobiological basis of ADHD is generally believed to be a dysfunction in the noradrenergic or dopaminergic activating systems, especially in the frontal basal ganglia circuitry. Psychomotor stimulants such as methylphendiate (Ritalin) act to increase brain levels of noradrenaline and dopamine and are widely used for treating ADHD. About 70 percent of children show improvement of attention and hyperactivity symptoms with treatment, but there is little evidence that drugs directly improve academic achievement. This is important because about 40 percent of children with ADHD fail to get a high-school diploma, even though many receive special education for their condition.

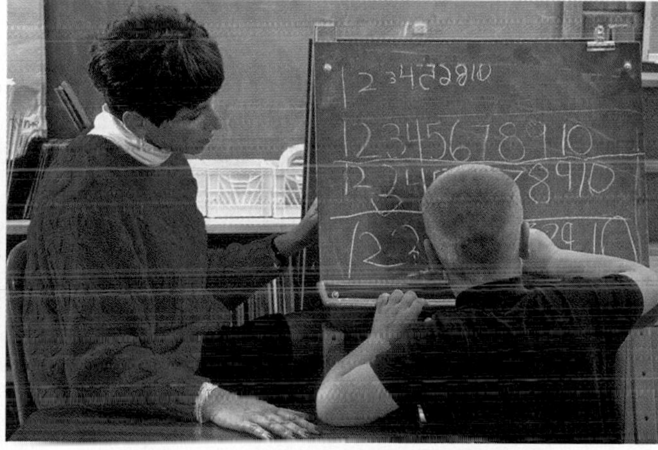
Ellen B. Senisi/The Image Works

ADHD children often have learning disabilities and may require full- or part-time school aides to keep up with their peers.

A common view that ADHD is a cultural phenomenon reflecting the tolerance of parents and teachers to children's behavior has been challenged by a scholarly review by Faraone et al. (2003). These investigators conclude that the prevalence of ADHD worldwide is remarkably similar when the same rating criteria are used. Little is known about incidence in developing countries, however. It is entirely possible that the incidence may actually be higher in developing countries given that the learning environment for children is likely to be less structured than it is in developed nations.

The cause of ADHD is unknown, but it probably involves dopamine receptors in the forebrain. The most likely areas are the frontal lobe and basal ganglia. Evidence of reduced brain volumes in these regions in ADHD patients is growing, as is evidence of an increase in the dopamine transporter. The dopamine transporter increase would mean that dopamine reuptake into the presynaptic neuron occurs faster than it does in the brains of people without ADHD. The result is a relative decrease in dopamine. Ritalin would then be effective because it blocks dopamine reuptake.

ADHD is believed to be highly heritable, a conclusion supported by twin studies showing a concordance of about 75 percent in identical twins. Molecular genetic studies have identified at least seven candidate genes, and several of them are related to the dopamine synapse, in particular to the D_4 receptor gene.

spond flexibly to the concerns of both the scientific community and the general public, through rapid and frequent amendments to its guidelines.

The Canadian Council on Animal Care endorses four principles as guidelines for reviewing protocols for experiments that will use animals:

1. The use of animals in research, teaching, and testing is acceptable only if it promises to contribute to the understanding of environmental principles or issues, fundamental biological principles, or development of knowledge that can reasonably be expected to benefit humans, animals, or the environment.
2. Optimal standards for animal health and care result in enhanced credibility and reproducibility of experimental results.
3. Acceptance of animal use in science critically depends on maintaining public confidence in the mechanisms and processes used to ensure necessary, humane, and justified animal use.

4. Animals are used only if the researcher's best efforts to find an alternative have failed. Researchers who use animals employ the most humane methods on the smallest number of appropriate animals required to obtain valid information.

Legislation concerning the care and use of laboratory animals in the United States is set forth in the Animal Welfare Act, which includes laws passed by Congress in 1966, 1970, 1976, and 1985. Legislation in other countries is similar and in some European countries much more strict. The U.S. act covers mammals, including rats, mice, cats, and monkeys, and birds, but it excludes farm animals that are not used in research. It is administered by the U.S. Department of Agriculture (USDA) through inspectors in the Animal and Plant Health Inspection Service, Animal Care.

In addition, the Office of Human Research Protections of the National Institutes of Health (NIH) administers the Health Research Extension Act (passed in 1986). The act covers all animal uses conducted or supported by the U.S. Public Health Service and applies to any live vertebrate animal used in research, training, or testing. The act requires that each institution provide acceptable assurance that it meets all minimum regulations and conforms with *The Guide for the Care and Use of Laboratory Animals* (National Research Council, 1996) before conducting any activity that includes animals. The typical method for demonstrating conformance with the Guide is to seek voluntary accreditation from the Association for Assessment and Accreditation of Laboratory Animal Care International.

All accredited U.S. universities that receive government grant support are required to provide adequate treatment for all vertebrate animals. Reviews and specific protocols for fish, reptiles, mice, dogs, or monkeys to be used in research, teaching, or testing are administered through the same process. Anyone using animals in a U.S. university submits a protocol to the university's institutional animal care and use committee, composed of researchers, veterinarians, people who have some knowledge of science, and laypeople from the university and the community.

Companies that use animals for research are not required to follow this process. In effect, however, if they do not, they will be unable to publish the results of their research, because journals require that research conforms with national guidlines on animal care. In addition, discoveries made using animals are not recognized by goverment agencies that approve drugs for clinical trials with humans if they do not follow the proscribed process. Companies therefore use standards described as Good Laboratory Practice (GLP) that are as rigorous as those used by government agencies.

U.S. regulations specify that researchers consider alternatives to procedures that may cause more than momentary or slight pain or distress to animals. Most of the attention on alternatives has focused on the use of animals in testing and stems from high public awareness of some tests for pharmacological compounds, especially toxic compounds. Testing of such compounds is now regulated by the National Institute of Environmental Health Sciences.

In spite of the legislation related to animal use, considerable controversy remains over using animals in scientific research. At the extremes, people on one side approve and people on the other side disapprove of using animals for any form of research. Others fall somewhere in between. The debate centers on issues of law, morals, custom, and biology.

Because researchers in many branches of science experiment with animals to understand the functions of the body, the brain, and behavior, the issues in this debate are important to them. Because many people benefit from this research, including those who have diseases of the nervous system or nervous system damage, this debate is important to them. Because many people are philosophically opposed to using animals for work or food, this debate is important to them. And, because you, as a student, encounter many experiments on animals in this book, these issues are important to you as well.

REVIEW: Using Animals in Brain–Behavior Research

- ✔ Laboratory animals can model such human dysfunction as Parkinson's disease, stroke, and schizophrenia, among myriad others.
- ✔ Some disorders are more difficult to model than others because it is difficult to determine whether laboratory animals experience the same symptoms that humans do. Nonetheless, animal models provide a way to investigate both the proposed neural bases of and putative treatments for behavioral disorders.
- ✔ Using laboratory animals in research leads to concerns about animal welfare and raises ethical issues about whether animals should be used in research and, if so, in what types of research.

Summary

Measuring Brain and Behavior

The brain's primary function is to produce behavior, so the fundamental technique of research in behavioral neuroscience is to study the direct relationship between brain and behavior in both human patients and laboratory animals with neurological problems. Behavioral measures were initially observational, but researchers later developed neuropsychological measures designed to study specific functions such as fine movements, memory, and emotion. These behavioral outcomes are then correlated with anatomical, physiological, chemical, and other molecular measures of brain organization.

Brain and behavioral relations can be manipulated by altering brain function, either permanently or temporarily. Permanent changes involve damaging the brain directly by removing or destroying brain tissue. Transient changes in brain activity can be induced either by using a mild electrical or magnetic current or by administering drugs.

Measuring the Brain's Electrical Activity

Electrical activity can be measured from thousands of neurons at once in electroencephalographic or magnetoencephalographic recordings or by recording from small numbers or even from individual neurons. EEG can reveal a gross relationship between brain and behavior, as when a person is alert and displays the beta-wave pattern versus when the person is resting or sleeping, as indicated by the slower alpha-wave patterns. On the other hand, event-related potentials tell us that, even though the entire brain is active during waking, certain parts are momentarily much more active than others. ERP records how the location of increased activity changes as information moves from one brain area to another.

Recording from single or multiple cells shows us that neurons employ a code and that cortical neurons are organized into functional groups that work as a coordinated network. Neurons in sensory areas respond to specific characteristics of stimuli, such as color or pitch, whereas neurons in other regions can code for more complex information such as location of an organism in space.

Static Imaging Techniques: CT and MRI

CT and MRI methods are sensitive to the density of different brain structures, ventricles, nuclei, and pathways. CT is a form of three-dimensional X-ray, whereas MRI works on the principle that hydrogen atoms behave like spinning bar magnets in the presence of a magnetic field. Although CT scans are less expensive and can be done quickly, MRI provides an exceptionally clear image both of nuclei and of fiber pathways in the

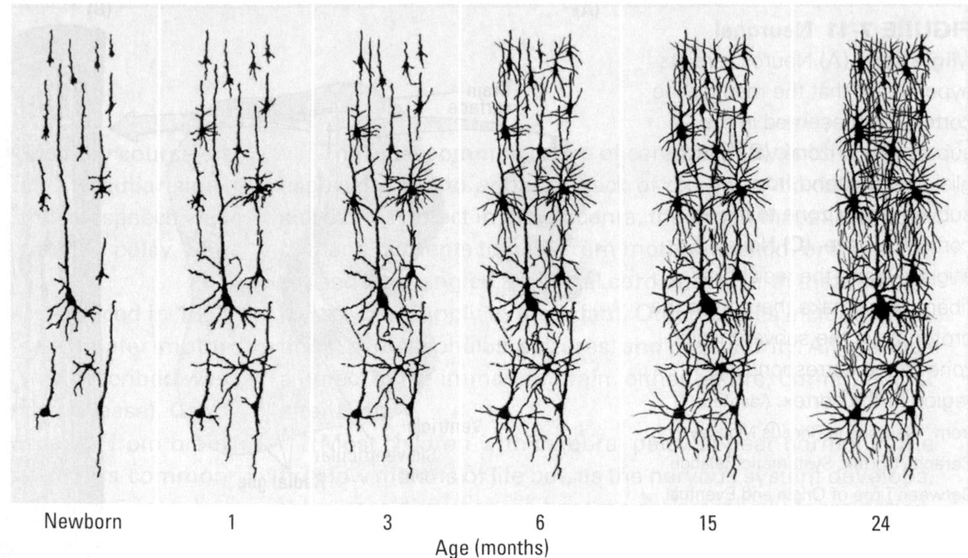

FIGURE 7-13 Neuronal Maturation in Cortical Language Areas. In postnatal differentiation of the human cerebral cortex—shown here around Broca's area, which controls speaking—neurons begin with simple dendritic fields that become progressively more complex until a child reaches about 2 years of age. Thus, brain maturation parallels the development of a behavior: the emergence of language.
Adapted from *Biological Foundations of Language* (pp. 160–161), by E. Lenneberg, 1967, New York: Wiley.

on the order of micrometers per day. Contrast this rate with that of the development of axons, which grow on the order of a millimeter per day, about a thousand times as fast. The disparate developmental rates of axons and dendrites are important because the faster-growing axon can contact its target cell before the dendrites of that cell are completely formed. In this way, the axon may play a role in dendritic differentiation and, ultimately, in neuron function—for example, as part of the visual, motor, or language circuitry of the brain.

Axon-appropriate connections may be millimeters or even centimeters away in the developing brain, and the axon must find its way through a complex cellular terrain to make them. Axon connections present a significant engineering problem for the developing brain. Such a task could not possibly be specified in a rigid genetic program. Rather, genetic–environmental interaction is at work again as the formation of axonic connections is guided by various molecules that attract or repel the approaching axon tip.

Santiago Ramón y Cajal was the first to describe this developmental process a century ago. He called the growing tips of axons **growth cones. Figure 7-14**A shows that, as these growth cones extend, they send out shoots, analogous to fingers reaching out to find a pen on a cluttered desk. When one shoot, known as a **filopod** (plural, *filopodia*), reaches an appropriate target, the others follow.

Growth cones are responsive to two types of cues (Figure 7-14B):

1. **Cell-adhesion molecules** (CAMs) are cell-manufactured molecules that either lie on the target cell's surface or are secreted into the intercellular space. Some CAMs

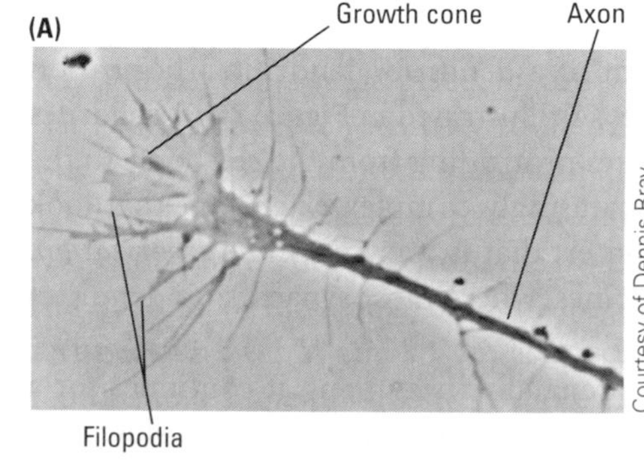

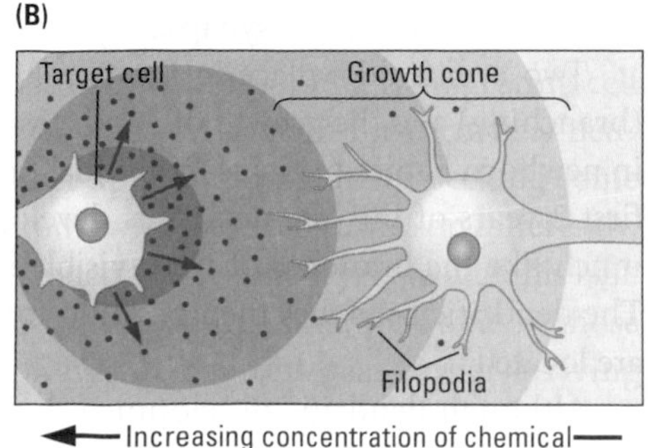

FIGURE 7-14 Seeking a Path. (A) At the tip of this axon, nurtured in a culture, a growth cone sends out filopodia seeking specific molecules to guide the axon's growth direction. (B) Filopodia guide the growth cone toward a target cell that is releasing cell-adhesion or tropic molecules, represented in the drawing by red dots.

provide a surface to which growth cones can adhere, hence their name, whereas others serve to attract or repel growth cones.

2. **Tropic molecules,** to which growth cones respond, are produced by the targets being sought by the axons (*tropic* means "to move toward"). Tropic molecules essentially tell growth cones to "come over here." They likely also tell other growth cones seeking different targets to "keep away."

As described in Chapter 5, ionotropic receptors in cell membranes guide ions either to flow through their pores or to block the flow. Tropic molecules likewise guide axons toward their targets. Do not confuse *tropic* (guiding) molecules with the *trophic* (nourishing) molecules, discussed earlier, that support the growth of neurons and their processes.

Although Cajal predicted tropic molecules more than 100 years ago, they have proved difficult to find. Only one group, **netrins** (from Sanskrit for "to guide"), has been identified in the brain so far. Given the enormous number of connections in the brain and the great complexity in wiring them, many other types of tropic molecules are likely to be found.

Synaptic Development

The number of synapses in the human cerebral cortex is staggering, on the order of 10^{14}, or 100,000 trillion. This huge number could not possibly be determined by a genetic program that assigns each synapse a specific location. Like all stages of brain development, only the general outlines of neural connections in the brain are likely to be genetically predetermined. The vast array of specific synaptic contacts is then guided into place by a variety of environmental cues and signals.

A human fetus displays simple synaptic contacts in the fifth gestational month. By the seventh gestational month, synaptic development on the deepest cortical neurons is extensive. After birth, the number of synapses increases rapidly. In the visual cortex, synaptic density almost doubles between age 2 months and age 4 months and then continues to increase until age 1 year.

Cell Death and Synaptic Pruning

Sculptors begin to create their statues with blocks of stone and chisel the unwanted pieces away. The brain does something similar by using cell death and synaptic pruning. The "chisel" in the brain could be of several forms, including a genetic signal, experience, reproductive hormones, and even stress. The effect of the "chisels" in the brain can be seen in changes in cortical thickness over time, as illustrated in **Figure 7-15**, a

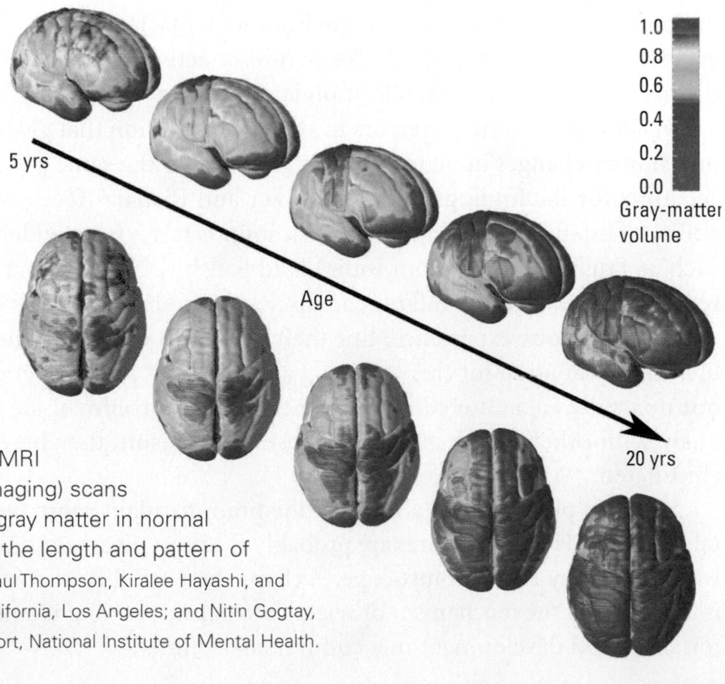

FIGURE 7-15 Progressive Changes in Cortical Thickness. MRI (magnetic resonance imaging) scans track the maturation of gray matter in normal development, revealing the length and pattern of maturation. Courtesy of Paul Thompson, Kiralee Hayashi, and Arthur Toga, University of California, Los Angeles; and Nitin Gogtay, Jay Gledd, and Judy Rappoport, National Institute of Mental Health.

Growth cone Growing tip of an axon.
Filopod (pl. filopodia) Process at the end of a developing axon that reaches out to search for a potential target or to sample the intercellular environment.
Cell-adhesion molecule (CAM) A chemical molecule to which specific cells can adhere, thus aiding in migration.
Tropic molecule Signaling molecule that attracts or repels growth cones.
Netrin Member of the only class of tropic molecules yet isolated.

As described in Chapter 6, brain atlases allow researchers to identify the precise spatial location of different brain regions.

brain-imaging atlas. The cortex actually becomes measurably thinner in a caudal–rostral (back-to-front) gradient, a process that is likely mostly due to the pruning of synapses.

The graph in **Figure 7-16** plots this rise and fall in synaptic density. Pasko Rakic estimated that, at the peak of synapse loss in humans, as many as 100,000 synapses may be lost per second. Synapse elimination is extensive. Peter Huttenlocher (1994) estimated it to be 42 percent of all synapses in the human cortex. We can only wonder what the behavioral consequence of this rapid synaptic loss might be. It is probably no coincidence that children, especially toddlers and adolescents, seem to change moods and behaviors quickly.

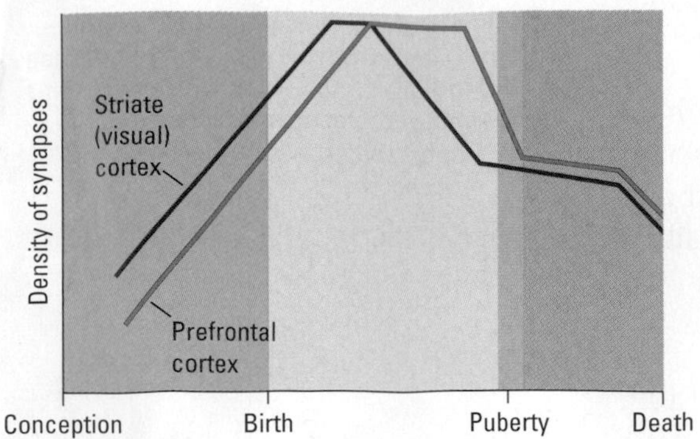

FIGURE 7-16 Synapse Formation and Pruning. Changes in the relative density of synapses in the human visual cortex and prefrontal cortex as a function of age.

Adapted from "Synaptogenesis in the neocortex of the newborn: The ultimate frontier for individuation?" by J.-P. Bourgeois, 2001, in *Handbook of Developmental Cognitive Neuroscience*, edited by C. A. Nelson and M. Luciana. Cambridge, MA: MIT Press.

How does the brain eliminate excess neurons? The simplest explanation is competition, sometimes referred to as **neural Darwinism.** Charles Darwin believed that one key to evolution is that it produces variation in the traits possessed by a species. Certain traits can then be selected by the environment as favorable in aiding survival. According to a Darwinian perspective, then, more animals are born than can survive to adulthood, and environmental pressures "weed out" the less-fit ones. Similar pressures cause neural Darwinism.

What exactly is causing this weeding out of cells in the brain? It turns out that, when neurons form synapses, they become somewhat dependent on their targets for survival. In fact, deprived of synaptic targets, they eventually die. Neurons die because target cells produce neurotrophic factors that are absorbed by the axon terminals and function to regulate neuronal survival. *Nerve growth factor* (NGF), for example, is made by cortical cells and absorbed by cholinergic neurons in the basal forebrain.

If many neurons are competing for a limited amount of a neurotrophic factor, only some of those neurons can survive. The death of neurons deprived of a neurotrophic factor is different from the cell death caused by injury or disease. When neurons are deprived of a neurotrophic factor, certain genes seem to be expressed, resulting in a message for the cell to die. This programmed process is called **apoptosis.**

Apoptosis accounts for the death of overabundant neurons, but it does not account for the pruning of synapses from cells that survive. In 1976, French neurobiologist Jean-Pierre Changeux proposed a theory for synapse loss that also is based on competition. According to Changeux, synapses persist into adulthood only if they have become members of functional neural networks. If they have not, they are eventually eliminated from the brain. We can speculate that environmental factors such as hormones, drugs, and experience would influence the formation of active neural circuits and thus influence the processes of synapse stabilization and pruning.

In addition to outright errors in synapse formation that give rise to synaptic pruning, subtler changes in neural circuits may trigger the same process. One such change accounts for the findings of Janet Werker and Richard Tees (1992), who studied the ability of infants to discriminate speech sounds taken from widely disparate languages, such as English, Hindi (from India), and Salish (a Native American language). Their results show that young infants can discriminate speech sounds of different languages without previous experience, but their ability to do so declines in the first year of life. An explanation for this declining ability is that synapses encoding speech sounds not normally encountered in an infant's daily environment are not active simultaneously with other speech-related synapses. As a result, they become unstable and are eliminated.

Synaptic pruning may also allow the brain to adapt more flexibly to environmental demands. Human cultures are probably the most diverse and complex environments with which any animal must cope. Perhaps the flexibility in cortical organization that is achieved by the mechanism of selective synaptic pruning is a necessary precondition for successful development in a cultural environment.

Neural Darwinism Hypothesis that the processes of cell death and synaptic pruning are, like natural selection in species, the outcome of competition among neurons for connections and metabolic resources in a neural environment.

Apoptosis Cell death that is genetically programmed.

Synaptic pruning may also be a precursor related to different perceptions that people develop about the world. Consider, for example, the obvious differences in "Eastern" and "Western" philosophies about life, religion, and culture. Given the obvious differences to which people in the East and West are exposed as their brains develop, we can only imagine how differently their individual perceptions and cognitions may be. Considered together as a species, however, we humans are far more alike than we are different.

An important and unique characteristic common to all humans is language. We considered its relevance to the increased size of the human brain in Research Focus 2-1. As illustrated in Figure 7-15, the cortex generally thins from age 5 to age 20. But there is one exception: the major language regions of the cortex actually show an *increase* in gray matter. **Figure 7-17** contrasts the thinning of other cortical regions with the thickening of language-related regions (O'Hare and Sowell, 2008). Finding a different pattern of cerebral development for brain regions critical in language processing may not be surprising, given the unique role of language in cognition as well as the protracted nature of the language-learning process.

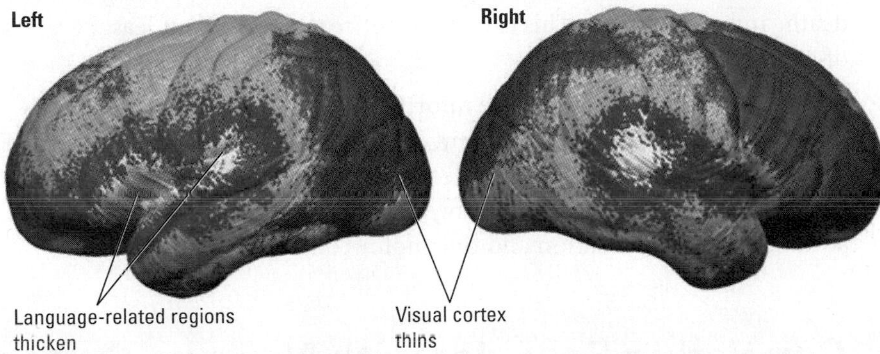

FIGURE 7-17 Gray-Matter Thickness. Brain maps showing the statistical significance of yearly change in cortical-thickness measures taken from MRIs. Color coding represents increasing (blue, white) or decreasing (yellow, green, red) cortical thickness. Red and white areas show statistically significant changes. Adapted from "Mapping Changes in the Human Cortex Throughout the Span of Life," by E. R. Sowell, P. M. Thompson, and A. W. Toga, 2004, *The Neuroscientist 10,* 372–392.

Glial Development

The birth of astrocytes and oligodendrocytes begins after most neurogenesis is complete and continues throughout life. Although CNS axons can function before they are myelinated, normal adult function is attained only after myelination is complete. Consequently, myelination is a useful rough index of cerebral maturation.

Astrocytes nourish and support neurons, and oligodendroglia form the myelin that surrounds axons in the spinal cord and brain. Table 3-1 lists the types and functions of these and other types of glia.

In the early 1920s, Paul Flechsig noticed that myelination of the cortex begins just after birth and continues until at least 18 years of age. He also noticed that some cortical regions were myelinated by age 3 to 4 years, whereas others showed virtually no myelination at that time. **Figure 7-18** shows one of Flechsig's cortical maps with areas shaded according to earlier or later myelination.

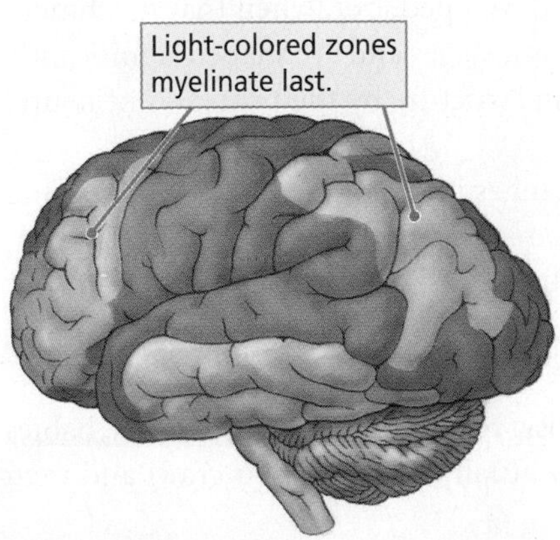

FIGURE 7-18 Progress of Myelination. The fact that the light-colored zones are very late to myelinate led Flechsig to propose that they are qualitatively different in function from those that mature earlier.

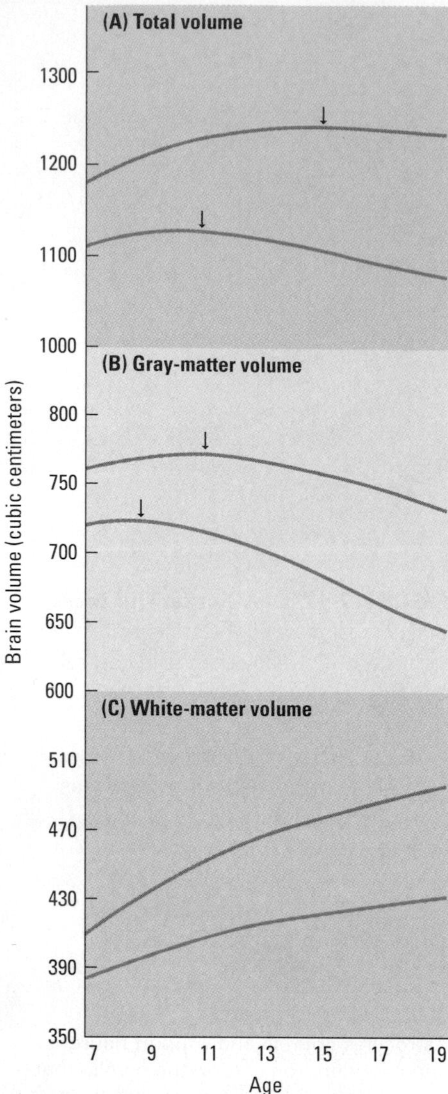

FIGURE 7-19 Sex Differences in Brain Development. Mean brain volume by age in years for males (pink) and females (purple). Females show more rapid growth than males, reaching maximum overall volume (A) and gray-matter volume (B) sooner (indicated by arrows). The decreasing gray matter corresponds to cell and synaptic loss. Increasing white-matter volume (C) largely corresponds to myelin development. Adapted from "Sexual Dimorphism of Brain Development Trajectories During Childhood and Adolescence, by R. K. Lenroot, N. Gogtay, D. K. Greenstein, et al., 2007, *NeuroImage 36,* 1065–1073.

Flechsig hypothesized that the earliest-maturing areas control simple movements or sensory analyses, whereas the latest-myelinating areas control the highest mental functions. MRI analyses of myelin development show that the thickness of white matter in the cortex largely does correspond to the progress of myelination, confirming Flechsig's ideas. Myelination continues until at least 20 years of age, as illustrated in **Figure 7-19,** which graphs total brain volume, gray-matter volume, and white-matter volume during brain development.

REVIEW: Neurobiology of Development

- ✔ The first neural stem cell heralds brain development in the 3-week-old human embryo. Beginning as a sheet of cells that folds to become the neural tube, nervous-system formation then proceeds rapidly; by about 100 days after conception, the brain begins to take a recognizably human form.
- ✔ Neurons and glia develop through a series of seven stages: birth, migration, differentiation, maturation, synaptic formation, synaptic pruning and cell death, and myelination. This process is not complete until at least 20 years of age.
- ✔ Neurons begin to process simple information before they are completely mature, but behavioral development is constrained by the maturation of CNS structures and circuits. For example, although infants and children are capable of complex movements, not until myelination is complete in adolescence are adult levels of coordination and fine motor control reached.

Correlating Behavior with Nervous-System Development

To predict that, as a particular brain area matures, a person exhibits behaviors corresponding to that particular mature brain structure is reasonable. The strongest advocate of this view has been Eric Lenneberg, who in 1967 published a seminal book, *Biological Foundations of Language.* A principal theme is that children's acquisition of language is tied to the development of critical language areas in the cerebral cortex.

This idea immediately stimulated debate about the merits of correlating brain and behavioral development. Now, more than 40 years later, the relation is widely accepted, although the influence of environmental factors such as experience and learning on behavior is still considered critical. That is, psychologists believe that behaviors cannot emerge until the neural machinery for them has developed, but, when that machinery is in place, related behaviors develop quickly through stages and are shaped significantly by experience. The new behaviors then alter brain structure by the processes of neural Darwinism.

Researchers have studied these interacting changes in the brain and behavior, especially in regard to the emergence of motor skills, language, and problem solving in children. We now explore development in all three areas.

Motor Behaviors

The development of locomotion skills is easy to observe in human infants. At first, babies are unable to move about independently but, eventually, they learn to crawl and then to walk.

Other motor skills develop in less obvious but no less systematic ways. Shortly after birth, infants are capable of flexing the joints of an arm in such a way that they can scoop something toward their bodies, and they can direct a hand such as occurs toward a breast when suckling. Between 1 and 3 months of age, babies also begin to make spontaneous hand and digit movements that consist of almost all the skilled finger movements that they might make as an adult, a kind of "motor babbling." These movements are then directed toward handling parts of their bodies and their clothes (Wallace and Whishaw, 2003). Only then are reaching movements directed toward objects in space. For example, Tom Twitchell (1965) studied and described how the ability to reach for objects and grasp them progresses in a series of stages, illustrated in **Figure 7-20.**

2 months
Orients hand toward an object and gropes to hold it.

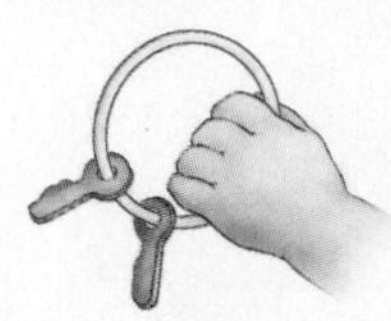
4 months
Grasps appropriately shaped object with entire hand.

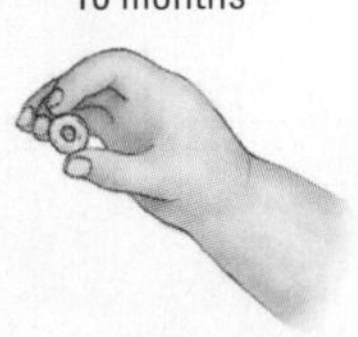
10 months
Uses pincer grasp with thumb and index finger opposed.

FIGURE 7-20 Development of the Grasping Response of Infants. Adapted from "The Automatic Grasping Response of Infants," by T. E. Twitchell, 1965, *Neuropsychologia, 3,* p. 251.

Between 8 and 11 months, infants' grasping becomes more sophisticated as the "pincer grasp," employing the index finger and the thumb, develops. The pincer grasp is a significant development because it allows babies to make the very precise finger movements needed to manipulate small objects. What we see, then, is a sequence in the development of grasping: first scooping, then grasping with all the fingers, and then grasping by using independent finger movements.

If the development of increasingly well coordinated grasping depends on the emergence of certain neural machinery, anatomical changes in the brain should accompany the emergence of these motor behaviors. Such changes do take place, especially in the development of dendritic arborizations and in connections between the neocortex and the spinal cord. And a correlation between myelin formation and the ability to grasp has been found (Yakovlev and Lecours, 1967).

One of the classic symptoms of damage to the motor cortex is the permanent loss of the pincer grasp, detailed in Chapter 11.

In particular, a group of axons from motor-cortex neurons become myelinated at about the same time that reaching and grasping with the whole hand develop. Another group of motor-cortex neurons, which are known to control finger movements, become myelinated at about the time that the pincer grasp develops. The results of MRI studies of changes in cortical thickness have shown that increased motor dexterity is associated with a decrease in cortical thickness in the hand region of the left motor cortex of right-handers (**Figure 7-21A**).

We can now make a simple prediction. If specific motor-cortex neurons are essential for adultlike grasping movements to emerge, the removal of those neurons should make an adult's grasping ability similar to that of a young infant, which is in fact what happens.

Language Development

The acquisition of speech follows a gradual series of developments that has usually progressed quite far by the age of 3 or 4. According to Lenneberg, children reach certain important speech milestones in a fixed sequence and at constant chronological ages. For example, children start to form a vocabulary by 12 months, and this 5-to-10-word

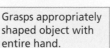

(A)
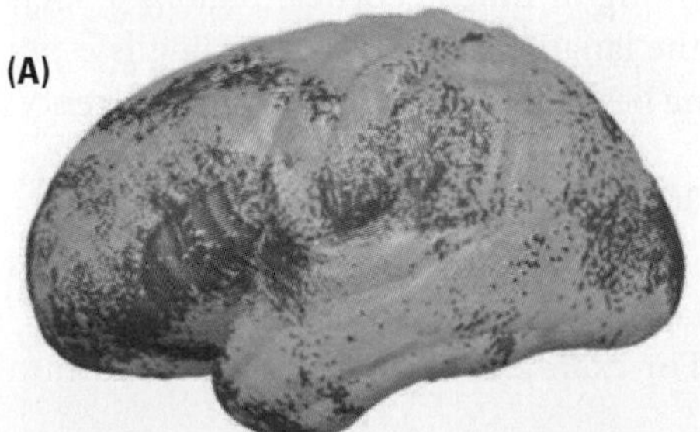

(B)
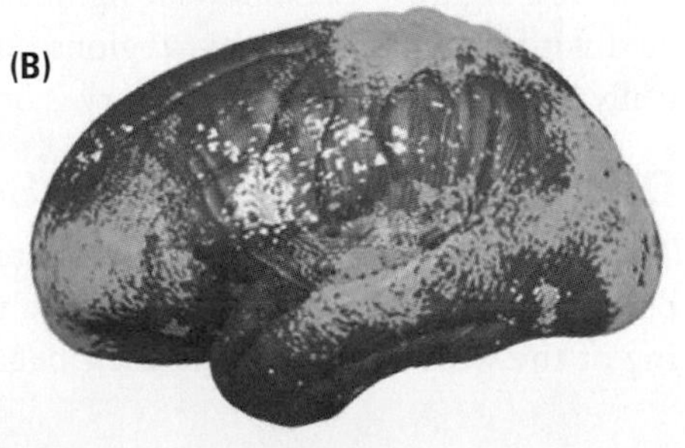

(C)
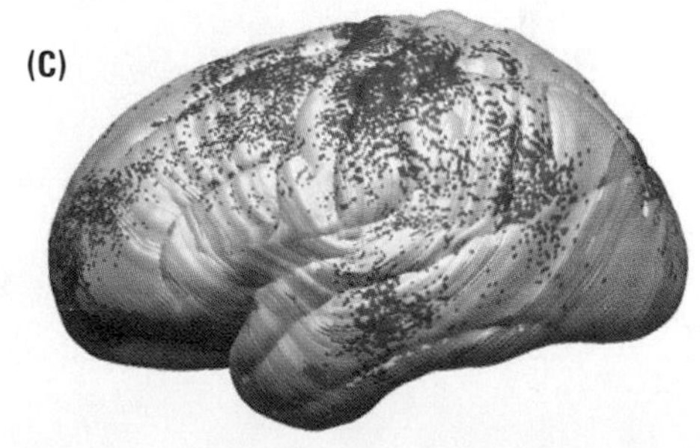

FIGURE 7-21 Correlations Between Gray-Matter Thickness and Behavior. (A) Red dots correspond to regions showing significant cortical thinning correlated with improved motor skills. (B) White dots correspond to regions showing significant cortical thickening correlated with improved language skills. (C) Red dots show regions of decreased cortical thickness correlated with improved vocabulary scores. (A and B) Adapted from "Normal Developmental Changes in Inferior Frontal Gray Matter Are Associated with Improvement in Phonological Processing: A Longitudinal MRI Analysis," by L. H. Lu, C. M. Leonard, P. M. Thompson, E. Kan, J. Jolley, S. E. Welcome, A. W. Toga, and E. R. Sowell, 2007, *Cerebral Cortex, 17,* 1092–1099. (C) Adapted from "Longitudinal Mapping of Cortical Thickness and Brain Growth in Normal Children, by E. R. Sowell, P. M. Thompson, C. M. Leonard, S. E. Welcome, E. Kan, and A. W. Toga, 2004, *Journal of Neuroscience, 24,* 8233–8223.

repertoire typically doubles over the next six months. By 2 years, the vocabulary will be from 200 to 300 words that include mostly everyday objects. In another year, the vocabulary approaches 1000 words and begins to include simple sentences. Six-year-old children have a vocabulary of about 2500 words and can understand more than 20,000 words en route to an adult vocabulary of more than 50,000 words.

Although language skills and motor skills generally develop in parallel, the capacity for language depends on more than just the ability to make controlled movements of the mouth, lips, and tongue. Precise movements of the muscles controlling these body parts develop well before children can speak. Furthermore, even when children have sufficient motor skill to articulate most words, their vocabularies do not rocket ahead but rather progress gradually.

A small proportion of children (about 1 percent) have normal intelligence and normal motor-skill development, yet their speech acquisition is markedly delayed. Such children may not begin to speak in phrases until after age 4, despite an apparently normal environment and the absence of any obvious neurological signs of brain damage. Because the timing of the onset of speech appears universal in the remaining 99 percent of children across all cultures, something different is likely to have taken place in the brain maturation of a child with late language acquisition. But it is hard to specify what that difference is.

Because the age of language onset is usually between 1 and 2 and language acquisition is largely complete by age 12, the best strategy is to consider how the cortex is different before and after these two milestones. By age 2, cell division and migration are complete in the language zones of the cerebral cortex. The major changes that take place between the ages of 2 and 12 are in the interconnections of neurons and the myelination of the speech zones.

The changes in dendritic complexity in these areas are among the most impressive in the brain. Recall from Figure 7-13 that the axons and dendrites of the speech zone called Broca's area are simple at birth but grow dramatically more dense between 15 and 24 months of age. This neural development correlates with an equally dramatic change in language ability, given that a baby's vocabulary starts to expand rapidly at about age 2.

We can therefore infer that language development may be constrained, at least in part, by the maturation of language areas in the cortex. Individual differences in the speed of language acquisition may be accounted for by differences in this neural development. Children with early language abilities may have early maturation of the speech zones, whereas children with delayed language onset may have later speech-zone maturation.

Results of MRI studies of the language cortex show that, in contrast with the thinning of the motor cortex associated with enhanced dexterity shown in Figure 7-21A, a *thickening* of the left inferior frontal cortex (roughly Broca's area) is associated with enhanced phonological processing (understanding speech sounds), as shown in Figure 7-21B. The unique association between cortical thickening and phonological processing is not due to a general relation between all language functions and cortical thickening, however. Figure 7-21C shows a significant thinning of diffuse cortical regions associated with better vocabulary—regions outside the language areas. This finding is especially intriguing because vocabulary is one of the best predictors of general intelligence.

Development of Problem-Solving Ability

The first person to try to identify discrete stages of cognitive development was Swiss psychologist Jean Piaget (1952). He realized that he could infer children's understanding of the world by observing their behavior. For example, a baby who lifts a cloth to

Doug Goodman/Monkmeyer

Courtesy of Don and Sandy Hockenbury

FIGURE 7-22 Two Stages of Cognitive Development. (*Top*) The infant shows that she understands object permanence—that things continue to exist when they are out of sight. (*Bottom*) This girl does not yet understand the principle of conservation of liquid volume. Beakers with identical volumes but different shapes seem to her to hold different amounts of liquid.

retrieve a hidden toy shows an understanding that objects continue to exist even when out of sight. This understanding, the concept of *object permanence,* is revealed by the behavior of the infant in the upper row of photographs in **Figure 7-22**.

An absence of understanding also can be seen in children's behavior, as shown by the actions of the 5-year-old girl in the lower row of photographs in Figure 7-22. She was shown two identical beakers with identical volumes of liquid in each and then watched as one beaker's liquid was poured into a taller, narrower beaker. When asked which beaker contained more liquid, she pointed to the taller beaker, not understanding that the amount of liquid remains constant despite the difference in appearance. Children display an understanding of this principle, the *conservation of liquid volume,* at about age 7.

By studying children engaged in such tasks, Piaget concluded that cognitive development is a continuous process. Children's strategies for exploring the world and their understanding of it are constantly changing. These changes are not simply the result of acquiring specific pieces of new knowledge. Rather, at certain points in development, fundamental changes take place in the organization of a child's strategies for learning about the world and for solving problems. With these developing strategies comes new understanding.

Piaget identified four major stages of cognitive development, which are summarized in **Table 7-2**:

- Stage I is the sensorimotor period, from birth to about 18 to 24 months of age. During this time, babies learn to differentiate themselves from the external world, come to realize that objects exist even when out of sight, and gain some understanding of cause-and-effect relations.
- Stage II, the preoperational period, extends from 2 to 6 years of age. Children gain the ability to form mental representations of things in their world and to represent those things in words and drawings.

TABLE 7-2 Piaget's Stages of Cognitive Development

Typical age range	Description of stage	Developmental phenomena
Birth to 18–24 months	*Stage I: Sensorimotor* Experiences the world through senses and actions (looking, touching, mouthing)	Object permanence Stranger anxiety
About 2–6 years	*Stage II: Preoperational* Represents things with words and images but lacks logical reasoning	Pretend play Egocentrism Language development
About 7–11 years	*Stage III: Concrete operational* Thinks logically about concrete events; grasps concrete analogies and performs arithmetical operations	Conservation Mathematical transformations
About 12+ years	*Stage IV: Formal operational* Reasons abstractly	Abstract logic Potential for mature moral reasoning

- Stage III is the period of concrete operations, typically from 7 to 11 years of age. Children are able to mentally manipulate ideas about material (concrete) things such as volumes of liquid, dimensions of objects, and arithmetic problems.
- Stage IV, the period of formal operations, is attained sometime after age 11. Children are now able to reason in the abstract, not just in concrete terms.

If we take Piaget's stages as rough approximations of qualitative changes that take place in children's thinking as they grow older, we can ask what neural changes might underlie them. One place to look for brain changes is in the relative rate of brain growth.

After birth, brain and body do not grow uniformly but rather tend to increase in mass during irregularly occurring periods commonly called **growth spurts.** In his analysis of brain-weight-to-body-weight ratios, Herman Epstein (1979) found consistent spurts in brain growth between 3 and 10 months (accounting for an increase of 30 percent in brain weight by the age of 1½ years) as well as from the ages of 2 to 4, 6 to 8, 10 to 12, and 14 to 16+ years. The increments in brain weight were from about 5 to 10 percent in each of these 2-year periods.

Brain growth takes place without a concurrent increase in the number of neurons, and so it is most likely due to the growth of glial cells and synapses. Although synapses themselves would be unlikely to add much weight to the brain, the growth of synapses is accompanied by increased metabolic demands, which cause neurons to become larger, new blood vessels to form, and new astrocytes to be produced for neuronal support and nourishment.

We would expect such an increase in the complexity of the cortex to generate more-complex behaviors, and so we might predict significant, perhaps qualitative, changes in cognitive function during each growth spurt. The first four brain-growth spurts identified by Epstein coincide nicely with the four main stages of cognitive development described by Piaget. Such correspondence suggests significant alterations in neural functioning with the onset of each cognitive stage.

At the same time, differences in the rate of brain development or perhaps in the rate at which specific groups of neurons mature may account for individual differences in the age at which the various cognitive advances identified by Piaget emerge. Although Piaget did not identify a fifth stage of cognitive development in later adolescence, the presence of a growth spurt then implies one.

Growth spurt Sporadic period of sudden growth that lasts for a finite time.

A difficulty in linking brain-growth spurts to cognitive development is that growth spurts are superficial measures of changes taking place in the brain. We need to know at a deeper level what neural events are contributing to brain growth and just where they are taking place. A way to find out is to observe children's attempts to solve specific problems that are diagnostic of damage to discrete brain regions in adults. If children perform a particular task poorly, then whatever brain region regulates the performance of that task in adults must not yet be mature in children. Similarly, if children can perform one task but not another, the tasks apparently require different brain structures, and these structures mature at different rates.

William Overman and Jocelyne Bachevalier (Overman et al., 1992) used this logic to study the development of forebrain structures required for learning and memory in young children and in monkeys. The Procedure section of **Experiment 7-1** shows the three intelligence-test items presented to their subjects. The first task was simply to learn to displace an object to obtain a food reward. When the subjects had learned this *displacement* task, they were trained in two more tasks believed to measure the functioning of the temporal lobes and the basal ganglia, respectively.

In the *nonmatching-to-sample* task, the subjects were shown an object that they could displace to receive a food reward. After a brief (15-second) delay, two objects were presented: the first object and a novel object. The subjects then had to displace the novel object to obtain the food reward. Nonmatching to sample is thought to measure object recognition, which is a function of the temporal lobes. The subject can find the food only by recognizing the original object and not choosing it.

In the third task, *concurrent discrimination,* the subjects were presented with a pair of objects and had to learn that one object in that pair was always associated with a food reward, whereas the other object was never rewarded. The task was made more difficult by sequentially giving the subjects 20 different object pairs. Each day, they were presented with one trial per pair. Concurrent discrimination is thought to measure trial-and-error learning of specific object information, which is a function of the basal ganglia.

Adults easily solve both the nonmatching and the concurrent tasks but report that the concurrent task is more difficult because it requires remembering far more information. The key question developmentally is whether there is a difference in the age at which children (or monkeys) can solve these two tasks.

EXPERIMENT 7-1

Question: In what sequence do the forebrain structures required for learning and memory mature?

Procedure

I. Displacement task

II. Nonmatching-to-sample learning task

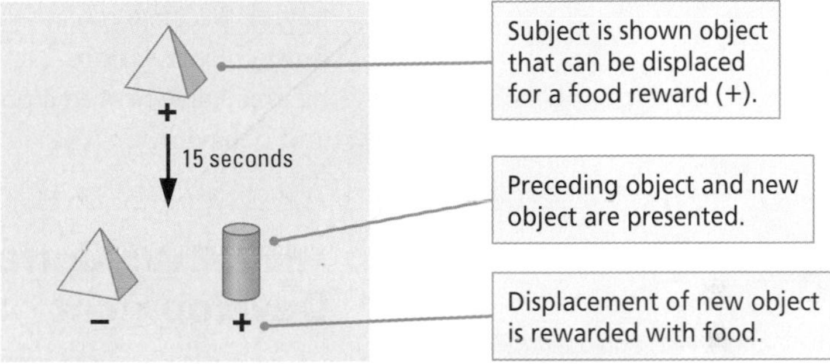
+
15 seconds
−
+
Subject is shown object that can be displaced for a food reward (+).
Preceding object and new object are presented.
Displacement of new object is rewarded with food.

III. Concurrent discrimination learning task

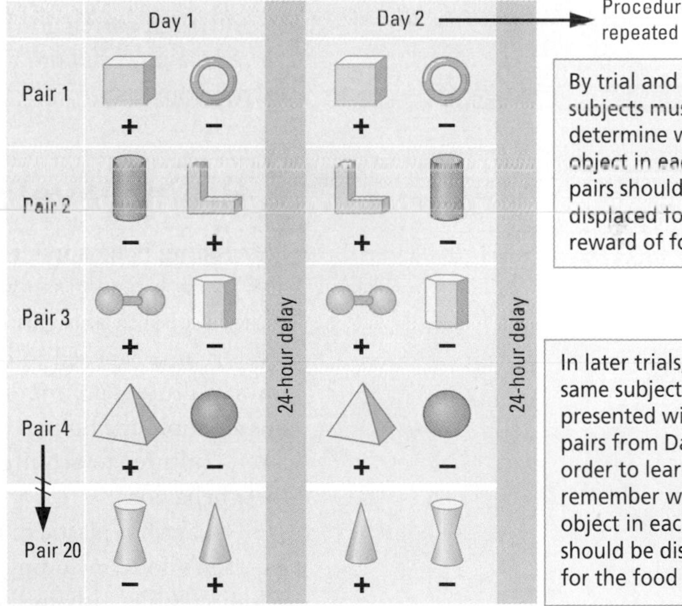
Day 1
Day 2
Procedure repeated
Pair 1
Pair 2
Pair 3
Pair 4
Pair 20
24-hour delay
24-hour delay
By trial and error, subjects must determine which object in each of 20 pairs should be displaced for a reward of food.
In later trials, the same subjects were presented with the 20 pairs from Day 1 in order to learn and remember which object in each pair should be displaced for the food reward.

Results

Both humans and monkey infants learn the concurrent-discrimination task at a younger age than the nonmatching-to-sample task.

Conclusion: Neural structures underlying the concurrent-discrimination task mature sooner than those underlying the nonmatching-to-sample task.

Adapted from "Object Recognition Versus Object Discrimination: Comparison Between Human Infants and Infant Monkeys," by W. H. Overman, J. Bachevalier, M. Turner, and A. Peuster, 1992, *Behavioral Neuroscience, 106,* p. 18.

It turns out that children can solve the concurrent task by about 12 months of age, but not until about 18 months of age can they solve what most adults believe to be the easier nonmatching task. These results imply that the basal ganglia, the critical area for the concurrent-discrimination task, mature more quickly than the temporal lobe, which is the critical region for the nonmatching-to-sample task.

A Caution about Linking Correlation to Causation

Throughout this section, we have described research that implies that changes in the brain cause changes in behavior. Neuroscientists assert that, by looking at behavioral development and brain development in parallel, they can make some inferences regarding the causes of behavior. Bear in mind, however, that just because two things correlate (take place together) does not prove that one of them causes the other.

The correlation–causation problem raises red flags in studies of the brain and behavior, because research in behavioral neuroscience, by its very nature, is often based on such correlations. Nevertheless, correlational studies, especially in the developmental area, have proved a powerful source of insight into fundamental principles of brain and behavior.

REVIEW: Correlating Behavior with Nervous-System Development

✔ Children develop increasingly mature motor, language, and cognitive behaviors in predictable sequences that correlate with neural changes in the brain.

✔ Although correlation does not prove causation, correlational research has proved to be a powerful predictor of behavioral milestones based on physical brain development.

Brain Development and the Environment

Developing behaviors are shaped not only by the emergence of brain structures but also by each person's environment and experiences. Neuroplasticity suggests that the brain is pliable and can be molded into different forms, at least at the microscopic level. Brains exposed to different environmental experiences are molded in different ways. Culture is an important aspect of the human environment, and so culture must help to mold the human brain. We would therefore expect people raised in widely different cultures to acquire differences in brain structure that have lifelong effects on their behavior.

The brain is plastic in response not only to external events but also to events within a person's body, including the effects of hormones, injury, and abnormal genes. The developing brain early in life is especially responsive to these internal factors, which, in turn, alter the way that the brain reacts to external experiences. In this section, we explore a whole range of external and internal environmental influences on brain development. We start with the question of exactly how experience manages to alter brain structure.

Experience and Cortical Organization

Researchers can study the effects of experience on the brain and behavior by placing laboratory animals in different environments and observing the results. In one of the earliest such studies, Donald Hebb (1947) took a group of young laboratory rats home

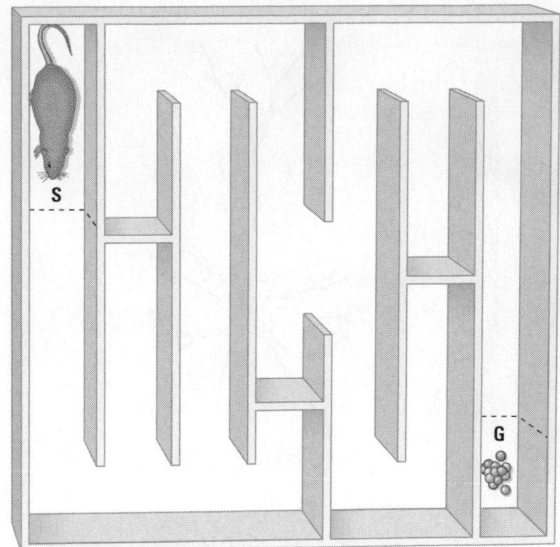

FIGURE 7-23 A Hebb–Williams Maze. In this version of the maze, a rat is placed in the start box (S) and must learn to find the food in the goal box (G). Investigators can reconfigure the walls of the maze to create new problems. Rats raised in complex environments solve such mazes much more quickly than do rats raised in standard laboratory cages.

and let them grow up in his kitchen. A control group grew up in standard laboratory cages at McGill University.

The "home rats" had many experiences that the caged rats did not, including being chased with a broom by Hebb's less-than-enthusiastic wife. Subsequently, Hebb gave both groups a rat-specific "intelligence test" that consisted of learning to solve a series of mazes, collectively known as Hebb–Williams mazes. A sample maze is shown in **Figure 7-23.** The home rats performed far better on these tasks than the caged rats did. Hebb therefore concluded that intelligence must be influenced by experience.

On the basis of his research, Hebb reasoned that people reared in "stimulating" environments will maximize their intellectual development, whereas people raised in "impoverished" environments will not reach their intellectual potential. Although Hebb's reasoning may seem logical, the problem lies in defining in what ways environments may be stimulating or impoverished.

People living in slums, for example, with few formal educational resources, are not in what we would normally call an enriched setting, but that does not necessarily mean that the environment offers no cognitive stimulation or challenge. On the contrary, people raised in this setting are better adapted for survival in a slum than are people raised in upper-class homes. Does this adaptability make them more intelligent in a certain way?

In contrast, slum dwellers are not likely to be well adapted for college life, which was probably closer to what Hebb had in mind when he referred to such an environment as limiting intellectual potential. Indeed, Hebb's logic led to the development of preschool television programs, such as *Sesame Street,* that offer enrichment for children who would otherwise have little preschool exposure to reading.

The exception proves the rule in the film *Slumdog Millionaire:* the life experience of a destitute young man enables him to win the Indian version of *Who Wants to Be a Millionaire?,* a television game show.

The idea that early experience can change later behavior seems sensible enough, but we are left with the question of why experience should make such a difference. One reason is that experience changes the structure of neurons, which is especially evident in the cortex. Neurons in the brains of animals raised in complex environments, such as that shown in **Figure 7-24A**, are larger and have more synapses than do those of animals reared in barren cages. Representative neurons are compared in Figure 7-24B.

Research Focus 5-5 describes some structural changes that neurons undergo as a result of learning.

Presumably, the increased number of synapses results from increased sensory processing in a complex and stimulating environment. The brains of animals raised in

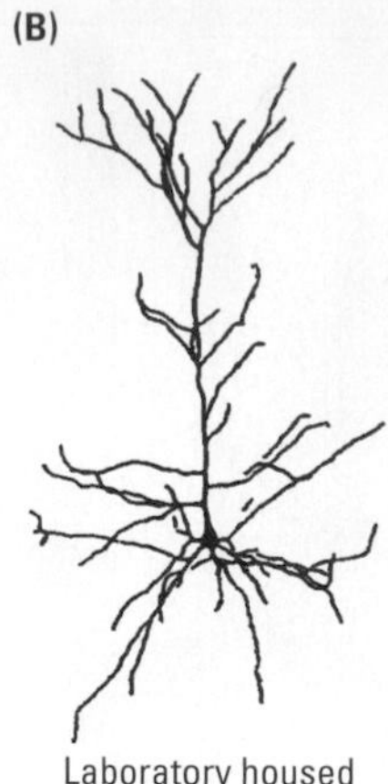

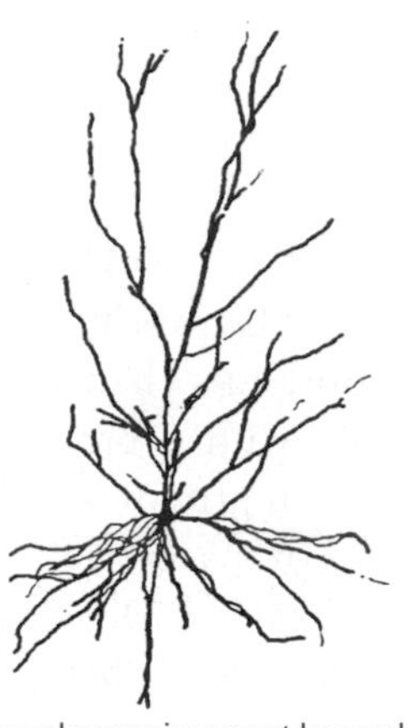

FIGURE 7-24 Enriched Environment, Enhanced Development. (A) A complex housing environment for a group of about six rats. The animals have an opportunity to move about and to interact with toys that are changed weekly. (B) Representative neurons from the parietal cortex of a laboratory-housed rat and that of a complex-environment-housed rat, the latter cortex being more complex and having about 25 percent more dendritic space for synapses.

complex settings also display more (and larger) astrocytes. Although complex-rearing studies do not address the effects of human culture directly, predictions about human development are easily made on the basis of their findings. We know that experience can modify the brain, and so we can predict that different experiences might modify the brain differently, which seems to be the case in language development, as explained in Research Focus 7-3, "Increased Cortical Activation for Second Languages."

Like exposure to language during development, early exposure to music also alters the brain. Perfect pitch, the ability to recreate a musical note without external reference, for example, is believed to require early musical training during a critical period. Similarly, people exposed to Western music since childhood usually find Eastern music peculiar, even nonmusical, on first encountering it when they are adults. In both examples, the neurons in the auditory system have been altered by early exposure to music.

Loss of plasticity does not mean that the adult human brain becomes fixed and unchangeable, however. Undoubtedly, the brains of adults are influenced by exposure to new environments and experiences, although probably more slowly and less extensively than the brains of children are. Findings from animal studies have shown plasticity in the adult brain. In fact, there is evidence that the brain is affected by experience well into old age, which is good news for those of us who are no longer children.

Chemoaffinity hypothesis Proposal that neurons or their axons and dendrites are drawn toward a signaling chemical that indicates the correct pathway.

Experience and Neural Connectivity

If experience can influence the structure of the cerebral cortex after a person is born, can it also sculpt the brain prenatally? It can. This prenatal influence of experience is very clearly illustrated in studies of the developing visual system.

RESEARCH FOCUS 7-3

Increased Cortical Activation for Second Languages

Most of the world is bilingual, but people rarely learn their second language as early as their first one. Denise Klein and her colleagues (2006) have used both PET (positron emission tomography) and fMRI (functional MRI) to determine whether native and second languages show differences in cortical activation.

Although the two languages overlap greatly in representation, there are differences. When subjects are asked to repeat words, the second language shows greater activation in the frontal and temporal regions as well as in the striatum and cerebellum. The investigators speculate that the second language has greater articulatory demands, which corresponds to the increased neural involvement in motor as well as language areas, as can be seen in the adjoining illustration.

The conclusions from these imaging studies are further supported by a review of cortical-mapping studies of bilingual patients undergoing neurosurgery. Carlo Giussani and his colleagues (2007) concluded that, although all studies show that language representation is grossly located in the same cortical regions, distinct language-specific areas exist in the language regions of the frontal and temporoparietal regions.

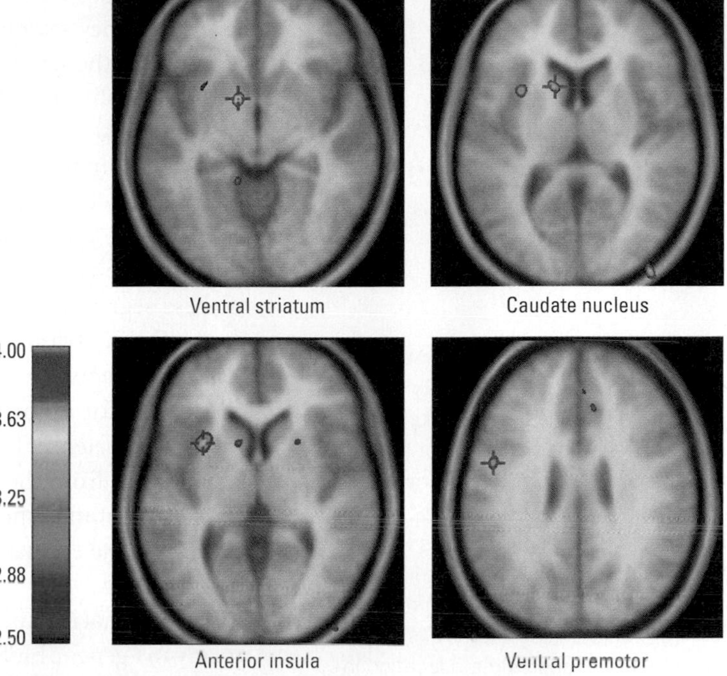

Blue regions show increased activation in motor structures when speaking a second language. From "Word and Nonword Repetition in Bilingual Subjects: A PET Study," by D. Klein, K. E. Watkins, R. J. Zatorre, and B. Milner, 2006, Human Brain Mapping, 27, 153–161.

Consider the problem of connecting the eyes to the rest of the visual system in development. A simple analogy will help. Imagine that students in a large lecture hall are each viewing the front of the room (the visual field) through a small cardboard tube, such as an empty paper-towel roll. If each student looks directly ahead, he or she will see only a small bit of the visual field.

This analogy essentially illustrates how the photoreceptor cells in the eyes act. Each cell sees only a small bit of the visual field. The problem is to put all the bits together to form a complete picture. To do so, analogously to students sitting side by side, receptors that see adjacent views must send their information to adjacent regions in the various parts of the brain's visual system, such as the midbrain. How do they accomplish this feat?

Chapter 9 explains how we see the world.

Roger Sperry (1963) suggested the **chemoaffinity hypothesis,** the idea that specific molecules exist in different cells in the various regions of the midbrain, giving each cell a distinctive chemical identity. Each cell, in other words, has an identifiable biochemical label. Presumably, incoming axons seek out a specific chemical, such as the tropic factors discussed earlier, and consequently land in the correct general region of the midbrain.

Structures in the midbrain, detailed in Figure 2-16, are critical in producing orienting movements, species-specific behaviors, and the perception of pain.

Many experiments have shown this process to take place prenatally as the eye and brain are developing. But the problem is that chemical affinity "directs" incoming axons only to a general location. To return to our two adjacent retinal cells, how do they now place themselves in the precisely correct position?

Here is where postnatal experience comes in: fine-tuning of neural placement is believed to be activity dependent. Because adjacent receptors tend to be activated at the same time, they tend to form synapses on the same neurons in the midbrain after chemoaffinity has drawn them to a general midbrain region. This process is illustrated in **Figure 7-25.** Neurons A and G are unlikely to be activated by the same stimulus, and so they seldom fire synchronously. Neurons A and B, in contrast, are apt to be activated by the same stimuli, as are B and C. Through this simultaneous activity with the passage of time, cells eventually line up correctly in the connections that they form.

Now consider what happens to axons coming from different eyes. Although the neural inputs from the two eyes may be active simultaneously, cells in the same eye are more likely to be active together than are cells in different eyes. The net effect is that inputs from the two eyes tend to organize themselves into neural bands, called *columns,* that represent the same region of space in each eye, as shown in **Figure 7-26.** The formation of these segregated cortical columns therefore depends on the patterns of coinciding electrical activity on the incoming axons.

If experience is abnormal—if one eye were covered during a crucial time in development, for example—then the neural connections will not be guided appropriately by experience. In fact, it is exactly what happens to a child who has a "lazy eye." Visual input from the lazy eye does not contribute to fine-tuning the neural connections as it should, and so the details of those connections do not develop normally, much as if the eye had been covered. The resulting loss of sharpness in vision known as **amblyopia.**

To summarize, the details of neural connections are modified by experience. An organism's genetic blueprint is vague in regard to exactly which connections in the brain go to exactly which neurons. Experience fine-tunes neural connectivity.

FIGURE 7-25 Chemoaffinity in the Visual System. Neurons A through G project from the retina to the tectum in the midbrain. The activities of adjacent neurons (C and D, say) are more likely to coincide than are the activities of widely separated neurons such as A and G. As a result, adjacent retinal neurons are more likely to establish permanent synapses on the same tectal neurons. By using chemical signals, axons grow to the approximate location in the tectum (*top*). The connections become more precise with the passage of time by the correlated activity (*bottom*).

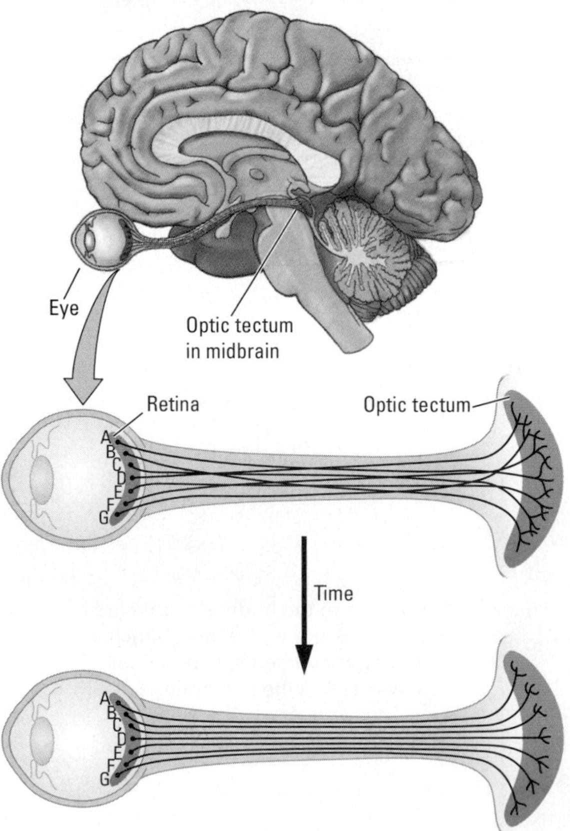

FIGURE 7-26 Ocular-Dominance Columns. In the postnatal development of the cat brain, axons enter the cortex, where they grow large terminal arborizations. (L, left eye; R, right eye).

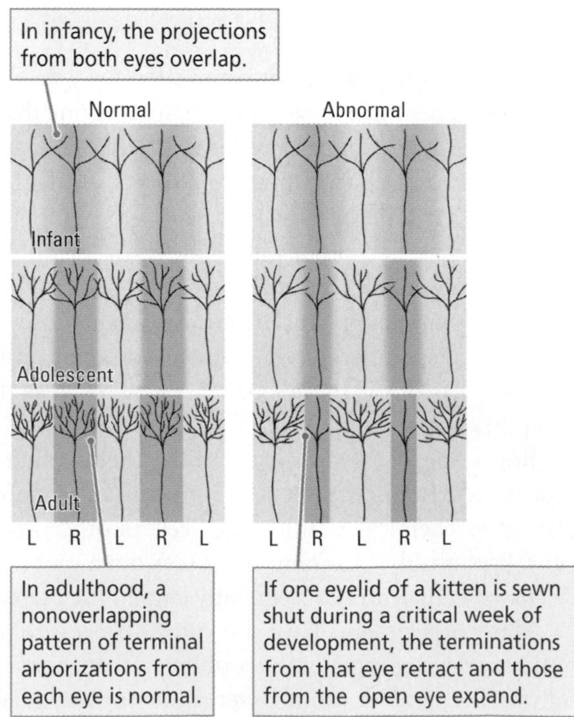

In infancy, the projections from both eyes overlap.
Normal
Abnormal
Infant
Adolescent
Adult
L R L R L
L R L R L
In adulthood, a nonoverlapping pattern of terminal arborizations from each eye is normal.
If one eyelid of a kitten is sewn shut during a critical week of development, the terminations from that eye retract and those from the open eye expand.

Critical Periods for Experience and Brain Development

At particular times in the course of brain development, specific experiences are especially important for development to be normal. In kittens, for example, the effect of suturing one eye closed has the most disruptive effect on cortical organization between 30 and 60 days after birth. A time span during which brain development is most sensitive to a specific experience is often called a **critical period.**

The absence of appropriate sensory experience during a critical period may result in abnormal brain development, leading to abnormal behavior that endures even into adulthood. Our colleague, Richard Tees, offered an analogy to help explain the concept of critical periods. He pictured the developing animal as a little train traveling past an environmental setting, perhaps the Rocky Mountains. All the windows are closed at the beginning of the journey (prenatal development), but, at particular stages of the trip, the windows in certain cars open, exposing the occupants (different parts of the brain) to the outside world. Some windows open to expose the brain to specific sounds, others to certain smells, others to particular sights, and so on.

This exposure affects the brain's development and, in the absence of any exposure through an open window, that development is severely disturbed. As the journey continues, the windows become harder to open until, finally, they are permanently closed. This closure does not mean that the brain can no longer change, but changes become much harder to induce.

Now imagine two different trains, one headed through the Rocky Mountains and another, the Orient Express, traveling across Eastern Europe. The "views" from the windows are very different, and the effects on the brain are correspondingly different. In other words, not only is the brain altered by the experiences that it has during a critical period, but the particular kinds of experiences encountered matter, too.

An extensively studied behavior that relates to the concept of critical periods is **imprinting,** a critical period during which an animal learns to restrict its social preferences to a specific class of objects, usually the members of its own species. In birds, such as chickens or waterfowl, the critical period for imprinting is often shortly after hatching. Normally, the first moving object that a young hatchling sees is a parent or sibling, and so the hatchling's brain appropriately imprints to its own species.

Appropriate imprinting is not inevitable, however. Konrad Lorenz (1970) demonstrated that, if the first animal or object that baby goslings encounter is a person, the goslings imprint to that person as though he or she were their mother. **Figure 7-27** shows a flock of goslings that imprinted to Lorenz and followed him wherever he went. Incorrect imprinting has long-term consequences for the hatchlings. They often direct their subsequent sexual behavior toward humans. A Barbary dove that had become imprinted to Lorenz directed its courtship toward his hand and even tried to copulate with the hand if it was held in a certain orientation.

Birds imprint not just to humans but also to inanimate objects, especially moving objects. Chickens have been induced to imprint to a milk bottle sitting on the back of a toy train moving around a track. But the brain is not entirely clueless when it comes to selecting a target to which to imprint. Given a choice, young chicks will imprint on a real chicken over any other stimulus.

Its rapid acquisition and permanent behavioral consequences suggest that, during imprinting, the brain makes a rapid change of some kind, probably a structural change, given the permanence of the new behavior. Gabriel Horn and his colleagues at Cambridge University (1985) tried to identify what changes in the brains of chicks during imprinting. The results of Horn's electron microscopic studies show that the

Amblyopia A condition in which vision in one eye is reduced as a result of disuse; usually caused by a failure of the two eyes to point in the same direction.

Critical period Developmental "window" during which some event has a long-lasting influence on the brain; often referred to as a *sensitive period.*

Imprinting Process that predisposes an animal to form an attachment to objects or animals at a critical period in development.

FIGURE 7-27 Strength of Imprinting. Ethologist Konrad Lorenz followed by goslings that imprinted on him. Because he was the first object that the geese encountered after hatching, he became their "mother."

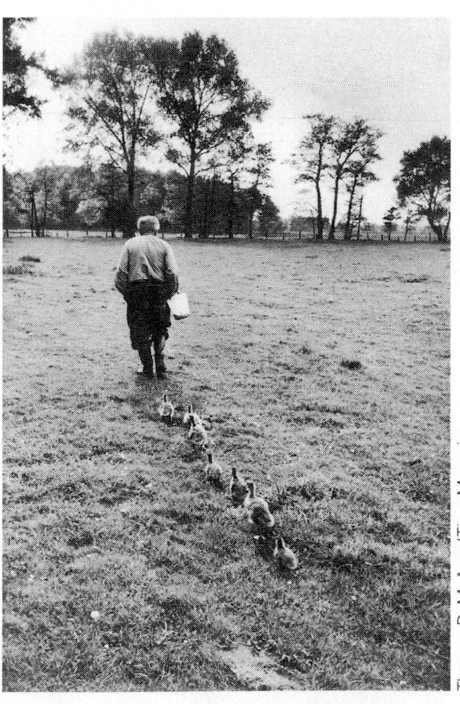

Thomas D. McAvoy/*Time Magazine*

synapses in a specific region of the forebrain enlarge with imprinting. Thus, imprinting seems a good model for studying brain plasticity during development, in part because the changes are rapid, related to specific experience, and localized in the brain.

Abnormal Experience and Brain Development

If complex experiences can stimulate brain growth and influence later behavior, severely restricted experiences seem likely to retard both brain growth and behavior. To study the effects of such restrictions, Donald Hebb and his colleagues (Clarke et al., 1951) placed young Scottish terriers in the dark with as little stimulation as possible and compared their behavior with that of dogs raised in a normal environment.

When the dogs raised in the barren environment were later removed from it, their behavior was very unusual. They showed virtually no reaction to people or other dogs, and they appeared to have lost the sensation of pain. Even sticking pins in them produced no response. When given a dog version of the Hebb–Williams intelligence test for rats, these dogs performed very poorly and were unable to learn some tasks that dogs raised in more-stimulating settings could learn easily.

The results of subsequent studies have shown that depriving young animals specifically of visual input or even of maternal contact has devastating consequences for their behavioral development and, presumably, for the development of the brain. For instance, Austin Riesen and his colleagues (Riesen, 1982) extensively studied animals raised in the dark and found that, even though the animals' eyes still work, they may be functionally blind after early visual deprivation. The absence of visual stimulation results in the atrophy of dendrites on cortical neurons, which is essentially the opposite of the results observed in the brains of animals raised in complex and stimulating environments.

Not only does the absence of specific sensory inputs adversely affect brain development, so do more-complex abnormal experiences. In the 1950s, Harry Harlow began the first systematic laboratory studies of analogous deprivation in laboratory animals. Harlow showed that infant monkeys raised without maternal (or paternal) contact have grossly abnormal intellectual and social behaviors in adulthood.

Harlow separated baby monkeys from their mothers shortly after birth and raised them in individual cages. Perhaps the most stunning effect was that, in adulthood, these animals were totally unable to establish normal relations with other animals. Unfortunately, Harlow did not analyze the brains of the deprived monkeys. We would predict atrophy of cortical neurons, especially in the frontal-lobe regions related to normal social behavior. Harlow's student, Stephen Suomi, continues to study early experiences in monkeys at the U.S. National Institute of Child Health and Human Development. Suomi has found a wide variety of hormonal and neurological abnormalities among motherless monkeys (see review by Stevens et al., 2009).

Children exposed to barren environments or to abuse or neglect will be at a serious disadvantage later in life. Proof can be seen in the retarded intellectual development of children raised in dreadful circumstances, as described in Clinical Focus 7-4, "Romanian Orphans." Although some argue that children can succeed in school and in life if they really want to, abnormal developmental experiences can clearly alter the brain irrevocably. As a society, we cannot be complacent about the environments to which our children are exposed.

Early exposure to stress also has a major effect on a child's later behavior. Stress can alter the expression of certain genes, such as those related to serotonin reuptake, as discussed in Research Focus 7-1. Early alteration in serotonin activity can severely alter how the brain responds to stressful experiences later in life.

CLINICAL FOCUS 7-4

Romanian Orphans

In the 1970s, the Communist regime governing Romania outlawed all forms of birth control and abortion. The natural result was thousands of unwanted pregnancies. More than 100,000 unwanted children were placed in state-run orphanages where the conditions were appalling.

The children were housed and clothed but given virtually no environmental stimulation. In most instances, they were confined to cots. There were few, if any, playthings and virtually no personal interaction with caregivers who were looking after 20 to 25 children at once. Bathing often consisted of being hosed down with cold water.

After the Communist government fell and the outside world was able to intervene, hundreds of these children were rescued and placed in adoptive homes throughout the world, especially in the United States, Canada, and the United Kingdom. Several studies of these severely deprived children document their poor physical state on arrival in their new homes. They were malnourished, they had chronic respiratory and intestinal infections, and they were severely developmentally impaired.

A British study by Michael Rutter and his colleagues (Rutter, 1998) found the orphans to be two standard deviations below age-matched children for weight, height, and head circumference. (Head circumference can be taken as a very rough measure of brain size.) Assessments using scales of motor and cognitive development showed most of the children to be in the retarded range.

The improvement in these children in the first 2 years after placement in their adoptive homes was nothing short of spectacular. Average height and weight became nearly normal, although head circumference remained below normal. Many of the children were now in the normal range of motor and cognitive development. A significant number, however, were still considered retarded. What caused these individual differences in recovery from the past deprivation?

The key factor was age at adoption. Those children adopted before 6 months of age did significantly better than those adopted later. In a Canadian study by Elenor Ames (1997), Romanian orphans who were adopted before 4 months of age had an average Stanford–Binet IQ score of 98 when tested at 4½ years of age. In comparison, age-matched Canadian controls had an average score of 109. Findings from brain-imaging studies showed the Romanian children adopted at an older age to have smaller-than-normal brains.

Charles Nelson and his colleagues (Nelson et al., 2007; Marshall et al., 2008) analyzed cognitive and social development as well event-related potential (ERP) measures in a group of Romanian children. Some had moved to foster homes in Romania; others remained in institutions. Regardless of their situation, the studies revealed severe abnormalites in these children at about 4 years of age.

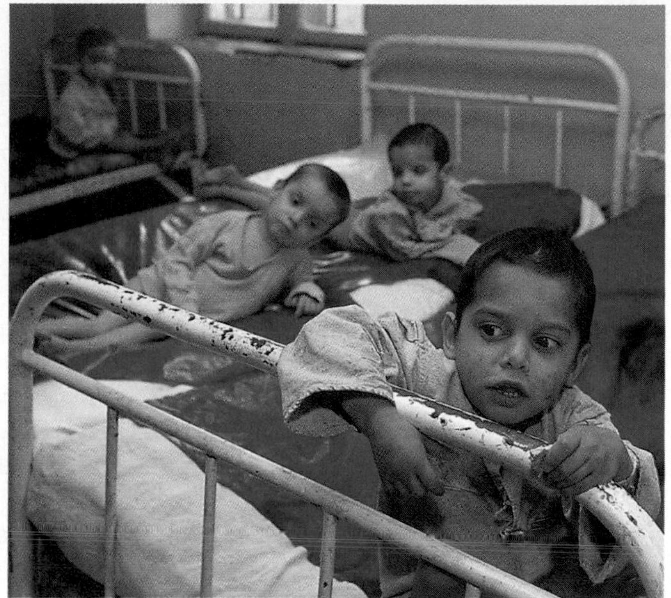

Johnson/Gamma-Liaison

Findings from studies of Romanian orphans who were warehoused in the 1970s and 1980s and endured the conditions shown in this photograph reveal that the lack of stimulation hampered normal brain development.

The inescapable conclusion emerging from the Romanian-orphanage experience is that the human brain may be able to recover from a brief period of extreme deprivation in early infancy, but periods longer than 6 months produce significant abnormalities in brain development that cannot be overcome completely. This conclusion is supported by the case study of an American girl named Genie, who experienced severe social and experiential deprivation as well as chronic malnutrition at the hands of her psychotic father (see Curtis, 1978).

Genie was discovered at the age of 13, after spending much of her life in a closed room. She was punished for making any noise. After her rescue, she, too, showed rapid growth and cognitive development, but her language development remained severely retarded.

To summarize, studies of the Romanian orphans, of orphans from other highly impoverished settings, and of cases such as that of Genie make it clear that the developing brain requires stimulation for normal development. Although the brain may be able to catch up after a short period of deprivation, more than a few months of severe deprivation results in a smaller-than-normal brain and associated behavioral abnormalities, especially in cognitive and social skills.

Chapter 5 introduces the possible roles of the noradrenergic and serotonergic activating systems in depression. You will find more detail on major depression in Chapter 8 and on anxiety disorders in Chapter 12.

Stress early in life may predispose people to develop various behavioral disorders, including depression (Sodhi and Sanders-Bush, 2004). Early stress can also leave a lasting imprint on brain structure: the amygdala is enlarged and the hippocampus is reduced in size (Salm et al., 2004). Such changes have been associated with the development of depressive and anxiety disorders.

Hormones and Brain Development

The determination of sex is largely genetic. In mammals, the Y chromosome present in males controls the process by which an undifferentiated primitive gonad develops into testes, as illustrated in Figure 7-8. The testes subsequently secrete testosterone, which stimulates the development of male reproductive organs and, in puberty, the appearance of male secondary sexual characteristics such as facial hair and the deepening of the voice.

Gonadal hormones also influence the development of neurons. Testosterone, the best-known **androgen** (the class of hormones that stimulates or controls masculine characteristics), is released during a brief period in the course of prenatal brain development and subsequently acts to alter the brain much as it alters the sex organs. This process is **masculinization.**

Just as testosterone does not affect all body organs, it does not affect all regions of the brain. It does, however, affect many brain regions and in many different ways. It affects the number of neurons formed in certain brain areas, reduces the number of neurons that die, increases cell growth, increases or reduces dendritic branching, increases or reduces synaptic growth, and regulates the activity of synapses, among other effects.

We have emphasized the role of testosterone in brain development, but **estrogens,** a variety of sex hormones responsible for the distinguishing characteristics of the female, also likely influence postnatal brain development. Jill Goldstein and her colleagues found sex differences in the volume of cortical regions that are known to have differential levels of receptors for testosterone (androgen receptors) and estrogen, respectively, as diagrammed in **Figure 7-28** (Goldstein et al., 2001). Clearly, hormones alter brain development: a male brain and a female brain are not the same.

Testosterone's effects on brain development were once believed to be unimportant, because this hormone was thought to primarily influence regions of the brain related to sexual behavior but not regions of "higher" functions. We now know that this belief is false. Testosterone changes the structure of cells in many regions of the cortex, with diverse behavioral consequences that include influences on cognitive processes. Clear sex differences appear in the rate of brain development shown in Figure 7-19.

Reconsider Experiment 7-1, described earlier. Jocelyne Bachevalier trained infant male and female monkeys in the concurrent-discrimination task. In this task, the subject has to learn which of two objects in a series of object pairs conceals a food reward. In addition, Bachevalier trained the animals in another task, *object-reversal learning.* The task is to learn that one particular object always conceals a food reward, whereas another object never does. After this pattern has been learned, the reward contingen-

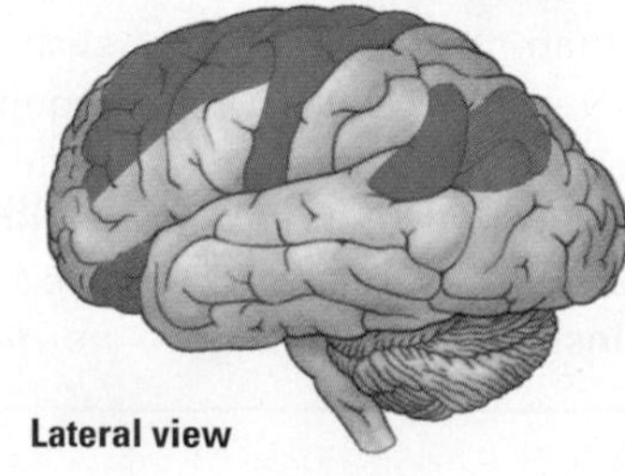

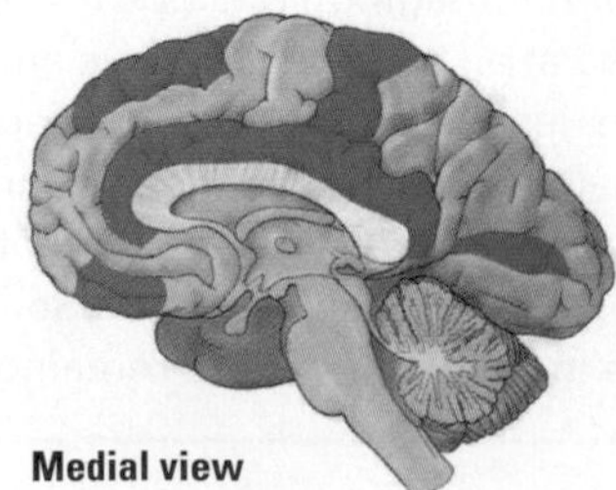

FIGURE 7-28 Sex Differences in Brain Volume. Cerebral areas related to sex differences in the distribution of estrogen (purple) and androgen (pink) receptors in the developing brain correspond to areas of relatively larger cerebral volumes in adult women and men. Adapted from Goldstein et al., 2001.

cies are reversed so that the particular object that has always been rewarded is now never rewarded, whereas the formerly unrewarded object now conceals the reward. When this new pattern has been learned, the contingencies are reversed again, and so on, for five reversals.

Bachevalier found that 2½-month-old male monkeys were superior to female monkeys on the object-reversal task, but females did better on the concurrent task. Apparently, the different brain areas required for these two tasks mature at different rates in male and female monkeys. Bachevalier later tested additional male monkeys whose testes had been removed at birth and so were no longer exposed to testosterone. These animals performed like females on the tasks, implying that testosterone was influencing the rate of brain development in areas related to certain cognitive behaviors.

Bachevalier and her colleague Overman (Overman et al., 1996) then repeated the experiment, this time using as their subjects children from 15 to 30 months old. The results were the same: boys were superior at the object-reversal task and girls were superior at the concurrent task. There were no such male–female differences in performance among older children (32–55 months of age). Presumably, by this older age, the brain regions required for each task had matured in both boys and girls. At the earlier age, however, gonadal hormones seemed to be influencing the rate of maturation in certain regions of the brain, just as they had in the baby monkeys.

Although the biggest effects of gonadal hormones may be during early development, their role is by no means finished in infancy. Gonadal hormones (including both testosterone and estrogen, which is produced in large quantities by the ovaries in females) continue to influence the structure of the brain throughout an animal's life. In fact, removal of the ovaries in middle-aged laboratory rats leads to marked growth of dendrites and the production of more glial cells in the cortex. This finding of widespread neural change in the cortex associated with loss of estrogen has implications for the treatment of postmenopausal women with hormone-replacement therapy.

Gonadal hormones also affect how the brain responds to events in the environment. For instance, among rats housed in complex environments, males show more dendritic growth in neurons of the visual cortex than do females (Juraska, 1990). In contrast, females housed in this setting show more dendritic growth in the hippocampus than do males. Apparently, the same experience can affect the male and female brain differently owing to the mediating influence of gonadal hormones.

This finding means that, as females and males develop, their brains continue to become more and more different from each other, much like coming to a fork in a road. After having chosen to go down one path, your direction of travel is forever changed as the roads diverge and become increasingly farther apart.

To summarize, gonadal hormones alter the basic development of neurons, shape the nature of experience-dependent changes in the brain, and influence the structure of neurons throughout our lifetimes. Those who believe that behavioral differences between males and females are solely the result of environmental experiences must consider these neural effects of sex hormones.

In part, it is true that environmental factors exert a major influence. But one reason that they do so may be that male and female brains are different to start with, and even the same events, when experienced by structurally different brains, may lead to different effects on the brain. In our view, the important task is not to deny the presence of sex differences in brain organization and function but rather to understand the degree to which those neurological differences contribute to observed differences in behavior.

Another key question related to hormonal influences on brain development is whether there might be sex differences in brain organization that are independent of

Androgen Class of hormones that stimulates or controls masculine characteristics.

Masculinization Process by which exposure to androgens (male sex hormones) alters the brain, rendering it identifiably male.

Estrogens Variety of sex hormones responsible for the distinguishing characteristics of the female.

FIGURE 7-29 A Gynandromorph. This rare zebra finch has dull female plumage on one side of the body and bright male plumage on the other side.

hormonal action. In other words, are differences in the action of sex-chromosome genes unrelated to sex hormones? Although little is known about such genetic effects in humans, the results of studies of birds clearly show that genetic effects on brain cells may indeed contribute to sex differentiation.

Songbirds have an especially interesting brain dimorphism: males sing and females do not. This behavioral difference between the sexes is directly related to a neural birdsong circuit that is present in males but not in females. Robert Agate and his colleagues (2003) studied the brain of a rare strain of zebra finch, a *gynandromorph* that exhibits physical characteristics of both sexes, as shown in **Figure 7-29.**

Genetic analysis shows that cells on one half of the brain and body are genetically female and cells on the other half are genetically male. Both sides of the gynandromorph's body and brain were exposed to the same hormones in the bloodstream during prenatal development. Thus, the effect of male and female genes on the birdsong circuit can be examined to determine how the genes and hormones might interact.

If the sex difference in the birdsong circuit were totally related to the presence of hormones prenatally, then both sides of the brain should be equally masculine or feminine. Agate's results confirm the opposite: the neural song circuit was masculine on the male side of the brain. Only a genetic difference in the brain that was at least partly independent of the effects of the hormones could explain such a structural difference.

Injury and Brain Development

Dating to the late 1800s, infants and children were generally believed to show better recovery from brain injury than adults. In the 1930s, Donald Hebb studied children with major birth-related injuries to the frontal lobes and found them to have severe and permanent behavioral abnormalities in adulthood. He concluded that brain damage early in life can alter the subsequent development of the rest of the brain and may be worse than injury later in life.

To what extent have other studies confirmed Hebb's conclusion? Few anatomical studies of humans with early brain injuries exist, but we can make some general predictions from studying laboratory animals. In general, early brain injuries do produce abnormal brains, especially at certain critical periods in development.

For humans, the worst time appears to be in the last half of the intrauterine period and the first couple of months after birth. Rats and cats that suffer injuries at a comparable time have significantly smaller brains than normal, and their cortical neurons show a generalized atrophy relative to normal brains, as illustrated in **Figure 7-30.**

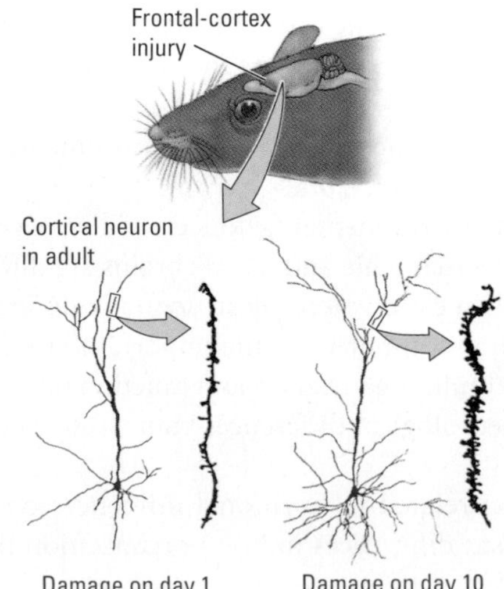

FIGURE 7-30 Time-Dependent Effects. In the rat, damage to the frontal cortex on the day of birth leads to cortical neurons with simple dendritic fields and a sparse growth of spines in the adult (*left*). In contrast, damage to the frontal cortex at 10 days of age leads to cortical neurons with expanded dendritic fields and denser spines than normal in adults (*right*). Adapted from "Possible Anatomical Basis of Recovery of Function After Neonatal Frontal Lesions in Rats," by B. Kolb and R. Gibb, 1993, *Behavioral Neuroscience, 107,* p. 808.

Behaviorally, these animals appear cognitively retarded, deficient in a wide range of skills.

The effect of injury to the developing brain is not always devastating, however. For example, researchers have known for more than 100 years that children with brain injuries in the first couple of years after birth almost never have the severe language disturbances common to adults with equivalent injuries. Animal studies help explain why.

Whereas damage to the rat brain in the developmental period comparable to the last few months of gestation in humans produces widespread cortical atrophy, damage at a time in the development of the rat brain roughly comparable to age 6 months to 2 years in humans actually produces more dendritic development in rats, as seen on the right in Figure 7-30. Furthermore, these animals show dramatic recovery of functions, implying that the brain has a capacity during development to compensate for injury. Parallel studies in cats have shown extensive reorganization or cortical-to-cortical connections after early injury to the visual cortex (see review by Payne and Lomber, 2001).

Anencephaly Failure of the forebrain to develop.

Drugs and Brain Development

The U.S. National Institute on Drug Abuse (NIDA) estimates that 25 percent of all live births in the United States today are exposed to nicotine in utero. Similar statistics on alcohol consumption by pregnant mothers are not available, but the effects of alcohol consumption in the etiology of fetal alcohol effects are well documented. Even low doses of commonly prescribed drugs, including antidepressants and antipsychotics, appear to alter prenatal neuron development in the prefrontal cortex. It manifests after birth in abnormalities in behaviors controlled by the affected regions (see review by Halliwell et al., 2009).

Chapter 8 describes the lasting effects of a mother's alcohol consumption on the developing brain of her child and details the actions of psychoactive drugs.

NIDA also estimates that 5.5 percent of all expectant mothers, approximately 221,000 pregnant women each year in the United States, use an illicit drug at least once in the course of their pregnancies. And what about caffeine? More than likely most children were exposed to caffeine (from coffee, tea, cola and energy drinks, and chocolate) in utero.

The precise effects of drug intake on brain development are poorly understood, but the overall conclusion from current knowledge is that children with prenatal exposure to a variety of psychoactive drugs have an increased likelihood of later drug use (Malanga and Kosofsky, 2003). Many experts suggest that, although, again, poorly studied, childhood disorders—learning disabilities and attention-deficit-hyperactivity disorder (ADHD) are examples—may be related to prenatal exposure to drugs such as nicotine or caffeine or both. Carl Malanga and Barry Kosofsky note poignantly that "society at large does not yet fully appreciate the impact that prenatal drug exposure can have on the lives of its children."

In the photo on page 199, bubbles fascinate a boy diagnosed with autism spectrum disorder. Focus 11-2 details ASD; see also Focus 15-2. Focus 6-4 details ADHD and Focus 14-1 details dyslexia. Chapter 16 contains more information about developmental disorders.

Other Kinds of Abnormal Brain Development

The nervous system need not be damaged by external forces to develop abnormally. For instance, many genetic abnormalities are believed to result in abnormalities in the development and, ultimately, the structure of the brain. *Spina bifida,* a condition in which the genetic blueprint goes awry and the neural tube does not close completely, leads to an incompletely formed spinal cord. After birth, children with spina bifida usually have serious motor problems.

Imagine what would happen if some genetic abnormality caused the front end of the neural tube not to close properly. Because the front end of the neural tube forms the brain, this failure would result in gross abnormalities in brain development. Such a condition exists and is known as **anencephaly.** Infants affected by this condition die soon after birth.

Abnormal brain development can be much subtler than anencephaly. For example, if cells do not migrate to their correct locations and these mispositioned cells do not subsequently die, they can disrupt brain function and may lead to disorders ranging from seizures to schizophrenia (see review by Guerrini et al., 2007). In a variety of conditions, neurons fail to differentiate normally. In certain cases, the neurons fail to produce long dendrites or spines. As a result, connectivity in the brain is abnormal, leading to developmental disabilities.

The opposite condition also is possible: neurons continue to make dendrites and form connections with other cells to the point at which these neurons become extraordinarily large. The functional consequences of all the newly formed connections can be devastating. Excitatory synapses in the wrong location effectively short-circuit a neuron's function.

A curious consequence of abnormal brain development is that behavioral effects may emerge only as the brain matures and the maturing regions begin to play a greater role in behavior. This consequence is especially true of frontal-lobe injuries. The frontal lobes continue to develop into early adulthood, and often not until adolescence do the effects of frontal-lobe abnormalities begin to be noticed.

As detailed in Chapter 16, the schizophrenic brain has many abnormalities, some of which are in the frontal lobes. Chapter 5 describes the possible relation between excessive dopamine or serotonin activity or both and schizophrenia.

Schizophrenia is a disease characterized by its slow development, usually not becoming obvious until late adolescence. Clinical Focus 7-5, "Schizophrenia," relates the progress and possible origin of the disease.

Developmental Disability

Impaired cognitive functioning accompanies abnormal brain development. Impairment may range from mild, allowing an almost normal life style, to severe, requiring constant care. As summarized in **Table 7-3**, such mental retardation can result from chronic malnutrition, genetic abnormalities such as Down syndrome, hormonal abnormalities, brain injury, or neurological disease. Different causes produce different abnormalities in brain organization, but the critical similarity across all types of developmental disability is that the brain is not normal.

Figure 3-23 illustrates trisomy, the chromosomal abnormality that causes Down syndrome.

Dominique Purpura (1974) conducted one of the few systematic investigations of the brains of developmentally disabled children. Purpura used Golgi stain to examine

TABLE 7-3 Causes of Developmental Disability

Cause	Example mechanism	Example condition
Genetic abnormality	Error of metabolism Chromosomal abnormality	Phenylketonuria (PKU) Down syndrome
Abnormal embryonic development	Exposure to a toxin	Fetal alcohol syndrome (FAS)
Prenatal disease	Infection	Rubella (German measles) Retardation
Birth trauma	Anoxia (oxygen deprivation)	Cerebral palsy
Malnutrition	Abnormal brain development	Kwashiorkor
Environmental abnormality	Sensory deprivation	Children in Romanian orphanages

CLINICAL FOCUS 7-5

Schizophrenia

> When Mrs. T. was 16 years old, she began to experience her first symptom of schizophrenia: a profound feeling that people were staring at her. These bouts of self-consciousness soon forced her to end her public piano performances. Her self-consciousness led to withdrawal, then to fearful delusions that others were speaking about her behind her back, and finally to suspicions that they were plotting to harm her.
>
> At first Mrs. T.'s illness was intermittent, and the return of her intelligence, warmth, and ambition between episodes allowed her to complete several years of college, to marry, and to rear three children. She had to enter a hospital for the first time at age 28, after the birth of her third child, when she began to hallucinate.
>
> Now, at 45, Mrs. T. is never entirely well. She has seen dinosaurs on the street and live animals in her refrigerator. While hallucinating, she speaks and writes in an incoherent, but almost poetic way. At other times, she is more lucid, but even then the voices she hears sometimes lead her to do dangerous things, such as driving very fast down the highway in the middle of the night, dressed only in a nightgown. . . . At other times and without any apparent stimulus, Mrs. T. has bizarre visual hallucinations. For example, she saw cherubs in the grocery store. These experiences leave her preoccupied, confused, and frightened, unable to perform such everyday tasks as cooking or playing the piano. (Gershon and Rieder, 1992, p. 127)

It has always been easier to identify schizophrenic behavior than to define what schizophrenia is. Perhaps the one universally accepted criterion for its diagnosis is the absence of other neurological disturbances or affective (mood) disorders that could cause a person to lose touch with reality—a definition by default.

The symptoms of schizophrenia are heterogeneous, suggesting that the biological abnormalities vary from person to person. Most patients appear to stay at a fairly stable level after the first few years of displaying schizophrenic symptoms, with little evidence of a decline in neuropsychological functioning. The symptoms come and go, much as for Mrs. T., but the severity is relatively constant after the first few episodes.

Numerous studies have investigated the brains of schizophrenia patients, both in autopsies and in MRI and CT scans. Although the results vary, most neuroscientists agree that the brains of people who develop schizophrenia are lighter in weight than normal and have enlarged ventricles. Research findings also suggest that schizophrenic brains have smaller frontal lobes (or at least a reduction in the number of neurons in the prefrontal cortex) and thinner parahippocampal gyri.

Joyce Kovelman and Arnold Scheibel (1984) found abnormalities in the orientation of neurons in the hippocampi of schizophrenics. Rather than the consistently parallel orientation of neurons in this region characteristic of normal brains, schizophrenic brains have a more haphazard organization, as shown in the accompanying drawings.

Evidence is increasing that the abnormalities observed in schizophrenic brains are associated with disturbances of brain development. William Bunney and his colleagues (1997) suggested that at least a subgroup of schizophrenia sufferers experience either environmental insults or some type of abnormal gene activity in the fourth to sixth month of fetal development.

These events are thought to result in abnormal cortical development, particularly in the frontal lobes. Later in adolescence, as the frontal lobes approach maturity, the person begins to experience symptoms deriving from this abnormal prenatal development.

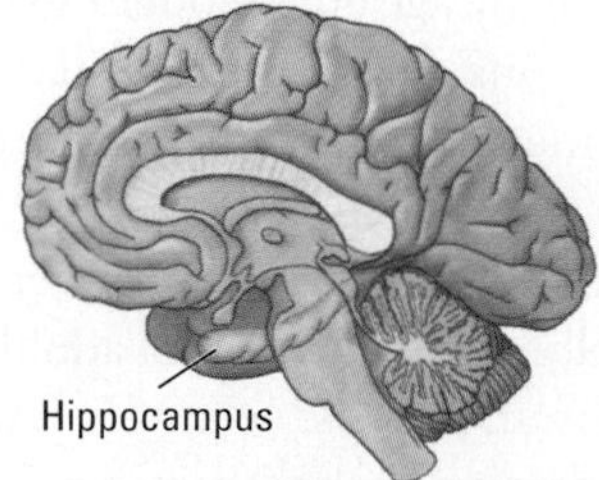

(A)

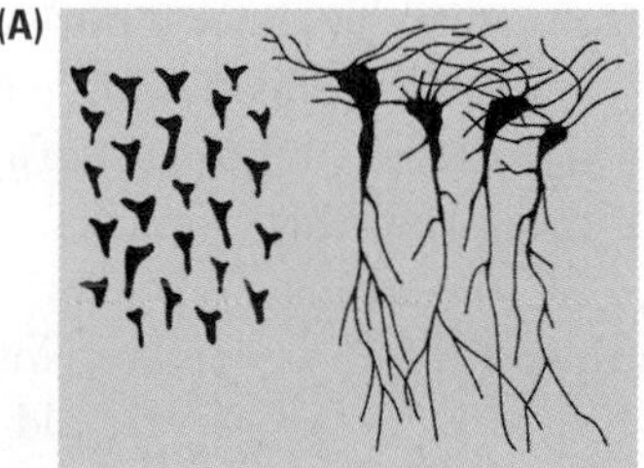

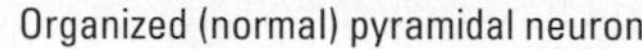

Organized (normal) pyramidal neurons

(B)

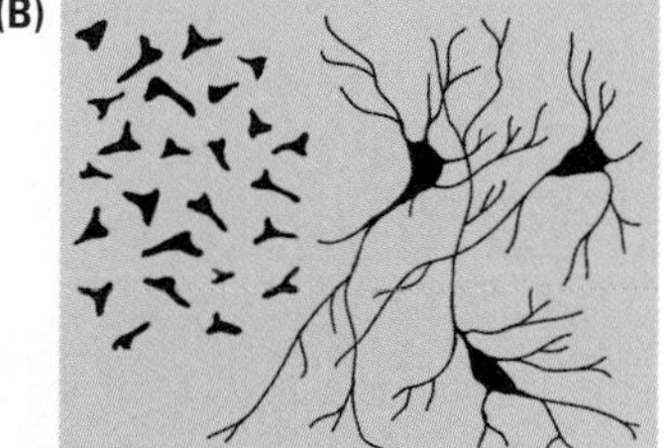

Disorganized (schizophrenic) pyramidal neurons

Pyramidal-cell orientation in the hippocampus of (A) a normal brain and (B) a schizophrenic brain. Adapted from "A Neurohistologic Correlate of Schizophrenia" by J. A. Kovelman and A. B. Scheibel, 1984, *Biological Psychiatry, 19*, p. 1613.

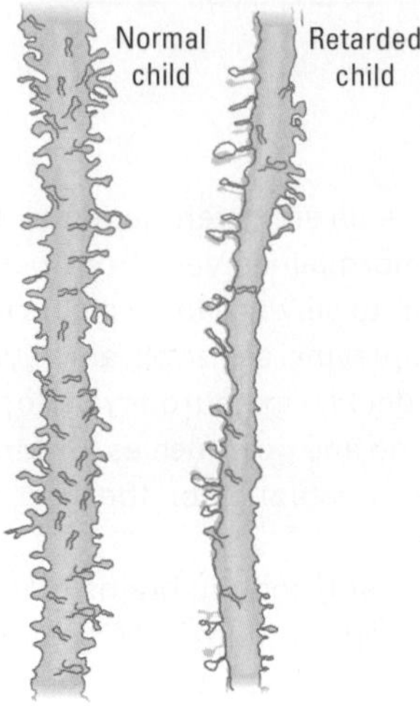

FIGURE 7-31 Neural Contrast. Representative dendritic branches from cortical neurons in a child of normal intelligence (*left*) and a developmentally disabled child (*right*), whose neurons are smaller and have far fewer spines. Adapted from "Dendritic Spine 'Dysgenesis' and Mental Retardation," by D. P. Purpura, 1974, *Science, 186*, p. 1127.

the neurons of children who had died from accident or disease unrelated to the nervous system. When he examined the brains of children with various forms of retardation, he found that dendrite growth was stunted and the spines were very sparse relative to dendrites from children of normal intelligence, as illustrated in **Figure 7-31.**

The simpler structure of these neurons is probably indicative of a marked reduction in the number of connections in the brain, which presumably caused the developmental disability. Variation in both the nature and the extent of neuronal abnormality in different children would lead to different behavioral syndromes.

REVIEW: Brain Development and the Environment

- ✔ The brain is especially plastic during its development and can therefore be molded by experience into different forms, at least at the microscopic level.
- ✔ Not only is the brain plastic in response to external events, but it may also be changed by internal events, including the effects of hormones, injury, abnormal genes, and drugs.
- ✔ The sensitivity of the brain to experience varies with time. At critical periods in development, specific parts of the brain are particularly sensitive to experience and environment.
- ✔ If experiences are abnormal, then the brain's development is abnormal, possibly leading to such disorders as schizophrenia or developmental disability.

How Do Any of Us Develop a Normal Brain?

When we consider the complexity of the brain, the less-than-precise process of brain development, and the number of factors that can influence the brain's development, we are left marveling at how so many of us end up with brains that pass for normal. All of us must have had neurons that migrated to wrong locations, made incorrect connections, were exposed to viruses or other harmful substances. If the brain were as fragile as it might seem, to end up with a normal brain would be almost impossible.

Apparently, animals have evolved a substantial capacity to repair minor abnormalities in brain development. Most people have developed in the range that we call "normal" because the human brain's plasticity and regenerative powers overcome minor developmental deviations. By initially overproducing neurons and synapses, the brain has the capacity to correct any errors that might have arisen accidentally.

These same plastic properties of the brain later allow us to cope with the ravages of aging. Neurons are dying throughout our lifetime. By age 60, we ought to be able to see significant effects of all this cell loss, especially considering the cumulative results of exposure to environmental toxins, drugs, traumatic brain injuries, and other neural insults. But this is not what happens.

Although teenagers may not believe it, very few 60-year-olds are demented. By most criteria, the 60-year-old who has been intellectually active throughout adulthood is likely to be much wiser than the 18-year-old whose brain has lost relatively few neurons. A 60-year old chess player will have a record of many more chess matches from which to draw game strategies than does an 18-year old.

Clearly, we must have some mechanism to compensate for loss and minor injury to our brain cells. This capacity for plasticity and change, for learning and adapting, is a most important characteristic of the human brain during development and throughout life.

We return to learning and memory in Chapter 14. Chapter 5 explores learning at the level of the synapse through habituation, sensitization, and associations.

Summary

Three Perspectives on Brain Development

Nervous-system development is more than the simple unfolding of a genetic blueprint. Development is a complex dance of genetic and environmental events that interact to sculpt the brain to fit within a particular cultural and environmental context. We can approach this dance from three different perspectives: (1) correlating nervous-system development with the emergence of behavior, (2) correlating the emergence of behavior and the likely maturing neurological structures, and (3) observing the relations among factors, such as music or injury, that influence both behavioral and neurological development.

Neurobiology of Development

Human brain maturation is a long process, lasting well into the 20s. Neurons, the units of brain function, develop a phenotype, migrate, and, as their processes elaborate, establish connections with other neurons even before birth. The developing brain produces many more neurons and connections than it needs and then prunes back in toddlerhood and again in adolescence to a stable adult level maintained by some neurogenesis throughout the life span.

Correlating Behavior with Nervous-System Development

Throughout the world, across the cultural spectrum, from newborn to adult, we all develop through similar behavioral stages. As infants develop physically, motor behaviors emerge in a predictable sequence from gross, poorly directed movements toward objects to controlled pincer grasps to pick up objects as small as pencils by about 11 months. Cognitive behaviors also develop through a series of testable stages of logic and problem solving. Researchers such as Jean Piaget have identified and characterized four or more distinct stages of cognitive development, each of which can be identified by specific behavioral tests.

Behaviors emerge as the neural systems that produce them develop. The hierarchical relation between brain structure and brain function can be inferred by matching the median timetables of neurodevelopment with observed behavior. Motor behaviors emerge in synchrony with the maturation of motor circuits in the cerebral cortex, basal ganglia, and cerebellum, as well as in the connections from these areas to the spinal cord. Similar correlations between emerging behaviors and neuronal development can be seen in the maturation of cognitive behavior, as circuits in the frontal and temporal lobes mature in early adulthood.

Brain Development and the Environment

The brain is most plastic during its development, and the structure of neurons and their connections can be molded by various factors throughout development. The brain's sensitivity to factors such as external events, quality of environment, drugs, gonadal hormones, and injury varies over time: at critical periods in the course of development, different brain regions are particularly sensitive to different events.

Perturbations of the brain in the course of development from, say, anoxia, trauma, or toxins can significantly alter brain development and result in severe behavioral abnormalities including retardation and cerebral palsy. The brain does have a substantial capacity to repair or correct minor abnormalities, however, allowing most people to develop normal behavioral repertoires and to maintain brain function throughout life.

Key Terms

amblyopia, p. 225
androgen, p. 229
anencephaly, p. 231
apoptosis, p. 212
cell-adhesion molecule (CAM), p. 211
cerebral palsy, p. 209
chemoaffinity hypothesis, p. 222
critical period, p. 225
estrogen, p. 229
filopod (pl. filopodia), p. 211
glioblast, p. 205
growth cone, p. 211
growth spurt, p. 218
imprinting, p. 225
masculinization, p. 229
netrin, p. 211
neural Darwinism, p. 212
neural plate, p. 202
neural stem cell, p. 205
neural tube, p. 202
neuroblast, p. 205
neurotrophic factor, p. 207
progenitor (precursor) cell, p. 205
radial glial cell, p. 207
sudden infant death syndrome (SIDS), p. 200
subventricular zone, p. 205
testosterone, p. 205
tropic molecule, p. 211

▶*Please refer to the Companion Web Site at* **www.worthpublishers.com/kolbintro3e** *for Interactive Exercises and Quizzes.*

Oliver Furrer/Brand X/Corbis

How Do Drugs and Hormones Influence the Brain and Behavior?

CLINICAL FOCUS 8-1

Addiction

My first experience was at age 14. Some friends of mine were doing it in a corner, and I said, "Gee, what is that?" So I did it, and that was intravenously. I didn't like it really at first, and it was a few years later that I tried it again, not really understanding why I was doing this, other than starting to remember things that had happened to me in my lifetime, being a survivor of incest and having a mother who didn't support me.

I'd use it each and every day. I would have to have some to wake up to in the morning. I remember being in the streets and not being able to keep my head up. I remember ugly stuff, uncontrollable stuff. When they talk about the insanity of the drug, it's true—it's really insane. I only had 5 years' sobriety time—5 years at one time. That's how bad it was.

I have a family—I want to see my grandchildren grow up, and I want to see what happens in their lives, and my daughter and my son.

My goal is to become drug free, maybe go back to school.

These are comments from Ms W, a 50-year-old woman who has spent most of her adult life addicted to intravenous heroin (O'Brien, 2008). In addition to using heroin, she has used crack cocaine, a variety of pills, LSD (lysergic acid diethylamide), and marijuana. For years she smoked about two packs of cigarettes a day. She tried many times to quit smoking and eventually did with the aid of a drug called bupropion (an atypical antidepressant that is as effective as nicotine patches in decreasing the desire to smoke).

Ms W is unusual among addicts in that she remained concerned about her health, avoided exposure to HIV and other infections, and stopped smoking. She remained drug free during her two pregnancies. She underwent numerous detoxification programs but always relapsed.

At age 50, Ms W was receiving methadone treatment, which was beneficial. Methadone is a synthetic opioid that acts at the same receptor sites as does heroin but does not produce the same euphoric effects and has a long action, usually more than a day. Treatment requires that she attend a clinic that ensures that she takes the drug.

Drug addiction is a complex individual, social, legal, and medical problem, and delivering treatment is beset by many problems. Ms W will likely need life-long support and treatment to cope with her drug problem. She observed, "I would like to know why it has taken so long for doctors and that type of community to want to help drug addicts, because this is an epidemic, and the kids are getting younger."

(A)

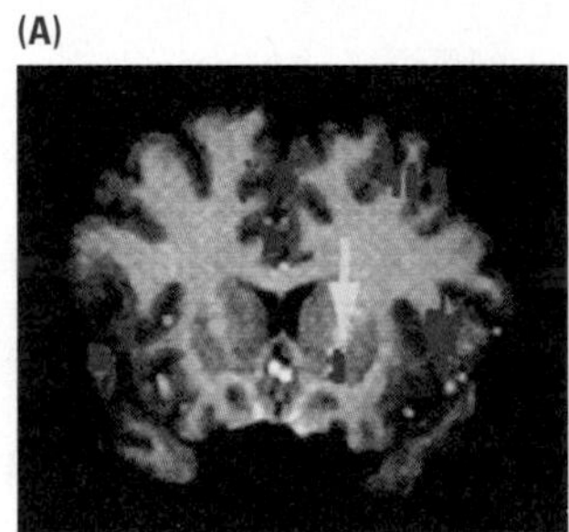

(B)

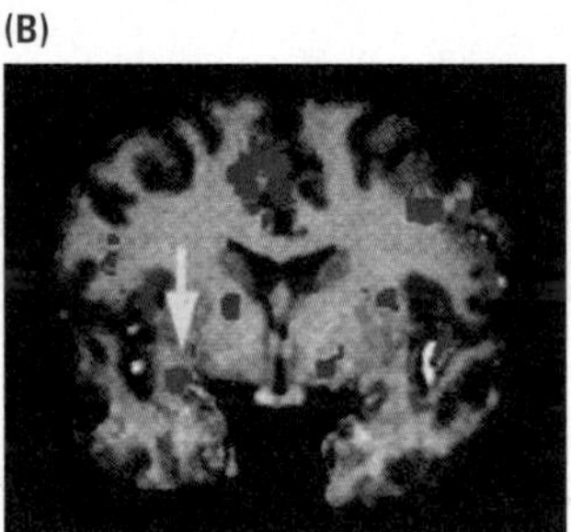

(C)

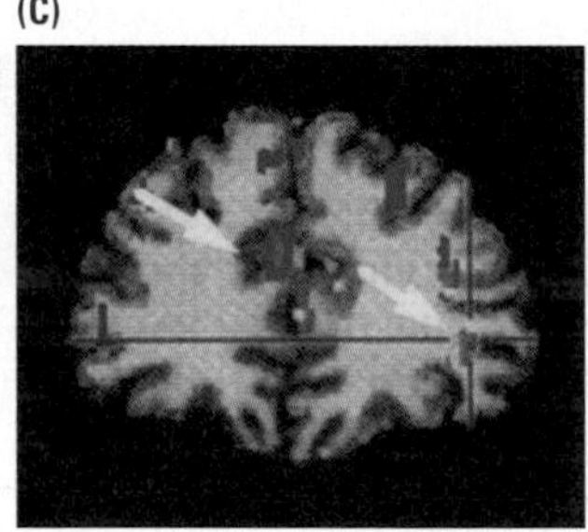

Functional MRI imaging of brain regions (yellow arrows) in the basal ganglia (A) and limbic system (B and C) that are activated by nicotine. All are targets of dopamine projections (red areas), consisent with the idea that the activation of dopamine systems is related to addiction. From "Nicotine-induced limbic cortical activation in the human brain: A functional MRI study," by F. A. Stein, J. Pankiewicz, H. H. Harsch, J. K. Cho, S. A. Fuller, R. G. Hoffmann, M. Hawkins, S. M. Rao, P. A. Bandettini, and A. S. Bloom, 1998, *American Journal of Psychiatry, 155,* 1009–1015.

PSYCHOPHARMACOLOGY IS THE STUDY of how drugs affect the nervous system and behavior. In this chapter, we group various drugs by their major behavioral effects. You will learn that the effects of drugs depend on how they are taken, in what quantities, and under what circumstances.

We begin by looking at the major ways that drugs are administered, what routes they take to reach the central nervous system, and how they are eliminated from the body. We consider how drugs act on neurons and why different people may respond differently to the same dose of a drug. Many principles related to drugs also apply to the action of hormones, the chapter's final topic.

Before we examine how drugs produce their effects on the brain for good or for ill, we must raise a caution: the sheer number of neurotransmitters, receptors, and possible sites of drug action is astounding. Psychopharmacology research has made important advances on principles of drug action, but neuroscientists do not know everything there is to know about any drug.

Psychopharmacology Study of how drugs affect the nervous system and behavior.

Psychoactive drug Substance that acts to alter mood, thought, or behavior and is used to manage neuropsychological illness.

Principles of Psychopharmacology

Drugs are chemical compounds administered to bring about some desired change in the body. Drugs are usually used to diagnose, treat, or prevent illness, to relieve pain and suffering, or to improve some adverse physiological condition. In this chapter, we focus on **psychoactive drugs**—substances that act to alter mood, thought, or behavior and are used to manage neuropsychological illness.

Many psychoactive drugs are taken for nonmedical reasons or recreationally, by some to the point at which they become substances of abuse. Such drug taking impairs the user's functioning, promotes craving, and may produce addiction. Some psychoactive drugs can also act as toxins, producing sickness, brain damage, or death.

Drug Routes into the Nervous System

To be effective, a psychoactive drug has to reach its nervous-system target. The way in which a drug enters and passes through the body to reach that target is called its *route of administration.* Drugs can be administered orally, inhaled into the lungs, administered through rectal suppositories, absorbed from patches applied to the skin, or injected into the bloodstream, into a muscle, or even into the brain.

Figure 8-1 illustrates the various routes of drug administration. Taking a drug orally (by mouth) is easy and convenient, but not all drugs can pass the barriers of the digestive-tract contents and walls. Drugs that are administered as gases or aerosols penetrate the cell linings of the respiratory tract easily and are absorbed across these membranes into the bloodstream nearly as quickly as they are inhaled. Presumably, such drugs of abuse as nicotine, cocaine, and marijuana, when administered as a gas or smoke, are absorbed in a similar way.

Our largest organ, the skin, has three layers of cells designed to be a protective body coat. Some small-molecule drugs (e.g., nicotine) penetrate the skin's barrier almost as easily as they penetrate the cell lining of the respiratory tract, whereas large-molecule drugs such as steroids do not. There are still fewer obstacles to a drug injected directly into the bloodstream. The fewest obstacles are encountered if a psychoactive drug is injected directly into the brain.

Figure 8-1 also summarizes the characteristics of drugs that allow them to pass through various barriers to reach their targets. Oral administration is the most-complex route. To reach the bloodstream, an ingested drug must first be absorbed through the lining of the stomach or small intestine. If the drug is liquid, it is absorbed more readily. Drugs taken in solid form are not absorbed unless they can be dissolved by the stomach's gastric juices and the large surface area of the intestine.

FIGURE 8-1 Routes of Drug Administration.

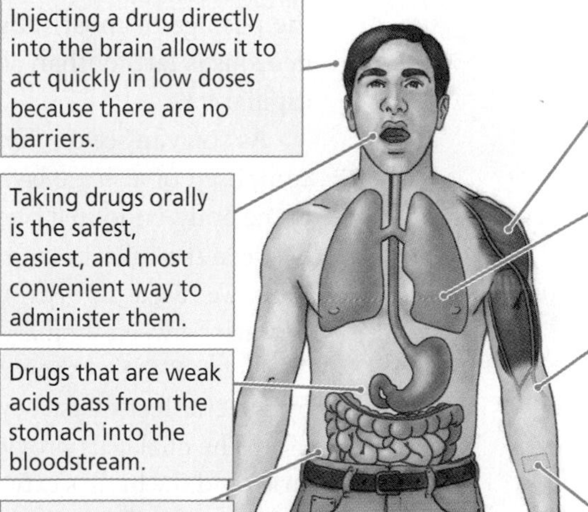

Injecting a drug directly into the brain allows it to act quickly in low doses because there are no barriers.
Taking drugs orally is the safest, easiest, and most convenient way to administer them.
Drugs that are weak acids pass from the stomach into the bloodstream.
Drugs that are weak bases pass from the intestines to the bloodstream.
Drugs injected into muscle encounter more barriers than do drugs inhaled.
Drugs inhaled into the lungs encounter few barriers en route to the brain.
Drugs injected into the bloodstream encounter the fewest barriers to the brain but must be hydrophilic.
Drugs contained in adhesive patches are absorbed through the skin and into the bloodstream.

In either form, liquid or solid, absorption is affected by the physical and chemical properties of the drug, as well as by the presence of other stomach or intestinal contents. In general, a drug that is a weak acid, such as alcohol, is readily absorbed across the stomach lining. A weak base such as phenobarbital, an anesthetic, cannot be absorbed until it passes through the stomach and into the intestine—a process that may destroy a weak base.

After it has been absorbed by the stomach or intestine, the drug must next enter the bloodstream. This part of the journey requires additional properties. Because blood has a high water concentration, a drug must be hydrophilic to be carried in the blood. A hydrophobic substance will be blocked from entering the bloodstream. After it is in the blood, a drug is then diluted by the approximately 6 liters of blood that circulate through an adult's body.

To reach its target, a drug must also travel from the blood into the extracellular fluid, which requires that its molecules be small enough to pass through the pores of capillaries, the tiny vessels that carry blood to the body's cells. Even if the drug makes this passage, it encounters other obstacles. The sheer volume of water in the body's extracellular fluid (roughly 35 liters) will dilute the drug even further. The drug is also at risk of being modified or destroyed by various metabolic processes taking place in cells.

1000 micrograms = 1 milligram

With each obstacle eliminated en route to the brain, the dosage of a drug can be reduced by a factor of 10. For example, 1000 micrograms, of amphetamine, a psychomotor stimulant, produces a noticeable behavioral change when ingested orally. If inhaled into the lungs or injected into the blood, thereby circumventing the stomach, a dose of just 100 micrograms produces the same results. If amphetamine is injected into the cerebrospinal fluid, thus bypassing both the stomach and the blood, 10 micrograms is enough to produce an identical outcome, as is merely 1 microgram if dilution in the cerebrospinal fluid also is skirted, and the drug is injected directly onto target neurons.

This math is well known to sellers and users of illicit drugs. Drugs that can be prepared to be inhaled or injected intravenously are much cheaper per dose because the amount required is so much smaller than that needed for an effective oral dose.

Revisiting the Blood–Brain Barrier

The passage of drugs across capillaries in the brain is made difficult by the *blood–brain barrier,* the tight junctions between the cells of blood vessels in the brain that prevent the passage of most substances. The brain has a rich capillary network. None of its neurons is farther than about 50 micrometers (one-millionth of a meter) away from a capillary.

As you can see on the left side of **Figure 8-2,** like all capillaries, brain capillaries are composed of a single layer of endothelial cells. In the walls of capillaries in most parts of the body, endothelial cells are not fused, and so substances can pass through the clefts between the cells. In contrast, in the brain (at least in most parts of it), endothelial cell walls are fused to form "tight junctions," and so molecules of most substances cannot squeeze between them.

Figure 8-2 also shows that the endothelial cells of brain capillaries are surrounded by the end feet of astrocytes attached to the capillary wall, covering about 80 percent of it. The glial cells provide a route for the exchange of food and waste between capillaries and the brain's extracellular fluid and from there to other cells, shown on the right in Figure 8-2. They may also play a role in maintaining the tight junctions between endothelial cells and in making capillaries dilate to increase blood flow to areas of the brain in which neurons are very active.

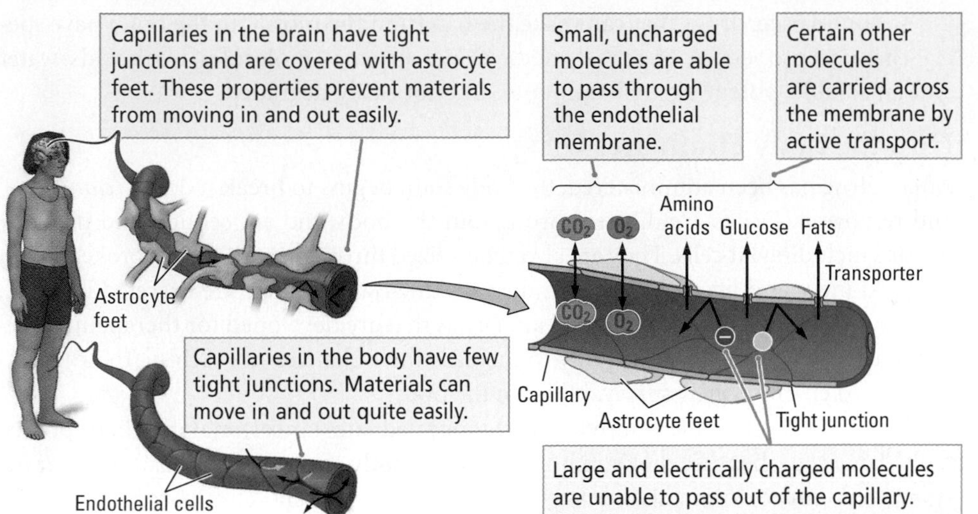

FIGURE 8-2 Blood–Brain Barrier. Capillaries in most of the body allow for the passage of substances between capillary cell membranes, but those in the brain, stimulated by the actions of astrocytes, form the tight junctions of the blood–brain barrier.

The cells of capillary walls in the three brain regions shown in **Figure 8-3** lack a blood–brain barrier. The pituitary is a source of many hormones that are secreted into the blood system, and their release is triggered in part by other hormones carried to the pituitary by the blood. The absence of a blood–brain barrier in the area postrema of the lower brainstem allows toxic substances in the blood to trigger a vomiting response. The pineal gland also lacks a blood–brain barrier, enabling hormones to reach it and modulate the day–night cycles controlled by this structure.

To carry out its work, the rest of the brain needs oxygen and glucose for fuel and amino acids to build proteins, among other substances. These fuel molecules must reach brain cells from the blood, just as carbon dioxide and other waste products must be excreted from brain cells into the blood. Molecules of these vital substances cross the blood–brain barrier in two ways:

1. Small molecules such as oxygen and carbon dioxide, which are not ionized and so are fat soluble, can pass through the endothelial membrane.
2. Molecules of glucose, amino acids, and other food components are carried across the membrane by active-transport systems or pumps—proteins specialized for the transport of a particular substance.

When a substance has passed from the capillaries into the brain's extracellular fluid, it can readily move into neurons and glia.

The blood–brain barrier protects the brain's ionic blance and prevents neurochemicals from the rest of the body from passing into the brain and disrupting communication between neurons. It protects the brain from the effects of many circulating hormones and from various toxic and infectious substances. Injury or disease can sometimes rupture the blood–brain barrier, letting pathogens through. For the most part, however, the brain is very well protected from substances potentially harmful to its functioning.

The blood–brain barrier has relevance for understanding drug actions on the nervous system. A drug can reach the brain only if its molecules are small and not ionized, enabling them to pass through endothelial cell membranes, or if the drug has a chemical structure that allows it to be carried across the membrane by an active-transport system. Because few drug molecules are small or have the correct chemical structure, few can gain access to the CNS. Because the blood–brain barrier works so well, it is difficult to find new drugs to use as treatments for brain diseases.

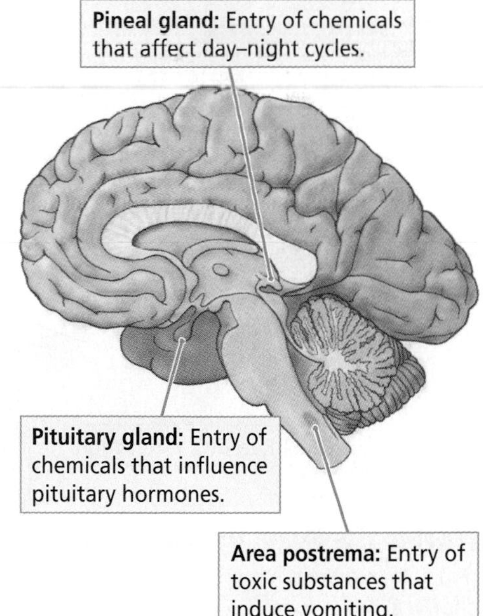

FIGURE 8-3 Barrier-Free Brain Sites. The pituitary gland is a target for many blood-borne hormones, the pineal gland is a target for hormones that affect circadian rhythms, and the area postrema initiates vomiting in response to noxious substances.

To summarize, drugs that can make the trip from the mouth to the brain have special chemical properties. The most effective ones are small molecules, weak acids, water and fat soluble, potent in small amounts, and not easily degraded.

How the Body Eliminates Drugs

Metabolic processes build up; catabolic processes break down.

After a drug has been administered, the body soon begins to break it down *(catabolize)* and remove it. Drugs are diluted throughout the body and are sequestered in many regions including fat cells. They are also catabolized throughout the body, broken down in the kidneys and liver, as well as in the intestine by bile. They are excreted in urine, feces, sweat, breast milk, and exhaled air. Drugs that are developed for therapeutic purposes are usually designed not only to increase their chances of reaching their targets but also to enhance their survival time in the body.

The body has trouble removing some ingested substances, making them potentially dangerous, because they can build up in the body and become poisonous. For instance, certain toxic metals, such as mercury, are not easily eliminated; when they accumulate, they can produce severe neurological conditions.

Even drugs that are eliminated from the body are problematic. They may remain in waste, enter the environment, and then be reingested in food and water by many animal species, including humans. When reingested, they may affect fertility, the development of embryos, and even the physiology and behavior of adult organisms. This problem requires radical redesign of waste-management systems to remove the many drugs and drug biproducts eliminated by humans as well as other animals (Radjenović et al., 2008).

Drug Action at Synapses: Agonists and Antagonists

Most drugs that have psychoactive effects do so by influencing the chemical reactions at synapses. So, to understand how drugs work, we must explore the ways in which they modify synaptic actions.

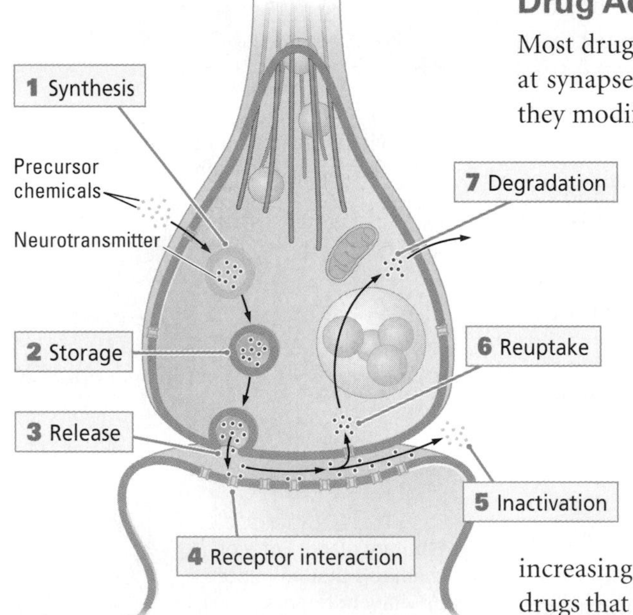

FIGURE 8-4 Points of Influence. In principle, a drug can modify seven major chemical processes, any of which results in enhanced or reduced synaptic transmission, depending on the drug's action as an agonist or an antagonist.

Figure 8-4 summarizes the seven major steps in neurotransmission at a synapse—each a site of drug action. Synthesis of the neurotransmitter can take place in the cell body, the axon, or the terminal. The neurotransmitter is then held in storage granules or in vesicles or in both until it is released from the terminal's presynaptic membrane.The amount of transmitter released into the synapse is regulated in relation to experience. When released, the transmitter acts on a receptor embedded in the postsynaptic membrane. It is then either destroyed or taken back up into the presynaptic terminal for reuse. The synapse also has mechanisms for degrading excess neurotransmitter and removing unneeded by-products from the synapse.

A drug can influence synaptic function in one of two ways: either by increasing the effectiveness of neurotransmission or by diminishing it. **Agonists** are drugs that increase the effectiveness of neurotransmission, whereas **antagonists** decrease its effectiveness. Agonists and antagonists can work in a variety of ways, as Figure 8-4 illustrates, but their respective end results are always the same. To illustrate, consider the acetylcholine synapse between motor neurons and muscles.

An Acetylcholine Synapse: Examples of Drug Action

Figure 8-5 shows how selected drugs and toxins act as agonists or antagonists at the acetylcholine synapse. Acetylcholine agonists excite muscles, making them rigid, whereas acetylcholine antagonists inhibit muscles, rendering them flaccid. Some of these substances may be new to you, but you have probably heard of others. Knowing their effects at the ACh synapse allows you to understand the behavioral effects that they produce.

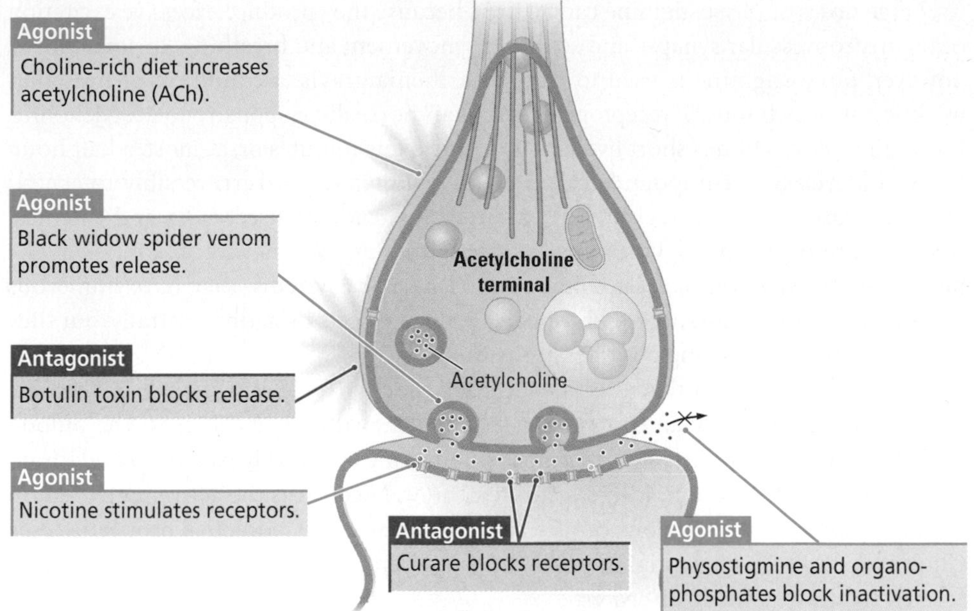
Agonist
Choline-rich diet increases acetylcholine (ACh).
Agonist
Black widow spider venom promotes release.
Antagonist
Botulin toxin blocks release.
Agonist
Nicotine stimulates receptors.
Acetylcholine terminal
Acetylcholine
Antagonist
Curare blocks receptors.
Agonist
Physostigmine and organophosphates block inactivation.

FIGURE 8-5 Acetylcholine Agonists and Antagonists. Drugs affect ACh transmission by affecting its synthesis, release, or binding to the postsynaptic receptor and by affecting its breakdown or inactivation.

Figure 8-5 shows two toxins that influence the release of ACh from the axon terminal. Black widow spider venom is an agonist because it promotes the release of acetylcholine to excess. A black widow spider bite contains enough toxin to paralyze an insect but not enough to paralyze a person, though a victim may feel some muscle weakness.

Botulin toxin, the poisonous agent in tainted foods such as canned goods that have been improperly processed, acts as an antagonist because it blocks the release of ACh. The effects of botulin toxin can last from weeks to months. A severe case can result in the paralysis of both movement and breathing and so cause death.

This action of botulin toxin has medical uses. If injected into a muscle, it can selectively paralyze that muscle. This selective action makes it useful in blocking excessive and enduring muscular twitches or contractions, including the spasms that makes movement difficult for people with cerebral palsy. Under the trade name Botox, botulin toxin is also used cosmetically to paralyze facial muscles that cause facial wrinkling.

Clinical Focus 7-2 describes the causes and range of outcomes for cerebral palsy.

Figure 8-5 also shows two drugs that act on receptors for acetylcholine. Nicotine's molecular structure is similar enough to that of ACh to allow nicotine to fit into the receptors' binding sites where it acts as an agonist. Curare acts as an antagonist by occupying cholinergic receptors and so preventing acetylcholine from binding to them. When curare binds to these receptors, it blocks their functioning. After having been introduced into the body, curare acts quickly, and it is cleared from the body in a few minutes. Large doses, however, arrest movement and breathing for a period sufficient to result in death.

As explained in Chapter 5, a single main receptor serves the somatic nervous system: the nicotinic ACh receptor (nAChr).

Early European explorers of South America discovered that the Indians along the Amazon River killed small animals by using arrowheads coated with curare prepared from the seeds of a plant. The hunters themselves did not become poisoned when eating the animals, because ingested curare cannot pass from the gut into the body. Many curare-like drugs have been synthesized. Some are used to briefly paralyze large animals so that they can be examined or tagged for identification. You have probably seen this use of these drugs in wildlife programs on television. Skeletal muscles are more sensitive to curare-like drugs than are respiratory muscles; an appropriate dose will paralyze an animal's movement temporarily but still allow it to breathe.

The fifth drug action shown in Figure 8-5 is that of physostigmine, a drug that inhibits cholinesterase, the enzyme that breaks down acetylcholine. Physostigmine therefore acts as an agonist to increase the amount of ACh available in the synapse. Physostigmine is obtained from an African bean and is used as a poison by native peoples in Africa.

Agonist Substance that enhances the function of a synapse.
Antagonist Substance that blocks the function of a synapse.

Clinical Focus 4-3, "Myasthenia Gravis," explains what happens when muscle receptors lose their sensitivity to motor-neuron messages.

Large doses of physostigmine can be toxic because they produce excessive excitation of the neuromuscular synapse and so disrupt movement and breathing. In small doses, however, physostigmine is used to treat myasthenia gravis, a condition of muscular weakness in which muscle receptors are less than normally responsive to acetylcholine. Physostigmine's action is short lived, lasting only a few minutes or, at most, a half hour.

Another class of compounds called *organophosphates* bind irreversibly to acetylcholinesterase and, consequently, are extremely toxic. Many insecticides and chemical weapons are organophosphates. Insects use glutamate as a neurotransmitter at the nerve–muscle junction but, elsewhere in their nervous systems, they have numerous nicotine receptors. Thus, organophosphates poison insects by acting centrally, but they poison chordates by acting peripherally as well.

Does a drug or toxin that affects neuromuscular synapses also affect acetylcholine synapses in the brain? That depends on whether the substance can cross the blood–brain barrier. For example, physostigmine and nicotine can readily pass the blood–brain barrier and affect the brain, whereas curare cannot. Nicotine is the active ingredient in cigarette smoke and its actions on the brain account for its addictive properties (see Clinical Focus 8-1). Physostigmine-like drugs are reported to have some beneficial effects in treating memory disorders.

Tolerance

Freshman roommates, B. C. and A. S., went to a party, then to a bar, and, by 3 A.M., were in a restaurant ordering pizza. A. S. decided that he wanted to watch the chef make his pizza, and off he went to the kitchen. A long and heated argument ensued between A. S., the chef, and the manager.

The roommates were headed away in A. S.'s car when a police officer, called by the manager, drove up and stopped them. A. S. failed a breathalyzer test, which estimates body-alcohol content, and was taken into custody. Surprisingly, B. C. passed the test, even though he had consumed the same amount of alcohol as A. S. had. Why this difference in their responses to the drinking bout?

In tolerance, as in habituation, a learned behavior results when a response to a stimulus weakens with repeated presentations (see Experiment 5-2).

The reason could be that B. C. had developed greater tolerance for alcohol than A. S. had. **Tolerance** is a decrease in response to a drug with the passage of time. Harris Isbell and coworkers (1955) show how such tolerance comes about. These researchers gave volunteers in a prison enough alcohol daily in a 13-week period to keep them in a constant state of intoxication. Yet they found that the subjects did not stay drunk for 3 months straight.

When the experiment began, all the subjects showed rapidly rising levels of blood alcohol and behavioral signs of intoxication, as shown in the Results section of **Experiment 8-1.** Between the 12th and 20th days of alcohol consumption, however, blood alcohol and the signs of intoxication fell to very low levels, even though the subjects maintained a constant alcohol intake. Interestingly, too, although blood-alcohol levels and signs of intoxication fluctuated in subsequent days of the study, one did not always correspond with the other. A relatively high blood-alcohol level was sometimes associated with a low outward appearance of intoxication. Why?

These results were likely the products of three different kinds of tolerance:

1. In the development of *metabolic tolerance,* the number of enzymes needed to break down alcohol in the liver, blood, and brain increases. As a result, any alcohol that is consumed is metabolized more quickly, and so blood-alcohol levels are reduced.
2. In the development of *cellular tolerance,* the activities of brain cells adjust to minimize the effects of alcohol present in the blood. This kind of tolerance can help explain why the behavioral signs of intoxication may be very low despite a relatively high blood-alcohol level.

Tolerance Decrease in response to a drug with the passage of time.

3. *Learned tolerance,* too, can help explain a drop in the outward signs of intoxication. As people learn to cope with the daily demands of living while under the influence of alcohol, they may no longer appear to be drunk.

That learning plays a role in tolerance to alcohol may surprise you, but this role has been confirmed in many studies. In an early description of the effect, John Wenger and his coworkers (1981) trained rats to walk on a narrow conveyor belt to prevent electric shock to their feet from a grid over which the belt slid. One group of rats received alcohol after training in walking the belt, whereas another group received alcohol before training. A third group received training only, and a fourth group received alcohol only.

After several days of exposure to their respective conditions, all groups were given alcohol before a walking test. The rats that had received alcohol before training performed well, whereas those that had received training and alcohol separately performed just as poorly as those that had never had alcohol before or those that had not been trained. Apparently, animals can acquire the motor skills needed to balance on a narrow belt despite alcohol intoxication. With the passage of time, in other words, they can learn to compensate for being drunk, as B. C. had.

All forms of tolerance are much more likely to develop with repeated drug use than with periodic drug use. B. C. came from a small town where he was the acclaimed local pool shark. He was accustomed to "sipping a beer" both while waiting to play and during play, which he did often. B. C.'s body, then, was prepared to metabolize alcohol, and his experience in drinking while engaging in a skilled sport had prepared him to display controlled behavior under the influence of alcohol.

Enhanced metabolism and controlled behavior are manifestations of tolerance of alcohol. In contrast with B. C., A. S. came from a large city and worked long hours assisting his father with his plumbing business. He seldom attended parties and was unaccustomed to the effects of alcohol.

EXPERIMENT 8-1

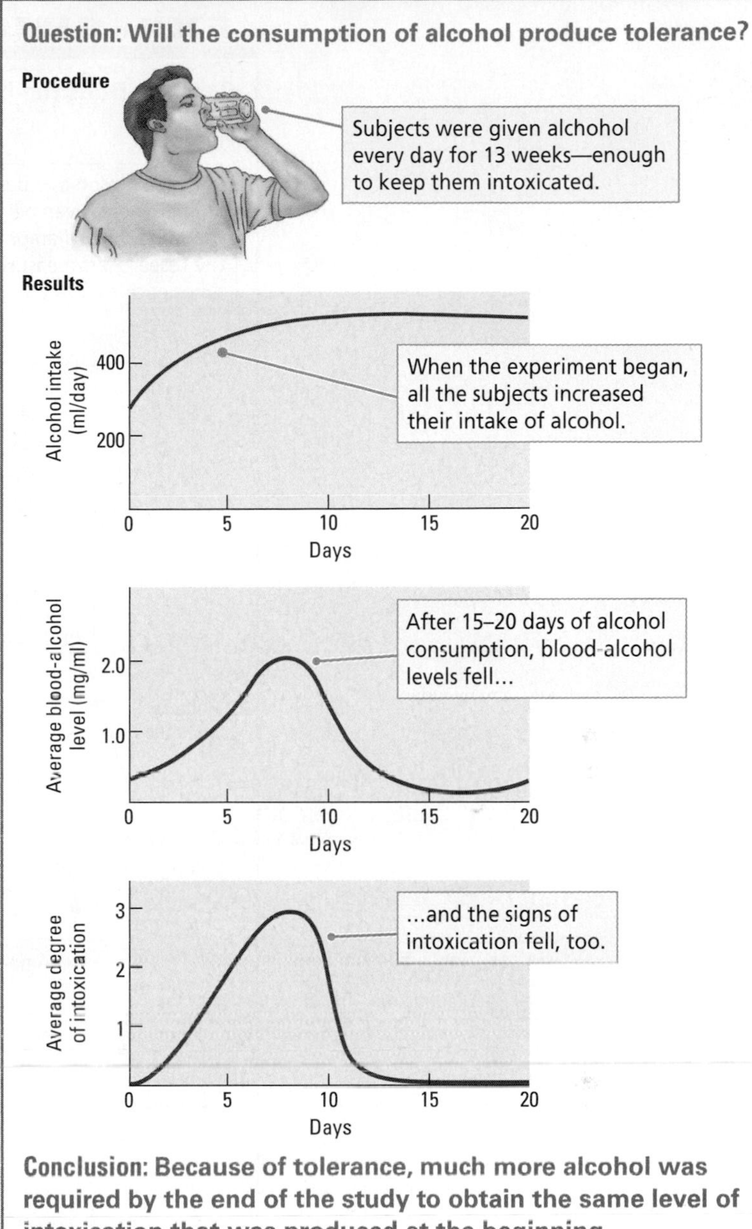
Question: Will the consumption of alcohol produce tolerance?
Procedure
Subjects were given alchohol every day for 13 weeks—enough to keep them intoxicated.
Results
Alcohol intake (ml/day)
400
200
0
5
10
15
20
Days
When the experiment began, all the subjects increased their intake of alcohol.
Average blood-alcohol level (mg/ml)
2.0
1.0
After 15–20 days of alcohol consumption, blood-alcohol levels fell...
Average degree of intoxication
3
2
1
...and the signs of intoxication fell, too.
Conclusion: Because of tolerance, much more alcohol was required by the end of the study to obtain the same level of intoxication that was produced at the beginning.

Adapted from "An Experimental Study of the Etiology of 'Rum Fits' and Delirium Tremens," by H. Isbell, H. F. Fraser, A. Winkler, R. E. Belleville, and A. J. Eisenman, 1955, *Quarterly Journal of Studies on Alcohol, 16,* pp. 1–21.]

Sensitization

Repeated exposure to the same drug does not always result in tolerance, which resembles habituation in that the response to the drug weakens with repeated presentations. The occasional drug taker may experience the opposite reaction, sensitization, or increased responsiveness to successive equal doses. Whereas tolerance generally develops with repeated use of a drug, sensitization is much more likely to develop with occasional use.

Experiment 5-3 describes sensitization at the level of neurons and synapses. Chapter 14 relates drug-induced behavioral sensitization to neuroplasticity and learned addictions.

To demonstrate drug sensitization, Terry Robinson and Jill Becker (1986) isolated rats in observation boxes and recorded their reactions to an injection of amphetamine, especially reactions such as increases in sniffing, rearing, and walking, which are typical rat responses to this drug. Every 3 or 4 days, the investigators injected the rats and found that the behavior of the rats was more vigorous with each administration of the drug, as graphed in Results 1 of **Experiment 8-2**.

EXPERIMENT 8-2

Question: Does the injection of a drug always produce the same behavior?

Procedure 1

In the Robinson and Becker study, animals were given periodic injections of the same dose of amphetamine. Then the researchers measured the number of times each rat reared in its cage.

Procedure 2

In the Whishaw study, animals were given different numbers of swims after being injected with Flupentixol. Then the researchers measured their speed to escape to a platform in a swimming pool.

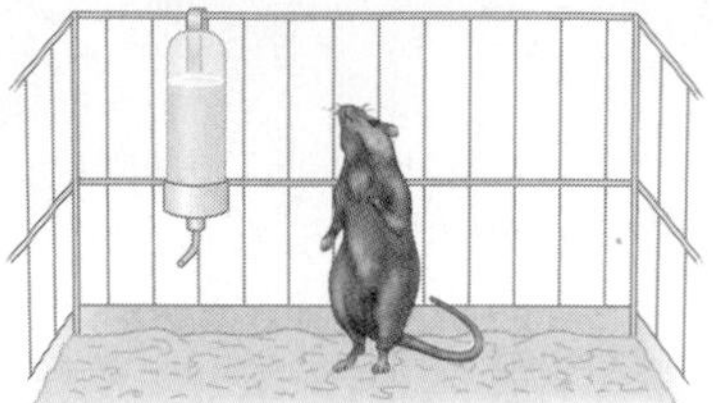

Agonist
Amphetamine

Antagonist
Flupentixol

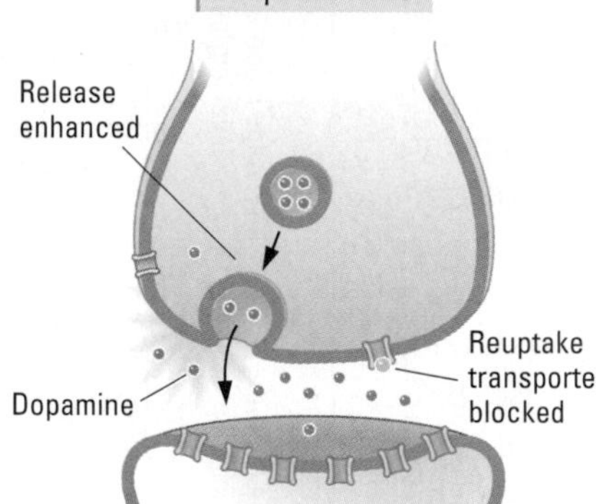

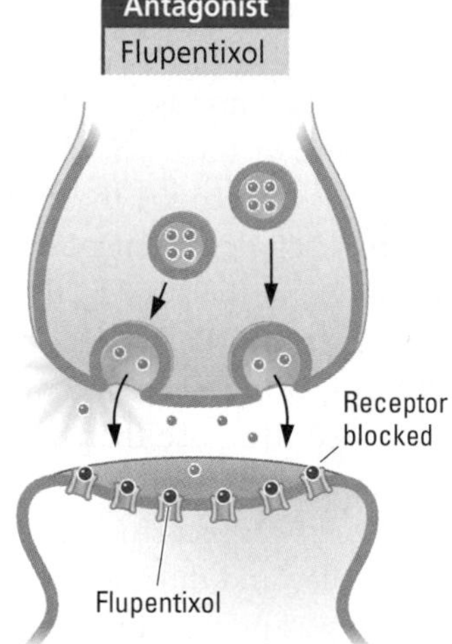

Results 1

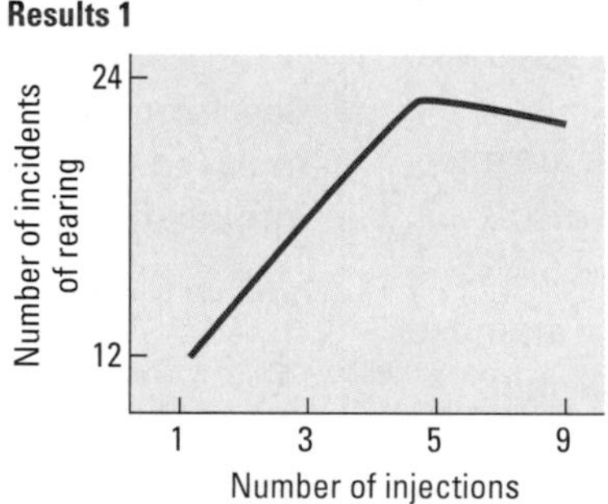

Results 2

Time to platform(s)
60
3
1
4
8
12
Number of trials

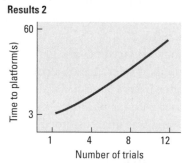

Conclusion 1: Sensitization, indicated by increased rearing, develops with periodic repeated injections.

Conclusion 2: Sensitization depends on the occurrence of a behavior: the number of swims increases the time that it takes the rat to reach the platform.

(*Left*) Adapted from "Enduring Changes in Brain and Behavior Produced by Chronic Amphetamine Administration: A Review and Evaluation of Animal Models of Amphetamine Psychosis," by T. E. Robinson and J. B. Becker, 1986, *Brain Research Reviews, 397,* pp. 157–198. (*Right*) Adapted from "Training-Dependent Decay in Performance Produced by the Neuroleptic *cis(Z)*-Flupentixol on Spatial Navigation by Rats in a Swimming Pool," by I. Q. Whishaw, G. Mittelman, and J. L. Evenden, 1989, *Pharmacology, Biochemistry, and Behavior, 32,* pp. 211–220.]

This increased response on successive tests was not due to the animals becoming comfortable with the test situation. Control animals that received no drug did not display a similar escalation in sniffing, rearing, and walking. Administering the drug to rats in their home cages did not affect exploration in subsequent tests. Moreover, the sensitization to amphetamine was enduring. Even when two injections of amphetamine were separated by months, the animals still showed an increased response to the drug. Even a single exposure to the drug produced sensitization.

Sensitization is not always characterized by an increase in an emmited behavior but may also manifest as a progressive decrease in behavior. One of us and his coworkers (Whishaw et al., 1989) administered Flupentixol, a drug that blocks dopamine receptors, to rats in a swimming task. As illustrated in Results 2 of Experiment 8-2, the rats displayed a decrease in swimming speed over successive trials when swimming to a refuge target. The trial-dependent decrease was similar when the trials were massed on the same day or spaced over days or weeks. Administering the drug to rats left in their home enviroment did not influence perfomance in subsequent swim tests.

The neural basis of sensitization lies in part in changes at the synapse. Studies on the dopamine synapse after sensitization to amphetamine show that more dopamine is released from the presynaptic terminal in sensitized animals. Sensitization can also be associated with changes in the number of receptors on the postsynaptic membrane, changes in the rate of transmitter metabolism in the synaptic space, changes in transmitter reuptake by the presynaptic membrane, and changes in the number and size of synapses.

Part of the basis of sensitization is that animals are showing a change in learned responses to the cues in their environment as senzitization progresses. Consequently, sensitization is difficult to achieve in an animal that is tested in its home cage. Sabina Fraioli and her coworkers (1999) gave amphetamine to two groups of rats and recorded the rats' behavioral responses to successive injections. One group of rats lived in the test apparatus; so, for that group, home was the test box. The other group was taken out of their normal home cage and placed in the test box for each day's experimentation. The "home" group showed no sensitization to amphetamine, whereas the "out" group displayed robust sensitization.

At least part of the explanation of the "home–out" effect is that the animals are accustomed to engaging in a certain repertoire of behaviors in their home environment, and so it is difficult to get them to change the behavior that "home" cues even in response to a drug. It is likewise difficult to condition new behavior to their familiar home cues. Presumably, humans, too, show sensitization to a drug when they periodically take it in novel contexts where new cues can be readily associated with the novel cognitive and physiological effects of the drug.

REVIEW: Principles of Psychopharmacology

- ✔ Drugs are chemical compounds administered to bring about some desired change in the body. Psychoactive drugs, substances that produce changes in behavior by acting on the nervous system, are one subject of psychoparmacology, the study of how drugs affect the nervous system and behavior.
- ✔ Drugs encounter various barriers on the journey between their entry into the body and their action at a CNS target. Perhaps the most important obstacle is the blood–brain barrier, which generally allows only substances needed for nourishing the brain to pass from the capillaries into the CNS.
- ✔ Most drugs that have psychoactive effects do so by crossing the blood–brain barrier and influencing chemical reactions at brain synapses. Drugs that influence

Antianxiety agent Drug that reduces anxiety; minor tranquillizers such as benzodiazepines and sedative-hypnotic agents are of this type.
Barbiturate Drug that produces sedation and sleep.
Cross-tolerance Response to a novel drug is reduced because of tolerance developed in response to a chemically related drug.

communication between neurons do so by acting either as agonists (increasing) or as antagonists (decreasing) the effectiveness of neurotransmission.

✔ Behavior may change in a number of ways with the repeated use of a psychoactive drug. These changes include tolerance and sensitization, in which the effect of the drug decreases or increases, respectively, with repeated use.

✔ The body eliminates drugs through feces, urine, sweat glands, the breath, and breast milk.

Classification of Psychoactive Drugs

Many psychoactive drugs used to treat mental illness are listed in **Table 8-1** along with the dates of their discovery and the names of their discoverers. You may be surprised to know that their therapeutic actions were all originally discovered by accident. Subsequently, scientists and pharmaceutical companies developed many forms of each drug in an effort to increase effectiveness and reduce side effects. At the same time, experimental researchers attempted to explain each drug's action on the nervous system—explanations that are as yet incomplete. We will consider the actions of some of these drugs in this section.

Drugs with similar chemical structures can have quite different effects, whereas drugs with different structures can have very similar effects. Hence, classifications based on a drug's chemical structure have not been successful. Classification schemes based on receptors in the brain also have been problematic, because a single drug can act on many different receptors. The same problem arises with classification systems based on the neurotransmitter affected by a drug, because many drugs act on many different transmitters.

The classification that we use is based on the most-pronounced behavioral or psychoactive effect produced by a drug—especially as it relates to medical applications.

TABLE 8-1 Drugs Used for the Treatment of Mental Illness

Illness	Drug class	Representative drug	Common trade name	Discoverer
Schizophrenia	Phenothiazines	Chlorpromazine	Largactile Thorazine	Jean Delay and Pierre Deniker (France), 1952
	Butyrophenone	Haloperidol	Haldol	Paul Janssen (Belgium), 1957
Depression	Monoamine oxidase (MAO) inhibitors	Iproniazid	Marsilid	Nathan S. Kline and J. C. Saunders (United States), 1956
	Tricyclic antidepressants	Imipramine	Tofranil	Roland Kuhn (Switzerland), 1957
	Selective serotonin reuptake inhibitors	Fluoxetine	Prozac	Eli Lilly Company, 1986
Bipolar disorder	Lithium (metallic element)			John Cade (Australia), 1949
Anxiety disorders	Benzodiazepines	Chlordiazepoxide Valium	Librium	Leo Sternbach (Poland), 1940
		Meprobamate Equanil	Miltown	Frank Berger and William Bradley (Czechoslovakia), 1946

The following classification apportions drugs into seven classes. Each class contains from a few to many thousands of different chemicals in its subcategories. With the discovery of new brain transmitters, new drugs, and advances in understanding behavior, this classification is subject to ongoing revision.

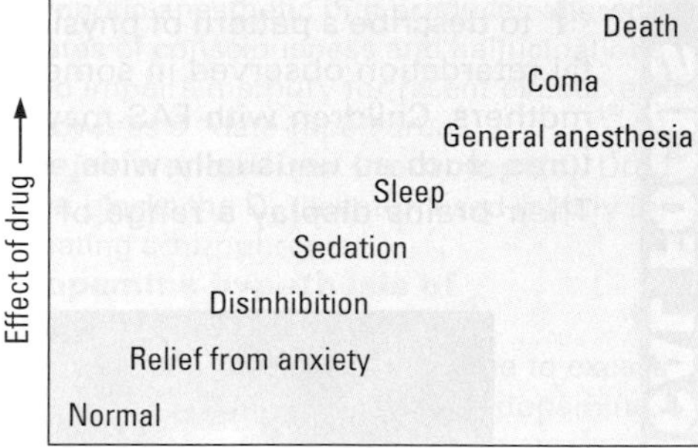

FIGURE 8-6 Behavioral Continuum of Sedation. Increasing doses of sedative-hypnotic and antianxiety drugs affect behavior: low doses reduce anxiety and very high doses result in death.

Class I: Antianxiety Agents and Sedative Hypnotics

At low doses, antianxiety drugs and sedative hypnotics reduce anxiety; at medium doses, they sedate; and, at high doses, they anesthetize or induce coma. At very high doses, they can kill (**Figure 8-6**). Antianxiety drugs differ from sedative hypnotics in their effects over their dose range and in their mechanisms of action.

The best-known **antianxiety agents,** also known as minor tranquilizers, are the benzodiazepines. An example is the widely prescribed drug Valium. Benzodiazepines are often used by people who are having trouble coping with a major life stress, such as a traumatic accident or a death in the family. They are also used as presurgical relaxation agents.

The sedative hypnotics include alcohol and barbiturates. Alcohol is well known to most people because it is so widely consumed. **Barbiturates** are sometimes prescribed as a sleeping medication, but they are mainly used to induce anesthesia before surgery. Whereas both alcohol and barbiturates can induce sleep, anesthesia, and coma at doses only slightly higher than those that sedate, the dose of benzodiazepines that produces sleep and anesthesia is substantially higher than that which is needed to relieve anxiety.

A characteristic feature of sedative hypnotics is that the user who takes repeated doses develops a tolerance for them. A larger dose is then required to maintain the drug's initial effect. **Cross-tolerance** results when the tolerance developed for one drug is carried over to a different member of the drug group.

Cross-tolerance suggests that antianxiety and sedative-hypnotic drugs are similar in their actions on the nervous system. Their common target is the receptor sites for the major inhibitory neurotransmitter gamma-aminobutyric acid, or GABA. One receptor affected by GABA is the $GABA_A$ receptor. As illustrated at the left in **Figure 8-7**, this receptor contains a chloride channel. Excitation of the receptor produces an influx of Cl^- ions through its pore. Remember that an influx of Cl^- ions increases the concentration of negative charges inside the cell membrane, hyperpolarizing it and making it less likely to initiate or propagate an action potential. The inhibitory effect of GABA, therefore, is to decrease a neuron's rate of firing.

As detailed in Chapter 5, neurons that contain GABA are inhibitory and are widely distributed in the nervous system.

The $GABA_A$ receptor has three binding sites called, respectively, the sedative-hypnotic site, a GABA site, and and antianxiety site. Excitation of the sedative-hypnotic site produces a GABA-like effect. Excitation of the antianxiety site enhances the natural action of GABA, as shown in the center of Figure 8-7. Because GABA is very quickly reabsorbed by the neurons that secrete it and by surrounding glial cells, GABA concentrations are never excessive, making it easy to overdose on sedative-hypnotic drugs and hard to overdose on antianxiety drugs.

Because of their different actions on the $GABA_A$ receptor, sedative-hypnotic and antianxiety drugs should not be taken together. A sedative hypnotic acts like GABA, but, unlike GABA, it is not quickly absorbed by surrounding cells. Thus, by remaining at the binding site, its effects are enhanced by an antianxiety drug, as shown on the right in Figure 8-7. The cumulative action of the two drugs will therefore exceed the individual action of either one. Even small combined doses of antianxiety and sedative-hypnotic drugs can produce coma or death.

FIGURE 8-7 Drug Effects at the $GABA_A$ Receptor. Sedative hypnotics, antianxiety agents, and GABA each have different binding sites.

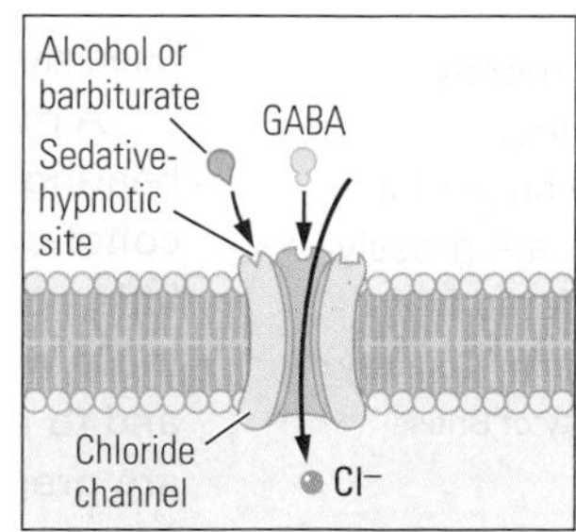

Sedative-hypnotic drugs (alcohol or barbiturates) act like GABA, causing increased chloride conductance.

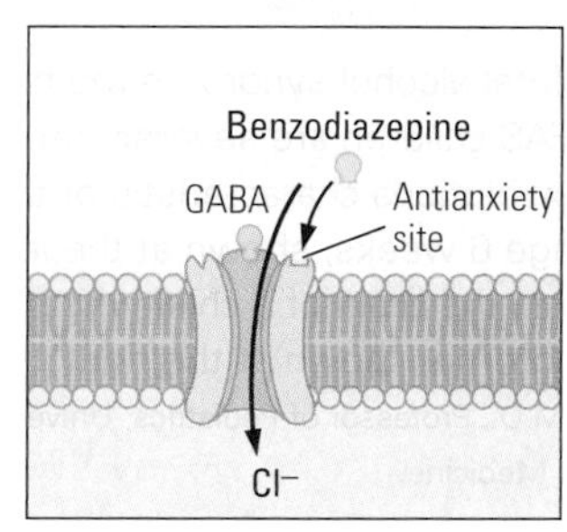

Antianxiety drugs (benzodiazepines) enhance the binding of GABA.

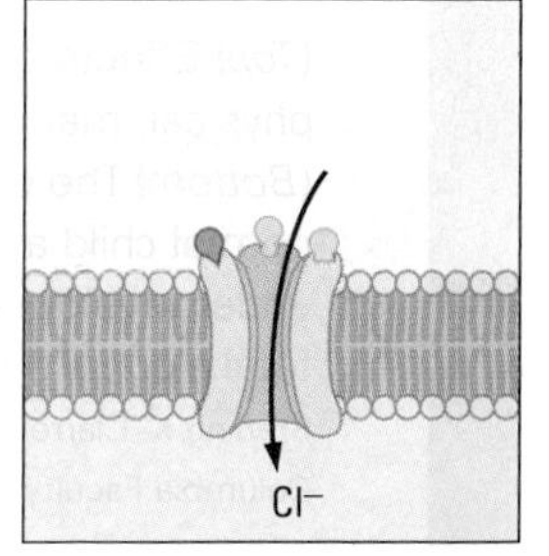

Because of their different actions, these drugs should not be taken together.

Disinhibition theory Explanation holding that alcohol has a selective depressant effect on the cortex, the region of the brain that controls judgment, while sparing subcortical structures responsible for more-primitive instincts, such as desire.
Alcohol myopia "Nearsighted" behavior displayed under the influence of alcohol: local and immediate cues become prominent, and remote cues and consequences are ignored.
Substance abuse Use of a drug for the psychological and behavioral changes that it produces aside from its therapeutic effects.
Addiction Desire for a drug manifested by frequent use of the drug, leading to the development of physical dependence in addition to abuse; often associated with tolerance and unpleasant, sometimes dangerous, withdrawal symptoms on cessation of drug use. Also called *substance dependence.*
Withdrawal symptom Physical and psychological behavior displayed by an addict when drug use ends.

recently, a seminar about the dangers of unprotected sexual intercourse was part of her college orientation, in which senior students provided the freshmen in her residence with free condoms and "safe sex" literature. Ellen and her former boyfriend were always careful to use latex condoms during intercourse.

At a homecoming party in her residence, Ellen has a great time, drinking and dancing with her friends and meeting new people. She is particularly taken with Brad, a sophomore at her college, and the two of them decide to go back to her room to order a pizza. One thing leads to another, and Ellen and Brad have sexual intercourse without using a condom. The next morning, Ellen wakes up, dismayed and surprised at her behavior and very concerned that she may be pregnant or may have contracted an STD. She is terrified that she may have contracted AIDS (MacDonald et al., 2000).

What happened to Ellen? What is it about drugs, especially alcohol, that makes people do things that they would not ordinarily do? Alcohol is associated with many harmful behaviors that are costly both to individual persons and to society. These risky behaviors include not only unprotected sexual activity but also drinking and driving, date rape, spousal or child abuse, and other forms of aggression and crime.

An early and still widely held explanation of the effects of alcohol is the **disinhibition theory.** It holds that alcohol has a selective depressant effect on the cortex, the region of the brain that controls judgment, while sparing subcortical structures, those areas of the brain responsible for more-primitive instincts, such as desire. Stated differently, alcohol presumably depresses learned inhibitions based on reasoning and judgment while releasing the "beast" within.

This theory often excuses alcohol-related behavior with such statements as, "She was too drunk to know better," or "The boys had a few too many and got carried away." Does disinhibition explain Ellen's behavior? Not really. Ellen had used alcohol in the past and managed to practice safe sex despite the effects of the drug. The disinhibition theory cannot explain why her behavior was different on this occasion. If alcohol is a disinhibitor, why is it not always so?

Craig MacAndrew and Robert Edgerton (1969) questioned disinhibition theory along just these lines in their book *Drunken Comportment.* They cite many instances in which behavior under the influence of alcohol changes from one context to another. People who engage in polite social activity at home when consuming alcohol may become unruly and aggressive when drinking in a bar.

Even their behavior at the bar may be inconsistent. Take Joe, for example. While drinking one night at a bar, he becomes obnoxious and gets into a fight. On another occasion, he is charming and witty, even preventing a fight between two friends, whereas, on a third occasion, he becomes depressed and only worries about his problems. McAndrew and Edgerton also cite examples of cultures in which people are disinhibited when sober only to become inhibited after consuming alcohol and cultures in which people are inhibited when sober and become more inhibited when drinking. How can all these differences in alcohol's effects be explained?

MacAndrew and Edgerton suggested that behavior under the effects of alcohol represents "time out" from the rules of daily life that would normally apply. This time out takes into consideration learned behavior that is specific to the culture, group, and setting. Time out can help explain Ellen's decision to sleep with Brad. In our culture, alcohol is used to facilitate social interactions, and so behavior while intoxicated represents time out from more-conservative rules regarding dating.

But time-out theory has more difficulty explaining Ellen's lapse in judgment regarding safe sex. Ellen had never practiced unsafe sex before and had never made it a part of her time-out social activities. So why did she engage in it with Brad?

Tara MacDonald and her coworkers (2000) suggest an explanation for alcohol-related lapses in judgment like Ellen's. **Alcohol myopia** (nearsightedness) is the tendency for people under the influence of alcohol to respond to a restricted set of immediate and prominent cues while ignoring more-remote cues and potential consequences. Immediate and prominent cues are very strong and obvious and are close at hand.

In an altercation, the person with alcohol myopia will be quicker than normal to throw a punch because the cue of the fight is so strong and immediate. Similarly, at a raucous party, the myopic drinker will be more eager than usual to join in because the immediate cue of boisterous fun dominates the person's view. Once Ellen and Brad arrived at Ellen's room, the sexual cues of the moment were far more immediate than concerns about long-term safety. As a result, Ellen responded to those immediate cues and behaved as she normally would not. Alcohol myopia can explain many lapses in judgment that lead to risky behavior, including aggression, date rape, and reckless driving.

Addiction and Dependence

B. G. started smoking when she was 13 years old. Now a university lecturer, she has one child and is aware that smoking is not good for her own health or for the health of her family. She has quit smoking many times without success. Recently, she used a nicotine patch that absorbs the nicotine through the skin, without the smoke.

After successfully abstaining from cigarettes for more than 6 months with this treatment, B. G. began to smoke again. Because the university where she works has a no-smoking policy, she has to leave the campus and stand across the street from the building in which she works to smoke. Her voice has developed a rasping sound, and she has an almost chronic "cold." She says that she used to enjoy smoking but does not any more. Concern about quitting dominates her thoughts.

B. G. has a drug problem. She is one of approximately 20 percent of North Americans who smoke. Most begin between the ages of 15 and 35, consuming an average of about 18 cigarettes a day, nearly a pack-a-day habit. Like B. G., most smokers realize that smoking is a health hazard, have experienced unpleasant side effects from it, and have attempted to quit but cannot. B. G. is exceptional only in her white-collar occupation. Today, most smokers are found within blue-collar occupations rather than among professional workers.

Substance abuse is a pattern of drug use in which people rely on a drug chronically and excessively, allowing it to occupy a central place in their lives. A more advanced state of abuse is *substance dependence,* popularly known as **addiction.** Addicted people are physically dependent on a drug in addition to abusing it. They have developed tolerance for the drug, and so an addict requires increased doses to obtain the desired effect.

Drug users may also experience unpleasant, sometimes dangerous, physical **withdrawal symptoms** if they suddenly stop taking the abused drug. Symptoms can include muscle aches and cramps, anxiety attacks, sweating, nausea, and, for some drugs, even convulsions and death. Withdrawal symptoms from alcohol or morphine can begin within hours of the last dose and tend to intensify over several days before they subside.

Although B. G. abuses the drug nicotine, she is not physically dependent on it. She smokes approximately the same number of cigarettes each day (she has not developed tolerance to nicotine), and she does not get sick if she is deprived of cigarettes (she does not suffer severe sickness on withdrawal from nicotine but does display some physical symptoms—irritability, anxiety, and increases in appetite and insomnia). B. G.

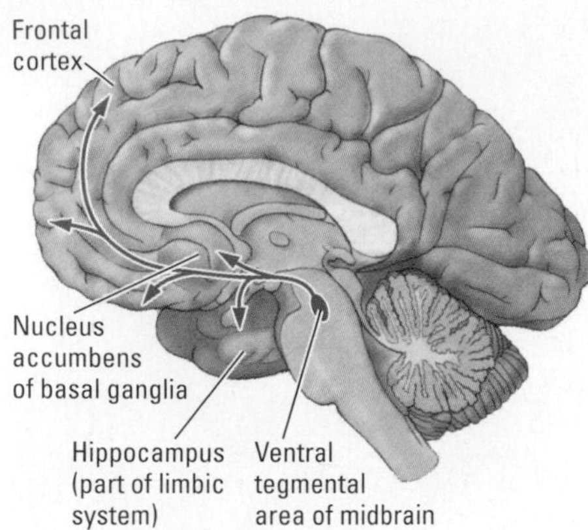

FIGURE 8-15 Mesolimbic Dopamine Pathways. Axons of neurons in the midbrain ventral tegmental area project to the nucleus accumbens, frontal cortex, and hippocampus.

illustrates that the power of psychological dependence can be as influential as the power of physical dependence.

Many different kinds of abused or addictive drugs—including sedative hypnotics, antianxiety agents, opioids, and stimulants—have a common property: they produce **psychomotor activation** in some part of their dose range. That is, at certain levels of consumption, these drugs make the user feel energetic and in control. This common effect has led to the hypothesis that all abused drugs may act on the same target in the brain.

One proposed target is dopamine neurons, because their stimulation is associated with psychomotor activity. Three lines of evidence support a central role in drug abuse for a specific part of this activating system, the mesolimbic dopamine system (**Figure 8-15**):

1. Animals will press a bar for electrical stimulation of the mesolimbic dopamine system in the brain, and they will no longer press it if the dopamine system is blocked or damaged. This finding suggests that the release of dopamine is somehow rewarding.
2. Abused drugs seem to cause the release of dopamine or to prolong its availability in synaptic clefts. Even drugs that have no primary action on dopamine synapses have been found to increase its level. Apparently, when activated, many brain regions that contain no dopamine neurons themselves may stimulate dopamine neurons elsewhere in the brain.
3. Drugs such as major tranquilizers, which block dopamine receptors or decrease its availability at dopamine receptors, are not abused.

Sex Differences in Addiction

Vast differences in individual responses to drugs are due to differences in age, body size, metabolism, and sensitivity to a particular substance. Larger people, for instance, are generally less sensitive to a drug than smaller people are: their greater volume of body fluids dilutes drugs more. Old people may be twice as sensitive to drugs as young people are. The elderly often have less-effective barriers to drug absorption as well as less-effective processes for metabolizing and eliminating drugs from their bodies. Individuals also respond to drugs in different ways at different times.

Females are about twice as sensitive to drugs as males on average, owing in part to their relatively smaller body size but also to hormonal differences. The long-held general assumption that human males are more likely to abuse drugs than are human females has led to a neglect of research on drug use and abuse in human females. The results of recent research support quite the opposite view: females are less likely to become addicted to some drugs than are males, but females are catching up and, for some drugs, are surpassing males in the incidence of addiction. Although the general pattern of drug use is similar in males and females, the sex differences are striking (Becker and Hu, 2008).

Females are also more likely than men are to abuse nicotine, alcohol, cocaine, amphetamine, opioids, cannabinoids, caffeine, and phencyclidine (PCP, or “angel dust”). Females begin to regularly self-administer licit and illicit drugs of abuse at lower doses than do males, use escalates more rapidly to addiction, and females are at greater risk for relapse after abstinence.

In experimental studies of drug effects on rats, females show more rapid and more pronounced sensitization to repeated drug administration than do males. The difference is in part due to circulating estrogen, which is greater in female rats. Nevertheless, female rats deprived of circulating hormones by ovariectomy still display greater sensitization than do male rats deprived of circulating hormones by castration. Sex differences in drug use must now be considered both in understanding and in treating drug abuse in humans.

Psychomotor activation Increased behavioral and cognitive activity; at certain levels of consumption, the drug user feels energetic and in control.

Incentive salience Quality acquired by drug cues that become highly desired and sought-after incentives in their own right.

REVIEW: Factors Influencing Individual Responses to Drugs

- ✔ Disinhibited behavior exhibited while a person is under the influence of alcohol can often be explained by the concepts of time out and alcohol myopia.
- ✔ The substance dependent abuse drugs; the addicted are physically dependent on a drug as well as abusing it. Many abused or addictive drugs induce psychomotor activation that makes the user feel energetic and in control.
- ✔ Females are more likely to abuse many drugs, becoming addicted to lower doses more rapidly than males. Female animals sensitize more rapidly to drugs, and estrogen is a contributing factor.

Explaining and Treating Drug Abuse

Why do people become addicted to drugs? An early explanation centered on dependence: habitual drug users experience psychological or physiological withdrawal symptoms when the effects of the drug wear off. They feel anxious, insecure, or just plain sick in the absence of the drug, and so they take the drug again to alleviate those symptoms. In this way, they get "hooked" on the drug.

Although this dependency hypothesis may account for part of drug-taking behavior, it has shortcomings as a general explanation. For example, an addict may abstain from a drug for months, long after any withdrawal symptoms have abated, and yet still be drawn back to using it. In addition, some psychoactive drugs, such as the tricyclic antidepressants, produce withdrawal symptoms when discontinued, but these drugs are not abused.

Researchers currently see addiction as a series of stages. The first stage is the pleasurable consequences of drug taking: the user likes the experience. In the second stage, associative learning links pleasure with mental representations of drug cues—the objects, acts, places, and events related to taking the drug. This associative learning may be achieved through *classical conditioning* (also called *Pavlovian conditioning*).

Recall from your introductory psychology course that classical conditioning consists of learning to associate some formerly neutral stimulus (such as the sound of a bell for a dog) with a stimulus (such as food in the mouth) that elicits some involuntary response (such as salivation). The pairing of the two stimuli continues until the formerly neutral stimulus alone triggers the involuntary reaction. In drug use, the sight of the drug and the drug-taking context and equipment are repeatedly paired with administering the drug, which produces the pleasurable reaction. Soon the visual cues alone are enough to elicit pleasure.

Neurochemistry is the basis for learned associations, explained in Chapter 5, and for classical conditioning.

The third stage in addiction attributes **incentive salience** to the cues associated with drug use. In other words, drug cues become highly desired and sought-after incentives in their own right. Stimuli that signal the availability of these incentives also become attractive. For instance, acts that led to the drug-taking situation in the past become attractive, as do acts that the drug taker predicts will lead again to the drug.

Drug users may even begin to collect objects that remind them of the drug. Pipe collecting by pipe smokers and decanter collecting by drinkers are examples. In this sequence of events, then, a number of repetitions of the drug-taking behavior lead from liking that act to seeking it out or wanting it, regardless of its current consequences.

A number of findings align with this explanation of drug addiction. For one thing, there is ample evidence that abused drugs initially have a pleasurable effect. There is also evidence that a habitual user continues to use his or her drug of choice even though taking it no longer produces any pleasure. Heroin addicts sometimes report that they are miserable, that their lives are in ruins, and that the drug is not even pleasurable anymore, but they still want it. Furthermore, desire for the drug is often greatest just when the addicted person is maximally high on the drug, not when he or she is withdrawing from it.

Wanting-and-Liking Theory

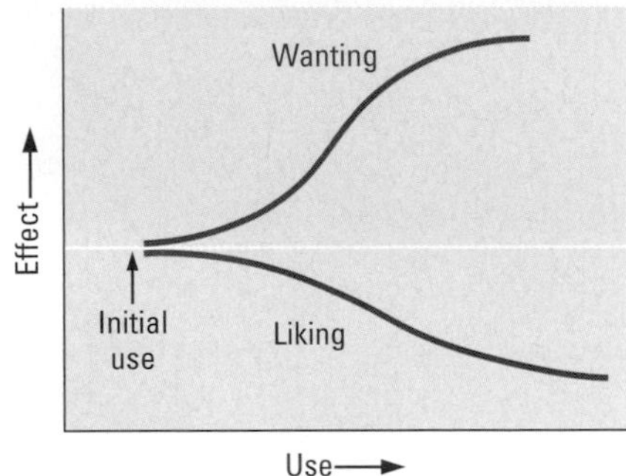

FIGURE 8-16 Wanting and Liking Theory. Wanting and liking a drug change in opposite directions with repeated drug use. Wanting (craving) is associated with drug cues.

Wanting-and-liking theory When a drug is associated with certain cues, the cues themselves elicit desire for the drug; also called *incentive-sensitization theory.*

To account for all the facts about drug abuse and addiction, Terry Robinson and Kent Berridge (2008) proposed the *incentive-sensitization theory.* This perspective is also called **wanting-and-liking theory** because wanting and liking are produced by two different brain systems. Wanting is equivalent to craving for a drug, whereas liking is the pleasure that drug taking produces. With repeated use, as illustrated in **Figure 8-16,** tolerance for liking develops, and, consequently, the expression of liking (pleasure) decreases. In contrast, the system that mediates wanting sensitizes, and wanting the drug (craving) increases.

The road to drug dependence begins at the initial experience when the drug affects a neural system associated with "pleasure." At this time, the user may experience liking the substance—including liking to take it in a social context. With repeated use, liking the drug may decline from its initial level. Now the user may also begin to show tolerance to the drug's effects and so may begin to increase the dosage to increase liking.

The drug also affects a neural system associated with wanting. With each use, the user increasingly associates the cues related to drug use—a hypodermic needle, the room in which the drug is taken, people with whom the drug is taken—with the drug-taking experience. The user makes this association because the drug enhances classically conditioned cues associated with drug taking. Later encounters with these wanting cues, rather than the expected liking (the pleasure derived from the drug's effects), initiates wanting or craving.

How can the wanting-and-liking theory explain B. G.'s smoking? B. G. reports that her most successful period of abstinence from cigarettes coincided with moving to a new town. She stopped smoking for 6 months and, during that time, felt as if she were free and in command of her life again. The wanting-and-liking theory would argue that her ability to quit at this time was promoted because she was separated from the many cues that had previously been associated with smoking.

Then one night after going out to dinner, B. G. and a few of her new colleagues went to a bar, where some of them began to smoke. B. G. reported that her desire for a cigarette became overpowering. Before the evening was over, she bought a package of cigarettes and smoked more than half of it.

On leaving the bar, she left the remaining cigarettes on the table, intending that this episode would be a one-time-only lapse. Shortly thereafter, however, she resumed smoking. The wanting-and-liking theory suggests that her craving for a cigarette was strongly conditioned to the social cues that she encountered again on her visit to the bar, which is why the wanting suddenly became overwhelming.

The learning related to wanting is unconscious: the person neither realizes that conditioning is taking place nor realizes the strength of the conditioning. The neural basis for liking may be due to the activity of opioid neurons, whereas wanting may be due to activity in the mesolimbic dopamine system (see Figure 8-15). In the mesolimbic pathways, the axons of dopamine neurons in the midbrain project to the nucleus accumbens, the frontal cortex, and the limbic system. When cues that have previously been associated with drug taking are encountered, the mesolimbic system becomes active, releasing dopamine. The release of dopamine is the neural correlate of the subjective experience of wanting or craving.

Many experimental studies demonstrate that the activation of mesolimbic dopamine, either by the presentation of cues previously associated with drug taking or by directly stimulating dopamine neurons, results in drug-seeking behavior by rats. The desire for the drug is not a conscious act. Rather, the craving derives from unconsciously acquired associations between drug taking and various cues related to it.

We can extend the wanting-and-liking theory of drug addiction to many life situations. Cues related to sexual activity, food, and even sports can induce a state of wanting, sometimes in the absence of liking. We frequently eat when prompted by the cue of other people eating, even though we may not be hungry and derive little pleasure from eating at that time. The similarities of these behaviors to drug addiction suggest that natural behaviors and addiction depend on the same learning and brain mechanisms. For this reason, any addiction is extremely difficult to treat.

Why Doesn't Everyone Abuse Drugs?

Observing that some people are more prone to drug abuse and dependence than other people are, scientists have investigated and found three lines of evidence suggesting a genetic contribution to differences in drug use:

1. In a pair of twins, if one twin abuses alcohol, the other twin is more likely to abuse it if those twins are identical (have the same genetic makeup) than if they are fraternal (have only some of their genes in common).
2. People adopted shortly after birth are more likely to abuse alcohol if their biological parents were alcoholic, even though they have had almost no contact with those parents.
3. Although most animals do not care for alcohol, the selective breeding of mice, rats, and monkeys can produce strains that consume large quantities of it.

Each line of evidence presents problems, however. Perhaps identical twins show greater concordance for alcohol abuse because they are exposed to more-similar environments than fraternal twins are. And perhaps the link between alcoholism in adoptees and their biological parents has to do with nervous-system changes due to prebirth exposure to the drug. Finally, the fact that animals can be selectively bred for alcohol consumption does not mean that human alcoholics have a similar genetic makeup. The evidence for a genetic basis of alcohol abuse will become compelling only when a gene or set of genes related to alcoholism is found.

Another avenue of research into individual differences associated with drug abuse has been to search for personality traits that drug abusers tend to have in common. One such trait is unusual risk taking. Consider the air surfer illustrated in the photograph at the beginning of this chapter.

Do people who love high-risk adventure have a genetic predisposition toward risk taking that will also lead them to experiment with drugs (Brody et al., 2009)? Possibly, but many people with no interest in risk taking also abuse drugs. In an attempt to find out if certain behavioral traits are related to drug abuse, Pier Vincenzo Piazza and his coworkers (1989) gave rats an opportunity to self-administer amphetamine.

Some rats were very quick to give themselves very large doses, whereas other rats avoided the drug. By examining the behavior of the rats in advance of the drug-taking opportunity, those rats that ran around the most when placed in an open area, thus seeming less cautious and self-restrained than other rats, were also the most likely to become addicted. Perhaps, the researchers concluded, such behavioral traits make some rats more prone to drug use.

The way in which a drug-taking experience is learned may influence conditioning to cues associated with drug use. Terry Robinson and Shelly Flagel (2008) tested rats in a Pavlovian learning situation. A retractable lever was inserted into the test cage for 8 seconds and then, after it was withdrawn, a computer delivered a food pellet into a food tray located nearby. Some of the rats, termed "sign trackers," approached the lever and bit and handled it and only went to the food tray when the lever was retracted. Other rats, termed "goal trackers," went directly to the food tray and mainly ignored the lever.

Thus, for the sign trackers, the the lever became a cue that took on incentive salience; for the goal tackers, it did not. With respect to addiction, for some people, a propensity to respond to cues—to be sign trackers—may make them susceptible to becoming conditioned to the cues associated with drug taking. This susceptibility in turn leads them to crave the drug on subsequent presentation of drug-related cues. Because goal trackers are not conditioned to drug-associated cues, they are less prone to addiction.

Although research on the characteristics that might influence becoming a drug user continues, no unequivocal evidence suggests that differences in the dopamine system make some people more prone to drug abuse than others. Nor is there unequivocal evidence that a specific gene determines substance abuse. And, even if a particular substance-abuse gene or genes were found, that genetic factor would not provide a full explanation of drug addiction. Identical twins have all their genes in common, and yet, when one becomes a drug abuser, the other does not necessarily become one, too. Clearly, learning also plays an important role in drug abuse and addiction.

Treating Drug Abuse

Figure 8-17 graphs the approximate number of people currently abusing different drugs in the United States. The two most abused drugs, tobacco and alcohol, are legal. The drugs against which laws are most harsh, cocaine and heroin, are much less abused in comparison. Nevertheless, the act of making a drug illegal is clearly not a solution to drug use, as is illustrated by the widespread use of marijuana, the third-most-used drug.

The treatment of drug abuse is difficult in part because legal proscriptions in relation to drug use are irrational. In the United States, the Harrison Narcotics Act of 1914 made heroin and a variety of other drugs illegal and made the treatment of addicted people by physicians in their private offices illegal. The Drug Addiction Treatment Act of 2000 has partly reversed this prohibition, allowing the treatment of patients but with a number of restrictions. In addition, the consequences of drug use vary greatly with the drug that is abused.

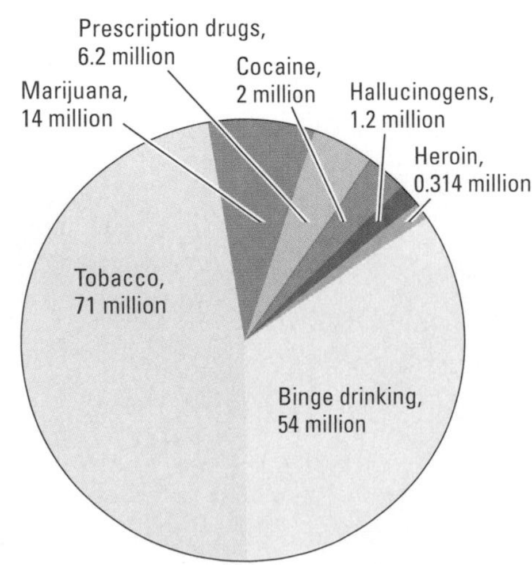

FIGURE 8-17 Incidence of Drug Abuse in the United States.

Using tobacco has much greater health risks than does using marijuana. The moderate use of alcohol is likely benign. The moderate use of opioids is likely impossible. Social coercion is useful in reducing tobacco use: there has been a marked decline in smoking as a result of the prohibition against smoking in public places. Medical intervention is necessary for providing methadone and other drug treatment of opioid abusers.

The numerous approaches to treating drug abuse vary, depending on the drug to which a person is addicted. Many Web sites support self-help groups and professional groups that address the treatment of various drug addictions. Importantly, because addiction is associated with unconscious conditioning to drug-related cues, relapse remains an enduring risk for people who have "kicked their habit."

Neuroscience research will continue to lead to a better understanding of the neural basis of drug use and to better treatment. Likely the best approach to any drug treatment recognizes that addiction will be a life-long problem for most people. Thus, addiction must be treated in the same way as other individual and medical problems are treated, analogous to recognizing that the control of weight with appropriate diet and exercise is a life-long problem for many people.

TABLE 8-2 Some Neurotoxins, Their Sources, and Their Actions

Substance	Origin	Action
Tetrodotoxin	Pufferfish	Blocks membrane permeability to Na^+ ions
Magnesium	Natural element	Blocks Ca^{2+} channels
Reserpine	Tree	Destroys storage granules
Colchicine	Crocus plant	Blocks microtubules
Caffeine	Coffee bean	Blocks adenosine receptors, blocks Ca^{2+} channels
Spider venom	Black widow spider	Stimulates ACh release
Botulin toxin	Food poisoning	Blocks ACh release
Curare	Plant berry	Blocks ACh receptors
Rabies virus	Infected animal	Blocks ACh receptors
Ibotenic acid	Mushroom	Similar to domoic acid, mimics glutamate
Strychnine	Plant	Blocks glycine
Apamin	Bees and wasps	Blocks Ca^{2+} channels

Can Drugs Cause Brain Damage?

Many natural substances can act as neurotoxins, and **Table 8-2** lists some of them. At first blush, some neurotoxins seem harmless. In the late 1960s, many reports circulated linking monosodium glutamate, MSG, a salty-tasting, flavor-enhancing food additive, to headaches in some people. In the process of investigating this effect, scientists placed large doses of MSG on cultured neurons and noticed that the neurons died. Subsequently, they injected MSG into the brains of experimental animals, where it also produced neuron death.

These findings raised the question of whether large doses of the neurotransmitter glutamate, which MSG resembles structurally, might also be toxic to neurons. It turned out that it is. Glutamate-receptor activation results in an influx of Ca^{2+} into the cell, and the influx of excessive Ca^{2+} may, through second messengers, activate a "suicide gene" in a cell's DNA leading to apoptosis (cell death).

As described in Chapter 7, apoptosis is a mechanism by which the brain disposes of sick cells.

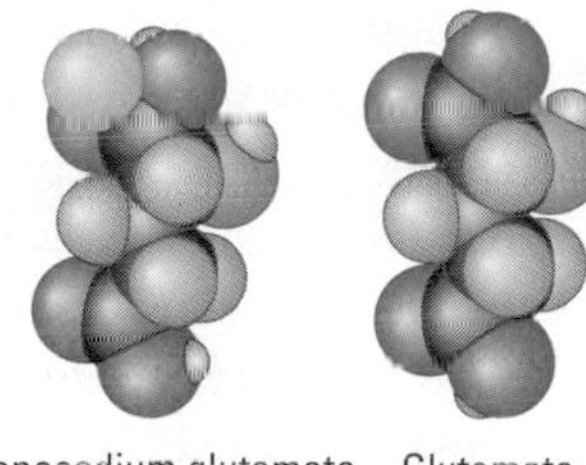

Thus, by acting like glutamate, MSG can be a neurotoxin. But this is not to say that people should totally avoid MSG, which is similar in chemical structure to glutamate. Only very large doses of glutamate analogs are harmful, just as glutamate itself is not harmful except in large doses. Glutamate, in fact, is an essential chemical in the body.

There are many reports of seaweed, plankton, mussels, and mushrooms causing sickness and death in animals, including humans, who injest them. For some of these outbreaks, the toxic substance has been found to be domoic acid, a chemical that is structurally similar to glutamate. Domoic acid binds to one of the glutamate receptors called the *kainate receptor,* so named because kainate, a chemical found in fertilizer, binds potently to it.

Domoic acid

Excessive activation of the glutamate receptor by domoic acid can produce brain damage, as is illustrated in **Figure 8-18.** Many glutamate-like chemicals, including kainate and ibotenic acid, which is found in some poisonous mushrooms, are now known to similarly kill neurons. Many of these glutamate analogs are now used to make experimental lesions in the brains of research animals.

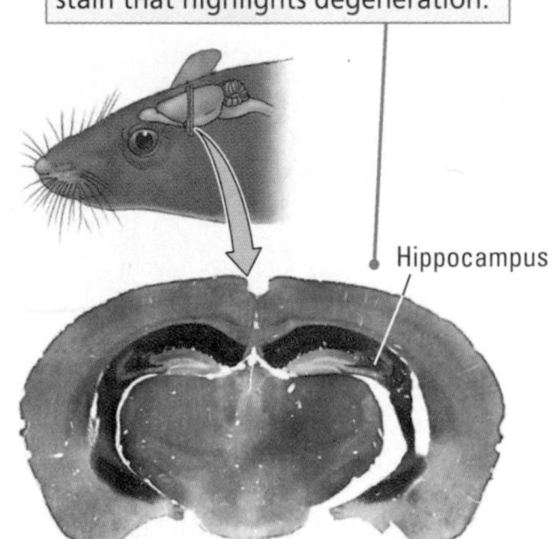

Domoic acid produces hippocampal damage, as shown by a dark silver stain that highlights degeneration.
Hippocampus

FIGURE 8-18 Neurotoxicity. Domoic acid damage, indicated by darker coloring, is not restricted to the hippocampus; it can be seen to a lesser extent in many other brain regions. Micrograph from NeuroScience Associates.

What about the many recreational drugs that affect the nervous system? Are any of them neurotoxic? The answer is not always easy to determine. Sorting out the effects of the drug itself from the effects of other factors related to taking the drug is a major problem. Although chronic alcohol use, for instance, can be associated with damage to the thalamus and limbic system, producing severe memory disorders, the alcohol itself does not seem to cause this damage but rather related complications of alcohol abuse, including vitamin deficiencies due to poor diet. Alcoholics typically obtain reduced amounts of thiamine (vitamin B_1) in their diets, and alcohol interferes with the absorption of thiamine by the intestine. Thiamine plays a vital role in maintaining cell-membrane structure.

Similarly, among the many reports of people who suffer some severe psychiatric disorder subsequent to their abuse of certain recreational drugs, in most cases, determining whether the drug initiated the condition or just aggravated an existing problem is difficult. Exactly determining whether the drug itself or some contaminant in the drug is related to a harmful outcome also is difficult. With the increasing sensitivity of brain-imaging studies, however, there is increasing evidence that many drugs used "recreationally" can cause brain damage.

Focus 5-4 reports the chilling case of heroin addicts who developed Parkinson's disease after using synthetic heroin. The disease was caused by a contaminant (MPTP) rather than by the heroin itself.

The strongest evidence that some recreational drugs can cause brain damage and cognitive impairments comes from the study of amphetamine, methamphetamine, and the synthetic amphetamine-like drug, MDMA, also called *ecstasy.* Although MDMA is structurally related to amphetamine, it produces hallucinogenic effects and is referred to as a "hallucinogenic amphetamine." Findings from animal studies show that doses of MDMA approximating those taken by human users result in the degeneration of very fine serotonergic nerve terminals. In monkeys, the terminal loss may be permanent, as shown in **Figure 8-19.** Memory impairments and brain damage revealed by MRI imaging have been reported in users of MDMA, which may be a result of similar neuronal damage (Cowan et al., 2008).

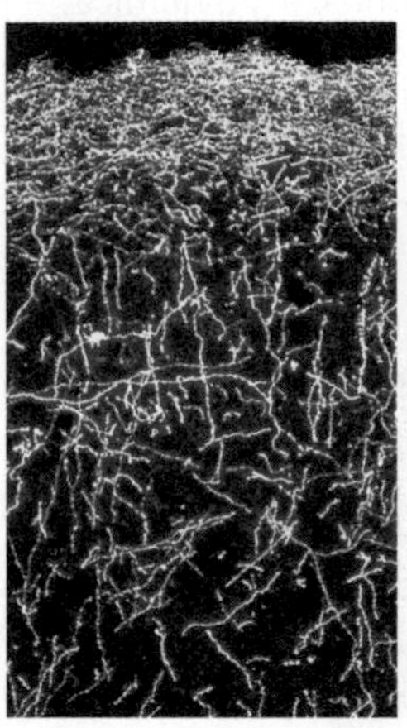

FIGURE 8-19 Drug Damage. The administration of MDMA changes the density of serotonin axons in the neocortex of a squirrel monkey: (*left*) normal monkey; (*right*) monkey 18 months after administration. From "Long-Lasting Effects of Recreational Drugs of Abuse on the Central Nervous System," by U. D. McCann, K. A. Lowe, and G. A. Ricaurte, 1997, *The Neurologist, 3,* p. 401.

The results of studies in rodents show that high doses of amphetamine can result in the loss of dopamine terminals. One form of amphetamine—methamphetamine, one of the most widely used recreational drugs—has been found to produce both brain damage in humans, as revealed by brain-imaging studies, and impaired memory performance, as indicated by neuropsychological tests (Yamamoto and Raudensky, 2008).

The psychoactive properties of cocaine are similar to those of amphetamine, and its possible deleterious effects have been subjected to intense investigation. The results of many studies show that cocaine use is related to the blockage of cerebral blood flow and other changes in blood circulation. Brain-imaging studies also suggest that cocaine use can be toxic to neurons (Sim et al., 2007).

Phencyclidine, or "angel dust," is an NMDA-receptor blocker that was originally developed as an anesthetic. Its use was discontinued after about half of treated patients were found to display psychotic symptoms for as long as a week after coming out of anesthesia. PCP users report perceptual changes and the slurring of speech after small doses, with high doses producing perceptual disorders and hallucinations. Some of the symptoms can last for weeks. The mechanisms by which PCP produces enduring behavioral changes are unknown, but John Olney and his colleagues (1971) reported that, after rats are given a related drug (MK-801), they undergo abnormal changes in neurons, as well as loss of neurons. This finding suggests that the altered behavior of PCP users may be related to neuron damage.

Some drugs that produce altered perceptual experiences and changes in mood do not appear to be linked to brain damage. For instance, LSD, a drug believed to act on serotonergic neurons, produces hallucinations but does not seem to cause enduring brain changes in rats. Similarly, although opiates produce mood changes, the results of long-term studies of opiate users have not revealed persistent cognitive impairments or brain damage.

Focus 6-3 explores the hypothesis that a genetic vulnerability predisposes some adolescents to develop a psychotic condition when exposed to cannabis.

A number of cases of chronic marijuana use have been associated with psychotic attacks. Clinical Focus 8-4, "Drug-Induced Psychosis," describes one. The marijuana plant contains at least 400 chemicals, 60 or more of which are structurally related to its active ingredient tetrahydrocannabinol. Determining whether a psychotic attack is related to THC or to some other ingredient contained in marijuana or to aggravation of an existing condition is almost impossible. Irrespective of whether THC can cause psychosis, there is no evidence that it is a result of brain damage (DeLisi, 2008).

CLINICAL FOCUS 8-4

Drug-Induced Psychosis

At age 29, R. B. S. smoked marijuana chronically. For years, he had been selectively breeding a particularly potent strain of marijuana in anticipation of the day when it would be legalized. R. B. S. made his living as a pilot, flying small-freight aircraft into coastal communities in the Pacific Northwest.

One evening, R. B. S. had a sudden revelation: he was no longer in control of his life. Convinced that he was being manipulated by a small computer implanted into his brain when he was 7 years old, he confided in a close friend, who urged him to consult a doctor. R. B. S. insisted that he had undergone the surgery when he participated in an experiment at a local university. He also claimed that all the other children who participated in the experiment had been murdered.

Jim Wilson/The New York Times/Redux

Employees fill prescriptions at a medical marijuana clinic in San Fransisco.

The doctor told R. B. S. that the computer implantation was unlikely but called the psychology department at the university and got confirmation that children had in fact taken part in an experiment conducted years before. The records of the study had long since been destroyed. R. B. S. believed that this information completely vindicated his story. His delusional behavior persisted and eventually cost him his pilot's license.

The delusion seemed compartmentalized in R. B. S.'s mind. When asked why he could no longer fly, he intently recounted the story of the implant and the murders, asserting that its truth had cost him the medical certification needed for a license. Then he happily discussed other topics in a normal way.

R. B. S. was suffering from a mild focal psychosis: he was losing contact with reality. In some cases, this break is so severe and the capacity to respond to the environment so impaired and distorted that the person can no longer function. People in a state of psychosis may experience hallucinations or delusions or they may withdraw into a private world isolated from people and events around them.

A variety of drugs can produce psychosis, including LSD, amphetamine, cocaine, and, as shown by this case, marijuana. At low doses, the active ingredient in marijuana, tetrahydrocannabinol, has mild sedative-hypnotic effects similar to those of alcohol. At the high doses that R. B. S. used, THC can produce euphoria and hallucinations.

Marijuana comes from the leaves of the hemp plant, *Cannabis sativa.* Humans have used hemp for thousands of years to make rope, paper, cloth, and a host of products. And marijuana has beneficial medical effects: THC alleviates nausea and vomiting associated with chemotherapy in cancer and AIDS patients, controls the brain seizures symptomatic of epilepsy, reduces intraocular pressure in patients with glaucoma, and relieves the symptoms of some movement disorders. In the Pacific Northwest, marijuana is the largest agricultural crop and makes a larger contribution to the economy than does forestry.

R. B. S.'s heavy marijuana use certainly raises the suspicion that the drug had some influence on his delusional condition. *Cannabis* use has been reported to moderately increase the risk of psychotic symptoms in young people and has a much stronger effect in those with a predisposition for psychosis (Henquet et al., 2008). There is no evidence that marijuana use produces brain damage.

R. B. S.'s delusions might have eventually arisen anyway, even if he had not used marijuana. Furthermore, any of the 400 or so compounds besides THC present in marijuana could trigger psychotic symptoms. Approximately 10 years after his initial attack, R. B. S.'s symptoms subsided, and he returned to flying.

REVIEW: Explaining and Treating Drug Abuse

- ✔ Wanting drugs and liking them are produced by two different brain systems. With repeated use, tolerance for liking develops, but the liking itself (pleasure) decreases. In contrast, the system that mediates wanting sensitizes, and wanting the drug (craving) increases.
- ✔ Addicts want drugs because they become conditioned to cues associated with drug taking. Treating drug abuse requires multifaceted approaches that consider individual, social, and medical factors as well as the drug that is abused.
- ✔ Scientists are still investigating the potential deleterious effects on the brain of different psychedelic drugs. So far, their findings have been mixed, with some drugs producing brain damage and others apparently not doing so.

Hormones

Berthold performed the first experiment demonstrating the existence and function of *hormones*—chemicals released by *endocrine glands,* cell groups in the body that secrete hormones into the bloodstream to circulate to a body target and affect it. The endocrine glands operate under the influence of the CNS and the ANS (review Figure 2-28).

In 1849, European scientist A. A. Berthold removed the testes of a rooster and found that the rooster no longer crowed; nor did it engage in sexual or aggressive behavior. Berthold then reimplanted one testis in the rooster's body cavity. The rooster began crowing and displaying normal sexual and aggressive behavior again. The reimplanted testis did not establish any nerve connections, and so Berthold concluded that it must release a chemical into the rooster's circulatory system to influence the animal's behavior.

That chemical, we now know, is **testosterone,** the sex hormone secreted by the testes and responsible for the distinguishing characteristics of the male. The effect that Berthold produced by reimplanting the testis can be mimicked by administering testosterone to a castrated rooster, or capon. The hormone is sufficient to make the capon behave like a rooster with testes.

Normal rooster

Capon (rooster with gonads removed)

Testosterone's influence on the rooster illustrates some of the ways that this hormone produces male behaviors. Testosterone also initiates changes in the size and appearance of the mature male body. In a rooster, for example, testosterone produces the animal's distinctive plumage and crest, and it activates other sex-related organs.

Hierarchical Control of Hormones

Figure 8-20 shows that the control and action of hormones operate within a hierarchy that begins when the brain responds to sensory experiences and cognitive activity. The hypothalamus produces neurohormones that stimulate the pituitary to pump "releasing hormones" into the circulatory system. The pituitary hormones, in turn, influence the remaining endocrine glands to release appropriate hormones into the bloodstream. These hormones then act on various targets in the body, also providing feedback to the brain about the need for more or less hormone release.

Hormones not only affect body organs but also target the brain and neurotransmitter-activating systems there. Almost every neuron in the brain contains receptors on which various hormones can act. In addition to influencing sex organs and physical appearance in a rooster, testosterone may have neurotransmitter-like effects on the brain cells that it targets, especially neurons that control crowing, male sexual behavior, and aggression.

In these neurons, testosterone is transported into the cell nucleus, where it activates genes. The genes, in turn, trigger the synthesis of proteins needed for cellular processes that produce the rooster's male behaviors. Thus, the rooster receives not only a male body but a male brain as well.

In subsequent chapters, we take up the story of hormones again as we examine motivation and emotion, including eating, in Chapter 12 and the relation between learning and memory in Chapter 14.

Although many questions remain about how hormones produce complex behavior, the diversity of testosterone's functions clarifies why the body uses hormones as messengers: their targets are so widespread that the best possible way of reaching all of them is to travel in the bloodstream, which goes everywhere in the body.

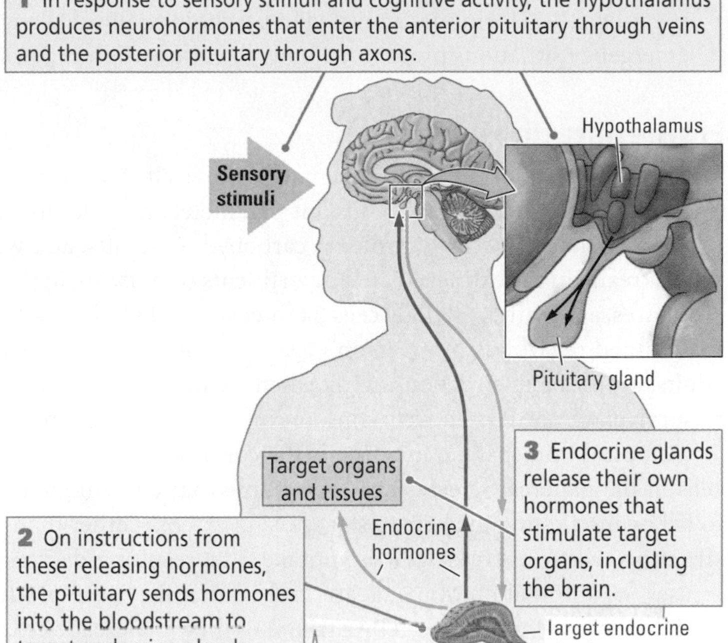

1 In response to sensory stimuli and cognitive activity, the hypothalamus produces neurohormones that enter the anterior pituitary through veins and the posterior pituitary through axons.
Sensory stimuli
Hypothalamus
Pituitary gland
Target organs and tissues
Endocrine hormones
3 Endocrine glands release their own hormones that stimulate target organs, including the brain.
2 On instructions from these releasing hormones, the pituitary sends hormones into the bloodstream to target endocrine glands.
Target endocrine gland

FIGURE 8-20 Hormonal Hierarchy.

Testosterone Sex hormone secreted by the testes and responsible for the distinguishing characteristics of the male.

Steroid hormone Fat-soluble chemical messenger synthesized from cholesterol.

Peptide hormone Chemical messenger synthesized by cellular DNA that acts to affect the target cell's physiology.

Homeostatic hormone One of a group of hormones that maintain internal metabolic balance and regulate physiological systems in an organism.

Gonadal (sex) hormone One of a group of hormones, such as testosterone, that control reproductive functions and bestow sexual appearance and identity as male or female.

Glucocorticoid One of a group of steroid hormones, such as cortisol, secreted in times of stress; important in protein and carbohydrate metabolism.

Classes and Functions of Hormones

Hormones can be used as drugs to treat or prevent disease. People take synthetic hormones as replacement therapy if the glands that produce those hormones are removed or malfunction. People also take hormones, especially sex hormones, to counteract the effects of aging, and they take them to increase physical strength and endurance and to gain an advantage in sports. As many as 100 hormones in the human body are classified chemically as either steroids or peptides.

Steroid hormones, such as testosterone and cortisol, are synthesized from cholesterol and are lipid (fat) soluble. Steroids diffuse away from their sites of synthesis in glands, including the gonads, adrenal cortex, and thyroid, easily crossing the cell membrane. They enter target cells in the same way and act on the cells' DNA to increase or decrease the production of proteins.

Peptide hormones, such as insulin, growth hormone, and the endorphins, are made by cellular DNA in the same way as other proteins are made. They influence their target cell's activity by binding to metabotropic receptors on the cell membrane, generating a second messenger that affects the cell's physiology.

Steriod and peptide hormones fall into one of three main functional groups with respect to behavior, and they may function in more than one of these groups:

1. **Homeostatic hormones** maintain a state of internal metabolic balance and the regulation of physiological systems in an organism. Mineralocorticoids (e.g., aldosterone) control both the concentration of water in blood and cells and the levels of sodium, potassium, and calcium in the body, and they promote digestive functions.
2. **Gonadal (sex) hormones** control reproductive functions. They instruct the body to develop as male (e.g., testosterone) or female (e.g., estrogen), influence sexual behavior and the conception of children, and, in women, control the menstrual cycle (e.g., estrogen and progesterone), the birthing of babies, and the release of breast milk (e.g., prolactin, oxytocin).
3. **Glucocorticoids** (cortisol and corticosterone are examples), a group of steroid hormones secreted in times of stress, are important in protein and carbohydrate

The term *homeostasis* comes from the Greek words *stasis* (standing) and *homeo* (in the same place).

metabolism and in controlling sugar levels in the blood and the absorption of sugar by cells. Hormones activated in psychologically challenging events or emergency situations prepare the body to cope by fighting or fleeing.

Homeostatic Hormones

The homeostatic hormones are essential to life itself. The body's internal environment must remain within relatively constant parameters in order for us to function. An appropriate balance of sugars, proteins, carbohydrates, salts, and water is required in the bloodstream, in the extracellular compartments of muscles, in the brain and other body structures, and within all body cells. Homeostasis of the internal environment must be maintained regardless of a person's age, activities, or conscious state. As children or adults, at rest or in strenuous work, when we have overeaten or when we are hungry, to survive, we need a relatively constant internal environment.

The normal concentration of glucose in the bloodstream varies between 80 and 130 milligrams per 100 milliliters of blood.

A typical homeostatic function is the control of blood-sugar levels. One group of cells in the pancreas releases insulin, a homeostatic hormone that causes blood sugar to fall by instructing the liver to start storing glucose rather than releasing it and by instructing cells to increase glucose uptake. The resulting decrease in glucose then decreases the stimulation of pancreatic cells so that they stop producing insulin.

Diabetes mellitus is caused by a failure of these pancreatic cells to secrete enough insulin or any at all. As a result, blood-sugar levels can fall (hypoglycemia) or rise (hyperglycemia). In hyperglycemia, blood-glucose levels rise because insulin does not instruct cells of the body to take up that glucose. Consequently, cell function, including neural function, can fail through glucose starvation, even in the presence of high levels of glucose in the blood. In addition, chronic high blood-glucose levels cause damage to the eyes, kidneys, nerves, heart, and blood vessels. In hypoglycemia, inappropriate diet can lead to to low blood sugar, which can be so severe as to cause fainting. Eric Steen and his coworkers (2005) propose that insulin resistance in brain cells may be related to Alzheimer's disease. They raise the possibility that Alzheimer's disease may be a third type of diabetes.

Gonadal Hormones

We are prepared for our adult reproductive roles by the gonadal hormones that give us our sexual appearance, mold our identity as male or female, and allow us to engage in sex-related behaviors. Sex hormones begin to act on us even before we are born and continue their actions throughout our lives.

The male Y chromosome contains a gene called the sex-determining region or *SRY* gene. If cells in the undifferentiated gonads of the early embryo contain an *SRY* gene, they will develop into a testes and, if they do not, they will develop into an ovary. In the male, the testes produce the hormone testosterone, which in turn masculinizes the body, producing the male body and genital organs and the male brain.

The **organizational hypothesis** proposes that actions of hormones in the course of development alter tissue differentiation. Thus, testosterone masculinizes the brain early in life by being taken up in brain cells, where it is converted into estrogen by the enzyme aromatase. Estrogen then acts on estrogen receptors to initiate a chain of events that include the activation of certain genes in the cell nucleus. These genes then contribute to the masculinization of brain cells and their interactions with other brain cells.

That estrogen, a hormone usually associated with the female, masculinizes the male brain may seem surprising. Estrogen does not have the same effect on the female brain, because females have a blood enzyme that binds to estrogen and prevents its entry into the brain. Hormones play a somewhat lesser role in producing the female body as well as the female brain, but they control the mental and physical aspects of menstrual cycles, regulate many facets of pregnancy and birth, and stimulate milk production for breastfeeding babies.

Hormones contribute to surprising differences in the brain and in cognitive behavior. The male brain is slightly larger than the female brain after corrections are made for body size, and the right hemisphere is somewhat larger than the left in males. The female brain has a higher rate both of cerebral blood flow and of glucose utilization. There are also a number of differences in brain size in different regions of the brain including nuclei in the hypothalamus that are related to sexual function, parts of the corpus callosum that are larger in females, and a somewhat larger language region in the female brain.

Recall that sex hormones play a role in male–female differences in drug dependence and addiction. Chapter 7 explains the roles of gonadal hormones in sexual differentiation, Chapter 12 describes their effects on sexual behavior, and Chapter 14 recounts sex differences in thinking patterns.

Three lines of evidence, summarized by Elizabeth Hampson and Doreen Kimura (2005), support the conclusion that sex-related cognitive differences result from these brain differences. These cognitive differences also depend in part on the continuing circulation of the sex hormones. The evidence:

1. The results of spatial and verbal tests given to females and males in many different settings and cultures show that males tend to excel in the spatial tasks tested and females in the verbal tasks.
2. The results of similar tests given to female subjects in the course of the menstrual cycle show fluctuations in test scores with various phases of the cycle. During the phase in which the female sex hormones estradiol (metabolized from estrogen) and progesterone are at their lowest levels, women do comparatively better on spatial tasks, whereas, during the phase in which levels of these hormones are high, women do comparatively better on verbal tasks.
3. Tests comparing premenopausal and postmenopausal women, women in various stages of pregnancy, and females and males with varying levels of circulating hormones all provide some evidence that hormones affect cognitive function.

These sex-hormone-related differences in cognitive function are not huge. A great deal of overlap in performance scores exists between males and females. Yet, statistically, the differences seem reliable. Similar influences of sex hormones on behavior are found in other species. Berthold's rooster experiment described earlier shows the effects of testosterone on that animal's behavior. Findings from a number of studies demonstrate that motor skills in female humans and other animals improve at estrus, a time when progesterone levels are high.

Anabolic–Androgenic Steroids

A class of synthetic hormones related to the male sex hormone testosterone have both muscle building (anabolic) and masculinizing (androgenic) effects. These *anabolic–androgenic steroids,* commonly known simply as **anabolic steroids** (known on the street as Boids), were synthesized originally to build body mass and enhance endurance. Russian weight lifters were the first to use them, in 1952, to enhance performance and win international competitions.

Synthetic steroid use rapidly spread to other countries and sports, eventually leading to a ban from track and field and then from many other sports as well. These bans are enforced by drug testing. Testing policy has led to a cat-and-mouse game in which new anabolic steroids and new ways of taking them and masking them are devised to evade detection.

Today, the use of anabolic steroids is about equal among athletes and nonathletes. More than 1 million people in the United States have used anabolic steroids not only to enhance athletic performance but also to enhance physique and appearance. Anabolic steroid use in high schools may be as high as 7 percent for males and 3 percent for females.

The use of anabolic steroids carries health risks. Their administration results in the body reducing its manufacture of the male hormone testosterone, which in turn reduces male fertility and spermatogenesis. Muscle bulk is increased and so is male

Organizational hypothesis Proposal that actions of hormones in development alter tissue differentiation; for example, testosterone masculinizes the brain.

Anabolic steroid Belongs to a class of synthetic hormones related to testosterone that have both muscle-building (anabolic) and masculinizing (androgenic) effects; also called *anabolic–androgenic steroid.*

Aggressive episodes attributed to anabolic-steroid use have come to be called "'roid rage."

aggression. Cardiovascular effects include increased risk of heart attacks and stroke. Liver and kidney function may be compromised and the risk of tumors may increase. Male pattern baldness may be enhanced, and females may experience clittoral enlargement, acne, an increase in body hair, and a deepened voice.

Anabolic steroids also have approved clinical uses. Testosterone replacement is a treatment for hypogonadal males. It is also useful for treating muscle loss subsequent to trauma and for the recovery of muscle mass in malnourished people. In females, anabolic steriods are used to treat endometriosis and fibrocystic disease of the breast.

Stress Hormones

"Stress" is a term borrowed from engineering to describe a process in which an agent exerts a force on an object. Applied to humans and other animals, a *stressor* is a stimulus that challenges the body's homeostasis and triggers arousal. Stress responses are not only physiological but also behavioral and include both arousal and attempts to reduce stress. A stress response can outlast a stress-inducing incident and may even occur in the absence of an obvious stressor. Living with constant stress can be debilitating.

Surprisingly, the body's response is the same whether the stressor is exciting, sad, or frightening. Robert Sapolsky (1992) uses the vivid image of a hungry lion chasing down a zebra to illustrate the stress response. The chase elicits very different reactions in the two animals, but their physiological stress responses are exactly the same. The stress response begins when the body is subjected to a stressor and especially when the brain perceives a stressor and responds with arousal. The response consists of two separate sequences, one fast and the other slow.

The left side of **Figure 8-21** shows the fast response. The sympathetic division is activated to prepare the body and its organs for "fight or flight," and the parasympathetic division for "rest and digest" is turned off. In addition, the sympathetic division stimulates the medulla on the interior of the adrenal gland to release epinephrine. The epinephrine surge (often called the adrenaline surge after epinephrine's original name) prepares the body for a sudden burst of activity. Among its many functions, epinephrine stimulates cell metabolism so that the body's cells are ready for action.

FIGURE 8-21 Activating a Stress Response. Two pathways to the adrenal gland control the body's response to stress. The fast-acting pathway primes the body immediately for fight or flight. The slow-acting pathway both mobilizes the body's resources to confront a stressor and repairs stress-related damage. Abbreviations: CRH, corticotropin-releasing hormone; ACTH, adrenocorticotropic hormone.

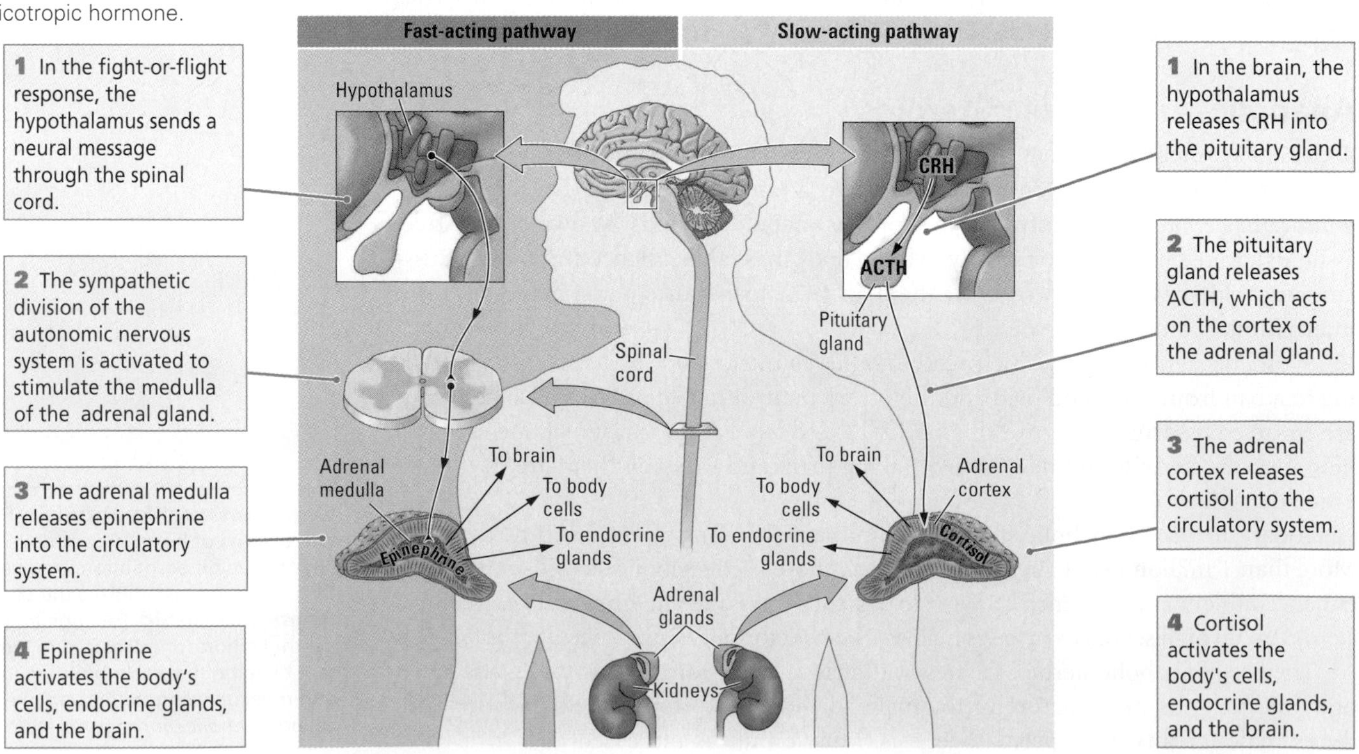

Fast-acting pathway

1 In the fight-or-flight response, the hypothalamus sends a neural message through the spinal cord.

2 The sympathetic division of the autonomic nervous system is activated to stimulate the medulla of the adrenal gland.

3 The adrenal medulla releases epinephrine into the circulatory system.

4 Epinephrine activates the body's cells, endocrine glands, and the brain.

Slow-acting pathway

1 In the brain, the hypothalamus releases CRH into the pituitary gland.

2 The pituitary gland releases ACTH, which acts on the cortex of the adrenal gland.

3 The adrenal cortex releases cortisol into the circulatory system.

4 Cortisol activates the body's cells, endocrine glands, and the brain.

Hypothalamus
CRH
ACTH
Pituitary gland
Spinal cord
Adrenal medulla
Epinephrine
To brain
To body cells
To endocrine glands
Adrenal cortex
Cortisol
Adrenal glands
Kidneys

The hormone controlling the slow response is the steroid cortisol, a glucocorticoid released from the outer layer (cortex) of the adrenal gland, as shown on the right side of Figure 8-21. The cortisol pathway is activated more slowly, taking from minutes to hours. Cortisol has a wide range of functions, which include turning off all bodily systems not immediately required to deal with a stressor. For example, cortisol turns off insulin so that the liver starts releasing glucose, thus temporarily producing an increase in energy supply. It also shuts down reproductive functions and inhibits the production of growth hormone. In this way, the body's energy supplies can be concentrated on dealing with the stress.

Posttraumatic stress disorder (PTSD) Syndrome characterized by physiological arousal symptoms related to recurring memories and dreams related to a traumatic event—for months or years after the event.

Ending a Stress Response

Normally, stress responses are brief. The body mobilizes its resources, deals with the challenge physiologically and behaviorally, and then shuts down the stress response. Just as the brain is responsible for turning on the stress reaction, it is also responsible for turning it off. Consider what can happen if the stress response is not shut down:

- The body continues to mobilize energy at the cost of energy storage.
- Proteins are used up, resulting in muscle wasting and fatigue.
- Growth hormone is inhibited, and so the body cannot grow.
- The gastrointestinal system remains shut down, reducing the intake and processing of food to replace used resources.
- Reproductive functions are inhibited.
- The immune system is suppressed, contributing to the possibility of infection or disease.

Sapolsky (2005) argued that the hippocampus plays an important role in turning off the stress response. The hippocampus contains a high density of cortisol receptors, and it has axons that project to the hypothalamus. Consequently, the hippocampus is well suited to detecting cortisol in the blood and instructing the hypothalamus to reduce blood-cortisol levels.

There may, however, be a more-insidious relation between the hippocampus and blood-cortisol levels. Sapolsky and his coworkers observed wild-born vervet monkeys that had become agricultural pests in Kenya and had therefore been trapped and caged. They found that some of the monkeys became sick and died of a syndrome that appeared to be related to stress. Those that died seemed to have been subordinate animals housed with particularly aggressive, dominant monkeys. Autopsies showed high rates of gastric ulcers, enlarged adrenal glands, and pronounced hippocampal degeneration. The hippocampal damage may have been due to prolonged high cortisol levels produced by the unremitting stress of being caged with the aggressive monkeys.

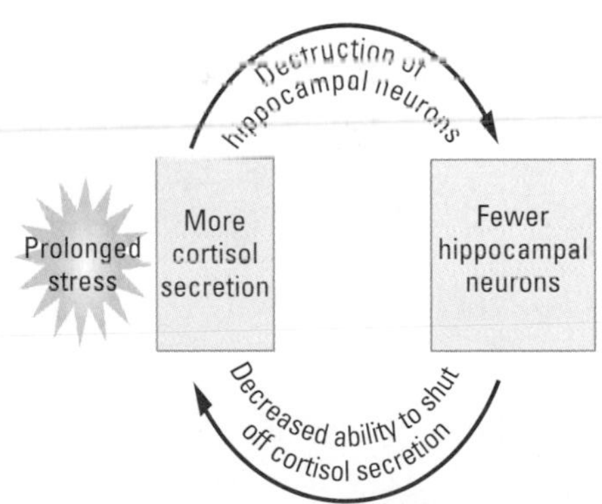

FIGURE 8-22 Vicious Cycle. Unrelieved stress promotes an excessive release of cortisol that causes damage to neurons in the hippocampus. The damaged neurons are unable to detect cortisol and therefore cannot signal the adrenal gland to stop producing it. The result is a feedback loop in which the enhanced secretion of cortisol further damages hippocampal neurons.

Cortisol levels are usually regulated by the hippocampus, but, if these levels remain elevated because a stress-inducing situation continues, the high cortisol levels eventually damage the hippocampus. The damaged hippocampus is then unable to do its work of reducing the level of cortisol. Thus, a vicious cycle is set up in which the hippocampus undergoes progressive degeneration and cortisol levels are not controlled (**Figure 8-22**).

Because stress-response circuits in monkeys are very similar to those in humans, the possibility exists that excessive stress in humans also can lead to damaged hippocampal neurons. Because the hippocampus is thought to play a role in memory, stress-induced damage to the hippocampus is postulated to result in impaired memory as well as in **posttraumatic stress disorder** (PTSD). PTSD is characterized by physiological arousal symptoms related to recurring memories and dreams related to a traumatic event—for months or years after the event. People with PTSD feel as if they are reexperiencing the trauma, and the accompanying physiological arousal enhances their belief that danger is imminent.

PTSD is among the anxiety disorders detailed in Chapter 12, with treatments discussed in Chapter 16.

Research has not led to a clear-cut answer to whether the cumulative effects of stress damage the human hippocampus. For example, research on women who were sexually abused in childhood and were diagnosed as suffering from PTSD yields some reports of no changes in memory or in hippocampal volume, as measured with brain-imaging techniques, compared with other reports of memory impairments and reductions in hippocampal volume (Bremner et al., 2008). That such different results can be obtained in what appear to be similar studies can be explained in a number of ways.

First, the amount of damage to the hippocampus that must occur to produce a stress syndrome is not certain. Second, brain-imaging techniques may not be sensitive to subtle changes in hippocampal-cell function or moderate cell loss. Third, large individual and environmental differences influence how people respond to stress. Finally, preexisting injury to the hippocampus or other brain regions could influence the probability of developing posttraumatic stress disorder (Gilbertson et al., 2002).

Humans are long lived and have many life experiences that complicate simple extrapolations from a single stressful event. Nevertheless, Patrick McGowan and his coworkers (2009) report that the glucocorticoid-receptor density in the hippocampi of suicide victims who had been sexually abused in childhood was decreased compared with that of suicide victims who had not been abused and with that of control subjects. The decrease in receptors and in glucorticoid mRNA suggests that childhood abuse induces epigenetic changes in the expression of glucorticoid genes. The decrease in glucocorticoid receptors presumably rendered the hippocampus less able to depress stress responses. The importance of the McGowan study is that it suggests a mechanism through which stress can influence hippocampal function without necessarily being associated with a decrease in hippocampal volume.

REVIEW: Hormones

✔ Hormonal activity is hierarchically controlled by the brain's response to sensory stimuli and cognitive activity. From the top down, the hypothalamus produces neurohormones that stimulate the pituitary gland to direct the endocrine glands to produce and secrete hormones to targets throughout the body. Levels of hormones circulating in the bloodstream then provide feedback to the brain.

✔ Because hormones often have such widespread targets, traveling through the bloodstream is an effective way to deliver their chemical messages.

✔ Hormones are of two types, steroid and peptide. Both types act within three functional groups:

1. Homeostatic hormones regulate body nutrients and metabolic processes.
2. Gonadal hormones regulate sexual behavior, pregnancy, and child bearing.
3. Stress hormones regulate the body's responses to challenging events.

✔ Synthetic anabolic–androgenic steroids increase muscle bulk and enhance appearance, but they also have adverse psychological and health effects.

Summary

Principles of Psychopharmacology

Psychoactive drugs—substances that alter mood, thought, or behavior—produce their effects by acting on neural receptors or on chemical processes in the nervous system, especially on processes of neural transmission at synapses. Drugs act either as agonists to stimulate neuronal activity or as antagonists to depress it. Psychopharmacology is the study of drug effects on the brain and behavior.

Drugs, chemicals taken to bring about some desired change in the body, are administered by mouth, by inhalation, by absorption through the skin, and by injection. To reach a target in the nervous system, a drug must pass a through numerous barriers posed by digestion, dilution, the blood–brain barrier, and cell membranes. Drugs are diluted by body fluids as they pass through successive barriers; are metabolized in the body; and excreted through sweat glands and in feces, urine, breath, and breast milk.

A common misperception about drugs is that they act specifically and consistently. But the body and brain rapidly become tolerant to many drugs, and so the dose must be increased to produce a constant effect. Alternatively, people may become sensitized to a drug: the same dose produces increasingly greater effects. Learning also plays an important role in a person's behavior under the influence of a drug.

Classification of Psychoactive Drugs

Psychoactive drugs are classified into seven groups according to their major behavioral effects: as sedative hypnotics and antianxiety agents, antipsychotic agents, antidepressants, mood stabilizers, opioid analgesics, psychomotor stimulants, and stimulants that have psychedelic and hallucinogenic effects. Each group contains natural or synthetic drugs or both, and they may produce their actions in different ways.

Factors Influencing Individual Responses to Drugs

A drug does not have a uniform action on every person. Physical differences—in body weight, sex, age, or genetic background—influence the effects of a given drug on a given person, as do behaviors, such as learning, and environmental context.

The influence of drugs on behavior varies widely with the situation and as a person learns appropriate drug-related behaviors. Some drugs, such as alcohol, can produce behavioral myopia such that a person is influenced primarily by prominent cues in the environment. These cues may encourage the person to act in ways in which he or she would not normally behave.

Females are more sensitive to drugs than are males, and recent evidence suggests that they become addicted more quickly to lower doses of drugs than do males. For many kinds of drug use, the incidence of female abuse equals or exceeds male drug abuse.

Explaining and Treating Drug Abuse

The neural mechanisms implicated in addiction are the same neural systems responsible for wanting and liking more generally. And so anyone is likely to be a potential drug abuser. Addiction develops in a number of stages as a result of repeated drug taking. Initially, drug taking produces pleasure, or liking, but, with repeated use, it becomes conditioned to associated objects, events, and places. Eventually, those conditioned cues acquire incentive salience, causing the drug user to seek them out, which leads to more drug taking. These subjective experiences associated with prominent cues and drug seeking promote craving for the drug. As addiction proceeds, the subjective experience of liking decreases while that of wanting increases.

Drug treatment varies by the drug that is abused. Whatever the treatment approach, success likely depends on permanent life-style changes. Considering how many people use tobacco, drink alcohol, use recreational drugs, or abuse prescription drugs, to find someone who has not used a drug when it was available is probably rare. But some people do seem vulnerable to drug use and addiction. Individual genetic differences could be influential, but drug availability and peer influences are likely more influential.

Excessive alcohol use can be associated with damage to the thalamus and hypothalamus, but the cause of the damage is poor nutrition rather than the direct actions of alcohol. Cocaine can harm brain circulation, producing brain damage by reducing blood flow or by bleeding into neural tissue. The drug "ecstasy," or MDMA, can result in the loss of fine axon collaterals of serotonergic neurons and in the associated impairments in cognitive function.

Psychedelic drugs such as marijuana and LSD can be associated with psychotic behavior. Whether this behavior is due to the direct effects of the drugs or to the aggravation of preexisting conditions is not clear.

Hormones

Steroid and peptide hormones produced by endocrine glands circulate in the bloodstream to affect a wide variety of targets. Interacting to regulate hormone levels are, at the top, a hierarchy of sensory stimuli and cognitive activity in the brain that stimulate the pituitary gland through the hypothalamus. The pituitary stimulates or inhibites the endocrine glands, and levels of hormones circulating in the blood send feedback to the brain.

Homeostatic hormones regulate the balance of sugars, proteins, carbohydrates, salts, and other substances in the body. Sex hormones regulate the physical features and behaviors associated with reproduction and the care of offspring. Anabolic steroids, used by both athletes and nonathletes, mimic the effects of testosterone and so increase muscle bulk and stamina but can have deleterious side effects.

Stress hormones regulate the body's ability to cope with arousing and challenging situations. Failure to turn stress responses off after a stressor has passed can contribute to susceptibility to posttraumatic stress disorder and other psychological and physical diseases. Stress may activate an epigenetic response that modifies genes that regulate hormonal responses to stress, so producing brain changes that persist long after the stress-provoking incident.

Key Terms

addiction, p. 260
agonist, p. 243
alcohol myopia, p. 260
amphetamine, p. 257
anabolic steroid, p. 273
antagonist, p. 243
antianxiety agent, p. 248
barbiturate, p. 248
bipolar disorder, p. 252
competitive inhibitor, p. 254
cross-tolerance, p. 248
disinhibition theory, p. 260
dissociative anesthetic, p. 251
dopamine hypothesis of schizophrenia, p. 251
endorphin, p. 254
fetal alcohol syndrome (FAS), p. 251
glucocorticoid, p. 271
gonadal (sex) hormone, p. 271
homeostatic hormone, p. 271
incentive salience, p. 263
major depression, p. 252
major tranquilizer, p. 251
monoamine oxidase (MAO) inhibitor, p. 252
mood stabilizer, p. 252
obsessive-compulsive disorder, p. 252
opioid analgesic, p. 254
organizational hypothesis, p. 273
peptide hormone, p. 271
posttraumatic stress disorder (PTSD), p. 275
psychedelic drug, p. 259
psychoactive drug, p. 239
psychomotor activation, p. 263
psychopharmacology, p. 239
second-generation antidepressant, p. 252
selective serotonin reuptake inhibitor (SSRI), p. 252
steroid hormone, p. 271
substance abuse, p. 260
testosterone, p. 271
tolerance, p. 243
tricyclic antidepressant, p. 252
wanting-and-liking theory, p. 264
withdrawal symptom, p. 260

▶*Please refer to the Companion Web Site at* **www.worthpublishers.com/kolbintro3e** *for Interactive Exercises and Quizzes.*

PhotoAlto/Getty Images

CHAPTER 9

How Do We Sense, Perceive, and See the World?

CLINICAL FOCUS 9-1

Migraines and a Case of Blindsight

D.B.'s recurring headaches began at about age 14. Before each headache, a visual aura warned D. B.: an oval-shaped area of flashing (scintillating) light appeared just to the left of center in his field of vision. Over the next few minutes, the oval enlarged. After about 15 minutes, the flashing light vanished, and D. B. was blind in the region of the oval.

D. B. described the oval as an opaque white area surrounded by a rim of color. A headache on the right side of his head followed and could persist for as long as 48 hours. D. B. usually fell asleep before that much time elapsed. When he awakened, the headache was gone and his vision was normal again.

D. B suffered from severe *migraine,* a recurrent headache usually localized to one side of the head. Migraines vary in severity, frequency, and duration and are often accompanied by nausea and vomiting. Migraine is perhaps the most common of all neurological disorders, afflicting some 5 to 20 percent of the population at some time in their lives.

Auras may be auditory or tactile, as well as visual, and may result in an inability to move or to talk. After the aura passes, most people suffer a severe headache caused by a dilation of cerebral blood vessels. The headache is usually loacalized to one side of the head, just as the aura is on one side of the field of vision. Left untreated, migraine headaches may last for hours or even days.

D. B.'s attacks continued at intervals of about 6 weeks for 10 years. After one attack, he was left with a small blind spot, or *scotoma,* illustrated in the accompanying photographs. When D. B. was 26 years old, a neurologist found that a collection of abnormal blood vessels at the back of his right occipital lobe was causing the migraine attacks—a most unusual cause.

By the time D. B. was 30, the migraines began to interfere with his family, social life, and job. No drug treatment was effective, and so D. B. had the malformed blood vessels surgically removed. The operation relieved his pain and generally improved his life, but a part of his right occipital lobe, deprived of blood, had died. D. B. became blind in the left half of his visual field: as he looks at the world through either eye, he is unable to see anything to the left of the midline.

Lawrence Weizkrantz (1986) made a remarkable discovery about D. B.'s blindness. D. B. could not identify objects in his blind area but could very accurately "guess" if a light had blinked on there and even where the light that he did not "see" was located. Apparently, D. B.'s brain knew when a light had blinked and where it appeared. This phenomenon is called *blindsight.* D. B.'s brain knew more than he was consciously aware of.

Novastock/StockConnection/PictureQuest

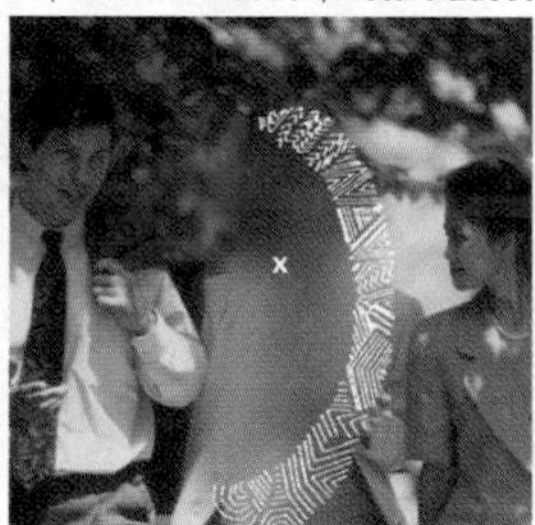

X = Fixation point

In the development of a migraine scotoma, a person looking at the small white "x" in the photograph at the far left first sees a small patch of lines. This striped area continues to grow outward, leaving an opaque area (scotoma) where the stripes had been. Within 15 to 20 minutes, the visual field is almost completely blocked. Normal vision returns shortly thereafter.

WHAT APPLIES to D. B. applies to everyone. You are consciously aware of only part of the visual information that your brain is processing. This selectivity is an important working principle behind human sensation and perception. Weizkrantz, a world-renowned visual neuroscientist at Oxford University, was able to detect it in the visual system because of D. B.'s injury.

Vision is not unique in this regard. We are also unaware of much of the sensory processing that takes place in the pathways for hearing, balance and touch, taste, and smell.

The function of all our senses is to convert energy into neural activity that has meaning for us. So we begin this chapter with a general summary of sensation and perception that explores how this energy conversion takes place.

The ability to lose conscious visual perception while retaining unconscious vision, as D.B. did, then leads us to the chapter's central question: How do we "see" the world? We begin to explore vision by overviewing the visual system's anatomy. Then, we consider the connections between the eyes and the brain and the sections of the brain that process visual information.

Turning next to the experience of sight, we focus on how neurons respond to visual input and enable the brain to perceive different features, such as color, shape, and movement. At the chapter's end, we explore the culmination of vision: to understand what we see. How do we infuse light energy with meaning, to grasp the meaning of written words or to see the beauty in a painting?

The Nature of Sensation and Perception

We may believe that we see, hear, touch, smell, and taste real things in a real world. In fact, the only input that our brains receive from the "real" world is a series of action potentials passed along the neurons of our various sensory pathways. Although we experience visual and body sensations as being fundamentally different from one another, the nerve impulses in the neurons of these two sensory systems are very similar, as are the neurons themselves.

Neuroscientists understand how nerves can turn energy, such as light waves, into nerve impulses. They also know the pathways taken by those nerve impulses to reach the brain. But they do not know how we end up perceiving one set of nerve impulses as what the world looks like and another set as what moves us.

How much of what you know comes through your senses? Taken at face value, this question seems reasonable. At the same time, we realize that our senses can deceive us—that two people can look at the same optical illusion and see very different images, that a person dreaming does not normally think that the dream images are real, that you often do not think that a picture of you looks like you. Many scientists think that much of what we know comes to us through our senses, but they also think that our brains actively transform sensory information into forms that help us to adapt and are thus behaviorally useful.

Our sensory systems are extremely diverse, and, at first blush, vision, audition, body senses, taste, and olfaction appear to have little in common. But, although our perceptions and behavior in relation to these senses are very different, each sensory system is organized on a similar, hierarchical plan. In this section, we consider the features common to the sensory systems, including their receptors, neural relays between the receptor and the neocortex, sensory coding and representation, and perception.

Sensory Receptors

Sensory receptors are specialized cells that transduce (convert) sensory energy—light, for example, into neural activity. Our wide range of sensory receptors have many common properties that allow them to provide us with a rich array of information about our world.

If we put flour into a sieve and shake it, the more finely ground particles will fall through the holes, whereas the coarser particles and lumps will not. Sensory receptors are designed to respond only to a narrow band of energy—analogous to particles of certain sizes—within each modality's energy spectrum. Each sensory system's receptors are specialized to filter a different form of energy:

- For vision, light energy is converted into chemical energy in the photoreceptors of the retina, and this chemical energy is in turn converted into action potentials.
- In the auditory system, air-pressure waves are converted first into mechanical energy, which activates the auditory receptors that produce action potentials.
- In the somatosensory system, mechanical energy activates receptor cells that are sensitive to touch, pressure, or pain. Somatosensory receptors in turn generate action potentials.
- For taste and olfaction, various chemical molecules carried by the air or contained in food fit themselves into receptors of various shapes to activate action potentials.

Were our visual receptors somewhat different, we would be able to see in the ultraviolet as well as the visible parts of the electromagnetic spectrum, as honeybees and butterflies can. The receptors of the human ear respond to a wide range of sound waves, but elephants and bats can hear and produce sounds far below and above the range in which humans hear. In fact, in comparison with those of other animals, human sensory abilities are rather average.

An animal's perception of the external world depends on the complexity and organization of the animal's nervous system.

Even our pet dogs have "superhuman" powers: they can detect odors, hear the low-range sounds of elephants, and see in the dark. We can hold up only our superior color vision. Thus, for each species and individual member, sensory systems filter the sensory world to produce an idiosyncratic representation of reality.

Receptive Fields

Every sensory-receptor organ and cell has a **receptive field,** a specific part of the world to which it responds. If you fix your eyes on a point directly in front of you, for example, what you see of the world is the scope of your eyes' receptive field. If you close one eye, the visual world shrinks, and what the remaining eye sees is the receptive field for that eye.

Each photoreceptor cell within the eye points in a slightly different direction and so has a unique receptive field. You can grasp the conceptual utility of the receptive field by considering that the brain uses information from the receptive field of each sensory receptor not only to identify sensory information but also to contrast the information that each receptor field is providing.

Receptive fields not only sample sensory information but also help locate sensory events in space. Because the receptive fields of adjacent sensory receptors may overlap, their relatively different responses to events help us localize sensations. The spatial dimensions of sensory information produce cortical patterns and maps of the sensory world that form, for each of us, our sensory reality.

Our sensory systems are organized to tell us both what is happening in the world around us and what we ourselves are doing. When you move, you change the perceived properties of objects in the world, and you experience sensations that have little to do with the external world. When we run, visual stimuli appear to stream by us, a stimulus configuration called **optic flow.** When you move past a sound source, you hear an **auditory flow,** changes in the intensity of the sound that take place because of your changing location. Optic or auditory flow is useful in telling us how fast we are going, whether we are going in a straight line or up or down, and whether it is we who are moving or an object in the world that is moving.

Try this experiment. Slowly move your hand back and forth before your eyes and gradually increase the speed of the movement. Your hand will eventually get a little blurry because your eye movements are not quick enough to follow its movement. Now keep your hand still and move your head back and forth. The image of the hand re-

Receptive field Region of the visual world that stimulates a receptor cell or neuron

Optic flow Streaming of visual stimuli that accompanies an observer's forward movement through space.

Auditory flow Change in sound heard as a person moves past a sound source or as a sound source moves past a person.

mains clear. When receptors in the inner ear inform your visual system that your head is moving, the visual system compensates for the head movements, and you observe the hand as a stationary image.

Receptor Density and Sensitivity

Receptor density is particularly important in determining the sensitivity of a sensory system. For example, the tactile receptors on the fingers are numerous compared with those on the arm. This difference explains why the fingers can discriminate touch remarkably well and the arm not so well.

Our sensory systems use different receptors to enhance sensitivity under different conditions. For example, the visual system uses different sets of receptors to respond to light and color. Color photoreceptors are small and densely packed to make sensitive color discriminations in bright light. The receptors for black–white vision are larger and more scattered, but their sensitivity to light—say, a lighted match at a distance of 2 miles on a dark night—is truly remarkable.

Differences in the density of sensory receptors determine the special abilities of many animals—the excellent olfactory ability in dogs and the excellent tactile ability in the digits of raccoons. Variations in receptor density in the human auditory-receptor organ may explain such abilities as perfect pitch displayed by some musicians.

Chapter 10 explains how we perceive music.

Neural Relays

Inasmuch as receptors are common to each sensory system, all receptors connect to the cortex through a sequence of three or four intervening neurons. The visual and somatosensory systems have three, for example, and the auditory system has four. Information can be modified at different stages in the relay, allowing the sensory system to mediate different responses.

Neural relays also allow sensory systems to interact. There is no straight-through, point-to-point correspondence between one neural relay and the next; rather, there is a recoding of activity in each successive relay. Sensory neural relays are central to the hierarchy of motor responses in the brain.

Recall the principle from Chapter 2: brain systems are organized both hierarchically and in parallel.

Some of the three to four relays in each sensory system are in the spinal cord, others are in the brainstem, and still others are in the neocortex. At each level, the relay allows a sensory system to produce relevant actions that define the hierarchy of our motor behavior. For example, the first relay for pain receptors in the spinal cord is related to reflexes that produce withdrawal movements of a body part from a painful stimulus. Thus, even after section of the spinal cord from the brain, a limb will still withdraw from a painful stimulus.

A dramatic effect of sensory interaction is the visual modification of sound. If a speech syllable such as "ba" is played by a recorder to a listener who at the same time is observing someone whose lips are articulating the syllable "ga," the listener hears not the actual sound ba, but the articulated sound da. The viewed lip movements modify the auditory perception of the listener.

The potency of this interaction effect highlights the fact that our perception of speech sounds is influenced by the facial gestures of a speaker. As described by Roy Hamilton and his coworkers (2006), the synchrony of gestures and sounds is an important aspect of our acquisition of language. A difficulty for people learning a foreign language can be related to the difficulty that they have in blending a speaker's articulation movements with the sounds the speaker produces.

Sensory Coding and Representation

After it has been transduced, all sensory information from all sensory systems is encoded by action potentials that travel along peripheral-system nerves until they enter the spinal cord or brain and, from there, on nerve tracts within the central nervous system. Every bundle carries the same kind of signal. How do action potentials encode the different kinds of sensations (how does vision differ from touch), and how do they encode the features of particular sensations (how does purple differ from blue)?

Parts of these questions seem easy to answer; others pose a fundamental challenge to neuroscience. The presence of a stimulus can be encoded by an increase or decrease in the discharge rate of a neuron, and the amount of increase or decrease can encode the stimulus intensity. As detailed later in this chapter, qualitative visual changes, such as from red to green, can be encoded by activity in different neurons or even by different levels of discharge in the same neuron (for example, more activity might signify redder and less activity greener).

Recall the principle from Chapter 2: the nervous system works by juxtaposing excitation and inhibition.

What is less clear is how we perceive such sensations as touch, sound, and smell as being different from one another. Part of the explanation is that these different sensations are processed in distinct regions of the cortex. Another part is that we learn through experience to distinguish them. A third part is that each sensory system has a preferential link with certain kinds of reflex movements, constituting a distinct wiring that helps keep each system distinct at all levels of neural organization. For example, pain stimuli produce withdrawal responses, and fine-touch and pressure stimuli produce approach responses.

The distinctions between the sensory systems, however, are not always clear: some people hear in color or identify smells by how the smells sound to them. This mixing of the senses is called *synesthesia.* Anyone who has shivered when hearing certain notes of a piece of music or at the noise that chalk or fingernails can make on a blackboard has "felt" sound.

You will find more information about synesthesia in Chapter 15.

In most mammals, the neocortex represents the sensory field of each modality—vision, hearing, touch, smell, or taste—as a spatially organized neural representation of the external world. Such a **topographic map** is a neural–spatial representation of the body or of the areas of the sensory world perceived by a sensory organ. All mammals have at least one primary cortical area for each sensory system. Additional areas are usually referred to as *secondary areas* because most of the information that reaches them is relayed through the primary area. Each additional representation is probably dedicated to encoding one specific aspect of the sensory modality. For vision, our focus in this chapter, different areas may take part in the perception of color, of movement, and of form.

FIGURE 9-1 Perceptual Illusions. (A) Edgar Rubin's ambiguous reversible image can be perceived as a vase or as two faces. (B) The top line of the Müller–Lyer illusion appears longer than the bottom line because of the contextual cues provided by the arrowheads.

(A)

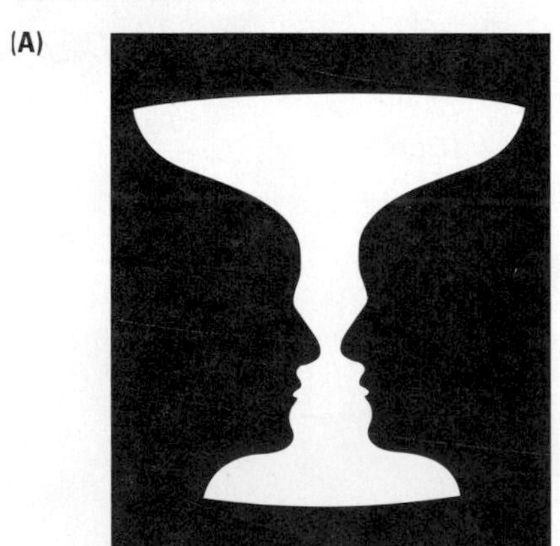

(B)

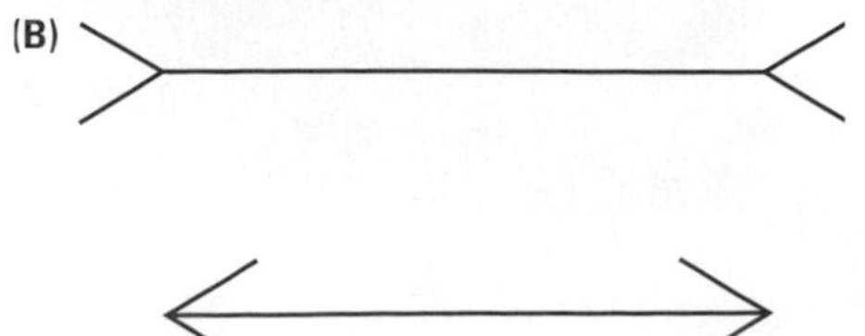

Perception

There is far more to **sensation** than the simple registration of physical stimuli from the environment by the sensory organs. When compared with the richness of actual sensation, our description of sensory neuroanatomy and function is bound to seem rather sterile. Part of the reason for the disparity is that our sensory impressions are affected by the contexts in which they take place, by our emotional states, and by our past experiences. All these factors contribute to **perception,** the subjective experience of sensation—how we interpret what we sense. Perception, rather than sensation, is of most interest to neuropsychologists.

As clear proof that perception is more than sensation, consider that different people transform the same sensory stimulation into totally different perceptions. The classic demonstration is an ambiguous image such as the well-known Rubin's vase shown in **Figure 9-1**A. This image may be perceived either as a vase or as two faces. If you fix your eyes on the center of the picture, the two perceptions will alternate, even though the sensory stimulation remains constant.

The Müller–Lyer illusion in Figure 9-1B demonstrates the influence of context on perception. The top line is perceived as longer than the bottom line, although both are exactly the same length. The contextual cues (the arrowheads) alter the perception of each line's length. Such ambiguous images and illusions demonstrate the workings of complex perceptual phenomena and are an enlightening source of insight into cognitive processes.

Topographic map Spatially organized neural representation of the external world.
Sensation Registration of physical stimuli from the environment by the sensory organs.
Perception Subjective interpretation of sensations by the brain.
Retina Light-sensitive surface at the back of the eye consisting of neurons and photoreceptor cells.

REVIEW: The Nature of Sensation and Perception

- ✔ Sensory receptors are energy filters that transduce incoming physical energy and identify change and constancy in the energy. Neural receptive fields locate sensory events, and receptor density determines sensitivity to sensory stimulation.
- ✔ Neural relays between sensory receptors and the brain modify messages and allow the senses to interact. Any sensory information that converges does so in higher cortical areas.
- ✔ The sensory systems all use a common code, sending information to the brain in the currency of action potentials. We distinguish one sensory modality from another by the source of the stimulation, its target in the brain, and by movements made in relation to the stimulation.
- ✔ The anatomical organization is similar for each sense in that each has many receptors, sends information to the cortex through a sequence of three or four neuron relays, and diverges into more than one pathway through the brain.
- ✔ D. B.'s surprising ability to locate lights shining in the blind side of his visual field makes clear that our sensory world is not unitary, despite what our conscious experience suggests. Vision is but one of a half dozen senses that allow us to act in the world that we perceive.

Functional Anatomy of the Visual System

Vision is our primary sensory experience. Far more of the human brain is dedicated to vision than to any other sense. Understanding the visual system's organization is therefore key to understanding human brain function. To build this understanding, we begin by following the routes that visual information takes to the brain and within it. This exercise is a bit like traveling a road to discover where it goes.

Structure of the Retina

Light energy travels from the outside world, through the pupil, and into the eye, where it strikes a light-sensitive surface on the back of the eye called the **retina.** From this stimulation of photoreceptor cells on the retina, we begin the process of creating a visual world. If you are familiar with the properties of the electromagnetic spectrum and with the structure of the eye, read on. To refresh your knowledge of these topics, read The Basics on pages 286–287 before you continue.

Figure 9-2 includes a photograph of the retina, which is composed of photoreceptors beneath a layer of neurons connected to them. Although the neurons lie in front of the photoreceptor cells, they do not prevent incoming light

FIGURE 9-2 Central Focus. This cross section through the retina shows the depression at the fovea—also shown in the scanning electron micrograph at bottom left—where receptor cells are packed most densely and where our vision is clearest.

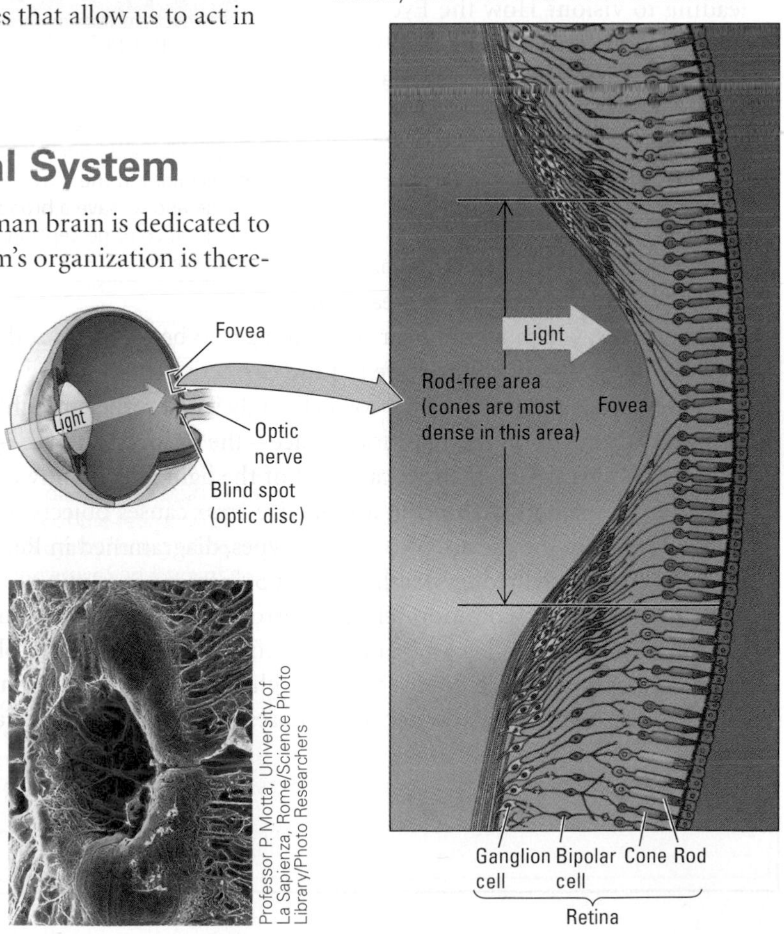

Professor P. Motta, University of La Sapienza, Rome/Science Photo Library/Photo Researchers

The neurons in the retina are insensitive to light and so are unaffected by the light passing through them.

from being absorbed by those receptors, because the neurons are transparent and the photoreceptors are extremely sensitive to light.

Together, the photoreceptor cells and the neurons of the retina perform some amazing functions. They translate light into action potentials, discriminate wavelengths so that we can distinguish colors, and work in a range of light intensities from very bright to very dim. These cells afford visual precision sufficient for us to see a human hair lying on the page of this book from a distance of 18 inches.

As in a camera, the image of objects projected onto the retina is upside down and backward. This flip-flopped orientation poses no problem for the brain. Remember that the brain is creating the outside world, and so it does not really care how the image is oriented initially. In fact, the brain can make adjustments regardless of the orientation of the images that it receives.

If you were to put on glasses that invert visual images and kept those glasses on for several days, the world would first appear upside down but then would suddenly appear right side up again because your brain would correct the distortion (Held, 1968). Curiously, when you removed the glasses, the world would temporarily seem upside down once more, because your brain at first would be unaware that you had tricked it another time. Eventually, though, your brain would solve this puzzle, too, and the world would flip back into the right orientation.

FIGURE 9-3 Acuity Across the Visual Field. To demonstrate the relative sizes of letters legible in the central field of vision compared with the peripheral field, focus on the plus sign in the middle of the chart. From *Basic Vision: An Introduction to Visual Perception* by R. Snowden, P. Thompson, and T. Troscianko, 2008, Oxford: Oxford University Press.

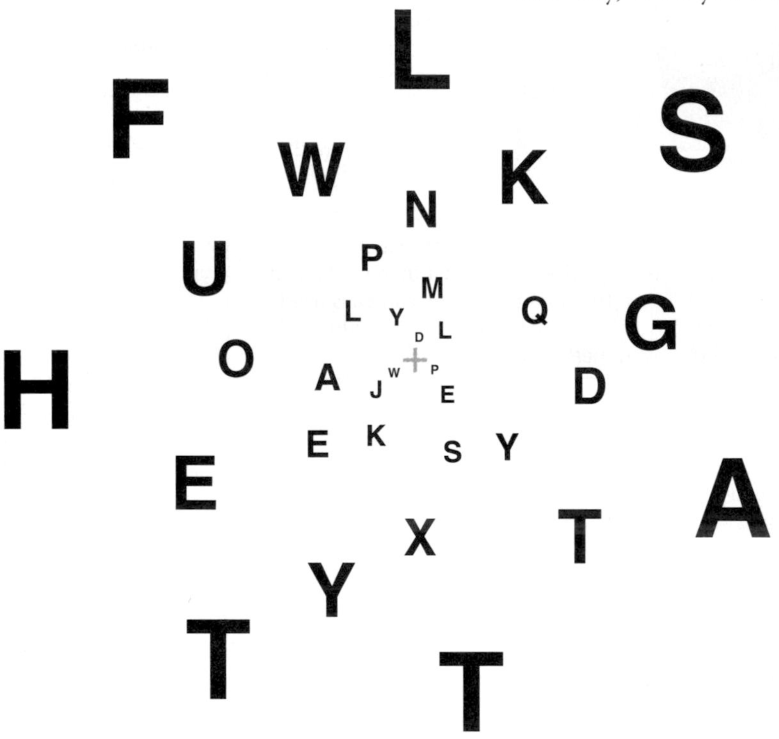

The Fovea

Try this experiment. Focus on the print at the left edge of this page. The words will be clearly legible. Now, while holding your eyes still, try to read the words on the right side of the page. It will be very difficult and likely impossible, even though you can see that words are there.

The lesson is that our vision is better in the center of the visual field than at the margins, or *periphery.* Letters at the periphery must be much larger than those in the center for us to see them as well. **Figure 9-3** shows how much larger. The difference is due partly to the fact that photoreceptors are more densely packed at the center of the retina, in a region known as the **fovea.** Figure 9-2 shows that the surface of the retina is depressed at the fovea. This depression is formed because many of the fibers of the optic nerve skirt the fovea to facilitate light access to its receptors.

The Blind Spot

Now try another experiment. Stand with your head over a tabletop and hold a pencil in your hand. Close one eye. Stare at the edge of the tabletop nearest you. Now hold the pencil in a horizontal position and move it along the edge of the table, with the eraser on the table. Beginning at a point approximately below your nose, move the pencil slowly along the table in the direction of the open eye.

When you have moved the pencil about 6 inches, the eraser will vanish. You have found your **blind spot,** a small area of the retina that is also known as the *optic disc.* As shown in Figure 9-2, the optic disc is the area where blood vessels enter and exit the eye and where fibers leading from retinal neurons form the optic nerve that goes to the brain. There are therefore no photoreceptors in this part of the retina, and so you cannot see with it. You can use **Figure 9-4** to demonstrate the blind spot in another way.

Fortunately, your visual system solves the blind-spot problem by locating the optic disc in a different location in each of your eyes. The optic disc is lateral to the fovea in

Fovea Region at the center of the retina that is specialized for high acuity; its receptive fields are at the center of the eye's visual field.

Blind spot Region of the retina where axons forming the optic nerve leave the eye and where blood vessels enter and leave; has no photoreceptors and is thus "blind."

Rod Photoreceptor specialized for functioning at low light levels.

Cone Photoreceptor specialized for color and high visual acuity.

each eye, which means that it is left of the fovea in the left eye and right of the fovea in the right eye. Because the visual world of the two eyes overlaps, the blind spot of the left eye can be seen by the right eye and vice versa.

Thus, using both eyes together, you can see the whole visual world. For people who are blind in one eye, the sightless eye cannot compensate for the blind spot in the functioning eye. Still, the visual system compensates for the blind spot in several other ways, and so they have no sense of a hole in their field of vision.

The optic disc that produces a blind spot is of particular importance in neurology. It allows neurologists to indirectly view the condition of the optic nerve that lies behind it while providing a window onto events within the brain. If intracranial pressure increases, as occurs with a tumor or brain abscess (an infection), the optic disc swells, leading to a condition known as *papilloedema* (swollen disc). The swelling occurs in part because, like all neural tissue, the optic nerve is surrounded by cerebrospinal fluid. Pressure inside the cranium can displace this fluid around the optic nerve, causing swelling at the optic disc.

Another reason for papilloedema is inflammation of the optic nerve itself, a condition known as *optic neuritis.* Whatever the cause, a person with a swollen optic disc usually loses vision owing to pressure on the optic nerve. If the swelling is due to optic neuritis, probably the most common neurological visual disorder, the prognosis for recovery is good.

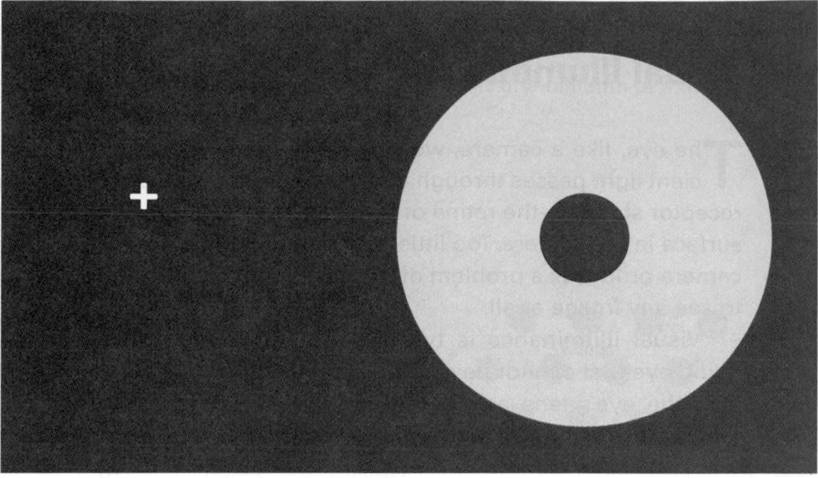

FIGURE 9-4 Find Your Blind Spot. Hold this book 30 centimeters (about 12 inches) away from your face. Shut your left eye and look at the cross with your right eye. Slowly bring the page toward you until the red dot disappears from the center of the yellow disc and is replaced by a yellow surface. The red spot is now in your blind spot and not visible. Your brain replaces the area with the surrounding yellow to fill in the image. Turn the book upside down to test your left eye.

Photoreceptors

The retina's photoreceptor cells convert light energy first into chemical energy and then into neural activity. When light strikes a photoreceptor, it triggers a series of chemical reactions that lead to a change in membrane potential (electrical charge). This change in turn leads to a change in the release of neurotransmitter onto nearby neurons.

Chapter 4 details the electrical activity of the cell membrane.

Rods and cones, the two types of photoreceptors, differ in many ways. As you can see in **Figure 9-5**, they are structurally different. Rods are longer than cones and cylindrically shaped at one end, whereas cones have a tapered end. **Rods** are more numerous than cones; are sensitive to low levels of brightness (luminance), especially in dim light; and function mainly for night vision (see Clinical Focus 9-2, "Visual Illuminance"). **Cones** do not respond to dim light, but they are highly responsive in bright light. Cones mediate both color vision and our ability to see fine detail.

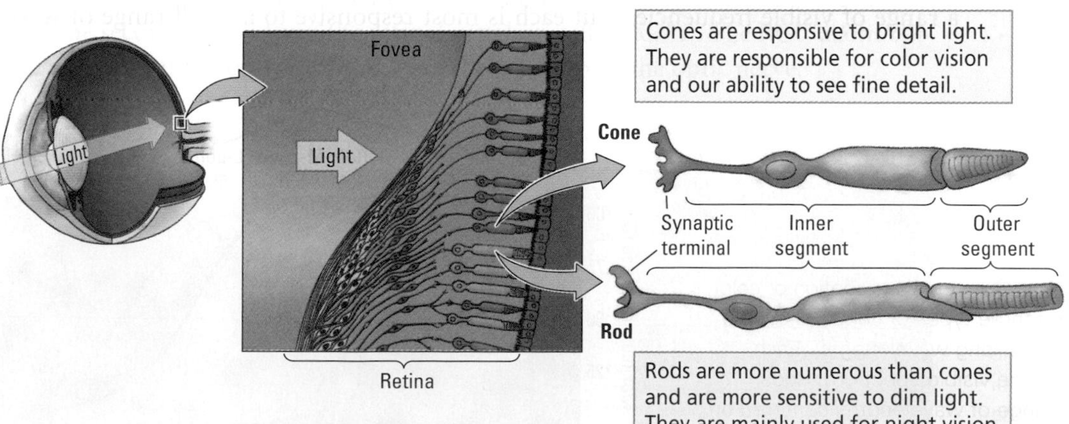
Light
Fovea
Light
Retina
Cones are responsive to bright light. They are responsible for color vision and our ability to see fine detail.
Cone
Synaptic terminal
Inner segment
Outer segment
Rod
Rods are more numerous than cones and are more sensitive to dim light. They are mainly used for night vision.

SPL/Photo Researchers

FIGURE 9-5 Photoreceptor Cells. Both rods and cones are tubelike structures, as the scanning electron micrograph shows, but they differ, especially in the outer segment, which contains the light-absorbing visual pigment. Rods are especially sensitive to broad-spectrum luminance, and cones are sensitive to particular wavelengths of light.

Retinal ganglion cells fall into two major categories that, in the primate retina, are called M and P cells. The designations derive from the distinctly different populations of cells in the visual thalamus to which these two classes of RGCs send their axons. As shown in **Figure 9-9,** one population consists of **magnocellular cells** (hence M); the other consists of **parvocellular cells** (hence P). The larger M cells receive their input primarily from rods and so are sensitive to light but not to color. The smaller P cells, receive their input primarily from cones and so are sensitive to color.

In Latin, *magno* means "large" and *parvo* means "small."

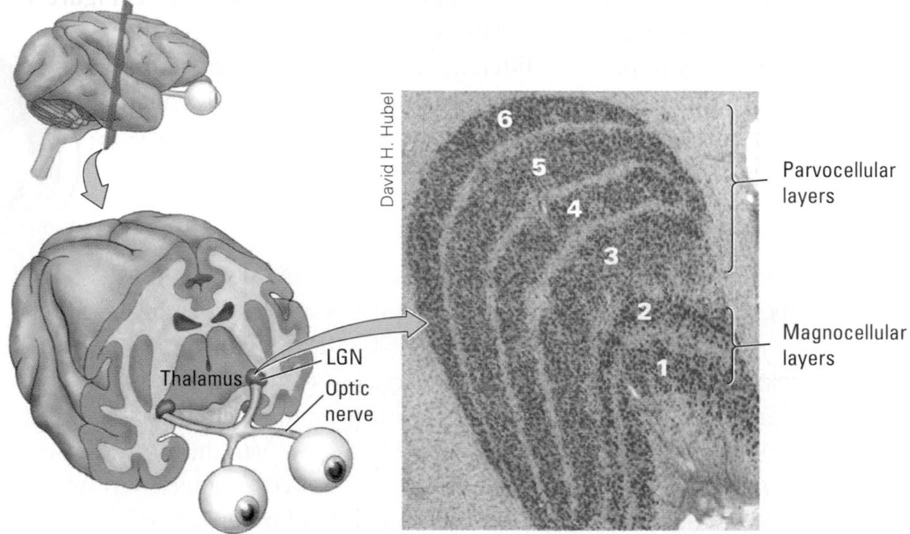

FIGURE 9-9 Visual Thalamus. The optic nerves connect with the lateral geniculate nucleus (LGN) of the thalamus. The LGN has six layers: two magnocellular layers that receive input mainly from rods and four parvocellular layers that receive input mainly from cones.

M cells are found throughout the retina, including the periphery, where we are sensitive to movement but not to color or fine details. P cells are found largely in the region of the fovea, where we are sensitive to color and fine details. A distinction between these two categories of RGCs is maintained throughout the visual pathways, as you will see next, as we follow the ganglion cell axons into the brain.

Visual Pathways

The retinal ganglion cells form the optic nerve, the road into the brain. This road leads to several places, each with a different visual function. By finding out the destinations of the branches, we can begin to guess what the brain is doing with visual input and how the brain creates our visual world. Let us begin with the optic nerves, one exiting from each eye. Just before entering the brain, the optic nerves partly cross, forming the **optic chiasm.**

The optic chiasm gets its name from the shape of the Greek letter χ (pronounced "ki," long "i"). Our visual system solves the challenge of representing the world seen through two eyes as a single perception by connecting both eyes with both hemispheres.

About half the fibers from each eye cross in such a way that the left half of each optic nerve goes to the left side of the brain, whereas the right half goes to the brain's right side, as diagrammed in **Figure 9-10.** The medial path of each retina, the *nasal retina,* crosses to the opposite side. The lateral path, the *temporal retina,* goes straight back on the same side. Because light that falls on the right half of each retina actually comes from the left side of the visual field, information from the left visual field goes to the brain's right hemisphere, whereas information from the right visual field goes to the left hemisphere. Thus, half of each retina's visual field is represented on each side of the brain.

On entering the brain, the RGC axons separate, forming the two distinct pathways charted in **Figure 9-11.** All the axons of the P ganglion cells and some of the M ganglion cells form a pathway called the **geniculostriate system.** This pathway goes from the retina to the lateral geniculate nucleus (LGN) of the thalamus and then to layer IV of the primary visual cortex in the occipital lobe.

FIGURE 9-10 Crossing the Optic Chiasm. This horizontal section shows the visual pathway from each eye to the primary visual cortex of each neural hemisphere. Information from the blue side of the visual field goes to the two left halves of the retinas and ends up in the left hemisphere. Information from the red side of the visual field hits the right halves of the retinas and travels to the right side of the brain.

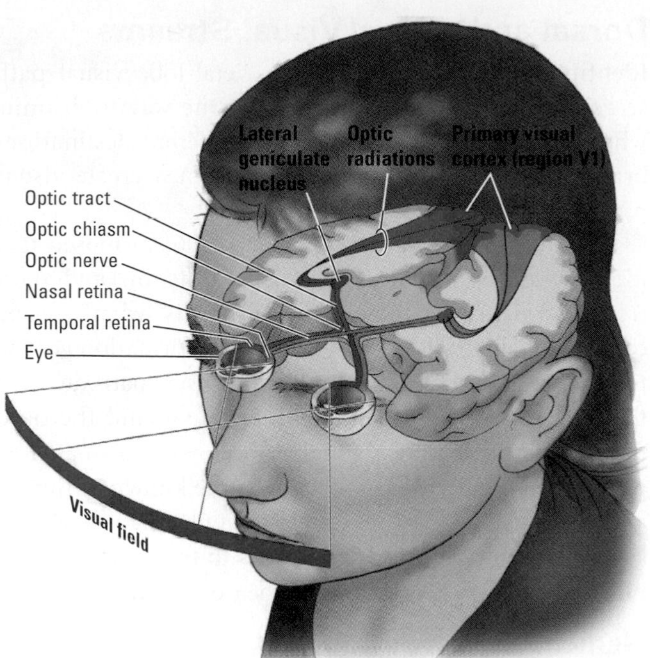

Magnocellular (M) cell Large-celled visual-system neuron that is sensitive to moving stimuli.
Parvocellular (P) cell Small-celled visual-system neuron that is sensitive to form and color differences.
Optic chiasm Junction of the optic nerves, one from each eye, at which the axons from the nasal (inside—nearer the nose) halves of the retinas cross to the opposite side of the brain.
Geniculostriate system Projections from the retina to the lateral geniculate nucleus to the visual cortex.
Striate cortex Primary visual cortex (V1) in the occipital lobe; its striped appearance when stained gives it this name.
Tectopulvinar system Projections from the retina to the superior colliculus to the pulvinar (thalamus) to the parietal and temporal visual areas.

Figure 9-12 shows that, when stained, the primary visual cortex appears to have a broad stripe across it in layer IV and so is known as **striate** (striped) **cortex.** The geniculostriate therefore bridges the thalamus (geniculate) and the striate cortex. From the striate cortex, the axon pathway now splits, with one route going to vision-related regions of the parietal lobe and another route going to vision-related regions of the temporal lobe.

The second pathway leading from the eye is formed by the axons of the remaining M ganglion cells. These cells send their axons to the superior colliculus, which sends connections to the pulvinar region of the thalamus. This pathway is therefore known as the **tectopulvinar system** because it runs from the eye through the tectum to the pulvinar (see Figure 9-11). The pulvinar then sends connections to the parietal and temporal lobes.

To summarize, two principal pathways, the geniculostriate and tectopulvinar, extend into the visual brain. Each pathway eventually leads either to the parietal or the temporal lobe. Our next task is to determine the respective roles of the parietal lobe and the temporal lobe in creating our visual world.

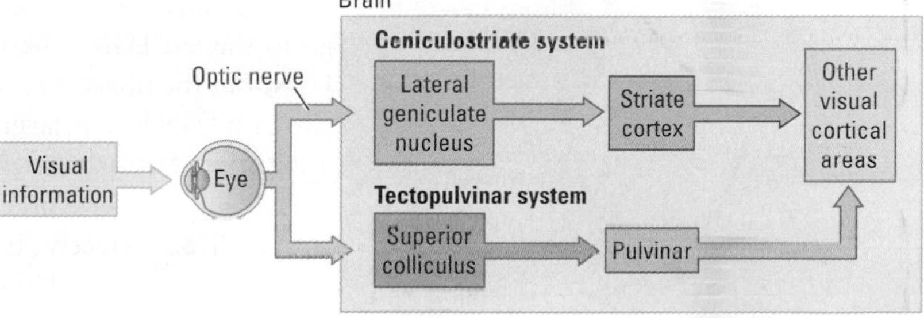

FIGURE 9-11 Flow of Visual Information into the Brain. The optic nerve's two main branches are (1) the geniculostriate through the LGN in the thalamus to the primary visual cortex and (2) the tectopulvinar through the superior colliculus of the tectum to the pulvinar region of the thalamus and then to the temporal and parietal lobes. (The thalamus, shown in Figure 2-17, is part of the diencephalon; the tectum forms part of the midbrain, shown in Figure 2-16.)

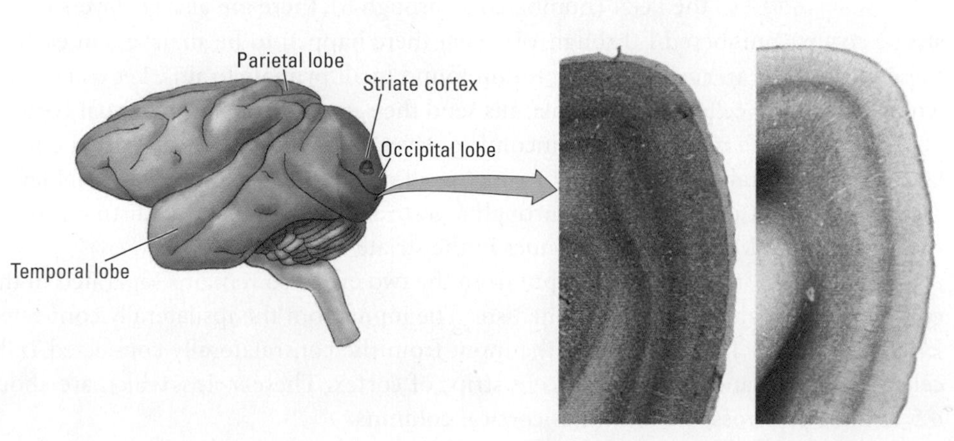

FIGURE 9-12 Striate Cortex. The primary visual cortex is also called the *striate cortex* because it appears to have striations (stripes) when sections are stained with either a cell-body stain (*left*) or a myelin stain (*right*). The sections shown here come from a rhesus monkey's brain.

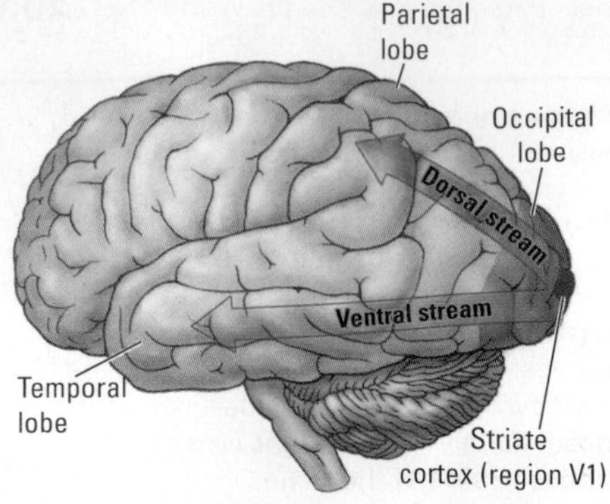

FIGURE 9-13 Visual Streaming. Visual information travels from the occipital visual areas to the parietal and temporal lobes, forming the dorsal and ventral streams, respectively.

Dorsal and Ventral Visual Streams

Identifying the temporal- and parietal-lobe visual pathways led researchers on a search for their possible functions. One way to examine these functions is to ask why evolution would produce two different destinations for these pathways in the brain. The answer is that each route must create visual knowledge for a different purpose.

David Milner and Mel Goodale (2006) proposed that these two purposes are to identify what a stimulus is (the "what" function) and to use visual information to control movement (the "how" function). This "what" compared with "how" distinction came from an analysis of where visual information goes when it leaves the striate cortex. **Figure 9-13** shows the two distinct visual pathways that originate in the striate cortex, one progressing to the temporal lobe and the other to the parietal lobe. The pathway to the temporal lobe has become known as the ventral stream, whereas the pathway to the parietal lobe has become known as the dorsal stream.

To understand how these two streams function, we return to the details of how visual input from the eyes contributes to them. Both the geniculostriate and the tectopulvinar pathways contribute to the dorsal and ventral streams.

Geniculostriate Pathway

The RGC fibers from the two eyes distribute their connections to the two lateral geniculate nuclei (left and right) of the thalamus in what at first glance appears to be an unusual arrangement. As seen in Figure 9-10, the fibers from the left half of each retina go to the left LGN, whereas those from the right half of each retina go to the right LGN. But the fibers from each eye do not go to exactly the same place in the LGN.

Each LGN has six layers, and the projections from the two eyes go to different layers, as illustrated in anatomical context in Figure 9-9 and diagrammed in **Figure 9-14.** Layers 2, 3, and 5 receive fibers from the ipsilateral eye (the eye on the same side), whereas layers 1, 4, and 6 receive fibers from the contralateral eye (the eye on the opposite side). This arrangement provides for combining the information from the two eyes and for segregating the information from the P and M ganglion cells.

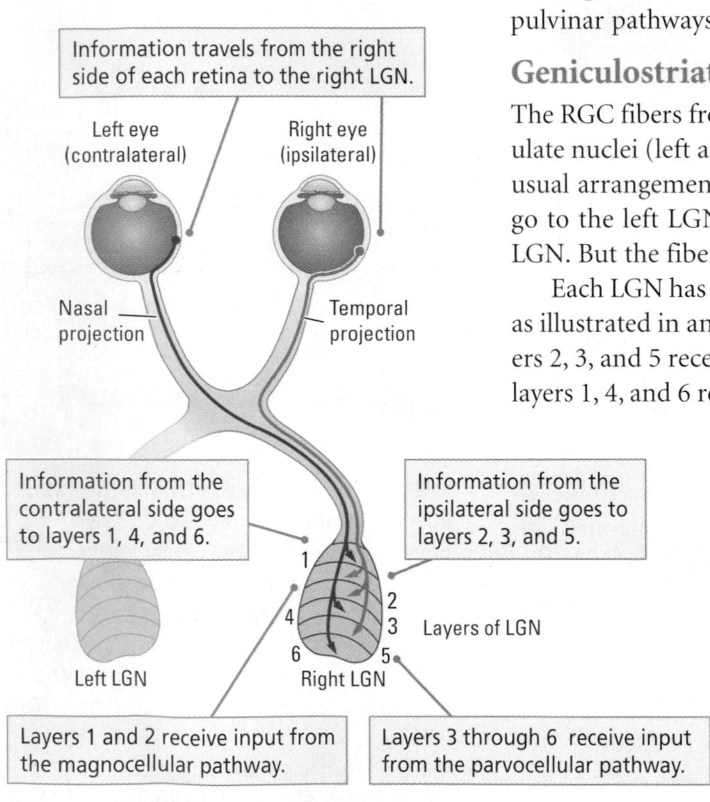

FIGURE 9-14 Geniculostriate Pathway.

Axons from the P cells go only to layers 3 through 6 (referred to as the parvocellular layers), whereas axons from the M cells go only to layers 1 and 2 (referred to as the magnocellular layers). Because the P cells are responsive to color and fine detail, layers 3 through 6 of the LGN must be processing information about color and form. In contrast, the M cells mostly process information about movement, and so layers 1 and 2 must deal with movement.

Before we continue, be aware that just as there are six layers of the LGN (numbered 1 through 6), there are also six layers of the striate cortex (numbered I through VI). That there happen to be six layers in each of these locations is an accident of evolution found in all primate brains. Let us now see where these LGN cells from the thalamus send their connections in the visual cortex.

You can review the functions of cortical layers I–VI in Figure 2-20.

Layer IV is the main afferent (incoming) layer of the cortex. In the visual cortex, layer IV has several sublayers, two of which are known as IVCa and IVCb. LGN layers 1 and 2 go to IVCα, and layers 3 through 6 go to IVCβ. As a result, a distinction between the P and M functions continues in the striate cortex.

As illustrated in **Figure 9-15,** input from the two eyes also remains separated in the cortex but through a different mechanism. The input from the ipsilaterally connected LGN cells (layers 2, 3, and 5) and the input from the contralaterally connected LGN cells (layers 1, 4, and 6) go to adjacent strips of cortex. These strips, which are about 0.5 millimeter across, are known as **cortical columns.**

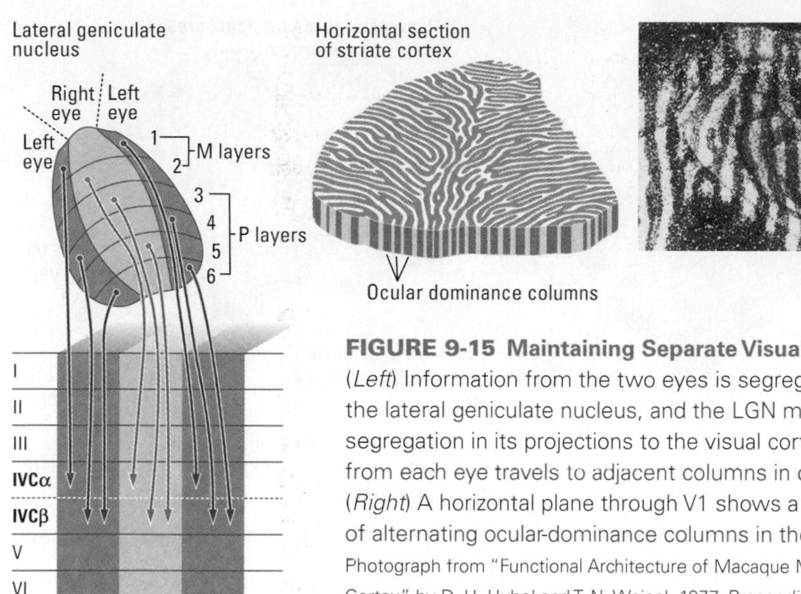

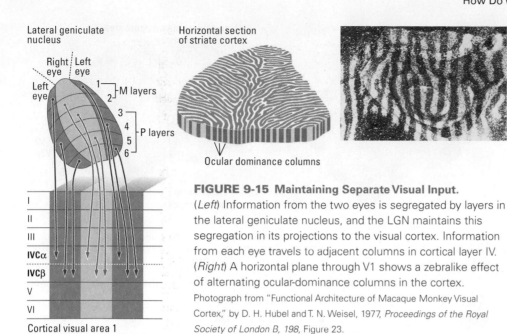

FIGURE 9-15 Maintaining Separate Visual Input. (*Left*) Information from the two eyes is segregated by layers in the lateral geniculate nucleus, and the LGN maintains this segregation in its projections to the visual cortex. Information from each eye travels to adjacent columns in cortical layer IV. (*Right*) A horizontal plane through V1 shows a zebralike effect of alternating ocular-dominance columns in the cortex. Photograph from "Functional Architecture of Macaque Monkey Visual Cortex," by D. H. Hubel and T. N. Weisel, 1977, *Proceedings of the Royal Society of London B, 198,* Figure 23.

Cortical column Cortical organization that represents a functional unit six cortical layers deep and approximately 0.5 millimeter square and that is perpendicular to the cortical surface.

Primary visual cortex (V1) Striate cortex that receives input from the lateral geniculate nucleus.

Extrastriate (secondary visual) cortex Visual cortical areas outside the striate cortex.

In summary, the P and M ganglion cells of the retina send separate pathways to the thalamus, and this segregation continues in the striate cortex. The left and right eyes also send separate pathways to the thalamus, and these pathways, too, remain segregated in the striate cortex.

Tectopulvinar Pathway

As already noted, the tectopulvinar pathway is formed by the axons of the remaining M retinal ganglion cells. These M cells send their axons to the superior colliculus in the midbrain's tectum, which functions to detect the location of stimuli and to shift the eyes toward stimuli. The superior colliculus sends connections to the region of the thalamus known as the pulvinar.

The pulvinar has two main divisions: medial and lateral. The medial pulvinar sends connections to the parietal lobe, and the lateral pulvinar sends connections to the temporal lobe. One type of information that these connections are conveying is related to "where," which is important in both the "what" and "how" visual streams.

Many textbooks emphasize the role of the "how" pathway as a "where" function. But "where" is a property of "what" a stimulus is as well as a cue for "how" to control movement to a place. We therefore use the "what–how" distinction suggested by Milner and Goodale.

The "where" function of the tectopulvinar system is useful in understanding D. B.'s blindsight, described in Clinical Focus 9-1. His geniculostriate system was disrupted by surgery, but his tectopulvinar system was not, thus allowing him to identify the location of stimuli (where) that he could not identify (what).

Occipital Cortex

Our route down the visual pathways has led us to now explore how visual information proceeds from the striate cortex through the rest of the occipital lobe to the dorsal and ventral streams. As shown in **Figure 9-16,** the occipital lobe is composed of at least six different visual regions, known as V1, V2, V3, V3A, V4, and V5. Region **V1** is the striate cortex, which, as already mentioned, is sometimes also referred to as the **primary visual cortex.** The remaining visual areas of the occipital lobe are called the **extrastriate cortex** or *secondary visual cortex.* Because each occipital region has a unique cellular structure (cytoarchitecture) and has unique inputs and outputs, we can infer that each must be doing something different from the others.

All mammals have at least one primary cortical area for each sensory system. Most of the information that reaches secondary areas is relayed through the primary area.

You already know that a remarkable feature of region V1 is its distinctly visible layers. When Margaret Wong-Riley and her colleagues (1993) stained region VI for the enzyme cytochrome oxidase, which has a role in cell metabolism, they were surprised

FIGURE 9-16 Visual Regions of the Occipital Lobe.

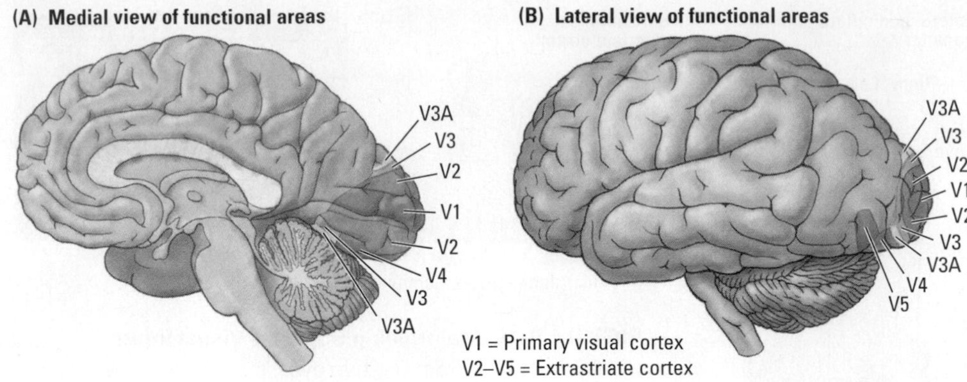

to find an unexpected heterogeneity. So they sectioned the V1 layers in such a way that each cortical layer was in one plane of section, much like peeling off the layers of an onion and laying them flat on a table. The surface of each flattened layer can then be viewed from above.

FIGURE 9-17 Heterogeneous Layering. Blobs in region V1 and stripes in region V2 are illustrated in this drawing of a flattened section through the visual cortex of a monkey. The blobs and stripes are revealed by a special stain for cytochrome oxidase, a marker for mitochondria, the organelles in cells that gather, store, and release energy.

As **Figure 9-17** illustrates, the heterogeneous cytochrome staining now appeared as random blobs in the layers of V1. These darkened regions have in fact become known as **blobs,** and the less-dark regions separating them have become known as *interblobs.* Blobs and interblobs serve different functions. Neurons in the blobs take part in color perception, whereas neurons in the interblobs participate in form and motion perception. So, within region V1, input that arrives in the parvo- and magnocellular pathways of the geniculostriate system is segregated into three separate types of information: color, form, and motion.

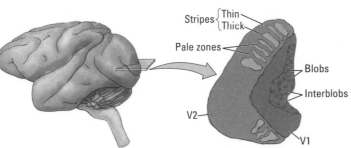

Information from region V1 moves next to region V2, which adjoins region V1. Here, the color, form, and motion inputs remain segregated, which can again be seen through the pattern of cytochrome oxidase staining. But the staining pattern in region V2 is different from that in region V1. Figure 9-17 shows that region V2 has a pattern of thick and thin stripes intermixed with pale zones. The thick stripes receive input from the movement-sensitive neurons in region V1; the thin stripes receive input from V1's color-sensitive neurons; and the pale zones receive input from V1's form-sensitive neurons.

As diagrammed in **Figure 9-18,** the visual pathways proceed from region V2 to the other occipital regions and then to the parietal and temporal lobes, forming the dorsal

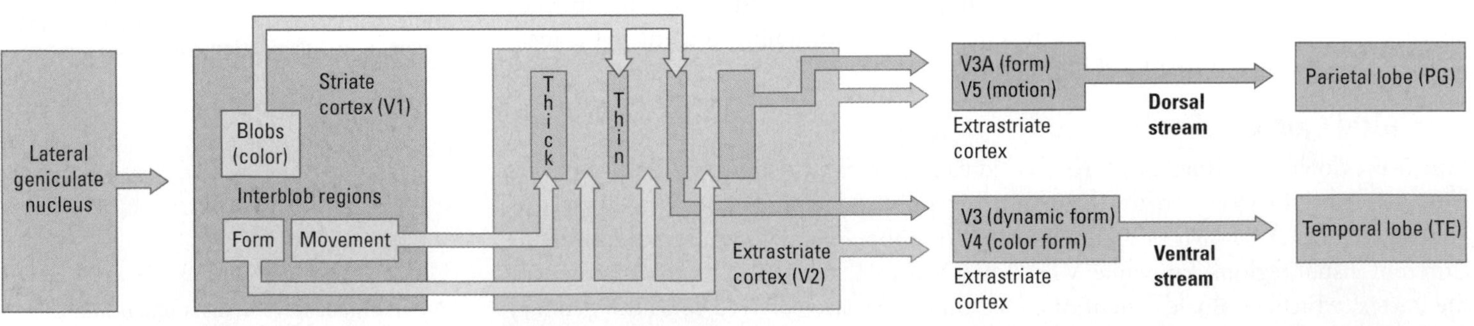

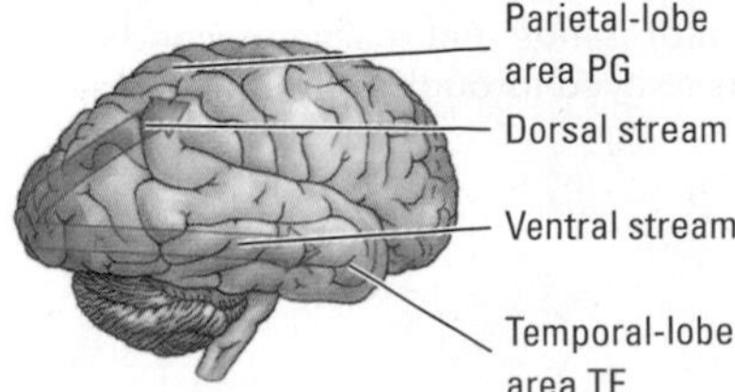

FIGURE 9-18 Charting the Dorsal and Ventral Streams. The dorsal stream, which controls visual action, begins in region V1 and flows through V2 to the other occipital areas and finally to the parietal cortex, ending in area PG. The ventral stream, which controls object recognition, begins in region V1 and flows through V2 to the other occipital areas and finally to the temporal cortex, ending in area TE. Information from the blobs and interblobs in V1 flows to the thick, thin, and pale zones of V2. Information in the thin and pale zones goes to regions V3 and V4 to form the ventral stream. That in the thick and pale zones goes to regions V3A and V5 to form the dorsal stream.

and ventral streams. Although many parietal and temporal regions take part, the major regions are region G in the parietal lobe (thus called region PG) and region E in the temporal lobe (thus called region TE).

Within the dorsal and ventral streams, the function of the visual pathways becomes far more complex than a simple record of color, form, and motion. Rather, the color, form, and motion information is assembled to produce a rich, unified visual world made up of complex objects, such as faces and paintings, and complex visuomotor skills, such as catching a ball. The functions of the dorsal and ventral streams are therefore complex, but they can be thought of as consisting of "how" functions and "what" functions. "How" is action to be visually guided toward objects, whereas "what" identifies what an object is.

Blob Region in the visual cortex that contains color-sensitive neurons, as revealed by staining for cytochrome oxidase.

Visual field Region of the visual world that is seen by the eyes.

REVIEW: Functional Anatomy of the Visual System

- ✔ Vision begins when photoreceptors in the retina at the back of the eye convert light energy into neural activity in neighboring ganglion cells, the axons of which form the optic nerve leading to the brain.
- ✔ P retinal ganglion cells receive input mostly from cones and carry information about color and fine detail, whereas M retinal ganglion cells receive input mostly from rods and carry information about light but not color.
- ✔ Visual input takes two routes into the brain. The geniculostriate pathway proceeds through the lateral geniculate nucleus of the thalamus to layer IV of the striate cortex in the occipital lobe. The tectopulvinar pathway runs from the tectum of the midbrain to the pulvinar of the thalamus and then to visual cortical areas.
- ✔ Both pathways contribute to the dorsal and ventral visual streams, which project to the parietal and temporal lobes, respectively. The dorsal stream to the parietal lobe processes the visual guidance of movements (the how), whereas the ventral stream to the temporal lobe processes the visual perception of objects (the what).

Location in the Visual World

As we move about, going from place to place, we encounter objects in specific locations. If we had no sense of location, the world would be a bewildering mass of visual information. The next leg of our journey down the neural roads traces how the brain constructs a spatial map.

The coding of location begins in the retina and is maintained throughout all visual pathways. To understand how this spatial coding is accomplished, imagine your visual world as seen by your two eyes. Imagine the large red and blue rectangles in **Figure 9-19** as a wall. Focus your gaze on the black cross in the middle of the wall.

All of the wall that you can see without moving your head is your **visual field.** The visual field can be divided into two halves, the left and right visual fields, by drawing a vertical line through the middle of the black cross.

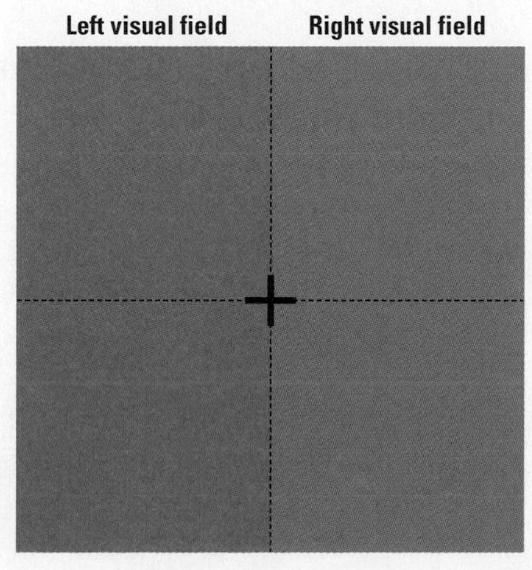

FIGURE 9-19 Visual-Field Demonstration. As you focus on the cross at the center, information at the left of this focal point forms the left visual field (red) and travels to the right hemisphere. Information to the right of the focal point forms the right visual field (blue) and travels to the left hemisphere. The visual field can be split horizontally as well: information above the focal point is in the upper visual field and that below the focal point is in the lower visual field.

Now recall from Figure 9-10 that the left half of each retina looks at the right side of the visual field, whereas the right half of each retina looks at the visual field's left side. Thus, input from the right visual field goes to the left hemisphere, whereas input from the left visual field goes to the right hemisphere.

Therefore, the brain can easily determine whether visual information is located to the left or right of center. If input goes to the left hemisphere, the source must be in the right visual field; if input goes to the right hemisphere, the source must be in the left visual field. This arrangement tells you nothing about the precise location of an object in the left or right side of the visual field, however. To understand how precise spatial localization is accomplished, we must return to the retinal ganglion cells.

Coding Location in the Retina

Look again at Figure 9-8 and you can see that each RGC receives input through bipolar cells from several photoreceptors. In the 1950s, Stephen Kuffler, a pioneer in studying visual-system physiology, made an important discovery about how photoreceptors and ganglion cells are linked. By shining small spots of light on the receptors, he found that each ganglion cell responds to stimulation on just a small circular patch of the retina, which is the ganglion cell's receptive field.

A ganglion cell's receptive field is therefore the region of the retina on which it is possible to influence that cell's firing. Stated differently, the receptive field represents the outer world as seen by a single cell. Each RGC sees only a small bit of the world, much as you would if you looked through a narrow cardboard tube. The visual field is composed of thousands of such receptive fields.

Now let us consider how receptive fields enable the visual system to interpret the location of objects. Imagine that the retina is flattened like a piece of paper. When a tiny light is shone on different parts of the retina, different ganglion cells respond. For example, when a light is shone on the top-left corner of the flattened retina, a particular RGC responds because that light is in its receptive field. Similarly, when a light is shone on the top-right corner, a different RGC responds.

By using this information, we can identify the location of a light on the retina by knowing which ganglion cell is activated. We can also interpret the location of the light in the outside world because we know where the light must come from to hit a particular place on the retina. For example, light from above hits the bottom of the retina after passing through the eye's lens, whereas light from below hits the top of the retina. Information at the top of the visual field will stimulate ganglion cells on the bottom of the retina, whereas information at the bottom of the field will stimulate ganglion cells on the top of the retina.

The cornea and lens of the eye, like the lens of a camera, focus light rays to project a backward, inverted image on a light-receptive surface (review How the Eye Works in The Basics).

Location in the Lateral Geniculate Nucleus and Cortical Region V1

Now consider the connection from the ganglion cells to the lateral geniculate nucleus. In contrast with the retina, the LGN is not a thin sheet; it is shaped more like a sausage. We can compare it to a stack of cards, with each card representing a layer of cells.

Figure 9-20 shows how the connections from the retina to the LGN can represent location. A retinal ganglion cell that responds to light in the top-left corner of the retina connects to the left side of the first card. A retinal ganglion cell that responds to light in the bottom-right corner of the retina connects to the right side of the last card. In this way, the location of left–right and top–bottom information is maintained in the LGN.

Like the ganglion cells, each LGN cell has a receptive field—the region of the retina that influences its activity. If two adjacent retinal ganglion cells synapse on a single LGN cell, the receptive field of that LGN cell will be the sum of the two ganglion cells' receptive fields. As a result, the receptive fields of LGN cells are bigger than those of retinal ganglion cells.

The LGN projection to the striate cortex (region V1) also maintains spatial information. As each LGN cell, representing a particular place, projects to region V1, a spatially organized neural representation, or topographic map, is produced in the cortex. As illustrated in **Figure 9-21,** this representation is essentially a map of the visual world.

The central part of the visual field is represented at the back of the brain, whereas the periphery is represented more anteriorly. The upper part of the visual field is represented at the bottom of region V1 and the lower part at the top of V1. The other regions of the visual cortex (such as V3, V4, and V5) also have topographical maps similar to that of V1. Thus the V1 neurons must project to the other regions in an orderly manner, just as the LGN neurons project to region V1 in an orderly way.

Within each visual cortical area, each neuron's receptive field corresponds to the part of the retina to which the neuron is connected. As a rule of thumb, the cells in the cortex have much larger receptive fields than those of retinal ganglion cells. This increase in receptive-field size means that the receptive field of a cortical neuron must be composed of the receptive fields of many RGCs, as illustrated in **Figure 9-22.**

There is one additional wrinkle to the organization of topographic maps. Jerison's principle of proper mass states that the amount of neural tissue responsible for a particular function is equivalent to the amount of neural processing required for that

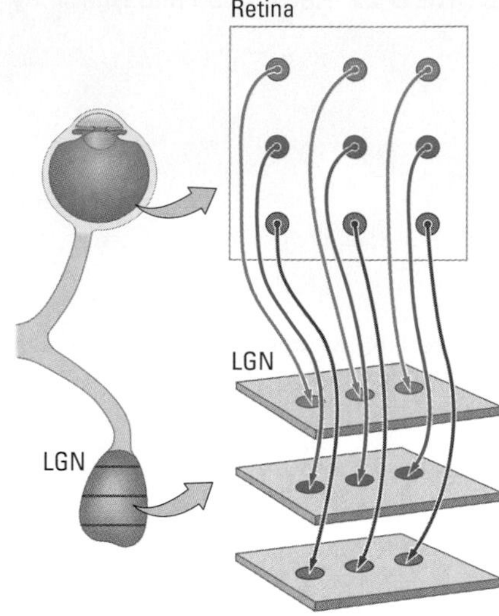
Retina
LGN
LGN

FIGURE 9-20 Receptive-Field Projection. The information from a receptive field in the retina retains its spatial relation when it is sent to the lateral geniculate nucleus. Here, information at the top of the visual field goes to the top of the LGN and information from the bottom of the visual field goes to the bottom of the LGN, and information from the left or right goes to the left or right of the LGN, respectively.

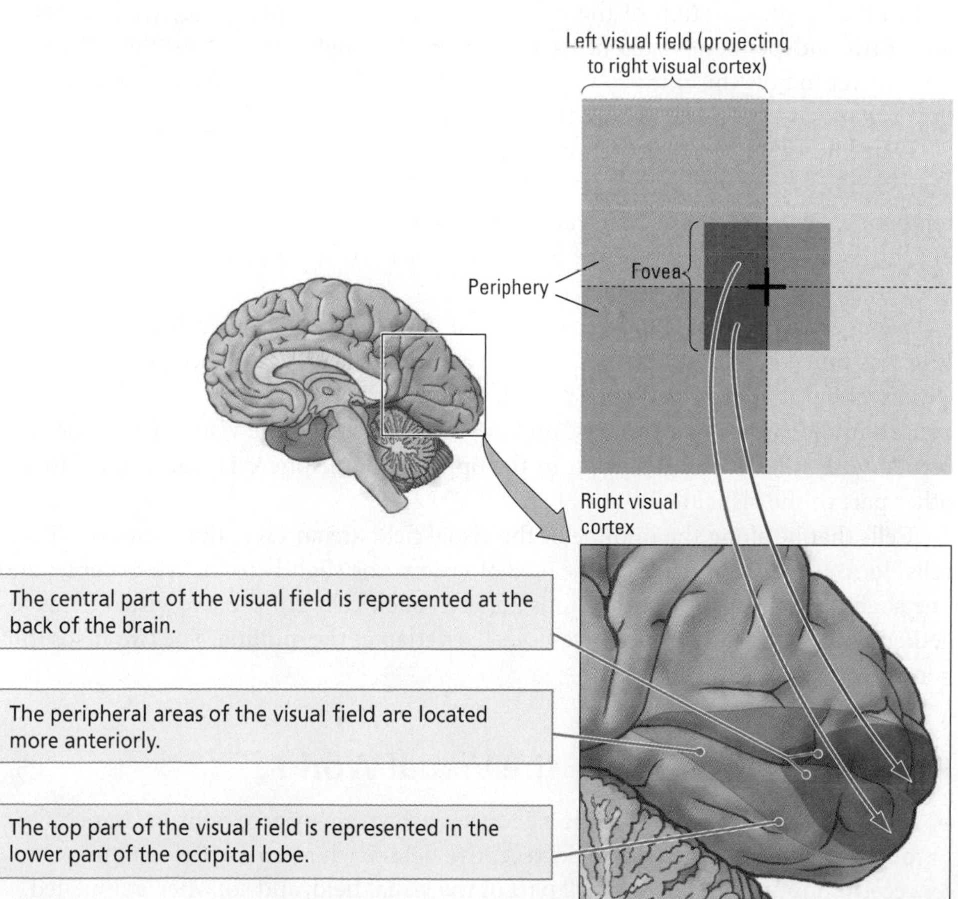
Left visual field (projecting to right visual cortex)
Periphery
Fovea
Right visual cortex
The central part of the visual field is represented at the back of the brain.
The peripheral areas of the visual field are located more anteriorly.
The top part of the visual field is represented in the lower part of the occipital lobe.

FIGURE 9-21 Topographic Organization of Region V1. The fovea occupies a disproportionately large part of the occipital cortex, which is why visual acuity is best in the central part of the visual field.

FIGURE 9-22 Receptive-Field Hierarchy.

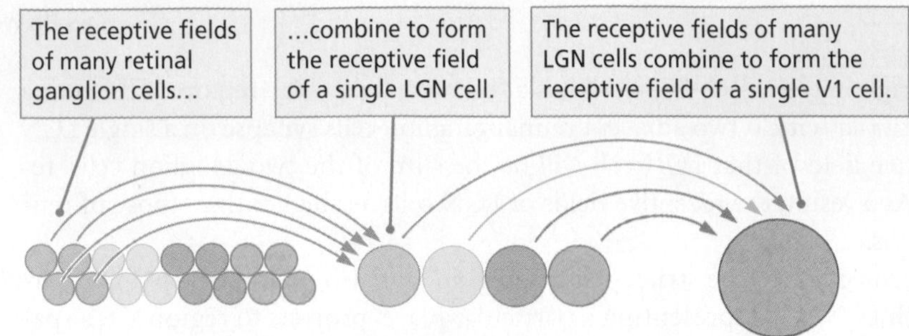
The receptive fields of many retinal ganglion cells...
...combine to form the receptive field of a single LGN cell.
The receptive fields of many LGN cells combine to form the receptive field of a single V1 cell.

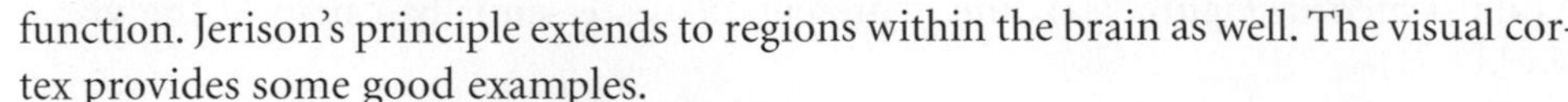

In Figure 1-14, we apply Jerison's principle to overall brain size.

function. Jerison's principle extends to regions within the brain as well. The visual cortex provides some good examples.

You can see in Figure 9-21 that not all parts of the visual field are equally represented in region V1. The small, central part of the visual field that is seen by the fovea is represented by a larger area in the cortex than the visual field's periphery, even though the periphery is a much larger part of the visual field. In accord with Jerison's principle, we would predict more processing of foveal information in region V1 than of peripheral information. This prediction makes intuitive sense because we can see more clearly in the center of the visual field than at the periphery. In other words, sensory areas that have more cortical representation provide a more-detailed creation of the external world.

The Visual Corpus Callosum

Corpus callosum

Creating topographic maps based on the receptive fields of neurons is an effective way for the brain to code the location of objects. But, if the left visual field is represented in the right cerebral hemisphere and the right visual field is represented in the left cerebral hemisphere, how are the two halves of the visual field ultimately bound together in a unified representation of the world? After all, we have the subjective impression not of two independent visual fields, but rather of a single, continuous field of vision. The answer to how this unity is accomplished lies in the corpus callosum, which binds the two sides of the visual field at the midline.

Until the 1950s, the function of the corpus callosum was largely a mystery. Physicians had occasionally cut it to control severe epilepsy or to reach a very deep tumor, but patients did not appear much affected by this surgery. The corpus callosum clearly linked the two hemispheres of the brain, but exactly which parts were connected was not yet known.

We now realize that the corpus callosum connects only certain brain structures. Whereas much of the frontal lobes have callosal connections, the occipital lobes have almost none, as shown in **Figure 9-23.** If you think about it, there is no reason for a neuron in the visual cortex that is "looking at" one place in the visual field to be concerned with what another neuron in the opposite hemisphere is "looking at" in another part of the visual field.

Cells that lie along the midline of the visual field are an exception, however. These cells "look at" adjacent places in the field of vision, one slightly to the left of center and one slightly to the right. Connections between such cells zip the two visual fields together by combining their receptive fields to overlap at the midline. The two fields thus become one.

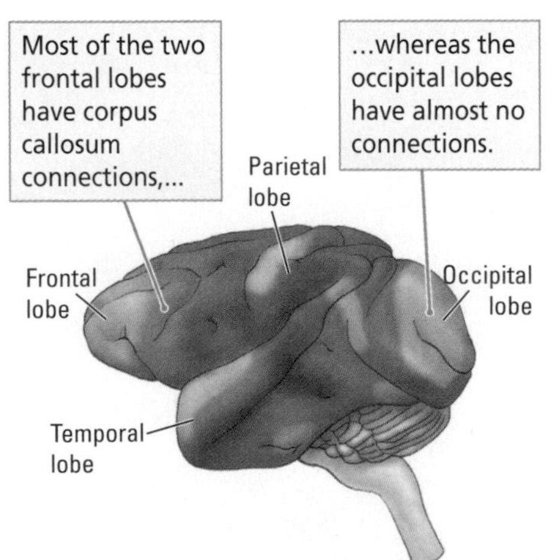
Most of the two frontal lobes have corpus callosum connections,...
...whereas the occipital lobes have almost no connections.
Parietal lobe
Frontal lobe
Occipital lobe
Temporal lobe

FIGURE 9-23 Callosal Connections. The darker areas indicate regions of the rhesus monkey cortex that receive projections from the opposite hemisphere through the corpus callosum.

REVIEW: Location in the Visual World

- ✔ The brain can determine location because each visual-system neuron connects to only a small part of the retina, its receptive field. Each receptive field, in turn, receives input from only a small part of the visual field, and so, when stimulated, can detect exactly where the light source is positioned in the environment.

- ✔ This location-detecting method is maintained at different levels in the visual system, from the ganglion cells of the retina to the neurons of the lateral geniculate nucleus in the thalamus to the neurons of the primary visual cortex.
- ✔ Inputs to different parts of cortical region V1 from different parts of the retina essentially form a topographic map of the visual world within the brain.
- ✔ Cells with receptive fields that lie along the midline of the field of vision are connected by the corpus callosum, binding the two sides of the visual world together as one perception.

Neuronal Activity

The pathways of the visual system are made up of individual neurons. By studying how these cells behave when their receptive fields are stimulated, we can begin to understand how the brain processes different features of the visual world beyond the location of a light. We first examine how neurons in the ventral stream respond to shapes and colors and then briefly consider how neurons in the dorsal stream direct vision for action.

Seeing Shape

Imagine that a microelectrode placed near a neuron somewhere in the visual pathway from retina to cortex is recording changes in the neuron's firing rate. This neuron occasionally fires spontaneously, producing action potentials with each discharge. Let us assume that the neuron discharges, on the average, once every 0.08 second. Each action potential is brief, on the order of 1 millisecond.

If we plot action potentials spanning a second, we see only spikes in the record because the action potentials are so brief. **Figure 9-24A** is a single-cell recording of 12 spikes in the span of 1 second. If the firing rate of this cell increases, we will see more spikes (Figure 9-24B). If the firing rate decreases, we will see fewer spikes (Figure 9-24C). The increase in firing represents excitation of the cell, whereas the decrease represents inhibition. Excitation and inhibition, as you know, are the principal mechanisms of information transfer in the nervous system.

Figure 4-14 graphs the effect of measuring action potentials generated over 30 milliseconds.

Now suppose we present a stimulus to the neuron by illuminating its receptive field in the retina, perhaps by shining a light on a blank screen within the cell's visual field. We might place before the eye a straight line positioned at a 45° angle. The cell could respond to this stimulus either by increasing or decreasing its firing rate. In either case, we would conclude that the cell is creating information about the line.

Note that the same cell could show excitation to one stimulus, inhibition to another stimulus, and no reaction at all. The cell could be excited by lines oriented 45° to the left and inhibited by lines oriented 45° to the right. Similarly, the cell could be excited by stimulation in one part of its receptive field (such as the center) and inhibited by stimulation in another part (such as the periphery).

Finally, we might find that the cell's response to a particular stimulus is selective. Such a cell would be telling us about the

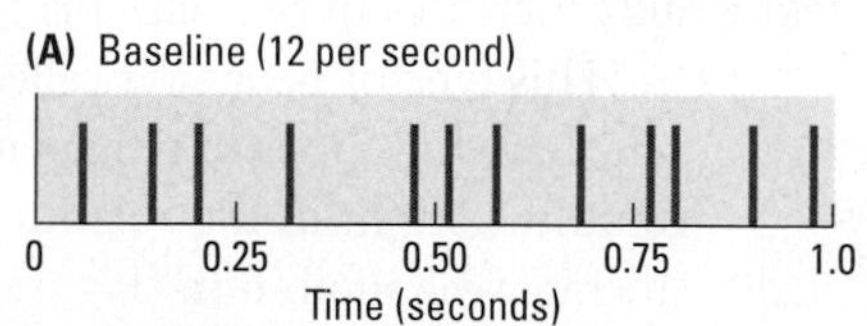

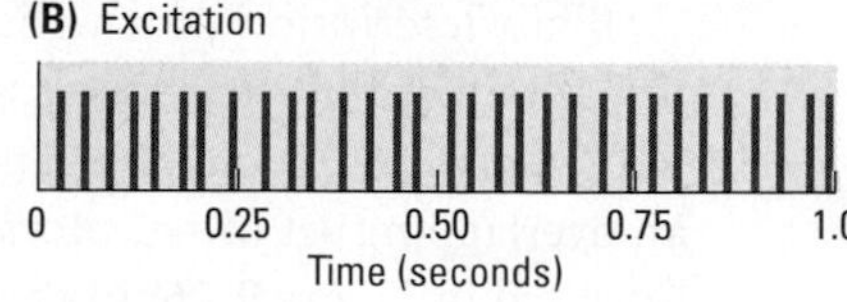

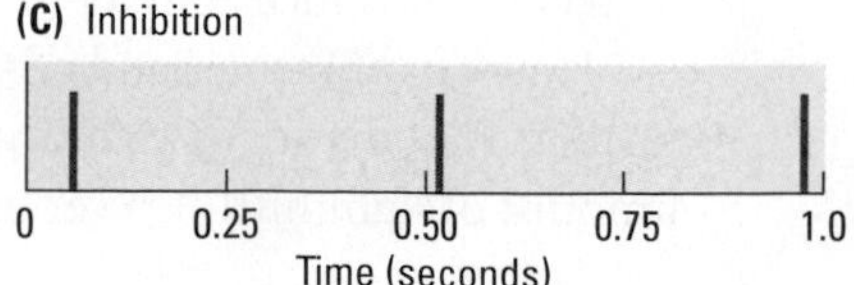

FIGURE 9-24 Recording Neural Stimulation. At the baseline firing rate of a neuron, each action potential is represented by a spike. In a 1-second time period, there were 12 spikes (A). Excitation is indicated by an increase in firing rate over baseline (B). Inhibition is indicated by a decrease in firing rate under baseline (C).

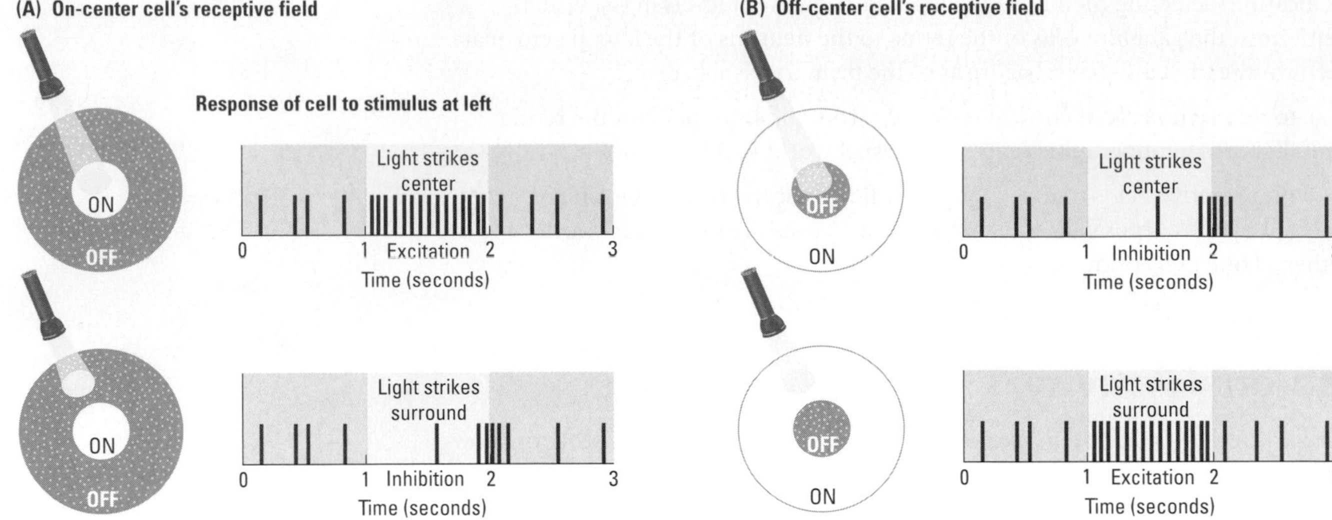

FIGURE 9-25 On–Off Receptivity. (A) In the receptive field of a retinal ganglion cell with an on-center and off-surround, a spot of light shining on the center excites the neuron, whereas a spot of light in the surround inhibits it. When the light in the surround region is turned off, firing rate increases briefly (called an "offset" response). A light shining in both the center and the surround would produce a weak increase in firing in the cell. (B) In the receptive field of a retinal ganglion cell with an off-center and on-surround, light in the center produces inhibition, whereas light on the surround produces excitation, and light across the entire field produces weak inhibition.

importance of the stimulus to the animal. For instance, the cell might be excited when a stimulus is presented with food but inhibited when the same stimulus is presented alone. In each case, the cell is selectively sensitive to characteristics in the visual world.

Neurons at each level of the visual system have distinctly different characteristics and functions. Our goal is not to look at each neuron type but rather to consider generally how some typical neurons at each level differ from one another in their contributions to processing shape. We focus on neurons in three areas: the ganglion-cell layer of the retina, the primary visual cortex, and the temporal cortex.

Processing in Retinal Ganglion Cells

Cells in the retina do not detect shape, because their receptive fields are very small dots. Each ganglion cell responds only to the presence or absence of light in its receptive field, not to shape. Shape is constructed by processes in the cortex from the information that ganglion cells pass on about events in their receptive fields.

The receptive field of a ganglion cell has a concentric circle arrangement, as illustrated in **Figure 9-25**A. A spot of light falling in the central circle of the receptive field excites some of these cells, whereas a spot of light falling in the surround (periphery) of the receptive field inhibits the cell. A spot of light falling across the entire receptive field weakly increases in the cell's firing rate.

FIGURE 9-26 Overlapping Receptive Fields.

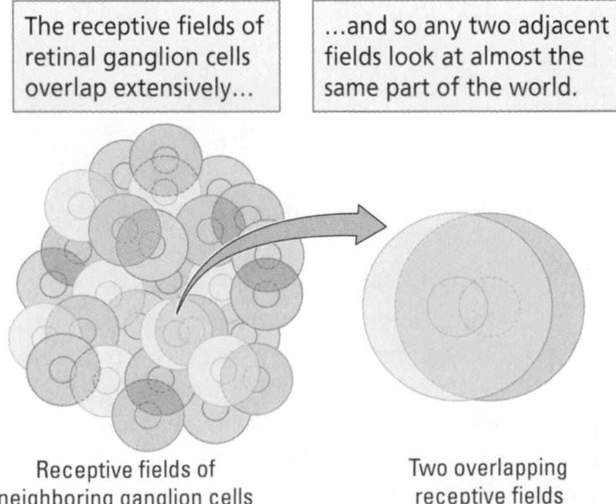

The receptive fields of retinal ganglion cells overlap extensively...
...and so any two adjacent fields look at almost the same part of the world.
Receptive fields of neighboring ganglion cells
Two overlapping receptive fields

This type of neuron is called an *on-center cell.* Other RGCs, called *off-center cells,* have the opposite arrangement, with light in the center of the receptive field inhibiting, light in the surround exciting, and light across the entire field producing weak inhibition (Figure 9-25B). The on–off arrangement of RGC receptive fields makes these cells especially responsive to very small spots of light.

This description of ganglion-cell receptive fields might mislead you into thinking that they form a mosaic of discrete little circles on the retina that do not overlap. In fact, neighboring retinal ganglion cells receive their inputs from an overlapping set of receptors. As a result, their receptive fields overlap, as illustrated in **Figure 9-26.** In this way, a small spot of light shining on the retina is likely to produce activity in both on-center and off-center ganglion cells.

How can on-center and off-center ganglion cells tell the brain anything about shape? The answer is that a ganglion cell is able to tell the brain about the amount of light hitting a certain spot on the retina compared with the average

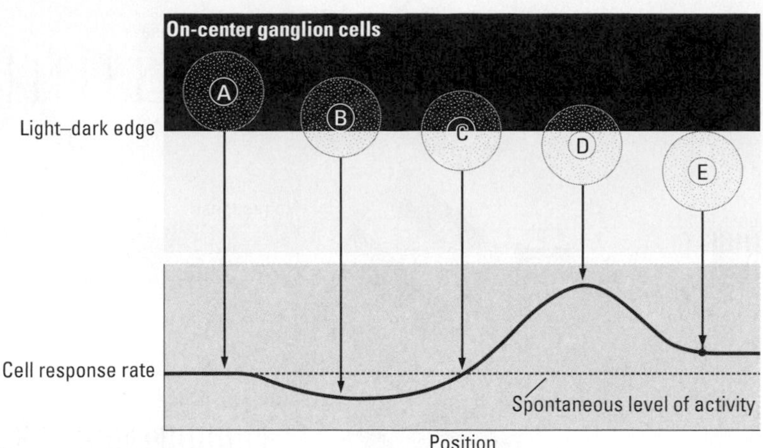

FIGURE 9-27 Activity at the Margins. Responses of a hypothetical population of on-center ganglion cells whose receptive fields (A–E) are distributed across a light–dark edge. The activity of the cells along the edge is most affected relative to those away from the edge. Adapted from *Neuroscience* (p. 195), edited by D. Purves, G. J. Augustine, D. Fitzpatrick, L. C. Katz, A.-S. LaMantia, and J. O. McNamara, 1997, Sunderland, MA: Sinauer.

amount of light falling on the surrounding retinal region. This comparison is known as **luminance contrast.**

To understand how luminance contrast tells the brain about shape, consider the hypothetical population of on-center ganglion cells represented in **Figure 9-27.** Their receptive fields are distributed across the retinal image of a light–dark edge. Some of the ganglion cells have receptive fields in the dark area, others have receptive fields in the light area, and still others have fields that straddle the edge of the light.

The ganglion cells with receptive fields in the dark or light areas are least affected because they experience either no stimulation or stimulation of both the excitatory and the inhibitory regions of their receptive fields. The ganglion cells most affected by the stimulus are those lying along the edge. Ganglion cell B is inhibited because the light falls mostly on its inhibitory surround, and ganglion cell D is excited because its entire excitatory center is stimulated but only part of its inhibitory surround is.

Consequently, information transmitted from retinal ganglion cells to the visual areas in the brain does not give equal weight to all regions of the visual field. Rather, it emphasizes regions containing differences in luminance. Areas with differences in luminance are found along edges. So retinal ganglion cells are really sending signals about edges, and edges are what form shapes.

Processing Shape in the Primary Visual Cortex

Now consider cells in region V1 that receive their visual inputs from LGN cells, which in turn receive theirs from retinal ganglion cells. Because each V1 cell receives input from multiple RGCs, the receptive fields of the V1 neurons are much larger than those of retinal neurons. Consequently, V1 cells respond to stimuli more complex than simply "light on" or "light off." In particular, these cells are maximally excited by bars of light oriented in a particular direction rather than by spots of light. These cells are therefore called *orientation detectors.*

Like the ganglion cells, some orientation detectors have an on–off arrangement in their receptive fields, but the arrangement is rectangular rather than circular. Visual cortex cells with this property are known as *simple cells.* Typical receptive fields for simple cells in the primary visual cortex are shown in **Figure 9-28.**

Simple cells are not the only kind of orientation detector in the primary visual cortex; several functionally distinct types of neurons populate region V1. For instance, the receptive fields of *complex cells,* such as those in **Figure 9-29,** are maximally excited by bars of light moving in a particular direction through the visual field. A *hypercomplex cell,* like a complex cell, is maximally responsive to moving bars but also has a strong inhibitory area at one end of its receptive field. As illustrated in **Figure 9-30,** a bar of

Luminance contrast The amount of light reflected by an object relative to its surroundings.

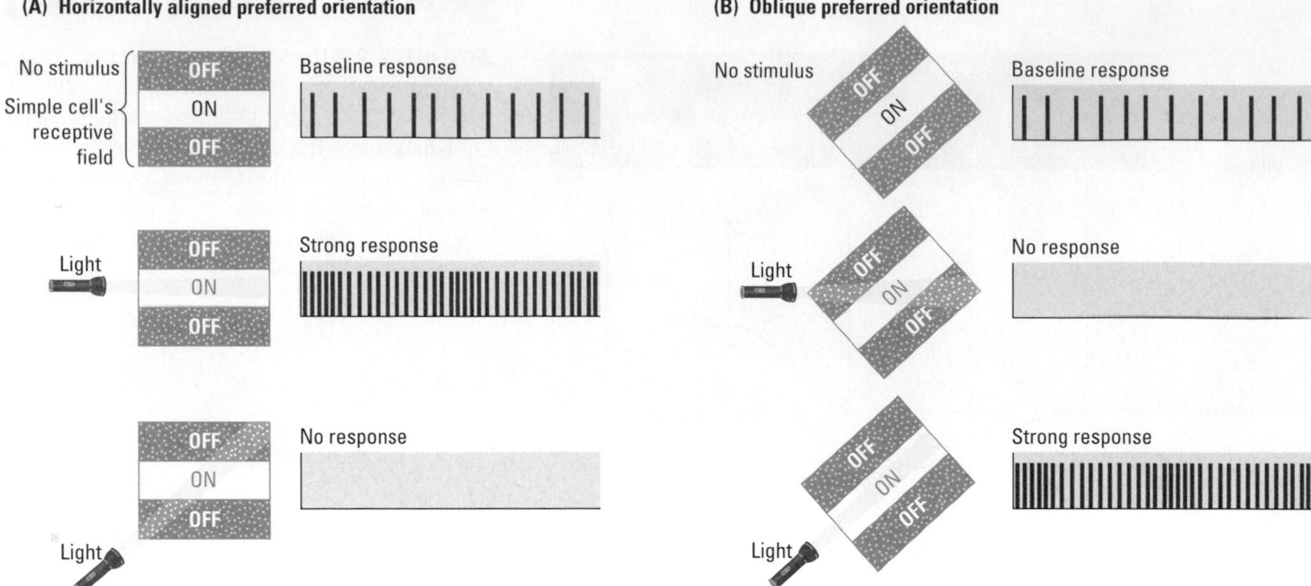

FIGURE 9-28 Typical Receptive Fields for Simple Visual-Cortex Cells. Simple cells respond to a bar of light in a particular orientation, such as horizontal **(A)** or oblique **(B)**. The position of the bar in the visual field is important, because the cell either responds (ON) or does not respond (OFF) to light in adjacent regions of the visual field.

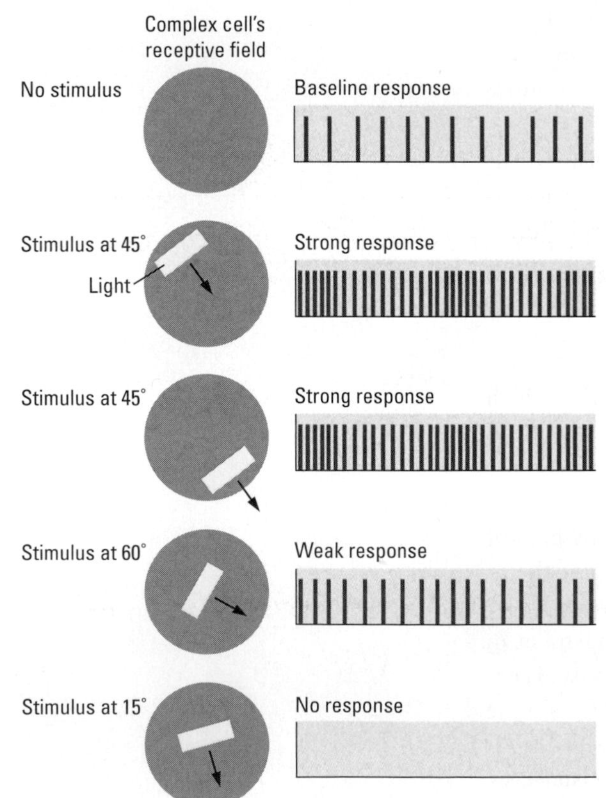

FIGURE 9-29 Receptive Field of a Complex Cell. Unlike a simple cell's on–off response pattern, a complex cell in the visual cortex shows the same response throughout its circular receptive field, responding best to bars of light moving at a particular angle. The response is reduced or absent with the bar of light at other orientations.

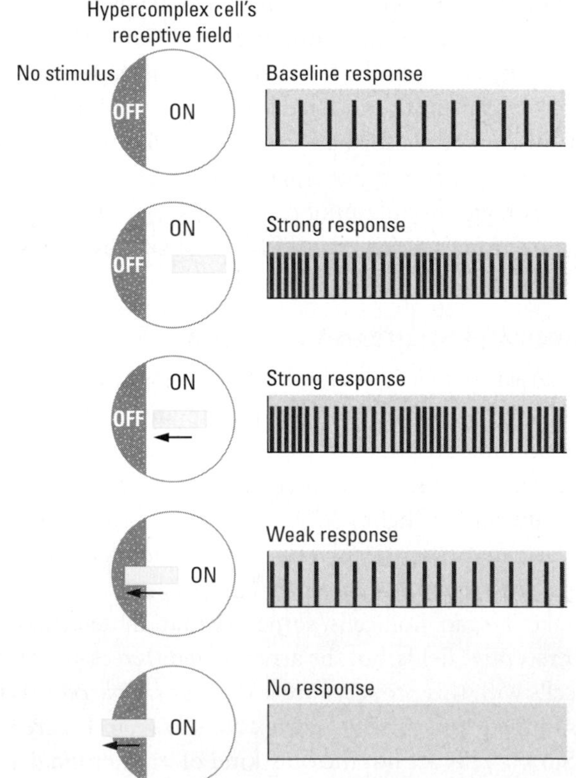

FIGURE 9-30 Receptive Field of a Hypercomplex Cell. A hypercomplex cell in the visual cortex responds to a moving bar of light in a particular orientation (horizontal, e.g.) anywhere in the excitatory (ON) part of its receptive field. If most of the bar extends into the inhibitory area (OFF), however, the response is inhibited.

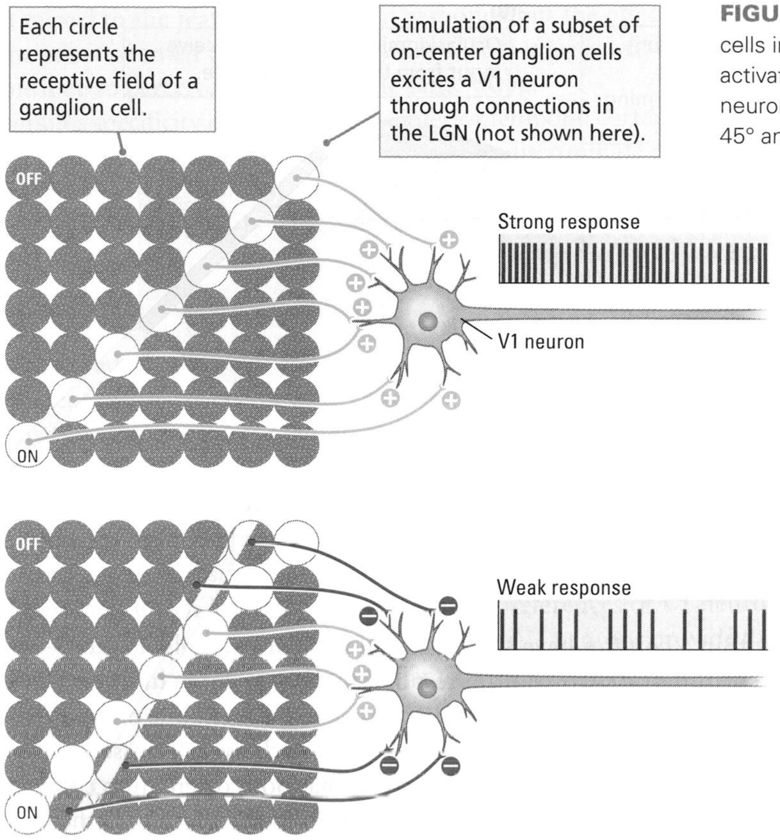

FIGURE 9-31 V1 Receptivity. A V1 cell responds to a row of ganglion cells in a particular orientation on the retina. The bar of light strongly activates a row of ganglion cells, each connected through the LGN to a V1 neuron. The activity of this V1 neuron is most affected by a bar of light at a 45° angle.

light landing on the right side of the hypercomplex cell's receptive field excites the cell; but, if, for example, the bar lands mainly on the inhibitory area to the left, the cell's firing is inhibited.

Note that each class of V1 neurons responds to bars of light in some way, yet this response results from input originating in retinal ganglion cells that respond maximally not to bars but to spots of light. How does this conversion from responding to spots to responding to bars take place? An example will help explain the process.

A thin bar of light falls on the retinal photoreceptors, striking the receptive fields of perhaps dozens of retinal ganglion cells. The input to a V1 neuron comes from a group of ganglion cells that happen to be aligned in a row, as in **Figure 9-31.** That V1 neuron will be activated (or inhibited) only when a bar of light hitting the retina strikes that particular row of ganglion cells. If the bar of light shines at a slightly different angle, only some of the retinal ganglion cells in the row will be activated, and so the V1 neuron will be excited only weakly.

Figure 9-31 illustrates the connection between light striking the retina in a certain pattern and the activation of a simple cell in the primary visual cortex, one that responds to a bar of light in a particular orientation. Using the same logic, we can also diagram the retinal receptive fields of complex or hypercomplex V1 neurons. Try it as an exercise yourself by adapting the format in Figure 9-31.

A characteristic of cortical structure is that the neurons are organized into functional columns. The pattern of connectivity in a column is vertical: inputs arrive in layer IV and then connect with cells in the other layers. **Figure 9-32** shows such a column, a 0.5-millimeter-diameter strip of cortex that includes representative neurons and their connections.

FIGURE 9-32 Neural Circuit in a Column in the Visual Cortex. In this three-dimensional view, sensory inputs terminate on stellate cells in layer IV. These stellate cells synapse with pyramidal cells in layers III and V in the same vertical column of tissue. Thus, the flow of information is vertical. The axons of the pyramidal cells leave the column to join with other columns or structures. Adapted from "The 'Module-Concept' in Cerebral Architecture," by J. Szentagothai, 1975, *Brain Research,* 95, p. 490.

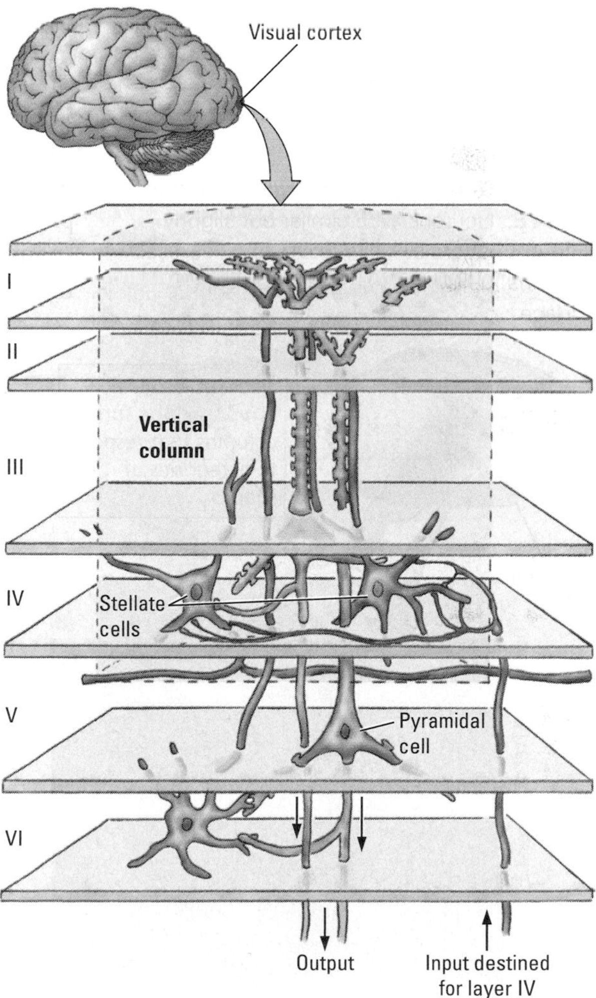

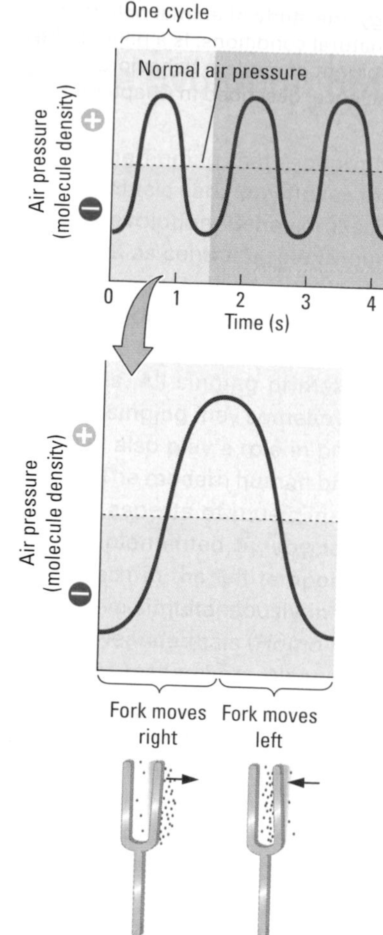

FIGURE 10-2 Visualizing a Sound Wave. Air-molecule density plotted against time at a particular point relative to the right prong of the tuning fork. Physicists call the resulting cyclical waves *sine waves.*

Properties of Sound Waves		
Frequency and pitch perception The rate at which sound waves vibrate is measured as cycles per second, or hertz (Hz).	Low frequency (low-pitched sound)	High frequency (high-pitched sound)
Amplitude and perception of loudness Intensity of sound is usually measured in decibels (dB).	High amplitude (loud sound)	Low amplitude (soft sound)
Complexity and timbre (perception of sound quality) Unlike the pure tone of a tuning fork, most sounds are a mixture of frequencies. A sound's complexity determines its timbre, allowing us to distinguish, for example, a trombone from a violin playing the same note.	Simple (pure tone)	Complex (mix of frequencies)

FIGURE 10-3 Physical Dimensions of Sound Waves. The frequency, amplitude, and complexity of sound-wave sensations correspond to the perceptual dimensions of pitch, loudness, and timbre.

The auditory system analyzes each property separately, just as the visual system analyzes color and form separately.

Sound-Wave Frequency

Although sound waves travel at a fixed speed of 1100 feet per second, sound energy varies in wavelength (frequency). More precisely, **frequency** is the number of cycles that a wave completes in a given amount of time. Sound-wave frequencies are measured in cycles per second, called **hertz** (Hz), named after the German physicist Heinrich Rudolph Hertz.

One hertz is 1 cycle per second; 50 hertz is 50 cycles per second; 6000 hertz is 6000 cycles per second; 20,000 hertz is 20,000 cycles per second; and so on. Sounds that we perceive as low in pitch have slower wave frequencies (fewer cycles per second), whereas sounds that we perceive as high pitched have faster wave frequencies (many cycles per second), as shown in the top panel of Figure 10-3.

Just as we can perceive light only at visible wavelengths, we can perceive sound waves in only a limited range of frequencies. These frequencies are plotted in **Figure 10-4.** Humans' hearing range is from about 20 to 20,000 hertz. Many animals communicate with sound, which means that their auditory systems are designed to interpret their species-typical sounds. After all, there is no point in making complicated songs or calls if other members of your species cannot hear them.

The range of sound-wave frequencies heard by different species varies extensively. Figure 10-4 shows that some species (such as frogs and birds) have rather narrow hearing ranges, whereas others (such as dogs, whales, and humans) have broad ranges. Some species use extremely high frequencies (bats are off the scale), whereas others use the low range (as do fish).

It is quite remarkable that the auditory systems of whales and dolphins are responsive to sound waves of such wide ranges. The characteristics at the extremes of these frequencies allow marine mammals to use them in different ways. Very-low-frequency sound waves travel long distances in water; whales produce them as a form of underwater communication over miles of distance. High-frequency sound waves create echoes and form the basis of sonar. Dolphins produce them in bursts, listening

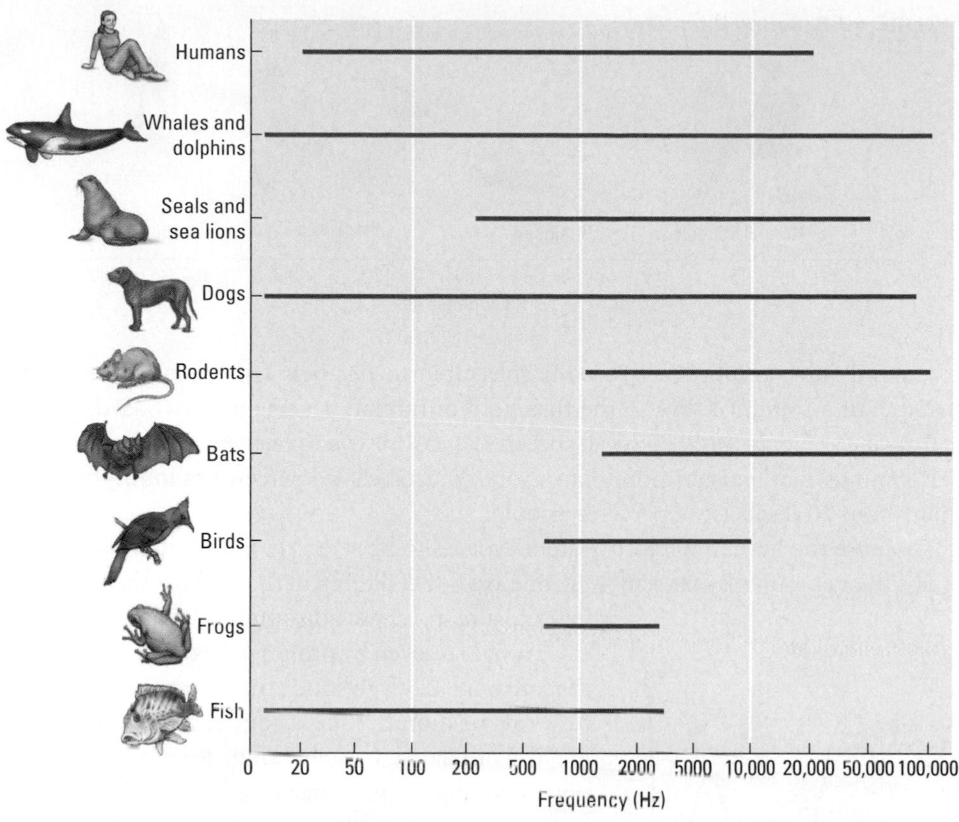

FIGURE 10-4 Hearing Ranges among Animals. Frogs and birds hear a relatively narrow range of frequencies; whales and dolphins have an extensive range, as do dogs. Although the human hearing range is fairly broad, we do not perceive many sound frequencies that other animals can both make and hear.

for the echoes that bounce back from objects and help the dolphins to navigate and locate prey.

As stated earlier, differences in the frequency of sound waves become differences in pitch when heard. Consequently, each note in a musical scale must have a different frequency because each has a different pitch. Middle C on the piano, for instance, has a frequency of 264 hertz.

Most people can discriminate between one musical note and another, but some can actually name any note that they hear (A, B flat, C sharp, and so forth). This *perfect* (or *absolute*) *pitch* runs in families, suggesting a genetic influence. On the side of experience, most people who develop perfect pitch also receive musical training in matching pitch to note from an early age.

The difference in the ability of people's auditory systems to distinguish pitch may be analogous to differences in the ability to perceive the color red, discussed in Chapter 9.

Sound-Wave Amplitude

Sound waves vary not only in frequency, causing differences in perceived pitch, but also in strength, or amplitude, causing differences in perceived *intensity,* or *loudness.* An example will help you understand the difference between the amplitude and the frequency of a sound wave.

If you hit a tuning fork lightly, it produces a tone with a frequency of, say, 264 hertz (middle C). If you hit it harder, you still produce a frequency of 264 hertz but you also transfer more energy into the vibrating prong. It now moves farther left and right but at the same frequency. This greater energy is due to an increased quantity of air molecules compressed in each wave, even though the same middle C frequency (number of waves) is created every second.

This new dimension of energy in the sound wave is **amplitude,** the magnitude of change in air-molecule density. Increased compression of air molecules intensifies the energy in a sound wave, which "amps" the sound—makes it louder. Differences in amplitude are graphed by increasing the height of a sound wave, as shown in the middle panel of Figure 10-3.

Frequency Number of cycles that a wave completes in a given amount of time.
Hertz (Hz) Measure of frequency (repetition rate) of a sound wave; 1 hertz is equal to 1 cycle per second.
Amplitude Intensity of a stimulus; in audition, roughly equivalent to loudness, graphed by increasing the height of a sound wave.

FIGURE 10-5 Sound Intensity.

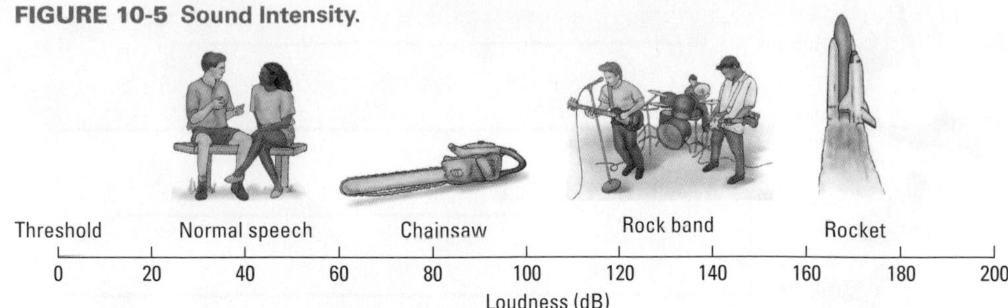

Sound-wave amplitude is usually measured in **decibels** (dB), a measure of the strength of a sound relative to the threshold of human hearing as a standard, pegged at 0 decibels (**Figure 10-5**). Normal speech sounds, for example, measure about 40 decibels. Sounds that register more than about 70 decibels we perceive as loud; those less than about 20 decibels we perceive as quiet.

Because the human nervous system evolved to be sensitive to soft sounds, it is literally "blown away" by extremely strong ones. People regularly damage their hearing by exposure to very loud sounds (such as rifle fire at close range) or even by prolonged exposure to sounds that are only relatively loud (such as at a live concert). As a rule of thumb, sounds louder than 100 decibels are likely to damage our hearing, especially if our exposure to them is prolonged.

Heavy-metal bands, among others, routinely play music that registers higher than 120 decibels and sometimes as high as 135 decibels. One researcher (Drake-Lee, 1992) found that rock musicians had a significant loss of sensitivity to sound waves, especially at about 6000 hertz. After a typical 90-minute concert, this loss was temporarily far worse—as much as a 40-fold increase in sound pressure was needed to reach a musician's hearing threshold. But the rock concert is not the only music venue that can damage hearing. Teie (1998) reports that symphony orchestras also produce dangerously high sound levels and that hearing loss is common among symphony musicians.

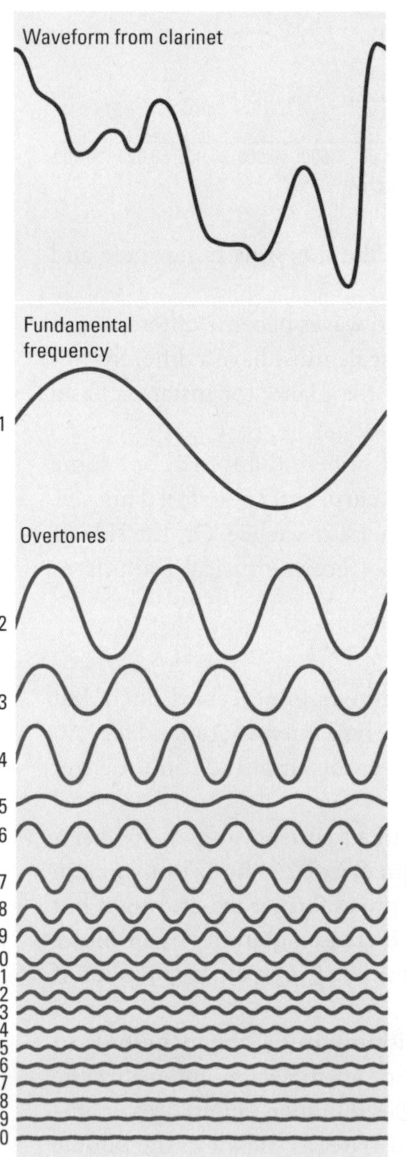
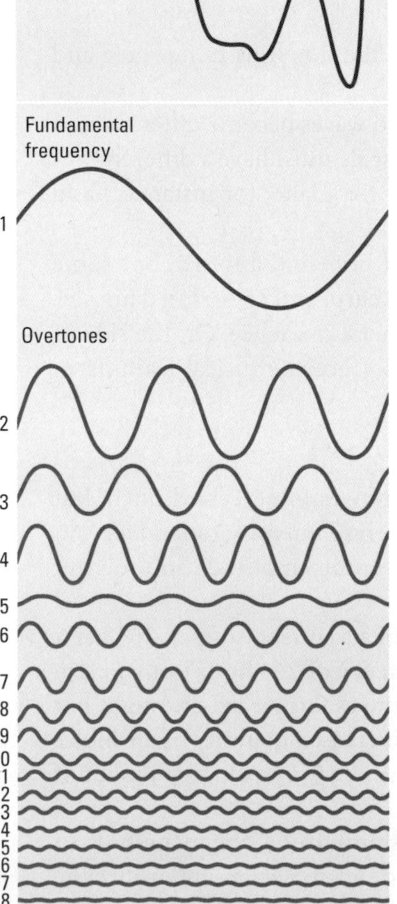

FIGURE 10-6 Breaking Down a Complex Tone. The wave shape of a single note from Don Byron's clarinet (*top*) and the component frequencies—the fundamental frequency (*middle*) and overtones (*bottom*)—that make up this complex tone. From *Stereo Review*, copyright 1977 by Diamandis Communications Inc.

Sound-Wave Complexity

Sounds with a single frequency wave are pure tones, much like those that emanate from a tuning fork or pitch pipe, but most sounds mix wave frequencies together in combinations and so are called *complex tones*. To better understand the blended nature of a complex tone, picture a clarinetist, such as Don Byron in **Figure 10-6,** playing a steady note. The upper graph in Figure 10-6 represents the sound wave produced by the clarinet.

Notice that the clarinet waveform has a more complex pattern than the simple, regular waves described earlier in this chapter. Even when a musician plays a single note, the instrument is making a complex, not a pure, tone. Using a mathematical technique known as Fourier analysis, we can break this complex tone into its many component pure tones, the numbered waves at the bottom of Figure 10-6.

The *fundamental frequency* (wave 1) is the rate at which the complex waveform pattern repeats. Waves 2 through 20 are *overtones,* a set of higher-frequency sound waves that vibrate at whole-number (integer) multiples of the fundamental frequency. Different musical instruments sound unique because they produce overtones of different amplitudes. Among the clarinet overtones, represented by the heights of the blue waves in Figure 10-6, wave 5 is low amplitude, whereas wave 2 is high amplitude.

Like primary colors, pure tones can be blended into complex tones in an almost infinite variety. In addition to emanating from musical instruments, complex tones emanate from the human voice, from birdsong, and from machines or repetitive mechanisms that give rise to rhythmic buzzing or humming sounds. A key feature of complex tones, besides being made up of two or more pure tones, is some sort of periodicity. The fundamental frequency repeats at regular intervals. Sounds that are aperiodic, or random, we call *noise.*

Figure 9-35 shows the primary colors used in additive and subtractive color mixing.

Perception of Sound

To better understand the relation between the energy of sound-wave sensations and sound perceptions, think about what happens when you toss a pebble into a pond. Waves of water emanate from the point where the pebble enters the water. These waves produce no audible sound. But, if your skin were able to convert the energy of the water waves into neural activity that stimulated your auditory system, you would "hear" the waves when you placed your hand into the rippling water. When you removed your hand, the "sound" would stop.

The pebble hitting the water is much like a falling tree, and the waves that emanate from the pebble's point of entry are like the air-pressure waves that emanate from the place where the tree strikes the ground. The frequency of the waves determines the pitch of the sound heard by the brain, whereas the height (amplitude) of the waves determines the sound's loudness.

Our sensitivity to sound waves is extraordinary. At the threshold of human hearing, we can detect the displacement of air molecules of about 10 picometers. We are rarely in an environment where we can detect such a small air-pressure change, because there is usually too much background noise. A very quiet rural setting is probably as close as we ever get to an environment suitable for testing the acuteness of our hearing. The next time you visit the countryside, take note of the sounds that you can hear. If there is no sound competition, you can often hear a single car engine miles away.

1 picometer = one-trillionth of a meter

In addition to detecting very small changes in air pressure, the auditory system is also adept at simultaneously perceiving different sounds. As you sit reading this chapter, you are able to differentiate all sorts of sounds around you—traffic on the street, people talking next door, your air conditioner humming, footsteps in the hall. If you are listening to music, you detect the sounds of different instruments and voices.

You can perceive different sounds simultaneously because the different frequencies of air-pressure change associated with each sound wave stimulate different neurons in your auditory system. The perception of sounds is only the beginning of your auditory experience. Your brain interprets sounds to obtain information about events in your environment, and it analyzes a sound's meaning. Your use of sound to communicate with other people through both language and music clearly illustrate these processes.

Decibel (dB) Unit for measuring the relative physical intensity of sounds.

Loomis Dean/Time Life Pictures/Getty Images

Elvis Presley's memory for lyrics suits his legend: while serving in the U.S. Army, he wagered all comers that he could sing any song they named. Elvis never lost a bet.

Properties of Language and Music As Sounds

Language and music differ from other auditory sensations in fundamental ways. Both convey meaning and evoke emotion. The analysis of meaning in sound is a considerably more complex behavior than simply detecting a sound and identifying it. The brain has evolved systems that analyze sounds for meaning, speech in the left temporal lobe and music in the right.

Infants are receptive to speech and musical cues before they have any obvious utility, suggesting the innate presence of these skills. Humans have an amazing capacity for learning and remembering linguistic and musical information. We are capable of learning a vocabulary of tens of thousands of words, often in many languages, and we have a capacity for recognizing thousands of songs.

Language facilitates communication. We can organize our complex perceptual worlds by categorizing information with words. We can tell others what we think and know and imagine. Imagine the efficiency that gestures and spoken language added to the cooperative food hunting and gathering behaviors of early humans.

All these benefits of oral language seem obvious, but the benefits of music may seem less straightforward. In fact, music helps us to regulate our own emotions and to affect the emotions of others. After all, when do people most commonly make music? We sing and play music to communicate with infants and put children to sleep. We play music to enhance social interactions and gatherings and romance. We use music to bolster group identification—school songs or national anthems are examples.

A sound segment is a distinct unit of sound.

Another characteristic that distinguishes speech and musical sounds from other auditory inputs is their delivery speed. Nonspeech and nonmusical noise produced at a rate of about 5 segments per second is perceived as a buzz. Normal speed for speech is on the order of 8 to 10 segments per second, and we are capable of understanding speech at nearly 30 segments per second. Speech perception at these higher rates is truly amazing, because the speed of input far exceeds the auditory system's ability to transmit all the speech as separate pieces of information.

Properties of Language

Experience in listening to a particular language helps the brain to analyze rapid speech, which is one reason why people who are speaking languages unfamiliar to you often seem to be talking incredibly fast. Your brain does not know where the foreign words end and begin, making them seem to run together in a rapid-fire stream.

This auditory constancy is reminiscent of the visual system's capacity for object constancy described in Chapter 9.

A unique characteristic of our perception of speech sounds is our tendency to hear variations of a sound as if they were identical, even though the sound varies considerably from one context to another. For instance, the English letter "d" is pronounced differently in the words "deep," "deck," and "duke," yet a listener perceives the pronunciations to be the same "d" sound.

The auditory system must therefore have a mechanism for categorizing sounds as being the same despite small differences in pronunciation. This mechanism, moreover, must be affected by experience, because different languages categorize speech sounds differently. A major obstacle to mastering a foreign language after the age of 10 is the difficulty of learning the categories of sound that are treated as equivalent.

Properties of Music

Like other sounds, musical sounds differ from one another in the subjective properties that people perceive in them. One subjective property is *loudness,* the magnitude of the sound as judged by a person. Loudness is related to the amplitude of a sound wave and is measured in decibels, but loudness is also subjective. What is "very loud" music for one person may be only "moderately loud" for another, whereas music that seems "soft" to one listener may not seem soft at all to someone else.

Prosody Melodical tone of the spoken voice.

Another subjective property of musical sounds is *pitch,* the position of each tone on a musical scale as judged by the listener. Although pitch is clearly related to sound-wave frequency, there is more to it than that. Consider the note middle C as played on a piano. This note can be described as a pattern of sound frequencies, as is the clarinet note in Figure 10-6.

Like the note played on the piano, any musical note is defined by its fundamental frequency. This is the lowest frequency of the sound-wave pattern, or the rate at which the overall pattern is repeated. For middle C, the fundamental frequency is 264 Hertz and the sound waves for notes C, E, and G, as measured by a spectrograph, are shown in **Figure 10-7.** Notice that, by convention, sound-wave spectrographs are measured in kilohertz (kHz), units of thousands of hertz. Thus, if we look at the fundamental frequency for middle C, it is the first large wave on the left, which is at 0.264 kilohertz. The fundamental frequencies for E and G are 0.330 and 0.392 kilohertz, respectively.

An important feature of the human brain's analysis of music is that middle C is perceived as being the same note regardless of whether it is played on a piano or on a guitar, even though the sounds made by these instruments are very different. The right temporal lobe has a special function in extracting pitch from sound, whether the sound is speech or music. In speech, pitch contributes to the perceived melodical tone of a voice, or **prosody.**

A final property of musical sound is *quality,* the characteristics that distinguish a particular sound from all others of similar pitch and loudness. We can easily distinguish the sound of a violin from that of a trombone even though the same note is being played on both instruments at the same loudness. The quality of their sounds differs. The French word *timbre* is normally used to describe perceived sound quality.

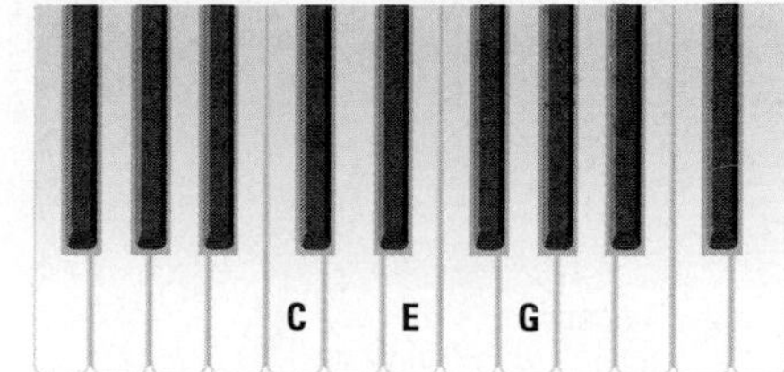

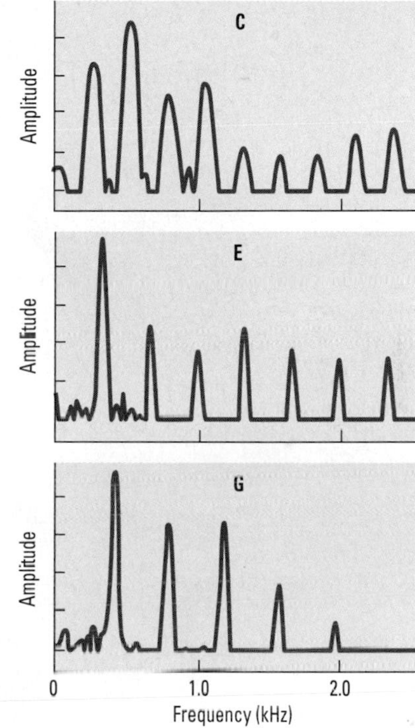

FIGURE 10-7 Fundamental Frequencies of Piano Notes. Waveforms of the notes C, E, and G as played on a piano and recorded on a spectrograph. The first wave in each graph is the fundamental frequency; the secondary waves are the overtones. Courtesy of D. Rendall.

REVIEW: Sound Waves: The Stimulus for Audition

- ✔ Sound energy, the physical stimulus for the auditory system, is produced by changes in pressure waves that are converted into neural activity in the ear.
- ✔ Sound waves have three key qualities: frequency, amplitude, and complexity.
- ✔ Combinations of these qualities allow the human auditory system to comprehend sounds as complex as language and music.
- ✔ Frequency is the rate at which the waves vibrate and roughly corresponds to the high or low pitch of the sound that we perceive.
- ✔ Amplitude, or wave height, is the magnitude of change in air-molecule pressure that the wave undergoes and roughly corresponds to perceived loudness.
- ✔ Complexity refers to the particular mixture of frequencies that create a sound's perceived uniqueness, or timbre.

Functional Anatomy of the Auditory System

To understand how the nervous system analyzes sound waves, we begin by tracing the pathway taken by sound energy to and through the brain. The ear collects sound waves from the surrounding air and converts their mechanical energy into electrochemical neural energy that begins a long route through the brainstem to the auditory cortex.

Before we can trace the journey from the ear to the cortex, we need to ask what the auditory system is designed to do. Because sound waves have the properties of frequency, amplitude, and complexity, we can predict that the auditory system is structured to code these properties. Most animals can tell where a sound comes from, so there must be some mechanism for locating sound waves in space. Finally, many animals, including

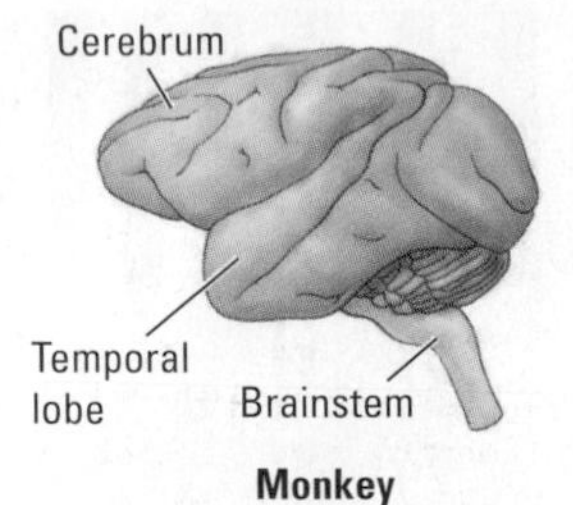

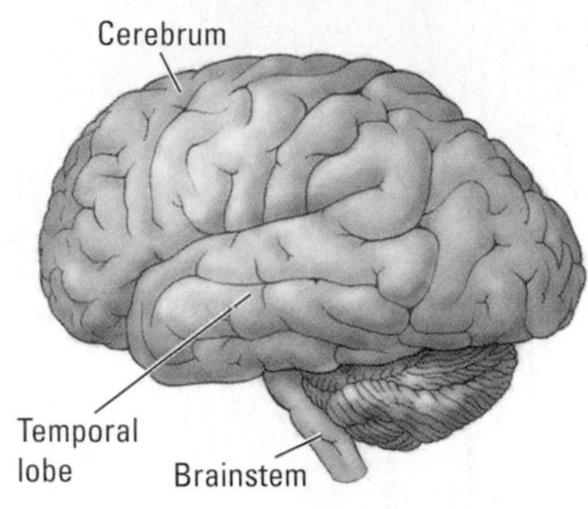

humans, not only analyze sounds for meaning but also themselves make sounds. Because the sounds they produce are often the same as the ones they hear, we can infer that the neural systems for sound production and analysis must be closely related.

In humans, the evolution of sound-processing systems for both language and music led to the enhancement of specialized cortical regions, especially in the temporal lobes. In fact, a major difference between the human and the monkey cortex is a marked expansion of auditory areas in humans.

Structure of the Ear

The ear is a biological masterpiece in three acts: the outer, middle, and inner ear, all illustrated in **Figure 10-8.**

Processing Sound Waves

Both the *pinna,* the funnel-like external structure of the outer ear, and the external ear canal, which extends a short distance from the pinna inside the head, are made of cartilage and flesh. The pinna is designed to catch sound waves in the surrounding environment and deflect them into the external ear canal.

The external canal, because it narrows from the pinna, amplifies sound waves somewhat and directs them to the *eardrum* at its inner end. When sound waves strike the eardrum, it vibrates, the rate of vibration varying with the frequency of the waves. On

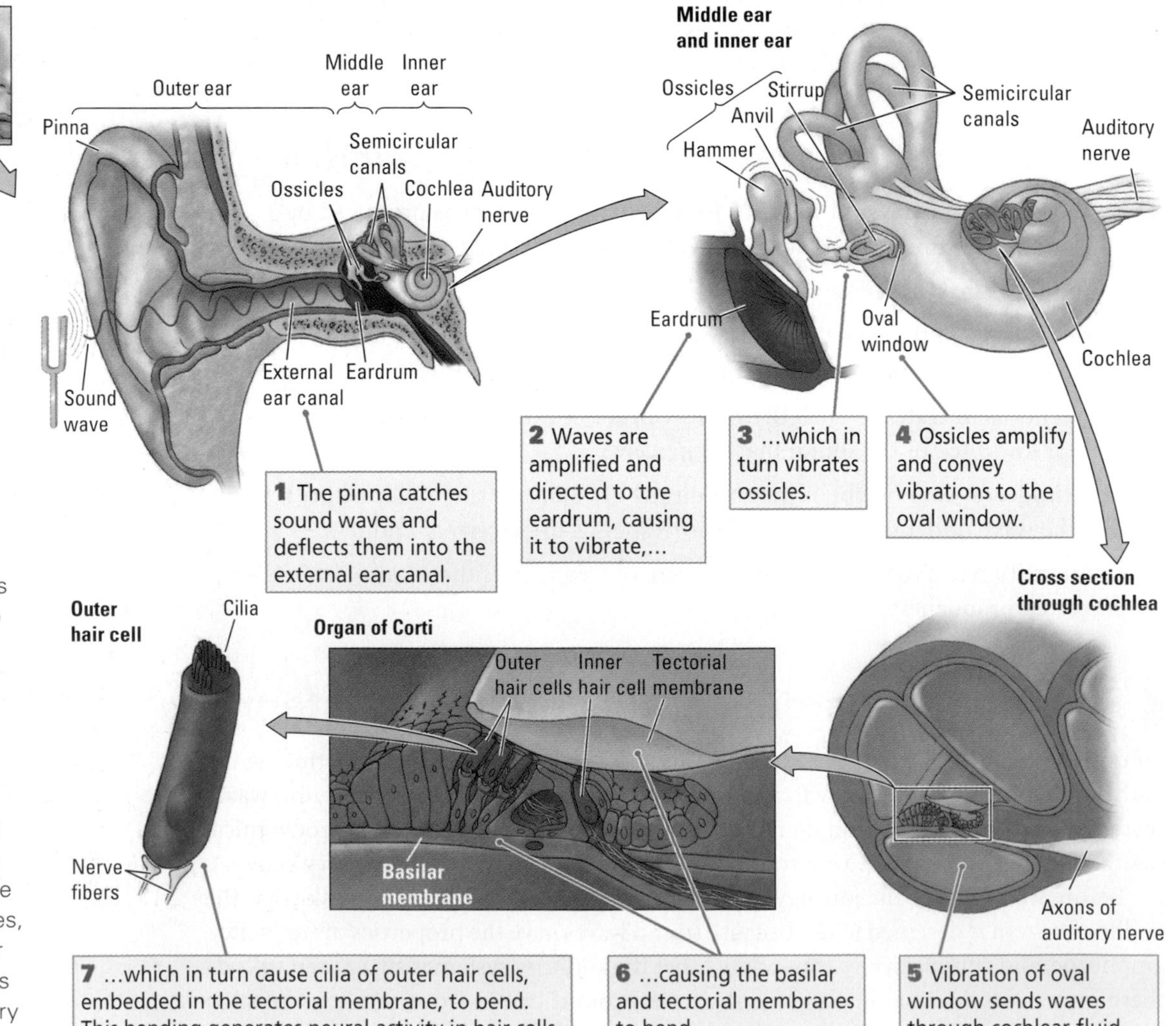

FIGURE 10-8 Anatomy of the Human Ear. Sound waves gathered into the outer ear are transduced from air pressure into mechanical energy in the middle-ear ossicles and into electrochemical activity in the inner-ear cochlea. Hair cells embedded in the basilar membrane (the organ of Corti) are tipped by cilia. The cilia are displaced by movements of the basilar and tectorial membranes, leading to changes in the inner hair cells' membrane potentials and resultant activity of auditory bipolar neurons.

the inner side of the eardrum, as depicted in Figure 10-8, is the middle ear, an air-filled chamber that contains the three smallest bones in the human body, connected to one another in a series.

These three **ossicles** are called the *hammer,* the *anvil,* and the *stirrup* because of their distinctive shapes. The ossicles attach the eardrum to the *oval window,* an opening in the bony casing of the **cochlea,** the inner-ear structure that contains the auditory receptor cells. These receptor cells and the cells that support them are collectively called the *organ of Corti,* shown in detail in Figure 10-8.

When sound waves vibrate the eardrum, the vibrations are transmitted to the ossicles. The ossicles' leverlike action conveys and amplifies the vibrations onto the membrane that covers the cochlea's oval window. As Figure 10-8 shows, the cochlea coils around itself and looks a bit like a snail shell. Inside its bony exterior, the cochlea is hollow, as the cross-sectional drawing reveals.

The hollow cochlear compartments are filled with a lymphatic fluid, and floating in its midst is the thin **basilar membrane.** Embedded in a part of the basilar membrane are outer and inner **hair cells.** At the tip of each hair cell are several filaments called *cilia,* and the cilia of the outer hair cells are embedded in an overlying membrane. The inner hair cells loosely contact this *tectorial membrane.*

Pressure from the stirrup on the oval window makes the cochlear fluid move because a second membranous window in the cochlea (the *round window*) bulges outward as the stirrup presses inward on the oval window. In a chain reaction, the waves that travel through the cochlear fluid cause the basilar and tectorial membranes to bend, and the bending membranes stimulate the cilia at the tips of the outer hair cells. This stimulation generates graded potentials in the inner hair cells, which act as the auditory receptor cells. The change in the membrane potential of the inner hair cells varies the amount of neurotransmitter that they release onto auditory neurons that go to the brain.

Ossicles Bones of the middle ear: malleus (hammer), incus (anvil), and stapes (stirrup).
Cochlea Inner-ear structure that contains the auditory receptor cells.
Basilar membrane Receptor surface in the cochlea that transduces sound waves into neural activity.
Hair cell Sensory neurons in the cochlea tipped by cilia; when stimulated by waves in the cochlear fluid, outer hair cells generate graded potentials in inner hair cells, which act as the auditory receptor cells.

The name *cochlea* derives from the Latin word for "snail."

Graded potentials are part of the cell membrane's electrical activity, as Chapter 4 explains.

Transducing Sound Waves into Neural Impulses

The key question is how the conversion of sound waves into neural activity codes the various properties of sound that we perceive. In the late 1800s, German physiologist Hermann von Helmholtz proposed that sound waves of different frequencies cause different parts of the basilar membrane to resonate. Von Helmholtz was not precisely correct. Actually, all parts of the basilar membrane bend in response to incoming waves of any frequency. The key is where on the basilar membrane the peak displacement takes place.

This solution to the coding puzzle was not determined until 1960, when George von Békésy was able to observe the basilar membrane directly. He saw that a traveling wave moves along the membrane all the way from the oval window to the membrane's apex. The structure and function of the basilar membrane are easier to visualize if the cochlea is uncoiled and laid flat, as in **Figure 10-9.**

The uncoiling structure in Figure 10-9A maps the frequencies to which each part of the basilar membrane is most responsive. When the oval window vibrates in response

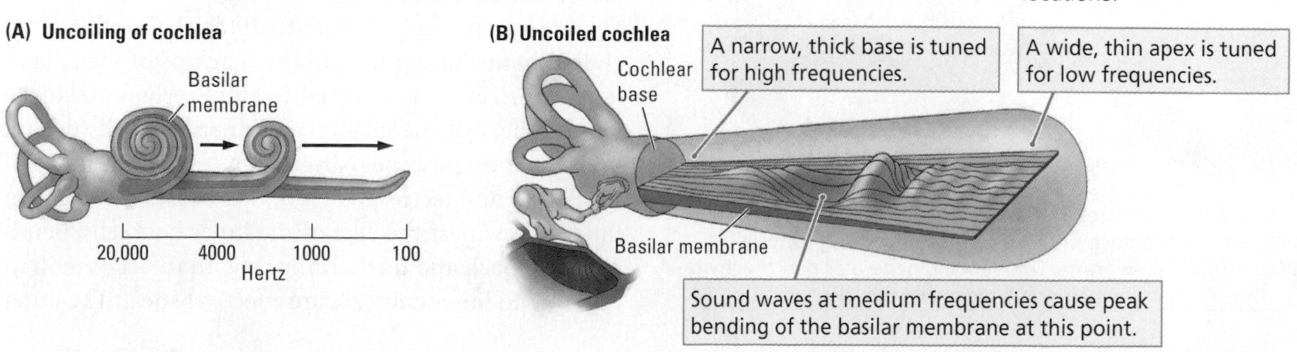
(A) Uncoiling of cochlea
Basilar membrane
20,000
4000
1000
100
Hertz
(B) Uncoiled cochlea
Cochlear base
A narrow, thick base is tuned for high frequencies.
A wide, thin apex is tuned for low frequencies.
Basilar membrane
Sound waves at medium frequencies cause peak bending of the basilar membrane at this point.

FIGURE 10-9 Anatomy of the Cochlea. (A) The frequencies to which the basilar membrane is maximally responsive are mapped as the cochlea uncoils. (B) Sound waves of different frequencies produce maximal displacement of the basilar membrane (shown uncoiled) at different locations.

Medial geniculate nucleus Major thalamic region concerned with audition.

Primary auditory cortex (area A1) Asymmetrical structures, found within Heschl's gyrus in the temporal lobes, that receive input from the ventral region of the medial geniculate nucleus.

to the vibrations of the ossicles, shown in Figure 10-9B, it generates waves that travel through the cochlear fluid. Békésy placed little grains of silver along the basilar membrane and watched them jump in different places with different frequencies of incoming waves. Faster wave frequencies caused maximum peaks of displacement near the base of the basilar membrane; slower wave frequencies caused maximum displacement peaks near the membrane's apex.

As a rough analogy, consider what happens when you shake a rope. If you shake it very quickly, the rope waves are very small and short and remain close to the hand holding the rope. But if you shake the rope slowly with a broader movement, the longer waves reach their peak farther along the rope. The key point is that, although both rapid and slow shakes of the rope produce movement along the rope's entire length, the maximum displacement of the rope is found at one end or the other, depending on whether the wave movements are rapid or slow.

This same response pattern is true of the basilar membrane to sound-wave frequency. All sound waves cause some displacement along the entire length of the basilar membrane, but the amount of displacement at any point varies with the frequency of the sound wave. In the human cochlea, shown uncoiling in Figure 10-9A, the basilar membrane near the oval window is maximally affected by frequencies as high as about 20,000 hertz, whereas the most effective frequencies at the membrane's apex register less than 100 hertz.

Intermediate frequencies maximally displace points on the basilar membrane between its two ends, as shown in Figure 10-9B. When a wave of a certain frequency travels down the basilar membrane, hair cells at the point of peak displacement are stimulated, resulting in a maximal neural response in those cells. An incoming signal composed of many frequencies causes several different points along the basilar membrane to vibrate and excites hair cells at all these points.

Not surprisingly, the basilar membrane is much more sensitive to changes in frequency than the rope in our analogy is. This degree of sensitivity is achieved because the basilar membrane varies in thickness along its entire length. It is narrow and thick at the base, near the oval window, and wider and thinner at its tightly coiled apex. The combination of varying width and thickness enhances the effect of small differences in frequency on the basilar membrane. As a result, the cochlear receptors can code small differences in sound-wave frequency as neural impulses.

FIGURE 10-10 Transducing Waves into Neural Activity. Movement of the basilar membrane creates a shearing force in the cochlear fluid that bends the cilia, leading to the opening or closing of calcium channels in the outer hair cells. The influx of calcium ions leads to the release of transmitter by the inner hair cells, which stimulates an increase in action potentials in auditory neurons.

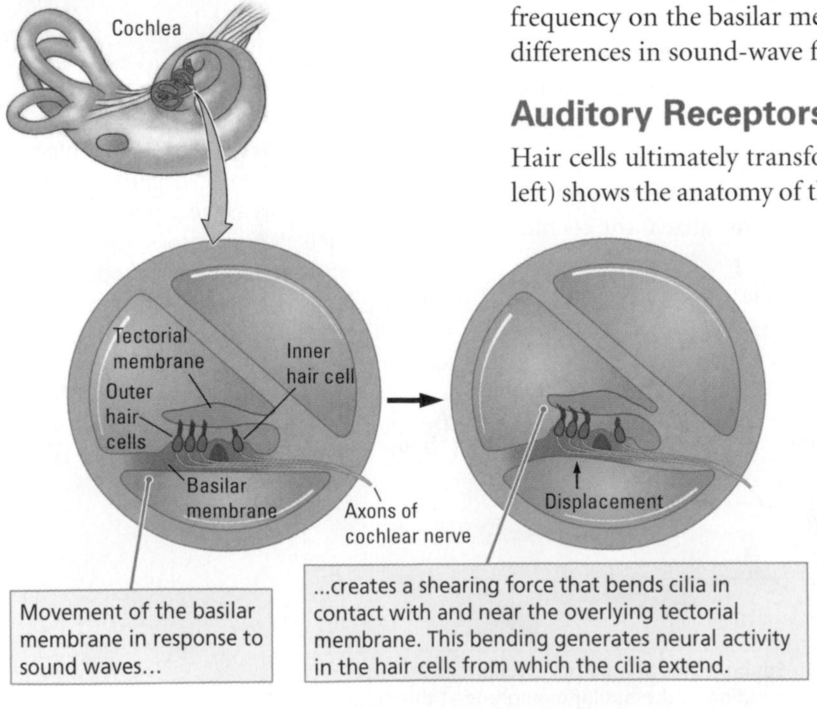

Movement of the basilar membrane in response to sound waves...

...creates a shearing force that bends cilia in contact with and near the overlying tectorial membrane. This bending generates neural activity in the hair cells from which the cilia extend.

Auditory Receptors

Hair cells ultimately transform sound waves into neural activity. Figure 10-8 (bottom left) shows the anatomy of the hair cells; **Figure 10-10** illustrates how sound waves stimulate them. The human cochlea has two sets of hair cells: 3500 inner hair cells and 12,000 outer hair cells. Only the inner hair cells are the auditory receptors. This total number of receptor cells is small, considering the number of different sounds we can hear.

As diagrammed in Figure 10-10, the hair cells are anchored in the basilar membrane. The tips of the cilia of outer hair cells are attached to the overlying tectorial membrane, but the cilia of the inner hair cells do not touch that membrane. Nevertheless, the movement of the basilar and tectorial membranes causes the cochlear fluid to flow past the cilia of the inner hair cells, bending them back and forth. Animals with intact outer hair cells but no inner hair cells are effectively deaf. The outer hair cells function simply to sharpen the resolving power of the cochlea by contracting or relaxing and thereby changing the stiffness of the tectorial membrane.

How this function of the outer hair cells is controlled is puzzling. What stimulates these cells to contract or relax? The answer seems to be that the outer hair cells, through connections with axons in the auditory nerve, send a message to the brainstem auditory areas and receive a message back that causes the outer hair cells to alter tension on the tectorial membrane. In this way, the brain helps the hair cells to create an auditory world.

A final question remains: How does movement of the cilia alter neural activity? The neurons of the auditory nerve have a spontaneous baseline rate of firing action potentials, and this rate is changed by how much neurotransmitter is released from the hair cells. It turns out that movement of the hair-cell cilia causes a change in polarization of the hair cell and a change in neurotransmitter release. Look at Figure 10-8 again and you'll notice that the cilia of a hair cell differ in height.

Movement of the cilia in the direction of the tallest results in depolarization, opening calcium channels and leading to the release of neurotransmitter onto the dendrites of the cells that form the auditory nerve, generating more nerve impulses. Movement in the direction of the shortest cilia hyperpolarizes the cell membrane and transmitter release decreases, thus decreasing activity in auditory neurons.

You can review the phases and propagation of the action potential in Chapter 4.

Hair cells are amazingly sensitive to the movement of their cilia. A movement sufficient to allow sound-wave detection is only about 0.3 nm, about the diameter of a large atom. We now can understand why our hearing is so incredibly sensitive.

Pathways to the Auditory Cortex

The inner hair cells in the organ of Corti synapse with neighboring bipolar cells, the axons of which form the auditory (cochlear) nerve. The auditory nerve in turn forms part of the eighth cranial nerve, which governs hearing and balance. Whereas ganglion cells in the eye receive inputs from many receptor cells, bipolar cells in the ear receive input from only a single hair-cell receptor.

Figure 2-25 lists and locates all the cranial nerves.

The cochlear-nerve axons enter the brainstem at the level of the medulla and synapse in the cochlear nucleus, which has ventral and dorsal subdivisions. Two other nearby structures in the brainstem, the superior olive (a nucleus in the olivary complex) and the trapezoid body, each receive connections from the cochlear nucleus, as charted in **Figure 10-11.** The projections from the cochlear nucleus connect with cells on the same side of the brain as well as with cells on the opposite side. This arrangement mixes the inputs from the two ears to form the perception of a single sound.

Both the cochlear nucleus and the superior olive send projections to the inferior colliculus in the dorsal midbrain. Two distinct pathways emerge from the inferior colliculus, coursing to the **medial geniculate nucleus,** which lies in the thalamus. The ventral region of the medial geniculate nucleus projects to the **primary auditory cortex (area A1),** whereas the dorsal region projects to the auditory cortical regions adjacent to area A1.

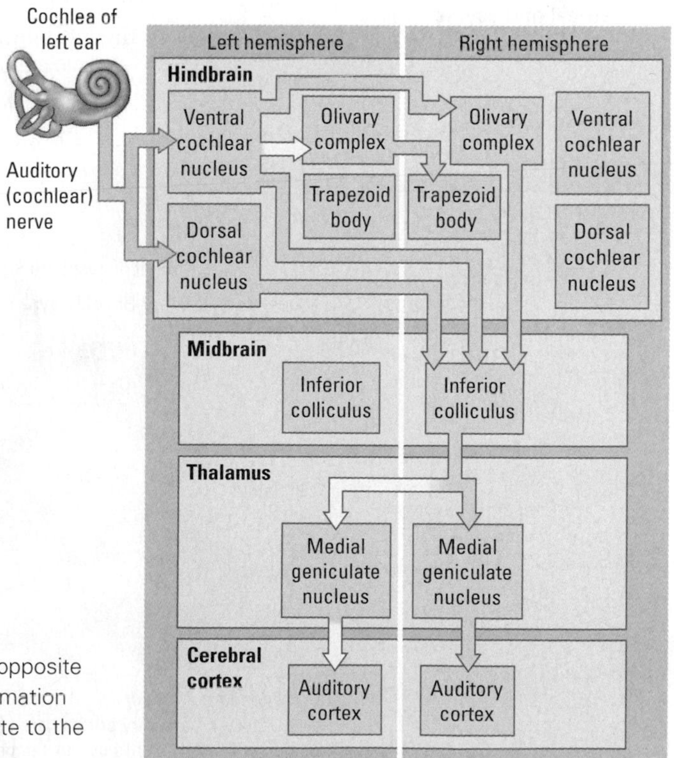

FIGURE 10-11 Auditory Pathway. Auditory inputs cross to the hemisphere opposite the ear in the hindbrain and midbrain, then recross in the thalamus so that information from each ear reaches both hemispheres. Multiple nuclei process inputs en route to the auditory cortex, charted here for the left ear.

Figure 9-13 maps the visual pathways through the cortex.

Analogous to the two distinct visual pathways—the ventral stream for object recognition and the dorsal stream for the visual control of movement—a similar distinction exists in the auditory cortex (Romanski et al., 1999). Just as we can identify objects by their sound characteristics, we can direct our movements by the sound that we hear. The role of sound in guiding movement is less familiar to sight-dominated people than it is to the blind. Nevertheless, the ability exists in us all. Imagine waking up in the dark and reaching to pick up a ringing telephone or to turn off an alarm clock. Your hand automatically forms the appropriate shape needed to carry out these movements just on the basis of the sound that you have heard.

That sound is guiding your movements much as a visual image guides them. Although relatively little is known about the what-how auditory pathways in the cortex, one appears to continue through the temporal lobe, much like the ventral visual pathway, and plays a role in identifying auditory stimuli. A second auditory pathway apparently goes to the posterior parietal region, where it forms a type of dorsal route for the auditory control of movement.

Auditory Cortex

In humans, the primary auditory cortex (A1) lies within Heschl's gyrus and is surrounded by secondary cortical areas (A2), as shown in **Figure 10-12**A. The secondary cortex lying behind Heschl's gyrus is called the *planum temporale* (meaning "temporal plane").

In right-handed people, the planum temporale is larger on the left side of the brain than it is on the right, whereas Heschl's gyrus is larger on the right side than on the left. The cortex of the left planum forms a speech zone, known as **Wernicke's area** (the posterior speech zone), whereas the cortex of the larger, right-hemisphere Heschl's gyrus has a special role in the analysis of music.

Recall the principle from Chapter 2: although the left and the right hemispheres look like mirror images, the brain is both symmetrical and asymmetrical.

These hemispheric differences mean that the auditory cortex is anatomically and functionally asymmetrical. Although cerebral asymmetry is not unique to the auditory system, it is most obvious here because the auditory analysis of speech takes place only in the left hemisphere of right-handed people. About 70 percent of left-handed people

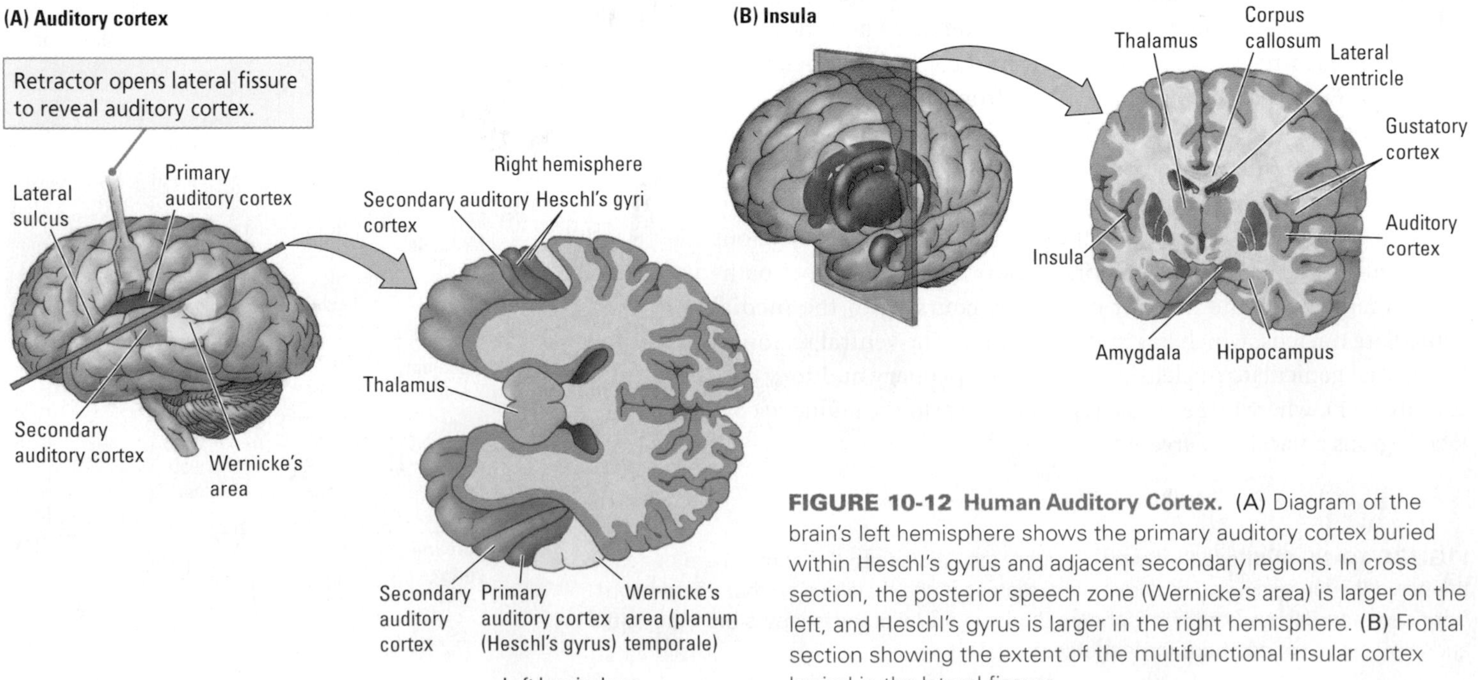

FIGURE 10-12 Human Auditory Cortex. (A) Diagram of the brain's left hemisphere shows the primary auditory cortex buried within Heschl's gyrus and adjacent secondary regions. In cross section, the posterior speech zone (Wernicke's area) is larger on the left, and Heschl's gyrus is larger in the right hemisphere. (B) Frontal section showing the extent of the multifunctional insular cortex buried in the lateral fissure.

have the same anatomical asymmetries as right-handers, an indication that speech organization is not related to hand preference. Language, which includes speech and other functions such as reading and writing, also is asymmetrical, although there are some right-hemisphere contributions to these broader functions.

The remaining 30 percent of left-handers fall into two distinct groups. The organization is opposite that of right-handers in about half of these people. The other half has some type of idiosyncratic bilateral representation of speech. That is, about 15 percent of all left-handed people have some speech functions in one hemisphere and some in the other hemisphere.

The localization of language on one side of the brain is an example of **lateralization.** Note here simply that, as a rule of thumb in neuroanatomy, if one hemisphere is specialized for one type of analysis, such as language in the left, the other hemisphere has a complementary function. Regarding audition, the right hemisphere appears to be lateralized for music.

We return to lateralization later in this chapter and again in Chapter 15 in connection with thinking.

The sulci of the temporal lobe enfold a large volume of cortical tissue more extensive than the auditory cortex alone (Figure 10-12B). The cortical tissue buried in the lateral fissure, called the **insula,** not only has lateralized regions related to language but also contains areas controlling the perception of taste (the gustatory cortex) and areas linked to the neural structures underlying social cognition. As you might expect, injury to the insula can produce diverse deficits, such as disturbance of both language and taste.

We consider both gustation and social cognition in Chapter 12.

REVIEW: Functional Anatomy of the Auditory System

- ✔ Incoming sound-wave energy vibrates the eardrum, which in turn vibrates the tiny bones of the middle ear. The innermost ossicle presses on the inner ear's oval window and sets in motion the cochlear fluid.
- ✔ The motion of this fluid vibrates cilia on the outer hair cells in the cochlea by displacing the basilar membrane. This bending generates membrane potential changes in the inner hair cells that alter their neurotransmitter release and the subsequent activity of auditory neurons, thus converting sound waves into changes in neural activity.
- ✔ The frequencies of incoming sound waves are largely coded by the surface areas on the basilar membrane that are most displaced.
- ✔ The axons of bipolar cells of the cochlea form the auditory (cochlear) nerve, which enters the brain at the medulla as part of cranial nerve 8 and synapses on cells in the cochlear nucleus.
- ✔ The neurons of each cochlear nucleus and associated regions in the medulla then begin a pathway that courses to the opposite-side midbrain (inferior colliculus), then recrosses in the thalamus (medial geniculate nucleus), and ends in the left and right auditory cortex.
- ✔ As in the visual system, two different cortical auditory pathways exist, one for sound recognition (like the ventral visual stream) and one for sound localization (like the dorsal visual stream).
- ✔ The auditory cortex on the left and right is asymmetrical, with the planum temporale being larger on the left and Heschl's gyrus being larger on the right in the brains of right-handed people. This anatomical asymmetry is correlated to a functional asymmetry: the left temporal cortex analyzes language-related sounds, whereas the right temporal cortex analyzes music-related ones. Most left-handed

Wernicke's area Secondary auditory cortex (planum temporale) lying behind Heschl's gyrus at the rear of the left temporal lobe that regulates language comprehension; also called posterior speech zone.

Lateralization Process whereby functions become localized primarily on one side of the brain.

Insula Located within the lateral fissure, multifunctional cortical tissue that contains regions related to language, to the perception of taste, and to the neural structures underlying social cognition.

people have a similar lateralization, although about 30 percent of left-handers have different patterns.

✔ The auditory cortex is part of the multifunctional cortex called the insula, which lies within the lateral fissure.

Neural Activity and Hearing

We now turn to the ways in which the activities of neurons in the auditory system create our perception of sounds. Neurons at different levels in this system serve different functions. To get an idea of what individual hair cells and cortical neurons do, we consider how the auditory system codes sound-wave energy so that we perceive pitch, loudness, location, and pattern.

Hearing Pitch

Recall that our perception of pitch corresponds to the frequency (repetition rate) of sound waves, which is measured in hertz (cycles per second). Hair cells in the cochlea code frequency as a function of their location on the basilar membrane. The cilia of hair cells at the base of the cochlea are maximally displaced by high-frequency waves that we hear as high-pitched sounds, and those at the apex are displaced the most by low-frequency waves that we hear as low-pitched sounds.

Tonotopic literally means "tone place."

This arrangement is a **tonotopic representation.** Because the axons of the bipolar cells that form the cochlear nerve are each connected to only one hair cell, they contain information about the spot on the basilar membrane, from apex to base, that is being stimulated.

If we record from single fibers in the cochlear nerve, we find that, although each axon transmits information about only a small part of the auditory spectrum, the cells do respond to a range of sound-wave frequencies. In other words, each hair cell is maximally responsive to a particular frequency but also responds to nearby frequencies, even though the sound wave's amplitude must be greater (louder) for the nearby frequencies to generate a change in the receptor's membrane potential.

The range of a hair cell's sound-wave curve is analogous to rods and cones in the retina responding to a range of light wavelengths (see Figure 9-6).

This range of hair-cell responses to different frequencies at different amplitudes can be plotted to form a tuning curve, as in **Figure 10-13.** Each type of receptor cell is maximally sensitive to a particular wavelength, but it still responds somewhat to nearby wavelengths.

The axons of the bipolar cells in the cochlea project to the cochlear nucleus in an orderly manner. Those entering from the base of the cochlea connect with one location, those entering from the middle connect to another location, and those entering from the apex connect to yet another. As a result, the tonotopic representation of the basilar membrane is reproduced in the cochlear nucleus.

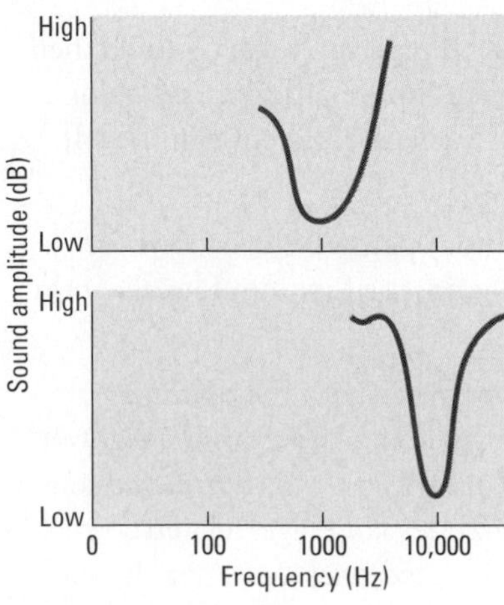

FIGURE 10-13 Tuning Curves. The graphs are plotted by the frequency and amplitude of sound-wave energy required to increase the firing rate of two different axons in the cochlear nerve. The lowest point on each curve is the frequency to which that hair cell is most sensitive. The upper tuning curve is centered on a midrange frequency of 1000 hertz, whereas the lower tuning curve is centered on a frequency of 10,000 hertz, in the high range of human hearing.

This systematic representation is maintained throughout the auditory pathways and can be found in the primary auditory cortex. **Figure 10-14** shows the distribution of projections from the base and apex of the cochlea across area A1. Similar tonotopic maps can be constructed for each level of the auditory system.

The systematic organization of tonotopic maps has enabled the development of **cochlear implants**—electronic devices surgically inserted in the inner ear to allow deaf people to hear (see

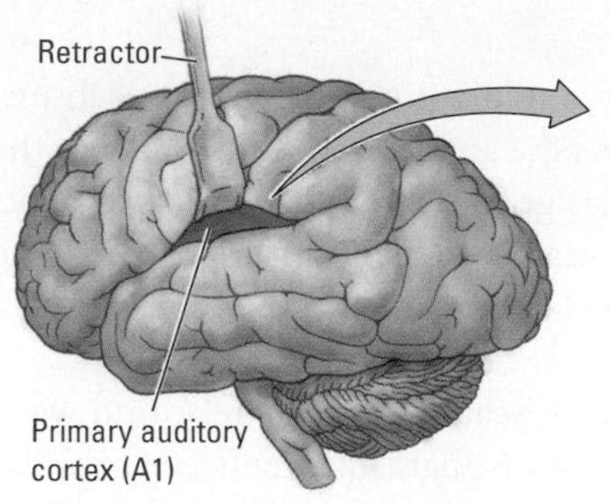

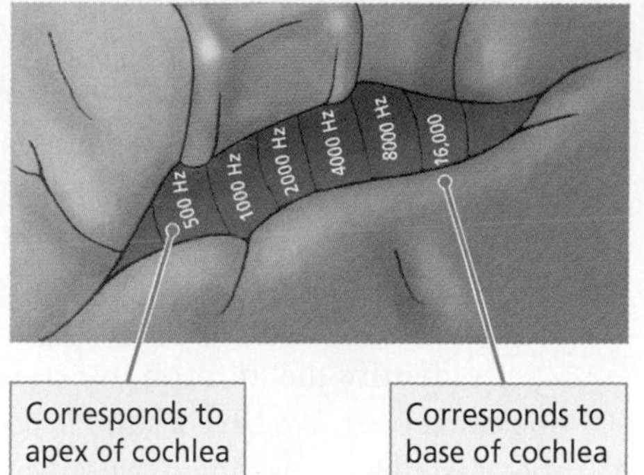

FIGURE 10-14 Tonotopic Representation of Area A1. A retractor holds the lateral fissure open to reveal the underlying auditory cortex, revealing Heschl's gyrus buried on the ventral side of the fissure. The anterior end of the primary auditory cortex corresponds to the apex of the cochlea and hence low frequencies, whereas the posterior end corresponds to the base of the cochlea and hence high frequencies.

Loeb, 1990). A miniature microphonelike processor detects the component frequencies of incoming sound waves and sends them to the appropriate place on the basilar membrane through tiny wires. The nervous system does not distinguish between stimulation coming from this artificial device, shown in **Figure 10-15**, and stimulation coming through the middle ear.

As long as appropriate signals go to the correct locations on the basilar membrane, the brain will "hear." Cochlear implants work very well, even allowing the deaf to detect the fluctuating pitches of speech. Their success corroborates the tonotopic representation of pitch in the basilar membrane.

One minor difficulty with the tonotopic theory of frequency detection is that the cochlea does not use this mechanism at the very apex of the basilar membrane, where hair cells, as well as the bipolar cells to which they are connected, respond to frequencies below about 200 hertz. At this location, all the cells respond to movement of the basilar membrane, but they do so in proportion to the frequency of the incoming wave. Higher rates of bipolar cell firing signal a relatively higher frequency, whereas lower rates of firing signal a lower frequency.

Why the cochlea uses a different system to differentiate pitches within this range of very-low-frequency sound waves is not clear. The reason probably has to do with the physical limitations of the basilar membrane. Although discriminating among low-frequency sound waves is not important to humans, animals such as elephants and whales depend on these frequencies to communicate. Most likely they have more neurons at this end of the basilar membrane than we humans do.

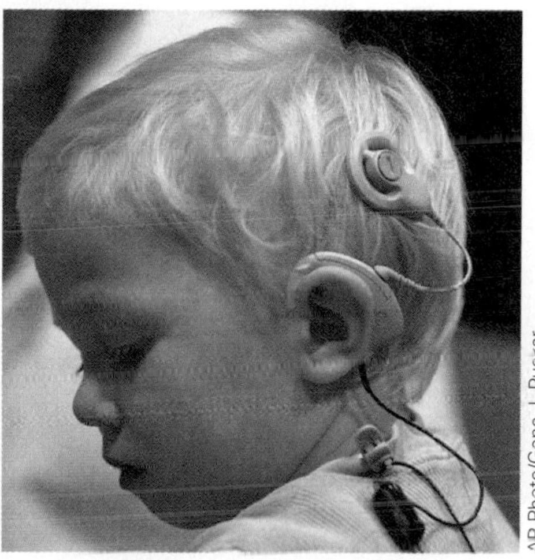
AP Photo/Gene J. Puskar

FIGURE 10-15 Tonotopic Technology. Cochlear implants bypass the normal route for sound-wave energy by electronically processing incoming stimulation directly to the correct locations on the basilar membrane via a microphone linked to a small speech-processing computer worn behind the ear.

Detecting Loudness

The simplest way for cochlear (bipolar) cells to indicate sound-wave intensity is to fire at a higher rate when amplitude is greater, which is exactly what happens. More intense air-pressure changes produce more intense vibrations of the basilar membrane and therefore greater shearing of the cilia. This increased shearing leads to more neurotransmitter released onto bipolar cells. As a result, the bipolar axons fire more frequently, telling the auditory system that the sound is getting louder.

Detecting Location

The fact that each cochlear nerve synapses on both sides of the brain provides mechanisms for locating the source of a sound. In one mechanism, neurons in the brainstem compute the difference in a sound wave's arrival time at each ear. Such differences in arrival time need not be large to be detected. If two sounds presented through earphones are separated in time by as little as 10 microseconds, the listener will perceive that a single sound came from the leading ear.

This computation of left-ear–right-ear arrival times is carried out in the medial part of the superior olivary complex (see Figure 10-11). Because these hindbrain cells receive inputs from each ear, they can compare exactly when the signal from each ear reaches them.

Tonotopic representation Property of audition in which sound waves are processed in a systematic fashion from lower to higher frequencies.
Cochlear implant Electronic device implanted surgically into the inner ear to transduce sound waves into neural activity and allow a deaf person to hear.

Extra distance that sound must travel to reach the right ear.

Figure 10-16 shows how sound waves originating on the left reach the left ear slightly before they reach the right ear. As the sound source moves from the side of the head toward the middle, a person has greater and greater difficulty locating it: the difference in arrival time becomes smaller and smaller until there is no difference at all. When we detect no difference, we infer that the sound is either directly in front of us or directly behind us.

To identify the location, we move our heads, making the sound waves strike one ear sooner. We have a similar problem distinguishing between sounds directly above and below us. Again, we solve the problem by tilting our heads, thus causing the sound waves to strike one ear before the other.

Another mechanism used by the auditory system to detect the source of a sound has to do not with the difference in arrival times of sound waves at the two ears but instead with the sound's relative loudness on the left or the right. The head acts as an obstacle to higher-frequency sound waves that do not easily bend around the head. As a result, higher-frequency sound waves on one side of the head are louder than on the other.

This difference is detected in the lateral part of the superior olive and the trapezoid body in the hindbrain. For sound waves coming from directly in front or behind or from directly above or below, the same problem of differentiation exists, requiring the same solution of tilting or turning the head.

FIGURE 10-16 Locating a Sound. Sound waves originating on the left side of the body reach the left ear slightly before the right, allowing us to locate the sound source. But the difference in arrival time is subtle, and the auditory system fuses the dual stimuli so that we perceive a single, clear sound coming from the left.

Horizontal orienting is called *azimuth detection;* vertical orienting is called *elevation detection.*

Head tilting and turning take time. Although not usually important for humans, time is important for other animals, such as owls, that hunt by using sound. Owls need to know the location of a sound simultaneously in at least two directions (e.g., left and below or right and above).

Owls, like humans, can orient in the horizontal plane to sound waves by using the different times at which sound waves reach the two ears. Additionally, the owl's ears have evolved to be slightly displaced in the vertical direction so that they can detect the sound waves' relative loudness in the vertical plane. This solution allows owls to hunt entirely by sound in the dark (**Figure 10-17**). Bad news for mice.

Detecting Patterns in Sound

Music and language are perhaps the primary sound-wave patterns that humans recognize. Perceiving sound-wave patterns as meaningful units is thus fundamental to auditory analysis. Because music and language are lateralized in the right and left temporal lobes, respectively, we can guess that neurons in the right and left temporal cortex take part in pattern recognition and analysis of these two auditory experiences. Studying the activities of auditory neurons in humans is not easy, however.

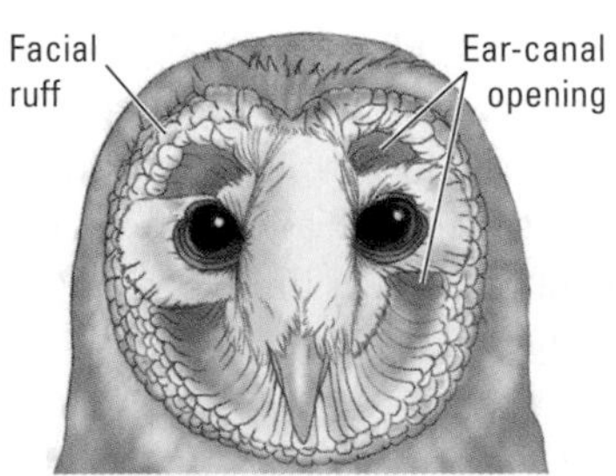

FIGURE 10-17 Hunting by Ear. (*Left*) For an owl, differences in perceived loudness yield clues to the elevation of a sound source, whereas inter-ear time differences serve to detect the source's horizontal direction. This barn owl has aligned its talons with the body axis of the mouse that it is about to catch in the dark. (*Right*) The owl's facial ruff extends from the relatively narrow skull down the length of the face to join below the beak. The ruff collects and funnels sound waves into ear-canal openings through tightly feathered troughs formed by the ruff above and below the eyes. The owl's left ear is more sensitive to sound waves from the left and below because the ear canal is higher on the left side and the trough is tilted down. The ear canal on the right is lower and the trough is tilted up, making the right ear more sensitive to sound waves from the right and above. Drawing adapted from "The Hearing of the Barn Owl," by E. I. Knudsen, 1981, *Scientific American, 245*(6), p. 115.

Most of the knowledge that neuroscientists have comes from studies of how individual neurons respond in nonhuman primates. For instance, Peter Winter and Hans Funkenstein (1971) found that neurons in the auditory cortex of the squirrel monkey are specifically responsive to squirrel monkey vocalizations. More recently, Joseph Rauschecker and his colleagues (1995) discovered that neurons in the secondary auditory areas of rhesus monkeys are more responsive to mixtures of sound waves than to pure tones.

Other researchers also have shown that removal of the temporal auditory cortex abolishes the ability to discriminate vocalizations made by other members of the species (Heffner and Heffner, 1990). Interestingly, discrimination of species-typical vocalizations in monkeys seems more severely disrupted by injury to the left temporal cortex than by injury to the right. This finding implies a possible functional asymmetry for the analysis of complex auditory material in nonhuman primates, such as the singing primates studied by Geissmann, cited at the beginning of this chapter.

REVIEW: Neural Activity and Hearing

- ✔ Neurons in the cochlea form tonotopic maps that code sound-wave frequencies and are maintained throughout the levels of the auditory system. The same cells in the cochlea vary their firing rate, depending on sound-wave amplitude.
- ✔ Detecting the location of a sound is a function of neurons in the superior olive and trapezoid body of the brainstem. These neurons compute differences in sound-wave arrival time and loudness in the two ears.
- ✔ Understanding the sound-wave patterns of music and language requires pattern recognition, which is performed by cortical auditory neurons.

Anatomy of Language and Music

This chapter began with the discovery of the Neanderthal flute and its evolutionary implications. The fact that Neanderthals made flutes implies not only that they processed musical sound-wave patterns but also that they made music. In the modern human brain, musical ability is generally a right-hemisphere specialization complementary to language ability, largely localized in the left hemisphere.

No one knows whether these complementary systems evolved together in the hominid brain, but it is certainly very possible that they did. Both language and music abilities are highly developed in the modern human brain. Although little is known about how language and music are processed at the cellular level, electrical stimulation and recording and blood-flow imaging studies have been sources of important insights into the regions of the cortex that process them. We investigate such studies next, focusing first on how the brain processes language.

You can survey dynamic brain imaging and methods for measuring the brain's electrical activity in Chapter 6.

Processing Language

More than 4000 human languages are spoken in the world today, and probably many more have gone extinct in past millennia. Researchers have wondered whether the brain has a single system for understanding and producing any language, regardless of its structure, or whether very different languages, such as English and Japanese, are processed in different ways. To answer this question, it helps to analyze languages to determine just how fundamentally similar they are, despite their obvious differences.

Uniformity of Language Structure

Foreign languages often seem impossibly complex to nonspeakers. Their sounds alone may seem odd and difficult to make. If you are a native speaker of English, for instance, Asian languages, such as Japanese, probably sound peculiarly melodic and almost without obvious consonants to you, whereas European languages, such as German or Dutch, may sound heavily guttural.

Even within related languages, such as Spanish, Italian, and French, marked differences can make learning one of them challenging, even if the student already knows another. Yet as real as all these linguistic differences may be, it turns out that they are superficial. The similarities among human languages, although not immediately apparent, are actually far more fundamental than their differences.

Noam Chomsky is usually credited with being the first linguist to stress similarities over differences in human language structure. In a series of books and papers written in the past 45 years, Chomsky has made a sweeping claim, as have researchers such as Steven Pinker (1997) more recently. They argue that all languages have common structural characteristics because of a genetically determined constraint on the nature of human language. Humans, apparently, have a built-in capacity for creating and using language.

When Chomsky first proposed this idea in the 1960s, it was greeted with skepticism, but it has since become clear that human language does indeed have a genetic basis. An obvious piece of evidence: language is universal in human populations. All people everywhere use language.

The complexity of language is not related to the technological complexity of a culture. The languages of technologically primitive peoples are every bit as complex and elegant as the languages of postindustrial cultures. Nor is the English of Shakespeare's time inferior or superior to today's English; it is just different.

Another piece of evidence that Chomsky adherents cite in favor of a genetic basis of human language is that humans learn language early in life and seemingly without effort. By about 12 months of age, children everywhere have started to speak words. By 18 months, they are combining words, and, by age 3 years, they have a rich language capability.

A year-old baby's vocabulary of 5 to 10 words will double in the next 6 months and by 36 months blossom into a 900- to 1000-word repertoire that the child combines into simple 3- to 4-word sentences, as explained in Chapter 7.

Perhaps the most amazing thing about language development is that children are not formally taught the structure of their language. As toddlers, they are not painstakingly instructed in the rules of grammar. In fact, their early errors—sentences such as "I goed to the zoo"—are seldom even corrected by adults. Yet children master language rapidly. They also acquire language through a series of stages that are remarkably similar across cultures. Indeed, the process of language acquisition plays an important role in Chomsky's theory of the innateness of language, which is not to say that language development is not influenced by experience.

At the most basic level, for example, children learn the language they hear spoken. In an English household, they learn English; in a Japanese home, they learn Japanese. They also pick up the vocabulary and grammar (structure) of the people around them, which can vary from one speaker to another. Children go through a sensitive period for language acquisition, probably from about 1 to 6 years of age. If they are not exposed to language throughout this critical period, their language skills are severely compromised. If children learn two languages simultaneously, both are represented in the same part of Broca's area, as described in Research Focus 10-2, "Distinct Cortical Areas for Second Languages."

Chapter 7 describes such critical periods for experience and normal brain development.

A third piece of evidence that favors a genetic basis of language is the many basic structural elements that all languages have in common. Granted, every language has its own particular rules that specify exactly how the various parts of speech are positioned

RESEARCH FOCUS 10-2

Distinct Cortical Areas for Second Languages

Children generally find it easier than adults to acquire more than one language and to speak each one with a native accent. Karl Kim and his colleagues (1997), asking whether the age at language acquisition might influence the way in which the language is represented in the brain, used fMRI to determine the spatial relation between native and second languages in the cortex.

Bilingual subjects were instructed to describe in their minds, without speaking aloud, the events that had taken place during a certain period of the preceding day—in the morning, for example. On different scans, they expressed their thoughts in different languages. Some subjects had learned a second language as children, whereas others had learned a second language as adults.

As would be expected in a sentence-generation task, both Broca's and Wernicke's areas were activated. There was a difference between childhood and adult acquisition of the second language in the activation in Broca's area but not in Wernicke's area.

As shown in the illustration, activation in Broca's area overlapped virtually completely for the childhood-acquisition subjects, but the adulthood-acquisition group showed an anatomical separation of the two languages. This spatial separation of the two languages in Broca's area suggests that language acquisition may alter its functional organization.

Thus, as human infants learn languages, Broca's area undergoes modification according to the nature of the languages being learned. Once modified, the region appears to resist subsequent modification, which necessitates utilizing adjacent cortical areas for the second language learned as an adult.

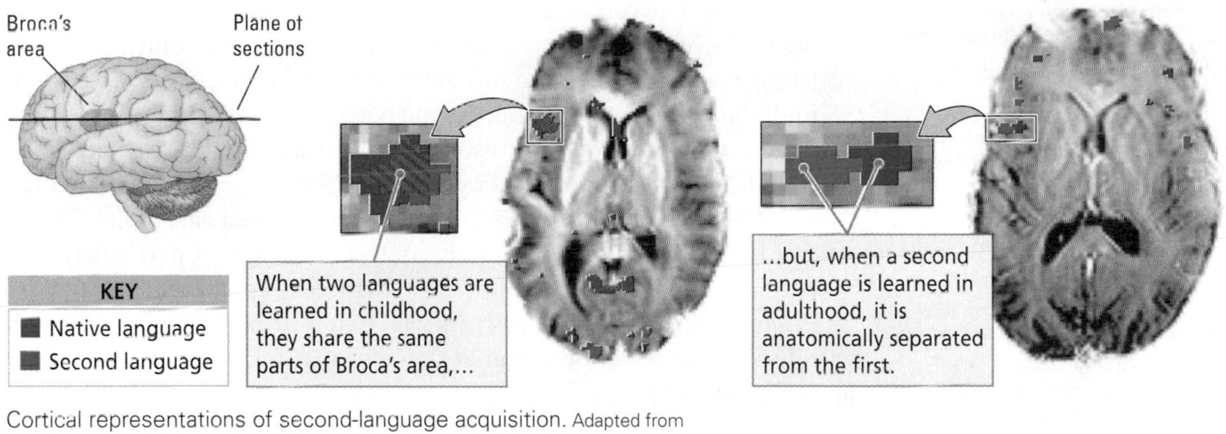
Broca's area
Plane of sections
KEY
Native language
Second language
When two languages are learned in childhood, they share the same parts of Broca's area,...
...but, when a second language is learned in adulthood, it is anatomically separated from the first.

Cortical representations of second-language acquisition. Adapted from "Distinct Cortical Areas Associated with Native and Second Languages," by K. H. S. Kim, N. R. Relkin, K. Young-Min Lee, and J. Hirsch, 1997, *Nature, 388*, pp. 171–174.

in a sentence (syntax), how words are inflected to convey different meanings, and so forth. But overarching rules also apply to all human languages.

For instance, all languages employ grammar, the parts of speech that we call subjects, verbs, and direct objects. Consider the sentence "Jane ate the apple." "Jane" is the subject, "ate" is the verb, and "apple" is the direct object. Syntax is not specified by any universal rule but rather is a characteristic of the particular language. In English, the order is subject, verb, object; in Japanese, the order is subject, object, verb; in Gaelic, the order is verb, subject, object. Nonetheless, all have both syntax and grammar.

The existence of these structural pillars in all human languages can be seen in the phenomenon of *creolization*—the development of a new language from what was formerly a very rudimentary language, or *pidgin*. Creolization took place in the seventeenth-century Americas when slave traders and the owners of colonial plantations brought together people from various African villages who lacked a common language. Because the new slaves needed to communicate, they quickly created a pidgin based on whatever language the plantation owners spoke—English, French, Spanish, or Portuguese.

The pidgin had a crude syntax (word order) but lacked a real grammatical structure. The children of the slaves who invented this pidgin were brought up by caretakers who spoke only pidgin to them. Yet, within a generation, these children had created their own creole, a language complete with a genuine syntax and grammar.

Clearly, the pidgin invented of necessity by adults was not a learnable language for children. Their innate biology shaped a new language similar in basic structure to all other human languages. All creolized languages seem to evolve in a similar way, even though the base languages are unrelated. This phenomenon could happen only if there were an innate, biological component to language development.

Do you think that, analogous to spoken language, text and twittered messages have evolved from pidgin to creole?

Localizing Language in the Brain

Finding a universal basic language structure set researchers on a search for an innate brain system that underlies language use. By the late 1800s, it had become clear that language functions were at least partly localized—not just within the left hemisphere but to specific areas there. Clues that led to this conclusion began to emerge in the early part of the nineteenth century, when neurologists observed patients with frontal-lobe injuries who suffered language difficulties.

Not until 1861, however, was the localization of certain language functions in the left hemisphere confirmed by the French physician Paul Broca, who concluded on the basis of several postmortem examinations that language functions are localized in the left frontal lobe in a region just anterior to the central fissure. A person with damage in this area is unable to speak despite both an intact vocal apparatus and normal language comprehension. The discovery of **Broca's area** was significant because it initiated the idea that the left and right hemispheres might have different functions.

You will find more about the process of Broca's observations and contributions to the emergence of neuropsychology in Chapter 6.

Other neurologists at the time believed that Broca's area might be only one of several left-hemisphere regions that control language. In particular, neurologists suspected a relation between hearing and speech. Proving this suspicion correct, Karl Wernicke later described patients who had difficulty comprehending language after injury to the posterior region of the left temporal lobe, identified as Wernicke's area in **Figure 10-18.**

FIGURE 10-18 Neurology of Language. (A) In Wernicke's model of speech recognition, stored sound images are matched to spoken words in the left posterior temporal cortex, shown in yellow. (B) Speech is produced through the connection that the arcuate fasciculus makes between Wernicke's area and Broca's area.

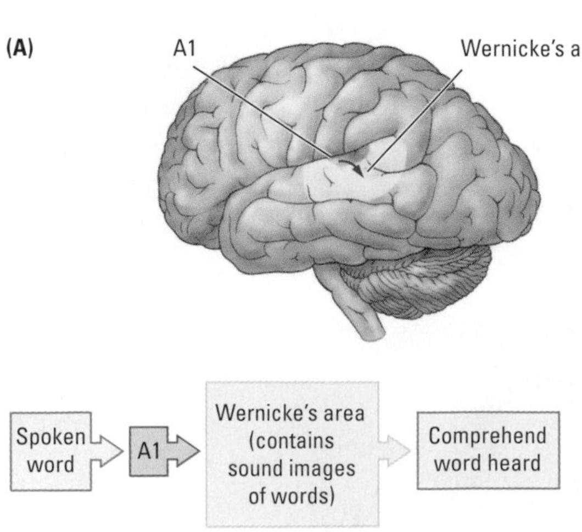

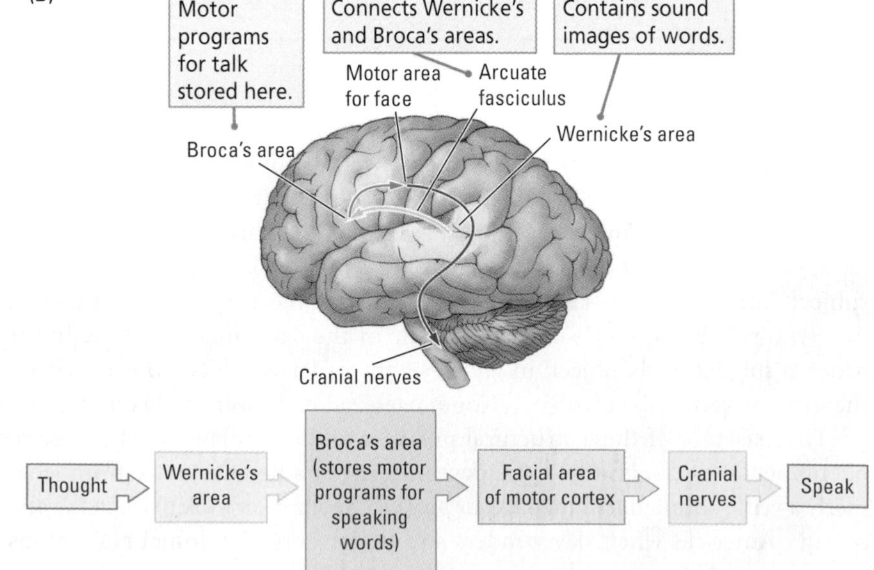

Broca's area Anterior speech area in the left hemisphere that functions with the motor cortex to produce the movements needed for speaking.

Aphasia Inability to speak or comprehend language despite the presence of normal comprehension and intact vocal mechanisms. Broca's aphasia is the inability to speak fluently despite the presence of normal comprehension and intact vocal mechanisms. Wernicke's aphasia is the inability to understand or to produce meaningful language even though the production of words is still intact.

We referred to Wernicke's area earlier as a speech zone (see Figure 10-12A). Damage to any speech area produces some form of **aphasia,** the general term for any inability to comprehend or produce language despite the presence of normal comprehension and intact vocal mechanisms. At one extreme, people who suffer *Wernicke's aphasia* can speak fluently, but their language is confused and makes little sense, as if they have no idea what they are saying. At the other extreme, a person with *Broca's aphasia* cannot speak despite normal comprehension and intact physiology.

Wernicke went on to propose a model, diagrammed in Figure 10-18A, for how the two language areas of the left hemisphere interact to produce speech. He theorized that images of words are encoded by their sounds and stored in the left posterior temporal cortex. When we hear a word that matches one of those sound images, we recognize it, which is how Wernicke's area contributes to speech comprehension.

To *speak* words, Broca's area in the left frontal lobe must come into play, because the motor program to produce each word is stored in this area. Messages are sent to Broca's area from Wernicke's area through a pathway, the *arcuate fasciculus,* that connects the two regions. Broca's area in turn controls the articulation of words by the vocal apparatus, as diagrammed in Figure 10-18B.

Wernicke's model provided a simple explanation both for the existence of two major language areas in the brain and for the contribution each area makes to the control of language. But the model was based on postmortem examinations of patients with brain lesions that were often extensive. Not until the pioneering studies of neurosurgeon Wilder Penfield, begun in the 1930s, were the language areas of the left hemisphere clearly and accurately mapped.

Auditory and Speech Zones Mapped by Brain Stimulation

It turns out, among Penfield's discoveries, that neither is Broca's area the independent site of speech production nor is Wernicke's area the independent site of language comprehension; electrical stimulation of either region disrupts both processes.

Penfield took advantage of the chance to map auditory and language areas of the brain when operating on patients undergoing elective surgery to treat intractable epilepsy. The goal of this surgery is to remove tissues where the abnormal discharges are localized. A major challenge is to prevent injury to critical regions that serve important functions. To determine the location of these critical regions, Penfield used a weak electrical current to stimulate the brain surface. By monitoring the response of the patient to stimulation in different locations, Penfield could map brain functions along the cortex.

Chapter 6 describes an array of brain-stimulation techniques used in neuroscience research.

Typically, two neurosurgeons perform the operation (Penfield is shown operating in **Figure 10-19**A), and a neurologist analyzes the electroencephalogram in an adjacent room. Because patients are awake, they can contribute during the procedure, and the effects of brain stimulation in specific regions can be determined in detail and mapped. Penfield placed little numbered tickets on different parts of the brain's surface where the patient noted that stimulation had produced some noticeable sensation or effect, producing the cortical map shown in Figure 10-19B.

When Penfield stimulated the auditory cortex, patients often reported hearing various sounds, a ringing that sounded like a doorbell, a buzzing noise, or a sound like birds chirping. This result is consistent with those of later studies of single-cell recordings from the auditory cortex in nonhuman primates. Findings in these later studies showed that the auditory cortex has a role in pattern recognition.

Penfield also found that stimulation in area A1 seemed to produce simple tones—ringing sounds, and so forth—whereas stimulation in the adjacent auditory cortex (Wernicke's area) was more apt to cause some interpretation of a sound—ascription of a

(A)

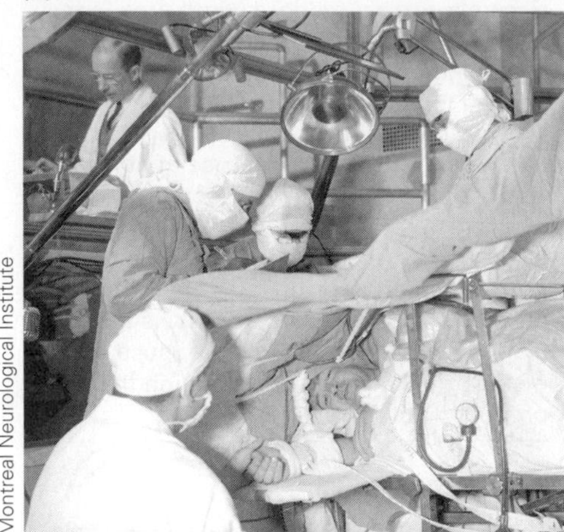

Montreal Neurological Institute

(B)

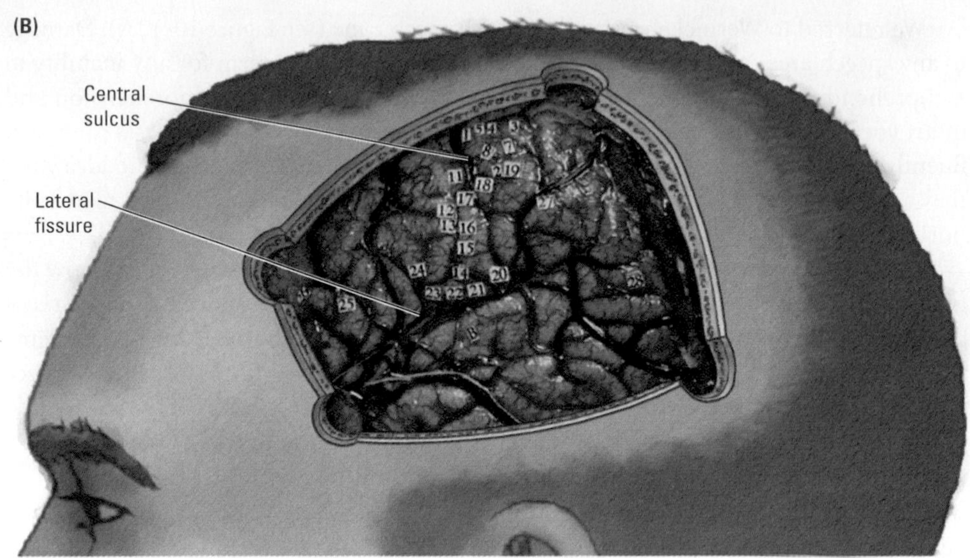

FIGURE 10-19 Mapping Cortical Functions. (A) The patient is fully conscious during neurosurgery for intractable epilepsy, lying on his right side and kept comfortable with local anesthesia. The left hemisphere of his brain is exposed as Wilder Penfield stimulates discrete cortical areas. In the background, the neurologist monitors the electroencephalogram recorded from each stimulated area, which will help in identifying the eleptogenic focus. The anesthetist (seated) observes the patient's response to the cortical stimulation. (B) A drawing of the entire skull overlies a photograph of the patient's exposed brain during surgery. The numbered tickets identify the points that Penfield stimulated to map the cortex. At points 26, 27, and 28, a stimulating electrode produced interference with speech. Point 26 is presumably in Broca's area, 27 (not shown) is the facial-control area in the motor cortex, and 28 is in Wernicke's area in this patient's brain.

buzzing sound to a familiar source such as a cricket, for instance. There was no difference in the effects of stimulation of the left or right auditory cortex, and the patients heard no words when the brain was stimulated.

Sometimes, however, stimulation of the auditory cortex produced effects other than the perception of sounds. Stimulation of one area, for example, might cause a patient to experience a sense of deafness, whereas stimulation of another area might produce a distortion of sounds actually being heard. As one patient exclaimed after a certain region had been stimulated, "Everything you said was mixed up!"

Penfield was most interested in the effects of brain stimulation not on simple sound-wave processing but on language. He and later researchers used electrical stimulation to identify four important cortical regions that control language. The two classic regions—Broca's area and Wernicke's area—are left-hemisphere regions. Located on both sides of the brain are the other two major regions of language use: the dorsal area of the frontal lobes and the areas of the motor and somatosensory cortex that control facial, tongue, and throat muscles and sensations. Although the effects on speech vary, depending on the region, stimulating any of them disrupts speech in some way.

Clearly, much of the left hemisphere takes part in audition, and **Figure 10-20** shows the areas of the left hemisphere that Penfield found engaged in some way in processing language. In fact, Penfield mapped cortical language areas in two ways, first by disrupting speech and then by eliciting speech. Not surprisingly, damage to any speech area produces some form of aphasia.

Supplementary speech area (vocalization or speech arrest)
Areas controlling facial movement or sensation (vocalization or speech arrest)
Aphasia
Broca's area (aphasia)
A1 (sounds heard)
Wernicke's area (aphasia)

FIGURE 10-20 Cortical Regions That Control Language. This map, based on Penfield's extensive study, summarizes areas in the left hemisphere where direct stimulation may interfere with speech or produce vocalization. Adapted from *Speech and Brain Mechanisms* (p. 201), by W. Penfield and L. Roberts, 1956. London: Oxford University Press.

Disrupting Speech Penfield expected that electrical current might disrupt ongoing speech by effectively "short-circuiting" the brain. He stimulated different regions of the cortex while the patient was in the process of speaking. In fact, the speech disruptions took several forms, including slurring, confusion of words, and difficulty in finding the right word. Such aphasias are detailed in Clinical Focus 10-3, "Left-Hemisphere Dysfunction."

Electrical stimulation of the **supplementary speech area** on the dorsal surface of the frontal

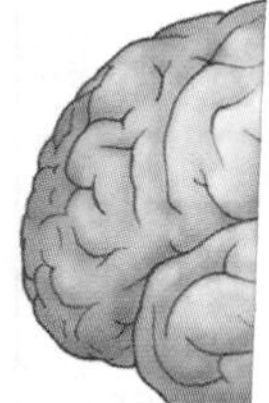

CLINICAL FOCUS 10-3

Left-Hemisphere Dysfunction

Susan S., a 25-year-old college graduate and mother of two, suffered from epilepsy. When she had a seizure, which was almost every day, she lost consciousness for a short period, during which she often engaged in repetitive behaviors, such as rocking back and forth.

Such psychomotor seizures can usually be controlled by medication, but the drugs were ineffective for Susan. The attacks were very disruptive to her life because they prevented her from driving a car and restricted the types of jobs she could hold. So Susan decided to undergo neurosurgery to remove the region of abnormal brain tissue that was causing the seizures.

The procedure has a very high success rate. Susan's surgery entailed the removal of a part of the left temporal lobe, including most of the cortex in front of the auditory areas. Although it may seem to be a substantial amount of the brain to cut away, the excised tissue is usually abnormal, so any negative consequences are typically minor.

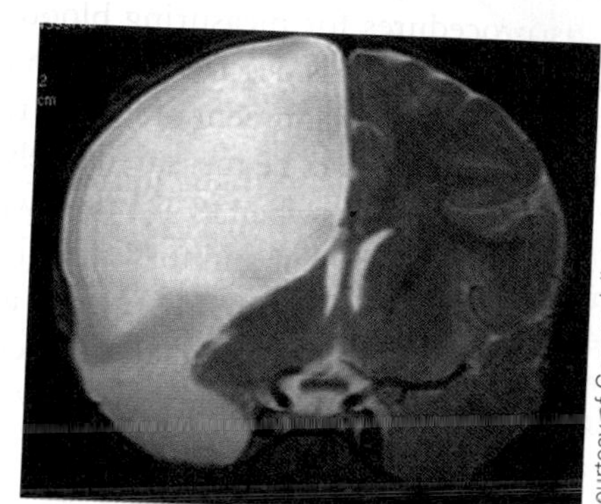

Postoperative MRI of a patient who has lost most of the left hemisphere.

Courtesy of George Jallo/Johns Hopkins Hospital

After the surgery, Susan did well for a few days, but then she suffered unexpected and unusual complications. As a result, she lost the remainder of her left temporal lobe, including the auditory cortex and Wernicke's area. The extent of lost brain tissue resembles that shown in the accompanying MRI.

Susan no longer understood language, except to respond to the sound of her name and to speak just one phrase: "I love you." Susan was also unable to read, showing no sign that she could even recognize her own name in writing.

To find ways to communicate with Susan, one of us (BK) tried humming nursery rhymes to her. She immediately recognized them and could say the words. We also discovered that her singing skill was well within the normal range and she had a considerable repertoire of songs.

Susan did not seem able to learn new songs, however, and she did not understand "messages" that were sung to her. Apparently, Susan's musical repertoire was stored and controlled independently of her language system.

lobes, shown in Figure 10-20, can even stop ongoing speech completely, a reaction that Penfield called *speech arrest.* Stimulation of other cortical regions well removed from the temporal and frontal speech areas has no effect on ongoing speech, with the exception of regions of the motor cortex that control movements of the face. This exception makes sense because talking requires movement of facial, tongue, and throat muscles.

Eliciting Speech The second way in which Penfield mapped language areas was to stimulate the cortex when a patient was not speaking to see if he could cause the person to utter a speech sound. Penfield did not expect to trigger coherent speech, because cortical stimulation is not physiologically normal and so probably would not produce actual words or word combinations. His expectation was borne out.

Stimulation of regions on both sides of the brain—for example, the supplementary speech areas—produces a sustained vowel cry, such as "Oh" or "Eee." Stimulation of the facial areas in the motor cortex and the somatosensory cortex produces some vocalization related to movements of the mouth and tongue. Stimulation outside these speech-related zones produces no such effects.

Supplementary speech area Speech-production region on the dorsal surface of the left frontal lobe.

Auditory Cortex Mapped by Positron Emission Tomography

Today, researchers use PET, a brain-imaging technique that detects changes in blood flow by measuring changes in the uptake of compounds such as oxygen or glucose, to study the metabolic activity of brain cells engaged in processing language. PET imaging is based on a surprisingly old idea.

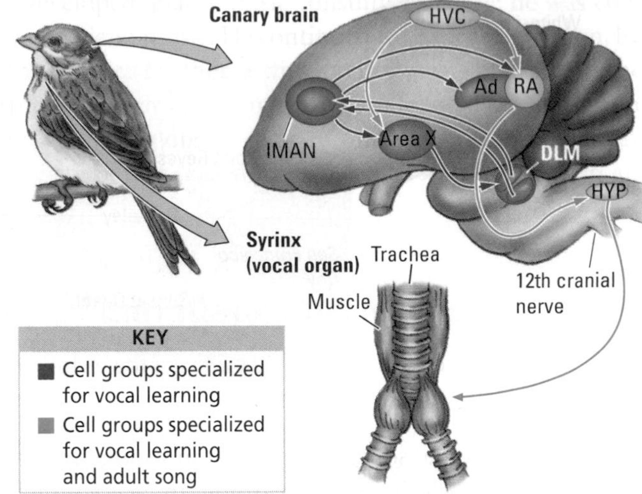

FIGURE 10-24 Avian Neuroanatomy. Lateral view of the canary brain shows several nuclei that control song learning, the two critical ones being the higher vocal control center (HVC) and the nucleus robustus archistriatalis (RA). These areas are necessary both for adult singing and for learning the song. Other regions necessary for learning the song during development but not required for the adult song include the dorsal archistriatum (Ad), the lateral magnocellular nucleus of the anterior neostriatum (IMAN), area X of the avian striatum, and the medial dorsolateral nucleus of the thalamus (DLM).

The neurobiology of birdsong has been a topic of intense research, partly because it provides an excellent model of changes in the brain that accompany learning and partly because it can be a source of insight into how sex hormones influence behavior. Fernando Nottebohm and his colleagues first identified the major structures controlling birdsong in the late 1970s (Nottebohm & Arnold, 1976). These structures are illustrated in **Figure10-24.** The largest are the higher vocal control center (HVC) and the nucleus robustus archistriatalis (RA). The axons of the HVC connect to the RA, which in turn sends axons to the 12th cranial nerve. This nerve controls the muscles of the *syrinx,* the structure that actually produces the song.

The HVC and RA have several important and some familiar characteristics:

- They are asymmetrical in some species, with the structures in the left hemisphere larger than those in the right hemisphere. In many cases, this asymmetry is similar to the lateralized control of language in humans: if the left-hemisphere pathways are damaged, the birds stop singing, but similar injury in the right hemisphere has no effect on song.
- Birdsong structures are sexually dimorphic. That is, they are much larger in males than in females. In canaries, they are five times as large in the male bird. This sexual difference is due to the hormone testosterone in males. Injection of testosterone into female birds causes the song-controlling nuclei to increase in size.
- The size of the birdsong nuclei is related to singing skill. For instance, unusually talented singers among male canaries tend to have larger HVCs and RAs than do less-gifted singers.
- The HVC and RA contain not only cells that produce birdsong but also cells responsive to hearing song, especially the song of a bird's own species.

Chapter 7 explains sexual dimorphism in humans and in birds and the effects of testosterone on brain development.

The same structures therefore play a role in both song production and song perception. This avian neural anatomy is comparable to the overlapping roles of Broca's and Wernicke's areas in language perception and production in humans.

Echolocation in Bats

Next to rodents, bats are the most numerous order of mammals. The two general groups, or suborders, of bats consist of the smaller echolocating bats (Microchiroptera) and the larger fruit-eating and flower-visiting bats (Megachiroptera), sometimes called flying foxes. The echolocating bats interest us here because they use sound waves to navigate, to hunt, and to communicate.

Bats are not unique in using sound waves for these purposes. Dolphins are among the marine mammals that use a similar system in water.

Microchiroptera
(an echolocating bat)

Megachiroptera
(a fruit-eating bat)

Most of the 680 species of echolocating bats feed on insects. Some others live on blood (vampire bats), and some catch frogs, lizards, fishes, birds, and small mammals. The auditory system of bats is specialized to use echolocation not only to locate targets in the dark but also to analyze the features of targets, as well as features of the environment in general. Through echolocation, a bat identifies prey, navigates through the leaves of trees, and locates surfaces suitable to land on. Perhaps a term analogous to visualization, such as "audification," would be more appropriate.

Echolocation works rather like sonar. The larynx of a bat emits bursts of sound waves at ultrasonic frequencies that bounce off objects and return to the bat's ears, allowing the animal to identify what is in the surrounding environment. The bat, in other words, navigates by the echoes that it hears, differentiating among the various characteristics of those echoes.

Objects that are moving (such as insects) have a moving echo, smooth objects give a different echo from rough objects, and so on. A key component of this echolocation system is the analysis of differences in the return times of echoes. Close objects return echoes sooner than more distant objects do, and the textures of various objects' surfaces impose minute differences in return times.

A bat's cries are of short duration (ranging from 0.3 to 200 milliseconds) and high frequency (from 12,000 to 200,000 hertz; see Figure 10-4). Most of this range lies at too high a frequency for the human ear to detect. Different bat species produce sound waves of different frequency that depend on the animal's ecology. Bats that catch prey in the open use different frequencies from those used by bats that catch insects in foliage and from those used by bats that hunt for prey on the ground.

The echolocation abilities of bats are impressive, as shown in **Figure 10-25.** Bats in the wild can be trained to catch small food particles thrown up into the air in the dark. These echolocating skills make the bat a very efficient hunter. The little brown bat, for instance, can capture very small flying insects, such as mosquitoes, at the remarkable rate of two per second.

Researchers have considerable interest in the neural mechanisms of bat echolocation. Each bat species emits sound waves in a relatively narrow range of frequencies, and a bat's auditory pathway has cells specifically tuned to echoes in the frequency range of its species. For example, the mustached bat sends out sound waves ranging from 60,000 to 62,000 hertz, and its auditory system has a cochlear fovea (a maximally sensitive area in the organ of Corti) that corresponds to that frequency range.

In this way, more neurons are dedicated to the frequency range used for echolocation than to any other range of frequencies. Analogously, our visual system dedicates

Steven Dalton/NHPA

FIGURE 10-25 Born with Sonar. A bat with a 40-centimeter wingspan can navigate through openings in a 14-by-14-centimeter mesh made of 80-millimeter nylon thread while flying in total darkness. The echolocating bat creates an accurate map of the world based entirely on auditory information.

Echolocation Ability to identify and locate an object by bouncing sound waves off the object.

You can review the structures of the retina and the fovea in Figure 9-2.

more neurons to the retina's fovea, the area responsible for our most detailed vision. In the cortex of the bat's brain, several distinct areas process complex echo-related inputs. For instance, one area computes the distance of given targets from the animal, whereas another area computes the velocity of a moving target. This neural system makes the bat exquisitely adapted for nighttime navigation.

REVIEW: Auditory Communication in Nonhuman Species

- ✔ The analysis of birdsong has identified several important principles of auditory functioning similar to those observed in human language, reinforcing the idea that many characteristics of human language may be innate:
  1. Underlying birdsong are specialized structures in the avian brain that produce and perceive vocal stimuli.
  2. These structures are influenced by early experience.
  3. An innate template imposes an important constraint on the nature of the songs that a bird produces and perceives.
- ✔ Insect-eating bats employ high-frequency sound waves as biological sonar that allows them to navigate in the dark and to catch insects on the fly as well as to communicate with others of their species.
- ✔ An echolocating bat's auditory world is easily as rich as our visual world because it contains information about the shape and velocity of objects—information that our visual system provides. Humans do not hear nearly as well as bats, but we see much better.

Summary

Although we take language and music for granted, both play central roles in our mental lives and in our social lives. Language and music provide us a way to communicate with other people—and with ourselves—and they facilitate social identification, parenting, and cultural transmission.

Sound Waves: The Stimulus for Audition

The stimulus for the auditory system is the mechanical energy of sound waves that results from changes in air pressure. The ear transduces three fundamental physical qualities of sound-wave energy: frequency (repetition rate), amplitude (size), and complexity. Perceptually, neural networks in the brain then translate these energies into the pitch, loudness, and timbre of the sounds that we hear.

Functional Anatomy of the Auditory System

Beginning in the ear, a combination of mechanical and electrochemical systems transform sound waves into auditory perceptions—what we hear. Changes in air pressure are conveyed in a mechanical chain reaction from the eardrum to the bones of the middle ear to the oval window of the cochlea and the cochlear fluid that lies behind it in the inner ear. Movements of the cochlear fluid produce movements in specific regions of the basilar membrane, leading to changes in the electrochemical activity of the auditory receptors, the inner hair cells found on the basilar membrane that send neural impulses through the auditory nerve into the brain.

Corbis

Neural Activity and Hearing

The basilar membrane has a tonotopic organization. High-frequency sound waves maximally stimulate hair cells at their base, whereas low-frequency sound waves maximally stimulate hair cells at the apex, enabling cochlear neurons to code various sound frequencies. Tonotopic organization of sound-wave analysis is found at all levels of the auditory system, and the system also detects both amplitude and location. Sound amplitude is coded by the firing rate of cochlear neurons, with louder sounds producing higher firing rates than softer sounds do. Location is detected by structures in the brainstem that compute differences in the arrival times and the loudness of a sound in the two ears.

The hair cells of the cochlea synapse with bipolar neurons that form the cochlear nerve, which in turn forms part of the eighth cranial nerve. The cochlear nerve takes auditory information to three structures in the hindbrain: the cochlear nucleus, the superior olive, and the trapezoid body. Cells in these areas are sensitive to differences in both sound-wave intensity and arrival times at the two ears. In this way, they enable the brain to locate a sound.

The auditory pathway continues from the hindbrain areas to the inferior colliculus of the midbrain, then to the medial geniculate nucleus in the thalamus, and finally to the auditory cortex. Like vision, dual pathways exist in the auditory cortex, one for pattern recognition and the other for controlling movements in auditory space. Cells in the cortex are responsive to specific categories of sounds, such as species-specific communication.

Anatomy of Language and Music

Despite differences in speech-sound patterns and structures, all human languages have the same basic foundation of a syntax and a grammar. This fundamental similarity implies an innate template for creating language. The auditory areas of the cortex in the left hemisphere play a special role in analyzing language-related information, whereas those in the right hemisphere play a special role in analyzing music-related information. The right temporal lobe also analyzes prosody, the melodical qualities of speech.

Among several language-processing areas in the left hemisphere, Wernicke's area identifies speech syllables and words and so is critically engaged in speech comprehension. Broca's area matches speech-sound patterns to the motor behaviors necessary to make them and so plays a major role in speech production. Broca's area also discriminates between closely related speech sounds. Aphasias result from an inability to speak (Broca's aphasia) or comprehend language (Wernicke's aphasia) despite the presence of normal comprehension and intact vocal mechanisms.

Auditory Communication in Nonhuman Species

Nonhuman animals have evolved specialized auditory structures and behaviors. One example is birdsong. Regions of songbirds' brains are specialized for producing and comprehending song. In many species, these regions are lateralized to the left hemisphere, analogous in a way to how language areas are lateralized to the left hemisphere in most humans. The similarities between the development of song in birds and the development of language in humans, as well as similarities in the neural mechanisms underlying both the production and the perception of song and language, are striking.

Both owls and bats can fly and catch prey at night by using only auditory information to guide their movement. Echolocating bats evolved a biological sonar that allows them to map the objects in their world, just as humans map their visual worlds. This mainly auditory reality we humans can only try to imagine.

How D
to Sti

Motor sequence Movement modules preprogrammed by the brain and produced as a unit.

Mirror neuron Cell in the primate premotor cortex that fires when an individual observes a specific action taken by another individual.

To refresh your knowledge of the chordate nervous system, review Figures 1-9 and 1-10.

The idea that the nervous system is hierarchically organized originated with the English neurologist John Hughlings-Jackson a century ago. He thought of the nervous system as being organized in a number of layers. Successively higher levels control more complex aspects of behavior by acting through the lower levels. The three major levels in Hughlings-Jackson's model are are those just mentioned: forebrain, brainstem, and spinal cord. He also proposed that further levels of organization exist within these divisions, an idea we will pursue when we describe the cortical control of movement.

Hughlings-Jackson adopted the concept of hierarchical organization from evolutionary theory. He knew that the chordate nervous system had evolved gradually: the spinal cord had developed in worms; the brainstem had developed in fish, amphibians, and reptiles; the forebrain had developed in birds and mammals. Because each level of the nervous system had developed at different times, Hughlings-Jackson reasoned, each must have some functional independence.

As we noted in describing how a cup is grasped, a hierarchically organized structure such as the mammalian nervous system does not operate piece by piece. It functions as a whole, with higher regions working through and influencing the actions of lower areas. To understand how all these regions work together, we consider the major components of the hierarchy one by one, starting at the top with the forebrain.

The Forebrain and Initiation of Movement

Complex movements consist of many components. Take painting a work of art. Your perceptions of what is appearing on the canvas must be closely coordinated with the brush strokes that your hand makes to achieve the desired effect.

The same high degree of control is necessary for other complex behaviors. Consider playing basketball. At every moment, decisions must be made and actions must be performed. Dribble, pass, and shoot are different categories of movement, and each can be carried out in many ways. Skilled players choose among the categories effortlessly and execute the movements seemingly without thought.

One explanation for how we control movements that was popular in the 1930s centers on the concept of feedback: after we perform an action, we wait for feedback about how well the action has succeeded; then we make the next movement accordingly. But Karl Lashley (1951), in an article titled "The Problem of Serial Order in Behavior," found fault with this explanation.

Lashley, a pioneering neuroscience researcher, argued that movements such as those required for skilled actions are performed too quickly to rely on feedback about one movement shaping the next movement. The time required to receive feedback about the first movement combined with the time needed to develop a plan for the subsequent movement and send a corresponding message to muscles is simply too long for effective action. Lashley suggested that movements must be performed as **motor sequences,** with one sequence of movements held in readiness while an ongoing sequence is being completed.

According to this view, all complex behaviors, including playing the piano, painting pictures, and playing basketball, require selecting and executing multiple movement sequences. As one sequence is being executed, the next sequence is being prepared so that the second can follow the first smoothly. The act of speaking seems to bear out Lashley's view. When people use complex rather than simple sequences of words, they are more likely to pause and make "umm" and "ahh" sounds, suggesting that it is taking them more time than usual to organize their word sequences.

The frontal lobe of each hemisphere is responsible for planning and initiating motor sequences. The frontal lobe is divided into a number of different regions, including the three illustrated in **Figure 11-2.** From front to back, they are the prefrontal cortex, the premotor cortex, and the primary motor cortex.

Premotor cortex organizes movement sequences.
Motor cortex produces specific movements.
Prefrontal cortex plans movements.
Prefrontal cortex plans
Premotor cortex sequences
Motor cortex executes actions

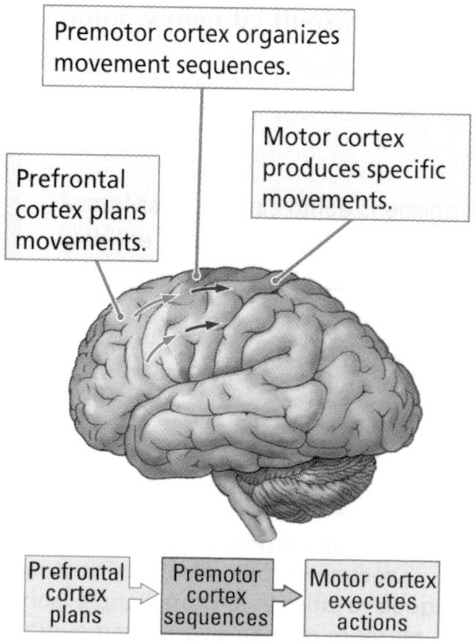

FIGURE 11-2 Initiating a Motor Sequence.

The areas of the frontal lobe are also hierarchically arranged. At the top of the hierarchy, the prefrontal cortex plans complex behavior, such as deciding to get up at a certain hour to arrive at work on time, deciding to stop at the library to return a book that is due, or deciding whether an action is right or wrong and thus whether it should be performed at all. Humans with prefrontal cortex injury often break social and legal rules not because they do not know them or the consequences of breaking them but because their decision making is faulty.

Chapter 15 explores the cognitive deficits created by frontal lobe injury.

The prefrontal cortex does not specify the precise movements to be made. It simply specifies the goal. To bring a plan to completion, the prefrontal cortex sends instructions to the premotor cortex, which produces the complex movement sequences appropriate to the task. If the premotor cortex is damaged, the sequences cannot be coordinated and the goal cannot be accomplished. For example, the monkey at the right in **Figure 11-3** has a lesion in the dorsal premotor cortex. The monkey has been given the task of extracting a piece of food wedged in a hole in a table (Brinkman, 1984). If the monkey simply pushes the food with a finger, the food will drop to the floor and be lost. The monkey has to catch the food by holding a palm beneath the hole as the food is being pushed out. But this brain-injured animal is unable to make the two complementary movements together. It can push the food with a finger and extend an open palm, but it cannot coordinate these actions of its two hands, as the normal monkey on the left can.

Recall the principle from Chapter 2: brain circuits are organized to process information both hierarchically and in parallel.

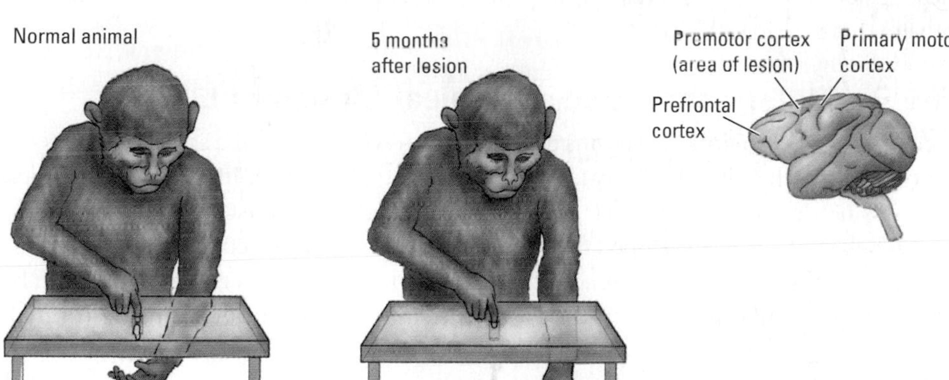

FIGURE 11-3 Premotor Control. On a task requiring both hands, the normal monkey can push the peanut out of a hole with one hand and catch it in the other, but 5 months after lesioning of the premotor cortex, the experimental monkey cannot. Adapted from "Supplementary Motor Area of the Monkey's Cerebral Cortex: Short- and Long-Term Effects after Unilateral Ablation and the Effects of Subsequent Callosal Section," by C. Brinkman, 1984, *Journal of Neuroscience, 4,* p. 925.

The primate premotor cortex also contains **mirror neurons** that discharge when the subject performs an action such as reaching for food or when the subject observes another individual performing the same movement. Mirror neurons allow a subject to observe, understand, and copy the movements of others (Aziz-Zadeh and Ivry, 2009).

Chapter 15 describes the evolutionary advantages of mirror neurons, and Clinical Focus 15-2 reports on the mirror neuron dysfunction in autism spectrum disorder.

The premotor cortex organizes movement sequences but does not specify how each movement is to be carried out. Those details are the responsibility of the primary motor cortex, which is responsible for executing skilled movements. To understand its role, consider some of the movements we use to pick up objects.

In using the pincer grip (**Figure 11-4A**), we hold an object between the thumb and index finger. This grip not only allows us to pick up small objects easily but also allows us to use whatever is held with considerable skill. In contrast, in using the power grasp (Figure 11-4B), we hold an object much less dexterously but with more power by simply closing the fingers around it.

FIGURE 11-4 Getting a Grip. The pincer grip (*left*), allows more skilled manipulation; the power grasp, or whole-hand grip (*right*), affords more power.

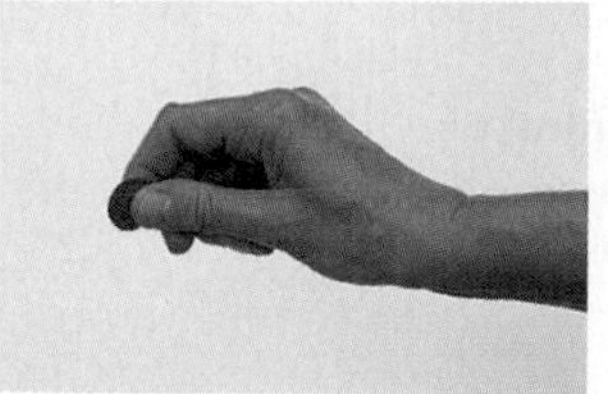

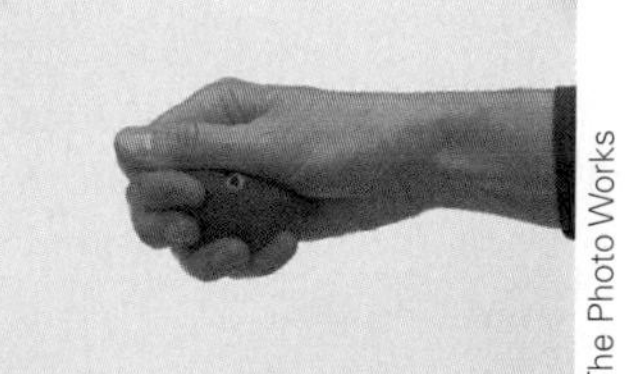

The Photo Works

Clearly, the pincer grip is a more demanding movement because the two fingers must be placed precisely on the object. People with damage

Cerebral palsy Group of brain disorders that result from brain damage acquired perinatally.

to the primary motor cortex have difficulty correctly shaping their fingers to perform the pincer grip, although they may perform a whole hand grasp easily. They also have difficulty in performing many skilled movements of the hands, arms, and trunk (Lang & Schieber, 2004).

In summary, the frontal lobe in each hemisphere plans, coordinates, and executes precise movements. The regions of the frontal cortex that perform these functions are hierarchically related. After the prefrontal cortex has formulated a plan of action, it instructs the premotor cortex to organize the appropriate sequence of behaviors, and the movements themselves are executed by the motor cortex.

Consult Chapter 6 for information on dynamic imaging methods that record and measure blood flow in the brain.

The hierarchical organization of frontal-lobe areas in producing movements is supported by findings from studies of cerebral blood flow, which serves as an indicator of neural activity. **Figure 11-5** shows the regions of the brain that were active as subjects in one such study performed different tasks (Roland, 1993).

As the subjects used a finger to push a lever, increased blood flow was limited to the primary somatosensory and primary motor cortex (Figure 11-5A). As the subjects executed a sequence of finger movements, blood flow also increased in the premotor cortex (Figure 11-5B). And, as the subjects used a finger to trace their way through a maze, a task that requires the coordination of movements in relation to a goal, blood flow increased in the prefrontal cortex, as well (Figure 11-5C). Notice that blood flow did not increase throughout the entire frontal lobe as the subjects were performing these tasks. Blood flow increased only in those regions taking part in the required movements.

The Brainstem and Species-Typical Movement

Species-typical behaviors are actions displayed by every member of a species—the pecking of a robin, the hissing of a cat, or the breaching of a whale. In a series of studies, the Swiss neuroscientist Walter Hess (1957) found that the brainstem controls species-typical behaviors. Hess developed the technique of implanting electrodes into the brains of cats and other animals and cementing them in place. These electrodes could then be attached to stimulating leads in the freely moving animal without causing it much discomfort.

By stimulating the brainstem, Hess was able to elicit the innate movements that the animal might be expected to make. A resting cat could be induced to suddenly leap up with an arched back and erect hair as though frightened by an approaching dog, for example. The movements elicited began abruptly when the stimulating current was turned on and ended equally abruptly when the stimulating current was

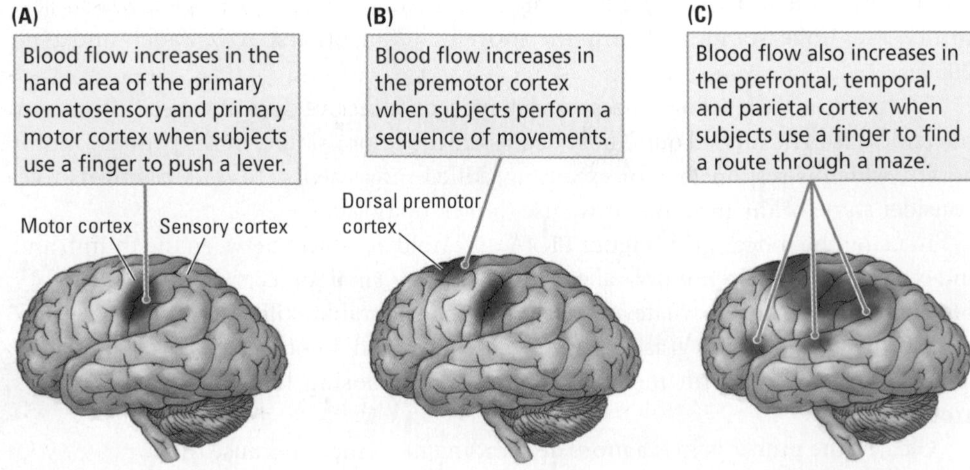

(A)
Blood flow increases in the hand area of the primary somatosensory and primary motor cortex when subjects use a finger to push a lever.
Motor cortex
Sensory cortex
(B)
Blood flow increases in the premotor cortex when subjects perform a sequence of movements.
Dorsal premotor cortex
(C)
Blood flow also increases in the prefrontal, temporal, and parietal cortex when subjects use a finger to find a route through a maze.

FIGURE 11-5 Hierarchical Control of Movement in the Brain. Adapted from *Brain Activation* (p. 63), by P. E. Roland, 1993, New York: Wiley-Liss.

turned off. The animal subjects performed such species-typical behaviors in a subdued manner when the stimulating current was low, but they increased in vigor as the stimulating current was turned up.

The actions varied, depending on the brainstem site that was stimulated. Stimulating some sites produced head turning, others produced walking or running, and still others elicited displays of aggression or fear. The animal's reaction toward a particular stimulus could be modified accordingly. For instance, when shown a stuffed toy, a cat responded to electrical stimulation of some sites by stalking the toy and to stimulation of other sites with a fearful response and withdrawal.

Hess's experiments have been confirmed and expanded by other researchers using many different animal species. For instance, **Experiment 11-1** shows the effects of brainstem stimulation on a chicken under various conditions (von Holst, 1973). Notice the effect of context: how the site stimulated interacts both with the presence of an object to which to react and with the stimulation's duration.

With stimulation of a certain site alone, the chicken displays only restless behavior. When a fist is displayed, the same stimulation elicits slightly threatening behavior. When the object displayed is then switched from a fist to a stuffed polecat, the chicken responds with vigorous threats. Finally, with continued stimulation in the presence of the polecat, the chicken flees, screeching.

Such experiments show that an important function of the brainstem is to produce species-typical adaptive behavior. Hess's classic experiments also gave rise to a sizable science-fiction literature in which "mind control" induced by brain stimulation figures centrally in the plot.

The brainstem also controls movements used in eating and drinking and in sexual behavior. Animals can be induced to display these survival-related behaviors when certain areas of the brainstem are stimulated. An animal can even be induced to eat nonfood objects, such as chips of wood, if the part of the brainstem that triggers chewing is stimulated. The brainstem is also important for maintaining posture, for standing upright, for making coordinated movements of the limbs, for swimming and walking, and for grooming the fur and making nests.

Grooming is a particularly complex movement pattern coordinated mainly by the brainstem (Kalueff et al., 2007). A grooming rat sits back on its haunches, licks its paws, wipes its nose with its paws, then wipes its paws across its face, and finally turns to lick the fur on its body. These movements are always performed in the same order, from the face to the shoulders and then toward the rear of the body. The next time you dry off after a shower or swimming, note the "grooming sequence" you use. Humans' grooming sequence is very similar to the one rats use.

The effects of damage to regions of the brainstem that organize specific-movement can be seen in the effects of **cerebral palsy.** A disorder primarily of motor function, cerebral palsy is caused by brain trauma in the course of fetal de-

EXPERIMENT 11-1

Question: What are the effects of brainstem stimulation under different conditions?

Procedures | **Results**

Stimulating electrode in brainstem

Electrical stimulation alone produces restless behavior.

Electrical stimulation in the presence of a fist produces slight threat.

Electrical stimulation in the presence of a stuffed polecat (a type of weasel) produces vigorous threat.

Continued electrical stimulation in the presence of the stuffed polecat produces flight and screeching.

Conclusion: Stimulation of some brainstem sites produces behavior that depends on context, suggesting that an important function of the brainstem is to produce appropriate species-typical behavior.

Adapted from *The Collected Papers of Erich von Holst* (p. 121), translated by R. Martin, 1973, Coral Gables, FL: University of Miami Press.

Clinical Focus 7-2 explores the causes and range of effects attendant to cerebral palsy.

Autism spectrum disorder (ASD) Range of cognitive symptoms, from mild to severe, that characterize autism; severe symptoms include greatly impaired social interaction, a bizarre and narrow range of interests, marked abnormalities in language and communication, and fixed, repetitive movements.

Quadriplegia Paralysis of the legs and arms due to spinal-cord injury.

Paraplegia Paralysis of the legs due to spinal-cord injury.

velopment or at birth. Trauma leading to cerebral palsy can sometimes happen in early infancy as well.

We examined E. S., a man who suffered a cold and infection when he was about 6 months old. Subsequently, he had great difficulty coordinating his movements. As he grew up, his hands and legs were almost useless and his speech was extremely difficult to understand. For most of his childhood, E. S. was considered retarded and was sent to a custodial school.

When he was 13 years old, the school bought a computer, and one of his teachers attempted to teach E. S. to use it by pushing the keys with a pencil that he held in his mouth. Within a few weeks, the teacher realized that E. S. was extremely intelligent and could communicate and complete school assignments on a computer. He was eventually given a motorized wheelchair that he could control with finger movements of his right hand.

Assisted by a computer and wheelchair, E. S. soon became almost self-sufficient and eventually attended college, where he achieved excellent grades and became a student leader. On graduation with a degree in psychology, he became a social worker and worked with children who suffered from cerebral palsy.

Clearly, a brain injury that causes cerebral palsy can be extremely damaging to movement while leaving sensory abilities and cognitive capacities unimpaired. Damage to the brainstem can also cause changes in cognitive function, such as occurs in the range of symptoms, from mild to severe, that mark **autism spectrum disorder** (ASD). Severe symptoms of autism include greatly impaired social interaction, a bizarre and narrow range of interests, marked abnormalities in language and communication, and fixed repetitive movements (see Clinical Focus 11-2, "Autism Spectrum Disorder").

The Spinal Cord and Execution of Movement

Christopher Reeve, a well-known actor who portrayed Superman in three films, was thrown from a horse during a riding competition in 1995. Reeve's spinal cord was severed near its upper end, at the C1–C2 level. The injury left Reeve's brain intact and functioning and his remaining spinal cord intact and functioning, too, but his brain and spinal cord were no longer connected.

To review the locations of the spinal-cord segments, see Figure 2-26.

As a result, other than movements of his head and slight movement in his shoulders, Reeve's body was completely paralyzed. He was even unable to breathe without assistance. A century ago such a severe injury would have been fatal, but modern and timely medical treatment allowed Reeve to survive for nearly a decade.

Cannon/The Kobal Collection

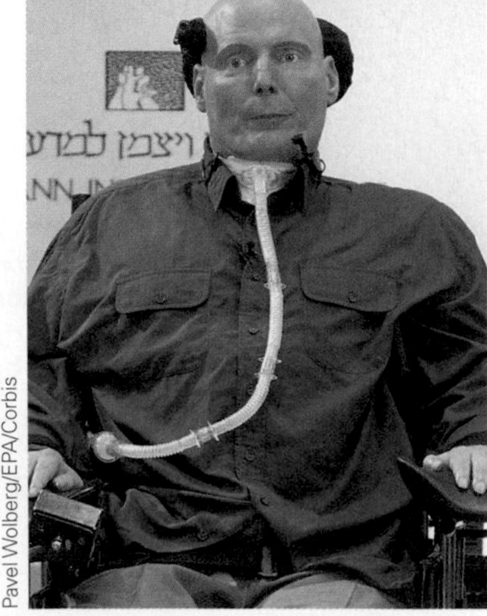

Pavel Wolberg/EPA/Corbis

The late actor Christopher Reeve (*left*) portraying Superman in 1984 and (*right*) nine years after his spinal-cord injury in 2004.

A cut high on the spinal cord, such as Christopher Reeve survived, entails paralysis and loss of sensation in the arms and legs, a condition called **quadriplegia.** If the cut is low, **paraplegia** results: paralysis and loss of sensation are confined to the legs and lower body, as described in Clinical Focus 11-3, "Spinal-Cord Injury." Christopher Reeve and his late wife Dana founded the Christopher and Dana Reeve Foundation for spinal-cord research. It is dedicated to improving the life and function of spinal-cord-injured people and also to searching for cures for spinal-cord injury.

Far from a mere relay between the body and brain, the spinal cord contains complex motor programs. A spinal-cord patient can walk on a conveyor belt if the body is supported. Indeed, Christopher Reeve was able to "walk" in a swimming pool in which his body was supported by water.

CLINICAL FOCUS 11-2

Autism Spectrum Disorder

Leo Kanner and Hans Asperger first used the term *autism* (from the Greek *autos,* meaning "self") in the 1940s to describe children who seem to live in their own self-created worlds. Although some of these children were classified as mentally retarded, the intellectual functioning of others was preserved. The current term, *autism spectrum disorder,* reflects this behavioral range to include children with either mild or severe symptoms.

An estimated 1 in 100 people has autism. Its incidence has increased over the last 40 years due to changes in diagnostic criteria, diagnosis of children at a younger age, and perhaps environmental influences on development. Although it knows neither racial nor ethnic nor social boundaries, the disorder is four times as prevalent in boys as in girls.

Many autistic children are noticeably different from birth. To avoid physical contact, these babies arch their backs and pull away from their caregivers or they grow limp when held. But approximately one-third of autistic children develop normally until somewhere between 1 and 3 years of age. Then the autistic symptoms emerge.

Perhaps the most recognized characteristic of autism spectrum disorder is failure to interact socially with other people. Some autistic children do not relate to other people on any level. The attachments that they do form are to inanimate objects, not to other human beings. Some are severely impaired, others learn to function quite well, and still others on the spectrum have exceptional abilities in music, art, or mathematics.

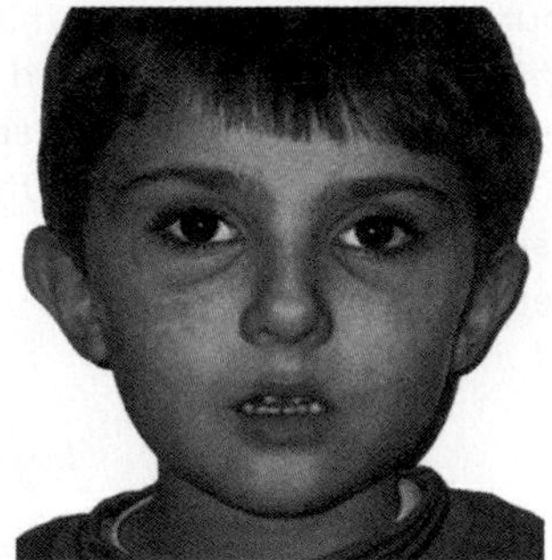

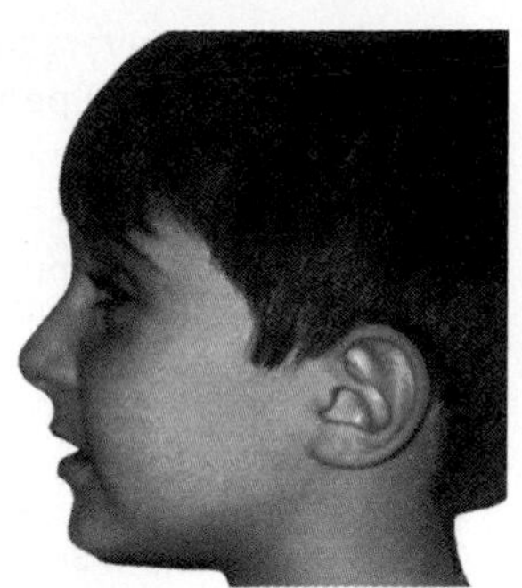

Photos courtesy of Susan L. Hyman

Although children with autism spectrum disorder often are normal in appearance, some physical anomalies characterize the disorder. The corners of the mouth may be low compared with the upper lip, and the tops of the ears may flop over (*left*). The ears may be a bit lower than normal and have an almost square shape (*right*).

Another common characteristic of autism is an extreme insistence on sameness. Autistic children vehemently resist even small modifications to their surroundings or their daily routines. Objects must always be placed in exactly the same locations, and tasks must always be carried out in precisely the same ways.

Autistic children also have marked impairments in language development. Many do not speak at all, and others repeat words aimlessly with little attempt to communicate or convey meaning. They may exhibit what seem like endlessly repetitive body movements, such as rocking, spinning, or flapping the hands. Some may engage as well in aggressive or self-injurious behavior.

At birth, children with autism spectrum disorder have relatively small heads compared with normal children, but, over the first year, 60 percent develop an excessive increase in head size, largely owing to an increase in the volume of the neocortex (Vaccarino et al., 2009). This finding suggests that the normal sculpturing of the brain in early infancy, in which there is normally a loss of cells, dendrites, and synapses to sculpture the adult brain, is abnormal in autistism.

Autism may have many different causes, including both genetic and environmantal causes (Charles et al., 2008). Women have an increased risk of giving birth to an autistic child if they are exposed to rubella (German measles) in the first trimester of pregnancy. Researchers also suspect that industrial toxins can trigger autism, but the evidence remains uncertain.

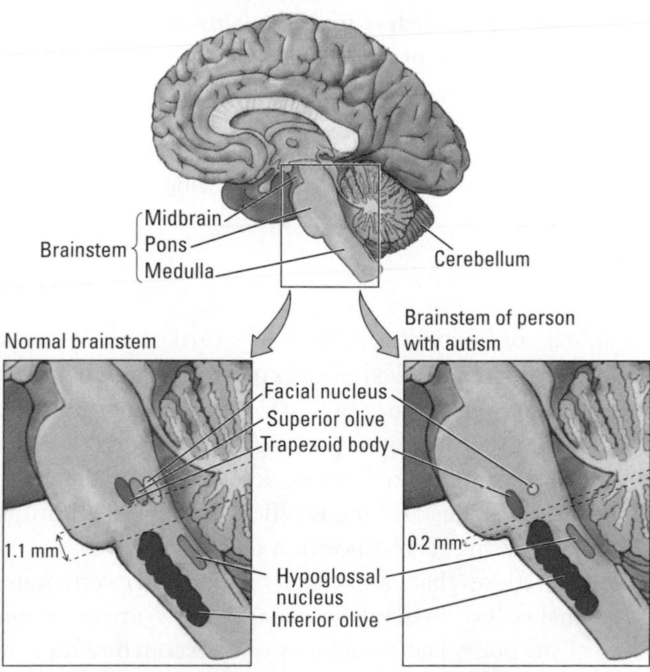

Autism affects the brainstem, where several nuclei in the posterior pons, including the facial nucleus, superior olive, and trapezoid body, are reduced in size.

CLINICAL FOCUS 11-3

Spinal-Cord Injury

Each year, on average, about 11,000 people in the United States and 1000 people in Canada suffer spinal-cord injury. Nearly 40 percent of these injuries occur in traffic accidents and another 40 percent occur as a result of falls. Often the spinal cord is completely severed, leaving the victim with no sensation or movement from the site of the cut downward.

Although 12,000 annual spinal-cord injuries may seem like a large number, it is small relative to the number of people in the United States and Canada who suffer other kinds of nervous-system damage each year. To increase public awareness about their condition and promote research into possible treatments, some, like Christopher Reeve and Canadian Rick Hansen, pictured here, have been especially active.

Courtesy of Nike/Rick Hansen Institute

Rick Hansen on the Man in Motion Tour in 1987.

Hansen's paraplegia resulted from a lower thoracic spinal injury in 1975. Twelve years later, to raise public awareness of the potential of people with disabilities, he wheeled himself 40,000 kilometers around the world to raise funds for the Man in Motion Legacy Trust Fund. The fund contributes to rehabilitation, wheelchair sports, and public-awareness programs. In 2008 it sponsored the Blusson Spinal Cord Centre in Vancouver, Canada, the largest institution dedicated to spinal-cord research in the world, housing over 300 investigators.

A severed spinal cord entails a cut that leaves the machinery on both sides of it intact. If only the cut could be bridged, function might be restored. Factors preventing nerve fibers from growing across a cut in a spinal cord are the formation of scar tissue, a lack of a blood supply, and the absence of appropriate growth factors to stimulate neuron growth. Normal tissue at the edge of the cut also actively repels regrowth.

It is encouraging that when a nerve fiber in the peripheral nervous system is cut, it regrows. Schwann cells that form the severed axon's myelin produce the chemical environment that facilitates regrowth. One focus of spinal-cord research is then to induce the same type of recovery in the spinal cord.

Research directed at this objective is searching for nerve-growth factors that might stimulate severed axons to regrow, ways of implanting Schwann cells that might enhance regrowth, and ways of implanting stem cells that could serve a like function. Another focus of spinal-cord research is to improve treatment, therapy, and the environment of spinal-injured people.

In the public arena, improved safety in automobiles and in sports, better emergency treatment to minimize the extent of injury, and improved assistance in movement and home care are all important in minimizing spinal-cord injury.

When the limb of a spinal-cord patient is moved backward on the conveyor belt, causing the foot to lose support, the limb reflexively lifts off the belt and swings forward underneath the body. As the foot then touches the surface of the belt again, tactile receptors initiate the reflex that causes the foot to push against the surface and support the body's weight. In this way, several spinal reflexes work together to facilitate the complex movement of walking. Because this walking is reflexive, even a preborn or newborn baby displays it when held in the correct position on a conveyor belt.

Scratch reflex

One of the more complex reflexes that can be observed in other vertebrates is the **scratch reflex.** Here, an animal reflexively scratches a part of its body in response to a stimulus from the surface of the body. The complexity of the scratch reflex is revealed in the accuracy of the movement. Without direction from the brain, the tip of a limb, usually a hind limb, can be correctly directed to the part of the body that is irritated.

In humans and other animals with a severed spinal cord, spinal reflexes still function, even though the spinal cord is cut off from communication with the brain. As a result, the paralyzed limbs may display spontaneous movements or spasms. But the brain can no longer guide the timing of these automatic movements. Consequently, reflexes related to bladder and bowel control may need to be artificially stimulated by caregivers.

Scratch reflex Automatic response in which an animal's hind limb reaches to remove a stimulus from the surface of the body.

REVIEW: Hierarchical Control of Movement

- ✔ The motor system is organized hierarchically.
- ✔ The forebrain, especially the frontal lobe, is responsible for selecting plans of action (prefrontal cortex), coordinating body parts to carry out plans (premotor cortex), and executing precise movements (primary motor cortex).
- ✔ The brainstem is responsible for species-typical movements, for survival-related actions, and for posture and walking.
- ✔ In addition to being a pathway between the brain and the rest of the body, the spinal cord is independently responsible for reflexive movements.
- ✔ Although lower-level functions in this hierarchical system can continue in the absence of higher-level ones, the higher levels provide voluntary control over movements. Consequently, when the brain is disconnected from the spinal cord, movement can no longer be controlled at will.

Organization of the Motor System

The use of different body parts to achieve skilled movements is widespread among animals. Dolphins and seals are adept at using their noses to carry and manipulate objects, elephants can perform a range of movements with their trunks, and dogs accomplish many actions using their mouths. Birds' beaks are specially designed for getting food, for building nests, and even for making and using tools.

Tails also are useful appendages. Some marsupials and some species of New World primates use their tails to pick up and carry objects. Among horses, the lips are dexterous enough to manipulate a single blade of grass of the type that a horse prefers from a patch of vegetation. Although we humans tend to rely primarily on our hands for manipulating objects, we can still learn to handle things with other body parts, such as the mouth or a foot, if we have to. Some people without arms become extremely proficient at using a foot for writing or painting or even for driving.

What properties of the motor system allow such versatility in carrying out skilled movements? In this section, you will find the answer to this question as we examine the organization of the motor cortex and its descending pathways to the brainstem and spinal cord, which in turn connects with the muscles of the body.

The Motor Cortex

In 1870, two Prussian physicians, Gustav Fritsch and Eduard Hitzig, discovered that they could electrically stimulate the neocortex of an anesthetized dog to produce movements of the mouth, limbs, and paws on the opposite side of the dog's body. They provided the first direct evidence that the neocortex controls movement. Later researchers confirmed the finding by using a variety of animals as subjects, including rats, monkeys and apes.

On the basis of this research background, beginning in the 1930s, Wilder Penfield used electrical stimulation to map the cortices of conscious human patients who were about to undergo neurosurgery. Penfield's aim was to use the results to assist in surgery.

Figure 10-19 shows Penfield using brain stimulation to map the cortex.

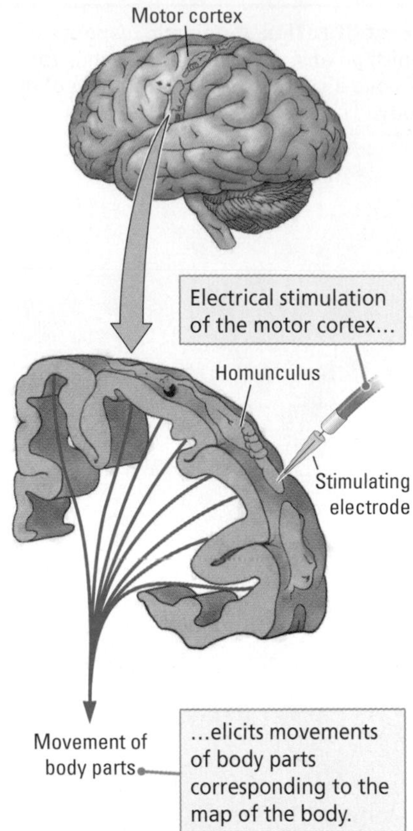
Motor cortex
Electrical stimulation of the motor cortex...
Homunculus
Stimulating electrode
Movement of body parts
...elicits movements of body parts corresponding to the map of the body.

FIGURE 11-6 Penfield's Homunculus. Movements are topographically organized in the motor cortex. Stimulation of the dorsal medial regions of the cortex produces movements in the lower limbs. Stimulation in ventral regions of the cortex produces movements in the upper body, hands, and face.

He and his colleagues confirmed that movements in humans also are triggered mainly in response to stimulation of the primary motor cortex.

Penfield summarized his results by drawing cartoons of body parts to represent the areas of the motor cortex that produce movement in those parts. The result was a **homunculus** (little person) that could be spread out across the motor cortex, as illustrated in **Figure 11-6.** Because the body is symmetrical, an equivalent motor homunculus is represented in the primary motor cortex of each hemisphere, and each mainly controls movement in the opposite side of the body. Penfield also identified another, smaller motor homunculus in the dorsal premotor area of each frontal lobe, a region sometimes referred to as the *supplementary motor cortex.*

The most striking feature of the motor homunculus is the disproportionate relative sizes of its body parts, shown in **Figure 11-7,** compared with the relative sizes of actual parts of the human body. As you can see, the homunculus has very large hands with an especially large thumb. Its lips and tongue are especially prominent, as well. In contrast, the trunk, arms, and legs, which constitute most of the area of a real body, are much smaller in relative size. These distortions illustrate the fact that large parts of the motor cortex regulate the hands, fingers, lips, and tongue, giving us precise motor control over these body parts. Areas of the body over which we have much less motor control have a much smaller representation in the motor cortex.

Another curious feature of the homunculus as laid out across the motor cortex is that the body parts are arranged much differently from those of an actual body. The area of the cortex that produces eye movements is located in front of the homunculus head on the motor cortex. As shown in Figure 11-6, the head is oriented with the chin up and the forehead down, and the tongue is located below the forehead.

Such details aside, the homunculus shows at a glance that relatively larger areas of the brain control the parts of the body that we use to make the most skilled movements. It is thus a useful concept for understanding the **topographic organization** (functional layout) of the primary motor cortex.

The discovery of the topographical organization of the motor cortex suggested how movements might be produced. Information from other regions of the neocortex could be sent to the motor homunculus, and neurons in the appropriate part of the homunculus could then execute the movements called for. If finger movements are needed, for example, messages can be sent to the finger area of the motor cortex, triggering the required activity there. If this model of how the motor system works is correct, damage to any part of the homunculus would result in loss of movement in the corresponding part of the body.

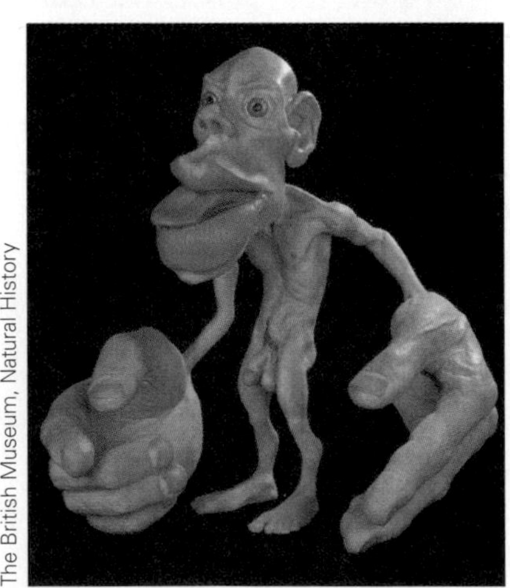
The British Museum, Natural History

FIGURE 11-7 Homuncular Man. An artist's representation illustrates the disproportionate areas of the sensory and motor cortices that control different parts of the body.

Although the general idea underlying this model is correct, more detailed mapping of the motor cortex and more detailed studies of the effects of damage to it reaveals that its functions may be even simpler. When researchers investigated the motor cortex in nonhuman primates using smaller electrodes than those used by Penfield to examine his patients, they discovered as many as ten motor homunculi. As many as four representations of the body may exist in the primary motor cortex, and a number of other representations may be found in the premotor cortex.

Using half-second-long trains of elecrical stimulation in conscious monkeys rather than the brief pulses of electrical stimulation used by Pen-

Homunculus Representation of the human body in the sensory or motor cortex; also any topographical representation of the body by a neural area.

Topographic organization Neural spatial representation of the body or areas of the sensory world perceived by a sensory organ.

Corticospinal tract Bundle of nerve fibers directly connecting the cerebral cortex to the spinal cord, branching at the brainstem into an opposite-side lateral tract that informs movement of limbs and digits and a same-side ventral tract that informs movement of the trunk; also called pyramidal tract.

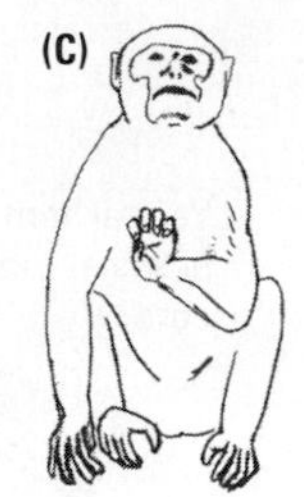

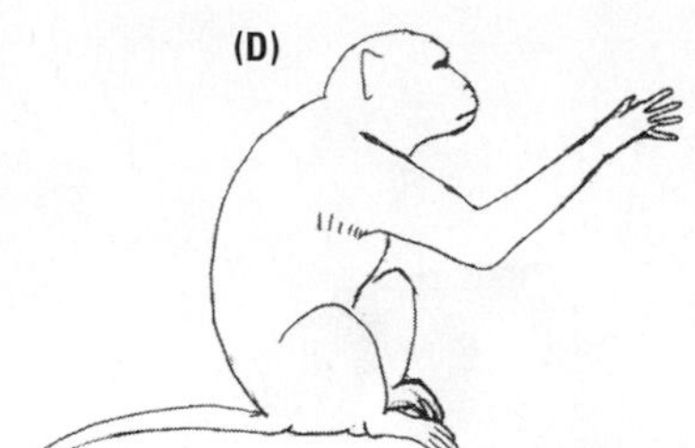

FIGURE 11-8 Motor Cortex Movement Categories. Five categories of movements evoked by electrical stimulation of the motor cortex in the monkey. Adapted from "The Organization of Behavioural Repertoire in Motor Cortex," by M. Graziano, 2006, *Annual Reviews of Neuroscience, 29,* 105–134.

field in humans, Michael Graziano found that stimulation elicits recognizable actions. The drawings in **Figure 11-8** illustrate the end points of a number of these categories: (A) defensive postures of the face, (B) movements of the hand to mouth, (C) manipulation and shaping of the hand and digits in central body space, (D) outward reach with the hand, and (E) climbing and leaping postures.

The movement categories observed by Graziano have the same end regardless of the location of a monkey's limb or its other ongoing behavior. Electrical stimulation that results in the hand coming to the mouth always recruits the hand. If a weight is attached to the monkey's arm, the evoked movement conpensates for the added load. Nevertheless, the movement is inflexible. When an obstacle is placed between the hand and the mouth, the hand hits the obstacle. Additionally, if stimulation continues after the hand has reached the mouth, the hand remains there for the duration of the stimulation.

Graziano proposes that the motor cortex represents three types of organization: the part of the body that is to be moved, the spatial location to which the movement is directed, and the movement's function. The motor representation of this organization implies many maps of the body, each represting somewhat different movements, the parts of space in which an action is to take place, and the function that action is intended to perform.

Nevertheless, movements of a certain type—for example, reaching—cluster together with respect to the part of the motor cortex from which they are elicited, but reaching to different parts of space is elicited from slightly different points in the reaching map. Presumably, movements elicited from the motor cortex represent basic "types" that can be modified by learning and practice. In other words, the motor cortex encodes a lexicon, or dictionary, of movements that is not large but, when used in different combinations, is versatile.

Corticospinal Tracts

The main pathways from the motor cortex to the brainstem and spinal cord are the **corticospinal tracts.** The axons of the corticospinal tracts originate mainly in layer V pyramidal cells of the motor cortex. Axons also come from the premotor cortex and the sensory cortex. These axons descend into the brainstem, sending collaterals to a few brainstem nuclei and eventually emerging on the brainstem's ventral surface where they form a large bump on each side. These bumps, or "pyramids," give the corticospinal tracts their alternate name, the *pyramidal tracts.*

Bundles of nerve fibers within the central nervous system are called *tracts;* outside the CNS they are called *nerves* (see Chapter 2). The term *corticospinal* indicates that these fiber bundles begin in the neocortex and terminate in the spinal cord. Figure 2-20 diagrams the six layers of the neocortex.

At this point, most of the axons descending from the left hemisphere cross over to the right side of the brainstem. Likewise, most of the axons descending from the right hemisphere cross over to the left side of the brainstem. The rest of the axons stay on their original sides. This division produces two corticospinal tracts, one uncrossed and the other crossed, entering each side of the spinal cord. **Figure 11-9** illustrates the division of tracts originating in the left-hemisphere cortex. The dual tracts on each side of the brainstem then descend into the spinal cord, forming the two spinal cord tracts.

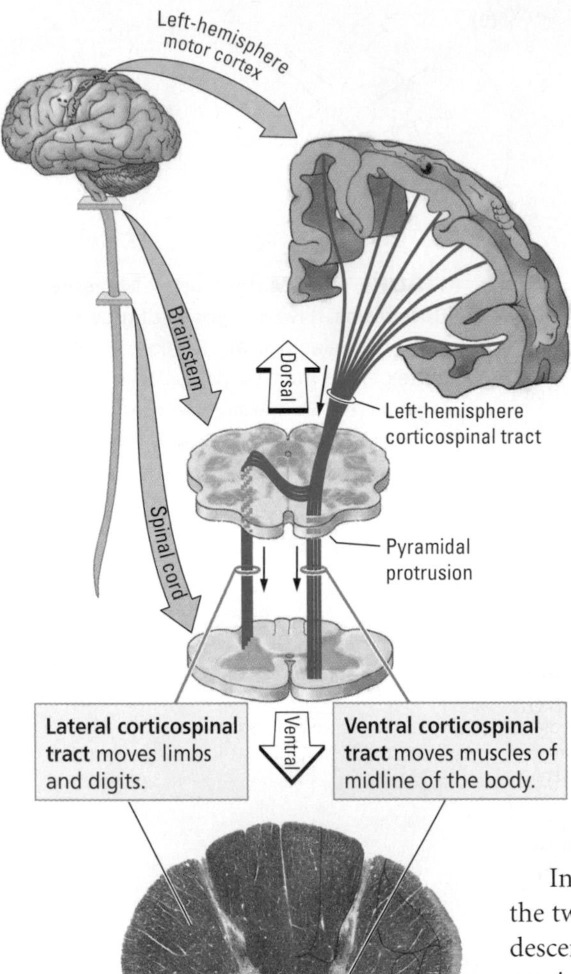

FIGURE 11-9 Corticospinal Tract. Nerve fibers from each hemisphere (only the left-hemisphere tract is shown here) descend from the motor cortex to the brainstem, where the tract branches into the spinal cord. A lateral tract crosses the midline to the opposite side of the spinal cord, and a ventral tract remains on the same side. Fibers in the lateral tract are represented by the limbs and digits of the cortical homunculus and are destined to move muscles of the limbs and digits. Fibers of the ventral tract are represented by the midline of the homunculus and are destined to move muscles at the body's midline.
Photograph of spinal cord reproduced from *The Human Brain: Dissections of the Real Brain,* by T. H. Williams, N. Gluhbegovic, and J. Jew, on CD-ROM. Published by Brain University, brain-university.com 2000.

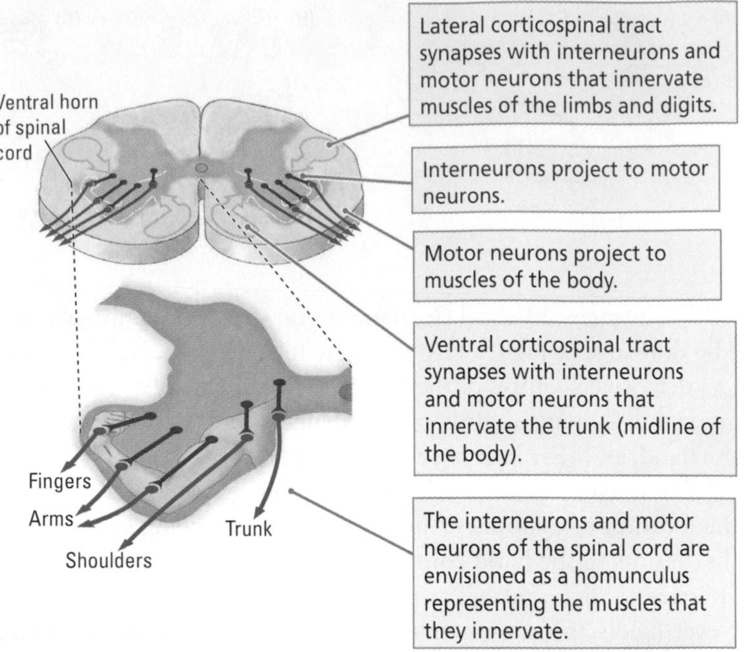

FIGURE 11-10 Motor-Tract Organization. The interneurons and the motor neurons of the ventral spinal cord are topographically arranged: the more lateral neurons innervate more distal parts of the limbs (those farther from the midline), and the more medial neurons innervate more proximal muscles of the body (those closer to the midline).

In the cross section of the spinal cord in **Figure 11-10,** you can see the location of the two tracts on each side. The fibers that cross to the opposite side of the brainstem descend the spinal cord in a lateral (side) position, giving them the name *lateral corticospinal tract.* The fibers that remain on their original side of the brainstem continue down the spinal cord in a ventral (front) position, giving them the name *ventral corticospinal tract.* As we will see, the two tracts eventually control different parts of the body.

Motor Neurons

The spinal-cord motor neurons that connect to muscles are located in the ventrolateral part of the spinal cord and jut out to form the spinal column's ventral horns. There are two kinds of neurons in the ventral horns. Interneurons lie just medial to the motor neurons and project onto them. The motor neurons send their axons to the muscles of the body. The fibers from the corticospinal tracts make synaptic connections with both the interneurons and the motor neurons, but all nervous system commands to the muscles are carried by the motor neurons.

Figure 11-10 shows that the more laterally located motor neurons project to muscles that control the fingers and hands, whereas intermediately located motor neurons project to muscles that control the arms and shoulders. The most medially located motor neurons project to muscles that control the trunk. Axons of the lateral corticospinal tract connect mainly with the lateral interneurons and motor neurons, and axons of the ventral corticospinal tract connect mainly to the medial interneurons and motor neurons. In other words, a homunculus of the body is represented again in the spinal cord.

To picture how the motor homunculus in the cortex is related to the motor neuron homunculus in the spinal cord, using Figure 11-9, place your finger on the index-finger region of the motor homunculus on the left side of the brain. Tracing the axons of the cortical neurons downward, your route takes you through the brainstem, across its midline, and down the right lateral corticospinal tract.

The journey ends at the interneurons and motor neurons in the most lateral region of the spinal cord's right ventral horn—the horn on the opposite side of the nervous system from which you began. Following the axons of these motor neurons, you find that they synapse on muscles that move the index finger on the right-hand side of the body.

By the way, the neurons that your brain is using to carry out this task are the same neurons whose pathway you are tracing.

If you repeat the procedure by tracing the pathway from the trunk of the motor homunculus on the left side of the brain, you follow the same route through the upper part of the brainstem. However, you do not cross over to the brainstem's opposite side. Instead, you descend into the spinal cord on the left side, the same side of the nervous system on which you began, eventually ending up in the most medially located interneurons and motor neurons of the left side's ventral horn. In addition, some of these axons also cross over to the other side of the spinal cord. Thus, if you follow the axons of these motor neurons, you end up at their synapses with muscles that move the trunk on both sides of the body.

This visualization should help you to remember the routes taken by the axons of the motor system. The limb regions of the motor homunculus contribute most of their fibers to the lateral corticospinal tract. Because these fibers have crossed over to the opposite side of the brainstem, they activate motor neurons that move the arm, hand, leg, and foot on the opposite side of the body.

In contrast, the trunk regions of the motor homunculus contribute their fibers to the ventral corticospinal tract. These fibers do not cross over at the brainstem, although some do cross over in the spinal cord. In short, the neurons of the motor homunculus in the left-hemisphere cortex control the trunk on both sides of the body and the limbs on the body's right side. Similarly, neurons of the motor homunculus in the right-hemisphere cortex control the trunk on both sides of the body and the limbs on the body's left side.

Thus, one hemisphere of the cortex controls the hands and fingers of the opposite side of the body and the trunk on both sides of the body. If the motor cortex is organized in terms of a number of functional movements, such as reaching to a point in space, it follows that the spinal cord must have a similar organization. In this way, instructions from the motor cortex concerning a reach to a part of space can be faithfully produced by a similar template in the spinal cord.

In addition to the corticospinal pathways, there are actually about 24 other pathways from the brainstem to the spinal cord. The other pathways carry instructions such as information related to posture and balance, and they control the autonomic nervous system. For all these functions, however, the motor neurons are the final common path.

Control of Muscles

The muscles on which spinal-cord motor neurons synapse control body movements. For example, the biceps and triceps of the upper arm control movement of the lower arm. Limb muscles are arranged in pairs, as shown in **Figure 11-11.** One member of a pair, the *extensor,* moves (extends) the limb away from the trunk. The other member of the pair, the *flexor,* moves the limb toward the trunk.

Connections between the interneurons and motor neurons of the spinal cord ensure that the muscles work together so that, when one muscle contracts, the other relaxes. Thus, the interneurons and motor neurons of the spinal cord not only relay instructions from the brain but also, through their connections, cooperatively organize the movement of many muscles. As you know, the neurotransmitter at the motor-neuron–muscle junction is acetylcholine.

FIGURE 11-11 Coordinating Movement.

Triceps (extensor muscle) extends the lower arm away from the body.
Biceps (flexor muscle) moves the lower arm toward the body.
Acetylcholine is the neurotransmitter at the neuromuscular junction.
Spinal cord
Extensor motor neurons and flexor motor neurons project to muscles.
The spinal cord ventral horn contains interneurons and motor neurons.

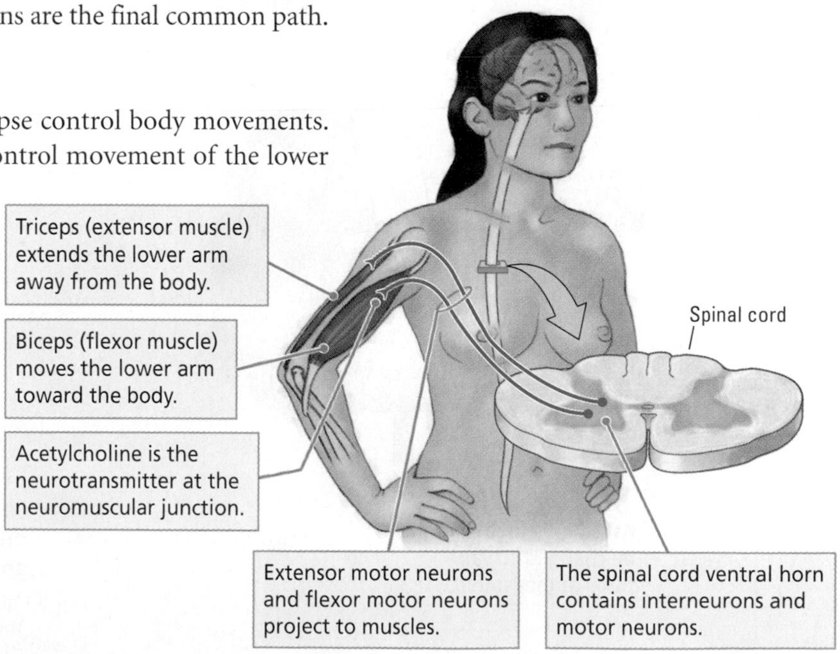

REVIEW: Organization of the Motor System

- ✔ The motor cortex is topographically organized as a homunculus in which parts of the body that are capable of the most skilled movements (especially the mouth, fingers, and thumb) are regulated by larger cortical regions.
- ✔ Instructions regarding movement travel from the motor cortex through the corticospinal tracts to interneurons and motor neurons in the ventral horn of the spinal cord. Many of the corticospinal-tract fibers cross to the opposite side of the spinal cord to form the lateral corticospinal tracts; some stay on the same side to form the ventral corticospinal tracts.
- ✔ The ventral corticospinal tracts carry instructions for trunk movements, whereas the lateral corticospinal tracts carry instructions for arm and finger movements. The axons of motor neurons in the spinal cord then carry instructions to muscles.
- ✔ Muscles are arranged in pairs in which one pair flexes a limb while the other extends the limb.

The Motor Cortex and Skilled Movement

In a study designed to investigate how the neurons of the motor cortex control movement, Edward Evarts (1968) used the simple procedure illustrated in **Experiment 11-2.** He trained a monkey to flex its wrist in order to move a bar to which different weights could be attached. An electrode implanted in the wrist region of the motor cortex recorded the activity of neurons there.

Evarts discovered that these neurons began to discharge even before the monkey flexed its wrist, as shown in the Results section of Experiment 11-2. Thus, they take

EXPERIMENT 11-2

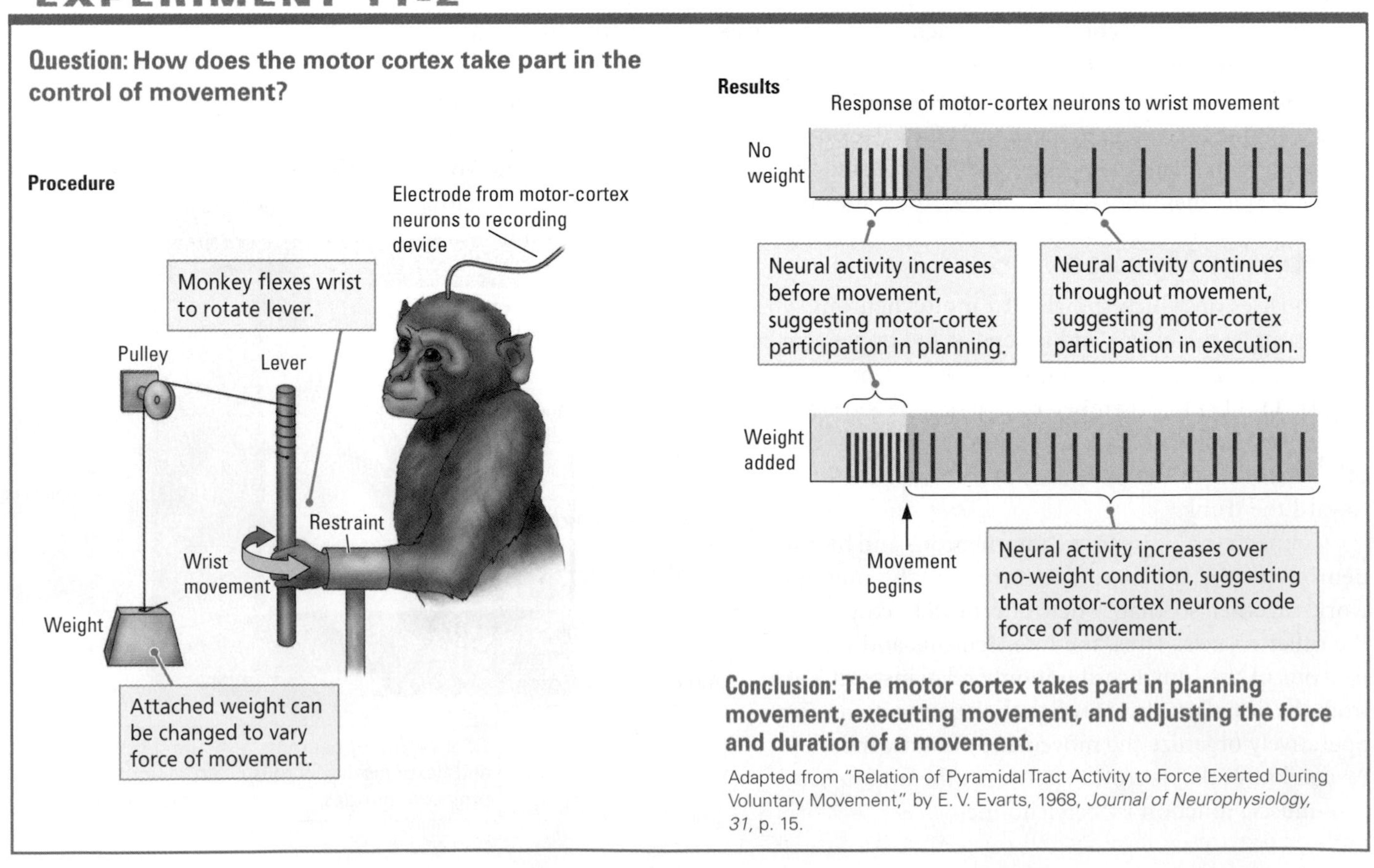
Question: How does the motor cortex take part in the control of movement?
Procedure
Electrode from motor-cortex neurons to recording device
Monkey flexes wrist to rotate lever.
Pulley
Lever
Restraint
Wrist movement
Weight
Attached weight can be changed to vary force of movement.
Results
Response of motor-cortex neurons to wrist movement
No weight
Neural activity increases before movement, suggesting motor-cortex participation in planning.
Neural activity continues throughout movement, suggesting motor-cortex participation in execution.
Weight added
Movement begins
Neural activity increases over no-weight condition, suggesting that motor-cortex neurons code force of movement.
Conclusion: The motor cortex takes part in planning movement, executing movement, and adjusting the force and duration of a movement.

Adapted from "Relation of Pyramidal Tract Activity to Force Exerted During Voluntary Movement," by E. V. Evarts, 1968, *Journal of Neurophysiology, 31*, p. 15.

part in planning the movement as well as initiating it. The neurons also continued to discharge as the wrist moved, confirming that they play a role in producing the movement. Finally, the neurons discharged at a higher rate when the bar was loaded with a weight. This finding shows that motor-cortex neurons increase the force of a movement by increasing their rate of firing and its duration, as stated in the Conclusion of the experiment.

Evarts's findings also revealed that the motor cortex has a role in specifying the direction of a movement. The neurons of the motor-cortex wrist area discharged when the monkey flexed its wrist inward but not when the wrist was extended back to its starting position. These on–off responses of the neurons, depending on whether the flexor or extensor muscle is being used, are a simple way of coding the direction in which the wrist is moving.

Control of Skilled Movement in Nonhuman Species

Humans are far from the only species that makes skilled movements. Kamala, a female Indian elephant at the Calgary Zoo in Canada, paints works of art with her trunk, and primates other than humans are very skilled with their hands. How is the motor cortex in other species organized to enable these skilled movement patterns?

The results of studies of a wide range of animals show that their motor cortices are organized to correspond to the skilled movements of their species. Just as in humans, larger parts of the motor cortex regulate body parts that carry out these movements. **Figure 11-12** shows cartoons representing the human homunculus and comparable drawings of four other animals—rabbit, cat, monkey, and elephant.

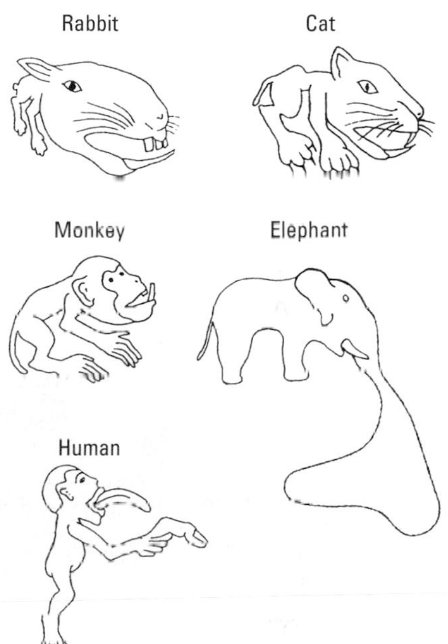

FIGURE 11-12 Motor-Control Cartoons. The size of the cortical area regulating a body part in these motor-cortex representations corresponds to the skill required in moving that body part. The representation for the elephant is only surmised. Adapted from *Principles of Neural Science* (3rd ed., p. 373), by E. R. Kandel, J. H. Schwartz, and T. M. Jessel, 1991, New York: Elsevier.

As you can see, rabbits have a large motor-cortex representation for the head and mouth, cats for the mouth and front claws, and monkeys for the hands, feet, and digits. Although no one has mapped the motor cortex of an elephant, it is likely that a disproportionately large area of its motor cortex is dedicated to regulating the trunk.

How did these specialized representations of the motor cortex evolve? One possibility is that they were adapted from the outside inward. Chance mutations caused an adaptive increase in the number of muscles in a particular part of the body, which led to more motor neurons in the spinal cord. Concurrent with this increase in motor neurons, the area of the motor cortex controlling the corresponding spinal-cord motor neurons increased. The larger motor-cortex representation, along with an increased possibility of making connections between the cortical neurons, led to an evolved capacity for making new and more complex movements. That is, after the motor cortex had expanded, evolutionary pressure could then select for subregions to become specialized for new behaviors.

Let us apply this scenario to the evolution of the elephant's trunk. First, chance mutations led to the expansion of muscles in the elephant's lip and nose and the spinal-cord motor neurons needed to move them. These developments were retained because they were useful, perhaps because the trunk was longer than it was in the elephant's ancestors. The area of the motor cortex coexpanded to represent the new muscles of the trunk. The cortical area for the trunk motor cortex expanded and differentiated to enable fine control of different trunk muscles that enabled selectively advantageous behaviors, such as feeding on new food sources.

How Motor-Cortex Damage Affects Skilled Movement

Scientists first mapped the motor cortex in the 1930s. A number of researchers got slightly different results when they repeated the mapping procedures on the same subjects. These findings led to a debate.

Some scientists held that motor-cortex topography was capable of changing—that areas controlling particular body parts might not always stay in exactly the same place and retain exactly the same dimensions. But other researchers felt that this view was unlikely. They argued that, given the enormous specificity of topographic maps of the motor cortex, the maps must surely be quite stable. If they appeared to change, it must be because the large electrodes used for stimulating and recording from cortical neurons were producing inexact results.

As cortical-mapping procedures improved, however, and as smaller and smaller electrodes were used, it became clear that motor maps can indeed change. They can change as a result of sensory or motor learning, and they can change when part of the motor cortex is damaged, as the following example shows.

Chapter 14 explores how motor maps change in response to learning.

A study by Randy Nudo and his coworkers (1996), summarized in the Procedure section of **Experiment 11-3,** illustrates change in a map of the motor cortex due to cortical damage. These researchers mapped the motor cortices of monkeys to identify the hand and digit areas. They then surgically removed a small part of the cortex that represents the digit area. After the surgery, the monkeys used the affected hand much less, relying mainly on the good hand.

Three months later, the researchers examined the monkeys. They found that the animals were unable to produce many movements of the lower arm, including the wrist, the hand, and the digits surrounding the area with the lesion. They also discovered that much of the area representing the hand and lower arm was gone from the cortical map. The shoulder, upper arm, and elbow areas had spread to take up what had formerly been space representing the hand and digits. The Results section of Experiment 11-3 shows this topographic change.

The experimenters wondered whether the change could have been prevented had they forced the monkeys to use the affected arm. To find out, they used the same procedure on other monkeys, except that, during the postsurgery period, they made the animals rely on the bad arm by binding the good arm in a sling.

Three months later, when the experimenters reexamined the motor maps of these monkeys, they found that the hand and digit area retained its large size, even though there was no neural activity in the spot with the lesion. Nevertheless, the monkeys had gained some function in the digits that had formerly been connected to the damaged spot. Apparently, the remaining digit area of the cortex was now controlling the movement of these fingers.

The property of the motor cortex that allows it to change as a result of experience, as you know, is plasticity. Thus, plasticity in the motor cortex underlies our ability to acquire new motor skills as well as our ability to recover from brain injury. Most likely plasticity is enabled by the formation of new connections among different parts of the homunculus in the motor cortex.

The motor-cortex reorganization that Nudo and his colleagues observed in monkeys probably explains recovery from brain damage observed in humans. Humans who suffer a stroke to the motor cortex may at first be completely unable to use their contralateral forelimb, but with time and practice they may recover a great deal of movement. One way to enhance re-

EXPERIMENT 11-3

Question: What is the effect of rehabilitation on the cortical representation of the forelimb after brain damage?

Procedure

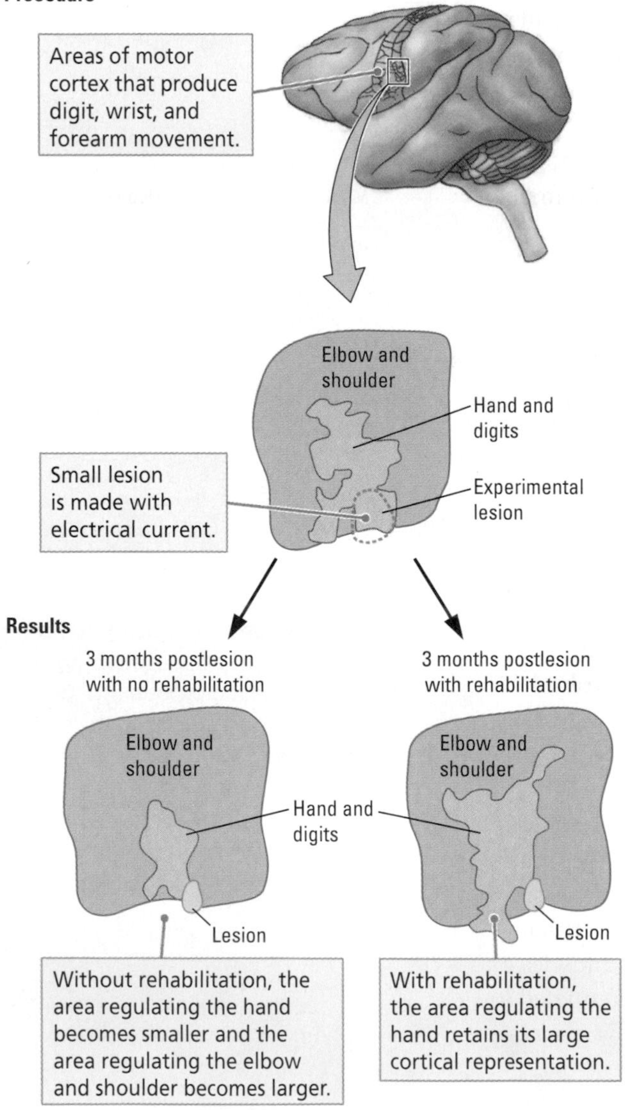

Areas of motor cortex that produce digit, wrist, and forearm movement.
Elbow and shoulder
Hand and digits
Experimental lesion
Small lesion is made with electrical current.

Results

3 months postlesion with no rehabilitation
3 months postlesion with rehabilitation
Elbow and shoulder
Hand and digits
Lesion
Elbow and shoulder
Lesion
Without rehabilitation, the area regulating the hand becomes smaller and the area regulating the elbow and shoulder becomes larger.
With rehabilitation, the area regulating the hand retains its large cortical representation.

Conclusion: Rehabilitation prevents both a loss of movement in the hand and a decrease in the hand's cortical representation.

Adapted from "Neural Substrates for the Effects of Rehabilitative Training on Motor Recovery after Ischemic Infarct," by R. J. Nudo, B. M. Wise, F. SiFuentes, and G. W. Milliken, 1996, *Science, 272,* p. 1793.

covery is to restrain the good limb. **Restraint-induced therapy**, which forces the person to use the affected limb, is a major therapy for stroke-induced limb paralysis. Its effectivness depends on the the neural plasticity identified by Nudo and his colleagues in monkeys.

Restraint-induced therapy Procedure in which restraint of a healthy limb forces a patient to use an impaired limb to enhance recovery of function.

REVIEW: The Motor Cortex and Skilled Movement

- ✔ The discharge patterns of motor-cortex neurons suggest that these neurons take part in planning and initiating movements as well as in carrying them out. Their discharge rate is related both to the force of muscle contraction and to the direction of a movement.
- ✔ The topographic map of the motor cortex of a particular species is related to the body parts that are capable of making the most skillful movements.
- ✔ The relation between neurons in the motor cortex and the movement of specific muscles is plastic. Considerable change can take place in the cortical motor map and in recovery of function after injury to the motor cortex.

The Basal Ganglia and the Cerebellum

The main evidence that the basal ganglia and the cerebellum perform motor functions is that damage to either structure impairs movement. Both structures also have extensive connections with the motor cortex, further suggesting their participation in movement. After an overview of the anatomy of the basal ganglia and cerebellum, we look at some symptoms that arise after they are damaged. Then we consider some experiments that illustrate the roles that these structures might play in controlling movement.

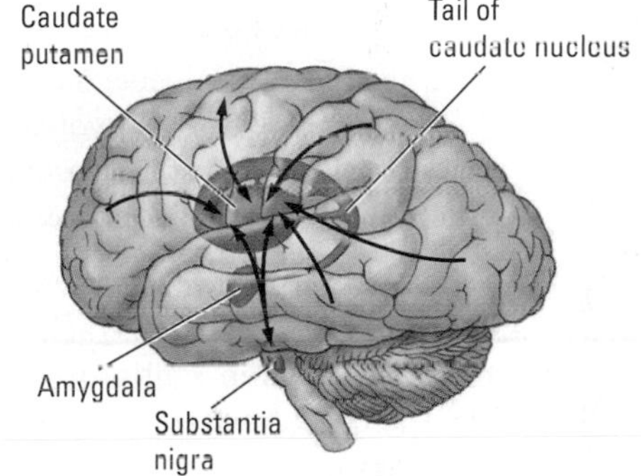

FIGURE 11-13 Basal Ganglia Connections. The caudate putamen in the basal ganglia connects to the amygdala through the tail of the caudate nucleus. The basal ganglia also make reciprocal connections with the substantia nigra, receive input from most regions of the cortex, and send input into the frontal lobes through the thalamus.

The Basal Ganglia and Movement Force

Our control over movement is remarkable. We can manipulate objects as light as a needle, to sew, or swing objects as heavy as a baseball bat to drive a ball more than 100 yards. The brain areas that allow us to adjust the force of our movements in these ways include the basal ganglia, a collection of subcortical nuclei within the forebrain that make connections with the motor cortex and with the midbrain. As shown in **Figure 11-13**, a prominent structure in the basal ganglia is the caudate putamen, a large cluster of nuclei that extends as a "tail" into the temporal lobe, ending in the amygdala.

The basal ganglia receive inputs from two main sources:

1. All areas of the neocortex and limbic cortex, including the motor cortex, project to the basal ganglia.
2. The nigrostriatial dopaminergic activating system projects to the basal ganglia from the substantia nigra, a cluster of darkly pigmented cells in the midbrain.

Figure 5-17 traces the nigrostriatial pathways and highlights their importance in maintaining normal motor behavior.

Basal ganglia nuclei project back to both the motor cortex and the substantia nigra.

Two different, in many ways opposite, kinds of movement disorders result from damage to the basal ganglia. If cells of the caudate putamen are damaged, unwanted choreiform (writhing and twitching) movements result. For example, Huntington's chorea, in which cells of the caudate putamen are destroyed, is characterized by involuntary and exaggerated movements. Other examples of involuntary movements related to caudate putamen damage are the unwanted tics and vocalizations peculiar to Tourette's syndrome, which is discussed in Clinical Focus 11-4, "Tourette's Syndrome."

Clinical Focus 3-4 describes the genetic basis of Huntington's chorea.

CLINICAL FOCUS 11-4

Tourette's Syndrome

The neurological disorder Tourette's syndrome (TS) was first described in 1885 by Georges Gilles de la Tourette, a French neurologist. Here is how he described the symptoms as they appeared in Madame de D., one of his patients:

> Madame de D., presently age 26, at the age of 7 was afflicted by convulsive movements of the hands and arms. These abnormal movements occurred above all when the child tried to write, causing her to crudely reproduce the letters she was trying to trace. After each spasm, the movements of the hand became more regular and better controlled until another convulsive movement would again interrupt her work. She was felt to be suffering from over-excitement and mischief, and because the movements became more and more frequent, she was subject to reprimand and punishment. Soon it became clear that these movements were indeed involuntary and convulsive in nature. The movements involved the shoulders, the neck, and the face, and resulted in contortions and extraordinary grimaces. As the disease progressed, and the spasms spread to involve her voice and speech, the young lady made strange screams and said words that made no sense. (Friedhoff & Chase, 1982)

The incidence of Tourette's syndrome is fewer than 1 in 1000 people. It affects all racial groups and seems to be hereditary. The age range of onset is between 2 and 25 years. The most frequent symptoms are involuntary tics and involuntary complex movements, such as hitting, lunging, or jumping. People with TS may also suddenly emit cries and other vocalizations or inexplicably utter words that do not make sense in the context, including scatology and swearing.

Tourette's syndrome is thought to be due to an abnormality of the basal ganglia, especially in the right hemisphere, because its symptoms can be controlled with haloperidol, which blocks dopamine synapses in the basal ganglia. Using fMRI to correlate resting activity in different regions of the brain, Church and colleagues (2009) documented cortical changes associated with TS: increases in connectivity mainly in the parietal cortex of Tourette's patients and decreases in connectivity between the parietal and frontal cortex. This finding, diagrammed in the illustration, suggests alterations in the function of dorsal-stream circuits that control relatively automatic visual–motor actions.

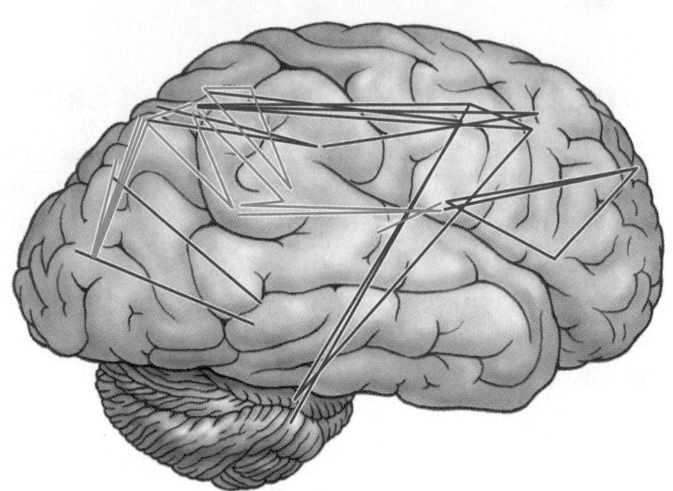

Areas of the brain that show enhanced connectivity (green) or decreased connectivity (red) in fMRI analysis of young adults with Tourette's syndrome suggest abnormalities in dorsal-stream structures linking the parietal cortex to the frontal cortex. Adapted from "Control Networks in Paediatric Tourette Syndrome Show Immature and Anomalous Patterns of Functional Connectivity," by J. A. Church, D. A. Fair, N. U. Dosenbach, et al., 2009, *Brain, 32*, pp. 225–238.

Many people with TS function quite well, coping successfully with their symptoms. They inhabit all walks of life, even surgical medicine, in which they must perform delicate operations. The efforts of the Tourette's Society over the past quarter-century have contributed to increased public awareness of the disorder. Children with TS are now less likely than in the past to be diagnosed as having a psychiatric condition, being hyperactive, or being "troublemakers."

You will find detailed coverage of Parkinson's disease in Chapters 5, 6, and 16.

In addition to causing involuntary movements, or **hyperkinetic symptoms,** damage to the basal ganglia can result in a loss of motor ability, or **hypokinetic symptoms.** Parkinson's disease, caused by the loss of dopamine cells in the substantia nigra, is characterized by hypokinetic symptoms that lead to rigidity and difficulty in initiating and producing movement. The two different kinds of symptoms that arise subsequent to basal ganglia damage—hyperkinetic and hypokinetic—suggest that a major function of these nuclei is to modulate movement.

Neuroscientists have attempted to relate these opposing symptoms by suggesting that the underlying function of the basal ganglia is to generate the force required for

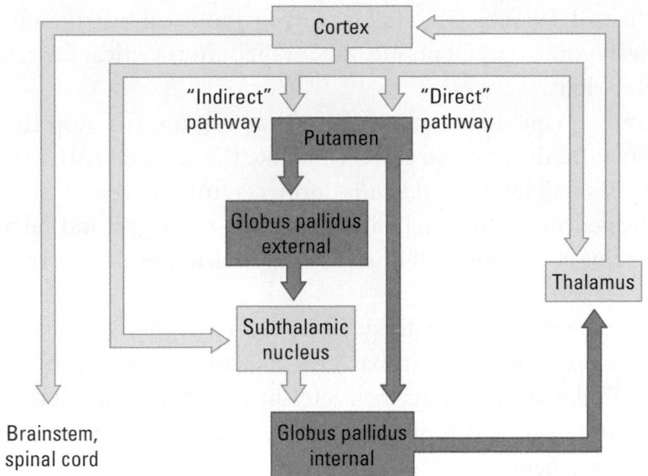

FIGURE 11-14 Regulating Movement Force. Two pathways in the basal ganglia modulate cortically produced movements. Here the green pathways are excitatory and the red are inhibitory. The indirect pathway has an excitatory effect on the GPi whereas the direct pathway has an inhibitory effect. If activity in the indirect pathway dominates, the thalamus shuts down and the cortex is unable to produce movement. If direct-pathway activity dominates, the thalamus can become overactive, thus amplifying movement. Adapted from "Functional Architecture of Basal Ganglia Circuits: Neural Substrates of Parallel Processing," by R. E. Alexander and M. D. Crutcher, 1990, *Trends in Neuroscience, 13,* p. 269.

each particular movement (Aparicio et al., 2005). The idea is that some types of basal ganglia damage cause errors of too much force and so result in excessive movement, whereas other types of damage cause errors of too little force and so result in insufficient movement. Other neuroscientists suggest that the basal ganglia are involved in initiating movements that are selected for action by the motor cortex and for learning how to make movements at the appropriate time and place.

What neural pathways enable the basal ganglia to select movements or modulate the force of movements? Basal ganglia circuits are quite complex, but one theory holds that two pathways affect the activity of the motor cortex: an inhibitory pathway and an excitatory pathway (Kreitzer and Malenka, 2008). Both pathways converge in the basal ganglia area called the GP_i (internal part of the globus pallidus), as charted in **Figure 11-14.**

The GP_i in turn projects into the the ventral thalamic nucleus, and the thalamus projects to the motor cortex. The thalamic projection modulates the size or force of a movement that the cortex produces and is influenced by the GP_i. The GP_i acts like the volume dial on a radio: its output determines whether a movement will be weak or strong.

The inputs to the GP_i are shown in red and green in Figure 11-14 to illustrate how they affect movement. If activity in the inhibitory pathway (red) is high relative to that in the excitatory pathway (green), inhibition of the GP_i will predominate, and the thalamus will be free to excite the cortex, thus amplifying movement force. If, on the other hand, activity in the excitatory pathway is high relative to that in the inhibitory pathway, excitation of the GP_i will predominate, and the thalamus will be inhibited, thus reducing input to the cortex and decreasing the force of movements.

The idea that the GP_i acts like a volume control over movement is the basis for one type of treatment for Parkinson's disease. If the GP_i is surgically destroyed in Parkinson patients—the equivalent of activating the green pathway—muscular rigidity is reduced and the ability to make normal movements is improved. Similarly, deep brain stimulation of the GP_i inactivates it, thus freeing movement. Consistent with this "volume hypothesis," recordings made from cells of the globus pallidus show that they are excessively active in people with Parkinson's disease.

Research Focus 1-2 describes and illustrates the DBS procedure.

Hyperkinetic symptom Symptom of brain damage that results in excessive involuntary movements, as seen in Tourette's syndrome.
Hypokinetic symptom Symptom of brain damage that results in a paucity of movement, as seen in Parkinson's disease.

The Cerebellum and Movement Skill

Musicians have a saying: "Miss a day of practice and you're OK; miss two days and you notice; miss three days and the world notices." Apparently, some change must take place in the brain when we neglect to practice a motor skill. The cerebellum may be the part of the motor system that is affected. Whether the skill is playing a musical instrument, pitching a baseball, or text-messaging on a cell phone, the cerebellum is critical for acquiring and maintaining motor skills.

The cerebellum, a large and conspicuous part of the motor system, sits atop the brainstem, clearly visible just behind the cerebral cortex, and like the cerebral cortex, is divided into two hemispheres. A small lobe, the *flocculus,* projects from its ventral surface. Although smaller than the neocortex, the cerebellum has many more gyri and sulci than the neocortex, and it contains about one-half of all the neurons in the entire nervous system.

As **Figure 11-15** shows, the cerebellum can be divided into several regions, each specialized in a different aspect of motor control. At its base, the flocculus receives projections from the middle-ear vestibular system, described later in the chapter, and takes part in controlling balance. Many of its projections go to the spinal cord and to the motor nuclei that control eye movements.

Just as the motor cortex has a homuncular organization and a number of homunculi, the hemispheres of the cerebellum have at least two, as shown in Figure 11-15. The most medial part of each homunculus controls the face and the midline of the body. The more lateral parts are connected to areas of the motor cortex and are associated with movements of the limbs, hands, feet, and digits. The pathways from the hemispheres project to nuclei of the cerebellum, which in turn project to other brain regions, including the motor cortex.

To summarize the cerebellum's topographic organization, the midline of the homunculus is represented in its central part, whereas the limbs and digits are represented in the lateral parts. Tumors or damage to midline areas of the cerebellum disrupt balance, eye movement, upright posture, and walking but do not substantially disrupt other movements such as reaching, grasping, and using the fingers. For example, a person with medial damage to the cerebellum may, when lying down, show few symptoms. Damage to lateral parts of the cerebellum disrupts arm, hand, and finger movements much more than movements of the body's trunk.

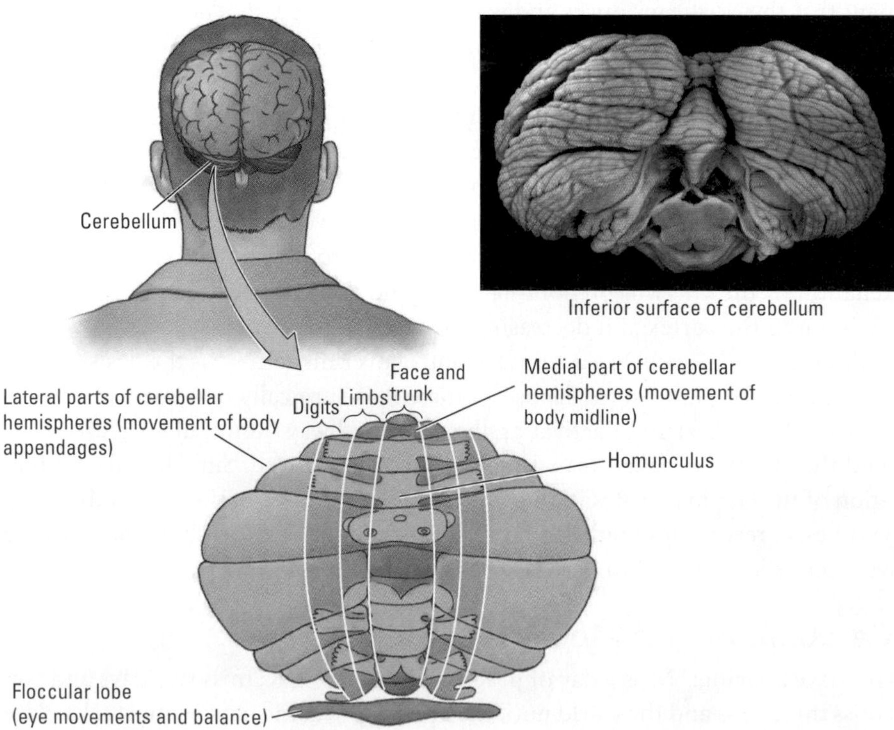

FIGURE 11-15 Cerebellar Homunculus. The cerebellar hemispheres control body movements, and the flocculus controls eye movements and balance. The cerebellum is topographically organized: its more medial parts represent the midline of the body and its more lateral parts represent the limbs and digits. Photograph of cerebellum reproduced from *The Human Brain: Dissections of the Real Brain,* by T. H. Williams, N. Gluhbegovic, and J. Jew, on CD-ROM. Published by Brain University, brain-university.com 2000.

Attempts to understand how the cerebellum controls movement have centered on two major ideas: that the cerebellum (1) plays a role in the timing of movements and (2) maintains movement accuracy. The cerebellum may act as a clock, or pacemaker, to ensure that both movements and perceptions are appropriately timed (Schlerf et al., 2007). In a motor test of timing, subjects are asked to tap a finger to keep time with a metronome. After a number of taps, the metronome is turned off and the subjects are to maintain the beat. Those with damage to the cerebellum, especially to the lateral cerebellum, are impaired on the task.

Tom Thach (2007) argues for the second role for the cerebellum: to help make the adjustments needed to keep movements accurate. Thach gathered evidence in support of this view by having subjects throw darts at a target, as shown in the Procedure section of **Experiment 11-4.** After a number of throws, which allowed the subjects to become reasonably accurate, the subjects put on glasses containing wedge-shaped prisms that displaced the apparent location of the target to the left. Now when the subjects threw a dart, it landed to the left of the intended target.

All subjects showed this initial distortion in aim. But then came an important difference, graphed in the Results section of Experiment 11-4. When normal subjects saw the dart miss the mark, they adjusted each successive throw until reasonable accuracy was restored. In contrast, subjects with damage to the cerebellum could not correct for this error. Time after time, they missed the target far to the left.

Next, the control subjects removed the prism glasses and threw a few more darts. Again, a significant difference emerged. The first dart thrown by each normal subject was much too far to the right (owing to the previous adjustment that the subject had learned to make), but soon each adjusted once again until his or her former accuracy was regained.

In contrast, subjects with damage to the cerebellum showed no aftereffects from having worn the prisms, as if they had never compensated for the glasses to begin with. This experiment suggests that many movements that we make—whether throwing a dart, hitting a ball with a bat, writing neatly, or painting a work of art—depend on moment-to-moment learning and adjustments that are made by the cerebellum.

To better understand how the cerebellum improves motor skills by adjusting movements, imagine throwing a dart yourself. Suppose you aim at the bull's eye, throw the dart, and find that it misses the board completely. You then aim again, this time adjusting your throw to correct for the original error. Notice that there are actually two versions of your action: (1) the movement that you intended to make and (2) the actual movement as recorded by sensory receptors in your arm and shoulder.

EXPERIMENT 11-4

Question: Does the cerebellum help to make adjustments required to keep movements accurate?

Procedure

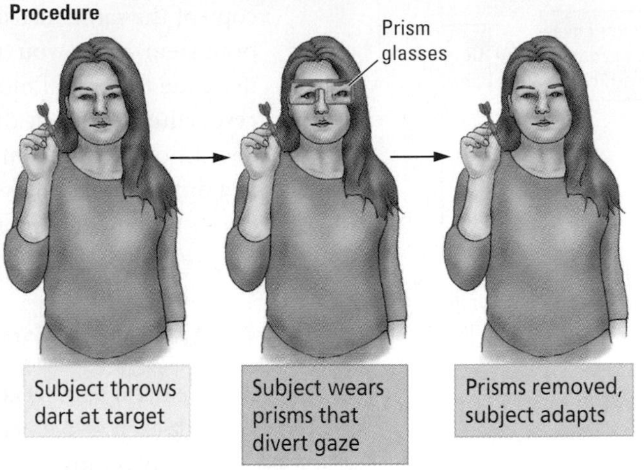

Prism glasses

Subject throws dart at target

Subject wears prisms that divert gaze

Prisms removed, subject adapts

Results

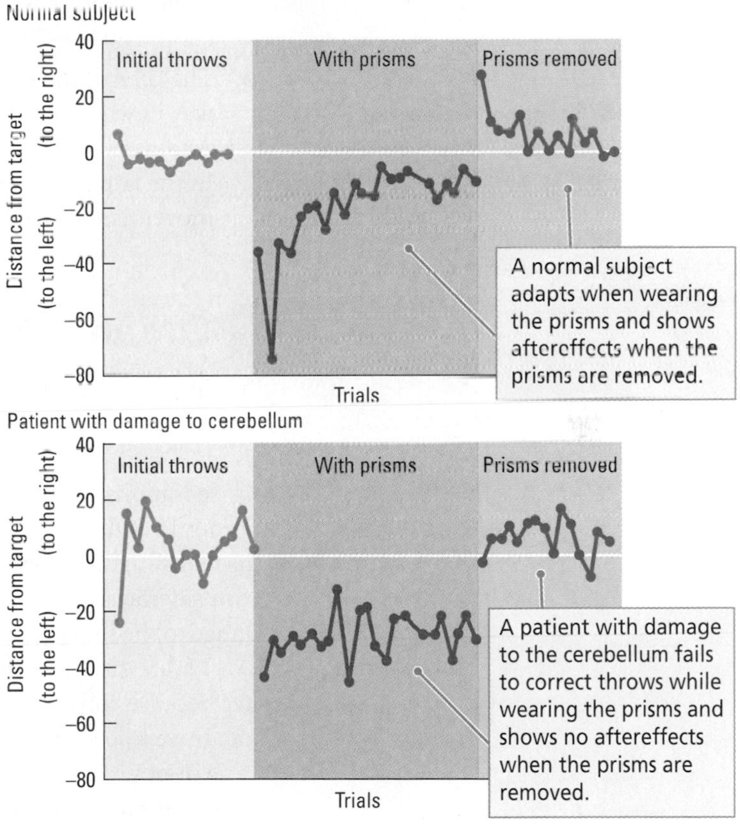

Normal subject

Distance from target (to the left) (to the right)

40, 20, 0, −20, −40, −60, −80

Initial throws | With prisms | Prisms removed

Trials

A normal subject adapts when wearing the prisms and shows aftereffects when the prisms are removed.

Patient with damage to cerebellum

Distance from target (to the left) (to the right)

40, 20, 0, −20, −40, −60, −80

Initial throws | With prisms | Prisms removed

Trials

A patient with damage to the cerebellum fails to correct throws while wearing the prisms and shows no aftereffects when the prisms are removed.

Conclusion: Many movements we make depend on moment-to-moment learning and adjustments made by the cerebellum.

Adapted from "The Cerebellum and the Adaptive Coordination of Movement," by W. T. Thach, H. P. Goodkin, and J. G. Keating, 1992, *Annual Review of Neuroscience, 15,* p. 429.

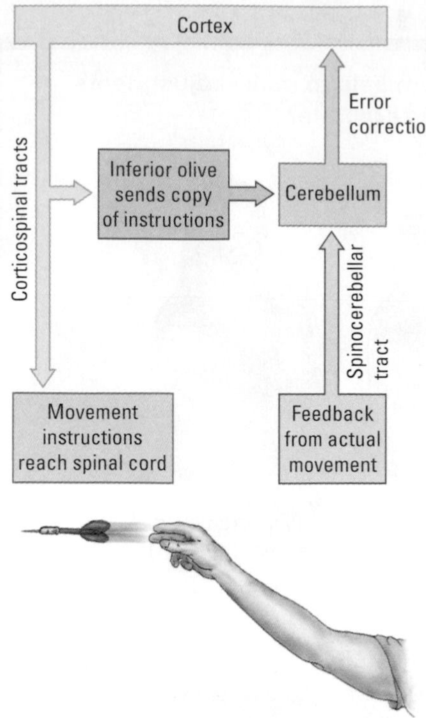

FIGURE 11-16 Intention, Action, and Feedback. By comparing the message for the intended movement with the movement that was actually performed, the cerebellum sends an error message to the cortex to improve the accuracy of a subsequent movement.

If the intended movement is successfully carried out, you need make no correction on your next try. But if you miss, an adjustment is called for. One way in which the adjustment might be made is through the feedback circuit shown in **Figure 11-16.**

The cortex sends instructions to the spinal cord to throw a dart at the target. A copy of the same instructions is sent to the cerebellum through the inferior olive in the brainstem. When you then throw the dart, the sensory receptors in your arm and shoulder code the actual movement that you make and send a message about it back to the cerebellum through the spinocerebellar tract. The cerebellum now has information about both versions of the movement—what you intended to do and what you actually did—and can now calculate the error and tell the cortex how to correct the movement. When you next throw a dart, you incorporate the correction into your throw.

REVIEW: The Basal Ganglia and the Cerebellum

✔ The basal ganglia contribute to motor control by adjusting the force associated with each movement. Consequently, damage to the basal ganglia results either in unwanted, involuntary hyperkinetic movements (too much force being exerted) or in such hypokinetic rigidity that movements are difficult to perform (too little force being exerted).

✔ The cerebellum contributes to motor control by improving movement skill. One way in which it may do so is by keeping track of the timing of movements. Another way is by making adjustments in movements to maintain their accuracy. In the latter case, the cerebellum compares an intended movement with an actual movement, calculates any necessary corrections, and informs the cortex.

Organization of the Somatosensory System

The motor system is responsible for producing movements, but without sensation movement would quickly become impaired. The somatosensory system tells us what the body is up to and what's going on in the environment by providing information about bodily sensations, such as touch, temperature, pain, position in space, and movement of the joints. In addition to helping us learn about the world, the somatosensory system allows us to distinguish what the world does to us from what we do to it: when someone pushes you sideways, your somatosensory system tells you that you have been pushed. If you lunge to the side yourself, your somatosensory system tells you that you moved yourself.

We are exploring the somatosensory system and the motor system in the same chapter because somatosensation has a closer relation to movement than the other senses do. If we lose sight or hearing or even both, we can still move around, and the same is true of other animals. Fish that inhabit deep, dark caves cannot see at all yet are able to move about normally. Animals that cannot hear, such as the butterfly, can still move very well. If an animal were to lose its body senses, however, its movements would quickly become impaired. Some aspects of somatosensation are absolutely essential to movement.

In considering the motor system, we started at the cortex and followed the motor pathways out to the spinal cord. This efferent (outward) route makes sense because it follows the direction that instructions regarding movements flow. As we explore the somatosensory system, we will proceed in the opposite direction because afferent sensory information flows inward from sensory receptors in various parts of the body through sensory pathways to the cortex.

Somatosensation is unique among sensory systems. It is not localized in the head as are vision, hearing, taste, and smell but rather is distributed throughout the entire body. Somatosensory receptors are found in all parts of the body, and neurons from these receptors carry information to the spinal cord.

Within the spinal cord, two somatosensory pathways project to the brain and eventually to the somatosensory cortex. One part of the somatosensory system, however, is confined to a single organ, the inner ear, which houses the vestibular system that contributes to our sense of balance and head movement. Before we detail its workings, we investigate the anatomy of the somatosensory system and how it contributes to movement.

Somatosensory Receptors and Perception

Our bodies are covered with sensory receptors that include our skin and body hair and are embedded in both surface layers and deeper layers of the skin and in muscles, tendons, and joints. Some receptors consist simply of the surface of a sensory neuron dendrite. Other receptors include a dendrite and other tissue, such as the dendrite attached to a hair or covered by a special capsule or attached by a sheath of connective tissue to adjacent tissue.

The density of sensory receptors in the skin, muscles, tendons, and joints varies greatly in different parts of the body. The variation in density is one reason why different parts of the body are more or less sensitive to stimulation. Body parts that are very sensitive to touch—including the hands, feet, lips, and eyes—have many more sensory receptors than other body parts do. Sensitivity to different somatosensory stimuli is also a function of the kinds of receptors that are found in a particular region.

Humans have two kinds of skin, hairy skin and **glabrous skin.** Glabrous skin, which includes the skin on the palms of the hands and feet, the lips, and the tongue is hairless and exquisitely sensitive to a wide range of stimuli. The need for heightened sensitivity in glabrous skin is due to the fact that it covers the body parts that we use to explore objects, including the lips, tongue, and hands.

The touch sensitivity of skin is often measured with a two-point sensitivity test. This test consists of touching the skin with two sharp points simultaneously and observing how close together the points can be placed while still being detected as two points rather than one. On glabrous skin, we can detect the two points when they are as close as 3 mm apart.

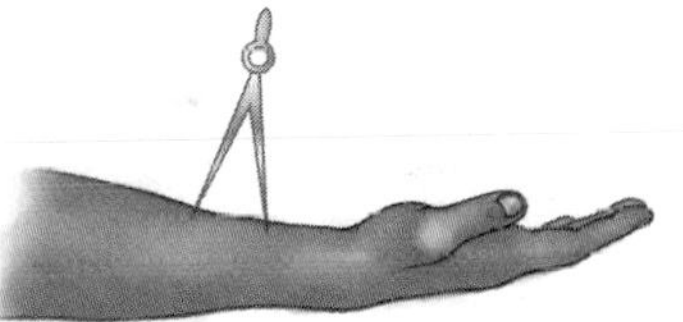

Two-point sensitivity test

On hairy skin, two-point sensitivity is much weaker. The two points seem to merge into one below a separation distance ranging from 2 to 5 cm, depending on exactly which part of the body is tested. You can confirm these differences in sensitivity on your own body by touching two sharp pencil points to a palm and to a forearm, varying the distances that you hold the points apart. Be sure not to look as you touch each surface.

Figure 11-17 samples the various somatosensory receptors located in the skin. There may be as many as 20 or more kinds of somatosensory receptors in the human body, but they can all be classified into the three groupings in Figure 11-17, depending on the type of perception they enable. Three types of perception and the receptors that mediate them follow.

- **Nocioception,** perception of pain and temperature. Nocioceptors consist of free nerve endings. When these endings are damaged or irritated, they secrete chemicals, usually peptides, which stimulate the nerve to produce an action potential. The action potential then conveys a message about pain or temperature to the central nervous system.

Glabrous skin Skin that does not have hair follicles but contains larger numbers of sensory receptors than do other skin areas.
Nocioception Perception of pain and temperature.

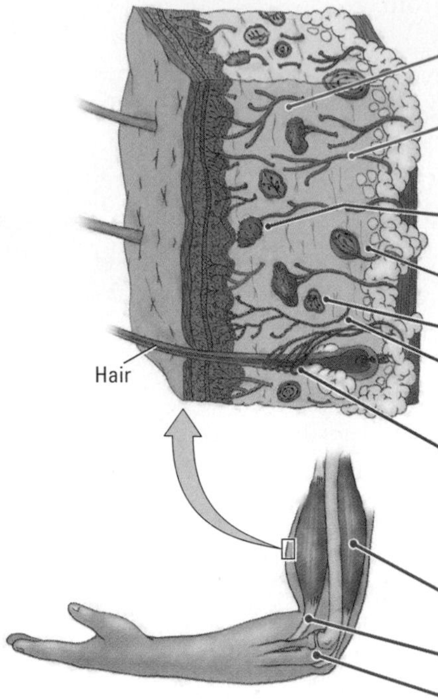

Nocioception (pain and temperature)	Adaptation
Free nerve endings for pain (sharp pain and dull pain)	Slow
Free nerve endings for temperature (heat or coldness)	Slow

Damage to the dendrite or to surrounding cells releases chemicals that stimulate the dendrite to produce action potentials.

Hapsis (fine touch and pressure)	Adaptation
Meissner's corpuscle (touch)	Rapid
Pacinian corpuscle (flutter)	Rapid
Ruffini corpuscle (vibration)	Rapid
Merkel's receptor (steady skin indentation)	Slow
Hair receptors (flutter or steady skin indentation)	Slow

Pressure on the various types of tissue capsules mechanically stimulates the dendrites within them to produce action potentials.

Proprioception (body awareness)	Adaptation
Muscle spindles (muscle stretch)	Rapid
Golgi tendon organs (tendon stretch)	Rapid
Joint receptors (joint movement)	Rapid

Movements stretch the receptors to mechanically stimulate the dendrites within them to produce action potentials.

FIGURE 11-17 Somatosensory Receptors. Perceptions derived from the body senses of nocioception, hapsis, and proprioception depend on different receptors located in different parts of the skin, muscles, joints, and tendons.

- **Hapsis,** perception of fine touch and pressure—that is, perception of objects that we grasp and manipulate or that contact the body. Haptic receptors are found both in superficial layers and in deep layers of the skin and are attached to body hairs as well. A haptic receptor consists of a dendrite attached to a hair or to connective tissue or a dendrite encased in a capsule of tissue. Mechanical stimulation of the hair, tissue, or capsule activates special channels on the dendrite, which in turn initiate an action potential. Differences in the tissue forming the capsule determine the kinds of mechanical energy conducted through the haptic receptor to the nerve. For example, pressure that squeezes the capsule of a Pacinian corpuscle is the necessary stimulus for initiating an action potential.
- **Proprioception,** perception of the location and movement of the body. Proprioceptors, which also are encapsulated nerve endings, are sensitive to the stretch of muscles and tendons and the movement of joints. In the Golgi tendon organ shown at the bottom of Figure 11-17, for instance, an action potential is triggered when the tendon moves, stretching the receptor attached to it.

Somatosensory receptors are specialized to tell us two things about a sensory event: when it occurs and whether it is still occurring. Information about when a stimulus occurs is handled by **rapidly adapting receptors** that respond to the beginning and the end of a stimulus and produce only brief bursts of action potentials. As shown in Figure 11-17, Meissner's corpuscles (which respond to touch), Pacinian corpuscles (which respond to fluttering sensations), and Ruffini corpuscles (which respond to vibration) are all rapidly adapting receptors.

To review how tactile stimulation produces nerve impulses, see Figure 4-26.

In contrast, **slowly adapting receptors** detect whether a stimulus is still occurring. These receptors continue to respond as long as a sensory event is present. For instance, after you have put on an article of clothing and become accustomed to how it feels, only slowly adapting receptors (such as Merkel's receptors and hair receptors) remain active. The difference between a rapidly adapting and a slowly adapting receptor is due in part to the way in which each is stimulated and in part to the way in which ion channels in the membrane of the dendrite respond to mechanical stimulation.

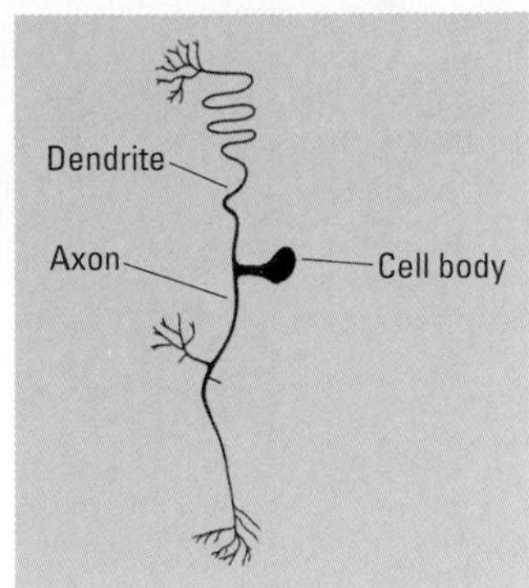
Dendrite
Axon
Cell body

Somatosensory neuron

Dorsal-Root Ganglion Neurons

The dendrites that carry somatosensory information belong to neurons whose cell bodies are located just outside the spinal cord in dorsal-root ganglia. Their axons enter the spinal cord. As illustrated in **Figure 11-18,** a *dorsal-root ganglion neuron* contains a single long dendrite, only the tip of which is responsive to sensory stimulation. This dendrite is continuous with the somatosensory neuron's axon, which enters the spinal cord.

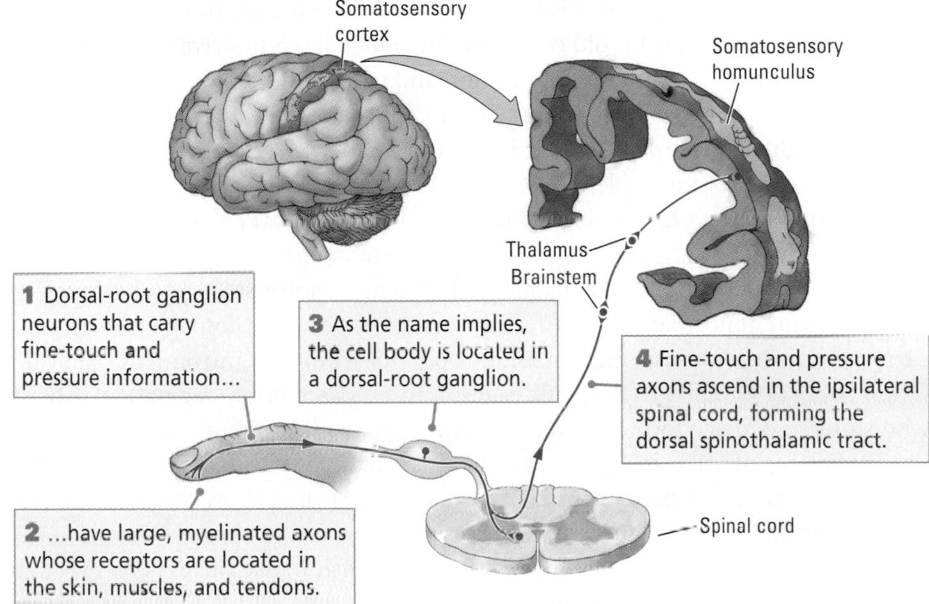
Somatosensory cortex
Somatosensory homunculus
Thalamus
Brainstem
1 Dorsal-root ganglion neurons that carry fine-touch and pressure information...
3 As the name implies, the cell body is located in a dorsal-root ganglion.
4 Fine-touch and pressure axons ascend in the ipsilateral spinal cord, forming the dorsal spinothalamic tract.
2 ...have large, myelinated axons whose receptors are located in the skin, muscles, and tendons.
Spinal cord

FIGURE 11-18 Haptic Dorsal-Root Ganglion Neuron. The dendrite and axon of this dorsal-root ganglion neuron are contiguous and carry sensory information from the skin to the central nervous system. The large, myelinated dorsal-root axons travel up the spinal cord to the brain in the dorsal column, whereas the small axons synapse with neurons whose axons cross the spinal cord and ascend on the other side (shown in Figure 11-19).

Each segment of the spinal cord has one dorsal-root ganglion on each side containing many dorsal-root ganglion neurons, each of which responds to a particular kind of somatosensory information. In the spinal cord, the axons of dorsal-root ganglion neurons may synapse with other neurons or continue to the brain or both.

The axons of dorsal-root ganglion neurons vary in diameter and myelination. These structural features are related to the kind of information the neurons carry. Proprioceptive (location and movement) information and haptic (touch and pressure) information are carried by dorsal-root ganglion neurons that have large, well-myelinated axons. Nocioceptive (pain and temperature) information is carried by dorsal-root ganglion neurons that have smaller axons with little or no myelin.

Figure 2-27 diagrams the structure of the spinal cord. As explained in Chapter 3, myelin is the coating around axons, formed by glial cells, that speeds neurotransmission.

Because of their size and myelination, the larger neurons carry information faster than the smaller neurons do. One explanation of why proprioceptive and haptic neurons are designed to carry messages quickly is that their information requires rapid response. For instance, the nervous system must react to moment-to-moment changes in posture and to the equally rapid sensory changes that take place as we explore an object with our hands. In contrast, a rapid response to stimulation that usually continues for quite some time, as when the body is injured or cold, is not as essential.

We can support the claim that sensory information is essential for movement by describing what happens when dorsal-root ganglion cells do not function. A clue comes from a visit to the dentist. If you have ever had a tooth "frozen" for dental work, you have experienced the very strange effect of losing sensation on one side of your

Hapsis Perceptual ability to discriminate objects on the basis of touch.
Proprioception Perception of the position and movement of the body, limbs, and head.
Rapidly adapting receptor Body sensory receptor that responds briefly to the onset of a stimulus on the body.
Slowly adapting receptor Body sensory receptor that responds as long as a sensory stimulus is on the body.

face. Not only do you lose pain perception, you also seem to lose the ability to move your facial muscles properly, making it awkward to talk, eat, and smile. So even though the anesthetic is blocking only sensory nerves, your movement ability is affected as well.

In much the same way, damage to sensory nerves affects both sensory perceptions and motor abilities. John Rothwell and his coworkers (1982) described a patient, G. O., who was **deafferented** (had lost afferent sensory fibers) by a disease that destroyed sensory dorsal-root ganglion neurons. G. O. had no somatosensory input from his hands. He could not, for example, feel when his hand was holding something. However, G. O. could still accurately produce a range of finger movements, and he could outline figures in the air even with his eyes closed. He could also move his thumb accurately through different distances and at different speeds, judge weights, and match forces by using his thumb. Nevertheless, his hands were relatively useless to him in daily life. Although G. O. could drive his old car, he was unable to learn to drive a new one. He was also unable to write, to fasten shirt buttons, and to hold a cup.

G. O. could begin movements quite normally, but, as he proceeded, the movement patterns gradually fell apart, ending in failure. Part of G. O.'s difficulties lay in maintaining muscle force for any length of time. When he tried to carry a suitcase, he would quickly drop it unless he continually looked down to confirm that he was carrying it. Clearly, although G. O. had damage only to his sensory neurons, he suffered severe motor disability as well, including the inability to learn new motor skills.

Movement abnormalities also result from more selective damage to neurons that carry proprioceptive information about body location and movement. Neurologist Oliver Sacks (1998) gives a dramatic example in his description of a patient, Christina, who suffered damage to proprioceptive sensory fibers throughout her body after taking megadoses of vitamin B_6. Christina was left with very little ability to control her movements and spent most of each day lying prone. Here is how she describes what a loss of proprioception means:

"What I must do then," she said slowly, "is use vision, use my eyes, in every situation where I used—what do you call it?—proprioception before. I've already noticed," she added, musingly, "that I may lose my arms. I think they are in one place, and I find they're in another. This proprioception is like the eyes of the body, the way the body sees itself. And if it goes, as it's gone with me, it's like the body's blind. My body can't see itself if it's lost its eyes, right? So I have to watch it—be its eyes." (Sacks, 1998, p. 46)

Clearly, although Christina's motor system is intact, she is almost completely immobilized without a sense of where her body is in space and what her body is doing. Jonathan Cole (1995) has described the case of Ian Waterman, who lost proprioception after a presumed viral infection at age 19. He is the only person reported to have learned how to move again and this relearning took a period of years. He was even able to drive. All this movement was mediated by vision, without which he was as helpless as Christina.

Deafferentation Loss of incoming sensory input usually due to damage to sensory fibers; also loss of any afferent input to a structure.

Dorsal spinothalamic tract Pathway that carries fine-touch and pressure fibers.

Ventrolateral thalamus Part of the thalamus that carries information about body senses to the somatosensory cortex.

Ventral spinothalamic tract Pathway from the spinal cord to the thalamus that carries information about pain and temperature.

Monosynaptic reflex Reflex requiring one synapse between sensory input and movement.

Somatosensory Pathways to the Brain

As the axons of somatosensory neurons enter the spinal cord, they divide, forming two pathways to the brain. The haptic-proprioceptive axons ascend the spinal cord ipsilaterally (on the same side of the body on which they enter), whereas nocioceptive fibers synapse with neurons whose axons cross to the contralateral side of the spinal cord before ascending to the brain. **Figure 11-19** shows these two routes through the spinal cord. The haptic-proprioceptive pathway is shown as a solid red line, the nocioceptive pathway as a dashed red line.

The haptic-proprioceptive axons are located in the dorsal portion of the spinal cord and form the **dorsal spinothalamic tract.** These axons synapse in the dorsal-column nuclei located at the base of the brain. Axons of neurons in the dorsal-column nuclei then cross over to the other side of the brainstem and ascend through the brainstem as part of a pathway called the *medial lemniscus.* These axons synapse in the **ventrolateral thalamus.** The neurons here send most of their axons to the somatosensory cortex, but some axons go to the motor cortex. Thus, three neurons are required to carry haptic-proprioceptive information to the brain: dorsal-root ganglia neurons, dorsal-column nuclei neurons, and thalamic neurons.

The nociceptive axons take a different route to the brain. They synapse with neurons in the dorsal part of the spinal cord's gray matter. These neurons, in turn, send their axons to the ventral part of the other side of the spinal cord, where they form the **ventral spinothalamic tract.** This tract joins the medial lemniscus in the brainstem to continue on to the ventrolateral thalamus. Some thalamic neurons receiving input from axons of the ventral spinothalamic tract also send their axons to the somatosensory cortex. So again, three neurons are required to convey nociceptive information to the brain: dorsal-root neurons, spinal-cord gray-matter neurons, and ventrolateral thalamic neurons.

Notice that two separate pathways in the spinal cord convey somatosensory information: the haptic-proprioceptive and the nociceptive pathways enter the spinal cord together, separate in the spinal cord, and join again in the brainstem. Because of this arrangement, unilateral spinal-cord damage results in distinctive sensory losses to both sides of the body below the site of injury.

As is illustrated in **Figure 11-20,** loss of hapsis and proprioception occurs on the side of the body where the damage occurred, along with a loss of nociception on the opposite side of the body. Unilateral damage to the dorsal roots or in the brainstem or the thalamus affects hapsis, proprioception, and nociception equally because these parts of the pathways for hapsis and proprioception and that for nociception lie in close proximity.

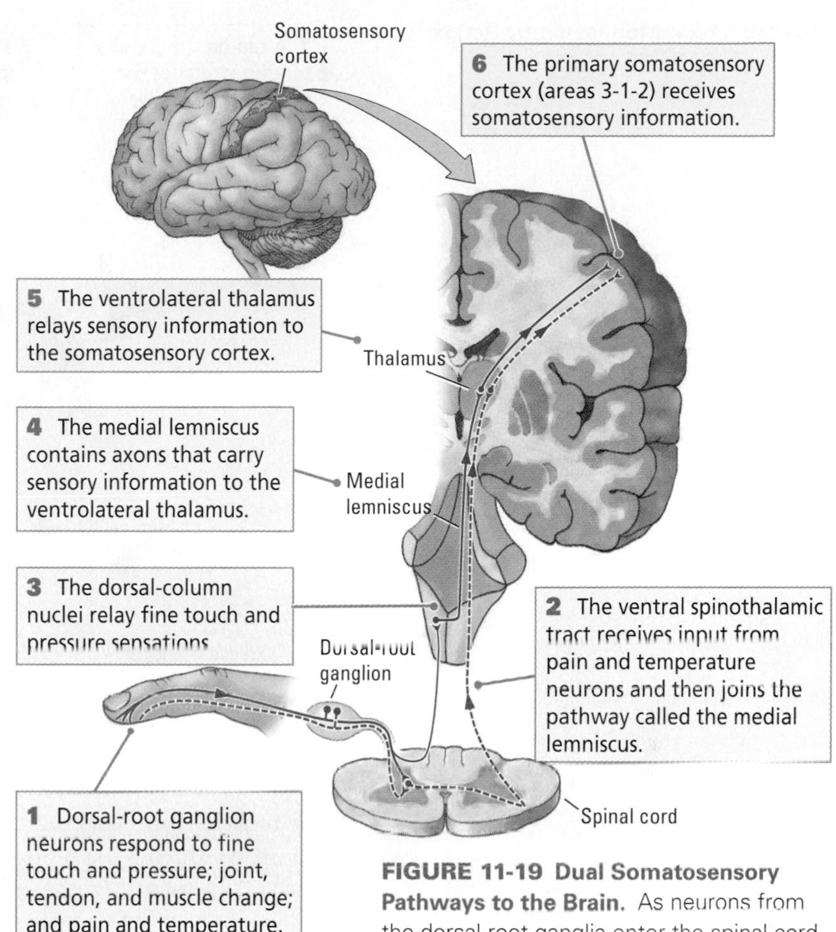
Somatosensory cortex
6 The primary somatosensory cortex (areas 3-1-2) receives somatosensory information.
5 The ventrolateral thalamus relays sensory information to the somatosensory cortex.
Thalamus
4 The medial lemniscus contains axons that carry sensory information to the ventrolateral thalamus.
Medial lemniscus
3 The dorsal-column nuclei relay fine touch and pressure sensations
Dorsal-root ganglion
2 The ventral spinothalamic tract receives input from pain and temperature neurons and then joins the pathway called the medial lemniscus.
1 Dorsal-root ganglion neurons respond to fine touch and pressure; joint, tendon, and muscle change; and pain and temperature.
Spinal cord

FIGURE 11-19 Dual Somatosensory Pathways to the Brain. As neurons from the dorsal-root ganglia enter the spinal cord, the somatosensory pathways to the brain diverge.

FIGURE 11-20 Effects of Unilateral Injury.

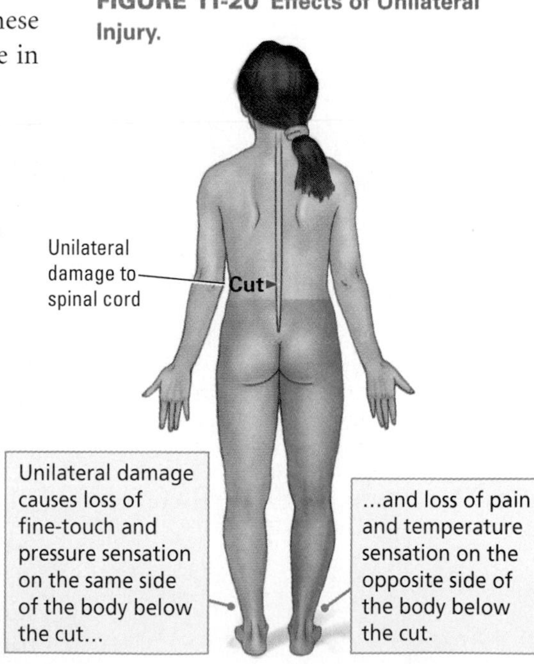
Unilateral damage to spinal cord
Cut
Unilateral damage causes loss of fine-touch and pressure sensation on the same side of the body below the cut...
...and loss of pain and temperature sensation on the opposite side of the body below the cut.

Spinal Reflexes

Somatosensory nerve fibers not only convey information to the cortex, they participate in behaviors mediated by the spinal cord and brainstem as well. Spinal-cord somatosensory axons, even those ascending in the dorsal columns, give off axon collaterals that synapse with interneurons and motor neurons on both sides of the spinal cord. The circuits made between sensory receptors and muscles through these connections mediate spinal reflexes.

The simplest spinal reflex is formed by a single synapse between a sensory neuron and a motor neuron. **Figure 11-21** illustrates such a **monosynaptic reflex,** the knee jerk that affects the quadriceps muscle of the thigh, which is anchored to the leg bone by the patellar tendon. When the lower leg hangs free and this tendon is tapped with a small hammer, the quadriceps muscle is stretched, activating the stretch-sensitive sensory receptors embedded in it. The sensory receptors then send a signal to the spinal cord through sensory neurons that synapse with motor neurons projecting back to the same thigh muscle. The discharge

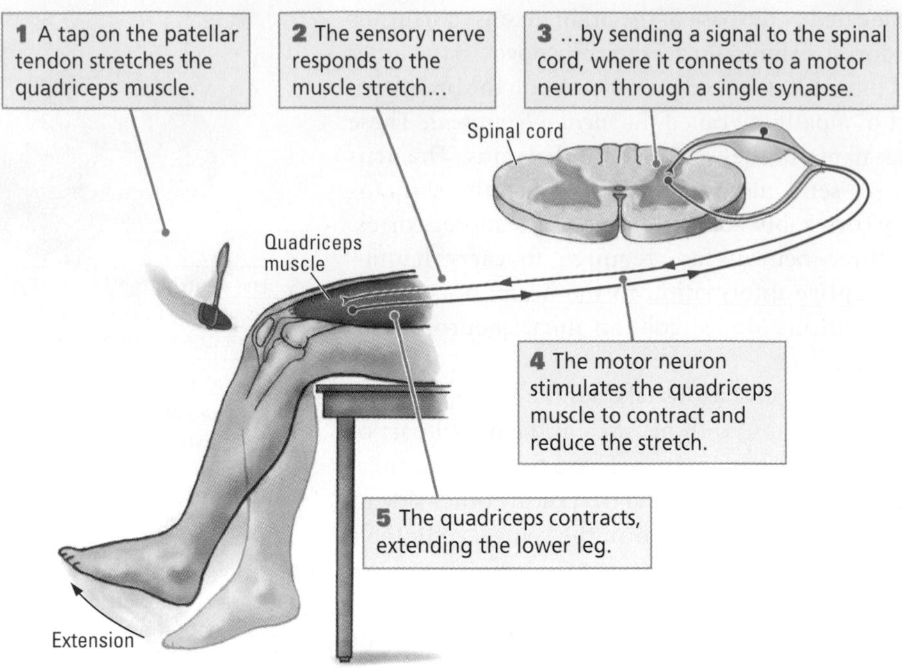

1 A tap on the patellar tendon stretches the quadriceps muscle.
2 The sensory nerve responds to the muscle stretch...
3 ...by sending a signal to the spinal cord, where it connects to a motor neuron through a single synapse.
Spinal cord
Quadriceps muscle
4 The motor neuron stimulates the quadriceps muscle to contract and reduce the stretch.
5 The quadriceps contracts, extending the lower leg.
Extension

FIGURE 11-21 Monosynaptic Reflex.

from the motor neurons stimulates the muscle, causing it to contract to resist the stretch. Because the tap is brief, the stimulation is over before the motor message arrives, and the muscle contracts even though it is no longer stretched. This contraction pulls the leg up, producing the reflexive knee jerk.

This simplest of reflexes entails monosynaptic connections between single sensory neurons and single motor neurons. Somatosensory axons from other receptors, especially those in the skin, make much more complex connections with both interneurons and motor neurons. These multisynaptic connections are responsible for more complex spinal reflexes that include many muscles on both sides of the body.

Feeling and Treating Pain

One survey concerning complaints about pain reports that the average person will suffer the equivalent of 10 years of pain in his or her lifetime. Another survey reports that 36 percent of patients visiting a physician's office—more than a third—complain of chronic pain. Pain symptoms may be related to arthritis, myalgias (muscle pains), migraine, cancer, nocioceptive pain (due to irritation of pain receptors), or neuropathic pain (due to irritation of pain nerves). People suffer pain as a result of acute injuries—including sprains, broken bones, cuts, burns—and stiffness due to exercise. Women experience pain during menstruation, pregnancy, and childbirth.

People can also experience "central pain" in a part of the body that is not obviously injured. One type, described in Research Focus 11-5, "Phantom Limb Pain," seems to occur in a limb, but the limb has been lost. People suffering pain would happily dispense with it. But pain is necessary: the occasional person born without pain receptors experiences body deformities through failure to adjust posture and acute injuries through failure to avoid harmful situations.

Pain perception results from the synthesis of a number of kinds of sensory information. There may be as many as eight different kinds of pain fibers, judging from the peptides and other chemicals released by these nerves when irritated or damaged. Some of the chemicals irritate surrounding tissue, stimulating it to release other chemicals to stimulate blood flow and to stimulate the pain fibers themselves. These reactions contribute to pain, redness, and swelling at the site of an injury.

RESEARCH FOCUS 11-5

Phantom-Limb Pain

Up to 80 percent of people who have had a limb amputated also endure phantom-limb phenomena. These include pain and other sensations and motor phantoms such as phantom movement and cramps (Kern et al., 2009). Phantom sensations and movements are puzzling and indicate that the source of the illusions is the brain.

Various techniques have been used to minimize phantom-limb pain, including typical pain management with opioids as well as the injecton of pain treatments into the spinal cord. An innovative method of treating phantom limb sensations is to assist the patient in creating an illusion that the limb is still intact and is providing normal sensory input to the brain.

V. S. Ramachandran devised a mirror box into which an amputee inserts an intact arm and then observes a reflection of that arm in the mirror. The mirror-image reflection provides the illusion that the missing arm is intact, as shown in the illustration. The image and movement of the arm provide the illusion that the missing arm is present and and can be controlled and serves as a therapy for phantom-limb sensations including pain and cramps.

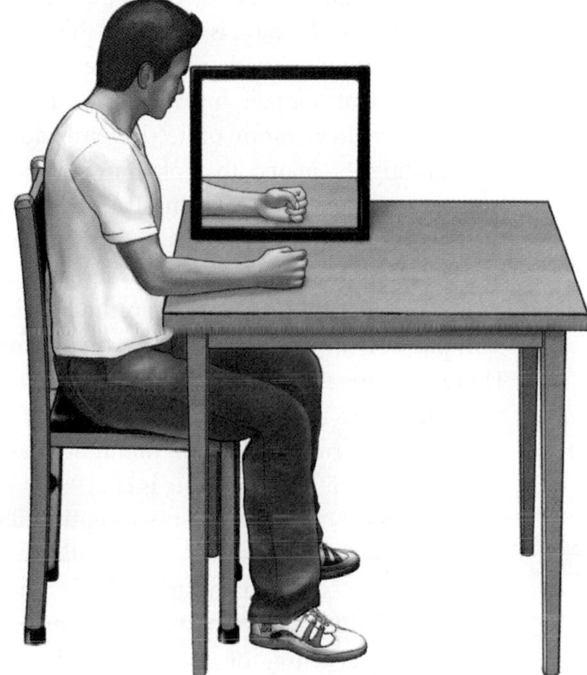

Stimulated by Ramachandran's mirror, researchers have developed other illusions in which the intact limb is seen as the amputated limb through virtual-reality goggles attached to computer simulations. Another method uses stump movement to produce an illusion of the movement of the entire limb. The so-called "rubber limb" phenomenon can be used to create the illusion that a missing limb is present. To induce this phenomenon, the intact stump of the limb is stimulated tactually while the subject observes a prosthetic limb being touched. All the illusions suggesting that the missing limb is present lessen phantom-limb pain and cramps.

Phantom-limb phenomena suggest that our perception of our limbs is hardwired in our neocortex. Indeed, people born without a limb can experience phantom-limb phenomena. In an imaginative application of ideas related to phantom limbs, Ramachandran has suggested that transsexuals may have "phantom genitalia" that are inconsistent with their actual genitalia. This may account for the mismatch that they perceive between their body image and their own body.

In addition, haptic information contributes to the perception of pain. For example, people can accurately report the location and characteristics of various kinds of pain, but in the absence of fine-touch and pressure information, pain is more difficult to identify and localize.

As described earlier, the ventral spinothalamic tract is the main pain pathway to the brain, but as many as four other pathways may carry pain information from the spinal cord to the brain. These pathways are both crossed and uncrossed and project to the reticular formation of the midbrain, where they may produce arousal; to the amygdala, where they may produce emotional responses; and to the hypothalamus, where they activate hormonal and cardiovascular responses. The fact of multiple pain pathways in the spinal cord makes it difficult to treat chronic pain by selectively cutting the ventrospinothalamic tract. The multiple pathways also explain the association between pain sensation and arousal, emotion, and other physiological responses.

Circuits in the spinal cord also allow haptic-proprioceptive and nocioceptive pathways to interact. Such interactions may be responsible for our very puzzling and variable responses to pain. For example, people who are engaged in combat or intense athletic competition may receive a serious injury to the body but start to feel the pain only much later.

A friend of ours was attacked by a grizzly bear while hiking and received 200 stitches to bind his wounds. When friends asked if it hurt to be bitten by a grizzly bear, he surprisingly answered no, explaining, "I had read the week before about someone who was killed and eaten by a grizzly bear. So I was thinking that this bear was going to eat me unless I got away. I did not have time for pain. I was fighting for my life. It was not until the next day that I started feeling pain—and fear."

Pain is puzzling in the variety of ways in which it can be lessened. The primacy of our friend's fear over his pain is related to the stress he was under. Failure to experience pain in a fight-or-flight-situation may be related to the activation of endogenous brain opioids. Treatments for pain include opioid drugs (such as morphine), acupuncture (which entails the rapid vibration of needles embedded in the skin), and simply rubbing the area surrounding the injury. To explain in part how pain can be suppressed in so many different ways, Ronald Melzack and Patrick Wall (1965) proposed a "gate" theory of pain.

Chapter 8 contrasts naturally occuring and synthethic opioids.

The essence of the Melzack and Wall gate is that activity due to haptic-proprioceptive stimulation can reduce pain, whereas the absence of such stimulation can increase pain. They argued that activity in the haptic-proprioceptive pathway can inhibit the pain pathway in the spinal cord through axon collaterals to spinal-cord interneurons. These neurons in turn inhibit pain neurons. For example, if the fine-touch and pressure pathway is active, it will excite the interneuron, which will in turn inhibit the second-order neurons in the pain and temperature pathway.

The action of this **pain gate** is charted in **Figure 11-22.** Notice that both the haptic-proprioceptive fibers and the nocioceptive fibers synapse with the interneuron. Collaterals from the haptic-proprioceptive pathway excite the interneuron, whereas collaterals from the nocioceptive pathway inhibit it. The interneuron, in turn, inhibits the neuron that relays pain information to the brain. Consequently, when the haptic-proprioceptive pathway is active, the pain gate partly closes, reducing the sensation of pain.

The gate theory helps to explain how different treatments for pain work. When you stub your toe, for instance, you feel pain because the pain pathway to the brain is open. Rubbing the toe activates the haptic-proprioceptive pathway and reduces the flow of information in the pain pathway because the pain gate partly closes, relieving the pain sensation.

Similarly, acupuncture may produce its pain-relieving effects because the vibrating needles used in this treatment selectively activate haptic and proprioceptive fibers, closing the pain gate. Moreover, the interneurons in the pain gate use opioid peptides as a neurotransmitter. Thus, the gate theory can also explain how endogenous opoids reduce pain.

The gate theory even suggests an explanation for the "pins and needles" that we feel after sitting too long in one position. Loss of oxygen from reduced blood flow may first

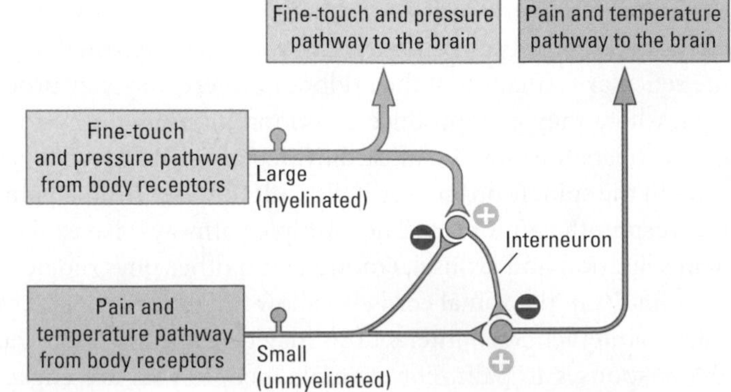

FIGURE 11-22 A Pain Gate. An interneuron in the spinal cord receives excitatory input (plus sign) from the fine-touch and pressure pathway and inhibitory input (minus sign) from the pain and temperature pathway. The relative activity of the interneuron then determines whether pain and temperature information is sent to the brain. Adapted from *The Puzzle of Pain* (p. 154), by R. Melzack, 1973, New York: Basic Books.

deactivate the large myelinated axons that carry touch and pressure information, leaving the small unmyelinated fibers that carry pain and temperature messages unaffected. As a result, "ungated" sensory information flows in the pain and temperature pathway, leading to the pins-and-needles sensation.

Melzack and Wall propose that pain gates may be located in the brainstem and cortex in addition to the spinal cord. These additional gates could help to explain how other approaches to pain relief work. For example, researchers have found that feelings of severe pain can be lessened when people have a chance to shift their attention from the pain to other stimuli. Dentists have long used this technique by giving their patients something soothing to watch or listen to while undergoing procedures.

The influence of attention on pain sensations may work through a cortical pain gate. Electrical stimulation in a number of sites in the brainstem also can reduce pain, perhaps by closing brainstem pain gates. Another way in which pain perceptions might be lessened is through descending pathways from the forebrain and the brainstem to the spinal-cord pain gate.

The presence in the spinal cord of relatively complex neural circuits, such as the pain gate, may be related both to the variable nature of pain and to some successful treatments and some problems in treating pain. In response to noxious stimulation, pain neurons in the spinal cord can undergo sensitization. In other words, successive pain experience can produce an escalating response to a similar noxious stimulus. Spinal-cord neurons thus learn to produce a larger pain signal.

One of the most successful treatments for pain is the injection of small amounts of morphine under the dura mater, the outer layer of the meninges that protects the spinal cord. This epidural anesthesia is mediated by the action of morphine or other opioid drugs on pain neurons in the spinal cord. Although morphine is a very useful treatment for pain, its effects lessen with continued use. This form of habituation may be related to changes that take place on the receptors of pain neurons in the spinal cord and brain.

The brain can also influence the pain signal it receives from the spinal cord. Electrical stimulation in a region of the midbrain called the **periaqueductal gray matter** (PAG) is surprisingly effective in suppressing pain. The cell bodies of PAG neurons surround the cerebral aqueduct connecting the third and fourth ventricles.

Neurons in the PAG excite brainstem-activating systems (including serotonin and noradrenaline neurons) that project to the spinal cord and inhibit neurons there that form the ascending pain pathways. Activation in these inhibitory circuits may explain in part why the sensation and perception of pain is lessened during sleep. Stimulation of the PAG by implanted microelectrodes is one way of treating pain that proves resistant to all other therapies, including treatment with opioid drugs.

Many internal organs of the body, including the heart, the kidneys, and the blood vessels, have pain receptors, but the ganglion neurons carrying information from these receptors do not have their own pathway to the brain. Instead, they synapse with spinal-cord neurons that receive nocioceptive information from the body's surface. Consequently, the neurons in the spinal cord that relay pain and temperature messages to the brain receive two sets of signals: one from the body's surface and the other from the internal organs.

These spinal-cord neurons cannot distinguish between the two sets of signals—nor can we. As a result, pain in body organs is often felt as **referred pain** coming from the body surface. For example, pain in the heart associated with a heart attack may be felt as pain in the left shoulder and upper arm (**Figure 11-23**). Pain in the stomach is felt as pain in the midline of the trunk; pain in the kidneys is felt as pain in the lower back. Pain in blood vessels in the head is felt as diffuse pain that we call a headache (remember that the brain has no pain receptors).

Pain gate Hypothetical neural circuit in which activity in fine-touch and pressure pathways diminishes the activity in pain and temperature pathways.

Periaqueductal gray matter (PAG) Nuclei in the midbrain that surround the cerebral aqueduct joining the third and fourth ventricles; PAG neurons contain circuits for species-typical behaviors (e.g., female sexual behavior) and play an important role in the modulation of pain.

Referred pain Pain felt on the surface of the body that is actually due to pain in one of the internal organs of the body.

Turn to Experiments 5-2 and 5-3 to review the habituation and sensitization responses.

Figure 2-16 shows the location of the PAG in the midbrain.

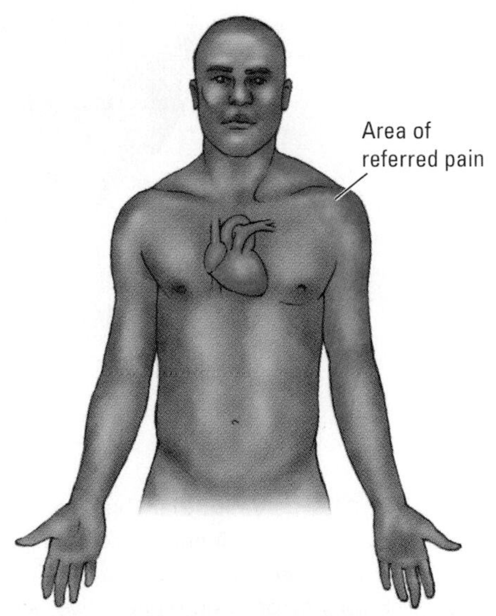

FIGURE 11-23 Referred Pain. During a heart attack, pain from receptors in the heart is felt in the left shoulder and upper arm.

The Vestibular System and Balance

The only localized part of the somatosensory system, the **vestibular system,** consists of two organs, one located in each inner ear. As **Figure 11-24**A shows, each vestibular organ is made up of two groups of receptors: the three *semicircular canals* and the *otolith organs,* the *utricle* and the *saccule.* These vestibular receptors do two jobs: (1) they tell us the position of the body in relation to gravity and (2) they signal changes in the direction and the speed of head movements.

You can see in Figure 11-24A that the semicircular canals are oriented in three different planes that correspond to the three dimensions in which we move through space. Each canal furnishes information about movement in its particular plane. The semicircular canals are filled with a fluid called *endolymph.* Immersed in the endolymph is a set of hair cells.

The vestibular hair cells work on the same principles as the coclear hair cells that mediate hearing, described in Chapter 10.

When the head moves, the endolymph also moves, pushing against the hair cells and bending the cilia at their tips. The force of the bending is converted into receptor potentials in the hair cells and action potentials that are sent over vestibular nerve axons to the brain. These axons are normally quite active: bending the cilia in one direction increases neurotransmitter release, consequently increasing vestibular nerve axon activity; bending them in the other direction decreases vestibular afferent axon activity. These responses are diagrammed in Figure 11-24B. Typically, when the head turns in one direction, the receptor message on that side of the body increases neural firing. The message on the body's opposite side leads to a decrease in firing.

The utricle and saccule lie stacked just beneath the semicircular canals. They also contain hair cells, but these receptors are embedded in a gelatinlike substance that contains small crystals of the salt calcium carbonate called *otoconia.* When you tilt your head, the gelatin and otoconia press against the hair cells, bending them. The mechanical action of the hair bending modulates the rate of action potentials in vestibular afferent axons that convey messages about the position of the head in three-dimensional space.

The receptors in the vestibular system tell us about our location relative to gravity, about acceleration and deceleration of our movements, and about changes in move-

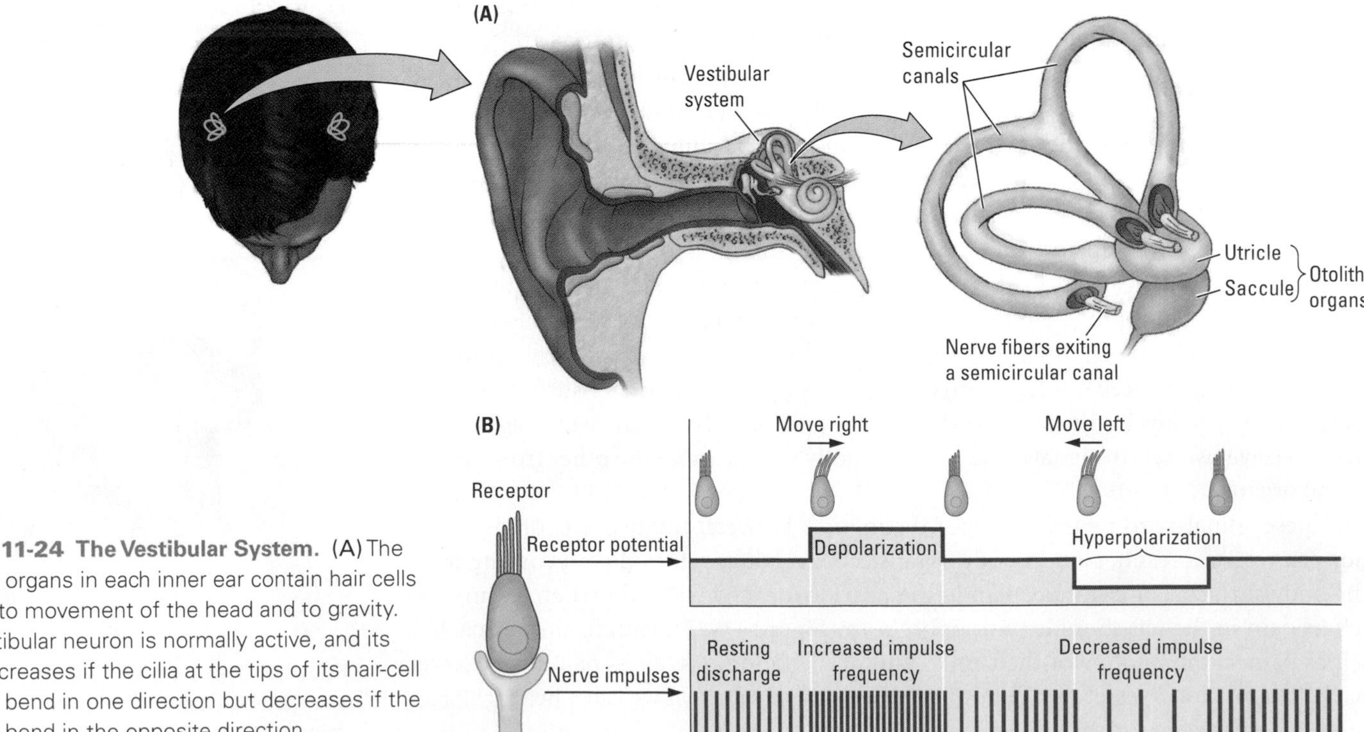

FIGURE 11-24 The Vestibular System. (A) The vestibular organs in each inner ear contain hair cells sensitive to movement of the head and to gravity. (B) A vestibular neuron is normally active, and its activity increases if the cilia at the tips of its hair-cell receptors bend in one direction but decreases if the receptors bend in the opposite direction.

ment direction. They also allow us to ignore the otherwise very destabilizing influence that our movements might have on us. When you are standing on a moving bus, for example, even slight movements of the vehicle could potentially throw you off balance, but they do not. Similarly, when you make movements yourself, you easily avoid tipping over, despite the constant shifting of your body weight. Your vestibular system enables your stability.

Vestibular system Somatosensory system that comprises a set of receptors in each inner ear that respond to body position and to movement of the head

To demonstrate the role of vestibular receptors in helping you to compensate for your own movements, try this experiment. Hold your hand in front of you and shake it. Your hand appears blurry. Now shake your head instead of your hand, and the hand remains in focus. Compensatory signals from your vestibular system allow you to see the hand as stable even though you are moving around.

REVIEW: Organization of the Somatosensory System

- ✔ Body senses contribute to the perception of hapsis (touch and pressure), proprioception (location and movement), and nocioception (temperature and pain).
- ✔ Haptic-proprioceptive information is carried by the dorsal spinothalamic tract; nocioceptive information is carried by the ventral spinothalamic tract.
- ✔ The two systems interact in the spinal cord to regulate pain perception via a pain gate. In the midbrain, the periaqueductal gray matter effectively suppresses pain by activating neuromodulatory circuits that inhibit pain pathways.
- ✔ The only localized somatosensory system, the vestibular system, helps us to maintain balance by signaling information about the head's position and our movement through space.

Exploring the Somatosensory Cortex

Somatosensory neurons do more than convey sensation to the brain: they enable our perceptions of things that we describe as pleasant or unpleasant, of the shape and texture of objects, of the effort required to complete tasks, and even of our spatial world. These perceptual abilities are mediated by the somatosensory cortex.

As illustrated in **Figure 11-25,** there are two main somatosensory areas in the cortex. The primary somatosensory cortex is the area that receives projections from the thalamus. It consists of Brodmann's areas 3-1-2 (all shaded red in the figure). The primary somatosensory cortex begins the process of constructing perceptions from somatosensory information. It mainly consists of the postcentral gyrus just behind the central fissure in the parietal lobe, which means that the primary somatosensory cortex is adjacent to the primary motor cortex in the frontal lobe. The secondary somatosensory cortex (Brodmann's areas 5 and 7, shaded orange and yellow in the figure), located in the parietal lobe just behind the primary somatosensory cortex, continues the construction of perceptions and sends information to the frontal cortex.

Brodmann's century-old map of the cortex, shown in Figure 2-21, was based on cell staining.

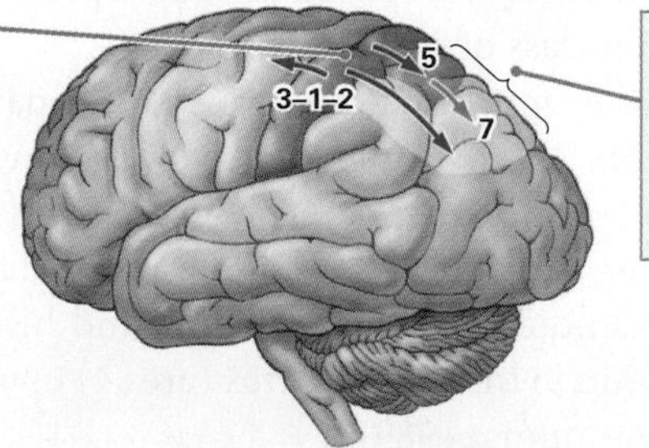
Primary somatosensory cortex receives sensory information from the body.
3-1-2
5
7
Secondary somatosensory cortex receives sensory information from the primary somatosensory cortex.

FIGURE 11-25 Somatosensory Cortex. Stimulation of the primary somatosensory cortex in the parietal lobe produces sensations that are referred to appropriate body parts. Information from the primary somatosensory cortex travels to the secondary somatosensory cortex for further perceptual analysis and to contribute to movement sequences mediated in the frontal lobes.

(A) Penfield's single-homunculus model

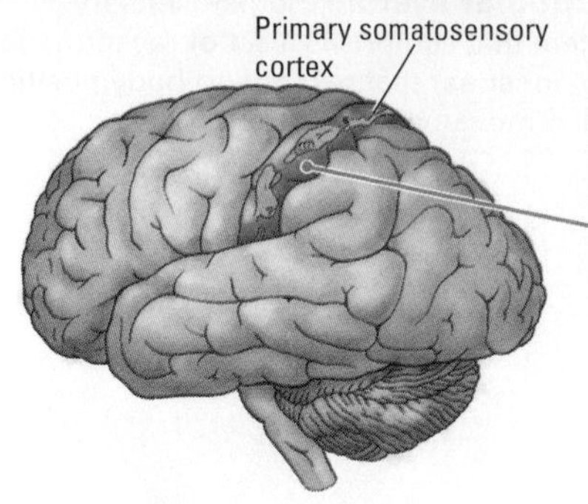

(B) Four-homunculus model

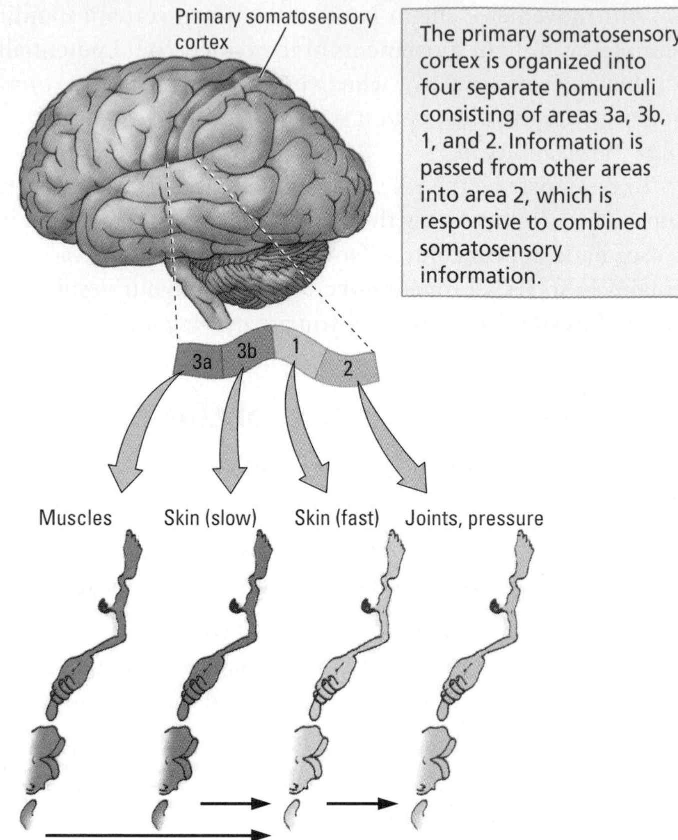

Primary somatosensory cortex
The primary somatosensory cortex is organized into four separate homunculi consisting of areas 3a, 3b, 1, and 2. Information is passed from other areas into area 2, which is responsive to combined somatosensory information.
3a
3b
1
2
Muscles
Skin (slow)
Skin (fast)
Joints, pressure

FIGURE 11-26 Two Models of Somatosensory Cortex Organization.

The Somatosensory Homunculus

In his studies of human patients undergoing brain surgery, Wilder Penfield electrically stimulated the somatosensory cortex and recorded the patients' responses. Stimulation at some sites elicited sensations in the foot, whereas stimulation of other sites produced sensations in a hand, the trunk, or the face. By mapping these responses, Penfield was able to construct a somatosensory homunculus in the cortex, shown in **Figure 11-26A**.

Penfield's work demonstrates, for example, that a dorsal-root ganglion neuron carrying fine-touch and pressure information from a finger through its connections sends information to the finger region of the somatosensory cortex. The sensory homunculus looks very similar to the motor homunculus in that the areas of the body most sensitive to sensory stimulation are accorded a relatively larger cortical area.

Using smaller electrodes and more precise recording techniques in monkeys, Jon Kaas (1987) proposed that the somatosensory cortex does not consist of a single homunculus, as proposed in Penfield's original model. Kaas stimulated sensory receptors on the body and recorded the activity of cells in the sensory cortex. He found that the somatosensory cortex is actually composed of four representations of the body. Each is associated with a certain class of sensory receptors.

The progression of these representations across the human cortex from front to back is shown in Figure 11-26B. Area 3a cells are responsive to muscle receptors; area 3b cells are responsive to slow-responding skin receptors. Area 1 cells are responsive to rapidly adapting skin receptors, and area 2 cells are responsive to deep tissue pressure and joint receptors. In other studies, Hiroshi Asanuma and his coworkers found still another sensory representation in the motor cortex (area 4) in which cells respond to muscle and joint receptors (Asanuma, 1989).

Perceptions constructed from sensations depend on a hierarchical organization in the somatosensory cortex, with basic sensations combining to form more complex perceptions. This combining of information takes place as areas 3a and 3b project onto area 1, which in turn projects onto area 2. Whereas a cell in area 3a or 3b may respond to activity in only a certain area on a certain finger, for example, cells in area 1 may respond to similar information from a number of different fingers.

At the next level of synthesis, cells in area 2 may respond to stimulation in a number of different locations on a number of different fingers as well as to stimulation from different kinds of somatosensory receptors. Thus, area 2 contains *multimodal neurons* that are responsive to movement force, orientation, and direction. We perceive all these properties when we hold an object in our hands and manipulate it.

With each successive relay of information, both the size of the pertinent receptive fields and the synthesis of somatosensory modalities increase. That the different kinds of somatosensory information are both separated and combined in the cortex raises the question of why both segregation and synthesis are needed. One reason that sensory information remains segregated at the level of the cortex could be that we often need to distinguish among different kinds of sensory stimuli coming from different sources. For example, we need to be able to tell the difference between tactile stimulation on the surface of the skin, which is usually produced by some external agent, and stimulation coming from muscles, tendons, and joints, which is probably produced by our own movements.

Yet at the same time, we also often need to know about the combined sensory properties of a stimulus. For instance, when we manipulate an object, it is useful to "know" the object both by its sensory properties, such as temperature and texture, and by the movements we make as we handle it. For this reason, the cortex provides for somatosensory synthesis too. The tickle sensation seems rooted in an "other versus us" somatosensory distinction, as described in Research Focus 11-6, "Tickling."

Research by Vernon Mountcastle (1978) showed that cells in the somatosensory cortex are arranged in functional columns running from layer I to layer VI, similar to columns found in the visual cortex. Every cell in a column responds to a single class of receptors. Some columns are activated by rapidly adapting skin receptors, others by slowly adapting skin receptors, still others by pressure receptors, and so forth. All neurons in a column receive information from the same local area of skin. In this way, neurons lying within a column seem to be an elementary functional unit of the somatosensory cortex.

Effects of Damage to the Somatosensory Cortex

Damage to the primary somatosensory cortex impairs the ability to make even simple sensory discriminations and movements. Suzanne Corkin and her coworkers (1970) demonstrated this effect by examining patients with cortical lesions that included most of areas 3-1-2 in one hemisphere. The researchers mapped the sensory cortices of these patients before they underwent elective surgery for removal of a carefully defined piece of that cortex, including the hand area. The patients' sensory and motor skills in both hands were tested on three different occasions: before the surgery, shortly after the surgery, and almost a year afterward.

The tests included pressure sensitivity, two-point touch discrimination, position sense (reporting the direction in which a finger was being moved), and haptic sense (using touch to identify objects, such as a pencil, a penny, eyeglasses, and so forth). For all the sensory abilities tested, the surgical lesions produced a severe and seemingly permanent deficit in the contralateral hand. Sensory thresholds, proprioception, and hapsis were all greatly impaired.

RESEARCH FOCUS 11-6

Tickling

Everyone knows the effects and consequences of tickling. The perception of tickling is a curious mixture of pleasant and unpleasant sensory stimulation. The tickle sensation is experienced not only by humans but also by other primates, cats, rats, and probably most mammals. Play in rats is associated with 50-kilohertz vocalizations, and tickling body regions that are targets of the rats' own play also elicits 50-kilohertzvocalizations (Panksepp, 2007). Tickling is rewarding in that people and animals will solicit tickles from others, but it is also noxious because they will attempt to avoid the stimulation when it becomes too intense.

LWA-Dann Tardif/Corbis

Using a robot and brain-imaging techniques, Sarah Blakemore and her colleagues (1998) explained why we cannot tickle ourselves. Using a robot, Blakemore delivered one of two kinds of identical tactile stimuli to the palm of the subject's hand. In one condition, the robot delivered the stimulus that the subject commanded. In the other condition, the robot introduced an unpredictable delay in the stimulus. Only the unpredictable stimulus was perceived as a tickle. Thus, it is not the stimulation itself but its unpredictability that accounts for the tickle perception. This is why we cannot tickle ourselves.

Tickling sensations may may activate neural circuits in the brain that underly social behavior more generally (Blakemore, 2008). These networks are activated by all sorts of social play, both in humans and in other animals. The same neural systems may be functionally impaired in autism spectrum disorder, a condition characterized by decreased social play. Thus, tickling may enhance social bonding through brain circuits that subserve the body senses.

The results of other studies in both humans and animals have shown that damage to the somatosensory cortex also impairs simple movements. For example, limb use in reaching for an object is impaired, as is the ability to shape the hand to hold an object (Leonard et al., 1991). Nevertheless, the somatosensory cortex is plastic, as is the motor cortex. It can dramatically reorganize itself after deafferentation.

In 1991, Tim Pons and his coworkers reported a dramatic change in the somatosensory maps of monkeys in which the ganglion cells for one arm had been deafferented a number of years earlier. The researchers had wanted to develop an animal model of damage to sensory nerves that could be a source of insight into human injuries, but they were interrupted by a legal dispute with an animal advocacy group. Years later, as the health of the animals declined, a court injunction allowed the mapping experiment to be conducted.

Pons and his coworkers discovered that the area of the somatosensory cortex that had formerly represented the arm no longer did so. Light touches on the lower face of a monkey now activated cells in what had formerly been the cortical arm region. As illustrated in **Figure 11-27**, the facial area in the cortex had expanded by as much as 10 to 14 millimeters, virtually doubling its original size by entering the arm area.

This massive change was completely unexpected. The stimulus–response patterns associated with the new expanded facial area of the cortex appeared indistinguish-

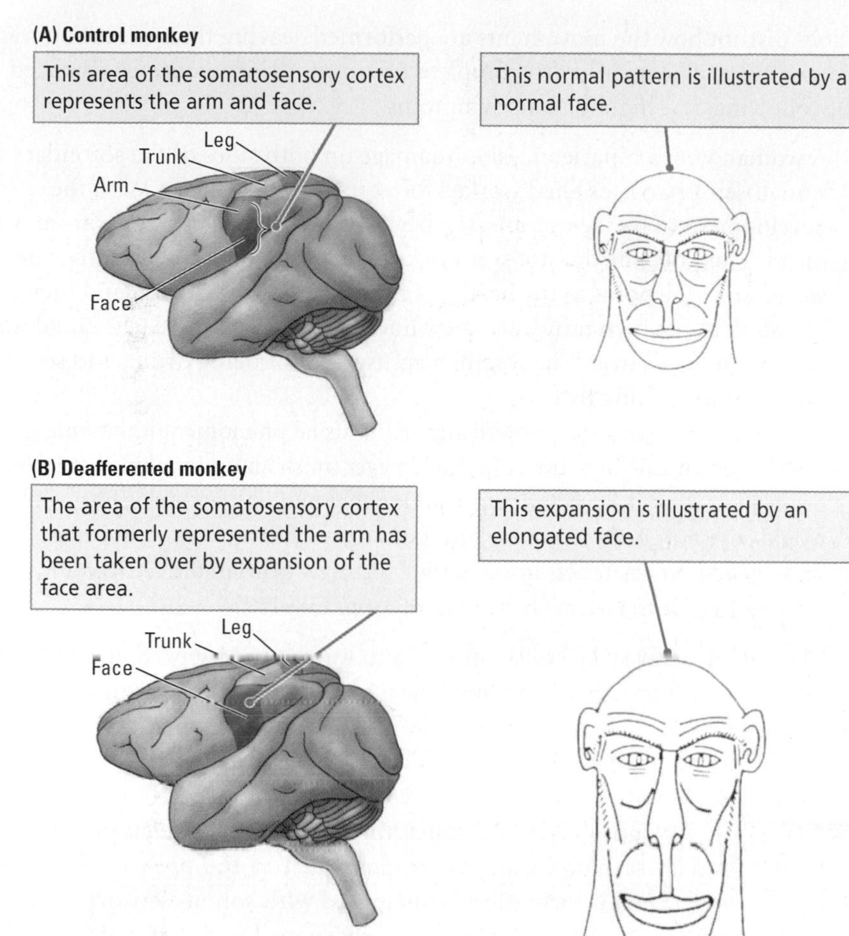
(A) Control monkey
This area of the somatosensory cortex represents the arm and face.
This normal pattern is illustrated by a normal face.
Leg
Trunk
Arm
Face
(B) Deafferented monkey
The area of the somatosensory cortex that formerly represented the arm has been taken over by expansion of the face area.
This expansion is illustrated by an elongated face.
Leg
Trunk
Face

FIGURE 11-27 Somatosensory Plasticity. Adapted from "Massive Cortical Reorganization after Sensory Deafferentation in Adult Macaques," by T. P. Pons, P. E. Garraghty, A. K. Ommaya, J. H. Kaas, and M. Mishkin, 1991, *Science*, 252, p. 1858.

able from those associated with the original facial area. Furthermore, the trunk area, which bounded the other side of the cortical arm area, did not expand into the vacated arm area.

What could account for this expansion of the face area into the arm area? One possibility is that axons grew across the cortex from the face area into the arm area, but no evidence supports this possibility. Another possibility is that the thalamic neurons representing the facial area projected axon collaterals to the cortical neurons representing the arm area. These collaterals might be preexisting or they might be new growths subsequent to deafferentation.

There is evidence for preexisting collaterals that are not normally active, but these collaterals would probably not be able to extend far enough to account for all the cortical reorganization. A third possibility is that, within the dorsal cortical columns, facial-area neurons projected collaterals to arm-area neurons. These neurons are close together, so the collaterals need travel only a millimeter or so. Whatever the mechanism, the very dramatic cortical reorganization observed in this study eventually had far-reaching consequences for understanding other remarkable phenomena, including phantom-limb sensations.

We return to this story in Chapter 14, where we look at how the brain changes in response to experience.

The Somatosensory Cortex and Complex Movement

This chapter has outlined the mechanics of our abilities to move and to interpret stimulation on our body. How are the abilities related? The somatosensory cortex plays an important role in confirming that movements have taken place. Damage to the secondary somatosensory cortex does not disrupt the plans for making movements, but

The word apraxia derives from the Greek words for "no" and "action."

it does disrupt how the movements are performed, leaving their execution fragmented and confused. The inability to complete a plan of action accurately is called **apraxia.** The following case highlights its symptoms.

> A woman with a biparietal lesion [damage on both sides of the secondary somatosensory cortex] had worked for years as a fish-filleter. With the development of her symptoms, she began to experience difficulty in carrying on with her job. She did not seem to know what to do with her knife. She would stick the point in the head of a fish, start the first stroke, and then come to a stop. In her own mind she knew how to fillet fish, but yet she could not execute the maneuver. The foreman accused her of being drunk and sent her home for mutilating fish.
>
> The same patient also showed another unusual phenomenon that might possibly be apraxic in nature. She could never finish an undertaking. She would begin a job, drop it, start another, abandon that one, and within a short while would have four or five uncompleted tasks on her hands. This would cause her to do such inappropriate actions as putting the sugar bowl in the refrigerator, and the coffeepot inside the oven. (Critchley, 1953, pp. 158–159)

Chapter 9 explains how visual information from the dorsal and ventral streams contributes to movement.

The somatosensory cortex contributes to movement by participating in both the dorsal and the ventral visual streams. The dorsal (how) stream, working without conscious awareness, provides vision for action, as when we automatically shape a hand to form as we reach to grasp a cup. The ventral (what) stream, in contrast, works with conscious awareness to identify the object as a cup.

As **Figure 11-28** illustrates, the dorsal visual stream projects to the secondary somatosensory cortex and then to the prefrontal cortex. In this way, visual information is integrated with somatosensory information to produce movements appropriately shaped and directed for their targets. Much less is known about how the secondary somatosensory cortex contributes to the ventral stream, but it is likely that somatosensory information about the identity of objects and completed movements is relayed by the ventral stream to the prefrontal cortex. The frontal cortex can then select the appropriate actions that should follow from those that are already complete.

Remember that the motor cortex contains regions that produce different movements, including the movement of reaching to a location in space. The visual cortex provides the target for the reach while the somatosensory cortex confirms that the appropriate movement occurs. In short, an interaction among the visual cortex (which identifies a target), the motor cortex (which produces the action), and the sensory cortex (which monitors what is being done) is central to how the brain produces movement in the here and now.

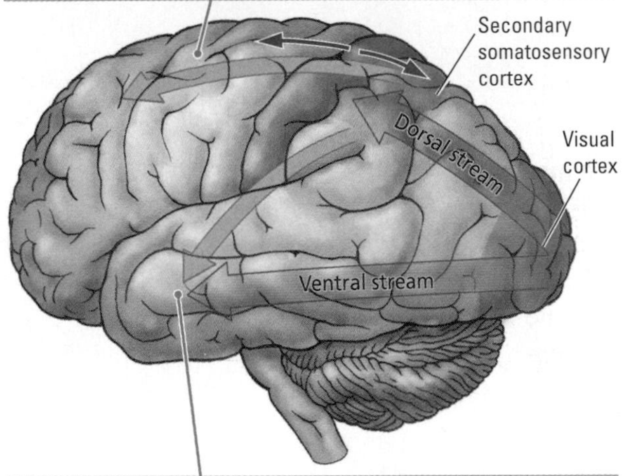
Information from the secondary somatosensory cortex contributes to the dorsal stream by specifing the movement used for grasping a target.
Secondary somatosensory cortex
Dorsal stream
Visual cortex
Ventral stream
Information from the secondary somatosensory cortex contributes to the ventral stream by providing information about object size and shape.

FIGURE 11-28 Visual Aid.

REVIEW: Exploring the Somatosensory Cortex

- ✔ The primary somatosensory cortex, arranged as a series of homunculi, feeds information to the secondary somatosensory cortex, which in turn contributes to the dorsal (how) and ventral (what) visual streams.
- ✔ Damage to the secondary somatosensory cortex produces apraxia, an inability to complete a series of movements. In enacting a movement sequence, a person with apraxia has trouble knowing both what action has just been completed and what action should follow in the sequence.

Apraxia Inability to make voluntary movements in the absence of paralysis or other motor or sensory impairment, especially an inability to make proper use of an object

Summary

Hierarchical Control of Movement

Movement is organized hierarchically, using the entire nervous system in some way (review Figure 11-1). The forebrain plans, organizes, and initiates movements, whereas the brainstem coordinates regulatory functions, such as eating and drinking, and controls neural mechanisms that maintain posture and produce locomotion. Many reflexes are organized at the level of the spinal cord and occur without the brain's involvement.

Organization of the Motor System

Maps produced by stimulating the motor cortex show that it is organized topographically as a homunculus, with the parts of the body capable of fine movements associated with large regions of motor cortex. Two pathways emerge from the motor cortex to the spinal cord.

The lateral corticospinal tract consists of axons from the digit, hand, and arm regions of the motor cortex. The tract synapses with spinal interneurons and motor neurons located laterally in the spinal cord, on the side of the cord opposite the side of the brain on which the corticospinal tract started.

The ventral corticospinal tract consists of axons from the trunk region of the motor cortex. This tract synapses with interneurons and motor neurons located medially in the spinal cord, on the same side of the cord as the side of the brain on which the corticospinal tract started.

Interneurons and motor neurons of the spinal cord also are topographically organized: more laterally located motor neurons project to digit, hand, and arm muscles, and more medially located motor neurons project to trunk muscles.

Organization of the Motor System

Movements innate to a species are organized as synergies, or movement patterns. Motor-cortex neurons initiate movement, produce movement, control the force of movement, and indicate movement direction.

Different species of animals have topographic maps in which areas of the body capable of the most skilled movements have the largest motor-cortex representation. Disuse of a limb, such as might follow motor-cortex injury, results in shrinkage of that limb's representation in the motor cortex. This shrinkage can be prevented, however, if the limb can be somehow forced into use.

The Basal Ganglia and the Cerebellum

Damage to the basal ganglia or to the cerebellum results in movement abnormalities. This tells us that both brain structures participate in movement control. The results of experimental studies suggest that the basal ganglia regulate the force of movements, whereas the cerebellum plays a role in movement timing and in maintaining movement accuracy.

Organization of the Somatosensory System

The somatosensory system is distributed throughout the entire body and consists of more than 20 types of specialized receptors, each sensitive to a particular form of mechanical energy. Each somatosensory receptor projecting from skin, muscles, tendons, or joints is associated with a dorsal-root ganglion neuron that carries the sensory information into the brain.

Fibers carrying proprioceptive (location and movement) information and haptic (touch and pressure) information ascend the spinal cord as the dorsal spinothalamic tract. These fibers synapse in the dorsal-column nuclei at the base of the brain, at which point axons cross over to the other side of the brainstem to form the medial lemniscus, which ascends to the ventrolateral thalamus. Most of the ventrolateral thalamus cells project to the somatosensory cortex. Nociceptive (pain and temperature) dorsal-root ganglion neurons synapse on entering the spinal cord. Their relay neurons cross the spinal cord to ascend to the thalamus as the ventral spinothalamic tract.

Because the two somatosensory pathways take somewhat different routes, unilateral spinal-cord damage impairs proprioception and hapsis ipsilaterally below the site of injury and nociception contralaterally below the site.

Exploring the Somatosensory Cortex

The somatosensory system is represented topographically as a homunculus in the primary somatosensory region of the parietal cortex (areas 3-1-2) such that the most sensitive parts of the body are accorded the largest regions of neocortex. A number of homunculi represent different sensory modalities, and these regions are hierarchically organized. If sensory input from a part of the body is cut off from the cortex by damage to sensory fibers, adjacent functional regions of the sensory cortex can expand into the now-unoccupied region.

The somatosensory system and the motor system are interrelated at all levels of the nervous system. At the level of the spinal cord, sensory information contributes to motor reflexes; in the brainstem, sensory information contributes to complex regulatory movements. At the level of the neocortex, sensory information is used to record just-completed movements as well as to represent the sizes and shapes of objects.

The somatosensory cortex contributes to the dorsal visual stream to direct hand movements to targets. The somatosensory cortex also contributes to the ventral visual stream to create representations of external objects.

Key Terms

apraxia, p. 392
autism spectrum disorder (ASD), p. 360
brain–computer interface (BCI), p. 354
cerebral palsy, p. 358
corticospinal tract, p. 364
deafferentation, p. 380
dorsal spinothalamic tract, p. 380
glabrous skin, p. 377
hapsis, p. 379
homunculus, p. 364
hyperkinetic symptom, p. 373
hypokinetic symptom, p. 373
mirror neuron, p. 356
monosynaptic reflex, p. 380
motor sequence, p. 356
nociception, p. 377
pain gate, p. 385
paraplegia, p. 360
periaqueductal gray matter (PAG), p. 385
proprioception, p. 379
quadriplegia, p. 360
rapidly adapting receptor, p. 379
referred pain, p. 385
restraint-induced therapy, p. 371
scratch reflex, p. 363
slowly adapting receptor, p. 379
topographic organization, p. 364
ventral spinothalamic tract, p. 380
ventrolateral thalamus, p. 380
vestibular system, p. 387

▶*Please refer to the Companion Web Site at* **www.worthpublishers.com/kolbintro3e** *for Interactive Exercises and Quizzes.*

John Henley/Corbis

CHAPTER 12

What Causes Emotional and Motivated Behavior?

RESEARCH FOCUS 12-1

The Pain of Rejection

We use words like *sorrow, grief,* and *heartbreak* to describe a loss. Loss evokes painful feelings, and the loss or absence of contact that comes with social exclusion leads to "hurt" feelings. To discover whether painful or hurtful feelings are manifested in the brain's neural circuitry, Naomi Eisenberger and colleagues (2003) performed an experiment.

Participants were scanned in an fMRI apparatus while they played a virtual ball-tossing video game. Initially, the subjects believed that they were merely observing the game, but during the experimental phase, they became active participants. Within a few throws, the other "players" (actually computerized stooges) stopped throwing the ball to the participants, leading them to feel excluded.

The question the researchers asked is whether the experience and regulation of both physical and social pain have a common neuroanatomical basis. Two regions of the forebrain are affected by physical pain: the anterior cingulate (limbic) cortex, becomes more active when physical pain is inflicted, and the **orbitofrontal cortex** lying above your eyes becomes more active when physical distress is low.

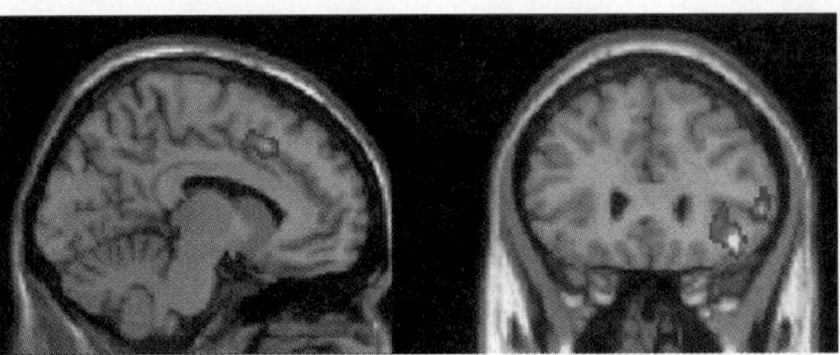

These fMRI scans result from averaging many individual images and then using the subtraction process to produce a representative image showing that activation in the anterior cingulate (left) and orbitofrontal cortex (right) occurs whether pain is physical or emotional. From "Does Rejection Hurt? An fMRI Study of Social Exclusion," by N. I. Eisenberger, M. D. Lieberman, and K. D. Williams, 2003, *Science,* 302, 290–292.

The Eisenberger team found that emotional pain activates the opposing reactions of these areas in exactly the same way physical pain does. Participants' fMRI scans revealed that activation in the anterior cingulate cortex may act to suppress the feelings of social distress, shown in the fMRI scan on the left, as does inhibition in the orbitofrontal cortex in the scan at right.

These results suggest that emotional pain activates the same neural systems normally activated when people feel physical pain. Findings from this study are the source of two insights about the range of emotional feelings, or *affective states:*

1. The same pattern of brain activation accompanies both physical and emotional pain—in this case, "hurt feelings." Other investigators have shown parallel neural correlates for a range of pleasant feelings, including the craving for chocolate, winning the lottery, and sexual arousal.
2. Normalizing the activity of these brain regions probably provides a basis for both physical and mental restorative processes. Seeing the similarity in brain activation during both social and physical pain helps us to understand why social support can reduce physical pain, much as it soothes emotional pain.

A later study by Eisenberger's team (2006) confirmed the hypotheses that (1) baseline sensitivity to physical pain will predict sensitivity to social rejection and (2) experience with social distress will reduce the threshold for physcial pain. Experience with one form of pain can influence our experience of the other form.

KNOWING THAT THE BRAIN makes emotional experience real—more than mere metaphors of "hurt" or "pain"—how do we incorporate our thoughts and reasons for behaving as we do? Clearly, our subjective feelings and thoughts influence our actions. The cognitive interpretation of subjective feelings are **emotions**—anger, fear, sadness, jealousy, embarrassment, joy—but these feelings can operate outside our immediate awareness as well.

This chapter begins by exploring the causes of behaviors in which human beings and other animals engage. Sensory stimulation, neural circuits, and hormones are of primary importance in explaining behavior. We focus both on emotions and on the underlying reasons for **motivation**—behavior that seems purposeful and goal-directed.

Like emotion, motivated behavior is both inferred and subjective and can occur without awareness or intent. Motivated behaviors include both regulatory behaviors, such as eating, which are essential for survival, and nonregulatory behaviors, such as curiosity, which are not required to meet the basic needs of an animal.

Research on the neuroanatomy responsible for emotional and motivated behavior focuses on a neural circuit formed by the hypothalamus, the limbic system, and the frontal lobes. But behavior is influenced as much by the interaction of our social and natural environments and by evolution as it is by biology. To explain all this interaction in regard to how the brain controls behavior, we concentrate on the specific examples of feeding and sexual activity. Our exploration leads finally to the topic of reward, which plays a key role in explaining emotional and motivated behaviors.

Identifying the Causes of Behavior

We may think that the most obvious explanation for why we behave as we do is simply that that we act in a state of free will: we do what we want to and we always have a choice. But free will is not a likely cause of behavior.

Consider Roger. We first met in the admissions ward of a large mental hospital when 25-year-old Roger approached us and asked if we had any snacks. We had chewing gum, which he accepted eagerly. We thought little about this encounter until 10 minutes later when we noticed Roger eating the flowers from the vase on a table. A nurse took the flowers away but said little to Roger.

Later, as we wandered about the ward, we encountered a worker replacing linoleum floor tiles. Roger was watching the worker and, as he did, he dipped his finger into the pot of gluing compound and licked the glue from his finger, as if he were sampling honey from a jar. When we asked Roger what he was doing, he said that he was really hungry and that this stuff was not too bad. It reminded him of peanut butter.

One of us tasted the glue and concluded not only that it did not taste like peanut butter but that it tasted awful. Roger was undeterred. We alerted a nurse, who quickly removed him from the glue. Later, we saw him eating another flower bouquet.

Neurological testing revealed that a tumor had invaded Roger's hypothalamus at the base of his brain. He was indeed hungry all the time and in all likelihood could consume more than 20,000 calories a day if allowed to do so.

Would you say that Roger had free will regarding his appetite and food preferences? Probably not. Roger seemed compelled to eat whatever he could find, driven by a ravenous hunger. In this case, the nervous system, not an act of free will, has produced behavior. If the nervous system can produce one such behavior, it can undoubtedly produce many others.

If free will does not adequately explain why we act as we do, what does? One possibility is the brain's inherent need for stimulation. Psychologists Donald Hebb and Woodburn Heron (Hebb, 1955; Heron, 1957) conducted a fascinating series of experiments to support their view that people are motivated to interact with the environment to maintain at least a minimum level of brain stimulation.

Behavior for Brain Maintenance

Hebb and his coworkers studied the effects of **sensory deprivation**, depriving people of nearly all sensory input. They wanted to see how well-fed, physically comfortable college students who were paid handsomely for their time would react if they did

Orbitofrontal cortex Prefrontal cortex located behind the eye sockets (or orbits) that receives projections from the dorsomedial nucleus of the thalamus; plays a central role in a variety of emotional and social behaviors as well as in eating.

Emotion Cognitive interpretation of subjective feelings.

Motivation Behavior that seems purposeful and goal-directed.

Sensory deprivation Experimental setup in which a subject is allowed only restricted sensory input; subjects generally have a low tolerance for deprivation and may even display hallucinations.

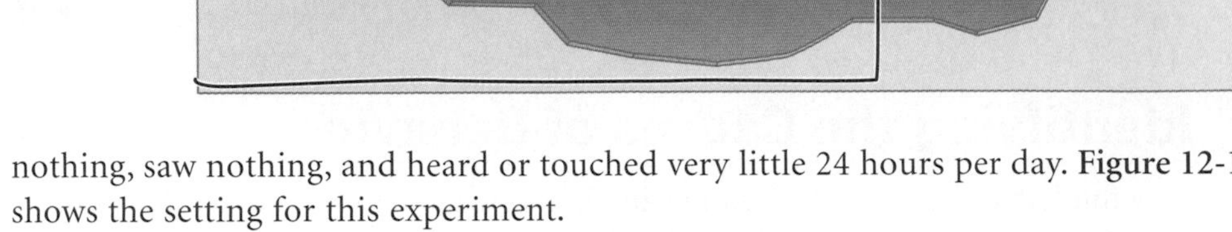

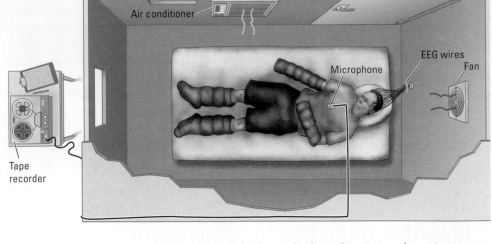

FIGURE 12-1 Sensory Deprivation. Experimenters record the EEG of a subject lying on a bed in a dimly lit environmental cubicle 24 hours a day, with time out only for meals and bathroom breaks. A translucent plastic visor restricts the subject's vision; a U-shaped pillow and the noise of a fan and air conditioner limit hearing. The sense of touch is restricted by cotton gloves and long cardboard cuffs. Adapted from "The Pathology of Boredom," by W. Heron, 1957, *Scientific American, 197*(4), p. 52.

nothing, saw nothing, and heard or touched very little 24 hours per day. **Figure 12-1** shows the setting for this experiment.

Each student lay on a bed in a small sound-proofed room with his ears enveloped by a hollowed-out pillow that muffled the monotonous hums of a nearby fan and air conditioner. Cardboard tubes covered his hands and arms, cutting off his sense of touch, and a translucent visor covered his eyes, blurring the visual world. The participants were given food on request and access to bathroom facilities. Otherwise, they were asked simply to enjoy the peace and quiet. For doing so, they would receive $20 per day, which was about four times what a student could earn even for a hard day's labor 60 years ago.

Wouldn't you think the participants would be quite happy to contribute to scientific knowledge in such a painless way? In fact, they were far from happy. Most were content for perhaps 4 to 8 hours; then they became increasingly distressed. They developed a need for stimulation of almost any kind. In one version of the experiment, the participants could listen, on request, to a talk for 6-year-old children on the dangers of alcohol. Some of them asked to hear it 20 times a day. Few subjects lasted more than 24 hours in these conditions.

The results of sensory deprivation studies are curious. After all, the participants' basic needs were being met, except perhaps the need for sexual gratification. (But Hebb assumed that, at the risk of insulting their virility, most of the young men in his study were accustomed to stretches of at least 3 or 4 days without engaging in sexual activity.)

So what was the cause of their distress? Why did they find sensory deprivation so aversive? The answer, Hebb and his colleagues concluded, must be that the brain has an inherent need for stimulation.

Psychologists Robert Butler and Harry Harlow (1954) came to a similar conclusion through a series of experiments they conducted at about the same time Hebb conducted his sensory-deprivation studies. Butler placed rhesus monkeys in a dimly lit room with a small door that could be opened to view an adjoining room. As shown in **Figure 12-2,** the researchers could vary the stimuli in the adjoining room so that the monkeys could view different objects or animals each time they opened the door.

Monkeys in these conditions spent a lot of time opening the door and viewing whatever was on display, such as toy trains cir-

FIGURE 12-2 Brain Maintenance. Monkeys quickly learn to solve puzzles or perform other tricks to gain access to a door that looks out from their dimly lit quarters into an adjacent room. A toy train is a strong visual incentive for the monkey peeking through the door; a bowl of fruit is less rewarding. From "Persistence of Visual Exploration in Monkeys," by R. A. Butler and H. F. Harlow, 1954, *Journal of Comparative and Physiological Psychology, 47,* p. 260.

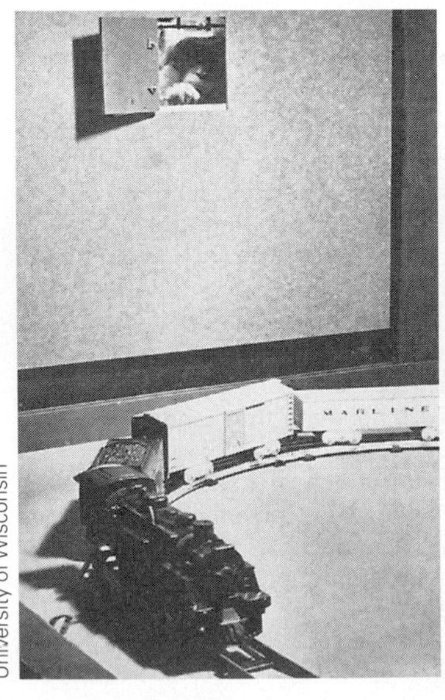

University of Wisconsin

cling a track. The monkeys were even willing to perform various tasks just for an opportunity to look through the door. The longer they were deprived of a chance to look, the more time they spent looking when finally given the opportunity.

The Butler and Harlow experiments, together with Hebb and colleagues' research on sensory deprivation, show that, in the absence of stimulation, the brain will seek it out.

Drives and Behavior

A pet cat living in a house or apartment awakes in the morning, stretches, wanders to its feeding place, and has a drink of water and some food. Then it sits and cleans itself. Next, it wanders around and spots its favorite toy mouse, which it pounces on and throws in the air. It may pounce and throw again and again for a number of minutes.

Seemingly bored with the toy, the cat wanders about looking for attention. It sits in its owner's lap, starts to purr, and falls asleep. Shortly thereafter, it gets up and walks away, passes its food and mouse toy, and meows. It explores the apartment, sniffing here and there, before napping in a sunbeam. On waking, the cat returns to the food bowl, eats heartily, bats once at the toy in passing, and searches for its wool ball, which it chases for a while. Later, it stares out the window and eventually settles down for a long sleep.

This cat's seemingly unremarkable actions provide three clues to the causes of behavior:

1. The cat's response to a particular stimulus is not the same each time. Both the food and the toy mouse elicit behavior on some occasions but not on others.
2. The strength of the cat's behaviors varies. For instance, the mouse toy stimulates vigorous behavior at one time and none at another.
3. The cat engages not only in behaviors that satisfy obvious biological needs (eating, drinking, sleeping) but also in behaviors that are not so obviously necessary (playing, affection seeking, exploring).

The same behavior patterns are typical of dogs and of people. People can be amused by a puzzle or a book at one moment and completely bored by it the next. They also respond to a certain object or situation vigorously on some occasions and half-heartedly on others. And they engage in many behaviors that do not seem to have any obvious function, such as tapping their toes to music. What generates all these different behaviors?

As psychologists and biologists began to ponder the causes of behavior in the 1930s, they concluded that some sort of internal energy must drive it. This internal energizing factor had many names, including instinct, but the name that stuck was **drives.** The concept gave rise to drive theories of behavior.

Instincts and drives are not identical, but for our purposes that does not matter.

Drive theorists assumed that, because animals perform many different behaviors, they must have many different drives—a sexual drive, a curiosity drive, a hunger drive, a thirst drive, and so on. An animal engages in a particular behavior because its drive for it is high, and it ceases engaging in that behavior because its drive for it becomes low. Our cat, for example, played vigorously with the toy mouse when its play drive was high and ceased playing when its play drive diminished to zero.

Drive theory suggests that the brain is storing energy for behavior. The energy builds up until it reaches a level where it is released in action, thereby becoming a cause of behavior. Ethologists offer an interesting analogy to describe this process: they compare behavior caused by drives to the flushing of a toilet.

When the water reservoir of a toilet is full, depressing the handle leads to a "whoosh" of water that, once begun, cannot be stopped. When the reservoir is only partly full, depressing the handle still produces a flush, but a less vigorous one. If the reservoir is empty, no amount of handle pressing will cause the toilet to flush. Applying this "flush

Drive Hypothetical state of arousal that motivates an organism to engage in a particular behavior.

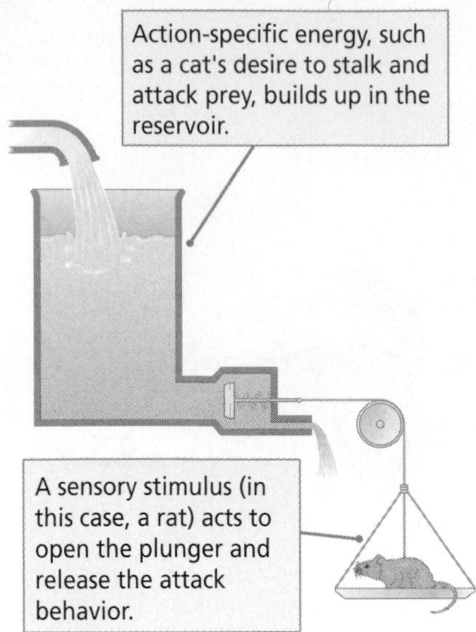

Action-specific energy, such as a cat's desire to stalk and attack prey, builds up in the reservoir.
A sensory stimulus (in this case, a rat) acts to open the plunger and release the attack behavior.

FIGURE 12-3 Flush Model of Motivation. Drive theories maintain that reservoirs of action-specific energies, once released, flow out and produce behavior. The greater the behavior's energy store, the longer it persists. Without an energy store, there is no behavior.

model" to our cat with the toy mouse, the cat will play vigorously if the play reservoir is full, less vigorously if it is partly full, and not at all if the reservoir is empty.

The flush model makes a couple of assumptions about drive-induced behavior (**Figure 12-3**). It assumes that a drive-induced behavior, once started, will continue until all the energy in its reservoir is gone. Our cat keeps playing, although with decreasing vigor, until all the energy held in reserve for play is depleted.

The flush model also assumes separate stores of energy for different behaviors. For instance, cats have a drive to play, and they have a drive to kill. Engaging in one of these behaviors does not reduce the energy stored for the other. That is presumably why a cat may play with a mouse that it has caught for many minutes before finally killing it. The cat will pounce and attack the mouse repeatedly until all its energy for play is used up, and only then will it proceed to the next drive-induced behavior, feeding.

The flush model can be applied to many different behaviors and makes some intuitive sense. We do seem to behave as if there were energy reserves for various behaviors. Males of most mammalian species, for instance, typically enter a refractory period subsequent to sexual intercourse when they no longer have interest in (or possibly energy for) sex. Later, the interest or energy returns. It is as though a pent-up sexual urge, once satisfied, vanishes for a time, awaiting a new energy buildup.

Neural Circuits and Behavior

Researchers once assumed that physiologists would quickly discover how the brain executes drives, but they were unable to establish a link between drives and brain activity. As researchers searched inside the brain for drives, they discovered instead the problem with drive theory: behavioral change correlates with biological changes in hormones and cellular activity.

Researchers studying the sexual drive, for example, found that a man's frequency of copulation correlates with his levels of **androgens** (male hormones). Unusually high androgen levels are related to very high sexual interest, whereas abnormally low androgen levels are linked to low sexual interest or perhaps no interest at all. The concept of sexual drive no longer seemed needed.

Researchers now sought to explain the action of androgens on neural circuits. Such physiological analysis provides more powerful explanations of behavior than does simply invoking drives. It allows us to say exactly what particular events in the brain can trigger a certain kind of behavior. An electrode used to stimulate the brain cells activated by androgens can induce sexual behavior. Such brain stimulation can produce amazing sexual activity in male rats, sometimes allowing 50 ejaculations over a couple of hours. Clearly, neuronal activity is responsible for the behavior, not some hidden energy reservoir as drive theories presumed.

The idea of a neural basis for behavior has wide application. For instance, we can say that Roger had such a voracious and indiscriminate appetite either because the brain circuits that initiated eating were excessively active or because the circuits that terminated eating were inactive. Similarly, we can say that Hebb's subjects were highly upset by sensory deprivation because the neural circuits that respond to sensory inputs were forced to be abnormally underactive. So the main reason why a particular thought, feeling, or action occurs lies in what is going on in brain circuits.

The Nature of Behavior: Why Cats Kill Birds

Although neural circuits are somewhat plastic as they form during brain development, they are not so easily changed later in life. It therefore follows that behaviors caused by these neural circuits also are going to be slow to adapt. Modifying the killing of prey by cats is a good example.

Androgen Male hormone related to level of sexual interest.

One of the frustrating things about being a cat owner is that even well-fed cats kill birds—often lots of birds. Most people are not too bothered when their cats kill mice, because they view mice as a nuisance. But birds are different. People enjoy watching birds in their yards and gardens. Many cat owners wonder why their pets keep killing birds.

To provide an answer, we can look to the activities of neural circuits. Cats must have a brain circuit that controls prey killing. When this circuit is active, a cat makes an appropriate kill. Viewed in an evolutionary context, it makes sense for cats to have such a circuit because, in the days when cats were not owned by doting human beings, they did not have food dishes that were regularly being filled.

Why does this prey-killing circuit become active when a cat does not need food? One explanation is that, to secure survival, the activity of circuits such as the prey-killing circuit have become rewarding in some way—they make the cat "feel good." As a result, the cat is likely to engage in the pleasure-producing behavior often, which helps to guarantee that it will usually not go hungry.

In the wild, after all, a cat that did not like killing would probably be a dead cat. The idea of behaviors such as prey killing being rewarding was first proposed by Steve Glickman and Bernard Schiff in the early 1960s. Because it is important to our understanding of the causes of behavior, we will return to reward at the end of this chapter.

Killing behavior by cats is innate, not learned. It is triggered automatically in the presence of the right stimulus. The innateness of killing in cats is demonstrated by a motherless cat named Hunter that was found abandoned as a tiny kitten. Hunter was bottle fed and raised without a mother cat to "teach" her to hunt.

Hunter did not need such education. She got her name from her innate and deadly skill at catching mice and other small prey. The prey-killing circuits in her brainstem worked without training. They no doubt were influenced by practice, however, because Hunter became more proficient at killing as she grew older. But the ultimate underlying cause of the behavior is a neural circuit that, when activated, produces stalking and killing responses.

REVIEW: Identifying the Causes of Behavior

- ✔ Free will is a not an adequate explanation of behavior because the nervous system can produce behaviors over which an organism has neither choice nor control.
- ✔ Researchers have investigated causes of behavior, including the apparent need of the brain to maintain at least a minimum level of stimulation and the behavioral control exerted by the nervous system.
- ✔ The earlier idea that internal, energizing drives build up and are released in behavior gave way to a more powerful explanation: behavior results from the activity of hormonal and neural circuits inside the brain that control how we think, act, and feel.

Biology, Evolution, and Environment

Why does the sight of a bird or a mouse trigger stalking and killing in a cat? Why does the human body stimulate sexual interest? We can address such questions by investigating the evolutionary and environmental influences on brain-circuit activity that contribute to behavior. Because the chemical senses (odor and taste) play a fundamental role in the biology of motivated behavior, we consider them here as well.

(A)

(B)

FIGURE 12-4 Innate Releasing Mechanism in Cats. (A) Displaying the "Halloween cat" stimulates cats to respond defensively, with raised fur, arched backs, and bared teeth. This behavior appears at about 6 weeks of age in kittens who have never seen such a posture before. (B) The "Picasso" cat evokes no response at all.

Evolutionary Influences on Behavior

The evolutionary explanation hinges on the concept of **innate releasing mechanisms** (IRMs), activators for inborn, adaptive responses that aid in an animal's survival. IRMs help an animal to successfully feed, reproduce, and escape predators. The concept is best understood by analyzing its parts.

The term *innate* implies that the mechanisms have proved adaptive for the species and therefore have been maintained in the genome. Innate releasing mechanisms are present from birth rather than acquired through experience. The term *releasing* indicates that IRMs act as triggers on behaviors for which there are internal programs.

Let us return to our cat. The brain of a cat must have a built-in mechanism that triggers appropriate stalking and killing in response to stimuli such as a bird or a mouse. Similarly, a cat must also have a built-in mechanism that triggers appropriate mating behavior in the presence of a suitable cat of the opposite sex. Although not all of a cat's behaviors are due to IRMs, you can probably think of other innate releasing mechanisms that cats possess, such as arching and hissing on encountering a threat. For all these IRMs, the animal's brain must have a set of norms against which it can match stimuli to trigger an appropriate response.

The existence of such innate, internalized norms is suggested in the following experiment. One of us (B. K.) and Arthur Nonneman allowed a litter of 6-week-old kittens to play in a room and become familiar with it. After this adjustment period, we introduced a two-dimensional image of an adult cat in a "Halloween posture," as shown in **Figure 12-4.**

The kittens responded with raised fur, arched backs, and bared teeth, all signs of being threatened by the image of the adult. Some even hissed at the model. These kittens had no experience with any adult cat except their mother, and there was no reason to believe that she had ever shown them this behavior. Rather, some sort of template of this posture must be prewired in the kitten brain. When the kittens saw the model that matched the preexisting template, a threat response was automatically triggered. This innate triggering mechanism is an IRM.

The IRM concept also applies to humans. In one study, Tiffany Field and her colleagues (1982) had an adult display to young infants various exaggerated facial expressions, such as happiness, sadness, and surprise. As **Figure 12-5** shows, the babies responded with very much the same expressions as the adults displayed. These newborns were too young to be imitating the adult faces intentionally. Rather, babies must have an innate ability to match these facial expressions to internal templates, which in turn triggers some prewired program to reproduce the expressions in their own faces. Such an IRM would have adaptive value if these facial expressions serve as important social signals for humans.

Evidence for a prewired motor program related to facial expressions also comes from the study of congenitally blind children. These children spontaneously produce the very same facial expressions that sighted people do, even though they have never seen them in others. IRMs such as these are prewired into the brain, but they can be modified by experience. Our cat Hunter's stalking skills were not inherited fully developed at birth but rather matured functionally as she grew older. The same is true of many human IRMs, such as those for responding to sexually arousing stimuli.

Different cultures may emphasize different stimuli as arousing, and even within a single culture, there is variation in what different people find sexually stimulating. Nonetheless, some human attributes are universally found to have sexually arousing value. An example is the hip-to-waist ratio of human females for most human males. This ratio is probably part of an IRM.

Review Darwin's theory and the philosophy of materialism in Chapter 1.

The IRM concept can be related to the Darwinian view of how the nervous system evolves. Natural selection favors behaviors that prove adaptive for an organism, and these behaviors are passed on to future generations. Because behavior patterns are produced by the activity of neurons in the brain, the natural selection of specific behaviors is really the selection of particular brain circuits.

Animals that survive long enough to reproduce and have healthy offspring are more likely to pass on the genes for making their brain circuits than are animals with traits that make them less likely to survive and successfully reproduce. Thus, cats with brain circuits that made them adept at stalking prey or responding fiercely to threats were more likely to survive and produce many offspring, passing on those adaptive brain circuits and behaviors to their young. In this way, the behaviors became widespread in the species over time.

Although the Darwinian view seems straightforward when considering how cats evolved brain circuits for stalking prey or responding to threats, it is less obvious when applied to many complex human behaviors. For instance, why have humans evolved the behavior of killing other humans? At first glance, this behavior would seem counterproductive to the survival of the human species. Why has it endured?

Evolutionary psychologists assume that any behavior, including homocide, exists because natural selection has favored the neural circuits that produce it. **Evolutionary psychology** applies principles of natural selection to explanations of human behavior. When two men fight a duel, one commonsense explanation might be that they are fighting over grievances. But evolutionary psychologists would instead ask why a behavior pattern that risks people's lives is sustained in a population. Their answer is that fights are about social status.

Men who fought and won duels passed on their genes to future generations, whereas those who lost duels did not. Through time, therefore, the traits associated with successful dueling—strength, aggression, agility—became more prevalent among humans, and so, too, did dueling itself. Martin Daly and Margot Wilson (1988) extended this evolutionary analysis to further account for homicide. In their view, homicide may endure in our society despite its severe punishment because it is related to behaviors that were adaptive in the human past.

Suppose, for example, that natural selection favored sexually jealous males who effectively intimidated their rivals and bullied their mates so as to guarantee their own paternity of any offspring produced by their mates. As a result, male jealousy would become a prevalent motive for interpersonal violence, including homicide. Homicide itself does not help a man produce more children. But men who are apt to commit homicides are more likely to engage in other behaviors (bullying and intimidation) that improve their social status and therefore their reproductive fitness. Homicide therefore is related to adaptive traits that have been selected through millennia.

Evolutionary theory cannot account for all human behavior, perhaps not even homicide. But evolutionary psychologists can generate intriguing hypotheses about how natural selection might have shaped the brain and behavior and provide an evolutionary perspective on the neurological bases of behavior.

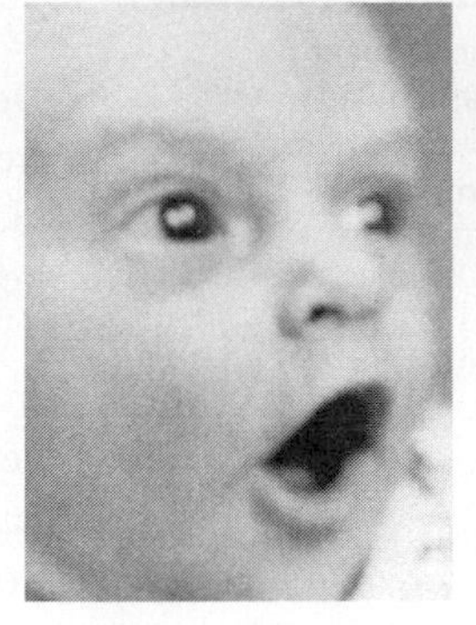

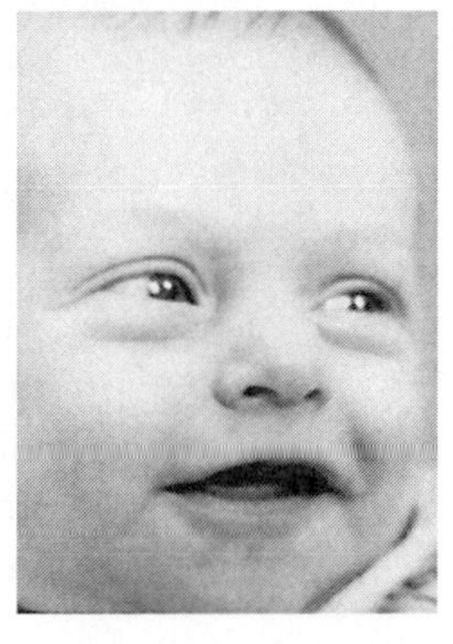

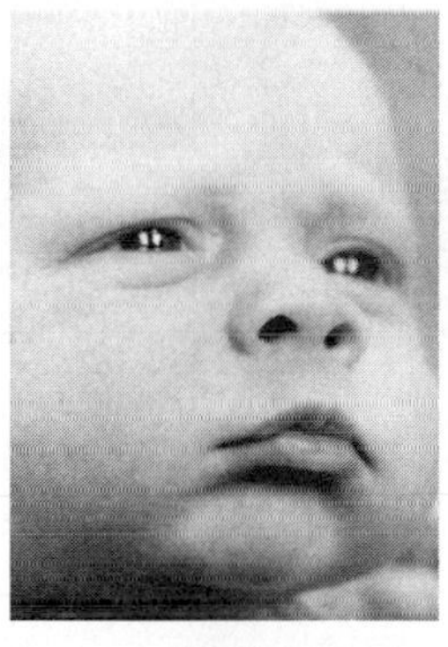
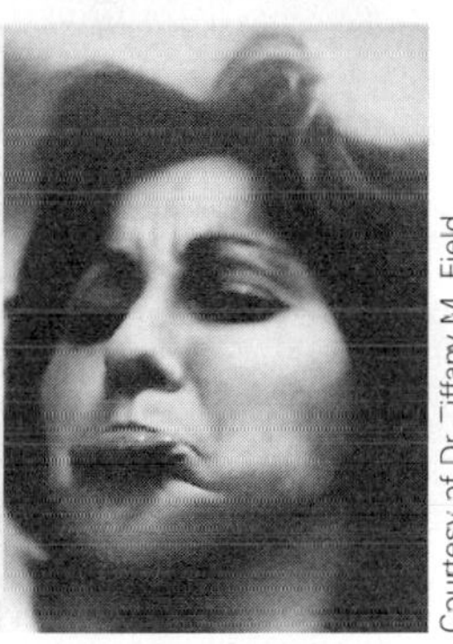

Courtesy of Dr. Tiffany M. Field

FIGURE 12-5 Innate Releasing Mechanism in Humans. Facial expressions made by young infants in response to expressions made by the experimenter. From "Discrimination and Imitation of Facial Expression by Neonates," by T. M. Field, R. Woodson, R. Greenberg, and D. Cohen, 1982, *Science, 218,* p. 180.

The Chemical Senses

Chemical reactions play a central role in nervous system activity, and *chemosignals* (chemical signals) play a central role in motivated and emotional behavior. Mammals identify group members by odor, mark their territories with urine and other odorants, identify favorite and forbidden foods by taste, and form associations among odors, tastes, and emotional events. We thus consider the chemical senses here in the context of mammalian emotional and motivated behavior.

Innate releasing mechanism (IRM) Hypothetical mechanism that detects specific sensory stimuli and directs an organism to take a particular action.

Evolutionary psychology Discipline that seeks to apply principles of natural selection to understand the causes of human behavior.

Pheromone Odorant biochemical released by one animal that acts as a chemosignal and can affect the physiology or behavior of another animal.

Olfaction

Odor is the most puzzling sensory system. We can discriminate thousands of odors, yet we have great difficulty finding words to describe what we smell. We may like or dislike smells or compare one smell to another, but we lack a vocabulary for our olfactory perceptions.

Wine experts rely on olfaction to tell them about wines, but they must learn to use smell to do so. Courses for training people in wine sniffing typically run one full day per week for a year, and most people who take the courses still have great difficulty in passing the final test. The degree of difficulty contrasts with that of vision and audition, which are designed to analyze specific qualities of the sensory input (such as pitch in audition or color in vision). In contrast, olfaction seem to be designed to determine whether information is familiar—for example, is the smell from an item of edible food or is it from a friend or a stranger?—or to identify a signal such as a receptive mate.

Receptors for Smell Identifying chemosignals is conceptually similar to identifying other sensory stimuli (light, sound, touch) except that, instead of converting physical energy such as light or sound waves into receptor potentials, scent interacts with chemical receptors. This constant chemical interaction appears to be tough on the receptors and so, in contrast with the receptors for light, sound, and touch, chemical receptors are constantly being replaced. The life of an olfactory receptor is about 60 days.

The receptor surface for olfaction is the olfactory epithelium, which lies in the nasal cavity, as illustrated in **Figure 12-6.** The epithelium is composed of receptor cells and support cells. Each receptor cell sends a process, which ends in 10 to 20 cilia, into a mucous layer known as the olfactory mucosa. Chemicals in the air that we breathe dissolve in the mucosa to interact with the cilia. If the receptors are affected by an olfactory chemosignal, metabotropic activation of a specific G protein leads to an opening of sodium channels and a change in membrane potential.

Figure 5-14A illustrates the activity of a metabotropic receptor coupled to an ion channel.

The receptor surface of the epithelium varies widely across species. In humans, the area is estimated to range from 2 to 4 square centimeters, in dogs the area is about 18 square centimeters, and in cats it is about 21 square centimeters. No wonder our sensitivity to odors is less acute than that of dogs and cats: they have 10 times as much receptor area as humans have. Roughly analogous to the tuning characteristics of cells in the auditory system, olfactory receptor neurons in vertebrates do not respond to specific odors but rather to a range of odors.

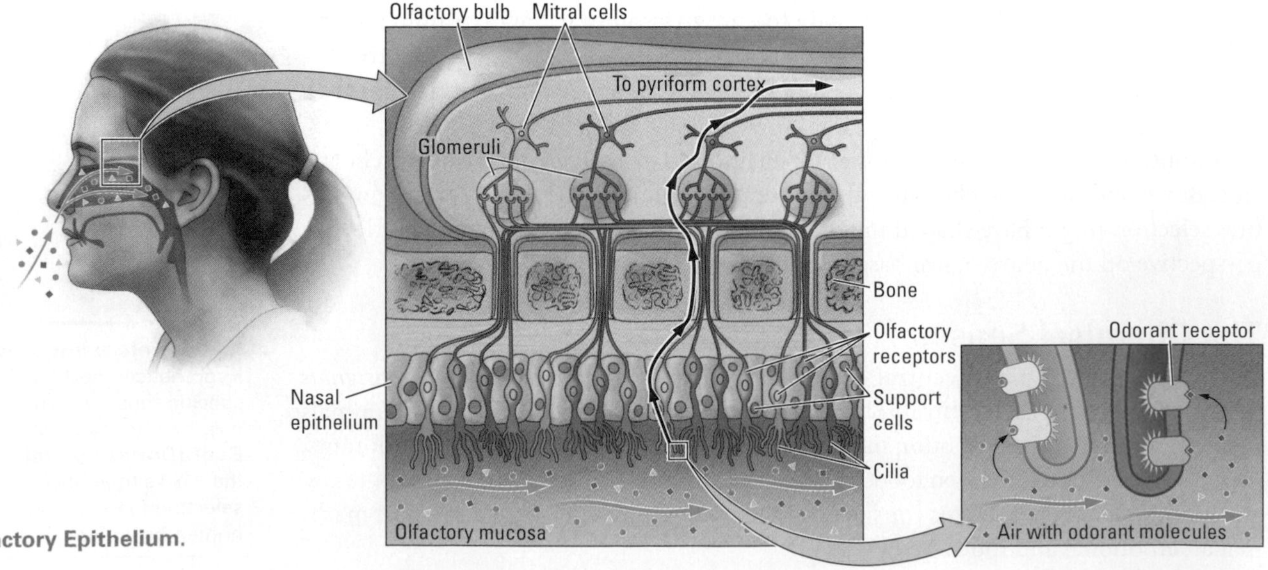

FIGURE 12-6 Olfactory Epithelium.

How does a limited number of receptor types allow us to smell many different odors? The simplest explanation is that any given odorant stimulates a unique pattern of receptors, and the summed activity, or pattern of activity, produces our perception of a particular odor. Analogously, the visual system enables us to identify many different colors with only three receptor types in the retina: the summed activity of the three cones leads to our rich color life.

A fundamental difference, however, is that there are far more receptors in the olfactory system than in the visual system. Richard Axel and Linda Buck won the Nobel Prize in medicine in 2004 for their discovery that a novel gene family (about 350 genes in humans) encodes a very large and diverse set of olfactory receptors. The combination of these receptors allows us to discriminate about 10,000 different smells.

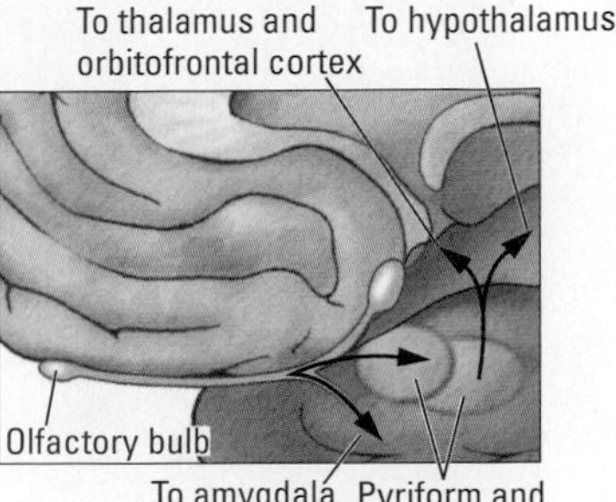

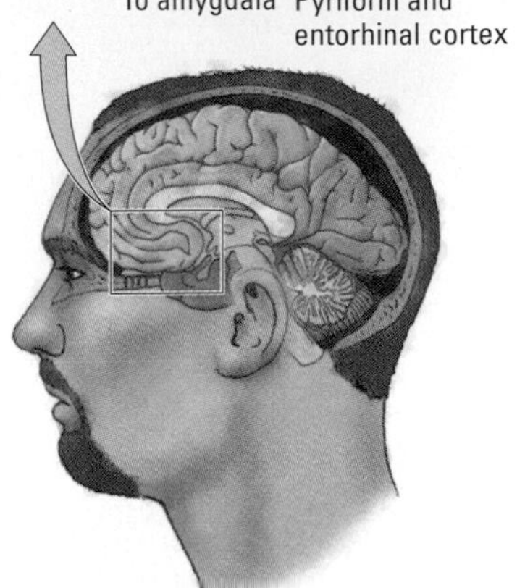

FIGURE 12-7 Olfactory Pathways.

Olfactory Pathways Olfactory receptor cells project to the olfactory bulb, ending in ball-like tufts of dendrites called glomeruli, shown in Figure 12-6. There they form synapses with the dendrites of mitral cells. The mitral cells send their axons from the olfactory bulb to a broad range of forebrain areas, summarized in **Figure 12-7.** Many olfactory targets, such as the amygdala and pyriform cortex, have no connection *through* the thalamus, as do other sensory systems. However, a thalamic connection (to the dorsomedial nucleus) does project to the orbitofrontal cortex, which plays a central role in a variety of emotional and social behaviors as well as in eating.

Accessory Olfactory System A unique class of odorants are **pheromones,** biochemicals released by one animal that act as chemosignals and can affect the physiology or behavior of another animal. For example, Karen Stern and Martha McClintock (1998) found that when women reside together they begin to cycle together. Furthermore, the researchers found that the synchronization of menstrual cycles is conveyed by odors.

The phenomenon of synchronizing menstrual cycles is called the *Whitten effect.*

Pheromones appear able to affect more than sex-related behavior. A human chemosignal, androstadienone, has been shown to alter glucose utilization in the neocortex—that is, how the brain uses energy (Jacob et al., 2001). Thus, a chemosignal appears to affect cortical processes even though the signal was not actually detected consciously. The puzzle is why we would evolve such a mechanism and how it might actually affect cerebral functioning.

Pheromones are unique odors because they are detected by a special olfactory receptor system known as the *vomeronasal organ,* which is made up of a small group of sensory receptors connected by a duct to the nasal passage. The receptor cells in the vomeronasal organ send their axons to the accessory olfactory bulb, which lies adjacent to the main olfactory bulb. The vomeronasal organ connects primarily with the amygdala and hypothalamus by which it likely plays a role in reproductive and social behavior.

The vomeronasal organ probably participates not in general olfactory behavior but rather in the analysis of pheromones such as those in urine. You may have seen bulls or cats engage in a behavior known as *flehmen,* illustrated in **Figure12-8.** When exposed to novel urine from a cat or human, cats raise their upper lip to close off the nasal passages and suck air into the mouth. The air flows through the duct on the roof of the mouth en route to the vomeronasal organ.

Courtesy Arthur Nonneman and Bryan Kolb

FIGURE 12-8 Response to Pheromones. (*Left*) A cat sniffs a urine-soaked cotton ball, (*center*) raises its upper lip to close off the nasal passages, and (*right*) follows with the full gape response characteristic of flehmen, a behavior mediated by the accessory olfactory system.

Human Olfactory Processing One common misperception is that people have a miserable sense of smell relative to other mammals. Our threshold for detecting many smells is certainly inferior to that of our pet dogs, cats, and horses, but humans have a surprisingly acute sensitivity to smells that are behaviorally relevant.

Several studies show convincingly that people can identify their own odor, the odor of kin versus non-kin, and the odor of friends versus strangers with accuracy well above chance (e.g., Olsson et al., 2006). Johan Lundstrom and colleagues (2008) used PET scans to identify the neural networks that process human body odors. They made two surprising findings.

First, the brain analyzes common odors and body odors differently. Although both activate primary olfactory regions, body odors also activate structures that were not previously believed to be involved in olfactory processing, including the posterior cingulate cortex, occipital cortex, and anterior cingulate cortex—regions that are also activated by visually emotional stimuli. Considered in an evolutionary perspective, the ability to identify human odors is likely uniquely important to safety.

Second, smelling a stranger's odor activates the amygdala and insular regions, similar to activation observed for fearful visual stimuli such as masked or fearful faces. The investigators also asked participants to rate the intensity and pleasantness of odors and found that the odors of strangers rated as stronger and less pleasant.

Lundstrom and colleagues conclude that processing body odors is mostly unconscious and represents an automatic process that matches odors to a learned "library" of smells. Similar unconscious processes seem to occur during visual and auditory information processing and to play an important role in our emotional reactions.

Gustation

Research reveals significant differences in taste preferences both between and within species. Humans and rats like sucrose and saccharin solutions, but dogs reject saccharin and cats are indifferent to both, inasmuch as they do not detect sweetness at all. The failure of cats to taste sweet may not be surprising: they are pure carnivores, and nothing that they normally eat is sweet.

Similarly, within the human species, clear differences in taste thresholds and preferences are obvious. An example is the preference for or dislike of bitter tastes—the flavor of brussels sprouts, for instance. People tend either to love them or hate them. Linda Bartoshuk (2000) showed absolute differences among adults: some perceive certain tastes as very bitter, whereas others are indifferent to them. Presumably, the latter group is more tolerant of brussels sprouts.

The sensitivity to bitterness is related to genetic differences in the ability to detect a specific chemical (6-n-propylthiouracil, or PROP). People who are able to detect minute quantities find the taste extremely bitter and are sometimes referred to as *supertasters.* The advantage of being a supertaster is that bitter foods are often poisonous. The disadvantage is that supertasters avoid many nutritious fruits and vegetables that they find bitter.

Differences in taste thresholds also emerge as we age. Children are much more responsive than adults to tastes and are often intolerant of spicy foods because they have more taste receptors than adults have. By age 20, humans have lost at least an estimated 50 percent of their taste receptors. No wonder children and adults have different food preferences.

Receptors for Taste Taste receptors are found within taste buds located on the tongue, under the tongue, on the soft palate on the roof of the mouth, on the sides of the mouth, and at the back of the mouth on the nasopharynx. Each of the five different taste-receptor types responds to a different chemical component of food. The four most familiar are sweet, sour, salty, and bitter. The fifth type, called the *umami* recep-

Reinforcer In operant conditioning, any event that strengthens the behavior it follows.

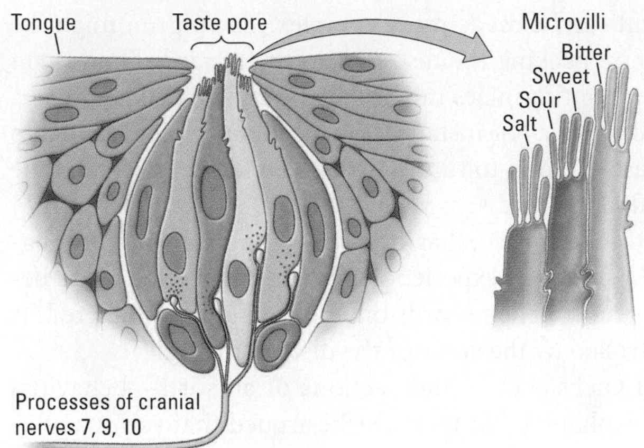

FIGURE 12-9 Anatomy of a Taste Bud. Adapted from "Chemical Senses: Taste and Olfaction," by D. V. Smith and G. M. Shepherd, 2003, in *Fundamental Neuroscience* (2nd ed., pp. 631–667), L. R. Squire, F. E. Bloom, S. K. McConnell, J. L. Roberts, N. C. Spitzer, & M. J. Zigmond (Eds.), New York: Academic Press.

tor, is specially sensitive to glutamate, a neurotransmitter molecule, and perhaps to protein.

Taste receptors are grouped into taste buds, each containing several receptor types, as illustrated in **Figure 12-9.** Gustatory stimuli interact with the receptor tips, the *microvilli,* to open ion channels, leading to changes in membrane potential. The base of the taste bud is contacted by the branches of afferent nerves that come from cranial nerves 7 (facial nerve), 9 (glossopharyngeal nerve), or 10 (vagus nerve).

Figure 2-25 lists and illustrates the cranial nerves.

Gustatory Pathways Cranial nerves 7, 9, and 10 form the main gustatory nerve, the *solitary tract.* On entering the brainstem, the tract divides in two as illustrated in **Figure 12-10.** One route travels through the posterior medulla to the ventroposterior medial nucleus of the thalamus. This nucleus in turn sends out two pathways, one to the primary somatosensory cortex and the other to a region just rostral to the secondary somatosensory cortex in the gustatory cortex of the insula.

The gustatory region is dedicated to taste, whereas the primary somatosensory region is also responsive to tactile information and is probably responsible for localizing tastes on the tongue and for our reactions to a food's texture. The gustatory cortex sends a projection to the orbital cortex in a region near the input of the olfactory cortex. It is likely that the mixture of olfactory and gustatory input in the orbital cortex gives rise to our perception of flavor.

The second pathway from the gustatory nerve projects through the pons to the hypothalamus and amygdala. Researchers hypothesize that this input plays some role in feeding behavior.

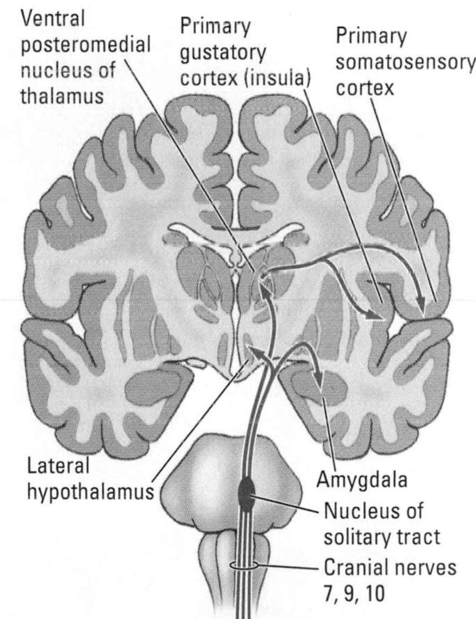

FIGURE 12-10 Gustatory Pathways.

Environmental Influences on Behavior

Many psychologists have emphasized learning as a cause of behavior. No one would question that we modify our behavior as we learn, but B. F. Skinner went much further. He believed that behaviors are selected by environmental factors.

Skinner's argument is simple. Certain events function as rewards, or **reinforcers,** and when a reinforcing event follows a particular response, similar responses are more likely to occur again. Skinner argued that reinforcement can be manipulated to encourage the display of complex behaviors.

The power of experience to shape behavior by pairing stimuli and rewards is typified by one of Skinner's experiments. A pigeon is placed in a box that has a small disc on one wall (the stimulus). If the pigeon pecks at the disc (the response), a food tray opens and the pigeon can feed (the reinforcement or reward). The pigeon quickly learns the association between the stimulus and the response, especially if the disc has a small spot on it. It pecks at the spot and, within minutes, it has mastered the response needed to receive a reward.

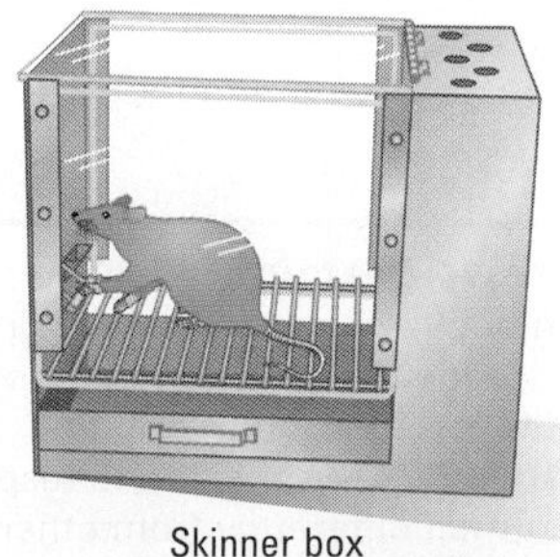

Skinner box

Now the response requirement can be made more complex. The pigeon might be required to turn 360 degrees before pecking the disc to gain the reward. The pigeon can learn this response, too. Other contingencies might then be added, making the response requirements even more complex. For instance, the pigeon might be trained to turn in a clockwise circle if the disc is green, to turn in a counterclockwise circle if the disc is red, and to scratch at the floor if the disc is yellow.

If you suddenly came across this complex behavior in a pigeon, you would probably be astounded. But if you understood the experience that had shaped the bird's behavior, you would understand its cause. The rewards offered to the pigeon altered its behavior: its responses were controlled by the color of the disc on the wall.

Skinner extended behavioral analysis to include actions of all sorts—behaviors that at first do not appear easily explained. For instance, he argued that various phobias could be accounted for by understanding a person's reinforcement history. Someone who once was terrified by a turbulent plane ride thereafter avoids air travel and manifests a phobia of flying. The avoidance of flying is rewarding because it lowers the person's anxiety level, so the phobic behavior is maintained. Skinner also argued against the commonly held view that much of human behavior is under our own control. From Skinner's perspective, free will is only an illusion, because behavior is controlled not by the organism but rather by the environment through experience.

Although our intent is not to debate the pros and cons of Skinner's ideas here, we can conclude that many complex behaviors are learned. It is also true that learning takes place in a brain that has been selected for evolutionary adaptations. This combination of learning and inherited brain circuits can lead to some surprising results. A case in point can be seen again in pigeons.

A pigeon in a Skinner box can quickly learn to peck a disc to receive a bit of food, but it cannot learn to peck a disc to escape from a mild electric shock to its feet. Why not? Although the same simple pecking behavior is being rewarded, apparently the pigeon's brain is not prewired for this second kind of association. The bird is prepared genetically to make the first association, for food, but not prepared for the second, which makes adaptive sense.

For a pigeon, pecking is a behavior that in a natural environment is widely linked with obtaining food. Learning associations between pecking and food come easily to a pigeon. By contrast, learning to peck to prevent electric shock is not part of the pigeon's inborn brain circuitry, so mastering this association does not come easily to the bird. Typically, it flies away from noxious situations.

The specific nature of the behavior–consequence associations that animals are able to learn was first shown in 1966 by psychologist John Garcia. He observed that farmers in the western United States are constantly shooting at coyotes for attacking lambs; yet, despite the painful consequences, the coyotes never seem to learn to stop killing lambs in favor of safer prey. The reason, Garcia speculated, is that a coyote's brain is not prewired by adaptation to make this kind of association.

So Garcia proposed an alternative to deter coyotes from killing lambs—one that uses an association that a coyote's brain is prepared to make: the connection between eating something that makes one sick and avoiding that food in the future. Garcia gave the coyotes a poisoned lamb carcass, which made them sick but did not kill them. With only one pairing of lamb and illness, most coyotes learned not to eat sheep for the rest of their lives.

Many humans have similarly acquired food aversions because the taste of a certain food—especially a novel one—was subsequently paired with illness. This **learned taste aversion** is acquired even when the food that was eaten is in fact unrelated to the later illness. As long as the taste and the nausea are paired in time, the brain is prewired to make a connection between them.

Learned taste aversion Acquired association between a specific taste or odor and illness; leads to an aversion to foods that have the taste or odor.

Preparedness Predisposition to respond to certain stimuli differently from other stimuli.

One of us ate his first Caesar salad the night before coming down with a stomach flu. A year later, he was offered another Caesar salad and, to his amazement, felt ill just at the smell of it. Even though his earlier illness had not been due to the salad, he had formed an association between the novel flavor and the illness. This strong and rapid associative learning makes adaptive sense. Having a brain that is prepared to make a connection between a novel taste and subsequent illness helps an animal avoid poisonous foods and so aids in its survival. A curious aspect of taste-aversion learning is that we are not even aware of having formed the association until we encounter the taste and/or smell again.

The fact that the nervous system is often prewired to make certain associations but not to make others has led to the concept of **preparedness** in learning theories. Preparedness can help account for some complex behaviors. For example, if two rats are paired in a small box and exposed to a mild electric shock, they will immediately fight with one another, even though neither was responsible for the shock.

Apparently, the rat brain is prepared to associate injury with nearby objects or other animals. Perhaps you have occasionally felt your own temper flare toward someone who was near you when you were accidentally hurt or in pain for some reason unrelated to that person. The extent to which we might extend this idea to explain such human behaviors as bigotry and racism is an interesting topic for debate. But the point here is that environmental events are working on a brain that is prewired to make certain types of associations.

Inferring Purpose in Behavior: To Know a Fly

A pitfall in studying the causes of behavior is the tendency to assume that behavior is intentional. The problems in inferring purpose from an organism's actions are illustrated in a wonderful little book, *To Know a Fly,* by Vincent Dethier.

When a fly lands on a kitchen table, it wanders about, occasionally stomping its feet. Eventually, it finds a bit of food and sticks its proboscis (a trunklike extension) into the food and eats. The fly may then walk to a nearby place and begin to groom by rubbing its legs together quickly. Finally, it spends a long period motionless.

If you observed a fly engaged in these behaviors, it might appear to have been initially searching for food because it was hungry. When it found food, you might assume that it gorged itself until it was satisfied, and then it cleaned up and rested. In short, the fly's behavior might seem to you to have some purpose or intention.

Dethier studied flies for years to understand what a fly is actually doing when it engages in these behaviors. His findings have little to do with purpose or intention. When a fly wanders about a table, it is not deliberately searching; it is tasting things that it walks on.

As **Figure 12-11** shows, a fly's taste receptors are on its feet. Tasting is automatic when a fly walks. An adult fly's nervous system has a built-in preference for sweet tastes and aversions to sour, salty, or bitter flavors. Therefore, when a fly encounters something sweet, it automatically lowers its proboscis and eats—or drinks if the sweet is liquid.

The taste preferences of a fly are interesting. When humans eat very sweet foods, they normally eat smaller portions than they eat of foods that are not as sweet. To the fly, the sweeter the food, the more it will consume. The fly's taste preference can be measured by comparing how much it drinks of sugar solutions of different concentrations. The fly has a lower preference for weak sugar solutions and drinks less of them than of very strong solutions.

The fly's preference for sweet is so great that it will choose food that tastes very sweet over food that is less sweet but nutritionally better. For instance, when given a choice between regular glucose and an exceptionally sweet sugar called fucose, which a fly cannot digest, the fly will always choose the fucose, presumably because it tastes better to the fly. In fact, given the opportunity, a fly will literally die of starvation by eating nothing but fucose, even though nutritious glucose is available only centimeters away.

FIGURE 12-11 Feeding System of the Fly. After sampling by taste buds on the fly's feet, food is taken in through the proboscis and passes through the esophagus to the gut. Stretch receptors at the entrance to the gut determine when the esophagus is full. The recurrent nerve alerts the brain to signal cessation of eating.

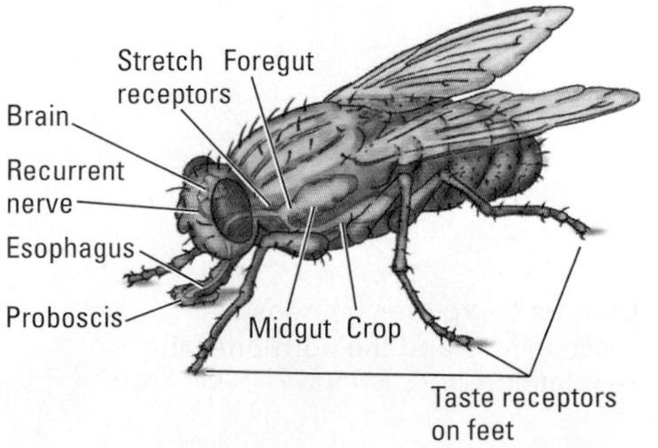

Homeostatic mechanism Process that maintains critical body functions within a narrow, fixed range.
Regulatory behavior Behavior motivated to meet the survival needs of the animal.

Why does a fly stop eating? A logical possibility is that its blood-sugar level rises to some threshold. If this were correct, injecting glucose into the circulatory system of a fly would prevent the fly from eating. But that does not happen. Blood-glucose level has no effect on a fly's feeding. Furthermore, injecting food into the animal's stomach or intestine has no effect either. So what is left? The upper part of the digestive tract.

It turns out that flies have a nerve (the recurrent nerve) that extends from the neck to the brain and carries information about whether any food is present in the esophagus. If the recurrent nerve is cut, the fly is chronically "hungry" and never stops eating. Such flies become so full and fat that their feet no longer reach the ground, and they become so heavy that they cannot fly.

Even though a fly appears to act with a purpose in mind, a series of very simple mechanisms actually control its behavior—mechanisms not remotely related to our concept of thought. A fly walks because it is tasting, it eats because its esophagus is devoid of food, and it stops when its esophagus has some food in it. When the nerve connecting the esophagus to the brain is cut, a fly keeps on eating even though the food is flattening its internal organs against the sides of its body.

Hunger is simply the activity of the nerve, not some drive. Clearly, we should not assume simply from appearances that a behavior carries intent. Behavior can have very subtle causes that do not include conscious purpose. How do we know that any behavior is purposeful? That question turns out to be difficult to answer.

REVIEW: Biology, Evolution, and Environment

- ✔ Behavior can have multiple causes that can vary from one behavior to another, and it may occur without intent.
- ✔ Behavior results from the interaction of evolution and environment with neurobiological events. Learned behaviors can be selected and influenced by an individual's unique experiences as well.
- ✔ The brain of a species is prewired to produce IRMs to specific sensory stimuli selected by evolution to prompt associations between certain environmental events.
- ✔ Human taste and smell receptors react chemically with olfactory and gustatory sensations. Their diverse pathways into the brain eventually merge in the orbitofrontal cortex, leading to the perception of flavor, the blending of smells and tastes in food.
- ✔ On the evolutionary end and outside conscious awareness, pheromones, chemosignals that convey information about the sender, can influence the physiology of the reciever.

Neuroanatomy of Motivated Behavior

The neural circuits that control behavior encompass regions at all levels of the brain, but the critical neural structures in emotional and motivated behavior are the hypothalamus and associated pituitary gland, the limbic system, and the frontal lobes. In this section, we investigate the anatomical and functional organization of these major, functionally interrelated structures.

Although the hypothalamus plays a central role in controlling motivated behavior, it takes its instructions from the limbic system and the frontal lobes. The limbic and frontal regions project to the hypothalamus, which houses many basic neural circuits for controlling behavior and for autonomic processes that maintain critical body functions within a narrow, fixed range—that is, **homeostatic mechanisms.** In

Chapter 8 explores homeostatic mechanisms and the hormones that regulate them.

Figure 12-12, the hypothalamus is represented by the neck of a funnel, and the limbic system and the frontal lobes form the funnel's rim. To produce behavior, the hypothalamus sends axons to other brainstem circuits.

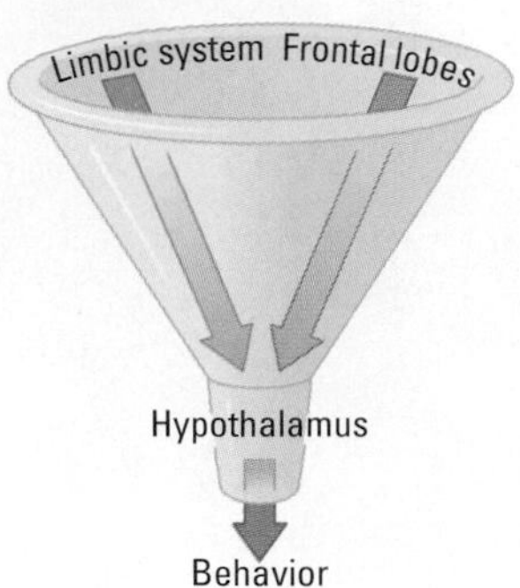

FIGURE 12-12 Funneling Signals. In this model, inputs from the frontal lobes and limbic system are funneled through the hypothalamus, which sends its axons to control brainstem circuits that produce motivated behaviors.

Regulatory and Nonregulatory Behavior

We seek mates, food, or sensory stimulation because of brain activity, but it is convenient to talk about such behavior as being "motivated." Like drives, however, motivated behaviors are not something that we can point to in the brain. Rather, motivations are inferences that we make about why someone, ourselves included, engages in a particular behavior. The two general classes of motivated behaviors are regulatory and nonregulatory. In this section we explore both categories before exploring the neuroanatomy of motivation.

Regulatory Behaviors

Regulatory behaviors, those motivated by an organism's survival, are controlled by homeostatic mechanisms. By analogy, consider a house where the thermostat is set at 18 degrees Celsius, like the one in **Figure 12-13.** When the temperature falls below a certain tolerable range (say, to 16 degrees Celsius), the thermostat turns the furnace on. When the temperature rises above a certain tolerable level (say, 20 degrees Celsius), the thermostat turns on the air conditioner.

Some Regulatory Behaviors

Some Regulatory Behaviors
Internal body temperature
Eating and drinking
Salt consumption
Waste elimination

Human body temperature is controlled in a somewhat similar manner by a "thermostat" in the hypothalamus that holds internal temperature at about 37 degrees Celsius, a temperature referred to as *setpoint.* Even slight variations cause us to engage in various behaviors to regain the setpoint. For example, when body temperature drops slightly, neural circuits that increase temperature are turned on. These neural circuits might induce an involuntary response such as shivering or a seemingly voluntary behavior such as moving closer to a heat source. Conversely, if body temperature rises slightly, we sweat or move to a cooler place.

Similar mechanisms control many other homeostatic processes, including the amount of water in the body, the balance of dietary nutrients, and the level of blood sugar. The control of many of these homeostatic systems is quite complex, requiring both neural and hormonal mechanisms. However, in some way, all the body's homeostatic systems include the activity of the hypothalamus.

Imagine that specific cells are especially sensitive to temperature. When they are cool, they become very active; when they are warm, they become less active. These cells could function as a thermostat, telling the body when it is too cool or too warm. A

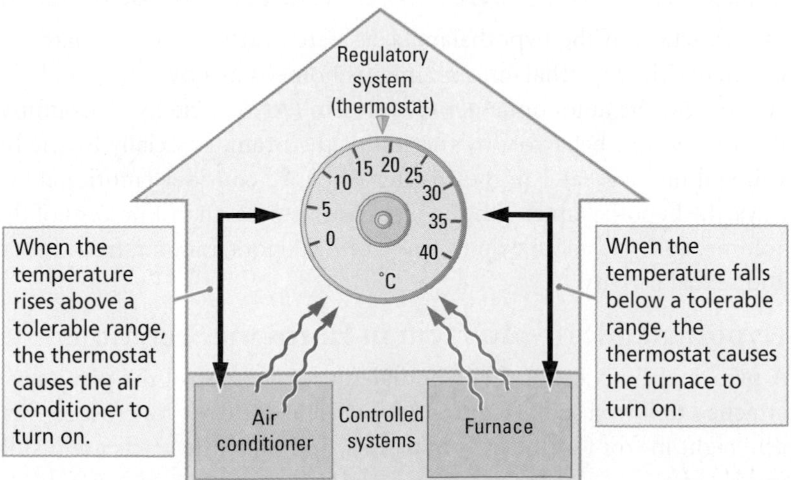

FIGURE 12-13 Regulatory Mechanism. A thermostat controls temperature inside a house. An analogous mechanism could control temperature in the body.

similar set of cells could serve as a "glucostat," controlling the level of sugar in the blood, or as a "waterstat," controlling the amount of H_2O in the body. In fact, the body's real homeostatic mechanisms are slightly more complex than this imagined one, but they work on the same general principle.

Mechanisms to hold conditions such as temperature constant have evolved because the body, including the brain, is a chemical "soup" in which thousands of reactions are taking place all the time. Maintaining constant temperature becomes critical. When temperature changes, even by such a small amount as 2 degrees Celsius, the rates at which chemical reactions take place change.

Such changes might be tolerable, within certain limits, if all the reaction times changed to the same extent. But they do not do so. Consequently, an increase of 2 degrees might increase one reaction by 10 percent and another by only 2 percent. Such uneven changes would wreak havoc with finely tuned body processes such as metabolism and the workings of neurons.

A similar logic applies to maintaining homeostasis in other body systems. For instance, cells require certain concentrations of water, salt, and glucose to function properly. If the concentrations were to fluctuate wildly, they would cause a gross disturbance of metabolic balance and a subsequent biological disaster.

Nonregulatory Behaviors

In contrast with regulatory behaviors, such as eating or drinking, **nonregulatory behaviors** are neither required to meet the basic survival needs of an animal nor controlled by homeostatic mechanisms. Thus, nonregulatory behaviors include everything else that we do—from sexual intercourse to parenting to such curiosity-driven activities as conducting psychology experiments. Some nonregulatory behaviors, such as sexual intercourse, entail the hypothalamus, but most of them probably do not. Rather, such behaviors entail a variety of forebrain structures, especially the frontal lobes. Presumably, as the forebrain evolved and enlarged, so did our range of nonregulatory behaviors.

Some Nonregulatory Behaviors

Sex	Food preference
Parenting	Curiosity
Aggression	Reading

Most nonregulatory behaviors are strongly influenced by external stimuli. As a result, sensory systems must play some role in controlling them. For example, the sexual behavior of most male mammals is strongly influenced by the pheromone emitted by receptive females. If the olfactory system is not functioning properly, we can expect abnormalities in sexual behavior. We will return to the topic of sexual behavior later in this chapter when we investigate it as an example of how a nonregulatory behavior is controlled. But first we explore the brain structures that take part in motivated behaviors—both nonregulatory and regulatory.

The Regulatory Function of the Hypothalamic Circuit

One function of the hypothalamus, as stated earlier, is to regulate our internal environment. The hypothalamus maintains homeostasis by acting on both the endocrine system and the autonomic nervous system (ANS). The hypothalamus also influences the selection of behaviors by the rest of the brain, especially by the limbic system, as you will discover later in the chapter when we consider emotional behavior. In these ways, the hypothalamus, although it constitutes less than 1 percent of the human brain's volume, controls an amazing variety of behaviors, ranging from heart rate to feeding and sexual activity.

Hypothalamic Involvement in Hormone Secretions

A principal function of the hypothalamus is to control the **pituitary gland,** which is attached to it by a stalk (**Figure 12-14A**). The optic nerves cross to form the optic chiasm right in front of the hypothalamus, and the optic tracts are just lateral to it (Figure 12-14B).

Nonregulatory behavior Behavior unnecessay to the basic survival needs of the animal.
Pituitary gland Endocrine gland attached to the bottom of the hypothalamus; its secretions control the activities of many other endocrine glands; known to be associated with biological rhythms.
Medial forebrain bundle (MFB) Tract that connects structures in the brainstem with various parts of the limbic system; forms the activating projections that run from the brainstem to the basal ganglia and frontal cortex.

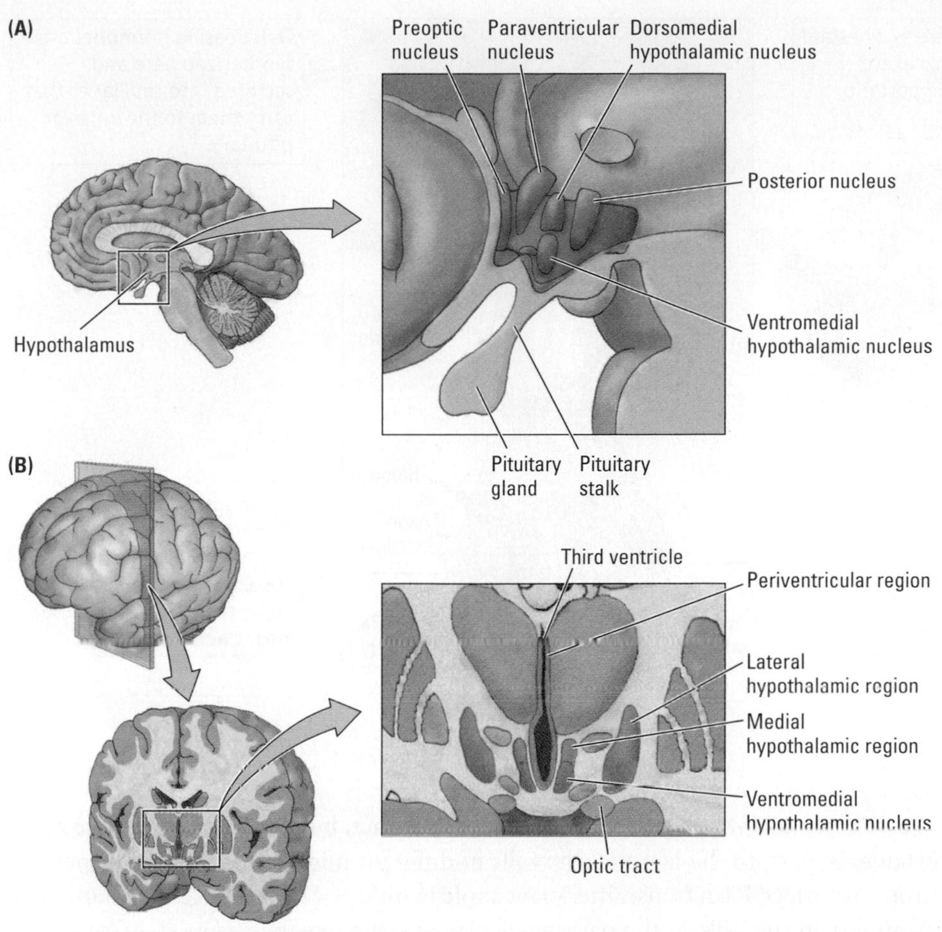

FIGURE 12-14 The Nuclei and Regions of the Hypothalamus. (A) Medial view shows the relation between the hypothalamic nuclei and the rest of the brain. (B) In the frontal section, the relation between the hypothalamus and the third ventricle can be seen. The three principal hypothalamic regions are the periventricular, the lateral, and the medial.

The hypothalamus can be divided into three regions: lateral, medial, and periventricular, illustrated in frontal view in Figure 12-14B. The lateral hypothalamus is composed both of nuclei and of nerve tracts running up and down the brain, connecting the lower brainstem to the forebrain. The principal tract, shown in **Figure 12-15,** is the **medial forebrain bundle** (MFB).

The MFB, which connects structures in the brainstem with various parts of the limbic system, forms the activating projections that run from the brainstem to the basal ganglia and frontal cortex. Fibers that ascend from the dopamine- and noradrenaline-containing cells of the lower brainstem form a significant part of the MFB. The dopamine-containing fibers of the MFB contribute to the control of many motivated behaviors, including eating and sex.

Chapter 8 elaborates on dopamine's importance in rewarding experiences related to drug use.

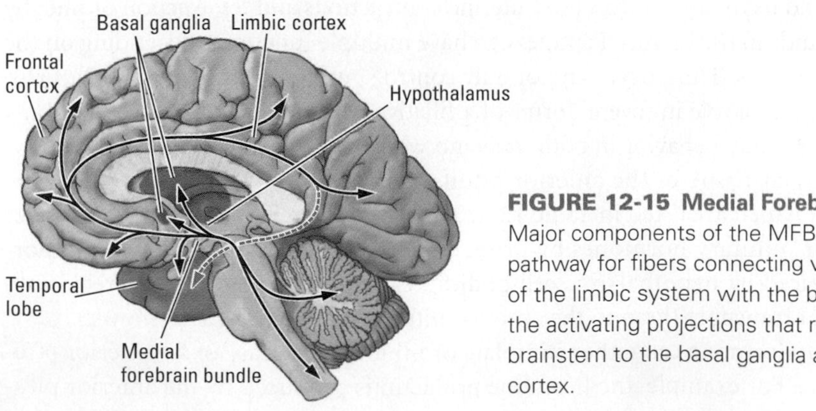

FIGURE 12-15 Medial Forebrain Bundle. Major components of the MFB, a major pathway for fibers connecting various parts of the limbic system with the brainstem, are the activating projections that run from the brainstem to the basal ganglia and frontal cortex.

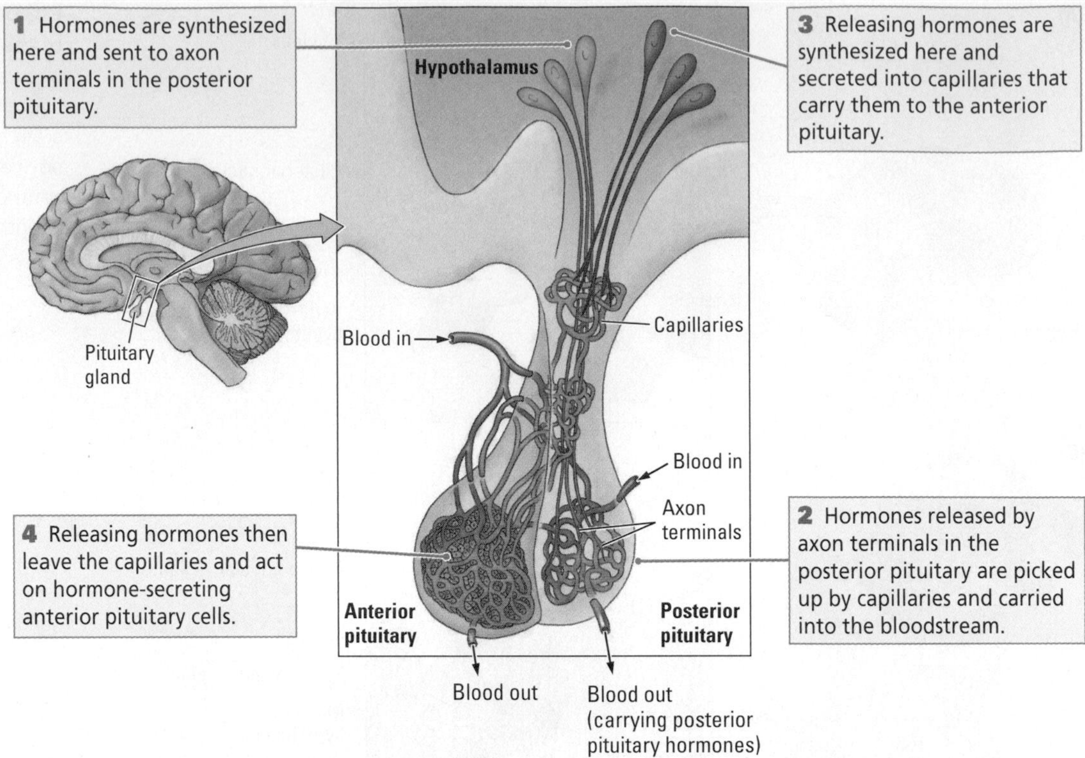
1 Hormones are synthesized here and sent to axon terminals in the posterior pituitary.
Hypothalamus
3 Releasing hormones are synthesized here and secreted into capillaries that carry them to the anterior pituitary.
Pituitary gland
Blood in
Capillaries
Blood in
Axon terminals
2 Hormones released by axon terminals in the posterior pituitary are picked up by capillaries and carried into the bloodstream.
4 Releasing hormones then leave the capillaries and act on hormone-secreting anterior pituitary cells.
Anterior pituitary
Posterior pituitary
Blood out
Blood out (carrying posterior pituitary hormones)

FIGURE 12-16 Hypothalamus and Pituitary Gland. The pituitary has two divisions: anterior and posterior. The anterior pituitary is connected to the hypothalamus by a system of blood vessels that carry hormones from the hypothalamus to the pituitary. The posterior pituitary receives input from axons of hypothalamic neurons. Both regions respond to hypothalamic input by producing hormones that travel in the bloodstream to stimulate target organs.

Each hypothalamic nucleus is anatomically distinct, but most have multiple functions due, in part, to the fact that the cells in different nuclei contain various peptide neurotransmitters. Each transmitter plays a role in different behaviors. For instance, the transmitters in the cells in the paraventricular nucleus may be vasopressin, oxytocin, or various combinations of other peptides (such as enkephalin and neurotensin).

Review the structure and functions peptide neurotransmitters in Chapter 5.

The production of various neuropeptides hints at the special relation between the hypothalamus and the pituitary. The pituitary consists of distinct anterior and posterior glands, as shown in **Figure 12-16.** The posterior pituitary is composed of neural tissue and is essentially a continuation of the hypothalamus.

Neurons in the hypothalamus make peptides (e.g., oxytocin and vasopressin) that are transported down their axons to terminals lying in the posterior pituitary. If these neurons become active, they send action potentials to the terminals, causing them to release the peptides stored there. But rather than affecting another neuron, as occurs at most synapses, these peptides are picked up by capillaries (tiny blood vessels) in the posterior pituitary's rich vascular bed.

The peptides then enter the body's bloodstream. The blood carries them to distant targets, where they have their effects. For example, vasopressin affects water resorption by the kidneys, and oxytocin controls both uterine contractions and the ejection of milk by mammary glands in the breasts. Peptides can have multiple functions, depending on the location of receptors. Thus, oxytocin not only controls milk ejection in females but also plays a more general role in several forms of affiliative behavior, including parental care, grooming, and sexual behavior in both men and women (Insel and Fernald, 2004).

The glandular tissue of the anterior pituitary synthesizes various hormones, the major ones of which are listed in **Table 12-1.** The hypothalamus controls the release of these anterior pituitary hormones by producing chemicals known as **releasing hormones.** Produced by hypothalamic cell bodies, releasing hormones are secreted into capillaries that transport them to the anterior pituitary, as Figure 12-16 shows.

Releasing hormones Peptides that are released by the hypothalamus and act to increase or decrease the release of hormones from the anterior pituitary.

A releasing hormone can either stimulate or inhibit the release of an anterior pituitary hormone. For example, the hormone prolactin is produced by the anterior pitu-

TABLE 12-1 Major Hormones Produced by the Anterior Pituitary

Hormone	Function
Adrenocorticotrophic hormone (ACTH)	Controls secretions of the adrenal cortex
Thyroid-stimulating hormone (TSH)	Controls secretions of the thyroid gland
Follicle-stimulating hormone (FSH)	Controls secretions of the gonads
Luteinizing hormone (LH)	Controls secretions of the gonads
Prolactin	Controls secretions of the mammary glands
Growth hormone (GH)	Promotes growth throughout the body

itary, but its release is controlled by a prolactin-releasing factor and a prolactin release–inhibiting factor, both synthesized in the hypothalamus. The release of hormones by the anterior pituitary in turn provides a means by which the brain can control what is taking place in many other parts of the body. Three factors control hypothalamic hormone-related activity: feedback loops, neural regulation, and responses based on experience.

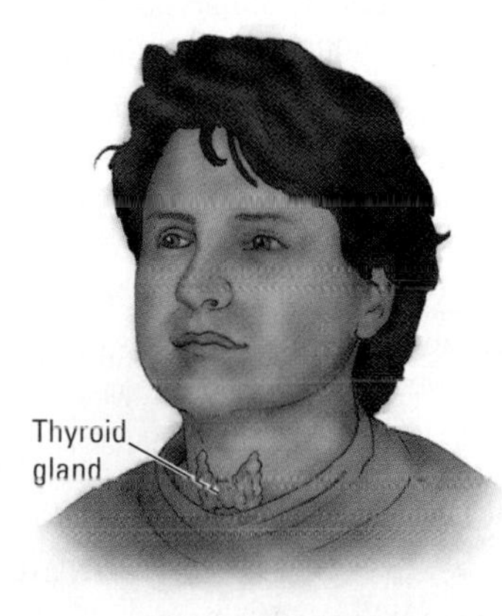

Feedback Loops When the level of, say, thyroid hormone is low, the hypothalamus releases thyroid-stimulating hormone–releasing hormone (TSH–releasing hormone) that stimulates the anterior pituitary to release TSH. TSH then acts on the thyroid gland to secrete more thyroid hormone.

There must, however, be some control over how much hormone is secreted, and the hypothalamus has receptors to detect the level of thyroid hormone. When that level rises, the hypothalamus lessens its secretion of TSH–releasing hormone. This type of system is essentially a form of homeostatic control that works as a feedback mechanism, a system in which a neural or hormonal loop regulates the activity of neurons, initiating the neural activity or hormone release, as illustrated in **Figure 12-17A**.

The hypothalamus initiates a cascade of events that result in the secretion of hormones, but it pays attention to how much hormone is released. When a certain level is reached, it stops its hormone-stimulating signals. Thus, the feedback mechanism in the hypothalamus maintains a fairly constant circulating level of certain hormones.

Neural Control A second control over hormone-related activities of the hypothalamus requires regulation by other brain structures, such as the limbic system and the frontal lobes. Figure 12-17B diagrams this type of control in relation to the effects of oxytocin released from the paraventricular nucleus of the hypothalamus. As stated earlier, one

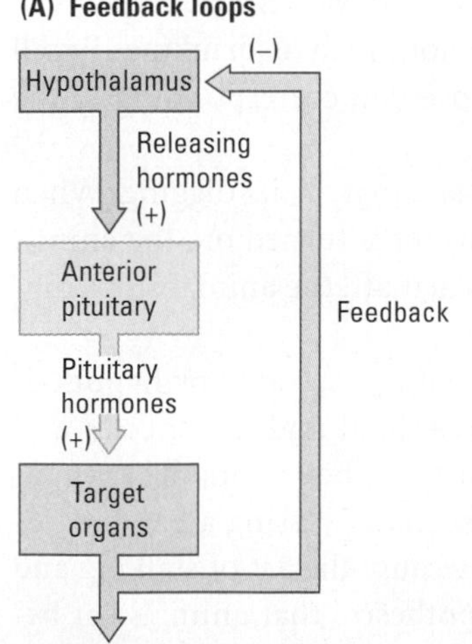

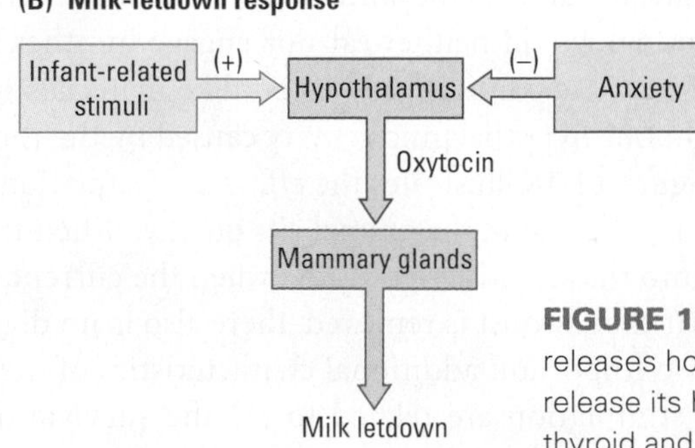

FIGURE 12-17 Hypothalamic Controls. (A) The hypothalamus releases hormones, which stimulate the anterior pituitary to release its hormones, which stimulate target organs such as the thyroid and adrenal gland to release their hormones. Those hormones act, in turn, to influence the hypothalamus to decrease its secretion of the releasing hormone. (B) Oxytocin stimulates the mammary glands to release milk. Oxytocin release from the hypothalamus is enhanced by infant-related stimuli and inhibited by maternal anxiety.

Hippocampus Distinctive, three-layered subcortical structure of the limbic system lying in the medial region of the temporal lobe; plays a role in species-specific behaviors, memory, and spatial navigation and is vulnerable to the effects of stress.

function of oxytocin is to stimulate cells of the mammary glands to release milk. As an infant suckles the breast, the tactile stimulation causes hypothalamic cells to release oxytocin, which stimulates milk letdown. In this way, the oxytocin cells participate in a fairly simple reflex that is both neural and hormonal.

Other stimuli also can influence the release of oxytocin, however, which is where control by other brain structures comes in. For example, the sight, sound, or even thought of her baby can trigger a lactating mother to eject milk. Conversely, as diagrammed in Figure 12-17B, feelings of anxiety in a lactating woman can inhibit milk ejection. These excitatory and inhibitory influences exerted by cognitive activity imply that the cortex can influence neurons in the paraventricular region. It is likely that projections from the frontal lobes to the hypothalamus perform this role.

Experiential Responses A third way in which the hormone-related activities of the hypothalamus are controlled is by the brain's responses to experience. In response to experience, neurons in the hypothalamus undergo structural and biochemical changes just as cells in other brain regions do. In other words, hypothalamic neurons are like neurons elsewhere in the brain in that they can be changed by prolonged demands placed on them.

Recall the principle of neuroplasticity from Chapter 2: the details of nervous system functioning are constantly changing.

Such changes in hypothalamic neurons can affect the output of hormones. For instance, when a woman is lactating, the cells producing oxytocin increase in size to promote oxytocin release to meet the increasing demands of a growing infant for more milk. Through this control, which is mediated by experience, the baby is provided with sufficient milk over time.

Hypothalamic Involvement in Generating Behavior

So far, we have considered the role of the hypothalamus in controlling hormone systems, but equally important is its role in generating behavior. This function was first demonstrated by studies in which stimulating electrodes were placed in the hypothalami of various animals, ranging from chickens to rats and cats. When a small electric current was delivered through a wire electrode, an animal suddenly engaged in some complex behavior. The behaviors included eating and drinking, digging, and displaying fear, attack, predatory, or reproductive behavior. The particular behavior depended on which of many sites in the hypothalamus was stimulated. All the behaviors were smooth, well integrated, and indistinguishable from normally occurring ones. Furthermore, all were goal directed.

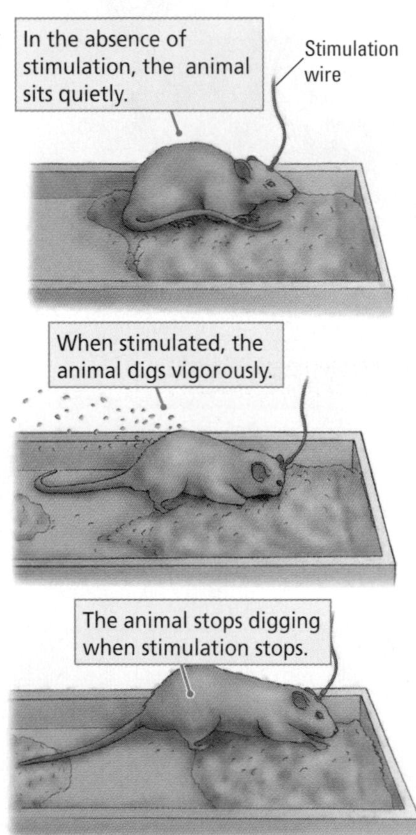
In the absence of stimulation, the animal sits quietly.
Stimulation wire
When stimulated, the animal digs vigorously.
The animal stops digging when stimulation stops.

FIGURE 12-18 Generating Behavior. When rats receive electrical stimulation to the hypothalamus, they produce goal-directed behaviors. This rat is stimulated to dig when and only when the electricity is turned on. Note also that, if the sawdust is removed (not shown in the bottom drawing), there is no digging.

The onset and termination of the behaviors depended entirely on the hypothalamic stimulation. For example, if an electrode in a certain location elicited feeding behavior, the animal would eat as soon as the stimulation was turned on and would continue to eat until the stimulation was turned off. If the food was removed, however, the animal would neither eat nor engage in other behaviors such as drinking. Recall that Roger ate continuously if foodlike materials were present, corresponding to the continuous hypothalamic activity caused by the tumor.

Figure 12-18 illustrates the effect of stimulation at a site that elicits digging. When there is no current, the animal sits quietly. When the current is turned on, the animal digs into the sawdust vigorously; when the current is turned off, the animal stops digging. If the sawdust is removed, there also is no digging.

Two important additional characteristics of the behaviors generated by hypothalamic stimulation are related to (1) the survival of the animal and the species and (2) reward. Animals apparently find the stimulation of these behaviors pleasant, as suggested by the fact that they willingly expend effort, such as pressing a bar, to trigger the stimulation. Recall that cats kill birds and mice because the act of stalking and killing prey is rewarding to them. Similarly, we can hypothesize that animals eat because eating is rewarding, drink because drinking is rewarding, and mate because mating is rewarding.

The Organizing Function of the Limbic Circuit

We now turn our attention to parts of the brain that interact with the hypothalamus in generating motivated behaviors. These brain structures evolved as a ring around the brainstem in early amphibians and reptiles. Nearly 150 years ago, Paul Broca was impressed by this evolutionary development and called these structures the "limbic lobe."

The primitive limbic cortex, introduced in Chapter 2, derives its name from the Latin word *limbus,* meaning "border" or "hem."

Known collectively as the *limbic system* today, these structures are actually a primitive cortex. In mammals, the limbic cortex encompasses the cingulate gyrus and the hippocampal formation, as shown in **Figure 12-19.** The hippocampal formation includes the **hippocampus,** a cortical structure that plays a role in species-specific behaviors, memory, and spatial navigation and is vulnerable to the effects of stress, and the *parahippocampal cortex* adjacent to it.

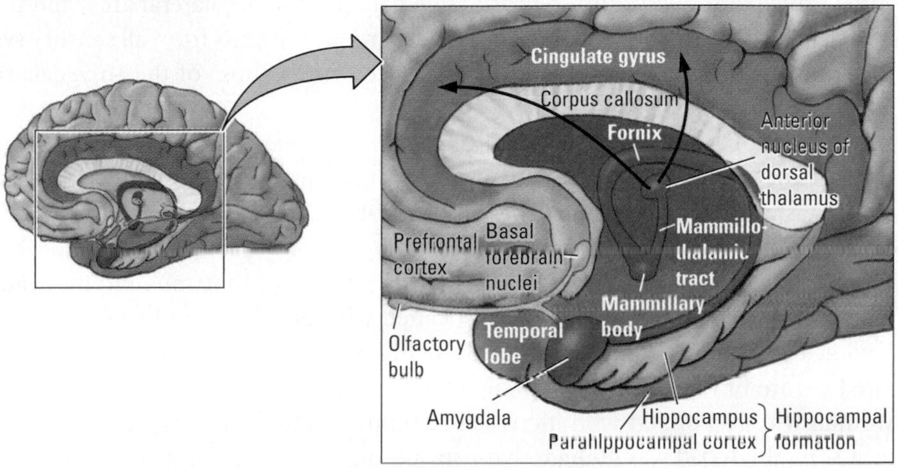

FIGURE 12-19 Limbic Lobe. Encircling the brainstem, the limbic lobe as described by Broca consists of the cingulate gyrus and hippocampal formation (the hippocampus and parahippocampal cortex), the amygdala, the mammillothalamic tract, and the anterior thalamus.

Organization of the Limbic Circuit

As anatomists began to study the limbic-lobe structures, connections to the hypothalamus became evident. It also became apparent that the limbic lobe has a role in emotion. For instance, in the 1930s, James Papez observed that people with rabies display radically abnormal emotional behavior, and postmortems showed that the rabies had selectively attacked the hippocampus.

The definitive proof of rabies is still a postmortem examination of the hippocampus.

Papez concluded from his observations that the limbic lobe and associated subcortical structures provide the neural basis of emotion. He proposed a circuit, traced in **Figure 12-20A**, now known as the *Papez circuit,* whereby emotion could reach consciousness, which was presumed to reside in the cerebral cortex. Papez's limbic-circuit concept was expanded by Paul MacLean in 1949 to include the amygdala and prefrontal cortex as well. Figures 12-19 and 12-20A show the amygdala lying adjacent to the hippocampus in the temporal lobe, with the prefrontal cortex lying just anterior.

Figure 12-20B charts the limbic circuit schematically. The hippocampus, amygdala, and prefrontal cortex all connect with the hypothalamus. The mammillary nucleus of the hypothalamus connects to the anterior thalamus, which in turn connects with the cingulate cortex, which then completes the circuit by connecting with the hippocampal formation, amygdala, and prefrontal cortex. This anatomical arrangement can be compared to the funnel in Figure 12-20C, which shows the hypothalamus as the spout leading to motivated behavior.

There is now little doubt that most structures of the limbic system, especially the amygdala and hypothalamus, take part in emotional behaviors, as detailed later in the chapter. But most limbic structures are now known to play an important role in various motivated behaviors as well, especially in motivating species-typical behaviors such as feeding and sexual activity. The critical structures for such motivated behaviors, as well as for emotion, are the amygdala and the hypothalamus. Having already considered the hypothalamus, we now turn to the amygdala.

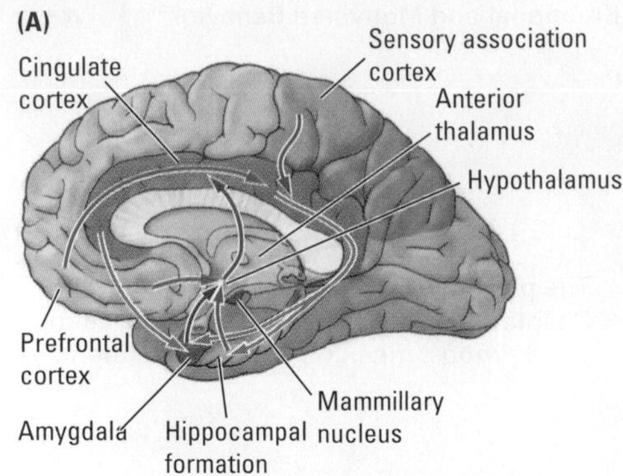

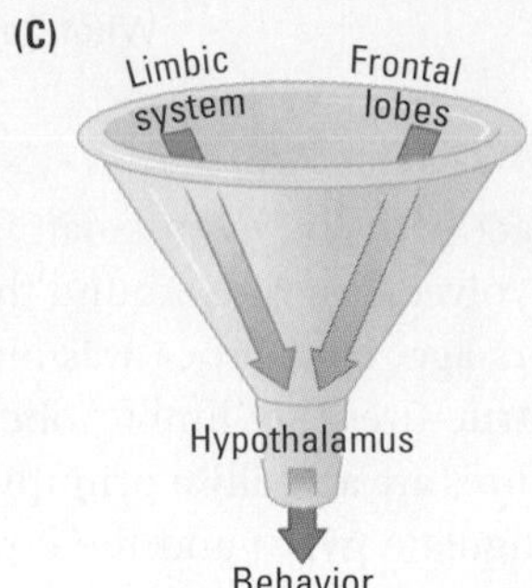

FIGURE 12-20 Limbic System. (A) In this contemporary conception of the limbic system, an interconnected network of structures, the Papez circuit, controls emotional expression. (B) A schematic representation, coded to brain areas shown in part A by color, charting the major connections of the limbic system. (C) A reminder that parts A and B can be conceptualized as a funnel of outputs through the hypothalamus.

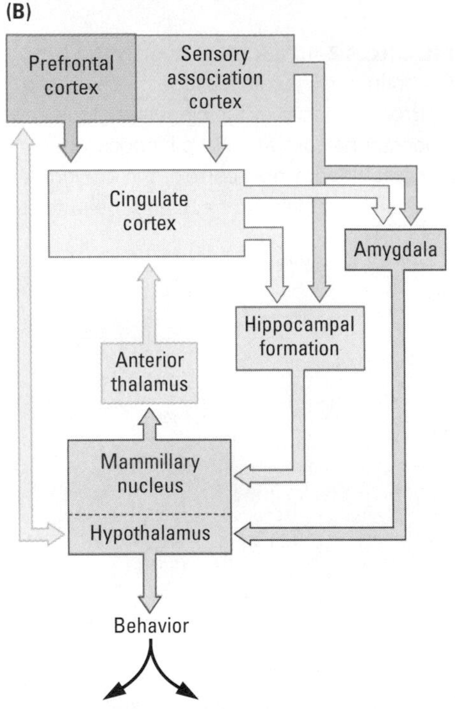

The Amygdala

Named for the Greek word for "almond" because of its shape, the **amygdala** consists of three principal subdivisions: the corticomedial area, the basolateral area, and the central area. Like the hypothalamus, the amygdala receives inputs from all sensory systems. But, in contrast with the neurons of the hypothalamus, those of the amygdala require more complex stimuli to be excited.

In addition, many amygdala neurons are *multimodal:* they respond to more than one sensory modality. In fact, some neurons in the amygdala respond to sight, sound, touch, taste, and smell stimuli. These cells must create a rather complex image of the sensory world.

The amygdala sends connections primarily to the hypothalamus and the brainstem, where it influences neural activity associated with emotions and species-typical behavior. For example, when the amygdalae of epileptic patients are electrically stimulated before brain surgery, the patients become fearful and anxious. We observed a woman who responded with increased respiration and heart rate, saying that she felt as if something bad was going to happen, although she could not specify what.

Amygdala stimulation can also induce eating and drinking. We observed a man who drank water every time the stimulation was turned on. (There happened to be a pitcher of water on the table next to him.) Within 20 minutes, he had consumed about 2 liters of water. When asked if he was thirsty, he said, "No, not really. I just feel like drinking."

The amygdala's role in eating can be seen in patients with lesions in the amygdala. These patients, like Roger as a result of his tumor, are often much less discriminating in their food choices, eating foods that were formerly unpalatable to them. Lesions of the amygdala may also give rise to hypersexuality.

The Executive Function of the Frontal Lobes

The amygdala is intimately connected with the functioning of the frontal lobes that constitute all cortical tissue in front of the central sulcus. This large area is made up of several functionally distinct cortical regions. **Figure 12-21** shows the three main regions: the motor cortex, the premotor cortex, and the prefrontal cortex.

Chapter 11 explains the interactions of these three frontal-lobe regions with regard to movement.

The motor cortex controls fine movements, especially of the fingers, hands, toes, feet, tongue, and face. The premotor cortex participates in the selection of appropriate movement sequences. For instance, a resting dog may get up in response to its owner's

Amygdala Almond-shaped collection of nuclei located within the limbic system; plays a role in emotional and species-typical behaviors.
Prefrontal cortex The cortex lying in front of the motor and premotor cortex of the frontal lobe; the prefrontal cortex is particularly large in the human brain.

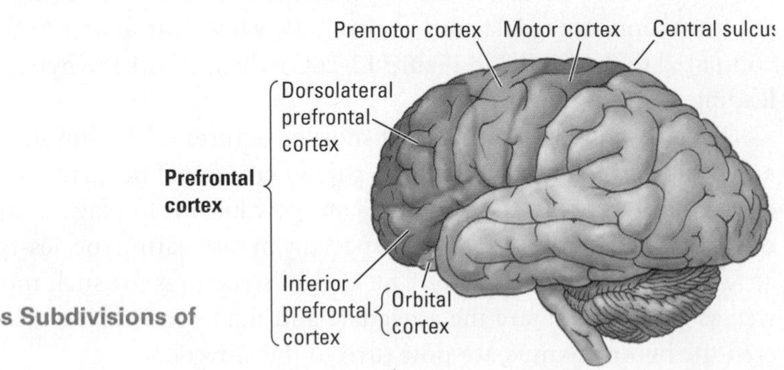

FIGURE 12-21 Gross Subdivisions of the Frontal Lobe.

call, which serves as an environmental cue for a series of movements processed by one region of the premotor cortex. Or a dog may get up for no apparent reason and wander about the yard, a sequence of actions in response to an internal cue, this time processed by a different region of the premotor cortex.

Finally, the **prefrontal cortex** is anterior to the premotor cortex. It is made up of two primary areas: the dorsolateral region and the inferior region, which includes the orbitofrontal cortex. The prefrontal cortex plays a role in specifying the goals toward which movement should be directed. It controls the processes by which we select movements that are appropriate for the particular time and place. This selection may be cued by internal information (such as memory and emotion) or it may be made in response to context (environmental information).

Prefrontal literally means "in front of the front."

Like the amygdala, the frontal lobes, particularly the prefrontal cortex, receive highly processed information from all sensory areas. Many neurons in the prefrontal cortex, like those in the amygdala, are multimodal. As shown in **Figure 12-22,** the prefrontal cortex receives connections from the amygdala, the dorsomedial thalamus, the posterior parietal (sensory association) cortex, and the dopaminergic cells of the ventral tegmental area.

The dopaminergic input plays an important role in regulating how prefrontal neurons react to stimuli, including emotional ones. Abnormalities in this dopaminergic projection may account for some disorders, including schizophrenia, in which people have little emotional reaction to normally arousing stimuli.

Chapter 16 elaborates on the causes of and treatments for schizophrenia.

Figure 12-22 also shows the areas to which the prefrontal cortex sends connections. The inferior prefrontal region projects axons to the amygdala and the hypothalamus in particular. These axons provide a route for influencing the autonomic system, which controls changes in blood pressure, respiration, and other internal processes. The dorsolateral prefrontal region sends its connections primarily to the posterior parietal cortex, the cingulate cortex, the basal ganglia, and the premotor cortex.

These connections provide a route for influencing movement, discussed in Chapter 11, as well as certain memory functions, considered in Chapter 14.

As already stated, the prefrontal cortex takes part in selecting behaviors appropriate to the particular time and place. Selection may be cued by internal information or made in response to the environmental context. Disruption to this selection function can be seen in people with injury to the dorsolateral frontal lobe. They become overly dependent on environmental cues to determine their behavior. Like small children, they can be easily distracted by what they see or hear. We have all experienced this kind of loss of concentration to some extent, but for a frontal-lobe patient, the problem is exaggerated and persistent. Because the person becomes so absorbed in irrelevant stimuli, he or she is unable to act on internalized information most of the time.

A good example is J. C., whose bilateral damage to the dorsolateral prefrontal cortex resulted from having a tumor removed. J. C. would lie in bed most of the day fixated on television programs. He was aware of his wife's opinion of this behavior, but only the opening of the garage door when she returned home from work in the evening would stimulate him into action. Getting out of bed was controlled by this specific environmental cue, and without it he seemed to lack motivation. Television completely distracted him from acting on internal knowledge of things that he could or should do.

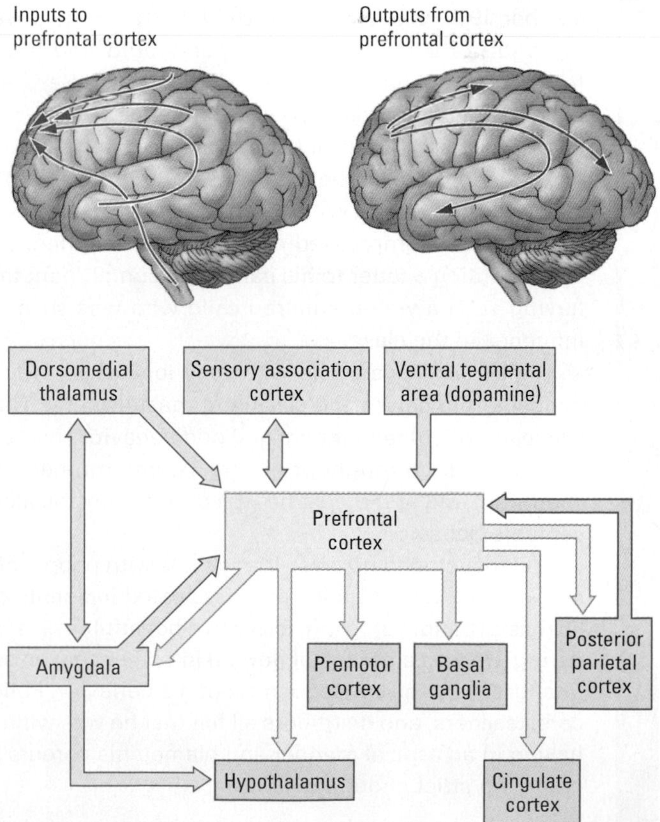

FIGURE 12-22 Prefrontal Connections. The prefrontal cortex receives inputs from all sensory systems, the amygdala, the dorsal medial thalamus, and the dopamine-rich cells of the ventral tegmentum. The prefrontal cortex sends connections to the amygdala, premotor cortex, basal ganglia, posterior parietal cortex, and hypothalamus.

Adapting behavior appropriately to the environmental context also is a function of the prefrontal cortex. Most people readily change their behavior to match the situation at hand. We behave one way with our parents, another with our friends, another with our children, and yet another with our coworkers. Each set of people creates a different context, and we shift our behaviors accordingly. Our tone of voice, our use of slang or profanity, and the content of our conversations are quite different in different contexts.

Even among our peers we act differently, depending on who is present. We may be relaxed in the presence of some people and ill at ease with others. It is therefore no accident that the size of the frontal lobes is related to the sociability of a species' behavior. Social behavior is extremely rich in contextual information, and humans are highly social.

Controlling behavior in context requires detailed sensory information, which is conveyed from all the sensory regions to the frontal lobes. This sensory input includes not only information from the external world but internal information from the ANS as well. People with damage to the inferior prefrontal cortex, which is common in traumatic brain injuries, have difficulty adapting their behavior to the context, especially the social context. Consequently, they often make social gaffes.

Clinical Focus 1-1 recounts some behavioral effects of brain trauma, Chapter 13 details recovery from TBI, and Chapter 16 explores symptoms and treatments.

In summary, the role of the frontal lobes in selecting behaviors is important in considering what causes behaviors. The frontal lobes act much like a composer but, instead of selecting notes and instruments, they select our actions. Not surprisingly, the

CLINICAL FOCUS 12-2

Agenesis of the Frontal Lobes

The role of the frontal lobes in motivated behavior is perhaps best understood by looking at J. P.'s case, described in detail by Stafford Ackerly (1964). J. P., who was born in December 1914, was a problem child. Early on, he developed the habit of wandering. Policemen would find him miles from home, as he had no fear of being lost. Severe whippings by his father did not deter him.

J. P.'s behavioral problems continued as he grew older, and by adolescence, he was constantly in trouble. Yet J. P. also had a good side. When he started school, his first-grade teacher was so impressed with his polite manners that she began writing a letter to his parents to compliment them on having such a well-mannered child who was such a good influence in the class.

As she composed the letter, she looked up to find J. P. exposing himself to the class and masturbating. This contradiction of polite manners and odd behavior characterized J. P.'s conduct throughout his life. At one moment he was charming, and at the next he was engaged in socially unacceptable behavior.

J. P. developed no close friendships with people of either sex, in large part because of his repeated incidents of public masturbation, stealing, excessive boastfulness, and wandering. He was a person of normal intelligence who seemed unaffected by the consequences of his behavior. Police officers, teachers, and neighbors all felt that he was willfully behaving in an asocial manner and blamed his parents for not enforcing strict enough discipline.

Perhaps as a result, not until he was 19 years old was J. P.'s true condition detected. To prevent him from serving a prison term for repeated automobile theft, a lawyer suggested that J. P. undergo psychiatric evaluation. He was examined by a psychiatrist, who ordered a brain scan. The image revealed that J. P. lacked a right frontal lobe. Furthermore, his left frontal lobe was about 50 percent of normal size. It is almost certain that he simply never developed frontal lobes.

The failure of a structure to develop is known as *agenesis;* J. P.'s condition was agenesis of the frontal lobes. His case offers an unusual opportunity to study the role of the frontal lobes in motivated behavior.

Clearly, J. P. lacked the "bag of mental tricks" that most people use to come to terms with the world. Normally, behavior is affected both by its past consequences and by current environmental input. J. P. did not seem much influenced by either factor. As a result, the world was simply too much for him. He always acted childlike and was unable to formulate plans for the future or to inhibit many of his behaviors. He acted on impulse. At home, he was prone to aggressive outbursts about small matters, especially with regard to his mother.

Curiously, J. P. seemed completely unaware of his life situation. Even though the rest of his brain was working fairly well—his IQ was normal and his language skills were very good—the functional parts of his brain were unable to compensate for the absence of the frontal lobes.

frontal lobes are sometimes described as housing the brain's executive functions. To grasp the full extent of frontal-lobe control of behavior, see Clinical Focus 12-2, "Agenesis of the Frontal Lobe."

Chapter 15 considers the role of the frontal lobe in the executive function of planning.

REVIEW: Neuroanatomy of Motivated Behavior

- ✔ Regulatory behavior is controlled by a homeostatic mechanism that keeps a vital aspect of body function within a narrow, fixed range. The hypothalamus provides this simplest, largely homeostatic, control.
- ✔ Nonregulatory behaviors—everything else we do—have both direction and purpose. Many nonregulatory behaviors are controlled partly by external cues. Within the brain, the hypothalamus, the limbic system, and the frontal lobes house the major behavioral circuitry involved in motivation.
- ✔ The limbic system stimulates emotional reactions and species-typical behaviors, whereas the frontal lobes generate the rationale for behavior at the right time and place, taking factors such as external events and internal information into account.

Stimulating Emotion

It is easier to identify how emotions are expressed than it is to define them. We all know what emotions are, but the concept is difficult to define because emotion, like motivation, is intangible: it is an inferred state. The expression of emotions includes physiological changes, in heart rate, blood pressure, and hormone secretions. It also includes certain motor responses, especially movements of the facial muscles that produce facial expression (see Figure 12-5).

The importance of emotion to our everyday lives is hard to underestimate. Emotion inspires artistic expression, from poetry to filmmaking to painting. Many people enjoy the arts simply because they evoke emotions. We can conclude that people find certain emotions pleasant. On the other hand, severe and prolonged negative emotions, especially anxiety and depression, can cause clinical disorders. So much of human life revolves around emotions that understanding them is central to understanding our humanness.

Explanations for Emotion

To explore the neural control of emotions, we must first specify the types of behavior we want to explain. Think of any significant emotional experience you've had recently. Perhaps you had a serious disagreement with a close friend. Maybe you just became engaged to be married.

A common characteristic of such experiences is that they include autonomic responses such as rapid breathing, sweating, and dry mouth. They may also entail strong subjective feelings that we often label as anger, fear, or love. Finally, emotions typically entail thoughts or plans related to the experience, which may take the form of replaying conversations and events in your mind, anticipating what you might say or do under similar circumstances in the future, or planning your married life.

These three forms of experience suggest the influence of different neural systems. The autonomic component must include the hypothalamus and associated structures. The feelings' components are more difficult to localize but clearly include the amygdala and probably parts of the frontal lobes. And the cognitions are likely to be cortical.

What is the relation between our cognitive experience of an emotion and the physiological changes associated with it? One view is that the physiological changes (such as trembling and rapid heartbeat) come first, and the brain then interprets these changes as an emotion of some kind. This perspective implies that the brain (most likely the cortex) creates a cognitive response to autonomic information.

Figure 2-28 summarizes the divisions of the autonomic nervous system.

That response varies with the context in which the autonomic arousal occurs. For example, if we are frightened by a movie, we experience a weaker, more short-lived emotion than if we are frightened by a real-life encounter with a gang of muggers. Variations of this perspective have gone by many names, beginning with the *James-Lange theory,* named for its originators. All assume that the brain concocts a story to explain bodily reactions.

Two lines of evidence support the James-Lange theory and similar points of view. One is that the same autonomic responses can accompany different emotions. In other words, particular emotions are not tied to their own unique autonomic changes. This line of evidence leaves room for interpreting what a particular pattern of arousal means, even though particular physiological changes may suggest only a limited range of possibilities. The physiological changes experienced during fear and happiness are unlikely to be confused with one another, for instance.

The second line of evidence supporting the view that physiological changes are the starting point for emotions comes from people with reduced information about their own autonomic arousal, owing to spinal-cord injury, for example. These people suffer a decrease in perceived emotion, the severity of which depends on how much sensory input they have lost. **Figure 12-23** illustrates this relation. It shows that people with the greatest loss of sensory input, which occurs with injuries at the uppermost end of the spinal cord, also have the greatest loss of emotional intensity. In contrast, people with low spinal injuries retain most of their visceral input and have essentially normal emotional reactions.

Christopher Reeve's spinal cord was severed at the cervical level (high), as described in Chapter 11. Although Reeve's emotions may have been blunted, his motivation clearly remained intact.

FIGURE 12-23 Losing Emotion. Spinal-cord injury reduces the experience of emotion. Loss of emotionality is greatest when the lesion is high on the spine. Adapted from *Principles of Behavioral Neuroscience* (p. 339), by J. Beatty, 1995, Dubuque, IA: Brown & Benchmark.

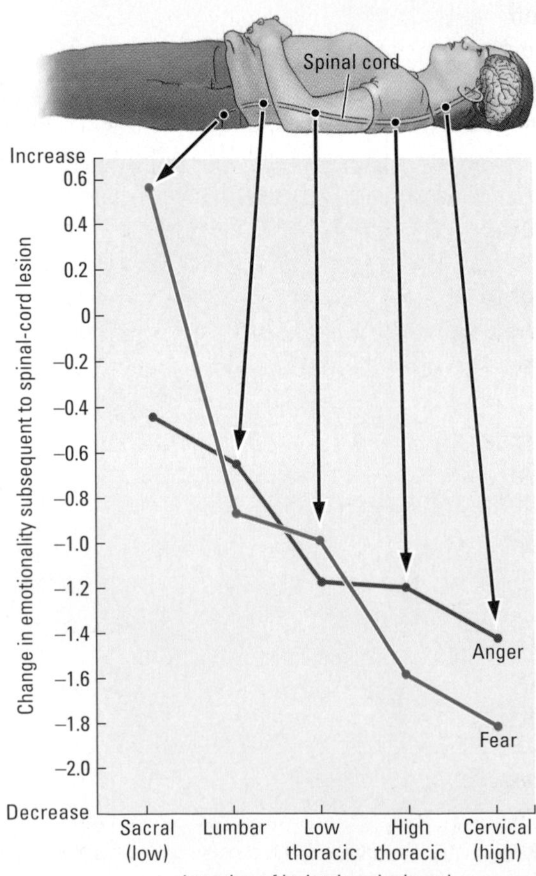

Antonio Damasio (1999) emphasized an important additional aspect of the link between emotion and cognitive factors in his **somatic marker hypothesis.** When Damasio studied patients with frontal-lobe injuries, he was struck by how they could be highly rational in analyzing the world yet still make decidedly irrational social and personal decisions. The explanation, he argued, is that the reasoning of people with frontal-lobe injury is no longer affected, either consciously or unconsciously, by the neural machinery that underlies emotion. Cut off from critical emotional input, many social and personal decisions therefore suffer.

To account for these observations, Damasio proposed that emotions are responses induced by either internal or external stimuli not normally attended to consciously. For example, if you encounter a bear as you walk down the street, presuming that you live in a place where this event could take place, the stimulus is processed rapidly without conscious appraisal. In other words, a sensory representation of the bear in the visual cortex is transmitted directly to brain structures, such as the amygdala, that initiate an emotional response.

This emotional response includes actions on structures in the forebrain and brainstem and ultimately on the autonomic nervous system. As mentioned earlier, the amygdala has connections to the frontal lobes, so the emotional response can influence the frontal lobes' appraisal of the world. However, if the frontal lobes are injured, the emotional information is excluded from cognitive processing, so the quality of emotion-related appraisals suffers. In other words, the response to the bear might be inappropriate.

To summarize, Damasio's somatic marker hypothesis proposes how emotions are normally linked to a person's thoughts, decisions, and actions. In a typical emotional state, certain regions of the brain send messages to many other brain areas and to most of the rest of the body through hormones and the ANS. These messages produce a global change in the organism's state, and the altered state influences behavior, usually in an unconscious way.

The Amygdala and Emotional Behavior

In addition to controlling certain species-typical behaviors, the amygdala influences emotion (Davis et al., 2003). Its role can be seen most clearly in monkeys whose amygdalae have been removed. In 1939, Heinrich Klüver and Paul Bucy reported an extraordinary result, now known as the **Klüver-Bucy syndrome,** that followed the removal of the amygdalae and anterior temporal cortices of monkeys. The principal symptoms include the following:

1. Tameness and loss of fear
2. Indiscriminate dietary behavior (eating many types of formerly rejected foods)
3. Greatly increased autoerotic, homosexual, and heterosexual activity with inappropriate object choice (e.g., the sexual mounting of chairs)
4. Tendency to attend to and react to every visual stimulus
5. Tendency to examine all objects by mouth
6. Visual agnosia, an inability to recognize objects or drawings of objects

Chapter 9 describes several varieties of visual form agnosia, including a range of case studies.

Visual agnosia results from damage to the ventral visual stream in the temporal lobe, but the other symptoms are related to the amygdala damage. The tameness and loss of fear after amygdalectomy is especially striking. Monkeys that normally show a strong aversion to stimuli such as snakes show no fear of them whatsoever. In fact, amygdalectomized monkeys may pick up live snakes and even put them in their mouths.

Although the Klüver-Bucy syndrome is not common in humans because bilateral temporal lobectomies are rare, symptoms of the syndrome can be seen in people with certain forms of encephalitis, a brain infection. In some cases, an encephalitis centered on the base of the brain can damage both temporal lobes and produce many Klüver-Bucy symptoms, including especially indiscriminate sexual behavior and the tendency to examine objects by mouth.

Clinical Focus 2-2 examines some causes and symptoms of encephalitis.

The role of the amygdala in Klüver-Bucy syndrome points to its central role in emotion. So does electrical stimulation of the amygdala, which produces an autonomic response (such as increased blood pressure and arousal) as well as a feeling of fear. Although this production of fear by the brain in the absence of an obvious threat may seem odd, fear is important to a species' survival. To improve their chances of surviving, most organisms using fear as a stimulus minimize their contact with dangerous animals, objects, and places and maximize their contact with things that are safe.

Exploiting fear has proved an especially effective technique for controlling group behavior throughout human history.

The awareness of danger and safety has both an innate and a learned component, as Joe LeDoux (1996) emphasized. The innate component, much as in the IRMs, is the automatic processing of species-relevant sensory information—specifically, sensory inputs from the visual, auditory, and olfactory systems. The importance of olfactory inputs is not obvious to humans, whose senses are dominated by vision. But there is a major input of olfactory information directly into the amygdala (you can see this connection in the human brain in Figure 12-19). For other animals, olfactory cues often predominate.

Thus, a rat that has never encountered a ferret shows an immediate fear response to the odor of ferret. Other novel odors (such as peppermint or coffee) do not produce an innate fear reaction. The innate response triggers an autonomic activation that stimulates conscious awareness of danger.

In contrast, the learned component of fear consists of the avoidance of specific animals, places, and objects that the organism has come to associate with danger. The organism is not born with this avoidance behavior prewired. In a similar way, animals learn to increase contact with environmental stimuli that they associate with positive outcomes, such as food or sexual activity or, in the laboratory, drugs. Damage to the

Somatic marker hypothesis Posits that "marker" signals arising from emotions and feelings act to guide behavior and decision making, usually in an unconscious process.
Klüver-Bucy syndrome Behavioral syndrome, characterized especially by hypersexuality, that results from bilateral injury to the temporal lobe.

amygdala interferes with all these behaviors. The animal loses not only its innate fears but also its acquired fears and preferences for certain environmental stimuli.

To summarize, the amygdala is required for species survival. It influences autonomic and hormonal responses through its connections to the hypothalamus. It influences our conscious awareness of the positive and negative consequences of events and objects through its connections to the prefrontal cortex.

The Prefrontal Cortex and Emotional Behavior

At about the same time that Klüver and Bucy began studying their monkeys, Carlyle Jacobsen was studying the effects of frontal lobotomy on the cognitive capacities of two chimpanzees. A frontal lobotomy destroys a substantial amount of brain tissue as the result of inserting a sharp instrument into the frontal lobes and moving it back and forth.

In 1935, Jacobsen reported that one of the chimps that had been particularly neurotic before being subjected to this procedure became more relaxed after it. Incredibly, a leading Portuguese neurologist of the time, Egas Moniz, seized on this observation as a treatment for behavioral disorders in humans, and the frontal lobotomy, illustrated in **Figure 12-24,** was initiated as the first technique of **psychosurgery,** that is, neurosurgery intended to alter behavior.

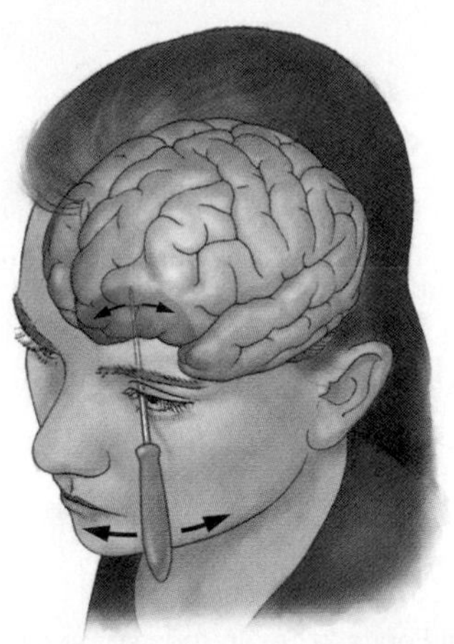

FIGURE 12-24 Transorbital Leukotomy. In this procedure, a leukotome is inserted through the bone of the eye socket and the inferior frontal cortex is disconnected from the rest of the brain.

The use of psychosurgery grew rapidly in the 1950s. In North America alone, nearly 40,000 people received frontal lobotomies as a treatment for psychiatric disorders. Not until the 1960s was any systematic research conducted into the effects of frontal lesions on social and emotional behavior. By this time, the frontal lobotomy had virtually vanished as a "treatment." There is now little doubt that prefrontal lesions in various species, including humans, have severe effects on social and emotional behavior.

Agnes is a case in point. We met Agnes at the psychiatric hospital where we met Roger, whose indiscriminate eating was described at the beginning of this chapter. At the time, Agnes, a 57-year-old woman, was visiting one of the nurses. Agnes had, however, once been a patient.

Agnes had been subjected to a procedure known as a *frontal leukotomy* because her husband, an oil tycoon, felt that she was too gregarious. Evidently, he felt that her "loose lips" were a detriment to his business dealings. He convinced two psychiatrists that she would benefit from psychosurgery, and her life was changed forever.

To perform a leukotomy, as illustrated in Figure 12-24, a surgeon uses a special knife called a leukotome to sever the connections of a region of the inferior frontal cortex, including especially the orbital cortex (see Figure 12-21). The first thing we noticed about Agnes was that she exhibited no outward sign of emotion. She had virtually no facial expression.

In our conversations with her, however, we quickly discovered that she had considerable insight into the changes brought about by the leukotomy. In particular, she indicated that she no longer had any feelings about things or most people, although, curiously, she was attached to her dog. She said that she often just felt empty and much like a zombie.

Agnes's only moment of real happiness in the 30 years since her operation was the sudden death of her husband, whom she blamed for ruining her life. Unfortunately, Agnes had squandered her dead husband's considerable wealth as a consequence of her inability to plan or organize. This inability, we have seen, is another symptom of prefrontal injury.

The orbital region of the inferior prefrontal area has direct connections with the amygdala and hypothalamus. Its stimulation can produce autonomic responses, and, as we saw in Agnes, damage to the orbital region can produce severe personality change characterized by apathy and loss of initiative or drive. The orbital cortex is probably responsible for the conscious awareness of emotional states that are produced by the rest of the limbic system, especially the amygdala.

Psychosurgery Any neurosurgical technique intended to alter behavior.

Agnes's loss of facial expression is also fairly typical of frontal-lobe damage. In fact, people with frontal-lobe injuries and people who suffer from schizophrenia or autism are usually impaired at both producing and perceiving facial expressions, including a wide range of expressions found in all human cultures—happiness, sadness, fear, anger, disgust, and surprise. As with J. P.'s frontal-lobe agenesis, described in Clinical Focus 12-2, it is difficult to imagine how such people can function effectively in our highly social world without being able to emote or to recognize the emotions of others.

Although facial expression is a key part of recognizing emotion, so is tone of voice, or *prosody*. Frontal-lobe patients are devoid of prosody, both in their own conversations and in understanding the prosody of others. The lost ability to comprehend or produce emotional expression in both faces and language partly explains the apathy of frontal-lobe patients. In some ways, they are similar to spinal-cord patients who have lost autonomic feedback and so can no longer feel the arousal associated with emotion. Frontal-lobe patients can no longer either read emotion in other people's faces and voices or experience it in their own.

Some psychologists have proposed that our own facial expressions may provide us with important clues to the emotions that we are feeling. This idea has been demonstrated in experiments reviewed by Pamela Adelmann and Robert Zajonc (1989). In one such study, people were required to contract their facial muscles by following instructions about which parts of the face to move. Unbeknown to the participants, the movements produced happy and angry expressions. Afterward, they viewed a series of slides and reported how the slides made them feel.

They said that they felt happier when they were inadvertently making a happy face and angrier when the face they were making was one of anger. Frontal-lobe patients presumably would have no such feedback from their own facial expressions, which could be a reason that their emotional experiences are dampened.

Emotional Disorders

A highly disruptive emotional disorder is major depression, characterized by prolonged feelings of worthlessness and guilt, the disruption of normal eating habits, sleep disturbances, a general slowing of behavior, and frequent thoughts of suicide. A depressed person feels severely despondent for a prolonged time. Depression is common in our modern world, with a prevalence of at least 10 percent of the population.

Consult Chapter 8 for detailed information on major depression and its treatment. We consider the neurobiology of depression in Chapter 16.

Depression has a genetic component. It not only runs in families but also frequently tends to be found in both members of a pair of identical twins. The genetic component in depression implies a biological abnormality, but the cause remains unknown.

The strongest evidence supporting a biological cause of depression comes from the fact that about 70 percent of depressed people can be treated with one of several antidepressant drugs. This success rate has made antidepressants among the most widely prescribed classes of drugs in the world. As summarized in **Table 12-2**, antidepressants act on synapses (especially noradrenaline- and serotonin-containing synapses) by increasing

Of all psychological disorders, major depression is one of the most treatable, and cognitive and intrapersonal therapies are as effective as drug therapies.

TABLE 12-2 Antidepressant Medications

Drug type	Action	Examples
Tricyclics	Block reuptake of serotonin and noradrenaline	Imipramine
MAO inhibitors	Block activity of monoamine oxidase	Iproniazid
Selective serotonin reuptake inhibitors (SSRIs)	Block reuptake of serotonin	Fluoxetine (Prozac) Sertraline (Zoloft) Paroxetine (Paxil)

CLINICAL FOCUS 12-3

Anxiety Disorders

Animals normally become anxious at times, especially when they are in obvious danger. But anxiety disorders are different. They are characterized by intense feelings of fear or anxiety that are inappropriate for the circumstances.

People with anxiety disorders have persistent and unrealistic worries about impending misfortune. They also tend to suffer multiple physical symptoms attributable to hyperactivity of the sympathetic nervous system.

G. B.'s case is a good example. He was a 36-year-old man with two college degrees who began to experience severe spells initially diagnosed as some type of heart condition. He would begin to breathe heavily, sweat, experience heart palpitations, and sometimes suffer pains in his chest and arms. During these attacks, he was unable to communicate coherently and would lie helplessly on the floor until an ambulance arrived to take him to an emergency room.

Extensive medical testing and multiple attacks in a period of about 2 years eventually led to the diagnosis of **generalized anxiety disorder.** Like most of the 5 percent of the U.S. population who suffer an anxiety disorder at some point in their lives, G. B. was unaware that he was overly anxious.

The cause of generalized anxiety is difficult to determine, but one likely explanation is related to the cumulative effect of general stress. Although G. B. appeared outwardly calm most of the time, he had been a prodemocracy activist in communist Poland, a dangerous position to adopt.

Because of the dangers, he and his family eventually had to escape from Poland to Turkey, and from there they went to Canada. G. B. may have had continuing worries about the repercussions of his political activities—worries (and stress) that eventually found expression in generalized anxiety attacks.

The most common and least disabling type of anxiety disorders are **phobias.** A phobia pertains to a clearly defined dreaded object (such as spiders or snakes) or some greatly feared situation (such as enclosed spaces or crowds). Most people have mild aversions to some types of stimuli. This kind of aversion becomes a phobia only when a person's feelings toward a disliked stimulus lead to overwhelming fear and anxiety.

The incidence of disabling phobias is surprisingly high: phobias are estimated to affect at least one in ten people. For most people with a phobia, the emotional reaction can be controlled by avoiding what they dread. Others face their fears in controlled settings, with the goal of overcoming them.

Michael Newman/Photo Edit

Up to 90 percent of people with animal phobias overcome their fears in a single exposure therapy session that lasts 2 or 3 hours.

Panic disorder has an estimated incidence on the order of 3 percent of the population. The symptoms of panic disorder include recurrent attacks of intense terror that come on without warning and without any apparent relation to external circumstances. Panic attacks usually last only a few minutes, but the experience is always terrifying. Sudden activation of the sympathetic nervous system, leads to sweating, a wildly beating heart, and trembling.

Although panic attacks may occur only occasionally, the victim's dread of another episode may be continual. Consequently, many people with panic disorders also experience *agoraphobia,* a fear of public places or situations in which help might not be available. This phobia makes some sense because a person with a panic disorder may feel particularly vulnerable to having an attack in a public place.

Freud believed that anxiety disorders are psychological in origin and treatable with talking therapies in which people confront their fears. Today, cognitive-behavioral therapies are used for this purpose, as shown in the accompanying photo, but anxiety disorders are known to have a clear biological link.

Pharmacologically, these disorders are most effectively treated with benzodiazepines, of which diazepam (Valium) is the best known. Alprazolam (Xanax) is the most commonly prescribed drug for panic attacks. Benzodiazepines act by augmenting GABA's inhibitory effect and are believed to exert a major influence on neurons in the amygdala.

Whether treatments are behavioral, pharmacological, or both, the general goal is to normalize brain activity in the limbic system.

the amount of available transmitter at them. The major projections of noradrenaline- and serotonin-containing cells to the limbic system imply that the activity of limbic regions, including the prefrontal cortex, is abnormal in depression.

Excessive anxiety is an even more common emotional problem than depression. Anxiety disorders, including posttraumatic stress disorder (PTSD), phobias, and obsessive-compulsive disorder (OCD), are estimated to affect from 15 to 35 percent of the population. Symptoms include persistent fears and worries in the absence of any direct threat, usually accompanied by various physiological stress reactions, such as rapid heartbeat, nausea, and breathing difficulty, as described in Clinical Focus 12-3, "Anxiety Disorders."

Generalized anxiety disorder Persistently high levels of anxiety often accompanied by maladaptive behaviors to reduce anxiety; the disorder is thought to be caused by chronic stress.
Phobia Fear of a clearly defined object or situation.
Panic disorder Recurrent attacks of intense terror that come on without warning and without any apparent relation to external circumstances.

As with depression, the root cause of anxiety disorders is not known, but the effectiveness of drug treatments implies a biological basis. The most widely prescribed anxiolytic (antianxiety) drugs are the benzodiazepines, such as Valium, Librium, and Xanax. These drugs are thought to be effective because of their agonistic action on the $GABA_A$ receptor. Although $GABA_A$ receptors are found throughout the brain, the amygdala has an especially high concentration. The infusion of benzodiazepines into the amygdala blocks fear, suggesting that the amygdala may be the site of their action.

Drug agonists enhance the function of a synapse; antagonists block function. Chapter 8 explains the actions of antianxiety agents, and Figure 8-7 illustrates their action at the $GABA_A$ receptor.

Why would the brain have a mechanism for benzodiazepine action? It certainly did not evolve to allow us to take Valium. Probably this mechanism is part of a system that both increases and reduces anxiety levels. The mechanism for raising anxiety seems to entail a compound known as diazepam-binding inhibitor. This compound appears to bind antagonistically with the $GABA_A$ receptor, resulting in greater anxiety.

There are times when such an increase in anxiety is beneficial, especially if we are drowsy and need to be alert to deal with some kind of crisis. Impairment of this mechanism or the one that reduces anxiety can cause serious emotional problems, even anxiety disorders.

Chapter 16 further explores causes for anxiety disorders and reviews treatments.

REVIEW: Stimulating Emotion

- ✔ Emotion and motivation have common autonomic responses (sweating and rapid heartbeat), subjective feelings (fear or trust, joy or pain), and a cognitive component—what we think about the arousing situation.
- ✔ The autonomic responses result from the activity of the hypothalamus and related structures. Psychologists have proposed that when the body experiences an autonomic reaction and intense feelings, the brain creates a story to explain the experiences.
- ✔ The amygdala and orbitofrontal-cortex circuits contribute to our feelings and our motives. It is likely that both our emotional thoughts and thinking that motivates us result from activity throughout the cerebral hemispheres.
- ✔ Abnormalities in the neural circuits that produce emotional and motivated behavior are responsible for society's most pervasive behavioral disorders—the anxiety disorders and depression.

Control of Regulatory Behavior

There is more to feeding behavior than sustenance alone. We must eat and drink to live, but we also derive great pleasure from eating and drinking. For many people, eating is a focus of daily life, if not for survival, for its centrality to social activities, from get-togethers with family and friends to business meetings and even to identification

Obesity Excessive accumulation of body fat.

Anorexia nervosa Exaggerated concern with being overweight that leads to inadequate food intake and often excessive exercising; can lead to severe weight loss and even starvation.

with a group. Are you a gourmet, a vegetarian, or a snack-food junkie? Do you diet? In this section, we focus mainly on the control of eating in humans, but we also consider how homeostatic mechanisms control our fluid intake.

Controlling Eating

Control over eating is a source of frustration and even grief for many people in the developed world. In 2000, the World Health Organization identified **obesity,** the excessive accumulation of body fat, as a worldwide epidemic. The United States is a case in point. From 1990 to 2010, the percentage of overweight people increased from about 50 percent to 65 percent of the population. The proportion of people considered obese increased from about 12 percent to 25 percent.

The increasing numbers of overweight and obese children and adults persist despite a substantial decrease in fat intake in American diets. What behaviors might cause persistent weight gain? One key to understanding weight gain in the developed world is evolutionary. Even 40 years ago, much of our food was only seasonally available. In a world with uncertain food availability, it makes sense to store excess body calories in the form of fat to be used later when food is scarce. Down through history and in many cultures today, plumpness was and is desirable as a standard of beauty and a sign of health and wealth.

In the postindustrial society of most of the world today, where food is continuously and easily available, being overweight may not be the healthiest strategy. People eat as though food will be scarce and fail to burn off the extra calories by exercising, and the result is apparent. About half of the U.S. population has dieted at some point in their lives. At any given time, at least 25 percent report that they are currently on a diet. For a comparison of how some well-known dieting programs perform, see Clinical Focus 12-4, "Weight-Loss Strategies."

Eating disorders entail being either underweight or overweight. Most Americans are overweight but live in a culture obsessed with slimness. The human control system for feeding has multiple neurobiological inputs, including cognitive factors such as thoughts about food. These cognitive factors also include the association between environmental cues (e.g., watching television or studying) and the act of eating. The constant pairing of such cues with eating can result in the cues alone becoming a motivation, or incentive, to eat. We return to this phenomenon in the discussion of rewards and addictions at the end of the chapter.

Anorexia nervosa is a disorder with a huge cognitive component—namely, self-image. Anorexia is especially identified with adolescent girls. A person's body image is highly distorted in anorexia. This misperception leads to an exaggerated concern with being overweight spiraling to excessive dieting, compulsive exercising, and severe, potentially life-threatening weight loss.

The neurobiological control of feeding behavior in humans is not as simple as it is in the fly described earlier in the chapter. The multiple inputs to the human control system for feeding come from three major sources: the cognitive factors already introduced, the hypothalamus, and the digestive system.

FIGURE 12-25 The Digestive System.

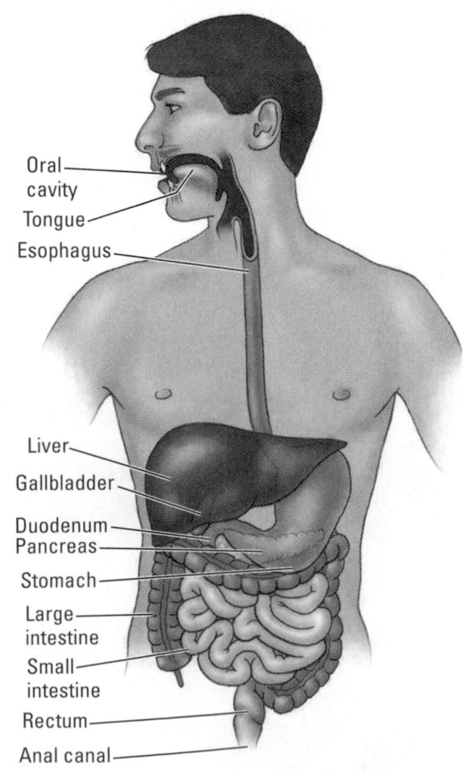

The Digestive System and Control of Eating

The digestive tract, illustrated in **Figure 12-25,** begins in the mouth and ends at the anus. Food travels from the oral cavity to the stomach through the esophagus. The stomach is a storage reservoir that secretes hydrochloric acid, to break food into smaller particles, and pepsin, an enzyme that breaks proteins down into amino acids.

The partly broken down food then moves to the upper part of the small intestine through the duodenum, where digestive enzymes produced in the gall bladder and pancreas further break the food down to allow the absorption of amino acids, fats, and

CLINICAL FOCUS 12-4

Weight-Loss Strategies

Among the wide range of diets and weight-loss strategies on the market, none has stopped the obesity epidemic. Diets range widely in their recommended proportions and the types of fats, carbohydrates, and proteins allowed. In the past few years, low-carbohydrate diets have become popular—Atkins, Zone, and South Beach are among them.

Proponents of these plans claim significant weight loss and good health, without hunger. What scientific evidence supports the claims made by these diets? Are they fads or do they really work? The difficulty in reaching scientific conclusions about a diet's effectiveness is that studies need to compare random samples of individuals on different diets over a period of at least 1 year. Few such studies have been designed.

The conclusion of a review by Arne Astrup and colleagues (2004) is that weight loss is associated with the restriction of energy intake and the duration of the diet but *not* with carbohydrate restriction. In one study, 63 participants followed either of two diets in which the proportions of nutrients are essentially reversed (Foster et al., 2003).

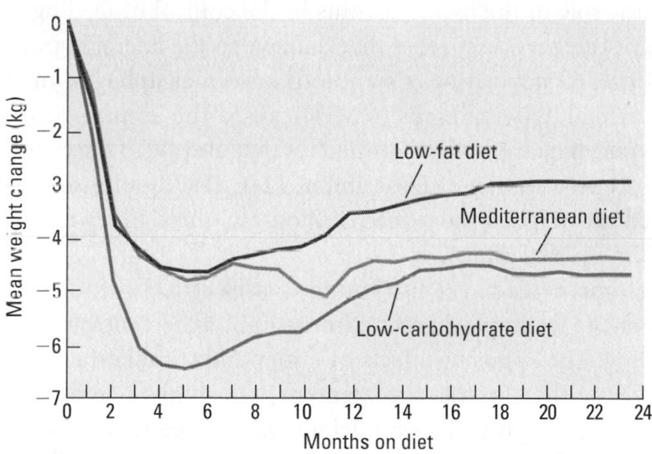

Benefits of Dieting. Changes in body weight over a 2-year period on three different diets. Low-carbohydrate and Mediterranean diets were equivalent after 1 year, and both led to more weight loss than did the low-fat diet. Adapted from "Weight Loss with a Low-Carbohydrate, Mediterranean, or Low-Fat Diet," by I. Shai, D. Schwarzfuchs, Y. Henkin, et al., 2008, *New England Journal of Medicine, 13,* 229–241.

In the low-carbohydrate–high-protein Atkins plan, the percentage of carbohydrates allowed ranges from 5 percent in the induction phase to a maximum of 19 percent in the maintenance phases. Protein is at least 36 percent and fat as much as 59 percent of the menu, depending on the phase. In an energy-restricted diet high in carbohydrates and low in protein, the allowable proportions are 60 percent carbohydrate and only 15 percent protein and 25 percent fat.

After 6 months, Foster and colleagues found that the low-carbohydrate group on Atkins had lost a larger percentage of body weight on average (7 percent versus 3 percent). But after 1 year, the difference was no longer statistically significant (4.4 percent versus 2.5 percent).

Thus, the low-carbohydrate diet was superior in the short run but not in the long run, a finding supported two other studies reviewed by Astrup's group. Two problems with all studies are that dropout rates tend to be high and ensuring compliance with the diets is difficult.

A more recent study by Iris Shai and her colleagues (2008) compared a low-fat diet, a low-carbohydrate diet, and the Mediterranean diet—one high in fruits, vegetables, legumes, and whole grains and including fish, nuts, and low-fat dairy products (Panagiotakos et al., 2004). This study lasted two years and had relatively low dropout rates (95.4 percent remained on their diets at 1 year and 84.6 percent at 2 years).

The accompanying figure shows that all three diets led to weight loss and, as in the Foster study, the low-carbohydrate diet produced the largest acute loss in weight. Over the 2-year period subjects gained back some weight, and in the second year the low-carbohydrate and Mediterranean dieters had similar weight loss. The low-carbohydrate diet had more favorable effects on lipid levels whereas the Mediterranean diet provided better control of glucose and insulin levels.

Shai and her colleagues concluded that health-care professionals might suggest more than one dietary approach based on individual preferences and metabolic needs, as long as the effort is sustained. At present, the only certain solution to weight loss appears to be a permanent switch to a diet reduced in *calories* and fat combined with increased physical activity.

simple sugars into the bloodstream. Most of the remaining water and electrolytes in food are absorbed by the large intestine, and the waste passes out of the body through the anus.

The digestive system extracts three types of nutrients for the body: lipids (fats), amino acids (the building blocks of proteins), and glucose (sugar). Each is a specialized energy reserve. Because we require varying amounts of these reserves depending on what we are doing, the body has detector cells to keep track of the level of each nutrient in the bloodstream.

Glucose is the body's primary fuel and is virtually the only energy source for the brain. Because the brain requires glucose even when the digestive tract is empty, the liver acts as a short-term reservoir of glycogen, a starch that acts as an inert form of glucose. When blood-sugar levels fall, as when we are sleeping, detector cells tell the liver to release glucose by converting glycogen into glucose.

Thus the digestive system functions mainly to break down food, and the body needs to be apprised of how well this breakdown is proceeding. Feedback mechanisms provide such information. When food reaches the intestines, it interacts with receptors there to trigger the release of at least 10 different peptide hormones, including one known as cholecystokinin (CCK).

The released peptides inform the brain (and perhaps other organs in the digestive system) about the nature and quality of the food in the gastrointestinal tract. The level of CCK appears to play a role in satiety, the feeling of having eaten enough. For example, if CCK is infused into the hypothalamus of an animal, the animal's appetite diminishes.

The Hypothalamus and Control of Eating

Review the general categories of hormones and how they work in Chapter 8.

Feeding behavior is influenced by hormones including insulin, growth hormone, and sex steroids. These hormones stimulate and inhibit feeding, and they aid in converting nutrients into fat and fat into glucose. Not surprisingly, the hypothalamus, which controls hormone systems, is the key brain structure in feeding.

Aphagia is derived from the Greek *a*, signifying "absent," and *phagein*, "to eat."

Investigation into the role of the hypothalamus in the control of feeding began in the early 1950s, when researchers discovered that damage to the lateral hypothalamus in rats caused the animals to stop eating, a symptom known as **aphagia.** In contrast, damage to the ventromedial hypothalamus (VMH) caused the animals to overeat, a symptom known as **hyperphagia.** A VMH-lesioned rat that overate to the point of obesity is shown in the Procedure section of **Experiment 12-1.** The Results section reveals that the VMH-lesioned rat weighed more than a kilogram, three times the weight of her normal sister, which was 340 grams.

At about the same time, researchers also found that electrical stimulation of the lateral hypothalamus elicits feeding, whereas stimulation of the ventromedial hypothalamus inhibits feeding. The opposing effects of injury and stimulation to these two hypothalamic regions led to the idea that the lateral hypothalamus signals "eating on," whereas the VMH signals "eating off." This model quickly proved to be too simple.

Not only does the lateral hypothalamus contain cell bodies, but also fiber bundles pass through it, and damage to either structure can produce aphagia. Similarly, damage to fibers passing through the VMH often causes injury as well to the paraventricular nucleus of the hypothalamus. And damage to the paraventricular nucleus alone is now known to produce hyperphagia. Clearly, then, there is more to the role of the hypothalamus in the control of feeding than the activities of the lateral and ventromedial hypothalamus alone.

In the half-century since the first studies on the role of the hypothalamus in feeding, researchers have learned that damage to the lateral and ventromedial hypothalamus and to the paraventricular nucleus has multiple effects. These effects include changes in hormone levels (especially insulin), in sensory reactivity (the taste and attractiveness of food is altered), in glucose and lipid levels in the blood, and in metabolic rate. The general role of the hypothalamus is to act as a sensor for the levels of lipids, glucose, hormones, and various peptides. For example, groups of hypothalamic neurons sense the level of glucose (glucostatic neurons) as well as the level of lipids (lipostatic neurons).

Aphagia Failure to eat; may be due to an unwillingness to eat or to motor difficulties, especially with swallowing.
Hyperphagia Disorder in which an animal overeats, leading to significant weight gain.

The sum of the activity of all such hypothalamic neurons creates a very complex homeostat that controls feeding. **Figure 12-26** shows that this homeostat receives inputs from three sources: the digestive system (such as information about blood-glucose levels), hormone systems (such as information about the level of CCK), and parts of the brain that process cognitive factors. We turn to these cognitive factors next.

Cognitive Factors and Control of Eating

Pleasure and its absence are cognitive factors in the control of eating. Just thinking about a favorite food is often enough to make us feel hungry. The cognitive aspect to feeding includes not only the images of food that we pull from memory but also external sensations, especially food-related sights and smells. In addition, learned associations, such as learned taste aversions discussed earlier, are related to feeding.

Neural control of the cognitive factors important for controlling eating in humans probably originates in multiple brain regions. Two structures are clearly important: the amygdala and the inferior prefrontal cortex. Damage to the amygdala alters food preferences and abolishes taste aversion learning. These effects are probably related to the amygdala's efferent connections to the hypothalamus.

The amygdala's role in regulating species-typical behaviors is well established, but the role of the inferior prefrontal cortex is more difficult to pin down. Rats and monkeys with damage to the orbital cortex lose weight, in part because they eat less. Humans with orbital injuries are invariably slim, but we know of no formal studies on their eating habits. The inferior prefrontal cortex receives projections from the olfactory bulb, and cells in this region do respond to smells. Because odors influence the taste of foods, it is likely that damage to the inferior prefrontal cortex decreases eating because of diminished sensory responses to food odor and perhaps to taste.

An additional cognitive factor in the control of eating is the pleasure we derive from it, especially from eating foods with certain tastes, such as chocolate. What pleasure is and how the brain produces it are topics discussed at the end of this chapter in the context of reward.

Randy Seeley and Stephen Woods (2003) have noted that, in spite of the problem people now appear to have with weight gain, adult mammals do a masterful job of matching their caloric intake to caloric expenditure. Consider that a typical man eats 900,000 calories per year. To gain just one extra pound requires him to eat 4000 calories more than are burned in that year. This increase amounts to only 11 calories per day, equivalent to a single potato chip.

According to Seeley and Woods, the average weight gain in the U.S population is less than 1 pound per year. This weight gain corresponds to an error in homeostasis of less than 0.5 percent, which is a rather small error. Seeley and Woods conjectured that the nervous sytem must juggle two competing challenges in weight control. The first is to maintain adequate stores of fuel and the second is to provide fuel for current cellular functions. They noted that the current obesity "epidemic" could be the result of factors that alter the sensing of stored fuel, the sensing of ongoing

EXPERIMENT 12-1

Question: Does the hypothalamus play a role in eating?

Procedure

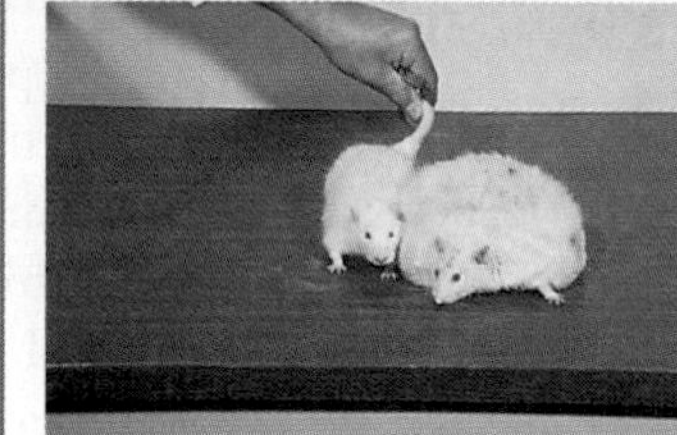

The ventromedial hypothalamus (VMH) of the rat on the right was damaged, and her body weight was monitored for a year. Her sister on the left is normal.

Intact brain of sister rat

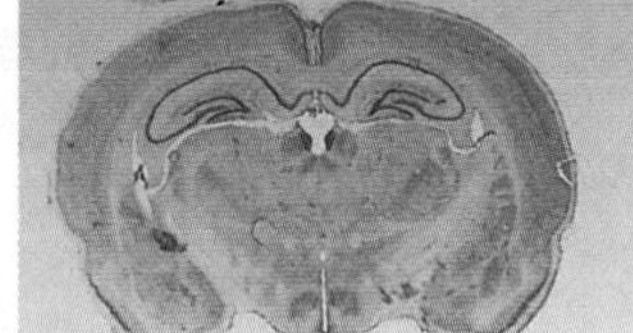

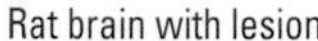

Rat brain with lesion

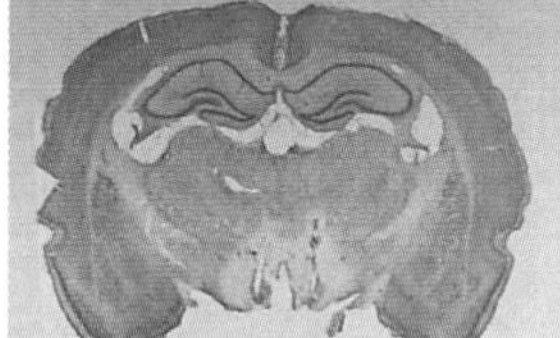

Results

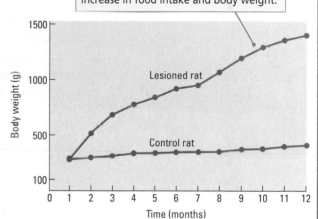

The VMH-lesioned rat showed a dramatic increase in food intake and body weight.

Body weight (g): 100, 500, 1000, 1500

Time (months): 0, 1, 2, 3, 4, 5, 6, 7, 8, 9, 10, 11, 12

Lesioned rat

Control rat

Conclusion: The VMH plays a role in controlling the cessation of eating. Damage to the VMH results in prolonged and dramatic weight gain.

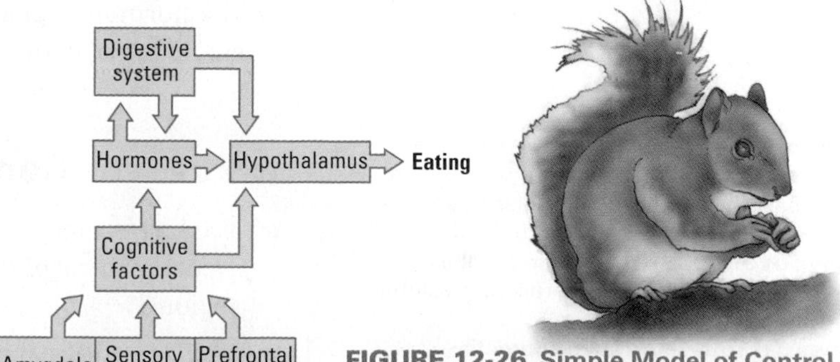

FIGURE 12-26 Simple Model of Control of Feeding Behavior.

fuel availability, or the integration of these two types of signal. Treatment strategies for obesity will require an understanding of what these factors are and how they operate.

Controlling Drinking

About 70 percent of the human body is composed of water that contains a range of chemicals that participate in the hundreds of chemical reactions involved in bodily functions. Homeostatic mechanisms control water levels (and hence chemical concentrations) within rather narrow limits. These mechanisms are essential because the rate of a chemical reaction is partly determined by how concentrated the supplies of participating chemicals are.

As with eating, we drink for many reasons. We consume some beverages, such as coffee, wine, beer, and juice, for an energy boost or to relax, as part of social activities, or just because they taste good. We drink water for its health benefits, to help wash down a meal or to intensify the flavor of dry foods. On a hot day, we drink water because we are thirsty, presumably because we have lost significant moisture through sweating and evaporation.

There are actually two kinds of thirst. **Osmotic thirst** results from an increase in the concentrations of dissolved chemicals, known as *solutes,* in the body fluids. **Hypovolemic thirst** results from a loss of overall fluid volume from the body.

Osmotic Thirst

The solutes found inside and outside cells in the body are ideally concentrated for the body's chemical reactions. Maintaining this concentration requires a kind of homeostat, much like the internal thermostat that controls body temperature. Deviations from the ideal solute concentration activate systems to reestablish the concentration.

When we eat salty foods, such as potato chips, the salt (NaCl) spreads through the blood and enters the extracellular fluid that fills the spaces between our cells. This shifts the solute concentration away from the ideal. Receptors in the hypothalamus along the third ventricle detect the altered solute concentration and relay the message "It's too salty" to various hypothalamic areas that, in turn, stimulate us to drink in response to osmotic thirst. Other messages are sent to the kidneys to reduce water excretion.

Hypovolemic Thirst

Unlike osmotic thirst, hypovolemic thirst arises when the total volume of body fluids declines, motivating us to drink more and replenish them. In contrast with osmotic thirst, however, hypovolemic thirst encourages us to choose something other than water, because water would dilute the solute concentration in the blood. Rather, we prefer to drink flavored beverages that contain salts and other nutrients.

Hypovolemic thirst and its satiation are controlled by a different hypothalamic circuit from the one that controls osmotic thirst. When fluid volume drops, the kidneys send a hormone signal (angiotensin) that stimulates midline hypothalamic neurons. These neurons, in turn, stimulate drinking.

Osmotic thirst Thirst that results from an increased concentration of dissolved chemicals, or *solutes,* in body fluids.
Hypovolumic thirst Thirst that is produced by a loss of overall fluid volume from the body.
Sexual dimorphism Differential development of brain areas in the two sexes.

REVIEW: Control of Regulatory Behavior

- ✔ Feeding is a regulatory behavior that has a large cognitive component in humans. Neural control of the cognitive factors in eating probably includes multiple brain regions.
- ✔ In the hypothalamus, the principal brain structure in control of eating, groups of neurons act as sensors to detect the levels of glucose, lipids, and peptides in the

blood. Three regions—the lateral hypothalamus, the ventromedial hypothalamus, and the paraventricular nucleus—play especially important roles.

✔ The brain also motivates us to drink whenever solutes in the blood deviate from ideal levels or whenever the body's volume of fluids drops significantly. Receptors detect these shifts, and neurons in the hypothalamus stimulate thirst.

Control of Nonregulatory Behavior

Individuals must feed repeatedly to survive, but sexual behavior is not essential for an individual organism's survival. Notwithstanding procreation, which is essential to the survival of the species, sexual activity is of enormous psychological importance to humans. Sexual themes repeatedly appear in our art, literature, and films. They also bombard us via advertising and other sales pitches. In Sigmund Freud's psychodynamic theory, sexual drives are central to human behavior. Such significance makes it all the more important to understand how human sexual behavior is controlled. The answer lies in both gonadal hormones and brain circuits.

Effects of Sex Hormones on the Brain

During the fetal stage of prenatal development, a male's Y chromosome controls the differentiation of embryonic gonad tissue into testes, which in turn secrete testosterone. This process is an organizing effect of gonadal hormones. Testosterone masculinizes both the sex organs and the brain during development. A major organizing effect that gonadal hormones have on the brain is in the hypothalamus, especially the preoptic area of the medial hypothalamus. Organizing effects also operate in other nervous system regions, notably the amygdala, the prefrontal cortex, and the spinal cord.

Sex-related differences in the nervous system make sense behaviorally. After all, animal courtship rituals differ between the sexes, as do copulatory behaviors, with females engaging in sexually receptive responses and males in mounting ones. The production of these sex differences in behaviors depends on the action of gonadal hormones on the brain during both development and adulthood.

The actions of hormones on the adult brain are referred to as *activating effects,* in contrast with the developmental organizing effects. Here we consider organizing and activating effects separately.

Chapter 7 explains the organizing influences of gonadal hormones and critical periods on the developing brain. Chapter 8 explains the activating effects of sex hormones on the behaviors of males and females.

Organizing Effects of Sex Hormones

During fetal development, as you know, a male's testes produce male hormones, the androgens. In the developing rat, androgens are produced during the last week of fetal development and the first week after birth. The androgens produced at this time greatly alter both neural structures and later behavior. For example, the hypothalamus and prefrontal cortex of a male rat differ structurally from both those of female rats and those of males that were not exposed to androgens during their development.

The organizing effects of gonadal hormones have been studied most extensively in rats.

Furthermore, in adulthood, males with little exposure to the androgen testosterone during development behave like genetically female rats. If given estrogen and progesterone, they become sexually "receptive" and display typical female behaviors when mounted by males. Male rats that are castrated in adulthood do not act in this way.

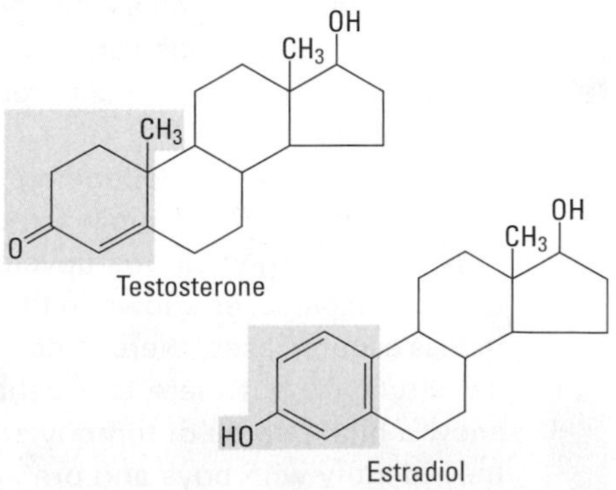

Sexual dimorphism, the differential development of brain areas in the two sexes, arises from a complex series of steps. Cells in the brain produce aromatase, an enzyme that converts testosterone into estradiol, one of the female sex hormones called estrogens. Therefore a female hormone, estradiol, actually masculinizes a male brain.

OH CH_3 CH_3 O

Testosterone

OH CH_3 HO

Estradiol

Females are not masculinized by the presence of estrogens because the fetuses of both sexes produce a liver enzyme (*alpha fetoprotein*) that binds to estrogen, rendering it incapable of entering neurons. Testosterone is unaffected by alpha fetoprotein, so it enters neurons and is converted into estradiol.

The organizing effects of testosterone are clearly illustrated in the preoptic area of the hypothalamus, which plays a critical role in the copulatory behavior of male rats. Comparing this area in males and females, Roger Gorski and his colleagues found a nucleus about five times as large in the males as in the females (Gorski, 1984). Significantly, the sexual dimorphism of the preoptic area can be altered by manipulating gonadal hormones during development. Castrating male rats at birth leads to a smaller preoptic area, whereas treating infant females with testosterone increases its size.

The organizing effects of gonadal hormones are more difficult to study in humans. The work of John Money and Anke Ehrhardt (1972), however, revealed an important role of these hormones in human development (see Clinical Focus 12-5, "Androgen-Insensitivity Syndrome and the Androgenital Syndrome").

CLINICAL FOCUS 12-5

Androgen-Insensitivity Syndrome and the Androgenital Syndrome

After the testes of a male fetus have formed, sexual development depends on the actions of testicular hormones. This dependence is made extremely clear by studying people with *androgen-insensitivity syndrome.* In this syndrome, an XY (male) fetus produces androgens, but the body is not able to respond to them.

Such a genetic male therefore develops a female appearance, or phenotype, as shown in the photograph on the left. Because estrogen receptors are not affected by the syndrome, these people are still responsive to estrogen produced both by the adrenal gland and by the testes. As a result, they develop female secondary sexual characteristics during puberty, even without additional hormone treatment. A person with androgen-insensitivity syndrome is therefore a genetic male who appears to be female.

If no Y chromosome is present to induce the growth of testes, a fetus develops ovaries and becomes a female. In some cases, however, the female fetus is exposed to androgens, producing a syndrome known both as *congenital adrenal hyperplasia* and as the *androgenital syndrome.* This exposure to androgens can occur if the adrenal glands of either the mother or the infant produce an excessive amount of androgens.

The effects vary, depending on when the androgens are produced and how much exposure there is. In extreme cases, an enlarged clitoris develops that can be mistaken for a small penis, as shown in the photograph on the right. In less severe cases, there is no gross abnormality in genital structure, but there is a behavioral effect: these girls show a high degree of tomboyishness. In early childhood, they identify with boys and prefer boys' clothes, toys, and games. One explanation for this behavioral effect is that the developing brain is masculinized, thus changing later behavior.

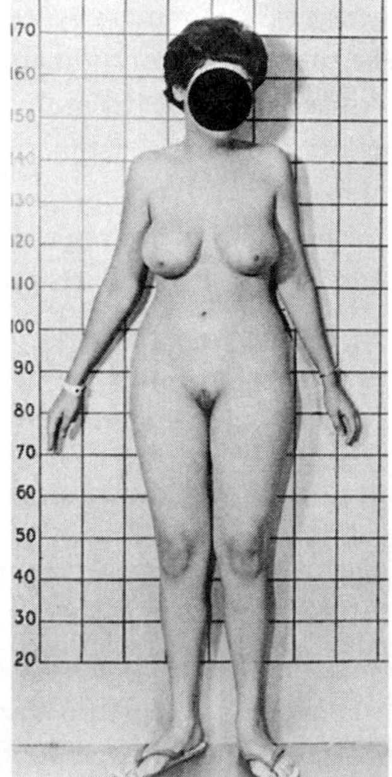

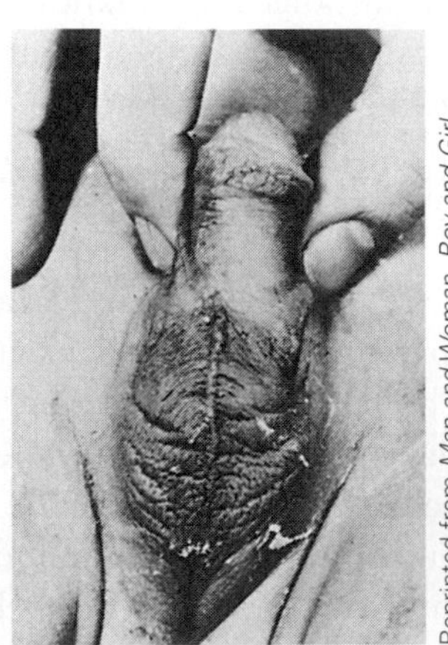

Reprinted from *Man and Woman, Boy and Girl* by John Money and Anke A. Ehrhardt

(*Left*) In androgen-insensitivity syndrome, a genetic male (XY) is insensitive to gonadally produced androgens but remains sensitive to estrogens, leading to the development of a female phenotype. (*Right*) In congenital adrenal hyperplasia, a genetic female (XX) is exposed to androgens produced by the adrenal gland embryonically, leading to the partial development of male external genitalia.

Activating Effects of Sex Hormones

The sexual behavior of both males and females also depends on the actions that gonadal hormones have on the adult brain. In most vertebrate species, female sexual behavior varies in the course of an estrous cycle during which the levels of hormones that the ovaries produce fluctuate. The rat's estrous cycle is about 4 days long, with sexual receptivity being only in the few hours during which the production of the ovarian hormones estrogen and progesterone peaks. These ovarian hormones alter brain activity, which in turn alters behavior. Furthermore, in female rats, various chemicals are released after mating, and these chemicals inhibit further mating behavior.

The activating effect of ovarian hormones can be seen clearly in cells of the hippocampus. **Figure 12-27** compares hippocampal pyramidal neurons taken from female rats at two points in the estrous cycle: one when estrogen levels are high and the other when they are low. When estrogen levels are high, more dendritic spines and presumably more synapses emerge. These neural differences during the estrous cycle are all the more remarkable when we consider that cells in the female hippocampus are continually changing their connections to other cells every 4 days throughout the animal's adulthood.

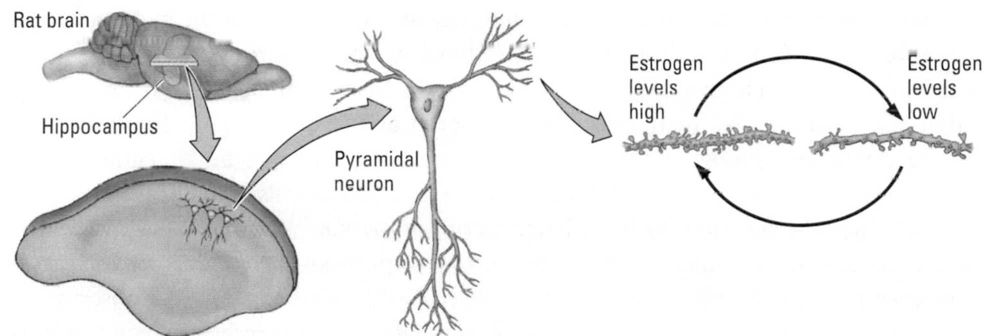

FIGURE 12-27 Hormonal Effects. A comparison of the dendrites of hippocampal pyramidal neurons at high and low levels of estrogen in the rat's (4-day) estrous cycle reveals far fewer dendritic spines in the low period. Adapted from "Naturally Occurring Fluctuation in Dendritic Spine Density on Adult Hippocampal Pyramidal Neurons," by C. S. Woolley, E. Gould, M. Frankfurt, and B. McEwen, 1990, *Journal of Neuroscience, 10,* p. 1289.

In males, testosterone activates sexual behavior in two distinctly different ways. First, the actions of testosterone on the amygdala are related to the motivation to seek sexual activity. Second, the actions of testosterone on the hypothalamus are needed to produce copulatory behavior. In the next section, we look at both processes.

The Hypothalamus, the Amygdala, and Sexual Behavior

The hypothalamus is the critical structure controlling copulatory behaviors in both males and females. The ventromedial hypothalamus controls the female mating posture, which in quadrapedal animals is called *lordosis:* arching the back and elevating the rump while the female otherwise remains quite still. Damage to the VMH abolishes lordosis. The role of the VMH is probably twofold: it controls the neural circuit that produces lordosis, and it influences hormonal changes in the female during coitus.

In males, the neural control of sexual behavior is somewhat more complex. The medial preoptic area, which is larger in males than in females, controls copulation. Damage to the medial preoptic area greatly disrupts mating performance, whereas electrical stimulation of this area activates mating, provided that testosterone is circulating in the bloodstream. Curiously, although destruction of the medial preoptic area stops males from mating, they continue to show interest in receptive females. For instance, monkeys with lesions in the medial preoptic area will not mate with receptive females, but they will masturbate while watching them from across the room.

Barry Everitt (1990) designed an ingenious apparatus that allows male rats to press a bar to deliver receptive females. After males were trained in the use of this apparatus, shown in **Figure 12-28,** lesions were made in their medial preoptic areas. Immediately, their sexual behavior changed. They would still press the bar to obtain access to females but would no longer mate with them.

Courtesy of Barry J. Everitt

FIGURE 12-28 Studying Sexual Motivation and Mating. In this experiment, a male rat is required to press the bar 10 times to gain access to a receptive female who "drops in" through a trap door. The copulatory behavior of the male rat illustrates mating behavior, whereas the bar pressing for access to a female rat illustrates sexual motivation. Adapted from "Sexual Motivation: A Neural and Behavioral Analysis of the Mechanisms Underlying Appetitive and Copulatory Responses of Male Rats," by B. J. Everitt, 1990, *Neuroscience and Biobehavioral Reviews, 14,* p. 227.

Apparently, the medial preoptic area controls mating, but it does not control sexual motivation. That brain structure responsible appears to be the amygdala. When Everitt trained male rats in the apparatus and then lesioned their amygdalae, they would no longer press the bar to gain access to receptive females, but they would mate with receptive females that were provided to them.

In summary, the hypothalamus controls copulatory behavior in both males and females. In males, the amygdala influences sexual motivation, and it probably plays a key role in human female sexual motivation as well, as it may among females of other species in which sexual activity is not tied to fluctuations in ovarian hormones.

Sexual Orientation, Sexual Identity, and Brain Organization

Does **sexual orientation**—a person's sexual attraction to the opposite sex or to the same sex or to both sexes—have a neural basis? Research to answer this question has been limited in scope, but it appears that differences in the structure of the hypothalamus may form a basis not only for sexual orientation but also for **sexual identity**—a person's feeling either male or female.

Like rats, humans have sex-related differences in the structure of the hypothalamus. The preoptic area of male humans can have twice as many neurons as does that of females, and a region known as the bed nucleus of the stria terminalis is 2.5 times as large in males (Swaab and Hofman, 1995; Swaab, Gooren, and Hofman, 1995). Similarly, a hypothalamic region known as INAH3 is two times as large in males, and a region known as the *suprachiasmatic nucleus* (SCN) contains twice as many cells in males as in females.

The SCN, shown in Figure 13-6, acts as a biological clock that instructs other neural structures when to produce behavior.

One hypothesis is that the hypothalamus of homosexual men should be more similar to the norm for females than for males. This hypothesis turns out to be incorrect, however. First, no difference between heterosexual and homosexual men is observed in the size of the preoptic area. Second, the SCN is twice as large in homosexual men as in heterosexual men.

Some evidence suggests a role for the SCN in sexual behavior in both male and female rats, and there is strong evidence that manipulating gonadal hormones alters the structure of the SCN. In contrast with the larger SCN in homosexual men, the INAH3 area in the hypothalamus is twice as large in the heterosexual brain as in the homosexual brain. These findings suggest that homosexual men form, in effect, a "third sex" because their hypothalami differ from those of both females and heterosexual males, (Swaab, Gooren, and Hofman, 1995).

No research has been published on the hypothalami of homosexual women. Paul Vasey (2002) described homosexual behavior in Japanese macaque monkeys. He compared the hypothalami of this species to data collected in purely heterosexual monkey species. To date, he has found no unique pattern of hypothalamic organization in homosexual female Japanese macaques, but we must wonder: Does the homosexual behavior of these monkeys and human females have a similar basis?

In contrast to homosexuals, transsexuals feel strongly that they have been born the wrong sex. Their desire to be the opposite sex can be so strong that they undergo sex-change surgery. Little is known about the causes of transsexuality, but it is generally assumed to result from a disturbed interaction between brain development and circulating hormones.

Swaab and Hofman (1995) found that the bed nucleus of the stria terminalis was female-sized in a small group of five male-to-female transsexuals. This finding suggests the possibility of a biological basis for transsexuality. We must, however, be wary of drawing cause-and-effect conclusions, especially in such a small sample of people.

Research Focus 11-5 reports the provocative idea that transsexuals may experience "phantom genitalia" that are inconsistent with their actual genitalia.

If differences in brain organization do exist in people with nontraditional sexual orientations and sexual identities, what might give rise to the differences? Dean Hamer

Sexual orientation A person's sexual attraction to the opposite sex or to the same sex or to both sexes.
Sexual identity A person's feeling of being either male or female.

and his colleagues (1993) studied the incidence of homosexuality in the families of 114 homosexual men. They recorded a higher-than-average incidence of male homosexuality on the maternal side of the men's families but not on the paternal side.

This maternal–paternal difference is most easily explained if a gene on the mother's X chromosome is implicated. Further investigation revealed that a large percentage of homosexual brothers had in common one small area at the tip of the X chromosome (area Xq28). This finding suggests that at least one subtype of male sexual orientation may be genetically influenced.

We must be cautious in drawing this conclusion, however. William Byne (1994) argued that, even if certain configurations of genes and neurotransmitters are correlated with homosexuality, correlation does not prove causation. After all, genes specify proteins, not sexual behavior.

Conceivably, particular sequences of DNA might cause the brain to be wired in ways that lead to a particular sexual orientation. But it is equally possible that these genes could influence the development of certain personality traits that in turn influence the way in which social experiences contribute to learning a certain sexual orientation. Clearly, establishing the cause-and-effect connections is not an easy task.

Cognitive Influences on Sexual Behavior

People think about sex, dream about sex, make plans about sex. These behaviors may include activity in the amygdala or the hypothalamus, but they must certainly also include the cortex. This is not to say that the cortex is essential for sexual motivation and copulation.

In studies of rats whose entire cortices have been removed, both males and females still engage in sexual activity, although the males are somewhat clumsy. Nevertheless, the cortex must play a role in certain aspects of sexual behavior. For instance, imagery about sexual activity must include activity in the ventral visual pathway of the cortex. And thinking about sexual activity and planning for it must require the participation of the frontal lobes.

As you might expect, these aspects of sexual behavior are not easily studied in rats, and they remain uncharted waters in research on humans. However, changes in the sexual behavior of people with frontal-lobe injury are well documented. And recall J. P.'s case, described in Clinical Focus 12-2.

Although J. P. lost his inhibition about sexual behavior, frontal-lobe damage is just as likely to produce a loss of libido (sexual interest). The wife of a man who, 5 years earlier, had a small tumor removed from the medial frontal region, complained that she and her husband had since had no sexual contact whatsoever. He was simply not interested, even though they were both still in their 20s.

The husband said that he no longer had sexual fantasies or sexual dreams and, although he still loved his wife, he did not have any sexual urges toward her or anyone else. Such cases clearly indicate that the human cortex has an important role in controlling sexual behaviors. The exact nature of that role is still poorly understood.

REVIEW: Control of Nonregulatory Behavior

- ✔ Sexual behavior is controlled by a combination of gonadal hormones, neurons in the hypothalamus and limbic system, and cognitive factors. The hypothalamus controls the details of copulation in both males and females, whereas the motivation for sexual behavior is controlled by the amygdala.
- ✔ In contrast with an onoing regulatory behavior such as feeding, hormones organize, by their activating effects, nonregulatory neural control of sexual behavior during development and in adulthood.

- ✔ Gonadal hormones influence the size of subregions and the structure of cells in the hypothalamus, as well as in the cerebral hemispheres.
- ✔ Anatomical differences promoted by gonadal hormones presumably account for variety in sexual behaviors, orientations, and identities between males and females and among individuals.

Reward

Survival for most animals depends on minimizing contact with certain stimuli and maximizing contact with others. Contact is minimized when an animal experiences fear or anxiety, but sometimes an animal avoids a stimulus that is not fear-arousing. Why? And why do animals maintain contact with other stimuli?

A simple answer is that animals maintain contact with stimuli that they find rewarding in some way and ignore or avoid stimuli that they find neutral or aversive. According to this view, reward is a mechanism that evolved to help increase the adaptive fitness both of entire species and of individual members of a species.

But what exactly is reward? One rather circular definition is that reward is the activity of neural circuits that function to maintain an animal's contact with certain environmental stimuli, either in the present or in the future. Presumably, an animal perceives the activity of these circuits as pleasant. This pleasantness would explain why reward can help maintain not only adaptive behaviors such as feeding and sexual activity but also potentially nonadaptive behaviors such as drug addiction. After all, evolution would not have prepared the brain specifically for the eventual development of psychoactive drugs.

The first clue to the presence of a reward system in the brain came with an accidental discovery by James Olds and Peter Milner in 1954. They found that rats would perform behaviors such as pressing a bar to administer a brief burst of electrical stimulation to specific sites in their brains. This phenomenon is called *intracranial self-stimulation* or *brain-stimulation reward.*

Chapter 6 describes how brain stimulation is used as a treatment as well as a research tool.

Typically, rats will press a lever hundreds or even thousands of times per hour to obtain this brain stimulation, stopping only when they are exhausted. Why would animals engage in such a behavior when it has absolutely no value to their survival or to that of their species? The simplest explanation is that the brain stimulation is activating the system underlying reward (Wise, 1996).

After more than 50 years of research on brain-stimulation reward, investigators now know that dozens of sites in the brain will maintain self-stimulation. Some especially effective regions are the lateral hypothalamus and medial forebrain bundle. Stimulation along the MFB tract activates fibers that form the ascending pathways from dopamine-producing cells of the midbrain tegmentum, shown in **Figure 12-29.** This

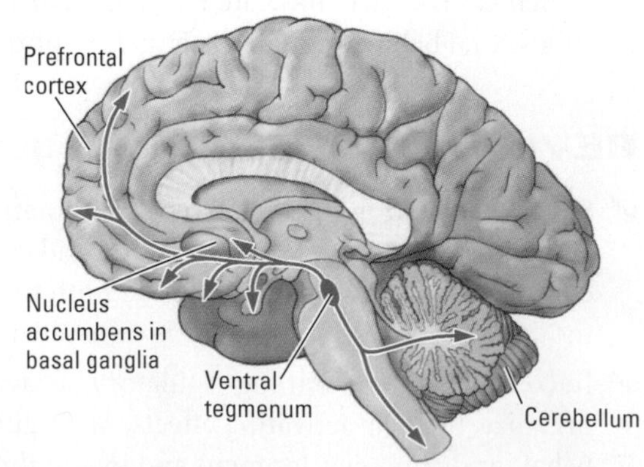

FIGURE 12-29 Mesolimbic Dopamine System. Axons emanating from the ventral tegmentum (blue arrows) project diffusely through the brain to synapse on their targets. Dopamine release in the mesolimbic pathways has a role in feelings of reward and pleasure. The nucleus accumbens is a critical structure in this "reward system."

mesolimbic dopamine pathway sends terminals to various sites, including especially the nucleus accumbens in the basal ganglia and the prefrontal cortex.

Neuroscientists believe that the mesolimbic dopamine system is central to circuits mediating reward for several reasons:

1. Dopamine release shows a marked increase when animals are engaged in intracranial self-stimulation.
2. Drugs that enhance dopamine release increase self-stimulation, whereas drugs that decrease dopamine release decrease self-stimulation. It seems that the amount of dopamine released somehow determines how rewarding an event is.
3. When animals engage in behaviors such as feeding or sexual activity, dopamine release rapidly increases in locations such as the nucleus accumbens.
4. Highly addictive drugs such as nicotine and cocaine increase the level of dopamine in the nucleus accumbens.

Even opiates appear to affect at least some of an animal's actions through the dopamine system. Animals quickly learn to press a bar to obtain an injection of opiates directly into the midbrain tegmentum or the nucleus accumbens. The same animals do not work to obtain the opiates if the dopaminergic neurons of the mesolimbic system are inactivated. Apparently, then, animals engage in behaviors that increase dopamine release.

Note, however, that dopamine is not the only reward compound in the brain. For example, Rainer Spanagel and Friedbert Weiss (1999) stressed that drugs can be rewarding in the absence of dopamine, and Keith Trujillo and his colleagues (1993) found that the reinforcing actions of opiates take place through activation of both dopaminergic and nondopaminergic systems. These findings suggest the existence of more than one reward-related system in the brain.

Robinson and Berridge (2008) propose that reward contains separable psychological components, corresponding roughly to "wanting," which is often called "incentive," and "liking," which is equivalent to an evaluation of pleasure. This idea can be applied to discovering why we increase contact with a stimulus such as chocolate.

Chapter 8 details Robinson and Berridge's wanting-and-liking theory of addiction, including the idea that reward has multiple parts.

Two independent factors are at work: our desire to have the chocolate (wanting) and the pleasurable effect of eating the chocolate (liking). This distinction is important. If we maintain contact with a certain stimulus because dopamine is released, the question becomes whether the dopamine plays a role in the wanting or the liking aspect of the behavior. Robinson and Berridge proposed that wanting and liking processes are mediated by separable neural systems and that dopamine is the transmitter in wanting. Liking, they hypothesize, entails opioid and benzodiazepine–GABA systems.

According to Robinson and Berridge, wanting and liking are normally two aspects of the same process, so rewards are usually wanted and liked to the same degree. However, it is possible, under certain circumstances, for wanting and liking to change independently.

Consider rats with lesions of the ascending dopaminergic pathway to the forebrain. These rats do not eat. Is it simply that they do not desire to eat (a loss of wanting) or has food become aversive to them (a loss of liking)? To find out which factor is at work, the animals' facial expressions and body movements in response to food can be observed to see how liking is affected. After all, when animals are given various foods to taste, they produce different facial and body reactions, depending on whether they perceive the food as pleasant or aversive.

For example, when a normal person tastes something sweet, he or she usually responds by licking the fingers or the lips, as shown at the top of **Figure 12-30.** In contrast, if the taste is unpleasantly salty, say, as shown in the bottom panel, the reaction

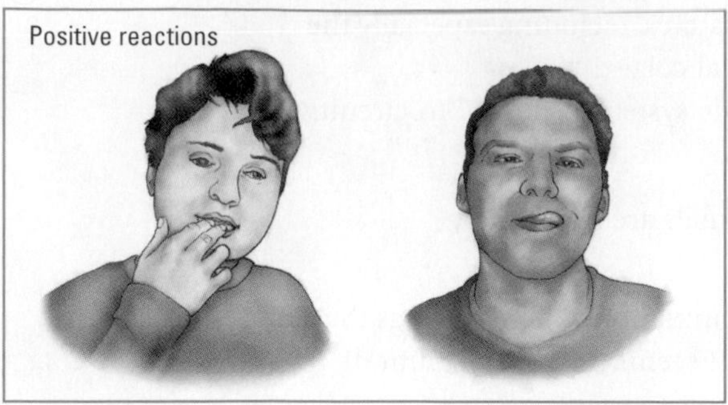

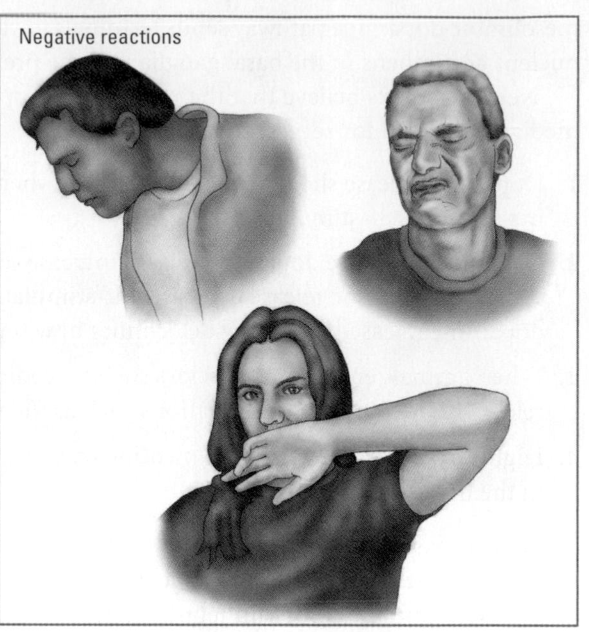

FIGURE 12-30 Human Reactions to Taste. Positive (hedonic) reactions are elicited by sucrose and other palatable tastes. Hedonic reactions include licking the fingers and licking the lips. Negative (aversive) reactions are elicited by quinine and other nonpalatable tastes. Aversive reactions include spitting, making a face of distaste, and wiping the mouth with the back of the hand. Adapted from "Food Reward: Brain Substrates of Wanting and Liking," by K. C. Berridge, 1996, *Neuroscience and Biobehavioral Reviews, 20,* p. 6

is often spitting, grimacing, or wiping the mouth with the back of the hand. Rats, too, show distinctive positive and negative responses to pleasant and unpleasant tastes.

By watching the responses when food is squirted into the mouth of a rat that otherwise refuses to eat, we can tell to what extent a loss of liking for food is a factor in the animal's food rejection. Interestingly, rats that do not eat after receiving lesions to the dopamine pathway act as though they still like food.

Now consider a rat with a self-stimulation electrode in the lateral hypothalamus. This rat will often eat heartily while the stimulation is on. The obvious inference is that the food must taste good—presumably even better than it does usually. But what if we squirt food into the rat's mouth and observe its behavior when the stimulation is on versus when it is off?

If the brain stimulation primes eating by evoking pleasurable sensations, we would expect that the animal would be more positive in its facial and body reactions toward foods when the stimulation is turned on. In fact, the opposite is found. During stimulation, rats react more aversively to tastes such as sugar and salt than when stimulation is off. Apparently, the stimulation increases wanting but not liking.

In conclusion, experiments of this sort show that what appears to be a single event—reward—is actually composed of at least two independent processes. Just as our visual system independently processes "what" and "how" information in two separate streams, our reward system appears to include independent processes of wanting and liking. Reward is not a single phenomenon any more than the processes of perception or memory are.

REVIEW: Reward

- ✔ Rewards are the effects that events have on the behavior of animals. Neural circuits maintain contact with rewarding environmental stimuli in the present or in the future through liking and wanting subsystems.
- ✔ The challenge for neuroscience researchers, as well as their reward, lies in segregating the neural subsystems that take part in reward and in accounting for how rewarding effects of environmental events influence liking or wanting.

Summary

Identifying the Causes of Behavior

Our inner, subjective feelings (emotions) and goal-directed thoughts (motivations) influence how we behave and adapt as individuals and as a species. We interpret subjective feelings as a range of emotion—the gamut from love at first sight to deeply burning hatred. Motivation is triggered by drives as universal as hunger or as characteristic of many individuals as curiosity. These behaviors seem purposeful.

Emotion and motivation are inferred states that can escape conscious awareness or intent. Such unconscious emotions and motives make the case for free will difficult to argue.

Biology, Evolution, and Environment

Biologically, reward motivates animals to engage in behavior. Sensory stimulation leads to hormone activity and to dopamine activity in the brainstem. Neural circuits organized in the brainstem control species-typical behaviors such as mouse killing by cats and singing by birds.

These brainstem circuits manifest their evolutionary advantage: they are rewarding. Rewarding behavior motivates living beings. When animals disengage from behaviors that motivate their species, they go extinct.

Behavior is controlled by its consequences as well as by its biology. Consequences may affect the evolution of the species or the behavior of an individual animal. Behaviors selected by evolution are often triggered by innate releasing mechanisms. Behaviors selected only in an individual animal are shaped by that animal's environment and are learned.

In the olfactory and gustatory senses, chemical neuroreceptors in the nose and tongue interact with chemosignals, leading to neural activity in cranial nerve 1 for olfaction and cranial nerves 7, 9, and 10 for taste. The cranial nerves enter the brainstem, and through a series of synapses, pass into the forebrain. Smell and taste input merges in the orbitofrontal cortex to produce our perception of flavor.

Neuroanatomy of Motivated Behavior and Stimulating Emotion

The neural structures that initiate emotional and motivated behaviors are the hypothalamus, the pituitary gland, the amygdala, the dopamine and noradrenaline pathways from nuclei in the lower brainstem, and the frontal lobes.

The experience of both emotion and motivation is controlled by activity in the ANS, hypothalamus, and forebrain, especially the amygdala and frontal cortex. Emotional and motivated behavior may be an unconscious response to internal or external stimuli and be controlled by the activity of innate releasing mechanisms or be a cognitive response to events or thoughts.

Control of Regulatory and Nonregulatory Behavior

The two distinctly different types of motivated behaviors are (1) regulatory (homeostatic) behaviors that maintain vital body-system balance and (2) nonregulatory behaviors, basically consisting of all other behaviors. Nonregulatory behaviors are not controlled by a homeostatic mechanism and is not reflexive. Feeding is a regulatory behavior controlled by the interaction of the digestive and hormonal systems and the hypothalamic and cortical circuits. Sexual activity is a nonregulatory behavior motivated by the amygdala. Copulatory behavior is controlled by the hypothalamus (the ventromedial hypothalamus in females and the preoptic area in males).

Reward

Survival depends on maximizing contact with some environmental stimuli and minimizing contact with others. Reward is a mechanism for controlling this differential. Two independent features of reward are wanting and liking. The wanting component is thought to be controlled by dopaminergic systems, whereas the liking component is thought to be controlled by opiate–benzodiazepine systems.

Key Terms

amygdala, p. 418
androgen, p. 401
anorexia nervosa, p. 428
aphagia, p. 430
drive, p. 399
emotion, p. 397
evolutionary psychology, p. 403
generalized anxiety disorder, p. 427
hippocampus, p. 416
homeostatic mechanism, p. 410
hyperphagia, p. 430
hypovolumic thirst, p. 432
innate releasing mechanism (IRM), p. 403
Klüver-Bucy syndrome, p. 423
learned taste aversion, p. 408
medial forebrain bundle (MFB), p. 412
motivation, p. 397
nonregulatory behavior, p. 412
obesity, p. 428
orbitofrontal cortex, p. 397
osmotic thirst, p. 432
panic disorder, p. 427
pheromone, p. 404
phobia, p. 427
pituitary gland, p. 412
prefrontal cortex, p. 418
preparedness, p. 408
psychosurgery, p. 424
regulatory behavior, p. 410
reinforcer, p. 406
releasing hormone, p. 414
sensory deprivation, p. 397
sexual dimorphism, p. 432
sexual identity, p. 437
sexual orientation, p. 437
somatic marker hypothesis, p. 423

▶*Please refer to the Companion Web Site at* **www.worthpublishers.com/kolbintro3e** *for Interactive Exercises and Quizzes.*

Bob Thomas/Getty Images

CHAPTER 13

Why Do We Sleep and Dream?

COMPARATIVE FOCUS 13-1

Biological Clocks

If animal behavior were affected only by seasonal and daily changes, the neural mechanisms that account for changes in behavior would be much simpler to study than they are. Behavior would be driven by external cues, which would be easy to identify, and the neural processes that respond to those cues also would be easy to identify.

That behavior is not driven simply by external cues was first recognized in 1729 by the French geologist Jean Jacques d'Ortous de Mairan (see Raven et al, 1992). In an experiment similar to the one illustrated in the Procedure section of **Experiment 13-1,** de Mairan isolated a plant from daily light and dark cues and from temperature cues. He noted that the rhythmic movements of its leaves continued, as graphed in the Results section of the experiment.

What concerned investigators who came after de Mairan's report was the possibility that some undetected external cue stimulates the rhythmic behavior of the plant. Such cues could include changes in gravity, in electromagnetic fields, and even in the intensity of rays from outer space. But further experiments showed that the daily fluctuations are endogenous—they come from within the plant. In fact, experiments show that most organisms have an internal **biological clock** that matches the temporal passage of a real day.

Your desk clock and calendar enable you to plan and schedule your time. Your biological clock performs these functions too. An endogenous biological clock allows an animal, in effect, to anticipate events: to migrate before it gets cold rather than waiting until it gets cold and to mate at the correct time of the year. The clock allows animals to arrive at the same place at the same time if they are to mate or to begin a migration. Most important, a biological clock signals to an animal that, if daylight lasts for about 12 hours today, it will last for about 12 hours tomorrow.

Plants and animals evolved internal clocks through natural selection to avoid being tricked by external cues into displaying maladaptive behavior. Plant bulbs that begin growing during a January thaw only to be killed by a subsequent freeze exemplify such maladaptive behavior.

EXPERIMENT 13-1

Question: Is plant movement exogenous or endogenous?

Procedure

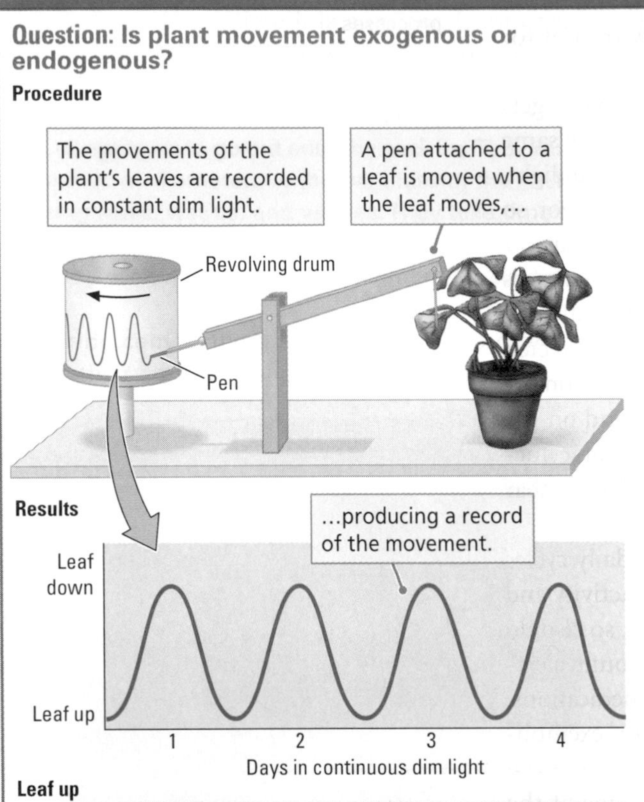
The movements of the plant's leaves are recorded in constant dim light.
A pen attached to a leaf is moved when the leaf moves,...
Revolving drum
Pen
Results
...producing a record of the movement.
Leaf down
Leaf up
1
2
3
4
Days in continuous dim light

Leaf up

Leaf down

Conclusion: Movement of the plant is endogenous. It is caused by an internal clock that matches the temporal passage of a real day.

Biological Rhythms

Although the existence of endogenous biological clocks was demonstrated nearly 300 years ago, the detailed study of biorhythms had to await the development of procedures that could analyze ongoing behavior over a long period of time. Behavior analysis requires a method for counting behavioral events and a method for displaying the events in a meaningful way. For example, the behavior of a rodent can be measured by giving the animal access to a running wheel in which it can exercise (**Figure 13-2A**).

A chart recorder or a computer records each turn of the wheel and displays the result (Figure 13-2B). Because most rodents are nocturnal, sleeping during light hours and becoming active during dark hours, their wheel-running activity takes place in the dark (Figure 13-2C). If each day's activity is plotted under the preceding day's activity in a column, we can observe a pattern, or cycle, of activity over a period of

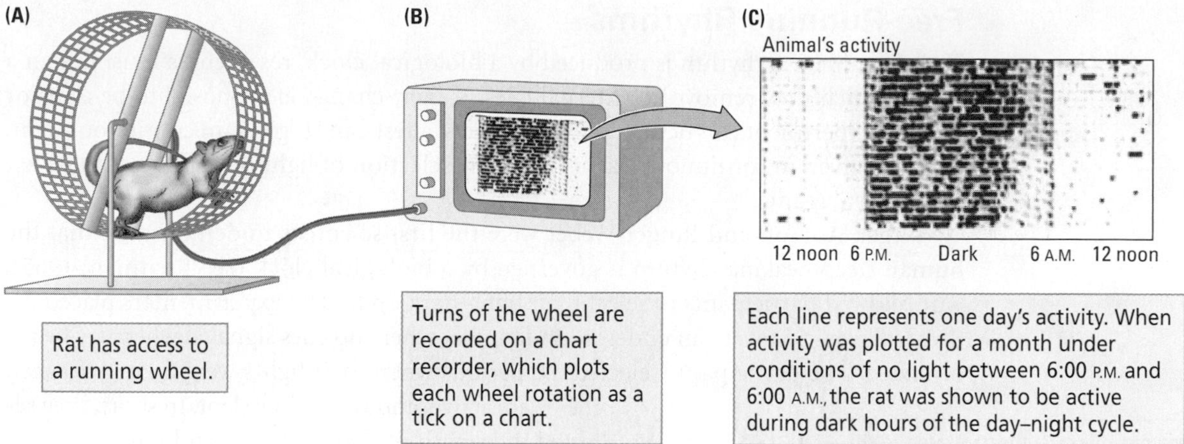

(A)
(B)
(C)
Animal's activity
12 noon 6 P.M. Dark 6 A.M. 12 noon
Rat has access to a running wheel.
Turns of the wheel are recorded on a chart recorder, which plots each wheel rotation as a tick on a chart.
Each line represents one day's activity. When activity was plotted for a month under conditions of no light between 6:00 P.M. and 6:00 A.M., the rat was shown to be active during dark hours of the day–night cycle.

FIGURE 13-2 Recording the Daily Activity Cycle of a Rat. Adapted from *Biological Clocks in Medicine and Psychiatry* (pp. 12–15), by C. P. Richter, 1965, Springfield, IL: Charles C. Thomas.

time. Details of the chart can then be examined, including when the animal was active and how active it was.

The cycle of activity is perhaps the most important piece of information charted by an activity record. The time required to complete a cycle of activity is called a **period.** The activity period of most rodents is about 24 hours in an environment in which the lights go on and off with regularity. Our own sleep–wake period also is about 24 hours. Many other kinds of behaviors, however, have periods that are longer or shorter than 24 hours.

Animals have a surprising number of biological clocks, and those clocks have varying periods. Two rhythms typical of most animals are *circannual rhythms* (the yearly migratory cycles of sea bears and Arctic terns are examples) and **circadian rhythms,** the day–night rhythms found in almost all animals and cellular processes. These two are not the only kinds of rhythms, however.

In Latin, *circa* means "about," *annum* means "year," and *dies* means "day."

Ultradian rhythms have a period of less than one day. Our eating behavior, which takes place about every 90 minutes to 2 hours, including snacks, is one ultradian rhythm. Rodents, although active throughout the night, display an ultradian rhythm in being most active at the beginning and end of the dark period.

Biological rhythm	Time frame	Example
Circannual	Yearly	Migratory cycles of birds
Circadian	Daily	Human sleep–wake cycle
Ultradian	Less than a day	Human eating cycles
Infradian	More than a day	Human menstrual cycle

Many sea-dwelling animals' rhythms cycle at about 12-hour intervals, which matches the twice-daily changes in tides produced by the pull of the moon on the earth and its oceans. Therefore, an ultradian rhythm is embedded within their circadian rhythm. Our eye-blink rate, our heart rate, and even the rhythmic action potentials of some of our neurons are other examples of ultradian rhythms.

Other biorhythms have monthly or seasonal periods greater than a day but less than a year. These are *infradian rhythms.* The menstrual cycle of female humans, with an average period of about 28 days, is an infradian biorhythm linked to the cycle of the moon and thus also referred to as a *circalunal cycle.*

We focus in this chapter on the circadian rhythm, which is central to our sleep–waking behavior. Note, however, that the fact that a behavior appears to be rhythmic does not mean that it is ruled by a biological clock. Sea bears will remain on the ice as long as the ice pack and food supplies last, and many migrating birds will postpone their migrations as long as they have a food supply. Therefore, whether a rhythmic behavior is produced by a biological clock must be demonstrated experimentally. A definitive experiment to support the conclusion that the sea bear does have a clock would be methodologically difficult to conduct, but such demonstrations are not difficult to make with other animals, including ourselves.

Biological clock Neural system that times behavior.
Period Time required to complete a cycle of activity.
Circadian rhythm Day–night rhythm.

Free-Running Rhythms

To determine if a rhythm is produced by a biological clock, researchers must design a test in which they remove all external cues. If light change is proposed to be a major cue, the experiment can be set up in three ways: a test can be given in continuous light, it can be given in continuous darkness, or the selection of light or darkness can be left to the participant.

Jurgen Aschoff and Rutger Weber were the first scientists to demonstrate that the human sleep–waking rhythm is governed by a biological clock (see Kleitman, 1965), who allowed participants to select their light–dark cycle. The experimenters placed individual participants in an underground bunker where no cues signaled when day began or ended. The participants selected the periods when their lights were on or off, when they were active, and when they slept. In short, they selected the length of their own day and night.

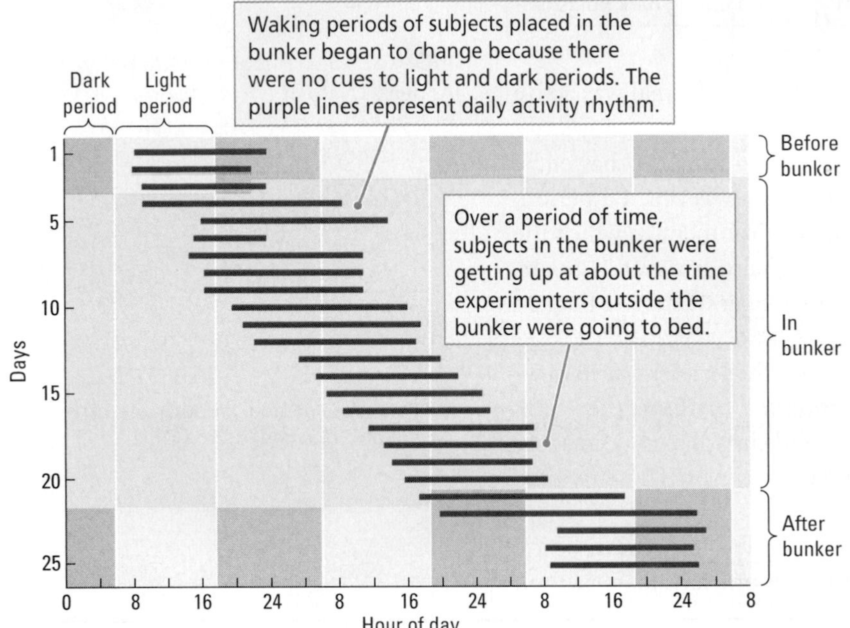

FIGURE 13-3 Free-Running Rhythm in a Human Subject. The record for days 1 through 3 shows the daily sleep period under normal day–night conditions. That for days 4 through 20 shows the free-running rhythm that developed while the subject was isolated in a bunker and allowed to control day and night length. The daily activity period shifts from 24 hours to 25.9 hours. On days 21 through 25, the period returns to 24 hours when the subject is again exposed to a normal light-and-dark cycle. Adapted from *Sleep* (p. 33), by J. A. Hobson, 1989, New York: Scientific American Library.

By measuring ongoing behavior and recording sleeping periods with sensors on the beds, Aschoff and Weber found that the participants continued to show daily sleep–activity rhythms. This finding demonstrated that humans have an endogenous biological clock that governs sleep–waking behavior.

Figure 13-3 shows, however, that the biorhythms recorded by Aschoff and Weber were peculiar when compared with the rhythms before and after isolation. Although the period of the participants' sleep–wake cycles approximated a normal period of 24 hours before and after the test, during the test they progressively deviated from clock time. Rather than being 24 hours, the period in the bunker ranged from about 25 to 27 hours, depending on the participant.

The participants were choosing to go to bed from 1 to 2 hours later every "night." A shift by an hour or so of sleeping time is not remarkable for a few days, but its cumulative effect quickly became evident: soon the participants were getting up at about the time the experimenters outside the bunker were going to bed. Clearly, the participants were displaying their own personal cycles. A rhythm that runs at a frequency of the body's own devising when environmental cues are absent is called a **free-running rhythm.**

The period of free-running rhythms depends on the way in which external cues are removed. When hamsters, a nocturnal species, are tested in constant darkness, their free-running periods are a little shorter than 24 hours; when they are tested in constant light, their free-running periods are a little longer than 24 hours. This test dependency in hamsters is typical of nocturnal animals.

As **Figure 13-4** shows, the opposite free-running periods are typical of diurnal animals (Binkley, 1990). When sparrows, which are diurnal birds, are tested in constant darkness, their free-running periods are a little longer than 24 hours; when they are tested in constant light, their free-running periods are a little shorter than 24 hours. Why periods change in different lighting conditions is not clear, but a rule of thumb is that animals expand and contract their sleep periods as the sleep-related lighting period—light for hamsters and dark for sparrows—expands or contracts.

Understanding this point enables you to predict how artificial lighting influences human circadian periods: our sleep periods contract. You can also offer an explanation of why Aschoff and Weber's participants displayed periods that were longer than 24 hours: they controlled the light switches, so they chose to go to bed a little later each

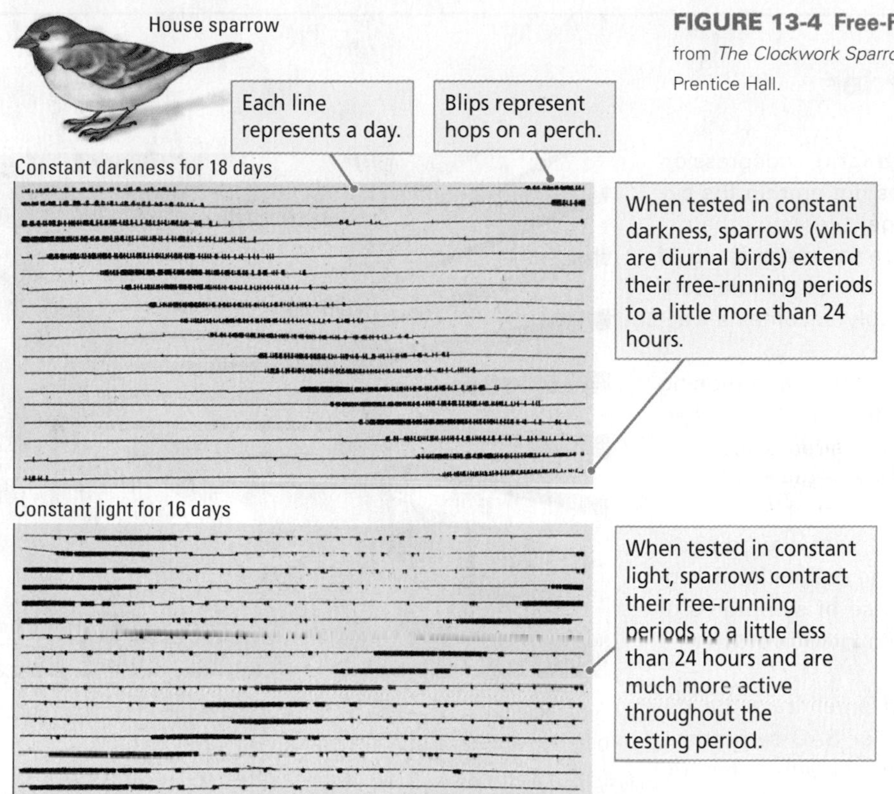

House sparrow
Each line represents a day.
Blips represent hops on a perch.
Constant darkness for 18 days
When tested in constant darkness, sparrows (which are diurnal birds) extend their free-running periods to a little more than 24 hours.
Constant light for 16 days
When tested in constant light, sparrows contract their free-running periods to a little less than 24 hours and are much more active throughout the testing period.

FIGURE 13-4 Free-Running Rhythms of a Diurnal Animal. Adapted from *The Clockwork Sparrow* (p. 16), by S. Binkley, 1990, Englewood Cliffs, NJ: Prentice Hall.

day. Endogenous rhythmicity is not the only factor that contributes to circadian periods, however. An endogenous rhythm that is just a little slow or a little fast would be useless because the error would accumulate. There must also be a mechanism for setting rhythms to correspond to environmental events.

Zeitgebers

Because Aschoff and Weber's participants had a sleep–wake cycle of 24 hours before and after they entered the experiment and because humans usually have a 24-hour rhythm, we might wonder how normal rhythms are maintained. The biological clock must keep to a time that matches changes in the day–night cycle. If a biological clock is like a slightly defective wristwatch that runs either too slow or too fast, it will eventually provide times that are inaccurate by hours and so become useless.

If we reset an errant wristwatch each day, however—say, when we awaken—it will then provide useful information even though it is not perfectly accurate. There must be an equivalent way of resetting a free-running biological clock. In experiments to determine how clocks are set, researchers have found that cues such as sunrise and sunset, eating times, and other activities can all set the circadian clock.

Normally, light is the most potent stimulus. Aschoff and Weber called a clock-setting cue a ***Zeitgeber*** ("time giver" in German). When a clock is reset by a Zeitgeber, it is said to be **entrained.** Clinical Focus 13-2, "Seasonal Affective Disorder" on page 450, explains the importance of light in entraining circadian rhythms.

Biological clocks are flexible. They can be reset each day so that they accurately correspond to the season. In polar regions, you'll recall, the time of onset and the length of day and night change as the seasons progress. At the higher latitudes, daylight begins very early in the morning in summer and very late in the morning in winter. To adjust to these changes, an animal responds both to daylight and to how long the day will last.

Free-running rhythm Rhythm of the body's own devising in the absence of all external cues.
Zeitgeber Environmental event that entrains biological rhythms: a "time giver."
Entrainment Determination or modification of the period of a biorhythm.

CLINICAL FOCUS 13-2

Seasonal Affective Disorder

In *seasonal affective disorder* (SAD), a form of depression associated with winter, sunlight does not entrain the circadian rhythm. The perception of longer nights by the circadian pacemaker stimulates pressure for more sleep. If not satisfied, cumulative sleep deprivation can result. Consequently, a person's biorhythm probably becomes a free-running rhythm.

Because people vary in the duration of their free-running rhythms, the lack of entrainment affects individuals differently. Some are phase-retarded, with desired sleep time coming earlier each day; some are phase-delayed, with desired sleep time coming later each day.

The cumulative changes associated with altered circadian rhythms can result in depression. The suggestion is supported by the finding that the incidence of symptoms of depression increase as a function of the latitude at which a person lives.

Researchers report that light can ameliorate the depression of SAD, and one treatment for SAD symptoms, *phototherapy,* uses light to entrain the circadian rhythm. The idea is to increase the short winter photoperiod by exposing a person to artificial bright light in the morning or both morning and evening. Typical room lighting is not bright enough.

Complicating the understanding of SAD, living in at a northern latitude in winter and so being deprived of sunlight is associated with decreased Vitamin D synthesis, which may also cause depression. In addition, increased consumption of carbohydrates and fats, reduced sensitivity of retinal receptors that convey light-entraining signals to the superchiasmatic nucleus, and structural damage in noradrenergic and serotinergic neurons in the brain all may contribute to changes in circadian rhythms and SAD (Gonzalez and Aston-Jones, 2008).

Louie Psihoyos/Science Faction/Corbis

A participant in research on SAD designed to investigate how differing amounts of full-spectrum light affect mood.

A biological clock that is reset each day tells an animal that daylight will begin tomorrow at approximately the same time that it began today and that tomorrow will last approximately as long as today did. But when should the clock be reset? Current research holds that light Zeitgebers work best when exposure occurs near the beginning or the end of the cycle, which is why sunrise and sunset are effective.

Hamster

If a hamster happens to blink during this Zeitgeber, the light will still penetrate its closed eyelids and entrain its biological clock.

The very potent entraining effect of light Zeitgebers is illustrated by laboratory studies of Syrian hamsters, perhaps one of the most compulsive animal timekeepers. When given access to running wheels, hamsters exercise during the night segment of the laboratory day–night cycle. A single brief flash of light is an effective Zeitgeber for entraining their biological clocks.

Considering the somewhat less compulsive behavior that most of us display, we should shudder at the way that we entrain our own clocks when we stay up late in artificial light, sleep late some days, and get up early by using an alarm clock on other days. **Light pollution,** the extent to which we are exposed to artificial lighting, disrupts circadian rhythms and accounts for a great deal of inconsistent behavior associated with accidents, daytime fatigue, and fluxuations in emotional states.

Entrainment works best if the adjustment to the biological clock is not too large. People who work shifts are often subject to huge adjustments, especially when they work the graveyard shift (11:00 P.M. to 7:00 A.M.), the period when they would normally sleep.

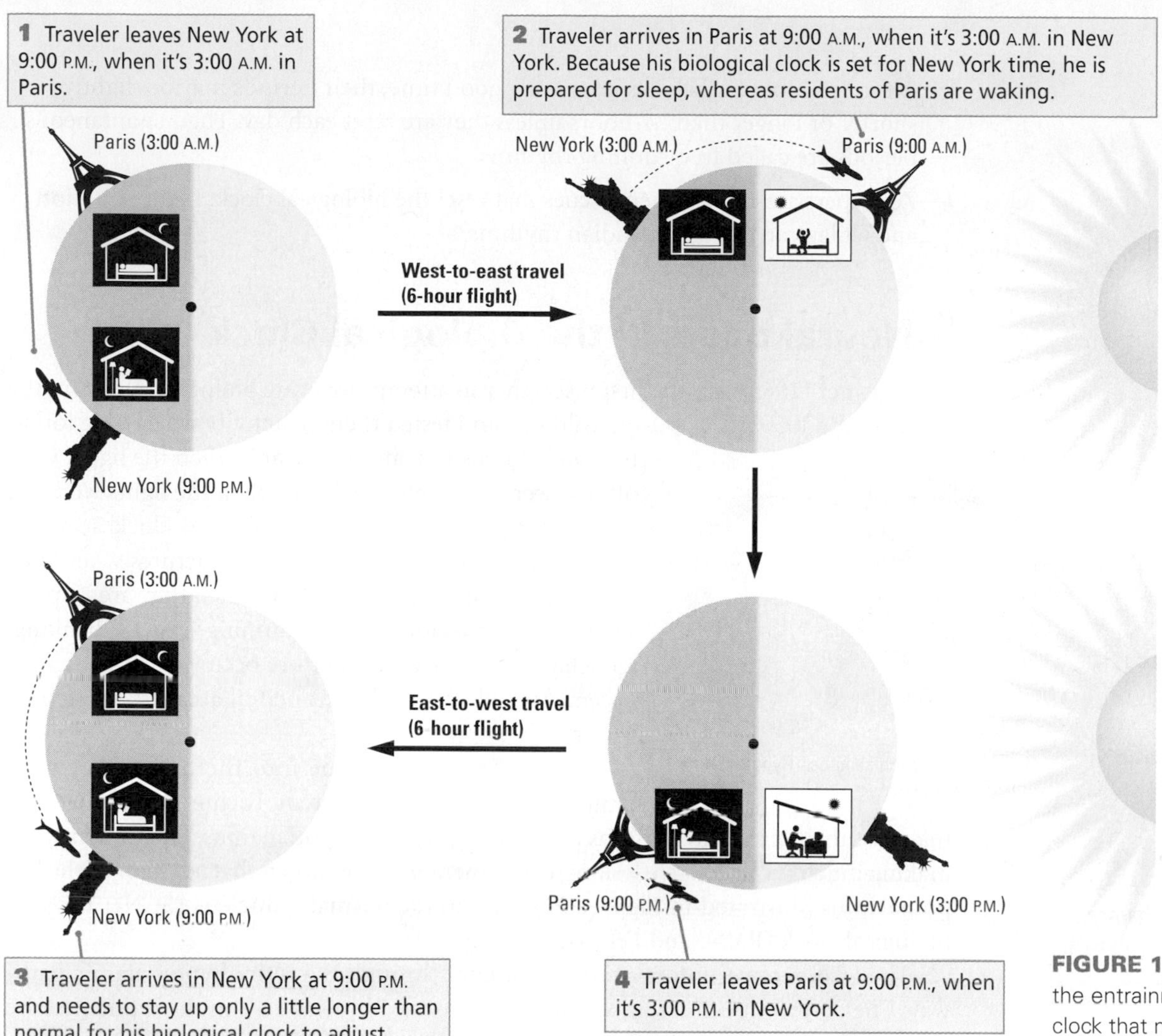
1 Traveler leaves New York at 9:00 P.M., when it's 3:00 A.M. in Paris.
2 Traveler arrives in Paris at 9:00 A.M., when it's 3:00 A.M. in New York. Because his biological clock is set for New York time, he is prepared for sleep, whereas residents of Paris are waking.
Paris (3:00 A.M.)
New York (9:00 P.M.)
West-to-east travel (6-hour flight)
New York (3:00 A.M.)
Paris (9:00 A.M.)
Paris (3:00 A.M.)
East-to-west travel (6 hour flight)
New York (9:00 P.M.)
Paris (9:00 P.M.)
New York (3:00 P.M.)
3 Traveler arrives in New York at 9:00 P.M. and needs to stay up only a little longer than normal for his biological clock to adjust.
4 Traveler leaves Paris at 9:00 P.M., when it's 3:00 P.M. in New York.

FIGURE 13-5 Jet Lag. Disruption in the entrainment of a person's biological clock that may be brought on by jet travel is undoubtedly more pronounced in west-to-east travel because the disruption in the person's circadian rhythm is dramatic. On the return journey, the traveler's biological clock has a much easier adjustment to make.

The results of studies show that adapting to such a change is difficult and stressful. Adaptations to shift work are better if people first work the evening shift (3:00 P.M. to 11:00 P.M.) for a time before beginning the graveyard shift.

Long-distance air travel—say, from North America to Europe or Asia—also demands a large and difficult time adjustment. For example, travelers flying east from New York to Paris will begin their first European day just when their biological clocks are signaling that it time for sleep (**Figure 13-5**). The difference between a person's circadian rhythm and the daylight cycle in a new environment can produce the feeling of disorientation and fatigue called **jet lag.**

The west-to-east traveler generally has a more difficult adjustment than does the east-to-west traveler, who needs to stay up only a little longer than normal. The occasional traveller may cope with jet lag quite well, but frequent travellers, such as airline personnal, face a substantial adaptive challenge.

REVIEW: A Clock for All Seasons

- ✔ Many behaviors occur in a rhythmic pattern in relation to time. These biorhythms may display a yearly cycle (circannual rhythms) or a daily cycle (circadian rhythms).
- ✔ Biological rhythms are timed internally by regions of the nervous system that serve as biological clocks to regulate most of our circadian rhythms, especially our sleep–wake cycles.

Light pollution Exposure to artifical light that changes activity patterns and so distrupts circadian rhythms.
Jet lag Fatigue and disorientation resulting from rapid travel through time zones and exposure to a changed light–dark cycle.

✔ Although biological clocks keep fairly good time, their periods may be slightly shorter or longer than 24-hours unless they are reset each day. Their spontaneous periods are called free-running rhythms.

✔ Zeitgebers are environmental cues that reset the biological clock. Light pollution and jet lag can disrupt circadian rhythms.

Neural Basis of the Biological Clock

Curt Richter (1965) was the first researcher to attempt to locate biological clocks in the brain. In the 1930s, he captured wild rats and tested them in activity wheels. He found that the animals ran, ate, and drank when the lights were off and were relatively quiescent when the lights were on.

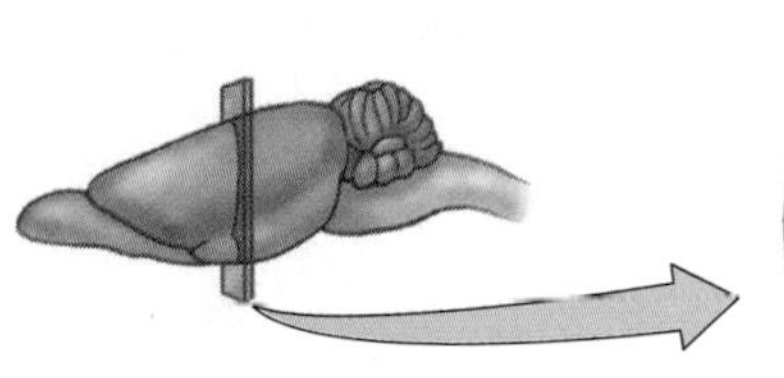
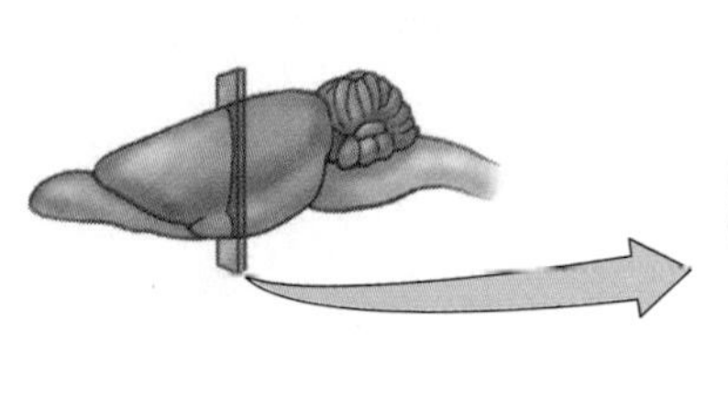

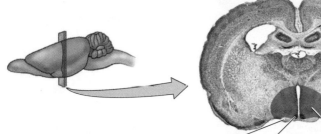

FIGURE 13-6 Suprachiasmatic Nucleus in a Rat Brain.

Richter proposed that the biological clock acts as a pacemaker to instruct other neural structures when they should produce the behaviors for which they are responsible. Thus, behaviors such as running, eating, drinking, and changes in body temperature occur when the master pacemaker tells their relevant neural areas that it is time to begin.

By inserting an electrode into the brain to damage brain tissue with electric current, Richter found that animals lost their circadian rhythms after damage to the hypothalamus. Subsequently, by making much more discrete lesions, experimenters have shown that a region of the hypothalamus illustrated in **Figure 13-6**, the **suprachiasmatic nucleus** (SCN), acts as a biological clock (Ralph and Lehman, 1991).

The SCN is located just above (*supra*) the optic chiasm; hence its name.

The SCN receives information about light through the **retinohypothalamic pathway.** The pathway begins with specialized cones and bipolar cells in the retina that are connected to ganglion cells. The ganglion cells project to SCN cells and use glutamate as their primary neurotransmitter in the SCN. When stimulated by light, the retinohypothalamic pathway excites the SCN and entrains its rhythm. Many other cellular pacemakers—in the retina and the pineal gland and all body cells—can oscillate, but the SCN is considered the master pacemaker.

Figure 9-8 diagrams the cellular structure of the retina. Visual fibers carrying information about light also go to an area of the thalamus (the intergeniculate leaflet), but we limit our consideration of rhythms to the role of the SCN.

The pineal gland can be directly activated by light to act as a pacemaker in some species of birds. When the heads of such birds are painted black, the pineal gland's pacemaker activities are blocked. Because the pineal gland can respond directly to light, it has been called the "third eye."

Chapter 1 recounts how, in the mid-1600s, Descartes chose the pineal gland, diagrammed in Figure 1-4, as the seat of the mind.

Suprachiasmatic Rhythms

Evidence for the SCN's role in circadian rhythms comes from a number of lines of evidence demonstrating that its neurons have intrinsic rhythmic activity (Schibler, 2009):

1. If the suprachiasmatic nuclei are selectively damaged in rodents, the animals still eat, drink, exercise, and sleep a normal amount, but they do things at haphazard times.
2. The metabolic activity of the SCN is higher during the light period of the day–night cycle than it is during the dark period. If a form of glucose that is taken up by metabolically active cells but is not used by them and cannot escape from them is tagged with a radioactive label, cells that are more active will subsequently give off more radioactivity. When this tracer is injected into rodents, more tracer is found in the SCN after injections given in the light period of the light–dark cycle

Suprachiasmatic nucleus (SCN) Main pacemaker of circadian rhythms located just above the optic chiasm.
Retinohypothalamic pathway Neural route from a subset of cone receptors in the retina to the suprachiasmatic nucleus of the hypothalamus; allows light to entrain the rhythmic activity of the SCN.

than after injections given in the dark period. This experiment demonstrates that suprachiasmatic cells have rhythmic metabolic activity and that the SCN is special in this respect.

3. Recording electrodes placed in the SCN confirm that neurons in this region are more active during the light period of the cycle than during the dark period.
4. If all the pathways into and out of the SCN are cut, the neurons of the suprachiasmatic nucleus maintain their rhythmic electrical activity.

Together, the results of these experiments show that the suprachiasmatic neurons have an intrinsically rhythmic pattern of activity.

Dual Clocks

How is SCN rhythmicity generated? When the SCN is removed from the brain, maintained in a laboratory dish, and subjected to electrical recording, the neurons maintain their rhythmic activity. Furthermore, if the neurons are isolated from one another, each is rhythmic, but some cells have a different rhythmicity than others.

This cellular individuality suggests that the SCN has components that produce rhythms with different periods. Findings from studies on the genes that control rhythms in fruit flies suggest that there are two separate groups of circadian neurons. *M-cells* control morning activity and need light for entrainment; *E-cells* control evening activity and need darkness for entrainment (Stoleru et al., 2007).

This finding shows that different pacemaker cells control different components of activity cycles. In mammals, the ventrolateral part of the SCN is controlled by the retinohypothalamic pathway and may be functionally equivalent to the M-cell system, while cells in the dorsomedial SCN are equivalnt to E cells. Individual differences in genes and activity in this dual system may explain why some people are "morning" and some are "evening" people (Lee et al., 2009).

Immortal Time

How do suprachiasmatic cells develop their rhythmic activity? The endogenous rhythm is not learned. In experiments in which animals are raised in constant darkness, their behavior still becomes rhythmic. In experiments in which animals have been maintained without entraining cues for a number of generations, each generation continues to display rhythmic behavior. Even if the mother has received a lesion of the SCN so that her behavior is not rhythmic, the behavior of the offspring is rhythmic.

A line of evidence supporting the idea that suprachiasmatic cells are genetically programmed for rhythmicity comes from studies performed in Canada by Martin Ralph and his coworkers with the use of transplantation techniques (Ralph and Lehman, 1991). **Figure 13-7** illustrates the experiment.

First, hamsters are tested in constant dim light or in constant darkness to establish their free-running rhythm. They then receive a suprachiasmatic lesion followed by another test to show that the lesion has abolished their rhythmicity. Finally, the hamsters receive transplants of suprachiasmatic cells obtained from hamster embryos. About 60 days later, the hamsters again show rhythmic activity, demonstrating that the transplanted cells have become integrated into the host brain and have reestablished rhythmic behavior.

FIGURE 13-7 Circadian Rhythms Restored by Neural Transplantation. Adapted from "Transplantation: A New Tool in the Analysis of the Mammalian Hypothalamic Circadian Pacemaker," by M. R. Ralph and M. N. Lehman, 1991 *Trends in Neurosciences, 14,* p. 363.

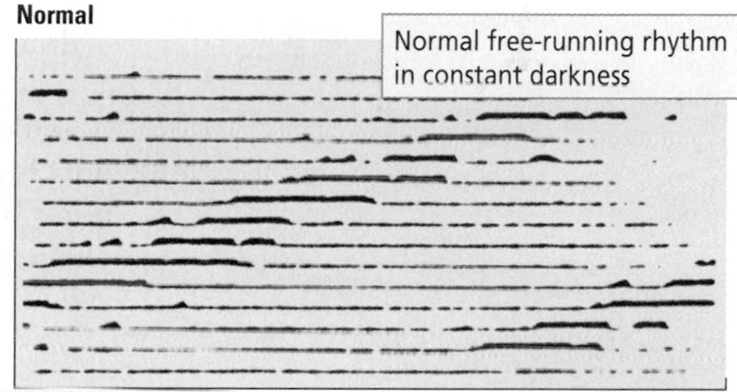

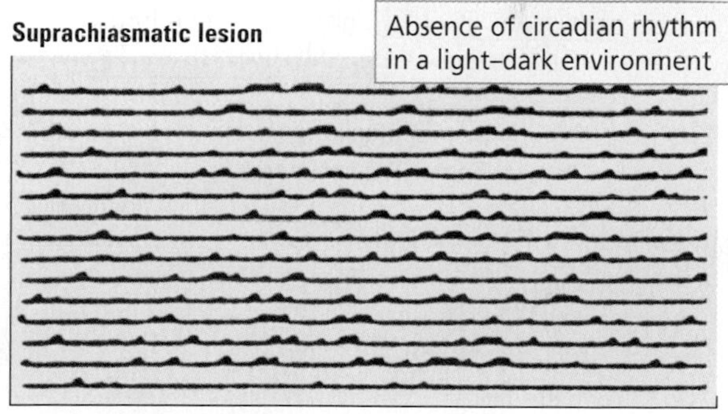

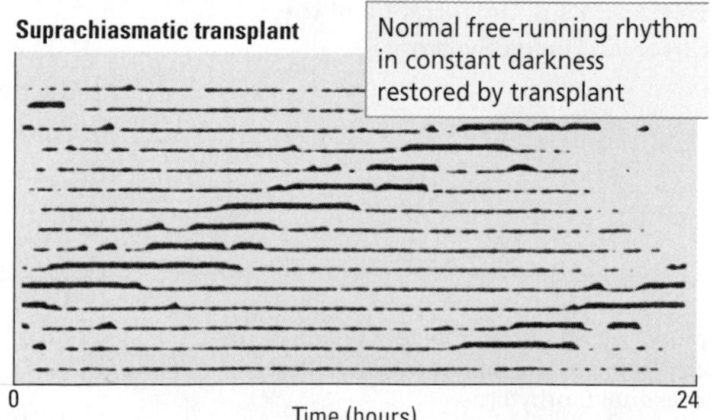

What Ticks?

Chapter 3 explains how genes code proteins, the building blocks of cells and of interaction among cells.

Considerable research is being directed toward determining what genes control the ticking of the circadian clock. Because a single suprachiasmatic neuron displays a circadian rhythm, the timing device must be in the neuron itself, possibly entailing an increase and decrease of one or more proteins made by the cell. Just as the back-and-forth swing of a pendulum makes a grandfather clock tick, the increase and decrease in this protein makes the cell tick once each day.

The actual way that the oscillation is produced is a little more complex than this description suggests.

According to this notion, a protein is made until it crests at a certain level. At that point it inhibits its own production. When its level falls to a critical point, production again rises. In turn, the electrical activity of the cell is linked to protein oscillation, allowing the cell to control other cells during a part of the oscillation.

Findings from a number of lines of evidence suggest that at least a half dozen genes and the proteins they make form two interlocking loops that produce the circadian rhythm of suprachiasmatic cells in mammals (Tournier et al., 2009). Although the mechanism is not fully understood, excitation of suprachiasmatic cells through the retinohypothalamic pathway degrades one of the proteins to entrain the sequence of biochemical steps in the interlocking loops.

Pacemaking Circadian Rhythms

The suprachiasmatic nucleus is of itself not responsible for directly producing rhythmic behavior. For example, after the SCN has been damaged, the behavioral activities of drinking and eating and of sleeping and wakefulness still occur. They no longer occur at appropriate times, however.

An explanation for how the SCN controls biological rhythms is illustrated in **Figure 13-8.** In this model, light entrains the SCN, and the pacemaker in turn drives a number of "slave" oscillators. Each slave oscillator is responsible for the rhythmic occurrence of one activity. In other words, drinking and eating, body temperature, and sleeping and waking are each produced by a separate slave oscillator.

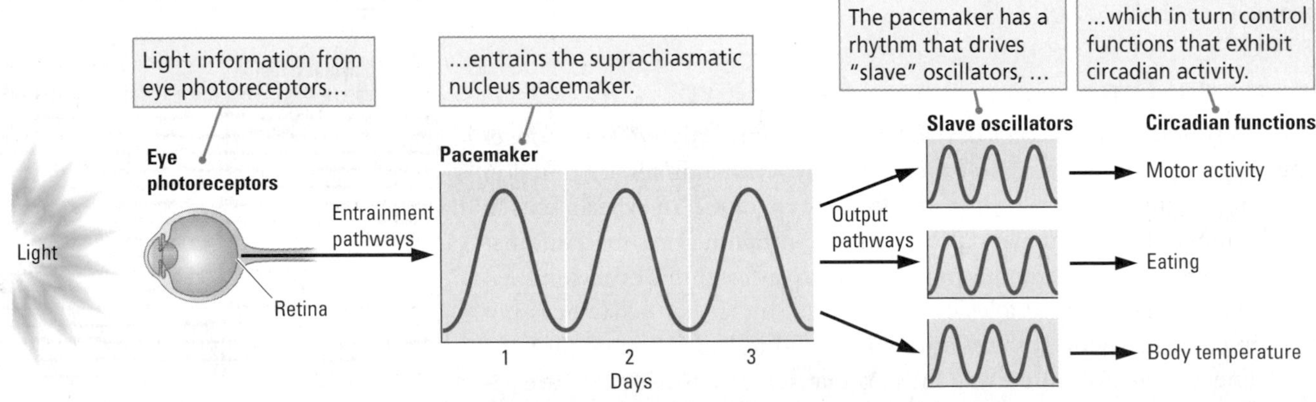

FIGURE 13-8 Organization of the Circadian Timing System.

The signal, or "chime," that synchronizes slave oscillators may be both hormonal and a neurotransmitter signal from axons of suprachiasmatic neurons. Evidence that a hormone takes part is discussed in Research Focus 13-3, "Synchronizing Biorhythms at the Molecular Level." A protein made and secreted by suprachiasmatic cells may be one chime; other rhythms may be driven by neural connections to slave oscillators.

Pacemaking Circannual Rhythms

Melatonin Hormone secreted by the pineal gland during the dark phase of the day–night cycle; influences daily and seasonal biorhythms.

The suprachiasmatic nucleus not only controls daily rhythms, it also can control circannual rhythms. Russel Reiter (1980) illustrates this form of pacemaking in hamsters. Hamsters are summertime (long-day) breeders. As the days lengthen in springtime,

RESEARCH FOCUS 13-3

Synchronizing Biorhythms at the Molecular Level

To be effective, a biological clock needs a Zeitgeber that tracks light changes during cycles of day and night, an oscillator for timekeeping, and a signal that can drive slave oscillators. The signal that tracks light changes is carried by the retinohypothalamic pathway that projects from special retinal receptors through ganglion neurons. These neurons have excitatory glutaminergic synapses onto the cells of the suprachiasmatic nucleus.

The retinohypothalamic pathway stimulates SCN neurons to be active during the light part of the cycle. Findings from molecular-genetic studies into the clockwork show that a number of genes and their protein products take part in timing the SCN oscillation. The genes *Period* and *Cryptochrome* encode the oscillator.

Period and *Cryptochrome* are switched on by the proteins Clock and Bmal and switched off by the protein complex of Per and Cry so that gene turn-on follows gene turn-off in an inexorable daily loop. Mutations either in *Period* or *Cryptochrome* can lead to inherited sleep disorders. Modifications in one gene that times the circadian oscillator can influence whether an individual will be "early to bed and early to rise" while changes in another gene can influence whether an individual will be "late to bed and late to rise."

The SCN sends neural projections as well as a chemical signal to slave oscillators in many other parts of the brain to synchronize body temperature, metabolic activity, growth-hormone release, sleep activity, and so forth, with the light–dark cycle. The chemical signal may be a protein called prokineticin 2 (PK2). Thus, PK2 SCN "chimes" to synchronize the oscillations of many brain regions with the ocillations of the SCN (Li et al., 2009).

Slave oscillators can be influenced by other Zeitgebers as well. These include motivation, schedules of food intake, exercise, and social influences (Amir and Stewart, 2009). For mothers with young children, the children's activity cycles serve as potent Zeitgiber for regulating her circadian oscillators. Consequently, it is possible to produce rhythmical circadian oscillations by introducing regularity into daily activities.

the gonads of male hamsters grow and release hormones that stimulate sexual behavior. As the days shorten in the winter, the gonads shrink, the amount of the hormones produced by the gonads decreases, and the males lose interest in sex.

During the dark phase of the day–night cycle, the pineal gland secretes the hormone **melatonin,** which influences daily and seasonal biorhythms. **Figure 13-9** shows that, when a hamster's melatonin level is low, the gonads enlarge and when it is high, the gonads shrink. The control that the pineal gland exerts over the gonads is in turn

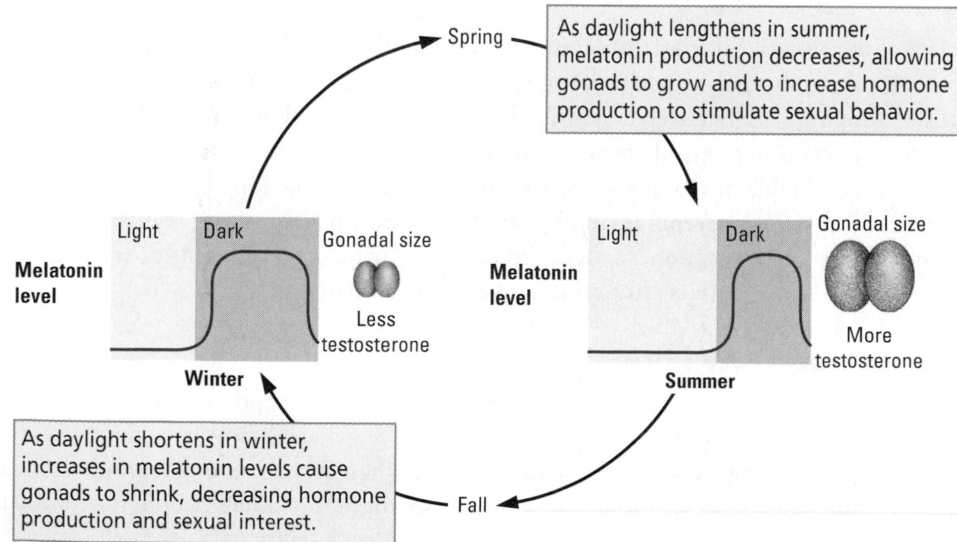

FIGURE 13-9 A Hamster's Circannual Pacemaker. Adapted from "The Pineal and Its Hormones in the Control of Reproduction in Mammals," by R. J. Reiter, 1980, *Endocrinology Review, 1*, p. 120.

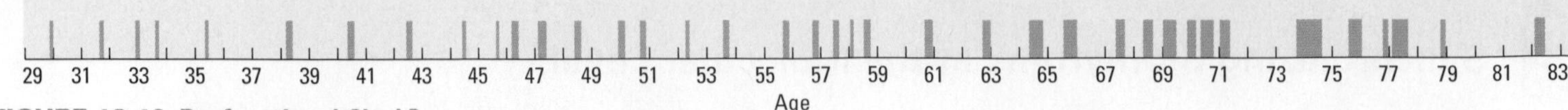

FIGURE 13-10 Dysfunctional Clock? Attacks of mental illness displayed by the English writer Mary Lamb through her adult life appear to have had a cyclical component. Such observations would be difficult to obtain today, because the drugs used to treat psychiatric disorders can mask abnormal biorhythms. Adapted from *Biological Clocks in Medicine and Psychiatry* (p. 92), by C. P. Richter, 1965, Springfield, IL: Charles C Thomas.

controlled by the suprachiasmatic nucleus. Through a rather indirect pathway, the SCN drives the pineal gland as a slave oscillator.

During the daylight period of the circadian cycle, the SCN inhibits melatonin secretion by the pineal gland. Thus, as the days become shorter, the period of inhibition becomes shorter and thus the period in which melatonin is released becomes longer. When the period of daylight is shorter than 12 hours, melatonin release becomes sufficiently long to inhibit the hamster's gonads, and they shrink.

Melatonin also influences the testes of animals that are short-day breeders, such as sheep and deer, which mate in the fall and early winter. The effect of melatonin on reproductive behavior in these species is the reverse of that in the hamster: their reproductive activities begin as melatonin release increases.

In his classic book *Biological Clocks in Medicine and Psychiatry,* Curt Richter (1965) hypothesized that many physical and behavioral disorders might be caused by "shocks," either physical or environmental, that upset the timing of biological clocks. For example, the record of psychotic attacks suffered by the English writer Mary Lamb, illustrated in **Figure 13-10,** is one of many rhythmic records that Richter thought represented the action of an abnormally functioning biological clock.

REVIEW: Neural Basis of the Biological Clock

- ✔ A number of nuclei in the brain serve as diurnal biological clocks, including the suprachiasmatic nucleus of the hypothalamus and the pineal gland of the thalamus.
- ✔ Cues from the environment called Zeitgebers entrain the suprachiasmatic nucleus to control daily rhythms. Light cues activate the SCN via the retinohypothalamic pathway. Damage to the SCN disrupts the rhythm of daily behaviors.
- ✔ Pacemaking produced by the suprachiasmatic nucleus is a product of its cells, which activate slave oscillators via both chemical signals and anatomical connections.

Sleep Stages and Dreaming

Most of us are awake during the day and asleep at night. Both behavioral states are more complex than our daily experiences suggest. Waking behavior encompasses some periods in which we are relatively inactive, other periods in which we are still but mentally active, and yet other periods in which we are physically active. Our sleeping behavior is similarly variable: it consists of periods of resting, napping, long bouts of sleep, and various sleep-related events including snoring, dreaming, thrashing about, and even sleepwalking. In this section, we describe some of the behavioral events of waking and sleeping and some of the neural processes that underlie them.

Measuring How Long We Sleep

A crude measure of sleeping and waking behavior is the self-report: people record in a diary when they wake and when they retire to sleep. The diaries show considerable variation in sleep–waking behavior. People sleep more when they are young than when they are old. Most people sleep about 7 to 8 hours per night, but some people sleep much more or much less than that, even as little as 1 hour each day.

Beta rhythm (β) Fast brain-wave activity pattern associated with a waking EEG.

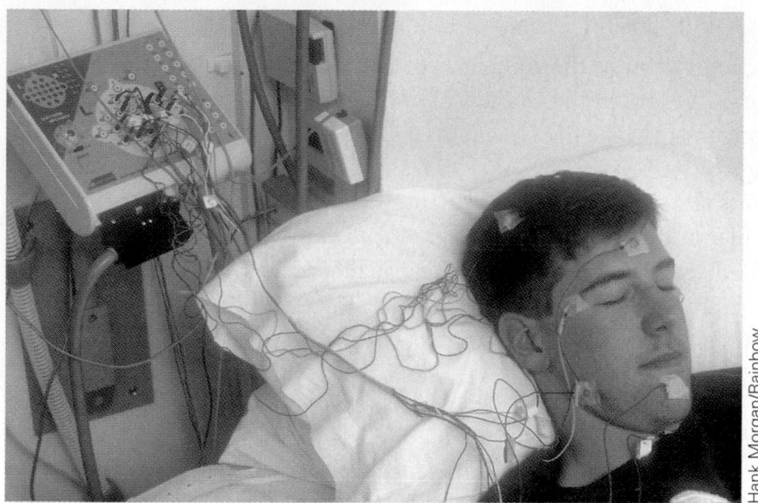

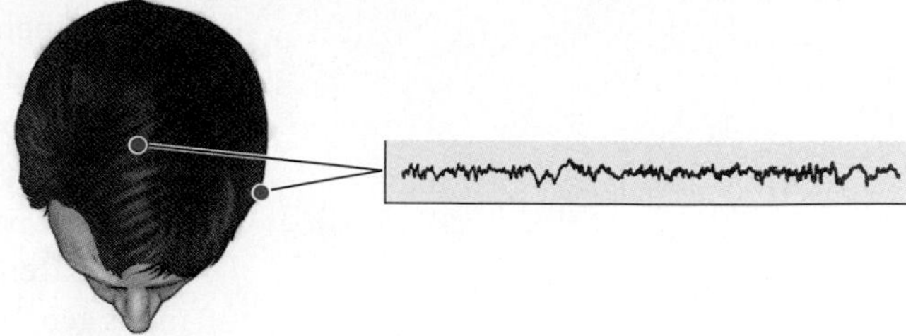

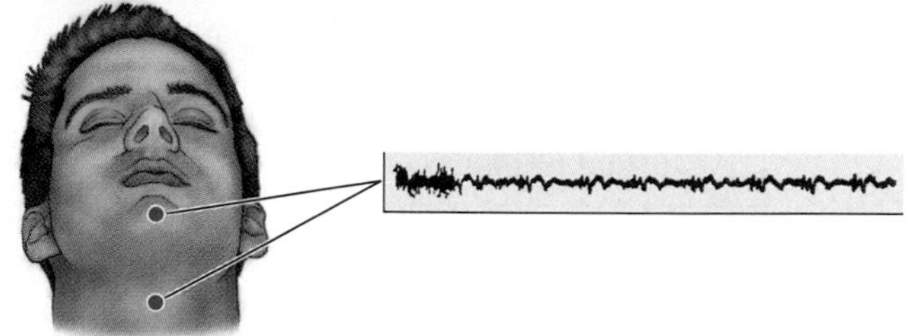

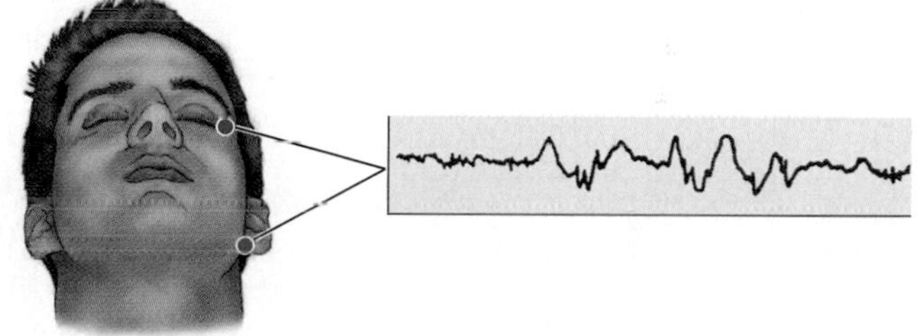

FIGURE 13-11 Sleep-Laboratory Setup. Electronic equipment records readouts from the electrodes attached to the sleeping subject. **(A)** Electroencephalogram made from a point on the skull relative to a neutral point on the ear. **(B)** Electromyogram made between two muscles, such as those on the chin and throat. **(C)** Electrooculogram made between the eye and a neutral point on the ear

Some people nap for a brief period in the daytime, and others never nap. Benjamin Franklin is credited with the aphorism "Early to bed and early to rise makes a man healthy, wealthy, and wise," but measures of sleep behavior indicate that the correlation that Franklin proposed does not actually exist. Apparently, variations in sleeping times are quite normal.

Measuring Sleep in the Laboratory

Laboratory sleep studies allow researchers to accurately measure sleep and to record physiological changes associated with sleep. Measurement of sleep requires recording a number of electrical body signals with a polygraph. **Figure 13-11** illustrates a typical polygraph setup in a sleep laboratory and some commonly used measures.

Chapter 6 reviews several methods for measuring the brain's electrical activity.

Electrodes pasted onto standard locations on the skull's surface yield an electroencephalogram (EEG), a record of brain-wave activity. Electrodes placed on muscles of the neck provide an electromyogram (EMG), a record of muscle activity. Electrodes located near the eyes provide an electrooculogram (EOG), a record of eye movements. A thermometer also may be used to measure body temperature.

Stages of Waking and Sleeping

Biological measurements show that sleep is not a unitary state but consists of a number of different stages. For example, the EEG recording shows distinct patterns of brainwave activity as the neocortex generates distinct rhythmic patterns from states categorized as awake, drowsy, sleeping, and dreaming.

Consult Figure 6-10 to review EEG brainwave patterns that reflect a range of conscious states in humans.

Waking State

When a person is awake, the EEG pattern consists of small-amplitude (height) waves with a fast frequency (repetition period). This pattern, the **beta rhythm** (β), is also called fast activity, activated EEG, or waking EEG. The waves of the beta rhythm have a frequency ranging from 15 to 30 Hz (times per second). The EMG is active, and the EOG indicates that the eyes move.

Drowsy State

When a person becomes drowsy, the EEG indicates that the fast-wave activity of the neocortex disappears. The amplitude of the EEG waves increases, and their frequency becomes slower. Concurrently, the EMG remains active, but the EOG indicates that the eyes are not moving.

When participants relax and close their eyes, they may produce the *alpha rhythm*—large, extremely regular brain waves that have a frequency ranging from 7 to 11 Hz. Humans generate alpha rhythms in the region of the visual cortex at the back of the brain, and the rhythms abruptly stop if a relaxed person is disturbed or opens his or her eyes. Not everyone displays alpha rhythms, and some people display them much better than others.

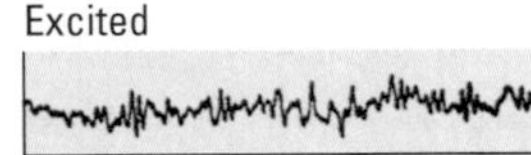

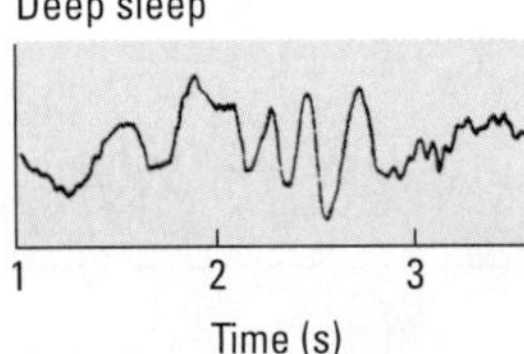

Sleeping State

As participants enter deep sleep, they produce yet slower, larger EEG waves known as **delta rhythms** (δ), also known as slow-wave activity or resting activity. Delta-rhythm waves have a frequency of 1 to 3 Hz. The slowing of brain-wave activity is also associated with the loss of consciousness that characterizes sleep. Still, the EMG indicates muscle activity, although the EOG indicates that the eyes do not move.

Dreaming State

Sleep consists of periods during which a sleeper is relatively still and periods when the mouth, fingers, and toes twitch. This behavior is readily observed in household pets and bed partners. In 1955, Eugene Aserinsky and Nathaniel Kleitman (Lamberg, 2003), working at the University of Chicago, observed that the twitching periods are also associated with rapid eye movements (REM). Other than twitches and eye movements, the EMG indicates that muscles are inactive.

REM coincides with distinct brain-wave patterns recorded on the EEG that suggest that the participant is awake, with the eyes flickering back and forth behind the sleeper's closed eyelids (see Dement, 1972). By accumulating and analyzing REM recorded on EEGs, the Chicago investigators were the first to identify **REM sleep,** the fast-wave pattern displayed by the neocortical EEG record, and its association with vivid dreams. The EEG and EOG record suggested that dreaming participants were awake, even though Aserinsky and Kleitman confirmed that they really were asleep.

The delta-rhythm sleep period during which the EEG pattern is slow and large and the EOG is inactive is called **NREM** (for non-REM) **sleep** to distinguish it from REM sleep. It is sometimes called **slow-wave sleep.** We use the terms REM and NREM sleep.

A Typical Night's Sleep

With this distinction between sleep phases in mind, **Figure 13-12**A displays the EEG patterns associated with waking, sleeping, and dreaming. NREM sleep is divided into four stages on the basis of EEG records. Notice that the main change that characterizes these stages is the increase in size and slowing in speed of brain waves in the progression from stage 1 sleep through stage 4 sleep.

The designation of these stages assumes that the sleeper moves from relatively shallow sleep in stage 1 to deep sleep in stage 4. Self-reports from participants who are awakened from sleep at different times suggest that stage 4 is the deepest sleep, and participants act groggy when disturbed during these periods. As described earlier, REM sleep is distinctive because, although a participant is asleep, EEG activity shows a waking pattern.

On the basis of a brain-activity record from one participant during a typical night's sleep, Figure 13-12B graphs when these different sleep stages actually occur and how long they last in the course of a night's sleep. Notice that the depth of sleep changes

Delta rhythm (δ) Slow brain-wave activity pattern associated with deep sleep.
REM sleep Fast brain-wave pattern displayed by the neocortical EEG record during sleep.
NREM (non-REM) sleep Slow-wave sleep associated with delta rhythms.
Slow-wave sleep NREM sleep.
Atonia No tone; condition of complete muscle inactivity produced by the inhibition of motor neurons.

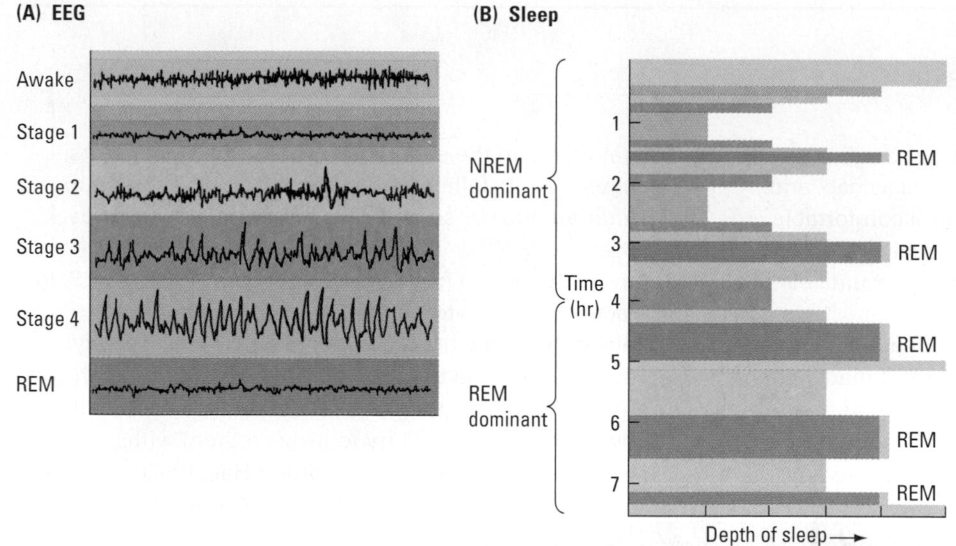

FIGURE 13-12 Sleep Recording and Revelations. (A) Electroencephalograph patterns associated with waking, with the four NREM sleep stages, and with REM sleep. (B) In a typical night's sleep, a person undergoes a number of sleep-state changes, roughly in 90-minute periods. NREM sleep dominates the early sleep periods, and REM sleep dominates later sleep. The duration of each sleep stage is reflected in the thickness of each bar, which is color-coded to the corresponding stage in part A. The depth of each stage is graphed as the relative length of the bar. Adapted from "Sleep and Dreaming," by D. D. Kelley, in E. R. Kandel, J. H. Schwartz, and T. M. Jessell (Eds.), *Principles of Neuroscience*, 1991, New York: Elsevier, p. 794.

several times. The participant cycles through the four stages of NREM sleep and then enters REM sleep. This NREM–REM sequence lasts approximately 90 minutes and is typically repeated about four times in the course of the sleep period.

The labels indicating REM sleep in Figure 13-12B tell us that the durations of the different sleep stages roughly divide the sleep period into two parts, the first dominated by NREM sleep, the second dominated by REM sleep. Body temperature is lowest (about 1.5 degrees below a normal temperature of 37.7 degrees Celsius during the first part of the sleep period and rises during the second part.

Findings from sleep-laboratory studies confirm that the sleep patterns of individual people are highly variable; they also confirm that REM sleep takes up a substantial proportion of sleep time. Adults who typically sleep about 8 hours spend about 2 of those hours in REM sleep. A person's REM durations may also vary at different times of life. Periods of REM sleep increase during growth spurts, in conjunction with physical exertion, and for women during pregnancy.

The time spent in REM sleep also changes dramatically over the life span. As is illustrated in **Figure 13-13**, most people sleep less as they grow older. Furthermore, in the first 2 years of life, REM sleep makes up nearly half of sleep time, but it declines proportionately until, in middle age, it constitutes little more than 10 percent of sleep time.

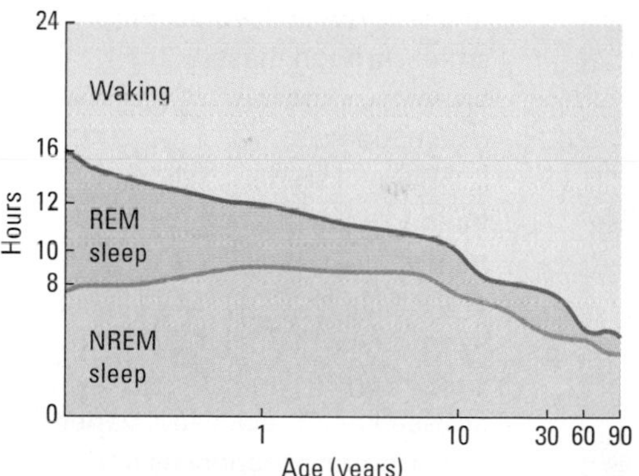

FIGURE 13-13 Sleeping and Waking over the Life Span. The amount of time that humans spend sleeping decreases with age. The proportion of REM sleep is especially high in the first few years of life. Adapted from "Ontogenetic Development of the Human Sleep-Dream Cycle," by H. P. Roffward, J. Muzio, and W. C. Dement (1966), *Science, 152,* 604-619.

NREM Sleep and REM Sleep

Although many people may think that sleep is an inactive period, a remarkable range of activities takes place during sleep. During NREM sleep, body temperature declines, heart rate decreases, blood flow decreases, body weight decreases because of water loss in perspiration, and levels of growth hormone increase.

NREM sleep is also the time during which we toss and turn in bed, pull on the covers, and engage in other movements (see Clinical Focus 13-4, "Restless Legs Syndrome"). If we talk in our sleep, we do so during NREM sleep. If we make flailing movements of the limbs, such as banging an arm or kicking a foot, we usually do so in NREM sleep. Some people even get up and walk while asleep, and this "sleepwalking" takes place during NREM sleep. It is remarkable that all these conditions occur during a period that is often described as quiet and inactive.

REM sleep is no less exciting and remarkable than NREM sleep. During REM sleep, our eyes move, our toes, fingers, and mouths twitch, and males have penile erections. Still, we are paralyzed, as indicated by **atonia** ("no tone"), the absence of muscle tone

CLINICAL FOCUS 13-4

Restless Legs Syndrome

I've always been a fairly untalented sleeper. Even as a child, it would take me some time to fall asleep, and I would often roll around searching for a comfortable position before going under. But my real difficulties with sleeping did not manifest themselves until early adulthood. . . .

Initially, my symptoms consisted of a mild tingling in my legs. It caused me to be fidgety and made it hard to fall asleep. Eventually, I went through a number of days without much sleep and reached a point where I simply could not function. I went to a doctor who prescribed a small course of sleeping medication (a benzodiazepine). I was able to get good sleep and my sleep cycle seemed to get back on track. Over the next decade I had periodic bouts of tingling in my legs which caused me to be fidgety and interfered with sleep. As time passed, the bouts occurred with increasing frequency and the symptoms became more noticeable and uncomfortable. I would simply suffer through these bouts, sleeping poorly and paying the consequences. . . .

Being a student, I did not have a regular doctor. Unfortunately, most physicians I met did not know about restless legs syndrom or RLS, and thought I was "drug seeking" or merely stressed out. I received a variety of patronizing responses and found these experiences insulting and demeaning. . . .

When I took my current position, I started seeing a doctor on a regular basis, and experimented with better medications. By this time, my sleep was being seriously affected by RLS. The sensations in my legs were something like a combination of an ache in my muscles (much like one gets after exercising) and an electrical, tingling sensation. They would be briefly relieved with movement, such as stretching, rubbing, contracting my muscles, or changing position, but would return within seconds. In fact, my wife says my cycle is about 13 to 15 seconds between movements. I do this either when awake or during sleep. Trying not to move greatly increases the discomfort—much like trying to not scratch a very bad itch. The symptoms get worse in the evening and at night. Most nights, I have trouble falling asleep. Other nights, I wake up after an hour or so and then have trouble going back under. . . .

I am very up front about the fact that I have RLS. In fact, whenever I teach the topic of sleep and sleep disorders in my brain and behavior classes, I always make some time to talk about my experiences with RLS. Occasionally, students approach me with their own difficulties, and I try to provide them with information and resources.) Stuart Hall, Ph.D., University of Montana)

B. W. Hoffmann/Envision

Restless legs syndrome (RLS) is a sleep disorder in which a person experiences unpleasant sensations in the legs described as creeping, crawling, tingling, pulling, or pain. The sensations are usually in the calf area but may be felt anywhere from the thigh to the ankle. One or both legs may be affected; some people also feel the sensations in their arms.

Many people with RLS have a related sleep disorder called *periodic limb movement in sleep.* PLMS is characterized by involuntary jerking or bending leg movements that typically occur every 10 to 60 seconds during the sleep period. Some people experience hundreds of such movements per night that can wake them, disturb their sleep, and annoy bed partners.

RLS may affect as much as 10 percent of the population and is more common in women than in men. In mild cases, massage, exercise, stretching, and hot baths may be helpful. For more severe cases, patients can restrict their intake of caffeine and take benzodiazepines to help them get to sleep.

L-dopa, a drug that is also used to treat Parkinson's disease, is an effective treatment, but there is no evidence that RLS is more frequent in Parkinson's patients, whose condition is related to low dopamine function. Nor is RLS associated with gross changes in dopamine cells in the brain (Thomas and Watson, 2008). RLS has been associated with poor iron uptake, especially in the substantia nigra, and some people have been helped by iron supplements. One focus of research into RSL is to improve iron absorption by the brain.

due to the inhibition of motor neurons. Atonia is recorded on an electromyogram as the absence of muscle activity.

You can get an idea of what REM sleep is like by observing a cat or dog. At the onset of REM sleep, the animal usually subsides into a sprawled posture as the paralysis of its muscles sets in. **Figure 13-14** illustrates the sleep postures of a horse. Horses can sleep while standing up by locking their knee joints, and they can sleep while lying down with their heads held slightly up. At these times, they are in NREM sleep. When they are completely sprawled out, they are in REM sleep.

During REM sleep, mammals' limbs twitch visibly, and, if you look carefully at the face of a dog or cat, you will also see the skin of the snout twitch and the eyes move behind the eyelids. It might seem strange that an animal that is paralyzed can make small twitching movements, but the neural pathways that mediate these twitches are presumably spared the paralysis. One explanation for the twitching movements of the eyes, face, and distal parts of the limbs is that such movements may help to maintain blood flow in those parts of the body.

An additional change resulting from atonia during REM sleep is that mechanisms that regulate body temperature stop working and body temperature moves toward room temperature. The sleeper may wake up from REM sleep feeling cold or hot, depending on the temperature of the room.

Courtesy of Ian Whishaw

FIGURE 13-14 Nap Time. Horses usually seek an open, sunny area for brief periods of sleep. I. Q. W.'s horse, Lady Jones, illustrates three sleep postures. (*Top*) She displays NREM sleep, standing with legs locked and head down. (*Middle*) She displays NREM sleep, lying down with head up. (*Bottom*) She is in REM sleep, in which all postural and muscle tone is lost.

Dreaming

The most remarkable aspect of REM sleep—dreaming—was discovered by William Dement and Nathaniel Kleitman in 1957 (Dement, 1972). When participants were awakened from REM sleep, they reported that they had been having vivid dreams. In contrast, participants aroused from NREM sleep were much less likely to report that they had been dreaming, and the dreams that they did report were much less vivid. Children may experience brief, very frightening dreams called *night terrors,* which also occur in NREM sleep. Night terrors can be so vivid that the child may continue to experience the dream and the fear after they awaken.

The technique of electrical recording from a sleeping participant in a sleep laboratory made it possible to subject dreams to experimental analysis, and such studies provided some objective answers to a number of interesting questions concerning dreaming.

The first question that studies of dreaming answered was How often do people dream? Reports by people on their dreaming behavior had previously suggested that dreaming was quite variable: some people reported that they dreamed frequently and others reported that they never dreamed. Waking participants up during periods of REM showed that everyone dreams, that they dream a number of times each night, and that dreams last longer as a sleep session progresses. Those who claimed not to dream were presumably forgetting their dreams. Perhaps people forget their dreams because they do not wake up in the course of a dream or immediately afterward, thus allowing subsequent NREM sleep activity to erase the memory of the dream.

Another interesting question that objective measures answered was How long do dreams last? There had been suggestions that dreams last but an instant. By waking people up at different intervals after the onset of REM sleep and matching the reported dream content to the previous duration of REM sleep, researchers were able to show that dreams appear to take place in real time. That is, an action that a person performed in a dream lasts about as long as it would take to perform while awake.

What We Dream About

The study of dreaming in sleep laboratories allows researchers to study some of the questions that have always intrigued people: Why do we dream? What do we dream about? What do dreams mean?

Past explanations of dreaming have ranged from messages from the gods to indigestion. The first modern treatment of dreams was described by the founder of psychoanalysis, Sigmund Freud, in *The Interpretation of Dreams,* published in 1900. Freud reviewed the early literature on dreams, described a methodology for studying them, and provided a theory to explain their meaning. We briefly consider Freud's theory because it remains popular in psychoanalysis and in the arts.

Freud suggested that the function of dreams was the symbolic fulfillment of unconscious wishes. His theory of personality was that people have both a conscious and an unconscious. Freud proposed that the unconscious contains unacknowledged desires and wishes, which are sexual. He further proposed that dreams have two levels of meaning. The *manifest content* of a dream consists of a series of often bizarre images and actions that are only loosely connected. The *latent content* of the dream contains its true meaning, which, when interpreted by a psychoanalyst, provides a coherent account of the dreamer's unconscious wishes.

Freud provided a method for interpreting manifest symbols and reconstructing the latent content of dreams. For example, he pointed out that a dream usually begins with an incident from the previous day, incorporates childhood experiences, and includes ongoing unfulfilled wishes. He also identified a number of types of dreams, such as those that deal with childhood events, anxiety, and wish fulfillment. The content of the dream was important to Freud and other psychoanalysts in clinical practice because, when interpreted, dreams served as a source of insight into a patient's problems.

Other psychoanalysts, unhappy with Freud's emphasis on sexual desire, developed their own methods of interpretation. The psychoanalyst Carl Jung, a contemporary of Freud, proposed that the symbolism of dreams signifies distant human memories encoded in the brain but long since lost to conscious awareness. Jung proposed that dreams allow a dreamer to relive the history of the human race, our "collective unconscious." As more theories of dream interpretation developed, their central weakness became apparent: it was difficult, if not impossible, to know which interpretation was correct.

The dream research of Freud and his contemporaries was impeded by their reliance on a subject's memory of a dream and by the fact that many of their subjects were patients. This situation unquestionably resulted in the selection of the unusual by both the patient and the analyst. Now researchers study dreams more objectively by waking participants and questioning them.

Most dreams are related to events that happened quite recently and concern ongoing problems. Colors of objects, symbols, and emotional content most often relate to events taking place in a person's recent waking period. Calvin Hall and his colleagues (1982) documented more than 10,000 dreams of normal people and found that more than 64 percent are associated with sadness, anxiety, or anger. Only about 18 percent are happy. Hostile acts against the dreamer outnumber friendly acts by more than two to one. Surprisingly, in regard to Freud's theory, only about 1 percent of dreams include sexual feelings or acts.

Contemporary researchers continue to attempt to interpret dream content. The two hypotheses that follow are polar opposites: one sees no meaning in dreams, and the other sees the content of dreams as reflecting biologically adaptive coping mechanisms.

Dreams as Meaningless Brain Activity

J. Allan Hobson (2004), proposed in his *activation–synthesis hypothesis* that, during a dream, the cortex is bombarded by signals from the brainstem, and these signals produce the pattern of waking (or activated) EEG. The cortex, in response to this excitation, generates images, actions, and emotion from personal memory stores. In the absence of external verification, these dream events are fragmented and bizarre and reveal nothing more than that the cortex has been activated.

Furthermore, Hobson proposed, on the basis of PET-imaging results, that part of the frontal cortex is less active in dreaming than in waking. The frontal cortex controls working memory, memory for events that have just happened, and attention. The dreamer has difficulty both in both remembering and linking dream events as they take place and in deciding what dream events should follow other events. On waking, the dreamer may attempt to create a story line for these fragmented, meaningless images.

According to Hobson's hypothesis, dreams are personal in that memories and experiences are activated, but they have no meaning. So, for example, the following dream, with its bizarre, delusional, and fragmented elements, represents images synthesized to accompany brain activation. Any meaning that the dream might seem to have is created by the dreamer after the fact, as was perhaps done by the middle-aged dreamer who recounted this dream:

> I found myself walking in a jungle. Everything was green and fresh and I felt refreshed and content. After some time I encountered a girl whom I did not know. The most remarkable thing about her was her eyes, which had an almost gold color. I was really struck by her eyes not only because of their unique color but also because of their expression. I tried to make out other details of her face and body but her eyes were so dominating that was all I could see. Eventually, however, I noticed that she was dressed in a white robe and was standing very still with her hands at her side. I then noticed that she was in a compound with wire around it. I became concerned that she was a prisoner. Soon, I noticed other people dressed in white robes and they were also standing still or walking slowly without swinging their arms. It was really apparent that they were all prisoners. At this time I was standing by the fence that enclosed them, and I was starting to feel more concerned. Suddenly it dawned on me that I was in the compound and when I looked down at myself I found that I was dressed in a white robe as well. I remember that I suddenly became quite frightened and woke up when I realized that I was exactly like everyone else. The reason that I remembered this dream is the very striking way in which my emotions seemed to be going from contentment, to concern, to fear as the dream progressed. I think that this dream reflected my desire in the 1970s to maintain my individuality. (Recounted by A. W.)

Dreams as a Coping Strategy

Anttio Revonsuo of Finland agrees with Hobson about the content of dreams, but he uses content analysis to argue that dreams are biologically adaptive in that they lead to enhanced coping strategies in dealing with threatening life events (Valli and Revonsuo, 2009). The evolutionary aspect of this "coping hypothesis" is that enhanced performance is especially important for people whose environment typically includes dangerous events that constitute extreme threats to reproductive success. Revonsuo notes that dreams are highly organized and are significantly biased toward threatening images, as was A. W.'s dream. People seldom dream about reading, writing, and calculating, even though these behaviors may occupy much of their day.

Dream threats are the same events that are threatening in waking life (**Figure 13-15**). For example, animals and strange men who could be characterized as "enemies" figure prominently in dreams. Dream content incorporates the current emotional problems of the dreamer and leads to improvements in and adjustments to life problems.

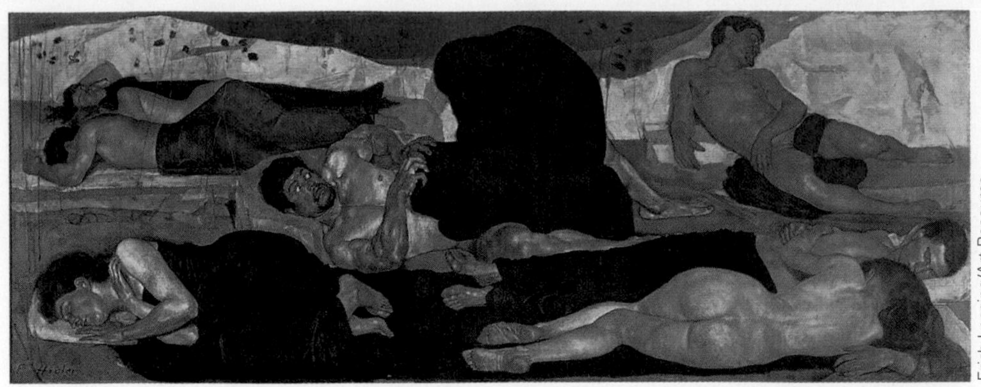

Erich Lessing/Art Resource

FIGURE 13-15 Dream Content. The terrifying visions that may persist even after awakening from a frightening dream are represented in *The Night,* by Swiss painter Ferdinand Hodler. *The Night,* by Ferdinand Hodler (1853–1918), oil on canvas, 116 × 299 cm, Kunstmuseum, Berne, Switzerland.

Recurrent dreams and nightmares generally begin in childhood, when a person is most vulnerable, and are associated with anxiety, threats, and pursuit. The dreamer is usually watching, hiding, or running away. Therefore, the experience of dealing with threats in dreams is adaptive because it can be applied to dealing with real-life threats. To illustrate, a student provided the following account of a dream from childhood that she had dreamed subsequently a few times:

> When I was five years old, I had a dream that at the time frightened me but that I now find somewhat amusing. It took place in the skating rink of my small hometown. There was no ice in the rink, but instead the floor consisted of sod. The women, my mother included, were working in the concession booth, and the men were in the arena, dressed in their work clothes. I was among the children of the town who were lined up in the lobby of the rink. None of the children, including myself, knew why we were lined up. The adults were summoning the children two at a time. I decided to take a peek through the window, and this is what I saw. There was a large circus-ride type metal chair that was connected to a pulley, which would raise the chair to about 20 feet into the air. The seat would be lowered and two children at a time would be placed in it. A noose was then placed around the neck of each and the chair was again raised. Once the chair reached its greatest height, the bottom would drop out of the chair and the children would be hanged (I did not see this but I thought that is what happened to them). At this point, I turned to a friend and said, "Here, Ursula, you can go ahead of me" and I went to my mother and told her what was going on. She smiled as if I were just being difficult and told me that I was to get back in the line. At this point I thought, "Forget it," and I found a place to hide underneath the big wooden bleachers in the lobby. It was dark and I could hear everyone out looking for me. (Recounted by N. W.)

When asked what she thought this dream meant, this student said that she really did not know. When told that it could be an anxiety dream, something common in children, that might represent an activity that she considered stressful, such as competing in figure skating and failing, she said that she did not think that was it. She volunteered, however, that her community's skating rink was natural ice and that it was bitterly cold whenever there was enough ice to go skating. When she had to skate, her feet got cold and her mother almost had to lift her up and drag her out onto the ice. Being dropped out of the chair may have been a symbolic representation of being pushed out onto the ice.

Elements of the dream did represent what went on at the skating rink. Men did prepare the ice and the women did run a concession booth, and she did resist being sent out to skate. The recurrence of the dream could be due to the conflict that she felt about having to do something that exposed her to the cold and her solution in hiding.

REVIEW: Sleep Stages and Dreaming

- ✔ The average length of a night's sleep is from 7 to 8 hours, but some people sleep much less or much more. Sleep consists of two states, rapid eye movement, or REM, sleep and non-REM, or NREM, sleep.
- ✔ Non-REM sleep is divided into four stages on the basis of the EEG record. Brain waves in stage 1 sleep resemble waking patterns and REM sleep. Those in stages 2 through 4 are characterized by progressive slowing of the EEG record. People may have less vivid dreams in non-REM sleep and will toss and turn.
- ✔ There are about four REM sleep periods each night, with each period lengthening as sleep progresses. REM sleep is also marked by muscle paralysis and dreams that are more vivid than those of NREM sleep.
- ✔ Among the various interpretations of the function of dreams, the activation–synthesis hypothesis suggests that they are simply a by-product of the brain's activity and so have no meaning, whereas the coping hypothesis suggests that dreams help people to work out solutions to threatening problems and events.

What Does Sleep Accomplish?

The simplest question that we can ask about sleep is Why do we sleep? Any satisfactory explanation has a lot to account for. As we have seen, sleep is complex and progresses through periodic stages. A variety of hypotheses advance somewhat different explanations for why we sleep.

Sleep As a Passive Process

One of the earliest explanations views sleep as a passive process that takes place as a result of a decrease in sensory stimulation. According to the theory, as evening approaches, there are fewer stimuli to maintain alertness, so sleep sets in.

This theory does not account for the complexity of sleep, nor is it supported by direct experimental investigations. It predicts that, if participants are deprived of all stimulation, they will go to sleep. But findings from sensory-deprivation research fail to bear out this prediction. And the results of sleep experiments reveal that, when participants are isolated in quiet bedrooms, they spend less, not more, time asleep. These results do not support the idea that sleep sets in because there is nothing else to do.

Consult Chapter 12 for more information about sensory-deprivation studies.

The passive-process theory of sleep originally did not consider biological rhythms as a contributing factor, but what we now know about biological rhythms provides some support for a weak version of this idea. The activities in which we engage before we sleep and after we wake up can become Zeitgebers by being associated with light–dark changes. Therefore, exposure to darkness and quiet in the evening and to light and other kinds of stimulation in the morning is one way of synchronizing biological rhythms.

Sleep As a Biological Adaptation

Another explanation holds that sleep is a biologically adaptive behavior influenced by the many ways in which a species adapts to its environment:

- Sleep is designed as an energy-conserving strategy to cope with times when food is scarce, as you learned in Comparative Focus 13-1. Each animal species gathers food at optimal times and conserves energy the rest of the time. If the nutrient value of the food that a species eats is high, the species can spend less time foraging and more time sleeping.

FIGURE 13-16 Do Not Disturb. Biological theories of sleep suggest that sleep is an energy-conserving strategy and serves other functions as well, such as staying safe during the night.

- An animal's behavior is influenced by whether the species is predator or prey. The predator can sleep at its ease; the prey's sleep time is reduced because it must remain alert and ready to fight or flee at unpredictable times (**Figure 13-16**).
- An animal that is strictly nocturnal or diurnal is likely to sleep when it cannot travel easily. Colloquially, Dement proposes: "We sleep to keep from bumping into things in the dark."

The sleep patterns of most animal species are consistent with the adaptive explanation. **Figure 13-17** charts the average sleep time of a number of common mammals. Herbivores, including donkeys, horses, and cows, spend a long time collecting enough food to sustain themselves, which reduces their sleep time. Because they are also prey, their sleep time is further reduced as they watch for predators. Carnivores, including domestic cats and dogs, eat nutrient-rich foods and usually consume most of a day's or even a week's food at a single meal. Because they do not need to eat constantly and because by resting they can conserve energy, carnivores spend a great deal of time each day sleeping.

The behavior of some animals does appear odd, however. Opossums, which spend much of their time asleep, may have specialized in energy conservation as a survival strategy. We humans are average among species in our sleep time, which is presumably indicative of an evolutionary pattern in which food gathering was not an overwhelming preoccupation and predation was not a major concern.

Sleep can contribute to energy conservation in a number of ways. During sleep, energy is not being expended in moving the body or supporting posture. The brain is a major energy user, so switching off the brain during sleep, especially NREM sleep, is another good way to conserve energy. The drop in body temperature that typically accompanies sleep slows metabolic activity, so it too contributes to energy conservation.

A good explanation of sleep must explain not only sleep but also NREM and REM sleep. Before the discovery of REM sleep, Kleitman suggested that animals have a **basic rest–activity cycle** (BRAC) that, for humans, has a period of about 90 minutes (see Dement, 1972). He based his hypothesis on the observation that human infants have frequent feeding periods between which they sleep.

FIGURE 13-17 Average Sleep Time. Sleep time is affected both by the amount of time required to obtain food and by the risk of predation.

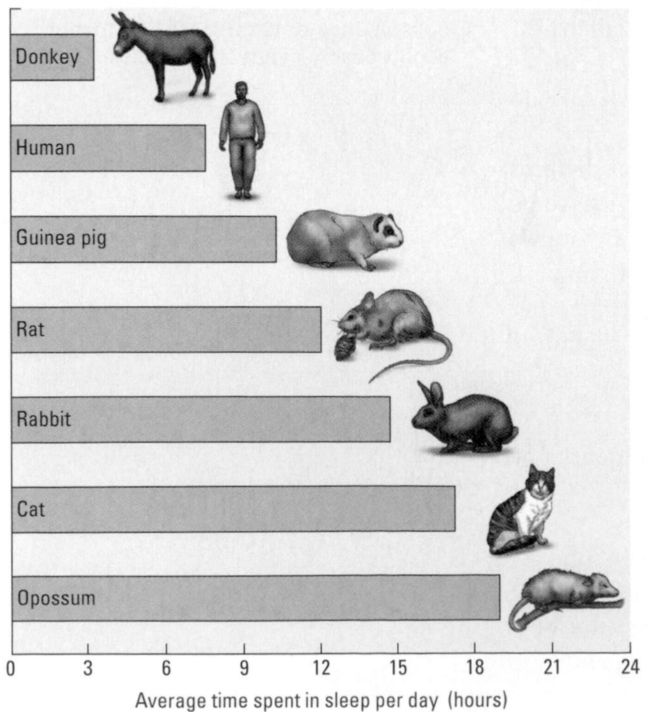

As is illustrated in **Figure 13-18**, the behavior of adult humans also suggests that activity and rest are organized into temporal packets. School classes, work periods, meal times, coffee breaks, and snack times appear to be divided into intervals of 90 minutes or so. The later discovery that REM sleep occurs at intervals of about 90 minutes added support to Kleitman's hypothesis, because the REM periods could be considered a continuation into sleep of the 90-minute BRAC cycle. The hypothesis now assumes that periods of eating are periods of high brain activity, just as are periods of REM.

Kleitman proposed that the BRAC rhythm is so fundamental that it cannot be turned off. Accordingly, in order for a night's sleep to be uninterrupted by periodic waking (and perhaps snacking), the body is paralyzed and only the brain is active. To use an analogy, rather than turning off your car's engine when you're stopped at a red light, you apply the brakes to keep the idling car from moving.

Sleep As a Restorative Process

The idea that sleep has a restorative function is widely held among poets, philosophers, and the public, as illustrated by Shakespeare in Macbeth's description of sleep:

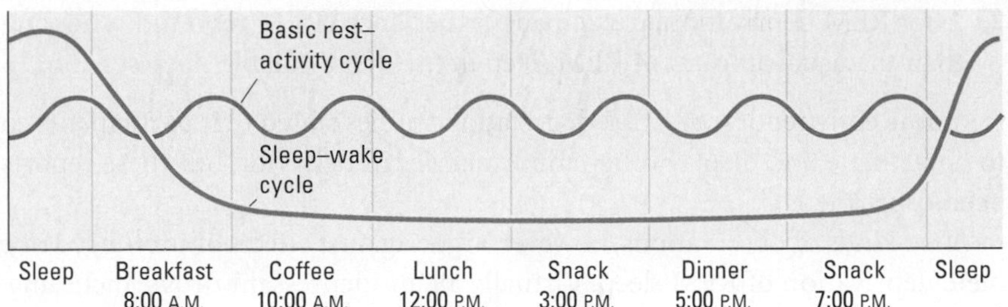

FIGURE 13-18 Behavioral Rhythms. Our behavior is dominated by a basic rest–activity cycle (red) through which our activity levels change in the course of the day and by an NREM–REM sleep cycle (purple) during the night.

Sleep that knits up the ravell'd sleave of care,
The death of each day's life, sore labour's bath,
Balm of hurt minds, great nature's second course,
Chief nourisher in life's feast.

Sleep as a restorative is also an idea that we can understand from a personal perspective. Toward the end of the day, we become tired, and, when we awaken from sleep, we are refreshed. If we do not get enough sleep, we often become irritable. One hypothesis of how sleep is restorative proposes that chemical events that provide energy to cells are reduced during waking and are replenished during sleep.

Nevertheless, fatigue and alertness may simply be aspects of the circadian rhythm and have nothing at all to do with wear and tear on the body or depletion of essential bodily resources. To evaluate whether sleep is essential for one or another bodily process, investigators have conducted sleep-deprivation studies. These studies have not clearly identified any function for which sleep is essential.

One case study on sleep deprivation in which Dement participated as an observer illustrates this point. In 1965, as part of a science-fair project, a student named Randy Gardner planned to break the world record of 260 hours (almost 11 days) of consecutive wakefulness with the help of two classmates, who would keep him awake. Gardner did break the record, then slept for 14 hours and reported no ill effects. The world record now stands at a little more than 18 days. It is important to note that one of the observers of Gardner reported that he experienced hallucinations and cognitive and memory lapses during deprivation, but these negative effects were not lasting. A number of reviews of sleep-deprivation research are consistent in concluding that, at least for these limited periods of sleep deprivation, no marked physiological alterations ensue.

Although sleep deprivation does not seem to have adverse physiological consequences, it is associated with poor cognitive performance. Decreased performance contributes to accidents at work and on the road. The sleep-deprivation deficit does not manifest itself in an inability to do a task, because sleep-deprived participants can perform even very complex tasks. Rather, the deficit is revealed when sustained attention is required and when a task is repetitive or boring.

Even short periods of sleep deprivation, amounting to the loss of a few hours of sleep, can increase errors on tasks requiring sustained attention. A confounding factor in cognitive performance is that sleep-deprived participants will take **microsleeps,** brief sleeps lasting a few seconds. During microsleep, participants may remain sitting or standing, but their eyelids droop briefly and they become less responsive to external stimuli. Many people who have driven a car while tired have experienced a microsleep and awakened just in time to prevent themselves from driving off the road.

Some studies have focused on the selective contributions of REM sleep. To deprive a participant of REM sleep, researchers allow participants to sleep but awaken them as they start to go into REM sleep. REM-sleep deprivation has two effects:

1. Participants show an increased tendency to go into REM sleep in subsequent sleep sessions, so awakenings must become more and more frequent.

Basic rest–activity cycle (BRAC) Recurring cycle of temporal packets, about 90-minute periods in humans, during which an animal's level of arousal waxes and wanes.

Microsleep Brief period of sleep lasting a second or so.

2. After REM deprivation, participants experience "REM rebound," showing more than the usual amount of REM sleep in the first available sleep session.

Some early reports of REM-deprivation studies stated that participants could begin to hallucinate and display other abnormalities in behavior, but these reports have not been confirmed.

Chapter 8 reviews the full spectrum of antidepressant drugs.

Two kinds of observations, however, argue against effects of prolonged or even complete deprivation of REM sleep. Virtually all antidepressant drugs, including MAO inhibitors, tricyclic antidepressants, and SSRIs, suppress REM sleep either partly or completely. The clinical effectiveness of these drugs may in fact derive from their REM-suppressant effects (Wilson and Argyropoulos, 2005). There are no reports of adverse consequences from prolonged REM deprivation as a consequence of treatment with antidepressants.

Research Focus 11-1 reports on the promise of brain–computer interfaces for helping locked-in patients communicate and move around.

In a number of reported cases, lower-brainstem damage resulted in a complete loss of REM sleep. Some of these people suffered from **locked-in syndrome:** they were fully conscious, alert, and responsive but quadriplegic and mute. Five of seven patients with locked-in syndrome were reported to have no REM sleep, without apparent ill effects (Markand and Dyken, 1976). Patients with more selective brainstem lesions reportedly remained ambulatory and verbally communicative, but their REM was abolished. They were reported to live quite satisfactorily without REM sleep (Osorio and Daroff, 1980).

Sleep and Memory Storage

A fourth explanation of sleep proposes that it plays a role in solidifying and organizing events in memory. One group of experimenters proposes that events are stored in permanent memory in NREM sleep, whereas another group proposes that REM sleep fulfills this function.

Figure 6-13 compares single-cell recordings of place cells in rodents of differing ages and genetic makeup.

Gerrard et al. (2008) made use of the finding that many hippocampal cells fire when a rat is in a certain location in an environment. These **place cells** are relatively inactive until the rat passes through a particular place in its environment; then they display a high rate of discharge. Recordings made from as many as 100 cells at the same time in three conditions—during NREM sleep, during a food-search task, and during NREM sleep after a food-search session—suggest that cell activity is correlated in waking and NREM sleep **Figure 13-19.** The result suggests that the memory of the previous food-searching experience is stored during NREM sleep.

To determine whether humans' dreams are related to memory, Pierre Maquet and his coworkers in Belgium trained participants on a serial reaction task and observed regional blood flow in the brain with PET scans during training and during REM sleep on the subsequent night (Maquet et al., 2000). The participants faced a computer screen displaying six positional markers. They were to push one of six keys when a corre-

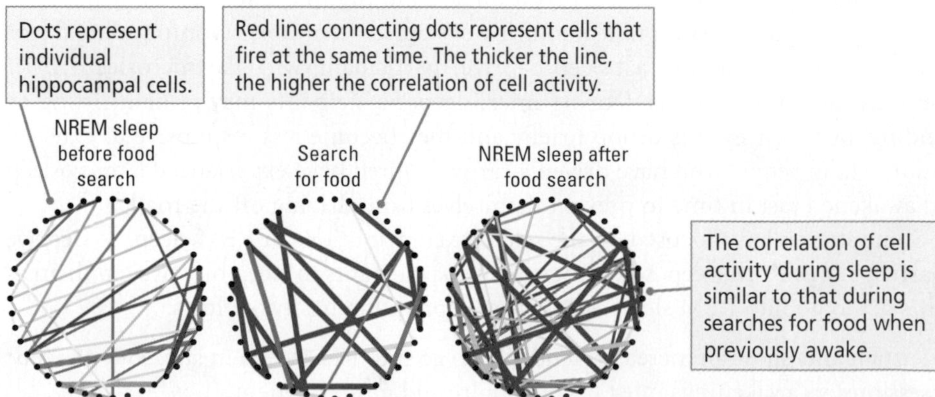
Dots represent individual hippocampal cells.
Red lines connecting dots represent cells that fire at the same time. The thicker the line, the higher the correlation of cell activity.
NREM sleep before food search
Search for food
NREM sleep after food search
The correlation of cell activity during sleep is similar to that during searches for food when previously awake.

FIGURE 13-19 Neural Replay? The activity of hippocampal cells suggests that rats dream about previous experiences. The dots on the periphery of the circles represent the activity of 42 hippocampal cells recorded at the same time during (*left*) slow-wave sleep before a food-searching task, (*middle*) the food-searching task, and (*right*) slow-wave sleep after the task. No strong correlations between cells emerged during the slow-wave sleep that preceded the food-searching task, but correlations between cells during the food search and during the subsequent slow-wave sleep were strong. Adapted from "Reactivation of Hippocampal Ensemble Memories During Sleep," by M. A. Wilson and B. L. McNaughton, 1994, *Science, 165,* p. 678.

Reaction-time task

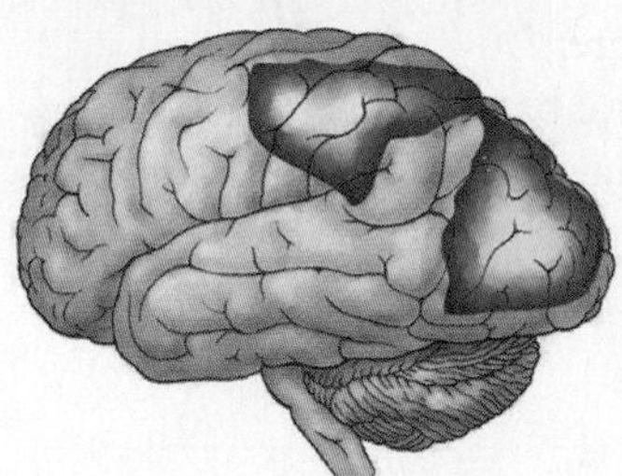

REM sleep that night

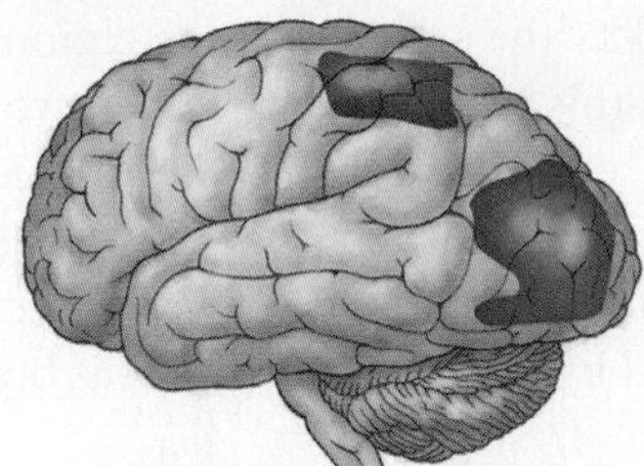

Subjects display a similar pattern of brain activity during subsequent REM sleep.

FIGURE 13-20 Do We Store Memories During REM Sleep? Adapted from "Experience Dependent Changes in Cerebral Activation During Human REM Sleep," by P. Maquet et al., 1998, *Nature Neuroscience,* 3, p. 832.

sponding positional marker was illuminated. They did not know that the sequence in which the positional markers were illuminated was predetermined.

Consequently, as training progressed, the participants indicated that they were learning because their reaction time improved on trials on which one positional marker was correlated with a preceding marker. On the PET-scan measures of brain activation, a similar pattern of neocortical activation was found during task acquisition and during REM sleep (**Figure 13-20**). On the basis of this result, Maquet and coworkers suggest first, that the participants were dreaming about their learning experience, and second, that the replay during REM strengthened the memory of the task.

Memory-storing explanations of sleep are extremely interesting, and the technology required for pursuing the question is quite new. Thus, there is considerable debate concerning the fate of memories during sleep (Brankačk et al., 2009). Among the more interesting speculations is a proposal that elaborate memories are formed during sleep and then pruned to more useful dimensions during waking. Another suggestion is that only certain events are likely to be consolidated during sleep and that these may become associated with unrelated events, thus risking creating a false or distorted memory of an event.

REVIEW: What Does Sleep Accomplish?

- ✔ Among the explanations put forward for why we sleep, the biological explanation—that sleep is an adaptive strategy for conserving energy during times when food resources are hard to obtain—has replaced the passive explanation—that sleep results from lack of sensory stimulation.
- ✔ Sleep may also be a restorative process and may have a role in storing and sorting memory.

Neural Bases of Sleep

The idea that the brain contains a sleep-inducing substance has long been popular and is reinforced by knowledge that a variety of chemical agents induce sleep. Such substances include sedative hypnotics and morphine. A twist on this idea held that the body secretes a chemical that induces sleep and that can be removed only by sleeping.

You can review the full range of sleep-inducing psychoactive drugs and how they work in Chapter 8.

The hormone melatonin, secreted from the pineal gland during the dark phase of the light–dark cycle, causes sleepiness and is taken as an aid for sleep, so it might be thought to be the sleep-producing substance. Sleep, however, survives the removal of the pineal gland. Thus, melatonin and many other chemical substances may only contribute to sleep, not cause it (see Research Focus 13-3).

In fact, experimenters have obtained evidence that sleep is not produced by a compound circulating in the bloodstream. When dolphins and birds sleep, only one brain hemisphere sleeps at a time. This ability presumably allows an animal's other hemisphere

Locked-in syndrome Lower brainstem damage that results in a fully conscious, alert, and responsive condition, but the patient is quadriplegic and mute.
Place cell Hippocampal neurons maximally responsive to specific locations in the world.

to remain behaviorally alert. This observation also strongly suggests that sleep is produced by the action of some region within each hemisphere.

In this section, we consider two points about the neural basis of sleep. First, we examine evidence that sleep is produced by the activity of a slave oscillator of the suprachiasmatic nucleus (see Figure 13-8). Second, we look at evidence that the various events associated with sleep, including events associated with REM and NREM sleep, are controlled by a number of different brainstem nuclei.

Reticular Activating System and Sleep

A dramatic experiment and a clever hypothesis by Giuseppe Moruzzi and Horace Magoun (1949) began to answer to the question of which areas of the brain regulate sleep. Moruzzi and Magoun were recording the cortical EEG from anesthetized cats while electrically stimulating the cats' brainstems. They discovered that, in response to the electrical stimulation, the large, slow cortical EEG typically produced by anesthesia was dramatically replaced by the low-voltage, fast-wave EEG typical of waking.

The waking pattern of EEG activity outlasted the period of stimulation, demonstrating that the pattern was produced by the activity of neurons in the region of the stimulating electrode. During the "waking period," the cat did not become behaviorally aroused, because it was anesthetized, but its cortical EEG appeared to indicate that it was awake.

Findings from subsequent experiments by Moruzzi and Magoun and by others show that a waking EEG can be induced from a large area running through the center of the brainstem. Anatomically, this area is composed of a mixture of cell nuclei and nerve fibers that form a *reticulum.* Moruzzi and Magoun named this brainstem area the **reticular activating system** (RAS) and proposed that it is responsible for sleep–waking behavior. **Figure 13-21** diagrams the location of the RAS.

A *reticulum,* derived from the Latin word *rete,* meaning "net," appears as a mottled mixture of gray matter and white matter. The RAS is also called the *reticular formation.*

If someone disturbs you when you are asleep, you usually wake up. To explain how sensory stimulation and the RAS are related, Moruzzi and Magoun proposed that sensory pathways entering the brainstem have collateral axons that synapse with neurons in the RAS. They proposed that sensory stimulation is conveyed to RAS neurons by these collaterals, and then RAS neurons produce the desynchronized EEG via axons that project to the cortex.

Because Moruzzi and Magoun could possibly have stimulated various sensory pathways passing through the brainstem, it was necessary to demonstrate that brainstem neurons, not sensory-pathway stimulation produced the waking EEG. When experimenters cut the brainstem just behind the RAS, thereby severing incoming sensory pathways, RAS stimulation still produced a desynchronized EEG.

The idea that the brainstem plays a role in waking behavior helps to explain why brainstem damage can result in **coma,** a prolonged state of deep unconsciousness resembling sleep. In a well-publicized case, after taking a minor tranquilizer and having a few drinks at a birthday party, a 21-year-old woman named Karen Ann Quinlan sustained RAS damage that put her in a coma (Quinlan and Quinlan, 1977). She was hospitalized, placed on a respirator to support breathing, and fed by tubes. Her family fought a protracted legal battle to have her removed from life support, which they finally won before the Supreme Court of New Jersey. Even after having been removed from life support, however, Quinlan lived for 10 more years in a perpetual coma.

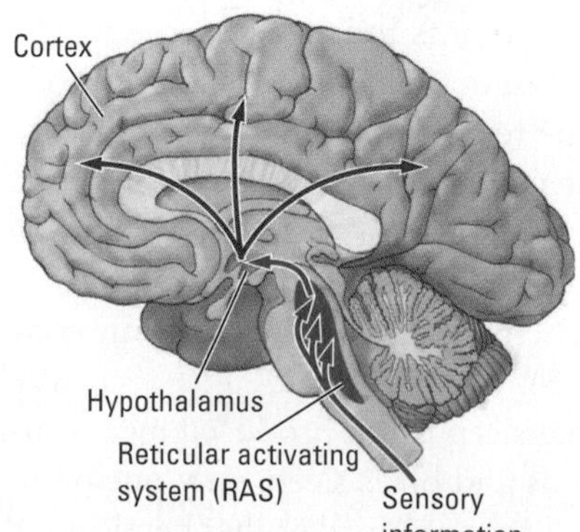

FIGURE 13-21 Sleep–Wake Controller. The reticular activating system, a region in the middle of the brainstem, is characterized by a mixture of cell bodies and fiber pathways. Stimulation of the RAS produces a waking EEG, whereas damage to it produces a slow-wave, sleeplike EEG.

Neural Basis of EEG Changes Associated with Waking

Building on the pioneering studies on the RAS, research has since revealed a number of neural systems in the brainstem that play a role in sleeping and waking behavior. A series of experiments performed on rats by Case Vanderwolf and his coworkers (Vanderwolf, 2002) suggest that two different systems in the brainstem influence waking EEG. **Figure 13-22** illustrates the locations of these structures. Both send neural pathways into the neocortex, where they make diffuse connections with cortical neurons.

Reticular activating system (RAS) Large reticulum (mixture of cell nuclei and nerve fibers) that runs through the center of the brainstem; associated with sleep–wake behavior and behavioral arousal; often called the *reticular formation.*

Coma Prolonged state of deep unconsciousness resembling sleep.

The basal forebrain contains large cholinergic cells. These neurons secrete acetylcholine (ACh) from their terminals onto neocortical neurons to stimulate a waking EEG (beta rhythm). The midbrain structure, the median raphé, contains serotonin (5-HT) neurons whose axons also project diffusely to the neocortex, where they also stimulate neocortical cells to produce a beta rhythm, recorded as a waking EEG.

Consult Figure 5-17 to review the major neural activating systems and their functions.

Although both pathways produce a very similar pattern of waking EEG activity, the relations of the two types of waking EEG to behavior are different. If the activity of the cholinergic projection is blocked by drugs or by lesions to the cells of the basal forebrain, the waking EEG normally recorded from an immobile rat is replaced by EEG activity resembling that of NREM sleep. If the rat walks or is otherwise active, a waking EEG is obtained from the neocortex. These findings suggest that the cholinergic EEG is responsible for the waking associated with being still yet alert, whereas the serotonergic activation is additionally responsible for the waking EEG when the animal moves.

Note that neither the basal forebrain system nor the median raphé system is responsible for behavior. In fact, if both structures are pharmacologically or surgically destroyed, a rat can still stand and walk around. Its neocortical EEG, however, resembles that of a sleeping animal.

As long as one of the activating systems is producing a waking EEG, rats can learn simple tasks. If both systems are destroyed, however, an animal, although still able to walk around, is no longer able to learn or display intelligent behavior. In a sense, the cortex is like a house in which the lights are powered by two separate power sources: both must fail for the house to be left in darkness, but, if at least one source is operating, the lights can be on.

It is likely that the basal forebrain and median raphé produce the same two desynchronized EEG patterns in humans as they do in rats. Consequently, when we are alert, the cholinergic neurons are likely to be active, and when we move, the serotonin neurons are likely to be additionally active.

You may have had the experience, when you felt sleepy in a class or behind the wheel of a car, of being able to wake yourself up by moving—shaking your head or stretching. Presumably, your arousal level decreased as your cholinergic neurons became inactive. When you moved, your serotonergic neurons became active and restored your level of arousal. When we enter sleep, both cholinergic and serotonergic neurons become less active, allowing slow waves to emanate in the cortex.

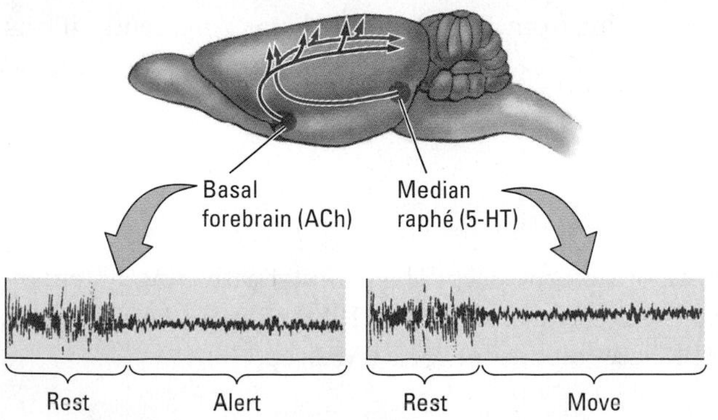

FIGURE 13-22 Brain Activators. In the rat, basal forebrain ACh neurons produce an activated EEG pattern when a rat is alert but immobile. The 5-HT raphé neurons of the midbrain produce an activated EEG pattern when the rat moves.

Neural Basis of REM Sleep

Barbara Jones (1993) and her colleagues have described a group of cholinergic neurons known as the **peribrachial area**, which appears to be implicated in REM sleep. This area is located in the dorsal part of the brainstem just anterior to the cerebellum (**Figure 13-23**). Jones selectively destroyed these cells by spraying them with the neurotoxin kainic acid. She found that REM sleep in her experimental animal subjects was drastically reduced. This result suggests that the peribrachial area is responsible for producing REM sleep and REM-related behaviors.

Figure 8-5 shows how selected drugs and toxins act as agonists or antagonists at the ACh synapse. Table 8-3 lists some natural substances that act as neurotoxins, their sources, and their actions.

Peribrachial area
Medial pontine reticular formation

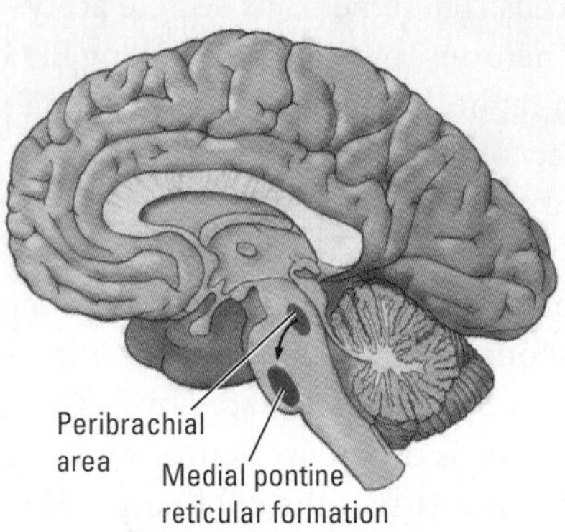

FIGURE 13-23 Brainstem Nuclei Responsible for REM. Damage to either the peribrachial area or the medial pontine formation reduces or abolishes REM sleep.

The peribrachial area extends into a more ventrally located nucleus called the **medial pontine reticular formation** (MPRF). Lesions of the MPRF also abolish REM sleep, and injections of cholinergic agonists (drugs that act like ACh) into the MPRF induce REM sleep. Thus, both the peribrachial area and the MPRF, illustrated in Figure 13-23, take part in producing REM sleep.

If these two brain areas are responsible for producing REM sleep, how do other events related to REM sleep take place? As you know, such events include the following:

- EEG pattern similar to waking EEG
- Rapid eye movements, or REM
- Atonia, the absence of muscle tone

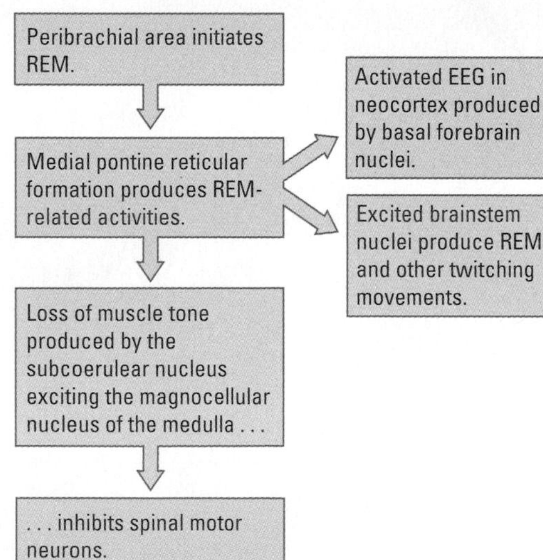
Peribrachial area initiates REM.
Medial pontine reticular formation produces REM-related activities.
Activated EEG in neocortex produced by basal forebrain nuclei.
Excited brainstem nuclei produce REM and other twitching movements.
Loss of muscle tone produced by the subcoerulear nucleus exciting the magnocellular nucleus of the medulla . . .
. . . inhibits spinal motor neurons.

FIGURE 13-24 Neural Control of REM Sleep.

Figure 13-24 charts a proposed explanation for how other REM-related activities take place via a number of neural areas that contribute to different aspects of REM sleep. The peribrachial area initiates REM sleep and activates the medial pontine reticular fromation. The MPRF then sends projections to activate basal forebrain cholinergic neurons, resulting in the activated EEG recorded from the cortex, and it also excites brainstem motor nuclei to produce rapid eye movements and other twitches. The atonia of REM sleep is produced by the MPRF through a pathway that sends input to the subcoerulear nucleus, located just behind it. Finally, the subcoerulear nucleus excites the magnocellular nucleus of the medulla, which sends projections to the spinal motor neurons to inhibit them so that paralysis is achieved during the REM-sleep period.

In support of such a neural arrangement, French researcher Michael Jouvet (1972) observed that cats with lesions in the subcoerulear nucleus display a remarkable behavior when they enter REM sleep. Rather than stretching out in the atonia that typically accompanies REM sleep, they stood up, looked around, and made movements of catching an imaginary mouse or running from an imaginary threat. Apparently, if cats with damage to this brain region dream about catching mice or escaping from a threat, then they act out their dreams.

REVIEW: Neural Bases of Sleep

✔ Separate neural regions are responsible for sleep. The reticular activating system in the central region of the brainstem is responsible for NREM sleep, whereas the peribrachial area and the MPRF are responsible for REM sleep.

✔ The peribrachial area and the MPRF, through activating pathways to the neocortex and spinal cord, are responsible for producing the waking EEG, rapid eye movements and other twitches, and the muscular paralysis associated with REM sleep.

Peribrachial area Cholinergic nucleus in the dorsal brainstem having a role in REM sleep behaviors; projects to medial pontine reticulum.
Medial pontine reticular formation (MPRF) Nucleus in the pons participating in REM sleep.
Insomnia Disorder of slow-wave sleep resulting in prolonged inability to sleep.
Narcolepsy Slow-wave sleep disorder in which a person uncontrollably falls asleep at inappropriate times.

Sleep Disorders

Occasional sleep disturbances are annoying and may result in impaired performance the following day. About 15 percent of people complain of ongoing sleep problems; an additional 20 percent complain of occasional sleep problems. As people age, the incidence of complaints increases.

In the extreme, a rare genetic condition, *fatal famial insomnia,* causes individuals to stop sleeping altogether. Their insomnia may contribute to death after a number of months of not sleeping (Synofzik et al., 2009). In this section, we consider more common abnormalities of NREM sleep and REM sleep.

Disorders of Non-REM Sleep

The two most common sleep disorders are **insomnia,** prolonged inability to sleep, and **narcolepsy,** uncontrollably falling asleep at inconvenient times. Both are considered disorders of slow-wave sleep. Insomnia and narcolepsy are related, as anyone who has stayed up late at night can confirm: a short night's sleep is often accompanied by a tendency to fall asleep at inconvenient times the next day.

The term *narcolepsy* derives from the Greek words meaning "numbness" and "to be seized."

Our understanding of insomnia is complicated by a large variation in how much time people spend asleep. Some short sleepers may think that they should sleep more, and some long sleepers may think that they should sleep less. Yet for each, the sleeping pattern may be appropriate.

It is also possible that some people's circadian rhythms are disrupted by subtle life-style choices. Staying up late, for example, may set a person's circadian rhythm forward, encouraging a cascade of late sleep followed by still later staying up. Indoors and outdoors, light pollution contributes to sleep disorders by disrupting circadian rhythms. Some sleep problems are brought on by shift work or by jet lag. Other common causes of sleep disorders are stress, long hours of work, and irregular life styles. Just worrying about insomnia is estimated to play a major role in 15 percent of cases.

People who are depressed may sleep too much or too little. Anxiety and depression may account for about 35 percent of insomnias. Quantitative differences also exist in the sleep of depressed patients, because they enter REM sleep very quickly. Entering REM sleep quickly, however, may be secondarily related to sleep deprivation rather than being related directly to depression, because people who are sleep-deprived also enter REM very quickly. Irregular sleeping patterns are also common in schizophrenia.

Insomnia may be brought on by sedative-hypnotic drugs, including seconal, sodium amytal, and many minor tranquilizers. These "sleeping pills" do help people get to sleep, but they cause additional problems. People may sleep under one of these drugs, but they are likely to feel groggy and tired the next day, which defeats the purpose of taking the drug. Sleeping pills may promote NREM sleep but at the same time deprive the user of REM sleep.

In addition, people develop tolerance to these medications, become dependent on them, and display rebound insomnia when they stop taking them. A person may increase the dose each time the drug fails to produce the desired effect. The syndrome in

Chapter 8 explains theories of drug tolerance and explores how sleep medications work.

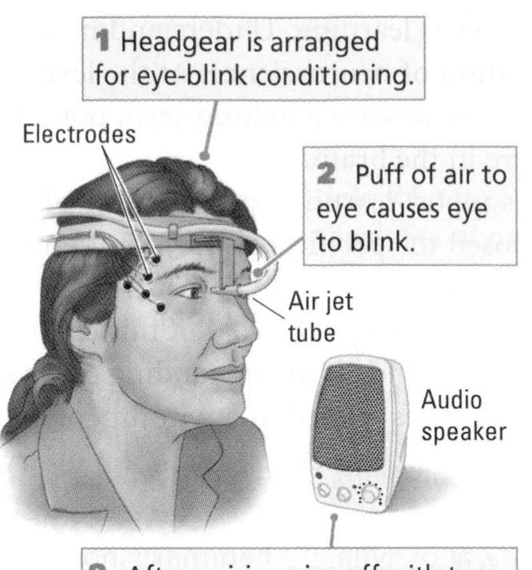

2 Puff of air to eye causes eye to blink.
Air jet tube
Audio speaker

FIGURE 14-1 Eye-Blink Conditioning. The participant's headgear contains an apparatus that delivers a puff of air to the eye, causing the participant to blink. When the air puff is paired with a tone, the participant learns the association and subsequently blinks to the tone alone. Circuits in the cerebellum mediate this form of stimulus–repsonse learning.

have learned it by giving the same response (such as salivation) to both stimuli. Pet owners are familiar with this type of learning: to a cat or dog, the sound of a can being opened is a clear stimulus for food. Two forms of Pavlovian conditioning are commonly used in experiments today: eye-blink conditioning and fear conditioning. Each is associated with neural circuits in discrete brain regions; thus both have proved especially useful.

Eye-blink conditioning has been used to study Pavlovian learning in rabbits and people (**Figure 14-1**). In these studies, a tone (or some other stimulus) is associated with a painless puff of air to the participant's eye. The tone is the **conditioned stimulus** (CS) that comes to elicit a blink produced initially by the air puff. The air puff is the **unconditioned stimulus** (UCS), because blinking is the normal reaction—the **unconditioned response** (UCR)—to a puff of air. Thus, the subject communicates to us that it has learned that the signal stimulus predicts the puff by blinking in response to the signal (the CS) alone—a **conditioned response** (CR).

Pavlovian learning is mediated by circuits in the cerebellum. The cerebellum does not have special circuits just for eye-blink conditioning, which is an artificial situation. Rather, the cerebellum has circuits designed to pair various motor responses with environmental events. Eye-blink conditioning experiments simply take advantage of this biological predisposition.

In the cerebellum, the flocculus controls eye movements. You can examine the cerebellar homunculus in Figure 11-15.

In **fear conditioning,** a noxious stimulus is used to elicit fear, an emotional response. A rat or other animal is placed in a box that has a grid floor through which a mild but noxious electric current can be passed. As shown in **Experiment 14-1,** a tone (the CS) is presented just before a brief, unexpected, mild electric shock.

When the tone is later presented without the shock, the animal acts afraid. It may become motionless and may urinate in anticipation of the shock. Presentation of a novel stimulus, such as a light, in the same environment has little effect on the animal. Thus, the animal communicates to us that it has learned the association between the tone and the shock.

The shock is roughly equivalent to a jolt of static electricity you might get when you rub your feet on a carpet and then touch a metal object or another person.

Because the CR is emotional, circuits of the amygdala rather than the cerebellum mediate fear conditioning. Although both eye-blink and fear conditioning are Pavlovian, different parts of the brain mediate the learning.

EXPERIMENT 14-1

Question: Does an animal learn the association between emotional experience and environmental stimuli?

Procedure and results

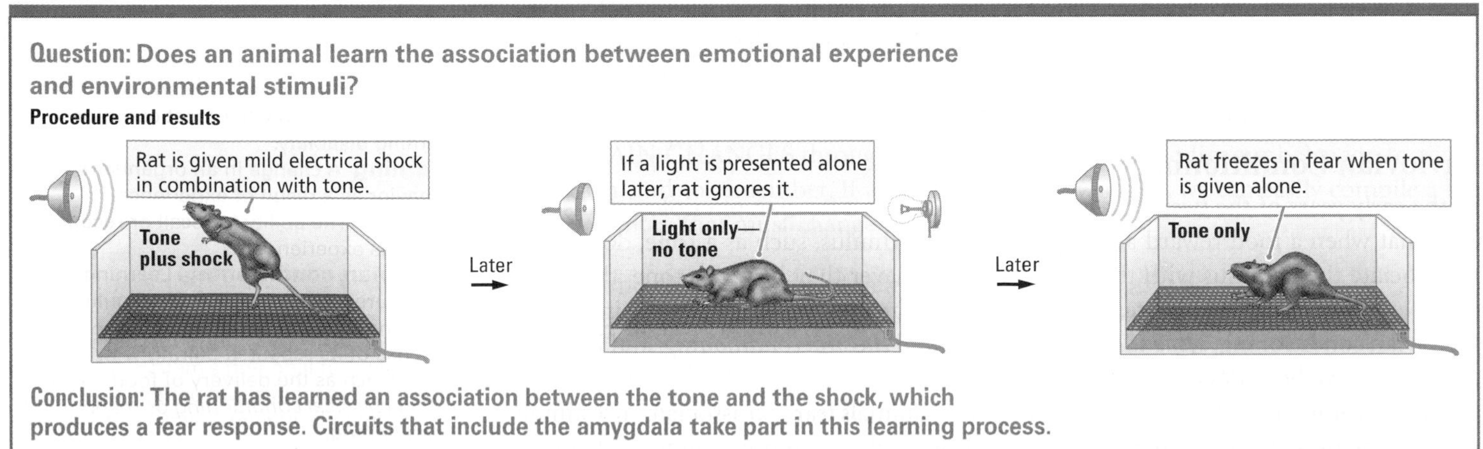

Rat is given mild electrical shock in combination with tone.
Tone plus shock
Later
If a light is presented alone later, rat ignores it.
Light only—no tone
Later
Rat freezes in fear when tone is given alone.
Tone only

Conclusion: The rat has learned an association between the tone and the shock, which produces a fear response. Circuits that include the amygdala take part in this learning process.

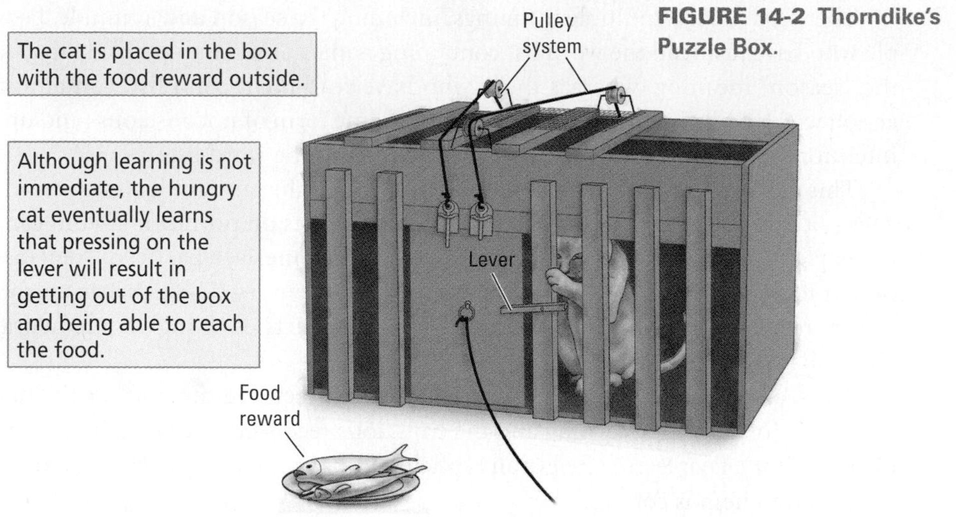

The cat is placed in the box with the food reward outside.
Although learning is not immediate, the hungry cat eventually learns that pressing on the lever will result in getting out of the box and being able to reach the food.
Pulley system
Lever
Food reward

FIGURE 14-2 Thorndike's Puzzle Box.

Eye-blink conditioning Commonly used experimental technique in which subjects learn to pair a formerly neutral stimulus with a defensive blinking response.

Conditioned stimulus (CS) In Pavlovian conditioning, an originally neutral stimulus that, after association with an unconditioned stimulus (UCS), triggers a conditioned response.

Unconditioned stimulus (UCS) A stimulus that unconditionally—naturally and automatically—triggers a response.

Unconditioned response (UCR) In classical conditioning, the unlearned, naturally occurring response to the unconditioned stimulus, such as salivation when food is in the mouth.

Conditioned response (CR) In Pavlovian conditioning, the learned response to a formerly neutral conditioned stimulus (CS).

Fear conditioning Learned association, a conditioned emotional response, between a neutral stimulus and a noxious event such as a shock.

Instrumental conditioning Learning procedure in which the consequences (such as obtaining a reward) of a particular behavior (such as pressing a bar) increase or decrease the probability of the behavior occurring again; also called operant conditioning.

Instrumental Conditioning

In the United States, Edward Thorndike (1898) began a second tradition of studying learning and memory. Thorndike was interested in how animals solve problems. In one series of experiments, he placed cats in a box with a plate of fish outside it (**Figure 14-2**). The only way for a hungry cat to get to the fish was to figure out how to get out of the box.

The solution was to press on a lever, which activated a system of pulleys that opened the box door. The cat gradually learned that its actions had consequences: on the initial trial, the cat touched the releasing mechanism only by chance as it restlessly paced inside the box. The cat apparently learned that something that it had done opened the door, and it tended to repeat the behaviors that had occurred just before the door opening. After a few trials, the cat took just seconds to get the door open so that it could devour the fish.

Later studies by B. F. Skinner (e.g., 1938) used a similar strategy of reinforcement to train rats to press bars or pigeons to peck keys to obtain food. Many animals will learn to bar press or key peck if they are simply placed in the apparatus and allowed to discover the response necessary to obtain the reward, just as Thorndike's cats learned to escape his puzzle boxes. This type of learning is **instrumental conditioning,** or *operant conditioning.* The subject demonstrates that it has learned the association between its actions and the consequences by the increasing speed at which it can perform the task.

Chapter 12 describes how Skinner used reinforcers to shape behavior.

The variety of instrumental associations is staggering: we are constantly learning associations between our behavior and its consequences. It should be no surprise, then, that instrumental learning is not localized to any particular circuit in the brain. The circuits needed vary with the actual requirements of the task. For example, olfactory tasks involve olfactory-related structures like the orbitofrontal cortex and the amygdala, spatial tasks recruit the hippocampus, and motor tasks require the basal ganglia.

Two Categories of Memory

Humans present a distinct challenge to the study of memory because so much of our learning is verbal. Psychologists have been studying human memory since the mid-1800s, and cognitive psychologists have developed sophisticated measures of learning and memory for neuropsychological investigations. Two such measures help to distinguish between two categories of memory in humans.

Experiments and examples throughout this book illustrate tests designed to measure the varieties of brain function. Chapters 6 and 15 detail the design of such measures by *neuropsychologists,* who study the relations between brain function and behavior in humans.

In one kind of task, a group of subjects is given a list of words to read, such as *spring, winter, car,* and *boat.* Another group of subjects read a list consisting of the words *trip, tumble, run,* and *sun.* All the subjects are then asked to define a series of words, one of which is *fall.*

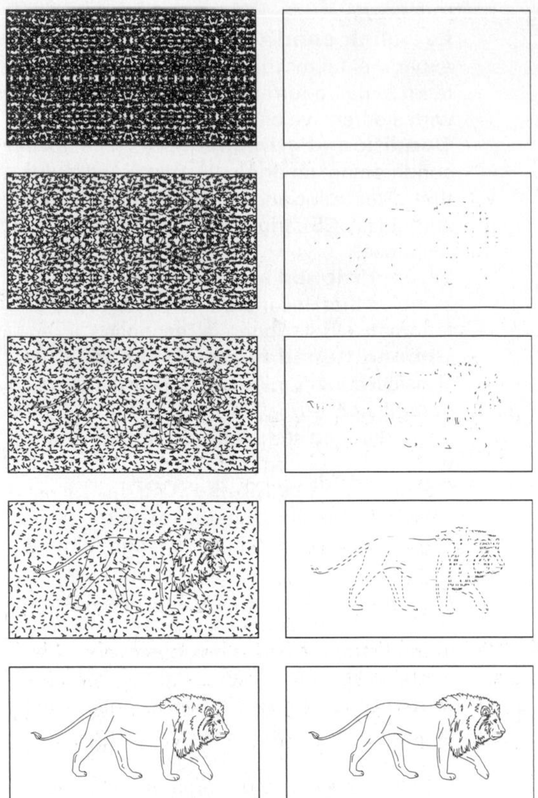

FIGURE 14-3 Gollin Figure Test. Participants are shown a series of drawings in sequence, from least to most clear, and asked to identify the image. Most people must see several panels before they can identify it. On a retention test some time later, however, participants identify the image sooner than they did on the first test, indicating some form of memory for the image. Amnesic subjects also show improvement on this test, even though they do not recall taking the test before.

The word *fall* has multiple meanings, including the season and a tumble. People who have just read the word list containing names of seasons are likely to give the "season" meaning, whereas those who have read the second list, containing action words, will give the "tumble" meaning. Some form of unconscious (and unintentional) learning takes place as the subjects read the word lists.

This word-list task measures **implicit memory:** subjects demonstrate knowledge—a skill, conditioned response, or recalling events on prompting—but cannot explicitly retrieve the information. People with **amnesia,** a partial or total loss of memory, perform normally on tests of implicit memory. The amnesic person has no recollection of having read the word list yet acts as though some neural circuit has been influenced by it.

Thus, a *dissociation*—a disconnect—occurs between the memory of the unconscious (or implicit) learning and the conscious recollection of training, or **explicit memory.** People can retrieve an explicit memory and indicate that they know the retreived item is correct.

This implicit–explicit distinction is not restricted to verbal learning; it is true of visual learning and motor learning tasks as well. For example, when people are shown the top panel of the Gollin figure test in **Figure 14-3** and asked what it shows, they are unlikely to be able to identify an image. They are then presented with a succession of more nearly complete sketches until they can identify the picture. When control participants and amnesics are later shown the same sketch, both groups can identify the figure sooner than they could the first time. Even though the amnesic subjects may not recall seeing the sketches before, they behave as though they had.

To measure implicit learning of motor skills, a person can be taught a skill, such as the pursuit-rotor task shown in **Figure 14-4.** A small metal disc moves in a circular pattern on a turntable that also is moving. The task is to hold a stylus on the small disc as it spins. This task is not as easy as it looks, especially when the turntable is moving quickly.

Nonetheless, with an hour's practice most people become reasonably proficient. If they are presented with the same task a week later, both normal participants and amnesics take less time to perform it. Here, too, the amnesics fail to recall performing the task before.

The distinction between tests of implicit and explicit memory is consistent and therefore must offer a key to how the brain stores information. Some theorists make subtle distinctions between the implicit–explicit dichotomy we use for categorizing unconscious and conscious memory and other terminologies. Many researchers prefer to distinguish between **declarative memory,** the specific contents of specific experiences that can be verbally recalled (times, places, or circumstances), and **procedural memory,** the ability to perform a task. As applied to humans there is little practical difference.

Table 14-1 lists commonly used dichotomies, the general distinction being that one memory category requires the recollection of specific information whereas the other refers to knowledge of which we are not consciously aware. We can include Pavlov's classi-

Rotating target
Stylus
Rotating disk

FIGURE 14-4 Pursuit-Rotor Task. The subject must keep the stylus in contact with the metal disc that is moving in a circular pattern on a turntable, which also is rotating in a circular pattern. Although the task is difficult, most people show significant improvement after a brief period of training. When given a second test at some later time, both normal participants and amnesics show retention of the task, but the amnesics typically do not recall learning the task before.

cal conditioning, Thorndike's instrumental learning, and Skinner's operant learning in this analysis too: all are forms of implicit learning.

Nonspeaking animals can display explicit memory. One of us owned a cat that loved to play with a little ball. One day, as the cat watched, the ball was temporarily put on a high shelf to keep it away from an inquisitive toddler. For weeks afterward, the cat sat and stared at the shelf where the ball had been placed, even though the ball was not visible—an example of explicit memory.

Animals also display explicit memory when they learn psychological tasks. Rats can be trained to find highly palatable food in a new location in a large compound each day. The task is to go the most recent location. This piece of information is explicit and can be demonstrably forgotten.

Suppose a well-trained rat is given one trial with the food at a new location for several trials and then retested an hour, a day, 3 days, or a week later. The rat has no difficulty with a delay of an hour or perhaps even a day. Some rats are flawless at 3 days, but most have forgotten the location by the time a week has elapsed. Instead, they wander around looking for the food. This behavior illustrates their implicit memory of the **learning set,** the "rules of the game"—an implicit understanding of how a problem can be solved with a rule that can be applied in many different situations—namely, here, that a desired food can be found with a certain type of search strategy.

TABLE 14-1 Differentiating the Two Categories of Memory

Term for conscious memory	Term for unconscious memory
Explicit	Implicit
Declarative	Nondeclarative
Fact	Skill
Memory	Habit
Knowing that	Knowing how
Locale	Taxon
Conscious recollection	Skills
Elaboration	Integration
Memory with record	Memory without record
Autobiographical	Perceptual
Representational	Dispositional
Episodic	Procedural
Semantic	Nonassociative
Working	Reference

Note: These paired terms have been used by various theorists to differentiate conscious from unconscious forms of memory. This list is intended to help you relate other discussions of memory that you may encounter to the one in this book, which favors the explicit–implicit distinction.

What Makes Explicit and Implicit Memory Different?

One reason explicit and implicit memories differ is that each type is housed in a different set of neural structures. Another reason they differ is that explicit and implicit information are processed differently.

Encoding Memories

Implicit information is encoded in very much the same way as it is perceived and can be described as data-driven, or "bottom up," processing. The idea is that information enters the brain through the sensory receptors and is then processed in a series of subcortical and cortical regions. For example, visual information about an object goes from the visual receptors (the "bottom") to the thalamus, the occipital cortex, and then through the ventral stream to the temporal lobe, where the object is recognized.

Explicit memory, in contrast, depends on conceptually driven, or "top down," processing: the subject reorganizes the data. For example, if you were searching for a particular object, such as your keys, you would ignore other objects. This is a top-down process because circuits in the temporal lobe (the "top") form an image that influences how incoming visual information (the "bottom") is processed, which in turn greatly influences information recall later.

Because a person has a relatively passive role in encoding implicit memory, he or she has difficulty recalling the memory spontaneously but recalls the memory more easily when there is **priming** by the original stimulus or some feature of it. Because a person plays an active role in processing information explicitly, the internal cues that were used in processing can also be used to initiate spontaneous recall.

Findings from studies of eyewitness testimony demonstrate the active nature of recalling an explicit memory—and its potential fallibility (e.g., Loftus, 1997). In a typical

Implicit memory Unconscious memory: subjects can demonstrate knowledge, such as a skill, conditioned response, or recalling events on prompting, but cannot explicitly retrieve the information.

Amnesia Partial or total loss of memory.

Explicit memory Conscious memory: subjects can retrieve an item and indicate that they know that the retreived item is the correct item.

Declarative memory Ability to recount what one knows, to detail the time, place, and circumstances of events; often lost in amnesia.

Procedural memory Ability to recall a movement sequence or how to perform some act or behavior.

Learning set The "rules of the game;" implicit understanding of how a problem can be solved with a rule that can be applied in many different situations.

Priming Using a stimulus to sensitize the nervous system to a later presentation of the same or a similar stimulus.

experiment, people are shown a video clip of an accident in which a car collides with another car stopped at an intersection. One group of participants is asked to estimate how fast the moving car was going when it "smashed" into the other car. A second group is asked how fast the car was going when it "bumped" into the other car.

Later questioning indicates that the memory of how fast the moving car was going is biased by the instruction: subjects looking at "smashing" cars estimate faster speeds than those estimated by subjects looking at "bumping" cars. In other words, the instruction causes the information to be processed differently. In both cases, the participants were certain that their memories were accurate.

Other experiments show that implicit memory also is fallible. For example, subjects are read the following list of words: *sweet, chocolate, shoe, table, candy, horse, car, cake, coffee, wall, book, cookie, hat.* After a delay of a few minutes, the subjects hear another list of words that includes some of the words from the first list and some that are new. Subjects are asked to identify which words were present on the first list and to indicate how certain they are of the identification.

One of the words on the second list is *sugar.* Most subjects indicate not just that *sugar* was on the first list but that they are certain it was. Although other sweet things were, *sugar* was not. This type of demonstration is intriguing, because it shows the ease with which we can form "false memories" and defend their veracity with certainty.

Processing Memories

Although we can distinguish memories generally as implicit or explicit, the brain does not process all implicit or all explicit memories in the same way. Memories can be divided according to categories that are different from those listed in Table 14-1. For example, we can make a distinction between memories for different types of sensory information.

Visual and auditory information is processed by different neural areas, so it is reasonable to assume that auditory memories are stored in different brain regions from those in which visual memories are stored. We can also make a distinction between information stored in so-called *short-term memory* and information held for a longer time in *long-term memory*. In short-term memory, information—such as the telephone number of a restaurant that we have just looked up—is held in memory only briefly, for a few minutes at most, and then discarded. In long-term memory, information—such as a close friend's name—is held in memory indefinitely, perhaps for a lifetime.

The frontal lobes play an important role in short-term memory, whereas the temporal lobe plays a central role in long-term storage of verbal information. The crucial point is that no single place in the nervous system can be identified as the location for memory or learning. Virtually the entire nervous system can be changed by experience, but different parts of an experience change different parts of the nervous system. One challenge for the experimenter is to devise ways of manipulating experience to demonstrate change in different parts of the brain.

Storing Memories

Accepting the idea that every part of the brain can learn influences how we view the neural circuits that mediate memory. We could expect that areas that process information also house the memory of that information. Areas that process visual information, for example, probably house visual memory. Since the temporal lobe has specialized regions for processing color, shape, and other visual characteristics of an object, we can predict that the memory for various visual attributes of objects is stored separately.

A series of PET studies by Alex Martin and colleagues (1995) at the U.S. National Institute of Mental Health has confirmed this prediction. In one study, participants were shown black-and-white line drawings of objects and asked to generate words denoting either colors or actions of the objects. The idea was that the processing of color and motion is carried out in different locations in the temporal lobe, and thus the activity associated with the memories of color and motion also might be dissociated.

Just such a dissociation was demonstrated. **Figure 14-5** shows that recall of colors activates a region in the ventral temporal lobe, just anterior to the area controlling color perception, whereas recall of action words activates a region in the middle temporal gyrus, just anterior to the area controlling motion perception. This distribution of neural activation shows not only that object memory is at least partly located in the temporal lobes but also that it is found in regions associated with the original perception of the objects.

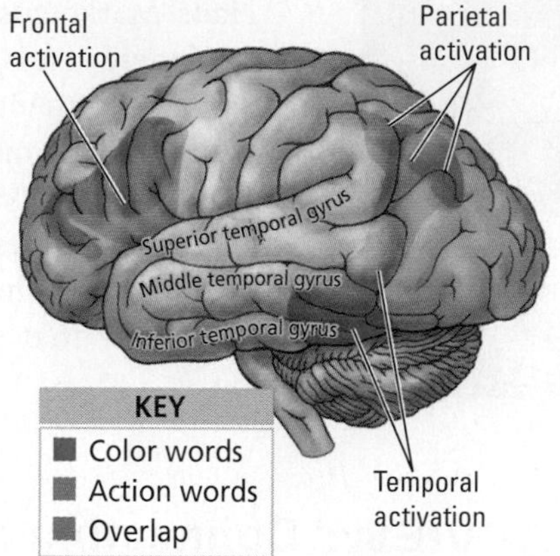

FIGURE 14-5 Memory Distribution. Blood flow in the left hemisphere increases when participants generate color words (red regions) and action words (blue regions) to describe objects shown to them in static, black-and-white drawings. Purple areas indicate overlap, and the red region extends into the ventral temporal lobe. These data suggest that object memory is organized as a distributed system. The attributes of an object are stored close to the cortical regions that mediate perceptions of those attributes. It is likely that activation in the parietal lobe is related to movements associated with action words and activation in the frontal lobe to the spontaneous generation of behavior. Adapted from "Discrete Cortical Regions Associated with Knowledge of Color and Knowledge of Action," by A. Martin, J. V. Haxby, F. M. Lalonde, C. L. Wiggs, and L. G. Ungerleider, 1995, *Science*, 270, p. 104.

What Is Special about Personal Memories?

One aspect of memory unique to each of us is our personal, or autobiographical, memory. This **episodic memory** includes not only a record of events (episodes) that took place but also of our presence and role in the events. Our personal experiences form the basis of who we are and the rules by which we live. That is, we have memories not only for events but also for their context at a particular time in a particular place. We thus have a concept of time and a sense of our personal role in a changing world.

Imagine what would happen if we lost our personal memories. We would still recall events that took place but would be unable to see our role in them. People with frontal-lobe injuries sometimes exhibit such symptoms, as illustrated in a case described by Endel Tulving (2002).

K. C. suffered a serious traumatic brain injury in a motorcycle accident that produced multiple cortical and subcortical lesions. What is remarkable about K. C. is that his cognitive abilities are intact and indistinguishable from those of most normal healthy adults. He can still play chess and the organ, and his short-term memory is intact. He knows who he is, when his birthday is, the names of schools he attended, the location of the family cottage, and so on.

What K. C. cannot do is recall any personally experienced events. This episodic amnesia covers his entire life, from birth until the present. Thus, whereas he knows facts about himself, he has no memory for events that included him personally. For example, he is unable to describe an event that took place in school that specifically included him, while at the same time recalling going to school and the knowledge he gained there.

Findings from neuroimaging studies of people with episodic amnesia suggest that they consistently have frontal-lobe injuries (Lepage et al., 2001), but exactly why these lesions produce episodic amnesia is still unclear. Nonetheless, Tulving made the interesting proposal that episodic memory is a marvel of nature: it transforms the brain into a kind of time machine that allows us to dwell on the past and make plans for the future. He goes further to suggest that this ability may be unique to humans and is presumably due to some novel evolutionary development of the frontal lobe.

Not all people with episodic amnesia have brain injury, however. Many case reports describe patients with massive memory disturbances resulting from some sort of "psychiatric" or "psychogenic" disorder. Such cases have been fodder for numerous movie plots.

Episodic memory Autobiographical memory for events pegged to specific place and time contexts.

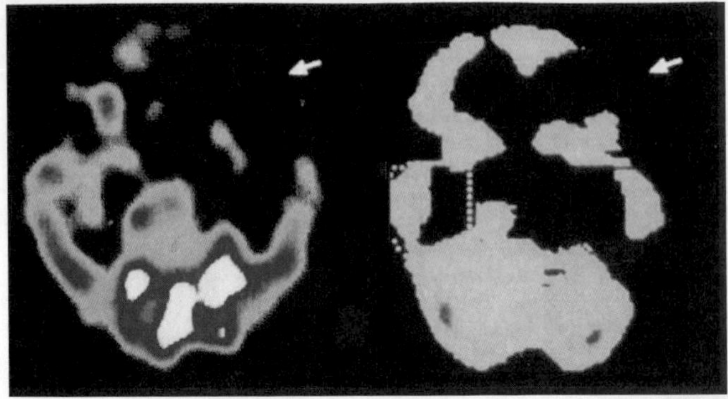

FIGURE 14-6 Lost Episodes. Horizontal sections of the brains of two patients with selective retrograde amnesia for autobiographical information. The section on the left is from an amnesic patient who had a brain infection (herpes simplex encephalitis). The section on the right is from the brain of a patient with psychogenic amnesia. In each case, the right frontal and temporal lobes are dark (white arrows), owing to a metabolic reduction in the right temporofrontal region. From "Functional Neuroimaging Correlates of Functional Amnesia," by H. J. Markowitsch, 1999, *Memory 7*, Plate 2. Reprinted by permission of Psychology Press Ltd., Hove.

Hans Markowitsch (2003) noted that the amnesia reported in some of these cases is remarkably similar to episodic amnesia seen in neurological patients. Neuroimaging of patients with psychogenic amnesia shows a massive reduction in brain activity in frontal regions that is remarkably similar to that seen in neurological patients with episodic amnesia (**Figure 14-6**). Therefore we can assume that patients with psychogenic amnesias have a dysfunction of frontal-brain activity that acts to block the retrieval of autobiographical memory.

REVIEW: Connecting Learning and Memory

- ✔ Among the multiple forms of learning, a primary distinction can be made between Pavlovian conditioning, in which some environmental stimulus (such as a tone) is paired with a reward, and operant conditioning, in which a response (such as pushing a button) is paired with a reward.
- ✔ The demands on the nervous system are different in classical and operant learning, and the brain regions each type activates are different. The cerebellum mediates classical conditioning, but the circuits required for operant conditioning vary with the learning requirements.
- ✔ Memory is the ability to recall or recognize previous experience, a definition that implies the existence of a memory trace, or mental representation, of a previous experience. Many forms of memory exist, each related to mental representations in different parts of the brain.
- ✔ One useful distinction is between implicit memory, in which information is unconsciously learned, and explicit memory, which is conscious memory for specific information. The mental representations of implicit and explicit memory are held in different regions of the brain.
- ✔ Episodic memory is autobiographical and unique to each person. Frontal-lobe injury or dysfunction is associated with both episodic amnesia and psychogenic amnesia.

Dissociating Memory Circuits

Beginning in the 1920s and continuing until the early 1950s, American psychologist Karl Lashley searched in vain for the neural circuits underlying memory for the solutions to mazes learned by laboratory rats and monkeys. Lashley's working hypothesis was that memories must be represented in the perceptual and motor circuitry used to learn solutions to problems. He believed that, if he removed bits of this circuitry or made knife cuts that disconnected it, amnesia should result.

In fact, neither procedure produced amnesia. Lashley found that the severity of the memory disturbance was related to the size of the injury rather than to its location. In 1951, after 30 years of searching, Lashley concluded that he had failed to find the location of the memory trace, although he did believe that he knew where it was *not* located (Lashley, 1960).

Chapter 10 describes how Penfield mapped the motor cortex using electrical stimulation as a means for sparing auditory and speech areas in patients undergoing surgery for intractable epilepsy.

Just two years later William Scoville made a serendipitous discovery that Lashley's studies had not predicted. Like Wilder Penfield, Scoville was a neurosurgeon who was attempting to rid people of seizures by removing the abnormal brain tissue that was causing them. On August 23, 1953, Scoville performed a bilateral medial-temporal-lobe

FIGURE 14-7 Extent of H. M.'s Surgery. H. M.'s brain viewed ventrally, with the right-hemisphere lesion highlighted. The lesion runs along the wall of the medial temporal lobe. The left side of the brain has been left intact to show the relative location of the medial temporal structures. Parts A, B, and C, based on MRI scans, depict a series of coronal sections of H. M.'s brain. Adapted from "H. M.'s Medial Temporal Lobe Lesion: Findings from Magnetic Resonance Imaging," by S. Corkin, D. G. Amaral, R. G. Gonzalez, K. A. Johnson, and B. T. Hyman, 1997, *Journal of Neuroscience, 17,* p. 3966.

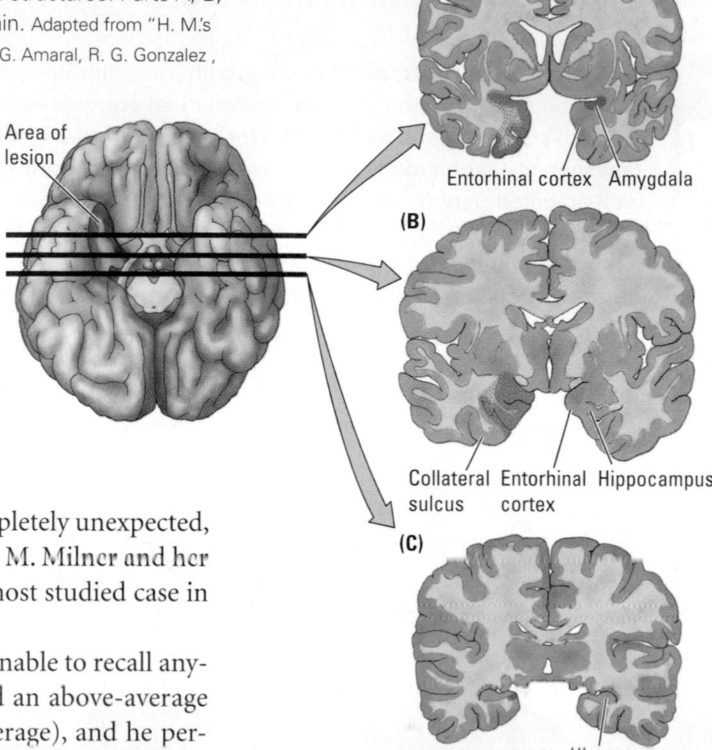

resection on a young man, Henry Molaison (H. M.), who had severe epilepsy that was not controlled by medication.

H. M.'s seizures originated in the medial temporal region, which includes the amygdala, hippocampal formation, and associated cortical structures, so Scoville removed the structures bilaterally, leaving the more lateral temporal-lobe tissue intact. As shown in **Figure 14-7,** the removal specifically included the anterior part of the hippocampus, the amygdala, and the adjacent cortex.

Disconnecting Explicit Memory

The behavioral symptoms Scoville noted after the surgery were completely unexpected, so he invited Brenda Milner, one of Penfield's associates, to study H. M. Milner and her colleagues studied H. M. for more than 50 years, making him the most studied case in neuroscience (e.g., Corkin, 2002). H. M. died in 2008.

H. M.'s most remarkable symptom was severe amnesia: he was unable to recall anything that had happened since his surgery in 1953. H. M. still had an above-average I.Q. score (118 on the Wechsler Adult Intelligence Scale; 100 is average), and he performed normally on perceptual tests. Furthermore, his recall of events from his childhood and school days was intact. Socially, H. M. was well mannered, and he engaged in sophisticated conversations. However, he had no recall for recent events. H. M. had no explicit memory.

In one study by Suzanne Corkin, H. M. was given a tray of hospital food, which he ate. A few minutes later, he was given another tray. He did not recall having eaten the first meal and proceeded to eat another. A third tray was brought, and this time he ate only the dessert, complaining that he did not seem to be very hungry.

To understand the implications and severity of H. M.'s condition, one need only consider a few events in his postsurgical life. His father died, but H. M. continued to ask where his father was, only to experience anew the grief of hearing that his father had passed away. (Eventually H. M. stopped asking about his father, suggesting that some type of learning had taken place.)

Similarly, when in the hospital, he typically asked, with many apologies, if the nurses could tell him where he was and how he came to be there. He remarked on one occasion, "Every day is alone in itself, whatever enjoyment I've had and whatever sorrow I've had." His experience was that of a person who perceives his surroundings but cannot comprehend the situation he is in because he does not remember what has gone before.

Formal tests of H. M.'s memory showed what one would expect: he had no recall for specific information just presented. In contrast, his implicit-memory performance was nearly intact. He performed normally on tests such as the incomplete-figure or pursuit-rotor tasks illustrated in Figures 14-3 and 14-4. Whatever systems are required for implicit memory must therefore have been intact, but the systems crucial to explicit memory were misssing or dysfunctional. Clinical Focus 14-2, "Patient Boswell's Amnesia," on page 492, describes a case similar to that of H. M.

Curiously, H. M. recognized faces, including his own, and he recognized that he aged. Face recognition depends on the parahippocampal gyrus, which was partly intact on H. M.'s right side.

Henry Molaison (H. M.).

Suzanne Corkin, reprinted with permission of The Wylie Agency

CLINICAL FOCUS 14-2

Patient Boswell's Amnesia

At the age of 48, Boswell developed herpes simplex encephalitis, a brain infection. Boswell had completed 13 years of schooling and had worked for nearly 30 years in the newspaper advertising business. By all accounts a normal, well-adjusted person, he was successful in his profession.

Boswell recovered from the acute symptoms of the disease, which included seizures and a 3-day coma. His post-disease intelligence was low average, probably owing to the neurological damage caused by the infection. Nonetheless, his speech and language remained normal in every respect, and he suffered no defects of sensory perception or of movement.

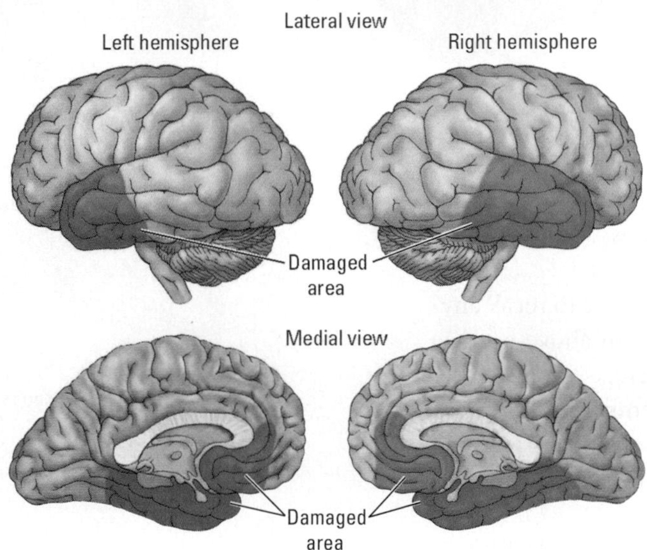

After a herpes simplex encephalitis infection, patient Boswell has great difficulty remembering events before and after his illness. Areas of damage in the medial temporal region, the basal forebrain, and the posterior orbitofrontal cortex are highlighted in red. Compare Figure 14-6.

But Boswell was left with a severe amnesic syndrome. If he hears a short paragraph and is asked to describe its main points, he routinely gets scores of zero. He can only guess the day's date and is unable even to guess what year it is. When asked what city he is in, he simply guesses.

Boswell does know his place of birth, and he can correctly recall his birth date about half the time. In sum, Boswell has a severe amnesia for events both before and since his encephalitis. He does show implicit memory, however, on tests such as the pursuit-rotor task (see Figure 14-4).

Boswell's amnesia has been extensively investigated by Antonio Damasio and his colleagues (1989), and his brain pathology is now well documented. The critical damage is a bilateral destruction of the medial temporal regions and a loss of the basal forebrain and the posterior part of the orbitofrontal cortex. In addition, Boswell has lost the insular cortex, which is found in the lateral fissure and not visible in the adjoining illustration.

In contrast, Boswell's sensory and motor cortices are intact, as are his basal ganglia. Boswell's injury is more extensive than H. M.'s. Like H. M., he has a loss of new memories, but, unlike H. M., he also has a severe loss of access to old information, probably because of his insular and prefrontal injuries. Nonetheless, again like H. M., Boswell has an intact procedural memory, a fact that illustrates the dissociation between neural circuits underlying explicit and implicit forms of memory.

Disconnecting Implicit Memory

There are probably several reasons why Lashley's research did not find a syndrome like that shown by H. M. Most important, Lashley did not use tests of explicit memory, so his animal subjects would not have shown H. M.'s deficits. Rather, Lashley's tests were mostly measures of implicit memory, with which H. M. had no problems. The following case illustrates that Lashley probably should have been looking in the basal ganglia for deficits revealed by his tests of implicit memory. The basal ganglia play a central role in motor control, and many compelling examples of implicit memory include motor learning—driving and playing instruments or games, to name a few.

J. K. was above average in intelligence and worked as a petroleum engineer for 45 years. In his mid-70s, he began to show symptoms of Parkinson's disease, in which the projections from the dopaminergic cells of the brainstem to the basal ganglia die. At about age 78, J. K. started to have memory difficulties.

Consult Chapters 5 and 6 for details about Parkinson's disease and Chapter 16 for a review of treatments.

Curiously, J. K.'s memory disturbance was related to tasks that he had done all his life. On one occasion, he stood at the door of his bedroom frustrated by his inability to recall how to turn on the lights. "I must be crazy," he remarked. "I've done this all my life and now I can't remember how to do it!" On another occasion, he was seen trying to turn the radio off with the television's remote control. This time he explained, "I don't recall how to turn off the radio so I thought I would try this thing!"

J. K. clearly had a deficit in implicit memory. In contrast, he was aware of daily events and could recall explicit events as well as most men his age. He could still speak intelligently on issues of the day that he had just read about. Once when we visited him, one of us entered the room first and he immediately asked where the other was, even though it had been 2 weeks since we told him that we would be coming to visit.

This intact long-term memory is very different from the situation of H. M., who would not have remembered that anybody was coming even 5 minutes after being told. Because Parkinson's disease primarily affects the basal ganglia, J. K.'s deficit in implicit memory was probably related to his basal ganglia dysfunction.

REVIEW: Dissociating Memory Circuits

- ✔ The circuits responsible for explicit memory and implicit memory are separate.
- ✔ Explicit memory relies on the anterior part of the hippocampus, the amygdala, and the adjacent cortex. These areas of H. M.'s brain were damaged, so he had no explicit memory.
- ✔ An implicit-memory deficit indicates deterioration of the basal ganglia characteristic of Parkinson's disease, as seen in patients such as J. K.

Neural Systems Underlying Explicit and Implicit Memories

Findings from laboratory studies largely on rats and monkeys have reproduced the symptoms of patients such as H. M. and J. K. in animals by injuring the medial temporal region and basal ganglia, respectively. Other structures, most notably in the frontal and temporal lobes, also play roles in certain types of explicit memory. We now consider the systems for explicit and implicit memory separately.

Neural Circuit for Explicit Memories

The dramatic amnesic syndrome discovered in H. M. in the 1950s led investigators to focus on the hippocampus, at the time regarded as a large brain structure in search of a function. But H. M. had other damaged structures, too, and the initial focus on the hippocampus as the location of explicit-memory processing turned out to be incorrect.

After several decades of anatomical and behavioral studies sorted out the complexities, by the mid-1990s consensus on the anatomy of explicit memory coalesced. The prime structures for explicit memory include the medial temporal region, the frontal cortex, and structures closely related to them.

If you consult books or reviews published before 1995, you may find explanations for memory quite different from those in this chapter (see Gazzaniga, 2000).

Before considering the model, we must first revisit the anatomy of the medial temporal region. Review Figure 14-5, which summarizes findings from the studies by Martin and colleagues showing that memories of the color and motion characteristics of objects reside in separate locations in the temporal lobe. The medial temporal region thus receives multiple sensory inputs.

The macaque monkey's medial temporal region shares many anatomical similarities with the human brain, and this monkey has been the principal subject of anatomical study of the region. In addition to the subcortical hippocampus and amygdala, three

FIGURE 14-8 Medial Temporal Cortex and Subcortical Structures. Ventral view of the rhesus monkey brain, showing the medial temporal regions on the left. Each plays a distinct role in processing sensory information for memory storage. The hippocampus and amygdala are not directly visible from the surface of the brain because they lie within the cortical regions illustrated on the left. All these cortical and subcortical structures are present on both sides of the brain.

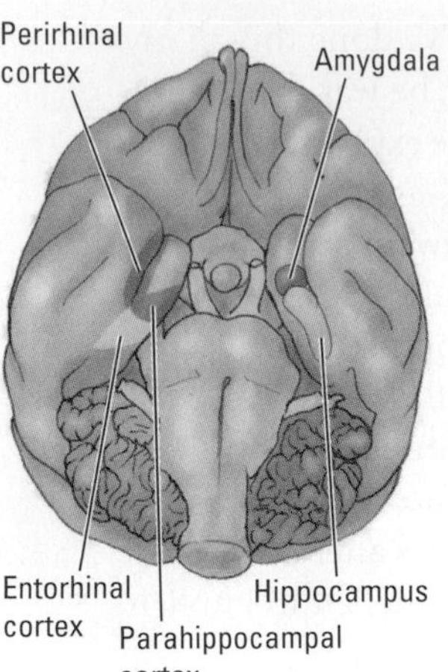

FIGURE 14-9 Reciprocal Medial Temporal Connections. Input from the sensory cortices flows to the parahippocampal and perirhinal regions, then to the entorhinal cortex, and finally to the hippocampus, which then feeds back to the medial temporal regions and on back to the sensory regions in the neocortex.

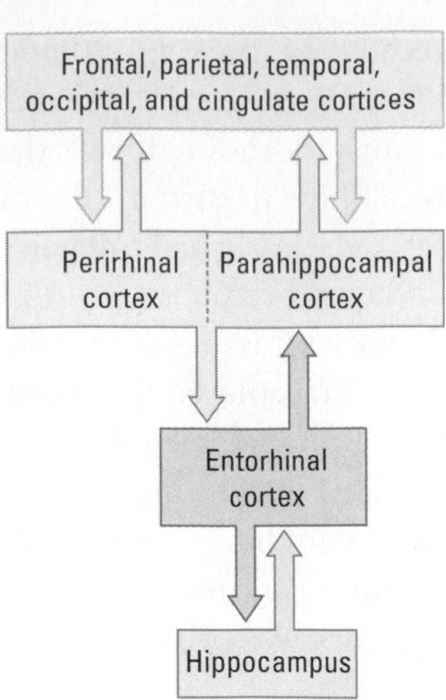

areas in the medial temporal cortex take part in explicit memory. As illustrated in **Figure 14-8,** these regions, lying adjacent to the hippocampus, are the **entorhinal cortex,** the **parahippocampal cortex,** and the **perirhinal cortex.** A sequential arrangement of two-way connections, charted in **Figure 14-9,** project from the major cortical regions into the perirhinal and parahippocampal cortices, which in turn project to the entorhinal cortex and then to the hippocampus.

In Greek, *para* means "beside" and *rhino* means "nose." The perirhinal cortex lies beside the rhinal sulcus on the bottom of the brain.

The prominent input from the neocortex to the perirhinal region is from the visual regions of the ventral stream coursing through the temporal lobe. The perirhinal region is thus a prime candidate for visual object memory. Similarly, the parahippocampal cortex has a strong input from regions of the parietal cortex believed to take part in visuospatial processing. Thus, the parahippocampal region likely has a role in **visuospatial memory,** that is, using visual information to recall an object's location in space.

Chapter 9 traces the visual pathways in detail.

Because both the perirhinal and the parahippocampal regions project to the entorhinal cortex, it is likely that this region participates in more integrative forms of memory. The entorhinal cortex is in fact the first area to show cell death in Alzheimer's disease, a form of dementia characterized by severe deficits in explicit memory (see Clinical Focus 14-3, "Alzheimer's Disease," on page 496).

Alzheimer's disease begins with minor forgetfulness, progresses to major memory dysfunction, and later develops into generalized dementia. Chapter 5 makes the link between Alzheimer's and acetylcholine, and Chapter 16 surveys treatments.

The Hippocampus and Spatial Memory

We are left with a conundrum. If the hippocampus is not the key structure in explicit memory yet is the recipient of the entorhinal connections, what does it do? The hippocampus is probably engaged in visuospatial memory processes required for places, such as recalling the location of an object. This idea was first advanced by John O'Keefe and Lynn Nadel in 1978.

Certainly, both laboratory animals and human patients with selective hippocampal injury have severe deficits in various forms of spatial memory. Similarly, monkeys with hippocampal lesions have difficulty learning the location of objects (i.e., *visuospatial learning*), as can be demonstrated in tasks such as those illustrated in **Figure 14-10.**

Monkeys are trained to displace objects to obtain a food reward (Figure 14-10A), then given one of two tasks. In the *visual-recognition task* shown in Figure 14-10B, the animal displaces a sample object to obtain a food reward. After a short delay, the animal is presented with two objects. One is novel. The task is to learn that the novel object must be displaced to obtain a food reward. This task is a test of explicit visual object memory. Monkeys with perirhinal lesions are impaired at the visual-recognition task.

In the *object-position task* in Figure 14-10C, the monkey is shown one object to be displaced for a food reward. Then the monkey is shown the same object along with a second, identical one. The task is to learn to displace the object that is in the same po-

Entorhinal cortex Located on the medial surface of the temporal lobe; provides a major route for neocortical input to the hippocampal formation; often degenerates in Alzheimer's disease.
Parahippocampal cortex Cortex located along the dorsal medial surface of the temporal lobe.
Perirhinal cortex Cortex lying next to the rhinal fissure on the base of the brain.
Visuospatial memory Using visual information to recall an object's location in space.

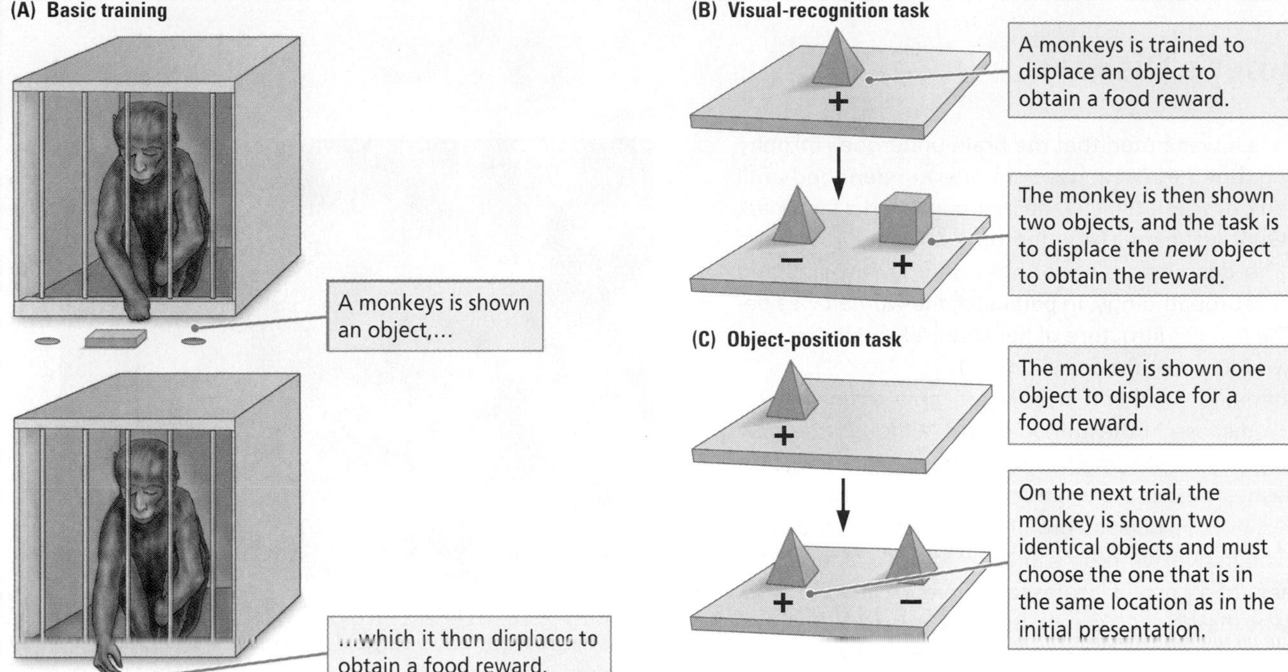

(A) Basic training
A monkeys is shown an object,...
...which it then displaces to obtain a food reward.
(B) Visual-recognition task
A monkeys is trained to displace an object to obtain a food reward.
The monkey is then shown two objects, and the task is to displace the *new* object to obtain the reward.
(C) Object-position task
The monkey is shown one object to displace for a food reward.
On the next trial, the monkey is shown two identical objects and must choose the one that is in the same location as in the initial presentation.
+
−
+
+
+
−

FIGURE 14-10 Two Memory Tasks for Monkeys. (A) In "basic training," a monkey learns to displace an object to obtain a food reward. (B) and (C) The plus and minus signs indicate whether the object is (+) or is not (−) associated with food.

sition as it was in the initial presentation. Monkeys with hippocampal lesions are selectively impaired at this object-position task.

From the results of these studies on the hippocampus, we would predict that animals with especially good spatial memories should have bigger hippocampi than do species with poorer spatial memories. David Sherry and his colleagues (1992) tested this hypothesis in birds.

Many birds are cachers: they harvest sunflower seeds and other favored foods and hide (cache) them to eat later. Some birds can find hundreds of items that they have cached. To evaluate whether the hippocampus plays a role in this activity, Sherry and his coworkers measured hippocampal size in closely related bird species, only one of which is a food cacher.

As shown in **Figure 14-11,** the hippocampal formation is larger in birds that cache food than in birds that do not. In fact, the hippocampi of food-storing birds are more than twice as large as expected for birds of their brain size and body weight.

Chapter 1 explains how Harry Jerison developed an index of brain-to-body-size ratios to allow for comparisons of different species' relative brain size even though their body sizes differ.

Sherry found a similar relation when he compared different species of food-storing rodents. Merriam's kangaroo rats, rodents that store food in various places throughout their territory, have larger hippocampi than bannertail kangaroo rats that store food only in their burrows. Hippocampal size in both birds and mammals appears to be related to the cognitive demands of two highly spatial activities, foraging for and storing food.

One prediction that we might make from the Sherry experiments is that people who have jobs with high spatial demands might have large hippocampi. Taxi drivers in London fit this category. Successful candidates for a cab driver's license in London must demonstrate that they know the location of every street in that huge and ancient city. Using MRI, Eleanor Maguire and her colleagues

Chickadee
Common sparrow
Relative volumetric ratio of hippocampus to forebrain
Food-storing Non-food-storing

FIGURE 14-11 Inferring Spatial Memory. This graph relates hippocampal volume to forebrain volume in 3 food-storing (*left*) and 10 non-food-storing (*right*) families of songbirds. The hippocampi of birds that cache food, such as the black-capped chickadee, are about twice as large as the hippocampi of birds that do not, such as the sparrow. Data from "Spatial Memory and Adaptive Specialization of the Hippocampus," by D. F. Sherry, L. F. Jacobs, and S. J. C. Gaulin, 1992, *Trends in Neuroscience, 15,* pp. 298–303.

CLINICAL FOCUS 14-3

Alzheimer's Disease

In the 1880s it was noted that the brain undergoes atrophy with aging, but the reason was not really understood until the German physician Alois Alzheimer published a landmark study in 1906. Alzheimer reported on a 51-year-old woman for whom he described a set of behavioral symptoms and associated neuropathology. In particular, the woman was demented. The cellular structure of her cerebral and limbic cortices showed various abnormalities.

An estimated 1 million people are now afflicted with Alzheimer's disease in the United States, although the only certain diagnostic test remains postmortem examination of cerebral tissue. The disease progresses slowly, and many people with Alzheimer's disease probably die from other causes before the cognitive symptoms become incapacitating.

We knew of a physics professor who continued to work until he was nearly 80 years old, at which time he succumbed to a heart attack. Postmortem examination of his brain revealed significant Alzheimer's pathology. His slipping memory had been attributed by his colleagues to "old-timer's disease."

The cause of Alzheimer's disease remains unknown, although it has been variously attributed to genetic predisposition, abnormal levels of trace elements (e.g., aluminum), immune reactions, and slow viruses. Two principal neuronal changes take place in Alzheimer's disease:

1. *Loss of cholinergic cells in the basal forebrain.* One treatment for Alzheimer's disease, therefore, is medication that increases acetylcholine levels in the forebrain. An example is Cognex, which is the trade name for tacrine hydrochloride, a cholinergic agonist that appears to provide temporary relief from the progression of the disease.
2. *Development of neuritic plaques in the cerebral cortex.* A **neuritic plaque** consists of a central core of homogeneous protein material (*amyloid*) surrounded by degenerative cellular fragments. The plaques, illustrated here, are not distributed evenly throughout the cortex but are concentrated especially in the temporal-lobe areas related to memory. Neuritic plaques are often associated with another abnormality, neurofibrillary tangles, which are paired helical filaments found in both the cerebral cortex and the hippocampus.

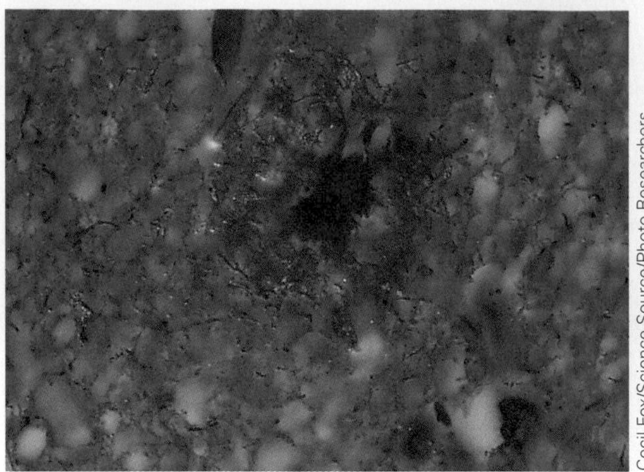
Cecil Fox/Science Source/Photo Researchers

Neuritic plaque, as often found in the cerebral cortices of Alzheimer patients. The amyloid is the dark spot in the center of the image, which is surrounded by the residue of degenerated cells.

Cortical neurons begin to deteriorate as the cholinergic loss, plaques, and tangles develop. The first cells to die are in the entorhinal cortex, and significant memory disturbance ensues.

An idea emerging from stroke neurologists is that dementia may reflect a chronic cerebrovascular condition, marginal high blood pressure. Marginal elevations in blood pressure can lead to cerebral microbleeds, especially in white matter. The cumulative effect of years or even decades of tiny bleeds would eventually lead to increasingly disturbed cognition.

(2000) found the posterior region of the hippocampus in London taxi drivers to be significantly larger than the same region in the control participants. This finding presumably explains why a select few pass a spatial-memory test that most of us would fail miserably.

Neuritic plaque Area of incomplete necrosis (dead tissue) consisting of a central protein core (amyloid) surrounded by degenerative cellular fragments; often seen in the cortex of people with senile dementias such as Alzheimer's disease.

Reciprocal Connections for Explicit Memory

The temporal pathway of explicit memory is reciprocal: connections from the neocortex run to the entorhinal cortex and then back to the neocortex (see Figure 14-9). Reciprocal connections have two benefits:

1. Signals from the medial temporal regions back to the cortical sensory regions keep the sensory experience alive in the brain: the neural record of an experience outlasts the actual experience.
2. The pathway back to the neocortex means that the neocortex is kept apprised of information being processed in the medial temporal regions.

Feedback to the cortex is not part of the basal ganglia systems that take part in implicit memory. This helps to explain the unconscious nature of implicit memory.

Although we have focused on the role of the medial temporal regions, other structures also are important in explicit memory. People with frontal-lobe injuries are not amnesic like H. M. or J. K., but they do have difficulties with memory for the temporal (time) order of events. Imagine that you are shown a series of photographs and asked to remember them. A few minutes later, you are asked whether you recognize two photographs and, if so, to indicate which one you saw first.

H. M. would not remember the photographs. People with frontal-lobe injuries would recall seeing the photographs but would have difficulty recalling which one they had seen most recently. The role of the frontal lobe in explicit memory is clearly more subtle than that of the medial temporal lobe.

The Frontal Lobe and Short-Term Memory All sensory systems in the brain send information to the frontal lobe, as do the medial temporal regions. This information is not used for direct sensory analysis, so it must have some other purpose. In general, the frontal lobe appears to have a role in many forms of short-term memory.

Joaquin Fuster (e.g., Fuster, Bodner, & Kroger, 2000) studied single-cell activity in the frontal lobe during short-term-memory tasks. For example, if monkeys are shown an object that they must remember for a short time before being allowed to make a response, neurons in the prefrontal cortex show a sustained firing during the delay. Consider the tests illustrated in **Figure 14-12:**

Single-cell recording, described in Chapter 6, can monitor the activity of a single neuron.

- In the general design for each test, a monkey is shown a light, which is the cue, and then must make a response after a delay to get a reward.
- In the *delayed-response task,* the monkey is shown two lights in the choice test and must choose the one that is in the same location as the cue.
- In the *delayed-alternation task,* the monkey is again shown two lights in the choice tests but now must choose the light that is *not* in the same location as the cue.
- In the *delayed-matching-to-sample task,* the monkey is shown, say, a red light and then, after a delay, is shown a red and a green light. The task is to choose the red light, regardless of its new location.

Fuster found that in each task certain cells in the prefrontal cortex fire throughout the delay. Animals that have not learned the task show no such cell activity. Curiously, if a trained animal makes an error, its cellular activity corresponds: the cells stop responding before the error occurs. They have "forgotten" the cue.

In the following tests, a monkey is shown a light, which is the cue, and then it makes a response after a delay.

Cue | Delay | Choice

Off

On

Delayed-response task: The monkey must choose the light that is in the same location as the cue.

Delayed-alternation task: The monkey must choose the light that is not in the same location as the cue.

Delayed-matching-to-sample task: The monkey must choose the light that is the same color as the cue.

Time →

FIGURE 14-12 Testing Short-Term Memory. A monkey performing a short-term memory task responds by pressing the disc to get a fruit juice reward (*top*). The correct disc varies, depending on the requirements of the task (*bottom*). The correct choice for each task is indicated by an arrowhead.
Adapted from *Memory in the Cerebral Cortex* (p. 178), by J. Fuster, 1995, Cambridge, MA: MIT

Tracing the Explicit Memory Circuit People who have chronically abused alcohol can develop an explicit-memory disturbance known as **Korsakoff's syndrome.** In some cases, severe deficits in explicit memory extend to implicit memory as well. Korsakoff's syndrome is caused by a thiamine (vitamin B_1) deficiency.

Thiamine deficiency results from poor nutrition. Alcohol abusers often neglect to eat, and even when they do, the alcohol in their system inhibits the body's ability to absorb vitamin B_1. Chapter 2 charts the anatomy of the diencephalon, or "between brain," at the top of the brainstem.

The B_1 deficiency kills cells in the medial part of the diencephalon, including the medial thalamus and mammillary bodies in the hypothalamus of Korsakoff patients. The frontal lobes of 80 percent show atrophy (loss of cells). The memory disturbance is probably so severe in many Korsakoff patients because the damage includes not only forebrain but also brainstem structures (see Clinical Focus 14-4, "Korsakoff's Syndrome").

Mortimer Mishkin and his colleagues (Mishkin, 1982; Murray, 2000) at the U.S. National Institute of Mental Health proposed a neural circuit for explicit memory. It incorporates the evidence from both humans and laboratory animals with injuries to the temporal and frontal lobes.

Figure 14-13 presents a modified version of the Mishkin model that includes not only the frontal and temporal lobes but also the medial thalamus, which is implicated in Korsakoff's syndrome, and the basal forebrain-activating systems that are implicated in Alzheimer's disease:

- The sensory neocortical areas send their connections to the medial temporal regions, which are in turn connected to the medial thalamus and prefrontal cortex.
- The basal forebrain structures are hypothesized to play a role in maintaining appropriate levels of activity in the forebrain structures so that they can process information.
- The temporal-lobe structures are hypothesized to be central to the formation of long-term explicit memories.

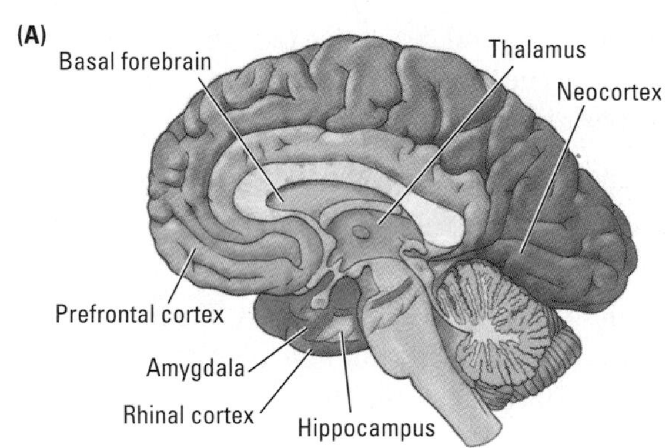

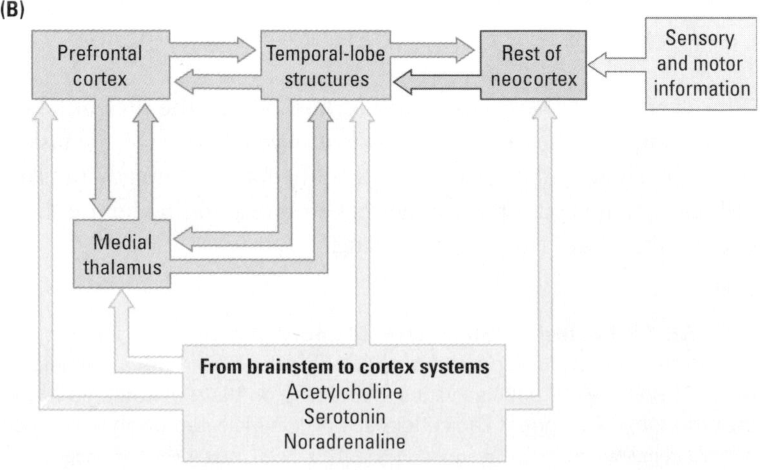

FIGURE 14-13 Reciprocal Neural Circuit Proposed for Explicit Mmory. (A) General neuroanatomical areas controlling explicit memory. (B) Circuit diagram showing the flow of information, beginning on the right with inputs from the sensory and motor systems, which are not considered part of the memory circuit.

Korsakoff's syndrome Permanent loss of the ability to learn new information (anterograde amnesia) and to retrieve old information (retrograde amnesia) caused by diencephalic damage resulting from chronic alcoholism or malnutrition that produces a vitamin B_1 deficiency.
Retrograde amnesia Inability to remember events that took place before the onset of amnesia.
Anterograde amnesia Inability to remember events subsequent to a disturbance of the brain such as head trauma, electroconvulsive shock, or certain neurodegenerative diseases.

CLINICAL FOCUS 14-4

Korsakoff's Syndrome

Over the long term, alcoholism, especially when accompanied by malnutrition, obliterates memory. When Joe R., a 62-year-old man, was hospitalized, his family complained that his memory had become abysmal. His intelligence was in the average range, and he had no obvious sensory or motor difficulties. Nevertheless, he was unable to say why he was in the hospital and usually stated that he was actually in a hotel.

When asked what he had done the previous night, Joe R. typically said that he "went to the Legion for a few beers with the boys." Although he had, in fact, been in the hospital, it was a sensible response because that is what he had done on most nights in the preceding 30 years.

Joe R. was not certain of what he had done for a living but believed that he had been a butcher. In fact, he had been a truck driver for a local delivery firm. His son was a butcher, however, so once again his story was related to something in his life.

Joe's memory for immediate events was little better. On one occasion, we asked him to remember having met us, and then we left the room. On our return 2 or 3 minutes later, he had no recollection of ever having met us or of having taken psychological tests that we administered.

Joe R. had Korsakoff's syndrome, a condition named after Sergei Korsakoff, a Russian physician who in the 1880s first called attention to a syndrome that accompanies chronic alcoholism. The most obvious symptom is severe loss of memory, including amnesia for both information learned in the past (**retrograde amnesia**) and information learned since the onset of the memory disturbance (**anterograde amnesia**).

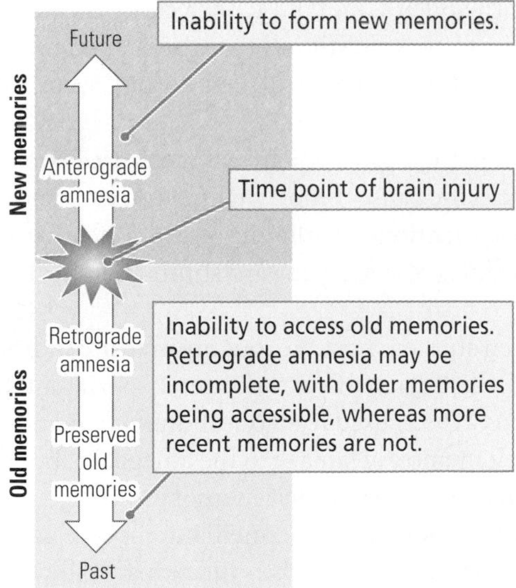

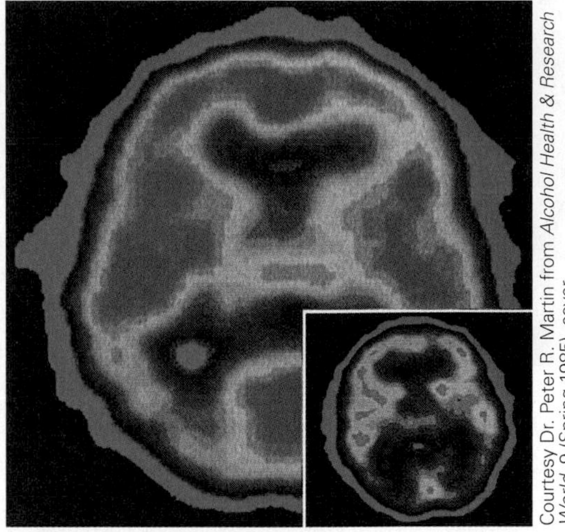

Courtesy Dr. Peter R. Martin from *Alcohol Health & Research World*, 9 (Spring 1985), cover.

These PET scans, from a normal patient (larger image) and a Korsakoff patient (inset), demonstrate reduced activity in the frontal lobe of the diseased brain. (The frontal lobes are at the bottom center of each scan.) Red and yellow represent areas of high metabolic activity versus the lower level of activity in the darker areas.

One unique characteristic of the amnesic syndrome in Korsakoff patients is that they tend to make up stories about past events rather than admit that they do not remember. These stories, like those of Joe R., are generally plausible because they are based on actual experiences.

Curiously, Korsakoff patients have little insight into their memory disturbance and are generally indifferent to suggestions that they have a memory problem. Such patients are generally apathetic to things going on around them too. Joe R. was often seen watching television when the set was turned off.

The cause of Korsakoff's syndrome is a thiamine (vitamin B_1) deficiency resulting from prolonged intake of large quantities of alcohol. Joe R. had a long history of drinking a 26-ounce bottle of rum every day, in addition to a "few beers with the boys." The thiamine deficiency results in the death of cells in the midline diencephalon, including especially the medial regions of the thalamus and the mammillary bodies of the hypothalamus.

Most Korsakoff patients also show cortical atrophy, especially in the frontal lobe. With the appearance of the Korsakoff symptoms, which can happen quite suddenly, prognosis is poor. Only about 20 percent of patients show much recovery after a year on a vitamin B_1–enriched diet. Joe R. has shown no recovery after several years and will spend the rest of his life in a hospital setting.

Emotional memory Memory for the affective properties of stimuli or events.

- The prefrontal cortex is central to the maintenance of temporary (short-term) explicit memories as well as memory for the recency (chronological order) of explicit events.

Neural Circuit for Implicit Memories

Hypothesizing that the basal ganglia are central to implicit memory, Mishkin and his colleagues also proposed a neural circuit for implicit memories (Mishkin, 1982; Mishkin et al., 1997). As **Figure 14-14** shows, the basal ganglia receive input from the entire neocortex and send projections to the ventral thalamus and then to the premotor cortex. The basal ganglia also receive widely and densely distributed projections from dopamine-producing cells in the substantia nigra. Dopamine appears necessary for circuits in the basal ganglia to function and may indirectly participate in implicit-memory formation.

The connection from the cortex to the basal ganglia in the implicit-memory system flows only in one direction. Most of the neocortex receives no direct information regarding the activities of the basal ganglia. Mishkin believes that this unidirectional flow accounts for the unconscious nature of implicit memories. For memories to be conscious, the neocortical regions involved must receive feedback, as they do in the explicit-memory system.

Mishkin's model shows why people with dysfunction of the basal ganglia, as occurs in Parkinson's disease, have deficits in implicit memory, whereas people with injuries to the frontal or temporal lobes have relatively good implicit memories, even though they may have profound disturbances of explicit memory. Some people with Alzheimer's disease are able to play games expertly, even though they have no recollection of having played them before.

Daniel Schacter (1983) wrote of a golfer with Alzheimer's disease. The golfer's medial temporal system was severely compromised by the disease, but his basal ganglia were unaffected. Despite impairment of his explicit knowledge, as indexed by his inability to find shots or to remember his strokes on each hole, the man retained his ability to play the game.

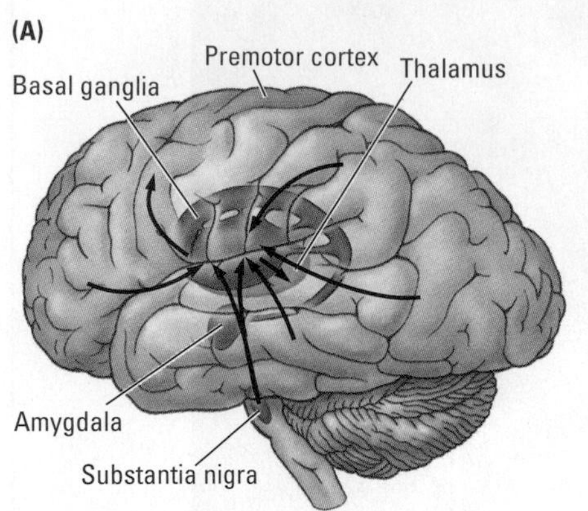

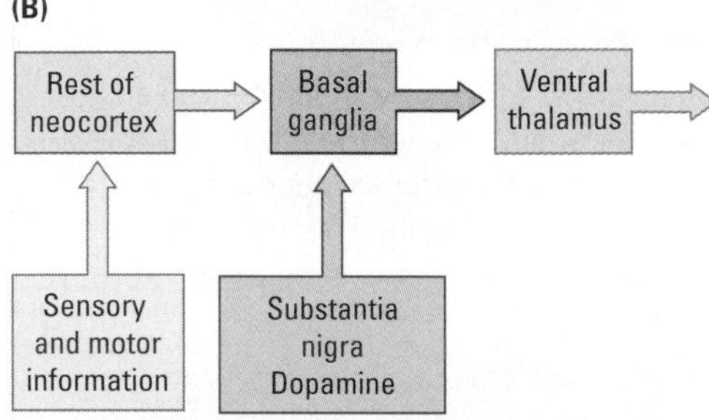

FIGURE 14-14 Unidirectional Neural Circuit Proposed for Implicit Memory. (A) General anatomical areas controlling implicit memory. (B) Circuit diagram showing the one-way flow of information beginning with inputs from the sensory and motor systems, which are not considered part of the memory circuit.

Neural Circuit for Emotional Memories

Whether a third type of memory, **emotional memory** for the affective properties of stimuli or events, is implicit or explicit is not altogether clear. It could be both. Certainly people can react with fear to specific stimuli that they can identify, and we have seen that they can also fear situations for which they do not seem to have specific memories.

Panic disorder is a common pathology of emotional memory. People show marked anxiety but cannot identify a specific cause. Emotional memory has a unique anatomical component—the amygdala, mentioned earlier in regard to fear conditioning. The amygdala seems to evoke our feelings of anxiety toward stimuli that by themselves would not normally produce fear.

Consult Chapter 12 for detail on the amygdala's function within the limbic system and its influence on emotional behavior.

Emotional memory has been studied most thoroughly in fear conditioning by pairing noxious stimuli, such as foot shock, with a tone (see Experiment 14-1). Michael Davis (1992) and Joseph LeDoux (1995) used fear conditioning to demonstrate that the amygdala is critical to emotional memory. Damage to the amygdala abolishes emotional memory but has little effect on implicit or explicit memory.

Chapter 11 reports on the PAG's role in perceiving pain. The autonomic nervous system, diagrammed in Figure 2-28, monitors and controls such life-support functions as blood pressure, glucose levels, and heart rate.

The amygdala has close connections with the medial temporal cortical structures as well as with the rest of the cortex. It also sends projections to the brainstem structures that control autonomic responses such as blood pressure and heart rate, to the hypothalamus that controls hormonal systems, and to the periaqueductal gray matter (PAG) that affects the perception of pain (**Figure 14-15**). The amygdala hooks in to the implicit-memory system through its connections with the basal ganglia.

Fear is not the only aspect of emotional memory coded by the amygdala. A study of severely demented patients by Bob Sainsbury and Marjorie Coristine (1986) nicely illustrates this point. The patients were believed to have severe cortical abnormalities but intact amygdalar functioning.

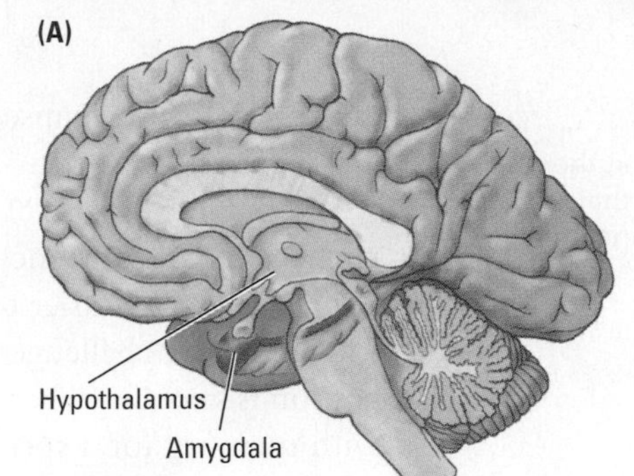

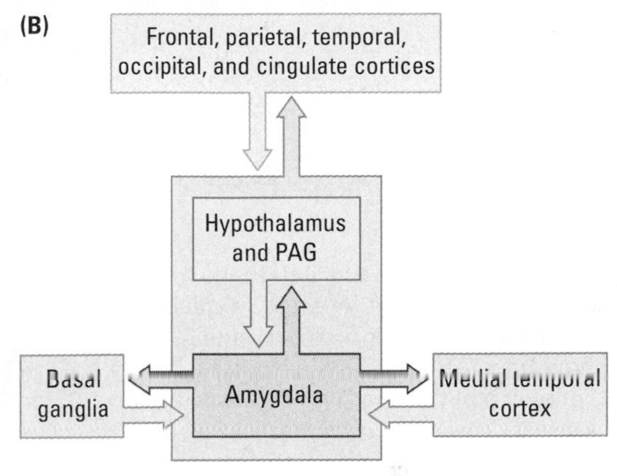

FIGURE 14-15 Neural Circuit Proposed for Emotional Memory. (A) The key structure in emotional memory is the amygdala. (B) Circuit diagram showing the flow of information in emotional memory.

The researchers first established that the ability of the patients to recognize photographs of close relatives was severely impaired. The patients were then shown four photographs, one of which depicted a relative (either a sibling or a child) who had visited in the past 2 weeks. The task was to identify the person whom they liked better than the others. Although the subjects were unaware that they knew anyone in the group of photographs, they consistently preferred the photographs of their relatives. This result suggests that, although the explicit and probably the implicit memory of the relative was gone, each patient's emotional memory guided his or her preference.

Emotionally arousing experiences tend to be vividly remembered, a fact confirmed by findings from both animal and human studies. James McGaugh (2004) concluded that emotionally significant experiences, both pleasant and unpleasant, must activate hormonal and brain systems that act to "stamp in" these vivid memories.

McGaugh noted that many neural systems probably take part, but the basolateral part of the amygdala is critical. The general idea is that emotionally driven hormonal and neurochemical activating systems (probably cholinergic and noradrenergic) stimulate the amygdala. The amygdala in turn modulates the laying down of memory circuits in the rest of the brain, especially in the medial temporal and prefrontal regions and the basal ganglia. We would not expect people with amygdala damage to have enhanced memory for emotion-laden events, and they do not (Cahill et al., 1995).

Figure 5-17 traces the connections of the neural activating systems, and Chapter 8 explains how hormones work.

REVIEW: Neural Systems Underlying Explicit and Implicit Memories

- ✔ Certain neural structures and circuits are associated with different types of learning and memory. The accompanying figure summarizes the broad categories of memory.
- ✔ Presumably, when we learn different types of information, changes take place in synapses in these systems, and these changes produce our memories of the experiences.
- ✔ One system, consisting of the prefrontal cortex and the medial temporal lobe and regions related to them, is the probable neural location of explicit memory.
- ✔ A second system, consisting of the basal ganglia and neocortex, forms the neural basis for implicit memory.
- ✔ A third system, which includes the amygdala and its associated structures, forms the neural basis for emotional memory.

Multiple Memory Systems.

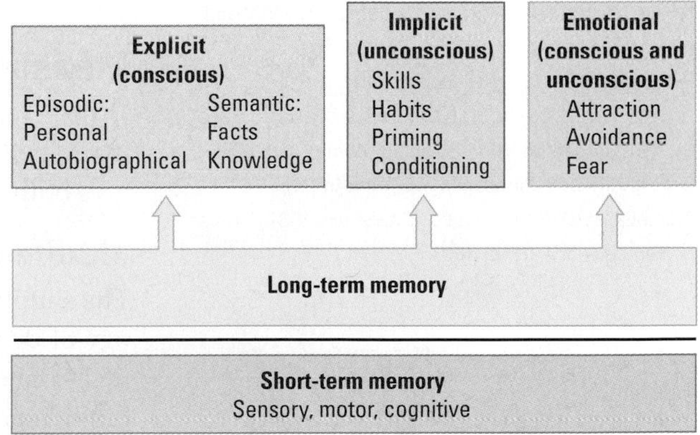

Structural Basis of Brain Plasticity

We have encountered three different categories of memory and the different brain circuits that underlie each type. Our next task is to consider how the neurons in the circuits change to store the memories. The consensus among neuroscientists is that the changes take place at the synapse, in part because that is where neurons influence one another. This idea dates back to 1928, when Spanish anatomist Santiago Ramón y Cajal suggested that the process of learning might produce prolonged morphological (structural) changes in the efficiency of the synapses activated in the learning process. This idea turned out to be easier to propose than to study.

Chapter 3 identifies Cajal as the author of the neuron hypothesis, the idea that neurons are the units of brain function.

The major challenge that researchers still encounter as they investigate Cajal's suggestion is knowing where in the brain to look for synaptic changes that might correlate with memory for a specific stimulus. This task is formidable. Imagine trying to find the exact location of the neurons responsible for storing your grandmother's name. You would face a similar challenge in trying to find the neurons responsible for the memory of an object in a monkey's brain as the monkey performs the visual-recognition task illustrated in Figure 14-10B.

Investigators have approached the problem of identifying synaptic change in two distinctly different ways. The first approach is to study simple neural systems. Study of the sea snail *Aplysia* revealed that changes in the properties of the synapse take place when animals learn the association between a noxious stimulus and a cue signaling the onset of the stimulus. In more complex animals, synaptic changes take place in hippocampal slices in which long-term potentiation (LTP) is induced. The identification of synaptic change is possible in *Aplysia* and in LTP because we know where in the nervous system to look. But we have little information about where to look for memory-storing synapses in mammals.

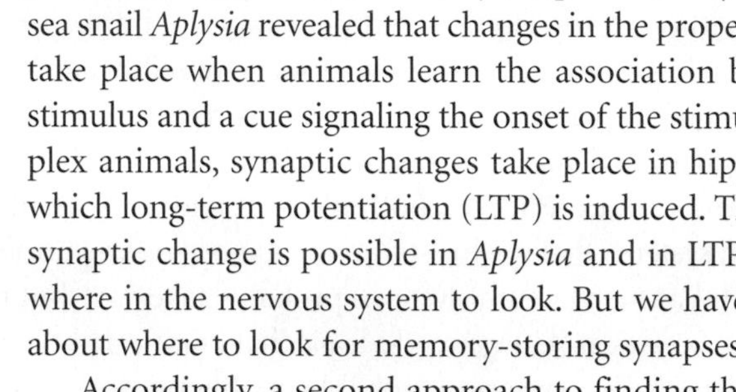

Aplysia

Experiment 5-2 explains habituation at the neuronal level, Experiment 5-3 explains sensitization, and Figures 5-18 and 5-19 show how LTP induces the synaptic changes that play a part in learning by association.

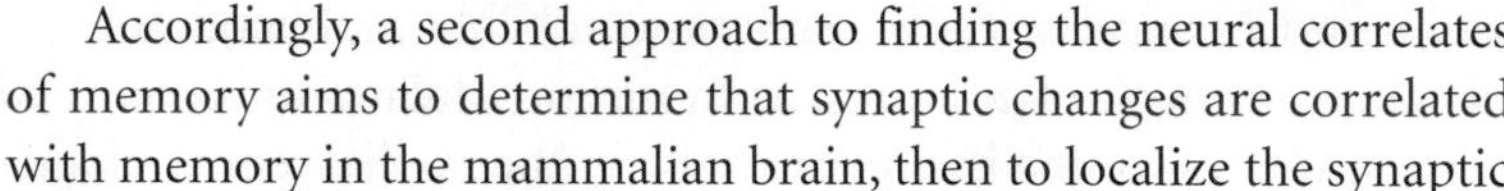

Accordingly, a second approach to finding the neural correlates of memory aims to determine that synaptic changes are correlated with memory in the mammalian brain, then to localize the synaptic changes to specific neural pathways and analyze the nature of the synaptic changes themselves. This section reviews the studies that have identified synaptic changes correlated with various types of experience. We first consider the general research strategy. We then look at the gross neural changes correlated with different forms of experience, ranging from living in specific environments to learning specific tasks or having specific experiences to the chronic administration of trophic factors, hormones, and addictive drugs. It turns out that the general synaptic organization of the brain is modified in a strikingly similar manner by each of these diverse forms of experience.

Measuring Synaptic Change

In principle, experience could cause the brain to change in either of two ways: by modifying existing circuitry or by creating novel circuitry. In actuality, the plastic brain uses both strategies.

Modifying Existing Circuits

The simplest way to find synaptic change is to look for gross changes in the morphology of dendrites. Dendrites and their spines are essentially extensions of the neuron membrane that allow more space for synapses. Cells that have few or no dendrites have limited space for inputs, whereas cells with complex dendritic structures may have space for tens of thousands of inputs. More dendrites mean more connections. Change in dendritic structure, therefore, implies change in synaptic organization. Complex neurons, such as pyramidal cells, have 95 percent of their synapses on the dendrites. Thus, measuring the extent of dendritic changes can infer synaptic change.

A striking feature of dendrites is that their shape is highly changeable. Dale Purves and his colleagues (Purves and Voyvodic, 1987) labeled cells in the dorsal-root ganglia of living mice with a special dye that allowed them to visualize the dendrites of the cells. When they examined the same cells at intervals ranging from a few days to weeks, they identified obvious qualitative changes in dendritic extent, as represented in **Figure 14-16.**

FIGURE 14-16 Dendritic Plasticity. Reconstructions of parts of the dendrites of three mouse superior cervical ganglion cells observed at an interval of 3 months. Changes in both the extension and the retraction of particular dendritic branches are evident. Adapted from "Imaging Mammalian Nerve Cells and Their Connections over Time in Living Animals," by D. Purves and J. T. Voyvodic, 1987, *Trends in Neuroscience, 10,* p. 400.

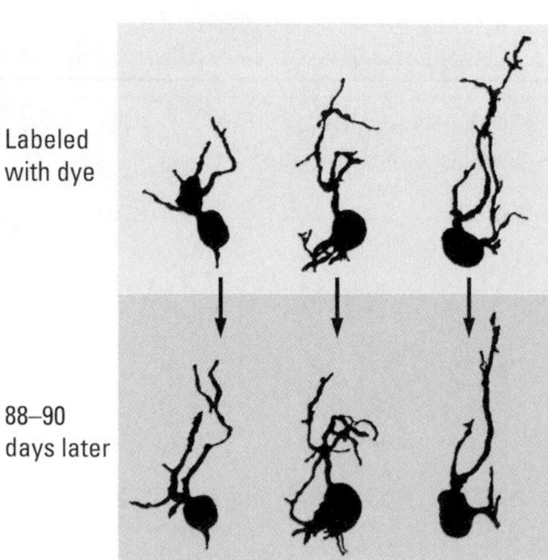

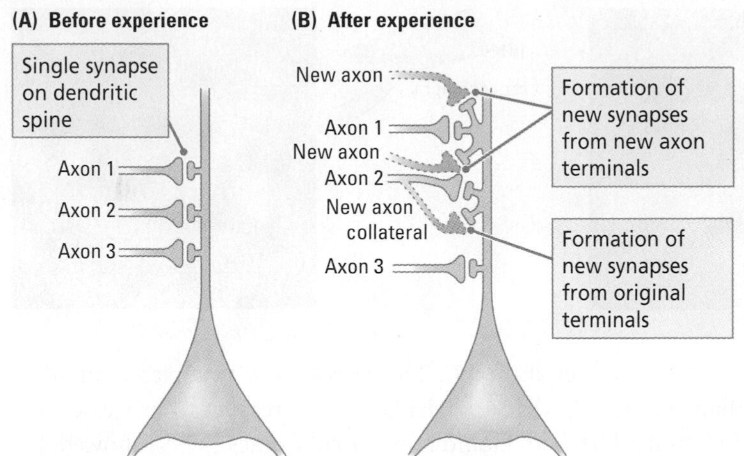

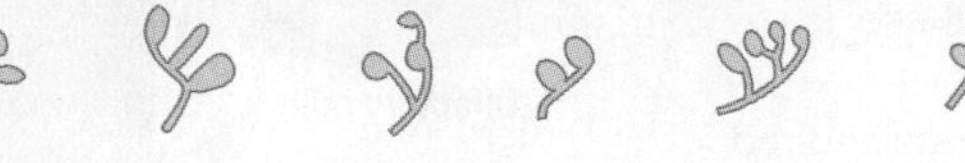

FIGURE 14-17 Effects of Experience. (A) Three inputs to a dendrite of a pyramidal cell. Each axon forms a synapse with a different dendritic spine. (B) Formation of multiple spine heads. Either the original axons may divide and innervate two spine heads or new axons or axon collaterals (dotted outlines) may innervate the new spine heads. (C) Single dendritic spines may sprout multiple synapses.

We can assume that new dendritic branches have new synapses and that lost branches mean lost synapses.

An obvious lesson from the Purves studies is that neuronal morphology is not static: neurons change their structure in response to their changing experiences. As they search for neural correlates of memory, researchers can take advantage of this changeability by studying variations in dendritic morphology that are correlated with specific experiences, such as learning some task.

What do changes in dendritic morphology reveal? Let us consider the case in which a given neuron generates more synaptic space. The new synapses can be either additional contacts between neurons that were already connected with the neuron in question or contacts between neurons that were not formerly connected. Examples of these distinctly different synapse types are illustrated in **Figure 14-17.**

Research Focus 5-5 explains how dendritic spines form and why they provide the structural basis for behavior.

New synapses can result either from the growth of new axon terminals or from the formation of synapses along axons as they pass by dendrites. In both cases, new synapses correspond to changes in the local circuitry of a region and not to the development of new connections between distant parts of the brain. Forming new connections between widely separated brain regions would be very difficult in a fully grown brain because of the dense plexus of cells, fibers, and blood vessels that lies in the way.

Thus, the growth of new synapses indicates modifications to basic circuits already in the brain. This strategy has an important implication for the location of synaptic changes underlying memory. During development, the brain forms circuits to process sensory information and to produce movement (behavior). These circuits are the most likely to be modified to form memories (see Figure 14-5).

Creating Novel Circuits

Before the mid-1990s, the general assumption was that the mammalian brain did not make new neurons in adulthood. The unexpected discovery in the 1970s that the brains of songbirds such as canaries grow new neurons to produce songs in the mating season led researchers to reconsider that the adult mammalian brain, too, might be capable of generating new neurons.

This possibility can be tested directly by injecting animals with a compound—bromode-oxyuridine (BrdU)—that is taken up by cells when they divide to produce new cells, including neurons. When the compound is injected into adult rats, dividing cells incorporate it into their DNA. In later analysis, a specific stain can be used to identify the new neurons. **Figure 14-18** shows such an analysis in the rat olfactory bulb and hippocampus.

The BrdU technique has yielded considerable evidence that the mammalian brain, including the primate brain, can generate neurons destined for the olfactory bulb, the hippocampal formation, and possibly even the neocortex of the frontal and temporal

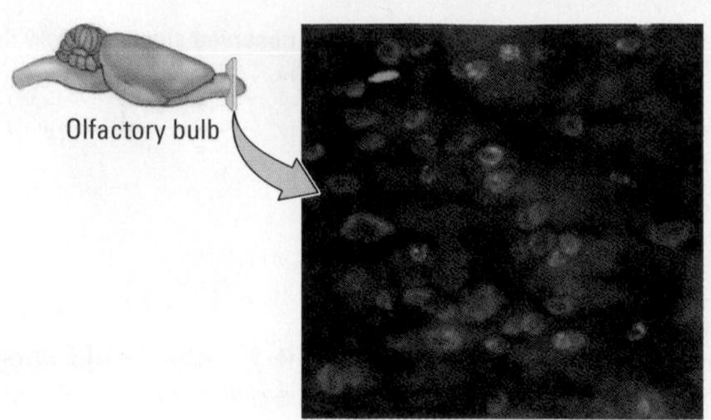

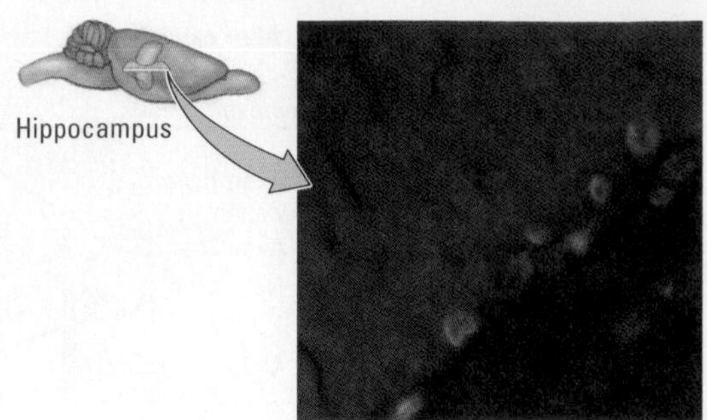

FIGURE 14-18 Neurogenesis in Adult Rats. In these confocal microscopic photographs, cells stained red with an antibody to neurons (called NeuN) are neurons; cells stained green with an antibody to bromode-oxyuridine (BrdU) are new cells, including both neurons and glia; cells stained yellow are positive for both red and green and are new neurons.

lobes (Eriksson et al., 1998; Gould et al., 1999). The reason is not yet clear, but adult neurogenesis may enhance brain plasticity, particularly with respect to processes underlying learning and memory. Elizabeth Gould and her colleagues (1999) showed, for example, that generation of new neurons in the hippocampus is enhanced when animals learn explicit-memory tasks. Furthermore, experience appears to increase the generation of these new neurons.

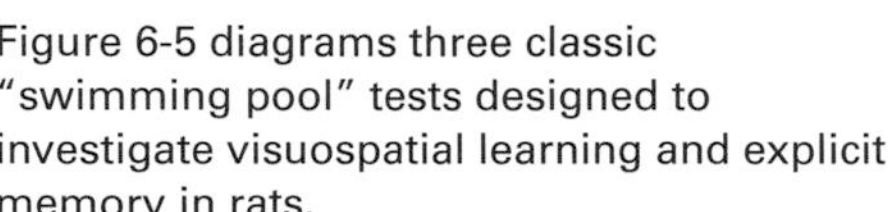
Figure 6-5 diagrams three classic "swimming pool" tests designed to investigate visuospatial learning and explicit memory in rats.

Enriched Experience and Plasticity

See Chapter 7 for more about Hebb's research, its effects on educational programs, and his wife's impact on the duration of the first enrichment exercise.

One way to stimulate the brain is to house animals in environments that provide sensory or motor experience. Donald Hebb took laboratory rats home and gave them the run of his kitchen. After an interval, Hebb compared the "enriched" rats with another group that had remained in cages in his laboratory at McGill University, by training both groups to solve various mazes. The enriched animals performed better, and Hebb concluded that one effect of the enriched experience is to enhance later learning. This important conclusion laid the foundation for the Head Start programs in the United States that provide academic experiences for disadvantaged preschool-aged children.

When subsequent investigators have worked with rats, they have opted for a more constrained procedure that uses some type of "enriched enclosure." For example, in our own studies, we place groups of six rats in enclosures. The enclosures give animals a rich social experience as well as extensive sensory and motor experience.

The most obvious consequence is an increase in brain weight that may be on the order of 10 percent relative to cage-reared animals, even though the enriched rats typically weigh less, in part because they get more exercise. The key question is What is responsible for the increased brain weight? A comprehensive series of studies by Anita Sirevaag and William Greenough (1988) used light- and electron-microscopic techniques to analyze 36 different aspects of cortical synaptic, cellular, and vascular morphology in rats raised either in cages or in complex environments. The simple conclusion: a coordinated change occurs not only in the extent of dendrites but also in glial, vascular, and metabolic processes in response to differential experiences (**Figure 14-19**).

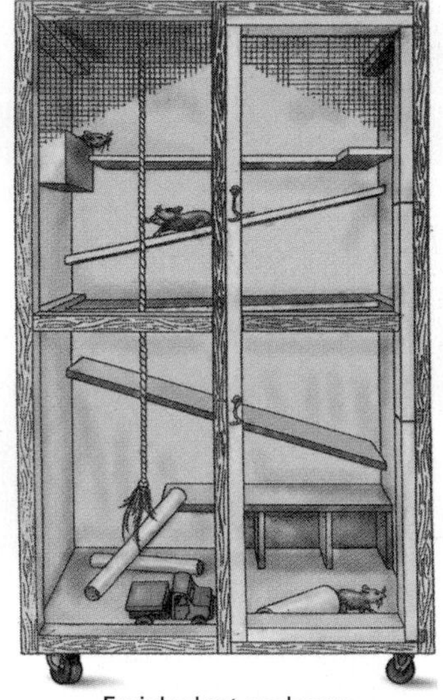

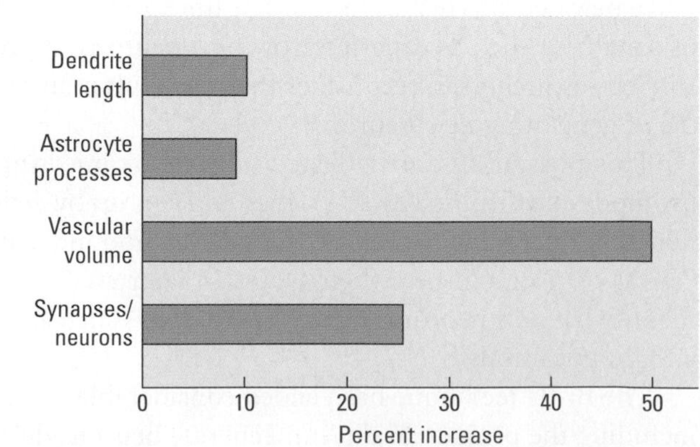

FIGURE 14-19 Consequences of Enrichment. Cortical changes that take place in response to experience are found not only in neurons but also in astrocytes and vasculature. Based on data from "Differential Rearing Effects on Rat Visual Cortex Synapses. I. Synaptic and Neuronal Density and Synapses per Neuron," by A. Turner and W. T. Greenough, 1985, *Brain Research, 329,* pp. 195–203; "Differential Rearing Effects on Rat Visual Cortex Synapses. III. Neuronal and Glial Nuclei," by A. M. Sirevaag and W. T. Greenough, 1987, *Brain Research, 424,* pp. 320–332; and "Experience-Dependent Changes in Dendritic Arbor and Spine Density in Neocortex Vary with Age and Sex," by B. Kolb, R. Gibb, and G. Gorny, 2003, *Neurobiology of Learning and Memory, 79,* pp. 1–10.

Animals with enriched experience have not only more synapses per neuron but also more astrocytes, more blood capillaries, and higher mitochondrial volumes. Clearly, when the brain changes in response to experience, the expected neural changes take place, and adjustments in the metabolic requirements of the now larger neurons take place as well.

Mitochondria gather, store, and release energy within the cell. Figure 3-10 diagrams the organelles and other internal components of a neuron.

Gerd Kempermann and his colleagues (1998) sought to determine whether experience actually alters the number of neurons in the brain. To test this idea, they compared the generation of neurons in the hippocampi of mice housed in complex environments with that of mice reared in laboratory cages. They located the number of new neurons by injecting the animals with BrdU several times in the course of their complex-housing experience.

The BrdU was incorporated into new neurons that were generated in the brain during the experiment. When the researchers later looked at the hippocampi, they found more new neurons in the complex-housed rats than in the cage-housed rats. Although the investigators did not look in other parts of the brain, such as the olfactory bulb, we can reasonably expect that similar changes took place in other structures. This result is exciting because it implies that experience not only can alter existing circuitry but also can influence the generation of new neurons and thus new circuitry.

Sensory or Motor Training and Plasticity

The studies showing neuronal change in animals housed in complex environments demonstrate that large areas of the brain can change with such experience. This finding leads us to ask whether specific experiences would produce synaptic changes in localized cerebral regions. One way to approach this question is to give animals specific experiences and then see how their brains have changed. Another way is to look at the brains of people who have had a lifetime of some particular experience. We will consider each research strategy separately.

Manipulating Experience Experimentally

Perhaps the most convincing manipulated-experience study was done by Fen-Lei Chang and William Greenough (1982). They took advantage of the fact that the visual pathways of the laboratory rat are about 90 percent crossed. That is, about 90 percent of the connections from the left eye to the cortex project through the right thalamus to the right hemisphere and vice versa for the right eye.

In humans, only about half the optic fibers cross. Figure 9-10 diagrams the pathways.

Chang and Greenough placed a patch over one eye of each rat and then trained the animals in a maze. The visual cortex of only one eye received input about the maze, but the auditory, olfactory, tactile, and motor regions of both hemispheres were equally active as the animals explored. A comparison of the neurons in the two hemispheres revealed that those in the visual cortex of the trained hemisphere had more extensive dendrites. The researchers concluded that some feature associated with the encoding, processing, or storage of visual input from training was responsible for forming new synapses because the hemispheres did not differ in other respects.

Chang and Greenough also severed the corpus callosum so that the two hemispheres could not communicate and share information about the world.

Complementary studies that mapped the motor cortex of monkeys have been conducted by Randy Nudo and his colleagues (1997), who noted striking individual differences in topography. The investigators speculated that the variability among individual monkeys might be due to each animal's experiences up to the time at which the cortical map was derived. To test this idea directly, they trained two groups of squirrel monkeys to retrieve banana-flavored food pellets from either a small or a large food well. A monkey was able to insert its entire hand into the large well but only one or two fingers into the small well, as illustrated in the Procedures section of **Experiment 14-2.**

The discussions of the sensory and motor systems in Chapters 9 through 12 explain that topographic cortical maps represent both these worlds. In the motor system, for example, and shown in Experiment 11-3, cortical maps of the body represent discrete muscles and movements.

Monkeys in the two groups were matched for number of finger flexions, which totaled about 12,000 for the entire study. The monkeys trained on the small well improved

EXPERIMENT 14-2

Question: Does the learning of a fine motor skill alter the cortical motor map?

Procedures

Difficult task	**Simple task**
One group of monkeys was trained to retrieve food from a small well.	Another group of monkeys was trained to retrieve food from a large well.

Both groups were allowed 12,000 finger flexions. The small-well task was more difficult and required the learning of a fine motor skill in order to match performance of the simpler task.

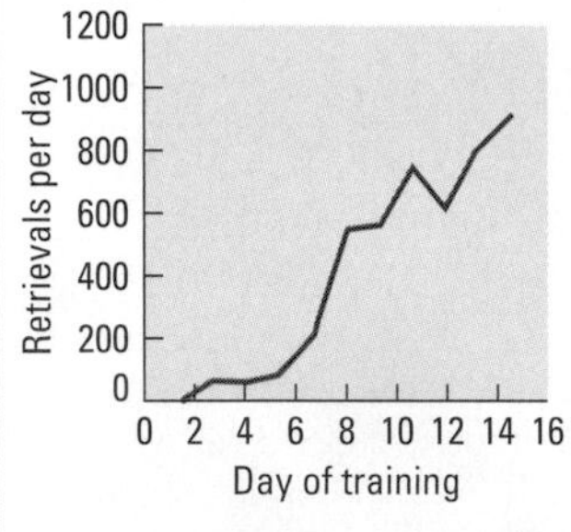

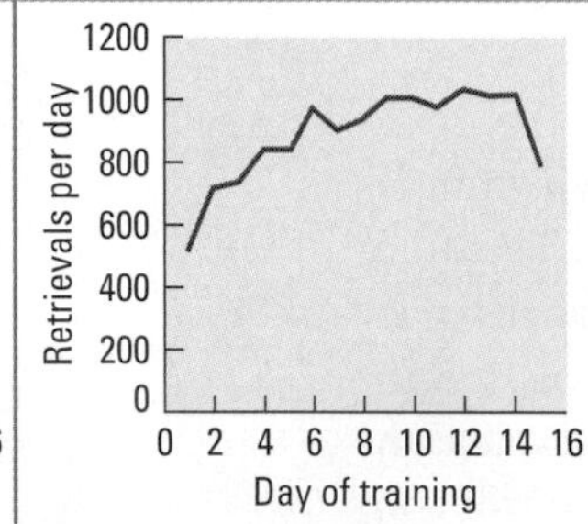

Results

The motor representation of digit, wrist, and arm was mapped.

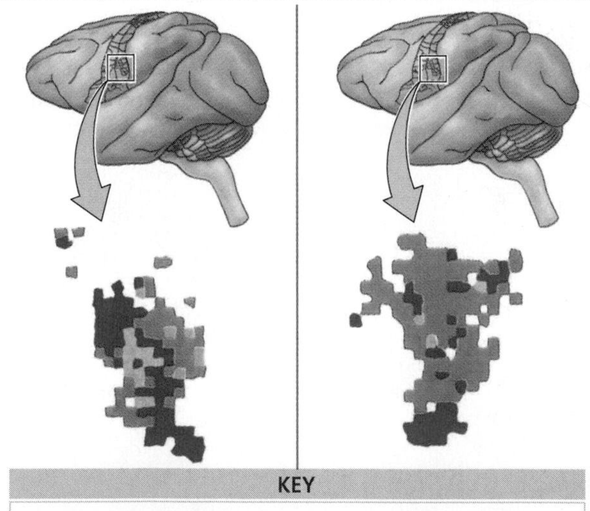

KEY

■ Digit ■ Wrist/forearm ■ Digit, wrist, and forearm

Conclusion: The digit representation in the brain of the animal with the more difficult task is larger, corresponding to the neuronal changes necessary for the acquired skill.

Adapted from "Adaptive Plasticity in Primate Motor Cortex as a Consequence of Behavioral Experience and Neuronal Injury," by R. J. Nudo, E. J. Plautz, and G. W. Milliken, 1997, *Seminars in Neuroscience, 9*, p. 20.

with practice, making fewer finger flexions per food retrieval as training proceded. Maps of forelimb movements were produced by microelectrode stimulation of the cortex.

The maps showed systematic changes in the animals trained on the small but not the large well. Presumably, these changes are due to the more demanding motor requirements of the small-well condition. The results of this experiment demonstrate that the functional topography of the motor cortex is shaped by learning new motor skills, not simply by repetitive motor use.

Most studies demonstrating plasticity in the motor cortex have been performed with laboratory animals in which the cortex was mapped by microelectrode stimulation. Today, imaging techniques such as transcranial magnetic stimulation (TMS) and functional magnetic resonance imaging (fMRI) make it possible to show parallel results in humans who have special motor skills. For example, musicians who play stringed instruments show an increased cortical representation of the fingers of the left hand and Braille readers an increased cortical representation of the reading finger.

Thus, the functional organization of the motor cortex is altered by skilled use in humans. It can also be altered by chronic injury in humans and laboratory animals. Jon Kaas (2000) showed that when the sensory nerves from one limb are severed in monkeys, large-scale changes in the somatosensory maps ensue. In particular, in the absence of input, the relevant part of the cortex no longer responds to stimulation of the limb, which is not surprising. But this cortex does not remain inactive. Rather, the deafferentated cortex begins to respond to input from other parts of the body. The region that formerly responded to the stimulation of the hand now responds to stimulation on the face, an area normally adjacent to the hand area.

Similar results can be found in the cortical maps of people whose limbs have been amputated. For example, Vilayanur Ramachandran (1993) found that when the face of a limb amputee is brushed lightly with a cotton swab, the person has a sensation of the amputated hand being touched. **Figure 14-20** illustrates the rough map of the hand that Ramachandran was actually able to chart on the face. The likely explanation is that the face area in the motor cortex has expanded to occupy the deafferentated limb cortex, but the brain circuitry still responds to the activity of this cortex as representing input from the limb. This response may explain the phantom limb pain often experienced by amputees.

The idea that experience can alter cortical maps can be demonstrated with other types of experience. For example, if animals are trained to make certain digit movements over and over again, the cortical representation of those digits expands at the expense of the remaining motor areas. Similarly, if animals are trained extensively to discriminate among different sensory stimuli such as tones, the auditory cortical areas responding to those stimuli increase in size.

As indicated in Research Focus 14-5, "Movement, Learning, and Neuroplasticity," on page 509, one effect of musical training is to alter the motor representations of the digits used to play different instruments. We can speculate that musical training probably alters the auditory representations of specific sound frequencies as well. Both

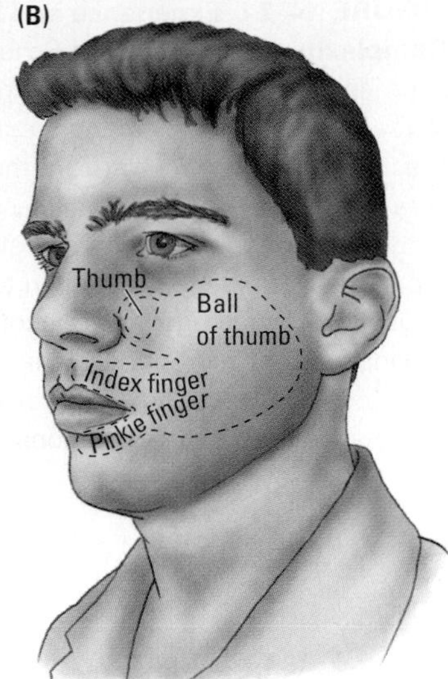

FIGURE 14-20 Cortical Reorganization. When the face of an amputee is stroked lightly with a cotton swab (A), the person experiences the touch as the missing hand being lightly touched (B) as well as experiencing touch to the face. The deafferentated cortex forms a representation of the amputated hand on the face. As in the normal map of the somatosensory cortex, the thumb is disproportionately large. Adapted from "Behavioral and Magnetoencephalographic Correlates of Plasticity in the Adult Human Brain," by V. S. Ramachandran, 1993, *Proceedings of the National Academy of Sciences (USA), 90,* p. 10418.

changes are essentially forms of memory, and it is likely that the underlying synaptic changes take place on the appropriate sensory or motor cortical maps.

Experience-Dependent Change in the Human Brain

According to the Ramachandran amputee study, the human brain appears to change with altered experience. But this study did not directly examine neuronal change; neuronal change was inferred from behavior. The only way to directly examine synaptic change is to look directly at brain tissue. Although experimental manipulation of experiences in people followed by an examination of their brains is not an option, the brains of people who died from nonneurological causes can be examined and the structure of their cortical neurons can be related to their experiences.

One way to test this idea is to look for a relation between neuronal structure and education. Arnold Scheibel and his colleagues conducted many such studies in the 1990s (Jacobs and Scheibel, 1993; Jacobs, Scholl, and Scheibel, 1993). In one study, they found a relation between the size of the dendrites in Wernicke's area and the amount of education. In the brains of deceased people with a college education, the cortical neurons from this language area had more dendritic branches than did those from people with a high-school education, which, in turn, had more dendritic material than did those from people with less education. People who have more dendrites may be more likely to go to college, but that possibility is not easy to test.

Wernicke's area, diagrammed in Figure 10-18, contributes to speech and to language comprehension.

Another way to look at the relation between human brain structure and behavior is to correlate the functional abilities of people with their neuronal structure. For example, one might expect to find differences in language-related areas between people with high and low verbal abilities. This experiment is difficult to conduct because it presupposes that behavioral measurements were taken before death, and such measures are not normally available.

However, Scheibel and his colleagues took advantage of the now well-documented observation that, on average, the verbal abilities of females are superior to those of males. When they examined the structure of neurons in Wernicke's area, they found that females have more extensive dendritic branching there than males do. In a subsequent study, they found that this sex difference was present as early as age 9, suggesting that such sex differences emerge within the first decade of life. In fact, on average, young girls tend to have significantly better verbal skills than young boys do.

Finally, these investigators approached the link between experience and neuronal morphology in a slightly different way. They began with two hypotheses. First, they suggested a relation between the complexity of dendritic branching and the nature of the computational tasks performed by a brain area. To test this hypothesis, they examined the dendritic structure of neurons in different cortical regions that handle different computational tasks. For example, when they compared the structure of neurons corresponding to the somatosensory representation of the trunk with those for the fingers,

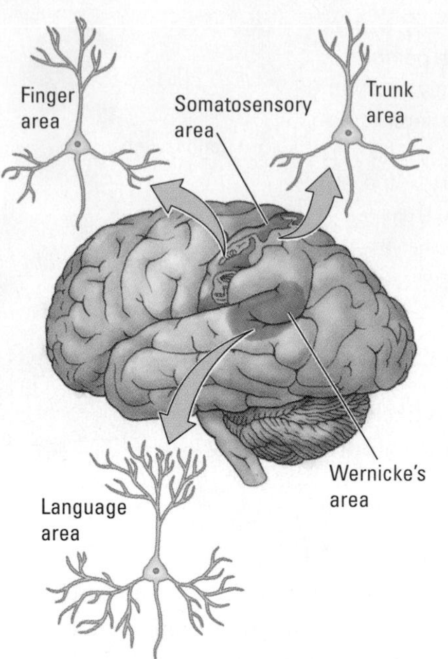

FIGURE 14-21 Experience and Neural Complexity. Confirmation of Scheibel's hypothesis that cell complexity is related to the computational demands required of the cell. Neurons that represent the trunk area of the body have relatively less computational demand than do cells representing the finger region. In turn, cells engaged in more-cognitive functions (such as language, as in Wernicke's area) have greater computational demand than do those engaged in finger functions.

they found the latter to have more complex cells. They reasoned that the somatosensory inputs from receptive fields on the chest wall would constitute less of a computational challenge to cortical neurons than would those from the fingers and that the neurons representing the chest would therefore be less complex.

This first hypothesis was proved correct (**Figure 14-21**). Similarly, when Scheibel's group compared the cells in the finger area with those in the supramarginal gyrus (SMG), a region of the parietal lobe associated with higher cognitive processes (thinking), they found the SMG neurons to be more complex.

The group's second hypothesis was that dendritic branching in all regions is subject to experience-dependent change. As a result, the researchers hypothesized that predominant life experience (e.g., occupation) should alter the structure of dendrites. Although they did not test this hypothesis directly, they did make an interesting observation. In their study comparing cells in the trunk area, the finger area, and the SMG, they found curious individual differences. For example, especially large differences in trunk and finger neurons were found in the brains of people who had a high level of finger dexterity maintained over long periods of time (for example, career word processors). In contrast, no difference between trunk and finger neurons was found in a sales representative. One would not expect a good deal of specialized finger use in this occupation, which would mean less complex demands on the finger neurons.

In summary, although the studies showing a relation between experience and neural structure in humans depend on correlations rather than actual experiments, the findings are consistent with those observed in experimental studies of other species. We are thus led to the general conclusion that specific experiences can produce localized changes in the synaptic organization of the brain and that it is likely that such changes form the structural basis of memory.

Plasticity, Hormones, Trophic Factors, and Drugs

The news media often report that drugs can damage your brain. Some drugs certainly do act as toxins and can selectively kill brain regions, but a more realistic mode of drug action is to *change* the brain. Although not many studies have looked at drug-induced morphological changes, there is evidence that some compounds can greatly change the synaptic organization of the brain. These compounds include hormones, neurotrophic factors, and psychoactive drugs. We briefly consider each category.

Hormones and Plasticity

Chapter 8 explains the classes, functions, and control exerted by hormones.

The levels of circulating hormones play a critical role both in determining the structure of the brain and in eliciting certain behaviors in adulthood. Although the structural effects of hormones were once believed to be expressed only in the course of development, current belief is that adult neurons also can respond to hormonal manipulations with dramatic structural changes. We consider the actions of gonadal hormones and stress-related hormones in this section.

RESEARCH FOCUS 14-5

Movement, Learning, and Neuroplasticity

Many lines of research show that practicing a motor skill—playing a musical instrument, for instance—induces change in the somatosensory and motor maps in the cortex. The mental maps generally become larger, at least for the finger and hand representations. Presumably, musical skill improves, but are other abilities enhanced too?

LaBrecht Music & Arts/Corbis

Patrick Ragert and colleagues (2003) showed that professional pianists have not only better motor skills in their fingers but enhanced somatosensory perception as well. When the researchers measured the ability to detect subtle sensory stimulation of the fingertips, they found that the pianists were more sensitive than controls. They also found that the enhancement in tactile sensitivity was related to the hours per day that the musicians spent practicing.

The investigators then asked whether the enhanced perceptual ability precluded further improvement in the musicians. Surprisingly, when both the musicians and controls were given a 3-hour training session designed to improve tactile sensitivity, the musicians showed more improvement than did the controls, and again the extent of improvement correlated with daily practice time. This result implies that well-practiced musicians not only learn to play music but also develop a greater capacity for learning. Rather than using up all the available synapses, they develop a capacity to make even more.

Not all motor learning is good, however. Many musicians develop *focal hand dystonia*—abnormal finger and hand positions, cramps, and difficulty in coordinating hand and finger movements. Dystonia can be so disabling that some musicians must give up their occupation.

Typically, dystonia afflicts musicians who practice trying to make perfect finger movements on their instruments. Musicians at high risk include string players, who receive vibratory stimulation at their fingertips. The constant practice has been suggested to lead not only to improved musical ability but also to distortion or disordering of the motor maps in the cortex. Synchronous activation of the digits by the vibration leads to this unwanted side effect.

Victor Candia and colleagues (2003) reasoned that musicians' dystonia was probably an example of disordered learning and could be treated by retuning the motor map. The investigators used magnetoencephalography to measure changes in sensory-evoked magnetic fields in the cortex.

At the beginning of the study, the musicians with dystonia had a disordered motor map: the finger areas overlapped one another. In training, each subject used a hand splint tailored to his or her hand. The splint allowed for the immobilization of different fingers while the subjects made independent movements of the others.

After 8 days of training for about 2 hours per day, the subjects showed marked alleviation in the dystonic symptoms, and the neuroimaging showed a normalization of the cortical map with distinct finger areas. Thus, training reversed the learned changes in the motor map and treated the dystonia. The musicians had actually "learned" a disorder and they were able to "unlearn" it.

Research findings have established that the differences in the structure of cortical neurons of male and female rats depend on gonadal hormones. What is more surprising, perhaps, is that gonadal hormones continue to influence cell structure and behavior in adulthood. Elizabeth Hampson and Doreen Kimura (1988) showed that women's performance on various cognitive tasks changes throughout the menstrual cycle as their estrogen levels fluctuate.

Chapter 7 explains the organizing effects of gonadal hormones during development, and Chapter 12 explains their activating effects in adulthood.

Changes in estrogen level appear to alter the structure of neurons and astrocytes in the neocortex and hippocampus, which probably accounts for at least part of the behavioral fluctuation. **Figure 14-22** illustrates changes in dendritic spines in the hippocampal cells of female rats at different phases of their 4-day estrous cycle. As the

FIGURE 14-22 Hormones and Neuroplasticity. Sections of dendrites from hippocampal cells during times of high and low levels of estrogen during the rat's 4-day estrous cycle reveal many more dendritic spines during the period when estrogen levels are high. Adapted from "Naturally Occurring Fluctuation in Dendritic Spine Density on Adult Hippocampal Pyramidal Neurons," by C. S. Woolley, E. Gould, M. Frankfurt, and B. S. McEwen, 1990, *Journal of Neuroscience, 10,* p. 4038.

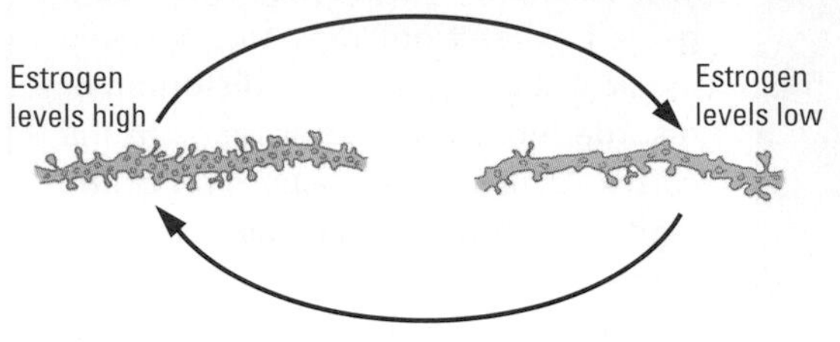

estrogen level rises, the number of synapses rises; as the estrogen level drops, the number of synapses declines.

Curiously, the influence of estrogen on cell structure may be different in the hippocampus and neocortex. Jane Stewart found, for example, that when the ovaries of middle-aged female rats are removed, estrogen levels drop sharply, producing an increase in the number of spines on pyramidal cells throughout the neocortex but a decrease in spine density in the hippocampus (Stewart and Kolb, 1994). How these synaptic changes might influence processes such as memory is not immediately obvious, but the question is reasonable—especially because menopausal women also experience sharp drops in estrogen levels and a corresponding decline in verbal memory ability.

This question is also relevant to middle-aged men, who show a slow decline in testosterone levels that correlates with a drop in spatial ability. Rats that are gonadectomized in adulthood show an increase in cortical spine density, much like the ovariectomized females, although we do not know how this change is related to spatial behavior. Nonetheless, a reasonable supposition is that testosterone levels might influence spatial memory throughout life.

Figure 8-22 illustrates the body's response to stress.

When the body is stressed, the pituitary gland produces adrenocorticotrophic hormone (ACTH), which stimulates the adrenal cortex to produce steroid hormones known as *glucocorticoids.* Important in protein and carbohydrate metabolism, controlling sugar levels in the blood, and the absorption of sugar by cells, glucocorticoids have many actions on the body, including the brain. Robert Sapolsky (1992) proposed that glucocorticoids can sometimes be neurotoxic.

In particular, he found that, with prolonged stress, glucocorticoids appear to kill cells in the hippocampus. Elizabeth Gould and her colleagues (1998) showed that even brief periods of stress can reduce the number of new granule cells produced in the hippocampi of monkeys, presumably through the actions of stress hormones. Evidence of neuron death and reduced neuron generation in the hippocampus has obvious implications for the behavior of animals, especially for processes such as spatial memory.

In sum, hormones can alter the brain's synaptic organization and even the number of neurons in the brain. Little is known today about the behavioral consequences of such changes, but it is likely that hormones can alter the course of plastic changes in the brain.

Nerve growth factor (NGF) Neurotrophic factor that stimulates neurons to grow dendrites and synapses and, in some cases, promotes the survival of neurons.

Drug-induced behavioral sensitization Escalating behavioral response to the repeated administration of a psychomotor stimulant such as amphetamine, cocaine, or nicotine; also called *behavioral sensitization.*

Neurotrophic Factors and Plasticity

Neurotrophic factors, chemical compounds that signal stem cells to develop into neurons or glia (listed in **Table 14-2**), also act to reorganize neural circuits. The first neurotrophic factor, **nerve growth factor** (NGF), was discovered in the peripheral nervous system more than a generation ago. NGF is trophic (nourishing) in the sense that it stimulates neurons to grow dendrites and synapses, and in some cases, it promotes the survival of neurons.

Chapter 7 explains how neurotrophic factors signal stem cells to develop into specific types of neurons or glial cells.

Trophic factors are produced in the brain by neurons and glia and can affect neurons both through cell-membrane receptors and by actually entering the neuron to act internally on its operation. For example, trophic factors may be released postsynaptically to act as signals that can influence the presynaptic cell. Experience stimulates their production, and so neurotrophic factors have been proposed as agents of synaptic change. For example, brain-derived neurotrophic factor (BDNF) increases when animals solve specific problems such as mazes. This finding has led to speculation that release of BDNF may enhance plastic changes, such as the growth of dendrites and synapses.

As noted in Chapter 5, the Hebb synapse—one that changes with use so that learning takes place—is hypothesized to employ just such a mechanism.

Unfortunately, although many researchers would like to conclude that BDNF has a role in learning, this conclusion does not necessarily follow. The behavior of animals when they solve mazes differs from their behavior when they remain in cages, so we must first demonstrate that changes in BDNF, NGF, or any other trophic factor are actually related to the formation of new synapses. Nevertheless, if we assume that trophic factors do act as agents of synaptic change, then we should be able to use increased trophic factor activity during learning as a marker for where to look for changed synapses associated with learning and memory.

TABLE 14-2 Molecules Exhibiting Neurotrophic Activities

Proteins initially characterized as neurotrophic factors
Nerve growth factor (NGF)
Brain-derived neurotrophic factor (BDNF)
Neurotrophin 3 (NT-3)
Ciliary neurotrophic factor (CNTF)
Growth factors with neurotrophic activity
Fibroblast growth factor, acidic (aFGF or FGF-1)
Fibroblast growth factor, basic (bFGF or FGF-2)
Epidermal growth factor (EGF)
Insulinlike growth factor (ILGF)
Transforming growth factor (TGF)
Lymphokines (interleukin 1, 3, 6 or IL-1, IL-3, IL-6)
Protease nexin I, II
Cholinergic neuronal differentiation factor

Psychoactive Drugs and Plasticity

Many people regularly use stimulants such as caffeine, and some use more psychoactively stimulating drugs such as nicotine, amphetamine, or cocaine. The long-term consequences of abusing psychoactive drugs are now well documented, but the question of why these drugs cause problems remains to be answered. One explanation for the behavioral changes associated with chronic psychoactive drug abuse is that the drugs change the brain.

One experimental demonstration of these changes is **drug-induced behavioral sensitization,** often referred to simply as *behavioral sensitization*. Drug-induced behavioral sensitization is the progressive increase in behavioral actions in response to repeated administration of a drug, even when the amount given in each dose does not change. Behavioral sensitization occurs with most psychoactive drugs, including amphetamine, cocaine, morphine, and nicotine.

Aplysia becomes more sensitive to a stimulus after repeated exposure. Psychoactive drugs appear to have a parallel action: they lead to increased behavioral sensitivity to their actions. For example, a rat given a small dose of amphetamine may show an increase in activity. When the rat is given the same dose of amphetamine on subsequent occasions, the increase in activity is progressively larger. If no drug is given for weeks or even months, and then the amphetamine is given in the same dose as before, behavioral sensitization picks up where it left off and continues, which means that some type of long-lasting change must have taken place in the brain in response to the drug. Drug-induced behavioral sensitization can therefore be viewed as a memory for a particular drug.

Experiment 5-2 illustrates the neural basis of behavioral sensitization.

The parallel between drug-induced behavioral sensitization and other forms of memory leads us to ask if the changes in the brain after behavioral sensitization are similar to those found after other forms of learning. They are. For example, there is evidence of increased numbers of receptors at synapses and of more synapses in sensitized animals.

In a series of studies, Terry Robinson and his colleagues found a dramatic increase in dendritic growth and spine density in rats that were sensitized to amphetamine, cocaine, or nicotine relative to rats that received injections of a saline solution (Robinson and Kolb, 2004). **Experiment 14-3** compares the effects of amphetamine and saline treatments on cells in the nucleus accumbens, a structure in the basal ganglia. Neurons in the amphetamine-treated brains have more dendritic branches and increased spine density. Repeated exposure to psychoactive stimulant drugs thus alters the structure of cells in the brain. These changes in turn may be related to "learned addictions."

EXPERIMENT 14-3

Question: What effect do repeated doses of amphetamine, a psychomotor stimulant, have on neurons?

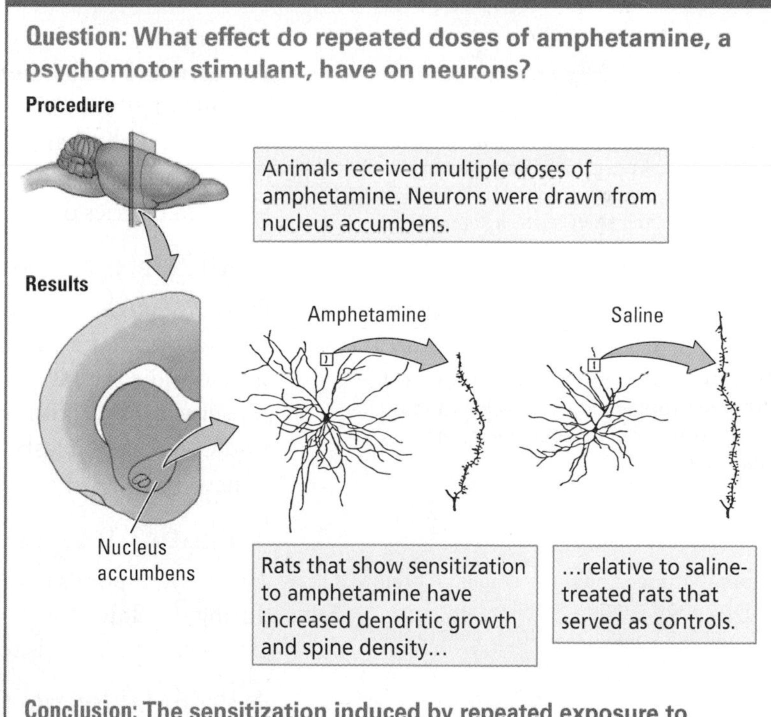
Procedure
Animals received multiple doses of amphetamine. Neurons were drawn from nucleus accumbens.
Results
Amphetamine
Saline
Nucleus accumbens
Rats that show sensitization to amphetamine have increased dendritic growth and spine density...
...relative to saline-treated rats that served as controls.

Conclusion: The sensitization induced by repeated exposure to amphetamine changes the structure of neurons in certain brain areas.

Adapted from "Persistent Structural Adaptations in Nucleus Accumbens and Prefrontal Cortex Neurons Produced by Prior Experience with Amphetamine," by T. E. Robinson and B. Kolb, 1997, *Journal of Neuroscience, 17,* p. 8495.

These plastic changes were not found throughout the brain. Rather, they were localized to such regions as the prefrontal cortex and nucleus accumbens that receive a large dopamine projection. Dopamine is believed to play a significant role in the rewarding properties of drugs (Wise, 2004). Other psychoactive drugs also appear to alter neuronal structure: marijuana, morphine, and certain antidepressants change dendritic length and spine density, although in somewhat different ways from those of stimulants. Morphine, for example, produces a decrease in dendritic length and spine density in the nucleus accumbens and prefrontal cortex (Robinson and Kolb, 2004).

What do changes in synaptic organization induced by drugs mean for later experience-dependent plasticity? If rats are given amphetamine, cocaine, or nicotine for 2 weeks before being placed in complex environments, the expected increases in dendritic length and spine density in the cortex do not happen (Kolb et al., 2003). This is not because the brain can no longer change: giving the animals additional drug doses can still produce change. Rather, something about prior drug exposure alters the way in which the brain later responds to experience. Why prior drug exposure has this effect is not yet known, but obviously drug taking can have long-term effects on brain plasticity.

Some Guiding Principles of Brain Plasticity

Brain plasticity will continue to be a fundamental concept underlying research into brain–behavior relationships through the coming decade. Much remains unknown, but some basic rules have emerged to guide this research (see Kolb and Gibb, 2008 for more details). Here we list seven.

1. Behavioral Change Reflects Change in the Brain

The primary function of the brain is to produce behavior, but behavior is not static. We learn and remember, we create new thoughts or images, and we change throughout our lifetimes. All these processes require changes in neural networks. Whenever neural networks change, then behavior, including mental behavior, also changes. A corollary of this principle is especially important as neuroscientists search for treatments for brain injuries or behavioral disorders: *To change behavior we must change the brain.*

2. All Nervous Systems Are Plastic in the Same General Way

Even the simplest animals, such as the roundworm *C. elegans,* can show simple learning that correlates with neuronal plasticity. The molecular details may differ between simple and complex systems, but the general principles of neuroplasticity appear to be conserved across both simple and complex animals. This conservation will allow more studies of neural plasticity among a wider range of animal species than in most areas of neuroscience.

Over the next decade, investigators will study neuroplasticity in species ranging from worms and insects to fish, birds, and mammals.

3. Plastic Changes Are Age-Specific

The brain responds to the same experiences differently at different ages—and especially during development. The prefrontal cortex is late to mature, for example, so the same experience affects this region differently in infancy than it does in adolescence.

Chapter 7 traces how the details of brain organization change rapidly—and sometimes critically—during development.

4. Prenatal Events Can Influence Brain Plasticity Throughout Life

We have emphasized plastic changes during postnatal development and beyond, but even prenatal experiences alter brain organization. Potentially negative experiences, such as prenatal exposure to recreational or prescription drugs, as well as positive experiences, such as tactile stimulation of the mother's skin, may alter gene expression and produce enduring effects on brain organization.

5. Plastic Changes Are Brain-Region Dependent

Although we are tempted to expect plastic changes in neuronal networks to be fairly general, it is becoming clear that many experience-dependent changes are highly specific. We saw this in the effects of psychoactive drugs on the prefrontal cortex but not on other cortical regions. Not only do drugs selectively change the prefrontal cortex but the dorsolateral and orbital prefrontal areas also show opposite changes—the precise changes varying with the particular drug. For example, stimulants such as amphetamine increase the spine density in the dorsolateral region but decrease it in the orbital region.

6. Experience-Dependent Changes Interact

As animals travel through life, an almost infinite number of experiences can alter brain organization. It is not surprising that a lifetime's experiences might interact. Housing animals in complex environments produces profound changes in the organization of their neural networks, but prior exposure to psychoactive drugs completely blocks the enrichment effect. Conversely, although complex housing does not block the effects of drugs, the effects are markedly attenuated. Prenatal events can also affect later drug effects: prenatal tactile stimulation of the mother, for example, reduces the later effect of psychoactive drugs on the child.

7. Plastic Events Are Not Always a Good Thing

Up to this point, we have mainly emphasized the plastic changes in the brain that can support improved motor and cognitive function. But plastic changes can also interfere with behavior. Drug addicts whose prefrontal cortex has been altered are prone to making very poor judgments in their personal lives. People who have posttraumatic stress disorders show altered blood flow in the amygdala and cingulate cortex. Reversing these alterations is associated with a loss of the disorder. Age-related dementia is related to synaptic loss that various forms of cognitive therapy can reverse (e.g. Mahncke, Bronstone, and Merzenich, 2006).

REVIEW: Structural Basis of Brain Plasticity

- ✔ Experience produces plastic changes in the brain. Dendrites grow, synapses form, and new neurons develop.
- ✔ Like environmental stimulation, neurochemicals in the form of hormones, neurotrophic factors, and psychoactive drugs appear to produce long-lasting effects on brain morphology. The effects are strikingly similar to those observed when animals show evidence of memory for sensory events.
- ✔ Structural changes include not only changes in synaptic organization, as inferred from the dendritic analyses, but also changes in the numbers of neurons, at least in the hippocampus. Thus, the neural changes that correlate with memory are similar to those observed in other types of behavioral change.
- ✔ The adjoining table summarizes seven basic principles that guide research about brain plasticity and behavior.

Some Guiding Principles of Brain Plasticity

1. Behavioral change reflects change in the brain.
2. All nervous systems are plastic in the same general way.
3. Plastic changes are age-specific.
4. Prenatal events can influence brain plasticity throughout life.
5. Plastic changes are brain-region dependent.
6. Experience-dependent changes interact.
7. Plastic events are not always a good thing.

Recovery from Brain Injury

The nervous system appears to be conservative in its use of mechanisms related to behavioral change. This message is important: it implies that, if neuroscientists wish to change the brain, as after injury or disease, then they should look for treatments that

Traumatic brain injury (TBI) Damage to the brain that results from a blow to the head.

will produce the types of neural changes related to learning, memory, and other forms of behavioral change.

Partial recovery of function is common after brain injury, and the average person would probably say that the process of recovery requires the injured person to relearn lost skills, whether walking, talking, or using the fingers. But what exactly does recovery entail? After all, a person with brain trauma or brain disease has lost neurons, so the brain may be missing structures critical for learning or memory.

Recall, for example, that H. M. showed no recovery of his lost memory capacities, even after 55 years of practice in trying to remember information. He had lost the requisite neural structures, so relearning was simply not possible. But other people do show some recovery.

Donna's Experience with Traumatic Brain Injury

Donna began dancing lessons when she was 4 years old, and she was a "natural." By the time she finished high school she had the training and skill necessary to apprentice with, and later join a major dance company. Donna remembers vividly the day she was chosen to dance a leading role in *The Nutcracker*. She had marveled at the costumes as she watched the popular Christmas ballet as a child, and now she would dance in those costumes!

Although her career as a dancer was interrupted by the births of two children, Donna never lost interest in dancing. In 1968, when both her children were in school, she began dancing again with a local company. To her amazement, she could still perform most of the movements, although she was rusty on the choreography of the classical dances that she had once memorized so meticulously. Nonetheless, she quickly relearned. In retrospect, she should not have been so surprised, because she had always had an excellent memory.

One evening in 1990, while on a bicycle ride, Donna was struck by a drunk driver. Although she was wearing a helmet, she suffered a **traumatic brain injury** (TBI), damage to the brain that results from a blow to the head. She was comatose for several weeks. As she regained consciousness, she was confused and had difficulty talking and understanding others. Her memory was very poor, she had spatial disorientation and often got lost, she had various motor disturbances, and she had difficulty recognizing anyone but her family and closest friends.

Clinical Focus 1-1 and Research Focus 1-2 introduce some consequences of and treatments for TBI, which are elaborated in Chapter 16.

In the ensuing 10 months, Donna regained most of her motor abilities and language skills, and her spatial abilities improved significantly. Nonetheless, she was short-tempered and easily frustrated by the slowness of her recovery, symptoms typical of people with brain trauma. She suffered periods of depression. She also found herself prone to inexplicable surges of panic when doing simple things. On one occasion early in her rehabilitation, she was shopping in a large supermarket and became overwhelmed by the number of salad dressing choices. She ran from the store, and only after she sat outside and calmed herself could she go back inside to continue shopping.

Two years later, Donna was dancing once again, but she now found it very difficult to learn and remember new steps. Her emotions were still unstable, which was a strain on her family, but her episodes of frustration and temper outbursts became much less frequent. A year later, they were gone and her life was not obviously different from that of other middle-aged women.

Digital Stock

The brain changes in response to these dancers' new experiences and new abilities. After her accident, Donna's brain had to change to allow her to regain her lost abilities, but she never recovered the ability that these young women have to learn new dances.

Some cognitive changes persisted, however. Donna seemed unable to remember the names or faces of new people she met and was unable to concentrate if there were distractions such as a television or radio playing in the background. She could not dance as she had before her injury, although she did work at it diligently. Her balance on sudden turns gave her the most difficulty. Rather than risk falling, she retired from her life's first love.

Donna's experiences demonstrate the human brain's capacity for continuously changing its structure and ultimately its function throughout a lifetime. From what we have learned in this chapter, we can identify three different ways in which Donna could recover from her brain injury: she could learn new ways to solve problems, she could reorganize the brain to do more with less, and she could generate new neurons to produce new neural circuits. We briefly examine these three possibilities.

Three-Legged Cat Solution

The simplest solution to recovery from TBI we call the "three-legged cat solution." Cats that lose a leg to accident (and subsequent veterinary treatment) quickly learn to compensate for the missing limb and once again become mobile; they can be regarded as showing recovery of function. The limb is gone, but behavior has changed to compensate.

A similar explanation can account for many instances of apparent recovery of function after brain trauma. Imagine a right-handed person who has a stroke that leads to the loss of the use of the right hand and arm. Unable to write with the affected limb, she switches to her left hand. This type of behavioral compensation is presumably associated with some sort of change in the brain. After all, if a person learns to use the opposite hand to write, some changes in the nervous system must underlie this new skill.

New-Circuit Solution

A second way to recover from brain damage is for the brain to change its neural connections to overcome the loss. This way is most easily accomplished by processes that are similar to those that we considered for other forms of plasticity. That is, the brain forms new connections that allow it to "do more with less."

Although this kind of change in the brain seems logical, the changes appear to be fairly small. As a result, without some form of intervention, recovery from most instances of brain injury is relatively modest. However, recovery can be increased significantly if the person engages in some form of behavioral, pharmacological, or brain-stimulation therapy that encourages the brain to make new connections and to do more with less.

Behavioral therapy, such as speech therapy or physiotherapy, presumably increases brain activity, which facilitates the neural changes. In a pharmacological intervention, the patient takes a drug known to influence brain plasticity. An example is nerve growth factor. When NGF is given to animals with strokes that damaged the motor cortex, their motor functions improve (**Experiment 14-4**). The behavioral changes are correlated with a dramatic increase in dendritic branching and spine density in the remaining, intact motor regions. The morphological changes are correlated with improved motor functions, such as reaching with the forelimb to obtain food, as

EXPERIMENT 14-4

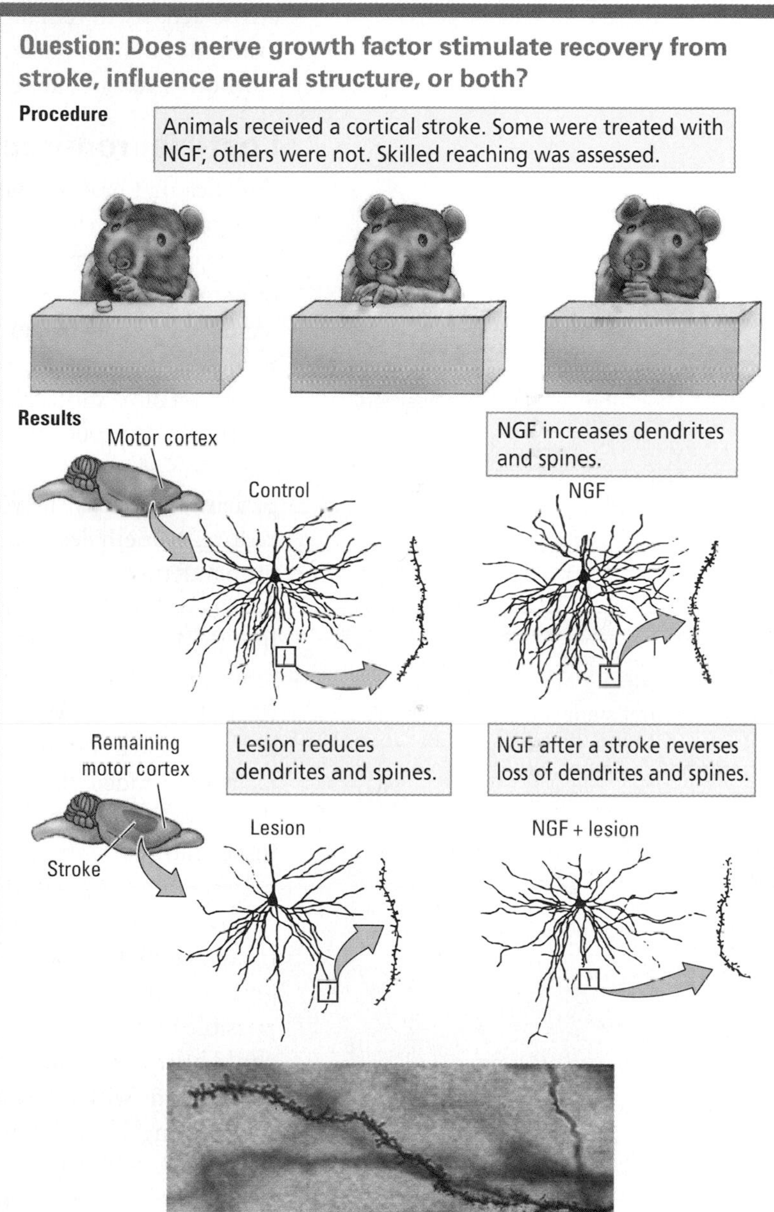

Question: Does nerve growth factor stimulate recovery from stroke, influence neural structure, or both?
Procedure
Animals received a cortical stroke. Some were treated with NGF; others were not. Skilled reaching was assessed.
Results
Motor cortex
Control
NGF increases dendrites and spines.
NGF
Remaining motor cortex
Lesion reduces dendrites and spines.
NGF after a stroke reverses loss of dendrites and spines.
Lesion
NGF + lesion
Stroke

Conclusion: Nerve growth factor stimulates dendritic growth and increased spine density in both normal and injured brains. These neuronal changes are correlated with improved motor function after stroke.

Adapted from "Nerve Growth Factor Treatment Prevents Dendritic Atrophy and Promotes Recovery of Function after Cortical Injury," by B. Kolb, S. Cote, A. Ribeiro-da-Silva, and A. C. Cuello, 1997, *Neuroscience, 76,* p. 1146.

illustrated in Experiment 14-2 (Kolb et al., 1997). Recovery is by no means complete, which is not surprising because brain tissue is still missing.

In principle, we might expect that any drug that stimulates the growth of new connections would help people recover from brain injury. However, the neural growth must occur in regions of the brain that can influence a particular lost function. A drug that stimulates the growth of synapses on cells in the visual cortex, for example, would not enhance recovery of hand use. The visual neurons play no direct role in moving the hand.

A third strategy to generate new circuits uses elecrical stimulation of perilesional regions or deep brain stimulation. The goal of elecrical stimulation is to directly increase activity in remaining parts of specific neural networks. In DBS, it is to put the brain into a more plastic ("trainable") state so that rehabiliation therapies work better. Both strategies are currently in preliminary clinical trials.

Lost-Neuron-Replacement Solution

The idea that brain tissue could be transplanted from one animal to another goes back a century. The evidence is good that tissue from fetal brains can be transplanted and will grow and form some connections in the new brain. Unfortunately, in contrast with transplanted hearts or livers, transplanted brain tissue functions poorly. The procedure seems most suited to conditions in which a small number of functional cells are required, such as in the replacement of dopamine-producing cells in Parkinson's disease or in the replacement of suprachiasmatic cells to restore circadian rhythms.

Clinical Focus 5-4 recounts a successful case of fetal stem cell transplantation, and Chapter 13 describes SCN cell replacement.

In fact, by 2004, dopamine-producing cells had been surgically transplanted into the striata of many Parkinson patients. Although the disease has not been reversed, some patients, especially the younger ones, have shown functional gains that justify the procedure. Nonetheless, ethical issues remain because the tissue is taken from aborted human fetuses.

There is a second way to replace lost neurons: adult stem cells. Investigators know that the brain is capable of making neurons in adulthood. The challenge is to get the brain to do so after an injury. The first breakthrough in this research was made by Brent Reynolds and Sam Weiss (1992). Cells lining the ventricles of adult mice were removed and placed in a culture medium. The researchers demonstrated that if the correct trophic factors are added, the cells begin to divide and can produce new neurons and glia. Furthermore, if the trophic factors—particularly **epidermal growth factor** (EGF)—are infused into the ventricle of a living animal, the subventricular zone generates cells that migrate into the striatum and eventually differentiate into neurons and glia.

In adults, neural stem cells line the brain's ventricles, forming the subventricular zone, diagrammed in Figure 7-11. This region apparently contains a primitive map of the cortex that predisposes cells formed in a particular part of the zone to migrate to a specific cortical location.

In principle, it ought to be possible to use trophic factors to stimulate the subventricular zone to generate new cells in the injured brain. If these new cells were to migrate to the site of injury and essentially regenerate the lost area, then it might be possible to restore at least some lost function. It seems unlikely that all lost behaviors could be restored, however, because the new neurons would have to establish the same connections with the rest of the brain that the lost neurons once had. This task would be daunting, because the connections would have to be formed in an adult brain that already has billions of connections.

Nonetheless, such a treatment might someday be feasible. Cocktails of trophic factors are effective in stimulating neurogenesis in the subventricular zone after brain injury, and the new cells can migrate to the injured region, as illustrated in **Figure 14-23.** The new cells can influence behavior and lead to improvement. Although the mechanism of influence is poorly understood (e.g., Kolb et al., 2007), preliminary clinical trials are under way.

Epidermal growth factor (EGF) Neurotrophic factor that stimulates the subventricular zone to generate cells that migrate into the striatum and eventually differentiate into neurons and glia.

There may be another way to use trophic factors to stimulate neurogenesis and enhance recovery. The hippocampus and olfactory bulb are among the regions that normally produce new neurons in adulthood, and the numbers of neurons can be influenced by experience. It is possible, therefore, that researchers could stimulate the

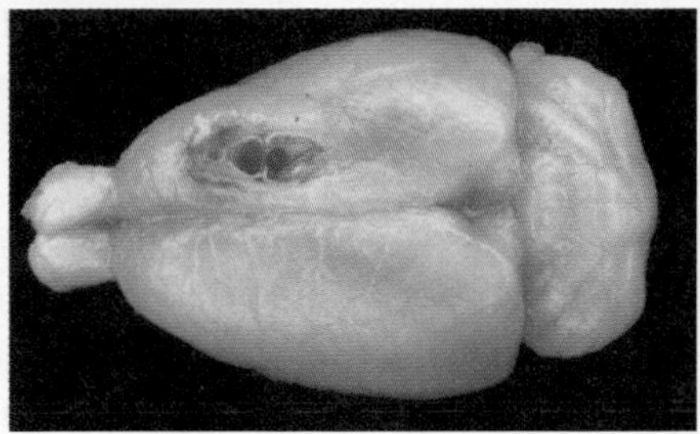

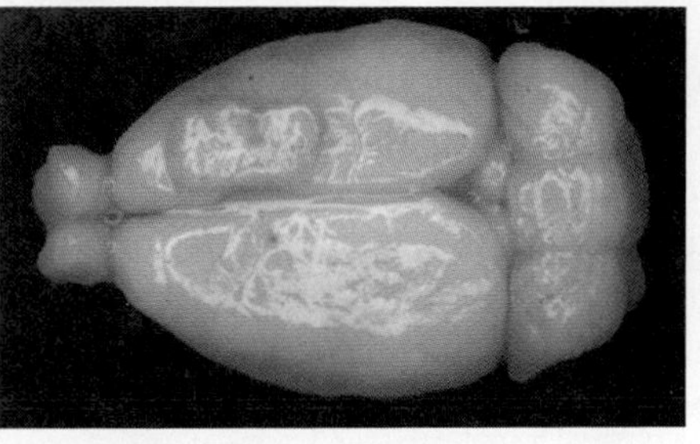

Courtesy of Bryan Kolb

FIGURE 14-23 Stem Cells Do the Trick. After cortical stroke (*left*), infusion of epidermal growth factor into the lateral ventricle of a rat induced neurogenesis in the subventricular zone. The stem cells migrated to the site of injury and filled in the damaged area (*right*).

generation of new neurons in intact regions of an injured brain and that these neurons could help the brain develop new circuits to restore partial functioning. Experience and trophic factors are likely to be used in combination in studies of recovery from brain injury in the coming years.

REVIEW: Recovery from Brain Injury

- ✔ Recovery from brain injury poses a special problem, because the brain may lose large areas of neurons and their associated functions.
- ✔ Three ways to compensate for the loss of neurons are (1) learn new ways to solve problems, (2) reorganize the brain to do more with less, and (3) replace the lost neurons. Although complete recovery is not currently practicable, all three strategies can enhance recovery from TBI.
- ✔ Rehabilitation programs are beginning to integrate all three compensating strategies. Recovery entails taking advantage of the brain's neuroplasticity.

Summary

Connecting Learning and Memory

Learning is a change in an organism's behavior as a result of experience. Memory is the ability to recall or recognize previous experience. Over a century of laboratory studies using animals have uncovered two fundamentally different types of learning: Pavlovian and operant (or instrumental).

The two basic types of memory are implicit (unconscious) and explicit (conscious). Episodic memory includes not only a record of events (episodes) that occurred but also our presence there and our role in the events. It is likely that the frontal lobe plays a unique role in this autobiographical memory.

Dissociating Memory Circuits

Multiple subsystems within the explicit and implicit systems control different aspects of memory. People with damaged explicit memory circuits have impaired recall of facts and events, whereas people with damaged implicit memory circuits show impairments in their recall of skills and habits.

Neural Systems Underlying Explicit and Implicit Memories

The neural circuits underlying implicit and explicit memory are distinctly different: the reciprocal system for explicit memory includes medial temporal structures; the unidirectional system for implicit memory includes the basal ganglia.

Emotional memory has characteristics of both implicit and explicit memory. The neural circuits for emotional memory are unique in that they include the amygdala.

Structural Basis of Brain Plasticity

The brain has the capacity for structural change, which is presumed to underlie functional change. The brain changes in two fundamental ways in response to experience. First, changes take place in existing neural circuits. Second, novel neural circuits are formed, both by new connections among existing neurons and by the generation of new neurons.

Neural activity is the key to brain plasticity; through it, synapses form and change. Neural activity can be induced by general or specific experience as well as by electrical or chemical stimulation of the brain. Chemical stimulation may range from hormones and neurotrophic compounds to psychoactive drugs. Much of the brain is capable of plastic change with experience. Different experiences lead to changes in different neural systems.

Brain plasticity underlies behavioral change. Plasticity is found in all nervous systems, differs across one's lifetime, is brain-region specific, and can lead to both normal and abnormal behavior. Plastic changes also interact with one another over a lifetime.

Recovery from Brain Injury

Plastic changes after brain injury parallel those seen when the brain changes with experience. Changes related to recovery do not always occur spontaneously, however, and must be stimulated either by behavioral training or by the effects of psychoactive drugs, neurotrophic factors, or electrical brain stimulation. The key to stimulating recovery from brain injury is to produce an increase in the plastic changes underlying the recovery.

Key Terms

amnesia, p. 487
anterograde amnesia, p. 498
conditioned response (CR), p. 485
conditioned stimulus (CS), p. 485
declarative memory, p. 487
drug-induced behavioral sensitization, p. 510
dyslexia, p. 483
emotional memory, p. 500
entorhinal cortex, p. 494
epidermal growth factor (EGF), p. 516
episodic memory, p. 489
explicit memory, p. 487
eye-blink conditioning, p. 485
fear conditioning, p. 485
implicit memory, p. 487
instrumental conditioning, p. 485
Korsakoff's syndrome, p. 498
learning, p. 483
learning set, p. 487
memory, p. 483
nerve growth factor (NGF), p. 510
neuritic plaque, p. 496
parahippocampal cortex, p. 494
Pavlovian conditioning, p. 483
perirhinal cortex, p. 494
priming, p. 487
procedural memory, p. 487
retrograde amnesia, p. 498
unconditioned response (UCR), p. 485
unconditioned stimulus (UCS), p. 485
traumatic bain injury (TBI), p. 514
visuospatial learning, p. 494

▶*Please refer to the Companion Web Site at* **www.worthpublishers.com/kolbintro3e** *for Interactive Exercises and Quizzes.*

Courtesy of Cognitive Evolution Group, University of Louisiana at Lafayette, New Iberia Research

CHAPTER 15

How Does the Brain Think?

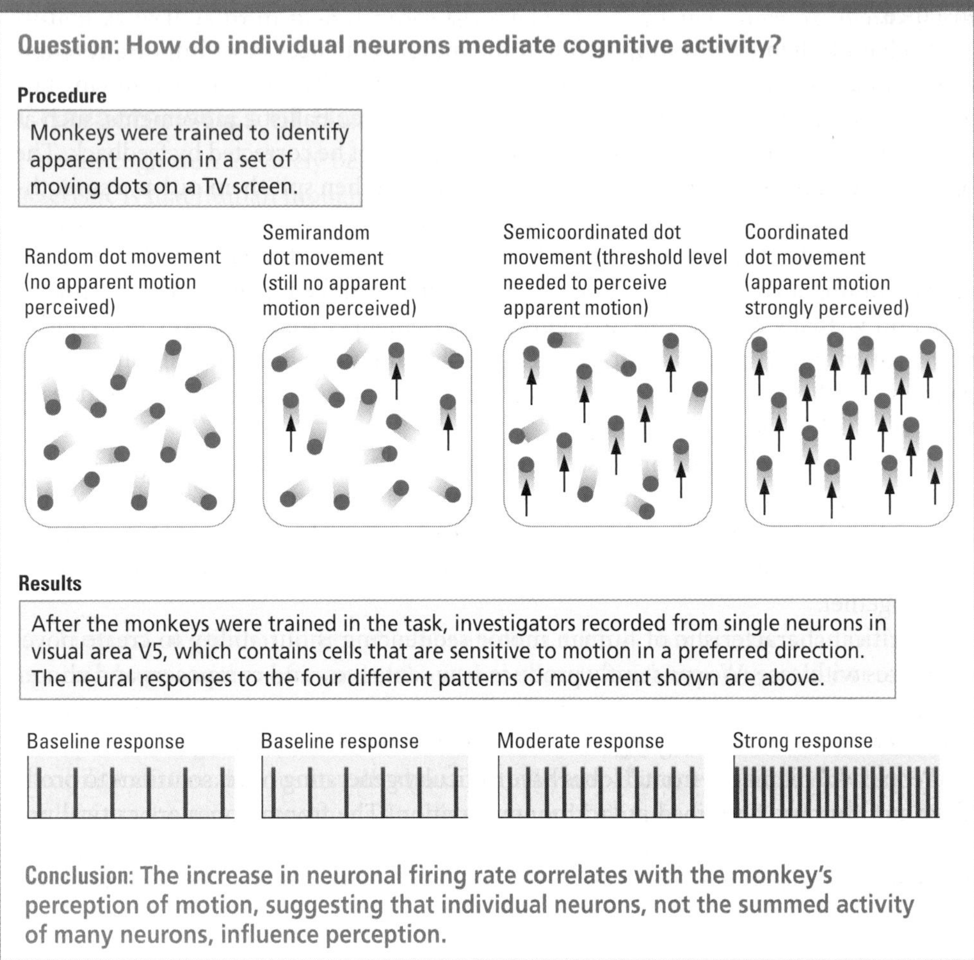

the neuron. If at some point the random activity of the dots increases to a level that obscures movement in a neuron's preferred direction, the neuron will stop responding because it does not detect any consistent pattern.

EXPERIMENT 15-1
Question: How do individual neurons mediate cognitive activity?
Procedure
Monkeys were trained to identify apparent motion in a set of moving dots on a TV screen.
Random dot movement (no apparent motion perceived)
Semirandom dot movement (still no apparent motion perceived)
Semicoordinated dot movement (threshold level needed to perceive apparent motion)
Coordinated dot movement (apparent motion strongly perceived)
Results
After the monkeys were trained in the task, investigators recorded from single neurons in visual area V5, which contains cells that are sensitive to motion in a preferred direction. The neural responses to the four different patterns of movement shown are above.
Baseline response
Baseline response
Moderate response
Strong response
Conclusion: The increase in neuronal firing rate correlates with the monkey's perception of motion, suggesting that individual neurons, not the summed activity of many neurons, influence perception.

So the question becomes How does the activity of any given neuron correlate with the perceptual threshold for apparent motion? On the one hand, if our perception of apparent motion results from the summed activity of many dozens or even thousands of neurons, little correlation would exist between the activity of any one neuron and the perception. On the other hand, if our perception of apparent motion is influenced by individual neurons, then a strong correlation would exist between the activity of a single cell and the perception.

The results of the experiment were unequivocal: the sensitivity of individual neurons was very similar to the perceptual sensitivity of the monkeys to apparent motion. As shown in the Results section of Experiment 15-1, if individual neurons failed to respond to the stimulus, the monkeys behaved as if they did not perceive any apparent motion. This finding is curious. Given the large number of V5 neurons, one would think that perceptual decisions are based on the responses of a large pool of neurons. But Newsome's results show that the activity of individual cortical neurons is correlated with perception.

Still, Hebb's idea of a cell assembly—an ensemble of neurons that represents a complex concept—suggests some way of converging the inputs of individual neurons to

Association cortex Neocortex outside the primary sensory and motor cortices that functions to produce cognition.

arrive at a consensus. In this case, the neuronal ensemble represents a sensory event (apparent motion) that the activity of the ensemble detects. Cell assemblies could be distributed over fairly large regions of the brain or they could be confined to smaller areas, such as cortical columns.

Figure 9-15 illustrates how cortical columns keep information from the two eyes separated in the visual cortex. Figures 9-32 through 9-34 diagram functional columns in the visual and temporal cortices.

Cognitive scientists have developed computer models of cell assembly circuits and have demonstrated their capacity for sophisticated statistical computations. The performance of other complex tasks, such as Alex the parrot's detection of an object's color, also are believed to entail ensembles of neurons. Cell assemblies provide the basis for cognition. Different ensembles come together, much like words in language, to produce coherent thoughts.

What is the contribution of individual neurons to a cell assembly? Each neuron acts as a computational unit. As Experiment 15-1 shows, even one solitary neuron can decide on its own when to fire if its summed inputs indicate that movement is taking place. Neurons are the only elements in the brain that combine evidence and make decisions. They are the foundation of thought and cognitive processes.

The combination of individual neurons into novel neural networks produces complex mental representations, such as ideas. Our next step is to determine where the cell assemblies for various complex cognitive processes are located in the human brain.

REVIEW: The Nature of Thought

- ✔ Thought is the act of attending to, identifying, and making meaningful responses to stimuli. Many animals, probably including all mammals and birds, are capable of thought.
- ✔ Unlike thought in other animals, human thought has the added flexibility of language, which influences the nature of human thinking. Human thought is also characterized by the ability to generate strings of ideas, many of which are novel.
- ✔ The basic unit of thought is the neuron. The cell assembly is the vehicle by which neurons interact to influence behavior and to produce cognitive processes.

Cognition and the Association Cortex

All together, the primary cortical regions responsible for deciphering inputs from sensory receptors and for executing movements occupy about a third of the cortex (**Figure 15-1**). The remainder, located in the frontal, temporal, parietal, and occipital lobes, is often referred to as **association cortex.** The association areas function to produce cognition.

Chapter 9 examines the neural basis of vision; Chapter 10, hearing; Chapter 11, body senses and movement; Chapter 12, smell and taste.

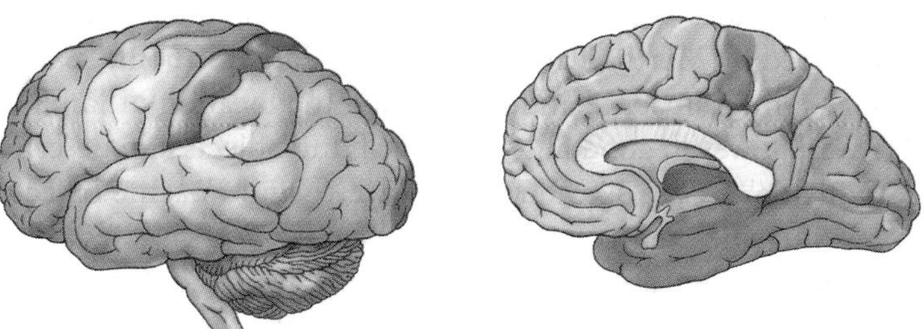

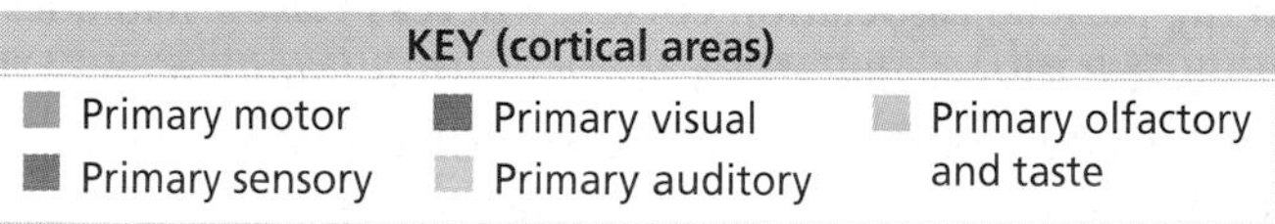

FIGURE 15-1 Cortical Functions. Lateral and medial views of the left and right hemisphere, respectively, showing the primary motor and sensory areas. All remaining cortical areas are collectively referred to as association cortex, which functions in thinking.

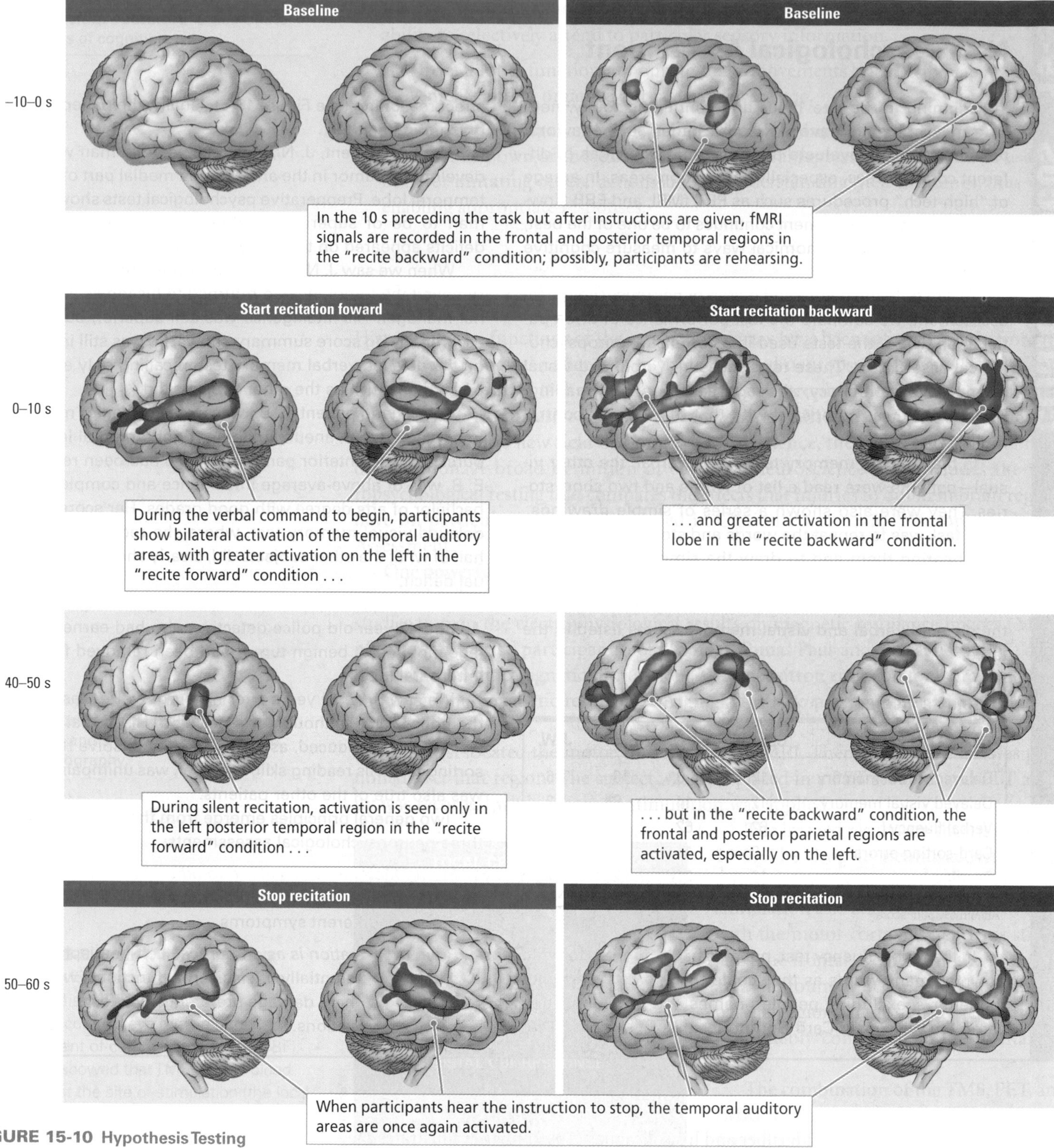

Baseline
Baseline
–10–0 s
In the 10 s preceding the task but after instructions are given, fMRI signals are recorded in the frontal and posterior temporal regions in the "recite backward" condition; possibly, participants are rehearsing.
Start recitation foward
Start recitation backward
0–10 s
During the verbal command to begin, participants show bilateral activation of the temporal auditory areas, with greater activation on the left in the "recite forward" condition . . .
. . . and greater activation in the frontal lobe in the "recite backward" condition.
40–50 s
During silent recitation, activation is seen only in the left posterior temporal region in the "recite forward" condition . . .
. . . but in the "recite backward" condition, the frontal and posterior parietal regions are activated, especially on the left.
Stop recitation
Stop recitation
50–60 s
When participants hear the instruction to stop, the temporal auditory areas are once again activated.

FIGURE 15-10 Hypothesis Testing with fMRI. Summary of fMRI-measured cerebral activation when normal participants silently recite the names of the months either forward (left column) or backward (right column). Adapted from "Dynamic Pattern of Brain Activation During Sequencing of Word Strings Evaluated by fMRI," by D. Wildgruber et al., 1999, *Cognitive Brain Research, 7,* pp. 285–294.

active during the reverse-serial-order task but not during the forward task, likely reflecting the greater complexity of the reverse task.

To evaluate the role of the frontal cortex in serial ordering, fMRI was conducted on normal participants who silently recited the names of the months either forward or backward. **Figure 15-10** summarizes the major findings of the study. The top row diagrams scans from the right and left hemispheres when the participants were lying quietly for 10 seconds before the task began. The second row shows scans during the first

10 seconds after the verbal instructions to start reciting were given, and the third row shows scans during the next 40 to 50 seconds while the silent recitation was going on. The bottom row shows scans during the 10 seconds after the participants were told to stop reciting.

Two major results emerge from the Wildgruber study. First, when the participants heard and analyzed the verbal instructions, increased blood flow to the temporal auditory areas was larger in the left (language-processing) hemisphere than in the right. This activation did not last, however, because the participants heard nothing new during the task.

Second, reciting the months activated the brain differently, depending on whether the recitation was in a forward or backward direction. During the forward recitation, activation was largely restricted to the posterior temporal cortex in the left hemisphere. During the backward recitation, in contrast, bilateral activation of the frontal and parietal cortex occurred, although activation was greater on the left side. Clearly, fMRI is a highly valuable method for analyzing changes in brain activity as they take place.

Although the major goal of the Wildgruber study was to examine the role of the frontal lobes in serial-ordering tasks, it also showed involvement of the parietal and posterior temporal regions, as well as a left–right asymmetry in cerebral activity. In the next section, we consider the differential role of the two hemispheres in thinking.

Chapter 10 explains the cerebral asymmetry particular to auditory processing of language and music.

REVIEW: Cognitive Neuroscience

- ✔ The development of noninvasive imaging techniques enabled cognitive psychologists to investigate the neural bases of thought, leading to a new field, cognitive neuroscience.
- ✔ The concurrent use of multiple methods, including ERP, fMRI, and PET, makes it possible to gather converging evidence on how the normal brain thinks.

Cerebral Asymmetry in Thinking

A fundamental discovery in behavioral neuroscience was the finding by Paul Broca and his contemporaries in the mid-1800s that language is lateralized to the left hemisphere. But the implications of lateralized brain functions were not really understood until the 1960s, when Roger Sperry (1968) and his colleagues began to study people who had undergone surgical separation of the two hemispheres as a treatment for intractable epilepsy.

It soon became apparent that the two cerebral hemispheres were more specialized in their functions than researchers had previously realized. Before considering how the two sides of the brain cooperate in generating cognitive activity, we look at the anatomical differences between the left and right hemispheres.

The media seized on Sperry's findings in the 1980s with an avalanche of self-help books about "left-brained" and "right-brained" people. Some claimed to teach left-brained people how to improve their right-hemisphere skills by using nonverbal strategies to solve cognitive problems. The novelty has worn off, but the concept of cerebral asymmetry is still important to understanding how the human brain thinks.

Anatomical Asymmetry

Building on Broca's findings, investigators have learned how the language- and music-related areas of the left and right temporal lobes differ anatomically. In particular, the primary auditory area is larger on the right, whereas the secondary auditory areas are larger on the left in most people. Other brain regions also are asymmetrical.

Figure 15-11 shows that the lateral fissure, which partly separates the temporal and parietal lobes, has a sharper upward course in the right hemisphere relative to the left.

Another clue that the left hemisphere's specialization for language may be related to its special role in controlling fine movements comes from investigating where certain parts of speech are processed in the brain. Recall that cognitive systems for representing abstract concepts are likely to be related to systems that produce more-concrete behaviors. Consequently, we might expect that the left hemisphere would have a role in forming concepts related to fine movements.

Concepts that describe movements are the parts of speech that we call verbs. Interestingly, a fundamental difference between left- and right-hemisphere language abilities is that verbs seem to be processed only in the left hemisphere, whereas nouns are processed in both hemispheres. In other words, not only does the left hemisphere have a special role in controlling the production of actions, it also controls the production of mental representations of actions in the form of words.

If the left hemisphere excels at language because it is better at controlling fine movements, what is the basis of the right hemisphere's abilities? One idea is that the right hemisphere has a special role in controlling movements in space. In a sense, this role is an elaboration of the functions of the dorsal visual stream (diagrammed in Figure 15-2).

Once again, we can propose a link between movement at a concrete level and movement at a more abstract level. If the right hemisphere is producing movements in space, then it is also likely to produce mental images of such movements. We would therefore predict that right-hemisphere patients would be impaired both at making spatially guided movements and at thinking about such movements. And they are.

Bear in mind that theories about the reasons for hemispheric asymmetry are highly speculative. Because the brain has evolved to produce movement and to create a sensory reality, the observed asymmetry must be somehow related to these overriding functions. In other words, more recent functions, such as language, are likely to be extensions of preexisting functions. The fact that language is represented asymmetrically does not mean that the brain is asymmetrical because of language. After all, brains are asymmetrically organized in other species that do not talk. Once again, we see evidence that more recent adaptations, such as mirror neurons, probably play an important role in the emergence of unique human functions.

The Left Hemisphere, Language, and Thought

We end our examination of brain asymmetry by considering one other provocative idea. Michael Gazzaniga (1992) proposed that the superior language skills of the left hemisphere are important in understanding the differences in thinking between humans and other animals. He called the speaking hemisphere the "interpreter." What he meant is illustrated in the following experiment, using split-brain patients as subjects.

Each hemisphere is shown the same two pictures—a picture of a match followed by a picture of a piece of wood, for example. A series of other pictures is then shown, and the task is to pick out a third picture that has an inferred relation to the other two. In this example, the third related picture might be a bonfire. The right hemisphere is incapable of making the inference that a match struck and held to a piece of wood could create a bonfire, whereas the left hemisphere can easily arrive at this interpretation.

An analogous task uses words. One or the other hemisphere might be shown the words *pin* and *finger* and then be asked to pick out a third word that is related to the other two. In this case, the correct answer might be *bleed*.

The right hemisphere is not able to make this connection. Although it has enough language ability to pick out close synonyms for *pin* and *finger* (*needle* and *thumb*, respectively), it cannot make the inference that pricking a finger with a needle will result in bleeding. Again, the left hemisphere has no difficulty with this task. Apparently, the left hemisphere's language capability gives it a capacity for interpretation that the right hemisphere lacks. One reason may be that language serves to label and express the computations of other cognitive systems.

Gazzaniga goes even farther. He suggests that the addition of the language abilities possessed by the left hemisphere makes humans a "believing" species. That is, humans can make inferences and have beliefs about sensory events.

In contrast, Alex, the gray parrot, would not have been able to make inferences or hold beliefs about things because he did not have a system analogous to our left-hemisphere language system. Alex could use language but could not make inferences about sensory events with language. Gazzaniga's idea is certainly intriguing. It implies a fundamental difference in the nature of cerebral asymmetry—and therefore in the nature of cognition—between humans and other animals because of the nature of human language.

REVIEW: Cerebral Asymmetry in Thinking

- ✔ The two cerebral hemispheres process information differently, which means that they think differently.
- ✔ The right hemisphere plays a role in spatial movements and spatial cognition as well as in music. The left hemisphere plays a role in controlling voluntary movement sequences and in language.
- ✔ The addition of verbal mediation to left-hemisphere thinking may confer a fundamental advantage to the left hemisphere because language can label the computations of the brain's various cognitive systems. As a result, the left hemisphere is able to make inferences that the right hemisphere cannot.

Variations in Cognitive Organization

No two brains are identical. Brains differ in gyral patterns, cytoarchitectonics, vascular patterns, and neurochemistry, among other things. Some of these differences are genetically determined; others result from plastic changes such as those created by experience and learning. Some brain differences are idiosyncratic (unique to a particular person), whereas many other variations are systematic and common to whole categories of people. In this section, we consider two systematic variations in brain organization, those related to sex and handedness, and one idiosyncratic variation.

Cytoarchitectonics refers to the organization, structure, and distribution of brain cells. Figure 2-21, for example, reproduces Brodmann's cytoarchitectonic map of the cortex.

Sex Differences in Cognitive Organization

The idea that men and women think differently is likely to have originated with the first men and women. Science backs up this view. Books, including one by Doreen Kimura (1999), have compiled considerable evidence for marked sex differences in the way men and women perform on many cognitive tests. As illustrated in **Figure 15-15**, paper-and-pencil tests consistently show that, on average, females have better verbal fluency than males do, whereas males do better on tests of spatial reasoning. Our focus here is on how such differences relate to the brain.

Neural Basis of Sex Differences

Many investigators have searched without success for gross differences in the structures of the male and female cortices. If such differences exist, they must be subtle. The stronger evidence points to the influence that gonadal hormones exert over the structure of cells in the brain, including cortical cells.

For example, gonadal hormones were found to influence the structures of neurons in the prefrontal cortices of rats (Kolb and Stewart, 1991). The cells in one prefrontal region,

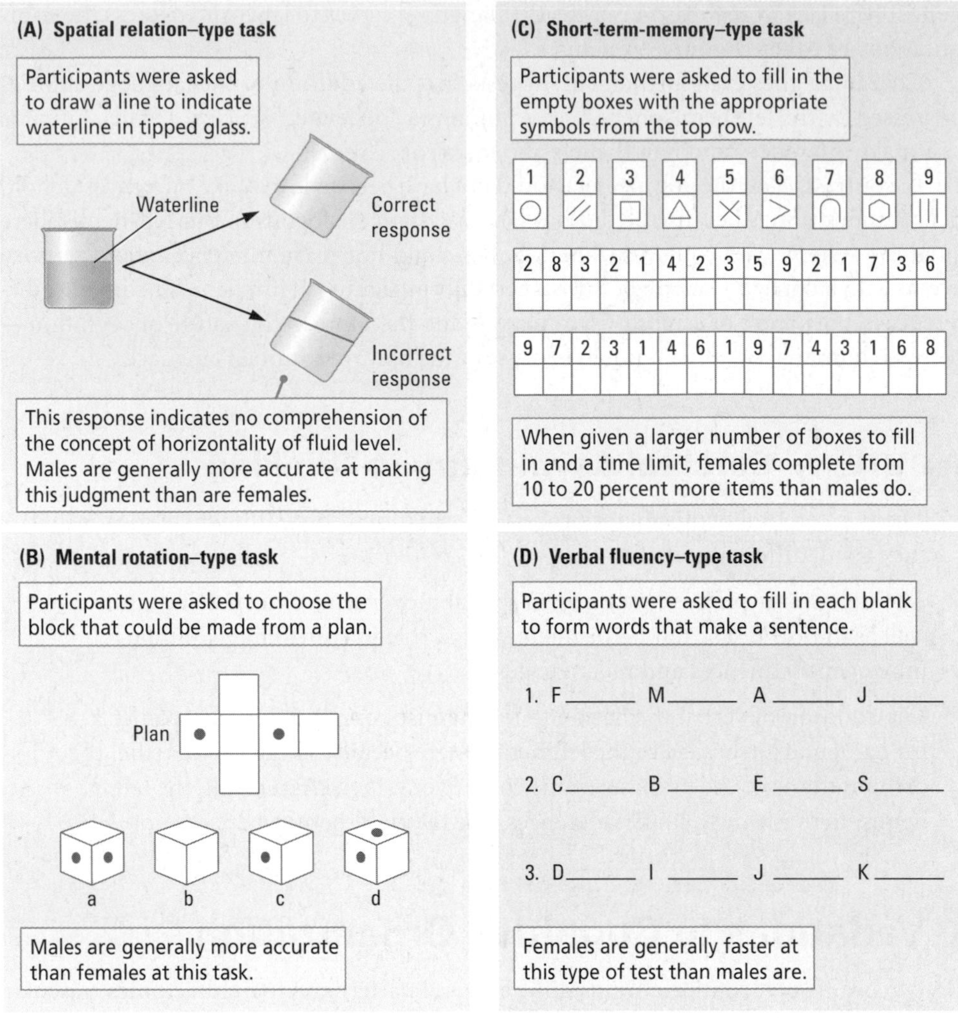

(A) Spatial relation–type task
Participants were asked to draw a line to indicate waterline in tipped glass.
Waterline
Correct response
Incorrect response
This response indicates no comprehension of the concept of horizontality of fluid level. Males are generally more accurate at making this judgment than are females.
(B) Mental rotation–type task
Participants were asked to choose the block that could be made from a plan.
Plan
a
b
c
d
Males are generally more accurate than females at this task.
(C) Short-term-memory–type task
Participants were asked to fill in the empty boxes with the appropriate symbols from the top row.
1 2 3 4 5 6 7 8 9
2 8 3 2 1 4 2 3 5 9 2 1 7 3 6
9 7 2 3 1 4 6 1 9 7 4 3 1 6 8
When given a larger number of boxes to fill in and a time limit, females complete from 10 to 20 percent more items than males do.
(D) Verbal fluency–type task
Participants were asked to fill in each blank to form words that make a sentence.
1. F___ M___ A___ J___
2. C___ B___ E___ S___
3. D___ I___ J___ K___
Females are generally faster at this type of test than males are.

FIGURE 15-15 Tasks That Reliably Show Sex-Related Cognitive Differences.

located along the midline, have larger dendritic fields (and presumably more synapses) in males than in females, as shown in the top row of **Figure 15-16.** In contrast, the cells in the orbitofrontal region have larger dendritic fields (and presumably more synapses) in females than in males, as shown in the bottom row. These sex differences are not found in rats that have had their gonads or ovaries removed at birth. Presumably, sex hormones somehow change the brain's organization and ultimately its cognitive processing.

Findings from a second study showed that the presence or absence of gonadal hormones affects the brain not only in early development but also in adulthood. In the course of this study, which focused on how hormones affect recovery from brain damage, the ovaries of middle-aged female rats were removed (Stewart and Kolb, 1994). When the brains of these rats and those of control rats were examined some months later, the cortical neurons (especially the prefrontal neurons) of the rats whose ovaries had been removed had undergone structural changes. Specifically, the cells had grown 30 percent more dendrites, and their spine density increased compared with the cells in control rats. Clearly, gonadal hormones can affect the neuronal structure of the brain at any point in an animal's life.

What do these hormonal effects mean in regard to how neurons process information and ultimately how the brain thinks? One possibility is that gonadal hormones may influence the way in which experience changes the brain. Evidence in support of this possibility came from a study by Robbin Gibb and her colleagues (Gibb, Gorny, and Kolb, 2009). These investigators placed male and female rats in complex environments.

See Chapters 7 and 14 for more information on research using complex, or enriched, environments and on the practical implications of this research.

After 4 months, they examined the animals' brains and found a sex difference in the effects of experience. Both sexes showed experience-dependent changes in neural structure, but the details of the changes differed.

Females exposed to the enriched environment showed a greater increase in dendritic branching in the cortex, whereas males housed in the same environment showed a greater increase in spine density. In other words, although experience changed the brains of both sexes, they were changed in different ways, presumably mediated by the animals' exposure to different gonadal hormones. These differences almost certainly affect cognitive processing in one sex relative to the other, although exactly how remains a matter for speculation.

Another way to investigate the effects of sex hormones on how neurons process information is to relate differences in hormone exposure to particular human cognitive abilities. This type of study presents obvious problems, because we cannot control hormone types and levels in people. We can, however, take advantage of naturally occurring hormone variations within a single sex.

Using these naturally occurring variations is rather simple in women. We can use the age of onset of the first menstrual cycle (known as *menarche*) as a marker for the presence of female gonadal hormones. This age varies considerably (from as early as 8 years old to as late as 18), offering ample opportunity to relate the presence of female hormones to women's cognitive abilities.

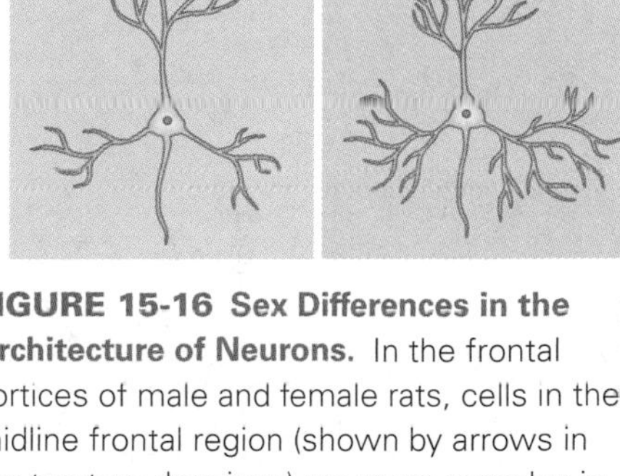

FIGURE 15-16 Sex Differences in the Architecture of Neurons. In the frontal cortices of male and female rats, cells in the midline frontal region (shown by arrows in the top two drawings) are more complex in males than in females, whereas the opposite is true of the orbitofrontal region (shown by arrows in the bottom two drawings).

In a study by Sharon Rowntree (2009), girls had been recruited at age 8 to take part in a 10-year longitudinal study of the relation between age at menarche and body type. The age at which each started to menstruate was known to within 1 month. At age 16, all the participants were given tests of verbal fluency (such as writing in 5 minutes as many words as possible that start with the letter *d*) and of spatial manipulation (such as the one illustrated in Figure 15-5).

Rowntree reasoned that, if hormones alter cortical neurons, then the age at which the neurons are changed may influence cognitive processing, which is exactly what she found evidence for. As summarized in **Figure 15-17**, girls who reached menarche earlier (age 12 or younger) were generally better at the verbal tasks than were girls who began to menstruate later. Girls who reached menarche later were generally better at the spatial tasks. In short, the age at which gonadal hormones affect the brain may be the critical factor in the development of cognitive skills.

Deborah Waber (1976) examined this idea in another way. She conducted a retrospective study in which both boys and girls estimated their age at the onset of puberty. She found that, regardless of sex, early-maturing adolescents performed better on tests

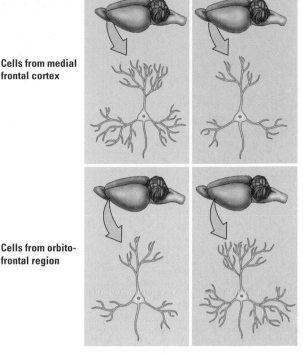

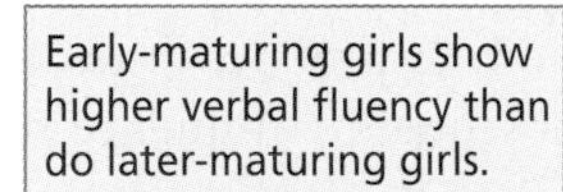

Early-maturing girls show higher verbal fluency than do later-maturing girls.

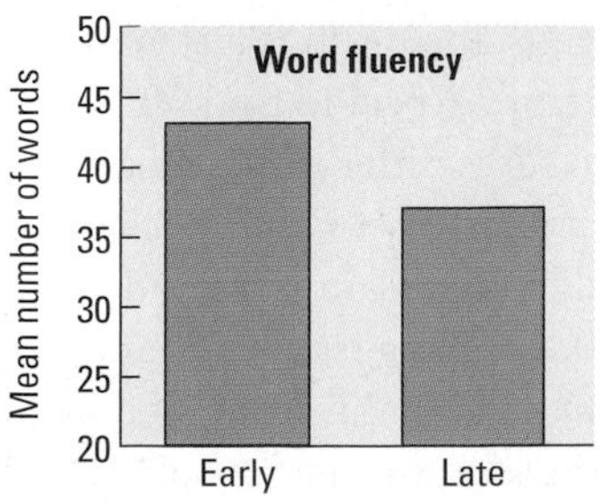

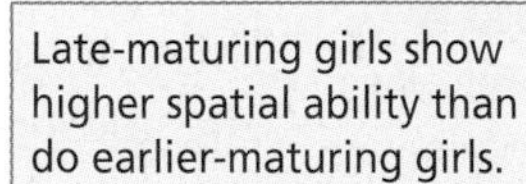

Late-maturing girls show higher spatial ability than do earlier-maturing girls.

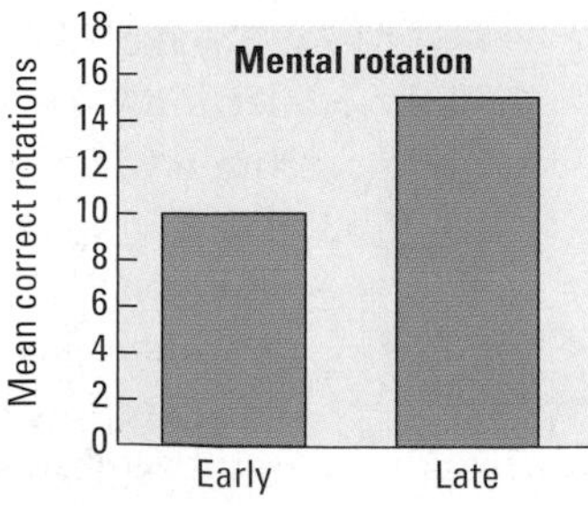

FIGURE 15-17 Effects of Sex Hormones. Girls who reach menarche early (before age 12) have better verbal skills but weaker spatial skills than do girls who reach menarche late (after age 14). Data courtesy of S. Rowntree, from "Spatial and Verbal Ability in Adult Females Vary with Age at Menses," by S. Rowntree, 2009, unpublished data.

of verbal abilities than they did on tests of spatial abilities, whereas late-maturing subjects showed the opposite pattern. Waber argued that sex differences in mental abilities result from differences in the organization of cortical function that are related to differential rates of physical maturation. Because boys usually mature later than girls, they show a different pattern of cognitive skills from that of girls.

The advantage of using same-sex participants in such studies is to reduce the probability that different experiences before puberty account either for the girls' age differences at menarche or for their different cognitive abilities. Rather, the gonadal hormones of puberty seem more likely to influence the structure of cortical neurons and ultimately cognitive processing.

Chapter 7 discusses more organizing effects of gonadal hormones during brain development.

The postpubertal experiences of the girls could have affected the brains of early maturers differently from those of late maturers, but gonadal hormones would still have played an important mediating role. Interestingly, boys reach puberty later than girls, and boys, on average, do better at spatial tasks and worse on verbal tasks than girls do at any age. Perhaps the age at which hormones affect the brain is the critical factor here.

An additional way to consider the neural basis of sex differences is to look at the effects of cortical injury in men and women. If there are sex differences in the neural organization of cognitive processing, there ought to be differences in the effects of cortical injury in the two sexes. Doreen Kimura (1999) conducted this kind of study and showed that the pattern of cerebral organization within each hemisphere may in fact differ between the sexes.

Investigating people who had sustained cortical strokes in adulthood, Kimura tried to match the location and extent of injury in her male and female subjects. She found that, although men and women were almost equally likely to be aphasic subsequent to left-hemisphere lesions of some kind, men were more likely to be aphasic and apraxic after damage to the left posterior cortex, whereas women were far more likely to be aphasic and apraxic after lesions to the left frontal cortex. These results, summarized in **Figure 15-18**, suggest a difference in intrahemispheric organization between the two sexes.

FIGURE 15-18 Evidence for Sex Differences in Cortical Organization. Apraxia and aphasia are associated with frontal damage to the left hemisphere in women and with posterior damage in men. Adapted from *Sex and Cognition*, by D. Kimura, 1999, Cambridge, MA: MIT Press.

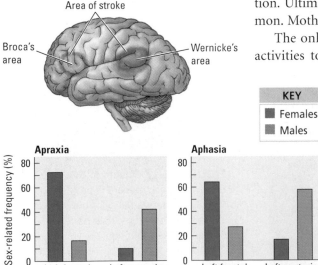

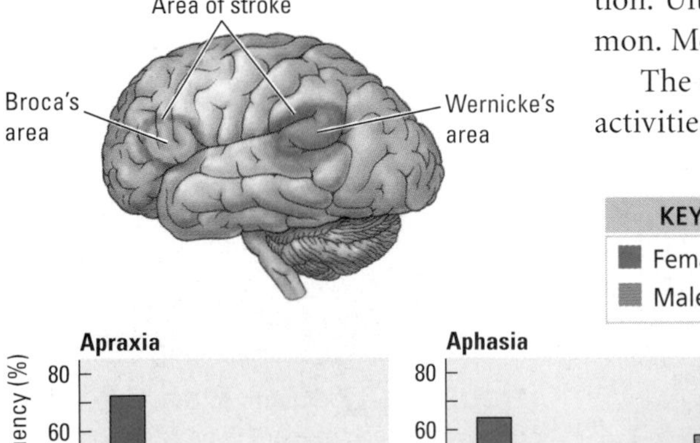

Evolution of Sex-Related Cognitive Differences

Although the role of gonadal hormones has taken center stage in explaining sex differences in cognitive function, we are still left with the question of how these differences arose in the first place. To answer this question, we must look back at human evolution. Ultimately, males and females of a species have virtually all their genes in common. Mothers pass their genes to both sons and daughters, and fathers do the same.

The only way in which a gene can affect one sex preferentially is for that gene's activities to be influenced by the animal's gonadal hormones, which in turn are determined by the presence or absence of the Y chromosome. The Y chromosome carries a gene called the *testes-determining factor* (TDF). This gene stimulates the body to produce testes, which then manufacture androgens, which subsequently influence the activities of other genes.

Like other body organs, the brain is a potential target of natural selection. We should therefore expect to find sex-related differences in the brain whenever the two sexes differ in the adaptive problems they have faced in the evolutionary history of the species. The degree of aggressive behavior produced by the brain is a good example.

Males are more physically aggressive than females in most mammalian species. This trait presumably improved males' reproductive success, reinforcing natural selection for greater aggressiveness in males.

Producing higher levels of aggression entails male hormones. We know from studies of nonhuman species that aggression is related directly to the presence of androgens and to their effects on gene expression both during brain development and later in life. In this case, therefore, natural selection has worked on gonadal hormone levels to favor aggressiveness in males.

Explaining sex-related differences in cognitive processes, such as language or spatial skills, is more speculative than explaining sex-related differences in aggressive behavior. Nevertheless, some hypotheses come to mind. We can imagine, for instance, that in the history of mammalian evolution, males have tended to range over larger territories than females have. This behavior requires spatial abilities, so these skills would have been favored in males.

Support for this hypothesis comes from comparing spatial problem-solving abilities in males of closely related mammalian species—species in which the males range over large territories versus species in which the males do not have such extensive ranges. Pine voles, for example, have restricted ranges and no sex-related difference in range, whereas meadow voles have ranges about 20 times as large as those of pine voles, with the males ranging more widely than the females.

When the spatial skills of pine voles and meadow voles are compared, meadow voles are far superior. Furthermore, a sex difference in spatial ability among meadow voles favors males, but no such sex difference exists among pine voles. The hippocampus is implicated in spatial navigation skills. Significantly, the hippocampus is larger in meadow voles than in pine voles, and it is larger in meadow vole males than females (Gaulin, 1992). A similar logic could help explain sex-related differences in spatial abilities between human males and females.

Chapter 14 explains how visuospatial learning and visuospatial memory both recruit the hippocampus.

Explaining sex-related differences in language skills also is speculative. One hypothesis holds that, if males were hunters and often away from home, the females left behind in social groups would be selectively favored to develop tools for social interaction, one of which is language. We might also argue that females were selected for fine motor skills (such as foraging for food and making clothing and baskets). Because of the relation between language and fine motor skills, enhanced language capacities also might have evolved in females.

Although such speculations are interesting, they are not testable. We will probably never know with certainty why sex-related differences in brain organization developed.

Handedness and Cognitive Organization

Nearly everyone prefers one hand over the other for writing or throwing a ball. Most people prefer the right hand. In fact, left-handedness has historically been viewed as odd. But it is not rare. An estimated 10 percent of the human population worldwide is left-handed. This proportion represents the number of people who write with the left hand. When other criteria are used to determine left-handedness, estimates range from 10 percent to 30 percent of the population.

Because the left hemisphere controls the right hand, the general assumption is that right-handedness is somehow related to the presence of speech in the left hemisphere. If this were so, then language would be located in the right hemispheres of left-handed people. This hypothesis is easily tested, and it turns out to be false.

In the course of preparing epileptic patients for surgery to remove the abnormal tissue causing their seizures, Ted Rasmussen and Brenda Milner (1977) injected the left or right hemisphere with sodium amobarbital (see Clinical Focus 15-4, "The Sodium Amobarbital Test," on page 550). This drug produces a short-acting anesthesia of the entire hemisphere, making it possible to determine where speech is located. For instance, if a person becomes aphasic when the drug is injected into the left hemisphere but not when the drug is injected into the right, then speech must reside in that person's left hemisphere.

CLINICAL FOCUS 15-4

The Sodium Amobarbital Test

Guy, a 32-year-old lawyer, had a vascular malformation over the region corresponding to the posterior speech zone. The malformation was beginning to cause neurological symptoms, including epilepsy. The ideal surgical treatment was removal of the abnormal vessels.

The complication with this surgery is that removing vessels sitting over the posterior speech zone poses a serious risk of permanent aphasia. Because Guy was left-handed, his speech areas could be in the right hemisphere. If so, the surgical risk would be much lower.

To achieve certainty in such doubtful cases, Jun Wada and Ted Rasmussen (1960) pioneered the technique of injecting sodium amobarbital, a barbiturate, into the carotid artery to produce a brief period of anesthesia of the ipsilateral hemisphere. (Injections are now normally made through a catheter inserted into the femoral artery.) This procedure enables an unequivocal localization of speech because injection into the speech hemisphere results in an arrest of speech lasting as long as several minutes. As speech returns, it is characterized by aphasic errors.

Injection into the nonspeaking hemisphere may produce no or only brief speech arrest. The amobarbital procedure has the advantage of allowing each hemisphere to be studied separately in the functional absence of the other (anesthetized) hemisphere. Because the period of anesthesia lasts several minutes, a variety of functions, including memory and movement, can be studied to determine a hemisphere's capabilities.

The sodium amobarbital test is always performed bilaterally, with the second cerebral hemisphere being injected several days after the first one to make sure that there is no residual drug effect. In the brief period of drug action, the patient is given a series of simple tasks requiring the use of language, memory, and object recognition. Speech is tested by asking the patient to name some common objects presented in quick succession, to count and to recite the days of the week forward and backward, and to spell simple words.

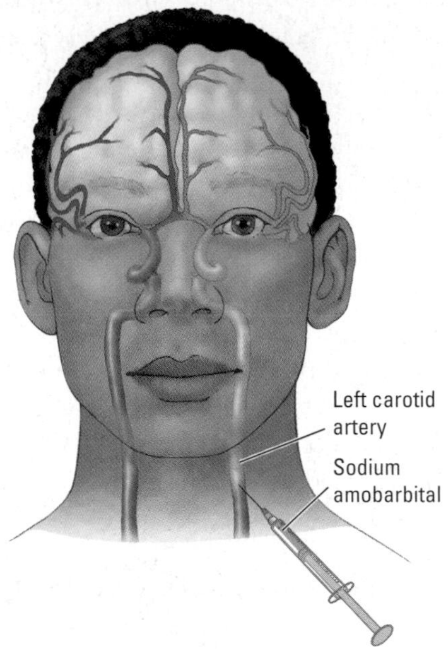

To avoid damaging speech zones in patients about to undergo brain surgery, surgeons inject sodium amobarbital into the carotid artery. The drug anesthetizes the hemisphere where it is injected (here, the left hemisphere), allowing the surgeon to determine if that hemisphere is dominant for speech.

If the injected hemisphere is nondominant for speech, the patient may continue to carry out the verbal tasks, although there is often a period as long as 30 seconds during which he or she appears confused and is silent but can resume speech with urging. When the injected hemisphere is dominant for speech, the patient typically stops talking and remains completely aphasic until recovery from the anesthesia is well along, somewhere in the range of 4 to 10 minutes.

Guy was found to have speech in the left hemisphere. During the test of his left hemisphere, he could not talk. Later, he said that, when he was asked about a particular object, he wondered just what that question meant. When he finally had some vague idea, he had no idea of what the answer was or how to say anything. By then he realized that he had been asked all sorts of other questions to which he had also not responded.

When asked which objects he had been shown, he said he had no idea. However, when given an array of objects and asked to choose with his left hand, he was able to identify the objects by pointing because his nonspeaking right hemisphere controlled that hand. In contrast, his speaking left hemisphere had no memory of the objects, because it had been asleep.

Rasmussen and Milner found that virtually all right-handed people had speech in the left hemisphere, but the reverse was not true for left-handed people. About 70 percent of left-handers also had speech in the left hemisphere. Of the remaining 30 percent, about half had speech in the right hemisphere and half had speech in both hemispheres.

Findings from anatomical studies have subsequently shown that left-handers with speech in the left hemisphere have anatomical asymmetries similar to those of right-handers. In contrast, in left-handers with speech located in the right hemisphere or in both hemispheres—known as **anomalous speech representation**—the anatomical symmetry is reversed or there is no obvious anatomical asymmetry at all.

Sandra Witelson and Charlie Goldsmith (1991) asked whether any other gross differences might exist in the brain structure of right- and left-handers. One possibility is that the connectivity of the cerebral hemispheres may differ. To test this idea, the investigators studied the hand preference of terminally ill subjects on a variety of one-handed tasks. They later did postmortem studies of these patients' brains, paying particular attention to the size of the corpus callosum. They found that the callosal cross-sectional area was 11 percent greater in left-handed and ambidextrous (no hand preference) people than in right-handed people.

Whether this enlarged callosum is due to a greater number of fibers, to thicker fibers, or to more myelin remains to be seen. If the larger corpus callosum is due to more fibers, the difference would be on the order of 25 million more fibers. Presumably, such a difference would have major implications for the organization of cognitive processing in left- and right-handers.

Anomalous speech representation Condition in which a person's speech zones are located in the right hemisphere or in both hemispheres.

Synesthesia Ability to perceive a stimulus of one sense as the sensation of a different sense, as when sound produces a sensation of color; literally, "feeling together."

Synesthesia

Some variations in brain organization are idiosyncratic. **Synesthesia** is an individual's capacity to join sensory experiences across sensory modalities, as discussed in Clinical Focus 15-5, "A Case of Synesthesia." Examples include the ability to hear colors and to

CLINICAL FOCUS 15-5

A Case of Synesthesia

Michael Watson tastes shapes. He first came to the attention of the neurologist Richard Cytowic over dinner. After tasting a sauce that he was making for roast chicken, Watson blurted out, "There aren't enough points on the chicken."

When Cytowic quizzed him about this strange remark, Watson said that all flavors had shape for him. "I wanted the taste of this chicken to be a pointed shape, but it came out all round. Well, I mean it's nearly spherical. I can't serve this if it doesn't have points" (Cytowic, 1998, p. 4).

Watson has synesthesia, which literally means "feeling together." All his life Watson has experienced the feeling of shape when he tastes or smells food. When he tastes intense flavors, he reports an experience of shape that sweeps down his arms to his fingertips. He experiences the feeling of weight, texture, warmth or cold, and shape, just as though he were grasping something.

The feelings are not confined to his hands, however. Watson experiences some taste shapes, such as points, over his whole body. He experiences others only on the face, back, or shoulders. These impressions are not metaphors, as other people might use when they say that a cheese is "sharp" or that a wine is "textured." Such descriptions make no sense to Watson. He actually feels the shapes.

Cytowic systematically studied Watson to determine whether his feelings of shape were always associated with particular flavors and found that they were. Cytowic devised the set of geometric figures shown here to allow Watson to communicate which shapes he associated with various flavors.

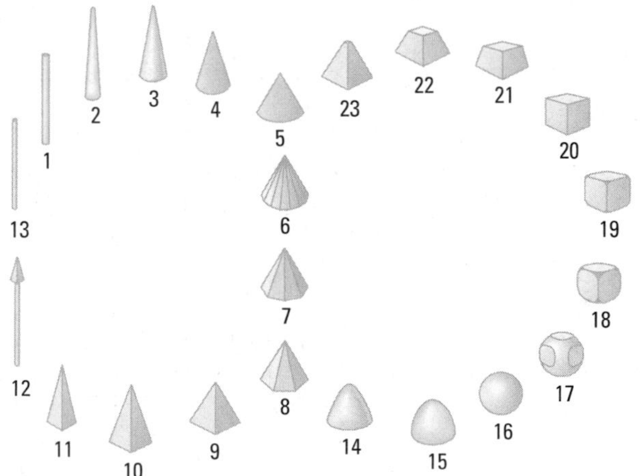

The neurologist Richard Cytowic devised this set of figures to help Michael Watson communicate the shapes that he senses when he tastes food.

Musician and composer Stevie Wonder is synesthetic, as were music legends Duke Ellington and Franz Liszt and the physicist Richard Feynman, who won the Nobel Prize.

taste shapes. Edward Hubbard (2007) estimated the incidence of synesthesia at about 1 in every 23 people, although it is likely to be limited in scope for most people.

Synesthesia runs in families, the most famous case being the family of Russian novelist Vladimir Nabokov. As a toddler, Nabokov complained to his mother that the letter colors on his wooden alphabet blocks were "all wrong." His mother understood what he meant, because she too perceived letters and words in particular colors. Nabokov's son is synesthetic in the same way.

If you recall shivering on hearing a particular piece of music or the noise of fingernails scratching across a chalkboard, you have "felt" sound. Even so, other sensory blendings may be difficult to imagine. How can sounds or letters possibly produce colors? Studies of people with this sensory ability show that the same stimuli always elicit the same synesthetic experiences for them.

The most common form of synesthesia is colored hearing. For many synesthetics, colored hearing means hearing both speech and music in color, the experience being a visual mélange of colored shapes, movement, and scintillation. The fact that colored hearing is more common than other types of synesthesia is curious.

The five primary senses (vision, hearing, touch, taste, and smell) all generate synesthetic pairings. Most, however, are in one direction. For instance, whereas synesthetic people may see colors when they hear, they do not hear sounds when they look at colors. Furthermore, some sensory combinations occur rarely, if at all. In particular, taste or smell rarely triggers a synesthetic response.

The neurological basis of synesthesia is difficult to study because each case is idiosyncratic. Few studies have related synesthesia directly to brain function or brain organization, and different people may experience it for different reasons. Various hypotheses have been advanced to account for synesthesia:

- Extraordinary neural connections between the different sensory regions are related in a particular synesthetic person.
- Activity is increased in multimodal areas of the frontal lobes that receive inputs from more than one sensory area.
- Particular sensory inputs elicit unusual patterns of cerebral activation.

Whatever the explanation, the brains of synesthetic people clearly think differently from the brains of other people when it comes to certain types of sensory inputs.

REVIEW: Variations in Cognitive Organization

- ✔ No two brains are alike, and no two people think the same.
- ✔ Although many individual differences in brain structure and thinking are idiosyncratic, systematic variations, such as those related to sex and handedness, also exist.
- ✔ Differences in the cerebral organization of thinking are undoubtedly related to differences in the synaptic organization of the neural circuits that underlie different types of cognitive processing.

Intelligence

Most people would probably agree that intelligence is one of the biggest influences on anyone's thinking ability. Intelligence is easy to identify in people and even easy to observe in other animals. Yet intelligence is not at all easy to define. Despite years of studying human intelligence, researchers have not yet reached agreement on what intelligence entails. We therefore begin this section by reviewing some hypotheses of intelligence.

The Concept of General Intelligence

In the 1920s, Charles Spearman proposed that although there may be different kinds of intelligence, there is also an underlying general intelligence, which he called the "g" factor. Consider for a moment what a general factor in intelligence might mean for the brain. Presumably, brains with high or low "g" would have some general difference in brain architecture.

This difference could not be something as simple as size, because human brain size (which varies from about 1000 to 2000 grams) correlates poorly with intelligence. Another possibility is that "g" is related to some special characteristic of cerebral connectivity or even to the ratio of neurons to glia. Still another possibility is that "g" is related to the activation of specific brain regions, possibly in the frontal lobe (Duncan et al., 2000; Gray and Thompson, 2004).

Chapter 1 reveals the fallacies inherent in attempting to correlate human brain size with intelligence.

The results of preliminary studies of Albert Einstein's brain imply that cerebral connectivity and glia-to-neuron ratio may play important roles. Sandra Witelson and her colleagues (Witelson, Kigar, and Harvey, 1999) found that, although Einstein's brain is the same size and weight as the average male brain, its lateral fissure is short, and both the left and the right lateral fissures take a particularly striking upward deflection (**Figure 15-19** and compare Figure 15-11). This arrangement essentially fuses the inferior parietal area with the posterior temporal area.

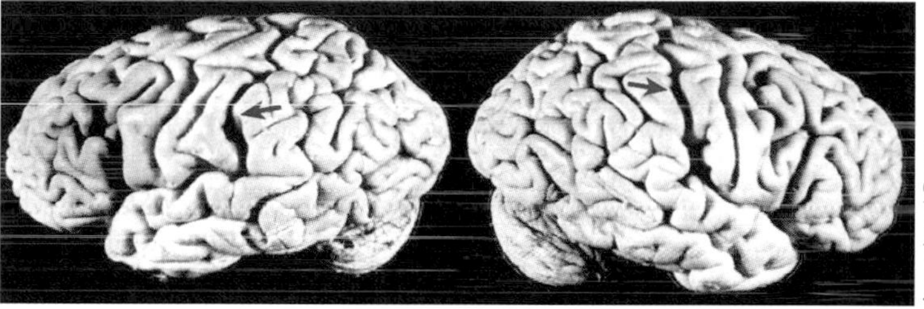

FIGURE 15-19 Einstein's Brain. The lateral fissure (at arrows) takes an exaggerated upward course relative to its course in typical brains, essentially fusing the posterior temporal regions with the inferior parietal regions. Reprinted with the permission of S. Witelson, D. Kigar, T. Harvey, and *The Lancet*, June 19, 1999.

The inferior parietal cortex is known to have a role in mathematical reasoning, and so it is tempting to speculate that Einstein's mathematical abilities were related to rearrangements of this area. But there may be another important difference in Einstein's brain. Marion Diamond and her colleagues (1985) looked at its glia-to-neuron ratio versus the mean for a control population. They found that Einstein's inferior parietal cortex had a higher glia-to-neuron ratio than average: each of his neurons in this region had an unusually high number of glial cells supporting them.

The glia-to-neuron ratio was not unusually high in any other cortical areas of Einstein's brain measured by these researchers. Possibly, then, certain types of intelligence could be related to differences in cell structure in localized regions of the brain. But, even if this hypothesis proves correct, it still offers little neural evidence in favor of a general factor in intelligence.

A neuropsychological possibility is that the "g" factor is related to language processes in the brain. Recall that language ability qualitatively changes the nature of cognitive processing in humans. So perhaps people with very good language skills also have an advantage in general thinking ability.

Multiple Intelligences

Many other hypotheses of intelligence have been set forth since Spearman's, but few have considered the brain directly. One exception is a proposal by Howard Gardner, a neuropsychologist at Harvard. Gardner (1983) considered the effects of neurological injury on people's behavior. He concluded that there are seven distinctly different forms of intelligence and that each form can be selectively damaged by brain injury. This view that there are multiple human intelligences should not be surprising, given the many different types of cognitive operations that the human brain is capable of performing.

TABLE 16-4 Factors That May Precipitate Seizures in Susceptible Persons

Drugs
Alcohol
Analeptics
Excessive anticonvulsants
Phenothiazines
Tricyclic antidepressants
Emotional stress
Fever
Hormonal changes
Adrenal steroids
Adrenocorticotrophic hormone (ACTH)
Menses
Puberty
Hyperventilation
Sensory stimuli
Flashing lights
Laughing
Reading, speaking, coughing
Sounds: music, bells
Sleep
Sleep deprivation
Trauma

Source: Adapted from *Behavioral Neurobiology* (p. 5), by J. H. Pincus and G. J. Tucker, 1974. New York: Oxford University Press.

to describe a basic set of symptoms to be expected in all or even most people with epilepsy. Nevertheless, three particular symptoms are found within the variety of epileptic episodes:

1. An *aura*, or warning, of impending seizure may take the form of a sensation—an odor or a noise—or it may simply be a "feeling" that the seizure is going to occur.
2. *Loss of consciousness* ranges from complete collapse in some people to simply staring off into space in others. The period of lost consciousness is often accompanied by amnesia, including forgetting the seizure itself.
3. Seizures commonly have a *motor component,* but as noted, the movement characteristics vary considerably. Some people shake; others exhibit automatic movements, such as rubbing the hands or chewing.

A diagnosis of epilepsy usually is confirmed by EEG. Some seizures, however, are difficult to document except under special circumstances (e.g., an EEG recorded during sleep). Moreover, not all persons with an EEG that suggests epilepsy actually have seizures. Some statistics estimate that as many as 4 people in 20 simply have abnormal EEG patterns, many more than the 1 in 200 thought to suffer from epilepsy. Among the many types of epileptic seizures, we compare only two here: focal and generalized seizures.

Focal Seizures

Focal seizures begin in one place and then spread out. John Hughlings-Jackson hypothesized in 1870 that focal seizures probably originate from the point (focus) in the neocortex representing the region of the body where the movement is first seen. He was later proved correct. In *Jacksonian focal seizures,* for example, the attack begins with jerking movements in one part of the body—a finger, a toe, or the mouth—and then spreads to adjacent parts. If the attack begins with a finger, the jerks might spread to other fingers, then the hand, the arm, and so on, producing so-called "Jacksonian marches."

Complex partial seizures, another focal type, originate most commonly in the temporal lobe and somewhat less frequently in the frontal lobe. Complex partial seizures are characterized by three common manifestations:

1. Subjective experiences—for example, forced, repetitive thoughts, alterations in mood, feelings of déjà vu, or hallucinations—before the attack
2. **Automatisms**—repetitive stereotyped movements such as lip smacking or chewing or activities such as undoing buttons during the attack
3. Postural changes, such as when the person assumes a **catatonic,** or frozen, **posture,** during the attack

Generalized Seizures

Generalized seizures lack focal onset and often occur on both sides of the body. The **grand mal** ("big bad") attack is characterized by loss of consciousness and stereotyped motor activity. Patients typically go through three stages, diagrammed in **Figure 16-8:** (1) a tonic stage, in which the body stiffens and breathing stops, (2) a clonic stage, in which there is rhythmic shaking, and (3) a postseizure **postictal depression** during which the patient is confused. About 50 percent of grand mal seizures are preceded by an aura.

The **petit mal** ("little bad") attack is a loss of awareness with no motor activity except for blinking, turning the head, or rolling the eyes. Petit mal attacks are of brief duration, seldom exceeding about 10 seconds. The typical EEG recording of a petit mal seizure has a 3-per-second spike-and-wave pattern.

Focal seizure Begins locally (at a focus) and then spreads out to adjacent areas.
Automatism Unconscious, repetitive, stereotyped movement characteristic of seizure.
Catatonic posture Rigid or frozen pose resulting from a psychomotor disturbance.
Grand mal seizure Seizure characterized by loss of consciousness and stereotyped motor activity.
Postictal depression Postseizure state of confusion and reduced affect.
Petit mal seizure Seizure of brief duration, characterized by loss of awareness with no motor activity except for blinking, turning the head, or rolling the eyes.

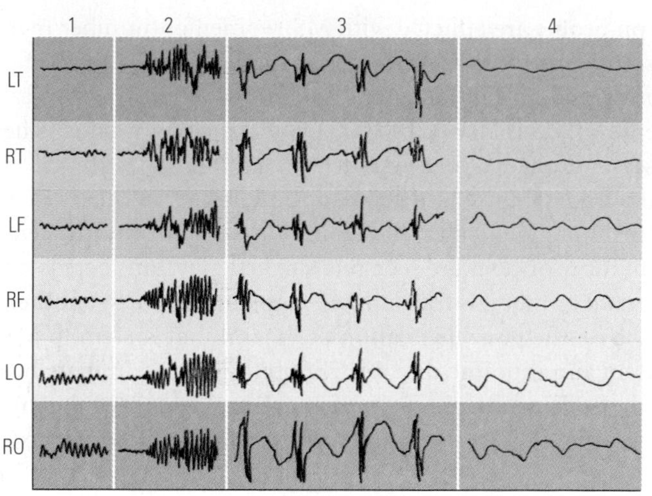

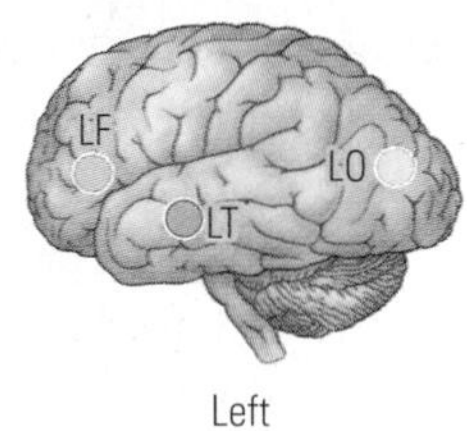

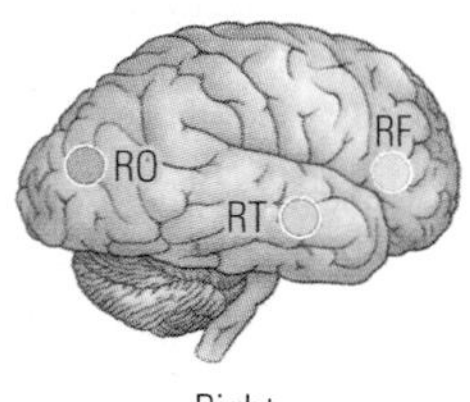

FIGURE 16-8 Grand Mal Seizure Patterns. Examples of electroencephalographic patterns recorded during a grand mal seizure. Abbreviations: LT and RT, left and right temporal; LF and RF, left and right frontal; LO and RO, left and right occipital. Dots on the hemispheres indicate the approximate recording sites. Column numbers refer to the stages of the seizure: (1) normal record before the attack; (2) onset of the attack; (3) clonic phase, in which the person makes rhythmic movements in time with the large abnormal discharges; and (4) period of coma after the seizure ends.

Treatment of Epilepsy

The treatment of choice for epilepsy is an anticonvulsant drug such as diphenylhydantoin (DPH, Dilantin), phenobarbital, or one of several others (Rogawski and Loscher, 2004). These drugs are anesthetic agents when given in low doses, and patients are advised not to drink alcohol. Although the mechanism by which these drugs act is uncertain, they presumably inhibit the discharge of abnormal neurons by stabilizing the neuronal membrane, especially in inhibitory neurons.

If medication fails to alleviate the seizure problem satisfactorily, surgery can be performed to remove the focus of abnormal functioning in patients with focal seizures. The abnormal tissue is localized by the surgeon by both EEG and cortical stimulation. It is then removed with the goal of eliminating the cause of the seizures. Many patients show complete recovery and are seizure free, although some must remain on anticonvulsants after the surgery to ensure that the seizures do not return.

Figure 10-19 shows the neurosurgeon Wilder Penfield using brain stimulation to map a patient's motor cortex as another neurologist monitors an EEG recorded from each stimulated area.

Multiple Sclerosis

In multiple sclerosis (MS), myelin is damaged, and the functions of the neurons whose axons it encases are disrupted. Multiple sclerosis is characterized by the loss of myelin, largely in motor tracts but also in sensory nerves. The myelin sheath and in some cases the axons are destroyed. Brain imaging with MRI, as shown in **Figure 16-9,** allows areas of sclerosis to be identified in the brain and spinal cord.

Sclerosis comes from the Greek word for "hardness."

Remissions and relapses are a striking feature of MS: in many cases, early symptoms are initially followed by improvement. The course varies, running from a few years to as long as 50 years. Paraplegia, however, the classic feature of MS, may eventually confine the affected person to bed.

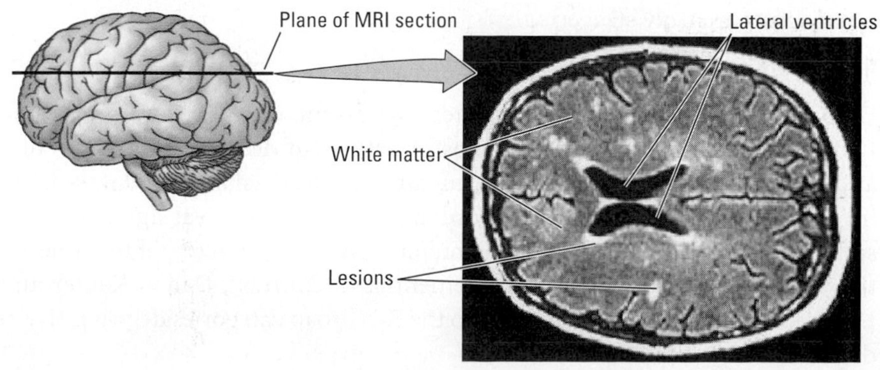

FIGURE 16-9 Diagnosing MS. Imaged by MRI, discrete multiple sclerosis lesions appear around the lateral ventricles and in the white matter of the brain. Adapted from "Disability and Lesion Load in MS: A Reassessment with MS Functional Composite Score and 3D Fast Flair," by P. A. Ciccarelli, A. J. Brex, A. J. Thompson, and D. H. Miller, 2000, *Journal of Neurology, 249,* pp. 18–24.

Worldwide, about 1 million people are afflicted with MS; women outnumber men about two to one. Multiple sclerosis is most prevalent in northern Europe, somewhat less prevalent in North America, and rare in Japan and in more southerly or tropical countries. The overall incidence of MS is 50 per 100,000 people, making it one of the most common structural diseases of the nervous system.

The cause of MS is still not known. Proposed causes include bacterial infection, a virus, environmental factors including pesticides, and an immune response of the central nervous system. Often a number of cases are seen in a single family, but there is no clear evidence that MS is inherited or that it is transmitted from one person to another.

Clinical Focus 4-3 describes the autoimmune disease myasthenia gravis.

Recent research has focused on the possible relation of the immune system to MS and the possibility that MS is an **autoimmune disease.** The ability to discriminate between a foreign pathogen in the body and the body itself is a central feature of the immune system. If this discrimination fails, the immune system makes antibodies to a person's own body.

As the genomes of various organisms have been sequenced in recent years, it has become apparent that all biological organisms have many genes in common, and thus the proteins found in different organisms are surprisingly similar. And here is the problem for the human immune system: a foreign microbe may have proteins that are very similar to the body's own proteins. If the microbe and human have a common gene sequence, the immune system can mistakenly attack itself, a process known as *horror autotoxicus*. Many microbial protein sequences are homologous with structures found in myelin, which leads to an attack against the microbe and a person's own myelin.

The work showing the important role of the immune system in MS has led to intense research to develop new treatments (Steinman et al., 2002). One strategy is to build up tolerance in the immune system by the injection of DNA encoding myelin antigens as well as DNA encoding specific molecules that are in the cascade of steps that leads to the death of myelin cells.

Neurodegenerative Disorders

The demographics now developing in North America and Europe have never been experienced by human societies. Since 1900, the percentage of older people has increased steadily. In 1900, about 4 percent of the population had attained 65 years of age. By 2030, about 20 percent of the population will be older than 65—about 50 million in the United States alone.

Dementias affect from 1 to 6 percent of the population older than age 65 and from 10 to 20 percent older than age 80. For every person diagnosed with dementia, it has been estimated that several others suffer undiagnosed cognitive impairments that affect their quality of life (Larrabee and Crook, 1994). Currently, about 6 million people in the United States are diagnosed with dementia. This number is projected to rise to about 15 million by 2050, at which time there will be 1 million new cases per year. When this projection is extended across the rest of the developed world, the social and economic costs are truly staggering.

Types of Dementia

Dementia is an acquired and persistent syndrome of intellectual impairment. The DSM defines the two essential diagnostic features of dementia as (1) loss of memory and other cognitive deficits and (2) impairment in social and occupational functioning. Dementia is not a singular disorder, but there is no clear agreement on how to split up subtypes. The DSM sees the memory symptom as central to amnesic dementia, which it contrasts to vascular dementia. In contrast, Daniel Kaufer and Steven DeKosky (1999) divide dementias into the two broad categories degenerative and nondegenerative (**Table 16-5**).

Autoimmune disease Illness resulting from the loss of the immune system's ability to discriminate between foreign pathogens in the body and the body itself.
Dementia Acquired and persistent syndrome of intellectual impairment characterized by memory and other cognitive deficits and impairment in social and occupational functioning.

TABLE 16-5 Degenerative and Nondegenerative Dementias

Degenerative	Nondegenerative
Alzheimer's disease	Vascular dementias (e.g., multi-infarct dementia)
Extrapyramidal syndromes (e.g., progressive supernuclear palsy)	Infectious dementia (e.g., AIDS dementia)
Wilson's disease	Neurosyphillis
Huntington's disease	Posttraumatic dementia
Parkinson's disease	Demyelinating dementia (e.g., multiple sclerosis)
Frontal temporal dementia	Toxic or metabolic disorders (e.g., vitamin B_{12} and niacin deficiencies)
Corticobasal degeneration	Chronic alcohol or drug abuse (e.g., Korsakoff's syndrome)
Leukodystrophies (e.g., adrenoleukodystrophy)	
Prion-related dementias (e.g., Creutzfeld-Jakob disease)	

Source: Adapted from "Diagnostic Classifications: Relationship to the Neurobiology of Dementia," by D. I. Kaufer and S. T. DeKosky, 1999, in *The Neurobiology of Mental Illness* (p. 642), edited by D. S. Charney, E. J. Nestler, and B. S. Bunney. New York: Oxford University Press.

Nondegenerative dementias are a heterogeneous group of disorders with diverse etiologies, including diseases of the vascular or endocrine systems, inflammation, nutritional deficiency, and toxic conditions, as summarized in the right column of Table 16-5, although the most prevalent cause is vascular. The most significant risk factors for nondegenerative dementias are chronic hypertension, obesity, sedentary lifestyle, smoking, and diabetes, all of which are risk factors for cardiovascular disease as well.

In contrast to the nondegenerative dementias, many *degenerative dementias* listed in the left column of the table presumably have a degree of genetic transmission. Here we review two degenerative dementias in detail, Parkinson's disease and Alzeimer's disease. Both pathological processes are primarily intrinsic to the nervous system and tend to affect certain neural systems selectively.

Parkinson's Disease

Parkinson's disease is fairly common; estimates of its incidence vary from 0.1 percent to 1.0 percent of the population, and the incidence rises sharply in old age. In view of the increasingly aging population in western Europe and North America, the incidence of Parkinson's disease is certain to rise in the coming decades. Parkinsonism is also of interest for several other reasons:

- Parkinson's disease seems related to the degeneration of the substantia nigra and to the loss of the neurotransmitter dopamine produced there and released in the striatum. The disease is therefore the source of an important insight into the role of this brainstem nucleus and its dopamine in the control of movement.

Figure 6-2 diagrams the degeneration of the substantia nigra associated with Parkinson's symptoms.

- Although Parkinson's disease is described as a disease entity, symptoms vary enormously among people, thus illustrating the complexity in understanding a behavioral disorder. A well-defined set of cells degenerates in Parkinson's disease, yet the symptoms are not the same in every sufferer.
- Many symptoms of Parkinson's disease strikingly resemble changes in motor activity that take place as a consequence of aging. Thus the disease is a source of indirect insight into the more general problems of neural changes in aging.

The symptoms of Parkinson's disease begin insidiously, often with a tremor in one hand and slight stiffness in the distal parts of the limbs. Movements may then become slower, the face becoming masklike with loss of eye blinking and poverty of emotional expression. Thereafter the body may become stooped, and the gait becomes a shuffle with the arms hanging motionless at the sides. Speech may become slow and monotonous, and difficulty in swallowing may cause drooling.

Although the disease is progressive, the rate at which the symptoms worsen is variable, and only rarely is progression so rapid that a person becomes disabled within 5 years; usually from 10 to 20 years elapse before symptoms cause incapacity. A most curious aspect of Parkinson's disease is its on-again–off-again quality: symptoms may appear suddenly and disappear just as suddenly.

Partial remission may also occur in response to interesting or stimulating situations. The neurologist Oliver Sacks (1998) recounts an incident in which a stationary Parkinson patient leaped from his wheelchair at the seaside and rushed into the breakers to save a drowning man, only to fall back into his chair immediately afterward and become inactive again. Although remission of some symptoms in activating situations is common, remission is not usually as dramatic as this case.

The four major symptoms of Parkinson's disease are tremor, rigidity, loss of spontaneous movement (*akinesia*), and disturbances of posture. Each symptom may be manifest in different body parts in different combinations. Because some symptoms entail the appearance of abnormal behaviors (positive symptoms) and others the loss of normal behaviors (negative symptoms), we consider the symptoms in these two major categories.

Positive symptoms are behaviors not seen in normal people or seen only so rarely—and then in such special circumstances—that they can be considered abnormal. *Negative symptoms* are marked by the absence of a behavior or by the inability to engage in an activity.

Positive Symptoms Because positive symptoms are common in Parkinson's disease, they are thought to be held in check, or inhibited, in normal people but released from inhibition in the process of the disease. Following are the most common positive symptoms:

- *Tremor at rest.* Tremor consists of alternating movements of the limbs when they are at rest; these movements stop during voluntary movements or during sleep. The tremors of the hands often have a "pill rolling" quality, as if a pill were being rolled between the thumb and forefinger.
- *Muscular rigidity.* Muscular rigidity consists of increased muscle tone simultaneously in both extensor and flexor muscles. Rigidity is particularly evident when the limbs are moved passively at a joint; movement is resisted, but with sufficient force, the muscles yield for a short distance and then resist movement again. Thus, complete passive flexion or extension of a joint occurs in a series of steps, giving rise to the term *cogwheel rigidity*. The rigidity may be severe enough to make all movements difficult, like moving in slow motion and being unable to speed up the process.
- *Involuntary movements.* Small movements or changes in posture, sometimes referred to as **akathesia** or "cruel restlessness," may be concurrent with general inactivity to relieve tremor and sometimes to relieve stiffness but often occur for no apparent reason. Other involuntary movements are distortions of posture, such as occur during *oculogyric crisis* (involuntary turns of the head and eyes to one side), which last for periods of minutes to hours.

Negative Symptoms After detailed analysis of negative symptoms, Jean Prudin Martin (1967) divided patients severely affected with Parkinson's disease into five groups:

1. *Disorders of posture.* A *disorder of fixation* presents as an inability or difficulty in maintaining a part of the body in its normal position in relation to other parts. A person's head may droop forward or a standing person may gradually bend forward, ending up on the knees. *Disorders of equilibrium* create difficulties in standing or even sitting unsupported. In less severe cases, people

may have difficulty standing on one leg, or if pushed lightly on the shoulders, they may fall passively without taking corrective steps or attempting to catch themselves.

2. *Disorders of righting.* A person has difficulty in achieving a standing position from a supine position. Many advanced patients have difficulty even in rolling over.
3. *Disorders of locomotion.* Normal locomotion requires support of the body against gravity, stepping, balancing while the weight of the body is transferred from one leg to the other, and pushing forward. Parkinson patients have difficulty initiating stepping, and when they do walk, they shuffle with short footsteps on a fairly wide base of support because they have trouble maintaining equilibrium when shifting weight from one leg to the other. On beginning to walk, Parkinson patients often demonstrate **festination:** they take faster and faster steps and end up running forward.
4. *Speech disturbances.* One symptom most noticeable to relatives is the almost complete absence of prosody (rhythm and pitch) in the speaker's voice.
5. *Akinesia.* Poverty or slowness of movement may also manifest itself in a blankness of facial expression or a lack of blinking, swinging the arms when walking, spontaneous speech, or normal fidgeting. Akinesia is also manifested in difficulty in making repetitive movements, such as tapping, even in the absence of rigidity. People who sit motionless for hours show akinesia in its most striking manifestation.

Akathesia Small, involuntary movements or changes in posture; motor restlessness.

Festination Tendency to engage in a behavior, such as walking, at faster and faster speeds.

Cognitive Symptoms Although Parkinson's disease is usually thought of as a motor disorder, changes in cognition occur as well. Psychological symptoms in Parkinson patients are as variable as the motor symptoms. Nonetheless, a significant percentage of patients show cognitive symptoms that mirror their motor symptoms.

Oliver Sacks (1998), for example, reports the negative effects of Parkinsonism on cognitive function: impoverishment of feeling, libido, motive, and attention; people may sit for hours, apparently lacking the will to begin or continue any activity. In our experience, thinking seems generally to be slowed and is easily confused with dementia because patients do not appear to be processing the content of conversations. In fact, they are simply processing very slowly.

Cognitive slowing in Parkinson patients has some parallels to Alzheimer's disease. Postmortem studies show clear Alzheimerlike brain abnormalities in most Parkinson patients, even those who showed no obvious signs of dementia. We return to these parallels later.

Causes of Parkinsonism The ultimate cause of Parkinson's disease—loss of cells in the substantia nigra—may be due to disease, such as encephalitis or syphilis, to drugs such as MPTP, or to unknown causes. Idiopathic causes may be familial or may be part of the aging process. *Idiopathic* causes may include environmental pollutants, insecticides, and herbicides. Demographic studies of patient admission in the cities of Vancouver, Canada, and Helsinki, Finland, show an increased incidence of patients contracting the disease at ages younger than 40. This finding has prompted the suggestion that water and air might contain environmental toxins that work in a fashion similar to MPTP (1-methyl-4-phenylpyridinium).

Clinical Focus 5-2 details the etiology of Parkinson's disease, Clinical Focus 5-3 explains how L-dopa acts to relieve muscular rigidity, and Clinical Focus 5-4 tells the story of Parkinson symptoms triggered by MPTP, a neurotoxin.

Treating Parkinson's Disease No known cure for Parkinson's disease exists, and it will not be possible to develop one until the factors that produce the progressive deterioration of the substantia nigra are known. Thus, treatment is symptomatic and directed toward support and comfort.

The major symptoms of Parkinsonism are influenced by psychological factors: a person's outcome is affected by how well he or she copes with the disability. Consequently, patients should seek behaviorally oriented treatment early, including counseling on the meaning of symptoms, the nature of the disease, and the potential for most to lead long and productive lives. Physical therapy should consist of simple measures

The photo on page 133 shows Parkinson's patients participating in a dance class.

such as heat and massage to alleviate painful muscle cramps and training and exercise to cope with the debilitating changes in movement.

Pharmacological treatment has two main objectives:

1. To increase the activity in whatever dopamine synapses remain
2. To suppress the activity in structures that show heightened activity in the absence of adequate dopamine action

L-Dopa is converted into dopamine in the brain and enhances effective dopamine transmission, as do drugs such as amantadine, amphetamine, monoamine oxidase inhibitors, and tricyclic antidepressants. Naturally occurring anticholinergic drugs, such as atropine and scopolamine, and synthetic anticholinergics, such as benztropine (Cogentin) and trihexyphenidyl (Artane), block the cholinergic systems of the brain that seem to show heightened activity in the absence of adequate dopamine activity.

A drawback of drug therapies is that, as the disease progresses, they become less effective and the incidence of side effects increases. Some drug treatments that stimulate dopamine receptors directly have been reported to result in increased sexuality and an increased incidence of compulsive gambling.

A number of treatments for Parkinson's disease focus on treating its positive symptoms. Two surgical treatments described earlier in the chapter are based on the idea that an increase in the activity of globus pallidus neurons inhibits motor function. Lesioning the internal part of the globus pallidis (GP_i) has been found to reduce rigidity and tremor. Hyperactivity of GP_i neurons can also be reduced neurosurgically by electrically stimulating the neurons via deep brain stimulation (see Figure 16-4). A stimulating electrode is permanently implanted in the GP_i or an adjacent brain area, the subthalamic nucleus. Patients carry a small electrical stimulator that they can turn on to produce DBS and so reduce the symptoms of rigidity and tremor. These two treatments may be used sequentially: when DBS becomes less effective as the disease progresses, a GP_i lesion may be produced.

Figure 11-14 charts how the GP_i, a structure in the basal ganglia, regulates the force of movements.

A promising treatment involves increasing the number of dopamine-producing cells. The simplest way to do so is to transplant embryonic dopamine cells into the basal ganglia. In the 1980s and 1990s, this treatment was used with varying degrees of success.

A newer course of treatment proposes to increase the number of dopamine cells either by transplanting stem cells that could then be induced to take a dopaminergic phenotype or by stimulating the production of endogenous stem cells and their migration to the basal ganglia. The advantage of stem cells is that they do not have to be derived from embryonic tissue but can come from a variety of sources including the person's own bone marrow. Another source of dopamine cells is retinal endothelial cells that can be harvested from neonatal tissue.

All these treatments are highly experimental. At present, neonatal retinal cells have probably been the most successful. Curiously, perhaps because this treatment is the least controversial, the media have basically ignored it and have focused on the more contentious issue of using embryological tissue.

Retinas are harvested from newborn infants who die. Since a single retina can generate cells for thousands of patients, very few donors are necessary.

Anatomical Correlates of Alzheimer's Disease

Clinical Focus 14-3 reports on the etiology of Alzheimer's disease.

Alzheimer's disease accounts for about 65 percent of all dementias. Its cause is unknown. Given the increasing population of elderly people and thus of Alzheimer's disease, research is being directed toward potential causes, including genetic predisposition, environmental toxins, high levels of trace elements such as aluminum in the blood, an autoimmune response, a slow-acting virus, and reduced blood flow to the cerebral hemispheres. Risk factors include the presence of the Apoe4 gene, below average IQ, poor education, and TBI. It is proposed that better educated and/or more intelligent people and those who carry the Apoe2 gene are better able to compensate for the cell death in degenerative dementia.

A decade ago, the only way to identify and to study Alzheimer's disease was to study postmortem pathology. This approach was less than ideal, however, because determining which brain changes came early in the disease and which followed as a result of the early changes was impossible. Nonetheless, it became clear that widespread changes take place in the neocortex and limbic cortex and associated changes take place in a number of neurotransmitter systems. None alone can be correlated simply with Alzheimer's clinical symptoms. Interestingly, most of the brainstem, cerebellum, and spinal cord are relatively spared its major ravages.

The principal neuroanatomical change in Alzheimer's disease is the emergence of neuritic (amyloid) plaques, chiefly in the cerebral cortex. Increased plaque concentration in the cortex has been correlated with the magnitude of cognitive deterioration. Neuritic plaques are generally considered nonspecific phenomena in that they can be found in non-Alzheimer patients and in dementias caused by other known events.

Another anatomical correlate of Alzheimer's disease is neurofibrillary tangles—paired helical (spiral) filaments found in both the cerebral cortex and the hippocampus. The posterior half of the hippocampus is affected more severely than the anterior half. Light-microscopic examination reveals that the filaments have a double-helical configuration. They have been described mainly in human tissue and have also been observed in patients with Down syndrome, Parkinson's disease, and other dementias.

Finally, neocortical changes that correlate with Alzheimer's disease are not uniform. Although the cortex atrophies (shrinks), losing as much as one-third of its volume as the disease progresses, some areas are relatively spared. **Figure 16-10** shows lateral and medial views of the human brain; color shading indicates the areas of degeneration. The darker the shading, the more severe is the degeneration.

As is clearly shown in Figure 16-10A, the primary sensory and motor areas of the cortex, especially the visual cortex and the sensory–motor cortex, are spared. The frontal lobes are less affected than the posterior cortex, but the areas of most extensive change are the posterior parietal areas, inferior temporal cortex, and limbic cortex. The limbic system undergoes the most severe degenerative changes in Alzheimer's disease, and of the limbic structures, the entorhinal cortex is affected earliest and most severely (Figure 16-10B).

A number of investigators agree that the entorhinal cortex shows the clearest evidence of cell loss. This loss has important implications for understanding some of the disease symptoms. The entorhinal cortex is the major relay through which information from the neocortex gets to the hippocampus and related structures and is then sent back to the neocortex. Damage is associated with memory loss. Given that memory loss is an early and enduring symptom of Alzheimer's disease, it is most likely caused by the degenerative changes that take place in this area of the cortex.

Many studies describe loss of cells in the cortices of Alzheimer patients, but this finding is disputed. There seems to be a substantial reduction in large neurons, but these cells may shrink rather than disappear. The more widespread cause of cortical atrophy appears to be a loss of dendritic arborization (**Figure 16-11**).

In addition to a loss of cells are changes in the neurotransmitters of the remaining cells. In the 1970s, researchers believed that a treatment for Alzheimer's disease could be found to parallel the L-dopa treatment of Parkinson's disease, and the prime candidate neurotransmitter was

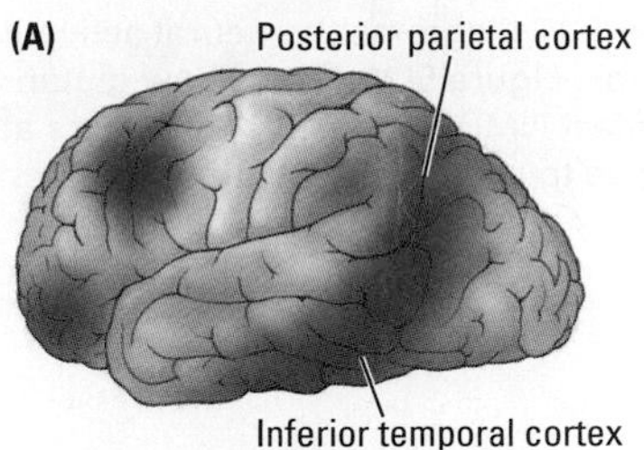

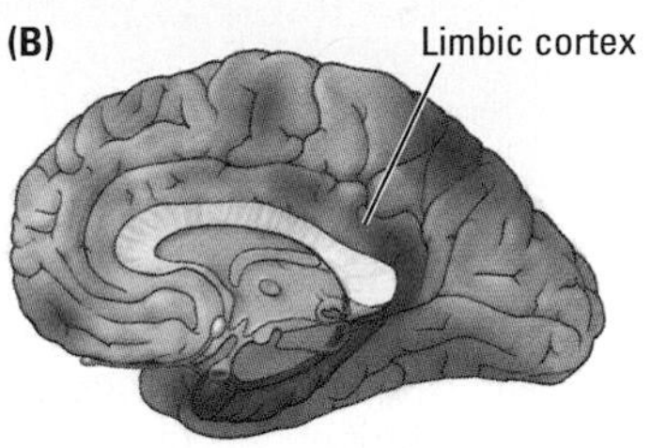

FIGURE 16-10 Cortical Degeneration in Alzheimer's Disease. Representative distribution and severity of degeneration in an average Alzheimer case shown in (A) lateral and (B) medial views. The darker the area, the more pronounced the degeneration. Areas in white are largely spared, with only basic changes discernible. Adapted from "An Overview of Light and Electron Microscopic Changes," by A. Brun, 1983, in *Alzheimer's Disease* (pp. 127–143), edited by B. Reisberg. New York: The Free Press.

FIGURE 16-11 Stripped Branches. As their dendritic trees degenerate and neurons atrophy, patients with Alzheimer's disease experience worsening symptoms, including memory loss and personality changes. Neurons drawn from Golgi-stained sections in "Age-Related Changes in the Human Forebrain," by A. Scheibel, 1982, *Neuroscience Research Program Bulletin, 20,* pp. 577–583.

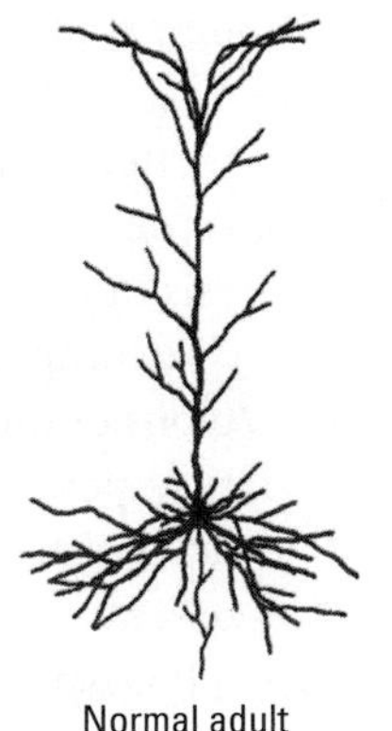
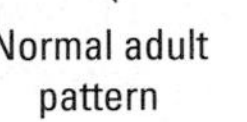

Figure 5-17 diagrams the neural activating systems; Figure 5-20 shows how glutamate can affect NMDA and AMPA receptors at the synapse to promote learning by association.

acetylcholine. Unfortunately, Alzheimer's has proved far more complex because other transmitters clearly are changed as well. Noradrenaline, dopamine, and serotonin are reduced, as are the NMDA and AMPA receptors for glutamate.

Are Parkinson's and Alzheimer's Aspects of One Disease?

Striking similarities in the pathologies of Parkinson's and Alzheimer's diseases led Donald Calne to ask whether the diseases are in fact syndromes resulting from various neurodegenerative processes in the brain (Calne and Mizuno, 2004). Their pathologies are far more similar than was previously recognized. For example, we have seen already is that all cases of Parkinson's disease have in common a loss of cells in the substantia nigra. The Parkinsonian brain suffers a larger loss, but the brains of Alzheimer patients also have nigral cell loss. Other anatomical correlates between the diseases also exist.

Neurofilaments are one of many types of *tubules,* cellular components that reinforce the cell's structure, aid in its movement, and transport proteins to their destinations inside and outside the cell. Figure 3-10 diagrams the internal components of a typical cell.

The best studied is the **Lewy body,** a circular fibrous structure that forms within the cytoplasm of neurons and is thought to correspond to abnormal neurofilament metabolism (**Figure 16-12**). Until recently, the Lewy body was believed to be a hallmark of Parkinson's disease, and it was most often found in the brainstem in the region of the substantia nigra. It is now clear, however, that Lewy bodies are found in several neurodegenerative disorders, including Alzheimer's disease. There are even reports of people with Alzheimer's-like dementias who do not have plaques and tangles but have extensive Lewy bodies in the cortex.

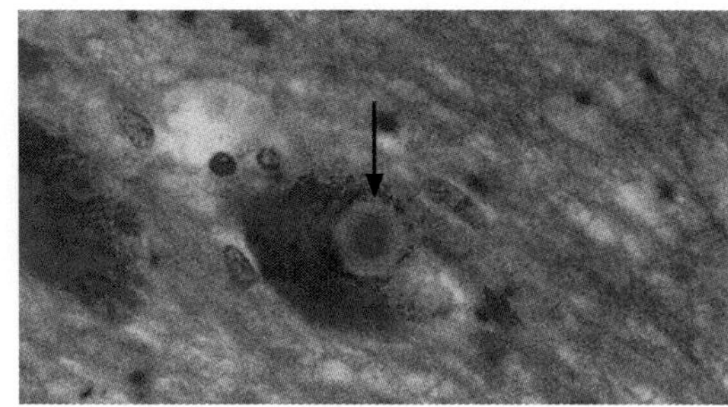

FIGURE 16-12 Midbrain Lewy Body. Lewy bodies (arrow) are characteristic of Parkinson's disease and are found in the brains of patients with other disorders as well. Courtesy of J. T. Stewart, MD, University of South Florida College of Medicine.

Calne noted that, when investigators went to Guam at the end of World War II to investigate a report of widespread dementia described as similar to Alzheimer's disease, they did indeed report a high incidence of Alzheimer's disease. Many years later, Calne and his colleagues, experts in Parkinson's disease, examined the same general group of people and found that they had Parkinson's disease. Calne noted that, if you look for Alzheimer symptoms in these people, you find them and miss the Parkinson symptoms. And vice versa.

Indeed, as we age, we all show a loss of cells in the substantia nigra, but only after we have lost about 60 percent of them will we start to show Parkinson symptoms. From this perspective, we begin to understand Calne's powerful argument and its important implications for treating both syndromes.

Age-Related Cognitive Loss

Most people who grow old do not become demented, but virtually everyone shows an age-related cognitive loss, even while living active, healthy, productive lives. Aging is associated with declines in perceptual functions, especially vision, hearing, and olfaction, and declining motor, cognitive, and executive (planning) functions as well. Older people tend to learn at a slower pace and typically do not attain the same mastery of new skills as younger adults.

Noninvasive imaging studies reveal that aging is correlated with a decrease in white-matter volume probably related to myelin loss. This condition is reparable. There is little evidence of neuronal loss in normal aging, although there is a reduction in neurogenesis in the hippocampus.

Compared with younger participants, older participants tend to activate larger regions of their attentional and executive networks (parietal and prefrontal cortex) when they perform complex cognitive and executive tasks. This increased activation correlates with reduced performance on tests of working memory as well as attentional and executive tasks.

Despite the depressing evidence that normal aging is associated with neurological and cognitive decline, at least two different forms of treatment offer encouraging reasons to believe that declines in both areas can be reduced or reversed. The first is aerobic exercise to enhance general health. The goal is to improve the brain's capacity for neural plasticity via increased neurogenesis, gliogenesis, and trophic factor support. The second treatment is exercise for the brain, employing training strategies that enhance neural plasticity and reverse learned nonuse.

Sandy Huffaker/The New York Times/Redux

Brain Stimulation. Engaging in cognitively stimulating activities can keep neural networks and general cognitive functions from declining with age. From "At the Bridge Table: Clues to a Lucid Old Age," *New York Times*, May 22, 2009 (pp. A1, A18).

Most of us have experienced the frustration of losing a skill (whether it's trigonometry or tennis) after having not done it for some time, perhaps not for decades. Loss of skill does not reflect dementia but simply a "use it or lose it" scenario. Training programs designed to stimulate plasticity in the appropriate cerebral circuitry include motor-, auditory-, or visual-system–based cognitive and/or attentional training (e.g., Bherer et al., 2008; Tang and Posner, 2009). Brain training is designed to stimulate plasticity rather than to rehabilitate specific losses.

William Milberg and his colleagues (e.g., Kuo et al., 2005; Leritz et al., 2008) have been exploring the interesting idea that aging changes in the brain take place in the context of the entire body's change with aging. They asked, for example, whether changes in the body such as weight gain, high cholesterol, or hypertension might be related to cognitive change and brain structure in people who show no dementia. Both hypertension and obesity were related to decreased cortical thickness in the frontal lobe, which was correlated with decreased performance on tests of frontal lobe function. In contrast, high cholesterol was associated with temporal lobe cortical thickening and impaired temporal lobe functioning. These results are especially interesting given that cognitive studies of aging never measure metabolic markers as cofactors.

REVIEW: Understanding and Treating Neurological Disorders

- ✔ The combined incidence of five common neurological disorders—TBI, stroke, epilepsy, MS, and the neurodegenerative syndromes Parkinson's disease and Alzheimer's disease—is so great that each of us in our lifetimes is likely to know a person who has one of these disorders. Chances are that we will know people who have each disorder.
- ✔ The cause of TBI is obvious—namely, a blow to the head—but the pathology is far more difficult to identify, even with fancy imaging techniques. The pathology of the other neurological disorders is equally elusive and the causes are poorly understood.
- ✔ Stroke results from an interruption of blood supply to the brain, leading to damage to gray and/or white matter; treatments are more effective if there is limited involvement of white matter. Epilepsy is a chronic neurological syndrome of recurrent seizures; it can be treated with antiepileptic drugs or in extreme cases with neurosurgery. Multiple sclerosis is an autoimmune disease in which the body's immune system attacks the myelin in the central nervous system; there is no known cure for MS.
- ✔ Parkinson's and Alzheimer's may actually be syndromes of a single disease. Effective treatments must wait until the causes are far better understood than they are today.
- ✔ Normal aging is associated with neurological and behavioral changes that are preventable or reversible by stimulating neural plasticity.

Lewy body Circular fibrous structure found in several neurodegenerative disorders; forms within the cytoplasm of neurons and is thought to result from abnormal neurofilament metabolism.

Understanding and Treating Behavioral Disorders

The DSM summarizes a wide range of psychiatric disorders. We focus on the three general categories—psychoses, mood disorders, and anxiety disorders—that are the best studied and understood. **Figure 16-13** summarizes the prevalence of specific disorders and lists common symptoms. Added together, nearly 50 percent of the U.S. population is experiencing behavioral disorders. The statistic holds even when we account for those who acquire more than one disorder.

Psychotic Disorders

Psychoses are psychological disorders in which a person loses contact with reality, experiencing irrational ideas and distorted perceptions. Although there are many psychotic disorders (schizophrenia, schizoaffective disorder, and schizophreniform disorder

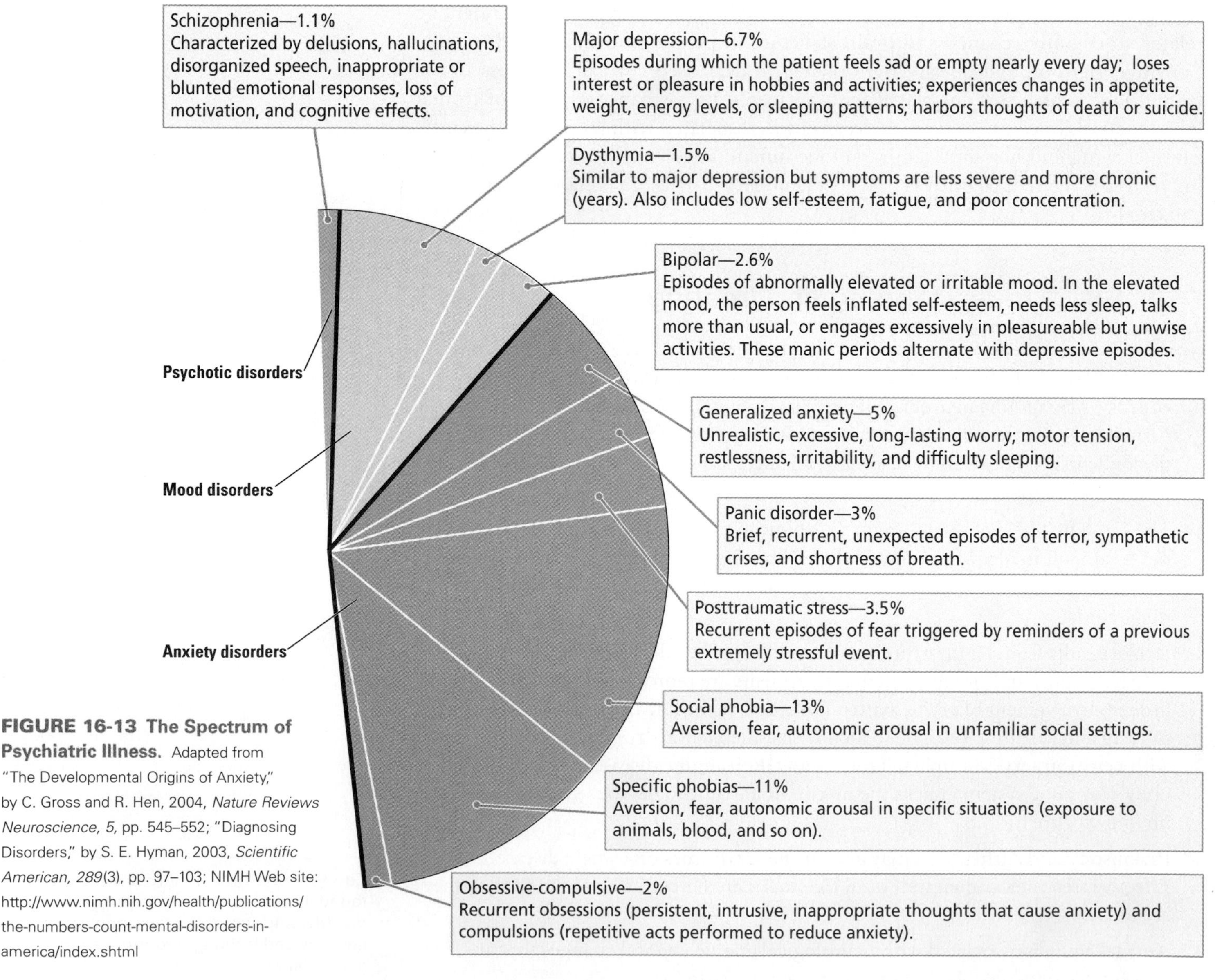

Schizophrenia—1.1%
Characterized by delusions, hallucinations, disorganized speech, inappropriate or blunted emotional responses, loss of motivation, and cognitive effects.
Major depression—6.7%
Episodes during which the patient feels sad or empty nearly every day; loses interest or pleasure in hobbies and activities; experiences changes in appetite, weight, energy levels, or sleeping patterns; harbors thoughts of death or suicide.
Dysthymia—1.5%
Similar to major depression but symptoms are less severe and more chronic (years). Also includes low self-esteem, fatigue, and poor concentration.
Bipolar—2.6%
Episodes of abnormally elevated or irritable mood. In the elevated mood, the person feels inflated self-esteem, needs less sleep, talks more than usual, or engages excessively in pleasureable but unwise activities. These manic periods alternate with depressive episodes.
Generalized anxiety—5%
Unrealistic, excessive, long-lasting worry; motor tension, restlessness, irritability, and difficulty sleeping.
Panic disorder—3%
Brief, recurrent, unexpected episodes of terror, sympathetic crises, and shortness of breath.
Posttraumatic stress—3.5%
Recurrent episodes of fear triggered by reminders of a previous extremely stressful event.
Social phobia—13%
Aversion, fear, autonomic arousal in unfamiliar social settings.
Specific phobias—11%
Aversion, fear, autonomic arousal in specific situations (exposure to animals, blood, and so on).
Obsessive-compulsive—2%
Recurrent obsessions (persistent, intrusive, inappropriate thoughts that cause anxiety) and compulsions (repetitive acts performed to reduce anxiety).
Psychotic disorders
Mood disorders
Anxiety disorders

FIGURE 16-13 The Spectrum of Psychiatric Illness. Adapted from "The Developmental Origins of Anxiety," by C. Gross and R. Hen, 2004, *Nature Reviews Neuroscience, 5*, pp. 545–552; "Diagnosing Disorders," by S. E. Hyman, 2003, *Scientific American, 289*(3), pp. 97–103; NIMH Web site: http://www.nimh.nih.gov/health/publications/the-numbers-count-mental-disorders-in-america/index.shtml

among them), schizophrenia is the most common and best understood. The complexity of the behavioral and neurobiological factors that characterize schizophrenia makes it especially difficult to diagnose and classify. Understanding schizophrenia is an evolving process that is far from complete.

Type I schizophrenia Disorder characterized predominantly by positive symptoms (e.g., behavioral excesses such as hallucinations and agitated movements) likely due to a dopaminergic dysfunction and associated with acute onset, good prognosis, and a favorable response to neuroleptics.

Type II schizophrenia Disorder characterized by negative symptoms (behavioral deficits) and associated with chronic affliction, poor prognosis, poor response to neuroleptics, cognitive impairments, enlarged ventricles, and cortical atrophy, particularly in the frontal cortex.

Diagnosing Schizophrenia

The DSM lists six diagnostic symptoms of schizophrenia:

1. Delusions—beliefs that distort reality
2. Hallucinations—distorted perceptions—such as hearing voices
3. Disorganized speech, such as incoherent statements or senselessly rhyming talk
4. Disorganized behavior or excessive agitation
5. The opposite extreme: catatonic behavior
6. Negative symptoms, such as blunted emotions or loss of interest and drive, all characterized by the absence of some normal response

The DSM criteria are subjective. They are more helpful in clinical diagnoses than in relating schizophrenia to measurable brain abnormalities.

Classifying Schizophrenia

Timothy Crow addressed the classifying difficulties by looking for a relation between brain abnormalities and specific schizophrenia symptoms. He proposed two distinct syndromes, which he called type I and type II (Crow, 1980, 1990).

- **Type I schizophrenia** is characterized predominantly by positive symptoms that manifest behavioral excesses, such as hallucinations and agitated movements. It is likely that type 1 schizophrenia is due to a dopaminergic dysfunction. It is also associated with acute onset, good prognosis, and a favorable response to neuroleptics.
- **Type II schizophrenia**, by contrast, is characterized by negative symptoms that entail behavioral deficits. Type II schizophrenia is associated with chronic affliction, poor prognosis, poor response to neuroleptics, cognitive impairments, enlarged ventricles, and cortical atrophy, particularly in the frontal cortex (see Figure 16-3).

Neuroleptics are antipsychotic drugs and are covered in Chapter 8.

Crow's analysis had a major effect on clinical thinking about schizophrenia. Between 20 and 30 percent of patients, however, show a pattern of mixed type I and type II symptoms. The types may actually represent points along a continuum of biological and behavioral manifestations of schizophrenia.

Neuroanatomical Correlates of Schizophrenia

Another approach to investigating schizophrenia deemphasizes typing and focuses instead on individual psychotic symptoms. Alan Breier (1999) stated that findings from a growing number of brain-imaging studies suggest a neuroanatomical basis for some diagnostic symptoms described by the DSM. For example, researchers found abnormalities in the auditory regions of the temporal lobe and in Broca's area in patients with auditory hallucinations (McGuire, Shah, and Murray, 1993).

Similarly, structural abnormalities in Wernicke's area are often found among patients with thought disorders (Shenton et al., 1992). The schizophrenic brain also generally has large ventricles and thinner cortex in the medial temporal regions. The

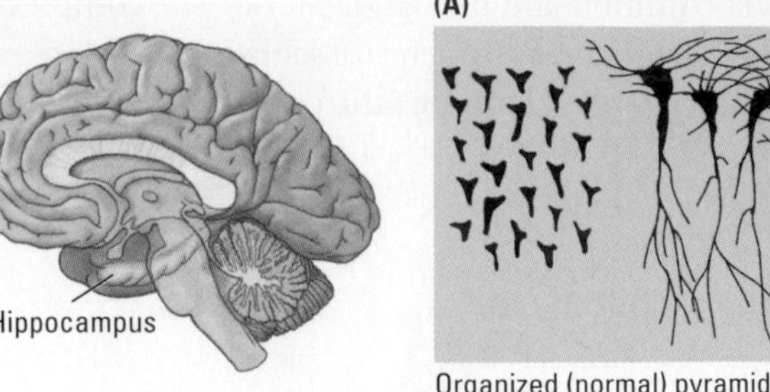

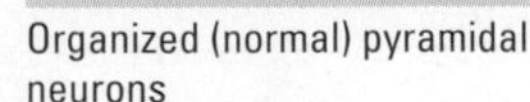

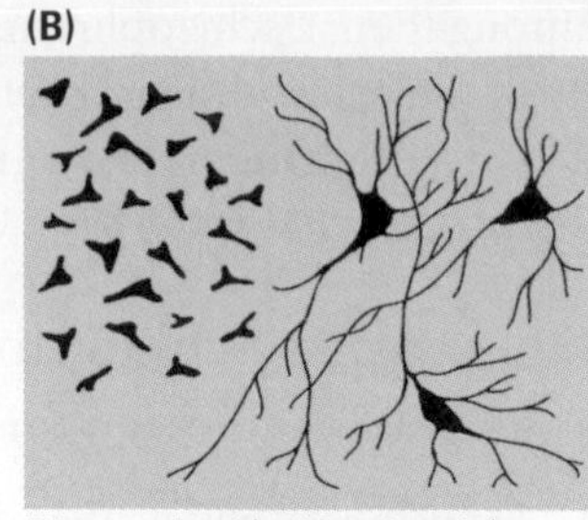

FIGURE 16-14 Organic Dysfunction. Rather than (A) the consistently parallel orientation of hippocampal neurons characteristic of normal brains, (B) hippocampal neurons in the schizophrenic brain have a haphazard organization Adapted from "A Neurohistologic Correlate of Schizophrenia," by J. A. Kovelman and A. B. Scheibel, 1984, *Biological Psychiatry, 19,* p. 1613.

dendritic fields of cells in the dorsal prefrontal regions and hippocampus are abnormal (Cho, Gilbert, and Lewis, 2004), as are those in the entorhinal cortex (Arnold, Rushinsky, and Han, 1997). These regions participate in various forms of memory. Deficits in verbal and spatial memory among people with schizophrenia will quite possibly turn out to be correlated with these medial temporal abnormalities (**Figure 16-14**).

Another correlation is frequently seen in schizophrenia between an abnormally low blood flow in the dorsolateral prefrontal cortex and deficits in executive functions, such as those measured by the Wisconsin Card Sorting Test (for a review, see Berman and Weinberger, 1999). Interestingly, when Daniel Weinberger and Barbara Lipska (1995) studied pairs of identical twins in which only one twin had been diagnosed as having schizophrenia, they found that the twin with schizophrenia always had a lower blood flow in the prefrontal cortex while taking this card-sorting test.

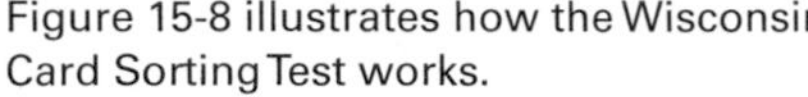
Figure 15-8 illustrates how the Wisconsin Card Sorting Test works.

Neurochemical Correlates of Schizozphrenia

Neuroscientists also consider the neurochemical correlates of brain–behavior relations in schizophrenia. Dopamine abnormalities were the first to be linked to schizophrenia, and the fact that most neuroleptic drugs act on the dopamine synapse was taken as evidence that schizophrenia is a disease of the ventral tegmental dopamine system. Similarly, drugs that enhance dopaminergic activity, such as amphetamine, can produce psychotic symptoms reminiscent of schizophrenia.

The dopamine theory of schizophrenia now appears too simple, however, because many other neurochemical abnormalities, summarized in **Table 16-6,** are also associated with schizophrenia—in particular, abnormalities in dopamine and dopamine receptors, glutamate and glutamate receptors, and GABA and GABA-binding sites. Considerable variability exists among patients in the extent of each abnormality, however. How these neurochemical variations might relate to the presence or absence of specific symptoms is not yet known.

TABLE 16-6 Biochemical Changes Associated with Schizophrenia

Decreased dopamine metabolites in cerebrospinal fluid
Increased striatal D_2 receptors
Decreased expression of D_3 and D_4 mRNA in specific cortical regions
Decreased cortical glutamate
Increased cortical glutamate receptors
Decreased glutamate uptake sites in cingulate cortex
Decreased mRNA for the synthesis of GABA in prefrontal cortex
Increased $GABA_A$-binding sites in cingulate cortex

Source: Adapted from "The Neurochemistry of Schizophrenia," by W. Byne, E. Kemegther, L. Jones, V. Harouthunian, and K. L. Davis, 1999, in *The Neurobiology of Mental Illness* (p. 242), edited by D. S. Charney, E. J. Nestler, and B. S. Bunney. New York: Oxford University Press.

To summarize, schizophrenia is a complex disorder associated with both positive and negative symptoms, with abnormalities in brain structure and metabolism (especially in the prefrontal and temporal cortex), and with neurochemical abnormalities in dopamine, glutamate, and GABA. Given the complexity of all these behavioral and neurobiological factors, it is not surprising that schizophrenia is so difficult to characterize and to treat.

Mania Disordered mental state characterized by excessive euphoria.
Bipolar disorder Mood disorder characterized by alternating periods of depression and mania.

Mood Disorders

In the past 50 years, researchers have debated whether mood disorders are psychological or biological in origin. In those with genetic predispositions to stress, environmental factors seem likely to act on the brain to produce biological changes related to people's moods and emotions. Although the precise nature of a genetic reactivity to stress is not fully understood, several genes have been implicated (Lohoff and Berrettini, 2009).

The DSM identifies a continuum of mood disorders, but the ones of principal interest here—depression and mania—represent the extremes of affect. The main symptoms of *major depression* are prolonged feelings of worthlessness and guilt, disruption of normal eating habits, sleep disturbances, a general slowing of behavior, and frequent thoughts of suicide.

Clinical Focus 8-3 explains the threat of suicide attendant to major depression that is left untreated.

Mania, the opposite affective extreme from depression, is characterized by excessive euphoria. The affected person often formulates grandiose plans and is uncontrollably hyperactive. Periods of mania often change, sometimes abruptly, into states of depression and back again to mania. Little is known about the neurobiology of this condition, called **bipolar disorder.**

Our emphasis here is on extending your knowledge about depression. Findings from clinical studies suggest that monoamine systems, particularly both the norepinephrine and the serotonin systems, have roles in depression. Many monoamine theories of depression have been proposed. To date, however, no unifying theory fully explains either the development of depression in otherwise normal people or how antidepressant medications treat it.

As detailed in Chapter 8, antidepressants, including selective serotonin reuptake inhibitors (SSRIs) and monoamine oxidase (MAO) inhibitors, are thought to act by improving chemical transmission in serotonin, noradrenaline, histamine, and acetylcholine receptors.

Neurobiology of Depression

Neuroscientists have known for nearly 40 years that antidepressant drugs acutely increase the synaptic levels of norepinephrine and serotonin. This finding led to the idea that depression results from a decrease in the availability of one or both neurotransmitters. Lowering their levels in normal participants does not produce depression, however. And while antidepressant medications increase the level of norepinephrine and serotonin within days, it takes weeks for drugs to start relieving depression.

Various explanations for these results have been suggested, none completely satisfactory. Ronald Duman (2004) reviewed evidence to suggest that antidepressants act, at least in part, on signaling pathways, such as on cAMP, in the postsynaptic cell. Neurotrophic factors appear to affect the action of antidepressants and furthermore may underlie the neurobiology of depression. Investigators know, for example, that brain-derived neurotrophic factor (BDNF) is down-regulated by stress and up-regulated by antidepressant medication.

Chapter 14 explores the relations of hormones, trophic factors, and psychoactive drugs to neuroplasticity.

Given that BDNF acts to enhance the growth and survival of cortical neurons and synapses, BDNF dysfunction may adversely affect noreprinephrine and serotonin systems through the loss of either neurons or synapses. Antidepressant medication may increase the release of BDNF through its actions on cAMP signal transduction. The key point here is that the cause is most likely not just a simple decrease in transmitter levels. Rather, explaining both the biochemical abnormalities in depression and the actions of antidepressants is probably far more complex than it seemed a generation ago.

HPA axis Hypothalamic-pituitary-adrenal circuit that controls the production and release of hormones related to stress.

Chapter 8 explains the neurobiology of the stress response—how it begins and ends.

Mood and Reactivity to Stress

A significant psychological factor in understanding depression is reactivity to stress. Monoamines—the noradrenergic and serotoninergic activating systems diagrammed in **Figure 16-15A**—modulate hormone secretion by the hypothalamic-pituitary-adrenal system—the **HPA axis**—illustrated in Figure 16-15B. When we are stressed, the HPA axis is stimulated to produce stress hormones, steroids such as cortisol (hydrocortisone).

The best-established abnormality in the HPA-axis modulation is an oversecretion of cortisol from the adrenal gland. Normally when you are stressed, the hypothalamus secretes corticotropin-releasing hormone, which stimulates the pituitary to produce adrenocorticotropic hormone. ACTH circulates through the blood and stimulates the adrenal medulla to produce cortisol.

The hypothalamic neurons that begin this cascade are regulated by norepinephrine neurons in the midbrain locus coeruleus. If the cortisol release is too large, the norepinephrine neurons fail to regulate it. High levels of cortisol are bad for neurons, and chronic increases lead to neuronal death in the hippocampus.

Charles Nemeroff (2004) showed that during critical periods in early childhood, abuse or other severe environmental stress can permanently disrupt the reactivity of the HPA axis. Chronic stress can lead to the oversecretion of cortisol, an imbalance associated with depression in adulthood. Nemeroff found, for example, that 45 percent of adults with depression lasting 2 years or more had experienced abuse, neglect, or parental loss as children.

More recently, Patrick McGowan and colleagues (2009) wondered if early experiences could alter gene expression related to the activity of cortisol in the HPA axis. They compared, postmortem, hippocampi obtained from suicide victims with a history of childhood abuse and hippocampi from other suicide victims with no childhood abuse

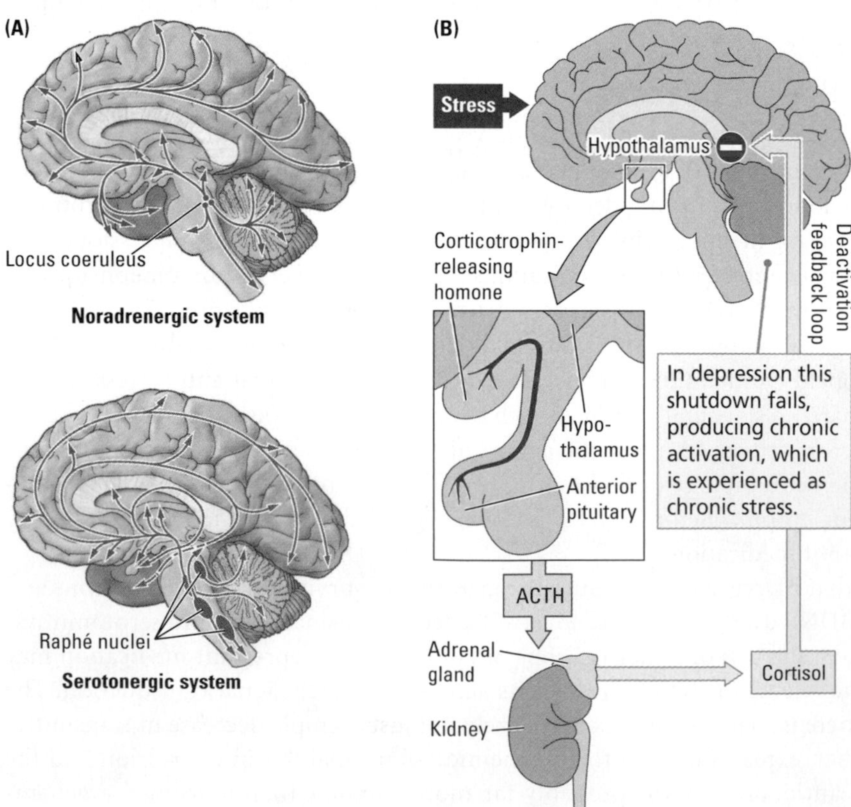

FIGURE 16-15 HPA axis. (A) In this medial view of the stress-activating system, the locus coeruleus contains the cell bodies of norepinephrine (noradrenaline) neurons (*top*), and cell bodies of the serotonergic activating system emanate from the Raphé nuclei (*bottom*). (B) When activated, the HPA system affects mood, thinking, and indirectly, secretion of cortisol by the adrenal glands. HPA deactivation begins when cortisol binds to hypothalamic receptors.

or from controls. Abused suicide victims showed decreased gene expression for cortisol receptor relative to the other people. These results, derived from epigenetics, confirm that early neglect or abuse alters the HPA axis.

Epigenetics refers to differences in gene expression that are caused by experience; see Chapter 6.

Fluoxetine (Prozac), a major drug for treating depression, is an SSRI that effectively increases the amount of serotonin in the cortex. But independent of serotonin production, fluoxetine stimulates both BDNF production and neurogenesis in the hippocampus, resulting in a net increase in the number of granule cells (see Research Focus 16-3, "Antidepressant Action in Neurogenesis").

To summarize, the diffuse distribution of the noreprinephrine- and serotonin-activating systems makes relating depression to a single brain structure impossible. Findings from neuroimaging studies show that depression is accompanied by increased blood flow and glucose metabolism in the orbitofrontal cortex, the anterior cingulate cortex, and the amygdala. Blood flow drops as the symptoms of depression remit when a patient takes antidepressant medication (Drevets, Kishore, and Krishman, 2004). The participation of these brain structures in affect should not be surprising, given their role in emotional behavior.

Chapter 12 traces the brain circuits involved in emotional and motivated behavior.

RESEARCH FOCUS 16-3

Antidepressant Action in Neurogenesis

A puzzle in treating depression pharmacologically is this: even though antidepressant drugs create an almost immediate increase in monoamines in the brain when people begin taking them, it typically takes from 3 to 4 weeks for the medication to affect the depression. If low levels of monoamines cause depression, then why does it take so long to see and feel improvement? One explanation is that the increased monoamine levels initiate a slow reparative process in their target areas in the brain.

In fact, findings from postmortem studies of the brains of depressed people show cell loss in the prefrontal cortex and hippocampus. The antidepressants' actions may reverse some of this loss. Furthermore, exposure to chronic stress can cause cell death and dendritic shrinkage in the hippocampus, changes that probably result from high levels of cortisol. The possibility arises, therefore, that antidepressant drugs act to reverse cell loss, at least in the hippocampus. In fact, there is good evidence that fluoxetine (Prozac) and other SSRIs stimulate neurogenesis in the hippocampi of rats and mice.

Luca Santarelli and colleagues (2003) conducted an experiment to test whether antidepressants are capable of reversing the behavioral symptoms when neurogenesis is prevented in depressed animals. They used a mouse bred with a genetic knockout manipulation that omitted a specific serotonin receptor (5-HT-1A). This receptor is thought to be stimulated by antidepressants such as fluoxetine.

The mice were tested in two behavioral procedures, including one that the investigators proposed as a model of depression. In this test, animals exposed to chronic, unpredictable stress developed a general deterioration in the state of their fur coat; this deterioration could be reversed by chronic but not acute treatment with antidepressants.

Santarelli's team hypothesized that, if the action of fluoxetine on depression was to increase neurogenesis in the hippocampus, then mice without the necessary 5-HT-1A receptor would not respond to the drug treatment. In contrast, animals with the serotonin receptor would show both a reversal in cell loss in the hippocampus and in the associated behavioral changes. This is exactly what the researchers found. It is important to note that the effect of the drug was not seen after only 5 days of drug treatment; it was seen after 11 to 28 days of treatment.

Santarelli and his team concluded that the hippocampus has a role in mood regulation and that interfering with hippocampal neurogenesis impairs this mood regulation. They proposed that antidepressants act, at least in part, to increase neurogenesis and thus relieve the impairment in hippocampal mood regulation. It is important to note that humans with hippocampal damage are not typically depressed, so the way in which neurogenesis in the hippocampus might relieve depression remains puzzling.

This study demonstrates how environmental factors such as chronic stress may alter the human brain's homeostatic regulator. Santarelli's animal model further explains how a class of drugs (in this case, antidepressants) act at the cellular level to reverse both anatomical and behavioral symptoms.

Cognitive-behavioral therapy (CBT) Problem-focused, action-oriented, structured, treatment for eliminating dysfunctional thoughts and maladaptive behaviors.

Although we have emphasized the biological cause of depression, once again we must emphasize that the best treatment need not be a direct biological intervention. **Cognitive-behavioral therapy** (CBT) focuses on challenging the reality of the patient's beliefs and perceptions. The objective is to identify dysfunctional thoughts and beliefs that accompany negative emotions and replace them with more realistic ones.

Simply pointing out to a person that the person's beliefs are faulty is not likely to be effective, however, because it probably took months or years to develop the beliefs. The neural circuits underlying the beliefs must be changed, just as the strategies of developing new ones must be changed. In a real sense, CBT is effective if it can induce neural plasticity and change brain activity. And in fact, CBT is at least as effective as medication as a treatment for depression.

Anxiety Disorders

We all experience anxiety at some time, usually acutely as a response to a stressful stimulus or, less commonly, as a chronic reactivity—an increased anxiety response—even to seemingly minor stressors. Anxiety reactions certainly are not pathological, and it is likely that they were an evolutionary adaptation for coping with adverse conditions. But anxiety can become pathological to the point of making life miserable.

Clinical Focus 12-3 describes the symptoms of three anxiety disorders: panic, phobia, and generalized anxiety; Chapter 8 describes how stress-induced damage contributes to posttraumatic stress disorder; Chapter 5 explains increased serotonergic activity accompanying symptoms observed in obsessive-compulsive disorder.

Anxiety disorders are among the most common psychiatric conditions. The DSM lists six classes of anxiety disorders that together affect an estimated 37.5 percent of the U.S. population at some point in their lifetimes (see Figure 16-13). The annual economic cost attributed to anxiety disorders is estimated at about $44 billion (Gross and Hen, 2004).

Imaging studies of people with anxiety disorders record increased baseline activity in the cingulate cortex and parahippocampal gyrus and an enhanced response to anxiety-provoking stimuli in the amygdala and prefrontal cortex. The likely culprit is excessive excitatory neurotransmission in the anterior cingulate cortex, prefrontal cortex, amygdala, and parahippocampal region. Researchers hypothesize that, because drugs that enhance the inhibitory transmitter GABA are particularly effective in reducing anxiety, excessive excitatory neurotransmission may enhance anxiety. But what is the cause?

Considerable interest has developed in investigating why some people show a pathological level of anxiety to stimuli to which others have a much-attenuated response. One hypothesis, just covered in the section on depression, is that stressful experiences early in life increase a person's susceptibility to a variety of behavioral abnormalities, especially anxiety disorders. Findings from studies on laboratory animals confirm that early experience can alter the stress response in adulthood.

Michael Meaney and his colleagues (e.g., Weaver et al., 2004) demonstrated a range of maternal licking-and-grooming behavior among rat mothers. Pups raised by mothers that display low levels of licking and grooming show more anxiety-related behaviors, including an enhanced corticosterone response in response to mild stressors, than do pups raised by mothers that display high levels of licking and grooming.

What is particularly intriguing in these studies is that rat pups raised by low or high lickers and groomers themselves show the same behavior toward their own infants. This link is not a direct genetic one, however, because pups raised by adoptive mothers show the behaviors of their adoptive mothers rather than their biological mothers.

Meaney's group showed that the licking-and-grooming behaviors alter the expression of certain genes, thus showing that early experiences can alter the phenotype. More exciting, the researchers have reversed the adverse effects of early experience with chemical treatments. This promising line of inquiry will undoubtedly lead to new forms of treatment for anxiety disorders in coming years.

Although anxiety disorders used to be treated primarily with benzodiazepines such as Valium, now they are effectively treated with SSRIs such as Prozac, Paxil, Celexa, and

Zoloft. Antidepressant drugs do not act immediately, however, suggesting that SSRI treatment must stimulate some gradual change in brain structure, much as these drugs act in treating depression.

Finally, medicating people does nothing to encourage the coping skills they may need to get better. This is especially true for anxiety disorders. The treatment of obsessive-compulsive disorders in particular requires an integrated approach, including both medications and cognitive-behavioral therapy.

In the case of anxiety disorders, CBT focuses on challenging the reality of the patients' obsessions and the behavioral necessity for their compulsions. The most effective behavioral therapies expose and reexpose patients to their fears. For example, treating a phobic fear of germs requires that the patient be exposed repeatedly to potentially germy environments, such as public washrooms, until the discomfort abates (Abramowitz, 1998). In general, CBT has proved as effective as medications in treating chronic anxiety disorders.

One more time: a pill is not a skill.

REVIEW: Understanding and Treating Behavioral Disorders

- ✔ Understanding psychiatric disorders such as psychosis, mood disorders, and anxiety disorders is best viewed as work in progress. Significant progress has been made in understanding the neurobiology of these disorders.
- ✔ Schizophrenia is correlated with abnormalities in dopamine, GABA, and glutamate systems. Structural abnormalities and low blood-glucose utilization are observed in both the prefrontal cortex and the temporal cortex. Treatments emphasize normalizing the dopaminergic abnormalities.
- ✔ The monoamine systems are abnormal in mood disorders, particularly in signal transduction in postsynaptic cells. And in depression, abnormally high levels of blood flow and glucose utilization show up in the prefrontal and anterior cingulate cortex and in the amygdala. Antidepressant treatments aim largely at normalizing the monoaminergic systems, which in turn normalizes glucose utilization.
- ✔ It is likely that anxiety disorders are related to GABA systems and abnormally high levels of blood flow in the cingulate cortex, amygdala, and parahippocampal cortex. Treatments aim to reverse the GABAergic abnormalities and to help people learn to modify their behaviors.

Is Misbehavior Always Bad?

You know this movie plot: a person sustains some sort of blow to the head and becomes a different (and better) person. You might wonder whether pathological changes in the brain and behavior sometimes lead to improvement. A report by Jim Giles (2004) on Tommy McHugh's case is thought provoking.

McHugh, a heroin addict, had committed multiple serious crimes and had spent a great deal of time in jail. He suffered a cerebral hemorrhage (bleeding into the brain) from an aneurysm. The bleeding was repaired surgically by placing a metal clip on the leaking artery. After he recovered from the injury, McHugh showed a dramatic change in personality, took up painting, which he had never done before, and has become a successful artist. His life of crime now exists only in the record books.

McHugh's injury-induced brain changes appear to have been beneficial. The exact nature of McHugh's brain injury is not easy to identify, because the metal clip in his

Neurocognitive enhancement Brain-function enhancement by pharmacological, physiological, or surgical manipulation.

brain precludes the use of MRI. Aspects of his cognitive behavior suggest that he may have frontal-lobe damage.

Bruce Miller has studied a larger group of 12 patients who, like Tommy McHugh, have frontal or temporal injury or both. All developed new musical or artistic talents after their injuries (Miller et al., 2000). Miller speculates that loss of function in one brain area sometimes can release new functions elsewhere.

The general idea that manipulating the brain might be beneficial is clearly a slippery slope. The idea behind psychosurgery, neurosurgical techniques intended to alter behavior, was based on this general idea. Today, it might be possible to influence brain function more scientifically through a strategy loosely described as **neurocognitive enhancement.** The general idea is that, by using our knowledge of pharmacology, brain plasticity, brain stimulation, neurogenetics, and so on, it will one day be possible to manipulate brain functioning.

Chapter 12 recounts the disturbing history of psychosurgery; Figure 12-24 diagrams one procedure, the transorbital leucotomy.

Many people already use drugs to alter brain function. But what about such treatments as genetic manipulation? Michael Meaney and his collaborators have demonstrated that specific behavioral manipulations can alter the expression of genes in rats. Serious moral and ethical issues certainly need discussion before neuroscientists begin to offer routes to neurocognitive enhancement. (See reviews of these issues by Caplan, 2003, and Farah et al., 2004).

Research Focus 11-1 describes the current and potential benefits offered by brain–computer interfaces. Is the BCI a form of neuroenhancement?

Summary

Freud's theories have been out of favor in behavioral neuroscience for about 50 years, but modern neuroimaging studies are reviving a Freudianlike theory of the self, a neuropsychoanalysis more in keeping with current scientific knowledge about brain organization and function. As a new, unifying model of the self develops, researchers and practitioners may begin to identify the neural basis of diseases now labeled as "mental" or "psychiatric."

Multidisciplinary Research on Brain and Behavioral Disorders

Most behavioral disorders have multiple causes—genetic, biochemical, anatomical, and social–environmental variables—all of them interacting. Research methods directed toward these causes include family studies designed to find a genetic abnormality that might be corrected, biochemical anomalies that might be reversed by drug or hormone therapy, anatomical pathologies that might account for behavioral changes, and social–environmental variables.

Investigators rely increasingly on neuroimaging (fMRI, PET, TMS, ERP) to examine brain–behavior relations in vivo in normal participants as well as in people experiencing disorders. Interest in more refined behavioral measurements is growing, especially for cognitive behavior, the better to understand behavioral symptoms.

Classifying and Treating Brain and Behavioral Disorders

Disorders can be classified according to presumed etiology (cause), symptomatology, or pathology. The primary etiological classification, neurological versus psychiatric, is artificial because it presupposes that two categories accommodate all types of disorders. In fact, as more is learned about etiology, more disorders fall into the neurological category.

The symptomatological classification requires a checklist, such as the DSM. The problem with such diagnosis is that symptoms of psychiatric disorders overlap. The checklist of likely symptoms for disorders is thus open to interpretation. Symptoms may appear more or less prominent, depending on the perceptions of the person doing the classifying.

The pathological classification of behavioral disorders may be possible with MRI or other scans but often requires postmortem examination. In either event, it is becoming clear that disorders have more overlap in pathology than was previously recognized.

Understanding and Treating Neurological Disorders

The treatment of behavioral disorders is usually tied to the presumed causes. If a disorder is presumed to be primarily one of biochemical imbalance, such as depression, the treatment is likely to be pharmacological. If the disorder has a suspected anatomical cause, the treatment may include the removal of pathological tissue (as in epilepsy) or the use of implanted electrodes to activate underactive regions (as in Parkinson's disease and stroke). Brain activation with TMS is promising and noninvasive. Many disorders, however, require medical treatment concurrent with behavioral therapy, including physiotherapy or cognitive rehabilitation for stroke or trauma and cognitive-behavioral therapies for depression and anxiety disorders.

Understanding and Treating Psychiatric Disorders

The number of people with hidden diseases of behavior, especially the neurodegenerative disorders and stroke, will increase as the population of the Western world ages. Like other plagues in human history, dementias affect not only the person who has the disease but also the caregivers. About half of the caregivers for people with disorders linked to aging will seek psychiatric care themselves.

Is Misbehavior Always Bad?

In rare cases, people with disordered behaviors may inadvertently benefit from neurological disease, suggesting that some brain misbehavior can prove beneficial.

The logic of psychosurgery is that, by altering brain organization, it might be possible to alter behavior. The history of psychosurgery is horrific, but the general principle of using our knowledge to influence brain function holds promise. Such neurocognitive enhancement could employ genetic manipulations, transplants, and brain stimulation.

Key Terms

akathesia, p. 587
autoimmune disease, p. 584
automatism, p. 582
behavioral therapy, p. 575
bipolar disorder, p. 595
catatonic posture, p. 582
cognitive-behavioral therapy (CBT), p. 598
cognitive therapy, p. 575
deep brain stimulation (DBS), p. 571
dementia, p. 584
diaschisis, p. 580
DSM, p. 568
festination, p. 587
focal seizue, p. 582
grand mal seizure, p. 582
HPA axis, p. 596
idiopathic seizure, p. 580
ischemia, p. 579
Lewy body, p. 591
magnetic resonance spectroscopy (MRS), p. 579
mania, p. 595
neurocognitive enhancement, p. 600
neuroprotectant, p. 580
neuropsychoanalysis, p.563
petit mal seizure, p. 582
phenylketonuria (PKU), p. 565
postictal depression, p. 582
posttraumatic stress disorder (PTSD), p. 563
psychotherapy, p. 575
real-time fMRI (rtfMRI), p. 576
symptomatic seizure, p. 580
tardive dyskinesia, p. 575
type I schizophrenia, p. 593
type II schizophrenia, p. 593

▶*Please refer to the Companion Web Site at* **www.worthpublishers.com/kolbintro3e** *for Interactive Exercises and Quizzes.*

Glossary

absolutely refractory Refers to the state of an axon in the repolarizing period during which a new action potential cannot be elicited (with some exceptions), because gate 2 of sodium channels, which is not voltage sensitive, is closed.

acetylcholine (ACh) The first neurotransmitter discovered in the peripheral and central nervous systems; activates skeletal muscles in the somatic nervous system and may either excite or inhibit internal organs in the autonomic system.

action potential Large, brief reversal in the polarity of an axon.

activating system Neural pathways that coordinate brain activity through a single neurotransmitter; cell bodies are located in a nucleus in the brainstem and axons are distributed through a wide region of the brain.

addiction Desire for a drug manifested by frequent use of the drug, leading to the development of physical dependence in addition to abuse; often associated with tolerance and unpleasant, sometimes dangerous, withdrawal symptoms on cessation of drug use. Also called *substance dependence.*

afferent Conducting toward a central nervous system structure.

agonist Substance that enhances the function of a synapse.

akathesia Small, involuntary movements or changes in posture; motor restlessness.

akinesia Slowness or absence of movement.

alcohol myopia "Nearsighted" behavior displayed under the influence of alcohol: local and immediate cues become prominent, and remote cues and consequences are ignored.

allele Alternate form of a gene; a gene pair contains two alleles.

alpha rhythm Regular wave pattern in an electroencephalogram; found in most people when they are relaxed with closed eyes.

Alzheimer's disease Degenerative brain disorder related to aging that first appears as progressive memory loss and later develops into generalized dementia.

amblyopia A condition in which vision in one eye is reduced as a result of disuse; usually caused by a failure of the two eyes to point in the same direction.

amnesia Partial or total loss of memory.

amphetamine Drug that releases the neurotransmitter dopamine into its synapse and, like cocaine, blocks dopamine reuptake.

amplitude Intensity of a stimulus; in audition, roughly equivalent to loudness, graphed by increasing the height of a sound wave.

amusia Tone deafness—an inability to distinguish between musical notes.

amygdala Almond-shaped collection of nuclei located within the limbic system; plays a role in emotional and species-typical behaviors.

anabolic steroid Belongs to a class of synthetic hormones related to testosterone that have both muscle-building (anabolic) and masculinizing (androgenic) effects; also called *anabolic–androgenic steroid.*

androgen Class of hormones that stimulates or controls masculine characteristics and that in males is related to level of sexual interest.

anencephaly Failure of the forebrain to develop.

anomalous speech representation Condition in which a person's speech zones are located in the right hemisphere or in both hemispheres.

anorexia nervosa Exaggerated concern with being overweight that leads to inadequate food intake and often excessive exercising; can lead to severe weight loss and even starvation.

antagonist Substance that blocks the function of a synapse.

anterograde amnesia Inability to remember events subsequent to a disturbance of the brain such as head trauma, electroconvulsive shock, or certain neurodegenerative diseases.

antianxiety agent Drug that reduces anxiety; minor tranquillizers such as benzodiazepines and sedative-hypnotic agents are of this type.

aphagia Failure to eat; may be due to an unwillingness to eat or to motor difficulties, especially with swallowing.

aphasia Inability to speak or comprehend language despite the presence of normal comprehension and intact vocal mechanisms. *Broca's aphasia* is the inability to speak fluently despite the presence of normal comprehension and intact vocal mechanisms. *Wernicke's aphasia* is the inability to understand or to produce meaningful language even though the production of words is still intact.

apoptosis Cell death that is genetically programmed.

apraxia Inability to make voluntary movements in the absence of paralysis or other motor or sensory impairment, especially an inability to make proper use of an object

association cortex Neocortex outside the primary sensory and motor cortices that functions to produce cognition.

associative learning Linkage of two or more unrelated stimuli to elicit a behavioral response.

astrocyte Glial cell with a star-shaped appearance that provides structural support to neurons in the central nervous system and transports substances between neurons and capillaries.

atonia No tone; condition of complete muscle inactivity produced by the inhibition of motor neurons.

attention Selective narrowing or focusing of awareness to part of the sensory environment or to a class of stimuli.

attention-deficit/hyperactivity disorder (ADHD) Developmental disorder characterized by core behavioral symptoms of impulsivity, hyperactivity, and/or inattention.

auditory flow Change in sound heard as a person moves past a sound source or as a sound source moves past a person.

autism spectrum disorder Range of cognitive symptoms, from mild to severe, that characterize autism; severe symptoms include greatly impaired social interaction, a bizarre and narrow range of interests, marked abnormalities in language and communication, and fixed, repetitive movements.

autoimmune disease Illness resulting from the loss of the immune system's ability to discriminate between foreign pathogens in the body and the body itself.

automatism Unconscious, repetitive, stereotyped movement characteristic of seizure.

autonomic nervous system (ANS) Part of the PNS that regulates the functioning of internal organs and glands.

autoreceptor "Self-receptor" in a neural membrane that responds to the transmitter released by the neuron.

axon "Root," or single fiber, of a neuron that carries messages to other neurons.

axon collateral Branch of an axon.

axon hillock Juncture of soma and axon where the action potential begins.

back propagation Reverse movement of an action potential into the dendritic field of a neuron; postulated to play a role in plastic changes that underlie learning.

barbiturate Drug that produces sedation and sleep.

basal ganglia Subcortical forebrain nuclei that coordinate voluntary movements of the limbs and body; connected to the thalamus and to the midbrain.

basic rest–activity cycle (BRAC) Recurring cycle of temporal packets, about 90-minute periods in humans, during which an animal's level of arousal waxes and wanes.

basilar membrane Receptor surface in the cochlea that transduces sound waves into neural activity.

behavioral neuroscience Study of the biological basis of behavior.
behavioral therapy Treatment that applies learning principles, such as conditioning, to eliminate unwanted behaviors.
beta rhythm (β) Fast brain-wave activity pattern associated with a waking EEG.
bilateral symmetry Body plan in which organs or parts present on both sides of the body are mirror images in appearance. For example, the hands are bilaterally symmetrical, whereas the heart is not.
binding problem Philosophical question focused on how the brain ties single and varied sensory and motor events together into a unified perception or behavior.
biological clock Neural system that times behavior.
biorhythm Inherent timing mechanism that controls or initiates various biological processes.
bipolar disorder Mood disorder characterized by alternating periods of depression and mania.
bipolar neuron Sensory neuron with one axon and one dendrite.
blind spot Region of the retina where axons forming the optic nerve leave the eye and where blood vessels enter and leave; has no photoreceptors and is thus "blind."
blob Region in the visual cortex that contains color-sensitive neurons, as revealed by staining for cytochrome oxidase.
blood–brain barrier The tight junctions between the cells that compose blood vessels in the brain, providing a barrier to the entry of large molecules into the brain.
brain–computer interface (BCI) Neuroprosthetic technology that uses electrical signals from the brains of people with movement impairments to operate computer-controlled devices that replace lost biological function.
brainstem Central structures of the brain, including the hindbrain, midbrain, thalamus, and hypothalamus, responsible for most unconscious behavior.
Broca's area Anterior speech area in the left hemisphere that functions with the motor cortex to produce the movements needed for speaking.

carbon monoxide (CO) Acts as a neurotransmitter gas in the activation of cellular metabolism.
cataplexy Form of narcolepsy linked to strong emotional stimulation in which an animal loses all muscle activity or tone, as if in REM sleep, while awake.
catatonic posture Rigid or frozen pose resulting from a psychomotor disturbance.
cell-adhesion molecule (CAM) A chemical molecule to which specific cells can adhere, thus aiding in migration.
cell assembly Hypothetical group of neurons that become functionally connected because they receive the same sensory inputs. Hebb proposed that cell assemblies were the basis of perception, memory, and thought.
cell body (soma) Core region of the cell containing the nucleus and other organelles for making proteins.
central nervous system (CNS) The brain and spinal cord that together mediate behavior.
cerebellum Major structure of the brainstem specialized for coordinating and learning skilled movements. In large-brained animals, it may also have a role in the coordination of other mental processes.
cerebral cortex Outer layer of brain-tissue surface composed of neurons; the human cerebral cortex is heavily folded.
cerebral palsy Group of brain disorders that result from brain damage acquired perinatally (at or near birth).
cerebral voltammetry Technique used to identify the concentration of specific chemicals in the brain as animals behave freely.
cerebrospinal fluid (CSF) Clear solution of sodium chloride and other salts that fills the ventricles inside the brain and circulates around the brain and spinal cord beneath the arachnoid layer in the subarachnoid space.
cerebrum Major structure of the forebrain, consisting of two virtually identical hemispheres (left and right) and responsible for most conscious behavior.
channel Opening in a protein embedded in the cell membrane that allows the passage of ions.
chemical synapse Junction at which messenger molecules are released when stimulated by an action potential.
chemoaffinity hypothesis Proposal that neurons or their axons and dendrites are drawn toward a signaling chemical that indicates the correct pathway.
cholinergic neuron Neuron that uses acetylcholine as its main neurotransmitter. The term *cholinergic* applies to any neuron that uses ACh as its main transmitter.
chordate Animal that has both a brain and a spinal cord.
circadian rhythm Day–night rhythm.
cladogram Phylogenetic tree that branches repeatedly, suggesting a taxonomy of organisms based on the time sequence in which evolutionary branches arise.
clinical trial Approved experiment directed toward developing a treatment.
cochlea Inner-ear structure that contains the auditory receptor cells.
cochlear implant Electronic device implanted surgically into the inner ear to transduce sound waves into neural activity and allow a deaf person to hear.
cognition Act or process of knowing or coming to know; in psychology, used to refer to the processes of thought.
cognitive-behavioral therapy (CBT) Problem-focused, action-oriented, structured treatment for eliminating dysfunctional thoughts and maladaptive behaviors.
cognitive neuroscience Study of the neural bases of cognition.
cognitive therapy Psychotherapy based on the perspective that thoughts intervene between events and emotions, and thus the treatment of emotional disorders requires changing maladaptive patterns of thinking.
color constancy Phenomenon whereby the perceived color of an object tends to remain constant relative to other colors, regardless of changes in illumination.
coma Prolonged state of deep unconsciousness resembling sleep.
common ancestor Forebearer from which two or more lineages or family groups arise and so is ancestral to both groups.
competitive inhibitor Drug such as nalorphine and naloxone that acts quickly to block the actions of opiods by competing with them for binding sites; used to treat opiod addiction.
computerized tomography (CT) X-ray technique that produces a static, three-dimensional image of the brain in cross section—a *CT scan.*
concentration gradient Differences in concentration of a substance among regions of a container that allow the substance to diffuse from an area of higher concentration to an area of lower concentration.
conditioned response (CR) In Pavlovian conditioning, the learned response to a formerly neutral conditioned stimulus (CS).
conditioned stimulus (CS) In Pavlovian conditioning, an originally neutral stimulus that, after association with an unconditioned stimulus (UCS), triggers a conditioned response.
cone Photoreceptor specialized for color and high visual acuity.
consciousness Level of responsiveness of the mind to impressions made by the senses.
contralateral neglect Ignoring a part of the body or world on the side opposite (contralateral to) that of a brain injury.
convergent thinking Form of thinking that searches for a single answer to a question (such as 2 + 2 = ?); contrasts with divergent thinking.
corpus callosum Fiber system connecting the two cerebral hemispheres to provide a route for direct communication between them.
cortical column Cortical organization that represents a functional unit six cortical layers deep and approximately 0.5 millimeter square and that is perpendicular to the cortical surface.
corticospinal tract Bundle of nerve fibers directly connecting the cerebral cortex to the spinal cord, branching at the brainstem into an opposite-side lateral tract that informs movement of limbs and digits and a same-side ventral tract that informs

movement of the trunk; also called pyramidal tract.

cranial nerve One of a set of 12 nerve pairs that control sensory and motor functions of the head, neck, and internal organs.

critical period Developmental "window" during which some event has a long-lasting influence on the brain; often referred to as a *sensitive period.*

cross-tolerance Response to a novel drug is reduced because of tolerance developed in response to a chemically related drug.

culture Learned behaviors that are passed on from one generation to the next through teaching and experience.

cytoarchitectonic map Map of the neocortex based on the organization, structure, and distribution of the cells.

deafferentation Loss of incoming sensory input usually due to damage to sensory fibers; also loss of any afferent input to a structure.

decibel (dB) Unit for measuring the relative physical intensity of sounds.

declarative memory Ability to recount what one knows, to detail the time, place, and circumstances of events; often lost in amnesia.

deep brain stimulation (DBS) Neurosurgery in which electrodes implanted in the brain stimulate a targeted area with a low-voltage electrical current to facilitate behavior.

delta rhythm (δ) Slow brain-wave activity pattern associated with deep sleep.

dementia Acquired and persistent syndrome of intellectual impairment characterized by memory and other cognitive deficits and impairment in social and occupational functioning.

dendrite Branching extension of a neuron's cell membrane that greatly increases the surface area of the cell and collects information from other cells.

dendritic spine Protrusion from a dendrite that greatly increases the dendrite's surface area and is the usual point of dendritic contact with the axons of other cells.

depolarization Decrease in electrical charge across a membrane, usually due to the inward flow of sodium ions.

dermatome Area of the skin supplied with afferent nerve fibers by a single spinal-cord dorsal root.

diaschisis Neural shock that follows brain damage in which areas connected to the site of damage show a temporary arrest of function.

dichotic listening Experimental procedure for simultaneously presenting a different auditory input to each ear through stereophonic earphones.

diencephalon The "between brain" that integrates sensory and motor information on its way to the cerebral cortex.

diffusion Movement of ions from an area of higher concentration to an area of lower concentration through random motion.

disinhibition theory Explanation holding that alcohol has a selective depressant effect on the cortex, the region of the brain that controls judgment, while sparing subcortical structures responsible for more-primitive instincts, such as desire.

dissociative anesthetic Sedative-hypnotic anesthetic that produces altered states of consciousness and hallucinations and impairs memory for recent events; also known as a "date-rape" drug.

diurnal animal Organism that is active chiefly during daylight.

divergent thinking Form of thinking that searches for multiple solutions to a problem (such as How many different ways can a pen be used?); contrasts with convergent thinking.

dopamine (DA) Amine neurotransmitter that plays a role in coordinating movement, in attention and learning, and in behaviors that are reinforcing.

dopamine hypothesis of schizophrenia Proposal that schizophrenia symptoms are due to excess activity of the neurotransmitter dopamine.

dorsal spinothalamic tract Pathway that carries fine-touch and pressure fibers.

Down syndrome Chromosomal abnormality resulting in mental retardation and other abnormalities, usually caused by an extra chromosome 21.

drive Hypothetical state of arousal that motivates an organism to engage in a particular behavior.

drug-dependency insomnia Condition resulting from continuous use of "sleeping pills"; drug tolerance also results in deprivation of either REM or NREM sleep, leading the user to increase the drug dosage.

drug-induced behavioral sensitization Escalating behavioral response to the repeated administration of a psychomotor stimulant such as amphetamine, cocaine, or nicotine; also called *behavioral sensitization.*

DSM Abbreviation for *Diagnostic and Statistical Manual of Mental Disorders,* the American Psychiatric Association's classification system for psychiatric disorders.

dualism Philosophical position that holds that both a nonmaterial mind and the material body contribute to behavior.

dyslexia Impairment in learning to read and write; probably the most common learning disability.

echolocation Ability to identify and locate an object by bouncing sound waves off the object.

efferent Conducting away from a central nervous system structure.

electrical stimulation Passage of an electrical current from the uninsulated tip of an electrode through tissue, resulting in changes in the electrical activity of the tissue.

electrical synapse Fused presynaptic and postsynaptic membrane that allows an action potential to pass directly from one neuron to the next.

electroencephalogram (EEG) Graph that records electrical activity through the skull or from the brain and represents graded potentials of many neurons.

embodied consciousness Hypothesis that the movements that we make and those that we perceive in others are essential features of our conscious behavior.

emotion Cognitive interpretation of subjective feelings.

emotional memory Memory for the affective properties of stimuli or events.

encephalization quotient (EQ) Jerison's quantitative measure of brain size obtained from the ratio of actual rain size to expected brain size, according to the principle of proper mass, for an animal of a particular body size.

endorphin Peptide hormone that acts as a neurotransmitter and may be associated with feelings of pain or pleasure; mimicked by opioid drugs such as morphine, heroin, opium, and codeine.

end plate On a muscle, the receptor–ion complex that is activated by the release of the neurotransmitter acetylcholine from the terminal of a motor neuron.

entorhinal cortex Located on the medial surface of the temporal lobe; provides a major route for neocortical input to the hippocampal formation; often degenerates in Alzheimer's disease.

entrainment Determination or modification of the period of a biorhythm.

ependymal cell Glial cell that makes and secretes cerebrospinal fluid; found on the walls of the ventricles in the brain.

epidermal growth factor (EGF) Neurotrophic factor that stimulates the subventricular zone to generate cells that migrate into the striatum and eventually differentiate into neurons and glia.

epigenetics Changes in gene expression related to experience.

epinephrine (EP, or adrenaline) Chemical messenger that acts as a hormone to mobilize the body for fight or flight during times of stress and as a neurotransmitter in the central nervous system.

episodic memory Autobiographical memory for events pegged to specific place and time contexts.

estrogens Variety of sex hormones responsible for the distinguishing characteristics of the female.

event-related potentials (ERPs) Complex electroencephalographic waveforms related in time to a specific sensory event.

evolutionary psychology Discipline that seeks to apply principles of natural selection to understand the causes of human behavior.

excitation Increase in the activity of a neuron or brain area.

excitatory postsynaptic potential (EPSP) Brief depolarization of a neuron membrane in response to stimulation, making the neuron more likely to produce an action potential.

explicit memory Conscious memory: subjects can retrieve an item and indicate that they know that the retreived item is the correct item.

extinction In neurology, neglect of information on one side of the body when it is presented simultaneously with similar information on the other side of the body.

extrastriate (secondary visual) cortex Visual cortical areas outside the striate cortex.

eye-blink conditioning Commonly used experimental technique in which subjects learn to pair a formerly neutral stimulus with a defensive blinking response.

fear conditioning Learned association, a conditioned emotional response, between a neutral stimulus and a noxious event such as a shock.

festination Tendency to engage in a behavior, such as walking, at faster and faster speeds.

fetal alcohol syndrome (FAS) Pattern of physical malformation and mental retardation observed in some children born of alcoholic mothers.

filopod Process at the end of a developing axon that reaches out to search for a potential target or to sample the intercellular environment.

focal seizure Begins locally (at a focus) and then spreads out to adjacent areas.

forebrain Evolutionarily the newest part of the brain; coordinates advanced cognitive functions such as thinking, planning, and language; contains the limbic system, basal ganglia, and the neocortex.

fovea Region at the center of the retina that is specialized for high acuity; its receptive fields are at the center of the eye's visual field.

free-running rhythm Rhythm of the body's own devising in the absence of all external cues.

frequency Number of cycles that a wave completes in a given amount of time.

frontal lobe Cerebral cortex often generally characterized as performing the brain's "executive" functions, such as decision making, lying anterior to the central sulcus and beneath the frontal bone of the skull.

functional magnetic resonance imaging (fMRI) Magnetic resonance imaging in which changes in elements such as iron or oxygen are measured during the performance of a specific behavior; used to measure cerebral blood flow during behavior or resting.

gamma-aminobutyric acid (GABA) Amino acid neurotransmitter that inhibits neurons.

ganglia Collection of nerve cells that function somewhat like a brain.

gate Protein embedded in a cell membrane that allows substances to pass through the membrane on some occasions but not on others.

generalized anxiety disorder Persistently high levels of anxiety often accompanied by maladaptive behaviors to reduce anxiety; the disorder is thought to be caused by chronic stress.

geniculostriate system Projections from the retina to the lateral geniculate nucleus to the visual cortex.

glabrous skin Skin that does not have hair follicles but contains larger numbers of sensory receptors than do other skin areas.

glial cell Nervous-system cell that provides insulation, nutrients, and support and that aids in repairing neurons and eliminating waste products.

glioblast Product of a progenitor cell that gives rise to different types of glial cells.

glucocorticoid One of a group of steroid hormones, such as cortisol, secreted in times of stress; important in protein and carbohydrate metabolism.

glutamate (Glu) Amino acid neurotransmitter that excites neurons.

gonadal (sex) hormone One of a group of hormones, such as testosterone, that control reproductive functions and bestow sexual appearance and identity as male or female.

G protein Belongs to a family of guanyl-nucleotide-binding proteins coupled to metabotropic receptors that, when activated, bind to other proteins.

graded potential Small voltage fluctuation in the cell membrane restricted to the vicinity on the axon where ion concentrations change to cause a brief increase (hyperpolarization) or decrease (depolarization) in electrical charge across the cell membrane.

grand mal seizure Seizure characterized by loss of consciousness and stereotyped motor activity.

gray matter Areas of the nervous system composed predominantly of cell bodies and blood vessels that function either to collect and modify information or to support this activity.

growth cone Growing tip of an axon.

growth spurt Sproradic period of sudden growth that lasts for a finite time.

gyrus (pl. gyri) A small protrusion or bump formed by the folding of the cerebral cortex.

habituation Learning behavior in which a response to a stimulus weakens with repeated stimulus presentations.

hair cell Sensory neurons in the cochlea tipped by cilia; when stimulated by waves in the cochlear fluid, outer hair cells generate graded potentials in inner hair cells, which act as the auditory receptor cells.

hapsis Perceptual ability to discriminate objects on the basis of touch.

hemisphere Literally, half a sphere, referring to one side of the cerebral cortex or one side of the cerebellum.

hemispherectomy Surgical removal of a cerebral hemisphere.

hertz (Hz) Measure of frequency (repetition rate) of a sound wave; 1 hertz is equal to 1 cycle per second.

heterozygous Having two different alleles for the same trait.

hindbrain Evolutionarily the oldest part of the brain; contains the pons, medulla, reticular formation, and cerebellum structures that coordinate and control most voluntary and involuntary movements.

hippocampus Distinctive, three-layered subcortical structure of the limbic system lying in the medial region of the temporal lobe; plays a role in species-specific behaviors, memory, and spatial navigation and is vulnerable to the effects of stress.

histamine Neurotransmitter that controls arousal and waking; can cause the constriction of smooth muscles and so, when activated in allergic reactions, contributes to asthma, a constriction of the airways.

homeostatic hormone One of a group of hormones that maintain internal metabolic balance and regulate physiological systems in an organism.

homeostatic mechanism Process that maintains critical body functions within a narrow, fixed range.

hominid General term referring to primates that walk upright, including all forms of humans, living and extinct.

homonymous hemianopia Blindness of an entire left or right visual field.

homozygous Having two identical alleles for a trait.

homunculus Representation of the human body in the sensory or motor cortex; also any topographical representation of the body by a neural area.

HPA axis Hypothalamic-pituitary-adrenal circuit that controls the production and release of hormones related to stress.

Huntington's chorea Hereditary disease characterized by chorea (ceaseless, involuntary, jerky movements) and progressive dementia, ending in death.

hydrocephalus Buildup of pressure in the brain and, in infants, swelling of the head caused if the flow of cerebrospinal fluid is blocked; can result in retardation.

hyperkinetic symptom Symptom of brain damage that results in excessive involuntary movements, as seen in Tourette's syndrome.

hyperphagia Disorder in which an animal overeats, leading to significant weight gain.

hyperpolarization Increase in electrical charge across a membrane, usually due to the inward flow of chloride ions or the outward flow of potassium ions.

hypnogogic hallucination Dreamlike event at the beginning of sleep or while a person is in a state of cataplexy.

hypokinetic symptom Symptom of brain damage that results in a paucity of movement, as seen in Parkinson's disease.

hypothalamus Diencephalon structure that contains many nuclei associated with temperature regulation, eating, drinking, and sexual behavior.

hypovolumic thirst Thirst that is produced by a loss of overall fluid volume from the body.

idiopathic seizure Appears spontaneously and in the absence of other diseases of the central nervous system.

implicit memory Unconscious memory: subjects can demonstrate knowledge, such as a skill, conditioned response, or recalling events on prompting, but cannot explicitly retrieve the information.

imprinting Process that predisposes an animal to form an attachment to objects or animals at a critical period in development.

incentive salience Quality acquired by drug cues that become highly desired and sought-after incentives in their own right.

inhibition Decrease in the activity of a neuron or brain area.

inhibitory postsynaptic potential (IPSP) Brief hyperpolarization of a neuron membrane in response to stimulation, making the neuron less likely to produce an action potential.

innate releasing mechanism (IRM) Hypothetical mechanism that detects specific sensory stimuli and directs an organism to take a particular action.

insomnia Disorder of slow-wave sleep resulting in prolonged inability to sleep.

instrumental conditioning Learning procedure in which the consequences (such as obtaining a reward) of a particular behavior (such as pressing a bar) increase or decrease the probability of the behavior occurring again; also called operant conditioning.

insula Located within the lateral fissure, multifunctional cortical tissue that contains regions related to language, to the perception of taste, and to the neural structures underlying social cognition.

intelligence A Hebb's term for innate intellectual potential, which is highly heritable and cannot be measured directly.

intelligence B Hebb's term for observed intelligence, which is influenced by experience as well as other factors in the course of development and is measured by intelligence tests.

interneuron Association neuron interposed between a sensory neuron and a motor neuron; thus, in mammals, interneurons constitute most of the neurons of the brain.

ionotropic receptor Embedded membrane protein with two parts: a binding site for a neurotransmitter and a pore that regulates ion flow to directly and rapidly change membrane voltage.

ischemia Lack of blood to the brain as a result of stroke.

jet lag Fatigue and disorientation resulting from rapid travel through time zones and exposure to a changed light–dark cycle.

Klüver-Bucy syndrome Behavioral syndrome, characterized especially by hypersexuality, that results from bilateral injury to the temporal lobe.

Korsakoff's syndrome Permanent loss of the ability to learn new information (anterograde amnesia) and to retrieve old information (retrograde amnesia) caused by diencephalic damage resulting from chronic alcoholism or malnutrition that produces a vitamin B_1 deficiency.

lateralization Process whereby functions become localized primarily on one side of the brain.

law of Bell and Magendie The general principle that sensory fibers are located dorsally and motor fibers are located ventrally.

learned taste aversion Acquired association between a specific taste or odor and illness; leads to an aversion to foods that have the taste or odor.

learning set The "rules of the game"; implicit understanding of how a problem can be solved with a rule that can be applied in many different situations.

learning Relatively permanent change in behavior that results from experience.

Lewy body Circular fibrous structure found in several neurodegenerative disorders; forms within the cytoplasm of neurons and is thought to result from abnormal neurofilament metabolism.

light pollution Exposure to artifical light that changes activity patterns and so distrupts circadian rhythms.

limbic system Disparate forebrain structures lying between the neocortex and the brainstem that form a functional system controlling affective and motivated behaviors and certain forms of memory; includes cingulate cortex, amygdala, hippocampus, among other structures.

locked-in syndrome Lower brainstem damage that results in a fully conscious, alert, and responsive condition, but the patient is quadriplegic and mute.

long-term potentiation (LTP) In response to stimulation at a synapse, changed amplitude of an excitatory postsynaptic potential that lasts for hours to days or longer and plays a part in associative learning.

luminance contrast The amount of light reflected by an object relative to its surroundings.

magnetic resonance imaging (MRI) Technique that produces a static, three-dimensional brain image by passing a strong magnetic field through the brain, followed by a radio wave, then measuring the radiation emitted from hydrogen atoms.

magnetic resonance spectroscopy (MRS) Modification of MRI to identify changes in specific markers of neuronal function; promising for accurate diagnosis of traumatic brain injuries.

magnetoencephalogram (MEG) Magnetic potentials recorded from detectors placed outside the skull.

magnocellular (M) cell Large-celled visual-system neuron that is sensitive to moving stimuli.

major depression Mood disorder characterized by prolonged feelings of worthlessness and guilt, the disruption of normal eating habits, sleep disturbances, a general slowing of behavior, and frequent thoughts of suicide.

major tranquilizer (neuroleptic) Drug that blocks the D_2 receptor; used mainly for treating schizophrenia.

mania Disordered mental state of extreme excitement.

masculinization Process by which exposure to androgens (male sex hormones) alters the brain, rendering it identifiably male.

materialism Philosophical position that holds that behavior can be explained as a function of the nervous system without explanatory recourse to the mind.

medial forebrain bundle (MFB) Tract that connects structures in the brainstem with various parts of the limbic system; forms the activating projections that run from the brainstem to the basal ganglia and frontal cortex.

medial geniculate nucleus Major thalamic region concerned with audition.

medial pontine reticular formation (MPRF) Nucleus in the pons participating in REM sleep.

melatonin Hormone secreted by the pineal gland during the dark phase of the day–night cycle; influences daily and seasonal biorhythms.

memory The ability to recall or recognize previous experience.

meninges Three layers of protective tissue—dura mater, arachnoid, and pia mater—that encase the brain and spinal cord.

mentalism Of the mind; an explanation of behavior as a function of the nonmaterial mind.

metabotropic receptor Embedded membrane protein, with a binding site for a neurotransmitter but no pore, linked to a G protein that can affect other receptors or act with second messengers to affect other cellular processes.

microdialysis Technique used to determine the chemical constituents of extracellular fluid.

microelectrode A microscopic insulated wire or a salt-water-filled glass tube of which the uninsulated tip is used to stimulate or record from neurons.

microglia Glial cells that originate in the blood, aid in cell repair, and scavenge debris in the nervous system.

microsleep Brief period of sleep lasting a second or so.

midbrain Central part of the brain that contains neural circuits for hearing and seeing as well as orienting movements.

mind Proposed nonmaterial entity responsible for intelligence, attention, awareness, and consciousness.

mind–body problem Quandary of explaining a nonmaterial mind in command of a material body.

minimally conscious state (MCS) Condition in which a person can display some rudimentary behaviors, such as smiling, or utter a few words but is otherwise not conscious.

mirror neuron Cell in the primate premotor cortex that fires when an individual observes a specific action taken by another individual.

monoamine oxidase (MAO) inhibitor Antidepressant drug that blocks the enzyme monoamine oxidase from degrading neurotransmitters such as dopamine, noradrenaline, and serotonin.

monosynaptic reflex Reflex requiring one synapse between sensory input and movement.

mood stabilizer Drug for treatment of bipolar disorder that mutes the intensity of one pole of the disorder, thus making the other pole less likely to recur.

motivation Behavior that seems purposeful and goal-directed.

motor neuron Neuron that carries information from the brain and spinal cord to make muscles contract.

motor sequence Movement modules preprogrammed by the brain and produced as a unit.

multiple sclerosis (MS) Nervous-system disorder that results from the loss of myelin (glial-cell covering) around neurons.

mutation Alteration of an allele that yields a different version of that allele.

myelin Glial coating that surrounds axons in the central and peripheral nervous systems.

narcolepsy Slow-wave sleep disorder in which a person uncontrollably falls asleep at inappropriate times.

natural selection Darwin's theory for explaining how new species evolve and how existing species change over time. Differential success in the reproduction of different characteristics (phenotypes) results from the interaction of organisms with their environment.

near-infrared spectroscopy (NIRS) Noninvasive technique that gathers light transmitted through cortical tissue to image blood-oxygen consumption; form of optical tomography.

neocortex (cerebral cortex) Newest, outer layer (new bark) of the forebrain and composed of about six layers of gray matter that creates our reality.

neoteny Process in which maturation is delayed, and so an adult retains infant characteristics; idea derived from the observation that newly evolved species resemble the young of their common ancestors.

nerve Large collection of axons coursing together outside the central nervous system.

nerve growth factor (NGF) Neurotrophic factor that stimulates neurons to grow dendrites and synapses and, in some cases, promotes the survival of neurons.

nerve impulse Propagation of an action potential on the membrane of an axon.

nerve net Simple nervous system that has no brain or spinal cord but consists of neurons that receive sensory information and connect directly to other neurons that move muscles.

netrin Member of the only class of tropic molecules yet isolated.

neural Darwinism Hypothesis that the processes of cell death and synaptic pruning are, like natural selection in species, the outcome of competition among neurons for connections and metabolic resources in a neural environment.

neural plate Thickened region of the ectodermal layer that gives rise to the neural tube.

neural stem cell A self-renewing, multipotential cell that gives rise to any of the different types of neurons and glia in the nervous system.

neural tube Structure in the early stage of brain development from which the brain and spinal cord develop.

neuritic plaque Area of incomplete necrosis (dead tissue) consisting of a central protein core (amyloid) surrounded by degenerative cellular fragments; often seen in the cortex of people with senile dementias such as Alzheimer's disease.

neuroblast Product of a progenitor cell that gives rise to any of the different types of neurons.

neurocognitive enhancement Brain-function enhancement by pharmacological, physiological, or surgical manipulation.

neuron A specialized "nerve cell" engaged in information processing.

neuropeptide Multifunctional chain of amino acids that acts as a neurotransmitter; synthesized from mRNA on instructions from the cell's DNA; peptide neurotransmitters can act as a hormones and may contribute to learning.

neuroplasticity The nervous system's potential for physical or chemical change that enhances its adaptability to environmental change and its ability to compensate for injury.

neuroprotectant Drug used to try to block the cascade of poststroke neural events.

neuropsychoanalysis Movement within neuroscience and psychoanalysis to combine the insights of both to yield a unified understanding of mind and brain.

neuropsychology Study of the relations between brain function and behavior.

neurotransmitter Chemical released by a neuron onto a target with an excitatory or inhibitory effect.

neurotrophic factor A chemical compound that acts to support growth and differentiation in developing neurons and may act to keep certain neurons alive in adulthood.

nitric oxide (NO) Acts as a chemical neurotransmitter gas—for example, to dilate blood vessels, aid digestion, and activate cellular metabolism.

nocioception Perception of pain and temperature.

node of Ranvier The part of an axon that is not covered by myelin.

nonregulatory behavior Behavior unnecessay to the basic survival needs of the animal.

noradrenergic neuron From *adrenaline,* Latin for epinephrine; a neuron containing norepinephrine.

norepinephrine (NE, or noradrenaline) Neurotransmitter found in the brain and in the sympathetic division of the autonomic nervous system.

NREM (non-REM) sleep Slow-wave sleep associated with delta rhythms.

nucleus (pl. **nuclei**) A group of cells forming a cluster that can be identified with special stains to form a functional grouping.

obesity Excessive accumulation of body fat.

obsessive-compulsive disorder (OCD) Behavior disorder characterized by compulsively repeated acts (such as hand washing) and repetitive, often unpleasant, thoughts (obsessions).

occipital lobe Cerebral cortex where visual processing begins, lying at the back of the brain and beneath the occipital bone.

ocular-dominance column Functional column in the visual cortex maximally responsive to information coming from one eye.

oligodendroglia Glial cells in the central nervous system that myelinate axons.

opioid analgesic Drug like morphine, with sleep-inducing (narcotic) and pain-relieving (analgesic) properties; originally *narcotic analgesic.*

opponent-process theory Explanation of color vision that emphasizes the importance of the opposition of pairs of colors: red versus green and blue versus yellow.

optic ataxia Deficit in the visual control of reaching and other movements.

optic chiasm Junction of the optic nerves, one from each eye, at which the axons from the nasal (inside—nearer the nose) halves of the retinas cross to the opposite side of the brain.

optic flow Streaming of visual stimuli that accompanies an observer's forward movement through space.

orbitofrontal cortex Prefrontal cortex located behind the eye sockets (or orbits) that receives projections from the dorsomedial nucleus of the thalamus; plays a central role in a variety of emotional and social behaviors as well as in eating.

organizational hypothesis Proposal that actions of hormones in development alter tissue differentiation; for example, testosterone masculinizes the brain.

orienting movement Movement related to sensory inputs, such as turning the head to see the source of a sound.

oscilloscope Device that serves as a sensitive voltmeter by registering the flow of electrons to measure voltage.

osmotic thirst Thirst that results from an increased concentration of dissolved chemicals, or *solutes,* in body fluids.

ossicles Bones of the middle ear: malleus (hammer), incus (anvil), and stapes (stirrup).

pain gate Hypothetical neural circuit in which activity in fine-touch and pressure pathways diminishes the activity in pain and temperature pathways.

panic disorder Recurrent attacks of intense terror that come on without warning and without any apparent relation to external circumstances.

parahippocampal cortex Cortex located along the dorsal medial surface of the temporal lobe.

paralysis Loss of sensation and movement due to nervous-system injury.

paraplegia Paralysis of the legs due to spinal-cord injury.

parasympathetic division Part of the autonomic nervous system; acts in opposition to the sympathetic division—for example, preparing the body to rest and digest by reversing the alarm response or stimulating digestion.

parietal lobe Cerebral cortex that functions to direct movements toward a goal or to perform a task, such as grasping an object, lying posterior to the central sulcus and beneath the parietal bone at the top of the skull.

Parkinson's disease Disorder of the motor system correlated with a loss of dopamine in the brain and characterized by tremors, muscular rigidity, and a reduction in voluntary movement.

parvocellular (P) cell Small-celled visual-system neuron that is sensitive to form and color differences.

Pavlovian conditioning Learning procedure whereby a neutral stimulus (such as a tone) comes to elicit a response because of its repeated pairing with some event (such as the delivery of food); also called *classical conditioning* or *respondent conditioning.*

peptide hormone Chemical messenger synthesized by cellular DNA that acts to affect the target cell's physiology.

perception Subjective interpretation of sensations by the brain.

periaqueductal gray matter (PAG) Nuclei in the midbrain that surround the cerebral aqueduct joining the third and fourth ventricles; PAG neurons contain circuits for species-typical behaviors (e.g., female sexual behavior) and play an important role in the modulation of pain.

peribrachial area Cholinergic nucleus in the dorsal brainstem having a role in REM sleep behaviors; projects to medial pontine reticulum.

period Time required to complete a cycle of activity.

peripheral nervous system (PNS) All the neurons in the body located outside the brain and spinal cord; provides sensory and motor connections to and from the central nervous system.

perirhinal cortex Cortex lying next to the rhinal fissure on the base of the brain.

persistent vegetative state (PVS) Condition in which a person is alive but unable to communicate or to function independently at even the most basic level.

petit mal seizure Seizure of brief duration, characterized by loss of awareness with no motor activity except for blinking, turning the head, or rolling the eyes.

phenylketonuria (PKU) Behavioral disorder caused by elevated levels of the amino acid phenylalanine in the blood and resulting from a defect in the gene for the enzyme phenylalanine hydroxylase; the major symptom is severe mental retardation.

pheromone Odorant biochemical released by one animal that acts as a chemosignal and can affect the physiology or behavior of another animal.

phobia Fear of a clearly defined object or situation.

pituitary gland Endocrine gland attached to the bottom of the hypothalamus; its secretions control the activities of many other endocrine glands; known to be associated with biological rhythms.

place cell Hippocampal neuron maximally responsive to specific locations in the world.

positron emission tomography (PET) Imaging technique that detects changes in blood flow by measuring changes in the uptake of compounds such as oxygen or glucose; used to analyze the metabolic activity of neurons.

postictal depression Postseizure state of confusion and reduced affect.

postsynaptic membrane Membrane on the transmitter-input side of a synapse.

posttraumatic stress disorder (PTSD) Syndrome characterized by prolonged physiological arousal symptoms related to recurring memories and dreams linked to a traumatic event—for months or years after the event.

prefrontal cortex The cortex lying in front of the motor and premotor cortex of the frontal lobe; the prefrontal cortex is particularly large in the human brain.

preparedness Predisposition to respond to certain stimuli differently from other stimuli.

presynaptic membrane Membrane on the transmitter-output side of a synapse.

primary auditory cortex (area A1) Asymmetrical structures, found within Heschl's gyrus in the temporal lobes, that receive input from the ventral region of the medial geniculate nucleus.

primary visual cortex (V1) Striate cortex that receives input from the lateral geniculate nucleus.

priming Using a stimulus to sensitize the nervous system to a later presentation of the same or a similar stimulus.

procedural memory Ability to recall a movement sequence or how to perform some act or behavior.

progenitor cell Precursor cell derived from a stem cell; it migrates and produces a neuron or a glial cell.

proprioception Perception of the position and movement of the body, limbs, and head.

prosody Melodical tone of the spoken voice.

psyche Synonym for mind, an entity once proposed to be the source of human behavior.

psychedelic drug Drug that can alter sensation and perception; lysergic acid diethylmide, mescalin, and psilocybin are examples.

psychoactive drug Substance that acts to alter mood, thought, or behavior and is used to manage neuropsychological illness.

psychological construct Idea, resulting from a set of impressions, that some mental ability exists as an entity; examples include memory, language, and emotion.

psychomotor activation Increased behavioral and cognitive activity; at certain levels of consumption, the drug user feels energetic and in control.

psychopharmacology Study of how drugs affect the nervous system and behavior.

psychosurgery Any neurosurgical technique intended to alter behavior.

psychotherapy Talking therapy derived from Freudian psychoanalysis and other psychological interventions.

pump Protein in the cell membrane that actively transports a substance across the membrane.

Purkinje cell Distinctive interneuron found in the cerebellum.

pyramidal cell Distinctive interneuron found in the cerebral cortex.

quadrantanopia Blindness of one quadrant of the visual field.

quadriplegia Paralysis of the legs and arms due to spinal-cord injury.

quantum (pl. **quanta**) Quantity, equivalent to the contents of a single synaptic vesicle, that produces a just observable change in postsynaptic electric potential.

radial glial cell Path-making cell that a migrating neuron follows to its appropriate destination.

radiator hypothesis Idea that selection for improved brain cooling through increased blood circulation in the brains of early hominids enabled the brain to grow larger.

rapidly adapting receptor Body sensory receptor that responds briefly to the onset of a stimulus on the body.

rate-limiting factor Any enzyme that is in limited supply, thus restricting the pace at which a chemical can be synthesized.

real-time fMRI (rtfMRI) Technique for imaging the brain as behavior occurs.

receptive field Region of the visual world that stimulates a receptor cell or neuron.

referred pain Pain felt on the surface of the body that is actually due to pain in one of the internal organs of the body.

regulatory behavior Behavior motivated to meet the survival needs of the animal.

reinforcer In operant conditioning, any event that strengthens the behavior it follows.

relatively refractory Refers to the state of an axon in the later phase of an action potential during which increased electrical current is required to produce another action potential; a phase during which potassium channels are still open.

releasing hormones Peptides that are released by the hypothalamus and act to increase or decrease the release of hormones from the anterior pituitary.

REM sleep Fast brain-wave pattern displayed by the neocortical EEG record during sleep.

resting potential Electrical charge across the cell membrane in the absence of stimulation; a store of energy produced by a greater negative charge on the intracellular side relative to the extracellular side.

restraint-induced therapy Procedure in which restraint of a healthy limb forces a patient to use an impaired limb to enhance recovery of function.

reticular activating system (RAS) Large reticulum (mixture of cell nuclei and nerve fibers) that runs through the center of the brainstem; associated with sleep–wake behavior and behavioral arousal; often called the *reticular formation.*

reticular formation Midbrain area in which nuclei and fiber pathways are mixed, producing a netlike appearance; associated with sleep–wake behavior and behavioral arousal.

retina Light-sensitive surface at the back of the eye consisting of neurons and photoreceptor cells.

retinal ganglion cell (RGC) One of a group of retinal neurons with axons that give rise to the optic nerve.

retinohypothalamic pathway Neural route from a subset of cone receptors in the retina to the suprachiasmatic nucleus of the hypothalamus; allows light to entrain the rhythmic activity of the SCN.

retrograde amnesia Inability to remember events that took place before the onset of amnesia.

reuptake Deactivation of a neurotransmitter when membrane transporter proteins bring the transmitter back into the presynaptic axon terminal for subsequent reuse.

rod Photoreceptor specialized for functioning at low light levels.

saltatory conduction Propagation of an action potential at successive nodes of Ranvier; *saltatory* means "jumping" or "dancing."

schizophrenia Behavioral disorder characterized by delusions, hallucinations, disorganized speech, blunted emotion, agitation or immobility, and a host of associated symptoms.

Schwann cell Glial cell in the peripheral nervous system that forms the myelin on sensory and motor axons.

scotoma Small blind spot in the visual field caused by migraine or by a small lesion of the visual cortex.

scratch reflex Automatic response in which an animal's hind limb reaches to remove a stimulus from the surface of the body.

second messenger Chemical that carries a message to initiate a biochemical process when activated by a neurotransmitter (the first messenger).

second-generation antidepressant Drug whose action is similar to that of tricyclics (first-generation antidepressants) but more selective in its action on the serotonin reuptake transporter proteins; also called *atypical antidepressant.*

segmentation Division into a number of parts that are similar; refers to the idea that many animals, including vertebrates, are composed of similarly organized body segments.

selective serotonin reuptake inhibitor (SSRI) Tricyclic antidepressant drug that blocks the reuptake of serotonin into the presynaptic terminal.

sensation Registration of physical stimuli from the environment by the sensory organs.

sensitization Learning behavior in which the response to a stimulus strengthens with repeated presentations of that stimulus because the stimulus is novel or because the stimulus is stronger than normal—for example, after habituation has occurred.

sensory deprivation Experimental setup in which a subject is allowed only restricted sensory input; subjects generally have a low tolerance for deprivation and may even display hallucinations.

sensory neuron Neuron that carries incoming information from sensory receptors into the spinal cord and brain.

serotonin (5-HT) Amine neurotransmitter that plays a role in regulating mood and aggression, appetite and arousal, the perception of pain, and respiration.

sexual dimorphism Differential development of brain areas in the two sexes.

sexual identity A person's feeling of being either male or female.

sexual orientation A person's sexual attraction to the opposite sex or to the same sex or to both sexes.

sleep apnea Inability to breathe during sleep; person has to wake up to breathe.

sleep paralysis Inability to move during deep sleep owing to the brain's inhibition of motor neurons.

slowly adapting receptor Body sensory receptor that responds as long as a sensory stimulus is on the body.

slow-wave sleep NREM sleep.

small-molecule transmitter Belongs to a class of quick-acting neurotransmitters synthesized in the axon terminal from products derived from the diet.

somatic marker hypothesis Posits that "marker" signals arising from emotions and feelings act to guide behavior and decision making, usually in an unconscious process.

somatic nervous system (SNS) Part of the PNS that includes the cranial and spinal nerves to and from the muscles, joints, and skin that produce movement, transmit incoming sensory input, and inform the CNS about the position and movement of body parts.

somatosensory neuron Brain cell that brings sensory information from the body into the spinal cord.

sound wave Undulating displacement of molecules caused by changing pressure.

spatial summation Graded potentials that occur at approximately the same location and time on a membrane are summated.

species Group of organisms that can interbreed.
species-typical behavior Behavior that is characteristic of all members of a species.
spinal cord Part of the central nervous system encased within the vertebrae (spinal column) that provides most of the connections between the brain and the rest of the body.
split brain Surgical disconnection of the two hemispheres in which the corpus callosum is cut.
stereotaxic apparatus Surgical instrument that permits the researcher to target a specific part of the brain.
steroid hormone Fat-soluble chemical messenger synthesized from cholesterol.
storage granule Membranous compartment that holds several vesicles containing a neurotransmitter.
stretch-sensitive channel Ion channel on a tactile sensory neuron that activates in response to stretching of the membrane, initiating a nerve impulse.
striate cortex Primary visual cortex (V1) in the occipital lobe; its striped appearance when stained gives it this name.
striatum Caudate nucleus and putamen of the basal ganglia.
stroke Sudden appearance of neurological symptoms as a result of severe interruption of blood flow.
substance abuse Use of a drug for the psychological and behavioral changes that it produces aside from its therapeutic effects.
subventricular zone Lining of neural stem cells surrounding the ventricles in adults.
sudden infant death syndrome (SIDS) Unexplained death of a seemingly healthy infant less that 1 year old while asleep.
sulcus (pl. **sulci**) A groove in brain matter, usually a groove found in the neocortex or cerebellum.
supplementary speech area Speech-production region on the dorsal surface of the left frontal lobe.
suprachiasmatic nucleus (SCN) Main pacemaker of circadian rhythms located just above the optic chiasm.
Sympathetic division Part of the autonomic nervous system; arouses the body for action, such as mediating the involuntary fight-or-flight response to alarm by increasing heart rate and blood pressure.
symptomatic seizure Identified with a specific cause, such as infection, trauma, tumor, vascular malformation, toxic chemicals, very high fever, or other neurological disorders.
synapse Junction between one neuron and another neuron, usually between an end foot of the axon of one neuron and a dendritic spine of the other neuron.
synaptic cleft Gap that separates the presynaptic membrane from the postsynaptic membrane.
synaptic vesicle Organelle consisting of a membrane structure that encloses a quantum of neurotransmitter.
synesthesia Ability to perceive a stimulus of one sense as the sensation of a different sense, as when sound produces a sensation of color; literally, "feeling together."
syntax Ways in which words are put together to form phrases, clauses, or sentences; proposed to be a unique characteristic of human language.

tardive dyskinesia Inability to stop the tongue from moving; motor side effect of neuroleptic drugs.
Tay-Sachs disease Inherited birth defect caused by the loss of genes that encode the enzyme necessary for breaking down certain fatty substances; appears 4 to 6 months after birth and results in retardation, physical changes, and death by about age 5.
tectopulvinar system Projections from the retina to the superior colliculus to the pulvinar (thalamus) to the parietal and temporal visual areas.
tectum Roof (area above the ventricle) of the midbrain; its functions are sensory processing, particularly visual and auditory, and the production of orienting movements.
tegmentum Floor (area below the ventricle) of the midbrain; a collection of nuclei with movement-related, species-specific, and pain perception functions.
temporal lobe Cortex that functions in connection with hearing, language, and musical abilities and lies below the lateral fissure, beneath the temporal bone at the side of the skull.
temporal summation Graded potentials that occur at approximately the same time on a membrane are summated.
terminal button (end foot) Knob at the tip of an axon that conveys information to other neurons.
testosterone Sex hormone secreted by the testes and responsible for the distinguishing characteristics of the male.
thalamus Diencephalon structure through which information from all sensory systems is integrated and projected into the appropriate region of the neocortex.
threshold potential Voltage on a neural membrane at which an action potential is triggered by the opening of Na+ and K+ voltage-sensitive channels; about −50 millivolts relative to extracellular surround.
tolerance Decrease in response to a drug with the passage of time.
tonotopic representation Property of audition in which sound waves are processed in a systematic fashion from lower to higher frequencies.
topographic map Spatially organized neural representation of the external world.
topographic organization Neural spatial representation of the body or areas of the sensory world perceived by a sensory organ.
torpor Inactive condition resembling sleep but with a greater decline in body temperature.
Tourette's syndrome Disorder of the basal ganglia characterized by tics; involuntary vocalizations (including curse words and animal sounds); and odd, involuntary movements of the body, especially of the face and head.
tract Large collection of axons coursing together within the central nervous system.
transcranial magnetic stimulation (TMS) Procedure in which a magnetic coil is placed over the skull to stimulate the underlying brain; used either to induce behavior or to disrupt ongoing behavior.
transgenic animal Product of the genetic-engineering procedure of taking a gene from one species and introducing it into the genome of another species.
transmitter-activated receptor Protein that has a binding site for a specific neurotransmitter and is embedded in the membrane of a cell.
transmitter-sensitive channel Receptor complex that has both a receptor site for a chemical and a pore through which ions can flow.
transporter Protein molecule that pumps substances across a membrane.
traumatic brain injury (TBI) Damage to the brain that results from a blow to the head.
trichromatic theory Explanation of color vision based on the coding of three primary colors: red, green, and blue.
tricyclic antidepressant First-generation antidepressant drug with a chemical structure characterized by three rings that blocks serotonin reuptake transporter proteins.
tropic molecule Signaling molecule that attracts or repels growth cones.
tumor Mass of new tissue that grows uncontrolled and independent of surrounding structures.
type I schizophrenia Disorder characterized predominantly by positive symptoms (e.g., behavioral excesses such as hallucinations and agitated movements) likely due to a dopaminergic dysfunction and associated with acute onset, good prognosis, and a favorable response to neuroleptics.
type II schizophrenia Disorder characterized by negative symptoms (behavioral deficits) and associated with chronic affliction, poor prognosis, poor response to neuroleptics, cognitive impairments, enlarged ventricles, and cortical atrophy, particularly in the frontal cortex.

unconditioned response (UCR) In classical conditioning, the unlearned, naturally occurring response to the unconditioned stimulus, such as salivation when food is in the mouth.

unconditioned stimulus (UCS) A stimulus that unconditionally—naturally and automatically—triggers a response.

ventral spinothalamic tract Pathway from the spinal cord to the thalamus that carries information about pain and temperature.

ventricle One of four cavities in the brain that contain cerebrospinal fluid that cushions the brain and may play a role in maintaining brain metabolism.

ventrolateral thalamus Part of the thalamus that carries information about body senses to the somatosensory cortex.

vertebrae (sing. **vertebra**) The bones, or segments, that form the spinal column.

vestibular system Somatosensory system that comprises a set of receptors in each inner ear that respond to body position and to movement of the head.

visual field Region of the visual world that is seen by the eyes.

visual-form agnosia Inability to recognize objects or drawings of objects.

visuospatial memory Using visual information to recall an object's location in space.

voltage gradient Difference in charge between two regions that allows a flow of current if the two regions are connected.

voltage-sensitive channel Gated protein channel that opens or closes only at specific membrane voltages.

voltmeter Device that measures the flow and the strength of electrical voltage by recording the difference in electrical potential between two bodies.

wanting-and-liking theory When a drug is associated with certain cues, the cues themselves elicit desire for the drug; also called *incentive-sensitization theory.*

Wernicke's area Secondary auditory cortex (planum temporale) lying behind Heschl's gyrus at the rear of the left temporal lobe that regulates language comprehension; also called posterior speech zone.

white matter Areas of the nervous system rich in fat-sheathed neural axons that form the connections between brain cells.

wild type Refers to a normal (most common in a population) phenotype or genotype.

withdrawal symptom Physical and psychological behavior displayed by an addict when drug use ends.

zeitgeber Environmental event that entrains biological rhythms: a "time giver."

References

Chapter 1

Benitez-Burraco, A. (2007). The molecular bases of dyslexia. *Reviews of Neurology, 45,* 491–502.

Bronson, R. T. (1979). Brain weight–body weight scaling in dogs and cats. *Brain, Behavior and Evolution, 16,* 227–236.

Coren, S. (1994). *The intelligence of dogs.* Toronto: The Free Press.

Darwin, C. (1963). *On the origin of species by means of natural selection, or the preservation of favored races in the struggle for life.* New York: New American Library. (Original work published 1859.)

Darwin, C. (1965). *The expression of the emotions in man and animals.* Chicago: University of Chicago Press. (Original work published 1872.)

Descartes, R. (1972). *Treatise on man* (T. S. Hall, Trans.). Cambridge, MA: Harvard University Press. (Original work published 1664.)

Eibl-Eibesfeldt, I. (1970). *Ethology: The biology of behavior.* New York: Holt, Rinehart and Winston.

Falk, D. (2004). Hominid brain evolution: New century, new directions. *Collegium antroplogicum, 228* (Suppl. 2), 59–64.

Gardner, H. (2006). *Multiple intelligences: New horizons.* New York: Basic Books.

Gardner R. A., & Gardner B. T. (1969). Teaching sign language to a chimpanzee. *Science 165,* 664–672.

Geshwind, N., & Galaburda, A. M. (1985). *Cerebral lateralization.* Cambridge, MA: MIT Press.

Goodall, J. (1986). *The chimpanzees of Gombe.* Cambridge, MA: Harvard University Press.

Gordon, A. D., Nevell, L., & Wood, B. (2008). The *Homo floresiensis* cranium (LB1): Size, scaling, and early *Homo* affinities. *Proceedings of the National Academy of Sciences of the United States of America, 105,* 4650–4655.

Gould, S. J. (1981). *The mismeasure of man.* New York: Norton.

Hebb, D. O. (1949). *The organization of behavior: A neuropsychological theory.* New York: Wiley.

Heron, W. (1957). The pathology of boredom. *Scientific American, 196*(1), 52–56.

Iwaniuk, A. N., Lefebvre, L., & Wylie, D. R. W. (2006). Comparative morphology of the avian cerebellum III: Correlations with tool use. *Brain, Behavior and Evolution, 68,* 113.

Jacobson, E. (1932). Electrophysiology of mental activities. *American Journal of Psychology, 44,* 677–694.

Jerison, H. J. (1973). *The evolution of the brain and intelligence.* New York: Academic Press.

Johnson, D., & Blake, E. (1996). *From Lucy to language.* New York: Simon & Schuster.

Kolb, B., & Whishaw, I. Q. (2009). *Fundamentals of human neuropsychology* (6th ed.). New York: Worth Publishers.

Lewin, R. (1998). *The Origin of Modern Humans.* New York: Scientific American Library.

Linge, F. R. (1990). Faith, hope, and love: Nontraditional therapy in recovery from serious head injury, a personal account. *Canadian Journal of Psychology, 44,* 116–129.

Lorenz, K. Z. (1981). *The foundations of ethology.* New York: Springer Verlag.

Martin, R. D. (1990). *Primate origins and evolution: A phylogenetic reconstruction.* Princeton, NJ: Princeton University Press.

McKinney, M. L. (1998). The juvenilized ape myth: Our "overdeveloped" brain. *Bioscience, 48,* 109–116.

Milton, K. (2003). The critical role played by animal source foods in human *(Homo)* evolution. *Journal of Nutrition, 133* (Suppl. 2), 3886S–3892S.

Murdock, G. P. (1965). *Culture and society: Twenty-four essays.* Pittsburgh: University of Pittsburgh Press.

Parchman, T. L., & Benkman, C. W. (2008). The geographic selection mosaic for ponderosa pine and crossbills: a tale of two squirrels. *Evolution, 62,* 348–360.

Prinz, J. (2008). Is consciousness embodied? In P. Robbins and. M. Aydede (Eds.), *Cambridge Handbook of Situated Cognition.* Cambridge: Cambridge University Press.

Sarà, M., Sacco, S., Cipolla, F., Onorati, P., Scoppetta, C., Albertini, G., & Carolei, A. (2007). An unexpected recovery from permanent vegetative state. *Brain Injury, 21,* 101–103.

Savage-Rumbaugh, S. (1999). *Ape communication: Between a rock and a hard place* in *origins of language—What non-human primates can tell us.* School of American Research Press.

Schiff, N. D., & Fins, J. J. (2007). Deep brain stimulation and cognition: Moving from animal to patient. *Current Opinion in Neurology, 20,* 638–642.

Schuiling, G. A. (2005). On sexual behavior and sex-role reversal. *Journal of Psychosomatic and Obstetric Gynaecology, 26*(3), 217–223.

Stedman, H. H., Kozyak, B. W., Nelson, A., Thesier, D. M., Su, L. T., Low, D. W., Bridges, C. R., Shrager, J. B., Minugh-Purvis, N., & Mitchell, M. A. (2004). Myosin gene mutation correlates with anatomical changes in the human lineage. *Nature, 428,* 415–418.

Taglialatela, J. P., Savage-Rumbaugh, S., & Baker, L. A. (2003). Vocal production by a language-competent Pan paniscus. *International Journal of Primatology, 24,* 1–17.

Taglialatela, J. P., Russell, J. L., Schaeffer, J. A., & Hopkins, W. D. (2008). Communicative signaling activates "Broca's" homolog in chimpanzees. *Current Biology, 18,* 343–348.

Terkel, J. (1995). Cultural transmission in the black rat: Pinecone feeding. *Advances in the Study of Behavior, 24,* 119–154.

Van Meir, V., Pavlova, D. Verhoye, R., Pinxten R., Balthazart, J., Eens, M., & Van der Linden, A. (2006). In vivo MR imaging of the seasonal volumetric and functional plasticity of song control nuclei in relation to song output in a female songbird. *Neuroimage 31,* 981–992.

Weiner, J. (1995). *The beak of the finch.* New York: Vintage.

Wijdicks, E. F. (2006). Minimally conscious state vs. persistent vegetative state: The case of Terry (Wallis) vs. the case of Terri (Schiavo). *Mayo Clinic Proceedings, 81,* 1155–1158.

Wilson, E. O. (1980). *Sociobiology.* Cambridge, MA: Belknap Press of Harvard University Press.

Chapter 2

Axel, R. (1995). The molecular logic of smell. *Scientific American, 273*(4), 154–159.

Brodmann, K. (1909). *Vergleichende Lokalisationlehr der Grosshirnrinde in ihren Prinzipien dargestellt auf Grund des Zellenbaues.* Leipzig: J. A. Barth.

Chiu, D., Krieger, D., Villar-Cordova, C., Kasner, S. E., Morgenstern, L. B., Bratina, P. L., Yatsu, F. M., & Grotta, J. C. (1998). Intravenous tissue plasminogen activator for acute ischemic stroke: Feasibility, safety, and efficacy in the first year of clinical practice. *Stroke, 29,* 18–22.

Chklovskii, D. B., Schikorski, T., & Stevens, C. F. (2002). Wiring optimization in cortical circuits. *Neuron, 34,* 341–347.

Diamond, M. C., Scheibel, A. B., & Elson, L. M. (1985). *The human brain coloring book.* New York: Barnes & Noble.

Elliott, H. (1969). *Textbook of neuroanatomy.* Philadelphia: Lippincott.

Everett, N. B. (1965). *Functional neuroanatomy.* Philadelphia: Lea & Febiger.

Felleman, D. J., & van Essen, D. C. (1991). Distributed hierarchical processing in the primate cerebral cortex. *Cerebral Cortex, 1,* 1–47.

Frackowiak, R. S. J., Friston, K. J., Frith, C. D., Dolan, R. J., & Mazziotta, J. C. (1997). *Human brain function.* New York: Academic Press.

Hamilton, L. W. (1976). *Basic limbic system anatomy of the rat.* New York and London: Plenum.

Heimer, L. (1995). *The human brain and spinal cord: Functional neuroanatomy and dissection guide* (2d ed.). New York: Springer Verlag.

Herrick, C. J. (1926). *Brains of rats and men.* Chicago: University of Chicago Press.

Jerison, H. J. (1991). *Brain size and the evolution of mind.* New York: American Museum of Natural History.

Kandel, E. R., Schwartz, J. H., & Jessell, T. M. (Eds.). (1995). *Essentials of neural science and behavior.* East Norwalk, CT: Appleton & Lange.

Luria, A. R. (1973). *The working brain.* Harmondsworth, UK: Penguin.

Netter, F. H. (1962). *The Ciba collection of medical illustrations:* Vol. 1. *Nervous system.* New York: Ciba.

Papez, J. W. (1937). A proposed mechanism of emotion. *Archives of Neurology and Psychiatry, 38,* 724–744.

Passingham, R. (2008). *What is special about the human brain?* Oxford: Oxford University Press.

Penfield, W., & Jasper, H. H. (1954). *Epilepsy and the functional anatomy of the human brain.* Boston: Little, Brown.

Purves, D., Augustine, G. J., Fitzpatrick, D., Katz, L. C., LaMantia, A.-S., & McNamara, J. O. (1997). *Neuroscience.* Sunderland, MA: Sinauer.

Ranson, S. W., & Clark, S. L. (1959). *The anatomy of the nervous system.* Philadelphia: Saunders.

Salter, K. L., Teasell, R. W., Foley, N. C., & Jutai, J. W. (2007). Outcome assessment in randomized controlled trials for stroke rehabilitation. *American Journal of Physical and Medical Rehabilitation, 86,* 1007–1012.

Shepherd, G. M. (1990). *The synaptic organization of the brain* (3rd ed.). New York: Oxford University Press.

Sporns, O., Tononi, G., & Edelman, G. M. (2002). Theoretical neuroanatomy and the connectivity of cerebral cortex. *Behavioural Brain Research, 135,* 69–74.

Truex, R. C., & Carpenter, M. B. (1969). *Human neuroanatomy.* Baltimore: Williams & Wilkins.

Whiting, B. A., & Barton, R. A. (2003). The evolution of cortico-cerebellar complex in primates: Anatomical connections predict patterns of correlated evolution. *Journal of Human Evolution, 44,* 3–10.

Zeki, S. (1993). *A vision of the brain.* London: Blackwell Scientific.

Chapter 3

Adar, E., Nottebohm, E. F., & Barnea A. (2008). The relationship between nature of social change, age, and position of new neurons and their survival in adult zebra finch brain. *Journal of Neuroscience, 28,* 5394–5400.

Ashrafi, K., Chang, F. Y., Watts, J. L., Fraser, A. G., Kamath, R. S., Ahringer, J., & Ruvkun, G. (2003) Genome-wide RNAi analysis of *Caenorhabditis elegans* fat regulatory genes. *Nature, 421,* 268–272.

Balaban, E. (1997). Changes in multiple brain regions underlie species differences in a complex, congenital behavior. *Proceedings of the National Academy of Sciences of the United States of America, 94,* 2001–2006.

Eisener-Dorman, A. F., Lawrence, D. A., & Bolivar, V. J. (2008). Cautionary insights on knockout mouse studies: The gene or not the gene? *Brain, Behavior, and Immunity,* September 12 e-publication.

Karlsson, E. K., Baranowska, I., Wade, C. M., Salmon Hillbertz, N. H., Zody, M. C., et al. (2007). Efficient mapping of Mendelian traits in dogs through genome-wide association. *Nature Genetics, 39,* 1321–1328.

Livet, J., Weissman, T. A., Kang, H., Draft, R. W., Lu, J., Bennis, R. A., Sanes, J. A., & Lichtman, J. W. (2007). Transgenic strategies for combinatorial expression of fluorescent proteins in the nervous system. *Nature, 450,* 56–62.

Niemann, H., & Kues, W. A. (2007). Transgenic farm animals: An update. *Reproduction, Fertility, and Development, 19,* 762–770.

Parker, H. G., Kim, L. V., Sutter, N. B., Carlson, S., Lorentzen,T. D., Malek, T. B., Johnson, G. S., DeFrance, H. B., Ostrander, E. A., & Kruglyak, L. (2004). Genetic structure of the purebred domestic dog. *Science, 304,* 1160–1164.

Ramón y Cajal, S. (1909–1911). *Histologie du système nerveux de l'homme et des vertébrés.* Paris: Maloine.

Reeve, R., van Schaik, A., Jin, C., Hamilton, T., Torben-Neilsen, B., & Webb, B. (2007). Directional hearing in a silicon cricket. *Biosystems, 87,* 307–313.

Riva, G., Gaggioli, A., & Mantovani, F. (2008). Are robots present? From motor simulation to "being there." *Cyberpsychology and Behaviour, 11,* 631–636.

van Dellen, A., Cordery, P. M., Spires, T. L., Blakemore, C., & Hannan, A. J. (2008). Wheel running from a juvenile age delays onset of specific motor deficits but does not alter protein aggregate density in a mouse model of Huntington's disease. *BMC Neuroscience, 9,* 34.

Wahlsten, D., & Ozaki, H. S. (1994). Defects of the fetal forebrain in acallosal mice. In M. Lassonde & M. A. Jeeves (Eds.), *Callosal agenesis* (pp. 125–132). New York: Plenum.

Webb, B. (1996). A cricket robot. *Scientific American, 275*(6), 94–99.

Chapter 4

Bartholow, R. (1874). Experimental investigation into the functions of the human brain. *American Journal of Medical Sciences, 67,* 305–313.

Bi, A., Cui, J., Ma, Y. P., Olshevskaya, E., Pu, M., Dizhoor, A. M., & Pan, Z. H. (2006). Ectopic expression of a microbial-type rhodopsin restores visual responses in mice with photoreceptor degeneration. *Neuron, 6,* 23–33.

Descartes, R. (1972). *Treatise on man* (T. S. Hall, Trans.). Cambridge, MA: Harvard University Press. (Original work published 1664.)

Eccles, J. (1965). The synapse. *Scientific American, 21*(1), 56–66.

Hodgkin, A. L., & Huxley, A. F. (1939). Action potentials recorded from inside nerve fiber. *Nature, 144,* 710–711.

Jiang, Y., Ruta, V., Chen, J., Lee, A., & MacKinnon, R. (2003). The principle of gating charge movement in a voltage-dependent K^+ channel. *Nature, 423,* 42–48.

Liewald, J. F., Brauner, M., Stephens, G. J., Bouhours, M., Schultheis, C., Xhen, M., & Gottschalk, A. (2008). Optogenetic analysis of synaptic function. *Nature Methods, 10,* 895–902.

Nagel, G., Brauner, M., Liewald, J., Adeishvili, N., Bamberg, E., & Gottschalk, A. (2005). Light-activation of channel rhodopsin-2 in excitable cells of *Caenorhabditis elegans* triggers rapid behavioral responses. *Current Biology, 15,* 2279–2284.

Penfield, W., & Jasper, H. H. (1954). *Epilepsy and the functional anatomy of the human brain.* Boston: Little, Brown.

Posner, M. I., & Raichle, M. E. (1994). *Images of mind.* New York: W. H. Freeman and Company.

Ranck, J. B. (1973). Studies on single neurons in dorsal hippocampal formation and septum in unrestrained rats I: Behavioral correlates and firing repertoires. *Experimental Neurology, 41,* 461–531.

Ruta, V., Jiang, Y., Lee, A., Chen, J., & MacKinnon, R. (2003). Functional analysis of an archaebacterial voltage-dependent K^+ channel. *Nature, 422,* 180–185.

Siddique, N., & Siddique, T. (2008). Genetics of amyotrophic lateral sclerosis. *Physical Medicine and Rehabilibation and Clinical Neuroscience, 19,* 429–439.

Valenstein, E. S. (1973). *Brain control.* New York: Wiley.

Zhang, F., Aravanis, A. M., Adamantidis, A., de Lecea, L., & Deisseroth, K. (2007). Circuit-breakers: Optical technologies for probing neural signals and systems. *Nature Reviews Neuroscience, 8,* 577–581.

Chapter 5

Bailey, C. H., & Chen, M. (1989). Time course of structural changes at identified sensory neuron synapses during long-term sensitization in *Aplysia. Journal of Neuroscience, 9,* 1774–1780.

Ballard, A., Tetrud, J. W., & Langston, J. W. (1985). Permanent human Parkinsonism due to 1-methyl-4-phenyl-1,2,3,6-tetrahydropyridine (MPTP). *Neurology, 35,* 949–956.

Barbeau, A., Murphy, G. F., & Sourkes, T. L. (1961). Les catecholamines dans la maladie de Parkinson. Bel-Air Symposium on Monoamines and the Central Nervous System, Georg et Cie, Geneva.

Birkmayer, W., & Hornykiewicz, O. (1961). Der L-3,4-Dioxyphenylalanin (L-DOPA) Effekt bei der Parkinson A Kinase. *Wiener Klinische, 73,* 787–789.

Bliss, T. V. P., & Lømø, T. (1973). Long lasting potentiation of synaptic transmission in the dentate area of the anesthetized rabbit following stimulation of the perforant path. *Journal of Physiology (London), 232,* 331–356.

Cooper, J. R., Bloom, F. E., & Roth, R. H. (1991). *The biochemical basis of neuropharmacology.* New York: Oxford University Press.

Debello, W.M. (2008) Micro-rewiring as a substrate for learning. *Trends in Neurosciences, 31,* 577–584.

Ehringer, H., & Hornykiewicz, O. (1960/1974). Distribution of noradrenaline and dopamine (3-hydroxytyramine) in the human brain and their behavior in the presence of disease affecting the extrapyramidal system. In J. Marks (Ed.), *The treatment of Parkinsonism with L-dopa* (pp. 45–56). Lancaster, UK: MTP Medical and Technical Publishing.

Engert, F., & Bonhoeffer, T. (1999). Dendritic spine changes associated with hippocampal long-term synaptic plasticity. *Nature, 399,* 66–70.

Galef, B. G., Jr., Attenborough, K. S., & Wishin, E. E. (1990). Responses of observer rats *(Rattus norvegicus)* to complex, diet-related signals emmitted by demonstrator rats. *Journal of Comparative Psychology, 104,* 11–19.

Hebb, D. O. (1949). *The organization of behavior.* New York: Wiley.

Kandel, E. R. (2007). *In search of memory: The emergence of a new science of mind.* New York: Norton.

Kandel, E. R., Schwartz, J. H., & T. M. Jessell (Eds.). (2000). *Principles of neural science* (4th ed.). New York: McGraw-Hill.

Katz, B. (1970). On the quantal mechanism of neural transmitter release. In *Nobel Lectures, Physiology or Medicine 1963–1970* (pp. 485–492). Amsterdam; Elsevier.

Langston, J. W. (2008). *The case of the frozen addicts.* Pantheon Books, 1995. Original from the University of Michigan, digitized August 5, 2008.

Miniaci, M. C., Kim, J. H., Puthanveettil, S. V., Si, K., Zhu, H., Kandel, E. R., & Bailey, C. H. (2008). Sustained CPEB-dependent local protein synthesis is required to stabilize synaptic growth for persistence of long-term facilitation in *Aplysia. Neuron, 59,* 1024–1036.

Parkinson, J. (1817/1989). An essay on the shaking palsy. In A. D. Morris & F. C. Rose (Eds.), *James Parkinson: His life and times* (pp. 151–175). Boston: Birkhauser.

Sacks, O. (1976). *Awakenings.* New York: Doubleday.

Tréatikoff, C. (1974). Thesis for doctorate in medicine, 1919. In J. Marks (Ed.), *The treatment of Parkinsonism with L-dopa* (pp. 29–38). Lancaster, UK: MTP Medical and Technical Publishing.

Ungerstedt, U. (1971). Adipsia and aphagia after 6-hydroxydopamine induced degeneration of the nigrostriatal dopamine system in the rat brain. *Acta Physiologica (Scandinavia), 82* (Suppl. 367), 95–122.

Widner, H., Tetrud, J., Rehngrona, S., Snow, B., Brundin, P., Gustavii, B., Bjorklund, A., Lindvall, O., & Langston, J. W. (1992). Bilateral fetal mesencephalic grafting in two patients with Parkinsonism induced by 1-methyl-4-phenyl-1,2,3,6-tetrahydropyridine (MPTP). *New England Journal of Medicine, 327,* 1556–1563.

Chapter 6

Bueller, J. A., Aftab, M., Sen, S., Gomez-Hassan, D. Burmeister, M., & Zubieta, J.-K. (2006). BDNF Val66Met allele is associated with reduced hippocampal volume in healthy subjects. *Biological Psychiatry, 59,* 812–815.

Cacucci, F., Yi, M., Wills, T. J., Chapmans, P., & O'Keefe, J. (2008). Place cell firing correlates with memory deficits and amyloid plaque burden in Tg2576

Alzheimer mouse model. *Proceedings of the National Academy of Sciences (USA), 105,* 7863–7868.

Caspi, A., Moffitt, T. E., Cannon, M., McClay, J., Murray, R., Harrington, H., Taylor, A., Arseneault, L., Williams, B., Braithwaite, A., Poulton, R., & Craig, I. W. (2005). Moderation of the effect of adolescent-onset cannabis use on adult psychosis by a functional polymorphism in the catechol-O-methyltransferase gene: longitudinal evidence of a gene X environment interaction. *Biological Psychiatry, 57,* 1117–1127.

Chamberlain, S. R., Robbins, T. W., & Sahakian, B. J. (2007). The neurobiology of attention-deficit/hyperactivity disorder. *Biological Psychiatry, 61,* 1317–1319.

Damasio, H., & Damasio, A. R. (1989). *Lesion analysis in neuropsychology.* New York: Oxford University Press.

Faraone, S. V., Segeant, J., Gillberg, C., & Biederman, J. (2003). The worldwide prevalence of ADHD: is it an American condition? *World Psychiatry, 2,* 104–113.

Fox, P. T., and Raichle, M. E. (1986). Focal physiological uncoupling of cerebral blood flow and oxidative metabolism during somatosensory stimulation in human subjects. *Proceedings of the National Academy of Sciences (USA), 83,* 1140–1144.

Fraga, M. F., Ballestar, E., Paz, M. F., Ropero, S., Setien, F., Ballestar, M. L., et al. (2005). Epigenetic differences arise during the lifetime of monozygotic twins. *Proceedings of the National Academy of Sciences (USA), 102,* 10604–10609.

Gonzalez, C. L. R., Gharbawie, O. A., & Kolb, B. (2006). Chronic low-dose administration of nicotine facilitates recovery and synaptic change after focal ischemia in rats. *Neuropharmacology, 50,* 777–787.

Hoshi, Y. (2007) Functional near-infrared spectroscopy: current status and future prospects. *Journal of Biomedical Optics, 12,* 062106-1–062106-9.

Kolb, B., & Walkey, J. (1987). Behavioural and anatomical studies of the posterior parietal cortex of the rat. *Behavioural Brain Research, 23,* 127–145.

Kwong, K. K., et al. (1992). Dynamic magnetic resonance imaging of human brain activity during primary sensory stimulation. *Proceedings of the National Academy of Sciences (USA), 89,* 5678.

McGowan, P. O., Sasaki, A., D'Alessio, A. C., Dymov, S., Labonté, B., Szyf, M., Turecki, G., & Meaney, M. J. (2009). Epigenetic regulation of ghe glucocorticoid receptor in human brain associates with childhood abuse. *Nature Neuroscience, 12,* 342–348.

Morris, R. G. M. (1981) Spatial localization does not require the presence of local cues. *Learning and Motivation, 12,* 239–260.

National Research Council (1996). *The guide for the care and use of laboratory animals.* Washington, DC: National Academy Press.

Ogawa, S., Lee, T. M., Kay, A. R., & Tank, D. W. (1990). Brain magnetic resonance imaging with contrast dependent on blood oxygenation. *Proceedings of the National Academy of Sciences (USA), 87,* 9868–9872.

O'Keefe, J., & Dostrovksy, J. (1971). The hippocampus as a spatial map. *Brain Research, 34,* 171–175.

Penfield, W., & Jasper, H. H. (1954). *Epilepsy and the functional anatomy of the human brain.* Boston: Little, Brown.

Posner, M. I., & Raichle, M. E. (1997). *Images of mind.* New York: W. H. Freeman and Company.

Reza, M. F., Ikoma, K., Ito, T, Ogawa, T., & Mano, Y. (2007). N200 latency and P300 amplitude in depressed mood post-traumatic brain injury patients. *Neuropsychological Rehabilitation, 17,* 723–734.

Schallert, T., Whishaw, I. Q., Ramirez, V. D., & Teitelbaum, P. (1978). Compulsive, abnormal walking caused by anticholinergics in akinetic, 6-hydroxydopamine-treated rats. *Science, 199,* 1461–1463.

Scoville, W. B., & Milner, B. (1957). Loss of recent memory after bilateral hippocampal lesions. *Journal of Neurology, Neurosurgery, and Psychiatry, 20,* 11–21.

Spinney, L. (2005) Optical topography and the color of blood. *The Scientist, 19,* 25–27.

Sullivan, R. M., and Brake, W. G. (2003). What the rodent prefrontal cortex can tell us about attention deficit/hyperactive disorder: The critical role of early developmental events on prefrontal function. *Behavioural Brain Research, 146:* 43–55.

Szyf, M., McGowan, P., & Meaney, M. J. (2008). The social environment and the epigenome. *Environmental Molecular Mutagenetics, 49,* 46–60.

Taga, G., Asakawa, K., Maki, A., Konishi, Y., & Koizumi, H. (2003). Brain imaging in awake infants by near-infrared optical topography. *Proceedings of the National Academy of Sciences (USA), 100,* 10722–10777.

Tisdall, M. M., & Smith, M. (2006). Cerebral microdialysis: research technique or clinical tool. *British Journal of Anaesthesia, 97,* 18–25.

Watanabe, H., Homae, F., Nakano, T., & Taga, G. (2008). Functional activation in diverse regions of the developing brain in infants. *NeuroImage, 43,* 346–357.

Whishaw, I. Q. (1989). Dissociating performance and learning deficits in spatial navigation tasks in rats subjected to cholinergic muscarinic blockade. *Brain Research Bulletin, 23,* 347–358.

Whishaw, I. Q., & Kolb, B. (2005). *The behavior of the laboratory rat.* New York: Oxford University Press.

Chapter 7

Agate, R. J., Grisham, W., Wade, J., Mann, S., Wingfield, J., Schanen, C., Palotie, A., & Arnold, A. P. (2003). Neural, but not gonadal, origin of brain sex differences in a gynandromorphic finch. *Proceedings of the National Academy of Sciences of the United States of America, 100,* 4873–4878.

Ames, E. W. (1997). The development of Romanian orphanage children adopted to Canada. Final report to Human Resources Development, Canada.

Audero, E., Coppi, E., Mlinar, B., Rossetti, T., Caprioli, A., Banchaabouchi, A., Corradetti, R., & Gross, C. (2008). Sporadice autonomic dysregulation and death associated with excessive serontonin autoinhibition. *Science, 321,* 130–133.

Bourgeois, J.-P. (2001). Synaptogenesis in the neocortex of the newborn: The ultimate frontier for individuation? In Nelson, C. A,. & Luciaa, M., *Handbook of Developmental Cognitive Neuroscience.* Cambridge, MA: MIT Press.

Bunney, B. G., Potkin, S. G., & Bunney, W. E. (1997). Neuropathological studies of brain tissue in schizophrenia. *Journal of Psychiatric Research, 31,* 159–173.

Changeux, J.-P., & Danchin, A. (1976). Selective stabilization of developing synapses as a mechanism for the specification of neuronal networks. *Nature, 264,* 705–712.

Clarke, R. S., Heron, W., Fetherstonhaugh, M. L., Forgays, D. G., & Hebb, D. O. (1951). Individual differences in dogs. Preliminary report on the effects of early experience. *Canadian Journal of Psychology, 5*(4), 150–156.

Cowan, W. M. (1979). The development of the brain. *Scientific American, 241*(3), 116.

Curtis, S. (1978). *Genie: A psycholinguistic study of a modern-day "wild-child."* New York: Academic Press.

Edelman, G. M. (1987). *Neural darwinism: The theory of neuronal group selection.* New York: Basic Books.

Epstein, H. T. (1979). Correlated brain and intelligence development in humans. In M. E. Hahn, C. Jensen, & B. C. Dudek (Eds.), *Development and evolution of brain size: Behavioral implications* (pp. 111–131). New York: Academic Press.

Gershon, E. S., & Rieder, R. O. (1992). Major disorders of mind and brain. *Scientific American, 267*(3), 126–133.

Giussani, C., Roux, F. E., Lubrano, V., Gaini, S. M., & Bello, L. (2007). Review of language organization in bilingual patients: What can we learn from direct brain mapping? *Acta Neurochir (Wien), 149,* 1109–1116.

Goldstein, J. M., Seidman, L. J., Horton, N. J., Makris, N., Kennedy, D. N., Caviness, V. S., Jr., Faraone, S. V., & Tsuang, M. T. (2001). Normal sexual dimorphism of the adult human brain assessed by in vivo magnetic resonance imaging. *Cerebral Cortex, 11,* 490–497.

Guerrini, R., Dobyns, W. B., & Barkovich, A. J. (2007). Abnormal dvelopment of the human cerebral cortex: Genetics, functional consequences and treatment options. *Trends in Neurosciences, 31,* 154–162.

Halliwell, C., Comeau, W., Gibb, R., Frost, D. O., & Kolb, B. (2009). Factors influencing frontal cortex development and recovery from early frontal injury. In press.

Harlow, H. F. (1971). *Learning to love.* San Francisco: Albion.

Hebb, D. O. (1947). The effects of early experience on problem solving at maturity. *American Psychologist, 2,* 737–745.

Horn, G., Bradley, P., & McCabe, B. J. (1985). Changes in the structure of synapses associated with learning. *Journal of Neuroscience, 5,* 3161–3168.

Huttenlocher, P. R. (1994). Synaptogenesis in human cerebral cortex. In G. Dawson & K. W. Fischer (Eds.), *Human behavior and the developing brain* (pp. 137–152). New York: Guilford Press.

Juraska, J. M. (1990). The structure of the cerebral cortex: Effects of gender and the environment. In B. Kolb & R. Tees (Eds.), *The cerebral cortex of the rat* (pp. 483–506). Cambridge, MA: MIT Press.

Klein, D., Watkins, K. E., Zatorre, R. J., & Milner, B. (2006). Word and nonword repetition in bilingual subjects: A PET study. *Human Brain Mapping, 27,* 153–161.

Kolb, B., & Fantie, B. (2008). Development of the child's brain and behavior. In C. R. Reynolds & E. Fletcher-Janzen (Eds.), *Handbook of clinical child neuropsychology* (3rd ed., pp. 17–41). New York: Plenum.

Kolb, B., Forgie, M., Gibb, R., Gorny, G., & Rowntree, S. (1998). Age, experience, and the changing brain. *Neuroscience and Biobehavioral Reviews, 22,* 143–159.

Kolb, B., & Gibb, R. (1993). Possible anatomical basis of recovery of function after neonatal frontal lesions in rats. *Behavioral Neuroscience, 107,* 799–811.

Kolb, B., & Whishaw, I. Q. (1998). Brain plasticity and behavior. *Annual Review of Psychology, 49,* 43–64.

Kovelman, J. A., & Scheibel, A. B. (1984). A neurohistologic correlate of schizophrenia. *Biological Psychiatry, 19,* 1601–1621.

Lenneberg, E. H. (1967). *Biological foundations of language.* New York: Wiley.

Lenroot, R. K., Gogtay, N., Greenstein, D. K., et al. (2007). Sexual dimorphism of brain development trajectories during childhood and adolescence. *NeuroImage, 36,* 1065–1073.

Lorenz, K. (1970). *Studies on animal and human behavior* (Vols. 1 and 2). Cambridge, MA: Harvard University Press.

Lu, L. H., Leonard, C. M., Thompson, P. M., Kan, E., Jolley, J., Welcome, S. E., Toga, A. W., & Sowell, E. R. (2007). Normal developmental changes in inferior frontal gray matter are associated with improvement in phonological processing: A longitudinal MRI analysis. *Cerebral Cortex 17,* 1092–1099.

Malanga, C. J., & Kosofsky, B. E. (2003). Does drug abuse beget drug abuse? Behavioral analysis of addiction liability in animal models of prenatal drug exposure. *Developmental Brain Research, 147,* 47–57.

Marin-Padilla, M. (1988). Early ontogenesis of the human cerebral cortex. In A. Peters & E. G. Jones (Eds.), *Cerebral cortex,* Vol. 7: *Development and maturation of the cerebral cortex* (pp.1–34). New York: Plenum.

Marin-Padilla, M. (1993). Pathogenesis of late-acquired leptomeningeal heterotopias and secondary cortical alterations: A Golgi study. In A. M. Galaburda (Ed.), *Dyslexia and development: Neurobiological aspects of extraordinary brains* (pp. 64–88). Cambridge, MA: Harvard University Press.

Marshall, P. J., Reeb, .C., Fox, N. A., Nelson, C. A., & Zeanah, C. H. (2008). Effects of early intervention on EEG power and coherence in previously institutionalized children in Romania. *Developmental Psychopathology, 20,* 861–880.

Michel, G. F., & Moore, C. L. (1995). *Developmental psychobiology.* Cambridge, MA: MIT Press.

Moore, K. L. (1988). *The developing human: Clinically oriented embryology* (4th ed.). Philadelphia: Saunders.

Myers, D. G. (2010). *Psychology* (9th ed.). New York: Worth Publishers.

National Institute on Drug Abuse. (1995). NIDA survey provides first national data on drug use during pregnancy. *NIDA Research Findings, 10*(1), 1–2.

National Institute on Drug Abuse. (1998). Research report series: Nicotine addiction (pp. 1–8). NIH Publ. 01-4342.

National Institute on Drug Abuse. (1999). Prenatal cocaine exposure costs at least $352 million per year. *NIDA Research Findings, 13*(5), 1–2.

Nelson, C. A., Zeanah, C. H., Fox, N. A., Marshall, P. J., Smyke, A. T., & Guthrie, D. (2007). Cognitive recovery in socially deprived young children: The Bucharest Early Intervention Project. *Science, 318,* 1937–1940.

Nelson, C. A., & Luciana, M. (Eds.) (2008). *Handbook of developmental cognitive neuroscience,* 2nd ed. Cambridge, MA: MIT Press.

O'Hare, E. D., & Sowell, E. R. (2008). Imaging developmental changes in gray and white matter in the human brain. In C. A. Nelson and M. Luciana (Eds.), *Handbook of developmental cognitive neuroscience* (pp. 23–38), Cambridge, MA: MIT Press.

Overman, W., Bachevalier, J., Schuhmann, E., & Ryan, P. (1996). Cognitive gender differences in very young children parallel biologically based cognitive gender differences in monkeys. *Behavioral Neuroscience, 110,* 673–684.

Overman, W., Bachevalier, J., Turner, M., & Peuster, A. (1992). Object recognition versus object discrimination: Comparison between human infants and infant monkeys. *Behavioral Neuroscience, 106,* 15–29.

Paterson, D. S., Trachtenberg, F. L., Thompson, E. G., Belliveau, R. A., Beggs, A. H., Dranall, R., Chadwick, A. E., Krous, H. F., & Kinney, H. C. (2006). Multiple serotonergic brainstem abnormalities in sudden infant death syndrome. *Journal of the American Medical Association, 296,* 2124–2132.

Payne, B. R., & Lomber, S. G. (2001). Reconstructing functional systems after lesions of cerebral cortex. *Nature Reviews Neuroscience, 2,* 911–919.

Piaget, J. (1952). *The origins of intelligence in children.* New York: Norton.

Purpura, D. P. (1974). Dendritic spine "dysgenesis" and mental retardation. *Science, 186,* 1126–1127.

Rakic, P. (1974). Neurons in rhesus monkey cerebral cortex: Systematic relation between time of origin and eventual disposition. *Science, 183,* 425.

Rakic, P. (1995). Corticogenesis in human and nonhuman primates. In M. Gazzaniga (Ed.), *The cognitive neurosciences* (pp. 127–145). Cambridge, MA: MIT Press.

Riesen, A. H. (1982). Effects of environments on development in sensory systems. In W. D. Neff (Ed.), *Contributions to sensory physiology* (Vol. 6, pp. 45–77). New York: Academic Press.

Rutter, M. (1998). Developmental catch-up, and deficit, following adoption after severe global early privation. *Journal of Child Psychology and Psychiatry, 39,* 465–476.

Salm, A. K., Pavelko, M., Drouse, E. M., Webster, W., Kraszpulski, M., & Birkle, D. L. (2004). Lateral amygdala nucleus expansion in adult rats is associated with exposure to prenatal stress. *Developmental Brain Research, 148,* 159–167.

Shingo, T., Gregg, C., Enwere, E., Fujikawa, H., Hassam, R., Geary, C., Cross, J. C., & Weiss, S. (2003). Pregnancy-stimulated neurogenesis in the adult female forebrain mediated by prolactin. *Science, 299,* 117–120.

Sodhi, M. S., & Sanders-Bush, E. (2004). Serotonin and brain development. *International Review of Neurobiology, 59,* 111–174.

Sowell, E. R., Thompson, P. M., Leonard, C. M., Welcome, S. E., Kan, E., & Toga, A. W. (2004). Longitudinal mapping of cortical thickness and brain growth in normal children. *Journal of Neuroscience, 24,* 8223–8231.

Sowell, E. R., Thompson, P. M., & Toga, A.W. (2004). Mapping changes in the human cortex throughout the span of life. *The Neuroscientist, 10,* 372–392.

Sperry, R. W. (1963). Chemoaffinity in the orderly growth of nerve fiber patterns and connections. *Proceedings of the National Academy of Sciences of the United States of America, 50,* 703–710.

Stevens, H., Leckman, J., Coplan, J., & Suomi, S. (2009). Risk and resilience: Early manipulation of macaque social experience and persistent behavioral and neurophysiological outcomes. *Journal of the American Academy of Child and Adolescent Psychiatry,* in press.

Twitchell, T. E. (1965). The automatic grasping response of infants. *Neuropsychologia, 3,* 247–259.

Wallace, P. S., & Whishaw, I. Q. (2003). Independent digit movements and precision grip patterns in 1–5-month-old human infants: Hand-babbling, including vacuous than self-directed hand and digit movements, precedes targeted reaching. *Neuropsychologia, 41,* 1912–1918.

Weiss, S., Reynolds, B. A., Vescovi, A. L., Morshead, C., Craig, C. G., & van der Kooy, D. (1996). Is there a neural stem cell in the mammalian forebrain? *Trends in Neurosciences, 19*(9), 387–393.

Werker, J. F., & Tees, R. C. (1992). The organization and reorganization of human speech perception. *Annual Review of Neuroscience, 15,* 377–402.

Wiesel, T. N. (1982). Postnatal development of the visual cortex and the influence of environment. *Nature, 299,* 583–591.

Yakovlev, P. E., & Lecours, A.-R. (1967). The myelogenetic cycles of regional maturation of the brain. In A. Minkowski (Ed.), *Regional development of the brain in early life.* Oxford: Blackwell.

Chapter 8

Becker, J. B., & Hu, M. (2008). Sex differences in drug abuse. *Frontiers in Neuroendocrinology, 29*(1), 36–47.

Becker, J. B., Breedlove, S. M., Crews, D., & McCarthy, M. M. (2002). *Behavioral endocrinology* (2nd ed.). Cambridge, MA: Bradford.

Bremner, J. D., Elzinga, B., Schmahl, C., & Vermetten, E. (2008). Structural and functional plasticity of the human brain in posttraumatic stress disorder. *Progress in Brain Research, 167,* 171–186.

Brody, G. H., Beach, S. R. H., Philibert, R. A., Chen, Y., Lei, M.-K., Murry, V. McBride, R., & Brown, A. C. (2009). Parenting moderates a genetic vulnerability factor in longitudinal increases in youths' substance use. *Journal of Consulting and Clinical Psychology, 77,* 1–11.

Comer, R. J. (2007). *Fundamentals of abnormal psychology* (6th ed.). New York: Worth Publishers.

Cooper, J. R., Bloom, F. E., & Roth, R. H. (2002). *The biochemical basis of neuropharmacology.* New York: Oxford University Press.

Cowan, R. L., Roberts, D. M., & Joers, J. M. (2008). Neuroimaging in human MDMA (Ecstasy) users. *Annals of the New York Academy of Sciences, 1139,* 291–298.

DeLisi, L. E. (2008). The effect of *Cannabis* on the brain: Can it cause brain anomalies that lead to increased risk for schizophrenia? *Current Opinion in Psychiatry, 21*(2), 140–50.

Fattore, L., Altea, S., & Fratta, W. (2008). Sex differences in drug addiction: A review of animal and human studies. *Womens Health (London, England), 4,* 51–65.

Feldman, R. S., Meyer, J. S., & Quenzer, L. F. (1997). *Principles of neuropsychopharmacology.* Sunderland, MA: Sinauer.

Fraioli, S., Crombag, H. S., Badiani, A., & Robinson, T. E. (1999). Susceptibility to amphetamine-induced locomotor sensitization is modulated by environmental stimuli. *Neuropsychopharmacology, 20,* 533–541.

Freud, S. (1974). *Cocaine papers* (R. Byck, Ed.). New York: Penguin.

Gilbertson, M. W., Shenton, M. E., Ciszewski, A., Kasai, K., Lasko, N. B., Orr, S. P., & Pitman, R. K. (2002). Smaller hippocampal volume predicts pathologic vulnerability to psychological trauma. *Nature Neuroscience, 5,* 1242–1247.

McGowan, P. O., Sasaki, A., D'Alessio, A. C., Dymov, S., Labonté, B., Szyf, M., Turecki, G., & Meaney, M. J. (2009). Epigenetic regulation of the glucocorticoid receptor in human brain associates with childhood abuse. *Nature Neurosciences, 12,* 342–348.

Hampson, E., & Kimura, D. (2005). Sex differences and hormonal influences on cognitive function in humans. In J. B. Becker, S. M. Breedlove, & D. Crews (Eds.), *Behavioral endocrinology* (pp. 357–398). Cambridge, MA: MIT Press.

Henquet, C., Di Forti, M., Morrison, P., Kuepper, R., & Murray, R.M. (2008). Gene-environment interplay between cannabis and psychosis. *Schizophrenia Bulletin, 34,* 1111–1121.

Inturrisi, C. E. (2002). Clinical pharmacology of opioids for pain. *Clinical Journal for Pain, 18*(Suppl.), S3–S13.

Isbell, H., Fraser, H. F., Wikler, R. E., Belleville, R. E., & Eisenman, A. J. (1955). An experimental study of the etiology of "rum fits" and delirium tremens. *Quarterly Journal of Studies on Alcohol, 16,* 1–35.

Julien, R. M. (1998). *A primer of drug action* (8th ed.). New York: W. H. Freeman and Company.

Julien, R. M. (2008). *A primer of drug action* (11th ed.). New York: Worth Publishers.

Kutcher, S., & Gardner, D. M. (2008). Use of selective serotonin reuptake inhibitors and youth suicide: Making sense from a confusing story. *Current Opinion in Psychiatry, 21,* 65–69.

Liberzon, I., & Phan, K. L. (2003). Brain-imaging studies of posttraumatic stress disorder. *CNS Spectroscopy, 8,* 641–650.

MacAndrew, C., & Edgerton, R. B. (1969). *Drunken comportment: A social explanation.* Chicago: Aldine.

MacDonald, T. K., MacDonald, G., Zanna, M. P., & Fong, G. T. (2000). Alcohol, sexual arousal, and intentions to use condoms in young men: Applying alcohol myopia theory to risky sexual behavior. *Health Psychology, 19,* 290–298.

McCann, U. D., Lowe, K. A., & Ricaurte, G. A. (1997). Long-lasting effects of recreational drugs of abuse on the central nervous system. *The Neurologist, 3,* 399–411.

Medwar, C., & Hardon, A. (2004). *Medicines out of control: Antidepressants and the conspiracy of goodwill.* New York: Aksant, Transaction.

O'Brien, C. P. (2008). A 50-year old woman addicted to heroin. Review of treatment of heroin addiction. *Journal of the American Medical Association, 300,* 314–321.

Olney, J. W., Ho, O. L., & Rhee, V. (1971). Cytotoxic effects of acidic and sulphur-containing amino acids on the infant mouse central nervous system. *Experimental Brain Research, 14,* 61–67.

Piazza, P. V., Deminiere, J. M., LeMoal, M., & Simon, H. (1989). Factors that predict individual vulnerability to amphetamine self-administration. *Science, 29,* 1511–1513.

Phillips, P. E. M., Stuber, G. D., Helen, M. L. A. V., Wightman, R. M., & Carelli, R. M. (2003). Subsecond dopamine release promotes cocaine seeking. *Nature, 422,* 614–818.

Radjenović, J., Petrović, M., & Barceló, D. (2009). Fate and distribution of pharmaceuticals in wastewater and sewage sludge of the conventional activated sludge (CAS) and advanced membrane bioreactor (MBR) treatment. *Water Research, 43,* 831–841.

Robinson, T. E., & Becker, J. B. (1986). Enduring changes in brain and behavior produced by chronic amphetamine administration: A review and evaluation of animal models of amphetamine psychosis. *Brain Research Reviews, 11,* 157–198.

Robinson, T. E., & Berridge, K. C. (2008). Incentive sensitization theory. *Philosophical Transactions of the Royal Society of London, 363,* 3137–3146.

Robinson, T. E., & Flagel, S. B. (2008). Dissociating the predictive and incentive motivational properties of reward-related cues through the study of individual differences. *Biological Psychiatry,* October 17 e-publication ahead of print.

Sahay, A., & Hen, R. (2008). Hippocampal neurogenesis and depression. *Novartis Foundation Symposium, 289,* 152–160.

Sapolsky, R. M. (1992). *Stress, the aging brain, and the mechanisms of neuron death.* Cambridge, MA: MIT Press.

Sapolsky, R. M. (2004). *Why zebras don't get ulcers* (3rd ed.). New York: Henry Holt and Company.

Sapolsky, R. M. (2005). The influence of social hierarchy on primate health. *Science, 308*(5722) 648–652.

Sim, M. E., Lyoo, I. K., Streeter, C. C., Covell, J., Sarid-Segal, O., Ciraulo, D. A., Kim, M. J., Kaufman, M. J., Yurgelun-Todd, D. A., & Renshaw, P. F. (2007). Cerebellar gray matter volume correlates with duration of cocaine use in cocaine-dependent subjects. *Neuropsychopharmacology, 10,* 2229–2237.

Steen, E., Terry, B. M., Rivera, E. J., Cannon, J. L., Neely, T. R., Tavares, R., Xu, X. J., Wands, J. R., & de la Monte, S. M. (2005). Impaired insulin and insulin-like growth factor expression and signaling mechanisms in Alzheimer's disease: Is this type 3 diabetes? *Journal of Alzheimer's Disease, 7,* 63–80.

Stein, F. A., Pankiewica, J., Harsch, H. H., Cho, J. K., Fuller, S. A., et al. (1988). Nicotine-induced limbic cortical activation in the human brain: A functional MRI study. *American Journal of Psychiatry, 155,* 1009–1015.

Teitelbaum, J. S., Zatorre, R. J., Carpenter, S., Gendron, D., Evans, A. C., Gjedde, A., & Cashman, N. R. (1990). Neurologic sequelae of domoic acid intoxication due to the ingestion of contaminated mussels. *New England Journal of Medicine, 322,* 1781–1787.

Thompson, P. M., Hayashi, D. M., Simon, S. L., Gheaga, J. A., Hong, M. S., Sui, Y., Lee, J. Y., Toga, A. W., Ling, W., & London, E. D. (2004). Structural abnormalities in the brains of human subjects who use methamphetamine. *Journal of Neuroscience, 24,* 6028–6036.

Wenger, J. R., Tiffany, T. M., Bombardier, C., Nicholls, K., & Woods, S. C. (1981). Ethanol tolerance in the rat is learned. *Science, 213,* 575–577.

Whishaw, I. Q., Mittleman, G., & Evenden, J. L. (1989). Training-dependent decay in performance produced by the neuroleptic *cis*(Z)-flupentixol on spatial navigation by rats in a swimming pool. *Pharmacology, Biochemistry, and Behavior, 32,* 211–220.

Yamamoto, B. K., & Raudensky, J. (2008). The role of oxidative stress, metabolic compromise, and inflammation in neuronal injury produced by amphetamine-related drugs of abuse. *Journal of Neuroimmune Pharmacology, 3,* 203–217.

Zink, C. F., Pagnoni, G., Martin-Skurski, M. E., Chappelow, J. C., & Berns G. S. (2004). Human striatal responses to monetary reward depend on saliency. *Neuron, 42,* 509–517.

Chapter 9

Balint, R. (1909). Seelenlähmung des "Schauens," optische Ataxie, räumliche Störung der Aufmerksamkeit. *Monatschrift für Psychiatrie und Neurologie, 25,* 51–81.

Farah, M. J. (1990). *Visual agnosia.* Cambridge, MA: MIT Press.

Geschwind, N. (1972). Language and the brain. *Scientific American, 226*(4), 78–83.

Goodale, M. A., Milner, D. A., Jakobson, L. S., & Carey, J. D. P. (1991). A kinematic analysis of reaching and grasping movements in a patient recovering from optic ataxia. *Nature, 349,* 154–156.

Hamilton, R. H., J. T. Shenton, and H. B. Coslett. (2006). An acquired deficit of audiovisual speech processing. *Brain and Language, 98,* 66–73.

Held, R. (1968). Dissociation of visual function by deprivation and rearrangement. *Psychologische Forschung, 31,* 338–348.

Hubel, D. H. (1988). *Eye, brain, and vision.* New York: Scientific American Library.

Hubel, D. H., & Weisel, T. N. (1977). Functional architecture of macaque monkey visual cortex. *Proceedings of the Royal Society of London B, 198,* Figure 23.

Kline, D. W. (1994). Optimizing the visibility of displays for older observers. *Experimental Aging Research, 20,* 11–23.

Kuffler, S. W. (1952). Neurons in the retina: Organization, inhibition and excitatory problems. *Cold Spring Harbor Symposia on Quantitative Biology, 17,* 281–292.

Lashley, K. S. (1941). Patterns of cerebral integration indicated by the scotomas of migraine. *Archives of Neurology and Psychiatry, 46,* 331–339.

Merbs, S. L., & Nathans, J. (1992). Absorption spectra of human cone pigments. *Nature, 356,* 433–435.

Milner, A. D., & Goodale, M. A. (2006). *The visual brain in action* (2nd ed.). Oxford: Oxford University Press.

Milner, A. D., & Goodale, M. A. (1995). *The visual brain in action.* Oxford: Oxford University Press.

Posner, M. I., & Raichle, M. E. (1997). *Images of mind.* New York: Scientific American Library.

Purves, D., Augustine, G. J., Fitzpatrick, D., Katz, L. C., LaMantia, A.-S., & McNamara, J. O. (Eds.). *Neuroscience.* Sunderland, MA: Sinauer.

Sacks, O., & Wasserman, R. (1987). The case of the colorblind painter. *The New York Review of Books, 34,* 25–33.

Snowden, R., Thompson, P., & Troscianko, T. (2008). *Basic vision: An introduction to visual perception.* Oxford: Oxford University Press.

Szentagothai, J. (1975). The "module-concept" in cerebral cortex architecture. *Brain Research, 95,* 475–496.

Tanaka, K. (1993). Neuronal mechanisms of object recognition. Science, 262, 685–688.

Tanaka, K. (1996). Inferotemporal cortex and object vision. *Annual Review of Neuroscience, 19,* 100–139.

Weizkrantz, L. (1986). *Blindsight: A case study and implications.* Oxford: Oxford University Press.

Wong-Riley, M. T. T., Hevner, R. F., Cutlan, R., Earnest, M., Egan, R., Frost, J., & Nguyen, T. (1993). Cytochrome oxidase in the human visual cortex: Distribution in the developing and the adult brain. *Visual Neuroscience, 10,* 41–58.

Zeki, S. (1997). *A vision of the brain.* Oxford: Blackwell Scientific.

Zihl, J., von Cramon, D., & Mai, N. (1983). Selective disturbance of movement vision after bilateral brain damage. *Brain, 106,* 313–340.

Chapter 10

Alexander, R. E., & Crutcher, M. D. (1996). Functional architecture of basal ganglia circuits: Neural substrates of parallel processing. *Trends in Neuroscience, 13,* 269.

Belin, P., Zatorre, R. J., Lafaille, P., & Pike, B. (2000). Voice-selective areas in the human auditory cortex. *Nature, 403,* 309–312.

Bermudez, P., Lerch, J. P., Evans, A. C., & Zatorre, R. J. (2009). Neuroanatomical correlates of musicianship as revealed by cortical thickness and voxel-based morphometry. *Cerebral Cortex, 19,* 1583–1596.

Chomsky, N. (1965). Aspects of the theory of syntax. Cambridge, MA: MIT Press.

Church, J. A., Fair, D. A., Donsenbach, N. U., et al. (2009). "Control networks in paediatric Tourette syndrome show immature and anomalous patterns of functional connectivity. *Brain, 32,* 225–238

Drake-Lee, A. B. (1992). Beyond music: Auditory temporary threshold shift in rock musicians after a heavy metal concert. *Journal of the Royal Society of Medicine, 85,* 617–619.

Evarts, E. V. (1968). Relation of pyramidal tract activity to force exerted during voluntary movement. *Journal of Neurophysiology, 31,* 15.

Fiez, J. A., Raichle, M. E., Balota, D. A., Tallal, P., & Petersen, S. E. (1996). PET activation of posterior temporal regions during auditory word presentation and verb generation. *Cerebral Cortex, 6,* 1–10.

Fiez, J. A., Raichle, M. E., Miezin, F. M., & Petersen, S. E. (1995). PET studies of auditory and phonological processing: Effects of stimulus characteristics and task demands. *Journal of Cognitive Neuroscience, 7,* 357–375.

Frackowiak, R. S. J., Friston, K. J., Frith, C. D., Dolan, R. J., & Mazziotta, J. C. (1997). *Human brain function.* San Diego: Academic Press.

Gazzaniga, M. S. (1992). *Nature's mind.* New York: Basic Books.

Geissmann, T. (2001). Gibbon songs and human music from an evolutionary perspective. In N. L. Wallin, B. Merker, & S. Brown (Eds.), *The origins of music* (pp. 103–124). Cambridge, MA: MIT Press.

Heffner, H. E., & Heffner, R. S. (1990). Role of primate auditory cortex in hearing. In W. C. Stebbins & M. A. Berkeley (Eds.), *Comparative perception* (vol. 2, *Complex signals,* pp. 279–310). New York: Wiley.

Hirsh, I. J. (1966). Audition. In J. B. Sidowsky (Ed.), *Experimental methods and instrumentation in psychology* (pp. 247–272). New York: McGraw-Hill.

Hyde, K. L., Lerch, J. P., Zatorre, R. J., Griffiths, T. D., Evans, A. C., & Peretz, I. (2007). Cortical thickness in congenital amusia: When less is better than more. *Journal of Neuroscience, 27,* 13028–13032.

Kandel, E. R., Schwartz, J. H., & Jessel, T. M. (Eds.) (1991). *Principles of neural science* (3rd ed.). New York: Elsevier.

Kim, K. H. S., Relkin, N. R., Young-Min Lee, K., and Hirsch, J. (1997). Distinct cortical areas associated with native and second languages. *Nature 388,* 171–174.

Knudsen, E. I. (1981). The hearing of the barn owl. *Scientific American, 245*(6), 113–125.

Lewis, D. B., & Gower, D. M. (1980). Biology of communication. New York: Wiley.

Loeb, G. E. (1990). Cochlear prosthetics. *Annual Review of Neuroscience, 13,* 357–371.

Luria, A. R. (1972). *The man with a shattered world.* Chicago: Regnery.

Marler, P. (1991). The instinct to learn. In S. Carey and R. German (Eds.), *The epigenesis of mind: Essays on biology and cognition* (p. 39). Hillsdale, NJ: Erlbaum.

McFarland, D. (1985). *Animal behaviour.* Bath, UK: Pitman Press.

Melzack, R. (1973). *The Puzzle of Pain.* New York: Basic Books.

Neuweiler, G. (1990). Auditory adaptations for prey capture in echolocating bats. *Physiological Reviews, 70,* 615–641.

Nottebohm, F., & Arnold, A. P. (1976). Sexual dimorphism in vocal control areas of the songbird brain. *Science, 194,* 211–213.

Nudo, R. J., Wise, G. M., SiFuentes, F., & Milliken, G. W. (1996). Neural substrates for the effects of rehabilitative training on motor recovery after ischemic infarct. *Science, 272,* 1793.

Penfield, W., & Rasmussen, T. (1950). *The cerebral cortex of man.* New York: Macmillan.

Penfield, W., & Roberts, L. (1956). *Speech and brain mechanisms.* Oxford: London: Oxford University Press.

Penfield, W., & Roberts, L. (1959). *Speech and brain mechanisms.* Princeton, NJ: Princeton University Press.

Peretz, I., Kolinsky, R., Tramo, M., Labrecque, R., Hublet, C., Demeurisse, G., & Belleville, S. (1994). Functional dissociations following bilateral lesions of auditory cortex. *Brain, 117,* 1283–1301.

Pinker, S. (1997). *How the mind works.* New York: Norton.

Pons, T. P., Garraghty, P. E., Ommaya, A. K., Kaas, J. H., Taum, E., & Mishkin, M. (1991). Massive cortical reorganization after sensory deafferentation in adult macaques. *Science, 252,* 1858.

Posner, M. I., & Raichle, M. E. (1997). *Images of mind.* New York: W. H. Freeman and Company.

Purves, D., Augustine, G. J., Fitzpatrick, D., Katz, L. C., LaMantia, A.-S., & McNamara, J. O. (Ed.) (1997). *Neuroscience.* Sunderland, MA: Sinauer.

Rauschecker, J. P., Tian, B., & Hauser, M. (1995). Processing of complex sounds in the macaque nonprimary auditory cortex. *Science, 268,* 111–114.

Romanski, L. M., Tian, B., Fritz, J., Mishkin, M., Goldman-Rakic, P. S., & Rauschecker, J. P. (1999). Dual streams of auditory afferents target multiple domains in the primate prefrontal cortex. *Nature Neuroscience, 2,* 1131–1136.

Sacks, O. (2007). *Musicophilia: Tales of music and the brain.* New York: Knopf.

Shepherd, G. M. (1994). *Neurobiology* (3rd ed.). New York: Oxford University Press.

Teie, P. U. (1998). Noise-induced hearing loss and symphony orchestra musicians: risk factors, effects, and management. *Maryland Medical Journal, 47,* 13–18.

Thach, W. T., Goodkin, H. P., & Keating, J. G. (1992). The cerebellum and the adaptive coordination of movement. *Annual Review of Neuroscience, 15,* 429.

Trehub, S., Schellenberg, E. G., & Ramenetsky, G. B. (1999). Infants' and adults' perception of scale structures. *Journal of Experimental Psychology: Human Perception and Performance, 25,* 965–975.

Williams, T. H., Gluhbegovic, N., & Jew, J. (2000). *The human brain: Dissections of the real brain,* on CD-ROM. Published by Brain University, brain-university.com 2000.

Winter, P., & Funkenstein, H. (1971). The auditory cortex of the squirrel monkey: Neuronal discharge patterns to auditory stimuli. *Proceedings of the Third Congress of Primatology, Zurich, 2,* 24–28.

Yost, W. A. (1991). Auditory image perception and analysis: The basis for hearing. *Hearing Research, 56,* 8–18.

Zatorre, R. J., Evans, A. C., & Meyer, E. (1994). Neural mechanisms underlying melodic perception and memory for pitch. *Journal of Neuroscience, 14,* 1908–1919.

Zatorre, R. J., Evans, A. C., Meyer, E., & Gjedde, A. (1992). Lateralization of phonetic and pitch discrimination in speech processing. *Science, 256,* 846–849.

Zatorre, R. J., Meyer, E., Gjedde, A., & Evans, A. C. (1995). PET studies of phonetic processing of speech: Review, replication, and reanalysis. *Cerebral Cortex, 6,* 21–30.

Chapter 11

Alexander, R. E., & Critcher, M. D. (1990). Functional architecture of basal ganglia circuits: Neural substrates of parallel processing. *Trends in Neuroscience, 13,* 269.

Aparicio, P., Diedrichsen, J., & Ivry, R. B (2005). Effects of focal basal ganglia lesions on timing and force control. *Brain and Cognition, 58,* 62–74.

Asanuma, H. (1989). *The motor cortex.* New York: Raven Press.

Aziz-Zadeh, L., & Ivry, R. B. (2009) The human mirror neuron system and embodied representations. *Advances in Experimental Medicine and Biology, 629,* 355–376.

Bauman, M. L., & Kemper, T. L. (1994). *The neurobiology of autism.* Baltimore: Johns Hopkins University Press.

Blakemore, S. J. (2008) The social brain in adolescence. *Nature Reviews Neuroscience, 9,* 267–277.

Blakemore, S. J., Wolpert, D. M., & Frith, C. D. (1998). Central cancellation of self-produced tickle sensation. *Nature Neuroscience, 1,* 635–640.

Brinkman, C. (1984). Supplementary motor area of the monkey's cerebral cortex: Short- and long-term deficits after unilateral ablation and the effects of subsequent callosal section. *Journal of Neuroscience, 4,* 918–992.

Charles, J. M., Carpenter, L. A., Jenner W., & Nicholas, J. S. (2008). Recent advances in autism spectrum disorders. *International Journal of Psychiatry and Medicine, 38,* 133–140.

Church, J. A., Fair, D. A., Dosenbach, N. U., Cohen, A. L., Miezin, F. M., Petersen, S. E., & Schlaggar, B. L. (2009). Control networks in paediatric Tourette syndrome show immature and anomalous patterns of functional connectivity. *Brain, 32,* 225–238.

Cole, J. (1995). *Pride and a daily marathon.* Cambridge, MA: MIT Press.

Corkin, S., Milner, B., & Rasmussen, T. (1970). Somatosensory thresholds. *Archives of Neurology, 23,* 41–58.

Critchley, M. (1953). *The parietal lobes.* London: Arnold.

Crowe, D. A., Chafee, M. V., Averbeck, B. B., & Georgopoulos, A. P. (2004). Participation of primary motor cortical neurons in a distributed network during maze solution: Representation of spatial parameters and time-course comparison with parietal area 7a. *Experimental Brain Research, 158,* 28–34.

Evarts, E. V. (1968). Relation of pyramidal tract activity to force exerted during voluntary movement. *Journal of Neurophysiology, 31,* 14–27.

Fadiga, L., & Craighero, L. (2004). Electrophysiology of action representation. *Journal of Clinical Neurophysiology, 21,* 100–106.

Friedhoff, A. J., & Chase, T. N. (1982). Gilles de la Tourette syndrome. *Advances in Neurology, 35,* 1–17.

Galea, M. P., & Darian-Smith, I. (1994). Multiple corticospinal neuron populations in the macaque monkey are specified by their unique cortical origins, spinal terminations, and connections. *Cerebral Cortex, 4,* 166–194.

Graziano, M. (2006). The organization of behavioural repertoire in motor cortex. *Annual Reviews of Neuroscience, 29,* 105–134.

Hess, W. R. (1957). *The functional organization of the diencephalon.* London: Grune & Stratton.

Hughlings-Jackson, J. (1931). *Selected writings of John Hughlings-Jackson* (Vols. 1 and 2, J. Taylor, Ed.). London: Hodder.

Kaas, J. H. (1987). The organization and evolution of neocortex. In S. P. Wise (Ed.), *Higher brain functions* (pp. 237–298). New York: Wiley.

Kalueff, A. V., Aldridge, J. W., LaPorte, J. L., Murphy D. L., & Tuohimaa, P. (2007). Analyzing grooming microstructure in neurobehavioral experiments. *Nature Protocols, 25,* 38–44.

Kandel, E. R., Schwartz, J. H., & Jessel, T. M. (Eds.) (1991). *Principles of neural science* (3rd ed.). New York: Elsevier.

Kreitzer, A. C., & Malaenka, R. C. (2008) Striatal plasticity and basal ganglia circuit function. *Neuron, 60,* 543–554.

Kern, U., Busch, V., Rockland, M., Kohl, M., & Birklein, F. (2009). Prevalence and risk factors of phantom limb pain and phantom limb sensations in Germany: A nationwide field survey. *Schmerz, 23,* 479–488.

Lang, C. E., & Schieber, M. H. (2004). Reduced muscle selectivity during individuated finger movements in humans after damage to the motor cortex or corticospinal tract. *Journal of Neurophysiology, 91,* 1722–1733.

Lashley, K. S. (1951). The problem of serial order in behavior. In L. A. Jeffress (Ed.), *Cerebral mechanisms and behavior* (pp. 112–136). New York: Wiley.

Leonard, C. M., Glendinning, D. S., Wilfong, T., Cooper, B. Y., & Vierck, C. J., Jr. (1991). Alterations of natural hand movements after interruption of fasciculus cuneatus in the macaque. *Somatosensory and Motor Research, 9,* 61–75.

Levitt, J. J., Blanton, R. E., Smalley, S., Thompson, P. M., Guthrie, D., McCracken, J. T., Sadoun, T., Heinichen, L., & Toga, A. W. (2003). Cortical sulcal maps in autism. *Cerebral Cortex, 7,* 728–735.

Melzack, R. (1973). *The puzzle of pain.* New York: Basic Books.

Melzack, R., & Wall, P. D. (1965). Pain mechanisms: A new theory. *Science, 150,* 971–979.

Mountcastle, V. B. (1978). An organizing principle for cerebral function: The unit module and the distributed system. In G. M. Edelman & V. B. Mountcastle (Eds.), *The mindful brain* (pp. 7–50). Cambridge, MA: MIT Press.

Napier, J. (1980). *Hands.* Princeton, NJ: Princeton University Press.

Nudo, R. J., Wise, B. M., SiFuentes, F., & Milliken, G. W. (1996). Neural substrates for the effects of rehabilitative training on motor recovery after ischemic infarct. *Science, 272,* 1791–1794.

Panksepp, J. (2007). Neuroevolutionary sources of laughter and social joy: modeling primal human laughter in laboratory rats. *Behavioural Brain Research, 4,* 231–244.

Penfield, W., & Boldrey, E. (1958). Somatic motor and sensory representation in the cerebral cortex as studied by electrical stimulation. *Brain, 60,* 389–443.

Pons, T. P., Garraghty, P. E., Ommaya, A. K., Kaas, J. H., Taum, E., & Mishkin, M. (1991). Massive cortical reorganization after sensory deafferentation in adult macaques. *Science, 252,* 1857–1860.

Porter, R., & Lemon, R. (1993). *Corticospinal function and voluntary movement.* Oxford: Clarendon Press.

Ramachandran, V. S., & McGeoch, P. D. (2007). Occurrence of phantom genitalia after gender reassignment surgery. *Medical Hypotheses, 69,* 1001–1003.

Ramachandran, V. S., & Rogers-Ramachandran, D. (2000). Phantom limbs and neural plasticity. *Archives of Neurology, 57,* 317–320.

Roland, P. E. (1993). *Brain activation.* New York: Wiley-Liss.

Rothwell, J. C., Taube, M. M., Day, B. L., Obeso, J. A., Thomas, P. K., & Marsden, C. D. (1982). Manual motor performance in a deafferented man. *Brain, 105,* 515–542.

Sacks, O. (1974). *Awakenings.* New York: Vintage.

Sacks, O. W. (1998). *The man who mistook his wife for a hat: And other clinical tales.* New York: Touchstone Books.

Schlerf, J. E., Spencer, R. M., Zelaznik, H. N., & Ivry, R. B. (2007). Timing of rhythmic movments in patients with cerebellar degeneration. *Cerebellum, 6,* 221–231.

Thach, W. T. (2007). On the mechanism of cerebellar contributions to cognition. *Cerebellum, 6,* 163–167.

Thach, W. T., Goodkin, H. P., & Keating, J. G. (1992)."The cerebellum and the adaptive coordination of movement." *Annual Review of Neuroscience, 15,* 429.

Vaccarino, F. M., Grigorenko, E. L., Smith, K. M., & Stevens, H. E. (2009). Regulation of cerebral cortical size and neuron number by fibroblast growth factors: implications for autism. *Journal of Autism and Developmental Disorders, 39,* 511–520.

von Holst, E. (1973). *The collected papers of Erich von Holst* (R. Martin, Trans.). Coral Gables, FL: University of Miami Press.

Williams, T. H., Gluhbegovic, N., & Jew, J. (2000). *The human brain: Dissections of the real brain,* on CD-ROM. Published by Brain University, brain-university.com 2000.

Chapter 12

Ackerly, S. S. (1964). A case of paranatal bilateral frontal lobe defect observed for thirty years. In J. M. Warren & K. Akert (Eds.), *The frontal granular cortex and behavior* (pp. 192–218). New York: McGraw-Hill.

Adelmann, P. K., & Zajonc, R. B. (1989). Facial efferents and the experience of emotion. *Annual Review of Psychology, 40,* 249–280.

Astrup, A., Larsen, T. M., & Harper, A. (2004). Atkins and other low-carbohydrate diets: Hoax or an effective tool for weight loss? *Lancet, 364,* 897–899.

Bartoshuk, L. M. (2000). Comparing sensory experiences across individuals: Recent psychophysical advances illuminate genetic variation in taste perception. *Chemical Senses, 25,* 447–460.

Beatty, J. (1995). *Principles of behavioral neuroscience* (p. 339). Dubuque, IA: Brown & Benchmark.

Becker, J. B., Berkley, K. J., Geary, N., Hampson, E., Herman, J. P., & Young, E. A. (2008). *Sex differences in the brain: From genes to behavior.* New York: Oxford University Press.

Berridge, K. C. (1996). Food reward: Brain substrates of wanting and liking. *Neuroscience and Biobehavioral Reviews, 20,* 6

Butler, R. A., & Harlow, H. F. (1954). Persistence of visual exploration in monkeys. *Journal of Comparative and Physiological Psychology, 47,* 257–263.

Byne, W. (1994). The biological evidence challenged. *Scientific American, 270*(5), 50–55.

Daly, M., & Wilson, M. (1988). *Homicide.* New York: Aldine.

Damasio, A. R. (1994). *Descartes' error: Emotion, reason, and the human brain.* New York: Plenum.

Damasio, A. R. (1999). *The feeling of what happens: Body and emotion in the making of consciousness.* New York: Harcourt Brace.

Davis, M., Walker, D. L., & Myers, K. M., (2003). Role of the amygdala in fear extinction measured with potentiated startle. *Annals of the New York Academy of Sciences, 985,* 218–232.

Dethier, V. G. (1962). *To know a fly.* San Francisco. Holden-Day.

Eibl-Eibesfeldt, I. (1989). *Human ethology.* New York: Aldine de Gruyter.

Eisenberger, N. I., Lieberman, M. D., & Williams, K. D. (2003). Does rejection hurt? An fMRI study of social exclusion. *Science, 302,* 290–292.

Eisenberger, N. I., Jarcho, J. M., Lieberman, M. D., & Naliboff, B. D. (2006). An experimental study of shared sensitivity to physical pain and social rejection. *Pain, 126,* 132–138.

Everitt, B. J. (1990). Sexual motivation: A neural and behavioral analysis of the mechanisms underlying appetitive and copulatory responses of male rats. *Neuroscience and Biobehavioral Reviews, 14,* 217–232.

Field, T. M., Woodson, R., Greenberg, R., & Cohen, D. (1982), Discrimination and imitation of facial expression by neonates. *Science, 218,* 179–181.

Flegal, K. M., Carroll, M. D., Kuczmarski, R. J., & Johnson, C. L. (1998). Overweight and obesity in the United States: Prevalence and trends, 1960–1964. *International Journal of Obesity and Related Metabolic Disorders, 22,* 39–47.

Foster, G. D., Wyatt, H. R., Hill, J. O., McGuckin, B. G., Brill, C., Mohammed, B. S., Szapary, P. O., Rader, D. J., Edman, J. S., & Klein, S. (2003). A randomized trial of a low-carbohydrate diet for obesity. *New England Journal of Medicine, 348,* 2082–2090.

Garcia, J., & Koelling, R. A. (1966). Relation of cue to consequences in avoidance learning. *Psychonomic Science, 4,* 123–124.

Glickman, S. E., & Schiff, B. B. (1967). A biological theory of reinforcement. *Psychological Review, 74,* 81–109.

Gorski, R. A. (1984). Critical role for the medial preoptic area in the sexual differentiation of the brain. *Progress in Brain Research, 61,* 129–146.

Hamer, D. H., Hu, S., Magnuson, V. L., Hu, N., & Pattatucci, M. L. (1993). A linkage between DNA markers on the X chromosome and male sexual orientation. *Science, 261,* 321–327.

Hebb, D. O. (1955). Drives and the C.N.S. (conceptual nervous system). *Psychological Review, 62,* 243–254.

Heron, W. (1957). The pathology of boredom. *Scientific American, 196*(1), 52–56.

Insel, T. R., & Fernald, R. D. (2004). How the brain processes social information: Searching for the social brain. *Annual Review of Neuroscience, 27,* 697–722.

Jacob, S., Kinnunen, L. H., Metz, J., Cooper, M., & McClintock, M. K. (2001). Sustained human chemosignal unconsciously alters brain function. *Neuroreport, 12,* 2391–2394.

Jacobsen, C. F. (1936). Studies of cerebral function in primates. *Comparative Psychology Monographs, 13,* 1–68.

Klüver, H., & Bucy, P. C. (1939). Preliminary analysis of the temporal lobes in monkeys. *Archives of Neurology and Psychiatry, 42,* 979–1000.

Lundstrom, J. N., Boyle, J. A., Zatorre, R. J., & Jones-Gotman, M. (2008) Functional neuronal processing of body odors differs from that of similar common odors. *Cerebral Cortex, 18,* 1466–1474.

LeDoux, J. (1996). *The emotional brain.* New York: Simon & Schuster.

MacLean, P. D. (1949). Psychosomatic disease and the "visceral brain": Recent developments bearing on the Papez theory of emotion. *Psychosomatic Medicine, 11,* 338–353.

Money, J., & Ehrhardt, A. A. (1972). Man and woman, boy and girl. Baltimore: Johns Hopkins University Press.

Nieuwenhuys, R., Voogd, J., & van Huijzen, C. (1981). *The human central nervous system: A synopsis and atlas* (2nd ed.). Berlin: Springer Verlag.

Olds, J., & Milner, P. (1954). Positive reinforcement produced by electrical stimulation of septal area and other regions of rat brain. *Journal of Comparative and Physiological Psychology, 47,* 419–427.

Olsson, S. B., Barnard, J., & Turri, L. (2006) Olfaction and identification of unrelated individuals: Examination of the mysteries of human odor recognition. *Journal of Chemical Ecology, 32,* 1635–1645.

Panagiotakos, D. B., Pitsavos, C., Polychronopoulos, E., Chrysohoou, C., Zampelas, A., & Trichopoulou, A. (2004). Can a Mediterranean diet moderate the development and clinical progression of coronary heart disease? A systematic review. *Medical Science Monitor, 10,* RA193–RA198.

Robinson, T. E., & Berridge, K. C. (2008). Incentive sensitization theory. *Philosophical Transactions of the Royal Society of London; 363,* 3137–3146.

Seeley, R. J., & Woods, S. C. (2003). Monitoring of stored and available fuel by the CNS: Implications for obesity. *Nature Reviews Neuroscience, 4,* 885–909.

Shai, I., Schwarzfuchs, D., Henkin, Y., Shahar, D. R., Witkow, S., et al. (2008). Weight loss with a low-carbohydrate, Mediterranean, or low-fat diet. *New England Journal of Medicine, 13,* 229–241.

Skinner, B. F. (1938). *The behavior of organisms.* New York: Appleton-Century-Crofts.

Smith, D. V., & Shepherd, G. M. (2003). Chemical senses: Taste and olfaction. In L. R. Squiare, F. E. Bloom, S. K. McConnell, J. L. Roberts, N. C. Spitzer, & M. J. Zigmond (Eds.), *Fundamental Neuroscience* (2nd ed., pp. 631–667). New York: Academic Press.

Spanagel, R., & Weiss, F. (1999). The dopamine hypothesis of reward: Past and current status. *Trends in Neurosciences, 22,* 521–527.

Stern, K., & McClintock, M. K. (1998). Regulation of ovulation by human phermones. *Nature, 392,* 177–179.

Swaab, D. F., Gooren, L. J., & Hofman, M. A. (1995). Brain research, gender and sexual orientation. *Homosexuality, 28,* 283–301.

Swaab, D. F., & Hofman, M. A. (1995). Sexual differentiation of the human hypothalamus in relation to gender and sexual orientation. *Trends in Neurosciences, 18,* 264–270.

Trujillo, K. A., Herman, J. P., & Schafer, M.-H. (1993). Drug reward and brain circuitry: Recent advances and future directions. In S. G. Korenman & J. D. Barchas (Eds.), *Biological bases of substance abuse* (pp. 119–142). New York: Oxford University Press.

Vasey, P. L. (2002). Sexual partner preference in female Japanese macaques. *Archives of Sexual Behavior, 31,* 51–62.

Wise, R. A. (1996). Addictive drugs and brain stimulation reward. *Annual Review of Neuroscience, 19,* 319–340.

Woolley, C. S., Gould, E., Frankfurt, M., & McEwen, B. (1990). Naturally occurring fluctuation in dendritic spine density on adult hippocampal pyramidal neurons. *Journal of Neuroscience, 10,* 4035–4039.

World Health Organization. (2000). *Obesity: Preventing and managing the global epidemic.* WHO Technical Report Series, No. 894, 1–253.

Chapter 13

Amir, S., & Stewart, J. (2009). Motivational Modulation of Rhythms of the Expression of the Clock Protein PER2 in the Limbic Forebrain. *Biological Psychiatry, 65,* 829–834.

Binkley, S. (1990). *The clockwork sparrow.* Englewood Cliffs, NJ: Prentice Hall.

Brankačk, J., Platt B., & Riedel, G. (2009). Sleep and hippocampus: Do we search for the right things? *Progress in Neuro-Psychopharmacology and Biological Psychiatry, 33,* 806–812.

Clark, E. L., Baumann, C. R., Cano, G., Scammell, T. E., & Mochizuki, T. (2009). Feeding-elicited cataplexy in orexin knockout mice. *Neuroscience, 161,* 970–977.

Dement, W. C. (1972). *Some must watch while some must sleep.* Stanford, CA: Stanford Alumni Association.

Freud, S. (1990). *The interpretation of dreams.* Leipzig and Vienna: Franz Deuticke.

Gerrard, J. L., Burke, S. N., McNaughton, B. L., & Barnes, C. A. (2008). Sequence reactivation in the hippocampus is impaired in aged rats. *Journal of Neuroscience 30,* 7883–7890.

Gonzalez, M. M., & Aston-Jones, G. (2008). Light deprivation damages monoamine neurons and produces a depressive behavioral phenotype in rats. *Proceedings of the National Academy of Sciences (USA), 105,* 4898–4903.

Hall, C. S., Domhoff, G. W., Blick, K. A., & Weesner, K. E. (1982). The dreams of college men and women in 1950 and 1980: A comparison of dream contents and sex differences. *Sleep, 5,* 188–194.

Hobson, J. A. (1989). *Sleep.* New York: Scientific American Library.

Hobson, J. A. (2002). Sleep and dream suppression following a lateral medullary infarct: A first-person account. *Consciousness and Cognition, 11,* 377–390.

Hobson, J. A. (2004). *13 dreams Freud never had: A new mind science.* New York: Pi Press.

Jones, B. E. (1993). The organization of central cholinergic systems and their functional importance in sleep-waking states. *Progress in Brain Research, 98,* 61–71.

Jouvet, M. (1972). The role of monoamines and acetylcholine-containing neurons in the regulation of the sleep–waking cycle. *Ergebnisse der Physiologie, 64,* 166–307.

Kelley, D. D. (1991). Sleep and dreaming. In E. R. Kandel, J. H. Schwartz, & T. M. Jessell (Eds.), *Principles of Neuroscience* (3rd ed., p. 794). New York: Elsevier.

Kleitman, N. (1965). *Sleep and wakefulness.* Chicago: University of Chicago Press.

Lamberg, L. (2003). Scientists never dreamed finding would shape half-century of sleep research. *Journal of the American Medical Association, 290,* 2652–2654.

Lavie, P., Pratt, H., Scharf, B., Peled, R., & Brown, J. (1984). Localized pontine lesion: Nearly total absence of REM sleep. *Neurology, 34,* 118–120.

Lee, M. L., Swanson, B. E., & de la Iglesia, H. O. (2009). Circadian timing of REM sleep is coupled to an oscillator within the dorsomedial suprachiasmatic nucleus. *Current Biology, 19,* 848–852.

Li, J. D., Hu, W. P., and Zhou, Q. Y. (2009). Disruption of the circadian output molecule prokineticin 2 results in anxiolytic and antidepressant-like effects in mice. *Neuropsychopharmacology, 34,* 367–373.

Maquet, P., Laureys, S., Peigneux, P., Fuchs, S., Petiau, C., et al. (2000). Experience-dependent changes in cerebral activation during human REM sleep. *Nature Neuroscience, 3,* 831–836.

Markand, O. N., & Dyken, M. L. (1976). Sleep abnormalities in patients with brain stem lesions. *Neurology, 26,* 769–776.

Mignot, E. (2004). A year in review: Basic science, narcolepsy, and sleep in neurological diseases. *Sleep, 27,* 1209–1212.

Moruzzi, G., & Magoun, H .W. (1949). Brain stem reticular formation and activation of the EEG. *Electroencephalography and Clinical Neurophysiology, 1,* 455–473.

Osorio, I., & Daroff, R. B. (1980). Absence of REM and altered NREM sleep in patients with spinocerebellar degeneration and slow saccades. *Annals of Neurology, 7,* 277–280.

Quinlan, J., & Quinlan, J. (1977). *Karen Ann: The Quinlans tell their story.* Toronto: Doubleday.

Ralph, M. R., & Lehman, M. N. (1991). Transplantation: A new tool in the analysis of the mammalian hypothalamic circadian pacemaker. *Trends in Neurosciences, 14,* 363–366.

Raven, P. H., Evert, R. F., & Eichorn, S. E. (1992). *Biology of plants.* New York: Worth Publishers.

Reiter, R. J. (1980). The pineal and its hormones in the control of reproduction in Mammals. *Endocrinology Review, 1,* 120.

Richter, C. P. (1965). *Biological clocks in medicine and psychiatry.* Springfield, IL: Charles C Thomas.

Roffward, H. P., Muzio, J., & Dement, W. C. (1966). Ontogenetic development of the human sleep–dream cycle. *Science, 152,* 604–619.

Rosen, C. L., Storfer-Isser, A., Taylor, H. G., Kirchner, H. L., Emancipator, J. L., Schenck, C. H., Bundlie, S. R., Ettinger, M. G., & Mahowald, M. W. (1986). Chronic behavioral disorders of human REM sleep: A new category of parasomnia. *Sleep, 9,* 293–308.

Schibler, U. (2009). The 2008 Pittendrigh/Aschoff lecture: peripheral phase coordination in the mammalian circadian timing system. *Journal of Biological Rhythms, 24,* 3–15

Siegel, J. (2004). Brain mechanisms that control sleep and waking. *Naturwissenschaften, 91,* 355–365.

Synofzik, M., Bauer, P., & Schöls, L. (2009). Prion mutation D178N with highly variable disease onset and phenotype. *Journal of Neurology, Neurosurgery and Psychiatry, 80,* 345–346.

Stoleru, D., Nawathean, P., Fernández, M. P., Menet, J. S., Ceriani, M. F., & Rosbash, M. (2007). The *Drosophila* circadian network is a seasonal timer. *Cell, 6*(129), 207–219.

Thomas, K., & Watson, C. B. (2008). Restless legs syndrome in women: A review. *Journal of Women's Health (Larchmt), 17,* 859–868.

Tournier, B. B., Birkenstock, J., Pévet, P., & Vuillez, P. (2009). Gene expression in the suprachiasmatic nuclei and the photoperiodic time integration. *Neuroscience, 160,* 240–247

Valli, K., & Revonsuo, A. (2009). The threat simulation theory in light of recent empirical evidence: A review. *American Journal of Psychology, 122,* 17–38.

Vanderwolf, C. H. (2002). *An Odyssey Through the Brain, Behavior and the Mind.* Amsterdam: Kluwer Academic.

Wenner, J. B., Cheema, R., & Ayas, N. T. (2009). *Journal of Cardiopulmonay Rehabilation and Prevention, 29,* 76–83.

Wilson, M. A., & McNaughton, B. L. (1994). Reactivation of hippocampal ensemble memories during sleep. *Science, 265,* 676–679.

Wilson, S., & Argyropoulos, S. (2005). Antidepressants and sleep: A qualitative review of the literature. *Drugs, 65,* 927–947.

Chapter 14

Cahill, L., Babinsky, R., Markowitsch, H. J., & McGaugh, J. L. (1995). The amygdala and emotional memory. *Nature, 377,* 295–296.

Candia, V., Wienbruch, C., Elbert, T., Rockstroh, B., & Ray, W. (2003). Effective behavioral treatment of focal hand dystonia in musicians alters somatosensory cortical organization. *Proceedings of the National Academy of Sciences (USA), 100,* 7942–7946.

Chang, F.-L. F., & Greenough, W. T. (1982). Lateralized effects of monocular training on dendritic branching in adult split-brain rats. *Brain Research, 232,* 283–292.

Corkin, S. (2002). What's new with the amnesic patient H. M.? *Nature Reviews Neuroscience, 3,* 153–160.

Corkin, S., Amaral, D. G., Gonzalez, R. G., Johnson, K. A., & Hyman, B. T. (1997). H. M.'s medial temporal lobe lesion: Findings from magnetic resonance imaging. *Journal of Neuroscience, 17,* 3964–3979.

Damasio, A. R., Tranel, D., & Damasio, H. (1989). Amnesia caused by herpes simplex encephalitis, infarctions in basal forebrain, Alzheimer's disease and anoxia/ischemia. In F. Boller & J. Grafman (Eds.), *Handbook of neuropsychology* (Vol. 3, pp. 149–166). New York: Elsevier.

Davis, M. (1992). The role of the amygdala in fear and anxiety. *Annual Review of Neuroscience, 15,* 353–375.

Eriksson, P. S., Perfilieva, E., Bjork-Eriksson, T., Alborn, A. M., Nordborg, C., Peterson, D. A., & Gage, F. H. (1998). Neurogenesis in the adult human hippocampus. *Nature Medicine, 4,* 1313–1317.

Fuster, J. M. (1995). *Memory in the cerebral cortex.* Cambridge, MA: MIT Press.

Fuster, J. M., Bodner, M., & Kroger, J. K. (2000). Cross-modal and cross-temporal association in neurons of frontal cortex. *Nature, 405,* 347–351.

Gazzaniga, M. S. (Ed.). (2000). *The new cognitive neurosciences.* Cambridge, MA: MIT Press.

Geshwind, N., & Galaburda, A. M. (1985). *Cerebral lateralization.* Cambridge, MA: MIT Press.

Gould, E., Tanapat, P., Hastings, N. B., & Shors, T. J. (1999). Neurogenesis in adulthood: A possible role in learning. *Trends in Cognitive Sciences, 3,* 186–191.

Gould, E., Tanapat, P., McEwen, B. S., Flugge, G., & Fuchs, E. (1998). Proliferation of granule cell precursors in the dentate gyrus of adult monkeys is diminished by stress. *Proceedings of the National Academy of Sciences (USA), 95,* 3168–3171.

Hampson, E., & Kimura, D. (1988). Reciprocal effects of hormonal fluctuations on human motor and perceptual-spatial skills. *Behavioral Neuroscience, 102,* 456–459.

Hebb, D. O. (1947). The effects of early experience on problem solving at maturity. *American Psychologist, 2,* 737–745.

Hebb, D. O. (1949). *The organization of behavior: A neuropsychological theory.* New York: Wiley.

Jacobs, B., Schall, M., & Scheibel, A. B. (1993). A quantitative dendritic analysis of Wernicke's area in humans: II. Gender, hemispheric, and environmental factors. *Journal of Comparative Neurololgy, 327,* 97–111.

Jacobs, B., & Scheibel, A. B. (1993). A quantitative dendritic analysis of Wernicke's area in humans: I. Lifespan changes. *Journal of Comparative Neurololgy, 327,* 83–96.

Kaas, J. (2000). The reorganization of sensory and motor maps after injury in adult mammals. In M. S. Gazzaniga (Ed.), *The cognitive neurosciences* (pp. 223–236). Cambridge, MA: MIT Press.

Kempermann, G., Kuhn, H. G., & Gage, F. H. (1998). Experience-induced neurogenesis in the senescent dentate gyrus. *Journal of Neuroscience, 18,* 3206–3212.

Kolb, B. (1999). Towards an ecology of cortical organization: Experience and the changing brain. In J. Grafman & Y. Christen (Eds.), *Neuropsychology: From lab to the clinic* (pp. 17–34). Paris: Springer Verlag.

Kolb, B., Cote, S., Ribeiro-da-Silva, A., & Cuello, A. C. (1997). "Nerve growth factor treatment prevents dendritic atrophy and promotes recovery of function after cortical injury." *Neuroscience, 76,* 1146.

Kolb, B. & Gibb, R. (2008). Principles of brain plasticity and behavior. In D. Stuss, I. Robertson, & G. Winocur (Eds.), *Brain plasticity and rehabilitation.* New York: Oxford University Press.

Kolb, B., Gibb, R., & Gorny, G. (2003). Experience-dependent changes in dendritic arbor and spine density in neocortex vary with age and sex. *Neurobiology of Learning and Memory, 79,* 1–10.

Kolb, B., Gorny, G., Cote, S., Ribeiro-da-Silva, & Cuello, A. C. (1997). Nerve growth factor stimulates growth of cortical pyramidal neurons in young adult rats. *Brain Research, 751,* 289–294.

Kolb, B., Gorny, G., Li, Y., Samaha, A. N., & Robinson, T. E. (2003). Amphetamine or cocaine limits the ability of later experience to promote structural plasticity in the neocortex and nucleus accumbens. *Proceedings of the National Academy of Science (USA), 100,* 10523–10528.

Kolb, B., Morshead, C., Gonzalez, C., Kim, N., Shingo, T., & Weiss, S. (2007). Growth factor-stimulated generation of new cortical tissue and functional recovery after stroke damage to the motor cortex of rats. *Journal of Cerebral Blood Flow and Metabolism, 27,* 983–397.

Kolb, B., & Whishaw, I. Q. (1998). Brain plasticity and behavior. *Annual Review of Psychology, 49,* 43–64.

Lashley, K. S. (1960). In search of the engram. Symposium No. 4 of the Society of Experimental Biology. In F. A. Beach, D. O. Hebb, C. T. Morgan, & H. T. Nissen (Eds.), *The neuropsychology of Lashley* (pp. 478–505). New York: McGraw-Hill. (Reprinted from R. Sutton (Ed.), *Physiological mechanisms of animal behavior,* pp. 454–482, 1951. Cambridge: Cambridge University Press.)

LeDoux, J. E. (1995). In search of an emotional system in the brain: Leaping from fear to emotion and consciousness. In M. S. Gazzaniga (Ed.), *The cognitive neurosciences* (pp. 1047–1061). Cambridge, MA: MIT Press.

Lepage, M., McIntosh, A. R., & Tulving, E. (2001). Transperceptual encoding and retrieval process in memory: A PET study of visual and haptic objects. *Neuroimage, 14,* 572–584.

Loftus, E. F. (1997). Creating false memories. *Scientific American, 277*(3), 70–75.

Maguire, E. A., Gadian, D. G., Johnsrude, I. S., Good, C. D., Ashburner, J., Frackowiak, R. S., & Frith, C. D. (2000). Navigation-related structural change in the hippocampi of taxi drivers. *Proceedings of the National Academy of Sciences (USA), 97,* 4398–4403.

Mahncke, H. W., Bronstone, A., & Merzenich, M. M. (2006). Brain plasticity and functional losses in the aged: scientific bases for a novel intervention. *Progress in Brain Research, 157,* 81–109.

Markowitsch, H. J. (1999). Functional neuroimaging correlates of functional amnesia. *Memory 7,* Plate 2.

Markowitsch, H. J. (2003). Psychogenic amnesia. *Neuroimage, 20*(Suppl. 1), S132–S138.

Martin, A., Haxby, J. V., Lalonde, F. M., Wiggs, C. L., & Ungerleider, L. G. (1995). Discrete cortical regions associated with knowledge of color and knowledge of action. *Science, 270,* 102–105.

Martin, P. R. (1985). Cover, *Alcohol Health & Research World, 9* (Spring 1985).

McGaugh, J. (2004). The amygdala modulates the consolidation of memories of emotionally arousing experiences. *Annual Review of Neuroscience, 27,* 1–28.

Milner, B., Corkin, S., & Teuber, H. (1968). Further analysis of the hippocampal amnesic syndrome: 14 year follow-up study of HM. *Neuropsychologia, 6,* 215–234.

Mishkin, M. (1982). A memory system in the brain. *Philosophical Transactions of the Royal Society of London, Biological Sciences, 298,* 83–95.

Mishkin, M., Suzuki, W. A., Gadian, D. G., & Vargha-Khadem, F. (1997). Hierarchical organization of cognitive memory. *Philosophical Transactions of the Royal Society of London, Biological Sciences, 352,* 1461–1467.

Murray, E. (2000). Memory for objects in nonhuman primates. In M. S. Gazzaniga (Ed.), *The new cognitive neurosciences* (pp. 753–763). Cambridge, MA: MIT Press.

Nudo, R. J., Plautz, E. J., & Milliken, G. W. (1997). Adaptive plasticity in primate motor cortex as a consequence of behavioral experience and neuronal injury. *Seminars in Neuroscience, 9,* 13–23.

O'Keefe, J., & Nadel, L. (1978). *The hippocampus as a spatial map.* New York: Oxford University Press.

Purves, D., & Voyvodic, J. T. (1987). Imaging mammalian nerve cells and their connections over time in living animals. *Trends in Neurosciences, 10,* 398–404.

Ragert, P., Schmidt, A., Altenmuller, E., & Dinse, H. R. (2003). Superior tactile performance and learning in professional pianists: Evidence for meta-plasticity in muscicians. *European Journal of Neuroscience, 19,* 473–478.

Ramachandran, V. S. (1993). Behavioral and magnetoencephalographic correlates of plasticity in the adult human brain. *Proceedings of the National Academy of Sciences (USA),* 90, 10413–10420.

Ramón y Cajal, S. (1928). *Degeneration and regeneration of the nervous system.* London: Oxford University Press.

Reynolds, B., & Weiss, S. (1992). Generation of neurons and astrocytes from isolated cells of the adult mammalian central nervous system. *Science, 255,* 1707–1710.

Robinson, T. E., & Kolb, B. (1997). Persistent structural adaptations in nucleus accumbens and prefrontal cortex neurons produced by prior experience with amphetamine. *Journal of Neuroscience, 17,* 8491–8498.

Robinson, T. E., & Kolb, B. (2004). Structural plasticity associated with drugs of abuse. *Neuropharmacology, 47*(Suppl. 1), 33–46.

Sainsbury, R. S., & Coristine, M. (1986). Affective discrimination in moderately to severely demented patients. *Canadian Journal on Aging, 5,* 99–104.

Sapolsky, R. M. (1992). *Stress, the aging brain, and the mechanisms of neuron death.* Cambridge, MA: MIT Press.

Schacter, D. L. (1983). Amnesia observed: Remembering and forgetting in a natural environment. *Journal of Abnormal Psychology, 92,* 236–242.

Sherry, D. F., Jacobs, L. F., & Gaulin, S. J. C. (1992). Spatial memory and adaptive specialization of the hippocampus. *Trends in Neuroscience, 15,* 298–303.

Sirevaag, A. M., & Greenough, W. T. (1987). Differential rearing effects on rat visual cortex synapses: III. Neuronal and glial nuclei, boutons, dendrites, and capillaries. *Brain Research, 424,* 320–332.

Sirevaag, A. M., & Greenough, W. T. (1988). A multivariate statistical summary of synaptic plasticity measures in rats exposed to complex, social and individual environments. *Brain Research, 441,* 386–392.

Skinner, B. F. (1938). *The behavior of organisms.* New York: Appleton-Century-Crofts.

Temple, E., Deutsch, G. K., Poldrack, R. A., Miller, S. L., Tallal, P., Merzenich, M. M., & Gabrieli, J. D. E. (2003). Neural deficits in children with dyslexia ameliorated by behavioral remediation: Evidence from functional MRI. *Proceedings of the National Academy of Sciences (USA), 100,* 2860–2865.

Thorndike, E. L. (1898). Animal intelligence: An experimental study of the associative processes in animals. *Psychological Review Monograph Supplements, 2,* 1–109.

Tulving, E. (2002). Episodic memory: From mind to brain. *Annual Review of Psychology, 53,* 1–25.

Turner, A., & Greenough, W. T. (1985). Differential rearing effects on rat visual cortex synapses: I. Synaptic and neuronal density and synapses per neuron. *Brain Research, 329,* 195–203.

Wise, R. A. (2004). Dopamine, learning and motivation. *Nature Neuroscience Reviews, 5,* 483–494.

Woolley, C. S., Gould, E., Frankfurt, M., & McEwen, B. S. (1990). Naturally occurring fluctuation in dendritic spine density on adult hippocampal pyramidal neurons. *Journal of Neuroscience, 10,* 4035–4039.

Chapter 15

Acredolo, L. P. (1976). Frames of reference used by children for orientation in unfamiliar spaces. In G. Moore & R. Gooledge (Eds.), *Environmental knowing* (pp. 165–172). Stroudsburg, PA: Dowden, Hutchinson, and Ross.

Adolphs, R., Gjosselin, F., Buchanan, T. W., Tranel, D., Schyns, P., & Damasio, A. R. (2005). A mechanism for impaired fear recognition after amygdala damage. *Nature, 433,* 68–72.

Barlow, H. (1995). The neuron doctrine in perception. In M. Gazzaniga (Ed.), *The cognitive neurosciences* (pp. 415–435). Cambridge, MA: MIT Press.

Calvin, W. H. (1996). *How brains think.* New York: Basic Books.

Carr, L., Iacoboni, M., Dubeau, M. C., Mazziotta, J. C. & Lenzi, G. L. (2003). Neural mechanisms of empathy in humans: a relay from neural systems for imitation to limbic areas. *Proceedings of the National Academy of Sciences (USA), 100,* 5497–5502.

Castiello, U., Paulignan, Y., & Jeannerod, M. (1991). Temporal dissociation of motor responses and subjective awareness. *Brain, 114,* 2639–2655.

Chalmers, D. J. (1995). *The conscious mind: In search of a fundamental theory.* Oxford: Oxford University Press.

Crick, F., & Koch, C. (1998). Consciousness and neuroscience. *Cerebral Cortex, 8,* 97–107.

Cytowic, R. E. (1998). *The man who tasted shapes.* Cambridge, MA: MIT Press.

Diamond, M. C., Scheibel, A. B., Murphy, G. M., Jr., & Harvey, T. (1985). On the brain of a scientist: Albert Einstein. *Experimental Neurology, 88,* 198–204.

Duncan, J., Seitz, R. J., Kolodny, J., Bor, D., Herzog, H., Ahmed, A., Newell, F. N., & Emslie, H. (2000). A neural basis for general intelligence. *Science, 289,* 457–459.

Farah, M. J. (1995). The neural bases of mental imagery. In M. Gazzaniga (Ed.), *The cognitive neurosciences* (pp. 2963–2975). Cambridge, MA: MIT Press.

Frith, C., Perry, R., & Lumer, E. (1999). The neural correlates of conscious experience: An experimental framework. *Trends in Cognitive Sciences, 3,* 105–114.

Ghanzanfar, A. A., & Schroeder, C. E. (2006). Is neocortex essentially multisensory? *Trends in Cognitive Science, 10,* 278–285.

Gardner, H. (1983). *Frames of mind.* New York: Basic Books.

Gaulin, S. J. (1992). Evolution of sex differences in spatial ability. *Yearbook of Physical Anthropology, 35,* 125–131.

Gazzaniga, M. S. (1970). *The bisected brain.* New York: Appleton-Century-Crofts.

Gazzaniga, M. S. (1992). *Nature's mind.* New York: Basic Books.

Gazzaniga, M. S., Ivry, R. B., & Mangun, G. R. (1999). *Cognitive science: The biology of the mind.* New York: Norton.

Ghanzanfar, A. A., & Schroeder, C. E. (2006). Is neocortex essentially multisensory? *Trends in Cognitive Science, 10,* 278–285.

Gibb, R., Gorny, G., & Kolb, B. (2009). The therapeutic effects of complex rearing after frontal lesions in infancy are sex dependent. Manuscript submitted for publication.

Gray, J. R., & Thompson, P. M. (2004). Neurobiology of intelligence: Science and ethics. *Nature Reviews Neuroscience, 5,* 471–482.

Guilford, J. P. (1967). *The nature of human intelligence.* New York: McGraw-Hill.

Hebb, D. O. (1980). *Essay on mind.* Hillsdale, NJ: Lawrence Erlbaum.

Hubbard, E. W. (2007). Neurophysiology of synesthesia. *Current Psychiatry Reports, 9,* 193–199.

Iacoboni, M., & Dapretto, M. (2006). The mirror neuron sytem and the consequences of its dysfunction. *Nature Neuroscience Reviews, 7,* 942–951.

James, W. (1890). *Principles of psychology.* New York: Henry Holt.

Kimura, D. (1967). Functional asymmetry of the brain in dichotic listening. *Cortex, 3,* 163–178.

Kimura, D. (1973). The asymmetry of the human brain. *Scientific American, 228*(3), 70–78.

Kimura, D. (1999). *Sex and cognition.* Cambridge, MA: MIT Press.

Kolb, B., & Stewart, J. (1991). Sex-related differences in dendritic branching of cells in the prefrontal cortex of rats. *Journal of Neuroendocrinology, 3,* 95–99.

Kolb, B., & Whishaw, I. Q. (2009). *Fundamentals of human neuropsychology* (6th ed.). New York: Worth Publishers.

Moran, J., & Desimone, R. (1985). Selective attention gates visual processing in the extrastriate cortex. *Science, 229,* 782–784.

Mukerjee, M. (1996). Interview with a parrot [field note]. *Scientific American, 274*(4), 24.

Newsome, W. T., Shadlen, M. N., Zohary, E., Britten, K. H., & Movshon, J. A. (1995). Visual motion: Linking neuronal activity to psychophysical performance. In M. Gazzaniga (Ed.), *The cognitive neurosciences* (pp. 401–414). Cambridge, MA: MIT Press.

Paus, T., Jech, R., Thompson, C. J., Comeau, R., Peters, T., & Evans, A. (1997). Transcranial magnetic stimulation during positron emission tomography: A new method for studying connectivity of the human cerebral cortex. *Journal of Neuroscience, 17,* 3178–3184.

Pepperberg, I. M. (1990). Some cognitive capacities of an African grey parrot (*Psittacus erithacus*). In P. J. B. Slater, J. S. Rosenblatt, & C. Beer (Eds.), *Advances in the study of behavior* (Vol. 19, pp. 357–409). New York: Academic Press.

Pepperberg, I. M. (1999). *The Alex studies.* Cambridge, MA: Harvard University Press.

Pepperberg, I. M. (2006). Ordinality and inferential ability of a grey parrot (*Psittacus erithacus*). *Journal of Comparative Psychology, 120,* 205–216.

Rasmussen, T., & Milner, B. (1977). The role of early left brain injury in determining lateralization of cerebral speech functions. *Annals of the New York Academy of Sciences, 299,* 355–369.

Rizzolatti, G. (2007). *Mirrors on the mind.* New York: Oxford University Press.

Rizzolatti, G., & Craighero, L. (2004). The mirror-neuron system. *Annual Review of Neuroscience, 27,* 169–192.

Rowntree, S. (2009). Spatial and verbal abilities in adult females vary with age at menses. Manuscript submitted for publication.

Sacks, O. (1989). *Seeing voices.* Los Angeles: University of California Press.

Stein, B. E., & Stanford, T. R. (2008). Multisensory integration: current issues from the perspective of the single neuron. *Nature Reviews Neuroscience, 9,* 255–266.

Sperry, R. (1968). Mental unity following surgical disconnection of the cerebral hemispheres. *Harvey Lectures, 62,* 293–323.

Stewart, J., & Kolb, B. (1994). Dendritic branching in cortical pyramidal cells in response to ovariectomy in adult female rats: Suppression by neonatal exposure to testosterone. *Brain Research, 654,* 149–154.

Waber, D. P. (1976). Sex differences in cognition: A function of maturation rate? *Science,* 192, 572–574.

Wada, J., & Rasmussen, T. (1960). Intracarotid injection of sodium amytal for the lateralization of cerebral speech dominance: Experimental and clinical observations. *Journal of Neurosurgery, 17,* 266–282.

Wildgruber, D., Kischka, U., Ackermann, H., Klose, U., & Grodd, W. (1999). Dynamic pattern of brain activation during sequencing of word strings evaluated by fMRI. *Cognitive Brain Research, 7,* 285–294.

Witelson, S. F., & Goldsmith, C. H. (1991). The relationship of hand preference to anatomy of the corpus callosum in men. *Brain Research, 545,* 175–182.

Witelson, S. F., Kigar, D. L., & Harvey, T. (1999). The exceptional brain of Albert Einstein. *Lancet, 353,* 2149–2153.

Chapter 16

Abramowitz, J. S. (1998). Does cognitive-behavior therapy cure obsessive-compulsive disorder? A meta-analytic evaluation of clinical significance. *Behavior Therapy, 29,* 339–355.

American Psychiatric Association. (1994). *Diagnostic and statistical manual of mental disorders* (4th ed.). Washington, DC: American Psychiatric Association.

Andreasen, N. C., & Olsen, S. A. (1982). Negative versus positive symptoms in schizophrenia: Definition and validation. *Archives of General Psychiatry, 39,* 789–794.

Arnold, S. E., Rushinsky, D. D., & Han, L. Y. (1997). Further evidence of abnormal cytoarchitecture in the entorhinal cortex in schizophrenia using spatial point analyses. *Biological Psychiatry, 142,* 639–647.

Bherer, L., Kramer, A. F., Peterson, M. S., Colcombe, S., Erickson, K., & Becic, E. 2008. Transfer effects in task-set cost and dual-task cost after dual-task training in older and younger adults: Further evidence for cognitive plasticity in attentional control in late adulthood. *Experimental Aging Research, 34,* 188–219.

Berman, K. F., & Weinberger, D. R. (1999). Neuroimaging studies of schizophrenia. In D. S. Charney, E. J. Nestler, & B. S. Bunney (Eds.), *The neurobiology of mental illness* (pp. 246–257). New York: Oxford University Press.

Boucai, L., Cerquetti, D., & Merello, M. (2004). Functional surgery for Parkinson's disease treatment: A structured analysis of a decade of published literature. *British Journal of Neurosurgery, 18,* 213–222.

Breier, A. (1999). Diagnostic classification of the psychoses: Historical context and implications for neurobiology. In D. S. Charney, E. J. Nestler, & B. S. Bunney (Eds.), *The neurobiology of mental illness* (pp. 195–202). New York: Oxford University Press.

Brooks, W. M., Friedman, S. D., & Gasparovic, C. (2001). Magnetic resonance spectroscopy in traumatic brain injury. *Journal of Head Trauma and Rehabilitation, 16,* 149–164.

Brun, A. (1983). An overview of light and electron microscopic changes. In B. Reisberg (Ed.), *Alzheimer's disease* (pp. 127–143). New York: The Free Press.

Calne, D. B., & Mizuno, Y. (2004). The neuromythology of Parkinson's disease. *Parkinsonism and Related Disorders, 10,* 319–322.

Caplan, A. L. (2003). Is better best? *Scientific American, 289*(3), 104–105.

Charney, D. S., Nestler, E. J., & Bunney, B. S. (Eds.). (1999). *The neurobiology of mental illness.* New York: Oxford University Press.

Charney, D. S., & Nestler, E. J. (Eds.). (2004). *The neurobiology of mental illness* (2nd ed.). New York: Oxford University Press.

Charney, D. S., & Nestler, E. J. (Eds.). (2009). *The neurobiology of mental illness* (3rd ed.). New York: Oxford University Press.

Cho, R. Y., Gilbert, H., & Lewis, D. A. (2004). The neurobiology of schizophrenia. In D. S. Charney & E. J. Nestler (Eds.), *The neurobiology of mental illness* (2nd ed., pp. 299–310). New York: Oxford University Press.

Ciccarelli, P. A., Brex, A. J., Thompson, A. J., & Miller, D. H. (2000). Disability and lesion load in MS: A reassessment with MS functional composite score and 3D fast flair. *Journal of Neurology, 249,* 18–24.

Crow, T. J. (1980). Molecular pathology of schizophrenia: More than one disease process? *British Medical Journal, 280,* 66–68.

Crow, T. J. (1990). Nature of the genetic contribution to psychotic illness: A continuum viewpoint. *Acta Psychiatrica Scandinavia, 81,* 401–408.

deCharms, R. C. (2008). Applications of real-time fMRI. *Nature Reviews Neuroscience 9,* 720–729.

deCharms, R. C., Maeda, F., Glover, G. H., Ludlow, D., Pauly, J. M., et al. (2005). Control over brain activation and pain learned by using real-time functional MRI. *Proceedings of the National Academy of Sciences (USA), 102,* 18626–18631.

Drevets, W. C., Gadde, K. M., & Krishnan, K. R. (1999). Neuroimaging studies of mood disorders. In D. S. Charney, E. J. Nestler, & B. S. Bunney (Eds.), *The neurobiology of mental illness* (pp. 394–418). New York: Oxford University Press.

Drevets, W. C., Kishore, M. G., & Krishman, K. R. R. (2004). Neuroimaging studies of mood disorders. In D. S. Charney & E. J. Nestler (Eds.), *The neurobiology of mental illness* (2nd ed., pp. 461–490). New York: Oxford University Press.

Duman, R. S. (1999). The neurochemistry of mood disorders. In D. S. Charney, E. J. Nestler, & B. S. Bunney (Eds.), *The neurobiology of mental illness* (pp. 333–347). New York: Oxford University Press.

Duman, R. S. (2004). The neurochemistry of depressive disorders. In D. S. Charney & E. J. Nestler (Eds.), *The neurobiology of mental illness* (2nd ed., pp. 421–439). New York: Oxford University Press.

Elbert, T., Flor, H., Birbaumer, N., Knecht, S., Hampson, S., Larbig, W., & Taub, E. (1994). Extensive reorganization of the somatosensory cortex in adult humans after nervous system injury. *Neuroreport, 5,* 2593–2597

Farah, M. J., Illes, J., Cook-Deegan, R., Gardner, H., Kandel, E., et al. (2004). Neurocognitive enhancement: What can we do and what should we do? *Nature Reviews Neuroscience, 5,* 421–425.

Fitzgerald, P. B., Brown, T. L., Marston, N. A. U., Oxley, T., de Castella, A., Daskalakis, Z. J., & Kulkarni, J. (2004). Reduced plastic brain responses in schizophrenia: A transcranial magnetic stimulation study. *Schizophrenia Research, 71,* 17–26.

George, M. S., Wasserman, E. M., Kimbrell, T. A., & Little, I. T. (1997). Mood improvements following daily left prefrontal repetitive transcranial magnetic stimulation in patients with depression: A placebo-controlled crossover study. *American Journal of Psychiatry, 154,* 1752–1756.

Geuze, E., Westenber, H. G. M., Heinecke, A., de Kloet, C. S., Goebel, & Vermetten, E. (2008). Thinner prefrontal cortex in veterans with posttraumatic stress disorder. *NeuroImage, 41,* 675–681.

Gogtay, N., Lu, A., Leow, A. D., Klunder, A. D., Lee, A. D., Chavez, A., Greenstein, D., Giedd, J. N., Toga, A. W., Rapoport, J. L., & Thompson, P. M. (2008). Three-dimensional brain growth abnormalities in childhood-onset schizophrenia visualized by using tensor-based morphomeetry. *Proceedings of the National Academy of Sciences (USA), 105,* 15979–15984.

Giles J. (2004). Neuroscience: Change of mind. *Nature, 430,* 14.

Gross, C., & Hen, R. (2004). The developmental origins of anxiety. *Nature Reviews Neuroscience, 5,* 545–552.

Haraldsson, H. M., Ferrarelli, F., Kalin, N. H., & Tonomi, G. (2004). Transcranial magnetic stimulation in the investigation and treatment of schizophrenia: A review. *Schizophrenia Research, 71,* 1–16.

Heninger, G. R. (1999). Special challenges in the investigation of the neurobiology of mental illness. In D. S. Charney, E. J. Nestler, & B. S. Bunney (Eds.), *The neurobiology of mental illness* (pp. 89–98). New York: Oxford University Press.

Hoffman, R. E., Hawkins, K. A., Gueorguieva, R., Boutros, N. N., Rachid, F., Carroll, K., & Krystal, J. H. (2003). Transcranial magnetic stimulation of left temporoparietal cortex and medication-resistant auditory hallucinations. *Archives of General Psychiatry, 60,* 49–56.

Hyman, S. E. (2003). Diagnosing disorders. *Scientific American, 289*(3), 97–103.

Kaufer, D. I., & DeKosky, S. T. (1999). Diagnostic classifications: Relationship to the neurobiology of dementia. In D. S. Charney, E. J. Nestler, & B. S. Bunney (Eds.), *The neurobiology of mental illness* (p. 642). New York: Oxford University Press.

Kessler, R. C., McGonagle, K. A., Zhao, S., Nelson, C. B., Hughes, M., Eshleman, S., Wittchen, H., & Kendler, K. S. (1994). Lifetime and 12-month prevalence of DSM-III-R psychiatric disorders in the United States. *Archives of General Psychiatry, 51,* 8–19.

Kito, S., Fujita, K., & Koga, Y. (2008). Regional cerebral blood flow changes after low-frequency transcranial magnetic stimulation of the right dorsolateral prefrontal cortex in treatment-resistant depression. *Neuropsychobiology, 58,* 29-36.

Kondziolka, D., Steinberg, G. K., Wechsler, L., Meltzer, C. C., Elder, E., et al. (2005). Neurotransplantation for patients with subcortical motor stroke: a phase 2 randomized trial. *Journal of Neurosurgery, 103,* 6–8.

Kondziolka, D., Wechsler, L., Goldstein, S., Meltzer, C., Thulborn, K. R., et al. (2000). Transplantation of cultured human neuronal cells for patients with stroke. *Neurology, 55,* 565–569

Kuo, H.-K., Jones, R.N., Milberg, W.P., Tennstedt, S., Talbot, L., et al. (2005). Effect of blood pressure and diabetes mellitus on cognitive and physical functions in older adults: A longitudinal analysis of the advanced cognitive training for independent and vital elderly cohort. *Journal of the American Geriatrics Society, 53,* 1154–1161.

Larrabee, G. J., & Crook, T. H. (1994). Estimated prevalence of age-related memory impairment derived from standardized tests of memory function. International *Psychogeriatrics, 6,* 95–104.

Leritz, E. C., Salat, D. H., McGlinchey, R. E., Williams, V. J., Chapman, C. E., et al. (2008). Variation in risk for cerebrovascular disease is associated with thickness of the human cerebral cortex. 15th International Conference of the Organization for Human Brain Mapping.

Levin, H. S., Benton, A. L., & Grossman, R. G. (1982). *Neurobehavioral consequences of closed head injury.* New York: Oxford University Press.

Lezak, M. (2004). *Neuropsychological assessment* (4th ed.). New York: Oxford University Press.

Lohoff, F. W., & Berrettini, W. H. (2009). Genetics of mood disorders. In D. S. Charney & E. J. Nestler (Eds.), *The neurobiology of mental illness* (3rd edition, pp. 360–377). New York: Oxford University Press

Marcoux, J., McArthur, D. A., Miller, C., Glenn, T. C., Villablanca, P., et al. (2008). Persistent metabolic crisis as measured by elevated cerebral microdialysis lactate-pyruvate ratio predicts chronic frontal lobe brain atrophy after traumatic brain injury. *Critcal Care Medicine, 36,* 2952–2953.

Martin, J. P. (1967). *The basal ganglia and posture.* London: Ritman Medical Publishing.

Mateer, C. A., & Sira, C. S. (2006). Cognitive and emotional consequences of TBI: Intervention strategies for vocational rehabilitation. *NeuroRehabilitation, 21,* 315–326

Mayberg, H. (2009). Targeted electrode-based modulation of neural circuits for depression. *Journal of Clinical Investigations, 119,* 717–725.

McGowan, P. O., Sasaki, A., D'Alessio, A. C., Dymov, S., Labonté, B., et al. (2009). Epigenetic regulation of the glucocorticoid receptor in human brain associates with childhood abuse. *Nature Neuroscience, 12,* 342–348.

McGuire, P. K., Shah, G. M. S., & Murray, R. M. (1993). Increased blood flow in Broca's area during auditory hallucinations in schizophrenia. *Lancet, 342,* 703–706.

Miller, B. L., Boone, K., Cummings, J. L., Read, S. L., & Mishkin, F. (2000). Functional correlates of musical and visual ability in frontotemporal dementia. *British Journal of Psychiatry, 176,* 458–463.

National Institute of Mental Health Web site: http://www.nimh.nih.gov/health/publications/the-numbers-count-mental-disorders-in-america/index.shtml

Nemeroff, C. B. (2004). Early-life adversity, CRF dysregulation, and vulnerability to mood and anxiety disorders. *Psychopharmacology Bulletin, 38,* 14–20.

Pallanti, S., & Bernardi, S. (2009). Neurobiology of repeated transcranial magnetic stimulation in the treatment of anxiety: a critical review. *International Journal of Clinical Psychopharmacology, 24,* 163–173.

Rizzo, A. A., Difede, J., Rothbaum, B. O., Johnston, S., McLay, R. N., et al. (2009). VR PTSD exposure therapy results with active duty OIF/OEF combatants. *Studies in Health Technology Informatics, 142,* 277–282.

Rogawski, M. A., & Loscher, W. (2004). The neurobiology of antiepileptic drugs. *Nature Reviews Neuroscience, 5,* 553–564.

Rossi, S., & Rossini, P. M. (2004). TMS in cognitive plasticity and the potential for rehabilitation. *Trends in Cognitive Sciences, 8,* 273–279.

Sacks, O. (1998). *The man who mistook his wife for a hat: And other clinical tales.* New York: Touchstone.

Santarelli, L., Saxe, M., Gross, C., Surget, A., Battaglia, F., et al. (2003). Requirement of hippocampal neurogenesis for the behavioral effects of antidepressants. *Science, 301,* 805–809.

Shenton, M. E., Kikinis, R., Jolesz, F. A., Pollak, S. D., LeMay, M., et al. (1992). Abnormalities of the left temporal lobe and thought disorder in schizophrenia: A quantitative magnetic resonance imaging study. *New England Journal of Medicine, 327,* 604–611.

Sohlberg, M. M., & Mateer, C. (1989). *Introduction to cognitive rehabilitation.* New York: Guilford Press.

Solms, M. (2004). Freud returns. *Scientific American, 290*(5), 83–89.

Sowell, E. R., Thompson, P. M., & Toga, A. W. (2004). Mapping changes in the human cortex throughout the span of life. *The Neuroscientist, 10,* 372–392.

Sporn, J., Belanoff, J. K., Schatzberg, A., & Charney, D. S. (2004). Principles of the pharmacotherapy of depression. In D. S. Charney & E. J. Nestler (Eds.), *The neurobiology of mental illness* (2nd ed., pp. 491–511). New York: Oxford University Press.

Steinman, L., Martin, R., Bernard, C., Conlon, P., & Oksenberg, J. R. (2002). Multiple sclerosis: Deeper understanding of its pathogenesis reveals new targets for therapy. *Annual Review of Neuroscience, 25,* 491–505.

Tang, Y.-Y., & Posner, M. I. (2009). Attention training and attention state training. *Trends in Cognitive Sciences, 13,* 222–227.

Teskey, G. C., Flynn, C., Goertzen, C. D., Monfils, M. H., & Young, N. A. (2003). Cortical stimulation improves skilled forelimb use following a focal ischemic infarct in the rat. *Neurological Research, 25,* 794–800.

Tsai, G., & Coyle, J. T. (1995). N-Acetylaspartate in neuropsychiatric disorders. *Progress in Neurobiology, 46,* 531–540.

Weaver, I. C., Cervoni, N., Champagne, F. A., D'Alessio, A. C., Sharma, S., et al. (2004). Epigenetic programming by maternal behavior. *Nature Neuroscience, 7,* 847–854.

Weinberger, D. R., & Lipska, B. K. (1995). Cortical maldevelopment, anti-psychotic drugs and schizophrenia: A search for common ground. *Schizophrenia Research, 16,* 87–110.

Name Index

Subject Index

Note: Page numbers followed by f indicate illustrations; those followed by t indicate tables.